Yale Language Series

The Hausa Language
An Encyclopedic Reference Grammar

Paul Newman

Yale University Press   New Haven & London

Printed in the United States of America.

Library of Congress Cataloging-in-Publication Data

Newman, Paul, 1937-
    The Hausa language : an encyclopedic reference grammar / Paul Newman.
    p. cm.-- (Yale language series)
    Includes bibliographical references and index.
    ISBN 0-300-08189-8 (alk. paper)
    1. Hausa language--Grammar. I.Title. II. Series.

PL8232 .N43 2000
493'.725--dc21   99-054069

A catalogue record for this book is available from the British Library.

The paper in this book meets the guidelines for permanence and durability
of the committee on Production Guidelines for Book Longevity of the Council
on Library Resources.

10 9 8 7 6 5 4 3 2 1

for Roxana

Contents

List of Tables and Figures

I. Tables

II. Figures

Preface

THIS grammar has been a long time in the making. How many years depends on from whence one commences counting. One could say that the grammar dates from 1992, when I officially began working on it in earnest; but one could push it back a few years when Russell Schuh and I came up with the idea of doing this as a joint project. (He subsequently was forced to withdraw due to other professional obligations.) In another sense, one could say that the seed was planted twenty years earlier (in 1972), when I assumed the directorship of the Centre for the Study of Nigerian Languages, Bayero University, Kano (then part of Ahmadu Bello University), which resulted in my intellectual shift from a Chadicist, with a focus on comparative/historical work, to a Hausaist and Chadicist, and then gradually to a Hausaist. If I had not gone to Kano and inherited an ongoing dictionary project, eventually published as Newman and Newman (1977), I never would have delved into Hausa to the extent that I did and certainly would not have had the chance to be introduced to the richness and complexity of the language by the native Hausa-speaking researchers at the Centre. I cannot acknowledge individually all of my Nigerian colleagues and coworkers, but I must pay tribute to Dr. Ishaya Audu, then vice-chancellor of ABU, who brought me to Kano, and to Professor Ibrahim Yaro Yahaya, the creative and prolific Hausa scholar whose untimely death in an automobile accident was such a loss to Hausa studies. In searching for significant moments in the chain of events that led to the preparation of this grammar, one might consider the period at UCLA in the mid 1960s when Roxana Newman and I had the temerity to undertake an ambitious study of comparative Chadic (Newman and Ma 1966); or one could go back a few years earlier when I, then an untrained linguist teaching secondary school in Maiduguri, met Professor Johannes Lukas, who encouraged and inspired me to undertake the study of Tera, the Chadic language on which I later wrote my Ph.D. dissertation. Or perhaps the real starting point was in 1961 when I joined the first Peace Corps group to go to Nigeria, an event that changed the course of my professional and personal life.

The grammar project per se was carried out at Indiana University (Department of Linguistics and Institute for the Study of Nigerian Languages and Cultures) over a six-year period. Financial support was provided by generous grants from the U.S. Department of Education (PO-17A10037), the National Endowment for the Humanities (RT-21236), and the National Science Foundation (DBS-9107103), for which I am deeply grateful. Throughout the project, I depended on the assistance of a large number of people who carried out a myriad of tasks. William Anderson, Nancy Caplow, Robert Shull, and Ezra Simon helped with library research and data-entry matters. Wayne Martin and Michael Newman set up the database and provided the essential computer support without which a project of this scope would not have been possible. John Hollingsworth drew the maps; Carol Rhodes was responsible for preparing the figures and overseeing the formatting of the camera-ready manuscript; and Joyce Ippolito did the painstaking job of copy editing the work as a whole.

Dr. Mustapha Ahmad Isa served as the primary research assistant on the project while he was pursuing his Ph.D. in linguistics at Indiana University. He was ably succeeded by Dr. Lawan Danladi Yalwa. Alhaji Daiyabu Abdullahi, Alhaji Maina Gimba, and Ibro Chekaraou also assisted in verifying Hausa examples and suggesting analytical modifications.

I was extremely fortunate in being able to benefit from the input of Dr. Mahamane L. Abdoulaye and Dr. Ismail Junaidu, excellent Hausa scholars who came to Bloomington for a summer each to work on the project. They were able to provide both their intuition as native speakers and their expertise as sophisticated linguists.

Dr. Malami Buba served as the major research associate during the later stages of the project, collaborating in the work both in Bloomington and after returning to England. He worked closely with me in the preparation and checking of the first full draft of the grammar.

Finally, I cannot begin to express the extent of my obligation to Dr. Philip Jaggar of the School of Oriental and African Studies, University of London. During his sabbatical year in Bloomington, we spent endless hours discussing the intricacies of Hausa phonology, morphology, and syntax, discussions that often forced me to rethink analyses that I had been comfortable with or to consider facts that I had been unaware of. Although Phil was always good-natured about the amount of time he devoted to my project, it is clear that he unselfishly sacrificed progress on his own academic objectives for the year in order to help me with the grammar. And later when I had completed what I thought was the final draft, Phil provided a meticulous page by page reading of the entire grammar, catching typos, redundancies, contradictions in analysis, infelicities in translations, and downright mistakes. It is undoubtedly true that this grammar would have been finished sooner if Phil had not taken such an interest in it; but it would have been a much inferior product. It is standard in academic books to acknowledge the many colleagues, friends, and coworkers who helped out in some important way or other, and this acknowledgement is invariably well deserved. In Phil's case, however, the assistance that he provided truly went beyond the ordinary. Phil's deep involvement in the preparation of this grammar is a testimony to his friendship and his love of the Hausa language. What can I say but Phil (Malam Bala), I thank you and I indeed owe you one. Allah ya saka da alheri!

Symbols and Abbreviations

I. Symbols

°AN:	analytical note
◊HN:	historical note
ΔDN:	dialect note
( )	(1) optional; (2) English gloss not present in corresponding Hausa example
< >	dialect variant
« »	topicalized constituent
{ }	(1) focused constituent; (2) morphemic representation
//...//	underlying (base) representation
/.../	phonemic representation
[...]	phonetic representation
)±	polar tone
=	equals
≠	not equals
*	historical/hypothetical
**	ungrammatical
??	of questional grammaticality/acceptability
σ	syllable
$	syllable boundary
.	(1) indicator of syllable break, e.g., **han.tà** 'liver'; (2) indicator in glosses of separate morphemes within a word, e.g., **masà** 'to.him'
<	comes from (synchronically or historically)
>	changes to (historically)
→	(1) changes to (phonologically); (2) rewrites as (phrase structure)
⇒	becomes (morphologically or syntactically)
§	section (Note: A reference to §**5**:2.3, for example, with the first numeral in bold, indicates section 2.3 in chapter 5. An indication like §2.3 denotes section 2.3 in the chapter where the reference is found.)

II. Abbreviations

adj	adjective		AV	aspectual verb
adj.pp	adjectival past participle		BDVN	base-derived verbal noun
adv	adverb		C	consonant
allat	allative (TAM)		cf.	compare
Ar.	Arabic		comp	completive (TAM)
Aug-1	augmentative-1		COMP	complementizer
Aug-2	augmentative-2		cont	continuous (TAM)

cor.	coronal	N	noun
CP	complement clause	NP	noun phrase
CTE	complement-taking expression	obj	object
d.a.	definite article	OIC	oblique impersonal construction
dem	demonstrative	PAC	person-aspect-complex
det	determiner	pal.	palatal
dim	diminutive	pal-vel.	palatalized velar
dv	dialect variant	PC	Proto-Chadic
DVN	deverbal noun	pds	pre-dative suffix
Eng.	English	pl.	plural
esp.	especially	plurac.	pluractional (verb)
etc.	et cetera	pn	personal pronoun
f. = fem.	feminine	pot	potential future (TAM)
F	falling tone	pp	prepositional phrase
ff.	and following	pret	preterite (TAM)
fut	future (TAM)	psn	person
fv	finite verb	q	question morpheme
fve	finite-verb environment	Q-word	question word
G	geminate consonant)	Rcont1	relative-continuous1 (TAM)
Gen	general TAM or syntactic	Rcont2	relative-continuous2 (TAM)
	environment	RC	relative clause
gl	glottalized	re.	regarding
gr1, gr2...	grade 1, grade 2, etc.	redup	reduplication
	(= v1, v2...)	rel	relative (clause or pronoun)
H	high tone	Rel	relative TAM or syntactic
hab	habitual (TAM)		environment
HAVE	*have* construction	rhet	rhetorical (TAM)
HC	hypocoristic	S	sentence (excluding focus)
ICP	intransitive copy pronoun	S´	sentence (including focus)
id	ideophone	sbj	subject
imp	imperative	sg.	singular
intr.	intransitive	s.o.	someone
i.o.	indirect object	SH	Standard Hausa
IOM	indirect object marker	SDVN	stem derived verbal noun
IP	infinitive phrase	Skt	Sokoto (dialect)
Kts	Katsina (dialect)	STAB	stabilizer
L	(1) low tone; (2) genitive linker	sth	something
lab.	labial	sub	subjunctive (TAM)
lab-vel.	labialized velar	TAM	tense/aspect/mood
laryn.	laryngeal	tr.	transitive
lit.	literally	usu.	usually
LTR	low-tone raising	V	vowel
m.	masculine	v1, v2, etc.	verb grade 1, verb grade 2, etc.
MP	modal particle		(= gr1, gr2, etc.)
neg	negative	vb	verb
neut	neutral (TAM)	vd	voiced
nfv	nonfinite verb	vdat	dative verb
nfve	nonfinite verb environment	vel.	velar

VERB	verb whether finite or nonfinite	VP	verb phrase
v.i.	intransitive verb	WH	western Hausa
vl	voiceless	wsp	weak subject pronoun
VN	verbal noun	Y/N	yes/no question

Glossary of Hausa Words Untranslated in Examples

ajami	/àjàmi/	Arabic script used for writing Hausa.
bori	/bòrī/	the spirit possession cult of the Hausa
fura	/furā/	ball(s) of cooked flour (usu. millet) eaten (although Hausa uses the verb *drink*) mixed with milk
tuwo	/tuwō/	staple food consisting of boiled grain (usually guinea corn or millet, less often rice) served in the form of a hemisphere, accompanied by a stew or sauce

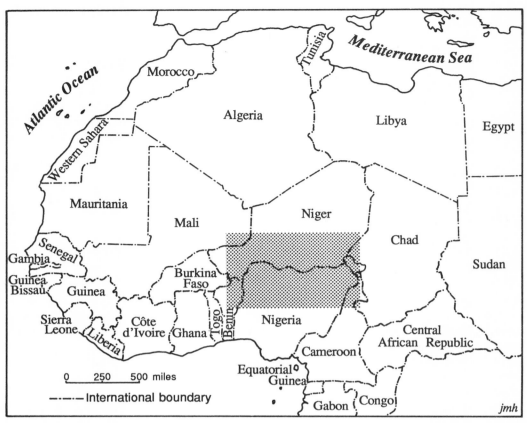

North and West Africa

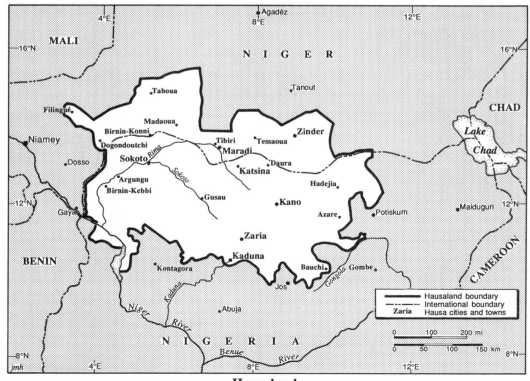

Hausaland

Introduction

THE Hausa language is spoken by upwards of thirty-five million speakers. It is the first language of ethnic Hausas and settled Fulanis in what one might call Hausaland proper (see map), which covers the traditional emirates of Kano, Katsina, Zaria, Daura, Sokoto, etc., in what is now Nigeria, and the Hausa-speaking areas of southern Niger, which consist of Gobir, Maradi, Damagaram, Tahoua, Dogondoutchi, etc. Hausa is also spoken as a first language by resident Hausa communities in Niamey (Niger), in Ibadan and Lagos (southern Nigeria), in Jos and Abuja (central Nigeria), in Ghana (especially in the north, but also in the capital Accra), and in the Blue Nile area of the Sudan. Hausa has probably been expanding for the past two hundred years, but its spread during the past half century has been particularly dramatic, particularly in northern Nigeria. Thus one finds that in urban areas like Bauchi, Gombe, Kaduna, and Potiskum, Hausa is rapidly establishing itself as a mother tongue for many of the inhabitants, or, if it is not replacing the indigenous language(s), it is at least being used on a day-to-day basis as a lingua franca.

Hausa is a member of the Chadic language family, which itself is a constituent member of the Afroasiatic phylum that also includes Semitic, Cushitic, Omotic, Berber, and Ancient Egyptian (Greenberg 1963; Newman 1980a). Within Chadic, Hausa's closest relatives are West Chadic languages belonging to the Bole-Tangale, Angas, and Ron groups (Newman and Ma 1966; Newman 1977a). Within West Chadic, Hausa essentially constitutes a group by itself. The only other member of the group, Gwandara, is a creolized offshoot of Hausa rather than a sister language (Newman 1985).

Hausa has a number of geographical dialects, marked by differences in pronunciation, grammatical formatives, and vocabulary (Ahmed and Daura 1970; Bello 1992). Roughly speaking, one can make a primary cut between western Hausa (WH), as spoken, for example, in Sokoto and Tahoua, and eastern Hausa, as spoken, for example, in Kano and Zinder, with the dialect of Katsina and Maradi falling somewhere inbetween. Within eastern Hausa, as so defined, one can distinguish Standard (Kano) Hausa (SH) from geographically more restricted dialects such as that of Daura in the north, Zaria in the south, or Bauchi in the far southeast. Cutting across the east-west division is a north-south division separating Hausa as spoken in Niger, characterized by the incorporation of loanwords from French, and Hausa in Nigeria, characterized by extensive influence from English.

This grammar is a description of "Standard Hausa", which essentially represents the dialect of Kano State, a dialect that has become recognized as the norm for the written language (as embodied in books and newspapers) and also for such media as radio and television. This is the dialect represented in the major dictionaries and grammars of the language prepared over the past century and in most pedagogical materials prepared for Americans and Europeans intending to learn the language. In the absence of precise information about Hausa dialectology, references to dialects other than SH are admittedly (and unfortunately) inexact. In some cases I have made reference to a particular town (e.g., Sokoto), where this seemed reasonably accurate given the available descriptions; in other cases I have used the broader designation [WH] (= western Hausa); and in other cases I have simply indicated [dv] (= dialect variant) (i.e., *not* SH).

1. HISTORY OF HAUSA LINGUISTICS

Hausa has been the subject of scholarly study for a century and a half. (For an overview see R. M. Newman 1974 and Newman 1991a.) The father of Hausa linguistics is clearly James Frederick Schön (1803–1889), who produced substantial dictionaries, grammars, and text collections in the language (Schön 1843, 1862, 1876, 1885). The explorer Heinrich Barth (1821–1865) played an important role in furthering the study of Hausa, not only through his own work (e.g., Barth 1862–66), but by bringing a young Hausa man back with him to Europe at the end of his travels across the Sahara to Borno, Hausaland, and Timbuctoo (see Kirk-Greene and Newman 1971). Important contributors to Hausa linguistics at the beginning of the twentieth century up until the Second World War include Adam Mischlich (1864–1948) (e.g., Mischlich 1906, 1911), Charles H. Robinson (1861–1925) (e.g., Robinson 1897, 1899–1900)—the fifth edition (1925) of whose grammar was reprinted as late as 1959!), Maurice Delafosse (1870–1926) (e.g., Delafosse 1901), Diedrich Westermann (1875–1956) (e.g., Westermann 1911), August Klingenheben (1886–1967) (e.g., Klingenheben 1920), and F. W. Taylor (1887–19??) (e.g., Taylor 1923), an expert on both Hausa and Fulani, who could claim credit for the discovery that Hausa is a tone language. One of the major accomplishments during these years was the publication in 1934 of the monumental *Hausa-English Dictionary* of G. P. Bargery (1876–1966). The last giant of Hausa linguistic scholarship whose work fell within this period was the remarkable lexicographer and grammarian R. C. Abraham (1890–1963), who not only produced significant works on Hausa (e.g., Abraham 1959b, Abraham and Kano 1949), but also on African languages as widely separated as Somali and Yoruba (see Jaggar 1992c).

Since the Second World War, there has been an efflorescence of Hausa scholarship. Without a doubt, the dominant figure during this period was F. W. Parsons (1908–1993), Reader at the School of Oriental and African Studies, University of London (see Parsons 1981); but extensive investigations and publications on the language have been carried out by scholars from around the world, like Joseph H. Greenberg, Carleton T. Hodge (1917–1998), and A. Neil Skinner (USA), Johannes Lukas (1901–1980) (Germany), Dmitrii Olderogge (1903–1987) (Russia), Claude Gouffé (France), and Petr Zima (Czech Republic). During the past quarter of a century, native Hausa-speaking linguists have increasing made their impact on Hausa scholarship, of whom special mention must be made of Muhammadu Hambali (Niger), and Dauda M. Bagari and M. K. M. Galadanci (1934–1996) (Nigeria).

2. RECENT PEDAGOGICAL WORKS ON HAUSA

In addition to the many analytical books and articles written on Hausa, the language is fortunate in having received the attention of scholars concerned with second-language learning and practical language use. The result has been the preparation of a number of pedagogical courses, dictionaries, readers, etc., e.g., Hodge and Umaru (1963); Skinner (1972); Kraft and Kirk-Greene (1973); Kraft and Kraft (1973); Cowan and Schuh (1976); Jungraithmayr and Möhlig (1976); Furniss (1991a); Leben et al. (1991a, 1991b); Ahmad and Botne (1992); and Jaggar (1992a, 1996), as well as practically-oriented dictionaries, e.g., Skinner (1968); Newman and Newman (1977); Herms (1987); R. M. Newman (1990); Mijinguini (1994); Awde (1996); and Caron and Amfani (1997).

3. DATA SOURCES FOR THE GRAMMAR

In this grammar, I have unapologetically borrowed ideas, analyses, and examples from the full range of previous publications on the language: old and new, reliable and questionable, theoretical and descriptive, focused and expansive. For a comprehensive bibliography of linguistic works on Hausa as well as on related Chadic languages, see Newman (1996). I have, however, particularly depended on a handful of essential works, without which this grammar would not have been possible. These are Abraham's dictionary and grammar (Abraham 1959b, 1962); Bargery's dictionary (1934); all of Parsons' published articles plus his collected papers (1981); Roxana Ma Newman's dictionary (1990); and H. Ekkehard Wolff's major reference grammar (1993).

In preparing the grammar, I have also drawn on the wealth of written materials now available in Hausa including elementary school readers, nonfiction books (health manuals, political tracts, history, etc.), books of fiction (novels, folktales, stories, etc.), pedagogical readers, and magazines and newspapers (especially the long-established *Gaskiya Ta Fi Kwabo*.) Finally, I have elicited basic data, dialect information, grammatical judgments, and analytical interpretations from a large number of linguistically well-trained native Hausa speakers.

Many (but not all) of the chapters in the *Grammar* conclude with a brief list of references. These constitute recommendations for *further* study, should someone care to dig deeper into some particular matter. They do not represent citations of the full range of works that I consulted and digested in preparing the chapters in question.

4. TRANSCRIPTION SYSTEM

Hausa examples are written using standard Hausa orthography (see §80:2) except for three additions needed for linguistic purposes. These are: (a) the use of diacritics (or occasionally double vowels) to indicate vowel length, (b) the use of diacritics to indicate tone, and (c) the use of a diacritic to distinguish between the two Rs found in the language. (Linguistic rather than orthographic practice is also followed in the use of lowercase rather than capital letters at the beginning of Hausa example sentences.)

Long vowels are normally indicated by means of a macron (but see below for the marking of length by means of a circumflex), e.g., **sūnā** 'name' (with long /ū/ and long /ā/) (cf. **ido** 'in the eye' (with short /i/ and short /o/)). Double vowels are occasionally used instead of a macron when needed to show optional length, e.g., **bà(a)** 'negative marker' (where the **a** can be long or short), or to specify and/or illustrate vowel shortening or lengthening rules more clearly, e.g., **ɗaa** 'son' + **-nsà** 'his' ⇒ *ɗaansà → ɗansà 'his son'; **àku** 'parrot' + **-naa** 'my' ⇒ **àkuunaa** 'my parrot'.

Low tone is indicated by a grave accent, e.g., **màcè** 'woman', **wàtò** 'that is to say'. Falling tone (which only occurs on heavy syllables) is indicated by a circumflex, e.g., **mântā** 'forget'. When occurring on a vowel in an open syllable, the circumflex indicates falling tone *and* length, e.g., **sû** 'fishing' (where the **û** is long); **shigôwā** 'entering' (where the **ô** is long); cf. **gyâffā** 'sides' (where the **â** is short). High tone is left unmarked, e.g., **ido** 'in the eye' (high-high); **sūnā** 'name' (high-high); **ràgō** 'ram' (low-high); **fuskà** 'face' (high-low).

The distinction between the two Rs (a retroflex flap vs. a coronal tap or roll) is indicated by a tilde over the latter, e.g., **garkā** 'small garden plot' vs. **farkà** 'wake up', **rīdà** 'action of grabbing or clutching' vs. **r̃ībà** 'profit'.

Most Hausa consonants have essentially the same value as their English counterparts, the major exception being **c**, which represents English *ch*, e.g., **cāca** 'gambling', pronounced as in English *chachacha*. The letter **g** is always hard, e.g., the initial syllable in **gēmù** beard is pronounced as in English *get*, not as in *gem*.

The Hausa alphabet uses five consonantal letters not found in English. These are the "hooked" letters ɓ, ɗ, and ƙ, which represent the laryngealized (sometimes implosive) bilabial and coronal consonants and the ejective velar consonant, respectively; the apostrophe ', which represents glottal stop (but not in non-initial position, where it is left unwritten); and **'y**, a laryngealized semivowel. (In addition, it employs the digraph **ts** to represent the ejective coronal sibilant, and, in WH only, **c'** for the ejective palatal affricate.)

Geminate consonants are indicated by double letters, e.g., **bàbba** 'big', **mannè** 'adhere to'. In the case of geminates of consonants represented by digraphs, however, only the first letter of the digraph is doubled, e.g., **sanasshē** 'inform (pre-pronoun form)' (with the geminate **sh**) = /sanashshē/, **tsattsafī** 'sprinkling of rain' (with the geminate **ts**) = /tsatstsafī/.

5. ORGANIZATION OF THE GRAMMAR

This grammar is designed as a reference work. The eighty topics covered are each treated in separate units and presented in alphabetical order. The expectation is that the grammar will be consulted like an encyclopedia or a dictionary rather than being read from beginning to end like a novel. This organizational format is a clear-cut departure from the usual grammar, where "abstract nouns", for example, would be included in the overall chapter on "Nominal Derivation" whereas a topic such as "causatives" would be embedded in the chapter on "Syntax" and/or "Morphology". This novel organization necessitates a slight amount of repetition/redundancy and a certain degree of cross-referencing, but on the whole the intention is that each unit be coherent and self-contained. The hope is that once the reader becomes accustomed to the approach adopted here, he or she will find this to be a user-friendly manner of presentation, one in which information is much easier to access than in the traditional grammar.

Each chapter provides a detailed description of some particular grammatical phenomenon as found in current-day Standard Hausa (SH). Advanced or specialized material, which the average reader may want to ignore, has been presented as notes in the text itself, distinguished by a smaller font size. There are three kinds of notes, which are indicated by °AN, ΔDN, and ◊HN. These are:

°AN: Analytical notes. These notes include information about lexical exceptions, clarification regarding orthographic practice, and acknowledgment of factual or analytical uncertainties, etc. General theoretical issues are raised and scholarly differences of opinion regarding treatments of Hausa linguistic phenomena are outlined and discussed (sometimes at length).

ΔDN: Dialect notes. It is here that information is generally presented about language features that are different from what one finds in Standard Hausa. (In a few instances, dialect characteristics are covered in the main text itself.) Dialect coverage has no pretense of being complete: notes are included on a somewhat ad hoc basis, depending on what is known and what appears to be interesting.

◊HN: Historical notes. These notes include established facts and hypotheses about the history of Hausa as well as comparative data from related Chadic languages. The intention in many cases is to provide a historical perspective that helps explain synchronic irregularities or anomalies in the language.

1. Abstract Nouns (Derived)

ABSTRACT nouns are derived from common nouns or adjectives by the use of three semiproductive suffixes: {-CI}, {-TA}, and {-TAKA}. Abstracts with the -CI suffix are masculine; those with the other two suffixes are feminine. These abstracts indicate the general state or condition or ascribed attributes associated with the underlying noun or adjective, e.g.,

(a) **ādalcì** justice, fairness < **ādàlī** just, honest, righteous (psn); **bambancì** difference, discrimination < **bambam** different; **butulcì** ingratitude, being a traitor < **bùtùlu** an ingrate; **shaiɗancì** misbehavior, recklessness < **shàiɗân** the devil
(b) **kuturtà** leprosy < **kuturū** leper; **sàbùntā** newness < **sābō** new; **wâutā** foolishness < **wāwā** a fool
(c) **dàngàntakà** relationship < **dangì** kin, relatives; **jàrùntakà** bravery < **jārùmī** brave man

> °AN: This chapter is devoted to a particular nominal derivation. Hausa also has a different morphological construction forming abstract nouns of sensory quality, e.g., **zurfī** 'depth', **fāɗī** 'width' (see chap. 2), as well as nonderived nouns that are syntactically and semantically abstract in nature, e.g., **rōwà** 'miserliness', **farī** 'whiteness' (see §52:1.2).
> ◊HN: The -CI and -TA suffixes are clearly variants of the same affix, the choice being determined by gender. That is, although synchronically it is probably correct to say that the forms with -CI are masculine and those with -TA are feminine, viewed historically, it is more accurate to say that those abstracts that were masculine suffixed -CI and those that were feminine suffixed -TA, i.e., gender was determinative, not determined. The ending -TAKA looks like a double suffix, i.e., -TA plus -KA; but this cannot be verified at this point.

On the whole, the three suffixes are essentially equivalent in meaning, the choice of one or the other being lexically determined. There are, however, some subtle differences in their use (§5 below). For example, abstracts indicating a professional activity are formed with -CI (or occasionally -TA) but not with -TAKA, e.g.,

alƙālancì judgeship; **dūkancì** leather working; **hākimcì** = **hākimtà** being a district head; **kār̃uwancì** prostitution; **līmancì** position and work of an imam

1. SEGMENTAL SHAPE OF THE ABSTRACT SUFFIXES

The essential forms of the three suffixes are -cī)^{HL}, -tā) [tone variable], and -takā)^{LHL}. Words containing -cī)^{HL} are minimally trisyllabic and words containing -takā)^{LHL} are minimally quadrisyllabic. Most words containing -tā are trisyllabic although some are longer and a few are disyllabic. With some words, these three suffixes attach directly to the base, i.e., the stem less the final vowel (examples in (a)); with others they are linked to the base by an intrusive -**Vn**- element (examples in (b)). Some words allow both options. Examples:

(a) **jāhilcì** illiteracy < **jāhìlī** ignorant psn; **la'ifcì** impotence < **là'īfī** impotent; **wâutā** foolishness < **wāwā** fool; **gajartà** shortness < **gàjērē** short; **sàmàrtakà** youthfulness, boyhood < **sàmàrī** young men

(b) **bōrancì** being an unfavored co-wife < **bōrà** unfavored co-wife; **wāwancì** (= **wâutā**) foolishness < **wāwā** fool; **gùrgùntā** lameness < **gurgù** a cripple; **kumāmantà** feebleness < **kùmāmà** feeble psn; **àbòkàntakà** friendship < **àbōkī** friend

There are two interrelated questions that need to be addressed regarding the suffix: first, whether the intrusive -**Vn**- element is used, and if so, the nature of the **V**. (A similar question regarding the presence or absence of the nasal comes up with the -**TA** verbalizing suffix, see chap. **79**.)

1.1. With disyllabic stems

CVCV words that have a glide (/**w**/ or /**y**/) as the second consonant drop the final vowel and append the -**tā** suffix directly. The glides then alter into /**u**/ and /**i**/, respectively, in accordance with automatic phonological representation rules (see §**54**:1.1.1), e.g.,

bàutā   slavery < //**bàwtā**// < **bāwà** slave
mâitā   witchcraft < //**mâytā**// < **māyè** witch

Three items found in the dictionaries, none of which is readily acceptable by modern SH speakers, connect the abstract suffix to a disyllabic base by a long vowel.

??**mātūcì**   femininity; female sexual organs < **màtā** wife, female
??**gabācì**   promotion < **gàbā** front
??**kusācì** (= **kusancì** = **kusantà**) closeness < **kusa** close

> °AN: At first sight, the words **lālācì** 'laziness, weakness' and **làlātà** 'immoral behavior, being a rogue' would appear on the basis of meaning and form to be abstract nouns. However, their correct analysis is more likely as verbal nouns derived from the verb **lālàtā** 'spoil, disgrace'.

All other simple disyllabic words use the -**Vn**- infix, e.g.,

mūzancì behaving like a simpleton < **mūzī** a simpleton; **wāwancì** foolishness < **wāwā** fool **bàràntā** being a servant < **barà** servant; **bèbàntakà** (= **bēbancì**) muteness < **bēbē** deaf mute **dògwàntakà** or **dògòntakà** tallness < **dōgō** tall; **gwànintà** expertise, skill < **gwànī** expert

If the final vowel of the lexical form is /**u**/, then the -**Vn**- is usually realized as /**un**/, although /**an**/ also occurs, e.g.,

(a) **gùrgùntā** lameness < **gurgù** a cripple; **mùgùntā** evil(ness) < **mūgù** evil (psn); **zumuncì** closeness, friendship < **zumù** close friend
(b) **dūkancì** leatherwork, cf. **bàdūkù** leatherworker; **hūtsantà** cantankerousness < **hūtsū** cantankerous

The /**un**/ realization of -**Vn**- is also found in some words that now end in /ō/ but that historically ended in */**u**/ (Newman 1990a).

bàƙuncì	being a guest < **bàƙō** (< ***bàƙu**) guest, stranger
gàɓùntā	immature behavior < **gāɓṑ** (< ***gāɓù**) simpleton
sàɓùntakà̀ (= **sàɓùntā**)	newness < **sābō** (< ***sābu**) new

If the final vowel is /ī/ or /ā/, then the -**Vn**- is generally realized as /**an**/, although in a few cases it appears as /**in**/. Examples:

(a) **bàràntā** being a servant < **barà̀** servant; **bōrancì** being an unfavored co-wife < **bōrà̀** unfavored co-wife; **dàngàntakà̀** relationship < **dangì̀** relatives; **gàřdancì** being a *gardi* < **gařdì̀** snake charmer; advanced Islamic student
(b) **gwànintà̀** expertise, skill < **gwànī** expert; **wòfintà̀** uselessness, being in a pitiful state < **wòfī** fool

With words ending in the mid vowels /ō/ (excluding the ones historically derived from ***u**) or /ē/, the -**Vn**- is realized as /**an**/, e.g.,

dōlancì foolishness < **dōlō** fool; **gwàřzàntakà̀** bravery, endurance < **gwařzō** brave man; **bēbancì** behaving as if one were a deaf mute < **bēbē** deaf mute; **shègàntakà̀** mischief, roguishness < **shègè** bastard, rogue
Exception: **gwà̀mùntā** being knock-kneed < **gwāmè̀** knock-kneed

◊HN: [i] Most likely, the original form of the -**Vn**- in e-final and o-final words was /**en**/ and /**on**/, and the change to /**an**/ was due to the general phonological rule that shortens and centralizes /ē/ and /ō/ to /a/ (phonetically [ə]) in closed syllables, e.g., **shègàntakà̀** < */**shègèntakà̀**/, **dōlancì** < */**dōloncì**/. The intuition of modern SH speakers, however, as reflected in spelling preferences, slow speech pronunciation, etc., suggests that the erstwhile phonological rule has become (or is becoming) morphologized and that /**an**/ is now selected directly as part of the abstract suffix, i.e., **dōlancì** < **dōl-ancì** (sg. **dōlō**) now parallels **mūzancì** < **mūz-ancì** (sg. **mūzì̀**). Another possibility is that */**an**/ was the original form and that other vowel realizations of -**Vn**- were due to assimilation, e.g., **zumuncì** 'friendship' < ***zumancì**.
[ii] The abstract **gwà̀mùntā** 'being knock-kneed', which appears on the surface to be formed irregularly, actually derives not from **gwāmè̀** 'knock-kneed', the current Kano pronunciation, but rather from **gwāmì̀**, a more widespread variant. The derivation is thus **gwāmì̀** ⇒ **gwà̀mìntā** → **gwà̀mùntā** (with common, though not automatic, rounding of the /i/ after the /**m**/).

Disyllabic words ending in a diphthong or a consonant—what one might called "latent trisyllabic words"—attach the suffix directly without the intrusive nasal, e.g.,

kaɗaicì	loneliness, being solitary < **kaɗai** only
kawaicì	taciturnity < **kawài** silently (cf. **kàwaità** be silent)
tàgwàtakà̀	twinship < **tagwai** [dv] twins
bambancì	difference, discrimination < **bambam** different
halaccì (< //halakcì̀//)	legitimacy, credibility, behaving honestly < **hàlâk** legitimate, lawful
mùtùntakà̀ (< //mùtùmtakà̀//)	human nature < **mùtûm** man

1.2. With polysyllabic stems

Quadrisyllabic (or longer) stems normally use the suffixal form with -an- regardless of the quality of the stem-final vowel. Trisyllabic stems occur both with and without -an-. The variant without -Vn- appears to be the originally preferred form, as evidenced by its choice with basic words and words undergoing archaic sound changes. The form with -Vn-, on the other hand, seems to be the more productive variant and the one that is spreading throughout the language. The intrusive -Vn- rarely (if ever?) occurs with the -TA suffix. Examples:

(a) **fataucì** (< //fatakcì//) trading < **fatàkē** traders; **gajartà** shortness < **gàjērē** short; **jàřùmtakà** = **jàřùmtā** bravery < **jàřùmī** brave man
Irregular: **sàràkutà** in-law relationship < **sàràkuwā** in-law
(b) **almubazzařancì** extravagance < **àlmùbazzàřī** extravagant psn; **hatsabībancì** recklessness < **hàtsàbībì** cantankerous psn, sorcerer; **kāsuwancì** marketing, trading < **kàsuwā** market; **miskilancì** contrariness < **miskìlī** contrary psn; **shūgabancì** leadership < **shùgàbā** leader (frozen compound < *shìg-gàba enter in front); **àbòkàntakà** friendship < **àbōkī** friend

2. TONE

2.1. The suffix -cī)^{HL}

The suffix -cī)^{HL} has a set H-L tone melody, i.e., L on the last syllable and H on all preceding syllables.

almubazzařancì extravagance; **bambancì** difference, discrimination; **dōlancì** foolishness; **fankashālancì** senselessness, stupidity; **jāgōrancì** leadership; **muhimmancì** importance

°AN: [i] There is a similar-looking suffix having the form -cī)^{H} with all H tone that is used to derive names of languages, e.g., **Jāmusancī** 'German' < **Jāmùs** 'Germany'. I have chosen to describe this formation in a separate unit (see chap. **41**) although some scholars prefer to relate it to the abstract derivation.
[ii] The words **àlbařkàcī** 'good fortune, blessing' and **tàkâicī** 'indignation' semantically could be considered abstract nouns; but given their tones, they probably do not contain the derivational suffix in question.

2.2. The suffix -takā)^{LHL}

The suffix -takā)^{LHL} has a set L-H-L melody, i.e., H-L on the last two syllables and L on all preceding syllables, e.g.,

jàřùntakà bravery; **shègàntakà** mischievousness; **tàgwàitakà** twinship, **'yàn'ùwàntakà** family relationship

2.3. The suffix -tā

The tone of abstracts with the -tā suffix is lexically determined and nonpredictable. With the few disyllabic abstract nouns that exist, F-H, L-H, and possibly H-L occur. Examples (complete):

F-H: **mâitā** witchcraft; **wâutā** foolishness, immature act by an adult
L-H: **bàutā** slavery; **cùtā** illness, disease
H-L: **tsaftà** cleanliness

°AN: Generally speaking, disyllabic words in Hausa with the tone pattern F-H can be viewed as compressed trisyllabic words with H-L-H tone (e.g., **dâbgī** 'anteater' = **dābùgī**). Given the existence of the forms **mâitā** 'witchcraft' and **wâutā** 'foolishness', it is thus strange that trisyllabic abstracts with -**tā** (to be described below) do *not* appear with H-L-H even though they exhibit a number of other tone patterns.

◊HN: [i] From an etymological point of view, the L-H words **bàutā** and **cùtā** could be viewed not as abstract nouns but rather as deverbal nouns containing the verbalizer -**TA**, where the L-H tone pattern is common.

[ii] The status of the word **tsaftà** (pronounced [tsaptà]) is unclear. On the surface it looks like an abstract noun, but this may be accidental. There are two main reasons for the doubt. First, the non-abstract common noun on which it should be built doesn't exist synchronically; instead all one has is a related ideophone **tsaf** (or **tsap**). Second, **tsaftà** has a derived verb **tsaftàcē** 'cleanse' using a -**TA** verbalizing suffix on top of the presumed -**tā** abstract suffix; no other abstract noun allows this. In short, either **tsaftà** is not an abstract noun, or else its derivation took place at a very early stage so that the suffix has now become lexically frozen.

Among the approximately fifty or so trisyllabic abstract nouns with -**tā** , H-H-L is the most common tone pattern. This is followed by L-L-H, and then L-H-L. A few words allow variant tones as equivalent alternatives. Examples:

H-H-L: **gajartà** shortness; **hūtsantà** cantankerousness; **kuturtà** leprosy; **shařiftà** being a holy man; **mālantà** = **màlàntà** scholarship, teaching
L-L-H: **bàràntā** = **barantà** being a servant; **àbôtā** friendship; **gàɓùntā** immature, foolish behavior; **nàgàřtā** goodness, uprightness
L-H-L: **bàjintà** bravery, achievement; **gwànintà** expertise, skill; **là'iftà** impotence

◊HN: There is some indication that L-L-H was the original tone pattern for polysyllabic abstract nouns with -**tā**, i.e., there was a tonal *and* segmental opposition between masculine abstracts, which were formed with -**cī** and H-L tone, and feminine abstracts, which were formed with -**tā** and L-H tone, e.g., **gàɓuncī** (m.) = **gàɓùntā** (f.) 'immaturity, naivete' (both < **gāɓò** 'immature psn'). It is significant that the abstracts with the L-H pattern are built on basic Hausa nouns and that they reflect historically older forms of the underlying bases, e.g., **sàɓùntā** 'newness' < **sābō** (< ***sābū**) 'new'. The explanation for the H-L tone, which includes abstracts built on Arabic loanwords, is probably influence from the extremely common and fully regular H-L -**cī** abstracts. The L-H-L forms would be due to confusion between the -**tā** abstract suffix and verbal nouns of verbs containing the denominative -**TA** suffix. If this is correct, a word like **mùzantà** 'being a simpleton', for example, would come not from **mūzī** simpleton + the abstract -**tā**, but rather from the verb **mùzantà** 'behave like or be treated like a simpleton'.

3. ABUTTING CONSONANT ADJUSTMENTS

When any of the abstract suffixes is attached directly to a base with final /**m**/, this /**m**/ typically undergoes assimilation to the following /**t**/ or /**c**/. (This rule is limited to SH.) Examples:

bàjìntakà = **bàjintà** bravery < **bàjimī** bull; **hukuncī** judgment, verdict < **hùkūmà** governing body; **ƙarantà** mean-mindedness < **ƙaramī** small ; **màlàntā/mālantà** scholarship, position or work of a teacher < **mālàm(ī)** teacher; **mùtùntakà** human nature < **mùtûm** man, person; **zāluncī** oppression, tyranny < **àzzàlùmī** tyrant

In SH, the distinction between /m/ and /n/ is generally neutralized in syllable-final position with a following abutting consonant. The nasal assimilates to the following consonant and appears on the surface as [m] before labials, [n] before coronals, and [ŋ] before velars. With some abstract nouns, however, SH speakers optionally block the assimilation rule and preserve underlying lexical /m/'s (as is the norm in other dialects), e.g.,

hařamcì (≠ ****hařancì** ?) unlawfulness < **hàřâm** not lawful (religiously)
hākimcì (≠ ****hākincì** ?)   being and sitting in the manner of a district head < **hākìmī** district head
jàřùmtā = (usu. SH) **jàřùntā** bravery < **jàřùmī** brave man
ƙàzâmtā = (usu. SH) **ƙàzântā** / **ƙazantà** filth, dirtiness < **ƙàzāmī** filthy
Musulumcì = (usu. SH) **Musuluncì** Islam < **Mùsùlmī** Muslim

With some non-nasal base-final consonants, one gets total assimilation, thereby producing a geminate, e.g.,

halaccì	legitimacy, credibility, behaving honestly < **hàlâk** legal + cì)^{HL}
ibiliccì	perverseness, naughtiness < **ìbìlîs** satan + cì)^{HL}
munāfuccì	hypocrisy < **mùnāfùkī** hypocrite + cì)^{HL}
wàlìttakà	sainthood < **wàliyyì** saint + takà)^{LHL}

The surface form of some abstract nouns exhibits the application of Klingenheben's Law changing syllable-final /k/ to /u/ (see §34:1.5), e.g.,

àbòtā	friendship < **àbōkī** friend + tā)^{LH} (with */k/ > /u/ and then */ou/ > /ō/)
fataucì (base //fatak-//)	trading < **fatàkē** traders + cì)^{HL}
sàrautà	being a ruler, kingship, cf. **sarkī** chief, **sàràkī** officeholder
talaucì	poverty < **talàkà** common man + cì)^{HL}

Interestingly, syllable-final labials, which in SH commonly alter into /u/ by Klingenheben's Law, do not undergo the expected weakening in abstract nouns. Rather, they remain as obstruents, with low-level assimilation to the voicing of the following /t/ or /c/ (not reflected in orthography), e.g.,

annabtà = **annabcì** (not ***annautà** nor ***annaucì**) prophethood < **ànnabì** prophet
la'ifcì impotence < **là'ìfì** impotent man
maƙwabtà = **màƙwàbtakà** neighborliness (< unknown root)
shařiftà = **shařifcì** being a holy man < **shàřîf** / **shàřīfì** holy man descended from the Prophet

4. SPECIAL FORMS OF THE BASE

The base generally has the form of the underlying lexical item less its final vowel and tone. There are, however, some deviations. Words with the feminative suffix drop the suffix in forming the base, e.g.,

àmàrtakà condition of being or acting like a newlywed < //amar-//, cf. **amaryā** bride
budurcì virginity, being a grown-up girl < //budur-//, cf. **bùdurwā** virgin, grown-up girl

Some abstracts are built on a base related to a feminine or plural form rather than the usually unmarked masculine singular form, e.g., makantằ (base //makam-//)   blindness < màkam-nìyā (= SH màkaunìyā) blind woman (*not* **makaftằ < màkāfồ blind man)

mazancì used in 'yan mazancì fearlessness < mazā males/men, pl. of mijì male, husband

sàmàrtakằ youthfulness, boyhood < sàmàrī youths, pl. of sauràyī

yằràntakằ childishness < yârā children, pl. of yārồ

Abstracts from trisyllabic words with reduplication use a shortened base with the final syllable lopped off, e.g.,

sūsancì (*not* **sūsūsancì)	foolishness < sūsùsū foolish psn
shāshancì	stupidity, silliness, acting witlessly < shāshầshā witless fool
dillancì	trade or brokerage < dìllālì broker
sĩ̀ràntakằ = sĩ̀rantầ	thinness < sĩ̀rĩ̀rĩ̀ thin

A few nonreduplicated words also use a shortened base in forming abstracts, e.g.,

galādancì (base //galād-//)	position of a galằdīmằ a traditional title
munāfuncì (base //munāf-//)	hypocrisy < munāfùkī hypocrite

The abstract noun derived from the word mūgù 'evil' is mùgùntā 'evilness', with a short vowel in the first syllable. The abstract derived from gwaurō 'bachelor' (historically derived from *gwagwrō by the application of Klingenheben's Law) is gwagwarcì or gwàgwàrtakằ 'bachelorhood' with recovery of the historically weakened obstruent.

5. ALTERNATIVE FORMS

Many words have alternative abstract forms employing the three different suffixes {-CI}, {-TA}, and {-TAKA}. In most cases, the alternative forms are essentially equivalent variants, as best as can be determined, the preference for one variant or another being dialectically or idiolectically determined. In the following examples, the numbers after the words give the order of preference indicated by the SH speakers with whom I worked:

gùrgùntā (1) =	gùrgùntakằ (2) =	gurguncì (3)	lameness
gwagwarcì (1) =	gwàuràntakằ (2)		being wifeless
gwànintầ (1) =	gwànìntakằ (2)		expertise, skill
hūtsancì (1) =	hūtsantầ (2) =	hùtsàntakằ (3)	cantankerousness
shaiɗancì (1) =	shaiɗantầ (2)		naughtiness, being strong willed
sĩ̀ràntakằ (1) =	sĩ̀rantầ (2)		thinness
zumuncì (1) =	zùmùntā (2)		closeness, friendship

In some cases, however, the words with different suffixes have different (or partially different) meanings and usage, e.g.,

amincì   friendship, trustworthiness, durability, vs. àmìntakằ intimacy

bằɓùntā (1) = bằɓùntakằ (2) being a guest, strangeness, unusualness, vs. bāɓuncì essentially limited to a greeting to a visitor, e.g., ìnā bāɓuncì? How are things going? How are you adjusting?

bàutā   slavery, vs. bautancì slaving for someone (e.g., being badly paid in a job)

bềbàntakằ   deaf-muteness, vs. **bēbancỉ** behaving as if one were a deaf-mute
ɗànyàntakằ   being uncooked, unripe, vs. **ɗanyancỉ** impulsiveness.
hākimtằ   being a district head (partially = **hākimcỉ**), vs. **hākimcỉ** being and sitting in the manner of a district head, e.g., **zaman hākimcỉ** sitting cross-legged (*not* = ****zaman hākimtằ**)
kaɗaicỉ   loneliness, being solitary, vs. **kàɗàitakằ** oneness, uniqueness
mùtùntakằ   human nature, treating other people in a good manner, vs. **mutuncỉ** decency, humaneness; dignity, prestige, reputation. Note idiom **ci mutuncỉ** humiliate s.o. (*not* ****ci mùtùntakằ**)
wàlìttakằ (1) = **walittằ** (2)   sainthood, vs. **waliccỉ** (1) = **walittằ** (2) being a representative of a bride or bridegroom (Note: **walittằ** partakes of the two meanings 'sainthood' *and* 'being a representative'.)

2. Abstract Nouns of Sensory Quality and Their Derivatives

1. ANSQs

THERE is a set of some 60 or so nouns indicating the qualities of touch, taste, size, strength, etc., comparable to English words with *-th*, e.g., *strength*, or *-ness*, e.g., *sweetness*. These words have been termed Abstract Nouns of Sensory Quality (ANSQ) (Parsons 1955). The words belonging to this class (a) are disyllabic, (b) have a heavy first syllable, either CVC or CVV, (c) end in -ī, and (d) have H-H tone, e.g., **zurfī** 'depth', **zāfī** 'heat'. Because of the final -ī, base-final coronals appear with their corresponding palatalized consonants, e.g., **ƙuncī** 'constrictedness' (< //ƙuntī//). The bases found in the ANSQs serve as the input to other derivations, namely that of Derived Adjectives of Sensory Quality (see §2) and Derived Verbs of Sensory Quality (see §3).

ANSQs are usually described as monomorphemic words with a common canonical shape. It is more accurate, however, to view them as derived bimorphemic words composed of an abstract base having the form CVVC- or CVCC- plus a tone-integrating suffix -ı)^{H}.

The full set of ANSQs found in the dictionaries and listed by Parsons includes a number of archaic and dialectal items with which current HS speakers are unfamiliar. The following are generally accepted, well-recognized items:

bāshī unpleasant smell of sth beginning to go bad; bad breath; **baurī** astringency (e.g., of unripe fruit, tree bark); **ɗācī** bitterness (e.g., medicine, neem bark, quinine); **ɗārī** cold (dry, windy); **dādī** pleasantness; **danshī** dampness, moistness (of soil, room, garment); **fādī** breadth, width (diameter, surface area, extent); **gautsī** brittleness (e.g., of cheap, flexible plastic shoes that crack when bent); disrespectful behavior; **kaifī** sharpness (of an edge); **ƙanshī** pleasant fragrance; **ƙarfī** strength (in physique or action); **ƙarnī** rank smelling (blood, meat, fish, nursing mother); **ƙuncī** constrictedness, narrowness, anger; **ƙwārī** strength (of substance or of construction); **lāmī** tastelessness; **laushī** softness (to the feel), fineness (flour, material); **nauyī** heaviness; **santsī** slipperiness, glossiness (e.g., silk cloth); **sanyī** (damp) coldness; **sauƙī** ease, cheapness; relief (from pain or illness); **saurī** speed, haste; **taurī** hardness; **tsāmī** sourness; **tsarkī** cleanliness, holiness; **wārī** foul odor; **yauƙī** viscosity, sliminess (e.g., of cooked okra); **zāfī** heat, difficulty; **zāƙī** sweetness; well seasoned (e.g., soup); **zařnī** acrid smell of urine; **zařtsī** brackishness; **zurfī** depth

> °AN: A few ANSQs have related common nouns, e.g., **zāƙò = bàzāƙìyā** 'very sweet cassava', cf. **zāƙī** 'sweetness'; **ɗātà** 'a bitter tomato', cf. **ɗācī** 'bitterness'.
>
> ◊HN: Hausa ANSQs have striking parallels in other Chadic languages. In Guruntum (Jaggar 1991), a West Chadic language, and Migama (Jungraithmayr and Adams 1992), a more distantly related East Chadic language, one finds abstract nouns characterized by a suffix -i and all H tone, e.g., Guruntum **ání** 'heat', **gíisí** 'heaviness'; Migama **gázáanyí** 'heat', **sáɗáamí** 'acidity'.

13

There is a strange phonotactic restriction with ANSQs. For unexplainable reasons, the consonant in base-final position is never a voiced obstruent nor is it /l/. (One also does not find base-final /r̃/. This restriction, however, is not surprising given that intervocalic /r̃/ is a newly introduced phoneme in the language.)

In addition to the regular ANSQs, there are three common "pseudo-ANSQs," i.e., words that do not have H-H tone but that semantically seem to fit into the class and phonologically end in -ī and are disyllabic with a heavy initial syllable:

ɗòyī   stench;   **mūnì**   ugliness, evil;   **tsìnī**   being sharp pointed

On semantic grounds, one could also include **ɗùmī** 'warmth' and **kyâu** (< **kyāwò**) 'goodness' as pseudo-ANSQs, but phonologically one is getting further afield.

Grammatically, ANSQs are abstract nouns, i.e., they have intrinsic gender and all other normal nominal properties. They often are used, however, in constructions where in English they correspond to and translate as attributive or predicative adjectives, e.g.,

rījìyā mài zurfī	a deep well (lit. well possessing depth)
kèkè maràs ƙwārī	a (structurally) unsound bicycle (lit. bicycle lacking strength)
fùren nàn yanà dà ƙanshī	This flower is aromatic. (lit. this flower has (is with) aroma)
yā fī nì ƙarfī	He is stronger than me. (lit. he exceeds me (in) strength)
kāyā sun cikà nauyī	The loads are too heavy. (lit. the loads fill heaviness)

The usual way that ANSQs enter into simple noun modification is by means of a **mài** (pl. **màsu**) phrase, e.g., **wuƙā mài kaifī / wuƙàƙē màsu kaifī** 'a sharp knife / sharp knives' (lit. knife/knives possessing sharpness). In a few cases, however, the modification is accomplished by direct genitive linking of the form N-L-ANSQ. For reasons that are not clear, this pattern is essentially restricted to phrases where the first word is **ruwā** 'water' or **lèmō** 'lemon', e.g.,

lèmon zāƙī	orange (lit. lemon.of sweetness); **lèmon tsāmī** bitter lemon
ruwan sanyī	cold water; **ruwan zāfī** hot water; **ruwan zaȓtsī** brackish water

ANSQs also enter into direct ANSQ-L-N genitive constructions, where the semantic role of the ANSQ is to modify the following noun. This is particularly common in, but not limited to, compounds. Examples:

gāfin-nōnò	ampleness of breasts or breast milk
kaifin-bàsīr̃à	quick intellect (lit. sharpness.of-intellect)
taurin-kâi	stubbornness (lit. hardness.of-head)
ƙarfin-halī	courageousness (lit. strength.of-character)
sanyin-râi	patience, gentleness (lit. coolness.of-life)
dāɗin-bàkī	sweet talk, lobbying (lit. sweetness.of-mouth)
ɗòyin-bàkī	bad breath (lit. stench.of-mouth)

1.1. Attenuation

As is the case with simple adjectives (see §4:2.3), ANSQs undergo semantic attenuation by full reduplication accompanied by final vowel shortening on both components. (The process also applies to **ɗùmī** 'warmth'.) Examples:

ɗācī →	ɗāci-ɗāci	somewhat bitterish
kaurī →	kauri-kauri	slight thickness
ƙwārī →	ƙwāri-ƙwāri	moderate strength
tsāmī →	tsāmi-tsāmi	sourishness
wārī →	wāri-wāri	slighly odorous
ɗùmī →	ɗùmi-ɗùmi	semiwarmth

Syntactically, these attenuated forms function more or less like corresponding nonreduplicated ANSQs, although they are unlikely to occur as clause subjects, e.g.,

rījìyā mài zurfi-zurfi	a somewhat deep well
wuƙàƙē màsu kaifi-kaifi	somewhat sharp knives
fùren nàn yanà dà ƙanshi-ƙanshi	This flower is somewhat aromatic.
but not **wannàn sanyi-sanyi yā dācè dà nī	**This somewhat coolness suits me.
cf. wannàn sanyī yā dācè dà nī	This coolness suits me.

Corresponding to ANSQs are two morphologically regular derivational formations: Derived Adjectives of Sensory Quality (DASQ) and Derived Verbs of Sensory Quality (DVSQ). These derivations, illustrated below, will be described in turn.

ANSQ		DASQ		DVSQ	
fāɗī	breadth	fàffāɗā	very broad	fāɗàɗā	broaden
zāƙī	sweetness	zàzzāƙā	very sweet	zāƙàƙā	sweeten
zurfī	depth	zùzzurfā	very deep	zurfàfā	deepen

2. DERIVED ADJECTIVES OF SENSORY QUALITY (DASQ)

Of the sixty or so ANSQs (including the few pseudo-ANSQs), some twenty-five have commonly occurring corresponding adjectival forms, which I refer to as Derived Adjectives of Sensory Quality (DASQ), e.g., (ANSQ) zāfī 'heat', (DASQ) zàzzāfā / zāfàfā 'very hot (sg./pl.)'. Semantically these words are characterized by an intensive quality and do not simply indicate a neutral adjective related to the ANSQ.

Singular DASQs have a set canonical shape. They are trisyllabic with all heavy syllables and L-H-H tone. The first syllable is CVC; the second is CVC or CVV, and the final syllable is Cā. They are formed by means of a low-tone reduplicative prefix C_1VC_2- or C_1VG - *and* a suffix $-ā)^H$, both of which are added to the ANSQ base. The second consonant of the prefix usually appears as G, i.e., it forms a geminate with the following consonant, although it sometimes copies and preserves the C_2 of the base, especially in the case of nasals. Examples:

$(kàG)^L$ + kaif + $-ā)^H$ →	kàkkaifā	very sharp
$(sàn)^L$ + sants + $-ā)^H$ →	sànsantsā	very smooth, slippery
$(zàG)^L$ + zāf + $-ā)^H$ →	zàzzāfā	very hot

°AN/◊HN: Historically, the G in the CVG- prefix undoubtedly comes from a copied C_2 plus assimilation to the following abutting consonant. Evidence that the G has become morphologized is provided by the fact that the geminate now appears where it synchronically is not required, e.g., ƙàƙƙarfā 'strong (psn)', not **ƙàrƙarfā, even though the phonological sequence /rƙ / is perfectly normal and acceptable.

The singular DASQ is not overtly marked for gender, i.e., it ends in -ā whether masculine or feminine. The gender distinction is, however, reflected in the form of the linker, e.g., **zàzzāfan ruwā** (m.) 'very hot water' vs. **zàzzāfaȓ miyà̄** (f.) 'very hot soup'.

Plural DASQs, which are trisyllabic with three heavy syllables, are formed by means of a suffix -āCā)^{HLH} (where C is a copy of the base-final consonant) with an associated H-L-H tone pattern, e.g., **zāfàfā** 'very hot (pl.)'. Note that the suffix is added to the base and not to the singular DASQ with its prefixal CVC-. Examples:

gàggautsā / gautsà̄tsā	very brittle (cf. **gautsī**)
kàkkaifā / kaifà̄fā	very sharp (cf. **kaifī**)
ȓàȓȓarfā / ȓarfà̄fā	very strong (psn) (cf. **ȓarfī**)
ràrraunā / raunà̄nā	pliant, weak, frail (cf. **raunī**)
sàssantsā = sànsantsā / santsà̄tsā	very smooth, slippery (cf. **santsī**)
zàzzaȓtsā / zaȓtsà̄tsā	very salty, brackish (water) (cf. **zaȓtsī**)

Two semantically qualitative "pseudo-ANSQs" that do not contain the normal -ī)^H ANSQ suffix also form DASQs according to the regular pattern, e.g.,

kyàkkāwā / kyāwà̄wā	good, beautiful < **kyâu** (< **kyāwò**) goodness, beauty
mùmmūnā / mūnà̄nā	evil, ugly < **mūnì** ugliness

Two additional words that are not ANSQs have related DASQs, but in the plural only, e.g.,

girmà̄mā (= **màsu girmā**)	large, important (pl. of **girmā**)
sīȓàȓā (= **siȓi-siȓi**)	thin (pl. of **sìȓīȓì**)

The formation of DASQs is morphologically regular, but synchronically it is far from productive, i.e., although close to half of the ANSQs have corresponding DASQs, the other half do not. Morphologically, one can easily create DASQs from ANSQs, but only certain lexically-specific items are actually used. In marginal cases, the singular DASQ is more readily accepted than the plural form. In the absence of a DASQ, the adjectival function is handled by a phrase consisting of **mài** (pl. **màsu**) 'possessing' + an ANSQ, e.g.,

mài /màsu bāshī	unpleasant smelling, not ****bàbbāsā**
mài / màsu ɗārī	cold (of weather), not ****ɗàɗɗārā**
mài / màsu galmī	tasteless (of leftover soup), not ****gàggalmā**
mài / màsu lāmī	tasteless, insipid, not ****làllāmā**
mài / màsu saurī	quick, not ****sàssaurā**

◊HN: It would appear that there has been a relatively recent change regarding the use of DASQs. According to Parsons (1955), who drew his data from older dictionaries, most ANSQs had corresponding DASQs. Modern SH speakers, on the other hand, accept a much smaller number, and some of these only reluctantly.

Where both a DASQ and a **mài** + ANSQ construction are possible, one finds a semantic difference. First, the DASQ generally has a stronger, more intensive meaning, e.g.,

zùzzurfaȓ rījìyā   a very deep well   **rījìyā mài zurfī**   a deep well

| zàzzāƙan ràkē | very sweet sugarcane | ràkē mài zāƙī | sweet sugarcane |

Second, the meaning of the DASQ tends to be restricted to the literal meaning of the quality, whereas the **mài** + ANSQ phrase allows for wider interpretations, e.g.,

ƙàƙƙarfan sarkī   a physically strong king

sarkī mài ƙarfī   a king who is either physically strong or is politically powerful and influential

zàzzāfan gàrī   a hot town (ref. to temperature)

gàrī mài zāfī   a town that is either hot in climate or dangerous and/or difficult to live in

tsàttsarkan mùhâllī   a clean place of abode

mùhâllī mài tsarkī   a place of abode that has been cleansed or purified

3. DERIVED VERBS OF SENSORY QUALITY (DVSQ)

Of the sixty or so ANSQs, only some twenty have commonly occurring corresponding verbal forms, the Derived Verbs of Sensory Quality (DVSQ), e.g., **fādī** 'breadth', **fādàɗā** 'broaden', **fàɗaɗà** 'become broad'. As with the DASQs, the morphological formation is regular but its use is lexically specific and not freely productive. The words that allow DVSQs are mostly the same as those that form DASQs. These derived verbs of sensory quality are formed from the ANSQ base by adding a suffix -aCa(a) (the length of the final vowel being determined by grade). The resulting verbs are all trisyllabic with the first two syllables having an alternating heavy-light rhythmic pattern (cf. the similar foot structure found with the verbalizer -TA described in §79:1.2).

The verb is normally gr1 if used transitively, and gr3 if used intransitively.

°AN: Parsons (1955) and most scholars following him have analyzed the suffix as consisting of -aC- with the final vowel being provided by the grade. My view is that the final -a(a) is an inherent part of the derivational suffix and that these verbs have been assigned to grades 1 and 3 *because* of the stem-final -a rather than vice versa.

kausàsā v1	roughen	kàusasà v3	become rough (cf. **kaushī** roughness)
sauƙàƙā v1	lessen	sàuƙaƙà v3	become easier, less (e.g., price) (cf. **sauƙī** ease)
tauràrā v1	harden	tàurarà v3	become hard (cf. **taurī** hardness)
tsarkàkā v1	purify	tsàrkakà v3	become clean, pure (cf. **tsarkī** cleanliness, purity)
yausàsā v1	cause to wilt	yàusasà v3	wilt, droop (cf. **yaushī** being withered, wilted)
zāfàfā v1	heat sth	zàfafà v3	become hot (cf. **zāfī** heat)
zāƙàƙā v1	sweeten	zàƙaƙà v3	become sweet (cf. **zāƙī** sweetness)
zurfàfā v1	deepen	zùrfafà v3	become deep (cf. **zurfī** depth)

(e.g., **munà sô mù zurfàfà ilìminmù** We want to deepen our knowledge.)

°AN: The verb **sauƙàƙā** is usually cited as having an equivalent form **sawwàƙā**. These verbs are not, in fact, synonymous, but rather relate to the two different meanings of **sauƙī** (1) ease, cheapness, (2) relief (e.g., from illness). The regular DVSQ **sauƙàƙā** means 'lessen', e.g., **kà sauƙàƙā minì kāyân** 'Lower the price of the goods for me' or **wàhalàr̃ tā sàuƙaƙà** 'The trouble has lessened.' The irregular DVSQ **sawwàƙā**—if it in fact is a DVSQ—means 'relieve, or let go of', e.g., **kà sawwàƙà kāyân** 'Get rid of, let go of the goods', **kadà kà sawwàƙà matà!** 'Don't divorce her!' It is also the verb used in the formulaic phrase said to someone on hearing of a problem or an illness, namely, **Allàh yà sawwàƙā** 'God forbid!'; 'May you get well soon!' (i.e., may God relieve you of your malady).

The pseudo-ANSQ **mūnì** 'ugliness, evil' has a corresponding DVSQ, as does the abstract noun **girmā** 'importance', e.g.,

mūnànā v1   render ugly, humiliate; **mùnanà** v3   become ugly or aggravated
girmàmā v1   honor, show respect to

> °AN: The verb **ɗaukàkā** 'exalt, promote' looks on the surface as if it ought to be a DVSQ; however it is derived not from an abstract noun but from the verb **ɗaukà** 'lift up'. It is possible that **girmàmā** 'honor, respect' should be treated in the same way, i.e., its correct source may not be the noun **girmā**, as given above, but rather the verb **gìrmā** 'be older than or senior to'.

[Reference: Parsons (1955)]

3. Adjectival Past Participles

1. FORM

ALL verbs (subject to semantic reasonableness) allow the derivation of corresponding adjectival past participles (adj.pp), e.g., **dafà** 'cook', **dàfaffē** 'cooked'. The formation, which is very regular, consists of the addition of a tone-integrating suffix $\text{-aCCē})^{\text{LHH}}$ (where CC represents a doubled/geminated copy of the preceding consonant). (Note that in transcribing geminates of consonants indicated by diagraphs, only the first letter is doubled, e.g., **ssh** = [shsh].)

◊HN: In Kanakuru (Newman 1974), adjectival past participles are formed by full reduplication, e.g., **tila-tìlà toro** 'a burnt farm' (< **tìle** 'burn'), **wura-wùrà yāwè** 'fried chicken' (< **wùri** 'fry'). It seems very likely that the suffixal geminate in Hausa reflects what was originally a reduplicated structure, i.e., a current-day past participle like **dàfaffē** would have come from a construction of the form *__dàfè-d(a)fe__ (with tones uncertain).

Because of the front vowel /-ē/ in the suffix, coronal consonants undergo the normal palatalization rules. (As is generally the case, palatalization of /**d**/ is less regular than for the other consonants.) The feminine form has final **-iyā** rather than **-ē**, this being the regular feminine ending corresponding to masculine stems with final **-ē**. Plural past participles use the common plural suffix $\text{-ū})^{\text{LH}}$. Examples:

	Masculine	*Feminine*	*Plural*
filled, full	cìkakkē	cìkakkiyā	cìkàkkū
cooked	dàfaffē	dàfaffiyā	dàfàffū
rebellious	gàgàrarrē	gàgàrarriyā	gàgàràrrū
roasted	gàsasshē	gàsasshiyā	gàsàssū
written	r̃ùbùtaccē	r̃ùbùtacciyā	r̃ùbùtàttū
stolen	sàtaccē	sàtacciyā	sàtàttū
tight, drawn in	tsùkakkē	tsùkakkiyā	tsùkàkkū
torn into pieces	yàgàlgàlallē	yàgàlgàlalliyā	yàgàlgàlàllū

ΔDN: In WH, the usual feminine formation is with **-ā** rather than **-iyā**. The plural is commonly formed with $\text{-ī})^{\text{LH}}$ instead of $\text{-ū})^{\text{LH}}$. Thus, in WH, the typical adj.pp formation is represented by a series like **cìkakkē/cìkakkā/cìkàkkī** 'filled' (m./f./pl.).

As in other derivations and grade forms, the past participle of **mutù** 'die' is built on a base //**mat**-// rather than //**mut**-//:

deceased	màtaccē	màtacciyā	màtàttū

The irregular verbs **gàji** 'tire' and **tàfi** 'go' build their adj.pp's on the fuller forms //**gàjìyà**// and //**tàfìyà**// from which they are derived. As with other words with base-final /y/, these items generally form feminines with -**ā** rather than -**iyā**.

tired	**gàjìyayyē**	**gàjìyayyā**	**gàjìyàyyū**
traveled	**tàfìyayyē**	**tàfìyayyā**	**tàfìyàyyū**

Monosyllabic verbs, such as **ci** 'eat', **jā** 'pull', and **sō** 'love', form their adj.pp's on bases containing an added epenthetic /y/.

eaten	**cìyayyē**	**cìyayyiyā**	**cìyàyyū**
pulled	**jàyayyē**	**jàyayyiyā**	**jàyàyyū**

In the following examples—and there probably are a few more of the same type—the adj.pp's are built on nouns (namely, **lāfiyà** 'health' and **màsîfà** 'misfortune', both Ar. loanwords) rather than on verbs.

healthy	**làfìyayyē**	**làfìyayyā**	**làfìyàyyū**
quarrelsome	**màsìfaffē**	**màsìfaffiyā**	**màsìfàffū**

2. USE

An adjectival past participle can be used in almost any construction where a simple adjective would be allowed. It thus can function, for example, as an equational predicate, a prenominal modifier (with a linker), or a postnominal modifier, e.g.,

shìnkāfâr̃ bà̀ dàfaffiyā ba cè	The rice is not cooked.
gàgàràrrun ɗàlìbai	rebellious students
wani hòtō sàtaccē	a stolen picture

As with normal adjectives, a head noun that is understood from the context can be omitted leaving the adj.pp standing on its own, e.g.,

af lōkàcin yāƙì nē, bâ àbîn dà zā sù yi gàme dà <u>gàjìyayyū</u> dà <u>r̃àunànnū</u>

It's wartime, there is nothing that one can do about the infirmed and injured.

bùɗè bùhun mangwàr̃òn nan kà kuma rabà <u>nùnànnū</u> dà <u>r̃ùɓàɓɓū</u>

Open that mango sack and separate the ripe (ones) from the rotten (ones).

3. EXPANSION

Adjectival past participles may be expanded by adverbial or prepositional phrase modifers. (These modifiers are the same as those that can accompany their underlying verbs.) When expanded, the adj.pp necessarily follows the head noun, e.g.,

mōtōcī wànkàkkū cikì dà bâi	cars that are washed inside and out
cf. **yā wankè mōtōcī cikì dà bâi**	He washed the cars inside and out.
cf. **mōtōcī sun wànku cikì dà bâi**	The cars have been well washed inside and out.
mōtà kòmàɗaɗɗiyā dàgà gēfè	a car buckled from the side

tsìrē k̃ùnsasshē à takàr̃dā	kebab wrapped in paper
cf. k̃ùnsasshen tsìrē	wrapped kebab
tagùwā yàgaggiyā ta bāya	a shirt torn down the back
cf. yàgaggiyar̃ tagùwā	a torn shirt
yārò tàɓaɓɓē na k̃în k̃āràwā	a really crazy boy (lit. boy touched of refusing of ending)
kātì r̃ùbùtaccē dà ruwan zīnār̃è	a card written in gold
fulāwà kwàɓaɓɓiyā dà mân gyàɗā	flour that is mixed with peanut oil
mâi tàtaccē dàgà Kàdūna	petrol that is refined in (lit. from) Kaduna

4. Adjectives

1. INTRODUCTION

ADJECTIVES in Hausa are defined *syntactically* by their use as nominal modifiers or predicators and semantically by their meaning. Morphologically simple adjectives are generally indistinguishable from nouns, which is why Parsons (1963) termed them "dependent nominals". They look like nouns, form feminines and plurals essentially like nouns, and use the same genitive linker as nouns. Moreover, many words exist both as nouns and as adjectives; compare, for example, the word **tsōhō** in the phrase **wani tsōhō** 'some elder' with **wani gwamnà tsōhō** 'some old governor'; **maròwàcī** 'tightwad' and **maròwàcin àlƙālī** 'a stingy judge'; **waccàn bàfādìyā** 'that courtier (female)' and **bàfādìyaȓ màganà** 'sycophantic speech'. A few adjectives, mainly core color terms, also function as abstract nouns, e.g., **farī** 'white or whiteness', **shūɗì** 'blue or blueness', contrast **sābō** 'new', a strict adjective that does not also mean 'newness', for which one has to use the derived noun **sàbùntā**. Note that when color terms serve as abstract nouns, they take the unmarked masculine form, e.g., **rìgaȓsà tā fi farī** 'His gown (f.) is the whitest.' (lit. exceeds in whiteness [m.]), whereas when functioning as adjectives they obligatorily agree in gender with the head noun, e.g., **rìgaȓsà farā cè** 'His gown (f.) is white (f.).' Lexically, some words occur more or less equally as adjectives and as nouns, e.g., **mahàukàcī** 'crazy or madman', **wāwā** 'foolish or fool'; some normally occur as nouns but can be used adjectivally, e.g., **bēbē** 'dumb or a deaf-mute', **gwànī** 'expert or an expert'; whereas others tend to be used exclusively or almost exclusively as adjectives, e.g., **manàgàȓcī** 'reliable, good', **zàzzāfā** 'very hot'.

Adjectives can, nevertheless, be distinguished from nouns. First, there are some derivations (to be described below) whose sole function is to create adjectives, not nouns. Second, adjectives have syntactic properties that set them apart from nouns, of which two are most important. Functionally, adjectives serve as noun modifiers rather than head words, i.e., they co-occur with and depend on nouns. Moreover, gender and number in adjectives are agreement features determined by the category of the head noun (whether simple or complex) rather than being intrinsic properties, as is the case with nouns, e.g.,

[farin]$_m$ [gidā]$_m$ (lit. white.L house)	= [gidā]$_m$ [farī]$_m$ (lit. house white)	white house
[faraȓ]$_f$ [mōtà]$_f$ (lit. white.L car)	= [mōtà]$_f$ [farā]$_f$ (lit. car white)	white car
[faràren]$_{pl}$ [hūlunà]$_{pl}$ (lit. white.L caps)	= [hūlunà]$_{pl}$ [faràrē]$_{pl}$ (lit. caps white)	white caps
[tsōhon]$_m$ [jàkìn-dōkì]$_m$	old mule	
[bàhagùwaȓ]$_f$ [bōlà-gajà]$_f$	left-handed (drive) wooden passenger truck	
[sàbàbbin]$_{pl}$ [jiràgen-samà]$_{pl}$	new airplanes	

2. MORPHOLOGICAL CLASSES OF ADJECTIVES

There are approximately ten different classes of adjectives. These include (1) simple/nonderived adjectives, and (2) adjectives derived by affixation, adjectives derived by reduplication, and compound adjectives. These will all be described here briefly; fuller discussion of the derived forms is found under

22

the separate entry for that derivation. The inventory of the classes of adjectives will be followed by a description of an attenuation process.

2.1. Simple adjectives

The so-called simple adjective class consists of morphologically nonderived words. The masculine singular constitutes the unmarked form. The corresponding feminine is formed by adding a toneless suffix {-ā} to the masculine stem (not to the underlying base). The surface output is determined in accordance with general feminine formation rules described in §31:3.1), but repeated below in simplified form.

-i(i) + -ā → -ā,	e.g., ƙulumī m. (f. ƙulumā) stingy
-e(e) + -ā → -iyā,	e.g., bēbē m. (f. bēbiyā) mute
-ì(i) or -è(e) + -ā → -ìyā,	e.g., màshàhūr̃ì m. (f. màshàhūr̃ìyā) famous; shēgè m. (f. shēgìyā) bastardly
-u(u) or -o(o) + -ā → -uwā,	e.g., huntū m. (f. huntuwā) naked; dōgō m. (f. dōguwā) tall
-ù(u) or -ò(o) + -ā → -ùwā,	e.g., gurgù m. (f. gurgùwā) lame; tsòlōlò m. (f. tsòlōlùwā) lanky

Adjectives with lexical final -a(a) have the same form regardless of gender, e.g., jā nè 'It's red (m.)', jā cè 'It's red (f.)', but the prenominal linkers will be gender sensitive, e.g., jan r̃àgō 'a red ram (m.)', jar̃ gōɗìyā 'a red mare (f.)'.

Adjectives inflect for plurality using essentially the same plural formatives as nouns of the same shape (compare farī 'white', pl. far̃àrē with wurī 'place', pl. wur̃àrē). There are, however, important restrictions as to which plural formations adjectives use. For reasons that are not at all evident, adjectives do not form plurals with the -uXa suffixes (e.g., -unà, -ukà, -uwà), the -aXi suffixes (-ànnī, -àki), nor with the very productive -ōCī ending. (See chap. 56 for a full discussion of plural formation and an explanation of these plural class abbreviations.)

Included under "simple adjective" are three subclasses.

(1) First, there are a small number of basic adjectives that are generally listed as such in pedagogical grammars. (In the lists below, only irregular feminines will be given; plurals, enclosed in < >, will be indicated by a shorthand plural class code unless the formation is irregular.)

algàshī <-ai> light green; baƙī <-aCe> black; ɗanyē (f. ɗanyā) <-u> raw, unripe; dōgō <-aye> tall; farī <-aCe> white; fatsī <-aCe> light red (complexion); gàjērē (f. gàjērā = gàjērìyā = gàjērùwā) <-u> short; huntū <-aye> naked, insufficiently clothed; hūtsū <-aye> cantankerous; jā <jājàyē> red; ƙātò <-Ca> huge; ƙanƙanè (f. ƙanƙanùwā) <ƙanānà> small; ƙàramī <ƙanānà> small; ƙàzāmī <-ai> dirty, filthy; ƙulumī <-aye> stingy; kōr̃è <-aye> green; kùmāmā <-ai> feeble; kùrurrùmī <-ai> broken-necked (e.g., pot), toothless; màtsōlò <-ai> cheap, stingy; mūgù (alt. f. mugunyà) < miyàgū, mūgàyē> evil, ugly; r̃àwayà <-u> yellow; sābō <sàbàbbī, sàbbī> new; sākar̃ai (f. sākar̃ai) <sākàr̃kar̃ī> witless; shūɗī̀ <-Ca, -aye> blue; tsagèrā <-u > bad-tempered (of child), unprincipled (of adult)

°AN: The adjectives gàjērē 'short' and ƙanƙanè 'small', which end in a front vowel, are unusual in having corresponding feminine forms with final -ùwā rather than (or as an alternative to) the expected final -ìyā. I have no explanation for why this occurs.

The very common adjective bàbba (f. bàbba) 'large, important, adult' has a suppletive plural mânyā, the singular and plural forms having distinct historical origins.

◊HN: The etymology of **bàbba**, which is doubly peculiar in having (a) a short final vowel and (b) a geminate stop, is a total mystery. The word **mânyā**, on the other hand, appears to have good cognates in other West Chadic languages, where the word is not restricted to the plural, e.g., Kanakuru **manjò** 'old' (sg.); Karekare **mayuwa** (tones not noted) 'big' (sg.). Interestingly, **mânyā** can in fact be used as a singular in certain special contexts, e.g., **wānè mânyā nè** 'So-and-so is an important psn'; **mânyan dawà** 'epithet for a lion' (lit. important one in the wild); **mânyan gàrī** 'term of address for a village head or other titleholder'. Abraham (1962: 52) refers to such examples as "plurals of majesty"; but they may reflect an earlier more general singular usage.

(2) Second, one has a miscellaneous open-ended list of noun/adjective items, including many Arabic loanwords, which have dual class membership. These words are usually glossed in dictionaries and grammars with a nominal reading but they also occur commonly as adjectives; compare **wani gurgù dà mukà sanì** 'a certain lame person whom we know' with **kadà kà sàyi gurgùn ràkumī** 'Don't buy a lame camel!'

àlmùbazzàrī <-ai> extravagant, spendthrift; **àshàr̄àr̄ù** (f. **àshàr̄àr̄ìyā**) <-ai> foul-mouthed, immodest (psn); **bēbē** <-aye> dumb, deaf-mute; **bàr̄ō** <**bàr̄ī**> strange(r), foreign(er); **bùtùlu** (f. **bùtùlu**) <-ai> ungrateful, an ingrate; **fàsìr̄ī** <-ai> profligate, immoral (psn); **gādìr̄ī** <-ai> deceitful, treacherous (psn); **guntū** <-aye> stub(by); **gurgù** <a-u> lame, a cripple; **gwāmè** <-aye> knock-kneed (psn); **gwar̄zō** <-aye> dauntless, energetic (psn); **jāhìlī** <-ai> ignorant, illiterate (psn); **kàmìlī** <-ai> gentle, well behaved (psn); **là'ìfī** <-ai> impotent (psn); **màkìr̄ī** <-ai> cunning, wily (psn); **mùnāfùkī** <-ai> hypocritical, hypocrite; **shēgè** <-u> bastard(ly), rascally; **tsōhō** <**tsòfàffī, tsòffī**> old (psn); **wāwā** (f. **wāwā**) <-aye> fool(ish)

> °AN: Some (esp. non-SH) speakers use **wāwā** (or **wāwiyā**) as a feminine adjective but **wāwanyà** as a derived feminine noun, e.g., **ita cè wāwar̄ sàraunìyā** 'She is a foolish queen', but **ita cè wāwanyà** 'She is a fool.'

(3) Third, there are a number of trisyllabic noun/adjective items with a frozen (cv-CVCV)^{LHL} shape (where cv-CVCV indicates that the last two syllables are segmentally identical). The initial vowel is occasionally short; the other two vowels are always long. This morphological class also includes many nouns that do not function adjectivally (see §62:3.2.1). In addition, there are a few fully reduplicated H-L-H words with all identical syllables. If these words form plurals—not all do—they employ the <-ai> suffix. Examples:

(a) **dàr̄īr̄ì** stupid (e.g., **dàr̄īr̄an ɗàlìbai** stupid students); **dòsōsò** ugly looking (of psn's face); **dùkūkù** glumly hesitant (e.g., **dùkūkùwar̄ màkaunìyā** a glum blind woman); **dùzūzù** unkempt (esp. hair); **gàɓūɓù** senseless (psn); **kwàtsātsà** tactless; **làɓūɓù** flabby, soggy; **sàrūrù** nincompoop, silly; **sìr̄īr̄ì** thin, slender; **tsòlōlò** tall and skinny; **zòlōlò** tall with a long neck (esp. a camel) (e.g., **zòlōlòn ràkumī** a tall camel)
(b) **shāshàshā** foolish, stupid (e.g., **wata shāshàshar̄ tsōhuwā** a foolish old woman); **sūsùsū** (f. **sūsùsū**) witless

2.2. Derived adjectives
2.2.1. Agential adjectives
The affix **ma-**...-**ī** with a set H-(L)-L-H tone pattern attaches to verb bases to form agentive nouns (see §7:1), e.g., **manòmī** m. 'farmer' (< //**nōm**-// 'to farm'). Many words of this form, especially those based on intransitive verbs, also (or primarily) function as adjectives, e.g.,

madàidàicī adj. average, medium-sized; matsìyằcī adj. poor, destitute

mahàukàcī adj. crazy, e.g., **wani mahàukàcin dìrēbà** a crazy driver; **mahàukàtan karnukằ** mad dogs, cf. **wannàn mahàukàcī** this madman

2.2.2. Ethnonymic adjectives

Ethnonyms formed with the singular prefix **bà-** (see chap. **24**) are most commonly used as nouns, e.g., **Bàhaushè** 'Hausa man', **bàdūkù** 'leather worker'. They can, however, also be used adjectivally, sometimes with the general ethnonymic meaning, more often, however, with a more specialized or figurative meaning, e.g.,

bàkanùwā adj.　　Kano-style (X), e.g., **bàkanùwar kwaryā** Kano-type calabash (n. = Kano woman)

bàfādìyā adj.　　sycophantic, e.g., **bàfādìyar màganà** sycophantic language

cf. **wata bàfādìyā**　a woman courtier

bàfàrishè adj.　　Persian, e.g., **bàfàrishèn bàrgō** Persian blanket (n. = a Persian)

2.2.3. Adjectival past participles

Adjectival past participles are productively formed from verbs by means of a tone-integrating suffix -aCCē)^{LHH} (where CC represents a doubled/geminated copy of the preceding consonant) (see chap. **3**). The feminine counterpart has final -**iyā** rather than -**ē**. Plural past participles use the normal -**ū**)^{LH} plural suffix. Examples:

dàfaffē / dàfaffiyā / dàfàffū　　　　　　　cooked < **dafà** cook

rùbùtaccē / rùbùtacciyā / rùbùtàttū　　　written < **rubùtā** write

yàgàlgàlallē / yàgàlgàlalliyā / yàgàlgàlàllū　torn into pieces < **yagalgàlā** tear into pieces

2.2.4. Derived adjectives of sensory quality

Corresponding to the Abstract Nouns of Sensory Quality is a set of trisyllabic intensive adjectives (DASQs) (see **2**:2), e.g., **zāfī** 'heat' (ANSQ), **zàzzāfā** 'very hot' (DASQ). The singular is formed by means of a reduplicative (CVC-)^L prefix plus a suffix -ā)^H. The plural makes use of a suffix -**āCā**)^{HLH}, which is added to the base rather than to the singular stem. Examples:

fàrfāɗā = fàffāɗā / fāɗàɗā　　　　very broad, wide (cf. **fāɗī** width)

kàkkaifā / kaifàfā　　　　　　very sharp (cf. **kaifī** sharpness)

mùmmūnā / mūnànā　　　　　evil, ugly (cf. **mūnì** ugliness)

2.2.5. Augmentative adjectives

The term *augmentative adjective* is used to describe a good-sized class of phonaesthetic, expressive adjectives where the notion of "very" or "excessively" is an integral part of the meaning of the word, e.g., **sundumēmè** (m.) 'overly big and swollen'; **santalēlìyā** (f.) 'extremely tall and slender'. Unlike agentives and ethnonyms, which occur both as independent nouns and as adjectives, all words of this class function exclusively as adjectives.

There are three subclasses of augmentative adjectives: those ending in a suffix -**ēCē**)^{HL}; those ending in -**ī**)^H, and those ending in -**ī** with an L-H-L-H reduplicated structure. (The corresponding feminine and plural forms are described in §11:1.) Examples:

tankwalēlè / tankwalēlìyā / tankwalā-tànkwàlà　large and round (m./f./pl.)

bullukī (= bullukēkè) / bullukā / bullukā-bùllùkà　huge (m./f./pl.)

bùgùzunzùmī / bùgùzunzùmā / bùgùzùnzùmai　big, fat, untidy, ungainly (m./f./pl.)

Being adjectives, augmentatives naturally occur as prenominal modifiers with a linker, e.g., **suntuɓeɓèn yārò** 'an oaf of a boy', **santalēlìyař yārinyà** 'a shapely girl'. They also occur postnominally. In this position, they are often extended by a **dà** 'with' plus pronoun phrase, e.g., **yārinyà santalēlìyā (dà ita)** (lit. girl shapely with her).

2.2.6. Diminutive adjectives

The term *diminutive adjective* is used for a small set of phonaesthetic reduplicated words emphasizing smallness in size, shape, or space (see §11:3). They are commonly preceded by the diminutive marker **ɗan/'yař/'yan** (m./f./pl.). Like augmentative adjectives, they can also be extended by a **dà** 'with' plus pronoun phrase when occurring postnominally, e.g.,

(**ɗan**) **mìtsītsìn gōřò**	a tiny kolanut
yārinyà ('yař) sìřīřìyā da ita	a slender girl
wasu yârā ("yan) mitsī-mitsī dà sū	some tiny boys

2.2.7. H-L reduplicated ideophonic adjectives

These is a good-sized class of H-L ideophonic adjectives that describe the color, texture, smell, look, or condition of their referents (see §35:1.2.11), e.g., **idànū ƙwalā-ƙwàlà** 'protruding or bulging eyes'. Many, but not all, of these adjectives are inherently plural. Examples:

batsō-bàtsò pl. poorly made, ugly looking; **buzū-bùzù** long, unkempt (of hair); **darā-dàrà** bold and beautiful (of eyes or writing); **falā-fàlà** broad and thin (e.g., leaves, paper, ears); **tsalā-tsàlà** pl. long and slender (esp. legs)

As with other reduplicated or complex adjectives, these adjectives only occur attributively in post-nominal position, where they are commonly extended by **dà** plus a pronoun. They may also be used in predicate adjective position and as the object of the verb **yi** 'do'. Examples:

wasu ƙuràjē ɓalō-ɓàlò dà sū sun fītō minì à kā	Some large boils appeared on my head.
wasu yârā sumū-sùmù sun wucè	Some despondent-looking chaps passed by.
hancìn Audù horō-hòrò	Audu's nostrils are very wide.
idònsà yā yi hulū-hùlù don kūkā	His eyelids got swollen from crying.
an bā nì gōřò ruƙū-rùƙù à wajen ɗaurìn auren Bàlā	
They gave me some large, round kolanuts at Bala's wedding.	

2.2.8. LL-HL reduplicated adjectives

Hausa has a considerable number of reduplicated quadrisyllabic nouns with final -a(a) and LL-HL tone (see §62:3.4), e.g., **àyà-ayà** 'wild tiger-nut grass and fruit', **zàngà-zangà** 'political demonstration'. A few words of this pattern function adjectivally, normally as postnominal modifiers, e.g.,

Lādì tā bā nì wata masàřā rùwà-ruwà	Ladi gave me soft (juicy) corn.
kâi, wà zâi àuri màzà-mazàř màce?	Who would marry a masculine woman?
aikì rànà-rānà bā yā daɗèwā	Late-morning work doesn't last.
yā yi hàntà-hantàř màganà	He has made a nasal utterance.

2.2.9. Reduplicated adjectives ('X-like')

Adjectives are formed from common nouns by full reduplication of the underlying noun, preserving the original tone. This is accompanied by shortening of the final vowel of both parts, e.g., **gishirī** 'salt' ⇒

gishiri-gishiri 'salty'. The resulting adjectives, which correspond to such English adjectives as 'powdery' or 'handlike', indicate a quality or characteristic of the source nouns. The formation appears to be extremely productive. Although the nouns from which the adjectives are derived are variably masculine or feminine (even plural), the derivatives themselves are invariant and do not have inflected feminine or plural forms.

bùhū sack, **bùhu-bùhu** sacklike (object); **gàrī** flour, **gàri-gàri** powdery; **gishirī** salt, **gishiri-gishiri** salty; **gùdàjī** lumps, **gùdàji-gùdàji** lumpy, in little chunks; **hannū** hand, **hannu-hannu** handlike (structure, shape); **hatsī** grain, **hatsi-hatsi** with specks (such as on a TV screen); **hòtō** picture, **hòto-hòto** picturelike; **kùřtū** small gourd, **kùřtu-kùřtu** gourdlike; **ƙōfà** door, **ƙōfà-ƙōfà** doorlike opening; **ƙuřjī** boil, **ƙuřji-ƙuřji** boillike swelling; **ruwā** water, **ruwa-ruwa** watery; **shirū** silence, **shiru-shiru** taciturn; **tsàkī** coarse part of flour, **tsàki-tsàki** coarse; **tsakuwà** stone, **tsakuwà-tsakuwà** stony (i.e., mixed with little stones); **yàshī** sand, **yàshi-yàshi** sandy; **wākē** black-eyed peas, **wāke-wāke** speckled black and white

Syntactically these words function just like other reduplicated adjectives, i.e., they can serve as predicate adjectives or as attributive (postnominal) modifiers, e.g.,

tsuntsàyen nàn wāke-wāke nè	These birds are speckled.
àbinci ruwa-ruwa	watery food
ƙasā yàshi-yàshi	sandy soil

°AN: Some speakers allow the use of the particle **mài** between the noun and the adjective, i.e., **ƙasā mài yàshi-yàshi = ƙasā yàshi-yàshi** 'sandy soil', i.e., they treat the derived forms like an attenuated ANSQ. This, however, is a less preferred alternative and one that is rejected as ungrammatical by other speakers.

Color terms derived by this derivation may have an additional '-ish' connotation, which relates to the attenuation function of this same reduplicative process (see §2.3 below), e.g.,

ɗòrawà locust bean tree, **ɗòrawà-ɗòrawà** yellowish; **ƙasā** earth, **ƙasa-ƙasa** brownish; **màkubà** mahogany tree, **màkubà-màkubà** dark brownish color; **tòkā** ashes, **tòka-tòka** gray (ash colored)

2.3. Attenuated reduplicated adjectives ('-ish')

When applied to adjectives (or sensory-quality nouns), the process of full reduplication with accompanying vowel shortening produces forms that are semantically "attenuated", i.e., have the quality of the simple adjective but to a lesser extent, e.g., **tsanwā** 'green', **tsanwa-tsanwa** 'light green, greenish'. The word **jā** 'red' uses a reduplicated base as the input to this derivation, e.g., **jā** (base //jājā//) ⟹ **jāja-jāja** 'reddish'. (A few words appear only in this form without an extant nonreduplicated stem, e.g., **řōɗî-řōɗî** 'spotty, speckled'.) The attenuation is often further (redundantly) indicated by use of the diminutive **ɗan/'yař/'yan** 'wee, small', e.g.,

baƙī black, (**ɗan**) **baƙi-baƙi** faded black		**dōgō** tall, (**ɗan**) **dōgo-dōgo** medium height
farī white, (**ɗan**) **fari-fari** off-white		**gàjērē** short, (**ɗan**) **gàjēre-gàjēre** a bit short
shūɗî dark blue, **shūɗî-shūɗî** light blue, bluish		**yalò** yellow, **yalò-yalò** yellowish

°AN: The productivity of the attenuation process is illustrated by its use with the recent English loanword **yalò** 'yellow'.

Corresponding feminine and plural adjectives also undergo the process, e.g.,

baƙā f. black, **baƙa-baƙa** blackish, gray   dōguwā f. tall, **dōguwa-dōguwa** somewhat tall
farārē pl. white, **farâre-farâre** off-white   shūɗâyē pl. blue, **shūɗâye-shūɗâye** bluish

> °AN: Note that in a form like **dōguwa-dōguwa** 'somewhat tall' (f.) (< **dōgō** 'tall') the feminine
> inflection precedes the attenuation derivation, and similarly, in **farâre-farâre** 'off-white' (pl.), the
> inflection has to precede the derivation.

The reduplicated form **mânya-mânya** 'large (things), important (people)' (< **mânyā** 'large (pl.)', does
not usually have the attenuated meaning but it may, e.g.,

bà ni waɗànnân 'yan mânya-mânya, kà ajìyè 'yan ƙanānàn
    Give me these largish ones and put aside the little ones.

Attenuated forms are most often encountered with simple, basic adjectives. The process can, however,
apply to the range of derived adjectives, including their inflected feminine and plural forms, e.g.,

dàfaffē / dàfaffe-dàfaffe   somewhat cooked (adj.pp)
tsàgaggē / tsàgagge-tsàgagge   somewhat cracked (adj.pp)
tsàttsāmā / tsàttsāma-tsàttsāma   somewhat sour (DASQ)
kàkkaurā / kàkkaura-kàkkaura   somewhat stout (DASQ)
mahàukàcī / mahàukàci-mahàukàci   slightly crazy (**ma**-agent)
malàlâtā / malàlâta-malàlâta   lazyish (pl.) (**ma**-agent)
bàhagò / bàhagò-bàhagò   semi-left-handed (ethnonym)

The attenuated adjectives generally occur in postnominal position, e.g.,

mōtà jāja-jāja   reddish car
sōjà ɗan dōgo-dōgo   medium-height soldier
dōyà bùsasshiya-bùsasshiya   somewhat-dried yams
kāyā wànkàkku-wànkàkku   slightly washed clothes
yârā malàlâta-malàlâta   lazyish children
wata màcè mahaukacìya-mahaukacìya   slightly crazy woman
wata màcè bàgidājìya-bàgidājìya   somewhat naive, dim-witted girl

Some attenuated adjectives can occur prenominally (with the linker), but this option seems to be limited
to basic, phonologically short masculine forms, e.g., **wani fari-farin kèkè** 'some off-white bicycle' (=
wani kèkè fari-fari), but not ****mahaukacìya-mahaukacìyar màcè** 'a slightly mad woman'.

2.3.1. ANSQs
Because of their semantic attributes, abstract nouns of sensory quality (ANSQs) can also undergo this
attenuation derivation even though it normally applies only to adjectives. This is also true in the case of
a few other semantically appropriate words that are not ANSQs in the strict morphological sense, e.g.,

ɗācī bitterness / **ɗāci-ɗāci** somewhat bitter   **kaurī** thickness / **kauri-kauri** slightly thick
tsāmī sourness / **tsāmi-tsāmi** sourish   **ɗùmī** warmth / **ɗùmi-ɗùmi** semiwarm

The resulting attenuated forms are grammatically still nouns and thus function syntactically as nouns and not as adjectives. For example, they form modifying adjectival phrases with the particle **mài/màsu** rather than immediately following the noun, and they express semantic predication by means of HAVE sentences. Moreover, they do not inflect for number or gender.

māgànī mài ɗáci-ɗáci	somewhat bitter-tasting medicine
cf. **bàbûr̃ shūɗì-shūɗì**	a light blue motorcycle (with the attenuated adjective)
kàtīfà tanà dà laushi-laushi	The mattress is somewhat soft.
cf. **kàtīfàr̃ tsàgaggiya-tsàgaggiya cè**	The mattress is ripped. (with the attenuated adjective)
ɗākunà màsu wāri-wāri	somewhat smelly rooms

2.4. Compound adjectives
There are only some twenty or so compound adjectives (see §16:1.2). About half of these are nonbasic color terms having the structure **ruwan** X 'color-of-X', e.g.,

ruwan-hōdà pink (< **hōdà** face powder); **ruwan-ƙasā** brown (< **ƙasā** earth); **ruwan-tòkā** gray (< **tòkā** ashes)

These adjectives can undergo the attenuation process by reduplicating the second component and subjecting it to the vowel-shortening rule, e.g.,

ruwan-hōdà-hōdà pinkish; **ruwan-ƙasa-ƙasa** brownish; **ruwan-tòka-tòka** grayish

The remaining compound adjectives represent a mixed assortment of formations. Here are some examples:

awòn-igiyà extremely tall/long (lit. measure.L rope); **ci-kar̃-kà-mutù** tasteless (lit. eat don't you die); **dūkàn-iskà** mentally ill (lit. beating.L spirits); **gàgàrà-kòyo** mysterious, very hard to learn (lit. defy learning); **gàmà-gàri** common, ordinary (lit. combine town); **shā-kà-tàfi** stupid (lit. drink you go)

Compound adjectives do not inflect for number or gender. When used attributively, they occur only postnominally.

mōtōcī ruwan-azùr̃fā	silver-metallic-colored cars	**yādì ruwan-hōdà-hōdà**	pinkish cloth
wàndō ɗinkìn-kèke	machine-sewn trousers	**wani mùtûm shā-kà-tàfi**	some foolish man

3. SYNTAX

3.1. Predicate adjectives
Adjectives can function predicatively or attributively. As predicates, adjectives function as the Y in equational or identificational sentences of the form (X) Y STAB (see chap. 23). The Y obligatorily agrees in gender and number with the expressed or understood X subject, e.g.,

[yāròn]$_X$ [dōgō]$_Y$ nè	The boy is tall.
[gidàjen nàn]$_X$ [sàbàbbī]$_Y$ nè	These houses are new.
[kàrensà]$_X$ [mafàɗàcī]$_Y$ nè?	Is his dog vicious?
[wuƙātā]$_X$ [kàkkaifā]$_Y$ cè	My knife is very sharp.

[rìgâr̃ dà na sàyā]χ [rìnanniyā]γ cè   The gown that I bought was dyed.
[farā]γ cè   It's white. (referring to some feminine object)
tsàgaggē]γ nè   It's cracked . (referring to some masculine object)

3.2. Attributive adjectives
3.2.1. Alternative word orders

Simple, single-word adjectives occur both before and after the head noun. Prenominal adjectives obligatorily connect to the head by means of a genitive linker (-n or -r̃, depending on number and gender); postnominal adjectives are immediately juxtaposed to the head noun, e.g.,

farin gidā (lit. white.L house) =	gidā far̃ī (lit. house white)	white house
r̃ànjàmammen fur̃sùnà =	fur̃sùnà r̃ànjàmammē	thin prisoner
tsàttsāmar̃ furā =	furā tsàttsāmā	sour *fura*
mākēkèn dūtsè =	dūtsè mākēkè	huge stone
rùsàssun ɗākunà =	ɗākunà rùsàssū	razed rooms

Generally speaking, noun phrases with the two orders have the same essential meanings, although there are a few exceptions, e.g., **gwamnà tsōhō** 'old governor' vs. **tsōhon gwamnà** 'former governor (or old governor)'. Differences do exist, however, but at the pragmatic/stylistic level. Both orders are normal and quite common, although it is probably true that in the everyday language the prenominal adjective is the less marked of the two, i.e., postnominal simple adjectives tend to add a certain degree of emphasis or contrastiveness. Significantly, in compounds consisting of an adjective and a noun, the adjective always occurs prenominally, e.g., **bar̃in-cikì** 'sadness; jealousy' (lit. black.L belly), *not* ****cikì-bar̃ī**.

◊HN: The standard word-order pattern in Chadic is noun + adjective, which presumably was the original order in Hausa as well. Prenominal adjectives in such phrases as **farin gidā** 'white house' probably began as N of N constructions meaning 'whiteness of house'.

A noun may be modified by more than one adjective. (Three seems to be the maximum allowed without the phrase becoming excessively clumsy.) Each prenominal adjective will contain a linker, whereas the postnominal adjectives will simply be strung one after the other. In principle, multiple adjectives can occur both before and after the head noun, although multiple prenominal adjectives are dispreferred, e.g.,

bàbban r̃àr̃r̃arfan àlfadàr̃ī = àlfadàr̃ī bàbbā r̃àr̃r̃arfā   big strong mule
zungurēr̃ìyar̃ sābuwar̃ farar̃ mōtà = mōtà zungurēr̃ìyā sābuwā farā   long new white car

It is possible, and indeed quite common, for a noun to be modified by both pre- and postnominal adjectives. This is a normal strategy to avoid too many adjectives in front of the noun, e.g.,

gàjēr̃ìyar̃ yārinyà kyàkkyāwā   a short, good-looking girl (lit. short.L girl pretty)
mafàɗàcin kàrē bar̃ī   a vicious black dog (lit. vicious.L dog black)

3.2.2. Strictly postnominal adjectives

Unlike phonologically short one-word adjectives, which can occur either before or after a head noun, "heavy" adjectives are restricted to postnominal position. These heavy adjectives include fully reduplicated adjectives, compound adjectives, adjectives that are themselves modified, and adjectival phrases formed with MAI 'having' or related items (see chap. **45**). Examples:

mātā santalā-sàntàlà thin, shapely women; **mōtå jāja-jāja** reddish car; **ƙafâfū tsalā-tsàlà** longand skinny legs

rìgā ruwan-ɗòrawà yellow gown; **tāgùwā ɗinkìn-kèke** machine-sewn shirt; **littāfī gàgàrà-kòyo** mysterious, hard-to-learn book

tsìrē ƙùnsasshē à takàřdā kebab wrapped in paper, cf. **ƙùnsasshen tsìrē** wrapped kebab

tagùwā yàgaggiyā ta bāya shirt ripped in the back, cf. **yàgaggiyař tagùwā** torn shirt

kāyā mài nauyī heavy loads (lit. loads having heaviness)

hanyà marař kyâu a bad road (lit. road lacking goodness)

> °AN: With reduplicated ideophonic adjectives such as **tsalā-tsàlà**, prenominal modification i s viewed as possible, but less preferred, e.g., **??tsalā-tsàlàn ƙafâfū** 'long and slender legs'.
>
> ◊HN: The word **dàbam** 'different', which as a modifier occurs only postnominally, e.g., **hanyà dàbam** 'different road', appears on the surface to be a simple one-word adjective. However, it differs from true adjectives not only in its word-order syntax, but also in its lack of a corresponding feminine form. (It is also unusual in forming its "plural" by repetition, e.g., **ƙasàshē dàbam dàbam** 'different countries'.) The explanation is that historically **dàbam** derives from a prepositional *phrase* consisting of **dà** 'with' + ***bam** 'difference' (now usually **bambam**), e.g., **yā shā bambam dà sū** 'He differs from them (lit. he drinks difference with them).

Adjectives in postnominal position also permit the insertion of conjunctions or modal particles, which is not the case with prenominal adjectives, e.g.,

wani mùtûm farī ƙàtò <u>àmmā</u> gàjērē   a big, light-skinned man but short

rìgā ruwan-hōdà <u>kuma</u> sābuwā ta sìlikī   a pink gown also new of silk

3.2.3. Gender/number agreement with conjoined NPs
Conjoined nouns can each be modified by an adjective, e.g.,

baƙin kàrē dà farař kyânwā	black dog and white cat
baƙin kàrē dà baƙař kyânwā	black dog and black cat
mahàukàcin sarkī dà mafàɗàcin àlƙālī	crazy chief and a ferocious judge
dōguwař sàraunìyā dà gàjērìyař jàkādìyā	tall queen and short emissary
bàhagòn kèkè dà bàhagùwař mōtà	left-handed bike and a left-handed car
rìkìřkìtaccen dōkì dà rìkìřkìtaccen jàkī	confused horse and confused donkey
ɗanyen lèmō dà ɗanyen dabīnò	unripe orange and unripe date
tsōhuwař būtà dà tsōhon gwangwanī	old kettle and old can
tsōhuwař būtà dà tsōhuwař tukunyā	old kettle and old pot
tsàgaggiyař rìgā da tsàgaggiyař tagùwā	ripped gown and ripped shirt
ƙarfàfan sàmàrī dà ƙarfàfan 'yammātā	strong boys and strong girls
faràren mōtōcī dà faràren jiràgē	white cars and white planes

If the two nouns are modified by the same adjective(s) *and* the words have the same gender/number, then it is possible to delete the second occurrence of the adjective(s) and have the adjectival meaning spread over the two words. This deletion seems to apply most naturally when the two nouns belong to the same semantic class, e.g.,

rìkìřkìtaccen dōkì dà ~~rìkìřkìtaccen~~ jàkī	confused horse and donkey
ɗanyen lèmō dà ~~ɗanyen~~ dabīnò	unripe orange and date

tsōhuwař būtằ dà ~~tsōhuwař~~ tukunyā   old kettle and pot
tsàgaggiyař rìgā da ~~tsàgaggiyař~~ tagùwā   ripped gown and shirt
ƙarfàfan sàmàrī dà ~~ƙarfàfan~~ 'yammātā   strong boys and girls
farāren mōtōcī dà ~~farāren~~ jirầgē   white cars and planes
tsōhon farin zanī dà ~~tsōhon farin~~ mayāfī   old white wrapper and (old white) shawl
làlàtaccen tàɓaɓɓen sōjà dà ~~làlàtaccen tàɓaɓɓen~~ ɗan sàndā
       a perverted mad soldier and (perverted mad) policeman

The above sentences are all ambiguous because they allow the interpretation with the adjective modifying the first noun only, e.g., **tsàgaggiyař rìgā da tagùwā** could also mean 'a ripped gown and (a nonripped) shirt' (a reading preferred by some speakers).

The ellipsis of the second adjective does not work if the words do not match in gender, e.g., **baƙin kàrē dà kyânwā** would normally be understood to mean 'a black dog and a (color unspecified) cat', and **tsōhuwař būtằ dà gwangwanī** would be understood as 'old kettle and (age unspecified) can'.

The extension of the adjectival meaning works only from left to right. If the adjective precedes the second noun, the modification does not apply to the first noun, e.g., **būtằ dà tsōhuwař tukunyā** can only mean 'a kettle and an old pot', and **lèmō dà ɗanyen dabīnồ** can only mean 'oranges (unspecified for ripeness) and unripe dates'.

Instead of modifying conjoined nouns individually, the adjective can modify the coordinate structure as such, in which case it takes plural concord, e.g.,

[mafàɗàtan]$_{pl}$ [[mijì]$_{m}$ dà [màtā]$_{f}$]$_{pl}$ quarrelsome husband and wife (couple)
waɗànnân [[kàzā]$_{f}$ dà [zàkarằ]$_{m}$]$_{pl}$ [matsòràtā]$_{pl}$ this (lit. these) frightened hen and rooster
[kyāwàwan]$_{pl}$ [[kèke]$_{m}$ dà [bàbûř]$_{m}$]$_{pl}$ attractive bicycle and motorbike
[hàzìƙan]$_{pl}$ [[ɗālìbī]$_{m}$ dà [ɗālìbā]$_{f}$]$_{pl}$ outstanding male student and female student

3.2.4. Headless adjectives

Hausa does not have an overt pronominal 'one' to accompany adjectives; thus if the head **bàbûř** is deleted from the phrase **bàbûř sābō** (or **sābon bàbûř**) 'new motorcycle', the surface result is simply **sābō** 'new (one)'. Similarly **ƙaramař àkuyằ** 'small goat' becomes **ƙaramā** 'small (one)', and **miyằgun 'yan sìyāsà** 'evil politicians' becomes **miyằgū** 'evil (ones)'.

> °AN: In NPs with the structure [Ø adj]$_{NP}$ the adjective is the only element that appears on the surface and thus it has to serve as the host/head for definite articles and such, e.g., Ø **ƙanānà-n** 'the small (ones)'. It is thus understandable that previous scholars would have mistakenly interpreted headless adjectives like **sābō** and **ƙanānà** as nouns.

Headless adjectives, which are extremely common in the language, occur either because of syntactically favored ellipsis or because the head is understood from the context. Notice that because these words are adjectives (and not nouns), the gender is determined by the controlling noun (even if not expressed) rather than being an intrinsic property of the adjective itself. Examples:

Mūsā yā sayō baƙar mōtằ, Sāni kuma farā
       Musa bought a black car and Sani a white one. (f. **farā** refers to **mōtằ**)
kanà sôn ƙwai? I, sai dai sòyayyē
       Do you want an egg? Yes, but fried. (m. **sòyayyē** refers to **ƙwai**)
gà àlāmà dōguwā zā tà fāɗì
       There's indication that the tall one will fail. (f. **dōguwā** refers to an understood female)

Ƙanānàn sun fi saurā tsàdā
> The small ones are the most expensive. (pl. **Ƙanānà** refers to an understood group of things)

3.3. The "quality-with-pronoun" construction

Adjectives (and ideophones) can be strengthened by using them in a postnominal construction of the form X **dà** pn, where X is the adjective (or ideophone), **dà** is the preposition 'with' and pn is an independent pronoun coreferential with the head noun. Examples:

wata yārinyà dōguwā dà ita	a very tall girl (lit. some girl tall with her)
cf. **wata yārinyà dōguwā = wata dōguwaȓ yārinyà**	a tall girl
sun bā nì ruwā sàssanyā dà shī	They gave me some cool water.
gà shìnkāfā dàfaffiyā dà ita	Here's some well-cooked rice.

Although this construction can in principle be used with all adjectives, it is particularly common with semantically marked adjectives such as augmentatives, diminutives, or ideophonic adjectives. When the construction is used with regular adjectives, it tends to emphasize a contrast and/or indicate above-average attributes. For example, in **yārinyà kyàkkyāwā dà ita** 'a beautiful girl', the construction serves to contrast **kyàkkyāwā** 'beautiful' with the implied **mùmmūnā** 'ugly'. Examples:

ɓēȓā nè muȓgujèjè dà shī	a really big mouse
'yammātā santalā-sàntàlà dà sū	truly shapely girls
zanì ɗan ɗìgìgì dà shī	a skimpy, shrunk cloth
rìgā cè figil dà ita	a too-small gown
wasu yârā mitsī-mitsī dà sū	some wee little boys
mùtûm digìȓgìȓ dà shī (sai kà cê kwàɗō)	a shrimp of a man (such that you would say a frog)
wasu ƙuràjē ɓalō-ɓàlò dà sū	some large boils
ƙafàfū tsalā-tsàlà dà sū	fine, thin legs
wani sarkī tsōfai-tsòfài dà shī	a very old chief

4. COMPARATIVE/SUPERLATIVE

Comparatives and superlatives of adjectives and nouns of quality are expressed syntactically rather than morphologically. These are described in chap. **14**. Examples:

Mūsā yā fi Sulè tsawō	Musa is taller than Sule. (lit. Musa exceeds Sule (in) height)
cf. **Mūsā dōgō nè**	Musa is tall.
yārò mafì ƙarfī	the strongest boy (lit. boy exceeding strength)
cf. **yārò mài ƙarfī**	a strong boy (lit. boy possessing strength)

[References: Korshunova and Uspensky (1993); Parsons (1963)]

5. Adverbs

1. INTRODUCTION

ADVERBS and adverbial phrases (of time, place, manner, etc.) have a number of different functions. To begin with, they serve as predicates of nonverbal locative and stative sentences, e.g., **ɗākìnā yanà dab dà nātà** 'My room is right next to hers'; **fàɗàwā sunà zàune kusa dà sarkī** 'The councilors are seated close to the chief'. They appear as locative goals of motion verbs, e.g., **mù tàfi cân** 'Let's go there!' They serve as modifiers in phrases and compounds having the structure N of adverb, e.g., **shùgàban ɗàzu** 'the leader of the moment' (lit. leader.of now); **kīshìn-zūci** 'ambition' (lit. jealousy.of in heart) (cf. the noun **zūcìyā** 'heart'). In addition, they function readily as modifiers of predicates, in which case they typically occur towards the end of the sentence after the core arguments in the VP or nonverbal predicate.

inà sôntà ainùn	I love her very much.
mùtumìn yanà dà kuɗī ƙwařai dà gàske	This man is really and truly rich.
tanà aikì sànnu sànnu	She is working slowly and carefully.
sun dāwō jiyà dà yâmma	They returned yesterday afternoon.
munà sàyensù à Tamburāwā	We buy them at Tamburawa.
àkwai buřōdì cikin kwabàd?	Is there bread in the cupboard?

It is possible to string a number of adverbs in a single sentence, the order of the various adverbs being subject to some degree of flexibility, e.g.,

gidan Bellò yanà bāyan asìbitì kusa dà shāgòn kāfintà
house.of Bello he.cont back.of hospital close with workshop.of carpenter
    Bello's house is behind the hospital close to the carpenter's workshop.

tā dafà àbinci à ɗākìn girkī jiyà dà dàddare cikin saurī (or **dà gaggāwā**)
she.comp cook food at room.of cooking yesterday with evening in speed (with haste)
    She cooked the food in the kitchen yesterday evening in haste.

= **tā dafà àbinci jiyà dà dàddare à ɗākìn girkī cikin saurī**
    She cooked the food yesterday evening in the kitchen in haste.

Like most constituents in the language, adverbs can be fronted for the purpose of focus, e.g.,

jiyà dà yâmma (nè) sukà dāwō	It was *yesterday afternoon* they returned.
à Tamburāwā (nè) mukè sàyensù	It's *at Tamburawa* we buy them.
dà ƙyař mukà sāmù	*With difficulty* we got it.
à kàsuwā takè	It's *at the market* she is.

34

Temporal adverbs can optionally be used at the beginning of a sentence without connoting focus.

<u>jiyà</u> an yi ruwā   Yesterday it rained. (= an yi ruwā <u>jiyà</u>   It rained yesterday.)
<u>gòbe</u> màkānikè zâi zō yà gyārà makà bàbûr
   Tomorrow the mechanic will come and fix your mortorcycle.
= màkānikè zâi zō <u>gòbe</u> yà gyārà makà bàbûr
   The mechanic will come tomorrow and fix your motorcycle.
<u>shèkaràr àlif dà ɗàrī tarà dà sìttin</u> Nàjēriyà tā sàmi mulkìn kâi
   In 1960 Nigeria gained independence.
<u>dâ</u> inà iyà ciyar dà ìyālì, àmmā yànzu dai, inâ!
   Formerly I could provide for my family, but nowadays, no way!

In the case of adverbs that indicate sentence perspective, doubt, obligation, etc., sentence initial position is the norm, e.g.,

<u>wataƙīlà</u> Mūsā zâi tàimàkē kà dà mōtà   Perhaps Musa will help you out with a ride.
<u>lallē</u> yā màkarà   Definitely he's late.
<u>wai</u> Tùràwā sukàn ci ɗanyen ƙwai   It is said that Europeans eat raw eggs.
<u>bâ shakkà</u> maƙwàbcinkà yanà dà kuɗī   Without a doubt your neighbor is rich.
<u>yāwancī</u> sun sākè irìn àddīnìnsù   For the most part, they have changed their religion.

Adverbs can be viewed in terms of their function (time, manner, etc.) or in terms of their internal composition—namely, whether they are expressed by single words or by phrases. As far as lexical adverbs are concerned, one can distinguish those that are simple (non-derived) words as opposed to those that are morphologically derived from words belonging to some other part of speech.

2. BASIC/SIMPLE ADVERBS

The basic adverbs constitute a phonologically and semantically varied class. One common phonological feature that many of them share, as opposed to nouns or adjectives, is the absence of a monophthongal long final vowel. Typically, adverbs end in a short final vowel, a diphthong, or a consonant. Here is a selected list of adverbs grouped into rough semantic classes. (A few lexical compounds and universal forms are listed here even though they are not monomorphemic.)

2.1. Spatial

dāma   right-hand side, direction; **hagu = hagun**   left; contrary to expectation
arèwa   north; **kudù**   south; **gabàs**   east; **yâmma**   west
kusa   nearby; **ìnā**   where?; **kō'ìnā**   everywhere

2.2. Temporal

bàra   last year; **bàɗi**   next year; **bana**   this year; **città**   four days hence; **dâ (mā)**   formerly, once upon a time; **dàɗai**   ever, always; (with neg) never; **ɗàzu**   just now; **gātà**   three days hence; **gòbe** tomorrow; **jìbi**   day after tomorrow; **jiyà**   yesterday; **yâu**   today; **shēkaranjiyà**   day before yesterday; **kullum**   always, every day; **tùni**   long ago; **tùtur**   forever, always; **wàshègàrī** (= **kàshègàrī**)   the following day; **yànzu**   now, at present; **yàushè = yàushē**   when? **kōyàushè, kōyàushē**   whenever

◊HN: Etymologically, **shēkaranjiyà** 'day before yesterday' (lit. X (?) of yesterday) and **wàshēgàrī** 'the following day' (lit. clear out the town) were compounds. Synchronically, however, they constitute single words.

Some of the temporal adverbs can be specified by means of a demonstrative or a definite article, e.g., **ɗàzun nàn** (lit. now.of this) 'just a little while ago', **yànzun nàn** 'right now' (lit. now.of this); **yâu ɗin nàn** 'this very today', **gòbên** 'the tomorrow' (that we were referring to).

2.3. Deictics: Both spatial and temporal

nân   here, now;   **nan**   there near you, then
cân   there (not near you);   **can**   there (remote), then (later)

Because of their high frequency and importance, the four forms **nân**, **nan**, **cân**, and **can** deserve special comments on their own. (For a description of these items functioning as demonstratives meaning 'this/that', see §21:1.1.) Note that these items commonly accompany other locative adverbs or adverbial prepositional phrases. (If the immediately following preposition is **à** 'at', it is usually deleted.) Examples:

mun hàngi mayàƙā can nēsà	We saw warriors there afar (i.e., in the distance).
yanà nân (à) ɗākìn	It is here in the room.

2.3.1. Form
The segmental contrast is between NAN and CAN, the former being nearer in space or time than the latter.

◊HN: Assuming that the initial /c/ derives from /t/, then one ends up with the **n** / **t** contrast that is so common in Hausa and elsewhere in Chadic as a masculine/feminine opposition. My feeling is that this is not accidental and that what is now a spatial/temporal difference was originally one of gender.

The surface tonal contrast is between falling and high. The surface falling tone represents HL on a single syllable. The surface H tone is a manifestation (historical or underlying) of LH, the change from LH to H being a regular tonal rule in the language. (Hausa does not have rising tones.) Once the H-tone forms are understood to be LH, one is able to identify the iconic tonal opposition between an H-L pattern indicating relatively proximal and an L-H pattern indicating relatively distal.

2.3.2. Meaning
The primary meaning of these deictics can be thought of as spatial, i.e., 'here/there'. By extension, three of the items (**nân**, **nan**, and **can**) also serve to denote temporal closeness or distance. Some of them also carry an existential sense. Unlike English, which has a simple two-term system 'here' vs. 'there' (with a third 'yonder' in some dialects), Hausa has a four-term system. The four deictic forms will now briefly be described one by one.

2.3.2.1. The falling tone (HL) **nân** denotes 'here' defined as speaker proximal, e.g.,

yanà nân kusa dà nī	He is here close to me.
nân nē ƙafà kè yi minì cīwò	It is here that my leg is hurting me.

mù tsayà nân mù yi nazàr̃ī kân lamàr̃in   Let's stop here and look over the situation.

In expressions contrasting 'here' and 'there', one often uses a repeated **nân** rather than switching to **cân**, e.g., **tā dūbà nân tā dubà nân bà tà ga kōwā ba** 'She looked here, she look there, she didn't see anyone.'

The fundamental identity in meaning between **nân** as a demonstrative meaning 'this' and as an adverb meaning 'here' shows up in the following structurally distinct but semantically equivalent sentences, e.g.,

bâ wandà zâi ɗagà à (<u>nân wajên</u> = <u>wajen nàn</u>) sai an fàɗi gaskiyar̃ àl'amàr̃in
No one will move from *this place*, until the fact of the matter is stated.
(...here (at) the place... = ...(at) this place...)

When used temporally, **nân** indicates proximal time, i.e., now or soon, e.g.,

dàgà nân zuwà ƙàrshen wannàn mākò   from now until the end of this week
zân kammàlà aikìn nân bà dà jumàwā ba   I'll finish the work soon (lit. ...now neg with passing
time neg).

It is commonly used along with another temporal adverb or in the set expression **nân gàba** 'in the near future' (lit. now ahead), e.g., **ai nân jiyà nē ta haifù** 'Well, it was just yesterday she gave birth'; **zā à būɗè hanyàr̃ nân gàba** 'The road will be opened at some time in the future.' The phrase **nân dà X**, where X is a temporal expression, indicates within a period of time, e.g., **nân dà watà biyu** 'in two months' time', **nân dà shèkarà hàmsin** 'in the next fifty years', **nân dà 'yan mintōcī** 'a few minutes from now'.

2.3.2.2. The H-tone (< LH) **nan** denotes 'there', defined as hearer proximal, e.g.,

gà macìjī nan kusa dà kai   There is a snake there next to you.
zā tà sâ fìtilà nan à kân tēbùr̃   She will put a lamp there (next to you) on the table.
yā kàmātà kù tsayà nan indà kukè   You ought to stay there where you are.

Used temporally, **nan** denotes 'then', often in a successive sense, e.g., **nan (= can) akà ji wani àbin màmākì** 'Then [after sth else] one heard a wonderful thing.' The conjoined expression **nan dà nan** means 'at once', e.g., **nan dà nan sai sukà gudù** 'They fled at once', whereas **nan tàke** (lit. there stepped), followed by a clause in the preterite, means 'suddenly', e.g., **nan tàke sai sukà mutù** 'Suddenly they died.'

The H-tone **nan** also indicates 'here/there' in an existential sense, e.g.,

munà nan munà ta taɓàwā   We're here trying. (but not literally at this spot)
yàyà ìyālì? sunà nan lāfiyà lau   How's the family? They're fine.
(lit. they.cont there healthy very)
kàkātā tanà nan dà rântà   My grandmother is still alive and kicking.
(lit. grandmother.my she.cont there with life.of.her)
lìttàttàfai sunà nan; an kāwō jiyà
The books are here (in an existential sense, not necessarily physically near the speaker); they were brought yesterday.
yanà nan kân aikìnsà, sai akà zō masà dà làbār̃in ràsuwar̃ mahàifinsà
He was (there) working away at his job, when the news of his father's death reached him.

2.3.2.3. The falling-tone (HL) **cân** 'there' indicates a distance away from the speaker and the hearer, but not extremely far away, e.g.,

don Allàh kù kai sù cân	Please take them there.
gà ta cân à gidan su Bintà	There she is at the house of Binta et al.
bankì yanà cân à hanyàr̃ Wùdil	The bank is there on Wudil Road.

Unlike the other three members of the set, **cân** does not occur in nonspatial contexts, i.e., it is not used temporally or existentially or anaphorically.

2.3.2.4. The H-tone (< LH) **can** 'there (remote)' indicates a distance 'yonder (way far away)', e.g.,

Ƙasar̃ Jàpân tanà can Āsiyà	Japan is way out there in Asia.
can à garin Bauchi na ar̃ēwacin Nàjēr̃iyà	there (far away) in Bauchi in northern Nigeria
yanà tàfiye-tàfiye har̃ yā ìsa can cikin jējì	
He was traveling on and on until he reached there (distant) in the forest.	

When used temporally, **can** indicates distal time, i.e., it is the counterpart of **nân**, e.g.,

Fàsih ya kōmà zaurè. Can zuwà àzahàr̃ Wàzīr̃ì ya far̃kà
Fasih went back to the entrance room. Much later on, toward afternoon, Waziri woke up.
can zuwà tsakar̃-darē sai na ji yā fārà àbîn dà sarkin nàn ya bā dà làbār̃ì dà r̃āna
Much later on, toward midnight, I then heard him begin the thing that the chief talked about in the afternoon.
can jìm kàɗan sai na ga yā dùbi sāƙòn dà gāwar̃ nàn takè
A little while later, I saw him look at the corner where this corpse is.
tò àmmā tun dâ can bâ shi dà ànniyàr̃ cikà àlƙawàr̃în
But even then, he had no intention of fulfilling his promise.

Finally, H-tone **can** can be used anaphorically (or sometimes cataphorically). In this function, it serves sometimes as an alternative to **nan**, although **can** always implies the absence of the speaker from the location referred to, e.g.,

manòmā sunà can cikin talaucinsù	The farmers are there (i.e., exist) in their poverty.
kàr̃ùwai kullum sunà can à ƙōfàr̃ òtâl bâ ruwansù dà kōmē	
The prostitutes are always there by the hotel not mindful of anything.	

2.4. Manner, intensity, and other miscellaneous adverbs
The following items constitute a mixed assortment of adverblike words of different types.

ainùn very much, thoroughly; **àƙallà** at least; **daidai** exactly; **dindìndin** permanently, perpetually; **dōlè** perforce; **duk** entirely; **fàfùr̃àtan** entirely, completely; **fàufau** absolutely not, never, none; **gàlibàn = gàlìbī** usually; **haiƙàn** very much, exceedingly; **hakà = hakàn** thus, so. (adverb pro-form); **hàƙīƙà** surely, without a doubt; **kàsàfài** rarely, seldom; **kawài** only, merely; (with **sai**) suddenly, without warning; **kàzālikà** likewise, also; **kō** even; **kurùm** only, merely; silently, motionlessly; **ƙwar̃ai** very much so, surely; **làbuddà** definitely, for sure; **lallē** for sure, certainly; **maza** quickly, as quickly as possible; **mùsammàn** especially, expressly; **sar̃ai**

absolutely, very much; **sòsai** very well, correctly, perfectly; **tabbàs** undoubtedly; **tīlàs** perforce; **tùkùna** (not) yet; **wai** it is said that; **(wata)ƙīlà** perhaps, maybe; **wùlàƙài** contemptuously, harshly; **kōyàyà** however; **yàyà** how?; **yawancī** mostly

The emphasizer **ƙwaƙai** 'very much so' often appears in the phrase **ƙwaƙai dà gàske** (lit. very in truth), comparable to English 'really and truly'. The adverb **daidai** 'exactly' enters in the stronger phrase **daidai wà daidà** whereas **sòsai** 'very well' can be conjoined with itself for strengthening purposes, e.g., **aikìnkà yā yi kyâu sòsai dà sòsai** 'Your work was particularly good.'

Apart from manner adverbs and adverbial phrases, the expression of manner is often indicated by phonologically distinctive and semantically loaded ideophones (see chap. **35**), e.g.,

yanà tàfiyà <u>bàzàƙ-bazaƙ</u>	He is going about in a disorganized, raggedy manner.
tā zaunà <u>bòɗòɗò</u>	She sat down exposing herself.
yā fāɗà ruwa <u>fùnjùm</u>	It fell into the water with a splash.
sun ɗaurè shi <u>tam</u>	They tied it up tightly.

3. DERIVED ADVERBS

Apart from the inventory of basic adverbs, there are classes of adverbs that are morphologically derived in a more or less productive manner from nouns and verbs.

3.1. Denominal adverbs

Many body-part terms, some locational and temporal nouns, and a few other items have corresponding adverbial forms. These adverbial forms, which are phonologically overtly marked, commonly occur with the prepositions **à** 'at' or **dà** 'with', e.g.,

māshì yā sòkē shì à zūci	A sword pierced him in the heart.
nā yankè à yātsu	I cut my fingers. (lit. I.comp was cut at fingers)
yā zō à ƙafà	He came by foot.
sunà aikì bakà dà hanci	They are working tooth and nail. (lit. at mouth and at nose)
yā haddàcē shi dà kā	He memorized it by heart. (lit. by head)
kadà kà ci àbinci dà rāna!	Don't eat food during the day!
munà sônsù dà gàske	We truly like them.
zanè tsàgaggē dàgà kàrbu	a cloth torn at (lit. from) the selvage

These adverbs occur also in genitive constructions, including many compounds.

yāƙìn gàske a bitter war (lit. war.of in truth); **ɗan-kunne** earring (lit. little.of in ear); **rōmon-bakà** sweet talk, false promise (lit. broth.of in mouth); **gīwaƙ-ruwa** Nile-perch (lit. elephant.of in water); **ƙwallon-ƙafà** soccer (lit. ball.of at foot); **sà-ɗakà** concubine slave-girl (lit. put-in room); **kīshìn-zūci** ambition (lit. jealousy.of in heart)

The derivation involves the following morphophonological processes: (1) shortening of the final vowel (in all cases where the corresponding final vowel is long), (2) dropping of the feminative suffix (in almost all cases), (3) change of tone to H-H (generally accompanies (2), but otherwise lexically specific or optional); (4) addition of a tone-integrating suffix **-a**^{HL}. This fourth process is uncommon, in three cases being accompanied by a change in the length or quality of the internal vowel as well. Examples (with the applicable processes indicated in parentheses):

(a) Locatives

cíbìyā navel ⟹ cíbi on the navel (1, 2, 3)	zūcìyā heart ⟹ zūci in heart, mind (1, 2, 3)
idò eye ⟹ ido in/on the eye (1, 3)	kûnnē ear ⟹ kunne on the ear (1, 3)
bāyā back ⟹ bāya in/at the back, behind (1)	fiffìkè wing ⟹ fiffìkè on the wing (1)
gòshī forehead ⟹ gòshi on the forehead (1)	ƙafà foot ⟹ ƙafà by foot (1) (or (4) ?)
ruwā water ⟹ ruwa in the water (1)	bisā height ⟹ bisà above (4)
bàkī mouth ⟹ bakà in the mouth, by mouth (4) (= bàki (1))	
ɗàkī room, hut ⟹ ɗakà in the room (4)	jìkī body ⟹ jikà in/on the body (4)
ƙasā ground ⟹ ƙasà on the ground, below (4)	nīsā distance ⟹ nēsà distant (4)
Irregular: gidā house ⟹ gijì at home	kâi head ⟹ kā (= ka) on the head

°AN: The long-vowel variant **kā** is characterized by a glottal closure and phonetic vowel shortening in prepausal position, i.e., [ka·?] ; the short vowel variant is a new creation.
◊HN: Synchronically, the derivation of the adverbial form **gijì** looks as if it involves a vowel change from the noun **gidā**. In reality, **gidā** is the plural of *gijì (still used in some dialects), which is the source of the adverbial **gijì**.

(b) Temporals (and others)

darē night ⟹ dare at night (1)   rānā day, sun ⟹ rāna midday, in the day (1)
rānī dry season ⟹ rāni in the dry season (1)   sāfiyā morning ⟹ sāfe in the morning (1, 2)
yâmmā afternoon ⟹ yâmma in the afternoon (1) gàskiyā truth ⟹ gàske truly (1, 2)
(fārà begin) ⟹ fārì in the beginning (1)

◊HN: [i] The word for 'truth' is often pronounced **gaskiyā** with H-H-H tone. The related adverbial form shows that the all H pronunciation is an innovation and that the L-H-H variant was the historically original form.
[ii] The adverb **fārì** derives from a synchronically nonexistent H-L i-final verbal noun *fārì 'beginning'.

The various stem changes are lexically restricted. The vowel shortening, on the other hand, appears to be quite a general process and, in the case of body-part nouns, can be applied even to feminatives and plurals, e.g.,

dundūnìyā	heel ⟹	dundūnìya	on the heel
jījìyā	vein, artery ⟹	jījìya	in the vein, artery
hannàyē	hands ⟹	hannàye	in/on the hands
kunnuwà	ears ⟹	kunnuwà	in/on the ears
yātsū	fingers ⟹	yātsu	on the fingers

◊HN: Originally, common nouns in Hausa all ended in short final vowels. Later, the vowels were lengthened, due to various essentially morphological processes, including the addition of feminative endings with long final vowels (Greenberg 1978; Newman 1979a, 1979b). The lengthening did not, however, affect adverbial forms. Thus, the short vowels on the locatives that synchronically appear to be due to a shortening process actually represent retention of the original vowel length. Viewed historically, **tōzō** 'hump', for example, comes from *tōzo (= current adverb **tōzo** 'on the hump') and not vice versa. Note, similarly, that the addition of the feminine ending did not apply to adverbs; thus **sāfiyā** comes from a feminine noun *sāfe 'morning' (preserved as the adverb 'in the morning') and not vice versa. Old Hausa did have processes for deriving adverbs from nouns, but they did not involve final vowel shortening per se. Rather they consisted of either the uncommon addition of the suffix -à)^HL, e.g., *jìki (now jìkī) 'body' ⇒ jikà 'on the body', or a more general tone change (essentially the addition of a final H tone), e.g., *kuncì (now kuncì) 'cheek' ⇒ kunci 'on the cheek'. Synchronically, vowel shortening appears to be the primary element in the derivation, with the result that the tone change has become a redundant option, i.e., kunci = kuncì 'on the cheek', ido (< *idò 'eye' (now idò) = idò 'in the eye'.

3.2. Deverbal statives

Statives are derived productively from verbs (and occasionally from nouns) by means of a tone-integrating suffix -e)^LH (see chap. **67**), e.g.,

būɗè̀ to open ⇒ bùɗe open, ajar, unlocked; mutù die ⇒ màce deceased; yāgà tear ⇒ yàge torn; zaunà̀ to sit ⇒ zàune seated; **Hausa** Hausa ⇒ hàusànce in Hausa

°AN: The statives translate into English as verb forms, adjectival past participles, etc. In Hausa, they constitute adverbials.

These statives commonly function as predicates of sentences in the continuous, e.g., sunà̀ zàune 'They are sitting/seated', but they can serve also as adverbial modifiers, often with the preposition à, e.g.,

yā bar ƙōfà̀ à bùɗe	He left the door open.
tā gayà̀ minì à àsìr̃ce	She told me in secret.
kù kāwō shì nân kō à r̃àye kō à màce	Bring him here dead or alive.
mutànensà̀ sunà̀ jère rìƙe dà māshì	His men are lined up armed with spears.

4. REDUPLICATION

Adverbs commonly enter into reduplicated (or repeated) formations. (It is not always clear whether the output constitutes a word, in which case one would want to speak of reduplication, or whether it is a phrase, in which case "repetition" would be the more accurate term.) In most cases, the reduplication is total (with possible final vowel modification), but some reductions do occur, especially with the strengthening group. Standard orthography is not totally consistent on how to represent reduplicated forms. Normally, partially reduplicated forms are treated as one word, e.g., mar̃maza 'very quickly' < maza 'quickly', whereas fully reduplicated items are written as two words, usually without a hyphen, e.g., maza maza 'very quickly'. (Exceptions are lexicalized CVVCVV words such as daidai 'correct' or faufau 'never'.) Generally speaking the tone pattern of the simple form is also reduplicated, although in some cases the reduplicated output has its own distinct tone. Reduplication of adverbs serves a number of functions:

4.1. Strengthening

Some basic temporal adverbs, the locatives 'here' and 'there', and a few manner adverbs are strengthened by reduplication. Some exhibit full reduplication. Some undergo deletion of the final vowel of the first reduplicate, the deletion being optional in some cases, obligatory in others. (Resulting syllable-final obstruent consonants undergo either rhotacism or gemination in accordance with regular phonological rules.) In one case, the nonreduplicated form doesn't exist synchronically. Examples:

àsùbâ dawn / àsùssùbâ very early dawn; **can** there / **can can** far, far away; ɗàzu this moment / ɗàzu ɗàzu this very moment; gòbe tomorrow / gòbe gòbe as early as tomorrow; kusa close / kusa kusa (= kur̃kusa) very close; **maza** quickly / **maza maza** (= mar̃maza) very quickly; **nân** here /

nân nân   right here; **sànnu**   slowly, carefully / **sànnu sànnu**   very slowly, carefully; **wuri**   early /
wuri wuri (= **wurwuri**)   very early; **yànzu**   now / **yànzu yànzu**   just now; **yâu**   today / **yâu yâu**   this
very day;   / **jijjifī**   just before sunrise;
Tonally aberrant: **dare**   at night / **dàddare**   (late) at night;   **sāfe**   in the morning / **sassāfe** = **sassàfe**
in the early morning

4.2. Attenuation
Denominal adverbs (mostly locative) undergo semantic weakening when reduplicated. This is the same
attenuation process found with adjectives (see §4:2.3), e.g., **gàba** 'forward' **gàba gàba** 'a bit forward',
cf. **farī** 'white', **fari fari** 'whitish'. In some cases, the nonreduplicated adverb does not exist, i.e., one
has only the noun and the reduplicated adverb (which being an adverb has a short final vowel), e.g.,

bāya	behind	**bāya bāya**	a bit behind
dà dāmā	OK, fairly well	**dà dāma dāma**	so-so, slightly
gàba	forward	**gàba gàba**	a bit forward
gēfè	side (not ****gēfè** on the side)	**gēfè gēfè**	around the side
ƙasà	below	**ƙasà ƙasà**	a bit lower
nēsà (dà)	far (from)	**nēsà nēsà (dà)**	somewhat far (from)
samà	above	**samà samà**	a bit higher
tsakiyà	center	**tsakiyà tsakiyà**	around the center

4.3. Distributives
Full repetition of nouns creates adverbs that express the notion of distribution in time, space, or
manner. The forms often correspond to English adverbial phrases of the sort 'from X to X' or 'X by X'.

àsabàr̃ àsabàr̃   from Saturday to Saturday, every Saturday
lōkàcī lōkàcī (= **lōtò lōtò**)   from time to time, sometimes
e.g., **bā nà̀ kallon talàbijìn kōwàcè rānā sai dai lōkàcī lōkàcī**
    I don't watch television every day, just from time to time.
mākò̀ mākò̀ (= **sātī sātī**)   weekly
e.g., **jàrīdà̀ tanà̀ fitôwā mākò̀ mākò̀**   The newspaper appears weekly.
ɗākì ɗākì   from room to room
fallē fallē   singly, one by one (< **fallē**   one unit)
gidā gidā   from house to house
e.g., **sukà riƙà yāwò̀ gidā gidā sunà̀ neman wândà̀ zâi bā sù àbinci**
    They kept on walking from house to house looking for someone who would give them food.
kashì kashì   in different categories, classes
e.g., **sai à ƙasà su kashì kashì**   One should put them in appropriate groups.
lābà̀ lābà̀   in abundance (lit. pound (by) pound)
tītì tītì   street to street
e.g., **sōjōjī sunà̀ bîn 'yan tāwāyè̀ tītì tītì**   The soldiers were following the rebels from street to street.

The distributed form of the numeral **ɗaya** 'one' is **ɗai ɗai** 'one by one', which optionally can be
conjoined with itself, e.g., **kù ajìyè̀ kāyan nàn ɗai ɗai dà ɗai ɗai** 'Put these loads down one by one'.

A few items occur only as repeated distributives rather than singly, e.g.,

binì binì   repeatedly, often

jēfì jēfì	from time to time, here and there
dakì dakì	in order, item by item, evenly
e.g., **sun jèru dakì dakì**	They are lined up evenly.
dallā dallā	clearly, in an orderly manner
e.g., **yā faɗà minì làbārì dallā dallā**	He told me the story step by step.

In the expression **à kâi à kâi** 'continually' (lit. at head at head), it is a prepositional phrase rather than an individual word that is repeated.

   Distributives of phrases consisting of more than one word are formed by repeating the final word only, e.g.,

kàsuwaȓ ƙauyè ƙauyè	from village market to village market
bàkin kògī kògī	riverbank by riverbank

By contrast, the distributive of a true compound requires repetition of the entire compound, e.g.,

ƙōfàȓ-gidā ƙōfàȓ-gidā	front yard after front yard (**ƙōfàȓ-gidā** = front yard)

A few adverbial phrases indicating 'X after X' have the structure Noun$_{1\text{-sg}}$ **dà** 'and' Noun$_{1\text{-pl}}$, e.g.,

kwānā dà kwànàkī	day after day, it's been long since (lit. day and days)
shèkarà dà shèkàrū	year after year (lit. year and years)
watà dà wàtànnī	month after month (lit. month and months)

The expression **bî-da-bî** (lit. following-and-following), with the conjoined verbal nouns, indicates 'successively, in succession'.

5. PREPOSITIONAL PHRASES

Many constructions whose external syntactic and semantic function is that of an adverb, whether locative, temporal, manner, etc., are structurally prepositional phrases. Most often, the object of the preposition is a common noun or NP (or even a pp); but, as indicated earlier, some prepositional phrases prefer that the object morphologically be an adverb; compare **dà hankàlī** 'carefully' (lit. with care), with **à bakà** 'in the mouth' (where **bakà** is an adverb derived from the noun **bàkī** 'mouth').

5.1. Spatial

Prepositional phrases, whether formed with "true prepositions", "phrasal prepositions", or "genitive prepositions" (see chap. **57** for the distinction), serve as spatial adverbs. Such adverbs function as predicates of nonverbal locative sentences and as verbal or adverbial modifiers, e.g.,

Lēgàs tanà [nēsà dà Kanò]	Lagos is [far from Kano].
kāyân bā sà [cikin kwabàd]	The clothes are not [in the cupboard].
kàntī yanà [bāyan bankì]	The store is [behind the bank].
sunà zàune [dab dà bàƙôn]	They were sitting [right next to the guest].
zā sù binnè shi [à gìndin bishiyàȓ]	They will bury it [at the base of the tree].
yā wucè [gàba dà mū]	He passed [ahead of us]. (either in location or in rank)
gà mōtà kòmàɗaɗɗiyā [dàgà gēfè]	Here is a car dented [at the side].
yā fizgè jàkâȓ [dàgà hannuntà]	He snatched the purse [from her hand].

nā sầmē sù [à makařantā]   I found them [at school].

In certain contexts the extremely common preposition **à** 'in, at' is deleted, sometimes obligatorily, sometimes optionally. For example, in nonverbal locative sentences following a continuous TAM, the **à** is generally omitted, e.g.,

yanầ masallacī (< **yanầ à masallacī**)   He is at the mosque.
mutầnên dà kè fīlin wầsā (< **mutầnên dà kè à fīlin wầsā**)   the men who were at the playing field

In initial position, the **à** is optional, as it is when preceding a genitive preposition or when following a basic locative adverb such as **nân** 'here', e.g.,

(à) makařantā na sầmē sù   It was at school I found them.
(à) masallacī yakè   It's at the mosque he is.
nā gan tà (à) gàban asìbitì   I saw her in front of the hospital.
sunầ can (à) Landàn   They are there in London.

5.2. *Temporal*
Temporal adverb phrases are also formed with a range of prepositions, e.g.,

Shātā yā gamầ [dab dà zuwàn 'yan rawân]
        Shata finished just before the coming of the dancers.
mālàmîn yā gamầ [kàfin zuwàn ɗàlìbân]
        The teacher finished before the coming of the students.
bà zā à rufè ba [sai bāyan ƙarfè bìyař]   They won't close until after five o'clock.
[tun kàfin sù isō], mukà tāshì   Before they arrived, we had left.

5.3. *Manner*
Adverbs of manner are commonly expressed by a prepositional phrase consisting of **dà** 'with' plus a nominal or adverbial of quality, e.g.,

dà gàngan   deliberately (lit. with ill will) (cf. **aikìn gàngan** deliberately reckless work)
dà gaggāwā   quickly (with haste)
dà hankàlī   carefully (with care)
dà ƙarfī   strongly (with strength)
dà yawàn gàske   truly a lot (lit. with quantity.of truth)
dà kyař (= dà ƙyař) (only) with difficulty

Prepositional phrases consisting of **à** plus a stative adverb also serve as manner adverbials, e.g.,

yā fìta à gùje   He went out on the run.
yā ɓōyè kuɗîn à àsìřce   He hid the money on the sly.
nā îskē yāròn à mìmmìƙe à kân gadō   I saw the boy stretched out on the bed.

The preposition **à** is also used in phases comparable to English 'by foot'.

yā zō à ƙafà He came by foot; **yā zō à mōtà** He came by car.

°AN: One can say **yā zō dà mōtà** 'He came with his car', which is semantically similar to **yā zō à mōtà**; but one cannot say ****yā zō dà ƙafà**.

There are two ways to express the idea of speaking (or writing) in a particular language. The most straightforward way is by means of a prepositional phrase consisting of **dà** plus the name of the language, e.g.,

yā yi màganà dà Tūřancī	He spoke in English.
yā raɗà minì dà Fillancī	He whispered to me in Fulani.
zâi bayyànā mukù dà Hausa	He'll explain it to you in Hausa.
tā řubùtà kundintà dà Jāmusancī	She wrote her thesis in German.

Alternatively, one can use a prepositional phrase made up of **à** plus a stative variant of the language name. This formation often has an indirect, figurative connotation, e.g.,

yā yi màganà à Tùřance	He spoke in English (i.e., Englishly).
yā raɗà minì à Fìllànce	He whispered to me in Fulani (or in a shy manner).
zâi bayyànā mukù à Hàusànce	He'll explain it to you in Hausa (or in a clear manner).
(but not **tā řubùtà kundintà à Jàmùsànce)	

5.4. *Instrumental*

Instrumentals and related expressions also make use of the preposition **dà**, but with a concrete noun, e.g.,

sun ɗaurè shi dà igiyà	They tied him with a rope.
zā mù cikà dà gyàɗā	We will fill (it) with peanuts.
nā sārè shi dà gàtarī	I cut it down with an axe.

In principle one should be able to have an instrumental phrase formed with **dà** followed by a manner phrase with **dà**, although speakers tend to find such sentences stylistically unappealing, if not downright ungrammatical, e.g.,

??sun ɗaurè shi dà igiyà dà niyyà	They tied him with a rope on purpose.

6. NONPREPOSITIONAL PHRASAL ADVERBS

Hausa has a large number of idiomatic adverb phrases consisting of (a) a bare noun plus an adverb (often a stative) or (b) a pair of conjoined nouns or adverbs.

(a) **haɓà samà** head up (lit. chin skyward), e.g., **yanà tàfiyà haɓà samà** He was going along head held high; **bàkī bùɗe** mouth agape; **hankàlī kwànce** peacefully (lit. care lying down); **kâi ƙasà** head down; **râi ɓàce** in despair (lit. life spoiled); **karā-zùbe** in a disorganized manner (lit. stalks poured out)

(b) **bàkī dà hancī** (= **bakà dà hanci**) tooth and nail (lit. mouth and nose); **kâi dà fātà** adamantly (lit. head and skin); **ƙarfī dà yājì** forcefully (lit. strength and spice)

A few nouns accompanied by a determiner function as adverbial phrases, e.g.,

kōwàcè shèkarà every year; **kwānan nàn** at present (lit. day.of this); **wani lōkàcī** sometime

The phrase **saurā kàɗan** (lit. remainder little) is used in an equational sentence followed by a clause in the subjunctive to indicate 'almost' with regard to the action of that clause, e.g.,

saurā kàɗan (nè) tà gamà aikì   She almost finished the work.
(lit. it's a small remainder (that) she finish the work)
saurā kàɗan (nè) yà kāmà birìn   He almost caught the monkey.

Some negative existentials function as adverbials, e.g.,

bâ shakkà̀   there is no doubt (< **shakkà̀** doubt)
bâ wai   there's no question (< **wai(wai)** hearsay)

7. COMPOUNDS

Most compounds in Hausa are nouns. There are, however, a small number of compound words (or tightly bound phrases) that function syntactically as adverbs (see §16:1.3). Examples:

ruwā-à-jàllō (lit. water-at-bottle) desperately; **shēkaràn-città** (lit. ? of-four days hence) five days hence; **tàkànas-ta-Kanò** (purpose-of-Kano) purposely; **tsayìn-dakà̀** (lit. standing.of-pounding) with resolve; **wân-shēkarè̀** (lit. being beyond.of-?) the following day, day after tomorrow

8. EVEN

The word **kō** 'even' modifies NPs, VPs, prepositional phrases, etc. It occurs in front of the constituent that it is modifying. It is particularly common in negative sentences. Examples:

kō kwabò̀ bài bā nì ba   He didn't give me even a penny.
(lit. even a penny he didn't give me)
kō Lawàn bài sanî ba   Even Lawan doesn't know.
kō kèkè bâ mu dà shī, bàllē mōtà   Even a bicycle we don't have, much less a car.
bài cê kō sànnu ba   He didn't even say hello. (lit. he didn't say even hello)
bài kō dùbē mù ba   He didn't even look at us.
bā sà̀ kō sôn baɓin ruwā   They do not even want clean water.
cf. **bā sà̀ sôn kō kwabò̀**   They do not want even a penny.
kō Audù yanà̀ sôn *pizza*   Even Audu likes pizza.
kō jàrīrì yā san hakà   Even a baby knows that.
kō dà wuɓā bà zâi iyà kashè̀ shi ba He wouldn't be able to kill it even with a knife.
(lit. even with a knife he won't be able to kill it)

Instead of modifying the VP in situ, one commonly fronts **kō** plus the corresponding verbal noun or infinitive phrase, e.g.,

ukùnsù kō mōtsî bā sà̀ yî   Three of them weren't even budging.
(lit. three of them even movement they weren't doing)
kō rufè̀ shi bà tà yi ba   She didn't even close it. (lit. even close it she didn't do)

9. A LITTLE / A LOT / ENTIRELY

The diminutive markers **ɗan/'yař/'yan** (m./f./pl./), which are derived from 'son / daughter / children', commonly serve to modify nouns and accompany adjectives, e.g., **'yař ƙàramař àkuyà** 'a wee small goat'. The masculine form **ɗan** also functions adverbially as a VP modifier. It occurs between the PAC (person-aspect complex) and the VP (which may be a finite or nonfinite verbal noun form).

Kànde tā ɗan tàimàkē nì	Kande helped me a bit.
(more or less = **Kànde tā tàimàkē nì kàɗan kàɗan**, with the post VP adverb)	
kà ɗan dākàtā!	Wait a little! (lit. you.sub little wait)
nā ɗan taɓà aikì	I worked a little. (lit. I.comp little touch work)
munà ɗan hūtàwā	We were taking a little rest. (lit. we.cont little resting)

The semantic counterpart of **ɗan** is **yawàn** 'a lot' (< **yawà** 'quantity' plus the linker **-n**). This pseudo-adverb occurs between the PAC, which is always in the continuous, and a following verbal noun. Examples:

yanà yawàn mārìntà	He is slapping her a lot.
cf. **yanà mārìntà dà yawà / dà ƙarfī**	He is slapping her a lot / with strength.
tanà yawàn kallon talàbijìn	She watches television a lot.
(lit. she.cont lot.of watching.of television	
sunà yawàn zuwà gidanmù	They come to our house a lot.

Although **yawàn** in the above sentences semantically functions as an adverbial modifier, at an abstract syntactic level it is really the head of an NP that is the direct object of the pro-verb **yi** 'do'. Thus **sunà yawàn zuwà gidanmù** derives from **sunà (yîn) yawàn zuwà gidanmù** (lit. they are (doing.of) lots.of coming house.of.us).

Among its other syntactic roles, the universal quantifier **duk(à)** 'all' functions as an adverbial indicating 'entirely, completely' (see §53:2.3). In this function, it normally appears in the form **duk** (without the final vowel) either between the subject (if expressed) and the PAC or at the beginning of the sentence before the subject.

wurîn duk yā harmùtsē	The place became completely muddled.
(lit. the place all it became muddled)	
duk kā ɓātà minì lōkàcī à banzā	You have entirely wasted my time.
(lit. all you spoil to.me time uselessly)	
duk bàn dàmu ba	I'm not bothered at all. (lit. all neg.I be bothered neg)
duk tsòřō yā kāmà shi	He became entirely frightened. (lit. all fear it caught him)

10. EXACTLY

The word **daidai** 'exactly' has a range of modifying uses. It occurs after an NP containing a numeral, e.g.,

ƙarfè ukù daidai   exactly three o'clock;   **dalà gōmà daidai**   exactly ten dollars

By contrast, it occurs before an NP (or adverb phrase) containing a relative clause, e.g.,

daidai lōkàcîn dà sukà zō   exactly when (= the time that) they came
daidai wurîn dà (= daidai îndà) na bař shì   exactly the place that (= exactly where) I left him
daidai àbîn dà ka gayà masà   exactly what (= the thing that) you told him
daidai yâddà mukè̆ yî   exactly how we were doing (it)

11. ESPECIALLY

The semantic notion of 'especially' can be expressed lexically or syntactically.

(a) When followed by a prepositional phrase or subordinate purposive clause, 'especially, particularly, purposely' is indicated by means of items such as **mùsammàn** or **tàkànas ta Kanô**, e.g.,

wannàn mùhimmî nē mùsammàn gà ƙasàshên dà bâ su dà ařzìkī
     This is important especially for poor countries.
anà yankà ràgō nè̄ mùsammàn don bìkī
     One slaughters rams especially for festivals.
nā zō tàkànas ta Kanô don ìn yi makà màganà
     I came purposely to talk with you.

(b) With nouns or prepositional phrases (or even some clauses), 'especially' is indicated by enveloping the constituent concerned in the complex expression **tun bà̀ ...bâ**, which literally means 'since not'. The first **bà̀** is often followed by the modal particle **mā** 'indeed'. Examples:

yànzu mōtōcī sun yi tsàdā, [tun bà̀ Mařsandî bâ]
     Cars are expensive, especially Mercedes.
yârā sunà dà ban shà'awà̀, [tun bà̀ mā ƙanānà bâ]
     Children are enjoyable, especially the young ones.
àbinci yā gàgàrē shì cî, [tun bà̀ mā tuwō bâ]
     It was difficult for him to eat food, especially *tuwo*.
Màidugùři tanà dà zāfī, [tun bà̀ dà bazarā bâ]
     Maiduguri is hot, especially in the hot season.
kà riƙà sâ tàkàlmī [tun bà̀ in zā kà shìga wurī mài ƙazântā bâ]
     You should always wear shoes, especially if you go into a filthy place.

°AN: According to Abraham (1959b: 39), the final **bà̀** (presumably long, but not marked by him as such) has L tone. He states that this L-tone variant becomes **bâ** after a preceding L tone. Although I have not been able to confirm the L-tone variant firsthand, I am willing to grant that it exists. Abraham is almost certainly wrong, however, in his choice of the basic form. It is much more likely that the basic form is **bâ** and that the final **bà̀** (if it occurs) reflects the operation of a general tone simplification rule that changes F to L if the preceding tone is H (see §71:6.2.2). What remains unexplained is why the final **bâ** should have falling tone and a long vowel at all since the normal discontinuous negative has the form **bà̀ ...ba** with final H tone and a short final vowel.

[References: Jaggar and Buba (1994); R. M. Newman (1984); Parsons (1963)]

6. Afterthought (Right Dislocation)

MOST syntactic processes in Hausa, such as topicalization, focus, questioning, and relativization, involve fronting. Generally speaking, items are not moved to the end of the sentence., If, however, a noun or noun phrase has not been mentioned when it should have been, e.g., it has been pronominalized or omitted even though the semantic referent was not clear, it can be added at the end of the sentence. A single noun is often preceded by an independent pronoun functioning as a determiner/specifier. The afterthought is usually set off from the main sentence by an intonational pause, indicated here by a comma. Examples:

yā dāwō dàgà Kàtsinà jiyà, shī Bellòn
> He returned from Katsina yesterday, the Bello in question that is.

cf. **Bellò yā dāwō dàgà Kàtsinà jiyà**   Bello returned from Katsina yesterday.

wājìbī nè sù yi sallà sàu bìyar̃, sū fa Mùsùlmī
> It is obligatory that they perform the prayers five times, Muslims that is.

yanà yìwuwā kà àurē tà, ita Bintà	It is possible that you might marry her, she Binta.
cf. **yanà yìwuwā kà àuri Bintà**	It is possible that you might marry Binta.
yā kàmātà Tànî tà biyā shì, hàr̃ājìn fa	It is fitting that Tani should pay it, the taxes.
wàtàkīlà zâi sàyi baƙâr̃, ita mōtàr̃	It is possible that he will buy the black one, the car.
yā dācè, auren Bintà dà Gar̃bà	It is fitting, Binta's marriage with Garba.
cf. **auren Bintà dà Gar̃bà yā dācè**	Binta's marriage with Garba is fitting.
yā hàlattà, cîn nāmàn àgwàgwā	It is permitted, eating duck meat.
dōlè nē, zuwàn gwamnà Kanò	It is necessary, the governor's coming to Kano.
mài yìwuwā nè, auren Bintà dà Audù	It is possible, Binta's marriage with Audu.

In some cases a postposed independent pronoun serves to strengthen a weak pronoun occurring earlier in the sentence, e.g.,

yā fi kyâu [kà] àuri Bintà, [kai] dîn   It would be good for you to marry Binta, you that is.

mài yìwuwā nè [nà] sàyi sābuwar̃ mōtà, [nī dà kâinā]
> It is possible/likely that I might buy a new car, I myself.

zā à bā [tà] izìnin shìgā, [itân] (= ita dîn)
> They will give her permission to enter, she (whom we were talking about).

In equational sentences of the form Y (= predicate) Stabilizer X (= subject) (where the X is a noun preceded by a pronominal determiner/specifier), it is not always clear whether one is dealing with simple right dislocation of the X or whether the structure also entails fronting and focus of the predicate. Examples:

Ŕàramā cè, [ita yārinyàř]	She's small, she the girl. (lit. small STAB she girl.the)
(focus on *small* or afterthought mentioning of the girl or both?)	
cf. ita yārinyàř] Ŕàramā cè	She the girl is small.
dabbōbī nè, [sū sàmàrîn]	They're (like) animals, these youths.
cf. sū sàmàrîn dabbōbī nè	These youths are (like) animals.
tàurārùwā cè, [ita Madonna]	She's a star, she Madonna.
cf. ita Madonna tàurārùwā cè	She Madonna is a star.
bà àbin tsòrō bā nè, [shī fànkàm-fàyàu]	He is nothing to fear, this big bag of wind.
cf. shī fànkàm-fàyàu bà àbin tsòrō bā nè	He this big bag of wind is nothing to be afraid of.

7. Agent, Location, and Instrument (ma- Forms)

THERE are three related derivational formations that make use of a high-tone prefix **ma**-: agent, location, and instrument, e.g., **manòmī** 'farmer', **majēmā** 'tannery', **masassabī** 'harvesting tool'.

◊HN: This **m**- prefix is one of the more striking Afroasiatic retentions found in Hausa and other Chadic languages (Greenberg 1963).

These **ma**- forms are typically built on verb stems, although there are some exceptions. Where semantically appropriate, the same verb base can give rise to two or all three **ma**- derivatives, e.g.,

ma'àikàcī   worker, **ma'aikatā** factory, workplace
ma'aunā   place where grain is sold by measure, **ma'aunī** measuring device, scales
masàssàƙī   carpenter, **masassaƙā** carpenter's work area, **masassaƙī** adze, carpenter's tool

1. AGENT (ma-...-ī)

1.1. Form

Nouns of agent, which are comparable to words with the *-er* ending in English, have three forms depending on gender and number. (Many words formed according to this derivation function also as adjectives, see below, §1.7). All agent nouns use the same H-tone **ma**- prefix. In addition, masculine singulars add a suffix -ī)^{LH}, which results in an H-(L)-(L)-L-H tone pattern. Feminine singulars use the suffix -**iyā**)^{HLH}. The suffix for plural agents is -**ā**)^{LH} with the same tone melody used with the masculine singulars. Examples:

	masculine	*feminine*	*plural*
quarrelsome psn	**mafàɗàcī**	**mafaɗàcìyā**	**mafàɗàtā**
parent	**mahàifī**	**mahaifìyā**	**mahàifā**
beggar, praise singer	**maròƙī**	**marōƙìyā**	**maròƙā**
coward	**matsòràcī**	**matsōracìyā**	**matsòràtā**

The plural formation as such is entirely regular., A few frozen/lexicalized agent nouns, however, employ other plurals, e.g., **magàjìyā** / **magājiyōyī** 'a madam' f./pl.; **magūɗìyā** / **màsu gūɗà** = **'yan gūɗà** 'woman who ululates during festivities' f./pl.; **macìjī** / **màcìzai** 'snake' (lit. one who bites) m./pl.

°AN: Derivationally, **macìjī** is formed from the verb **cìzā** 'bite' even though in Hausa, snakes do not *bite* but rather *slash*, e.g., **macìjī yā sārè ta** 'A snake bit (lit. slashed) her'.

Monosyllabic verbs employ an epenthetic /**y**/ between the verb root and the suffixal ending, e.g.,

51

bi	follow	mabìyī / mabiyìyā / mabìyā	a follower of s.o. (m./f./pl.)
ƙi	dislike	maƙìyī / maƙiyìyā / maƙìyā	enemy (m./f./pl.)
shā	drink	mashâyī / mashāyìyā / mashâyā	drinker, alcoholic (m./f./pl.)

In the above feminine forms, the sequence /iyìyā/ is usually pronounced without the /i/ between the two /y/'s. The floating L tone attaches to the preceding syllable to produce a fall, i.e., **mabiyìyā** → [mabîyyā], **maƙiyìyā** → [maƙîyyā].

1.2. Verb stems with -TA

The **ma**- forms are built on verb stems. Many of these verb stems are derived from noun roots by means of the verbalizing suffix -**TA** (chap. **79**), e.g.,

mahàukàcī	crazy, madman, idiot	< **haukàtā** make s.o. crazy	< **hàukā** madness
mahùkùncī	judge, administrator	< **hukùntā** judge, administer	< **hùkūmà** governing body
maƙàryàcī	liar	< **ƙaryàtā** falsify	< **ƙaryā** a lie
mashâwàr̃cī	adviser, counselor	< **shāwàr̃tā** advise	< **shāwar̃à** advice
matsòràcī	coward(ly)	< **tsòratà** be afraid	< **tsòrō** fear

Agents are not built directly from the verbs **jirā** 'wait for' and **ƙaura** 'migrate'; rather they are built on coexisting longer stems containing the verbalizer -**TA**, e.g.,

majìràcī (not **majìrī)	watchman, overseer < **jìrātà** wait for
maƙàuràcī (not **maƙàurī)	emigrant/immigrant < **ƙauràcē** migrate from

°AN: The verb **ƙaura** 'migrate' is probably a backformation from the verbal noun **ƙaurā** 'migrating', from which **ƙauràcē** is derived. This explains the absence of an agent **maƙàurī. There is no reason, on the other hand, to assume that **jirā**, or its equivalent longer form **jìrāyà**, was ever anything but a verb, and thus the absence of **majìrī or **majìràyī is inexplicable.

Many agentives are built on *fictitious* -**TA** verb stems, i.e., the postulated stem either does not occur independently as a verb or only rarely so, e.g.,

maɓàr̃nàcī	destructive (psn) < *ɓàr̃nàta < **ɓàr̃nā** damage
magàbcī	enemy < *gabta < **gàbā** enmity
magìdàncī	householder < *gidanta < **gidā** home
mahàjjàcī	pilgrim intending to go to Mecca < *hajjata < **hajjì** hadj
maròwàcī	tightwad < *ròwata < **ròwà** stinginess
mazìnàcī	adulterer < *zināta < **zìnā** adultery

A very few agentives are built directly on noun stems (some of which historically are probably verbal nouns of verb roots), e.g.,

magūɗîyā	woman who ululates during festivities < **gūɗà** ululation
matsàfī	fetish-worshipper, magician < **tsāfì** fetish
mawàƙī	singer, poet < **wāƙà** song, poem

1.3. Meaning

The basic meaning of an agent noun is someone who customarily does the action of the underlying verb, commonly as a profession, e.g., **maɗìnkī** 'tailor' (< **ɗinkà** 'to sew'). The semantic connection between the agent nouns and their source words is generally evident, e.g., **ma'àskī** barber < **askè** 'shave'. In some cases, however, these words have a lexicalized meaning that is more specialized and restricted than that of the related verb. Examples:

mabìyī	a follower (esp. religious); younger brother or sister < **bi** follow
macìyī	voracious < **ci** eat
mafàshī (usu. **ɗan fashì**)	robber < **fasà** break, shatter; commit robbery
makàɗàicī	unique (referring to God) < **kàɗaità** sit apart; acknowledge the unity of God
manìyyàcī	an intending pilgrim < *niyyata < **niyyà** intention, wish
marìƙī	guardian, foster parent < **riƙè** grasp, hold
matàshī	adolescent, youth < **tāshì** rise, grow up

In a couple of special cases, the agent does not denote the doer of the action but rather the one affected by the action. The word **ma'àikī** (< **àikā** 'send') is used in the designation **ma'àikin Allàh** 'the Prophet Muhammad, i.e., the one who was sent by God', cf. **Allàh ma'àikī** 'God (lit. God the sender)'. The dictionaries also give the feminine agent word **makullìyā** with the meaning 'slave-concubine' (i.e., one who is locked up) < **kullè** 'lock'.

1.4. Gender restrictions

Morphologically, all agentives have three forms: masculine, feminine, and plural. With adjectival usage (see below), masculine and feminine forms are equally common. For example, **mahàukàcī** (m.) and **mahaukacìyā** (f.) 'mad, crazy' are both fully acceptable. With nouns, however, the agential tends to be restricted to one gender or the other. In many cases this restriction is determined by real-world culture and semantics, for example, **ma'àskī** 'barber' (not ****ma'askìyā**) is masculine only because this traditionally has been a masculine profession. In other cases, however, the agent occurs only in the masculine form even though there is no cultural reason why the feminine agent shouldn't be allowed, e.g., **mamàcī** 'the deceased' is normal but, for inexplicable reasons, ****mamacìyā** is not. Examples:

Masculine only
maɗìnkī tailor; **magìnī** builder, potter, cf. **magìnā tukunyà** pot makers (pl.) (m. and/or f.); cf. **mài tukwànē** potter (lit. owner of pots) (m. or f.); **mahàȓbī** hunter; **mahàucī** butcher, meat-seller; **majèmī** tanner; **mamàcī** the deceased; **manòmī** farmer; **masàssàƙī** carpenter, carver; **masùncī** (usu. **ɗan sû**) fisherman; **matàshī** youth, young man
Feminine only
magàjìyā a madam; older sister (cf. **magàjī** a prince) both < **gàdā** inherit; **magūɗìyā** woman who ululates; **makitsìyā** women's hairdresser; **makullìyā** (slave) concubine; **mashēƙìyā** winnower (used primarily in the idiomatic phrase/epithet **ƙàiƙàyī kòmà kân mashēƙìyā** (lit. chaff return on winnower) the hairy weed *Indigofera astragalina*, which causes a spell to recoil on a psn who sets it in action

1.5. Productivity and alternatives

Morphologically, the agent derivation is extremely regular. In principle, one could morphologically create an agent noun from almost any verb. In fact its occurrence is lexically quite restricted: some agentives are readily accepted and are commonly used, others are viewed as clumsy if not totally unacceptable. An alternative to the agentive is the MAI construction (see chap. **45**) made up of **mài** (pl. **màsu**) 'one having properties of' + NP (including verbal noun). Examples (where the notation =? indicates that the variant to the left is preferred):

mài askì	barber (< askì shaving) = ma'àskī	mài ba'à̀	a mocker = mabà'àncī
mài fassaȓà̀	translator =? mafàssàȓī	mài ȓafkanuwā	forgetful psn =? maȓàfkànī

1.6. Agent nouns with objects

In English, agent -er nouns allow the expression of the thematic direct object (in front of the noun), e.g., 'wheat farmer', 'bird watcher', 'lion hunter', etc. In Hausa, the expression of the object is also allowed in some cases, e.g., **mahàȓā kwâl** 'coal miners', but there are significant peculiarities and restrictions related to gender and number and to whether one uses a full form or a short form.

1.6.1. Full-form agentives with objects

Masculine singular agents that take thematic objects tend to be limited to fixed phrases or very close collocations. The agent is connected to the object by means of the linker -**n**, e.g.,

mashàyin giyà̀	a drinker, drunkard (lit. drinker of alcoholic beverages)
but not ****mashàyin kòfī**	a coffee drinker
mahàddàcin Kùȓ'ānì	someone who has memorized the Koran
matùȓin jirgī	a pilot (not ****matùȓin mōtà̀** a car driver)
masòyin Mànzō	devout Muslim, follower of the teachings of the Prophet Muhammad
(lit. lover of the Messenger)	

In most cases, one either uses the agent noun without explicitly mentioning the object, which is implied or understood anyway, or else employs a paraphrase, as with a **mài** construction, e.g.,

marìnī	a dyer (of cloth) (not ****marìnin yādī** a cloth dyer)
manìyyàcī	an intending pilgrim
= the full but less common **manìyyàcin aikìn hajjì** (lit. intender.of work.of hadj)	
mài ɗinkà̀ hūlunà̀	cap embroiderer (not ****maɗìnkin hūlunà̀**)

> °AN: In modern journalese, as practiced, for example, by BBC announcers, one commonly comes across agents with objects, e.g., **masànin Hausa** 'a Hausa scholar'. It remains to be seen whether this practice will become the norm or whether these agent phrases are ephemeral neologisms meeting the exigencies of news deadlines.

Feminine agentives cannot be followed by thematic objects, i.e., expressions such as ****mashāyìyaȓ giyà̀** 'a female drunk' are unacceptable.

1.6.2. Plural agentives with objects

Plural agentives, on the other hand, take objects much more readily than do the masculine singular forms. Interestingly, the plural agents do not require a linker before the object. The linker is allowed, but its use is the less common alternative. Examples:

manèmā làbāȓī	reporters (= **manèman làbāȓī**)
macìyā nāmà̀	meat-eaters (= **macìyan nāmà̀**)
mashàyā giyà̀	alcohol drinkers, drunkards
maȓèȓā mōtōcī	auto manufacturers
magìnā tukunyā	potters
mabùnȓùsā ȓasā	root-crops (potatoes, onions, etc.)
masòyā āmadà̀	lovers of the teachings of the Prophet

With the linkerless form some speakers allow phrases in which the plural agent is followed by an indirect object, e.g.,

??mabùgā manà rīgunà̀	the ones who beat gowns for us
??madàkā minì sàkwàrā	the ones who pound yams for me

1.6.3. Short-form agentives with objects

Some verbs, mostly grade 0 monoverbs, have special disyllabic short-form agents that can be used only if there is a following object (or locative goal). These are composed of **ma-** plus a monosyllabic verb stem with an overriding H-L tone pattern. **Ci** verbs, which underlyingly have a short vowel, lengthen the vowel in the agentive formation in keeping with the requirement that the syllable after the **ma-** must be heavy. Examples:

macì àmānà̀	treacherous person (lit. eater trust)
mabì sarkī	one who follows the emir
mazò̀ gàrī	one who comes to town
maƙì rawā	one who hates dancing
majà̀ hanyà̀	a guide (lit. puller road)
makàs dubū	king's assassin; killer of thousands (< **kashè̀** kill)
majè̀ sìlìmân	one who frequents the movies

> °AN: [i] The short form **majè̀** (from the irregular verb **jē** 'go to') does not have a full-form counterpart, i.e., ****majè̀yī** does not exist.
>
> [ii] Full-form agents constitute independent, self-standing nouns, e.g., [mabìyī]ₙ 'follower, younger brother' (< **bi** 'follow'). The short-form agents, on the other hand, are bound formatives that connect with the following word to form compoundlike NPs. Thus, whereas the phrase [mabì sarkī]ₙ 'one who follows the emir' constitutes an NP, **mabì** by itself does not qualify as a noun.

Short-form nouns of agent can be built with short-form grade 5 verbs, which take oblique objects introduced by **dà** rather than direct objects, e.g.,

mabà̀ dà nōnò̀	wet nurse (lit. giver (of) breast/milk) (< **bā dà** give (sth) < **bā** give to)
mabì dà aȓnā	one who subdues pagans (< **bī dà** subdue, control < **bi** follow)

Short-form agents are normally understood to be singular only (gender irrelevant). Overt expression of the plural requires use of the corresponding long-form plural, e.g.,

macìyā àmānà̀ treacherous people; **mabìyā sarkī** follows of the emir; **makàsā dubū** king's assassins, killers of thousands

Some speakers accept short-form agents with an indirect object. As with the plural agents, other speakers reject these formations, e.g.,

??macì minì àmānà̀	the one who cheats me
??mabì minì dà yârā	the man who controls the children for me

In many cases, the short-form agentives are found in set expressions and compounds, e.g.,

magà̰-takàr̃dā	scribe (one who sees-paper)
Magà̰-watà̰	proper name (lit. one who sees-moon)
majà̰-cikì	name of a spirit. (lit. puller-belly)
mashà̰-ruwā	rainbow (lit. drinker-water)
majḭ̀-dādī	luxurious psn, emir's private secretary (lit. feeler-pleasantness)
majà̰-sir̃dì	traditional title (lit. puller-saddle)

Three short-form agentives have become grammaticalized with special syntactic functions. The form **masò̰** (< **sō** 'want, like, love') indicates directions, e.g.,

kudù masò̰ gabàs	southeast (lit. south one that likes east)
arèwa masò̰ yâmma	northwest (lit. north one that likes west)

The short-form agentive **mafḭ̂** (< **fi** 'exceed') is used in superlative expressions. The plural uses the regular form **mafîyā** without the linker, e.g.,

mōtà̰ mafḭ̂ tsàdā	most expensive car
'yan k̃wallon rāgā mafîyā kyâu	the best basketball players

> °AN: Some speakers allow **mafḭ̂** as a number-neutral grammatical marker, e.g., **'yan k̃wallon rāgā mafḭ̂ kyâu** 'the best basketball players'; **sū nè mafḭ̂ yawà̰ nân gàrī** 'They are the majority in this town.'

The short-form agentive **maràs** (= **maràr̃** = **maràG** (where G geminates with the following consonant) = **marà**) (< **rasà̰** 'lack') functions as the negative counterpart to the particles **mài / màsu** 'having the quality of'. The full-form **maràsā**, which occurs without the linker, is required in the plural, e.g.,

yār̃ò̰ marà̰r̃ hankàlī	a senseless boy (cf. **yār̃ò̰ mài hankàlī** a sensible boy)
yârā maràsā hankàlī	senseless boys (cf. **yârā màsu hankàlī** sensible boys)
ɗākì marà̰r̃ tāgà̰	a room without windows
ɗākunà̰ maràsā tāgà̰	rooms without windows

1.7. Adjectival usage

Many **ma-** agent forms, especially those based on intransitive verbs, also function as adjectives, e.g., **wannàn mahàukàcin dir̃ēbà** 'this crazy driver' vs. **wannàn mahàukàcī** 'this madman'. Whether the nominal or adjectival usage is the more common varies from word to word. These adjectival items all tend to have masculine, feminine, and plural forms, e.g., **matsò̰ràcī / matsōracìyā / matsò̰ràtā** adj./n. 'coward(ly)'. Examples (given in the masculine singular only):

maɓàr̃nàcī adj./n.	destructive, a spendthrift		**mahò̰màcī** adj./n.	boastful, swanker
makwàɗàicī adj./n.	greedy (psn)		**mak̃àryàcī** adj./n.	lying, liar
mak̃ètàcī adj./n.	malicious, wicked (psn)		**mak̃ḭ̀wàcī** adj./n.	lazy, slacker
malàlàcī adj./n.	lazy (psn)		**marò̰wàcī** adj./n.	stingy, tightwad
matsìyàcī adj./n.	poor, destitute (psn)		**mawàdà̰cī** adj./n.	wealthy, contented (psn)
mayùnwàcī adj./n.	voracious, hungry (psn)		**mazàmbàcī** adj./n.	swindler, con man

Although one normally thinks of the **ma-** construction as a means of deriving nouns, there are some agent forms that function almost exclusively as adjectives and must be recognized as such. Examples:

madàidàicĪ adj.   average, medium-sized;   mafàɗàcĪ adj.   vicious, quarrelsome, cantankerous;   mafĪ̃fĪcĪ adj.   superior;   magàggàucĪ adj.   impetuous;   mahànkàlcĪ adj.   sensible;   maɼazàncĪ adj.   filthy; manàgàɼcĪ adj.   reliable, good (e.g., **manàgàɼcin yārȍ**   a reliable lad);   manì'ìmcĪ adj.   luxurious, fertile (land);   manĪ̀sàncĪ adj.   distant (e.g., **manĪ̀sàncin gàrĪ**   distant town);   matàbbàcĪ adj. permanent, enduring; reliable;   matàɼàicĪ adj.   restricted, reduced in scale;   matsànàncĪ adj.   severe, excessive, extreme (e.g., **matsànàncin àl'amàɼĪ**   a severe situation);   mawùyàcĪ adj.   difficult, troublesome (e.g., **àbù mawùyàcĪ**   difficult or impossible thing);   mayàlwàcĪ adj.   abundant, adequate; extensive (of area)

Like simple adjectives, agent adjectives obligatorily agree in gender and number with the head noun, e.g., **mafàɗàcin sâ** 'a vicious bull';   **mafaɗàcìyaɼ ɓaunà** 'a vicious buffalo'   **mafàɗàtan sōjōjĪ** 'vicious soldiers'. They occur both as pre-head modifiers (with a linker) and post-head modifiers, e.g.,

madàidàicin mùtûm = mùtûm madàidàicĪ	medium-sized man
mahàukàtan kaɼnukà̀ = kaɼnukà̀ mahàukàtā	mad dogs
malàlàcin ɗàlìbĪ = ɗàlìbĪ malàlàcĪ	a lazy student
matsanancìyaɼ wàhalà̀ = wàhalà̀ matsanancìyā	an extreme difficulty
mayàudàran mutànē = mutànē mayàudàrā	deceitful people
mawadācìyaɼ sàraunìyā = sàraunìyā mawadācìyā	a rich queen

It was pointed out above (§1.6.2), that the linker is optional (and typically not used) with plural agentives followed by an object, e.g., **makàsà kuɗĪ** 'squanderers' (i.e., money killers). When plural agentives function as prenominal adjectives, the linker is required, e.g.,

malàlàtan yârā (not **malàlà̀tā yârā)	lazy children
mawàdà̀tan 'yan kàsuwā (not **mawàdà̀tā 'yan kàsuwā)	rich businessmen

There are some phrases where the agentive adjectives appear to be restricted to post-head position. These, however, are not true noun-adjective constructions, despite the translations, but rather are noun-noun constructions where the second noun is in apposition to the first, e.g.,

wani mùtûm maɗìnkĪ	a certain tailor (lit. a certain man, a tailor)
dìɼēbà mashàyĪ (not **mashà̀yin dìɼēbà)	a drunkard of a driver (lit a driver, a drunkard)
Filà̀nĪ makìyà̀yā (not **makìyà̀yan Filà̀nĪ)	pastoral Fulani (lit. Fulani, pastoralists)
tsōhō makàɼàncĪ (not **makàɼàncin tsōhō)	an old man who has memorized the Koran

2. LOCATION (ma-...-ā / ma-...-ī)

Deverbal nouns of location containing the prefix **ma-** occur in two forms, both of which have all H tone. Most (about three-fourths) of the commonly occurring locationals end in -ā. These are feminine. The others end in -ī. These are masculine. The meaning of the derivative is the place generally associated with the activity of the base verb. Examples:

(a) **maɓuɓɓugā**   spring (of water);   **mafakā**   shelter;   **mafarautā**   hunting ground;   **majēmā**   tannery;   **makaɼantā**   school;   **makiyāyā**   pasture, grazing land;   **masussukā**   threshing floor
(b) **masallācĪ**   mosque (cf. **sàllàtà** perform daily prayer);   **masaukĪ**   lodging place, overnight quarters, guest room/house;   **mashigĪ**   opening, doorway; canal;   **matsayĪ**   position, post, status, place where psn or sth remains/stands;   **masai** (< *masāyĪ) cesspit (cf. **sàyè** fence in)

The derivative **mafitsārā** 'bladder' is built on the noun **fitsārī** 'urine' rather than a verb stem.

Many (but not all) location nouns containing final -ī have an alternative variant with final -ā. Where the two variants coexist, the ā-final form is the one that is generally preferred (indicated (1)).

maɓōyī = **maɓōyā** (1)	hiding place
macēcī (1) = **macētā**	place of refuge
magamī = **magamā** (1)	junction, crossroad, meeting place
magangarī = **magangarā** (1)	place of descent
makwarārī = **makwarārā** (1)	water-channel

◊HN: It is possible that at an earlier stage, location nouns with **ma-...-ī** were more common than at present. (Note that some of the most basic locationals, such as **masaukī** 'lodging place', have this form.) The motivation for the switch to **ma-...-ā** would have been to differentiate the locationals from the **ma-** instruments nouns, all of which are formed by **ma-...-ī**, e.g., **magirbī** 'harvesting tool' (*not* 'harvesting place').

In one instance—and there may be a few more—there is a semantic difference between a location noun with final -ā and the one with final -ī, e.g.,

matsayā	a stop (e.g., **matsayar̃ bâs** bus stop); a resting place for travelers
cf. **matsayī**	place where psn or thing remains, stands, position, post, status

As a class, these location nouns do not form plurals as readily as agents or instruments. (Common lexical items such as **makar̃antā** 'school' are an exception.) The formation of the plural, when used, can be described as follows. Locationals ending in -ī form their plurals with -ai)^{LH}, e.g.,

macēcī / màcêtai	place of refuge
makwancī / màkwàntai	sleeping place
masallācī / màsàllàtai	mosque

Locationals ending in -ā show greater variation in plural formation. Some require or prefer a plural with -u)^{LH}; others prefer the -ai)^{LH} plural suffix. Some words allow either plural type equally. A few words with final -iyā also allow the -ōCī)^H plural formative, this being the preferred plural choice for non-derived feminative nouns. Examples:

ma'aikatā / mà'àikàtū workplace, factory; **makar̃antā / màkàr̃àntū** school; **marāyā / màràyū** town (as opposed to village); **ma'auratā / mà'àuràtai** place for getting married; **mafakā / màfàkai** shelter; **mahayā / màhàyai** incline, place where one climbs up; **mashēk̃ā / màshèk̃ai** winnowing-floor; **mafarautā / màfàràutū** = **màfàràutai** hunting ground; **masukwānā / màsùkwànū** = **màsùkwànai** galloping place, race field; **maciyā / màcìyū** = **màcìyai** = **maciyōyī** small wayside eating place; **ma'ajiyā / mà'àjìyū** = **mà'àjìyai** = **ma'ajiyōyī** storeroom, place for safekeeping

◊HN: For many of the location nouns, the plural does not seem to be fixed but rather is determined by speaker preference with regard to individual items. The confusion is probably due to the choice between the two singular forms. For example, if one normally uses the form **mak̃ētarī** 'crossing-place' with the regular plural **màk̃ètàrai**, this form may become the preferred plural, rather than **màk̃ètàrū**, even if one switches to **mak̃etarā** in the singular. That is, originally there was probably a fully regular connection between -ā singulars and -ū plurals on the one hand and -ī singulars and -ai plurals on the other hand (the latter still being seen with the instrument forms).

3. INSTRUMENT (ma-...-ī)

Instruments containing the prefix **ma-** are formed by suffixing -ī)[H], with an all H tone pattern. All of these words are masculine. Examples:

madōshī   punch (tool); branding iron; **magirbī**   harvesting tool; **makaɗī**   musician's drumstick, spindle; **matōshī**   stopper, cork; **mazurārī**   funnel

The word **makarī** 'antidote', which semantically relates to the expression **karyà dafī** 'break poison', is built on the base //**kar-**// without the synchronically frozen -**ya** suffix.

The **ma-** prefix often assimilates to /**mu**/ when the vowel in the following syllable is /**u**/ (especially short /**u**/). This has become the preferred pronunciation in present-day SH.

mahūjī = muhūjī	boring tool	**magurjī = mugurjī**	stone for rubbing/scraping off
makullī = mukullī	key, lock	**mazurārī = muzurārī**	funnel
mahūcī = muhūcī	fan (cf. the variant **mafīcī**, which does not change into ****mufīcī**)		

For reasons that are not clear, the assimilation is much less common with **ma-** nouns of agent and location than it is with the instruments, e.g.,

magùjī ≠ **mugùjī   a runaway (agent);   **makūsā ≠ **mukūsā**   blemish (location)

The instrument **murfī** 'cover' (< **murufī** < **marufī** (< the verb **rufà** 'cover')) is now essentially fixed in the shortened form. The word **mur(i)ƙī** < **mariƙī** 'handle' is unusual in that **mu-** appears even though there is no /**u**/ in the following syllable.

The application of the /**a**/ to /**u**/ assimilation rule is not, however, automatic. Some instrument words resist the assimilation, especially when the following /**ū**/ is long, e.g., **mabūɗī** 'opener' is not normally pronounced as ??[mubūɗī], nor is **matūƙī** 'stirring stick' pronounced as ??[mutūƙī].

Plurals of instrument nouns are formed regularly by means of the -**ai**)[LH] suffix, e.g.,

madōshī / màdòsai	punch (tool); branding iron
magirbī / màgìrbai	harvesting tool
muburgī / mùbùrgai	swizzle stick, stick for stirring soup
murfī / mùrfai	lid, cover

Exception: **majanyī / màjànyai = màjànyū**   strap for tying a baby on the back

Generally speaking the meaning of the instruments is transparent, i.e., a tool or instrument for doing the action of the verb, e.g., **magirbī** 'harvesting tool' < **girbè** 'to harvest'. In some cases, the meaning is somewhat restricted or not so clearly instrumental, e.g.,

madūbī	mirror < **dūbà** to look
madōgarī	prop, support; one's means of livelihood < **dògarà** lean on
mafārī	origin, beginning; reason, cause < **fārà** start
makāmī	weapon < **kāmà** catch
mashimfiɗī	cloth placed over animal's back before saddle is put on < **shimfiɗà** spread
masōshī	thick pin used by women for hairdressing or scratching head < **sōsà** scratch
masakī	large calabash < **sakà** put

4. FROZEN **ma**- FORMS

There are a small number of words that have the shape of **ma**- derivatives but that synchronically must be treated as simple lexical items. The forms can generally be derived from verb (or noun) bases, but the semantic relation is often opaque or very specific.

These words are typically feminine and look exactly like feminine agents, e.g., **matāshìyā** 'reminder, headline' (< **tāshì** 'rise'); **maɗamfarìyā** 'tick' (< **ɗàmfarà** 'cling to'). Semantically, however, the words do not appear to be agents. If they relate to the underlying base in any systematic way it is as instruments, and, in principle, there is no reason why they couldn't be considered as feminine instruments. (In other words, the **ma**-...-**ìyā** H...LH forms would represent the feminine counterpart to the masculine instruments in the same way that they serve as feminine nouns corresponding to the masculine agents.) Synchronically feminine instruments do not exist as a productive derivational formative—all the productive instruments are masculine and end in -**ī**—but there is no reason why they could not have existed as such at an earlier period, these frozen items being the vestige.

Note that words of this group that allow plurals do *not* use the regular agent plural form. Rather, they either drop the final -**ìyā** and add -**ai** or else retain the -**ìyā** ending and add -**ōCī**. Here is a fairly complete list of these frozen **ma**-...-**ìyā** forms.

madōbìyā / màdòbai	rosewood tree (< ??)
madudduk̄ìyā	low (back) door (= **madudduk̄ā** (loc.) (< **duddùk̄ā** crouch)
maɗācìyā / màɗàtai	gall bladder (< noun **ɗācī** bitterness)
maɗamfarìyā	tick (< **ɗàmfarà** cling to)
magūɗìyā	the short high string on a lute (< noun **gūɗà** ululating)
majinācìyā / màjìnàtai	artery, jugular vein; a red-juiced weed (cf. **jinī** blood)
mak̄ar̄kashìyā / mak̄ar̄kashiyōyī	plot, conspiracy, sabotage (< noun **k̄ar̄kashī** underside)
mak̄ēk̄ashìyā	anemia (< **k̄ēk̄àshē** dry up)
mak̄ērìyā	flat-headed tool of blacksmith (< **k̄ērà** forge)
mak̄yūyacìyā	cramp (cf. **k̄yûyā** indolence, laziness)
makallacìyā	cornstalk, spindle (< **kàllatà** look at (?))
manūnìyā	sign, signal (< **nūnà** show)
marāɓìyā	spleen (< **rāɓà** stick to, prop against (?))
masanìyā	knowledge (< **sanì** know)
masōkìyā	spasm on the side of the body (< **sōkè** stab)
masōshìyā	itch inducing disease (< **sōsà** scratch)
matāshìyā / matāshiyōyī	reminder, headline (< **tāshì** rise)
mayank̄wanìyā	anemia (< **yank̄wànē** become emaciated, shrivelled)

In addition to the above feminine words, there is one common masculine singular agent form and one plural agent form that refer to things rather than persons, e.g.,

maɗàcī	mahogany tree (< **ɗācī** bitterness)
maràinā	testicles (< **rainà** have no respect for (?))

[References: McIntyre (1988a, 1988b, 1995); Parsons (1963)]

8. Apposition

1. INTRODUCTION

APPOSITION is indicated by immediate juxtaposition of two NPs without use of an overt morphological connector and normally without any noticeable phonological hiatus. The two NPs normally match in terms of number and gender. In some cases, the order of the two elements can be reversed without appreciable difference in meaning. Apposition is particularly common with proper nouns, but all kinds of nouns and NPs are possible, e.g.,

[Bàlā Mùhammàd] [àlƙālin gàrinmù]	Bala Muhammad, the judge of our town
[Lādì] [uwaȓgidansà]	Ladi, his senior wife
[Sànūsi] [Sarkin Kanò]	Sanusi, Emir of Kano
[Kanò] [bàbban biȓnin jihàȓ]	Kano, the capital of the state
[matåsā] ['yan cāca]	youths, gamblers
[Sulè] [sarkin tashå]	Sule, the station master
[Bellò] [gōganmù]	Bello, our hero (e.g., in this play)
[ƙasaȓmù] [Nìjēȓiyà]	our country, Nigeria
[wani mùtûm] [maɗînkī]	a certain man, a tailor
[wata yārinyà] [Bàfilātànā]	a certain Fulani girl (lit. certain girl, Fulani)
[mùtumìn nân] [ɗan ƙasaȓ Mālì]	this man, a Malian
[wannàn manòmī] [bāwàn Allàh]	this farmer, a simple man (lit. slave of God)
[dilā] [mālàminsù] dà [zākì] [sarkinsù]	jackal, their teacher and lion, their chief

°AN: Jaggar (personal communication) has pointed out that apposition, like relativization, can be restrictive or nonrestrictive, e.g., **Mālàm Mūsā mālàminmù yā yi ràsuwā** 'Malam Musa our teacher died' (where the restrictive apposition 'our teacher' tells which Malam Musa) vs. **Mālàm Mūsā mālàminmù yā yi ràsuwā** 'Malam Musa, our teacher, died' (where the nonrestrictive apposition 'our teacher' is extra, extraneous information. The nature and phonological marking of this distinction needs further study.

Instead of being juxtaposed directly, nouns in apposition can be introduced by particles, the most common being **wàtàu** (= **wàtò**) 'that is to say'. Examples:

Rabat, wàtàu bàbban biȓnin Màȓōkò	Rabat, i.e., the capital of Morocco
kànàri-bâ-kējì, wàtò kāȓùwà	a prostitute (lit. canary-without-cage), i.e., a prostitute
shùgàban tîm ɗîn, wàtò Gaȓbà Pele	the captain of the team, i.e., Garba Pele

2. WEAK PRONOUNS

Weak object pronouns and genitive object pronouns, which do not allow direct modification or coordination, can be followed by an appositional phrase containing a coreferential independent pronoun, e.g.,

yā tàimàkē [mù] [dà nĪ dà shĪ]	He helped us, me and him.
anǎ yàbon[sà] [shĪ àlƙālîn]	They are praising him, he the judge.
zân biyā [kù] [kū biyu]	I will pay you, you two.
don mè ka gayǎ ma[tà] [ita mâyyā]?	Why did you tell her, she the witch?
mun hàr̄bē [shì] [shĪ kânsà]	We shot him, he himself.
sunǎ gayǎ mi[nì] [nĪ kâinā]	They are telling me, me myself.

3. EMPHATIC REFLEXIVES

Emphatic reflexives (see §63:1.2) are formed by means of an independent pronoun followed by a reflexive pronoun in apposition, e.g.,

kàfîn [shĪ] [kânsà] yà yàr̄da dōlè yà tàmbàyi wânsà
   Before he himself agrees he should ask his older brother.
[ita] [kântà] tàurārùwā cè   She herself is a star.
[sū] [kânsù] nē sukà gòyi bāyan màganàr̄sà   They themselves supported his assertion.

Emphatic reflexives, which internally are appositional in structure, can themselves stand in apposition to a noun, e.g.,

[Bellò] [[shĪ] [kânsà]]	Bello himself (lit. Bello he himself)
[kūrā [[ita] [kântà]]	the hyena itself
[màlàmai] [[sū] [kânsù]]	the teachers themselves

As is the case with many other items in apposition, in appropriate circumstances the noun and the emphatic reflexive can be transposed, e.g.,

[gwamnatì] [ita kântà] zā tà ɓatar̄ dà kuɗī dà yawǎ
= [ita kântà] [gwamnatì] zā tà ɓatar̄ dà kuɗī dà yawǎ
   The government itself is going to spend a lot of money.
yā sâ [Kànde] [ita kântà] tā kōmǎ gidā = yā sâ [ita kântà] [Kànde] tā kōmǎ gidā
   He caused Kande herself to return home.

4. PRENOMINAL POSSESSIVES

Possessive pronouns consisting of a genitive linker plus a bound pronoun follow the head noun, e.g., gidanmù 'our house' (lit. house.of.us). One can foreground the possessive by using a free-form possessive pronoun in front of the noun (which usually will have a definite article attached) in an appositional construction, e.g.,

an rūshè [nāmù] [gidân]	They tore down *our* house. (lit. one.comp raze ours house.the)
zā mù shìga [tāsà] [mōtàr̄]	We will enter *his* car.

wằ kằ iyà hōrař dà [nāsù] [dawākī]?   Who could possibly train *their* horses?

°AN: Most grammars describe the above examples as simply having pre-head as opposed to post-head modifiers. This is inexact grammatically and misleading typologically. In Hausa, possessive modifiers qua modifiers occur *only* after the head noun; the semantically related sentences with the possessives in front represent an appositional structure.

5. 'KIND OF' PHRASES

Phrases indicating 'kind/type of' are indicated by an appositional structure, although the translation is not appositionlike. The special appositional phrase is formed with **irìn** 'the type' + linker (**na/ta**) + NP. Note that the linker agrees with the head noun and not with **irìn**, e.g.,

tufāfì [irìn na dâ]	old-style clothing (lit. clothing kind.the of formerly)
gàshìn-bàki irìn na Hitler	a mustache like Hitler's (lit. mustache type.the of Hitler)
mōtằ irìn tākà	a car like yours (lit. car type.the of.you)

6. UNIT MEASURES

Non-count nouns like water, grain, sand, etc. denote an undifferentiated mass and thus cannot be modified directly by a numeral. To express a quantity, one uses an appositional phrase consisting of a "unit measure" noun plus a numeral (or other quantifier), e.g.,

mâi galàn huɗu	four gallons of oil (lit. oil gallon four)
takàřdā fallē ɗaya	a single sheet of paper (lit. paper sheet one)
yàshī tīfằ takwàs	eight dump truck loads of sand (lit. sand dump trucks eight)

7. PRONOUNS WITH NUMERALS

Phrases consisting of a plural independent pronoun plus a numeral can stand in apposition to a head noun. In the third person, the exact semantic function of the appositional phrase as opposed to simply using the numeral is unclear, although the presence of the pronoun seems to add a degree of emphasis or specificity to the phrase, e.g.,

mawàllàfā kū bìyař	you five authors (lit. authors you (pl.) five)
'yan-jàřīdū mū ukù	we three reporters (lit. reporters we three)
shùgàbànnī sū huɗu	four leaders (lit. leaders they four) = (?) **shùgàbànnī huɗu**
ɓàrằyī sū gōmà	ten thieves (lit. thieves they ten) = (?) **ɓàrằyī gōmà**
ɗàlìbai sū shidà	six students (lit. students they six) = (?) **ɗàlìbai shidà**

[Reference: Galadanci (1969)]

9. Aspectual Verbs

1. INTRODUCTION

ASPECTUAL verbs (AVs), like **fārà** 'begin', **sākè** 'repeat', **cikà** 'do too much', require that they be followed by an embedded nonfinite VP with the same subject interpretation. The embedded VP consists of an infinitive phrase (IP) or a verbal noun (VN) or VN phrase. (The VP can also consist of a dynamic noun due to deletion of the pro-verb **yi** 'do'.) Aspectual verbs denote such concepts of verbal aspect, modality, or manner as inceptive, durative, repetitive, etc. Sentences with AVs can sometimes be translated with an English aspectual verb, but the best translation is often with an adverb or other modifier of the complement. Examples:

wà zâi sākè [harbà bindigàr]?	Who will fire the gun again? [IP]
yā kāsà [gyāràwā]	He was unable to fix (it). [VN]
sun nèmi [kòyon Lārabcī]	They tried to learn Arabic. [VN phrase]
Audù yā dingà [gayà matà tà tàfi]	Audu kept on telling her to go. [IP]
yā cikà [shân giyà]	He drinks too much. [VN phrase]
(lit. he filled drinking beer)	
yā kumà [zìyartàr 'yan'uwansà]	He visited his family again. [VN phrase]
(lit. he repeated visiting his family)	

> °AN: These verbs were formerly called "auxiliary" verbs by Hausaists. The term *aspectual* verb, used, for example, by Yalwa (1994), seems more in keeping with modern linguistic usage and the treatment of similar verbs in other languages. The term also avoids confusion with the AUX category often employed in the analysis of tense/aspect inflection.

There are some thirty or so aspectual verbs. (One cannot indicate an exact number because the dividing line between aspectual verbs and main verbs that take nonfinite VP complements is fuzzy.) Most AVs are transitive or sociative; some are intransitive. A few, e.g., **dingà** (= **rikà** = **rinkà**) 'keep on doing', **fayè** (= **fiyà**) 'do too much of', **kumà** 'do again' (cf. the adverb/modal particle **kuma** 'again'), occur exclusively as aspectual verbs. The large majority of AVs, however, exist also as simple main verbs, the primary meaning and the metaphorical/extensional meaning sometimes being close and sometimes more remote, e.g.,

(AV) **mun rasà [ganin sarkī]**	We were unable to see the chief.
(lit. we lacked seeing chief)	
(main) **mun rasà àbîn dà zā mù yi**	We didn't know what to do.
(lit. we lacked thing that we will do)	
(AV) **Wàzīrì Aku zâi kārà [bā shì mìsàlai]**	Vizier Parrot will give him more examples.
(lit. ... will increase give him examples)	

(main) yā ƙārà kuɗī	He increased the money.
(AV) yā cikà [shân giyà]	He drinks too much beer.
(main) tā cikà tùlū	She filled the water pot.
(AV) mun kāmà [shirìn yāƙì dà sū]	We have started preparing for war with them.
(main) mun kāmà ɓarāwòn	We caught the thief.
(AV) kā taɓà [cîn nāmàn kadà]?	Have you ever eaten crocodile meat?
(main) kā taɓà hòtôn?	Did you touch the photo?
(AV and main) kā taɓà [taɓà macìjī]?	Have you ever touched a snake?

The following is a list of the more common aspectual verbs. The largest number operate grade 1; the rest are scattered in other grades. AVs do not seem to fall into grade 5 or grade 6. Examples:

barì v* stop doing/leave off doing; ci gàba dà v0 carry on, continue doing; cikà v1 do too much of; daɗà v1 repeat/do again; dainà v1 stop/cease doing; dingà v1 keep on doing; dōsà v1 keep on doing; fārà (dà) v1 begin (with), fārā v2 initiate, introduce; fāsà v1 postpone/fail; fiyà v1 (= fayè v4) do too much; gamà v1 finish/complete; gazà v1 lack; ìsa v3 be capable of; iyà v1 be able to/know how to; jimà dà v1 be for a while; kāmà v1 begin doing; kammàlā v1 complete doing; kāsà v1 fail to do/be unable to; ƙārà (dà) v1 repeat/do again; ƙārè v4 finish doing; kōmà v1 go back to doing; kumà v1 repeat/do again; kusa v* be about to/almost; nèmā v2 try to, be about to; ràbu dà v7 time has passed since; ragè v4 do less than before; rasà v1 be unable to do; riƙà (= rinƙà) v1 keep on doing; sābà (dà) v1 be used to doing; sākè v4 repeat/do again; sāmù v2 manage to /succeed in doing; sōmà (dà) v1 begin (with) (= fārà (dà)); sōmā v2 initiate, introduce (= fārā); shā v0 do often/much; shìga v3 set about/begin/start/take on doing; taɓà v1 ever do; tārā v1 share doing; tàsā v2 (= tāshì v3b) set about, take steps toward doing; tsayà v1 persist in, stick to, persevere in; yi ta v0 keep doing

The gr7 aspectual verbs and a few others, including the phrasal verb ci gàba dà 'proceed with, continue to be' (lit. eat front with), function as sociatives with the prepositional particle dà. When sābà (dà) 'be accustomed to' is used as an AV, the dà is optional; otherwise it is obligatory. Examples:

nā ràbu dà ganinkà	I haven't seen you for some time.
(lit. I.comp separate with seeing you)	
yā sābà dà wàsā dà macìjī = yā sābà wàsā dà macìjī	He is accustomed to playing with snakes.
cf. yā sābà dà talaucìnsà	He is accustomed to his poverty.
Lādì tā fārà dà shirìn zàrē	Ladi started with preparing the thread.
Shàgàri yā ci gàba dà zamā shùgàbanmù	Shagari continued to be our president.

The phrasal verb yi ta 'keep on doing' is composed of the pro-verb yi 'do' plus the preposition ta 'via'. In the continuous TAMs, the yi is almost always dropped, e.g.,

sun yi ta ròƙonsà	They (completive) kept on begging him.
munà yi ta tàimakon talakāwā ⇒ munà ta tàimakon talakāwā	
We (continuous) keep on helping the needy.	
don mè kukè yi ta yàbonsà? ⇒ don mè kukè ta yàbonsà?	
Why do you (pl.) keep on praising him?	

Transitive AVs followed by an embedded object use the pre-direct object C-form of the verb, which in gr1 ends in short -a and in gr2 ends in short -i, e.g.,

kù <u>gamà</u> shārè ɗākìn	You (pl.) finish sweeping the room!
yā <u>cikà</u> shân giyà	He drinks too much beer.
yā <u>iyà</u> sāƙàr̃ tàbarmā	He is able to weave mats.
Rùmfa yā <u>fàr̃i</u> ginìn gānuwā à Kanò	Rumfa initiated the building of the Kano wall.
yā <u>tàshi</u> bugùn yārò	He set about beating the boy.

Grade 4 verbs normally have two alternative C-forms, one with a short final -e and one with a long -ē. When functioning as AVs, grade 4 verbs (in SH at least) use the short vowel variant only, e.g.,

sâ <u>sākè</u> faɗà makà	They will probably tell you again.
cf. sâ sākè(e) r̃īgunànsù	They will probably change their gowns.
tā <u>ragè</u> zuwà kàsuwā	She goes to the market less often.
cf. tā ragè(e) àlbâshinmù	She reduced our wages.

With intransitive AVs, the following nonfinite VP constitutes a complement rather than a direct object. The verb thus appears in its normal A-form, e.g.,

ya <u>ìsa</u> [hawan kèkè]	He is old enough to ride a bicycle. (< ìsa reach)
ya <u>kōmà</u> [kàr̃àtun Hausa]	He switched back to the study of Hausa. (< kōmà return)
kā <u>tsayà</u> [yi minì wani shìrmē]	You persisted in doing nonsense to me. (< tsayà stand, stay)

2. INDIRECT OBJECTS

Aspectual verbs do not take indirect objects. Verbs in an embedded infinitive clause, on the other hand, may take an i.o., e.g.,

tā <u>fàrà</u> [dakà [masà]$_{i.o.}$ hatsī]	She began pounding the grain for him.
not **tā <u>fàrà</u> [masà]$_{i.o.}$ [dakàn hatsī]	
sun <u>kāsà</u> [kāmà [wà wàzīr̃ì]$_{i.o.}$ dōkì]	They failed to catch the horse for the vizier.
not **sun <u>kāsà</u> [wà wàzīr̃ì]$_{i.o.}$ [kāmà dōkì]	
mun kusa [yi [musù]$_{i.o.}$ bìkī]	We were close to doing the celebration for them.
not **mun kusa [musù]$_{i.o.}$ [yi bìkī]	

In limited circumstances the object of an AV consisting of the pro-verb **yi** plus an i.o. plus a direct object allows deletion of **yi**. The result is a surface sequence of an AV followed immediately by an i.o. (Most AVs do not allow this.) Interestingly the AV followed by the i.o. uses the D (pre-i.o.) form of the verb (which has a long final vowel) and not the C (pre-d.o.) form with a short final vowel. This is so even though structurally the surface i.o. is not the i.o. of its adjacent AV. Examples:

nā <u>fàrà</u> [yi masà aikì] = nā <u>fārà</u> [masà aikì]   (fàrà is the C-form; fārà is the D-form)
    I began to work for him.
yā <u>sàbà</u> [yi wà yârā wàsā dà macìjī] = yā <u>sābà</u> [wà yârā wàsā dà macìjī]
    He is accustomed to playing with snakes for the children.
kadà kù <u>sākè</u> [yi manà munāfuncì] = kadà kù <u>sākè</u> [manà munāfuncì]
    Don't be treacherous to us again.

Sometimes **yi** followed by an i.o. undergoes fast speech contraction rather than being deleted, e.g.,

yā yi [ta yi] wà mutånē ɓàr̄nā (→) yā yi [tai] wà mutånē ɓàr̄nā
>He kept on causing damage for the people.

yā nèmi [yi] masà aikì̃ (→) yā nèmī masà aikì̃   He sought to work for him.

3. TAM

Subject to semantic appropriateness, the aspectual verb in the main clause can be in any TAM (tense/aspect/mood) or in the imperative, e.g.,

(fut) zâi ƙār̄à bā shì mìsålai   He will give him additional examples.
(pret) wândà ya shā ɗaukàr̄ kāyā   the one who is burdened with picking up the loads
(cont) yanà shìgā (yîn) kāsuwancì duk lōkàcîn dà kuɗī ya yankè̃ masà
>He goes in for trading whenever he runs short of money.

(sub) bài dācè̃ ba kà dingà wulākàntà talakāwā
>It is inappropriate that you should keep on belittling poor people.

(imp) fàr̄à kar̄àntà littāfìn!   Start reading the book!

In negative sentences using the discontinuous negative marker bà(a)...ba, the second ba goes at the end of the sentence after the embedded object/complement, e.g.,

bà tà fār̄à kar̄àntà littāfìn ba   She hasn't started reading the book.
bà zâi ƙār̄à bā shì mìsålai ba   He will not give him any more examples.
bà sù ìsa tàfiyà makar̄antà ba   They aren't old enough to go to school.

The verb nèmā is semantically varied depending on the choice of the TAM and the verb in the nonfinite clause. Normally it means 'try to'; however, in the continuous with a nonvolitional verb, it means 'be about to', e.g.,

yā nèmi shìgā makar̄antā   He tried to enter school.
zā mù nèmi biyàn kuɗin hayà   We will try to pay the rent.
tanà nēman cirè tàkàlmintà   She is trying to take off her shoes.
tunkìyā tanà nēman mutuwà̃   The ewe is about to die.
ɗākìn yanà̃ nēman fāɗō wà mutånē à kā   The room is about to fall on people's heads.

4. THE EMBEDDED COMPLEMENT AND yi DELETION

AVs are followed by three main types of embedded objects/complements: (1) general nonfinite verb phrases (infinitive phrases, nominalized verbs, and verbal nouns); (2) yîn (which is the verbal noun of yi 'do' plus the linker) followed by a nonverbal dynamic noun (e.g., barcī 'sleep', gar̄damà̃ 'disagreement'; sùr̄ūtù 'noise'), and (3) yîn followed by an abstract noun (e.g., sanyī 'coolness', nauyī 'heaviness', tsawō 'height'). Examples:

(1) yā fār̄à [kar̄àntà littāfìn]   He began to read the book. (lit. he started read book)
(1) sun cikà [sàyen yādì]   They bought too much cloth. (lit. they filled buying yardage)
(1) lìttàttàfan Lār̄abcī sun dainà [såmuwā à Los Angeles]
>Arabic books can no longer be found in L.A. (lit. ...have ceased (being) acquirable in L.A.)

(2) yā fār̄à [yîn màganà̃]   He began to talk. (lit. he started doing conversation)
(2) sun cikà [yîn sùr̄ūtù]   They make too much noise. (lit. they fill doing racket)

(3) yā fārà [yîn wārī]   It began to stink. (lit. it started doing stench)
(3) sun cikà [yîn nauyī]   They were too heavy. (lit. they filled doing heaviness)

A general feature of the language is the optional (but usual) deletion of the pro-verb **yi** in nonfinite predicates (see **§58:3**), e.g., **yanà̃ yîn aikì̃** (⟹) **yanà̃ aikì̃** 'He is working' (lit. he.cont (doing) work). As a consequence of this rule, AVs are commonly followed on the surface, not by verbal noun phrases, but rather by dynamic nouns or abstract nouns, e.g.,

yā fārà màganà̃	He began to talk.
sun cikà sù̃r̄ū̀tù̃	They make too much noise.
mun yi ta gar̄damà̃	We kept on arguing.
yā fārà wārī	It began to stink.
sun cikà nauyī	They were too heavy.
an yi ta sanyī	It kept on being cool.

The **yi** in the AV **yi ta** 'keep on' may undergo deletion in nonfinite clauses. When it is followed by a predicate containing **yi** plus a dynamic or abstract noun, one can get two instances of **yi** deletion in the same sentence, the first obligatory, the second optional, e.g.,

munà̃ yi ta yîn gar̄damà̃ ⟹ **munà̃ Ø ta (yîn) gar̄damà̃**   We were arguing continuously.

In most cases, sentences with and without the **yi** are essentially equivalent in meaning, e.g., **yā sā̀kè** [yîn barcī] = **yā sā̀kè** [barcī] 'He slept again', **an sṑmà yîn ruwā** = **an sṑmà ruwā** 'It began to rain'. In some instances, on the other hand, there tends to be a semantic difference, the sentence with **yi** having a more specific time reference than the one without it, e.g.,

wannàn mùtûm yā cikà yîn nauyī	This man is getting too heavy. (process)
wannàn mùtûm yā cikà nauyī	This man is too heavy. (state)
gàrī yā shìga yîn zāfī	This town has started to become difficult to live in.
gàrī yā shìga zāfī	The weather has started getting hot.

If the object of **yi** is fronted, the verb (in its verbal noun form) is usually required. Sometimes, however, it may still be deleted, depending on the specific nature of the AV. If the **yi** is deleted and the AV is not followed on the surface by an object, then the AV naturally appears in its A-form with a long final vowel.

ciyar̄ dà ìyālìnsà kàm, yā dainà yî = ciyar̄ dà ìyālìnsà kàm, yā dainà̃
       As for providing for his family, he has ceased doing it.
màganà̃ ya fārà yî = màganà̃ ya fārà   It was talking he began (to do).
sù̃r̄ū̀tùn dà sukà cikà yî ≠ **sù̃r̄ū̀tùn dà sukà cikà̃   the noise they made too much of
mè̃ kukà yi ta yî? ≠ **mè̃ kukà yi ta?   What did you keep on doing?

Similarly, if the nonfinite VP object of the AV is fronted, a resumptive dummy **yî** verbal noun is usually inserted after the AV, although in some cases the sentence without the **yî** is acceptable, e.g.,

wulā̃k̀àntà gàjìyàyyū ya yi ta yî	Bothering the unfortunate he kept on doing.
(< yā yi ta wulā̃k̀àntà gàjìyàyyū	He kept on bothering the unfortunate.)
sàyen mōtà̃ ya sā̀kè yî	Buying cars he did again. (< yā sā̀kè sàyen mōtà̃)

5. DELETION OF FULL VERBS IN THE EMBEDDED CLAUSE

Apart from **yi**, there are other nonfinite verb forms in the embedded clause after the AV that can sometimes be omitted. This deletion is allowed when the verb plus a semantically closely related object indicate a common, well-understood activity so that the meaning of the verb is recoverable from the context, e.g., **màtātā tā gamà dafà àbincin rāna** 'My wife finished cooking lunch' can be shortened to **màtātā tā gamà àbincin rāna** (lit. my wife finished lunch). Note that this sentence is still understood to mean 'My wife finished *cooking* lunch' and not, for example, 'My wife finished *eating* lunch'. Further examples:

yā iyà hawan dōkì (⇒) **yā iyà dōkì**
> He is a good horseman. / He knows how to ride. (lit. he is able to (riding.L) horse)

bà tà iyà dafà miyà ba (⇒) **bà tà iyà miyà ba**
> She doesn't know how to cook. (lit. she isn't able to (cook) soup)

Shātā yā fārà rērà Bàkandamìyā (⇒) **Shātā yā fārà Bàkandamìyā**
> Shata began (singing) the *Bakandamiya* (name of a song).

Audù yā kusa gamà nōman gōnařsà mākòn jiyà (⇒) **Audù yā kusa gamà gōnařsà mākòn jiyà**
> Audu almost finished (tilling) his farm last week.

nā ci gàba dà kařàntà Ruwan Bagajā yâu (⇒) **nā ci gàba dà Ruwan Bagajā yâu**
> I continued (reading) *Ruwan Bagaja* (title of a novel) today.

6. STACKING OF AVs

Where semantically appropriate the object/complement of an AV can itself contain an AV, i.e., AVs can in principle be stacked one after the other, although if there are too many (probably more than three) the sentence becomes clumsy, e.g.,

Tankò yā [kusa [gamà nōman gōnařsà]]
> Tanko almost finished tilling his farm.

Tankò zâi [iyà [fārà (yîn) kařàtū cikin watà ɗaya]]
> Tanko will be able to start reading in one month.

Tankò bà zâi [sākè [cî-gàba dà [(yîn) kařàtū kàfin mū]] ba
> Tanko will never again continue with the reading before us.

Tankò bà zâi [kārà [cî-gàba dà [fārà [(yîn) kařàtū kàfin mū]]] ba
> Tanko will not ever continue with beginning the reading before us.

Tankò bà zâi [iyà [kārà [sākè [(yîn) kařàtū kàfin mū]]] ba
> Tanko will not be able to repeat again the reading before us.

7. SUBJUNCTIVE COMPLEMENTS

Some AVs (often expressing modality) also serve as complement-taking verbs followed by a tensed sentence in the subjunctive, e.g., **Sāni zâi iyà [yà yi aikìn yâu]** 'Sani can do the work today' (lit. Sani will be able that he do the work today). These verbs are **ìsa** 'be up to', **iyà** 'be able to', **nèmā** 'attempt to', **ràbu dà** 'not do for some time', **sābà** 'be accustomed to', and, for some speakers, **fārà** 'begin'. For speakers who accept them—and not all do—the sentences with the subjunctive are semantically more or less equivalent to the comparable sentences with an AV followed by a nonfinite VP, e.g., **Sāni zâi iyà [yà yi aikìn yâu]** = Sāni zâi iyà [yîn aikìn yâu]** (lit. Sani will be able doing the work today) 'Sani can do the work today.' Curiously, the gr1 AVs followed by a complement sentence in the subjunctive appear in the A-form (with a long final vowel), which is the form used when no object follows, whereas the one gr2 AV appears in the pre-object C-form. Examples:

Gwamnằ yā ìsa [yà yankè hukuncì] (subjunctive clause) = **Gwamnằ yā ìsa [yankè hukuncì]** (IP)
    The Governor suffices (i.e., has the position or authority) to give the verdict.
mutằnên sun nèmi [sù bijìrē] (subjunctive clause) = **mutằnên sun nèmi [bijìrêwā]** (VN)
    The people wanted to revolt. (**nèmi** is a gr2 C-form)
yā sābằ [yà zìyàřci maràsā lāfiyằ] = **yā sābằ [zìyařtař maràsā lāfiyằ]**
    He is used to visiting sick people.
    (**sābằ** with the long final -**ằ** is a gr1 A-form; **sābà** with the short final -**à** is a gr1 C-form)
nā ràbu dà [ìn gan shì] = **nā ràbu dà [ganinsà]**
    I've not seen him for some time.
yā fằrà [yà yi zāgì] = **yā fằrà [(yîn) zāgì]**
    He began spouting insults.

[References: Abraham (1934); Jaggar (1977); Pilszczikowa (1960); Tuller (1986); Yalwa (1994)]

10. Associated Characteristics (Suffix -au)

THE major dictionaries of Hausa include large numbers of derived nouns containing a suffix -au and a fixed L-H tone pattern. These are normally built on verb bases, e.g., **màkàrau** 'dilatory psn' < **màkarà** (base //**makar**-//) 'be late' + -**au**)^{LH}. Generally speaking, the suffix is nonproductive and occurs fixed in lexically specific items. Many of the individual items found in the dictionaries (including a few of the examples below) are unknown to modern SH speakers. Derivatives with -**au**)^{LH} often have an expressive, adverblike, almost exclamatory function. It is hard to provide a single meaning for the suffix that covers all of its occurrences. The best that one can do is to group these words, which I will refer to simply as "-**au** words", into a small number of identifiable semantic categories or groups.

1. GROUP 1

In this most general category, the -**au** words indicate a person, action, or thing with the characteristics—often excessive—of the base verb. Examples:

àrau being prone to borrowing < **àrā** borrow (e.g., **yanà shân àrau dà yawà** 'He tends to borrow a lot, or tends to be borrowed from.'); **bìyau** child or animal that follows the psn it knows < **bi** follow); **dàgùlau** a spoiler < **dàgulà** be spoiled; **dàgàzau** a slovenly psn who overeats < **dàgazà** (usu. **dàgàr̃gazà** (with a short initial vowel!)) eat a large quantity of some particular food; **dàkùsau** psn who is invulnerable to knives, etc. < **dākùsā** make blunt; **fìddau** a reject (e.g., piece of paper spoiled while writing) < **fid dà** throw out; **fìƙau** a very sharp thing, state of being well sharpened < **fēƙè** / **fìƙu** sharpen / be sharpened (e.g., **wai! fìƙau, lallai wannàn fensìr̃ yā fìƙu** 'Sharp! Well this pencil has been truly sharpened.'); **fìtìnau** being very worrisome < **fìtinà** worry, bother (e.g., **kâi fìtìnau, wannàn mùtûm yā cikà fìtinàr̃ tsìyā** 'This man is a big nuisance.'); **gìgìtau** psn or thing that flusters people < **gìgìtā** fluster; **gìllau** telling huge lies < **gìllà ƙaryā** tell a big lie; **hàndàmau** glutton (with medial /a/) < **hàndumà** eat much of; **jìmrau** / **jùrau** energetic, tireless person/animal (also a personal name) < **jūrè** show fortitude; **kàràiràyau** a grass < **karairàyā** keep breaking; **kyànkyènau** officious psn; rainbow < **kyankyènē** be officious, monopolize conversation or work; **ƙàgau** a bucket jammed in well < **ƙagè** get stuck; **màntau** very forgetful psn < **mântā** forget; **sàgau** leather charm worn on the upper arm supposed to stiffen arm of one's opponent < **sagè** stiffen, paralyze; **tàfìyau** s.o. who travels a lot < base //**tafiy**-//, cf. **tàfi** go; **tàbàrau** eye-glasses < ??

◊HN: The word **tàbàrau** 'eyeglasses' would appear to be an -**au** word, but the source stem is missing. Another possibility is that the -**au** ending has nothing to do with this derivation, but rather is an archaic plural suffix now limited to just a few words like **kibiyà** 'arrow', pl. **kibau**.

In a few instances, the -**au** derivative is built on a noun or adjective rather than a verb, e.g.,

àsȋrau	a psn well known for being secretive < àsȋrȋ secret
gàngàmau	describes a huge psn < gangamēmè huge
sìyȁsau	s.o. overly involved in politics < sìyāsȁ politics

2. GROUP 2

The second category indicates doing the action of the verb for payment, e.g.,

càsau threshing grain for payment < càsā thresh; dàkau pounding grain for pay < dakȁ pound; ɗìnkau sewing for pay < ɗinkȁ sew; nìƙau grinding for payment < nikȁ grind; rìnau dyeing for wages < rinȁ dye with indigo; sùrfau pounding grain for payment < surfȁ pound moistened grain to remove bran

3. GROUP 3

A small number of insects and plants (especially harmful) appear with frozen -**au**, e.g.,

bùȓdìngau	sausage-fly < ??
hùrau	larvae of digger-wasp (= rùrau, bùrau, fùrau) < hūrȁ blow (on)
kùɗau	type of small water-beetle < kuɗȅ to draw back head, dive into water
shȁshȁtau	a weed supposed to ward off results of wrongdoing if put in criminal's mouth or in his bathwater < shāshȁtā treat as a fool, divert from topic
tsȋdau (= [Kts] tsàidau)	a thorny weed < tsai dà bring to a halt, stop
tùnkùyau	flea < tùnkuyȁ butt, gore

4. GROUP 4

Diseases constitute a fourth category of lexically fixed -**au** words:

fàsau	chapping, esp. of heels < fasȁ break
hàȓbau	blackquarter (cattle-disease) < hàȓbā shoot
kùȓkùzau	eczema on cow; mange on dog/donkey < kūjè fray, abrade, cause slit in material or skin
ƙàràmbau	chicken pox < ??
màƙarau	quinsy, diphtheria; anthrax < màƙarȁ strangle (?) (Note length of initial vowel.)
sànƙàrau (usu. cīwòn sànƙàrau or ànnòbaȓ sànƙàrau)	cerebro-spinal meningitis < sanƙàrē stiffen

5. GROUP 5

A common use of the -**au** suffix is in descriptive epithets, e.g.,

dàgùyau	epithet of a hyena < dàguyȁ gnaw at/eat much of (meat)
dàmàmùsau	epithet of an emir or brave warrior < damāmùshē eat up quickly
dìmau	epithet of storm; epithet of an emir < dimȁ plunge weapon into a psn
dìrkàkau	epithet of an emir < dìrkākȁ approach with determination
gàbȁtau	epithet of a paramount chief < gàbātȁ be leader of
gàgàrau	epithet or nickname of any Abubakar; epithet of a warrior or of a difficult, unbeatable psn or thing < gàgarà behave rebelliously
gìndau	epithet of a dog or a destitute person < ??

jìtau	epithet of a paramount chief < **jìtà** put on a lot of clothing
kêtau	epithet of any barber < **kētà** split, tear
kòrau	epithet of any **shâmaki** (official in charge of stables); a proper name < **kōrà** drive animals in front of oneself
mâk̄âsau	epithet of elephant, a burly psn, or an influential man < ?? (cf. ideophone **màk̄as** emphasizing fullness)
sûr̄au	epithet of a kite or hawk < **sûr̄à** swoop down

6. GROUP 6

The **-au** suffix also frequently occurs in descriptive proper names, most often personal names, but sometimes place names as well, e.g.,

Bàrau	proper name < **barì** leave
Dìbgau	name for any person called Bello < **ɗìbgā** drive away, take too much of
Gùsau	place name < ??
Hàk̄ùrau	proper name < **hàk̄urà** be patient
Kòsau	name for child born at harvesttime < **k̄ōsà** be well-fed
Mâkau	proper name; **Bāwâ Mâkau** name for a *bori* spirit < **mâkā** beat
Màntau	proper name (given to a child after previous infants have died) < **mântā** forget
Màyau	name for posthumous child < **màyā** replace
Sàllau	nickname for Salihu (boy born during a festival) < **sallà** festival
Shèkàrau	proper name (given to a boy supposed to have spent a year in the womb) < **shèkarà** spend a year
Tùnau	proper name (given to a boy whose mother was long childless) < **tunà** remember (cf. **Allàh yā tunà dà kē** God has remembered you, i.e., you have given birth to a child after all.)
Jâtau	proper name (for light-skinned boy) < **jā** red (?)

◊HN: I have no explanation for the medial /t/, unless this derivation is incorrect and **Jâtau** has a different etymological origin.

Names with **-au**)^LH are all masculine. The corresponding feminine names, if they exist, do not exhibit a regular morphological formation, e.g.,

Bàrau m., cf. **Barkò** f. or **Bàraukà** f.; **Màntau** m., cf. **Mantai** f.; **Shèkàrau** m., cf. **Shēkàrā** f.; **Tùnau** m., cf. **Tùne** f.; **Jâtau** m., cf. **'Yar̄-ja** (with short final vowel) f.

7. GROUP 7

In recent times, the **-au** suffix, which one would have thought was in a state of desuetude, has been employed to create new grammatical terminology (often as an alternative to loanwords from English or Arabic). Examples of these neologisms include the following:

àikàtau verb < **aikàtā** to work; **bàyânau** adverb < **bayyànā** explain (cf. **bàyānì** explanation); **dògàrau** relative, dependent (clause) < **dògarà** depend on; **hàddàsau** causative < **haddàsā** cause; **kàr̄ɓau** (direct) object < **kàr̄ɓā** receive

11. Augmentatives and Diminutives

1. AUGMENTATIVE ADJECTIVES

HAUSA has a good-sized class of phonaesthetic, expressive adjectives (referred to in the literature as "augmentatives" or "profusatives"), where the notion of "exceedingly" or "excessively" is an integral part of the meaning of the word, e.g., **sundumēmè** 'very big and swollen', **santalēlìyā** 'extremely tall and slender'; **dùgùzunzùmī** 'shaggy-haired, disheveled' (e.g., crazy person or animal). They primarily express expansiveness of size, shape, or space, often with negative connotations. Semantically these items correspond to such English words as 'voluminous', 'extensive', 'stupendous', 'colossal', etc., and often lend themselves to expressive translations like 'a whale of a fish', 'a scarecrow of a youth', 'a well-stacked woman', etc. These words tend to be somewhat coarse and thus are normally not found in "polite company" or formal situations.

Augmentatives are often narrowly restricted in their collations, e.g., **ŕingimēmè** indicates 'overly large and round', particularly of heads, whereas **shamɓarēŕìyā** 'bosomy' refers only to women's breasts. Most words of this class denote largeness, bountifulness, and/or beauty of some sort, but some—especially those belonging to the C-form, to be described below—connote abnormally small or stupid, being in effect augmentatives in reverse. Unlike agentives and ethnonyms, for example, many of which occur both as independent nouns and as adjectives, all words of this class function exclusively as adjectives.

Augmentative adjectives can be identified by a regular morphological formation involving a set final vowel and tone pattern plus in many cases an athematic stem-final consonant. In most cases the underlying base does not exist apart from these words. For example, **buŕɗumēmè** 'huge' (of animals) clearly contains a reduplicative suffix with an associated H-L tone pattern, but the base //**buŕɗum**-// doesn't exist elsewhere in the language.

> °AN: Out of some 140 or so augmentative adjectives, there are only a handful that could be analyzed as deriving from a base found in a possibly related extant verb. These include **gabjējè** 'bulky' < **gabzà** 'heap up a lot of sth'; **gamɓashēshè** 'huge and muscular' < **gàmɓasà** 'break off a large chunk'; **shimfiɗēɗè** 'extensive' < **shimfiɗā** 'spread'; **tsamfēfè** 'handsome' < **tsamfà** 'do task well'.

Following the convention initiated by Parsons (1963: 192–95), augmentatives are normally described as having three subclasses, referred to as forms A, B, and C. The implication is that these variant forms are essentially equivalent allomorphs of the same morpheme. Although the variant forms are semantically related and share common ideophonic and exclamatory derivations, the C-form (which I am labeling Aug(mentative)-2) is really different enough to be set apart from the A- and B-forms. These latter forms can be grouped together to form a subclass (called Aug(mentative)-1), although even this grouping is somewhat problematic.

1. 1. Augmentative-1 (A & B forms)

In describing the two Augmentative-1 variants, I present the B-form before the A-form because the B-form is the more active and productive.

1.1.1. Augmentative-1b: The B-form -ēCē)^{HL}

The B-form is built using a tone-integrating suffix -ēCē)^{HL} where C represents a copy of the base-final consonant. The fixed H-L tone pattern spreads from right to left over the entire word. The corresponding feminine forms end in -ìyā as determined by general feminine formation rules, e.g.,

sangamēmè m.	sangamēmìyā f.	huge (of living things)
ƙur̃shēshè m.	ƙur̃shēshìyā f.	large and round (of nuts)

About a quarter of the B-form augmentatives are trisyllabic words built on a base with a heavy initial syllable. The base has either the form CVVC-, where the long vowel is /ā/ or /ū/ (or /ī/ in one case), or CVCC-. The base-final consonant is occasionally a sonorant, but most often it is an obstruent. (Examples will be given only of the masculine forms since the corresponding feminine forms are fully predictable, e.g., **zūƙēƙè / zūƙēƙìyā** 'very beautiful'.)

ɓūlēlè	excessively fat	mākēkè	long and broad (e.g., room, farm)
wāgēgè	large	tīƙēƙè	huge (Note /tī/ without palatalization!)
burmēmè	ragged, disheveled	gabjējè	huge, plentiful
ribɗēɗè	huge and bulky	shabcēcè	wide and slitlike (e.g., mouth, cut)

About three-quarters of the B-forms are quadrisyllabic built on CVCCVC- (or occasionally CVCCVCC-) bases where both vowels are identical. (Again, examples will be given only of the masculine forms since the corresponding feminines with -ìyā are fully predictable, e.g., **sundumēmè** / f. **sundumēmìyā** 'very big and swollen'.)

(a) birkiɗēɗè	huge (e.g., cloth)	gansamēmè	tall and stout
bundumēmè	fat-bellied, plump	hangamēmè	huge, cavernous (esp. mouth)
ɓuɓɓukēkè	hefty	sangarmēmè	proportionately tall and strong
famfarērè	spacious (room, container)	zar̃taɓēɓè	big and strong
gamɓashēshè	huge and muscular, gigantic	zinƙir̃ērè	chock full
zungurmēmè (= zungurērè)	long (e.g., stick, car), tall (e.g., man)		

Synchronically the final consonant of the quadrisyllabic forms, which is most commonly /m/ (the second most common consonant being /l/), constitutes an intrinsic part of the lexical item, but in some ways it appears to be a base extension and not part of the root as such. There are, for example, a certain number of doublets with and without the final sonorant, as well as some examples where the final sonorant is dropped in the plural, e.g.,

fir̃ɗēɗè = fir̃ɗimēmè	huge (horse) / pl. fir̃ɗā-fìr̃ɗà
zandēdè = zandamēmè	tall and well built / pl. zandā-zàndà *or* zandamā-zàndàmà
zungurērè = zungurmēmè	long / pl. zungurā-zùngùrà
bambarmēmè	spacious (e.g., room, container) / pl. bambarā-bàmbàrà
dandarmēmè	huge and long / pl. dandarā-dàndàrà

°AN: Note that the /d/ in the example **zandēdè** does not palatalize, whereas /z/ in augmentatives always does, e.g., **gabjējè** 'huge' (< //gabzēzè//, pl. **gabzā-gàbzà**.

1.1.2. Plurals -ā x 2)$^{H-L}$

The plural formation of B-type augmentatives consists of the addition of a suffix -ā to the base (extended or plain), complete reduplication, and the imposition of a fixed H-L tone pattern, i.e., all H on the first reduplicate and all L on the second reduplicate. Consonants that appear palatalized in the singular because of the final -ē (or feminine -ìyā) "depalatalize" before the final -ā of the plural. Examples:

gabjējè / **gabzā-gàbzà** huge (people)		**gansamēmè** / **gansamā-gànsàmà** tall and stout	
ribɗēɗè / **ribɗā-rìbɗà** huge and bulky		**shaȓtaɓēɓè** / **shaȓtaɓā-shàȓtàɓà** long and sharp	
tsālēlè / **tsālā-tsàlà** tall, slender (usu. women)		**zungurērè** / **zungurā-zùngùrà** long, tall	

Being adjectives, augmentatives occur naturally as prenominal modifiers with an attached linker, e.g., **suntuɓēɓèn yārò** 'an oaf of a boy'; **santalēlìyaȓ yārinyà** 'a shapely girl'. They may also occur post-nominally, where they are usually extended by a prepositional phrase made up of **dà** plus a coreferential independent pronoun, e.g., **yārò suntuɓēɓè dà shī**; **yārinyà santalēlìyā dà ita**. The corresponding plural augmentatives, on the other hand, do not normally occur in prenominal position, i.e., the phrase **'yammātā santalā-sàntàlà (dà sū)** 'shapely girls' is fine but ??**santalā-sàntàlàn 'yammātā** is considered extremely clumsy. This limitation, however, is not a property of augmentatives per se but rather is due to a more general prohibition against over-heavy (including fully reduplicated) adjectives in prenominal position.

1.1.3. Augmentative-1a: The A-Form -ī)^{H}

About half of the quadrisyllabic B-form augmentatives have corresponding A-forms, e.g., **fandamēmè** (B) = **fandamī** (A) 'huge'. The trisyllabic B-forms do not have A-forms. There are no A-forms without corresponding B forms. Semantically the two forms are essentially equivalent, although native speakers have a sense that the heavier B-forms are slightly stronger and more expressive than the A-forms.

The A-forms contain a tone-integrating suffix -ī)^{H}, i.e., final -ī and an all H tone pattern. They all have the canonical shape CVCCVCī. Corresponding feminines replace the final -ī by -ā, this being the normal feminine marking for words ending in H tone -ī, e.g., **fankamī** m. / **fankamā** f. 'very broad and flat', **bulluƙī** m. / **bulluƙā** f. 'huge'. The A-forms share the same ā-final reduplicated plurals as the B-forms, e.g., **fankamī** m. (= **fankamēmè**) / **fankamā-fànkàmà** pl. Examples (giving the masculine and plural forms only):

gandamī (= **gandamēmè**) / **gandamā-gàndàmà**	long and strong (e.g., sword)
jimɓirī (= **jimɓirērè**) / **jirɓirā-jìmɓìrà**	heavy
samɓalī (= **samɓalēlè**) / **samɓalā-sàmɓàlà**	tall and well-formed psn
sangamī (= **sangamēmè**) / **sangamā-sàngàmà**	huge

According to the standard descriptions, the A-forms and the B-forms are syntactically as well as semantically the same in that they both function as normal adjectives, e.g.,

(a) **fankamēmèn kògī** = **fankamin kògī** (b) **kògī fankamēmè** = **kògī fankamī**
     an immensely broad river
(a) **santalēlìyaȓ yārinyà** = **santalaȓ yārinyà** (b) **yārinyà santalēlìyā** = **yārinyà santalā**
     a tall, shapely girl

Present-day Hausa speakers—at least as represented by most of the people with whom I worked—only allow the B-forms as adjectival NP modifiers, i.e., **fankamēmèn kŏgī** is acceptable but ****fankamin kŏgī** is not; **yārinyà santalēlìyā** is acceptable but ****yārinyà santalā** is not. For these speakers (and even others who would allow such expressions as **fankamin kŏgī** as grammatical), the A-forms are considered more nominal-like and stylistically/pragmatically restricted, i.e., **santalā** is better translated as 'a tall, shapely one' rather than 'tall/shapely'. This nominal character shows up in two ways. First, the A-forms (and not the B-forms) can stand as the descriptive head of a **kìrārì** (praise epithet). For example, epithets like **suntuɓī** (…) 'Oh heavy one (you are too difficult to lift)' or **kinkimī** (…) 'Oh large one [turban] (only an emir can enjoy you)' would be perfectly normal. Second, A-forms (but again, not the corresponding B-forms) can be used as nicknames, e.g., **Gundumī** (*not* ****Gundumēmè**) nickname for a strong, solid guy (name of a famous boxer), contrast **gundumēmèn mùtûm** 'a strong man', *not* = ****gundumin mùtûm**; **Santalā** (*not* ****Santalēlìyā**) nickname for a tall, shapely girl.

1.2. Augmentative-2: the C-form -ī)ᴸᴴᴸᴴ

Augmentative-2 adjectives constitute a small class of some two dozen or so words that denote unusual smallness, shortness, or compactness as well as largeness or expansiveness. They primarily, although not exclusively, serve to modify nouns referring to humans or other animates. They are often restricted to humans of one sex or the other. Some three words allow Aug-2 adjectives as an alternative to a corresponding Aug-1 form (A or B), namely, **bŏɗaɗɗàrī** (C) = **bōɗarērè** (B) 'having big buttocks'; **fànkankàmī** (C) = **fankamī** (A) = **fankamēmè** (B) 'very broad and flat (e.g., river)'; **wàngamgàmī** (C) = **wangamī** (A) = **wangamēmè** (B) 'extensive or broad (e.g., container, pond)'. This, however, is clearly the exception rather than the rule. Aug-2 adjectives are generally totally independent of Aug-1 forms and constitute a separate, if semantically related, word class.

> °AN: Presumably it was the existence of the triplets **fankamī** (A) = **fankamēmè** (B) = **fànkankàmī** (C), for example, that mislead Parsons into thinking that the A-, B-, and C-forms could be grouped together as a single class. As analysts, we often run the danger of generalizing on the basis of very common forms that later turn out to be atypical.

The canonical shape for Aug-2 adjectives, all of which have four or more syllables, is the reduplicative structure X-CVC-CVCī)ᴸᴴᴸᴴ (where X represents one syllable of any type (light or heavy) or two light syllables), and the antepenultimate CVC syllable is a copy of the first three segments of the final two syllables, e.g., **càkur̃kùr̃ī** 'short and slight (person or animal)'. The Aug-2 adjectives all exhibit the same (L)-L-H-L-H tone pattern.

> °HN: Historically these augmentatives were formed by two-syllable reduplication to the right as was the case with frozen reduplicated nouns (see §62:3.1). Thus **shìnkinkìmī** 'heavy, weak-minded', for example, came from ***shìnkìm(ī)** + **-kìmī** with dropping of the original stem-final vowel and simplification of the LH on the resulting antepenultimate closed syllable to H.

The feminine Aug-2 adjective is derived in a regular fashion by replacing the final -ī of the masculine stem by -ā, e.g., **càkur̃kùr̃ā** f. The plural is formed from the singular stem by adding the very common nominal plural suffix **-ai)ᴸᴴ**, e.g., **càkur̃kùr̃ai** pl. In cases where the masculine ends in a palatalized consonant plus -ī, the feminine and plural forms manifest the corresponding alveolars, e.g., **dàgir̃gìjī** (< ***dàgizgìzī**), f. **dàgir̃gìzā**, pl. **dàgir̃gìzai**) 'short and hairy (e.g., person or sheep)'. The vowel in the initial syllable(s) need not be identical to the other vowels, but it usually is, e.g., **kùtùɓur̃ɓùr̃ī** 'short, thickset, ugly (person)'. The reduplicated nature of the CVC in the antepenultimate syllable is often disguised because of phonological processes of assimilation, gemination, or rhotacism. This can be seen in the following examples, all of which form plurals with -ai)^{LH}:

bùgùzunzùmī (< *bùgùzumzùmī)	big, fat, untidy, ungainly (esp. woman), or animals
dàmɓaᵳɓàsā (< *dàmɓasɓàsā)	dumpy but of pleasant appearance (woman)
ɗàgwaᵳwàsā (< *ɗàgwaswàsā)	small-proportioned (girl)
kùduddùsā (< *kùdusdùsā)	short stout (woman)
lùkùtuttùɓā (< *lùkùtuɓtùɓā)	flabby, well-fatted (girl)
shìnkinkìmī (< *shìnkimkìmī)	heavy (psn or animal); weak-minded (psn)

There are in addition a few words that tonally and semantically would appear to fit into the Aug-2 class but do not exhibit the usual reduplicative structure. Like the regular Aug-2 adjectives, they form corresponding feminines with -ā and plurals with -ai)^{LH}.

dàndaɓàsā squat, well-built (girl); gàgārùmī (= gùrùngunɗùmī) loutish, important (affair, news); gàrànhōtsàmī = gàràngātsàmī pushy, unruly (psn); zàᵳāᵳùᵳī outstanding (psn)

2. RELATED DERIVATIONS

Augmentative adjectives (esp. the Aug-1 forms) have related exclamatory and ideophonic forms, e.g.,

gamɓashēshè	huge (chunks) [Aug-1]
gamɓàshi!	what huge chunks! [exclamation]
gàmɓàsɓàs sg. / gamɓas-gàmɓàs pl.	huge and chunky [ideophone]

2.1. Exclamations

Exclamations related to augmentatives are formed by adding a suffix -i)$^{HL(H)}$ to the base, i.e., short final -i and H-L tone if disyllabic and H-L-H tone if trisyllabic (see §25:2). Note that the base does not include the reduplicative -ēCè suffix of the B-form nor the CVC reduplication of the C-form. The formation is productive with the B-form augmentatives and sporadic/uncommon with the C-forms, e.g.,

fiᵳɗì	what a hulk! < fiᵳɗēdè large, esp. a horse (= fiᵳɗìmi! < fiᵳɗimēmè)
mākì!	how long and broad! < mākēkè
ɓuɓɓùki!	how hefty! < ɓuɓɓukēkè hefty
cākùᵳi!	how short and slight (psn or animal) < càkuᵳkùᵳī
shinkìmi!	how heavy (psn or animal); how weak-minded (psn) < shìnkinkìmī

2.2. Ideophonic qualifiers

Many four (and five) syllable augmentatives (both Aug-1 and Aug-2) have corresponding ideophonic qualifiers that characterize a manner, state, appearance, or other quality of some NP in the sentence, e.g., fànkànkàm / pl. fankam-fànkàm 'broadly spread out' < fankamēmè 'broad'. The singular ideophone is formed by adding -CVC)^L, i.e., by reduplicating the final CVC of the base with the imposition of an all L tone pattern, e.g., tangalēlè 'huge (head) (base //tangal-//) ⇒ tàngàlgàl. (Stem-final nasals automatically assimilate to the following C, e.g., //fànkàmkàm// → [fànkàŋkàm].) The corresponding plural is formed by full reduplication of the base with the imposition of an H-L tone pattern, e.g., base //tangal-// ⇒ tangal-tàngàl (pl.). Examples:

ɓangwalēlè	large/round (e.g., kolanuts) ⇒	ɓàngwàlgwàl / ɓangwal-ɓàngwàl

daṅƙwalēlě	large/round (e.g., raindrops, chickens) ⇒	dàṅƙwàlƙwàl / danƙwal-dàṅƙwàl
bundumēmè	fat-bellied, plump (pot, psn, pit) ⇒	bùndùndùm / bundum-bùndùm
řinɗimēmè	huge/round (e.g., potbelly) ⇒	řinɗìndîm / řinɗim-řìnɗîm
jimɓiřēřè	heavy ⇒	jìmɓìřɓìř / jimɓiř-jìmɓìř
bùgùzunzùmī	fat, untidy, ungainly (psn or animal) ⇒	bùgùzùnzùm / buguzum-bùgùzùm
cåkuřkùřī	short and slight (psn or animal) ⇒	cåkùřkùř / cākuř-cåkùř

The following two examples are interesting in that the syllable final /s/ undergoes rhotacism to /ř/ in the augmentative adjective but remains /s/ in the ideophonic qualifier.

càřařřàsā   petite, good-looking (girl) ⇒   cařasřas / cařas-cařas   (tonally irregular)

dàɓařɓàshī / dàɓařɓàsā   squat, dumpy (animal or woman) ⇒   dàɓàsɓàs / daɓas-dàɓàs

The ideophonic qualifiers serve to describe situations and events, but in a less restrictive, more adverbial way than the augmentatives, which are bona fide adjectives. Here are some examples of ideophonic qualifiers in a sentential context:

kògîn yanà dà fāɗī fànkànkàm	The river is broad, spread out flatly.
kōgunà sunà dà fāɗī fankam-fànkàm	The rivers are broad, spread out flatly.
kåzā nakè sô dàṅƙwàlƙwàl	It's a chicken I want, large and round.
cf. kåzā danƙwalēlìyā nakè sô	It's a large and round chicken I want. (with the Aug-1B)
ruwā yā saukō danƙwal-dàṅƙwàl	The rain fell in huge round drops.
mātā sunà tàfiyà shamɓař-shàmɓàř	The women were walking as buxom women do.
cf. mātā shaɓařā-shàmɓàřå	bosomy women (with the Aug plural)
kà yayyànkà nāmà gamɓas-gàmɓàs!	Cut up the meat in lots of big chunks!

3. DIMINUTIVE ADJECTIVES

A lexically very limited set of some ten ideophonic diminutive adjectives emphasizes the smallness in size, shape, or space of persons, places or things. The ideophonic nature of these words is shown by their expressive meaning (e.g., **tsìgìgìn yārò** 'a shrimp of a boy') and by various phonological features, such as the preservation of nonpalatalized /t/ before a front vowel and the appearance of intervocalic rolled /ř/ where flap /r/ would be expected. These adjectives generally describe things as being narrow, tiny, skinny, constricted, short, light (in weight), etc. They also serve to belittle the people or things referred to. Collocational restrictions often apply in the usage of these adjectives because of their specificity of meaning, e.g., **yisī-yisī** 'tiny' is always plural since it refers only to teeth.

The canonical shape for diminutives (masculine singular) is **cī-CīCī)**^{LHL}, i.e., trisyllabic with the last two syllables identical. The vowel in all three syllables is /ī/, e.g., **mìnìnī** 'small, tiny pieces (of food items)'. The feminine is formed by adding -**ìyā** to the masculine stem in accordance with regular inflectional rules, e.g., **mìnìnìyā**. The plural has a distinct reduplicated structure **CiCī-CiCī)**$^{H-H}$, e.g., **minī-minī**. The diminutive adjectives also have corresponding adjectival ideophones, which are invariant for gender and number. These have the segmental shape of the masculine singulars but with an all H tone pattern, e.g., **mītsītsī** 'tiny'. In some cases, these have become confused with and now function as an alternative to the true masculine singular adjectival forms.

°AN: The feminine singular will normally still take the proper adjectival form; thus one may find such pairs as **ɗan zīřīřin lungù** 'a narrow alley' (with all H), but **'yař zìřīřìyař hanyà** 'a narrow road' (with the correct feminine adjective tone pattern).

Table 1 contains a full list of diminutive adjectives with their corresponding ideophones. Empty cells mean that the forms in question do not occur.

Table 1: Diminutives

gloss	m.	f.	pl.	ideophone
small and plump			dìɓì-dìɓì	
skimpy, shrunk	ɗìgìgì	ɗìgìgìyā	ɗigì-ɗigì	ɗìgìgì
short, skimpy	fìtìtì	fìtìtìyā	fitì-fitì	fìtìtì
tiny (object)			ƙilì-ƙilì	ƙìlìlì
tiny (food)	mìnìnì	mìnìnìyā	minì-minì	mìnìnì
small, tiny	mìtsìtsì	mìtsìtsìyā	mitsì-mitsì	mìtsìtsì
skinny, narrow	sìřìřì	sìřìřìyā	siřì-siřì	sìřìřì
short and small	tsìgìgì	tsìgìgìyā	tsigì-tsigì	tsìgìgì
tiny (of teeth)			yisì-yisì	
narrow, thin	zìřìřì	zìřìřìyā		zìřìřì

°AN: The word **sìřìřì** has other plurals as well, namely, **sìřìřai**, with the regular -**ai** suffix, and **sìřàřā**, a regular DASQ-type plural.

ΔDN: [i] Some speakers pronounce the plural diminutives with a more ideophonic pattern with all short vowels, e.g., **mini-mini** 'tiny', **mitsi-mitsi** 'small', etc., cf. ideophones such as **caɓa-caɓa** 'pimpled, pockmarked', **dushi-dushi** 'hazy, dim, semiblind', etc.

[ii] The word for 'short, skimpy' is also found with /c/ instead of /t/, i.e., **fìcìcì / fìcìcìyā / ficì-ficì / fìcìcì**.

A striking feature of diminutive adjectives is the optional (but commonly employed) redundant use of the diminutive markers **ɗan/'yař/'yan** (m./f./pl.) along with them. (This is comparable to the nonstandard English usage 'wee small'.) The diminutive marker accompanies the diminutive adjective in prenominal as well as postnominal positions. Like other expressive adjectives, post-head diminutives may be extended by a phrase consisting of **dà** + a coreferential personal pronoun. Examples:

(ɗan) mìtsìtsìn gōřò	a tiny kolanut
zanè (ɗan) ɗìgìgì dà shì	a skimpy, shrunk cloth
yārinyà ('yař) sìřìřìyā dà ita	a slender girl
wasu yârā ('yan) mitsì-mitsì (dà sū) nè sukà bā mù tsòrō	Some tiny boys frightened us.

With the H-tone adjectival ideophones, the use of the preposed **ɗan/'yař/'yan** is generally obligatory, e.g.,

wani yārò ɗan tsìgìgì dà shì	a shrimp of a boy
lungunàn Yākàsai 'yan zìřìřì nè	The alleys of Yakasai quarters are very narrow.

[References: Mijinguini (1986); R. M. Newman (1988); Parsons (1963)]

12. Causatives (and Related Formations)

1. CAUSATIVES

CAUSATIVES are expressed analytically by a clause containing the verb **sâ** 'cause', which is etymologically the same as the verb 'put'. The complement may be a tensed sentence or an NP.

°AN: The Hausa grade 5 verb form (see §74:9), as in **yā sayař** 'He sold (it)' (cf. **yā sàyā** gr2 'He bought (it)'), has traditionally been labeled *causative*. This a serious misnomer, which is why I offered a new label for grade 5, namely *efferential*, see Newman (1983). The only causative in the language is the analytic causative being described here. Although Bagari (1977a) was saddled with the old terminology, he clearly outlined the very significant difference between what he termed "morphological causative" (i.e., the gr5 verb) and the analytic true causative with **sâ**.

ΔDN: In place of **sâ**, some speakers use **sânyā**, an alternative variant of the word 'put, cause', e.g., **nā sâ sun yi rawā = nā sânyā sun yi rawā** 'I made them dance' (lit. I caused they did dancing). The word 'put' has an additional variant **sakà**. This, however, is not used to mean 'cause'.

1.1. Causatives with finite-clause complements

Causatives are commonly expressed analytically by a sequence of full clauses. The initial clause with **sâ**, which constitutes the higher clause, indicates who did the causing (i.e., the controller). The second clause, which constitutes the lower clause, describes who was caused (i.e., the controllee) and what he/she/they were caused to do, e.g.,

[Bellò yā sâ] [Kànde tā kōmà gidā]
(lit. Bello he.comp cause Kande she.comp return home)
    Bello caused Kande to return home.
[rashìn ruwā yā sâ] [mutànên nan sù bař ƙauyènsù]
    Lack of water caused those people to leave their village.
[ganin hakà nē ya sâ] [sukà kai sōjōjîn (à) kân iyàkâř]
    Seeing thus caused them to post the soldiers on the border.

If the subject of the lower clause is a pronoun (represented on the surface by the weak subject pronoun), a pronoun identical in person, number and gender can be (and often is) expressed as the object of **sâ** in the higher clause. The two alternatives mean essentially the same thing. Examples:

kà sâ [tà gamà àbinci à kân lōkàcī] = kà sâ <u>ta</u> [tà gamà àbinci à kân lōkàcī]
    Make her finish (preparing) the food on time!
tā sâ [nā yi rawā] = tā sâ <u>ni</u> [nā yi rawā]   She made me dance.
yā sâ [tā shārè ɗ̄akìn] = yā sâ <u>ta</u> [tā shārè ɗ̄akìn]   He had her sweep the room.

°AN: Raising of the subject of the lower clause to object of the higher clause is possible with nouns as well as pronouns; but in the case of nouns it normally cannot be seen. With pronouns, one would get a derivation like the following: [yā sâ] [Pro$_i$ tā shārè ɗākìn] ⇒ [yā sâ ta$_i$] [Ø tā shārè ɗākìn], where the object pronoun, in this case 'her', has the features of the erstwhile subject pronoun. (The form tā in the lower clause is a weak subject pronoun (wsp) that copies the features of the underlying subject pronoun.) The resulting output is yā sâ ta tā shārè ɗākìn. Without raising, the original sentence surfaces as yā sâ tā shārè ɗākìn. With a noun subject in the lower clause, the derivation would be as follows: [yā sâ] [Kànde tā shārè ɗākìn] [he caused] [Kande she swept the room] ⇒ [yā sâ Kànde] [Ø tā shārè ɗākìn] [he caused Kande] [she swept the room]. The output is yā sâ Kànde tā shārè ɗākìn 'He had Kande sweep the room', which is exactly the same surface form one would get from the original sentence without raising. There are some constructions, however, that allow one to see whether raising of the noun subject of the lower clause has taken place or not. In these cases, some speakers have a clear preference for the variant with raising. (1) In the continuous, the verb sâ converts into a weak verbal noun with the suffix ˋwā when not followed by an object. Thus, one gets the following alternatives resulting from the presence or absence of raising: [yanà <u>sâ</u> yârā] [sunà yi masà aikì] = [yanà <u>sâwā</u>] [yârā sunà yi masà aikì] 'He was having the children do work for him.' (2) The verb sânyā, which some people use in place of sâ, has two syntactically conditioned allomorphs: sânyà with final L tone and a short final vowel, when followed by a direct object that is not a personal pronoun (the so-called C-form) and sânyā elsewhere. This distinction allows one to identify raising in noncontinuous constructions, which is not possible with the verb sâ, e.g., [yā sânyā] [Kànde tā shāre ɗākìn] ⇒ [yā sânyà Kànde] [Ø tā shāre ɗākìn] 'He had Kande sweep the room.'

The raising option is not available with the impersonal weak subject pronoun because there is no impersonal object pronoun, e.g.,

| yā sâ ( ) an kāmà ta | He caused that one catch her. |
| yanà sâwā ( ) anà kōrè su | He causes that one chase them away. |

Sentences with and without the raised object pronoun mean essentially the same thing but they are not identical. The sentence with the raised pronoun indicates more explicitly that the controller is directly causing the controllee to do something whereas the sentence without the d.o. pronoun could be interpreted to mean that the causation was more indirect or roundabout, e.g.,

| nā sâ <u>shi</u> [yā mayař dà littāfì] | I made him return the book. |
| nā sâ [yā mayař dà littāfì] | I made him return the book *or* I made it so (i.e., caused something to happen) such that he returned the book. |

The higher clause can have any TAM. With some TAMs, the lower clause can have either (a) a copy of the higher clause TAM, e.g., comp(letive) followed by comp, or (b) the sub(junctive), e.g.,

(a) nā sâ shi [yā mayař da littāfì] (comp...comp)	I made him return the book.
(b) nā sâ shi [yà mayař da littāfì] (comp...sub)	
(a) sū nè sukà sâ Kànde ta kōmà gidā dà wuri (pret...pret)	*They* made Kande return home early.
(b) sū nè sukà sâ Kànde tà kōmà gidā dà wuri (pret...sub)	
(a) yanà sâ ta tanà shārè ɗākìntà (cont...cont)	He is having her sweep the room.
(b) yanà sâ ta tà shārè ɗākìntà (cont...sub)	

In the completive, the choice of a copied TAM or a subjunctive in the lower clause corresponds to a difference in meaning. If the second clause is also in the completive, it indicates that the action was carried out; if the second clause is in the subjunctive, it is not clear whether the action was carried out (in which case the meaning is essentially the same as that with the completive) or whether it is yet to be done, e.g.,

sarkī yā sâ 'yammātā sun yi rawā (comp...comp)
    The chief caused the girls to dance (and they did).
sarkī yā sâ 'yammātā sù yi rawā (comp...sub)
    The chief caused the girls to dance (and either they did or did not yet).

With some TAMs (habitual, future, potential), one normally does not get a repeated TAM in the lower clause. Rather, one finds a bare weak subject pronoun (wsp), which may represent the subjunctive or, as in coordinate sentences, the neutral TAM, there being no way on the surface to determine which (see §19:2.1.1 and §70:18). Examples:

sukàn sâ ta tà tāshì dà wurwuri (hab...wsp) They make her get up early.
not ****sukàn sâ ta takàn tāshì dà wurwuri**
zā mù sâ su sù tàimàkē mù (fut...wsp) We will make them help us.
not ****zā mù sâ su zā sù tàimàkē mù** (not normal)
nâ sâ (ta) tà kōmà gidan mijìntà (pot...wsp) I intend for her to return to her husband's house.
??**nâ sâ (ta) tâ kōmà gidan mijìntà** (pot...pot) (possible for some speakers but very marginal)

If the higher clause is in the subjunctive or the imperative, the lower clause will normally be in the subjunctive, e.g.,

kì sâ ta tà zō dà wuri! (sub...sub) You (f.) make her come early!
Allàh yà sâ sù dāwō lāfiyà! (sub...sub) May God cause that they return safely!
sā Mūsā yà wankè tufāfī! (imp...sub) Have Musa wash the clothes!
sà ta tà lūřa dà gōyontà! (imp...sub) Make her look after her baby!

Although causative sentences most commonly have a copied TAM or a subjunctive in the lower clause, other TAMs are possible, e.g.,

nā sâ yanà shārè ɗākìnsà (comp...cont) I got him to clean his room.
nā sâ zâi bař ōfìs (comp...fut) I ordered him to leave the office.

A sequence of a subjunctive in the higher clause followed by a TAM other than the subjunctive in the lower clause is particularly common in formulaic expressions of the "God willing" type introduced by **Allàh (yà) sâ** (where the wsp **yà** is often omitted), e.g.,

Allàh yà sâ zā sù zō dà wuri! (sub...fut) May God have them come back soon!
Allàh yà sâ sun dāwō lāfiyà! (sub...comp) May God see to it that they return safely!
Allàh yà sâ an yi cikin yawancin râi! (sub...comp) May they have a long life together!
(greeting on a marriage) (lit. may God cause that one do in abundance.of life)

The TAMs in the higher and lower clauses must match in terms of the Rel feature, i.e., if the higher clause TAM is general completive or continuous, then the TAM in the lower may not be preterite or Rel-continuous; if the higher clause TAM is preterite or Rel-continuous, then the TAM in the lower clause may not be completive or general continuous, e.g.,

mằlàmai <u>sun</u> sâ yârā <u>sun</u> gōgè àllō (comp...comp)
> The teachers made the children wipe off the blackboard.

mằlàmai nè <u>sukà</u> sâ yârā <u>sukà</u> gōgè àllō (pret...pret)
> The *teachers* made the children wipe off the blackboard.

<u>nā</u> sâ shi <u>yā</u> shìga makařantā (comp...comp)	I made him enter school.
gằ wândà <u>na</u> sâ <u>ya</u> shìga makařantā (pret...pret)	Here is the one whom I made enter school.
<u>yanằ</u> sâwā <u>anà</u> yi masà aikì (cont...cont)	He was having them do work for him.
wằ <u>yakè</u> sâwā <u>takè</u> gamà àbinci? (Rcont1...Rcont1)	Who is causing her to be finishing the food?
<u>nā</u> sâ <u>yanà</u> shārè ɗākìnsà (comp...cont)	I made it happen that he is cleaning his room.
wằ <u>ka</u> sâ <u>yakè</u> shārè ɗākìnsà? (pret...Rcont1)	Who did you make clean his room?

°AN: The verb aikằ 'send' behaves much like sâ in taking sentential complement clauses with a matching Rel feature, e.g., janař <u>yā</u> aikằ <u>sun</u> kirāwō hākìmī 'The general sent (some people) to call the district head', i.e., 'The general had someone call the district head' (lit. general he sent they called district head); cf. jiyà nē janař <u>ya</u> aikằ <u>sukà</u> kirāwō hākìmī '*Yesterday* the general sent (some people) to call the district head.'

In most cases, the lower clause can be in the subjunctive, in which case the issue of Rel feature matching does not occur, e.g.,

mằlàmai <u>sun</u> sâ yârā <u>sù</u> gōgè àllō (comp...sub)
> The teachers made the children wipe off the blackboard.

mằlàmai nè <u>sukà</u> sâ yârā <u>sù</u> gōgè àllō (pret...sub)
> The *teachers* made the children wipe off the blackboard.

<u>yanằ</u> sâwā <u>à</u> yi masà aikì (cont...sub)	He was having them do work for him.
wằ <u>yakè</u> sâwā <u>tà</u> gamà àbinci? (Rcont1...sub)	Who is causing her to finish (cooking) the food?

1.1.1. Negation

Causatives permit negation of either the higher clause, the lower clause, or both.

Negation of the higher clause involves negating the TAM of the higher clause. The lower clause retains an affirmative TAM. The second ba of the bà(a)...ba discontinuous negative morpheme goes at the end of the whole sentence, e.g.,

bà mù sâ shi yā sayō àbinci ba	We didn't cause him to buy food.
bà nâ sâ Mařyàm tà kōmằ gidan mijìntà ba	I'll not make Maryam return to her husband's house.
Audù bài sâ mu mun kāsà cîn zàɓē ba	Audu didn't cause us to fail to win the election.
ìdan bā sằ sôn sìnīmằ, kadà kà sâ su sù jē	If they don't like movies, don't make them go.

Negation of the lower clause is often expressed by a paraphrase using a semantically negative lexical item, e.g., yā sâ mu mun ƙi biyàn hařājì 'He had us not pay taxes' (lit. he caused us we refused paying taxes). However, it is possible to negate the lower clause directly, e.g.,

sōkè zàɓēn dà gwamnatì ta yi yā sâ [bà à naɗà sābon shùgàban farař hùlā ba]
> Canceling the election that the government did caused one not to install a new civilian president.

rashìn lāfiyằ tā (or yā) sâ bà mù sằmi dāmař zuwằ gidankà ba
> Illness caused us not to be able to come to your house.

yāɓìn Tèkun Pāshà yā sâ bà à sằmi ìsasshen mâi à dūniyằ ba
> The Persian Gulf War caused that one not get enough oil in the world.

If the lower clause is negated, subject to object raising is disallowed (or at least dispreferred), e.g.,

Audù yā sâ bà mù ci zằɓē ba   Audu caused us not to win the election. (i.e., Audu caused we not win election), not **Audù yā sâ <u>mu</u> bà mù ci zằɓē ba)

It is also possible to negate both the higher and the lower clause. In such cases, the final **ba** of the discontinuous morpheme serves double duty for both occurrences of the negative, e.g.,

Audù [<u>bài</u> sâ [<u>bà</u> sù yi aurē <u>ba</u>]]   Audu didn't cause them not to get married.
Tankò <u>bài</u> sâ <u>bài</u> ɗinkà rìgâř <u>ba</u>   Tanko didn't cause him not to sew the gown.
<u>bà</u> yājìn aikìn nē zâi sâ <u>bà</u> zân zō <u>ba</u>, sai dai rashìn mōtằ
> It's not the strike that will cause me not to come, only lack of transport.

1.1.2. Adverbs
Adverbial modifiers may apply either to the higher or to the lower clause, the interpretation depending upon the position of the adverb in the sentence and the semantic context, e.g.,

[dà gàngan] ya sâ ta ta yi kūkā	He [purposely] caused her to cry.
yā sâ ta tā yi kūkā [dà gàngan]	He had her cry [on purpose]. (e.g., she was an actress)
yā sâ ta tā yi rawā à makařantā	He had her dance at school.

(not **It was at school where he caused that she should dance.)

1.1.3. Q-word questions
Causative sentences allow Q-word questions coming out of either (a) the higher or (b) the lower clause. Examples:

(a) **su wằ sukà sâ su sù ƙōnè cìyāwằ?**	Who (pl.) made them burn the grass?
wằ yakè sâwā takè gamà àbinci?	Who was causing her to be finishing the food?
don mè ta sâ ki kì yi kitsòn banzā?	Why did she make you do a useless hairdo?
(b) **wằcē cè sukà sâ ta gayằ wà mālàm làbārì?**	Who did they cause to tell the news to the teacher?
mè sukà sâ Kànde ta yi?	What did they cause Kande to do?
wằ sukà sâ Kànde ta gayằ wà/masà làbārì?	Whom did they cause Kande to tell the news to?

Occasionally, one cannot tell from the surface which clause the Q-word belongs to; for example, the sentence **yàushē ya sâ ta ta yi rawā?** 'When did he cause her to dance?' is ambiguous. It would normally be understood to be asking when he did the causing, but it could also be a question about when she did the dancing.

1.1.4. Relativization, focus, and topicalization
Causative sentences allow (a) relativization, (b) focus, and (c) topicalization of items coming out of either the higher or the lower clause. Examples:

(a) **mùtumìn dà ya sâ 'yammātā sukà yi rawā**   the man who caused the girls to dance

'yammātân dà sarkī ya sâ (su) sukà yi rawā	the girls whom the chief caused to dance
àbîn dà sarkī ya sâ 'yammātā sukà yi	the thing that the chief caused the girls to do
yārinyàř dà na sâ ta dafà manà àbinci	the girl whom I had cook food for us
yārinyàř dà na sâ yârā sù tàimàkē tà	the girl whom I had the children help
ita d̃în dà kàkā ta sâ tà kōmà wajen mijìntà	
she whom grandmother caused to return to her husband	
(b) [Sulè nē] ya sâ (ni) na shārè fālò	It was Sule who had me sweep the parlor.
[Sulè nē] na sâ (shi) ya shārè fālò	It was Sule I had sweep the parlor.
[fālò nē] na sâ Sulè ya shārè	It was the parlor that I had Sule sweep.
[cikin gaggāwā] na sâ shi yà shārè fālò	It was in haste I ordered him to sweep the parlor.
(c) shī kàm, nā sâ shi yā shārè fālò	As for him, I had him sweep the parlor.
fālò kàm, nā sâ Sulè yā shārè shi	As for the parlor, I had Sule sweep it.
sâwā kàm, nā yi (cêwař) Sulè yā shārè fālò	
As for causing, I caused (lit. did) that Sule sweep the parlor.	

°AN: Some speakers find the above sentence with topicalization of the causative verb to be awkward and only marginally acceptable.

If a VP is focused, it appears in nonfinite (infinitive or verbal noun) form and the pro-verb **yi** 'do' is inserted in its place.

[shārè fālò nē] na sâ Sulè ya yi	It was sweeping the parlor I had Sule do.
[sâ Sulè ya shārè fālò] na yi	It was having Sule sweep the parlor that I did.
[sâwā] na yi Sulè ya shārè fālò	It was causing I did that Sule sweep the parlor.
[sâ Sulè] na yi ya shārè fālò	Causing Sule I did that he sweep the parlor.

In the neutral sentence **nā sâ Sulè ya shārè fālò** 'I caused Sule to sweep the parlor', one cannot tell whether there has been subject to object raising or not. In the sentences with focus, however, differences emerge. In **sâwā na yi Sulè ya shārè fālò** (lit. causing I did Sule he sweep parlor), Sule is clearly the subject of the lower clause, whereas in **sâ Sulè na yi ya shārè fālò** (lit. causing Sule I did he sweep parlor), Sule is clearly the direct object of the verb in the higher clause.

1.2. Causatives with NP complements

Instead of being followed by a lower clause consisting of a tensed sentence, the causative verb **sâ** can be followed by two objects in a double-object construction. The first object is the person who is being caused; the second object, which is often a dynamic noun, is what is being caused, e.g.,

yunwà tā sâ [ka] [fushī]	Hunger has made you irritable.
mè ya sâ [shi] [àřàhā]?	What has made it so cheap?
rashìn wankà yā sâ [ni] [kwâřkwatà]	Lack of bathing has made me full of lice.
yakàn sâ [mùtûm] [fàriyà]	It makes people boastful.
sunà sâ [Bintà] [kūkā]	They are making Binta cry.

Either of the objects can be focused, e.g.,

[Bintà] sukè sâwā kūkā	It is Binta they are making cry.
[kūkā] sukè sâ Bintà	It is crying they are causing Binta (to do).

The above examples show that the first object is the "true" direct object and that the second "object" has a different status. Notice that when **Bintà**, the first d.o., is fronted, **sâ** takes the verbal noun form **sâwā**, which is required when no object follows. On the other hand, when **Bintà** stays in place immediately following the verb, the verb retains its pre-object form **sâ** whether **kūkā** is fronted or not.

If the second object is focused, the double-object construction is often replaced by a sentential complement with the pro-verb **yi** 'do', e.g.,

fushī sukà sâ shi   It was angry they made him. (< **sun sâ shi fushī** They made him angry.)
= **fushī sukà sâ shi yà yi** (< **sun sâ (shi)**] [**yà yi fushī**])   They made him be angry.

The second NP can be a simple noun, but it can also be a verbal noun (phrase) or even an infinitive phrase, e.g.,

shēgèn nan yā sâ [mu] [sātôwā]   That bastard had us steal. (lit. …caused us stealing) (VN)
cf. **shēgèn nan yā sâ [mu] [mù yi sātà]** (lit. …cause us that we do theft)
uwaŕgidā tā sâ [ki] [ɗībàŕ ruwā]?   Did Madam have you (f.) fetch water?
(lit. …cause you dipping water) (VN)
mālàmā tā sâ [su] [sāƙà tàbarmā]   The teacher had them weave mats.
(lit. …cause them weave mats) (IP)
cf. **mālàmā tā sâ (su) [sù sāƙà tàbarmā]** (lit. …cause (them) that they weave mats)
wà ya sâ [ku] [kashè tsuntsàyē]?   Who had you kill the birds? (lit. …cause you kill birds) (IP)

2. PERMISSIVES AND PROHIBITIVES

2.1. *Permissives*
The description of causatives applies equally to parallel "permissive" structures containing the verb **barì** 'permit, let, allow'. Consider the following:

màigidā yā baŕ màtaŕsà tā/tà tàfi bìkī   The husband allowed his wife to go to the ceremony.
cf. **màigidā yā sâ màtaŕsà tā/tà tàfi bìkī**   The husband made his wife go to the ceremony.

°AN: Similar sentences with other semantically permissive verbs are also possible, e.g., **nā ƙyālè shi yā tàfi** 'I let him go' (lit. I.comp ignore him he.comp go).

As with causatives, the lower clause in a permissive construction can be in the completive (or preterite when grammatically appropriate) or in the subjunctive. If the object of the lower clause appears as the object of the higher clause, then **barì** appears as **baŕ** (its normal pre-object form). Before nouns, one gets both **barì** or **baŕ** (but usually the latter), which is consistent with the interpretation that raising is optional even though one can't see it on the surface as one can with a direct object pronoun. In the continuous (and other nonfinite environments) one gets the verbal noun **barìn** with the linker instead of the finite form **baŕ**. In the case of an impersonal subject, where raising is not possible, one normally gets the form that is used when no object follows, namely, **barì**. Examples:

Sàlāmatù tā baŕ kì kì/kin yi matà kitsò?   Did Salamatu allow you to braid her hair?
màigidā bài baŕ màtaŕsà tà/tā tàfi ùnguwā ba
    The husband did not allow his wife to go to the quarter.
dòg̀arai bà sù barì jàma'à sù/sun taɓà àlkyabbàŕ sarkī ba
    The palace guards did not allow the people to touch the emir's robe.

bàban Mūsā bà zâi bař shì yà àuri bàtūřìyā ba
> Musa's father will not allow him to marry a white woman.

ìnā mutànên dà sukà bař yârā sù/sukà shā àlāwà?
> Where are the men who allowed the children to eat candy?

yā bař sù sun shā àlāwà = yā barì sun shā àlāwà   He allowed them to eat candy.

yanà barìn bàk̃ō yà yi aron mōtàřsà   He is letting the guest borrow his car.

gwamnatì tā barì à/an fàrà řajistàř jàm'ìyyun sìyāsà
> The government has allowed for political party registration to start.

The higher clause can be negated, but the lower clause cannot, presumably for pragmatic/semantic reasons, e.g.,

bā mà barìnsù sù shìga makařantā   We are not letting them enter school.
bài barì à/an kāmà su ba   He didn't allow them to be caught.
kadà kà barì sù yī wà kânsù ràunī!   Don't let them harm themselves!

The permissives differ from causatives in requiring finite-clause complements and not just bare NPs. Examples:

Bintà tā sâ ka [fushī]   Binta has made you irritable.
but not ****Bintà tā bař kà [fushī]**   Binta has let you irritable.
yakàn sâ [yârā] [dàriyā]   He makes children laugh.
but normally not ****yakàn bař yârā dàriyā**   He lets children laugh.
cf. **yakàn bař yârā sù yi dàriyā**   He lets the children laugh.
(lit. he allows children that they do laughter)

2.2. *Prohibitives*

Prohibitives are typically indicated by a double-object construction formed with the verb **hanà** 'prohibit, forbid, prevent'. The second object is usually a verbal noun (phrase). Examples:

an hanà mu shân tābà   We were forbidden to smoke.
(lit. one.comp forbid us drinking.L tobacco)
yā hanà Bintà sāmùnsà   He prevented Binta (from) getting it.
mahaifìyař yârā tā hanà su fìtā wàje   The children's mother forbade them to go outside.

With this verb, some speakers express the first object as an indirect object rather than as a direct object, e.g.,

yā hanà minì zuwà = yā hanà ni zuwà   He prevented me from coming.

Prohibitives also occur in biclausal structures of the type used in causatives and permissives, e.g.,

'yan makařantā sun yi yājì sābòdà màlàmai sun hanà su sù yi wàsan k̃wallō
> The students went on strike because the teacher prohibited them from playing soccer.

[Reference: Bagari (1977a)]

13. Cognate Accusative

VERBS may be accompanied in a sentence by a morphologically related verbal noun. Borrowing the term from Greek grammar, the related verbal noun will be referred to as a cognate accusative. There are three syntactically and semantically distinct formations using cognate verbal nouns.

1. COGNATE ACCUSATIVE TYPE 1 (ADVERBIAL)

In the cognate accusative type 1, a verb is followed later in the sentence by a cognate verbal noun that serves in an adverbial manner to narrow or intensify the basic meaning of the verb, e.g., **an kashè shi mūgùn kisà** 'He was killed violently' (lit. one.comp kill him horrible.L killing). (In literal glosses, the linker -n / -r̃, which often can be translated as 'of', will be indicated simply as L.) The cognate accusative construction is not terribly common—there is something literary about it—but it is not really esoteric and it does seem to be potentially quite productive.

> ◊HN: Parsons, among others, has suggested that this construction was borrowed from Arabic, where it is quite prevalent. (It is known as "maf'uul muTlaq" = absolute object, objective complement, etc.) However, since cognate accusative constructions are widespread in Chadic—a good description of this construction in Miya, for example, has been provided by Schuh (1998: 183–85)—it seems more likely that this represents an Afroasiatic inheritance rather than an Arabic borrowing.

1.1. Cognate accusative with modifier

In almost all cases the cognate accusative is postmodified in some way, e.g., by an adjective, a genitive phrase, or a **mài** 'possessor of, characterized by' phrase (which I gloss in the examples as 'having'). The cognate verbal noun can sometimes appear without an overt modifier, but in such cases the modifier is understood. The verb in sentences with the construction is not restricted with regard to grade nor is the verbal noun limited to any particular morphological type (i.e., both strong and weak verbal nouns can be used). With intransitive verbs, the cognate accusative follows directly upon the verb; with transitive verbs, it follows the direct object. Examples:

Audù yā shàhar̃à shàhar̃à̀ sànanniyā
Audu he.comp is famous fame known
Audu is extremely well known.

sun kōkà̀ kūkā mài tsōrat̃r̃wā
they.comp cry crying having frightening
They cried in a frightening manner.

mun gōdè̀ masà dà matukar̃ gòdiyā
we.comp thank to.him with enormous.L thanks
We thanked him profusely.

gidan nàn yā gìnu ginìn gaskiyā
house.L this it.comp built building.L truth
This house is well built.

tā zàgē shì zàgì na ɓātà hankàlī
she.comp insult him insulting of spoil sense
She hurled gross insults on him.

yā <u>dòkē</u> shì <u>dūkằ</u> na rashìn hankàlī   He beat him severely.
he.comp beat him beating of lack.L sense

yā <u>ci</u> àbinci mūgùn <u>cî</u> irìn na hàřâm   He ate the food horribly/maliciously.
he.comp eat food evil.L eating type.the of forbidden

tā <u>màrē</u> shi <u>màrì</u> mài cīwò   She slapped him a painful slap.
she.comp slap him slap having injury

sarkī yā <u>amìncē</u> ta dà iyằkař <u>amìncêwā</u>   The emir trusted her to the utmost limit.
emir he.comp trust her with limit.L trusting

gwamnatì tā <u>azabtař</u> dà sū mùmmūnař <u>àzābằ</u>   The government tortured them mercilessly.
government it.comp torture **dà** them ugly.L torture   [**dà** is a particle that accompanies gr5 verbs.]

wani macìjī yā <u>sàri</u> Audù mùmmūnan <u>sārā</u>   A snake has bitten Audu seriously.
some snake he.comp slash Audu ugly.L slashing

an <u>wankè</u> mîn kāyānā <u>wankì</u> mài kyâu   My clothes have been washed spanking clean.
one.comp wash to.me clothes.L.my washing having goodness

yā <u>tsōratař</u> dà sū <u>tsōratàřwā</u> mài ban tsòrō   He frightened them beyond description.
he.comp frighten **dà** them frightening having giving.L fear

māgànîn yā <u>warkař</u> dà nī <u>warkâřwā</u> sàhīhìyā   The medicine cured me completely.
medicine.the it.comp cure **dà** me curing pure

an <u>kằyař</u> dà Bàlā <u>kằyâřwā</u> mùmmūnā   Bala was thrown down in a humiliating manner.
one.comp throw **dà** Bala throwing ugly

yā <u>sai</u> dà mōtàřsà <u>sayâřwā</u> ta tīlàs   He was forced into selling his car.
he.comp sell **dà** car.of.his selling of perforce

yā <u>mutù</u> <u>mutuwàř</u> wulằkancì   He died a miserable death.
he.comp die death.L harshness

Mūsā yā <u>ɗàuru</u> ɗaurìn kằwō wuƙā   Musa is all tied up tightly.
Musa he.comp is tied tying.L bring knife

AN: The phrase **ɗaurìn kằwō wuƙā** (lit. tying.L bring knife) 'being tied up tightly' refers to the tying up of a ram that is about to be slaughtered.

The cognate accusative can modify the main verb in a contrastive manner using the conjunction **àmmā** 'but':

yā <u>yàbē</u> tà àmmā <u>yàbon</u> maròƙā   He praised her but in an insincere way.
(lit. he praised her but praise.of professional beggar)

sun <u>kwāna</u> à gidân àmmā <u>kwānan</u> zàune   They spent the night at the house but without any sleep.
(lit. ...but spending night.of seated)

munà <u>kòyon</u> Tūřancī àmmā <u>kòyon</u> gaggāwā   We are learning English but in a rushed manner.
(lit. ...but learning.of haste)

Audù yā <u>shā</u> ruwā àmmā <u>shâ</u> na ràƙumī   Audu drank water but in an impolite way.
(lit. ...but drinking of camel)

One can have negative sentences with cognate accusatives, although for pragmatic reasons such sentences are not very common, e.g.,

nā <u>san</u> Bàlā bằ <u>sanìn</u> shānū ba   I know Bala more than casually.
(lit. ...neg knowing of cattle neg)

(Better is **nā san Bàlā sanìn gàske**   I know Bala truly well.)

bà tà <u>màrē</u> shì <u>màrì</u> mài cīwǒ ba   She didn't slap him painfully.
(Better is **tā ɗan <u>màrē</u> shì** She slapped him a little bit.)

1.1.1. Focus and relativization
Cognate accusatives are allowed in clauses that are focused (including those with Q-word questions) and in relative clauses, e.g.,

ita cě ta <u>màrē</u> shì <u>màrì</u> mài cīwǒ   *She* slapped him painfully.
wǎ ta <u>màrā</u> <u>màrì</u> na rashìn hankàlī?   Whom did she slap in a thoughtless way?
wànè irìn macìjī ya <u>sàri</u> yāròn mùmmūnan <u>sārā</u>?
      What kind of snake gave the boy a horrible bite?
macìjī wândà ya <u>sàrē</u> shì mùmmūnan <u>sārā</u> kāsā cě
      The snake that bit him seriously is a puff-adder.

1.2. Cognate accusative with numeral
Instead of being modified adjectivally, the cognate accusative verbal noun can be followed by a numeral or other quantifier. The semantic reading is then 'so many times', e.g., **tā <u>màrē</u> shì <u>màrì</u> gōmà** 'She slapped him ten times' (lit. ten slappings), cf. the equivalent but more usual **tā màrē shì sàu gōmà** (where **sàu** is the normal word for 'times'). Examples:

yā <u>fēƙè</u> fensìrī <u>fīƙà</u> ukù   He sharpened the pencil three times. (i.e., three sharpenings)
mun <u>bugà</u> musù wayà <u>bugù</u> huɗu   We telephoned them four times. (i.e., beat...four beatings)
jirgin samà yā <u>tāshì</u> <u>tāshì</u> shidà   The plane took off six times. (i.e., six risings)
mun <u>zaunà</u> dà shī <u>zamā</u> ukù   We lived together three times. (i.e., three stayings)
matsòràcī zâi <u>mutù</u> <u>mutuwà</u> mài yawà   A coward will die many deaths.

2. COGNATE ACCUSATIVE TYPE 2 (DIRECT OBJECT)

In the second cognate accusative type, the direct object is a deverbal noun that is "accidentally" cognate with the verb. These are constructions like English 'He sang a song' or 'He built a building'. The cognate object can be modified, just like any other object NP, but this is not required. In these constructions, the direct object noun is just one of many direct objects that the verb could take, and the fact that it happens to be morphologically related to the verb does not carry any special semantic or expressive significance. The following are a few examples from the many one could provide. (The items in parentheses represent alternative objects.)

yā <u>ginà</u> <u>ginì</u> (ɗākì, masallācī) dà yawà   He built many buildings (rooms, mosques).
mun <u>ɗumàmà</u> <u>ɗùmàmē</u> (àbinci, shìnkāfà)   We heated up the leftovers (food, rice).
yā <u>cāshè</u> <u>càsā</u>   He threshed the grain.
yā <u>jiƙà</u> <u>jiƙò</u> mài ɗācī   He steeped a bitter infusion.
yā <u>dasà</u> <u>dàshē</u> dà yawà à gōnā   He transplanted a lot of seedlings in the farm.

2.1. Cognate accusative-2 plus cognate accusative-1
In the expressive cognate accusative-1 construction, the cognate verbal noun appears after the direct object. Because the cognate objects in cognate accusative-2 constructions are simple direct objects, there is nothing to prevent them from being followed by a cognate verbal noun in a cognate accusative-1 construction. Note that the direct object position could equally be filled by a noncognate object. Examples:

yā <u>shūkà shūkà</u> (irì) <u>shūkầwā</u> mài kyâu   He planted the crops (seeds) in a good manner.
tā <u>gồyi gōyontà</u> (jầrīrì) <u>gōyon</u> lālācì   She tied her baby (infant) on the back sloppily.
sun <u>dasà dàshē</u> (shìnkāfā) <u>dàsuwā</u> marầř àmfằnī
    They transplanted the seedlings (rice) in a useless manner.
yā <u>shânyà shanyà</u> (kāyā) <u>shanyầ</u> mài kyâu
    He spread out the laundry (clothes) in a careful manner.

3. COGNATE ACCUSATIVE TYPE 3 (na + VN)

Transitive verbs (including gr5 verbs, which strictly speaking take oblique objects) can take as their object a phrase made up of the linker **na/ta** plus a cognate verbal noun, e.g., **sun sàyi na sàyē** 'They bought the ones to be bought (and left the others)', lit. they bought of buying. The usual implication is that the things or people in question constitute the exclusive set affected by the verb as opposed to those that are not. Examples:

sun hàřbi na hařbì   They shot the ones who were supposed to be shot.
sunầ sūkàn na sūkầ   They are criticizing those who deserve to be criticized.
nā zàɓi na zàɓē   I chose those available to be chosen.
yā sayař dà na sayâřwā   He sold the sellable items.
munầ sàyen na sàyē   We are buying the one that can be bought.
an ƙyālè na ƙyālèwā   One ignored what could/should be ignored.
tā wārè na wārèwā   She separated the ones to be separated.
kunầ cîn na cî?   Are you (pl.) eating the edibles?
mun tsōratař dà na tsōratâřwā   We frightened the (timid) ones who were susceptible to fright.
mun tsāmè na tsầmā (= mun tsāmè na tsāmèwā)   We picked out the ones to be taken out.

The linker + VN phrase represents an NP with a missing head, e.g., Ø **na ɗaurèwā** 'the ones for tying', where the Ø stands for the understood things or animals or people to be tied. Because the understood head is semantically plural, the linker is usually **na**, not **ta**. Nevertheless, singular nouns in Hausa may be used in a plural or generic sense and thus the feminine linker **ta** can sometimes be employed if the understood referent is grammatically feminine, e.g.,

(gyàɗař Ràbo) mun cāsà <u>ta</u> <u>cāsầwā</u>, mun zubà ràgōwàř à rùmbunsà
    (As for Rabo's peanuts (f.)), we shelled the ones to be shelled, we poured the remainder in his bin.
(àyàbà), an sayař dà <u>ta</u> <u>sayâřwā</u>, an kōmầ dà saurā cikin gāřējì
    (Bananas (f.)), one sold the ones for sale, one put the rest back in the garage.

[Reference: Newman (1999)]

14. Comparison

COMPARATIVE statements are expressed by verbal sentences of the type X Verb Y Z, where X and Y represent the persons or things being compared, Z represents the quality being compared, and the verb indicates the nature of the comparison (higher, same, or lower), e.g., [Bàlā]$_X$ yā fi [Mūsā]$_Y$ [ƙarfī]$_Z$ 'Bala is stronger than Musa' (lit. Bala he.comp exceeds Musa strength); [wannàn]$_X$ bài kai [nāmù]$_Y$ [haskē]$_Z$ ba 'This one isn't as bright as ours' (lit. this neg.it reach ours brightness neg). (Comparative sentences are most often in the completive, preterite, or neg-completive.) The Z must be an abstract noun, a verbal noun, or a common noun having a generic meaning; it cannot be an adjective. Examples:

jirgī yā fi mōtà̄ girmā	A plane is bigger than a car.
(with the abstract verbal noun **girmā** 'largeness'), *not* **...bàbba** with the adjective 'big')	
kàkaṛ Bàlā tā fi tāmù tsūfā	Bala's grandmother is older than ours.
(with the abstract verbal noun **tsūfā** 'age'), *not* **...tsōhuwā** with the adjective (f.) 'old')	
wannàn bài fi wancàn sàbùntā ba	This is not newer than that.
(with the abstract noun **sàbùntā** 'newness') *not* **...sābō** with the adjective (m.) 'new'	
fātàṛ kadà̄ tā gazà̄ ta macìjī taushī	Crocodile skin is less soft than snake skin.
(with the abstract noun **taushī** 'softness'), *not* **...tàttausā** with the adjective 'very soft')	
kânsà yā fi nàwa tallèwā	His (shaved) head has more of a sheen than mine.
(with the verbal noun **tallèwā** 'shining'), *not* **...tallēlè̄** with the adjective (m.) 'very shiny'	
Gàmbo yā fī sù wàyō	Gambo is the most clever.
(with the quality noun **wàyō** 'cunning, cleverness')	

1. COMPARISON AT A HIGHER DEGREE

For comparison at a higher degree, the most common verb employed is **fi** 'exceed', e.g.,

kàṛàtū yā fi nōmā gajiyâṛwā	Reading/studying is more tiring than farming.
(lit. writing it exceeds farming tiring out)	
Audù yā fī nì kuɗī	Audu is richer than me.
(lit. Audu he exceeds me money/wealth)	
Kanò̄ tā fi Kàdūna yawàn mutằnē	Kano is bigger (i.e., is more populous) than Kaduna.
(lit. Kano it exceeds Kaduna quantity.of people)	
yā fī tà shāshancì̄	He is more of a simpleton than she is.
sàmàrin yànzu sun fi na dâ lālācì̄	Youth of today are lazier than those of former times.
mātā sun fi mazā butulcì̄	Women are more ungrateful than men.
yàɓen gidankù yā fi nāmù duhù̄	The plaster on your house is darker than ours.

93

In the case of the primary color terms, the same word functions as an abstract noun, a common noun, and as an adjective. The fact that these words can appear in comparative sentences thus does not constitute an exception to the requirement that the Z slot must be filled by an abstract noun and not an adjective. Note that when color terms appear in the Z slot, they are invariant for gender, whereas when they function as adjectives, they obligatorily agree with the head noun. Examples:

rìgātā tā fi tākà farī	My gown is whiter than yours. (with the m. noun **farī** 'whiteness')
cf. **rìgātā farā cè**	My gown is white. (with the f. adjective **farā**)
fentì yā fi bulà shūɗì	Paint is darker blue than washing-blue.

Compound color terms formed with the word **ruwā** 'color', e.g., **ruwan-hōɗà** 'pink' (lit. color.of powder), do not qualify as abstract nouns. To express them comparatively, one has to use paraphrases like the following:

gidānā ruwan-tòkā yā fi na Bàlā duhù   My house is grayer than Bala's.
(lit. house.my color.of-ashes it exceeds of Bala darkness)
rìgařtà ruwan-hōɗà tā fi tākì haskē   Her gown is pinker than yours.
(lit. gown.of.her color-powder it exceeds yours (f.) brightness)

There is no special construction for the superlative, either morphological or syntactic. Rather, one gets a superlative semantic interpretation from the choice of items compared, especially when the Y is a universal pronoun or quantifier, e.g.,

Mūsā yā fi kōwā tsawō	Musa is the tallest. (lit. Musa exceeds everyone height)
cf. **Mūsā yā fi Bàlā tsawō**	Musa is taller than Bala. (lit. Musa exceeds Bala height)
dōkìnā yā fi dukkànsù saurī	My horse is the fastest. (lit. my horse exceeds all of them speed)

In appropriate contexts, the direct object (Y), or the quality (Z) being compared, or both can be omitted, e.g.,

dògarà dà kânkù yā fi kyâu
      Depending on yourselves is best.
cikin yâran makařantā Bellò yā fi wàyō
      Among the schoolboys, Bello is the cleverest.
talaucì dà kwànciyař râi yā fi ařzìkī dà tāshìn hankàlī
      Being poor but living peacefully is better than being rich but with trouble.
Sāni yā fi
      Sani is (best/tallest/strongest/smartest, etc). (lit. Sani he.comp exceed)

1.1. Adverbial comparison

If the Z is a dynamic noun representing an action rather than an abstract concept, then the sentence corresponds to what in English would be adverbial comparison, e.g.,

sun fi nì ɗinkìn hùlā	They sew caps better than I do. (lit. they.comp exceed me sewing cap)
bài fi tà màganà ba	He doesn't speak better than she. (lit. neg.he exceed her talk neg)
dōkìn nân yā fi wancàn gudù	This horse is faster than that one.

(lit. horse.of this it.comp exceed that one running)

1.2. Agentive and stative phrases

In the absence of adjectives that inflect for degrees of comparison, attributive modifiers employ agent phrases with **mafì** (m. or f.) / **mafìyā** (pl.) 'the one(s) that exceed in Z)' (see §7:1.6.3), e.g.,

mōtà mafì tsàdā	most expensive car
gidan àbinci mafì tsabtà	the cleanest restaurant
yārinyà mafì kyâun ganī	the best-looking girl
'yan kwallon rāgā mafìyā tsawō	the tallest basketball players
mōtōcī mafìyā tsàdā	the most expensive cars

These agent phrases can also be used as the predicate in equational sentences, e.g.,

Audù nē mafì karfī	Audu is the stronger/strongest.
sū nè mafì /mafìyā yawà	They are the majority (lit. the most).

°AN: One sometimes finds the singular **mafì** with a plural referent.

Stative phrases (see chap. **67**) formed with with **fìye dà** generally indicate 'more' in a quantitative rather than qualitative sense, e.g.,

gidàjē fìye dà nāmù	more houses than we have
rìgā fìye dà tàwa	a more expensive gown than mine
talàbijìn fìye dà kusan dukà	a television better than (i.e., with more features than) most
zāfin rānā fìye dà kīmà	a hotter day (lit. heat.of day exceeding the ordinary)

1.3. Other 'exceed' verbs

Comparison to a higher degree can also be indicated by semantically appropriate verbs other than **fi**, such as **ɗarà** 'exceed slightly', e.g., **nā ɗarà ta tsawō** 'I am slightly taller than her.' With this verb (which takes a clipped form) the Y is often expressed as an indirect object, e.g., **nā ɗar matà shèkarà** 'I am slightly older than her' (lit. I slightly exceed to.her year).

The verb **gìrmā** v2 (plus a direct object) or **girmè** v4 (plus an indirect object), which means 'be older than', has the quality built in and thus expresses comparison with a simple object without the need for a Z (although the number of years can be mentioned by a prepositional phrase), e.g.,

nā gìrmē shì (dà shèkarà ukù) = nā girmè masà (dà shèkarà ukù)
   I am older than him (by three years).

2. COMPARISON AT AN EQUAL DEGREE

For comparison at an equal degree, one uses the verb **kai** 'reach', e.g.,

tàwadà tā kai àllō bakī   Ink is as black as a blackboard.
(lit. ink it.comp reaches blackboard blackness)
àmfànin gōnā na bana bài kai na bàra àlbarkà ba
   This year's crops are not as plentiful as last year's.

Another common way of expressing comparison at an equal degree is with sentences formed with the pro-verb **yi** plus an abstract noun with a genitive complement, i.e., X **yi** abstract.of Y, e.g.,

wannàn tēbùr̃ yā yi k̃wārin wancàn   This table is as strong as that one.
(lit. this table it does strength.of that)
gidānā bài yi girman nākà ba   My house is not as big as yours.
(lit. house.of.my neg.it does size.of yours neg)

°AN: Similar ideas can of course be expressed by other means, e.g., **zurfin rāmìn nân yā yi kàmā dà wancàn** 'This hole is as deep as that one' (lit. depth.of hole.of this it does like with that).

3. COMPARISON AT A LOWER DEGREE

For comparison at a lower degree, one uses the verb **gazà** 'fall short of' (or one of its synonyms, e.g., **kāsà**). Examples:

gidānā yā gazà nākà girmā   My house is not as large as yours.
(lit. house.of.my it falls short of yours size)
bà tà gazà ki hàk̃urī ba   She is not less patient than you.
(lit. neg she fall short of you patience neg)

4. CLAUSAL COMPARISON

Comparison at a clausal level is indicated by connecting two clauses by means of the subordinating conjunction **dà** 'than (that)'. (The clause following **dà** appears with a bare L-tone weak subject pronoun (wsp), which I interpret to be the neutral TAM although it could also be the subjunctive.) The two clauses can sometimes occur in either order. Examples:

gāra mù kōmà gidā dà mù shā irìn wannàn wàhalà
    We would rather go back home than experience this kind of difficulty.
= **dà mù shā irìn wannàn wàhalà, gāra mù kōmà gidā**
    Rather than experience this kind of difficulty, we would rather go back home.
sun fi sô sù zaunà dà sù kōmà wurinsà
    They prefer to stay where they are rather than return to him.
yā fi àr̃àhā à sàyē shì nân dà à tàfi Kanò
    It is cheaper to buy it here than to go to Kano.

15. Complementation

THIS chapter describes complementation by clauses (with reference, where appropriate, to equivalent infinitive or verbal noun phrases). The Hausa complement clauses sometimes correspond to finite clauses in English, e.g., **yā gayà manà zâi zō** 'He told us that he would come', whereas other times they are used where English might use an infinitive, e.g., **inà sô ìn àri fensìr̃** 'I want to borrow a pencil' (lit. I want (that) I borrow a pencil). In both cases, however, the Hausa complement has a clausal structure with a finite verb. The complements (CP) can be divided into two large categories: VP complements (as in (a)) and propositional complements (as in (b)):

(a) **mun ji làbār̃ì (wai) an sai dà ita**   We heard news that it was sold.
(b) **yā kàmātà kù kōmà gidā**   It is appropriate that you return home.

1. VP COMPLEMENTS

VP complements are full sentences that are embedded in the VP of the matrix sentence. For purposes of presentation, the VP complements can be divided into 'that' complements and 'to' complements.

1.1. 'That' complements
'That' complements sometimes follow an intransitive verb, other times a transitive verb with its object. The CP is commonly introduced by a complementizer (COMP), the most common being **cêwā** 'that' (lit. saying), but the usage depends on the specific verb or verbal expression in the matrix sentence. Both the matrix sentence and the CP allow a full range of TAMs, and both the matrix sentence and the CP allow negation. Examples:

yârân sun tsayà cêwā sun maidō manà dà kuɗinmù
      The children insisted that they had paid us back our money.
yârân sun tsayà cêwā mù mayar̃ musù dà kuɗinsù
      The children insisted that we should pay them back their money.
yā gayà wà 'yan-jàr̃ìdū cêwā jihàr̃sà bā tà sāmùn tàimakō ìsasshē
      He told the reporters that his state does not get enough aid.
hākìmī yâ gàr̃gàɗē sù cêwā sù biyā hàr̃ājìn
      The district head will likely admonish them that they should pay the taxes.
yā musà cêwā shī ɓàrāwò nē   He denied that he was a thief.
yā aikà dà sàƙō cêwā sù dainà yàƙe-yàƙe   He sent a message that they should stop fighting.

The grade 5 verb **tarar̃**, which has the basic meaning of 'overtake, come upon', occurs with an immediately following CP without an intervening COMP. In this usage it connotes 'find that'. (The same is true for the synonymous gr4 verb **îskē**.) Example:

dà sukà isō, sukà tarar̃ àbòkansù sun rìgā sun tàfi

 When they arrived they found that their friends had already gone.

If the matrix sentence contains the verb **cê** 'say' (or its verbal noun **cêwā**) then the COMP **cêwā** is not allowed. Examples:

Audù yā cê Ø Sulè zâi gàyyàcē shì	Audu said that Sule will invite him.
Audù yā cê Ø Sulè bà zâi gàyyàcē shì ba	Audu said that Sule will not invite him.

not ****Audù yā cê cêwā Sulè (bà) zâi gàyyàcē shì (ba)**

sarkī yā cê Ø kù biyā hàr̃ājìn	The emir said that you should pay the taxes.

not ****sarkī yā cê cêwā kù biyā hàr̃ājìn**

yā ƙàrà dà cêwā janàr̃ zâi hàlàr̃ci tàrôn dà kânsà

 He added (by saying) that the general would attend the meeting himself.

not ****yā ƙàrà dà cêwā cêwā janàr̃ zâi hàlàr̃ci tàrôn dà kânsà**

Certain verbs, like **ji** 'hear', **cê** 'say', and certain phrasal verbs, like **yi tsàmmānì** 'think' and **sâ râi** 'expect' (lit. put life), generally prefer the reportive particle **wai** 'hearsay, it is said that' as the COMP instead of **cêwā**, e.g.,

sun yi tsàmmānì wai zā sù sàmi hanyàr̃ shìgā

 They thought that they might find a means of getting in.

bà sù yi tsàmmānì (wai) zā sù sàmi hanyàr̃ shìgā ba

 They didn't think that they would find a means of getting in.

nā ji wai bà à naɗ'à shī sarkī ba tùkùna

 I heard that they haven't appointed him chief yet.

bā mà̀ jîn dāɗī wai bâ ta dà lāfiyà̀	We are not happy that she is not well.
nā sâ râi wai zâi zō	I expect that he will come.
Audù yā shā kân Hàlīmà(wai) tà tàfi	Audu persuaded Halima to leave.
bàn yi zàton (wai) zā tà zō wurin nàn ba	I didn't think that she would come to this place.
bàn ji làbārì (wai) bà à būɗ'è hanyàr̃ ba	

 I didn't hear the news that they didn't open up the road.

 °AN: [i] The genitive linker /n/ attached to the verbal noun **zàtō** 'thinking' is optional.

 [ii] In the last example, note that the final **ba** serves as the second element of the discontinuous **bà...ba** morpheme both for the matrix sentence and the CP sentence. One does *not* get ****[bàn ji làbārì (wai) [bà à būɗ'è hanyàr̃ ba] ba]**.

Certain verbs and verbal expressions normally employ the relativizer **dà** 'that' as the COMP, e.g.,

mun yi farin cikì dà kukà zō	We are happy that you came.
munà̀ baƙin cikì dà bà kà zō ba	We are sad that you didn't come.

yā yi kirà gà mutànē dà sù biyā hàr̃ājìn

 He called upon the people to pay (that they pay) their taxes.

'yan sìyāsà̀ sun tīlàstā wà shùgàbân dà yā yi rìtāyà̀ à wannàn shèkarà̀

 The politicians have forced the president to retire (that he retire) this year.

an amìncē wà Audù (dà/cêwā) yà zama sarkī

 Audu was allowed to become the chief. (lit. one agreed to Audu (that) he become chief)

1.2. 'To' complements

'To' complements follow immediately upon the VP of the matrix sentence and function as the NP object of the preceding word. (Verbs appear in their pre-direct object form.) They do not make use of a COMP. If that preceding word is a noun (or verbal noun), it obligatorily adds a linker. The CP, which always occurs in the "neutral" zero TAM, cannot be negated. If the subject of the matrix sentence and the CP are the same, a sentential CP can be replaced by a semantically (essentially) equivalent verbal noun or infinitive phrase, e.g.,

nā yi shāwafàf [ìn gudù]	I made the decision [to run away].
(lit. (that) I run away) = **nā yi shāwafàf gudù** (lit. I made the decision of running away)	
yanà shân wàhalàf [yà tāshì dà wuri]	He finds it difficult [to wake up early].
(lit. (that) he wake up early) = **yanà shân wàhalàf tāshì dà wuri** (lit. ...[of arising early])	
yanà ɗāri-ɗārin yà zìyàfci àbōkinsà	He is timid about visiting his friend.
= **yanà ɗāri-ɗārin zìyaftàf àbōkinsà**	
bàn yi ƙòƙarin ìn rabà su ba	I didn't make an effort to separate them.
= **bàn yi ƙòƙarin rabà su ba** (where **rabà su** is an infinitive phrase)	
sun ƙi sù yi aikì	They refused to work. = **sun ƙi yîn aikì**
nā tsàni Audù yà dingà yī minì ɗàriyā	I hate for Audu to keep on laughing at me.
bà sù baf Hàlīmà tà tàfi gidā ba	They didn't let Halima go home.
yanà dà sauƙī Tankò yà gyàrà halinsà	It is easy for Tanko to straighten up his behavior.
(lit. it is easy (that) Tanko he repair his character)	

°AN: Because the subjunctive and the neutral TAM are both phonologically zero (see §70:17–18), one cannot be sure in individual cases which one is present. Given the absence of distinctive subjunctive semantics in embedded CPs, such as in **yanà ɗāri-ɗārin [yà]**$_{neut}$ **zìyàfci àbōkinsà** 'He is timid about visiting his friend', I have provisionally opted to analyze the TAM as being the neutral form, although the matter is admittedly debatable. The absence of negative CPs supports this analysis because the neutral form cannot be negated whereas the subjunctive can.

If the verbal noun **sô** 'wanting' is followed by a sentential CP as object, it commonly occurs without the linker, although use of the linker is not ungrammatical. If it is followed by a verbal noun phrase constituting an NP, then the linker is required, e.g.,

munà sô(n) sù tàfi Kanò	We want them to travel to Kano.
bā yà sô(n) yà zìyàfci sùrùkansà = bā yà sôn zìyaftàf sùrùkansà	
He doesn't like visiting his in-laws.	

With certain expressions, one almost always gets a verbal noun CP rather than a sentential CP, e.g.,

yanà zāfin sôn yārinyàf nan	He is wild for that girl.
(lit. he.cont heat.L wanting.L girl.L that)	
munà ƙāwàf (sôn) tàfiyà Amìfkà	We eagerly want to go to America.
yanà fàfùtàkaf shìgā makarantā	He is straining every nerve to get into school.

2. PROPOSITIONAL COMPLEMENTS

Complex sentences involving complementation are composed of a matrix sentence, which constitutes the complement-taking expression (CTE), plus a sentential complement (CP). The CTE, which corresponds to English clauses such as 'It is appropriate that...', can be either in the affirmative or the negative. The sentential CP is most often in the subjunctive, but it need not be (see discussion below). The CP is optionally introduced by a complementizer, either **cêwā** 'saying', **wai** 'it is said that', or **dà** 'that'. Examples:

[yā kàmātà]$_{CTE}$ [(wai) sàmā̀rin nàn sù yi aurē]$_{CP}$
    It is desirable that these young men get married.
[bài kàmātà ba]$_{CTE}$ [Tankò yà ƙi biyàn hàr̃ājì]$_{CP}$
    It is not right that Tanko should refuse to pay taxes.
[yā dācè]$_{CTE}$ [(wai) yârân sù ci àbinci mài kyâu]$_{CP}$
    It is fitting that the children should eat nutritious food.
[yā kyàutu]$_{CTE}$ [(dà) kì gamà aikìnkì]$_{CP}$
    It is better/nice/desirable that you (f.) should finish your work.
[mài yìwuwā nề]$_{CTE}$ [(dà) nà sàyi sābuwar̃ mōtà]$_{CP}$ It is possible I might buy a new car.
[shìrmē nề]$_{CTE}$ [(cêwā/wai) nà yi r̃ītāyà yànzu fa]$_{CP}$?   Is it nonsense that I retire now?
[bā̀ àbin kunyà ba nề]$_{CTE}$ [mùtûm yà kwāna à gidan sùrùkansà]$_{CP}$
    It is not shameful for a person to sleep overnight at his in-laws' house.
[yanā̀ dà muhimmancì (kùwa)]$_{CTE}$ (dà) [mù gamà aikìn bana]$_{CP}$
    It is important (moreover) that we finish the work this year.

As best as one can determine, the sentences mean the same whether the COMP is present or not, but in many cases it is stylistically better without. Apparently **cêwā** and **wai** are mutually substitutable without substantially affecting the meaning. The use of **dà** with propositional complements appears to have a somewhat different status from **cêwā** and **wai**, but the details are yet to be worked out. (The COMP **dà** is the same as the relativizer **dà** that introduces relative clauses.)

    The semantic subject of the CP can often be expressed in the matrix sentence as the object of the preposition **gà(rē)** 'at, with'. (This preposition is unique in having distinct variants depending on the nature of the object. If it is a personal pronoun, one uses **gàrē**; otherwise one uses **gà**. The prepronominal form **gàrē** is optionally (but usually) preceded by the preposition **à** 'at'. This **à** is not used with **gà**.) If the CTE contains **gà** plus a noun, the noun cannot also appear as the subject of the CP. Whether the matrix sentence contains a prepositional phrase or not, the CP remains a tensed sentence, even though the most natural English translation is often with an infinitive, e.g.,

[yā kyàutu [gà yârā]] [sù ci àbinci mài kyâu]   It is good for children to eat nice food.
(lit. it is good for children (that) they eat good food) = [yā kyàutu] [yârā sù ci àbinci mài kyâu]
[yā hàr̃amtà [gà Mùsùlmī]] [sù ci nāman àladè]   It is unlawful for Muslims to eat pork.
(lit. ...that they eat pork) = yā hàr̃amtà cêwā [Mùsùlmī sù ci nāman àladè]
[yanā̀ dà ban shà'awā̀ [gà Tankò]] dà yà sā̀mi nasar̃ā̀
    It is pleasing to Tanko that he succeeded.
[yanā̀ dà muhimmancì [à gàrē kì]] kì àuri mijì nagàri
    It is important for you to marry a good husband.
[wājìbī nề [à gàrē mù]] cêwā mù yi sallà   It is incumbent on us that we should do the prayers.
[wâutā nề [gà Mūsā]] dà yà ci bāshì̀   It was foolish of Musa to take out a loan.

One also finds CTE phrases with prepositions other than **gà(rē)**. For example, the verb and verbal noun **dācè/dācêwā** 'be fitting' use **dà** 'with', whereas various other structures use **à kân** 'on', or **à wurin** 'at place of', e.g., [yā fì kyâu [à wurinkì]] kì kōmằ gà Tànīmù   It would be better for you to return to Tanimu.

[yā dācè [dà Mūsā]] yà shìga sōjà   It is fitting for Musa that he enter the army.

[zâi fì dācèwā [dà mū]] (dà) mù dingà zìyaŕtàŕ jūnā

    It will be more appropriate for us that we keep visiting each other.

[bàbban nauyī nề [à kânkù]] kù taimàkā wà jūnā

    It is a big responsibility on/upon you that you should help each other.

[wājìbī nề [à kânmù]] à kōwàcè rānā mù yi sallằ sàu bìyaŕ

    It is incumbent on us that we pray five times a day.

2.1. Kinds of complement-taking expressions (CTEs)

There are five main kinds of matrix sentences that can serve as CTEs: (1) Intransitive verbal sentences, (2) transitive verbal sentences with **yi** 'do' or **fì** 'exceed', (3) other transitive verbal sentences; (4) HAVE sentences with a nonconcrete predicate, and (5) Identificational sentences.

(1) [yā kyàutu] nà gamà aikīnā   It is desirable that I finish my work.

(2) [yā fì sauŕī] à sầmi gōŕò à Kanồ   It is easier to get kolanuts in Kano.

(3) [yanằ bā nì haushī] Audù yà dingà taunà cìngâm

    It annoys me that Audu keeps on chewing chewing gum.

[yā gằgàri Audù] yà fìd dà mōtàŕ dàgà gāŕējì

    It was impossible for Audu to get (lit. that he get) the car out of the garage.

(4) [yanằ dà muhimmancī gà Bàlā] (dà) yà tàfi yâu   It is important for Bala that he go today.

(5) [hàŕāmùn nē] mù shā giyằ   We are prohibited from drinking beer.

(lit. prohibition STAB we.sub drink beer)

[rashìn tùnằnī nề] kà ci bāshìn nan   It is a bad idea that you should take that loan.

(1) Intransitive CTEs typically contain a gr3 verb (less often, gr4 or gr7) that is preceded by a non-referential 3m weak subject pronoun (wsp). The verb is generally in the completive (or the corresponding preterite or negative-completive). Examples:

yā càncantà...	It is appropriate...	yā hàlattà (gà X)...	It is lawful (for X)...
yā fàskarà...	It is difficult to...	yā hàŕamtà (gà X)...	It is unlawful (for X)...
yā kàmātà...	It is fitting...	yā dācè (dà X)...	It's nice/suitable (for X)...
yā kyàutu...	It's better/nice...		

°AN: Unlike "weather" sentences, e.g., **anà ruwā** 'It is raining', the semantically impersonal CTEs use a nonreferential third person masculine wsp rather than the impersonal pronoun, e.g., **yā kàmātà...** 'It is necessary/fitting...', *not* ****an kàmātà**....

The gr7 verb **yìwu** (verbal noun **yìwuwā**) 'be possible' (< **yi** 'do') occurs in the potential and the continuous as well as in the completive, e.g.,

yā yìwu = [yâ]$_{pot}$ **yìwu** = (more or less) [yanằ]$_{cont}$ **yìwuwā**   It is/may be possible/likely that...

For totally unexplained reasons, some speakers allow **tā yìwu** and **tâ yìwu** with the 3f pronoun instead of the expected masculine pronoun.

The verb **dācè** 'be appropriate' may be either in the completive or in the future, e.g.,

yā dācè̀... It is appropriate...   **zâi dācè̀**... It will be appropriate...

(2) CTEs are commonly formed with the dummy verb **yi** 'do' or the verb **fi** 'exceed' plus a noun (or verbal noun) of quality. Sentences with **fi** often express the English comparative. Both the completive and the future occur naturally.

yā fi dācè̀wā...	It's more appropriate...
yā yi/fi kyâu (gà X)...	It is good/more suitable (for X)...
zâi fi sauƙī (gà X)...	It will be easier (for X)...
zâi yi wùyā (gà X)...	It will be difficult (for X)...

(3) Various other verbal sentences occur as CTEs. The semantic subject of the CP generally appears as an object (direct or indirect) of the verb in the matrix sentence, e.g.,

yanà̀ baƙàntā wà X râi...	It displeases X... (lit. ...blacken to X life)
yanà̀ faràntà rân X...	It pleases X that... (lit. ...whiten life.of X)
yā ragè ruwan X...	It is up to X... (lit. ...reduce water.of X)
yanà̀ bā (wà) X mà̀māki̇̀/haushī	It amazes/annoys X... (lit. ...give to X amazement/annoyance)
zâi tāyar̃ wà dà X hankàlī...	It will upset X...
yanà̀ dāmùn X...	It worries X...
yā gàgàri X...	It is impossible for X...

A few verbs that commonly occur as gr3 intransitives in CTEs can occur also as transitives (usually gr2) followed by a direct object with essentially the same meaning, e.g.,

[**yā kàmàci (v2) Bàrau**] (dà) **yà dainà kur̃ɓàwā**	It befits Barau to stop drinking (alcohol).
= [**yā kàmātà(v3) Bàrau yà dainà kur̃ɓàwa**	It is fitting that Barau stop drinking (alcohol).
[**yā càncànci (v2) mutà̀nên**] (dà) **sù taimàkā wà jūnā**	
It appropriate/desirable for the people to help each other.	
= [**yā càncantà (v3)**] (dà) **mutà̀nên sù taimàkā wà jūnā**	
It appropriate/desirable that the people help each other.	

(4) Some CTEs have the form of HAVE sentences with a 3m wsp. In many cases, the HAVE sentences have corresponding and semantically equivalent verbal sentences formed with the pro-verb **yi**, e.g.,

yanà̀ dà wùyā... = **yā yi wùyā**...	It is difficult...
(lit. it is with difficulty = it does difficulty)	
yanà̀ dà kyâu (gà X)... = **yā yi kyâu (gà X)**...	It is nice/better (for X)...
yanà̀ dà sauƙī... = **yā yi/fi sauƙī**...	It is easy...
yanà̀ dà wàhalà...	It is troublesome...
yanà̀ dà muhimmancì̀ (gà X)...	It is important/essential (for X)...
yanà̀ dà àmfàni̇̀ (gà X)...	It is useful (for X)...
yanà̀ dà ban shà'awà̀...	It is interesting...

(5) Identificational (i.e., reduced equational) sentences consisting of a predicate (Y) plus the stabilizer constitute another type of CTE. The stabilizer invariably takes the masculine form **nē** (with polar tone) regardless of the gender of the preceding word. A particularly common Y consists of a phrase made up of **àbin** 'thing of' plus a noun, e.g., **àbin kunyà̀ nē** 'it is shameful' (i.e., a thing of shame). If the

identificational sentence contains a prepositional phrase with **gà** (= (**à**) **gàrē** before a pronoun) it occurs after the stabilizer. Examples:

àbin àlfahàřī nè...	It's a matter of pride...	**dōlè nē (gà X)**...	It's obligatory (for X)...
àbin màmākì nē...	It is amazing...	**hàřāmùn nē (gà X)**	It is unlawful (for X)...
mài yìwuwā nè...	It's likely/possible...	**lâifī nè (gà X)**...	It's a sin/crime (for X)...
daidai nè...	It's right...	**shìřmē nè (gà X)**...	It's nonsense/foolish (for X)...
mūgùwař ɗàbī'à nē...	It's a bad habit...	**tīlàs nē (gà X)**...	It's obligatory (for X)...
nufìn X nē...	It is X's intention...	**wâutā nè (gà X)**...	It's foolish/stupid (for X)...
rashìn tùnằnī nè...	It's a bad idea...	**wājìbī nè (gà X)**...	It's incumbent (on X)...

wājìbī nè (à gàrē kù = à kânkù) kù tàimàki jūnankù

> It's incumbent on you to help each other.

rashìn kunyằ nē à ƙasàshen Afìřkà mùtûm yà ci àbinci dà hannun hagu

> It's lack of good manners in African countries for a person to eat with the left hand.

2.2. Negation

CTEs can be in the negative as well as in the affirmative. (The COMP is most often omitted in the negative.) Examples:

bâ shi dà àmfằnī à gàrē kà kà dingà zāgìn mutằnē

> It is valueless for you that you keep insulting people.

cf. yanà dà àmfằnī à gàrē kà dà kà dingà kàřàtū   It is useful for you to keep on studying.

bằ àbin kunyằ ba nè (wai) à kwāna à gidan sùrùkai

> It is not shameful for people to sleep overnight at their in-laws' house.

Negatives formed with the discontinuous marker **bà(a)...ba** have two options as to the position of the second **ba**. It can occur at the end of the matrix sentence before the CP or it can occur at the end of the entire sentence, e.g.,

bài kàmātà ba [Tankò yà ƙi biyàn hàřājì] = **bài kàmātà [Tankò yà ƙi biyàn hàřājì] ba**

> It is not right that Tanko should refuse to pay taxes.

bài kàmàci Bìlki ba [tà tàfi gidā yâu] = **bài kàmàci Bìlki [tà tàfi gidā yâu] ba**

> It isn't appropriate for Bilki to go home today.

bằ tabbàs ba nè [Audù yà zō yâu] = **bằ tabbàs nē [Audù yà zō yâu] ba**

> It is not certain that Audu will come today.

°AN: To my ear—which is that of a non-native speaker—sentences with **ba** at the end sound better when the matrix sentence contains a verb, whereas identificational matrix sentences sound better with the **ba** nearby. My guess is that the alternatives are not in free variation but rather vary according to dialectal or stylistic factors that have yet to be identified precisely.

The sentential CP clause normally expresses timeless volition, obligation, etc., and thus is usually in the subjunctive. If, however, the CP expresses a statement about an event that happened in the past or is to happen in the future, then one can employ a TAM other than the subjunctive, e.g.,

yā hàřamtà [kunằ]$_{cont}$ cîn nāmàn àladè   It was unlawful that you were eating pork.

yā kyàutu [tā]$_{comp}$ gyārà halintà

> It was nice that she behaved appropriately. (lit. repaired her character)

yanà bā nì màmākî (cêwā/wai) [kā]_{comp} kāsà gamà aikìn dà wuri

    It surprises me that you failed to finish the work early.

yā yìwu sun tāshì   It is possible that they left.

cf. yā yìwu sù (= zā sù) tāshì   It is possible that they will leave.

2.3. Question words, focus, topicalization
2.3.1. Constituents in the CP

Almost any item in the CP can be questioned, focused, or topicalized by moving it to the front of the
sentence. With questions and focus, which involve movement into the focus position, the TAM in the
following matrix clause requires a Rel form. Identificational matrix CTEs (such as **dōlè nē**... 'It is
necessary that...) drop their stabilizer when they are preceded by a focused item (itself usually marked by
a stabilizer). The deletion does not, however, apply to Q-word constructions. Examples:

(a) Question words

wā(nē nè) ya càncantà yà zama sarkinmù?

    Who is it appropriate for him to become our emir?

wàcē cè zâi yìwu tà zama sàraunìyā?

    Who is it that it is possible for her to become the queen?

su wàyê (nē) ya dācè sù yi aurē?

    Who (pl.) it is appropriate/proper for them to get married?

wàcè mōtà cē yakè dà muhimmancì Maŗyàm tà sāmù?

    Which car is it important for Maryam to get?

dàgà wànē nè dōlè (nē) mù kàŗɓi kuɗin hàŗājìn?

    From whom must we take/receive the tax money?

dà su wà ya dācè (cêwā) tà zaunà à Kanò?

    With whom (pl.) is it appropriate/suitable for her to live/stay in Kano?

dà wàcè màcè cē yakè dà wùyā (wai) Daudà yà yi zaman aŗzìkī?

    With which woman is it difficult for Dauda to live in peace?

gà wà yakè dà muhimmancì à gàrē mù mù bā dà kuɗîn?

    To whom is it important for us to give the money?

(b) Focus

Asshà cē zâi yìwu tà zama sàraunìyā

    It is Assha who it is possible that she become the queen.

Mustàfā (nè) ya càncantà yà zama sarkinmù

    It is Mustapha who is appropriate that he become our emir.

waɗànnân yârā (nè) ya dācè sù yi aurē

    It is these young people who it is appropriate for them to get married.

ita cè zâi yi kyâu à gàrē tà (dà) tà gamà aikìntà bana

    It is she who it is good for her to finish her work this year.

Bàrau nè ya kàmātà Asshà tà kai wà (= masà) àbincîn

    It is Barau who it is desirable that Assha should take the food to (him).

dà iyàyentà (nē) ya dācè (cêwā) tà zaunà à Kanò?

    Is it with her parents that it is appropriate for her to live/stay in Kano?

gà Bintà nē yakè dà muhimmancì mù bā dà kuɗîn

    It is to Binta that it is important for us to give the money.

kàŗàtū nè tīlàs mù yi à yâu ɗin nàn

    It is studying that we must do today. (not **kàŗàtū nè tīlàs nē...)

tàre dà kafìrì nè hàr̃āmùn Mùsùlmī yà shìga masallācī

> It is together with an unbeliever that it is forbidden for a Muslim to enter the mosque.

mū nè ya zama dōlè à gàrē mù mù tāshì yànzu

> It is we that it has become necessary that we should leave now.

(c) Topicalization

sarkī kàm, mài yìwuwā nè Sālisù yà zama

> As for emir, it is possible for Salisu to become (it).

kàr̃àtū dai, yanà dà àmfànī kà yī shì

> As for studying, it is useful that you do it.

waɗànnân yârā kàm, yā dācè sù yi aurē

> As for these boys, it is fitting (that) they get married.

hàr̃ājì kàm, yā kàmātà Tankò yà biyā (shì)

> As for taxes, it is desirable that Tanko pay (them).

sàyen sābon gidā (kàm), shī nè ya fī minì kyâu

> As for buying a new house, *it is that* which is better for me. (Topic *and* Focus)

2.3.2. The CP

The entire CP, usually with an overt COMP, can be fronted, for purposes of focus, indicated by { }, or topicalization, indicated by « ». In this position, the COMP cêwā typically has the form cêwar̃ with the linker attached.

{(wai) Tankò yà biyā hàr̃ājì nē} ya kàmātà

> *That Tanko should pay taxes* is appropriate.

«(cêwar̃) kà àuri Bintà», mài yìwuwā nè

> As for the assertion that you should marry Binta, it is possible.

If the CP is focused, the matrix sentence can appear as is or it can be followed by a resumptive clause consisting of a wsp + yi 'do', optionally preceded by the COMP dà. The wsp + yi expression tends to be used if it is followed by a contrastive clause. Examples:

(cêwar̃) Ābù tà rèni yār̃òntà nē ya càncantà   *That Abu should raise her child* is appropriate.

(wai) yârân sù yi aurē nè ya dācè   *That the youths should get married* is proper.

(cêwar̃) Ābù tà rèni yār̃òntà nē ya càncantà (dà) tà yi, bà tà bā dà shī gà mài rènō ba

> *That Abu should raise her child* is appropriate for her to do, not that she gives it to a nanny.

(wai) yârân sù yi aurē nè ya dācè (dà) sù yi màimakon (yîn) yāwòn banzā

> *That the youths should get married* is proper that they do instead of useless roaming about.

(cêwar̃) Tankò yà biyā hàr̃ājì nē ya kàmātà (dà) yà yi bà yà ƙi biyà ba

> *That Tanko should pay taxes* is appropriate, not that he refuse to pay.

When preceded by a topicalized CP, the matrix sentence, which usually has a zero subject indicating 'it', may appear with a pro-form subject like wannàn 'this', or hakà(n) 'thus'. Examples:

(cêwar̃) Tankò yà biyā hàr̃ājì, yā kàmātà

> (The assertion) that Tanko should pay taxes, it is desirable.

(wai) à tunà bāya, r̃òƙō nè

> That one should remember the past, it is one's wish.

(wai) Hasàn yà gyārà halinsà, <u>wannàn</u> zâi fi kyâu

> That Hassan should improve his behavior, this would be better.

(cêwař) **Audù yà sākè mōtà, wannàn yanà dà muhimmancì**

    That Audu should change his car, this is important.

(cêwař) **à yi sallà kullum, hakàn wājìbī nè**

    That one should pray every day, this is compulsory.

In sentences with a topicalized CP, one sometimes finds **wai** before the matrix CTE. In this case, however, it is not functioning as a COMP but rather as a reportive, point-of-view marker, e.g.,

cêwař Tankò yà àuri Bintà kàm, wai yā càncantà

    (As for) Tanko marrying Binta, (one could say that) it is desirable.

kà yi sallà kullum (kàm), wai wannàn wājìbī nè

    That you should pray every day, (as they say) this is obligatory.

2.3.3. The CTE

2.3.3.1.   It is possible to focus or topicalize the prepositional phrase (representing the thematic subject) out of the matrix CTE. (The English translations sound clumsy, but the Hausa sentences are normal.) Examples:

gà Tankò nē ya kàmātà yà biyā hàřājì	It is Tanko who ought to pay the taxes.
(lit. it is Tanko that it is better that he (Tanko) pay taxes)	
gà Audù nē tīlàs yà bā dà kuɗîn	Regarding Audu it is necessary that he give the money.
gà Tankò, yā kàmātà yà biyā hàřājì	As for Tanko, it is better that he pay taxes.
gà Mūsā, tīlàs nē yà kōmà gidā	As for Musa, it is necessary for him to return home.

2.3.3.2.   Some verbs in the matrix sentence also permit focus (more for stylistic that emphatic purposes). This is accomplished by fronting the corresponding verbal noun and inserting the pro-verb **yi** in the original verb position. The fronted verbal noun occurs without the stabilizer, but it does require that the following TAM be a Rel form. Examples:

dācèwā ya yi kì àuri Sulè (< yā dācè (dà) kì àuri Sulè)

    Appropriate it is that it is that you should marry Sule.

kyàutuwā ya yi kù tàimàki jūnankù (< yā kyàutu kù tàimàki jūnankù)

    It is nice for you to help each other.

kàmātà ya yi mù hau wannàn dūtsè (< yā kàmātà mù hau wannàn dūtsè)

    We ought to climb this mountain. (lit. obligation it do we climb this mountain)

2.3.3.3.   Alternatively, it is possible to emphasize the entire CTE by means of a focused pseudo-cleft construction with **àbîn dà** 'what, the thing that'), e.g.,

àbîn dà ya càncantà shī nè Ābù tà yi aurē	What is proper is that Abu should get married.
àbîn dà ya fi kyâu shī nè mù wāshè gàrinsù	What is better is that we sack their town.
àbîn dà ya kàmātà shī nè Tankò yà biyā hàřājì	What is fitting is that Tanko should pay taxes.
àbîn dà ya dācè shī nè yârân sù kōmà gidā	What is appropriate is that the children return home.

The following examples represent an alternative means of expressing the same idea:

àbîn dà ya kàmātà Tankò yà yi shī nè yà biyā hàřājì

    What is fitting that Tanko do is that he should pay taxes.

àbîn dà ya càncantà Ābù tà yi shī nè̀ tà yi aurē
> What is proper for Abu to do is that she should get married.

àbîn dà ya dācè̀ yârân sù yi shī nè̀ sù kōmà̀ gidā
> The thing that is appropriate for the children to do is that they return home.

The erstwhile subject of the CP can be moved even further forward immediately after the Rel clause marker, e.g.,

àbîn dà Tankò ya kàmātà yà yi shī nè̀ yà biyā hàrājì̀
> The thing that Tanko it is appropriate that he do is that he should pay taxes.

In this sentence, **Tankò** would appear on the surface to be the subject of **kàmātà**, but syntactically it is still actually the subject of the lower verb **yi**. This can be seen clearly in the following examples where the fronted noun is not masculine singular:

àbîn dà Ābù ya (*not* ****ta**) càncantà tà yi shī nè̀ tà yi aurē
> The thing that Abu (feminine name) it is appropriate that she do is that she should get married.

àbîn dà yârân ya (*not* ****sukà**) dācè̀ sù yi shī nè̀ sù kōmà̀ gidā
> The thing that children it is appropriate that they do is that they return home.

Focusing of the CTE by means of a pseudo-cleft construction can be combined with topicalization of the CP. Examples:

(cêwař) Tankò yà biyā hàrājì̀ (kàm), àbù nē dà ya kàmātà
> As for Tanko paying taxes, it is something that is appropriate.

Ābù tà gyārà halintà (fa), àbù nē dà ya càncantà
> As for Abu bettering herself, it is something that is proper.

2.4. Yes/No questions

Sentences with propositional complements can be in the interrogative, e.g.,

yā kàmātà (wai) sàmà̀rin nàn sù yi aurē? — Is it desirable that these young men get married?
yā hàřamtà gà Mùsùlmī sù ci nāmàn àladè̀? — Is it unlawful for Muslims to eat pork?
yanà̀ dà saukī à sà̀mi gōřò à Landàn? — Is it easy to get kolanuts in London?

Such questions can be introduced by the sentence-initial interrogative particle **kō̄**, e.g.,

kō̄ yā kàmātà (wai) Tànî tà biyā hàřājì̀? — Is it fitting that Tani should pay taxes?
kō̄ wājìbī nè̀ Mùsùlmī sù yi aikìn hajjì̀? — Is it obligatory for Muslims to do the hadj?

Another possibility is to treat the matrix clause and the CP as distinct sentences for purposes of question formation. In this case one can insert **kō̄** before the CP rather than before the matrix clause. The matrix clause will, nevertheless, carry the normal markers of questions, like question intonation, final vowel lengthening, and possibly a falling tone, e.g.,

yā kàmātà [kàmātà̀]? kō̄ Tànî tà biyā hàřājìn? — Is it fitting that Tani should pay taxes?
tīlàs nē [nê]? kō̄ yà yi azùmī [azùmî]? — Is it necessary that he should fast?
= kō̄ tīlàs nē yà yi azùmī?

bâ shi dà kyâu? kō ìn yi zànzarō?   Is it not good that I tuck in my shirt?
bà̀ àbin kunyà̀ ba nè̀? kō (wai) à kwāna à gidan sùrùkai?
          Is it not shameful that people should sleep overnight at their in-laws' house?

With topicalized CPs, one also has the option of placing **kō** in front of the questioned matrix sentence or else in front of the CP. In the latter case, the **kō** replaces the COMP, e.g.,

cêwař Tànî tà biyā hàřājì̀, kō yā kàmātà? = kō Tànî tà biyā hàřājìn? yā kàmātà?
          That Tani should pay taxes, is it fitting?
cêwař yà yi azùmī, kō tīlàs nē? = kō yà yi azùmī? tīlàs nē?
          That he should fast, is it necessary?

[References: Dimmendaal (1989); Yalwa (1995)]

16. Compounds

OMPOUNDS are sequences of two or more words that are bound together in such a way as to constitute a single word, e.g., **farař-hùlā** (lit. white.L cap) 'civilian'. (In literal glosses, the bound genitive linker (**-n / -ř**), which often can be translated as 'of', is indicated simply as L.) Polymorphemic words that are built with grammatical morphemes, e.g., **kōwā** 'everyone' < **kō** 'or' plus **wằ** 'who?', are treated elsewhere and are not included in this chapter. Standard orthography is inconsistent in the representation of compounds: some are written as single words, some as separate words, and some with hyphens. In this chapter only, I have made use of hyphens throughout so that the compounds are explicitly indicated as such regardless of the orthographic practice.

The essential feature that distinguishes compounds from similar phrases is their "lexical integrity." What this means is that the components of the compound necessarily appear *as is* without permitting permutations, insertions, substitutions, or deletions. For example, the phrase **farař hùlā** 'white cap' can be expressed as **hùlā farā**, with a postnominal adjective, whereas the compound **farař-hùlā** 'civilian' allows only the adjective-noun order. The phrase **gidan Mūsā** 'Musa's house' (lit. house.L Musa) allows an adjectival insertion, e.g., **gidā bàbba na Mūsā** 'Musa's big house' (lit. house big of Musa), whereas the compound **gidan-saurō** 'mosquito net' does not, i.e., one must say **gidan-saurō bàbba** 'big mosquito net' (lit. house.L-mosquito big) not ****gidā bàbba na saurō** (lit. house big of mosquito). In the phrase **fitsārin tsōhō** 'the old man's urine', one can substitute the synonym **bawàlī** without a change in meaning, i.e., **bawàlin tsōhō**, but this substitution is not allowed in the compound **fitsārin-gwaurō** 'type of boil on knee' (lit. urine.L bachelor), not ****bawàlin-gwaurō**. Finally, phrases allow gapping but compounds do not, e.g., with the phrase **jan kèke** 'red bicycle' one can say **nā fi sôn jan kèke dà kōřè** 'I prefer a red bicycle to a green (one)', but with the compound **jàn-bằki** 'lipstick' (lit. red.L-mouth) one cannot say ****nā fi sôn jàn-bằki dà kōřè** 'I prefer lipstick to green.'

> °AN: It needs to be pointed out that, notwithstanding the above factors, the exact dividing line between loose, semantically transparent compounds and close-knit phrases is not always so easy to determine. In this sense, Hausa is not different from English, where some items are clearly compounds, some are clearly phrases, and some, e.g., note pad, record player, or window washer, are debatable.

Some, but not all compounds, have clearly distinctive semantic and/or phonological characteristics. At the semantic end of the spectrum, one finds compounds that are semantically noncompositional in relation to the component parts, e.g., **kàren-mōtà** 'driver's mate' (lit. dog.L vehicle), **hànà-sallà** 'baseball cap, brimmed hat' (lit. prevent prayer). Note that this feature, however, does not uniquely define compounds because (a) there are compounds that are semantically transparent (as is sometimes the case in English), e.g., **rìgař-ruwa** 'raincoat' (lit. coat.L rain) and (b) there are semantically non-compositional idiomatic phrases, e.g., **jan aikì** 'difficult task' (lit. red.L work) = **aikì jā**. At the phonological level, one finds that some compounds are overtly marked, primarily by means of tone and vowel length, e.g., **gàshìn-bằki** 'mustache' (lit. hair.L mouth), where 'hair' is normally **gāshì** with H-L tone and mouth is normally **bàkī** with a long final vowel, whereas others are not, e.g., **farař-ƙasā** 'whitewash', which is indistinguishable on the surface from **farař ƙasā** (= **ƙasā farā**) 'white earth'.

Compounds can be looked at from two main perspectives, namely, external, i.e., the syntactic class and related grammatical features of the output, and internal, i.e., the morpho-syntactic structure and phonological characteristics of the compound per se.

1. EXTERNAL: PART OF SPEECH

1.1. Nouns
Approximately 95% of Hausa compounds (regardless of their internal structure) are nouns, e.g.,

àbōkin-gàbā	opponent (friend.L-enmity)
ban-gàskiyā	trust (giving.L-truth)
farin-cikì	happiness (white.L-belly)
hànà-ƙarya	hair grown under the lower lip (prevent-lying)
hùlař-kwānò	helmet (cap.L-bowl)

1.1.1. Gender
All compound nouns have gender. The gender is determined in three (perhaps four) different ways.

1.1.1.1. Sex reference. Compounds referring to humans (or other animates) have variable gender based on the sex of the real-world referent. The compounds formed with **ɗan** 'son/psn.of' have corresponding feminine forms with **'yar̃**. Morphologically, compounds with **àbōkin** 'friend.of' might be expected to allow corresponding feminines with **àbōkìyar̃**, but they rarely do. This is because in traditional Hausa culture, men do not have female friends, and the word for a woman's female friend is not **àbōkìyā**, but rather **ƙawā**, which does not enter into compounds. The other compounds are invariant in shape, the gender showing up in agreement rules, pronoun substitution, etc. Examples:

ɗan-hayà	male tenant / **'yar̃-hayà** female tenant
ɗan-ƙwàyā	drug user (male) / **'yar̃-ƙwàyā** drug user (female)
àbōkin-wàsā	playmate (male) / **àbōkìyar̃-wàsā** female cross cousin
àbōkin-aikì	coworker, colleague (not ****àbōkìyar̃ aikì**)
idòn-sanì	acquaintance (male or female) (eye.L-knowing)
tàttàɓà-kunne	great-grandchild (male or female) (touch repeatedly-ear)

e.g., **tàttàɓà-kunnen Sālè yā/tā shā ràunī** Sale's great-grandchild (m./f.) he/she was hurt.

1.1.1.2. Head determined. The gender of compound nouns of the form NP.L + X and Adj.L + NP is determined by the gender of the head noun. (In the Adj.L + NP compounds, the head noun also determines the gender of the adjective.) Examples:

(1) [[**fìtilàř**]$_f$ [**ƙwai**]$_m$]$_f$ lamp.L egg 'hurricane lamp'   [[**makar̃antař**]$_f$ [**àllō**]$_m$]$_f$ school.L slate 'Koranic school'
[[**ƙwan**]$_m$ [**fìtilà**]$_f$]$_m$ egg.L lamp 'light bulb'   [[**tùràren**]$_m$ [**wutā**]$_f$]$_m$ scent.L fire 'incense'

(2) [[**baƙař̃**]$_f$ [**zūcìyā**]$_f$]$_f$ black.L heart 'wickedness'   [[**farař̃**]$_f$ [**ƙasā**]$_f$]$_f$ white.L earth 'whitewash'
[[**baƙin**]$_m$ [**mâi**]$_m$]$_m$ black.L oil 'engine oil'   [[**jan**]$_m$ [**ƙarfè**]$_m$]$_m$ red.L iron 'copper'

1.1.1.3. Hyponomy, analogy, or semantic association. With other compounds gender is determined not by internal structure but by semantic connection between the referent of the compound as such and the gender of some other word, e.g.,

Compound (gender)		Referent (gender)
hànà-sallà (f.) 'baseball cap' prevent-prayer	is a type of	**hùlā** (f.) 'cap'
gàgàrà-gàsa (m.) 'special fabric' defy-competition	is a type of	**yādì** (m.) 'fabric'
gài-dà-yàya (m.) 'type of dish' greet-elder sister	is a type of	**kwānò̀** (m.) 'dish'
mashà̀-ruwā (m.) 'rainbow' one who drinks-rain	is a type of	**bàkā** (m.) 'arc'
fàɗi-tàshi (f.) 'struggle, effort' fall-rise	is a type of	**gwagwàr̃mayà̀** (f.) 'struggle'
dàfà̀-dukà (f.) 'jollof rice' cook-all	is a type of	**shìnkāfā** (f.) 'rice'

> °AN: The compound **dàfà̀-dukà** also denotes a station wagon van used for commercial transportation. (This is in reference to the passengers all squashed in together, i.e., 'everyone and the kitchen sink'.) With this meaning it is also feminine because it represents a type of **mōtà̀** (f.) 'vehicle'.

As is often the case with noncompound nouns, the intrinsic gender of items such as the above shows up not in the overt shape or internal make-up of the compound, but rather in agreement rules (e.g., with the stabilizer or adjectives or pronouns), e.g.,

hànà-sallà <u>cē</u>	It is a baseball cap. (f. STAB)
gài-dà-yàya <u>ƙàramī</u>	a small dish (m. adj.)
ƙwan-fìtilà̀ <u>yā</u> **fashè̀**	The light bulb broke. (m. wsp)

The only exception is the bound genitive linker (and segmentally identical definite article) whose form (-**n**/-**r̃** 'not f./f.') may be determined by the gender of the last item in the compound rather than by that of the compound as a whole (see discussion in §43:2.1.1), e.g.,

ƙwan-fìtilà̀r̃sà̀ ƙàramī	his small light bulb
gài-dà-yàyâr̃ = **gài-dà-yàyân**	the small dish

1.1.1.4. Masculine default. If there is no semantic basis for the assignment—and one can usually be found—compounds appear to be assigned masculine gender by default, e.g.,

fàɗà̀-wuta (m.)	moth (lit. fall into-fire)
fàsà-kwàri (m.)	spice-bark tree (lit. break-quiver (of arrows)).
[Note: Tree names in general are sometimes m. and sometimes f.]	
hànà-màkarà (m.)	rattle/chimes serving as an alarm clock (lit. prevent-lateness)
shà̀-jini (m.)	plant used as headache medicine (lit. drink-blood)
ban-hàƙuri (m.)	apology (lit. giving.of-patience)

1.1.2. Plurality

1.1.2.1. Compounds of the structure N.L + X can be pluralized by pluralizing the initial noun, e.g.,
rìgař-ruwa 'raincoat', pl. **rīgunàn-ruwa** 'raincoats'. Examples:

ɗan-fashì dà makāmī / 'yan-fashì dà makāmī	armed robber(s)
ɗan-kunne / 'yan-kunne	earring(s)
àbōkin-wàsā / àbòkan-wàsā	playmate(s)
kân-sarkī / kāwunàn-sarkī	postage stamp(s) (lit. head(s).L-king)
wàsan-kwaikwayō / wàsànnin-kwaikwayō	play(s), drama(s)
mūgùn-dawà / mûggan-dawà	wart hog(s) (lit. evil one(s).L-the bush)

°AN: Interestingly, **mûggan-dawà** is the preferred plural form for the compound even for speakers who otherwise use **mūgàyē** as the plural of **mūgù** 'evil, ugly'.

In a few cases, both members of a compound pluralize, e.g.,

ɗan-jàřīdằ / 'yan-jàřìdū	newspaper reporter(s)
ɗan-kwālī / 'yan-kwālàyē	head scarf/head scarves

1.1.2.2. Most compounds with the structure Adj.L + N do not undergo overt pluralization. Those that do pluralize generally inflect the adjective only while keeping the head noun in its singular form. A few loose compounds pluralize both parts.

farař-hùlā / faràren-hùlā	civilian(s) (lit. white.L-cap(s))
ƙaramin-àlhakī / ƙanānàn-àlhakī	a nonentity/nonentities (lit. small.L-being)
bàbbař-rìgā / mânyan-rīgunà	full gown(s) (lit. big.L-gown(s))
baƙař-màganà / baƙàƙen-màgàngànū	insult(s) (lit. black.L-talk)
sàbòn-shìga / sàbbin-shìga	recruit(s) (lit. new.L-enter)

°AN: The normal plural of **sābō** 'new' is **sàbàbbī**. In the compound, however, the truncated variant is preferred.

1.1.2.3. Other compounds do not overtly inflect for number. As with unmarked gender, semantic number is overtly shown by concord phenomena, e.g.,

bàbbā-dà-jàkā baƙī / bàbbā-dà-jàkā baƙàƙē	black maribou stork(s)
wata hànà-sallà / wasu hànà-sallà	a/some baseball cap(s)

1.1.2.4. A few erstwhile compounds have become so fused that they are now treated as ordinary non-compound nouns. As a result, these words now take regular suffixal plurals, e.g.,

magàtakařdā (< magà-takàřdā one who sees-paper) / màgàtàkàřdū	scribe(s)
sàɗakà (< sà-ɗakà put-in room) / sāɗakōkī	concubine(s)
shùgàbā (< shìg-gàba enter-in front) / shùgàbànnī	leader(s)

◊HN: Another possible example is **garwā** (< *gà-ruwā 'here is-water') / **garèwanī** 'four-gallon kerosene can(s)'. It is not certain, however, that this oft-cited etymology is in fact valid. It may be—although I have my doubts—but if so, then it has to be a very old creation, witness not only the unproductive **è…anī** plural formation but also the feminine gender (cf. **ruwā**, which is either plural or masculine). Note that there does exist a compound **gà-ruwa** 'water selling', which is used most often in **ɗan /'yan gà-ruwa** 'water-seller(s)'.

1.2. Adjectives

There are only some twenty compound adjectives, half of which are of the type **ruwan-X** 'color (lit. water).L-X'. Examples:

(a) **ruwan-azùřfā** silver colored, metallic colored (< -silver); **ruwan-ɗòrawà** yellow (< -locust bean); **ruwan-gōřò** orange (< -kolanut); **ruwan-gwâl** gold colored (< -gold); **ruwan-hōdà̀** pink (< -face powder); **ruwan-ƙasā** brown (< -earth); **ruwan-ƙwai** yellow-orange (< -egg (yolk)); **ruwan-mà̀kubà̀** mahogany colored (< -mahogany); **ruwan-madařā** milky white (< -milk); **ruwan-tòkā** gray (< -ashes); **ruwan-zīnāřè** gold colored (< -gold)

(b) **awòn-igiyà̀** extremely tall/long (measure.L-rope); **ci-kâř-kà-mutù** tasteless (food) (eat-don't-you-die); **cì-mà̀-zàune** lazy, jobless (eat-even-seated); **dūkàn-iskà̀** mentally ill (beating.L-spirits); **dūkàn-shāhò̀** mentally ill (beating.L-hawk); **ɗinkìn-kèke** machine-sewn (sewing.L-machine); **gà̀gàrà-kòyo** mysterious, hard to learn (defy-learning); **gàmà-gàri** common, ordinary (combine-town); **innà-rùdùdù** unruly (of crowd) (spirit-scattered movement); **shā-kà-tàfi** stupid (drink-you-go); **tāshìn-ƙauyè** ill-mannered (getting up.L-village); **yîn-hannu** handmade (doing.L (by) hand); **tàɓā-kà-lāshè** insufficient (esp. tasty food) (taste-you-lick up); **wankan-tařwaɗā** medium complexioned (of a black psn) (washing.L-mudfish)

When used attributively these compound adjectives occur only postnominally. They do not inflect for number or gender. If they co-occur with a simple adjective, the simple adjective goes first, e.g.,

wàndō ɗinkìn-kèke	machine-sewn trousers
rìgā yîn-hannu	handmade shirt
wasu yârā wankan-tařwaɗā	some medium-complexioned boys
wani mùtûm shā-kà-tàfi	a stupid man
yārò̀ gàjērē dūkàn-iskà̀	a short, mentally ill boy (lit. boy short mentally-ill)
hūlā ƙaramā ruwan-ƙasā	a small brown cap (lit. cap small brown)

1.3. Adverbs

There are only some twenty or so compound adverbs. With a number of them, it is not entirely clear whether they constitute true lexical compounds or whether they are close-knit phrases. Examples:

bàɗin-bàɗaɗà many years hence (next year.L-**bàɗaɗà** (ideophone)); **bà̀kī-dà-hancì** nearby (mouth-and-nose); **hannū-Rabbànā** empty-handed (hand-God); **idò̀-dà-idò̀** face to face (eye-and-eye); **kâi-dà-fātà** adamantly (head-and-skin); **kâi-tsàye** straight ahead, without hesitation (head-standing); **kân-karì** right on time (head.L-happening); **karā-zùbe** in a disorganized manner, randomly (cornstalks-poured); **ƙarfī-dà-yājì** forcefully (strength-and-spice); **ràbà-tsakà** halfway (divide-middle); **ruwā-à-jàllō** desperately (water-at-gourd bottle); **sanìn-shānū** casually (re. knowing s.o.) (knowing.L-cattle); **shēkàràn-città** five days hence (day after.L four days hence); **shēkaranjiyà** day before yesterday (day after.L yesterday); **tàkànas-ta-Kanò̀** purposely (purpose-of-Kano); **tsàkà̀-tsaki** in the middle of, halfway through (middle-middle); **tsakař-dare** midnight (lit. middle.L-night); **tsakař-rānā** noon (middle.L-day); **tsayìn-dakà** with resolve (standing.L-pounding); **wân-shēkarè** the following day (senior brother.L-day after?)

°AN: The essential meaning of **shēkarḕ** is hard to determine because it never occurs except in compounds, but it would appear to designate the next day following a specified day. (It may be related to **shèkarā̀** 'year', but the semantic connection is not evident.) Its use both in **shēkaran-jiyà** 'day *before* yesterday' and **shēkaràn-città** 'day *after* four days hence' makes sense if one takes a linear perspective moving from the present, the temporal center, outward toward the past or the future, i.e., the day *before* yesterday, for example, is the next day one gets to *after* having passed yesterday. The final high tone on **shēkaran-** in **shēkaranjiyà** is due to the phonological fusion of the two elements of the compound into a single unit.

Here are a few examples in context:

yanā̀ nēman aikī̀ ruwā-à-jàllō	He is desperately looking for work.
yāròn yā shìga gidân kâi-tsàye	The boy entered the house straightaway.
sun isō shēkaran-jiyà	They arrived the day before yesterday.

1.4. Verbs

There are no compound verbs in the strict sense of the term, i.e., one does not have compounds that constitute distinct verbal entities with the lexical integrity that characterizes words qua words. There are, on the other hand, phrasal verbs, primarily formed with the preposition **dà** 'with' or some other grammatical formative, e.g., **lṳ̀ra dà** 'look after', **ci karṑ (dà)** 'run/bump into someone' (lit. eat collision with), **yi ta** 'keep on doing' (lit. do via), and there are many fixed idiomatic verb phrases (see chap. **36**), e.g., **karyà kùmallō** 'have breakfast' (lit. break nausea), **zubà idṑ** 'wait in great anticipation' (lit. pour eye), **cikà bàkī** 'boast' (lit. fill mouth).

°AN: The expression **ci gàba** 'proceed, progress' (lit. eat front) is so common that it can almost be considered a compound verb; but even this can be shown to be phrasal. It can, for example, be broken up by a modal particle, e.g., **ci fa gàba na cè** 'I really told you to continue', and in nonfinite environments the verb is altered into the its corresponding verbal noun, e.g., **sunā̀ cî gàba dà bìncìkē** 'They were proceeding with the investigation.' The corresponding noun **cî-gàba** 'civilization, progress', on the other does appear to constitute a discrete lexical compound.

2. INTERNAL STRUCTURE OF COMPOUNDS

Compounds display a wide variety of internal structures, from simple two-word compounds to full sentences. The three most common structural types are: (a) N.L + N/Adv, (b) Adj.L + N, and (c) V + N/Adv. Other common types are (d) phrases with **dà** 'and/with' or other connectors, (e) simple juxtaposition, (f) agential formations, and (g) full sentences.

2.1. Noun-linked compounds (N.L + X)

The most common compound type by far has the structure of a regular N.L + X genitive phrase (i.e., noun of X) where the form of the linker (L) depends on the gender and number of the head noun (-ř̃ for feminines ending in -a(a), -n for others). The linker always takes the zero vowel form (i.e., -ř̃/-n, not **ta/na**), e.g., **cīwòn-zūcìyā** (sickness.L-heart) 'heart attack'; **tàwadàř̃-Allàh** (ink.L-God) 'dark pigment on skin'. The initial noun is either (a) a common noun or (b) a verbal noun. The X is either [i] a noun (or noun phrase) or a sentence, or [ii] an adverb (or, in just a few cases, an ideophone or a numeral). Note that the X is commonly an adverbial form of a noun (see §5:3.1), even though from the translation one might expect to find a common noun, e.g., **kīshìn-zūci** (N.L-adv) (desire.L-at heart) 'drive, determination', not **kīshìn-zūcìyā** (N.L-N) 'desire of the heart'. Examples:

(a) [i] ɗan-sàndā   policeman   (son.L-stick)

àbōkin-gàbā   enemy, foe   (friend.L-enmity)

àllon-kàfaɗà   shoulder blade   (slate.L-shoulder)

ɓēɼan-masàɼ   guineapig   (mouse.L-Egypt)

bàɼkònon-tsōhuwā   teargas   (pepper.L-old woman)

cācaɼ-bàkī   argument   (gambling.L-mouth)

dòkaɼ-tā-ɓàcì   state of emergency   (law.L-it-spoiled)

kujèɼaɼ-nā-ƙi   veto   (chair.L-I-refuse)

ƙarfin-gwīwà   courage, encouragement   (strength-L-knee)

uwaɼ-kuɗī   principal (money)   (mother.L-money)

[ii] ɓàrāwòn-zàune   a "fence"   (thief.L-seated)

jirgin-ruwa   ship   (vehicle.L -in water)

kīshìn-zūci   drive, determination   (desire.L-at heart)

rōmon-bakà   sweet talk, false promises   (broth.L-in mouth)

gàrin-buɗus   ground corn   (flour.L-**buɗus** [emphasizes fineness])

kāyan-aɼas   ceramic plates, etc.   (goods.L-**aɼas** [breaking sound])

'yan-biyu   twins   (children.L-two)

zàkaràn-wuyà   Adam's apple   (rooster.L-at neck)

(b) [i] bîn-watà   menstruation   (following.L-month)

ban-kāshī   punishment   (giving.L-excrement)

cîn-fuskà   humiliation, insult   (eating.L-face)

dūkàn-iskà   mentally ill   (beating.L-demon)

harbìn-àllūɼà   evil magic   (shooting.L-needle)

jân-ràgō   snoring   (pulling.L ram)

kāmùn-ƙafà   lobbying   (holding.L foot)

sôn-zūcìyā   selfishness, greed   (liking.L-heart)

[ii] awòn-gàba   head start   (weighing.L-front)

hàngen-nēsà   foresight, forecast   (espying.L-afar)

ganin-ƙwaf   inquisitiveness   (seeing.L-**ƙwaf** [looking about])

ɓatàn-ɓàkàtantàn   loss of both of two opportunities   (losing.L-**ɓàkàtantàn** [carelessness])

A few N.L + X compounds make use of a short, compressed form of the first noun, e.g., **ban-ɗākì** < *bāyan-ɗākì (lit. behind the room) 'toilet'; **san-ƙīrà** < *sarkin ƙīrà (lit. chief of smithing) 'head panegyrist'; **san-girmā** < saurin girmā (lit. speed of growing) 'growth spurt in children'.

    Most compounds of the N.L + X type are phonologically unmarked. Some, such as **zàkaràn-wuyà** 'Adam's apple' or **yîn-hannu** 'handmade', appear at first sight to be marked by a short final vowel, but the length of the vowel is actually due to the second word being an adverb. There are, however, some compounds of this type that are in fact marked. Some of these have a L-L tone on the first word and a short final vowel on the last, a feature combination characteristic of phonologically marked compounds in other structural types. A few only have final vowel shortening without the tone change. Examples:

fàrìn-shìga   novice (cf. **fārì** beginning, **shìgā** entering)

gàshìn-bàki   mustache (cf. **gāshì** hair, **bàkī** mouth)

jàkìn-dōkì   mule (cf. **jàkī** donkey, **dōkì** horse)

kàn-tàfi   carrying something on upturned palm (cf. **kâi** head, **tàfī** palm)

bàƙon-dàuro   measles (cf. **bàƙō** stranger, **dàurō** type of millet)

ɗan-wāke   small dumplings made of bean flour (cf. **wākē** black-eyed peas)

°AN: At one time, it was thought that vowel shortening in and of itself was a regular marker of compounds (cf. Gouffé 1965). This turns out to be inexact. Vowel shortening is found in compounds, but it interacts with and is dependent upon tone changes and structural class.

There are a couple of compounds with the linker **na/ta** where the head is an adverb or exclamation:

tàkànas-ta-Kanồ   purposely   **zūƙì-ta-màlle**   tall tale, blatant lie

2.2. Adjective–noun compounds (Adj.L + N)

Some very common compounds have the structure of a prenominal adjective (+ linker) plus a noun. Note that compounds never appear with the alternative N Adj order allowed in normal phrases, i.e., **farař-hùlā** 'civilian', not ****hùlā farā** (which only means 'white cap'). The adjectives used in compounds tend to be basic underived words, commonly, but not exclusively, color terms. One example, **gajen-hàƙurī** 'impatience, impetuousness' (< **gàjērē** 'short' + **hàƙurī** 'impatience'), uses an irregular short form of the adjective. Some three compounds of this type are phonologically marked by means of L tone on the initial adjective and a short vowel at the end. Examples:

(a) **baƙin-cikì**   sadness, jealousy (black-belly)
ɗanyen-kâi   savage act/behavior (raw-head)
dōgon-Tūřancī   beating around the bush (long-English language)
farař-ƙasā   whitewash (white-earth)
jan-ƙarfè   copper (red-metal)
mūgùn-ɗā   thief (wicked-son)
(b) **jàn-bàki**   lipstick (cf. **jā** red, **bàkī** mouth)
jàn-farcè   fingernail polish (cf. **jā** red, **farcè** fingernail)
sàbòn-shìga   recruit (cf. **sābō** new, **shìgā** entering)

2.3. V + X compounds

There are numerous verb-based compounds. The verb is typically followed by a direct object, an adverbial complement, or a **dà** 'with' phrase. These verb-based compounds are of three types. The first type uses a special compound verb form. The second type uses the imperative form of the verb. The third type uses an ordinary infinitive phrase.

2.3.1. Special L-tone compound form

In this structural type, the compound is overtly marked by L tone on the verb and a short final vowel on the last item in the compound, e.g., **hànà-sàllà** (prevent-prayer) 'baseball cap'; **zàunà-inuwà** (sit-(in) shade) 'type of dwarf guinea-corn', **kàs-kaifi** (kill-sharpness) 'medicine to serve as protection against sharp weapons'. Unlike noun-initial and adjective-initial compounds, where final vowel shortening is rare, with V + X compounds, it represents the norm. There are some exceptions. First, compounds that have become fused and are now treated synchronically as simple nouns tend to have long final vowels, as is typical of ordinary common nouns, e.g., **jàgōrà** 'guide', from earlier **jàgōrā** (< **jā** 'pull' + **gōrà** 'staff'); **shùgàbā** 'leader, president', from earlier **shùgàba** (< **shìg(a)** 'enter' + **gàba** 'front'). Second, in long or syntactically complex compounds, the final vowel generally preserves its lexical length, e.g., **gàyà-wà-jinī-nā-wucè** 'type of sharp sword' (lit. tell-to-blood-I.comp-pass by).

In addition to the general phonological features of low-tone V + X compounds, individual verb grades have specific characteristics. (a) In compounds, gr0 Ci monoverbs lengthen their vowel, e.g., **cì-fàra** (eat-locust) 'a type of bird', cf. **yā ci fàrā** 'It ate locusts.' The result is that all monosyllabic verbs that occur in compounds, whether intrinsic monoverbs or apocopated/shortened disyllabic verbs, are bimoraic. (b) Verbs belonging to grade 3 also manifest a long vowel. (c) Grade 5 verbs in compounds invariably appear in the short-form variant, which is always accompanied by the particle **dà** (which is here left untranslated), e.g., **tsài-dà-màganà** (stop-talk) 'hair under the lower lip' (not ****tsàyàr̃-dà-màganà**). (d) The one grade 7 verb occurring in a compound appears in an apocopated form accompanied by a **dà** 'with' phrase), e.g., **gàm-dà-yāк̃ì** (meet-with-war) 'black stork'. (e) Grade 1 verbs in these compounds exhibit the final vowel alternation found in normal sentences, i.e., short in the pre-direct object C-form, long elsewhere. (f) There are occasional exceptions, namely a few transitive verbs with a long final vowel and a few intransitives with a short vowel. (g) Grade 2 verbs are surprisingly, and inexplicably, rare in this formation type. In the few examples that occur, they function *as if* they were gr1 verbs, i.e., they have final -a in the C-form, -ā elsewhere. The v* verb **barì** 'let, allow', which is really an irregular gr2 verb, also appears with short -a before its object. Examples:

(a) **bà-ta-kāshi**	a turmoil, fight, severe combat (give-it-shit)
bì-bango	leakage from the roof along the wall, wall ivy (follow-wall)
cì-rāni	dry season work; migrant labor (eat-dry season)
cì-dà-к̃arfi	hard task/labor (eat-with-strength)
gà-ruwa	selling water in jerry-cans (here is-water)
к̃ì-bugù	a charm that makes a person invincible (refuse-beating)
sà-màigidā-tsalle	type of snack (make-husband-jumping)
shà-jìɓi	type of undershirt (drink-sweat)
bà-duhù	a charm that makes one invisible (give-darkness)
kàs-gaushì	fat meat (kill-embers)

°AN: [i] The verb **bā** 'give' normally requires a thematic indirect object, e.g., **yā bā nì kwabò** 'He gave me a penny', not ****yā bā kwabò**. 'He gave a penny.' In the compound **bà-duhù** (as well as in compounds with the verbal noun **ban** 'giving'), however, **bā** appears followed by the thing given without overt mention of the recipient.
[ii] The monosyllabic verb **kàs** is a clipped form derived from **kashè** 'kill'.

(b) **tàр̃ì-dà-gidankà**	mobile (e.g., home, truck) (go-with-your home)
tùmà-dà-gayyà	a biting black ant before the wings have dropped off (jump-with-malice)
tùmà-к̃asà	crocheted dish cover (jump-to ground)
(c) **ɓàd-dà-kàma**	disguise, camouflage (mislead-appearance)
gài-dà-yàya	small basin or basket for presents (greet- elder sibling)
kàu-dà-bàr̃a	a charm against attack (avert-aim)
(d) **gàm-dà-kàtar̃**	good luck (meet-with-luck)
(e) **àmsà-amo**	loudspeaker (return-sound)
ɗànɗànà-gànɗa	alveolar consonant (taste-palate)
fàsà-к̃wàuri	smuggling (smash-shins)
gàmà-gàri	common, ordinary thing (combine-town)
fàɗà-wuta	moth (fall into-fire)
kàryà-gàrma	deep-rooted plant (break-plough)
kòmà-bāya	reactionary ideology (return-back)
ràbà-daidai	equal share (divide-exactly)
rùfà-ido	magic (close-at eye)
tàkà-tsantsan	caution (tred-carefully)
(f) **dàfà-dukà**	Jollof rice; Peugeot station wagon used as intercity taxi (cook-all)
gògà-māsu	type of weed (rub-swords)

zàunà-gàrī-banzā	idle/unemployed psn (sit-town-useless)
(g) ɗaukǎ-wuyà	carrying someone on the shoulders (carry-on neck) (< ɗaukǎ v2 carry)
gàgàrà-gàsa	outstanding psn or thing (defy-competition) (< gàgarǎ v2 defy)
hàrǎrà-garkè	an eye syndrome (glance-flock) (< hàrārǎ v2 glance sideways)
bàrà-gurbì	unhatched egg ignored by hen (leave-hatching place) (< barì v* leave)

2.3.2. Imperative verb form

Numerous compounds are built on the imperative form of the verb. Some of these are simple compounds with the verb followed by a direct object noun, an adverb, or an ideophone. Some are expanded by a **dà** 'with' phrases. Others are composed of an imperative plus an imperative or an imperative plus a command in the subjunctive.

A number of the imperative verbs appear with final -i without an object expressed, e.g., **kwànci-tàshi** 'slowly, day by day'. With verbs belonging to grades 2 and 3b, the compound form is identical to the normal imperative form, e.g., **sǎri**! 'Slash (it)!'; **tàshi**! 'Get up!' With gr1 and gr3 verbs, however, the final -i represents either a rhyming vowel or an archaic imperative marker that is no longer functional outside of fixed compounds (cf. **kwànci** in the compound **kwànci-tàshi** with the regular gr1 imperative **kwàntā**! 'Lie down!').

Unlike the compounds above, where the final vowel is usually short, the final vowel in these imperative verb-based compounds generally preserves the lexical vowel length. Examples:

dǎgùri-gùrzau	charm for invulnerability (dig up-strong man)
sǎri-kutuf	an old gecko (slash-very old)
sàkō-tumāki	simpleton (release-sheep) [short final vowel!]
bàr̃-ni-dà-mūgǔ	pimples in adolescents (leave-me-with-ugliness)
fàɗi-kà-mutù	chinaware, dish (fall-you-die)
sā-dà-kūkā	tight bracelet put on wrist with help of soap (put-with-crying)
jè-ka-dà-kwàrinkà	type of marriage (go-you-with-your bow and arrows)
sàu-ta-gà-wāwā	beautiful girl divorced soon after marriage (release-her-to-foolishness)
bàlàgi-tsindir̃	precocious child (grow up-**tsindir̃** (emphasizes quickness)) (< bàlàgà v3)
dàki-bàri	strong and reliable thing (pound-leave)
gùntsi-fèsar̃	type of medicine (take sip-spray out)
shàci-fàɗi	wild guess, rumors (outline-tell)
tsùgùni-tàshi	struggle (squat-get up) (< tsugùnā v1)
ci-kar̃-kà-mutù	tasteless food (eat-don't-you-die)
tàɓā-kà-lāshè	insufficient, esp. tasty food (taste-you-lick)

°AN: In normal usage, transitive gr1 verbs have L-L tone in the imperative before a direct object noun, e.g., **dàfà shìnkāfà**! 'Cook rice!' Thus, many of the examples included in the special L-L category such as **hànà-sallà** (prevent-prayer) 'baseball cap' might seem to belong here. I have put them in the special category for two reasons, First, they pattern with the special L-L forms in having a final short vowel on the noun that follows. Second, the corresponding intransitive gr1 verbs found in compounds also have L-L tone whereas they would be expected to have L-H tone if they were imperatives.

In a few cases, the imperative clause is preceded by mention of an addressee, e.g.,

yàwō-dàɗō-miyà	a wide-sleeved blouse (bride-increase-soup)
mālàm-bùɗā-manà-littāfì	butterfly (teacher-open-for.us-book)

2.3.3. Infinitives

Some ten or so compounds have the structure of an infinitive phrase (see §40:1), i.e., the verb stem appears in its basic form even though there is no preceding PAC (person-aspect-complex). All words in these compounds preserve their lexical tone and vowel length. Examples:

bajè-kōlì	trade fair (spread-wares)
ɗaurè-fuskà	scowling (tie-face)
iyà-shēgè	inconsiderate, unacceptable behavior (abusive term) (be able-bastard)
rabà-màkāhò-dà-gōrà	a dirty trick, cheating, deception (separate-blind man-from-staff)
sâ-hannū	signature (put-hand)
sādà-zumuncì	keeping family ties (connect-family relationship)
shā-jinin-marà-gātā	wearing a cap low on the forehead (suffer-blood.of-lacking-support)
wāsà-ƙwaƙwalwā	riddle, puzzle (sharpen-brains)

2.4. *Phrasal compounds*

There are a good number of phrasal compounds formed using the connector **dà** 'and, with' and a few formed with **bâ** 'without, there is not' or **à** 'at'. These compounds are not overtly marked by modifications in tone or final vowel length. Examples:

bàbbā-dà-jàkā	maribou stork (Mr. Big-with-bag)
karò-dà-gōmà	brave person (collision-with-ten)
màcè-dà-gōyō	snap fastener (woman-with-baby on back)
ƙarfī-dà-yājì	forcefully (strength-and-spice)
yāƙì-dà-jāhilcì	adult literacy program (war-with-ignorance)
sùɓùl-dà-bakà	slip of the tongue (slipperiness-with-at mouth)
bāya-bâ-zanè	false security, false confidence (at back-without-cloth)
kànàr̃i-bâ-kējì	prostitute (canary-without-cage)
shìgā-bâ-biyà	caged police van (entering-without-paying)
kuturū-à-wāfà	type of rubber shoe (leper-at-Wapa [name of a night club])
ruwā-à-jàllō	desperately (water-at-bottle)

°AN: The adjective **bàbba** 'big' has a short final vowel; the corresponding proper name **Bàbbā** 'Mr. Big', however, has a long final vowel, which is reflected here.

2.5. *Juxtaposed compounds*

A small number of compounds are made up of two words (nouns or verbal nouns) that are directly juxtaposed without the use of a linker. Some preserve the phonological shape of the input words; others exhibit L-L tone on the initial word plus final vowel shortening. There are also a few ideophone-initial juxtaposed compounds. Examples:

[i] **bindigà-dāɗī**	trigger-happy (gun pleasantness)
birì-bōkò	big but ineffective psn or thing (monkey-trickery)
kōwā-mālàm	a type of leather slipper (everyone-teacher)
kwānā-rawā	tinkling ear-pendant (spending day-dancing)
sārā-sūkà	thuggery (slashing-stabbing)
zāƙì-banzā	type of brown sugarcane (sweetness-useless)
kàmà-r̃ùbùtu	homographs (< **kàmā** resemblance + **r̃ùbùtū** writing)

[ii] **fankàm-fayàu**	big but useless thing (big-weightless)
hàmburun-hàyà̰	person who eats anything (big mouthed-chaos)
ƙyàlƙyàl-banzā	sth shiny but valueless (twinkling-useless)

2.6. Agentive compounds

Some six compounds consist of a **ma-** agent formative plus an object. In one case, the agentive is a plural built on a polysyllabic verb. In the other cases, one has a short-form agentive (see §7:1.6.3) with a CVV verb stem. These compounds are becoming frozen and are being reinterpreted as monomorphemic words, i.e., they could be (and sometimes are) written without the hyphen.

magà̰-takàr̃dā	scribe (one who sees-paper)
Magà̰-watà̰	proper name (one who sees-moon)
majà̰-cikì	name of a spirit (one who pulls-in belly)
majḭ̀-dāɗi	a traditional title (one who feels-pleasantness)
mashà̰-ruwā	rainbow (one who drinks-rain)
mabùnƙùsā-ƙasā	root-crops (potatoes, onions, etc.) (ones who push up-earth)

2.7. Sentential compounds

Many compounds have the structure of regular sentences. (This is in addition to the imperative verb compounds described above (§2.3.2), which could have been included here as well.) Patterns that are most commonly attested include (a) an impersonal subject in the neutral TAM, (b) some other person in the neutral or subjunctive, (c) a second person subject in the completive, and (d) a negative existential. Other structures are exemplified in (e).

(a) **à-kòri-kūrā**	delivery truck (one-drive out-cart)
à-ji-garau	type of antidepressant pill (one-feel-clear headed)
(b) **kar̃-tà-kwāna**	traditional pony-express-type message system (don't-she-sleep)
mù-hàɗu-à-bankì	type of cap (we-meet-at-bank)
(c) **kā-fi-àllūr̃à**	type of drug/medicine (you-surpass-needle)
kun-ƙi-cî	a weevil found in sacks of corn (you (pl.)-refuse-eating)
(d) **bâ-hayà̰**	excrement (euphemism); public toilet (there is not-renting)
bâ-ruwānā	fragile part of branch (lit. there is not-my water, an idiom that means 'This is none of my business')
biyu-bābù	losing both opportunities or things (two-there is not)
(e) **bā-kà̰-zuwà̰-kògī**	unwashable fabric (neg-you.cont-going-river)
gāwā-tā-ƙi-rāmì	old and sickly, but courageous psn (corpse-it-refuse-grave)
ka-cè-na-cè	argument (you-say-I-say)
ƙàƙà-nikà̰-yi	dilemma, hard times (how-I.rhet-do)
mālàm-gòbe-dà-nīsā	type of sleeping drug (teacher-tomorrow-with-distance)
zâ-ka-zâ-ni	strong and tireless psn or horse (going-you-going-me)

3. FUSED COMPOUNDS

Some compounds have become so fused, phonologically and semantically, that native speakers now view them as simplex nouns on a par with other ordinary common nouns in the language. In orthography, these tend to be written as one word. Examples:

àbinci   food (thing.of eat); **ɗan'ùbā**   half brother (son.of father); **ɗan'uwā**   brother, cousin, mate, fellow (son.of mother); **ɗankwālī**   women's headscarf (small + ?); **fàr̃gàbā**   fear, nervousness, anxiety (< **fàɗ** < **fàɗì** fall + **gàba** front); **jàgōrà̀**   guide (pull staff); **kwàrjinī**   dignity (esp. of appearance), popularity (? + blood); **ƙishirwā**   thirst (probably < *ƙishìn-ruwā thirst.of water); **ƙyûyā**   indolence, laziness (< **ƙi** refuse + **wùyā** trouble, hardship); **sàɗakà** (pl. **sàɗàkū = sāɗakōkī**) concubine slave-girl (put in room); **shēkaranjiyà**   day before yesterday (day following + yesterday); **shùgàbā**   leader (< **shìu** < **shìg** < **shìga** enter + **gàba** front); **ùbangidā**   employer, master, boss (father.of household); **ùbangijì**   master; God. (father.of home); **wàshègàrī**   the next day, morning after (probably < **wāshè** clear + **gàrī** town); **'yammātā**   girls, young women (< diminutive (pl.) + women)

°AN: [i] The compound **àbinci** 'food' (lit. thing.of eat) is built using the finite verb **ci**; the phrase **àbin cî** (lit. thing.of eating), which contains the verbal noun **cî**, means 'edible thing'.
[ii] Many SH speakers have simplified the phonologically anomalous word **ƙyûyā**, with the long /ū/ after the palatalized velar, and pronounce it as **ƙîwā**, which totally disguises its compound origin.

That these words have made the transition from recognized compounds to integrated simplexes is shown in a number of different ways. First there are phonological factors. The item **shēkaranjiyà** 'day before yesterday' behaves as a single word with H-H-H-H-L tone (not **H-H-L-H-L) even though the component word **shēkarè** 'next in time' has H-H-L tone. (Interestingly, the underlying tone is preserved in the less common, nonfused compound **shēkaràn-città** 'five days hence'. Similarly, **ƙishirwā** 'thirst', which is presumably derived from **ƙishìn-ruwā** 'thirst of water' manifests simplification of the tone as well as segmental shortening of both components. For most young SH speakers, **jàgōrà̀** 'guide' and **shùgàbā** 'leader' now end in a long final vowel, which is typical of common nouns, rather than a short vowel, which would be expected of a compound. The lengthening is presumably also true of **wàshègàrī** 'the next day', assuming that the analysis of this as an erstwhile compound is correct. Second, there are morphological factors. A number of these words now allow regular suffixal pluralization: **sàɗakà / sàɗàkū = sāɗakōkī** 'concubine slave-girl' (sg. / pl.); **shùgàbā / shùgàbànnī** 'leader' (sg. / pl.). These words also enter into various secondary derivations, e.g., **jàgōrà̀** 'guide', **jàgōrantà̀** 'to guide, lead', **jàgorancì** 'guidance, leadership'; **ɗan'ùbā** (pl. **'yan'ùbā**) 'half brother', **'yan'ubancì** 'rivalry between half brothers'; **ɗan'uwā** 'brother, cousin, mate, fellow' (pl. **'yan'uwā** 'brothers'), **'yan'uwancì = 'yàn'ùwàntakà̀** 'brotherhood'. Third, there are grammatical factors relating to gender. The word **ƙishirwā** 'thirst' is feminine (probably by analogy with the large number of other **wā**-final feminine nouns) even though its presumed component parts **ƙishì** 'thirst' and **ruwā** 'water' are masculine and plural respectively. The word **ɗan'uwā** (son.of mother) functions as a masculine noun that invariably controls an -**n** linker even though the second component **'uwā** is feminine, e.g., **ɗan'uwa-n-sà** 'his cousin'. This is unlike the situation with active compounds where the form of the bound linker tends to be locally determined by the gender of the final element, e.g., **kàren-mōtàr̃sà** 'his driver's mate'.

4. LOANS

Among the loanwords that one finds in Hausa are a number of items that are compounds in the donor language. (I am limiting myself here to loanwords from English). Some of these could also be said to constitute compounds in Hausa, in the sense that the component parts of the word are recognizable. (These are transcribed with a hyphen.) Most, however, have become fused into simple monomorphemic words. Selected examples:

atòm-bôm atom bomb; **àtōnè-janàr̃** attorney-general; **bir̃kìlà** bricklayer; **būzāyè** bull's-eye; **cîf-jōjì** chief judge of high court; **cìngâm** chewing gum; **fambêl** = **fambèl** fanbelt; **fasà-ōfìs** post office; **fasàl-ōdà̀** postal money order; **gàdìr̃ûm** guard-room, jail; **gùr̃ûf-kyaftìn** group captain (military); **hedìmastà̀** = **hêdmastà̀** headmaster of a school; **iyàkwàndishàn** air conditioner, air conditioning; **kwalàshât** shirt with collar; **làmbàtû** = **làmbàtū** ditch, gutter (< number two); **làmbàwân** a poison (< number one); **lâskōfûr̃** lance-corporal; **monì-ōdà̀** money order; **sà̀manjà** sergeant-major; **shakàsōbà̀** = **cakàsōbà̀** = **shakàzōbà̀** shock absorber; **wanwê** = **wanwè̀** one-way street

5. PRODUCTIVITY

Compounds of most types are lexically restricted in terms of their membership and meaning. However, some formations constitute more or less open classes with a recurrent meaning. These all have a genitive linking structure X-L-Y, where the X is the common formative and the Y is an adverb or noun (including compounds) or verbal noun or nominal phrase. Four such classes will be presented here.

5.1. d'an-

The word **d'an** 'person of' (or the feminine counterpart **'yar̃**) / plural **'yan** enters into compounds that indicate a person associated with a particular profession, activity, or place of origin, e.g., **d'an-sìyāsà̀** 'politician' (lit. psn.of politics). (Etymologically **d'an** is a genitive form of the word **d'ā** 'son'.) For simplicity, I shall refer to these as **d'an** compounds with the understanding that they may use the corresponding feminine and plural forms, e.g., **d'an/'yar̃/'yan-k̃asā** 'citizen(s)' (m./f./pl.) (lit. psn.of (m./f./pl.) country). The plural form used in compounds is the short variant **'yan**, e.g., **'yan-kallō** 'spectators', and not the reduplicated form **'yā'yan** 'children of', which is the normal plural of **d'an** and **'yar̃** in their etymological meanings, e.g., **'yā'yan Mūsā** 'Musa's children'. (The noun following **'yan-** usually remains in the singular, e.g., **'yan-kà̀suwā** 'traders', not ** **'yan-kāsuwōyī**, but there are exceptions, e.g., **'yan-jàr̃ìdū** 'newspaper reporters', pl. of **d'an-jàr̃ĩdà̀**.) The **d'an** formative is semantically comparable to English *-man* in compounds like 'fireman', e.g., **d'an-sàndā** 'policeman' (lit. psn.of stick), or *-er* in derived agentials like 'trader', e.g., **d'an-dambe** 'boxer' (lit. psn.of boxing). Examples (where semantically appropriate, the masculine singular **d'an** can be replaced by the feminine **'yar̃** or the plural **'yan**):

d'an-adàm human being (d'an-Adam); **d'an-hayà̀** tenant (d'an-renting); **d'an-kallō** spectator (d'an-watching); **d'an-kà̀suwā** trader (d'an-market); **d'an-kwangilā** contractor (d'an-contract); **d'an-k̃wà̀yā** drug user (d'an-pill); **d'an-tēbùr̃** stall trader (d'an-table); **d'an-zāmànī** modern person (d'an-(modern)time); **d'an-fàsà-k̃wàuri** smuggler (d'an-smuggle (lit. smash shin)); **d'an-gudùn-hijìr̃ā** refugee (d'an-running of flight/migration); **'yar̃-kwàntà-k̃ùri** chaperone ('yar̃-lie in corner)

> ΔDN: In WH dialects, the words for daughter and children are **d'ìyā** and **d'iyā** respectively. In SH, the initial CVC has merged into the phoneme /'y/, the original L-H and H-H disyllabic words both coming out as monosyllabic H tone **'yā**. Interestingly, the WH dialects that use **d'ìyā** and **d'iyā** for the words 'daughter' and 'children' in the literal senses use the phonologically fused **'yar̃** and **'yan** forms as compound formatives, e.g., **'yan-adàm** 'human beings', but **d'iyan Mūsā** 'Musa's children'.

In addition to the above compounds indicating people who perform various actions, there are **d'an** compounds that denote names of things or events associated with the main noun or adverb. With many of these items, the initial **d'an** reflects its function as a diminutive marker. The choice of **d'an** or **'yar̃** in these compounds is fixed depending on the gender of the semantic referent. (Corresponding plurals are formed with **'yan**.) The meaning of these compounds is often not transparent from the meaning of the content word, but rather is derived in an indirect or specialized manner. Examples:

ɗan-gōyō cloth for securing baby when carried on the back (ɗan-tying baby); ɗan-itàcē fruit (ɗan-tree); ɗan-jīfà shuttle (in weaving) (ɗan-throwing); ɗan-kunne earring (ɗan-on ear); ɗan-mukullī key (ɗan-lock); ɗan-wāke small dumpling made of bean flour (ɗan-black-eyed peas); 'yař-Bùhāři hunger, poverty, (economic) depression ('yař-Buhari); 'yař-ciki light shirt worn under a gown ('yař-inside); 'yař-Jòs lightweight three-quarter-length shirt ('yař-Jos); 'yař-Muřtàlā twenty naira bill ('yař-Murtala); 'yař-rāni smallpox ('yař-in dry season); 'yař-shàřā type of sleeveless shirt ('yař-sweeping); 'yař-yâu cake made of cassava ('yař-today); 'yan-bakà facial marks on both sides of the lower cheek ('yan-on mouth)

°AN: The ₦20 bill is named **'yař-Muřtàlā** because it has a picture of the Nigerian former head of state General Murtala Muhammad. It is feminine by analogy with the feminine word **takàřdā** 'paper'. The compound **'yař-Bùhāři** relates to the time of General Buhari, a former head of state of Nigeria. It is feminine by analogy with **yunwà** 'hunger' or **fatařā** 'impoverishment', both of which are feminine.

5.2. àbōkin-

The word **àbōkī** 'friend' (pl. **àbòkai**) enters into a number of compounds that denote one's partner or counterpart, e.g., **àbōkin-tafìyà** / **àbòkan-tafìyà** 'traveling companion(s)'. These are loose compounds—barely distinguishable from close-knit phrases—whose meanings are generally quite transparent. Examples:

àbōkin-aikì coworker, colleague (friend.of-work); àbōkin-ařzìkī business partner (friend.of-wealth); àbōkin-cìnikī customer (friend.of-business); àbōkin-gàbā opponent (friend.of-enmity), àbōkin-hīřa conversation partner (friend.of-chatting); àbōkin-wàsā playmate (friend.of-play)

5.3. ruwan-

The word **ruwā** 'color, water' combines with names of various substances to produce color adjectives. Examples:

ruwan-tòkā gray (color.of-ash); ruwan-gōřò orange colored (color.of-kolanut); ruwan-gwâl gold colored (color.of-gold); ruwan-hōdà pink (color.of-face powder)

5.4. ban-

The word **ban** 'giving of' enters into a number of compounds with a considerable range of meanings, generally denoting actions or abstract qualities. Examples:

ban-fuskà welcoming expression on one's face (ban-face); ban-gàskiyā trust (ban-truth); ban-girmā respect (ban-age); ban-haushī outrage (ban-anger); ban-hannù handshake (ban-hand); ban-hàƙurī apology (ban-patience); ban-kwānā goodbye (ban-day); ban-màganà coaxing (ban-talk); ban-tàusàyī pity, sympathy (ban-pity)

°AN: For many SH speakers, the word **gaskiyā** 'truth' has either L-H-H tone or all H tone, the latter appearing to be in the process of becoming the norm. In the compound, however, it invariably has the historically original L-H-H tone (at least for Kano speakers), this being a further indication of the true compound as opposed to phrasal status of these items.

◊HN/◦AN: Jaggar (1992a: 36) suggests that the **ban** in these compounds derives from a fused imperative *bà-ni, i.e., **ban màganà** 'coaxing' (< *bà ni màganà 'Give me talk!'). Because the contraction of **bà-ni** to **ban** with the regular tone change of L-H to H is well attested, this proposal is not unreasonable; nevertheless, my feeling is that a more likely hypothesis is the one put forward by Abraham (1959b: 35), namely, that **ban** is a tonally irregular verbal noun (with H rather than falling tone) plus the linker, i.e., **ban màganà** < *bā-n (or *bai-n) + **màganà** 'giving of talk'. The fact that **bā** *synchronically* always requires a recipient as first (or only) object is no impediment to the verbal noun analysis as a historical/derivational explanation. (In the compound **bà-duhù** 'a charm that makes one invisible' (lit. give-darkness), the semantic recipient is also missing.) A third, never-mentioned, possibility, which is a variant of Jaggar's proposal, but which makes better sense semantically, is that **ban** in these compounds does indeed come from a fused imperative *bà-ni, but that **ni** is the old Chadic third person masculine pronoun 'him' (still seen in **wani** 'some' (m.)) rather than the first person pronoun 'me'.

[References: Ahmad (1994); Galadanci (1969, 1972); Gouffé (1975a, 1981a); Wysocka (1989)]

17. Conditionals and Concessives

T HIS chapter describes six kinds of subordinate clauses, which are labeled: (1) regular conditionals, (2) counterfactual conditionals, (3) concessive conditionals, (4) universal concessive conditionals, (5) hypothetical concessive conditionals, and (6) concessives.

1. REGULAR CONDITIONALS

1.1. Formation

Regular conditionals of the form "if X (then Y)" are expressed by a hypothetical clause (the protasis) introduced by the conjunction **ìdan** (= **in**) 'if' plus a full consequence clause (the apodosis), e.g.,

in mutầnē sun shiryầ, sai mù tàfī	If the people are ready, we'll go.
ìdan kin ci wannàn, bà zā kì ji dāɗī ba	If you eat this, you won't enjoy it.
in hùlầř tā yi makà kàɗan, zân kāwō wata	If the cap is too small, I'll bring another.
in zā kà hūtầ, kà zaunầ nân	It you are intending to rest, sit here.
ìdan yanầ barcī, kadà kà fařkař dà shī	If he is sleeping, don't wake him up.
in àkwai sukàřī, zân sakầ à shāyì̀	If there is sugar, I'll put some in the tea.
ìdan shī likità nē, zâi wařkař dà nī	It he is a doctor, he will cure me.
ìdan bài bā kà aron mōtầř ba, sai kà hàƙuřầ	
If he doesn't lend you the car, just put up with it.	
in bā yầ aikì̀, yā kàmātà kà kai shì wajen màkānikè̀	
If it's not working, you ought to take it to the mechanic.	
in kanầ dà kuɗī, bâ wândà zâi hanầ ka shìgā	
If you have money, no one will prevent you from entering.	

For pragmatic reasons, the hypothetical clause normally precedes the consequence clause. Sentences with the reverse order, however, are grammatical. In some cases, as in examples (c), (d), and (e), the hypothetical clause at the end would appear to be the most natural, e.g.,

(a) **zā kì fasầ shi in bà kì yi hankàlī ba**	You're going to break it if you're not careful.
(b) **kadà kà sàyā in yā yi tsầdā!**	Don't buy it if it's too expensive!
(c) **munầ zuwầ sìnīmầ in dà àkwai**	We go to the movies if (when) there is one.
(d) **Abdù yakàn hàsalà in an taɓầ kèkensà**	Abdu gets angry if anyone touches his bicycle.
(e) **zâi dācè̀ ìdan Audù yā àuri Bintầ**	It would be nice if Audu married Binta.

As illustrated in the examples presented above, hypothetical clauses can contain both verbal and nonverbal sentences. All TAMs (affirmative and negative) are allowed in the hypothetical clause with the exception of the potential and the subjunctive.

The completive and the preterite, which occur to some extent in complementary syntactic environments, are both allowed in the hypothetical clause and with very similar meanings.

in yârā <u>sun</u> / <u>sukà</u> dāwō zân bā sù kwabò kwabò

If the children come back (comp / pret), I'll give them a penny each.

in <u>an</u> / <u>akà</u> fārà ruwā, zā mù shìga ɗākìn

If it starts to rain (comp / pret), we'll go in the room.

°AN: Bagari (1987) claims that the conditional sentences with the completive are more conditional and less probable than those with the preterite, i.e., the distinction corresponds more or less to an 'if/when' difference. Most Hausa speakers agree that there is a semantic difference depending on whether the completive or the preterite is used, but there is remarkable lack of agreement on where the difference lies, and in some cases the alternatives even seem to be in free variation. The intuition of many speakers is exactly opposite that of Bagari, whereas others seem to look for a different semantic nuance altogether to distinguish between the alternatives.

The Rel-continuous TAMs can occur in a hypothetical clause, but only when grammatically called for in Rel environments (such as focus fronting), e.g.,

ìdan zīnārìyā [kakè]$_{Rcont1}$ sô, tô inā dà ita	If it's gold you want, I have it.
cf. **idan [kanà]$_{cont}$ sôn zīnārìyā, tô inā dà ita**	If you want gold, I have it.
ìdan shī nè [yakè]$_{Rcont2}$ dà kuɗī, sai mù sàmi tàimakō	
If he is the one who has money, we'll get some help.	

The consequence clause is often in the future. If the potential future is used (which some speakers tend to avoid), it indicates uncertainty and doubt about the consequence. As an alternative to the regular future, one can use a clause introduced by the particle **sai** followed by the neutral form, i.e., a weak subject pronoun without an overt TAM. (This is a structure that other scholars describe as the subjunctive.) Examples:

in an sâ musù kāyā dà yawà [zā sù]$_{fut}$ gàji

= **in an sâ musù kāyā dà yawà sai [sù]$_{neut}$ gàji**

If one puts too heavy a load on them, they'll tire.

ìdan mùtûm yā yi aikì mài kyâu [zâi]$_{fut}$ ci lādā

= **ìdan mùtûm yā yi aikì mài kyâu sai [yà]$_{neut}$ ci lādā**

If someone does good work, he'll get a reward.

in kā tàfi gòbe, kògī [yâ]$_{pot}$ ƙètàru	If you go tomorrow, the river is likely to be crossable.
in Allàh yā yàrda, [mâ]$_{pot}$ gamà aikìn gòbe	God willing, we will likely finish the work tomorrow.

1.2. Meaning

In most instances, the Hausa hypothetical clause corresponds to an English 'if' clause. Hausa, however, also uses the conditional where there is a greater degree of certainty about the future result and where English would use 'when' (see §69:1.2), e.g.,

in nā kòyi Hausa zâ ni Nàjēriyà	When I learn Hausa I'm going to Nigeria.
in sun dāwō, kà bā sù rūwā sù shā	When they return, give them water to drink.

Some sentences in which the hypothetical clause is in the completive and the consequence clause is formed with **sai** plus the neutral unmarked TAM express a generic situation. In these cases, **in/idan** often translates best as 'whenever' rather than 'if'. Examples:

ìdan mayàk̃ā sun kai wà gàrī hārì, sai sù kāmà bāyī
>Whenever warriors attacked the town, they would capture slaves.

in mùtûm yā ískē ɗan'uwansà yanà cîn àbinci sai yà cê dà shī "munà kwaryā", shī kò sai yà cê "àlhamdù lìllāhì"
>If (whenever) a person finds his pal eating, he (the pal) says to him, "Come and join me," whereupon he replies, "Thanks."

ìdan kiɗà yā sākè, rawā sai tà sākè
>Whenever the drumming changes, the dance changes. (i.e., keep in step with the times)

in mun kwāshè tāsōshī sai mù wankè su   Whenever we collect the dishes, we wash them.

2. COUNTERFACTUAL CONDITIONALS

2.1. Formation
The primary means of forming counterfactual conditionals is by use of **dà...dà**, the markers occurring at the beginning of both the hypothetical and consequence clauses, e.g.,

dà kun ci wannàn ganyē, dà kun mutù   If you had eaten these leaves you would have died.
dà nā sanì, dà bàn fàɗi hakà ba   Had I known, I would not have said that.
dà sunà faɗà, dà munà jîn īhù   If they were fighting, we would be hearing shouts.
dà mōtà tā lālàcē, dà bà mu isō yànzu ba
>Had the car broken down, we wouldn't have been here by now.

dà bā kà barcī, dà kā ga shigôwar̃sà
>If you hadn't been sleeping, then you would have seen him enter.

dà nī nè mùtumìn nan mài hankàlī, dà nā sayà makà jàkâr̃
>If I were that sensible man, I would have bought you the bag.

dà kanà dà kuɗī, dà mun shiryà
>If you had any money, we would have come to an arrangement.

dà shī sarkī nè, dà yā sâ an tumɓùkè wàzīr̃ì
>If he had been chief, then he would have had the vizier deposed.

The allowable TAMs in hypothetical clauses of counterfactual conditionals are not exactly the same as those in regular conditionals. In neither case can the subjunctive be used. The potential, however, is allowed. If it occurs, the consequence clause will normally also be in the potential. Similarly, if the hypothetical clause is in the future, then the consequent clause must also be in the future, e.g.,

dà [â]$_{pot}$ tàmbàyē nì, dà [nâ]$_{pot}$ yàr̃da   If one were to ask me, I would agree.
dà [zā sù]$_{fut}$ zàɓē shì, dà [zâi]$_{fut}$ cùcē sù   If they were to elect him, he would cheat them.

A striking difference between regular and counterfactual conditionals is the absence in the counterfactual case of the preterite as a free choice in the hypothetical clause. (The preterite can appear, but only when required in a Rel environment.) Examples:

dà [sun]$_{comp}$ tàimàkē mù, dà [mun]$_{comp}$ gamà   If they had helped us, we would have finished.
not ****dà [sukà]$_{pret}$ tàimàkē mù, dà [mukà]$_{pret}$ gamà**

cf. **dà gubà [sukà]**~pret~ **bā tà, dà [tā]**~comp~ **hadîyē**

> If it were poison that they had given her, she would have swallowed it.

The **dà** in the hypothetical clause can optionally be preceded by the conjunction 'if', usually the short form **in**, less commonly the full form **ìdan**, e.g.,

in dà Audù sarkī nè dà yā bā kà àlkyabbà

> If Audu were king, he would have given you a royal robe.

in dà kanà kallō sòsai dà kā ga ta îndà ta shigō

> If you had been looking carefully, you would have seen by which way she entered.

If the consequence clause is in the potential, the neutral, or the future, it is possible to omit the second **dà**, e.g.,

dà an tàmbàyē nì (dà) nâ yàřda (= sai ìn yàřda)   If they had asked me I would have agreed.

in dà àbōkinkà zâi zìyàřcē nì (dà) zân bā shì tuwon dawà

> If your friend were to visit me, I'd give him guinea-corn *tuwo*.

Another possibility is to use **in** without the **dà** before the hypothetical clause, especially if the clause is negative, e.g.,

in (dà) bà don hakà ba, dà nā yàřda   If not for this I would have agreed.

2.2. Meaning

Counterfactual conditionals indicate hypothetical propositions that are not true and/or are not likely to become true, e.g.,

dà nā san kanà zuwà, dà bà nâ tàfi ba

> If I had known that you were coming (but I didn't!) I wouldn't have gone.

dà kā sàmi fâm dubū hàmsin, dà zā kà sàyi Marsandî?

> If you were to get £50,000 [which you're not!] would you buy a Mercedes?

A hypothetical clause with **dà mā** that is not followed by a consequence clause forms an expression of regret or unfulfilled wish, e.g.,

dà mā nā ji shāwařàřsà   Would that I had followed his advice.

dà mā bàn kashè duk kudîn ba   If only I hadn't squandered all the money.

dà mā inà dà mōtà nē   If only I had a car.

3. CONCESSIVE CONDITIONALS

3.1. Formation

Concessive conditional clauses, which can usually be translated by 'even if', are formed with **kō** plus a full clause. It the clause is tensed, it uses a general TAM, e.g.,

kō an yi minì àzābà, bàn yàřda ba   Even if I were tortured, I would not agree.

kō bà kà san nì ba, nā dai san kà   Even if you don't know me, I know you.

kō bā nà̂ nân, kadà kà canzà masà sūnā   Even if I'm not here, don't change his name.

kō kanằ barcī, bâ shakkằ zā kà ji ƙāraƙ jirgī

Even if you are sleeping, you will hear the sound of the plane.

°AN: Note that the particle **kō** can also have the meaning 'even' in constructions other than concessives, e.g., **kō Audù yanằ sôn pizza** 'Even Audu likes pizza'; **bài cê kō sànnu ba** 'He didn't even say hello.'

3.2. *Meaning*

The essence of concessive conditionals is a semantic opposition between the first clause, which may or not be true, and the consequence clause, which is claimed to be so. Whereas in a regular conditional, the consequence depends on the truth of the hypothetical clause, in a concessive conditional, the reality of the event or situation in the first clause is irrelevant.

4. HYPOTHETICAL CONCESSIVE CONDITIONALS

Hypothetical concessive conditionals combine semantic properties of concessive conditionals with the element of doubt and unreality characteristic of counterfactual conditionals. (In some sentences, it is very hard to capture the semantic nuances separating a hypothetical concessive conditional from a simple concessive conditional.) The hypothetical concessive conditionals are expressed by clauses formed with **kō dằ** (plus a general TAM), e.g.,

kō dằ tā zō bà zā tà sằmē nì ba

Even if she were to come, she wouldn't meet me. [but she probably won't come]

cf. the concessive: **kō tā zō bà zā tà sằmē nì ba**

Even if she comes, she won't meet me. [so she shouldn't come]

cf. the counterfactual: **dằ tā zō dằ bà tà sằmē nì ba**

If she had come, she wouldn't have met me. [but she didn't come]

kō dằ yā zằgē kà kâƙ kà cê masà kōmē

Even if he were to insult you, don't say anything to him.

cf. **kō yā zằgē kà kâƙ kà cê masà kōmē**

Even if he insults you, don't say anything to him.

kō dằ Hāmidù zâi biyō ta nân, kì gayằ masà nā wucè

In case Hamidu comes this way, tell him I've gone.

kō dằ an bā kà kuɗī, bà zā kà baƙ mùtûm yà shìga ba?

[You mean] even if you were bribed, you wouldn't allow a person to enter?

kō dằ sun ƙi sayaƙ masà dà mōtàƙ, bằ daidai ba nè yà dingà zằge-zằge

Even if they refused to sell him the car, it is not right that he should keep on hurling insults.

The phrase **kō dằ akằ yi**, with the impersonal rhetorical TAM, has become a fixed expression meaning 'just in case', e.g.,

kà tàfi dà laimằ, kō dằ akằ yi

Take your umbrella, just in case.

gằ ɗan gùzurī kà shā ruwā, kō dằ akằ yi

Here's some pin money for you to spend on the way, just in case.

5. UNIVERSAL (INDEFINITE) CONCESSIVE CONDITIONALS

Universal concessive conditional constructions are built with universal generic relatives (**kō**-forms) (see chap. **73**) followed by a full clause. If the clause is tensed, it requires a Rel TAM like the preterite or the Rel-continuous, e.g., **kōmē kukè sô**... 'Whatever (= no matter what) you want...' (*not* ****kōmē kunà̀ sô**...). The concessive conditional clause specifies a class of possible persons, things, events, etc., the consequence relating to any and all of them. Examples:

kōwā ya ci wākē, cikìnsà zâi kùmburà	Whoever eats beans, his stomach will swell up.
kōwā mukà gàyyatà̀, zâi zō	Whoever we invite will come.
kōmē sukà yi makà, kadà kà dàmu	Whatever they do to you, don't worry.
kōmē kakè dà shī, sai kà rabà̀ ràbon Allàh	Whatever you have, you should distribute fairly.
kōyà̀yà̀ sukà yi, sai sun yi dà kyâu	However they did it, they would do it well.
kōwàɗànnē kikà bā nì, zân kàrɓā	Whichever ones you give me, I'll accept.

kōwàcè irìn rìgā zā kà sàyā, munà̀ dà ita
      Whatever kind of gown you'll buy, we have it.

kō'ìnā yakàn tàfi (= yakè̀ tàfiyà̀), yanà̀ tattàrà lìttàttàfai
      Wherever (i.e., no matter where) he goes, he collects books.

kōyàushè akà bugà ƙàrarrawā, sai ɗàlìbai sù fitō
      Whenever the bell was rung, students would come out.

The universal pro-forms built with **mè ya sâ** 'why?' and **nawà** 'how much, how many?' are generally restricted to universal concessive conditional constructions.

kō mè ya sâ sukè̀ ɓōyè àbinci, bà mù yàrda ba
      No matter why they are hoarding food, we don't agree to it.

kō nawà ka tayà̀, bā nà̀ sayầrwā
      However much you offer, I am not selling.

Universal concessive conditionals with 'whoever' and 'whatever', can be expressed either by use of the universal pronouns **kōwā** 'everyone' and **kōmē** 'everything', as in the examples above, or else by use of **kō** plus the Q-words **wà(nē nè)** (= **wà̀yê**) 'who? or **mè(nē nè)** (= **mèyê**) respectively. (If the concessive clause contains an equational predicate, then the Q-word variant is required.)

1.a. **kōwā ya yàr̄da mahàukàcī nè̀**	Whoever agrees is crazy.
1.b. **kō wà(nē nè) ya yàr̄da mahàukàcī nè̀**	Whoever agrees is crazy.
2.a. **kōmē ta ganī, tanà̀ sô**	Whatever she sees, she wants.
2.b. **kō mè(nē nè) ta ganī, tanà̀ sô**	Whatever she sees, she wants.
3. **kō wà̀nē nè shī, bà zân būɗè̀ masà àkwàtìnā ba**	

      Whoever he is, I won't open my box for him.

There is a slight difference in meaning depending on whether one uses the universal pronouns or not. Sentence 1a has the reading that everyone/anyone (i.e., all people in the world) who might agree are crazy, whereas 1b could be interpreted to refer to whoever from among a specific set of people such as the ones who might be in the room. Similarly in sentence 2a, one is indicating anything in the world that she might see, whereas 2b could be more limited, e.g., to the things that she sees when she goes to a toy store.

°AN: The distinction between the a and b sentences could be indicated by a translation difference, i.e., 'whoever / whatever' vs. 'no matter who / no matter what', although it is far from clear to me exactly what the semantic difference is in English.

Universal pro-forms are typically followed by a tensed clause. However, **kōmē** 'everything, whatever' can be followed by a genitive phrase, usually headed by an abstract noun, e.g.,

kōmē ƙarfin mùtûm, àkwai wândà ya fī shì
> No matter how strong a man is (i.e., whatever a man's strength), there is someone stronger.

kōmē zurfin rījìyā, zân shìga   However deep the well is, I'll enter it.
kōmē nīsan tàfiyằ, bà zā mù barì ba   No matter how long the journey is, we won't quit.

°AN: The construction consisting of **kōmē** followed by an N of N phrase is particularly common in proverbs (see Kirk-Greene 1966), e.g., **kōmē kyâun tàfaṟnuwā, bà tà yi kàmaṟ àlbasằ ba** 'However good the garlic is, it's not like an onion' (i.e., quality will tell); **kōmē nīsan darē, gàrī yâ wāyè** 'No matter how long the night, the day will dawn' (i.e., every cloud has a silver lining).

6. CONCESSIVES

Concessive clauses indicating 'although, even though' are formed with **kō dà yakè** (= **duk dà yakè** = **duk dà cêwā**) plus a full clause. It the clause is tensed, it uses a general TAM, e.g.,

kō dà yakè inằ rashìn lāfiyằ, bà zân jē asìbitì ba
> Although I'm sick, I won't go to the hospital.

kō dà yakè sun taɓà zuwằ gidānā sun ɓatà hanyằ
> Even though they had been to my house before, they got lost.

kō dà yakè tā ƙi jinin haushì, tā sayō kwīkwiyò
> Even though she hates barking, she bought a puppy.

kō dà yakè kinằ shirìn tāshì, inằ sôn màganằ dà kē
> Even though you are preparing to leave, I have something to say to you.

duk dà cêwā zā kà yi màmākìnsà, gaskiyā nè
> Although it may seem strange to you, it is true.

One can optionally shorten **kō dà yakè** to **kō dà**. If this is done, then the following TAM must be a Rel form, e.g.,

kō dà [mukà]pret **jē, bà mù gan shì ba**   Even though we went, we didn't see him.
kō dà [nikè]Rcont2 **dà laimằ, nā jiƙè**   Even though I had an umbrella, I got soaked.

[Reference: Bagari (1987)]

18. Conjunctions

CONJUNCTIONS can be classified into three main groups: (1) the basic coordinating conjunctions; (2) the special function words **haŕ** and **sai**; and (3) miscellaneous subordinating conjunctions.

1. BASIC COORDINATING CONJUNCTIONS

1.1. 'And'

The conjunction **dà** 'and' serves to conjoin two NPs or two postnominal adjectives. It is not used to conjoin sentences. Examples:

Bàlā dà Bābìyā sunà sôn wàsā   Bala and Babiya want to play.
sunà nēman wata yārinyà farā dà (kuma) dōguwā
  They are searching for a light-skinned and (also) tall girl.

The **dà** is often used in front of the first conjunct as well as between items, especially if the first item is a pronoun, e.g., **(dà) nī dà shī dà àbōkin Mūsā mun yàrda** 'He and I and Musa's friend agree.' With some items like question words, universals, etc., the conjunction serves to form pseudoplurals, e.g.,

tunà masà [kōmē dà kōmē] yā zama aikìnā nè
  Reminding him of everything (lit. everything and everything) has become my job.
(dà) wà dà wà zā sù zō?   Who (pl.) will come?
tàimakon kâi dà kâi yanà dà àmfànī   Self-help (lit. helping oneself and oneself) is useful.

1.2. 'Or'

The disjunctive conjunction **kō** 'or' serves to connect two NPs. One can optionally use **kō** in front of the first of the disjuncts, e.g., **kàwō manà (kō) kòfī kō tî!** 'Bring us (either) coffee or tea!' Unlike **dà** 'and', the conjunction **kō** can be used to connect sentences, e.g., **zâi dāwō nân dà awà biyu kō zâi bugà manà wayà** 'He'll return within two hours or he'll call us.' The discontinuous **kō...kō** with clauses generally indicates 'either/whether...or', e.g., **kō kā zō kō bà kà zō ba bài dàmē nì ba** 'Whether you come or not it doesn't bother me.'

  The same notion can also be expressed by **au...au**, e.g., **au kā zō au bà kà zō ba...** 'Whether you come or not...'.

  A more formal alternative is **ìmmā...kō** or **ìmmā...ìmmā** (followed by the subjunctive), e.g.,

ìmmā dai sù biyā nì yànzu kō kuma mù yi rìgimà
  Either they pay me right now or we're going to have a fight.
ìmmā kà yi hakà ìmmā kadà kà yi, òho
  Whether you do this or not, I don't care.

1.3. 'But'

The conjunction **àmmā** 'but, nevertheless', which is a loanword from Arabic, serves to connect sentences or phrases in which there is a contrast between the two constituents, e.g.,

inà sôntà àmmā bằ dà yawằ ba	I like her, but not a lot.
mun rồ̄ē shì àmmā yā ƙi	We begged him but he refused.

2. THE WORDS haȓ AND sai

The words **haȓ** 'up until' and **sai** 'until, except' are extremely high-frequency items that function both as prepositions (see chap. **57**) and as conjunctions.

> °AN: The multifunctional words **haȓ** and **sai** have extensive dictionary entries and have been the subject of individual lexical studies, e.g., Lukas (1955), Kraft (1970), Meyers (1974).

The conjunction **haȓ** indicates: as far as, up to; until; even, including; even though, even with; so much so that, etc. It serves to conjoin sentences where the first sentence is viewed as moving forward and leading into (sometimes resulting in) the second sentences, e.g.,

zân iyà tsayằwā haȓ kā gamằ	I can wait until you have finished.
cīwồ yā ci ƙarfìntà haȓ yā kashề ta	The illness weakened her to the point that it killed her.
sun yi aikì haȓ sun gàji	They worked until (with the result that) they got tired.

The word **haȓ** is unusual in that it allows preposing of a following noun subject, e.g.,

nā daɗề inà kàȓằtū haȓ <u>wuyằnā</u> yā ƙagề = nā daɗề inà kàȓằtū <u>wuyằnā</u> haȓ yā ƙagề
> I was reading for such a long time that my neck got stiff.

The conjunction **sai** '(not) until, except, only, unless, etc.' (which is sometimes accompanied by **dà**) differs from **haȓ** in connoting a terminal point in time or space. It often occurs with an expressed or implied negative, e.g.,

bà zân iyà hawan wannàn ginì ba sai an sakà tsānì
> I won't be able to climb this wall unless a ladder is put up.

yā cê, "sai kā gamà aikìn zā kà tàfi gidā"
> He said, "It is only after you have finished the work that you can go home."

bà zā kà ɗagà dàgà nân ba sai kā biyā	You're not going to leave here until you pay.
yanằ ta kàȓằtū sai dà ya shìga sōjà	He was studying until he joined the army.
cf. yanằ ta kàȓằtū haȓ yā sằmu dìgìȓî na biyu	He studied until he got his master's degree.

One often gets **haȓ** plus **sai** together in immediate succession to indicate 'up until', i.e., **haȓ** serves to lead the action forward, while **sai** serves to put on the brakes and specify an end point, e.g.,

zâi baȓ tà à gōnâȓ haȓ sai tā būshề	He will leave it in the farm up until it dries.
zā à yi tàfiyằ haȓ sai an kai Sằminàkà	One will keep going until one reaches Saminaka.
sunằ yîn kàȓằtun Àlƙuȓ'ānî haȓ sai sun girma	They study the Koran until they grow up.
tun dà yakè tanằ barcī, zā mù zaunà à wàje haȓ sai tā tāshì	
> Since she is sleeping we will sit outside until she gets up.

3. SUBORDINATING CONJUNCTIONS

The uses of the various subordinating conjunctions are described through the grammar in the sections in which different kinds of clauses are treated. Many of these subordinators introduce sentence-initial clauses. Here is a simple listing of the most common ones:

dà   (1) when, e.g., <u>dà</u> mukà gàbàcē sù sai sukà gudù   When we approached them, they fled. (2) rather than (that), e.g., yā fi àřàhā à sàyē shì nân <u>dà</u> à tàfi Kanò   It is cheaper to buy it here than to go to Kano.

bāyan (dà)   after, e.g., <u>bāyan</u> sun fita mun būɗè kwālîn   After they went out we opened the parcel.

dòmin (= don)   because, in order that, e.g., an ɗaurè shi <u>don</u> kadà yà gudù   They tied him up so that he wouldn't run away.

ìdan (= in)   if; when (in future), e.g., <u>ìdan</u> kā cùcē mù zā mù rāmà   If you cheat us, we'll get back at you.

kàfîn = kàfîn (= kàmìn = kàmin)   before, e.g., <u>kàfîn</u> mù hūtà sai mù kammàlà aikìn   Before we rest, we should finish the work.

kàmař (= tàmkař)   like, as if, e.g., nā ji <u>kàmař</u> zân yi amai   I felt as if I would vomit. (Etymologically **kàmař** is composed of the noun **kàmā** 'similarity' plus the feminine linker -ř. For some speakers, the word is **kàman** with the masculine linker.)

kō   even if, e.g., <u>kō</u> Audù yā gàji, yâ ƙāràsà aikìnsà   Even if Audu is tired, he will (likely) finish his work.

kō dà   as soon as, e.g., <u>kō dà</u> ya ɗagà hannū, yârā sukà dainà màganà   As soon as he raised his hand, the students stopped talking.

kō dà (yakè)   even though, e.g., <u>kō dà yakè</u> kinà shirìn tāshì inā dà màganà dà kē   Even though you are prepared to leave, I have sth to say to you.

màimakon   instead of (plus a clause in the neutral TAM), e.g., <u>màimakon</u> à kòrē shì hař zā à yi masà kyàutā   Instead of chasing him away, they are even going to give him a gift; <u>màimàkon</u> sù ràgu, ƙàruwā sukà yi   Instead of decreasing, they increased.

muddìn   as long as, provided that, e.g., <u>muddìn</u> yanà zuwà gidan nàn bà zā à ràbu da tāshìn hankàlī ba   As long as he keeps coming to this house, there will always be trouble.)

sabòdà   because, on account of, e.g., nā yi fushì <u>sabòdà</u> kā màkarà   I am angry because you are late.

tàmkař (= kàmař)   like, as, e.g., tanà tākàwā ɗai-ɗai <u>tàmkař</u> an naɗà ta sàraunìyā   She was walking around as if one had appointed her queen.

tun   (1) while, e.g., kà faɗà musù <u>tun</u> sunà nân!   Tell them while they're here!; (2) (followed by **kàfîn** 'before' or a neg clause) even before, e.g., nā gamà aikÌ <u>tun</u> kàfîn kà zō = nā gamà aikÌ <u>tun</u> bà kà zō ba   I finished the work (even) before you came.

tun dà   since (past temporal), e.g., <u>tun dà</u> mukà isō, bà mù gan shì ba   Since we arrived we haven't seen him.

tun (dà yakè)   since (factive), e.g., <u>tun dà yakè</u> bà kà rigā kā gayà masà ba, sai kà fàsà   Since you haven't told him yet, you might as well leave the matter alone.

19. Coordination

THIS chapter describes general issues of coordination affecting noun phrases, adjectives, verb phrases, and full sentences.

1. NP COORDINATION

1.1. 'And'

Simple coordination is accomplished by means of the conjunction **dà** 'and', e.g.,

gidā dà mōtà a house and a car; **farin tsuntsū dà dōguwar̃ bishiyà** a white bird and a tall tree; **r̃àgō ɗaya dà tumākī gōmà** one ram and ten sheep; **kàzā dà kàzā** such and such; **cîn nāmàn àladè dà shân giyà** eating pork and drinking beer

In principle, there is no limit as to the number of NPs that can be conjoined, e.g., **dāwà dà gērò dà shìnkāfā dà àlkamà**... 'guinea-corn and millet and rice and wheat...'. A modal particle can be inserted between the conjunction and the following NP, e.g., **ɗàlìbai dà kuma lēbur̃ōr̃ī** 'students and also workers'. The **dà** is often inserted before the first conjunct as well, e.g., **dà Bellò dà Mūsā** 'both Musa and Bello', **dà zākì dà dàmisà** 'both a lion and a leopard'. In conjoining nouns and pronouns, the latter normally occur first. In conjoining pronouns, the order is first person, then second, and then third. If both pronouns are second or third person, then the order is pragmatically determined, e.g.,

shī dà Mūsā	he and Musa	**ita dà Bintà**	she and Binta
dà nī dà shī/ita/sū	I and he/she/they	**mū dà sū**	we and they
kai dà ita	you (m.) and she	**kē dà shī**	you (f.) and he
kai dà kē *or* **kē dà kai**	you (m.) and you (f.) / you (f.) and you (m.)		
shī dà ita *or* **ita dà shī**	he and she / she and he		

Certain types of bound pronouns, specifically indirect objects and genitives, cannot be conjoined. One cannot, for example, say ****yā gayà minì dà masà** 'He told me and him.' Instead one would need a paraphrase like **yā gayà manà, (dà) nī dà shī** 'He told us, me and him.' Similarly, to express 'They were looking at her and Binta' (where looking is a dynamic noun taking a genitive object), one would need to say **sunà kallonsù, ita da Bintà** (lit. they.cont looking.of.them, her and Binta).

Adjectival modifiers are normally strung together without use of **dà**. In prenominal position, the adjectives are connected by linkers, e.g., **dōgon ƙàƙƙarfan ɗan-dambe** 'a tall, strong boxer'. In postnominal position the adjectives are simply juxtaposed, perhaps with the addition of the particle **kuma** 'also', e.g., **ɗan-dambe dōgō (kuma) ƙàƙƙarfā** 'a tall, strong boxer' (lit. boxer tall (also) strong). If **dà** is used before the second adjective, that adjective is generally interpreted as modifying a different referent, e.g., **ɗan-dambe dōgō dà (kuma) ƙàƙƙarfā** 'a tall boxer and a strong (one)'.

135

When used with numerals, **dà** serves both to connect independent numbers and also to form number combinations, e.g., **bìyař dà shidà** '5 and 6', cf. **tàlàtin dà huďu** '34' (lit. 30 and 4).

Certain NPs can be conjoined with themselves to indicate pseudo-plurals or distributives, e.g.,

yāƙî yā tāshì tsàkānin ƙàbīlà dà ƙàbīlà
> War broke out between the tribes. (lit. tribe and tribe)

dà wà dà wà sukà ƙi biyà?
> Who (pl.) refused to pay? (lit. and who and who)

sunà shân wàhalà shèkarà dà shèkàrū
> They have been suffering for years. (lit. year and years)

1.1.1. Ellipsis in coordinate phrases

Conjoined phrases in which the same noun appears with different modifiers permit deletion of the repeated noun, e.g.,

farař mōtà dà baƙař mōtà	a white car and a black car
(⇒) **farař mōtà dà baƙā Ø**	a white car and a black (one)
lìttàttàfai màsu kyâu dà Ø maràsā kyâu	good books and bad
hùlař yârā dà Ø ta mânyā	a cap of children and of adults
mìjìn Bintà dà Ø na Jummai	Binta's husband and Jummai's
tūtà jā dà tūtà shūďîyā	a red flag and a blue flag
(⇒) **tūtà jā dà Ø shūďîyā**	a red flag and a blue (one)
cf. **tūtà mài launìn jā dà shūďî**	a red and blue flag

(lit. flag possessing color.of redness and blueness)

1.1.2. Asymmetric coordination

When a singular pronominal is conjoined with another NP, the plurality of the conjoint is often anticipated and the initial pronoun appears in plural form, i.e., an English phrase like 'I and Musa' commonly appears in Hausa as **mū dà Mūsā** (lit. we and Musa), e.g.,

tsàkāninsù dà jīkàn sarkī, àbîn bài ƙò yi shèkarà ba
> Between him (lit. them) and the emir's grandson, there wasn't even one year's difference (in age).

nā san yâddà zân rabà su dà tsōhuwař nàn
> I know how I'm going to separate him (lit. them) and this old woman.

ràbonmù dà ganinkà yā daďè
> I haven't seen you for a long time. (lit. our separation with seeing you has been long)

It is especially common for weak subject pronouns to mark anticipatory plurality when a **dà** + NP phrase appears after the verb (or at the beginning of the sentence if focused), e.g.,

mun jē Kanò dà Audù	Audu and I went to Kano.

(lit. we went to Kano with Audu) (or 'Audu and we went to Kano' *or* 'We went to Kano with Audu')

dà Audù nē mukà jē Kanò	It was with Audu that I went to Kano.
mun daddàlē dà shī	He and I reached an agreement.

(lit. we reached agreement with him)

zā kù shiryà dà ita?	Are you (sg.) (lit. you (pl.)) going to make up with her?
mun shā ďawàiniyā dà shī	He and I suffered together (in doing sth).

(lit. we drank difficulties with him)

Note that all sentences displaying asymmetric coordination are potentially ambiguous because the referent for the plural pronoun could in fact be plural, thus **mun shā ɗàwàiniyā dà shī**, for example, could also mean 'We suffered putting up with him.'

1.1.3. Concord phenomena

If two (or more) singular nouns are conjoined, they become grammatically plural, e.g.,

yārinyā dà ƙawařtà sunà wàsā	The girl and her friend (they) are playing.
tùmātìř dà àlbasà ɗîn dà na sàyā sun ruɓè	
The tomato(es) and onion(s) that I bought (they) became rotten.	
ɓaunā dà gīwā nè mukà hàřbā	It was a buffalo and an elephant we shot.

(where the stabilizer **nè** is used because the head is plural, cf. **gīwā cè mukà hàřbā** 'It was an elephant (f.) we shot', with the feminine stabilizer **cè**)

The form of the bound linker is locally determined by the last conjunct rather than by the phrase as a whole, whereas the free linker agrees with the plural phrase (cf. the similar situation with compounds (see §43:2.1.1), e.g.,

gīwā dà ɓaunařsà = gīwā dà ɓaunā nāsà	his elephant and buffalo
gīwā dà ɓaunař nàn na (not **ta) **mahàřbîn**	this elephant and buffalo of the hunter
ɓaunā dà gīwâř dà mukà hàřbā	the buffalo and elephant that we shot

Some (but not all) speakers allow a plural demonstrative in front of a conjunct phrase consisting of two singular nouns, but the construction is considered to be awkward, e.g.,

??waɗànnân kujèrā dà tēbùř	??these chair and table

1.2. 'Or'

Disjunction, which makes use of **kō** '(either) or', essentially follows the rules just described with respect to order or elements, optional use of the conjunction in front of the first noun, etc. Examples:

Lìtìnîn kō Tàlātà kō Làřàbā	Monday or Tuesday or Wednesday
Kanò kō kùwa Kàtsinà	Kano or maybe Katsina

kō biyu kō ukù two or three; **kō ita kō Bintà** either she or Binta; **nī kō kai** you or I (lit. I or you)

kō Tankò kō Sulè bà zâi sàmi wurin shìgā ba
Either Tanko or Sule will not find room to get in. (but one will)

The negative '(neither) nor' does not make use of **kō**. Rather, the idea is expressed by the juxtaposition of negative clauses or else by a paraphrase, using, for example, the negative existential expression **bâ wândà** 'there is no one who', e.g.,

bâ yàbō bâ fàllasà	neither praise nor blame
(lit. there is not praise there is not blame)	
bài ga kōmē ba bài kuma ji kōmē ba	He neither saw anything nor heard anything.
(lit. neg.he see anything neg neg.he also hear anything neg)	
tsàkānin Tankò dà Sulè bâ wândà zâi sàmi wurin shìgā	
(lit. between Tanko and Sule there is not who.that fut.he get room.of entering)	

Neither Tanko nor Sule will find room to get in.

1.3. 'But'

Contrasting items are conjoined by means of **àmmā** 'but', e.g.,

shī sīr̄īr̄ī nè àmmā dà ƙarfī	He is thin but strong.
inā sôntà àmmā bā̀ dà yawā̀ ba	I like her, but not a lot.
mài kuɗī àmmā mài rōwā̀	rich but stingy

2. COORDINATION OF SENTENCES

2.1. 'And'

The conjunction **dà** is not used to conjoin sentences. Rather, sentences are directly juxtaposed (with possible adverbial connectors inbetween), e.g.,

mun ci mun sha	We ate and drank.
Mūsā yā jē yā dāwō	Musa went and came back.
jē-ka kà kāwō ruwā!	Go and bring some water!
munā̀ nan munā̀ ta taɓā̀wā	We're there (existential) (we are) trying.
rùfè tāgà̀ tùkùn, kānà mù tàfi	Close the window first, then we can go.
wata rānā sukà fitō dàgà gidā sukà nùfi makar̄antar̄sù	
	One day they left home and headed for their school.

It is common for stylistic effect to conjoin an active clause with a passive clause containing the same lexical verb. (This construction emphasize the thoroughness of an action.) Examples:

yā ɗaurè tunkìyā tā ɗàuru	He tied a sheep (such that) it was well tied up.
tā dafà àbinci yā dàfu	She cooked the food (so that) it was good and well cooked.

Conjoined sentences commonly make use of the connective **kuma** 'also, in addition'. It occurs either between the sentences or, more commonly, after the PAC (person-aspect-complex) of the second sentence, e.g.,

nā ci àbinci <u>kuma</u> [nā] shā ruwan lèmō = nā ci àbinci [nā] <u>kuma</u> shā ruwan lèmō
  I ate food and also drank juice.
dōlè kù būɗè tāgà̀ <u>kuma</u> [kù] shār̄è ɗākìn = dōlè kù būɗè tāgà̀ [kù] <u>kuma</u> shār̄è ɗākìn
  You must open the window and sweep the room.
Bintà tanà̀ kàr̄àtū <u>kuma</u> [tanà] sàurāren r̄ēdiyò = Bintà tanà̀ kàr̄àtū [tanà] <u>kuma</u> sàurāren r̄ēdiyò
  Binta was studying and listening to the radio.

In a string of conjoined sentences, **kuma** will show up only with the last, e.g.,

yā ci àbinci yā wankè hannunsà yā gōgè à r̀ìgar̄sà yā <u>kuma</u> yi hamdalà̀ dàgà ƙarshē
  He ate food, washed his hands, wiped them on his gown, and in addition gave thanks.

One can conjoin sentences both of which are negative or one of which is negative and the other affirmative, e.g.,

tàfi maza kuma kadà kà dāwō hannū sàke!	Go quick and don't return empty-handed!
Mūsā yā shigè bài cê masà kōmē ba	Musa passed by and didn't say anything to him.

tsōhuwā bā tà jî bā tà ganī	The old woman doesn't hear and doesn't see.
ƙārâr̃ bà tà ràgu ba kuma bà tà tsayà ba	The noise has neither decreased nor stopped.
bā yà̄ shân tî, nī kuma bā nà̄ shân kòfī	He doesn't drink tea and I don't drink coffee.
bà zā tà hàɗu dà ƙawà̀yen ba bà̀ kuma zā tà tàfi sìnīmà̄ ba	
She is not going to meet her friends and she is not going to go to the movies.	

As seen in the above examples, if two negative sentences are conjoined, each can carry its own negative marking. Alternatively, one can use only one (discontinuous) neg marker, which encompasses the full sentence. This option is particularly common if the two clauses are closely connected, e.g.,

<u>bàn</u> fìta nā ganī <u>ba</u>	I didn't go out and see (it).
<u>bà</u> yâ zō yà biyā bāshìn dà akè bînsà <u>ba</u>	He will probably not come and pay the loan.
<u>bà</u> zā tà hàɗu dà ƙawà̀yen tà kuma tàfi sìnīmà̄ <u>ba</u>	
She is not going to meet her friends and go to the movies.	

When a sentence in the past (preterite or completive) is conjoined with one in the allative or the future, one often gets an 'in order to' reading, e.g.,

sū ukù àbòkan jūnā [sukà] tāshì dàgà gàrinsù [zâ su] wani gàrī nēman aurē	
These three friends left their town to go to another town for marriage.	
[yā] ajìyè kuɗī [zâi] sàyi tikitìn jirgī	He saved money in order to buy a plane ticket.
(lit. he saved money he will buy a plane ticket)	

The use of the preterite (optionally preceded by the conjunction **sai**) in a clause after the completive denotes consecutive action as opposed to a comp + comp sequence, where the different actions are simply enumerated, e.g.,

[nā]comp hau kūkà̄ sai [na]pret ga ƙauyè	I climbed the baobab tree and then I saw the village.
[an]comp yi wata gar̃damà̄ [akà]pret cê wà ya fi wàyō cikin mutà̄nen nàn?	
There was a dispute and it was asked who was cleverest among these men?	

A continuous sentence followed by one in the preterite (optionally preceded by **sai**) indicates that the second action intruded into the first one, e.g.,

inà̀ kàr̃ātū mutà̄nē sukà shigō	While I was reading, people came in.
sunà̀ cikin cîn àbinci kūrà̀yen sukà far̃ musù	
As they were eating, the hyenas attacked them.	
anà̀ yāwò cikin jējì sai kwatsàm wani dòdō ya ɓullō	
They were wandering in the forest, when suddenly a monster appeared.	
yanà̀ nan kân aikìnsà, sai akà zō masà dà là̀bār̃ìn r̃àsuwar mahàifìnsà	
He was there working away at his job, when the news of his father's death reached him.	

Simultaneity or overlapping of two actions is indicated by conjoined sentences, the second of which is in the continuous. The best translation for the continuous clause is often that of an English subordinate participial phrase. Examples:

nā gan shì yanà̀ dūkàn dōƙì	I saw him beating a horse.
yanà̀ wàsā Bir̃nin Rûm yanà̀ ƙōnèwā	He was fiddling while Rome was burning.

bā yā shân ruwā yanằ cîn àbinci — He was not drinking water while eating his food.

gằ ni nan inằ ta aikì haữ ƙarfè gōmà na dare — There I was working until ten o'clock at night.

gằ cùnkōson mutằnē sunằ jiràn kàntōmằ
(lit. here is crowd of people they are waiting for the administrator)
    There was a crowd of people waiting for the government adminstrator.

Conjoined sentences that employ certain verbs in the first clause such as **daɗ'ề** or **jimằ** 'last long' or **rigā** (= **rìgā** = **rìgāyằ**) 'precede, have already done' have a an essentially unitary meaning, e.g.,

yā daɗ'ề yanằ aikì — He's been working for a long time.
(lit. he.comp last long he.cont working)

nā daɗ'ề bàn gan shì ba — I haven't seen him for a long time.
(lit. I.comp last long neg.I see him neg)

yā jimằ yanằ aikì — He has been working for some time.

bài jimằ yanằ kờyon Hausa ba — He hasn't been studying Hausa long.

bài rìgāyằ yā sằmi bīzằ ba — He hadn't already got the visa.

bà à rigā an fārằ ba — One hasn't begun yet.

mū nề mukà rigā mukà gan shì — *We* already saw him.

sun rìgā sun ji làbāữìn — They have already heard the news.
(lit. they.comp precede they.comp hear news.the)

°AN: When it indicates 'precede', **rigā** appears as a gr0 verb with H-H tone, e.g., **yā rigā mù** 'He preceded us.' When it is used in a conjoined sentence to indicate 'have already done', it appears either as **rigā** or as **rìgā** with L-H tone. This latter form appears to be in the ascendancy among young SH speakers.

Conjoined sentences in which the first consists of the pro-verb **yi** 'do' plus an ideophone also tend to have an essentially unitary meaning, i.e., the **yi** clause expresses what would be handled in English by an adverbial phrase. Examples:

tā yi faữat tā tāshì — She got up suddenly. (lit. she did *wup* she got up)

yā yi fùnjum yā fāɗ'ằ ruwa — He fell in the water *kerplunk*. (lit. he did *spash* he fell (in) water)

2.1.1. TAM deletion

If a sequence of sentences are both in the future, potential, habitual, or continuous (general or Rel), the repeated TAM marker may be deleted. (The process is similar to factoring in algebra.) What remains is a neutral PAC consisting only of the wsp (which takes default L tone), e.g.,

[zā mù] tàfi gidan Aishà [Ø mù] shā tî [Ø mù] yi hīữā
    We're going to Aisha's house and drink tea and chat. (fut + (fut) + (fut) $\Rightarrow$ fut + neut + neut)

[mâ] tàfi gidā [mù Ø] kāwō littāfìn
    We will likely go home and bring the book. (pot + (pot) $\Rightarrow$ pot + neut)

mutằnē [sukàn] jē masallācī [sù Ø] sàurằri huɗ'ubằ
    People go to the mosque and listen to the sermon (hab + (hab) $\Rightarrow$ hab + neut)

[yanằ] wankè mōtằ [yà Ø] gōgà mâi à jìkī
    He is washing the car and rubbing wax on it. (cont + (cont) $\Rightarrow$ cont + neut)

wằcē cề [takề] ɗ'inkà hùlā [tà Ø] kai kằsuwā?
    Who (f.) sews caps and takes them to market? (Rcont1 + (Rcont1) $\Rightarrow$ Rcont1 + neut)

2.1.2. Reduction of repeated NPs

Conjoined sentences with underlying identical subjects obligatorily drop the repeated subject in the second clause. The person/number/gender of the subject is then carried by the wsp, e.g.,

[Bintà] tanà kàr̃àtū [Ø] tanà kuma sàuràren r̃ēdiyò
    Binta is reading and also listening to the radio.
[Mustàphā] yā yi wankā [Ø] yā gyārà fuskà   Mustapha took a bath and shaved.

A direct object (or oblique object) noun that is repeated can be either deleted (favored with a nonpersonal antecedent) or replaced by a resumptive pronoun (preferred in the case of a personal/animate antecedent). A repeated pronoun is usually deleted. A repeated indirect object is usually pronominalized. Examples:

zâi wankè [mōtà] yà gōgè [(ta)] dà mâi   He will wash the car and wax it. (lit. rub it with oil)
zā mù ciyar̃ dà [shānunmù] mù kuma shāyar̃ dà [sū]   We will feed our cattle and water them.
dōlè kù kāmà [ta] kù ɗaurè [Ø]   You should catch it and tie it up.
wasu sunà yàbon [Fela], wasu sunà zāgìn[sà]
    Some are praising Fela, others are insulting him.
ta sàyi [ƙwai], ta kai [Ø] gidā, ta dafà [Ø], ta ci [Ø]
    She bought eggs, took (them) home, cooked (them), and ate (them).
yakàn tàfi wurin [wàzīr̃ì] yà gayà ma[sà] àbîn dà jīkàn sarkī yakè yî
    He would regularly go to the vizier and tell him what the chief's grandson was doing.

Another possibility (albeit an uncommon one) is to suspend mention of the object until after the verb in the second clause, e.g.,

nā sâ yârā sù shārè ( ) sù kuma wankè [gidân]
    I've asked the boys to sweep and wash the house.
mū nè mukà nēmō ( ) mukà kuma r̃ubùtà [làbār̃ìn]
    We're the ones who researched and wrote the story.
mijì shī nè zâi ciyar̃ ( ) yà kuma tufātar̃ dà [màtar̃sà]
    It is the husband who will feed and clothe his wife.
kàfin àzahàr̃ har̃ yā līƙè ( ) yā kuma ɗaurà [tāyàr̃]
    Before noon, he'd already patched and mounted the tire tube.
na yankà ( ) na kuma sōyà [ta]   I slaughtered and fried it.

Normally, as in the above examples, the objectless verb in the first clause appears in its A-form, i.e., the form used when no object follows. With grade 2 verbs, some speakers use the A-form whereas others anticipate the d.o. and use the pre-noun C-form, e.g.,

Mar̃yàm tā [kàr̃bi]$_C$ ( ) tā kuma r̃èni yārinyàr̃ = Mar̃yàm tā [kàr̃ɓā]$_A$ ( ) tā kuma r̃èni yārinyàr̃
    Maryam accepted and raised the girl.
Bellò yā [hàr̃bi]$_C$ ( ) yā kuma sòki bàrēwâr̃ = Bellò yā [hàr̃ɓā]$_A$ ( ) yā kuma sòki bàrēwâr̃
    Bello shot and stabbed the gazelle.

Although sentences with the object deferred until the second clause are considered grammatically possible, they are not normal and are seldom encountered in writing. They tend to represent an abrupt, impolite speech style.

2.1.3. Verbal ellipsis

A repeated verbal action can be replaced by the pro-form **hakà** 'thus' plus the modal particle **mā** 'also, indeed', as in the following example:

Audù yā biyā Bintà hakà mā Mūsā   Audu paid Binta and also (paid) Musa.

In many instances, the sentence is ambiguous as to whether the noun following **hakà mā** is the subject or the object of the understood action, e.g.,

Bellò yā tsōratař dà Kànde, hakà mā Daudà
>   (a) Bello frightened Kande and so did Dauda. (b) Bello frightened Kande and also (frightened) Dauda.

inà sôn Lādì, hakà mā Lawàn
>   (a) I like Ladi and Lawan also likes her. (b) I like Ladi and also (I like) Lawan.

2.2. 'Or'

Disjunctive sentences are formed with **kō** 'or' or **kō...kō** 'either...or'. The particle **kuma** 'also' or **mā** 'also, even' sometimes accompanies the **kō**, e.g.,

zā kà rakà mu kō zā kà zaunà à gidā?
>   Are you going to accompany us or are you going to stay home?

bâ shi dà kyâu kà zàgi mutànē kō (kuma) kà yi dà sū
>   It is not right for you to insult people or to back-bite them.

bà àbin kunyà ba nè à kwāna à gidan sùrùkai kō mā à shā furā à can
>   It is not shameful for someone to sleep at one's in-laws' house or even to drink *fura* there.

kō Tànî tà biyā hàřājî kō à ɗaurè ta, ôho
>   Whether Tani should pay the taxes or whether she should be imprisoned, I couldn't care less.

hàřāmùn nē mù shā giyà kō mù sayař dà ita kō mā mù bāyař dà ita gà wani
>   It is prohibited for us either to drink alcohol or to sell it or even to give it to someone.

2.3. 'But' and 'however'

Contrasting/oppositional sentences or phrases are conjoined by means of **àmmā** 'but' or **àmmā (duk dà hakà)** 'but nevertheless', e.g.,

mun ròkē shì àmmā yā ƙi   We begged him but he refused.
nā yi nā yi àmmā ìnâ!   I tried and tried, but no way!
tā zō àmmā bà tà daɗè ba   She came but she didn't stay long.
rānā tanà fāɗùwā àmmā bà zā mù tsayà ba   The sun is setting but we won't stop.
shī bà Mùsùlmī ba nè àmmā (duk dà hakà) yanà azùmī
>   He is not Muslim, however he is fasting.

sun yi iyā ƙòƙarinsù àmmā duk dà hakà bà sù ci ba
>   They did their best, nevertheless they failed.

[References: Schwartz (1989, 1991); Schwartz, Newman, and Sani (1988)]

20. Definite Article

THE definite article (d.a.) (= "previous reference marker") is an enclitic that indicates that the NP to which it is attached is a definite item previously referred to in the discourse or contextually inferable therefrom, e.g., **tùlûn yā fashè** 'The (known) water pot (which has some previous reference) broke', cf. **tā fasà tùlū** 'She broke a water pot.' The exact meaning and uses of the d.a. are not entirely clear: note that a noun without it may also translate into English with a definite article, e.g., **tùlū yā fashè** 'The/A water pot broke.' Looking at texts and older grammars, it appears that use of the d.a. was formerly restricted to sentences where one specifically wanted to emphasize the previous referential nature of the word in question. (This is apart from definite heads of relative clauses, where the d.a. is normally found.) Among modern SH speakers, on the other hand, use of the d.a. is extremely common and seems to be approximating the use of the definite article in English. Whether this is due to English influence or whether this is a natural historical development is hard to say.

°AN: I have adopted the familiar term *definite article* instead of the more cumbersome *previous reference marker*. Semantically, however, the latter designation is probably more accurate because it focuses on the language internal (as opposed to the real-world knowledge) determinant of its use. Thus, when a definite NP occurs for the first time in a text, one normally does not use the d.a., even if it would require a definite article in English. The Hausa d.a. is thus similar to the presumably cognate marker **nə** in Mupun, a related West Chadic language (see Frajzyngier 1991).

The d.a. can co-occur with (prenominal) demonstratives and with possessives and other genitives. The position of the d.a. is always immediately after the head noun, e.g.,

wannàn dōkì-n	this horse in question
wànnan sàraunìyâ-r̃	that queen in question
jàkî-n nàwa	the donkey of mine
àkuyà-r̃ ta wànnan tsōhuwâr̃	the goat of that old woman

Constructions indicating 'like that of' have the form N **irì-n** L N. The word **irì-n** 'the kind' (derived from 'seed'), which obligatorily contains the d.a., stands in apposition to the preceding noun, which governs the gender and number (**na** or **ta**) of the linker, e.g.,

wàndō irì-n na dâ	trousers like those of olden days
(lit. trousers type-the of formerly)	
mōtōcī irì-n na màsu hannū dà shūnī	cars like those of rich people
(lit. cars type-the of having hands with dye)	
rìgā irì-n ta yâu	a modern gown
(lit. gown type-the of today)	

1. FORM

The d.a. appears as ˋ-r̃ and ˋ-n, i.e., /r̃/ and /n/ preceded by a floating L tone. If the d.a. is attached to a word with final H tone, the floating L of the clitic combines with the H to produce a fall. (Final long vowels automatically shorten in the resulting closed syllables, see §54:3.) Examples:

bàkā + ˋ-n → bàkân   the bow   hùlā + ˋ-r̃ → hùlâr̃   the cap
manòmā + ˋ-n → manòmân   the farmers

If the word to which the d.a. is attached ends in a low tone (or falling = HL), the floating L attaches vacuously, e.g.,

watà + ˋ-n → watàn   the month   mōtà + ˋ-r̃ → mōtàr̃   the car
fàsfô + ˋ-n → fàsfôn   the passport   kwàmìtî + ˋ-n → kwàmìtîn   the committee

The use of ˋ-r̃ vs. ˋ-n and the form of the preceding word are the same as for the segmentally identical, but toneless, enclitic linker (see §43:2 for full details). In brief, ˋ-r̃ is attached to feminine singular nouns ending in the vowel /a(a)/; ˋ-n is attached elsewhere. (Note: In the examples, I have glossed the d.a. as 'the', with the understanding that its exact meaning cannot be equated with 'the' in English.) Examples:

gōd̃îyā f. mare / gōd̃îyâ-r̃   the mare   ùngùlu f. vulture / ùngùlû-n   the vulture
dōkì m.   horse / dōkì-n   the horse   nāmà m. meat / nāmà-n   the meat
gōd̃iyōyī pl. mares / gōd̃iyōyî-n   the mares
d̃aya m. or f. one / d̃ayâ-n / d̃ayâ-r̃   the (other) one (m. or f. referent)

> ΔDN: The masculine d.a. is ˋ-n in all dialects. The feminine counterpart shows considerable dialectal variation. In Daura, for example, where SH final /r̃/ generally appears as /l/, the d.a. appears as ˋ-l, e.g., rìgâl 'the gown'. In Katsina and Maradi, the feminine d.a. is ˋ-i, e.g., rìgâi, fuskài 'the face', etc. (What is not clear is whether this form represents a phonological weakening of ˋ-r̃ or whether it is an archaic retention of a common d.a. /-i/ found in related West Chadic languages like Kanakuru (Newman 1974: 86ff.).) In Sokoto, the d.a. for some speakers is indicated simply by the floating L tone with no segmental addition, e.g., rìgâ 'the gown', cf. rìgā 'a gown'.

With compounds—even some quite fixed compounds—the form of the d.a. is usually determined by the gender of the noun to which it is attached, not by the gender of the compound as a whole. (This latter controls all other gender-agreement rules.) Examples:

[gidan-[àshānâ]f-r̃]m   the matchbox (lit. house.of matches-the)
e.g., gidan-àshānâr̃ dà nakè dà shī   the matchbox that I have (lit. that I am with him)
[ƙwan-[fìtilà]f-r̃]m   the light bulb (lit. bulb.of lamp-the)
e.g., ƙwan-fìtilàr̃ yā fashè   The light bulb (he) broke.
but ['yan-[kàsuwâ]f-n]m   the traders (lit. people.of market-the)
e.g., 'yan kàsuwân sunà ta cìnikinsù   The traders are doing their buying and selling.
[tashàr̃-[jirgî]m-n]f   the airport (lit. station.of plane-the)
e.g., tashàr̃-jirgîn tanà nan kusa?   Is the airport nearby?
[uwar̃ [gidâ]m-n]f   the senior wife (lit. mother.of house-the)
e.g., uwar̃gidân bā tà nân   The wife is not here.

Personal pronouns in Hausa can affix a definite article, e.g., **shîn** 'he/him we were referring to' (< **shī** + **ˋ-n**). All pronouns take **ˋ-n** rather than **ˋ-r̃**, even the third person feminine pronoun that ends in /a/, e.g.,

ita she + d.a. → **itân**, e.g., **itân na bā wà**	It's she (the one in question) I gave it to.
wàtàk̃īlà zā à bā tà izìnin shìgā, itân	
	Perhaps they will give her permission to enter, the she (about whom we were discussing).
tātà hers + d.a. → **tātàn**	hers (f. thing previously referred to)

The general pro-form **hakà** 'thus' takes its gender from its antecedent/referent. However, it always takes **ˋ-n** as its d.a. regardless of the gender of its referent, e.g., **hakàn tā fi** 'Thus (referring to some understood f. antecedent) is better.'

Semantically definite nouns modified by a relative clause normally contain a d.a. (The feminine **ˋ-r̃** commonly assimilates to the initial /d/ of the relative marker **dà**.) Examples:

yār̃òn dà ya tàfi	the boy who went
yārinyàr̃ dà (often [yārinyàddà]) **bā tằ sôn tautàu**	the girl who doesn't like spiders
mōtàr̃ dà (often [mōtàddà]) **mukè gyār̃àwā**	the car that we were repairing
r̃īgunàn dà yakè dà sū	the gowns that he has

A final falling tone on a noun + d.a. often simplifies to H when followed by the L-tone relativizer **dà**, i.e., HL-L → H-L. In SH, this rule is optional; in some WH dialects, it appears to be obligatory, e.g.,

yârân dà sukà tàfi = yâran dà sukà tàfi	the children who went
mōtōcîn dà mukè gyār̃àwā = mōtōcin dà mukè gyār̃àwā	the car that we were repairing
r̃ìgâr̃ dà ta yāgè = r̃ìgar̃ dà ta yāgè	the gown that got ripped
hùlâr̃ dà na sàyā = hùlar̃ dà na sàyā	the cap that I bought

If something, e.g., a modal particle, is inserted between the noun and the relativizer, then the falling tone surfaces, even for speakers who normally apply the simplification rule, e.g.,

hùlâr̃ dai dà na sàyā	the cap indeed that I bought ≠ ****hùlar̃ dai dà…**
mōtōcîn kùwa dà mukè gyār̃àwā	the cars, moreover, that we were repairing
≠ ****mōtōcin kùwa dà…**	

Instead of attaching the d.a. directly, consonant-final words, foreign words, proper names, pronouns, numerals, and ideophones often make use of a connector **ɗi-** (= **ki-** in certain NW dialects). Because the connector ends in a vowel other than /a/, it takes **ˋ-n** regardless of the gender of the head word, e.g.,

bâs f.	bus	**bâs ɗîn**	the bus
thesis m.	thesis	*thesis* **ɗîn**	the thesis
ita f.	she	**ita ɗîn**	the she (= **itân**)
Gar̃bà m.	proper name	**Gar̃bà ɗîn**	the Garba in question (= **Gar̃bàn**)
mài shī m.	owner of it	**mài shī ɗîn**	the owner of it
wānè m.	so-and-so	**wānè ɗîn**	the so-and-so
dōkìnsà m.	his horse	**dōkìnsà ɗîn**	his horse we were talking about
k̃èr̃èr̃è id.	standing disrespectfully	**k̃èr̃èr̃è ɗîn**	the disrespectful standing

°AN: Because of the tightly bound nature of **ɗi-** plus the **⸜n**, and the fact that **ɗi-** does not occur as an independent word in the language, many native speakers tend to think of **ɗîn** as a monomorphemic word comparable to English 'the'. This falling tone **ɗîn** with the d.a. attached has a wider distribution and is less restricted phonologically and grammatically than is the same connector **ɗi** when used with the linker. Thus **ɗaya ɗîn** 'the one in question', for example, is readily accepted whereas ****ɗaya ɗin-sù** 'one of them' is disliked, **ɗayansù** without **ɗi** being much preferred. For a detailed description of the use of **ɗi-**, see Buba (1997b).

Use of **ɗi-** is a way of avoiding the gender anomaly in compounds where the compound as a whole is masculine but the final member is feminine. If the d.a. is suffixed directly, one has to choose between two unattractive alternatives: suffixing the feminine d.a. **⸜r̃** to a masculine compound or suffixing the masculine d.a. **⸜n** to a feminine word.

[sarkin-[tashà]]f]m	stationmaster	**sarkin-tashà ɗîn**	the stationmaster
(= sarkin-tashàr̃ = sarkin-tashàn)			
[ƙwan-[fitilà]]f]m	light bulb	**ƙwan-fitilà ɗîn**	the light bulb
(= ƙwan-fitilàr̃ = ƙwan-fitilàn)			

For many speakers, **ɗîn** is subject to the F → H tone simplification rule when preceding the relativizer **dà**, e.g.,

bâs ɗîn dà zā mù shìga = bâs ɗin dà zā mù shìga	the bus that we will enter
kanàr̃ ɗîn dà ya yi bòr̃ē = kanàr̃ ɗin dà ya yi bòr̃ē	the colonel who rebelled

2. DOUBLE DEFINITE ARTICLES

A definite head noun modified by a relative clause typically contains a d.a. Less common, but still quite normal, is to also use a d.a. at the end of the entire NP, i.e., after the relative clause. This second d.a. attaches to the final element, whatever that happens to be. Examples:

mutànê-n dà na gayà musù-n	the men that I told
(lit. men-the that I told to.them-the)	
Audù-n dà na san kàwunsà ɗî-n	the Audu whose uncle I know
(lit Audu-the that I know uncle.of.his ɗi-the)	
wândà sukà kāmà shî-n	the one they caught
(lit. who.the.that they caught him-the)	

°AN: An exactly parallel structure is found in Kanakuru (Newman 1974), where double marking is the norm rather than the exception.

[References: Jaggar (1985); Newman (1992c)]

21. Demonstratives and Determiners

1. THE wa- WORDS

THE label "demonstrative" is used as a cover term to include such grammatical items as 'this (one)', 'which (one)', 'some (one)', or 'the one who/that'. Some of these items function exclusively as pronouns, e.g., **wànnē?** 'which one', and some as determiners, e.g., **wànè dōkì?** 'which horse'. Others function both as pronouns and as determiners, e.g., **wannàn yā fi kyâu** 'This (one) is best'; **wannàn bīr̃ò yā fi kyâu** 'This ballpoint pen is best.'

Most of these items occur in what has traditionally been referred to as a long form. The definite demonstratives 'this, that, etc.' also appear postnominally in a short form, e.g., **waccàn kàsuwā = kàsuwar̃ càn** 'that market'.

The long form contains a prefix **wa-** (with variable surface tone), e.g., **wannàn** 'this', **wàccē** 'which one (f.)'. With a few phonologically conditioned exceptions, these demonstratives all have distinct masculine, feminine, and plural forms. A striking feature of the plural forms is the unusual infix **-ɗan-** (see below for tones), which is not a normal plural morpheme elsewhere in the language, e.g., **waɗànnân** 'these'.

◊HN: Although the **ɗan** morpheme is anomalous in that it does not function as a normal plural marker, there are possible cognate plural forms with **ɗ-** in other Chadic languages (Newman 1990b).

The full inventory of Hausa demonstratives is presented in table 2.

Table 2: Demonstratives

	m.	*f.*	*pl.*
1. this (by me)	wannàn	wannàn	waɗànnân
2. that (by you)	wànnan / wânnan	wànnan / wânnan	wàɗànnan / waɗànnan
3. that (there)	wancàn	waccàn	waɗàncân
4. that (distant)	wàncan / wâncan	wàccan / wâccan	wàɗàncan / waɗàncan
5. which?	wànè	wàcè	wàɗànnè
6. which one?	wànnē	wàccē	wàɗànnē
7. who, which, that	wândà / wandà / wàndà	wâddà / waddà / wàddà / waccè / wàccè	waɗàndà / wàɗàndà
8. some/other	wani	wata	wa(ɗan)su
9. so-and-so	wānè	wancè	su wānè / su wancè

147

The above items can be organized into five groups: the definite (deictic) demonstratives (rows 1–4), the interrogative demonstratives (rows 5–6), the relative pronouns (row 7), the specific indefinite demonstratives (row 8), and the unspecified pronouns (row 9).

1.1. Definite (deictic) demonstratives

The singular definite demonstratives in rows 1–4 all have the following form: **wa-** (with underlying H tone) + linker (underlyingly //n// or //t//) + locative adverb (segmentally **nan** 'here' or **can** 'there'), e.g., **wa- + n + cân** → **wancàn** 'that'.

> ΔDN: In WH, the speaker-proximal demonstratives corresponding to row 1 make use of the true determiner `-ga (which has an associated L-H tone pattern) instead of the erstwhile adverb **nân**, e.g., **wânga**, f. **wâgga**, pl. **waɗànga** 'this/these'.

The feminine linker //t// fully assimilates to the initial /n/ of the locative **nan**, with the result that the underlying distinction between the masculine and feminine demonstratives in rows 1 and 2 is not reflected in the surface form, e.g., //wa- + n + nân// → **wannàn** 'this' (m.) and //wa- + t + nân// → **wannàn** 'this' (f.).

> °AN: As a general phonological rule, syllable-final /t/ regularly changes to /r̃/, e.g., **'yā-tasà** = **'yar̃sà** 'his daughter'. In the case of the feminine demonstratives, one could thus have the /t/ pass through an intermediate /r̃/ stage before undergoing assimilation, i.e., //wa- + t + nân// → **war̃nàn* → **wannàn** 'this' (f.). It is not immediately clear whether anything is to be gained by this approach.

The plural demonstratives have the form **wa- + ɗàn** + the locative adverb, where the plural morpheme **ɗàn** can be analyzed either as having inherent L tone or as receiving that tone by default, e.g., **wa- + ɗàn + nân** → **waɗànnân** 'these'. Note that the linker used in the singular forms is omitted if the plural morpheme is present. (Alternatively, one could say that the linker is structurally present and that the /n/ of **ɗan** does double duty, serving both as the final consonant of the plural morpheme and as the linker.)

The demonstratives in row 1 contain the speaker-proximal adverb **nân** 'here', which has underlying H-L tone. The demonstratives in row 3 contain the distal adverb **cân** 'here', which is also H-L. In the singular forms, the H-L tone pattern of these adverbs spreads over the two available syllables, e.g., $(wa)^H$-n-nan)^{HL} → **wannan**^{HL}, i.e., /wánnàn/ 'this'; $(wa)^H$-t-can)^{HL} → **waccan**^{HL}, i.e., /wáccàn/ 'that'.

The demonstratives in rows 2 and 4 contain the hearer-proximal adverb **nan** 'there (near you)', and the distal adverb **can** 'there remote', respectively. These morphemes both have underlying L-H tone (which, in isolation, simplifies to H because there is no rising tone in the language). The demonstratives appear with two different tonal realizations depending on the nature of the tone spreading. The (L-)L-H surface variants result from the spreading of the L-H of **nan** and **can** in a tone-integrating fashion (which obliterates the initial H tone), e.g., $(wa-)^H + n + nan)^{LH}$ → **wannan**^{LH}, i.e., /wànnán/ 'that (near you)'; $(wa-)^H + (ɗàn)^L + can)^{LH}$ → **waɗancan**^{LH}, i.e., /wàɗàncán/ 'those yonder'. The F-H surface variants result from the spreading of the L-H of **nan** and **can** onto the syllable consisting of the **wa** + linker, but without destroying the underlying H tone. The H + L on the initial syllable surfaces as a fall, e.g., $(wa-)^H + t + nan)^{LH}$ → $(wan)^{HL} nan)^H$, i.e., /wânnán/ 'that (f.) (near you)'. In the plural forms, the light syllable **wa-** cannot serve as a host for two tones and thus remains H, e.g., $(wa-)^H + (ɗan)^L + can)^{LH}$ → $(wa)^H (ɗan)^{LL} + can)^H$, i.e., /wáɗàncán/ 'those yonder'.

> °HN: Some speakers (Buba 1997a and Galadanci 1969, for instance) feel that the L-H and F-H forms are not just equivalent phonological variants but rather have slightly contrastive meanings.

Historically this probably was not the case. Whereas it may be so for some speakers nowadays, it is almost certainly a secondary development making use of meaningless free variation preexisting in the language. (This would be an example of *exaptation*, to use the term borrowed into linguistics from biology by Lass 1990.)

The essential semantic difference between the four rows is as follows. (The distinction is essentially the same as that found with **nân/nan/cân/can** functioning as adverbs, see §5:2.3.) Row 1 (**wannàn** etc.) indicates speaker proximal, e.g., **wannàn kwālī** 'this carton (in my hands or next to me the speaker)'. It can also be used to denote proximity in time, e.g., **wannàn watà** 'this very month'. It also serves important anaphoric functions, e.g., **dâ an yi wata sàraunìyā..., wannàn sàraunìyā kùwa...** 'Formerly there was a queen..., this queen moreover...'. When repeated in a sentence, **wannàn** often indicates 'this other' (where in English we might use 'that'), e.g., **gà wannàn kà kai ōfìshin àkantà, wannàn kùwa na ōfìshin dàřektà nē** 'Here, take this one to the accountant's office; this other [one] is for the director's office'; **an kirā sù don sù fàhìmci jūnā sai wannàn mālàmī ya kāwō tāsà, wannàn mālàmī ya kāwō tāsà** 'They were called to come to an understanding; this teacher expressed his (opinion), this other (i.e., that) teacher expressed his.' Row 2 (**wànnan** etc.) indicates hearer proximal, e.g., **wàɗànnan awākī** 'those goats (near you the hearer)'. These L-H demonstratives also function as existential/referential/anaphoric markers, e.g., **wànnan làbāřì** 'that very story (we were talking about)'. Row 3 (**wancàn** etc.) indicates distal from both speaker and hearer, e.g., **waccàn kàsuwā** 'that market there'. Row 4 (**wàncan** etc.) indicates remoteness from speaker and hearer, e.g., **wàɗàncan garūruwà** 'those towns far away (yonder)'. It can also be used to denote distance in time, e.g., **wàncan ƙařnì** 'that century long ago'.

The definite demonstratives function both as pronouns and as prenominal determiners. In the latter function, they serve as (semantically not equivalent) alternatives to the postnominal short-form determiners, to be described below. Examples:

wàccan ita cè kàsuwařmù ta dâ	That one (yonder) is our former market.
wannàn yā fi wancàn kyâu	This one is better than that one.
kàwō wàɗànnan!	Bring those (near you)!
waɗànnân fensiřōřī nàwa nè	These pencils are mine.
wàccan mōtà cē na ganī ɗàzu	It was that car (way off) that I saw a moment ago.
yârā 'yan tāwāyè sun ɓàtà waccàn makařantà	The rebellious students vandalized that school.

The demonstratives in Hausa can co-occur with the definite article, e.g.,

wannàn yārò-n	this boy (that we were referring to) (lit. this boy-the)
wàccan jihà-ř	that state (that we were talking about) (lit. that state-the)

1.1.1. Short-form definite demonstratives

When functioning as determiners, the four groups of definite demonstratives may also be expressed by the locative adverbial forms **nân** 'here', **nan** 'there (speaker proximal)' **cân** 'there (distant)', and **can** 'there (remote)'. The structure of the short-form demonstratives is noun + linker + dem, where the linker is gender/number sensitive but the demonstrative determiner itself is not, e.g., **dōkìn nân** 'this horse', **rāgunàn nân** 'these rams', **àkuyàř nân** 'this goat'. The feminine linker /ř/ always assimilates fully to the abutting /n/, e.g., the preceding example, is pronounced [àkwiyànnân], but the orthographic rules dictate that it should be written as **r**. (One also gets assimilation of /ř/ to /c/, but this is less automatic, e.g., **àkuyàř cân** 'that goat' → [àkwiyàccân] or [àkwiyàřcân]. Strictly speaking the short-form demonstrative is a clitic that should be written together with its head, e.g., **dōkìn-nân**, but the convention is to write them as separate words. (In this section only, I shall use the hyphen; elsewhere I follow the orthographic rules.)

ΔDN: The short form of the speaker-proximal demonstrative in WH is formed with `-ga` instead of **nân**, e.g., **dōkìn-ga** 'this horse', **rìgâg-ga** 'this gown', **mōtōcîn-ga** 'these cars'.

As indicated earlier, **nân** and **cân** have underlying H-L tone. When preceded by a word with final L tone (or falling = HL), the demonstratives are realized with falling tone, e.g.,

yāròn-nân	this boy	**fàsfôn-nân**	this passport
tāgàř-cân	that window	**ɗākunàn-cân**	those rooms

When preceded by a word with final H tone, the H component of the H-L demonstrative is absorbed by the previous H tone, with the result that one ends up with an H-L melody on the final two syllables, e.g., $(\text{ràgō})^{LH} + \text{n} + (\text{nân})^{HL} \to (\text{ràgon-nàn})^{LHL}$ 'this ram'. Examples:

bàřgon-nàn	this blanket	**mōtōcin-nàn**	these cars
makařantař-càn	that school	**jiràgen-càn**	those planes

The formatives **nan** 'hearer proximal' and **can** 'remote' have underlying L-H tone. When attached to a word with final L tone, the L of the demonstrative is absorbed and one gets L-H spread over the final two syllables, e.g., $(\text{bīřò})^{HL} + \text{n} + \text{nan})^{LH} \to (\text{bīřòn-nan})^{HLH}$ 'this pen'. Examples:

yāròn-nan	that boy	**fàsfôn-nan**	that passport
tāgàř-can	that (remote) window	**ɗākunàn-can**	those (remote) rooms

When an L-H demonstrative is attached to a word with final H tone, the L tone spreads onto the preceding syllable thereby producing a surface fall, and the H remains on the demonstrative. The result is a final falling-high pattern, e.g., $(\text{kàrē})^{LH} + \text{n} + (\text{nan})^{LH} \to (\text{kàrên})^{L-HL} + (\text{nan})^{H} \to$ /kàrên-nan/ 'that dog'. Examples:

bàřgôn-nan	that blanket	**mōtōcîn-nan**	those cars
makařantâř-can	that yonder school	**jiràgên-can**	those planes yonder

1.1.2. Short-form and long-form definite demonstratives contrasted

Most descriptions state or imply that the long-form and the short-form demonstratives are equivalent, i.e., **wannàn bīřò̀ = bīřòn-nân** 'this ballpoint pen'. Although they are quite close in meaning, they are not in fact interchangeable. To begin with, the short form, which can be taken as the more basic, unmarked construction, can occur with words belonging to various parts of speech (e.g., adverbs or numerals) whereas the long forms can be used only with nouns. The following examples, thus, do not have long form demonstrative counterparts:

kū huɗun-nàn kù matsã̀ gēfè gùdā!	You four (lit. you four this) move to one side!
shī ɗin-nàn ɗan-iskã̀ nē	He this (guy) (lit. he this) is a bastard.
jiyà-jiyàn-nân ta haihù	Just yesterday (lit. yesterday yesterday this) she gave birth.
mun sāmù ɗàzun-nàn	We got it just a while ago. (lit. now this)
à 'yan kwãnàkin nàn gwamnatì tā shìga ƙafàř-wàndō dà 'yan sùmōgàl	
Recently (lit. few days these) the government has stepped up measures against smugglers.	

°AN: The compound **bàra-wàccan** 'the year before last' (lit. last year that) is unusual not only in containing the long-form demonstrative but also in having it after rather than before the head word.

Note that if one uses such words as day and night as common nouns rather than as temporal adverbs, then the prenominal long form is possible, e.g.,

sai gòdiyā gà Allàh à wannàn darē/rānā mài àlbařkà
> Let's give thanks to God on this (special) blessed eve/day.

In constructions where both the long and short variants can be used, they are semantically and pragmatically different. Roughly speaking, the short form is used as a determiner when the item referred to is known, previously referred to, presupposed, etc. In some cases with the speaker-proximal **nân**, the demonstrative means little more than the definite article 'the', e.g., **sìřdìn-nân** 'the/this saddle'. The pre-nominal long form is used when indicating a new and/or non-presupposed referent, e.g., **wannàn sìřdì** 'this saddle (new information, not one that we had been talking about)'. It commonly carries an explicit or implied contrast with another deictic marker, i.e., it is often accompanied by a pointing gesture, e.g., **wànnan ƙōfà** 'that doorway near you that I'm pointing to' as opposed to **waccàn ƙōfà** 'that doorway over there'. The difference between the two variants is illustrated in the following pairs of sentences:

(a) **màganàř-nân dà na faɗà mukù, bā nà̀ sôn kōwā yà jī tà**
> This matter that I told you (i.e., already known), I don't want anyone to hear it.

(b) **wannàn màganàř dà zân faɗà mukù, bā nà̀ sôn kōwā yà jī tà**
> This matter that I'm about to tell you (i.e., new information), I don't want anyone to hear it.

(a) **littāfìn-nan, nā san wandà ya řubùtā shi**
> That book (which perhaps you're showing me), I know who wrote it.

(b) **wànnan littāfì, nā san wandà ya řubùtā shi**
> That book (which perhaps I know about, but you don't), I know who wrote it.

(a) **gà takàřdař-nàn kà dūbà**   Here is the/this paper for you to look at. (to which the answer might be **nā gōdè** 'Thanks (for bringing it).')

(b) **gà wannàn takàřdā kà dūbà**   Here is a/this paper (that might interest you) for you to look at (to which the answer might be **mè̀ nē nè̀ wannàn kuma**? 'What is this again?')

(a) **mōtàř-nân tanà̀ bā nì wàhalà**   The/this car is giving me a hard time.

(b) **wannàn mōtà̀ tanà̀ bā nì wàhalà**   This car (which I just bought, or this car that I am pointing to as opposed to that car) is giving me a hard time.

(a) **Shēhùn-nân bâ shi dà kirkì**   This Shehu (whom we were talking about) is not nice.

(b) **wannàn Shēhù bài ci sūnansà ba**   This Shehu doesn't deserve to have such a (glorious) name.

(a) **dùbi jumlōlin-nàn sànnan kà yi bàyānìn bambancìnsù**
> Examine these sentences (we have been analyzing) and explain the differences between them.

(b) **dùbi waɗànnân jumlōlī sànnan kà yi bàyānìn bambancìnsù**
> Examine these sentences (here in this textbook) and explain the differences between them.

Because the prenominal long forms generally imply a contrast, they tend not to be used with words that have either a unique or a generic/nonspecific reference, e.g.,

ruwan-nàn (*not* ****wannàn ruwā**) **dà akè tafkà̀wā, zā sù ɗaukē kùwa?**
> This downpour, is it ever going to stop?

kuɗin-nàn (*not* ****wannàn/waɗànnân kuɗî**) na jàma'ậ hàřāmùn nē ậ taɓậ su
It's unlawful to touch (these) public funds.
(lit. money-this of people unlawful STAB one touch them)
Ƙasař-nàn tāmù tā lālậcē   This country of ours has gone to pot.
kàrɓi àbin-nàn!   Grab the thingamajig! cf. **kàrɓi wannàn àbù!**   Grab this very thing!

◊HN: The use of the long-form demonstratives as prenominal determiners is an innovation. Historically, they functioned only as pronouns, i.e., **wannàn**, for example, originally meant 'this one', e.g., **inậ sôn wannàn** 'I want this one.' A phrase such as **wannàn dōkî** would have been an appositional structure, which literally would have meant 'this one, a horse'. Later this must have been reinterpreted to mean 'this horse'. Before the change, the only way to express 'this horse' would have been **dōkìn-nân**, with the postnominal short form. But even this structure is historically an innovation. Originally, the postnominal demonstrative would have been a "true" determiner like the **ga** that one finds in the WH, e.g., **dōkìn-ga** 'this horse'. This original determiner very possibly had distinct allomorphs depending on gender and number. (In Kanakuru (Newman 1974: 86–87), the definite demonstrative appears with the following variants: **gamī mè** 'this ram' (m.), **gamî me** 'that ram'; **gunyoi jè** 'this girl', **gunyôi she** 'that girl'; **amboi mè** 'these children', **amboi mòi** 'those children'.) (The tonal opposition evidenced in **gamī mè** vs. **gamî me** is strikingly similar to what exists in Hausa, e.g., **ràgon-nàn** 'this ram' vs. **ràgôn-nan** 'that ram near you'.) The present-day short-form demonstratives, e.g., **dōkìn-nân** 'this horse', are paraphrases using the locative adverbs **nan** and **can** 'here, there, etc.' thus **dōkìn-nân** was literally 'horse.of-here' and **kàsuwař-càn** 'that market' was 'market.of-there', etc.

1.2. *Interrogative demonstratives*

The fifth and sixth rows in the table contain the interrogative demonstratives 'which'. The items in the fifth row have the form **wa** + (**ɗan**) + **ne/ce/ne** (where **ce** < ***te**) with an all L tone melody. They function solely as prenominal determiners, e.g.,

wànè sōjà? which soldier?   **wàcè kujềrā?** which chair?   **wàɗànnè mằlàmai?** which teachers?

The items in the sixth row have the form **wa** + (**ɗan**) linker + **nē/cē/nē** with an L-H tone pattern, e.g., **wa** + /t/ + **cē**)^LH → **wàccē** 'which one (f.)'. (As with the definite demonstratives, **ɗan** either supplants or incorporates the linker, depending on one's analysis.)

◊HN: It is possible that the tone pattern for the pronouns was also originally all L and that the L-H pattern is due to historical low-tone raising conditioned by the long final vowel (see §34:3.2), i.e., ***wànè** remained **wànè**, but the earlier form ***wànnè** changed to **wànnē**.

These L-H forms function solely as specific interrogative pronouns, e.g.,

wànnē/wàccē/wàɗànnē sukà zāɓā?   Which one(s) (m./f./pl.) did they choose?

These pronouns, especially the masculine singular form, are commonly extended by a partitive genitive phrase, e.g., **wànnensù kikề sô** 'Which of them do you (f.) want?' (Note that the shortening of the final /ē/ in the closed syllable is phonologically automatic.).

The interrogative demonstratives combine with the prefix **kō-** to form the universals **kōwànè / kōwàcè / (kōwàɗànnè)** 'whichever, each, every (m./f./pl.(rare))' and **kōwànnē / kōwàccē / kōwàɗànnē** 'whichever one(s) (m./ f./ pl.)' (see chap. 73). Examples:

àkwai kàsuwā à kōwànè gàrī	There is a market in every town.
kōwàɗànnē zā kà bā nì zân kàrɓā	Whichever ones you give me, I'll accept.
kōwàccensù tā sàmi dìflōmà	Each (f.) of them received a diploma.

1.3. Relative pronouns

The seventh row in the table contains the relative pronouns 'who, that, which'. These have the structure wa (+ ɗàn) + definite article (underlyingly // ˋn// (masculine or plural) or // ˋt// (feminine)) + dà (relativizer). The underlying feminine marker //t// automatically geminates with the following consonant, e.g., wa + ˋt + dà → wâddà.

The original tone pattern of the disyllabic singular forms was F-L (e.g., wânda and wâddà), where the F represents the attachment of the floating L tone of the definite article to the H-tone prefix wa. (In the plural, the floating L tone attaches to the already L tone plural morpheme ɗàn (e.g., waɗàndà).) Many SH speakers now simplify the F-L melody to H-L (e.g., wanda and wadda); in some dialects this simplification has become lexicalized so that only H-L is found. A further tone change is the weakening of these forms to all low, e.g., wàndà, wàddà, wàɗàndà.

°AN: All low is an uncommon tone pattern in Hausa. It is, however, found with "unstressed" grammatical morphemes, e.g., wànè 'which', dàgà 'from'. As with the case of the wànnan/wânnan pair described earlier, some speakers feel that there is a semantic difference between wandà and wàndà, the former being considered somewhat stronger than the latter. Jaggar (1998) has found that for some speakers the H-L and L-L forms also differ syntactically in that the latter are preferred—in some cases even required—in nonrestrictive relative clauses. My guess is that whatever differences may now exist between the coexisting variants are the result of secondary developments rather than being retentions of an old contrast.

The feminine variant waccè (which can also appear as wàccè with L-L tone) is anomalous since the final syllable ought to be dà. The explanation is probably not phonological, but rather analogical confusion with the other feminine demonstratives with surface geminate /cc/, e.g., waccē 'which one? (f.)' waccàn 'that (f.)'.

The relative demonstratives serve to introduce relative clauses. They may appear by themselves or with an overt head (especially one that is indefinite), e.g.,

mun biyā wasu yârā waɗàndà sukà yi manà aikì

> We paid some children who did work for us.

ànnòbar̃ kwalar̃à tā ɓarkè à ƙasàshên nan, wàɗàndà dukànsù à Afìr̃kà ta gabàs sukè

> A cholera epidemic has broken out in those countries, all of which are in East Africa.

màcè wâddà bā tà jîn màganà bà zā tà sàmi mijìn ƙwar̃ai ba

> A woman who doesn't listen won't find a good husband.

wâddà ta shā ràunī fa, an kai tà asìbitì

> As for the one who was injured, they took her to the hospital.

ìnā (mùtûm) wândà ya cè zâi iyà gamà aikìn nân?

> Where is the one (the man) who said he will be able to finish this job?

1.4. Specific indefinite demonstratives

The eighth row in the table contains the specific indefinite demonstratives wani, wata, wa(ɗan)su 'some(one) (m./f./pl.)'. These have the structure wa- plus a personal pronoun: ta 'her' in the case of wata, and su 'them' in the case of wasu. The ni in wani is *not* the first person pronoun 'me', as it appears to be but rather is a frozen vestige of what historically was a 3m pronoun **ni* 'him'. This third person pronoun **ni* is widespread in Chadic languages, where it often differs from the first person only in tone. It has been completely lost in Hausa except in this one archaism (Newman 1972a).

The plural demonstrative has two equivalent variants: **wasu** and **waɗansu**. The **wasu** variant possibly represents the original form. If this is so, the insertion of **ɗan** in **waɗansu** would be due to analogic pressure from the other plural demonstratives like **waɗànnân** 'these', **waɗàndà** 'the ones who', etc.

The indefinite demonstratives function both as prenominal determiners, where they sometimes correspond to the English indefinite article 'a/an'—note that Hausa doesn't have an indefinite article— and as self-standing pronouns, e.g.,

wata yārinyà tā zō	A girl came.
bâ ni dà wani àbōkī à nân gàrī	I don't have a friend in this town.
nā ga wasu ɓaunàyē bāyan gàrī	I saw some buffaloes behind the town.
wata rānā mâ shiryà	Some day we are going to settle this.
wani yā tsērè masà	Someone (m.) escaped from him.
wata tā iyà	Someone (f.) is able.
wasu sunà tàimakon jūnā	Some (pl.) are helping one another.

As determiners, the indefinite demonstratives often combine with the nouns **àbù** 'thing', **lōkàcī** 'time', and **wurī** 'place' to form semifixed compound expressions, e.g.,

wani àbù yā fàru	Something happened.
wani lōkàcī anà sāmùn ruwā	Sometimes one gets water.
yā tàfi wani wurī	He went somewhere.

In contexts in which there is an explicit or implied contrast, the indefinite demonstratives denote 'other' or 'another', e.g.,

wannàn kujèrā bâ ta dà kyâu; bà ni wata	This chair is not good; give me another.
wasu sun fi sôn *Fanta*, **wasu kuma** *Pepsi*	Some prefer Fanta, others Pepsi.
wasu (ɗàlìbai) sun shìga zàngà-zàngà, wasu sun zaunà à gidā kawài	
Some (students) entered the demonstration, others just stayed home.	
nā ga wani dòdō à hanyà; dàgà bāya wani ya ɓullō	
I saw a goblin on the road; after a bit another appeared.	

When followed by a plural possessive pronoun, the indefinite demonstratives function as partitives. (The feminine is only marginally acceptable.) Examples:

waninkù some one of you (pl); **watar̃sù** some one (f.) of them; **wasunmù** some of us

1.5. Unspecified pronouns

The ninth row in the table contains the 'so-and-so' pronouns. These pronouns morphologically differ from the others in a few respects. First, the final -**cè** in the feminine form does not entirely replace the masculine -**nè** but rather is added to a base containing a final /**n**/, i.e., the pairing is **wānè** / **wancè** m./f. 'Mr. so-and-so / Ms. so-and-so'. Second, these words do not have true plurals but rather form pseudo-plurals by prefixed the third plural personal pronoun to the masculine and feminine singular forms, e.g., su wānè / su wancè 'so-and-so's (m.) / so-and-so's (f.)'. These forms are used when a person referred to is known but is not mentioned by name. Examples:

wancè tanằ nēman fàsfô dà kântà	So-and-so is seeking a passport of her own.
ìnā wānè?	Where is so-and-so (m.)?

2. PRONOUNS AS DETERMINERS/SPECIFIERS

In Hausa, independent pronouns can function as pre-noun determiners/specifiers in a pseudo-appositional structure, e.g., **mū màlàmai** 'we teachers', **shī Bellò** 'he Bello'. It is possible to separate the pronoun from its noun by a modal particle, e.g., **mū fa màlàmai** 'we (indeed) teachers'. This pronoun can co-occur with a definite demonstrative or definite article, e.g., **mū màlàman-nàn** 'we these teachers', **sū mutằnê-n** 'they the men'. The determiner pronoun, which in principle can be of any person/number, has a particularizing function, i.e., it serves to pick out some particular person(s) or thing(s) as opposed to others. Here are some examples in sentential context:

shī Mūsā zâi tàimàkē nì dà mōtằ	He Musa will give me ride.
shī Abdù yanằ zuwằ Marằɗi gòbe?	Is (this particular) Abdu coming to Maradi tomorrow?
sū Hàusàwā sunằ dà ìyằlì màsu yawằ	They the Hausa have large families.
an yabằ wà shī àlƙālìn	They praised him the judge.
yanằ sô yà àuri ita sàraunìyầr̃ kântà	He wanted to marry she the queen herself.
kū sàmằrī, zā mù hàɗu dà kū nân gàba	You guys, I'm going to meet up with you in the future.

mū talakàwā munà r̃ôƙon gwamnatì tà ragè manằ kuɗin tākìn zāmànī

    We common people are appealing to the government to lower the cost of fertilizer.

mū màlàmai munằ shân wàhalằ sabồdà rashìn kuɗī

    We teachers are suffering because of a lack of money.

ita dai gyàɗā, Hàusàwā sunằ nōmằ ta sòsai

    As for peanuts (lit. she indeed peanut), Hausas farm them seriously.

3. ISOLATOR

Numerals normally follow their head nouns, e.g., **mōtằ ɗaya** 'one car', **mangwàr̃ò gōmà** 'ten mangoes'. The numeral **ɗaya** 'one', however, can occur in front of a singular noun with the meaning 'the other', and thus semantically, if not structurally, behaves as a demonstrative. (In this function, **ɗaya** is sometimes termed an *isolator*.) The noun necessarily contains a definite article, e.g.,

ɗaya littāfìn	the other book (cf. **littāfì ɗaya** one book)
ɗaya hùlâr̃	the other cap (cf. **hùlā ɗaya** one cap)

If the head noun is understood, it can be omitted and the isolator can appear by itself with the gender appropriate d.a. attached, e.g., **ɗayân** 'the other one' (e.g., a book); **ɗayâr̃** 'the other one' (e.g., a cap).

[References: Abdoulaye (1992); Buba (1997a); Galadanci (1969); Jaggar (1985, 1988b)]

22. Deverbal Nouns

1. DVNs WITH VERBAL NOUN MORPHOLOGY

IN "nonfinite environments" (see §77:1.1), the verb slot in a Hausa sentence is often filled by a participial-like "verbal noun" (VN) rather than a finite verb (vb), e.g., **yanà kòyon** (VN) **Hausa** 'He is learning Hausa', cf. **yā kòyi** (vb) **Hausa** 'He learned Hausa.' The complex and varied morphological formation of these verbal nouns is described in §77:3. As with an English '-ing' word like 'building', which functions as a simple noun meaning a structure as well as an inflected participial form of the verb 'to build', many Hausa words with verbal noun morphology have become lexicalized as common nouns, which we call "deverbal nouns" (DVNs).

> °AN: Ideally one would like to have a contrast between "deverbal nouns" and "nominalized verbs" (rather than "verbal nouns"), so as to emphasize the syntactically distinct functions of the two word classes. The term "verbal noun" (VN), however is too well established in Hausa scholarship to countenance a terminological change at this point.

Morphologically, DVNs are generally indistinguishable from corresponding active verbal nouns, i.e., they follow the same affixation rules and are found in the same formation classes. Semantically, on the other hand, the connection between a deverbal noun and its source verb is often more tenuous and specialized than that of a syntactic verbal noun. (This is especially true in the case of concrete DVNs, less so in the case of DVNs indicating an activity or event associated with the source verb.)

From a syntactic point of view, deverbal nouns function just like ordinary common nouns, e.g.,

kanà dà ḳyàstū?	Do you have a lighter? (< ḳyastà to strike flint)
cf. kanà dà àshānā?	Do you have a match? (with the simple noun àshānā)
yā yi minì tsìmē	He made me a type of ink. (< tsimà to soak)
cf. yā yi minì tàwadà	He made me ink. (with the simple noun tàwadà)
yanà sànye dà shìga maràř kunyà	He is wearing an outlandish outfit. (< shìga to enter)
cf. yanà sànye dà tagùwā maràř kunyà	He is wearing an outlandish shirt.
nā sàmi rāmuwā	I got revenge. (< rāmà to retaliate),
cf. nā sàmi lādā	I got a reward. (with the simple noun lādā)
kàwō minì ɗan burmì!	Bring me a small calabash.
	(< burmà to invert a small calabash on a large one)
àkwai mòlaḳà à mōtàřkà	There is a dent on your car. (< mòlaḳē to dent)
rūrìn zākì yā fìřgìtā mu	The lion's roar startled us. (< rūrà to roar, make fire)
zanè ban dà lāfì	wrapper without a hem (< lāfè to hem)
cf. yanà lāfìn zanèn	He is hemming the wrapper.
makàɗā sun yi manà cāshiyā	The drummers sped up the music for us.
	(lit. ...did for.us speeding up) (< cāshè to speed up)

DVNs can be found representing practically all (if not all) of the regular verbal noun formations in the language. The following is a selected list of deverbal nouns organized according to the formation classes set out in chap. 77. (Note: With few exceptions, which are overtly marked, DVNs ending in -ā are feminine; those not ending in -ā are masculine.)

1.1. Weak VNs
girmàmâwā   respect (< **girmàmā** to honor, to respect); **gudàwā** diarrhea (the runs) (< **gudà** hasten, cf. **gudù** run); **iyàwā** ability, mastery (< **iyà** be able to); **sādàwā** reconciliation (< **sādà** join); **ƙwarèwā** expertise (< **ƙwarè** be(come) an expert); **ràsuwā** death (< **ràsu** die, be lacking); **gabātār̃wā** introduction, preface (< **gabātar̃** introduce, promote); **sanar̃wā** announcement (< **sanar̃** inform)

1.2. Stem-derived VNs
àjiyà   trust, sth stored for safekeeping (< **ajìyē** put aside); **ɓarzā** corn that has been or is to be ground (< **ɓarzà** grind coarsely); **dànganà** resignation (< **dànganà** be resigned to); **ɗàmarā̀** belt (cf. **ɗaurè** (< **ɗamrè**) tie); **gàjiyà** tiredness, fatigue (< **gàji** (< *gàjiyà) tire); **kàrayà** a bone fracture (< **karyè** break); **kàrayà** loss of nerve (< **kàrayà** (= **kàrai**) be nervous, lose one's nerve); **kùr̃ɓā** a sip (< **kùr̃ɓā** sip); **sanì** knowledge (< **sanì** know); **shìgā** an outfit (< **shìga** enter); **sô** love, affection (< **sō** love); **wàdātà̀** wealth (< **wàdātà̀** enrich)

1.3. Base-derived VNs
1.3.1. -ī
cūr̃ì   a kneaded ball (< **cūr̃à** knead); **ɗaurì** knot, bundle/wad; an arrest (< **ɗaurè** tie, arrest); **fashì** robbery (< **fasà** break, rob); **gàr̃gàɗī** a warning, admonishment (< **gàr̃gaɗà̀** warn, admonish); **ginì** a building (< **ginà** build, make pottery); **kùmburī** a swelling (< **kùmburà** swell); **rabì** a half (< **rabà** divide); **ràiràyī** fine sand (< **ràirayà̀** sift); **tàusàyī** mercy, pity (< **tausàyā wà** sympathize with); **wankì** the wash/laundry (< **wankà̀** wash); **yāƙì** war (< **yàƙā** make war on); **zàr̃gī** accusation; reproach, blame (< **zàrgā** accuse)

1.3.2. -ū
kàftū   tool for making ridges on farm (< **kàftā** hack/scrape with shovel or hoe); **kāmù** an arrest (< **kāmà̀** catch); **ƙyàstū** steel for striking a fire, cigarette lighter (< **ƙyastà̀** strike (match, flint, etc.)); **musù** denial, contradiction, argument, debate (< **musà̀** deny); **yāgù** a fingernail scratch; tear on a piece of cloth (< **yāgà̀** tear, rip)

1.3.3. -ē
aurē   marriage (< **àurā** marry); **dàɓē** a floor (< **daɓè** pound a floor); **dàshē** transplanted seedling (< **dasà̀** transplant); **fàntsàrē** coarsely ground flour (< **fantsàrā** grind coarsely); **màrkàɗē** ground peppers / tomato puree (< **markàɗā** grind, e.g., peppers); **tsìmē** ink made by steeping (< **tsimà̀** steep); **wànkē** ink made by washing off soot on cooking pot (< **wankè** wash); **yàɓē** plaster (< **yāɓà̀** to plaster)

1.3.4. -ō
ɗigò   a drop; period (< **ɗigà** drip); **gōyō** baby (< **gòya** carry on the back); **karò** collision, encounter, occasion (< **karà dà** collide/clash with); **kitsò** a braid, coiffure (< **kitsà** braid hair) [the verb is uncommon]; **mahò** a patch on a garment (< **mafè** mend (cloth)); **yàbō** praise, eulogy (< **yàbā** to praise); **zàtō** assumption (< **zàtā** think)

1.3.5. -ā (variable gender)

askā f.   razor, penknife (< askḛ̀ shave);   girmā m.   size, status, prestige (< gìrmā̰ be older than);
ƙìdāyā f. census (< ƙidàyā count); rawā f. a dance, dancing (< rau dà shake); sātā f. theft (< sà̰tā
steal); shūkā̰ f. a plant (< shūkā̰̀ to plant); tsìnkāyā f. foresight (< tsìnkāyā̰̀ see from afar); hawā
m. durbar; a steep place (< hau mount)

2. DVNs WITHOUT REGULAR VERBAL NOUN MORPHOLOGY

Some deverbal nouns have distinctive forms other than those found with regular active verbal nouns.

2.1. DVNs with -iyā and -uwā

A small number of trisyllabic DVNs appear with the feminative endings -iyā and -uwā. The tone is
usually all H, but two words have L-H-H. There are also two words with final -ōwā and L-H-L tone.
Examples (complete):

dàriyā   laughter (< dārā̰̀ laugh); datsiyā   dam (< datsḛ̀ block sth); gòdiyā   thanks (< gōdḛ̀ thank);
tōshiyā   bribe (< tōshḛ̀ block up a hole); yāfiyā   addition given to corn purchaser (< yāfā̰̀ sprinkle);
tsintuwā   sth found by chance (< tsìntā luckily find sth);   baiwā (< *bāyuwā)   gift, betrothal (< bai
give); rantsuwā   oath, swearing (< rantsḛ̀ swear); cìkōwā̰   crowd, overcrowding, overflowing (< cìka
/ cikā̰ be full / fill up); ràgōwā̰   remainder, respect (< ragḛ̀ remain, be left over; reduce sth)

2.2. DVNs with -ē)^{HL}

There are some twenty trisyllabic verb-derived nouns ending in -ē and having H-H-L tone. In most cases,
the initial syllable is CVC. With two exceptions, namely, buwāyḛ̀ 'invincibility' (< bùwāyā̰̀ 'be
beyond one's strength or ability') and rinjāyḛ̀ 'victory, success' (< rìnjāyā̰̀ 'defeat, overcome'), the
medial syllable is CV with a short vowel. These deverbal nouns generally connote concrete things
resulting from or related to the action of the verb. In a number of the cases, the DVN is more common
than the source verb. Examples:

ɓangarḛ̀   fragment, part, chip; region (< ɓangàrē chip a piece off); dumbujḛ̀   a pile (< dumbùzā take
a pile of sth); dunƙulḛ̀   a kneaded ball (< dunƙùlā knead into a ball); gangarḛ̀   downward slope (<
gangàrā go down a slope); gēwayḛ̀   enclosure; latrine (< gēwàyā go around, encircle); gutsurḛ̀
fragment, piece broken off (< gutsùrē break piece off); kuskurḛ̀   mistake (< kùskurà be mistaken,
miss a target); ƙētarḛ̀   the other side (< ƙētàrē cross over); ƙwaȓzanḛ̀   a scratch (< ƙwàȓzanā̰̀
scratch, scrape); ƙyanƙyashḛ̀   embers falling from a torch (< ƙyanƙyàsā tap torch to knock off burnt
end); mulmulḛ̀   kneaded ball (< mulmùlā knead); sassaƙḛ̀   chip of wood, bark of tree cut off for
medicinal purposes (< sàssaƙā̰̀ carve); targaɗḛ̀   sprain, dislocation (< synchronically nonexistent
verb)

2.3. DVNs with -kō

A small number of nouns derived from verbs end in -kō. The nouns roughly connote the nature or result
of the activity represented by the underlying verb. There are two subclasses here, the first with a simple
suffix -kō, the second with a suffix -makō.

   Some eleven nouns end in -kō. The suffix is added to the simple verbal base (with reduplication in
some cases). Monosyllabic Ci verbs lengthen the vowel in order to add weight to the syllable preceding
the suffix. Four of the derived nouns have all H tone; the others have H-L tone: the choice is lexically
determined and cannot be accounted for by general rule. One example (rare, but listed in the dictionaries)
is reported with an L-H-L pattern in addition to all H.

baikō betrothal, engagement (< **bai** give); **bīkò** attempted reconciliation (by husband with wife) (< **bi** follow); **farkō** beginning (< **fārà** begin); **fīfīkò** superiority, favoritism (< **fi** exceed); **gankò** (= **gangankò**) crowd (< **gamà** meet, assemble); **īkò** (//**iykò**//) power, arrogance, ability (< **iyà** be able); **mankò** (rare) forgetfulness (< **màntā** forget); **rankō** restitution, revenge (< **rāmà** pay back (good for good, evil for evil); **tarkò** trap (< **tarè** intercept, catch up with); **tsaikò** roof frame (< **tsay(ař) dà** raise (roof)); **màmulkò** = **māmulkō** psn/mouth without teeth (< **māmùlā** eat without teeth)

Four verb-derived nouns end in the suffix -**makō**)^LHH with (L)-L-H-H tone. This is very likely a double suffix composed of -**ma** (elsewhere not attested as a derivational suffix in the language) and the deverbal formative -**kō**.

màimakō	replacement, substitute (< **màyā** replace, substitute)
sàkàmakō	result, outcome (reward or punishment) (< **sākà** pay back)
sàmmakō	early start in the morning (< **sàuka** alight ?)
tàimakō	help, aid (< **tàyā** help)

◊HN: [i] The word **sàmmakō** most likely comes from /**sàfmakō**/ by full assimilation of the /**f**/ to the abutting /**m**/. If so, its underlying base would be *//**saf**-//, which presumably is found in the verb **sàuka** (= WH **sàfka**) 'alight' and possibly also in the adverb **sāfe** 'in the morning'.

[ii] Synchronically **tàimakō** would look to be an -**ō** verbal noun formed in a regular manner from the gr2 verb **tàimakà**. Historically, however, **tàimakà** is probably a backformation from the noun **tàimakō**, which, as indicated above, derives from **tàyā** 'help' plus the suffix -**makō**.

[Reference: Gouffé (1981b), esp. §3, "Le nom verbal en haoussa: essai de mise au point"]

23. Equational Sentences

1. BASIC STRUCTURE

EQUATIONAL sentences, which in Hausa are nonverbal sentences (even though they usually translate as English copular sentences), have the core structure X Y STAB, where X is the subject NP, Y is a predicate nominal or adjective, and STAB is the gender/number sensitive stabilizer **nē/cē**, e.g., **bilbilō tsuntsū nè** 'A swallow is a bird.'

> °AN: In addition to its role in "equational" sentences, the stabilizer also functions as a focus marker, e.g., **Hàdīzà cē na ganī** 'It was *Hadiza* I saw', and as a sentence-level or VP-level reinforcing element, e.g., **lōkàcin kàkā yakàn zō nè̀ bāyan dàmunā** 'Harvest time comes after the rainy season' (see chap. **66**).

One can take X Y STAB as the "ideal" structure. Sentences without the X or without the stabilizer or with an alternative word order will be described in due course. Equational sentences are not inflected for tense or aspect, the temporal reading depending on the context, e.g.,

[Audù] [bāwà̀] nē	Audu is a slave.
[yārinyàr̃ dà ta 6atà] [ƙawar̃ Tàlātù] cē	The girl who got lost is Talatu's friend.
dâ mā [Mūsā dà Shēhù] [àbòkan gàske] nè̀	Musa and Shehu were already true friends.

The stabilizer takes the form **nē** when agreeing with words that are masculine singular or plural and **cē** when agreeing with feminine words. The tone of both forms is polar to that of the preceding tone, i.e., L if the preceding tone is H, and H if the preceding tone is L or falling (= HL), e.g., **wannàn jàkī nè / dōkì̀ nē / bàbûr̃ nē / rìgā cè / tāgà̀ cē / tàsî cē** 'This is a donkey / horse / motorcycle / gown / window / taxi.' The polarity shows up clearly with words that have alternative variants or in the case of different word orders, e.g., **wannàn tēbùr̃ī nè̀ / wannàn tēbùr̃ nē** 'This a table'; **Audù bà̀ yārò ba nè̀ = Audù bà̀ yārò nē ba** 'Audu is not a lad.'

> ΔDN: In WH, the stabilizers have the form **nā/tā**, also with polar tone. These variants with /ā/ represent the historically original shapes.

Equational sentences allow a full range of NPs as subjects (the X) and a full range of NPs and adjectives as predicates (the Y), e.g.,

yādìn farī nè	The cloth is white.	**màtar̃sà dōguwā cè̀**	His wife is tall.
mōtàr̃sà Hondà̀ cē	His car is a Honda.	**mōtōcîn ƙònànnū nè̀?**	Are the cars burnt?
idà̀nûn ƙwalā-ƙwàlà̀ nē	The eyes are bulging.	**ganinsà garma-garma nè̀**	His sight is poor.
zanèn shūɗì̀-shūɗì̀ nē	The wrapper is bluish.	**Bàlā shù̀gàbanmù nē**	Bala is our boss.

160

shī manajà nē?	Is he the manager?	kai gwànī nè	You are an expert.
sū kūrầyē nè	They are real cheats. (lit. they hyenas STAB)		
dầ nī kai nè, dầ nā yầřda	If I were you, I would have agreed.		

2. IDENTIFICATIONAL SENTENCES

Identificational sentences, which correspond to English 'it's (a) / they're ...', are equational structures without an expressed X, i.e., they have the surface structure Y STAB. Examples:

Mūsā nè It's Musa. **gwàdò nē** It's a blanket. **Kanò cē** It is Kano. **ƙafầ cē** It's a foot. **àljànū nè** They're jinns. **garūruwầ nē** They're towns. **Kànde dà Lādì nē** It is Kande and Ladi. **Sāni kō Bàlā nè** It is Sani or Bala. **ita cè** It is she/her. **mū nè** It is we/us. **shī dà kai nè** It is you and him. (lit. he and you STAB); **farī nè** It is white. **gàjēriyā cè** She's short. **ƙònànnū nè** They're burnt.

Identificational sentences with the structure Y STAB constitute one of the sentence types that take propositional complements. In this function, they are often extended by a prepositional phrase formed with **gà** + noun or **gàrē** + pronoun, which occurs after the STAB. These complement-taking expressions normally use the masculine STAB regardless of the intrinsic gender of the noun. Examples:

hàlâk nē kà shā madařā	It's permitted for you to drink milk.
shìrmē nè gàrē kà kà yi řitāyầ yànzu fa	It is nonsense for you to retire now.
wājìbī nè Mùsùlmī sù yi sallầ	Muslims must perform the daily prayers.
(lit. it's incumbent that Muslims do prayers)	
wâutā nè gà Mūsā dà yà ci bāshī	It was foolish of Musa to take out a loan.
(cf. wâutā cè It's foolishness.)	

3. ALTERNATIVE 'HAVE' EXPRESSIONS

Equational sentences with the structure Y STAB plus a prepositional phrase **dà** + NP 'with NP' semantically have a 'has/have' reading. The **dà** + NP phrase semantically constitutes the possessor and the NP preceding the STAB is the thing possessed, e.g.,

rashìn tàusàyī nè dà kàntōmầ	The administrator is without pity.
(lit. lack.of pity STAB with administrator)	
sābuwař munduwā cè dà ita	She has a new bracelet.
(lit. new bracelet STAB with her)	
littāfī nē dà shī à hannunsà	He has a book in his hand.
(lit. book STAB with him at hand.of.him)	
kuɗin gàske nè dà mùtumìn nân	This man has a lot of money.
(lit. money.of truth STAB with man.of this)	
gwâřřā rūsā-rùsầ nē dà ita	She has large kolanuts.
bầ gidầjē mânya-mânya ba nè dà Audù, ƙanānầ nē dà shī	
It's not big houses Audu has, it's small ones he has.	

The usual means of expressing HAVE is by a tensed sentence of the form X is with Y, e.g.,

| tanầ dà sābuwař munduwā | She has (lit. is with) a new bracelet. |
| mùtumìn nân yanầ dà kuɗin gàske | This man has a lot of money. |

Sentences formed with the equational structure and the **dà** phrase are colloquial Kano speech and are not accepted by all speakers. They are definitely marked as compared with the straightforward HAVE sentences; but the exact semantic/pragmatic nuances are far from clear.

4. PLEONASTIC INDEPENDENT PRONOUNS

Noun subjects in equational sentences, especially those referring to humans, may optionally be accompanied by a pleonastic independent pronoun. This pronoun adds a degree of prominence to the NP, e.g.,

Sāni (shī) mùtûm nē	Sani (he) is truly a man. (i.e., is a truly decent psn)
yārinyàr̃ (ita) gàjērìyā cè	The girl (she) is short.
mutànên (sū) wāwàyē nè	The people (they) are fools indeed.

°AN: The sentences with the pleonastic pronouns should not be confused with similar-looking sentences with topicalization, which have a distinct intonation including a slight pause and the possibility of using a modal particle, e.g., **Sānî, shī mùtûm nē / Sāni kàm, shī mùtûm nē** 'As for Sani, he is a true gentleman.' Nor should they be confused with prenominal pronouns that function as determiners, e.g., **shī Sāni mùtûm nē** 'He Sani (i.e., this Sani) is truly a gentleman'; **ita yārinyàr̃ bēbiyā cè** 'She the girl is deaf-mute.'

5. RESUMPTIVE INDEPENDENT PRONOUNS

Some equational sentences, especially with an adjectival predicate, allow the use of a resumptive pronoun agreeing with the subject at the end of the sentence after the STAB. The pronoun belongs to the independent set. The subject is generally in a definite form or else is a proper noun. The exact semantic contribution of the pronoun is not clear, but it seems to add a degree of insistence to the described attribution, sometimes with an element of contrast implied. A possible parallel in English would be sentences with a tag like, 'This kid is very bright, he is.' Examples:

mōtàr̃ farā cè <u>ita</u>	The car is white.
wannàn ɗālìbī dàr̃ìr̃ì nē <u>shī</u>	This student is dull.
masàr̃ar̃ gàrī cè <u>ita</u>	The corn/maize is powdery.
itàcên ɗanyē nè <u>shī</u>	The wood is green (i.e., not dry).
mutànên nan jàr̃ùmai nè <u>sū</u>	Those men are brave.
Sābo mālàmī nè <u>shī</u>, bà jāhìlī ba (nè)	Sabo is a teacher, not an illiterate.

6. CONCORD

If the X and Y in an equational sentence have the same gender and number, as is always the case whenever the Y is an adjective, then the choice of the stabilizer (**nē** or **cè**) is straightforward, e.g.,

[wàndōnā]ₘ [shūɗì]ₘ nē	My trousers are blue.
[tsōhuwâr̃]f [makitsìyā]f cè	The old woman is a hairdresser.
[yâran nàn]pl [àlmàjìr̃ai]pl nè	These children are pupils.
[mutànên nan]pl [gàjērū]pl nè	Those men are short.

If, on the other hand, the X and Y do not match, the determination of which stabilizer to use is more complicated and subject to considerable idiolectal and dialectal variation. There are two basic systems, with some shifting inbetween. There is what I shall refer to as the "subject-controlling" system, which seems to be favored by many SH speakers (although the exact dialectal or sociolectal distribution is yet to be determined), and there is the "prominence-controlling" system.

In the subject-controlling system, the gender of the X, i.e., the subject, determines the gender of the stabilizer, e.g.,

[bāsukùř ɗin Audù]ₘ [akwalā]f nè	Audu's bicycle is a piece of junk.
[itàcen nàn]ₘ [tsāmiyā]f nè	This tree is a tamarind.
[kàrē]ₘ [dabbàř-gidā]f nè	A dog is a domesticated animal.
[wàndō]ₘ [tufà]f nē	Pants are a (type of) clothing.
[jēmāgè]ₘ [dabbà]f nē kō tsuntsū	A bat is an animal or a bird.
[dabbàř dà na ganī]f [ràƙumin sarkī]ₘ cè	The animal I saw is the emir's camel.
[jìminā]f [bàbban tsuntsū]ₘ cè	An ostrich is a big bird.
[shìnkāfā]f [mùhimmin àbinci]ₘ cè	Rice is important food.

In the prominence-controlling system, the stabilizer can agree with the subject, but it can also agree with the predicate noun if the objective is to pay particular attention to that item.

[bāsukùř ɗinsà]ₘ [akwalā]f cè	His bicycle is a piece of junk.
(e.g., even though he just paid a lot of money for it)	
[itàcen nàn]ₘ [tsāmiyā]f cè	This tree is a tamarind.
[jēmāgè]ₘ [dabbà]f cè kō tsuntsū	A bat is an animal or a bird.
[dabbàř dà na ganī]f [ràƙumin sarkī]ₘ nè	The animal I saw is the emir's camel.
[jìminā]f [bàbban tsuntsū]ₘ nè	An ostrich is a big bird.
[shìnkāfā]f [mùhimmin àbinci]ₘ nè	Rice is important food.

If the stabilizer immediately follows the subject for purposes of focus, then the agreement is invariably with the subject, e.g.,

[bāsukùř ɗinsà]ₘ nē [akwalā]f	*His bicycle* is a piece of junk.
[shìnkāfā]f cè [mùhimmin àbinci]ₘ	*Rice* is important food.

In pseudo-cleft sentences in which the subject is semantically unmarked or nonspecific, the stabilizer agreement is generally with the predicate, even for speakers who normally use the subject-controlling system, e.g.,

àbîn dà nakè sô [àlāwà]f cē	The thing that I like is halvah.
wandà ya ci lambàř [Hàdīzà]f cē kō Mūsā	The one who won the medal is Hadiza or Musa.

7. NEGATION

The basic structure of negative equational and identificational sentences is (X) bà Y ba STAB, i.e., the Y is surrounding by the discontinuous marker bà...ba. Examples:

Audù bà yārò ba nè	Audu is not a small boy.
shī bà mahàukàcī ba nè	He is not crazy.
jàkař nàn bà tàwa ba cè	This bag is not mine.
mutànē sū bà wāwàyē ba nè	People are not stupid.

wànnan bằ amaryātā ba cề   That psn is not my bride.
Mūsā dà Shēhù bằ àbồkai ba nề   Musa and Shehu are not friends.
bằ lềmō ba nề It's not a soft drink. **bằ giyầ ba cề** It's not beer. **bằ mū ba nề** It's not us.

> ΔDN: A common alternative found in dialects other than SH is to have the final **ba** at the end of the
> sentence after the stabilizer, e.g., **shī bằ mahàukàcī nề ba** 'He is not crazy'; **wànnan bằ amaryātā**
> **cề ba** 'That psn is not my bride'; **mutầnē sū bằ wāwầyē nề ba** 'People are not stupid'; **bằ mū nề**
> **ba** 'It is not us.'

8. OMISSION OF THE STABILIZER

In normal equational sentences, affirmative or negative, the stabilizer is obligatory. There are some
structures, however, where the stabilizer is always, or almost always, left out.

8.1. *Names, times, places, occupations, numbers*
Sentences indicating someone's name or describing time, place, occupation, or number normally occur
without the stabilizer, although in some contexts it is allowed, e.g.,

sūnānā Sābo My name is Sabo. **sūnantà Màiřo** Her name is Mairo.
yâu àsabàř Today is Saturday. **jiyà ran kằsuwā (nề/cề)** Yesterday was market day.
gàrinsù Kàtsinà His (home)town is Katsina. **indà akà hàifē shì jējì** Where he was born was the
countryside.
sàna'àřsà nōmā His occupation is farming. **mùřāmìnsà fùřòfēsầ** His rank is professor.
cf. **Dr. Daudầ fùřòfēsầ nē** Dr. Dauda is a professor. (**nē** required)
àbincinsù dàbam, nāmù dàbam Their food is different, ours is different.
gồbe bằ ɗaya gà watầ ba Tomorrow is not the first of the month. **bàɗi shềkàrun Mūsā bìyař dà**
ràsuwā (nề) Next year will be the fifth anniversary of Musa's death. **mātansà huɗu (nề)** He has four
wives. (lit. wives.of.his four STAB) **'yan-bangànsà shâ-biyu** He has twelve bodyguards.

Certain adjectives can be expanded by a phrase made up of **dà** plus an independent pronoun copying the
number and gender of the head. If an equational predicate contains such an expansion, the stabilizer is
omitted, e.g.,

yāròn dōgō dà shī   The boy is tall. (cf. **yāròn dōgō nề**)
Fầtī kùduddùsā dà ita   Fati is short and stout.
'yammātan nàn santalā-sàntàlằ dà sū   The girls are shapely.

The question word **wầyê** (pl. **su wầyê**) 'who?' may occur with or without the stabilizer. If it is used, it
occurs immediately after 'who?' (as is required of all focused elements) rather than after the predicate Y,
e.g.,

wầyê (nē) ƙātòn nan dà kề kallonmù?   Who was that brute who was looking at us?
su wầyê (nē) bàƙîn?   Who are the strangers?

8.2. *Exclamatory expressions*
If the stabilizer is omitted from a sentence that normally requires one, the result is an exclamatory
expression, e.g.,

Mammàn bāwà!	What a slave Mamman is! (i.e., he works like a slave)
cf. Mammàn bāwà nē	Mamman is a slave.
ruwā lāfiyà!	How healthy water is!
talakāwā bāyin Allàh!	Poor people are masses!
Mūsā gwànī!	Musa is a real maven!
sàrautà bà àbar̃ wàsā ba!	Chieftaincy is not play!

The structure without the stabilizer is particularly prevalent in fixed expressions and proverbs, e.g.,

Allàh Sarkī!	How wonderful! (lit. God is the Lord)
namijì kàrē!	How useless is a man! (lit. a man is a dog)
màtar̃ mùtûm kabàr̃insà	A man's wife is his destiny. (lit. his grave)
àbincin wani gubàr̃ wani	One man's food is another man's poison.
gidā biyu māgànin gòbar̃ā	Two houses is the remedy for a house fire.
kā dà màge bà yankā ba	Knocking down a cat is not slaughtering (it).
bà cinyàr̃ ba, ƙafàr̃ bāya	It's not the thigh, it's the hind leg.

(i.e., six of one half a dozen of the other)

By contrast with the above, proverbs in which the X and the Y contain a repetition of the same word require the stabilizer, e.g.,

[mugunyàr̃ dàbār̃à] [dàbār̃à] cē	A bad plan is still a plan.
[ɗan bàjimī] [bàjimī] nè	The son of a bull-ox is himself a bull-ox.
[àbōkin ɓàrāwò] [ɓàrāwò] nē	The friend of a thief is himself a thief.

8.3. Reduction of multiple stabilizers

Identificational sentences functioning as complement-taking expressions normally appear with the STAB nē/nè, e.g.,

[mài yìwuwā nè] Bàlā tà sàyi sābuwar̃ mōtà   It is possible that Bala may buy a new car.

If, however, an item is extracted from the complement and focused (using the STAB), then the STAB that normally accompanies the complement-taking expression is deleted, e.g.,

Bàlā nè [mài yìwuwā ( )] yà sàyi sābuwar̃ mōtà
  It's Bala who it is possible that he may buy a new car.
sābuwar̃ mōtà cē mài yìwuwā ( ) Bàlā yà sàyā
  It's a new car that it is possible that Bala may buy.
Audù nē dōlè ( ) yà àuri Bintà   It is Audu who it is necessary that he marry Binta.

As far as negative complement-taking identificational sentences are concerned, the deletion rule is not applied and the STAB is retained, e.g.,

Fù'âd nē [bà dōlè ba nē] (wai) yà yi barcī cikin ɗākìnsà
  It is Fu'ad who it is not necessary that he must sleep in his room.
Bintà cē [bà mài yìwuwā ba nè] (wai) tà zama sàraunìyar̃mù
  It is Binta who it is not likely that she will become our queen.

9. POSITION OF THE STABILIZER

According to the general formula X Y STAB, the stabilizer occurs at the end of the sentence after the predicate constituting the Y. Deviations from this order result from two independent factors: focus and heavy predicates.

9.1. Focus

If the subject X of an equational sentence is focused, the STAB is placed immediately after the X and before the Y. This is true also of structures that normally occur without the stabilizer. Note that the pleonastic pronoun described above in §4 is commonly used along with focused NPs. Examples:

Audù nē mālàmī	It is *Audu* who is a teacher.
cf. Audù mālàmī nè	Audu is a teacher.
ɗàlìbai nè àbin tàusàyī	It is *students* who are pitiful.
shaddàř cē tòka-tòka	It is the *brocade* that is gray.
kèkên nē sābō fìl	It is the *bicycle* that is brand new.
sàna'àřsà ita cè nōmā	*His occupation* is farming.
cf. sàna'àřsà nōmā	His occupation is farming.
gwâřřā nè rūsā-rùsà dà sū	The *kolanuts* are really large.
Bintà ita cè wùlàƙàntacciyā	It is *Binta* who is disrespectful.
shī nè Mālàm Bellò	*He* is Malam Bello.
mū nè màsu rawā	It is *we* who are the dancers.

In negative sentences with focus, the first **bà** normally appears at the beginning of the sentence immediately in front of the focused constituent.

bà [mū]X nè mahàukàtā ba	It is not *we* who are crazy.
bà [shī]X nè Mālàm Sāni ba	It is not *he* who is Malam Sani.

9.1.1. Focusing of the Y

The predicate Y of an equational sentence is focused by moving it to the focus position at the beginning of the sentence. The fronted Y is immediately followed by the STAB. Examples:

Mālàm Bellò nē nī   It's *Malam Bello* who I am. (cf. **nī Mālàm Bellò nē**   I am Malam Bello.) **mài wàyō nè shī** He is a *clever*. **maƙaryacìyā cè ita** She is a *liar*. **'yan-lèƙen-àsīřī nè sū** They're *spies*.

When the X is a noun (rather than a pronoun) fronting of the Y for purposes of focus results in sentences that tend to be clumsy, e.g., **??àlƙālī nè Bàlā** 'Bala is a *judge*'. One strategy that solves the problem is to topicalize the subject. This can then be followed by a straightforward structure composed of the focused Y plus the stabilizer, followed optionally by a resumptive pronoun, e.g.,

Bàlā, àlƙālī nè (shī)	Bala, he's a *judge* (he is).
ɗàlìbîn, dàƙīƙì nē (shī)	The student, he's *dull*.
sàmàrîn fa, dabbōbī nè (sū)	As for the youths, (like) *animals* they are.

Corresponding negative sentences employ a pronoun either in the X position or optionally at the very end of the sentence. (Different speakers have different preferences regarding the alternative structures.)

mōtàȓ, ita bà̀ farā ba cě = mōtàȓ, bà̀ farā ba cě (ita)　　　　The car, it's not *white*.
ɗālìbîn, shī bà̀ dàȓīȓì ba nè̀ = ɗālìbîn, bà̀ dàȓīȓì ba nè̀ (shī)　　The student, he is not *dull*.

Another strategy when two nouns are involved is to front the Y + STAB and to right-shift the X (consisting of a noun preceded by a pronominal determiner/specifier) in an afterthought construction (see chap. **6**), e.g.,

tàurārùwā cě, [ita Madonna]　　　　She's *a star*, she Madonna.
cf. ita Madonna tàurārùwā cě　　　　She Madonna is a star.

9.1.2. Question words

The stabilizer occurs immediately next to question words, whether they appear in initial position or later in a sentence. (In the interrogative forms **wằnē nè̀** 'who', **mènē nè̀** 'what', etc., which contain two occurrences of the stabilizer, the orthographic convention is to write the first one attached to the Q-word and the second one separate.) Examples:

wằnē nè̀ ȓanìnkà?　　　　　　　　Who is your younger brother?
wàcē cě màtaȓ manajà?　　　　　　Who is the manager's wife?
su wằnē nè̀ bà̀ȓîn?　　　　　　　　Who are the strangers/guests?
kèkên nan na wằnē nè̀?　　　　　　Whose bicycle is that? (lit. bicycle.of that of who STAB)
kū su wằnē nè̀?　　　　　　　　　Who are you (pl.)?
mènē nè̀ aikìn bàbankà?　　　　　 What is your father's occupation?
wàccē cě gōɗìyaȓ lìmân?　　　　　Which one is the imam's mare?
kuɗin rīgunàn nawà-nawà nē? = nawà-nawà nē kuɗin rīgunàn?
　　　How much is the price of the gowns each?

9.2. *Heavy predicate shift*

If the Y is a simple adjective, or a single noun, with or without a prenominal modifier, or a simple genitive complex, then the basic word order is X Y STAB, e.g.,

shī ȓàtò̀ nē　He is very large. **Bellò màshàhūrìn likità nē**　Bello is a famous doctor. **waɗànnân zàbī nè**　These are guinea-fowls. **Tàlātù sàraunìyaȓ kyâu cē**　Talatu is the beauty queen. **mùtumìn cân kàwun Jummai nè̀**　That man is Jummai's uncle.

If the predicate noun is followed by a relatively simple postnominal modifier, then the STAB either can be placed after the full Y or it can be moved up after the head noun and before the modifier, e.g.,

Màtī dà Shēhù yârā nàgàȓtàttū nè̀ = Màtī dà Shēhù yârā nè̀ nàgàȓtàttū
　　　Mati and Shehu are well-behaved children.
àkuyà dabbà̀ ȓòsasshiyā cě = àkuyà dabbà̀ cē ȓòsasshiyā　　　A goat is a well-fed animal.
Ādaȓāwā mutằnē fīȓɗā-fīȓɗà̀ nē = Ādaȓāwā mutằnē nè̀ fīȓɗā-fīȓɗà̀　Ader people are hefty.
Yunūsà yârò̀ mài nàtsuwā nè̀ = Yunūsà yârò̀ nē mài nàtsuwā　　Yunusa is a composed boy.
Maȓsandî mōtà̀ mài tsằdā cě = Maȓsandî mōtà̀ cē mài tsằdā　　Mercedes is an expensive car.

Similarly, predicate adjectives modified by phonologically simple ideophones (underlined) or adverbs usually allow the STAB following the entire Y although the preferred position is immediately after the head, e.g.,

tukunyâr̃ baк̃ā cè к̃irin (= tukunyâr̃ baк̃ā к̃irin cè)	The pot is jet black.
kèkên sābō nè fil (= kèkên sābō fil nè)	The bicycle is brand new.
wannàn dōkì magùjī nè sòsai	This horse is really fast.
dâmman hatsī ɗànyū nè shar̃af (= dâmman hatsī ɗànyū shar̃af nè)	

The grain bundles are wet.

yārinyàr̃ kyàkkyāwā cè ainùn (≠ **yārinyàr̃ kyàkkyāwā ainùn cē)

The girl is very beautiful.

If, however, the modifier is "heavy," i.e., it consists of a prepositional phrase or a relative clause, etc., then the STAB is generally placed immediately after the head rather than after the Y as such, e.g.,

Audù ɗālìbī nè à jāmi'à	Audu is a student at the university.
(lit. Audu student STAB at university)	
mutuwà tabbàs cē gà kōwā	Death is a certainty for everyone.
(lit. death certain STAB to everyone)	
Kànde màtā cè dà bā tà rìgimà	Kande is a woman who isn't troublesome.
(lit. Kande woman STAB that neg 3f-Ncont trouble)	
ɗinkì bàbbar̃ sàna'ā̀ cē à к̃asar̃ Hausa	Tailoring is an important profession in Hausaland.
mōtàr̃sà akwalā cè dàgà gēfè	His car is wrecked from the side.
Shatù yārinyà̀ cē 'yar̃ shèkarā̀ bakwài	Shatu is a seven-year-old girl.
àljànū hàlìttū nè dà bā ā̀ ganī	Jinns are creatures that are not seen.
bàbban nauyī nè à kânkù kù taimàkā wà jūnā	

It is a big responsibility on/upon you that you should help each other.

Màtī yārò̄ nē dà akà hàifā bāyan an yi ta haihùwar̃ mātā

Mati is [the name of] a boy born after a series of females.

Audù shī mùtûm nē dà kè̀ sôn à kulà̀ dà shī   Audu is a person who likes to be looked after.

Sentences such as ??**Audù shī mùtûm dà kè̀ sôn à kulà̀ dà shī nè** with the STAB as the end are not considered totally ungrammatical, but they are felt to be very awkward and are definitely dispreferred.

Another strategy employed to avoid placing the STAB at the end of a heavy Y is to move the STAB up between the X and the Y, e.g.,

Àlhajì Mūsā nè mùtumìn dà sukà bā làbār̃ìn

Alhaji Musa is the man the story was told to.

Hàdīzà cē yārinyàr̃ dà akà yi wà aurē

Hadiza is the girl that one arranged the marriage for.

zākì nē dabbàr̃ dà ta fi kōwàcè dabbà̀ ban tsòrō

A lion is the animal that is most fearful of all.

There is difference of opinion among native speakers as to whether these sentences connote focus on the X or whether they are essentially equivalent to corresponding sentences with the STAB after the Y.

If the Y contains an NP consisting of conjoined or disjoined nouns, the natural place for the STAB is after the first noun. (In such cases, the STAB usually agrees with the immediately preceding noun rather than with the subject.) Examples:

Audù sākar̃ai nè kō mahàukàcī	Audu is either a fool or crazy.
àbîn dà ka ganī kāsā cè kō gànshèк̃ā?	Was the thing that you saw a puff-adder or a cobra?
àbōkîn nākà daktà nē kō kùwa daftàn?	Is your friend a (true) doctor or just a quack?

mùtûm nē kō àljan?	Is it a person or a jinn?
Bintà cē kō Lādì	It's Binta or Ladi.
kèkên akwalā cè kō gāwā	The bicycle is either a jalopy or totally useless.
waɗànnân tsuntsàyē ùngùlu cè dà shāhò	These birds are a vulture and an eagle.
waɗànnân yârā màkàfī nè dà kuma guràgū	

These children are (composed of the) blind and also the lame.

[References. Parsons (1963); Rufa'i (1977); Schachter (1966)]

24. Ethnonyms

1. BASIC FORM AND MEANING (bà-)

SINGULAR words indicating a person's place of origin, nationality, ethnicity, occupation, or social group (or qualities ascribed thereto) are formed by means of a low-tone prefix **bà-**, which is attached to the name of the ethnic group, language, or place in question. (I am using "ethnonym" as a cover term with the understanding that it is not semantically accurate in all cases.) In addition to the **bà-** prefix, masculine nouns typically utilize a vocalic suffix -ē)^{HL}. The H-L pattern of the suffix spreads to the left up to the initial **bà-**, which retains its intrinsic L tone, thereby producing a regular L-(H)H-L tone sequence, e.g.,

Bàgumalè man from Gumel (**Gumàl**)   **Bàzamfarè** man from Zamfara (**Zàmfàrà**)

A few ethnonyms end in /ū/, /ō/, or /ā/ instead of (or as an alternative to) the usual /ē/:

bàdūkǔ	leather worker (cf. **dūkancì** leather working)
bàfādà̀ (= **bàfādè̀**)	courtier (< **fādà** palace)
bàhagò̀	left-handed psn (< **hagu** left)
Bàkanò̀ (= **Bàkanè̀**)	man from Kano (**Kanò̀**)

Feminine singular ethnonyms add {-ā} to the masculine stem. The surface realization is determined by the following regular rules of feminine inflectional formation (see §31:3.1): -è + -ā → -ìyā and -ò + -ā → -ùwā, e.g., **Bàgumalè** m. / **Bàgumalìyā** f. 'man / woman from Gumel'; **Bàkanò̀** m. / **Bàkanùwā** f. 'man / woman from Kano'. The feminine counterpart of **bàfādà̀** 'courtier' is **bàfādìyā** (without palatalization of the /d/).

> ΔDN: In WH, the feminine ending for masculine words ending in -è is -à rather than -ìyā, e.g., [SH] **Bàkatsinìyā** = [WH] **Bàkatsinà** 'Katsina woman'; [SH] **Bàsakkwacìyā** = [WH] **Bàsakkwatà** 'Sokoto woman'; [SH] **Bàmāgujìyā** = [WH] **Bàmāguzà** 'pagan Hausa woman'. An exception is the feminine form of **Bàtūrè** 'European', which is **Bàtūrìyā** in WH just as it is in SH. Conversely, SH uses the WH form **Bàfillātà** 'Fulani woman' (without the -ìyā ending) as the feminine counterpart of **Bàfillācè** 'Fulani man'.

The plural forms of ethnonyms normally make use of a suffix -āwā, which is added to the lexical base without the final vowel and without the **bà-** prefix (see discussion below in §3.1), e.g., **Bàgumalè** m. / **Gumalāwā** 'man / people from Gumel'.

Here is a list of common ethnonyms divided into two rough semantic categories. Where the ethnonym is built on a place name, this is provided after the gloss, which is given in the singular only.

(1) Ethnic/geographical origin

m.	f.	pl.	
Bàfaȓanshè̩	Bàfaȓanshìyā	Faȓansāwā	French (Fàȓansà)
Bàhaushè̩	Bàhaushìyā	Hàusàwā	Hausa (Hausa)
Bàjāmushè̩	Bàjāmushìyā	Jāmusāwā	German (Jāmùs)
Bàkatsinè̩	Bàkatsinìyā	Katsināwā	psn from Katsina (Kàtsinà)
Bàlāȓabè̩	Bàlāȓabìyā	Lāȓabāwā	Arab
Bàmisiȓè̩	Bàmisiȓìyā	Misiȓāwā	Egyptian (Misiȓà)
Bàsakkwacè̩	Bàsakkwacìyā	Sakkwatāwā	psn from Sokoto (Sakkwato)
Bàtūȓè̩	Bàtūȓìyā	Tùȓàwā	European (Tūȓai)
Bàyaȓabè̩	Bàyaȓabìyā	Yaȓabāwā	Yoruba

°AN: [i] The word **bàtūȓè̩**, which originally meant 'white person (European or Arab)', has been semantically extended, especially in compounds and fixed phrases, to mean a government official, e.g., **bàtūȓèn-gōnā** 'agricultural extension worker' (lit. European.of-farm).

(2) Profession, adherent, status

m.	f.	pl.	
bàbambaɗè̩	bàbambāɗìyā	bambaɗāwā	praise singer
bàdūkù		dùkàwā	leather worker
bàfādà̩	bàfādìyā	fàdàwā	courtier
bàkwanīkè̩		kwanīkāwā	joker
bàmālikè̩		Mālikāwā	follower of Maliki school of Islamic law
	bàzawàrā	zawarāwā	widow, divorcee

°AN: The masculine word **bàbambaɗè̩** 'praise singer' has a less common variant **bàbambāɗè̩** with a long penultimate vowel. The feminine **bàbambāɗìyā**, on the other hand, normally occurs with the long /ā/.

◊HN: The prefix **bà-** is etymologically related to a root ***ba** meaning 'son/daughter', which one finds scattered throughout West Chadic. (The word is perhaps cognate with Semitic **bin**). The phonological similarity between the Hausa prefix **bà-** and the Bantu **ba-** class prefix for people is totally accidental and without significance.

A pair of polysyllabic place names with final /m/ treat the nasal as part of the nucleus, i.e., as a "nasal diphthong" (see §54:2.1.1), which is excluded from the base on which the ethnonym is formed, e.g.,

//damagaȓ-// ⇒ **Bàdamagaȓè̩** / **Bàdamagaȓìyā** / **Damagaȓāwā**   psn from Damagaram (**Dàmagàȓam**)

(*not* **//damagaȓam-// ⇒ ****Bàdamagaȓamè̩**, etc.)

//dungur-// ⇒ **Bàdungurè̩** / **Bàdungurìyā** / **Dungurāwā**   psn from Dungurum (**Dùngùrùm**)

In just a few cases, the ethnonym is built on a plural form of the underlying stem, e.g., **bàfatàkè̩** 'itinerant trader' is built on **fatàkē**, which is the plural of **faȓkē** (= **falkē**), a word that is equivalent in meaning to the ethnonym. Similarly, **bàgidājè̩** 'simpleton' comes from **gidàjē**, the plural of **gidā** 'home'. (Interestingly, the word **gidādancī** 'being a simpleton', which contains the -cī manner suffix, is also built on the plural stem.)

Some words, especially those with a stem-final consonant, form their ethnonyms by adding a non-integrating H-tone suffix -ī rather than -è̩)[HL]. The base generally retains its lexical tone. The corresponding feminine ends in -ā, in accordance with the general feminine formation rules (see §31:3.1), which specify that H-tone ī + -ā → -ā, e.g., **Bàgòbìrī** / **Bàgòbìrā** 'man / woman from Gobir area' (**Gòbìr**). Many speakers, however, have generalized the use of the -è)^{HL} suffix, so that it is now allowed or preferred in place of the final -ī ethnonyms cited in dictionaries and older sources. In SH, the feminines of these ī-final ethnonyms often take the -ìyā suffix built on the final -è variant even if the final -ī variant is preferred for the corresponding masculine form. Examples:

m.	*f.*	*pl.*	
Bà'azbìnī = Bà'azbìnè	Bà'azbìnā (= Bà'azbìnìyā)	Azbināwā	psn from Asben (**Azbìn**)
Bàdàurī	Bàdàurā	Daurāwā	psn from Daura (**Dàurā**)
Bàfulātànī	Bàfulātànā	Fulànī	Fulani psn
bàgabàshī = bàgabashè	bàgabàsā (= bàgabashìyā)	gabasāwā	easterner (**gabàs**)
Bàgumàlī = Bàgumalè	Bàgumalìyā (not **Bàgumàlā)	Gumalāwā	psn from Gumel
Bàjāhùnī = Bàjāhunè	Bàjāhunìyā (not **Bàjāhùnā)	Jāhunāwā	psn from Jahun
Bàtèrī = Bàtèrè	Bàtèrā	Tèrāwā	Tera psn
Bàzazzàgī	Bàzazzàgā	Zazzagāwā	psn from Zaria (**Zagzàg**)
Bàgwārè = Bàgwārè	Bàgwārìyā	Gwàrāwā	Gwari psn, psn who

speaks unintelligibly (cf. **Gwāri** member of the Gwari ethnic group)

ΔDN: The word **Bà'azbìnī** 'psn from Asben area' (along with its related forms) is commonly pronounced with metathesis of the medial /zb/, i.e., **Bà'abzìnī**, etc.

2. ALTERNATIVE CONSTRUCTIONS

Although the ethnonymic affixes are productive to some extent, they are not used freely with just any stem. In many cases, the normal way of forming an ethnonym is by using a genitive phrase with the word **mùtumìn** (f. **mùtūnìyař**, pl. **mutànen**) lit. 'man/woman/people of', or with **ɗan** (f. **'yař**, pl. **'yan**), lit. 'child/children of'. One often uses the **ɗan/ 'yař/ 'yan** forms with the word **ƙasař** 'country of' to indicate more explicitly 'psn of the country of', e.g.,

mùtumìn/mùtūnìyař/mutànen Azàre	psn from Azare
mùtumìn/mùtūnìyař/mutànen Gùsau	psn from Gusau
mùtumìn/mùtūnìyař/mutànen Màrōkò	Moroccan
mùtumìn/mùtūnìyař/mutànen Pàkìstân	Pakistani
ɗan/ 'yař/ 'yan (ƙasař) Cādì	Chadian
ɗan/ 'yař/ 'yan (ƙasař) Kwangò	Congolese
ɗan/ 'yař/ 'yan Ingìlà	Englishman
ɗan/ 'yař/ 'yan Nàjēřiyà	Nigerian

3. THE -āwā SUFFIX

3.1. Plural ethnonyms

Most **bà-** ethnonyms form their plurals by dropping the prefix and the final vowel and adding an **-āwā** suffix. Trisyllabic plurals with a heavy first syllable (and the one quadrisyllabic word **gìdàdàwā**) typically manifest L-H tone. Plurals of other shapes, e.g., those that have more than three syllables or that have a light first syllable, regardless of the number of syllables, have an all H tone pattern. A few trisyllabic heavy-syllable words allow either tone pattern. Examples:

(a) **Bàdàurī**	**Dàuràwā = Daurāwā**	people from Daura
bàfādà	**fàdàwā**	courtiers
bàgidājè	**gìdàdàwā**	simpletons
Bàgwārī	**Gwàràwā**	Gwari people
Bàhaushè	**Hàusàwā**	Hausas
Bàtūrè	**Tùràwā = Tūràwā**	Europeans, white people
(b) **Bàdamagàrè**	**Damagàrāwā**	people from Damagaram
Bàgòbirī	**Gòbirāwā**	people from Gobir
Bàkanò	**Kanāwā**	people from Kano
Bàlàrabè	**Làrabāwā**	Arabs

3.2. Singular/plural asymmetry

Although **bà-** singulars and **-āwā** plurals are commonly paired, there is not a perfect match between them. Some ethnonyms containing the prefix **bà-** form their plurals by means other than by **-āwā** or as an alternative to **-āwā**. In a few cases, the **bà-** prefix is retained in the plural, e.g.,

bàdūkù	**bàdùkai = dùkàwā**	leather workers
bàhagò	**bàhàgwai**	left-handed people
Bàbadè	**Badèbadī = Badāwā**	Bades
Bàbarbarè	**Barèbarī**	Kanuris
Bàdakkarè	**Dakàrkarī**	Dakarkaris
Bàfillācè / Bàfilātànī	**Filànī / Fulànī**	Fulanis
Bànasàrè	**Nàsàrū = Nàsāra**	white people, Christians
bàsarākè	**sàràkai**	title holders
bàtijjānè	**'yan Tìjjàniyyà**	Tijaniyya sect members

°AN: From a morphological perspective, the word **nàsāra** 'white people, Nazarenes', which is a loanword from Arabic, is better thought of as a collective noun rather than as a plural, even though it usually commands plural concord. (Neither the tone pattern nor the short final vowel is plural-like.) The word **nàsàrū**, on the other hand, is a true morphological plural containing the common **-ū** suffix.

Conversely, some words indicating professions or social positions form plurals with **-āwā** even though they do not use **bà-** in the singular, e.g.,

ànnabì	**annabāwā**	prophets
dògarì	**dōgarāwā = dògàrai**	emir's bodyguards
ɗan bàrikì	**bàrikāwā (='yan bàrikì)**	city slickers
gàrdì	**gàrdàwā**	advanced students in Koranic school
kìlākì	**kilākāwā (= kìlàkai)**	modern-day prostitutes
kūrì	**kùràwā**	young pupils
talàkà	**talakāwā**	poor people, commoners
yārì	**yārāwā**	chief jailers

The singular noun **dattījò** 'adult, mature individual', which is a loanword from Fulani, has two plurals, **dàttàwā** and **dàttìjai**, which earlier were equivalent alternatives. In modern usage, the plurals have diverged in meaning: the former generally denotes 'senators' whereas the latter is used more generally for 'gentlemen, older respectable men'.

In forming new ethnonyms, the plural form with -āwā seems much more productive than the corresponding singular with bà-, e.g.,

ɗan / mùtumìn Bosniyà	Bosniyāwā (='yan / mutànen Bosniyà)	Bosnians
ɗan / mùtumìn Pàlàsɗìnù	Palasɗīnāwā	Palestinians
ɗan / mùtumìn Sābiyà	Sābiyāwā (='yan / mutànen Sābiyà)	Serbs
ɗan / mùtumìn Sin	Sīnāwā (= mutànen Sin)	Chinese

3.3. Followers of

A special case where plural ethnonyms formed with -āwā occur readily without corresponding singular forms is the construction with personal names. (The -āwā forms have all H tone regardless of the segmental shape.) These derivatives indicate followers or adherents of someone, often in a political or religious context, e.g.,

Alāsāwā	people with connections to the family of Alhasan (Àlāsàn) Dantata
Kādiřāwā	followers of Abdulƙadir Jelani (i.e., members of this sect)
Mūsāwā	followers of Musa
Sanūsāwā	backers of the former Emir Sanusi
Yařīmāwā	people related to the royal family (< yàřīmà prince)

3.4. Toponyms

In addition to its function as a pluralizing suffix for ethnonyms, the -āwā ending (usually with all H tone) also serves to form place names (villages, towns, or quarters of towns). These -āwā toponyms are built on a wide variety of roots: personal names, titles, simple place names, and common nouns. What semantically ties these toponyms to the plural ethnonyms, especially the group above indicating followers of someone, is the notion of *community*. Examples:

Ādamāwā	name of a province	< Ādamà	personal name
Agadasāwā	a quarter in Kano	< Àgadàs	town name
Amaryāwā	a town/village	< amaryā	bride
Daurāwā	a quarter in Kano	< Dàurā	town name
Gabasāwā	a town/village	< gabàs	east
Gāgarāwā	a town/village	< Gàgarà	personal name
Gòbiřāwā	a quarter in Kano	< Gòbiř	name of an area/emirate
Hařūnāwā	a town/village	< Hařūnà	personal name
Kùrmàwā	a quarter in Kano	< kurmì	copse, wooded area
Tamburāwā	a town/village	< tamburà	ceremonial drums (for emir)
Tsanyāwā	a town/village	< tsanyà	cricket
Yařīmāwā	a town/village	< yàřīmà	prince

Although these place names are plural in form, grammatically they are all feminine singular, as is the norm for names of towns and quarters, e.g.,

[Tsanyāwā]f [tanà]f nan kuřkusa	Tsanyawa is there just nearby.
[Kùrmàwā]f [tā]f fi dukà yawàn mutànē	Kurmawa is the most populous.

4. ADJECTIVES

Up to this point, the ethnonyms formed with **bà-** have all been described and glossed as nouns. They can, however, also be used adjectivally, sometimes with the general ethnonymic meaning, more often with a more specialized or figurative meaning. When functioning as adjectival modifiers, whether attributive or predicative, they obligatorily agree in number and gender with the head noun, e.g.,

bàfār̃ishèn bàr̃gō	Persian blanket (= **bàr̃gō ɗan Fār̃isà**) (cf. **Bàfār̃ishè** a Persian)
bàfādìyar̃ màganà	sycophantic language (cf. **bàfādìyā** female courtier)
bàkanùwar̃ ƙwaryā	Kano-type calabash (cf. **Bàkanùwā** a Kano woman)
bàkanùwar̃ màganà	clever language, "fast-talk"
bàmāgujèn zāgì	a seriously obscene insult (cf. **bàmāgujè** a pagan Hausa man)
bàbarbarìyar̃ wuƙā	a Borno type of knife (which is always very sharp)
(cf. **Bàbarbarìyā** a woman from Borno)	
bàhagùwar̃ mōtà	car with a left-sided steering wheel, or an unusual or hard-to-handle car
(cf. **bàhagùwā** a left-handed woman)	
bà'abōr̃èn mùtûm	shy, unsophisticated man
(cf. **Bà'abōr̃è** man of the Abore pastoral Fulani clan)	
shī bàgwār̃è nē	He is incomprehensible, confused, unsophisticated.
(cf. **shī Gwāri nè** He is a Gwari.)	
Audù bàfilātànī nè	Audu is shy, modest. (adj.) *or* Audu is a Fulani. (n.)
(cf. **Bàfilātànī** a Fulani man)	

4.1. Plural of adjectival ethnonyms

Whereas nominal ethnonyms drop the **bà-** prefix in forming plurals, ethnonymic adjectives typically build their plurals on the stem complete with **bà-** in place. The most common plural suffixes employed are -ai or -ū. A few ethnonymic adjectives, however, do use the -āwā form. Examples:

bà'àzbìnan dàwàkai	Asben horse (*not* **azbināwan dàwàkai)
bàbàrbàrun wuƙàƙē	Borno knives (*not* **barèbarin wuƙàƙē)
bàr̃ūman takubbà	Roman swords (= **Rūmāwan takubbà**)
gìdàdàwan mutànē	unsophisticated people
ƙauyàwan manòmā	naive farmers

4.2. Common nouns from adjectival ethnonyms

In some instances, the collocation between an ethnonymic adjective and the noun it modifies has become so close that the noun is now generally left unexpressed. The result is a transition from an ethnonymic adjective into a common noun (cf. Chinaware → china). Examples:

bà'ingilà	long-grain rice (< **bà'ingilàr̃ shìnkāfà**) (lit. English rice)
bàbarbarà	type of knife or sword (Borno style)
bàgòbir̃ā	type of Mercedes (with grill design similar to Gobir facial markings)
bàzabar̃mè	fringed honeycomb cloth (presumably originating from **Zabar̃mā**)
bàzàmfàrī	a medicinal plant (presumably originating from **Zàmfàrà**)

[Reference: Newman (1984a)]

25. Exclamations / Interjections

1. NONDERIVED LEXICAL EXCLAMATIONS

EXCLAMATORY words can be divided into two groups: nonderived and derived. Included among the nonderived are a miscellany of lexical items (and phrases) that are used to express various emotions. As contrasted with most common nouns, but like adverbs, exclamations commonly end in a short vowel or a consonant. The words are difficult to define precisely because a great part of the meaning is pragmatically determined. Examples include the following:

a'a expression of surprise; **ā'à̃** no; **af** indicates sudden surprise; used for P.S. or Nota Bene; **àhiř** Never ever do that again! **ai** well yes, but…, oh; **Allàh?** Is that so? **Allàh wadai** God damn! **àkul** (= **kul**) Stop doing that! You'd better take heed! **ànâ = ìnâ** Is that really possible?! No way! **anyà̃** expression of strong doubt (often preceding questions); **ař** Damn it! **ash** expression of regret; **àshē** expression of surprise or doubt; expression of confirmation, e.g., **àshē Audù nē** So it was Audu after all; **àsshā** What a pity! How distressing! **àyyē** Great, I see; **bìsimillà̃** used when inviting s.o. to begin a meal or to come into a room or to sit down, etc.; **cabɗì̃ = caɓ = cabɗìján** (= **tabɗì̃ = tabɗìján**) expression of great surprise; **hā** Open your mouth! (said to children); **hâ** expression of anticipated fall, e.g., of a child or a boxer; **habà** used in negative persuasion or coaxing; used when sth is finally understood; used in contradicting; **habà̀wâ** expression of strong doubt; No, that's impossible! **ī** yes; **kâi** used to express mild disapproval, doubt, or surprise; **kaico** (= **kaito**) What a pity! What bad luck! **kash** Oh dear! **mādàllā** expression of thanks, agreement, or approval; **mànà** for sure, well, indeed (often used with an imperative, e.g., **shìgō mànà!** Come on in now!); **na'àm** yes that's so; **nà'am** yes (in reply to a call); **òho** I don't know! I don't care! Who gives a hoot? **òhô** I see! **sùbhānàllāhì** Goodness gracious! **tiř** What a bother! **tô = tò** OK, That's all right (e.g., **tô fa** There you have it); then, well then...; **ùbākà** (crude) Damn you! (lit. your father); **ungo** Here, take (it)! **uwākà** (crude) Screw you! (lit. your mother); **wâsh** (= **wash**) expression of concern over news of an unfortunate event; expression of relaxation by a tired psn; **wâyyō** (= **wâyyô**) expression of deep regret, sorrow, pain; cry for help

Generally speaking, exclamations are invariant and are used as full expressions in and of themselves, but there are some exceptions. For example, the words **kaico** (= **kaito**) 'What a pity!' and **wadai** (used in **Allàh wadai** 'God damn!') allow an attached genitive pronoun, e.g., **kaiconkù** 'What bad luck for you (pl.); it serves you right'; **kaicōnā!** 'Woe is me!' (with automatic lengthening of the final vowel before the first person possessive); **Allàh wadankà** 'God damn you!' The word **ungo** 'Here, take (it)!' behaves like a verb in allowing a (usually pronominal) direct object, e.g., **ungō tà!** 'Take it!' Note that the final vowel lengthens before the d.o. pronoun, as happens regularly with verbs. Some speakers go further and treat **ungo** plus its pronoun object like a grade 2 verb in the imperative by assigning an (L)-L-H tone pattern, e.g., **ùngò-ta!** 'Take it!' cf. **sàyè-ta!** 'Buy it!' The interjection **tiř** 'What a bother!' is commonly extended by a 'with' plus pronoun phrase, e.g., **tiř dà kē** 'the hell with you (f.)', **yā yi tiř dà mū** 'He disapproved of us.'

2. DERIVED EXCLAMATIONS -i)^HL(H)

Exclamations indicating 'what a large X' or 'what a lot of (doing) Y' (e.g., **fiřɗì!** 'What a hulk!' **birkìci!** 'What a mess!') are derived from augmentatives (see §11:2.1) and verbs by adding a suffix -i)^HL(H), i.e., they end in short -i and have H-L tone if disyllabic and H-L-H tone if trisyllabic. Because of the high front suffixal vowel, base-final coronals invariably appear as corresponding palatals. These words are typically pronounced with exclamatory intonation marked by stress and raised pitch on the first syllable. With the augmentatives, the suffix is added to the base without the -ēCè suffix or reduplication characteristic of these words. The derivation appears to be fairly regular with the augmentatives, but lexically more restricted with verbs. Examples:

(a) From augmentatives

mākì!	How long and broad! < **mākēkè** long and broad
rūshì!	How big (esp. kolanuts)! < **rūshēshè** big (esp. kolanuts)
ɗibgì!	How rotund! < **ɗibgēgè** huge, rotund
ɓuɓɓùki!	How hefty! < **ɓuɓɓukēkè** hefty
gamɓàshi!	What huge chunks! < **gamɓashēshè** huge (chunks)
řamɓàshi!	What a huge body! < **řamɓashēshè** huge
ringìmi!	What a huge head! < **ringimēmè** huge (re. head)
shařtàɓi!	How long and sharp! < **shařtaɓēɓè** long and sharp
zangàri!	How tall! < **zangarērè** very tall

(b) From verbs

ɗirkì	What a lot of drinking! < **ɗìrkā** drink a lot of
gillì!	What a lie! < **gillà** used in **yā gillà ƙaryā** He told a huge lie.
shārì	What a lot of sweeping! < **shārè** sweep
wuřgì	What a throw! < **wuřgà** hurl a projectile
yāɓì!	What a lot of plastering! < **yāɓà** plaster
danƙàri!	What a huge lot of packed material! < **danƙārē** compress tightly
ɗanɗàshi!	How befitting/elegant! < **ɗanɗàsā** do sth well
hargìtsi!	What a confusion! < **hargìtsā** muddle up
malàli!	What a flooding! < **màlālà** flood, overflow
shiřɓùni!	What a lot of oil rubbed on! < **shiřɓùnā** rub on oil

°AN: According to my information, the final -**i** is always short. Baba (1998), on the other hand, describes it as having variable length: long with disyllabic words but short with polysyllabic words.

These derived exclamations stand as self-contained utterances, i.e., they do not take subjects or objects. They may, however, be preceded by a simple exclamation plus a modal particle or followed by a semantically related clause, e.g.,

kâi ɗibgì!	Wow, how rotund!
ai kùwa birkìci!	Indeed what disorder!
gabjì an gàbjē shì	Yikes, he's been whacked!

26. Existential and Other Nonverbal Sentences

1. EXISTENTIAL SENTENCES

SIMPLE existential sentences are formed by means of a predicator **àkwai** 'there is / there are', e.g., **àkwai shìnkāfā** 'There is rice.' Alternatively, existentials can make use of the particle **dà**, which presumably is the same morpheme as the preposition **dà** 'with', e.g., **dà kuɗī** 'There is money.' Both **àkwai** and **dà** are invariant for number and gender, e.g.,

àkwai ruwā	There is water.
àkwai àlbasà	There are onions.
àkwai wani bàk̃ō à k̃ōfà	There is a stranger at the door.
dà dàlīlì	There is a reason.
dà ìsasshen shāyì?	Is there enough tea?

dà makullintà cikin àljīhūnā
   There is the key for it in my pocket.
àkwai mutằnē màsu yawằ dà bà sù san amsằ ba
   There are many people who don't know the answer.
àkwai lōkàcîn dà mutằnē zā sù gānè cêwā bâ Sarkī sai Allàh
   There is a time when people will understand that there is no Lord except God.
sàbàbbin mōtōcîn dà kè àkwai, yawancī anằ kāwôwā dàgà Jàpân
   New cars which there are, most have been brought from Japan.

The predicator **àkwai** makes use of the weak object pronoun set whereas **dà** is followed by an independent pronoun, e.g.,

àkwai tà = dà ita	There is it/her.
àkwai mù cikin màganàr̃	We were involved in the matter. (lit. there was us in the matter)

dà sū waɗàndà bà sù ji ba, bà sù ganī ba
   There are those (lit. them) who have nothing to do with the matter. (lit. ...who don't hear and don't see)

If no overt object is expressed immediately after the existential marker, **àkwai** must be used; **dà** cannot be stranded.

àkwai?	Is there any? (*not* ****dà?**)
àkwai saurā?	Is there some remaining? **Ī, àkwai** Yes, there is. (*not* ****ī, dà**)
àlbasàr̃ dà kè àkwai	the onions that there are (*not* ****àlbasàr̃ dà kè dà**)
cf. **dà àlbasà**	There are onions.

The only exception to the requirement that **dà** has to be followed directly by a complement is when it co-occurs with **àkwai** in the sequence **dà àkwai**, e.g.,

dà àkwai kuɗī	There is money.
dà àkwai sù cikin kwabàd	There are (some of) them in the cupboard.
dà àkwai mànà!	There are really!
àkwai ìsasshen àbinci?	Is there enough food? Ī, dà àkwai Yes, there is.

ΔDN: In some dialects **dà àkwai** has fused into a single word, **dàkwai**.

1.1. Existentials expressing attributes

An existential structure made up of **àkwai** plus a pronoun extended by **dà** plus an NP indicates possession. (This construction requires **àkwai** and not **dà** or **dà àkwai**.) The thing possessed, indicated by the **dà** phrase, is usually a quality rather than a concrete object (for which one would use the normal HAVE construction; see chap. 33). In general this construction is considered semantically more marked and expressive than the normal HAVE construction. Examples:

àkwai shì dà wàyō	He is very clever. (lit. there is him with cleverness)
mutànen nàn, àkwai sù dà rōwà	These men, they are misers.
(lit. men these, there is them with miserliness)	
àkwai tà dà ban màmākì	She is really amazing.
àkwai shì dà ban haushī	He is really aggravating.
àlƙālîn kàm, àkwai shì dà kuɗī	The judge, he really has money.
cf. the normal àlƙālîn kàm, yanà dà kuɗī	The judge, he has money. (lit. ...he is with money)

1.2. Negative

Negative existential sentences are expressed by **bābù** or **bâ** plus the predicate. In normal everyday language in SH, the short form **bâ** is likely to be used when a nominal object is present, although both variants are considered fully grammatical and equivalent in meaning. Examples:

bābù/bâ wùyā	It's not difficult. (lit. there is no difficulty)
bābu/bâ yârā à gidā	There are no children at home.
bābù/bâ sauran àbinci	There is no food remaining.
bābù/bâ dōkì dà zân hau?	Is there no horse for me to ride?
bābù/bâ ɗàlìbîn dà ya ci nasaràa kàmaɾ Mūsā	There are no students who succeeded like Musa.

The long form **bābù** tends to be preferred with pronoun predicates, which employ the independent set. With **bâ**, the independent pronoun paradigm is also usually employed, although the high-tone object set is attested as well. Examples:

bābù ita = bâ ita (= the less common bâ ta)	There isn't any of it.
bābù mū à lìssāfìn dà akà yi	We were not included in the counting that they did.
(lit. there was not us...) = bâ mū... (= the less common bâ mu...)	

If no overt object is expressed, only **bābù** can be used, e.g.,

àkwai saurā?	Is there some remaining? ā'ā̀, bābù No, there isn't. (not **ā'ā̀, bâ)
bābù?	Is there not any? (not ** bâ?)

The word **bābù** is sometimes used colloquially to mean 'no', generally as an elliptical response or as a sign of dispute or disagreement, e.g.,

kā sàmi mâi? bābù   Did you get any gas? No (I haven't got any).

◊HN: Etymologically, the relation between **bābù** and **bâ** is in dispute. One analysis takes **bābù** as original and interprets **bâ** as a phonologically reduced form restricted to certain syntactic environments (Eulenberg 1971). Support for this analysis comes from the fact that some WH dialects only have **bābù** but not **bâ** (Caron 1991, Malami Buba, personal communication). The other analysis, which is the traditional one and the one to which I subscribe, views **bābù** as a historically fused, grammaticalized word derived from **bâ** plus **àbù** 'thing' (Newman 1971a). (Skinner (1996) adopts this etymology without hesitation or discussion.) Comparative support for this view is provided by the existence of other Chadic languages, e.g., Gude (Hoskison 1983), in which the negative existential is made up of a negative marker plus the word for 'thing'. Internal evidence against the interpretation of **bābù** as a basic, monomorphemic function word comes from the fact that it uses independent rather than object pronouns as its object/complement. (Actually, in Sokoto, which does not use the **bâ** form, **bābù** takes the high-tone object pronouns rather than the independent set, e.g., [Skt] **bābù ta** = [SH] **bābù ita**. I take this to be an example of grammaticalization, I.e., once **bābù** developed into the one and only negative existential marker, it was natural to replace the independent pronoun by the grammatically more integrated object set.) Finally, there is also the possibility that **bâ** is a borrowing from Kanuri (whose negative existential has this same shape), which would preclude its having developed from **bābù** by internal means.

1.2.1. Times and numbers

The negative existentials **bābù** and **bâ** (usually the latter) have the sense of 'minus/subtraction' in forming the numerals 18 and 19 and the time expression 'a quarter of', e.g.,

àshìřin bâ ɗaya   19 (lit. 20 there is not 1) = **gōmà shâ tařà** (lit. 10 + 9)
àshìřin bâ biyu   18 (lit. 20 there is not 2) = **gōmà shâ takwàs** (lit. 10 + 8)
ƙarřè ukù bâ kwatà   2:45 (I.e., 3 o'clock there is not a quarter)

The numerals have an alternative formation with the negative existential at the end. In this case, the long form **bābù** is required, e.g.,

àshìřin ɗaya bābù   19   **àshìřin biyu bābù**   18

ΔDN: In Sokoto, where the **bâ** form is not used, the numbers 19 and 18 can be expressed only as **àshìřin ɗaya bābù** and **àshìřin biyu bābù**, respectively, with **bābù** at the end. To indicate 'a quarter of', one uses **saurā** 'remaining', e.g., **ƙarhè ukkù saurā kwatà** 'a quarter of three'.

1.2.2. Negative-HAVE

One means of expressing the negative counterpart of affirmative HAVE sentences is by a structure that on the surface looks like the negative existential **bâ** expanded with a **dà** phrase, e.g.,

bâ ta dà wàyō   She is not clever. (I.e., there is not her with cleverness)
cf. **tanà dà wàyō**   She is clever. (lit. ...is with cleverness) (= **àkwai tà dà wàyō**   She is clever.)
bâ shi dà kuɗī   He doesn't have money. (lit. there is not him with money)
cf. **yanà dà kuɗī**   He has money.

The negative of HAVE sentences ("Neg-HAVE" structure) differs synchronically from a "true" negative existential with a pronoun object in four respects: (1) Neg-HAVE only uses **bâ** whereas the negative existential before a pronoun prefers **bābù**, e.g., **bâ ta dà àbinci** 'She doesn't have food', vs. **bābù ita cikin waɗàndà sukà ci jaṝṝàbâwā** 'She was not among those who passed the exam.' (2) As illustrated in the previous examples, the pronouns after **bâ** in Neg-HAVE sentences belong to the H-tone CV set, whereas pronouns after the existential **bâ** usually belong to the independent set. (3) The 3rd person masculine singular pronoun after **bâ** in the Neg-HAVE construction may be expressed by the subject pronoun **ya** (which optionally reduces to /i/), whereas the 3m object of the existential **bâ** only allows the **shī** form, e.g., **bâ ya dà kuɗī** = **bâi dà kuɗī** = **bâ shi dà kuɗī** 'He doesn't have money' vs. **bâ shī** 'He's dead' (lit. there isn't him). (4) The impersonal pronoun (which exists only as a weak subject pronoun) can be used in Neg-HAVE sentences but not as an object of the existential **bâ**, e.g., **bâ a dà màkàmai** 'One doesn't have weapons', but not ****bâ ā** 'There aren't some (people).' Thus, although the Neg-HAVE construction *may* be derived historically from a negative existential, synchronically they have to be analyzed separately, the former involving a negative marker **bâ** plus a weak subject pronoun, the latter involving the negative existential **bābù/bâ** plus an object complement.

1.2.3. The **bâ** X **bâ** Y construction
The construction **bâ** X **bâ** Y with two negative existential clauses is used to indicate a serious incompatibility between people and things. It can also be used to warn or reprimand someone. Examples:

bâ kai bâ 'yātā   Don't come near my daughter again! You have no business with my daughter.
(lit. there is not you there is not my daughter)
bâ kū bâ Lādì   Don't you ever be with Ladi again! *or* You have no business with Ladi.
bâ nī bâ shī   I've parted ways with him.
bâ nī bâ kai   There is nothing more between you and me.
bâ nī bâ cîn ɗan-wākē dàgà yâu   As of today, I shall no longer eat **ɗan-wākē** beans.
(i.e., I've learned my lesson.) (lit. there is not me there is not eating **ɗan-wākē** from today)

There is an equivalent construction indicating incompatibility of the form **ìnā** X **ìnā** Y (lit. where is X where is Y?) (see §60:1.1.4), e.g., **ìnā nī ìnā Bàlā?** 'I have no business with Bala.'

2. PRESENTATIONAL SENTENCES

Presentational sentences ('here is/are / there is/are') call attention to or merely present a referent. They are formed with **gà** (which presumably is derived historically from an imperative of the verb **ga(nī)** 'see') plus an NP. (If the NP is a pronoun, it will belong to the strong high-tone d.o. set.) These sentences occur only in the affirmative. Examples:

gà yāròn	Here is the boy.
gà shi	Here he is.
gà tsōhuwā nân	Here is an old woman right here.
gà ni nan inā ta aikì haṝ ḳarfè gōmà	There I was working until ten o'clock.
Lādì kàm, gà ta can à bàkin kàsuwā	As for Ladi, there she is at the entrance to the market.
gà cùnkōson mutànē, sunà jìràn kàntōmà	

Hey, look at the crowd of people waiting for the government administrator.
gà mùtumìn dà ya tsìnci kuɗī dà dāmā lōkàcîn dà ya tàfi Landàn
Here is the man who found a lot of money when he went to London.

sunā̀ ràbuwā kè nan sai gā̀ Abdù

> They were in the process of separating when here appeared Audu.

It is possible, though not so common, to embed a presentational sentence in a relative clause, e.g.,

tsōhuwā̂r dà (takè) gā̀ ta nan râi gà Allàh   the old woman who is still here (but) really old
(lit. elder.L that (she.is) here is she there life with God)
Tankòn dà (yakè) gā̀ shi yanā̀ tā̀ɓamā̀ dà sābon kambàs mài tsā̀dā

> the Tanko who here he is showing off his new expensive sneakers

3. QUALITATIVE SENTENCES

Qualitative sentences, which translate into English as predicate adjective sentences, consist of an NP semantically representing a quality followed by a prepositional phrase made up of **gàrē** 'at/associated with' plus a pronoun, e.g.,

ɓarfī̀ gàrē sù	They are strong. (lit. strength at them)
bā̀ ɓarfī̀ gàrē kà ba	You are not strong. / It's not the case that you are strong.
ilìmī gàrē shì	He is erudite. (lit. knowledge at him)

The noun about which the quality is ascribed can be mentioned in topic position, e.g.,

àkûn (dai), hāziƙancì̀ gàrē shì   The parrot (well), he is clever.
(lit. parrot.the (indeed), cleverness at him)

These qualitative sentences can probably be subsumed under presentational or existential sentences, e.g., **hāziƙancì̀ gàrē shì** < **gā̀ hāziƙancì̀ gàrē shì** 'Here is cleverness with him' or **àkwai hāziƙancì̀ gàrē shì** 'There is cleverness with him.' Synchronically, however, the derivation is not transparent.

4. 'RATHER' SENTENCES

Sentences indicating 'rather, (it would be) better, etc.' are indicated by the particle **gāra** (or one of its essentially equivalent alternatives: **gwamma** (or **gwàmmà**); **gwàndà** (or **gwanda**)) plus an NP. These sentences occur only in the affirmative. If the NP is a pronoun, it takes the independent form. The 'rather' clause is often accompanied by a contrastive prepositional phrase formed with **dà** 'than', e.g.,

gāra kai dà shī   Better you than him.
gwàmmà màkarā̀ dà ƙin zuwā̀   Better lateness than refusing to come.
(i.e., 'Better late than never.')
dà mūgùwā̂r rawā, gāra ƙin tāshì   Rather than dance badly, it's better not to get up at all.
(lit. than bad.L dancing, better refusing.L arising) (i.e., 'Better leave well enough alone.')
gwàndà mutuwā̀ sai fa (in) àkwai mutuncì̀ mài gamsā̂rwā

> Death is preferable unless there is pleasing humanity.

> AN: The particle **gāra** (like its equivalent forms) also serves as an adverbial introducing clauses in the subjunctive, e.g., **gāra kà zaunā̀ à gidā** 'It would be better if you stayed at home'; cf. **dōlè kà zaunā̀ à gidā** 'You must stay at home'; **gāra mù yi saurī** 'It would be better if we hurried / We ought to hurry; cf. **yanā̀ dà muhimmancì̀ dà mù yi saurī** 'It is important that we hurry.'

27. Expressives of Contempt

1. INTRODUCTION

T HE label "expressives of contempt" has been adopted for a phrasal construction used to belittle or disregard something that has been mentioned in the discourse. In response to repeated pestering by a child about a **hùlā** 'cap', one could respond **hūlō matà** 'The hell with the cap!' Or if a child was complaining that a girl named **Hàdīzà** was getting special favors, one could answer **Hadīzō matà** 'Who cares about Hadiza?'

> °AN: The closest that one has to this in (American) English is the fairly restricted *shm* construction seen in *pickle / shmickle* or *maven / shmaven*. The comparison, however, is far from apt because the Hausa construction is considerably more open-ended.

The exact pragmatic and sociolinguistic rules for employing this construction have never been described, but it appears primarily to be used as a put-down by adults talking to children, although children can use it among themselves. Among adults, the construction would be considered very rude and insulting, except in the case of peers who were clearly joking with one another.

2. FORM

2.1. Basic formation

There are two parts to the expressive formation. First, the word in question is altered by the addition of a tone-integrating suffix $-\bar{o})^H$, I.e., final $-\bar{o}$ with all H tone. Second, the word is followed by **matà**, which presumably is the 3f indirect object pronoun 'to her'. In some cases the **matà** is omitted, although it is understood to be part of the expression, e.g., **gaȓgaɗō** = **gaȓgaɗō matà** 'I don't want to hear about a warning!' (< **gàȓgàɗī** 'warning, stern advice'). The omission somewhat lessens the abusive force of the expression.

> °AN: [i] It is likely that the 'her' originally referred to 'mother' (whether synchronically people recognize this or not). As is well known, the reference to 'mother' is abusive and insulting in many cultures of the world.
> [ii] According to Abdullahi Bature (personal communication), some people pronounce **mata** with H-H tone, thereby calling into question its interpretation as an indirect object form. My own guess is that this is a secondary development representing the spread of the H tone of the -ō suffix to the entire phrase.

The suffix $-\bar{o})^H$, which replaces the final vowel of the underlying stem, can be added to almost any word, simple or derived, singular or plural, common noun or proper noun, noun or verb, etc.

fire	**wutā**	**wutō**	rings	**zôbbā**	**zobbō**
Hamisu	**Hāmisù**	**Hāmisō**	read	**kařàntā**	**kařantō**
cooked	**dàfaffē**	**dafaffō**	drumming	**kìɗe-kìɗe**	**kiɗe-kiɗō**
in a mess	**kaca-kaca**	**kaca-kacō**	three	**ukù**	**ukō**
tomorrow	**gòbe**	**gōbō**	she	**ita**	**itō**

2.2. Compounds and phrases

With compounds, the high tone spreads from right to left over the entire word (whether written as one word or not), e.g.,

crockery	**fàɗi-kà-mutù**	**fāɗi-ka-mutō**
pimple	**bàř-ni-dà mūgù**	**bař-ni-da-mūgō**
peanut oil	**mân gyàɗā**	**man gyaɗō**

Short phrases are treated as compounds. With longer phrases, there is variation as to how far to the left the H tone will spread, e.g.,

Come! (lit. come you)	**yā kà**	**yā kō**
sixteen	**shâ shidà**	**shā shidō**
nineteen (lit. 20 1 there is not)	**àshìřin ɗaya bābù**	**àshìřin ɗaya bābō**
United Nations	**màjàlisàř ɗinkìn dūniyà**	**màjàlisàř ɗinkin dūniyō**

2.3. Consonant-final words

Consonant-final words (nasals excepted, see below) add -ō)^H to the stem, e.g.,

carrots	**kařàs**	**kařasō**	cricket (the sport)	**kuřkèt**	**kuřketō**
pencil	**fensìř**	**fensiřō**	Wudil	**Wùdil**	**Wudilō**

Stems ending in diphthongs replace the diphthong by -ō, I.e., the diphthongs are treated as complex vocalic nuclei rather than as vowel plus glide (VC) sequences, e.g.,

pennies	**kwàbbai**	**kwabbō** (*not* ****kwabbayō**)
Larai (fem. name)	**Lāřai**	**Lāřō**
Gusau (place name)	**Gùsau**	**Gusō**
patience	**jìmrau**	**jimrō**

2.4. Nasal-final words

With most words ending in a nasal (excluding monosyllabic words), the final -VN is treated not as a vowel plus consonant sequence to which -ō is added but rather as a vocalic "nasal diphthong" (see §54:2.1.1), which is thus replaced by -ō, e.g.,

chinaware	**tangaran**	**tangarō** (*not* ****tangaranō**)
envelope	**ambùlàn**	**ambulō**
fifty	**hàmsin**	**hamsō**
resident	**řazdàn**	**řazdō**
jet black	**baƙī ƙirin**	**baƙī ƙirō**

There is variation in the treatment of final -V**m**. Some speakers treat it as a nasal diphthong like -V**n**. (In SH the contrast between final /**m**/ and /**n**/ is usually neutralized, both nasals being pronounced as [ŋ].) Other speakers accord /**m**/ a stronger status than /**n**/ and treat it as a regular consonant to which -ō is added, e.g.,

Ringim (place name)	**Ringìm**	**Ringō** = **Ringimō**
Damagaram (place name)	**Dàmagàr̃am**	**Damagar̃ō** = **Damagar̃amō**

Nasal-final words with a "latent final vowel" retain the final nasal (whether /**m**/ or /**n**/), as do some recent loanwords, e.g.,

man	**mùtûm** (< **mùtumî**)	**mutumō**		Japan	**Jàpân**	**Japanō**
grape	**zàbûn** (< **zàbūnî**)	**zabūnō**		chewing gum	**cìngâm**	**cingamō**
teacher	**mālàm** (< **mālàmī**)	**mālamō**				

2.5. Monosyllabic words

The output of the contempt formation rule must have at least two syllables. With monosyllabic stems of the form CVC, the addition of -ō results naturally in the requisite shape.

bomb	**bâm**	**bamō**		cake	**kyât**	**kyatō**
course	**kwâs**	**kwasō**		ton	**tôn**	**tonō**

With vowel-final monosyllabic stems, the suffix -ō also attaches to the stem rather than replacing the final vowel, as is done with longer stems. An epenthetic glide (/**y**/ after a front vowel, /**w**/ elsewhere) provides a transition between the stem vowel and the suffix , e.g.,

drink	**shā**	**shāwō**		love (noun)	**sô**	**sōwō**
us	**mū**	**muwō**		eat	**ci**	**ciyō**
you (f.)	**kē**	**keyō**		oil	**mâi**	**mayō**
foot(print)	**sau**	**sawō**				

°AN: [i] As a general phonological rule, /**u**/ before /**w**/ is automatically short, thus the vowel length alternation seen in **mū** / **muwō**. Presumably a similar process accounts for the alternation in **kē** / **keyō**, although medial short /**e**/ is extremely rare in Hausa.
[ii] Etymologically, **sau** is an apocopated form of the word **sāwū**. The initial short vowel in **sawō** shows that the contempt form is based on the synchronically occurring variant **sau** and not on the disyllabic form **sāwū**.

2.6. Palatal(ized) consonants

The behavior of palatal(ized) consonants when the -ō replaces a front vowel exhibits peculiarities. If the final consonant is /**sh**/ or /**j**/, one regularly undoes the palatalization and recovers the corresponding /**s**/ or /**z**/, e.g.,

spear	**māshì**	**māsō**		countries	**ƙasàshē**	**ƙasāsō**
spice	**yājì**	**yāzō**		chest	**ƙìrjī**	**ƙirzō**

The treatment of final /**c**/ before -ō shows variation. A common pattern is to keep the /**c**/ in its palatal form with simple stems but to depalatalize /**c**/ to /**t**/ in inflected or derived forms, e.g.,

nose	**hancì**	**hancō**	Bici	**Bicì**	**Bicō**
food	**àbinci**	**abincō**	cars	**mōtōcì**	**mōtōtō**
stolen	**sàtaccē**	**sātattō**	Sokoto man	**bàsakkwacè**	**basakkwatō**

Depalatalization of /j/ to an etymological /d/ is not liked. Preferred is to keep the /j/ or even to depalatalize it to /z/! Examples:

houses	**gidàjē** (< **gidā** sg.)	**gidājō** = ??**gidādō** = **gidāzō**
a runaway	**gùdajjē** (< **gudù** run)	**gudajjō** = ??**gudaddō** = **gudazzō**

°AN: Although both /z/ and /d/ palatalize to /j/, the "natural" pairing in the language, as indicated here, is **z / j**.

Before a front vowel, the glide /w/ palatalizes to /y/, e.g., **hawā** 'riding', **mahàyī** 'rider'. However, /y/ before -ō never reverts back to /w/, e.g.,

slaves	**bāyī** (< **bāwà** sg.)	**bāyō** (*not* ****bāwō**)
markets	**kāsuwōyī** (< **kàsuwā** sg.)	**kāsuwōyō** (*not* ****kāsuwōwō**)

2.7. Prepausal glottal stop

This -ō suffix has an interesting phonetic property that it shares with the homophonous grade 6 ventive suffix, e.g., **kōmō** 'return here', namely, the addition of a phonetic glottal closure in prepausal position (see §54:1.2.2). As indicated earlier, in normal usage the contempt form is usually followed by **matà**, in which case it appears clearly with a long final vowel -ō. When, however, it is used by itself, and thus occurs sentence finally, it adds a glottal closure and appears as half-long [o·?], e.g.,

		Non-pre-pausal	Pre-pausal
paper	**takàrdā**	**takafdō matà**	[takafdo·?]
gowns	**rīgunà**	**rīgunō matà**	[rīguno·?]
hare	**zōmō**	**zōmō matà**	[zōmo·?]

[Reference: Newman (1988)]

28. Focus

1. INTRODUCTION

FOCUS involves the fronting of an NP, adverb, or prepositional phrase, in order to emphasize it or to contrast it with some other comparable constituent (which has the potential of being overtly expressed). The focus slot is a distinct syntactic position located at the beginning of the sentence, i.e., S′ → {Focus} S (where S consists of the normal NP VP etc.). This is illustrated in the following tree diagrams (fig. 1):

Figure 1: Focus structure

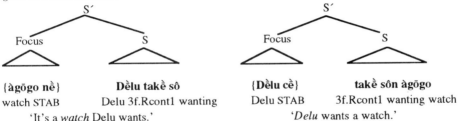

{àgōgo nè}	Dèlu takè sô	{Dèlu cè}	takè sôn àgōgo
watch STAB	Delu 3f.Rcont1 wanting	Delu STAB	3f.Rcont1 wanting watch
'It's a *watch* Delu wants.'		'*Delu* wants a watch.'	

Sentences with focus generally correspond to and translate as English cleft sentences, e.g.,

{Mūsā nè} ta àurā	It was *Musa* she married (not someone else).
{Kànde cè} ta ci jaȓȓàbâwā	*Kande* passed the exam (not someone else).
{Mutånen nàn} mukà gayà wà	It was these *men* we told it to.
{ƙwai} yârā sukè sàyē (bà gōȓò ba)	It's *eggs* the children are buying (not kolanuts).
{ɓēȓā nè} ya shìga kwabàd (bà jāɓā ba)	

      It was a *rat* that got in the cupboard (not a shrew-mouse).

bà Tàlātù ta zàgē shì ba (sai dai Zàinabù)

      It wasn't *Talatu* who insulted him (but rather Zainabu).

Focus shares a number of features with topicalization (see chap. **72**); but they are syntactically and semantically distinct categories, e.g., {**Hàdīzà cè**} **ta ci lambà** 'It was *Hadiza* who won the prize' (focus), cf. «**Hàdīzà kàm**», **tā ci lambà** 'As for Hadiza, she won the prize' (topicalization). Unlike topics, which have to be in absolute sentence-initial position, the requirement on focused elements is only that they occur at the front of *their* S, which need not be at the very beginning of the whole sentence. For examples, focus is allowed internally in a sentence following a subordinate clause or phrase, or in a sentence embedded in a relative clause, e.g.,

tsàkānin yâran nàn, {Sulè nē} ya fi ƙarfī
    Between these boys, it's *Sule* who is the strongest.

in kā yàr̃da, {baƙī nè̀} zân bā sù
    If you agree, it's the *black* one I'll give them.

màimakon sù ràgu, {ƙàruwā} sukà yi
    Instead of decreasing, they *increased*. (lit. increasing they did)

Fù'âd dîn wândà {shī nè̀} ya yi barcī cikin ɗākìn
    the *Fu'ad* who slept in the room (lit. Fu'ad the who {he is}he did sleeping in room.the)

màtâr̃ dà {ita cè̀} ya kàmātà tà biya hàr̃ājī à bana
    the woman who *she* is the one who ought to pay taxes this year

màlàmân waɗàndà {sū nè̀} zā mù zàɓā
    the teachers whom *they* are the ones we will choose

A sentence can contain more than one topicalized element, e.g., «Audù fa», «hùlā kàm», yā sàyā 'As for Audu, regarding the cap, he bought it.' This is not, however, possible with focus because the purpose of focus is to highlight one constituent, usually in a contrastive manner. Thus, a sentence like **{Audù nē}, {hùlā cè̀}, ya sàyā 'It is *Audu*, it's a *cap* he bought' is ungrammatical. There is no problem, however, in combining topicalization and focus, e.g.,

«Audù fa», {hùlā cè̀} ya sàyā
    As for Audu, it's a *cap* he bought.

«hùlā kàm», {Audù nē} ya sàyā
    As for the cap, it was *Audu* who bought it.

2. FORM AND STRUCTURE

A focused element is placed in the focus slot immediately followed by the stabilizer (STAB), i.e., Focus → Z + STAB (where Z is any constituent). This STAB, which has the form nē/cē/nē (m./f./pl.) with polar tone, can be optionally deleted. (Examples will generally be given with or without the STAB as found in my own notes or in other sources. Sentences collected both with and without the STAB will be indicated with the (STAB) in parentheses.) An essential characteristic of focus is the requirement that the TAM in the sentence that follows be a Rel form, e.g.,

{bāyan bishiyà̀} [yakè]$_{Rcont2}$
    It's behind the tree he is.

cf. [yanà̀]$_{cont}$ bāyan bishiyà̀
    He is behind the tree.

{Audù (nē)} [ya]$_{pret}$ tàfi kàsuwā
    It is Audu who went to the market.

cf. Audù [yā]$_{comp}$ tàfi kàsuwā
    Audu has gone to the market.

{sabò̀dà tsananin zāfī (nè̀)}[sukè]$_{Rcont1}$ sàyen fankà̀
    It's because of the terrible heat they are buying fans.

cf. [sunà̀]$_{cont}$ sàyen fankà̀ sabò̀dà tsananin zāfī
    They are buying fans because of the terrible heat.

°AN: It is not clear in the least what accounts for the presence or absence of the STAB in focus constructions nor what is its actual frequency of occurrence. My impression is that the STAB is more likely to appear if the focused element is a simple noun subject or object, e.g., **Bellò nē ya iyà** 'It's Bello who can do it' and less likely to appear if the focused element is an adverbial like a stative, e.g., **à zàune mukè** 'It's seated we were.' This question calls for a careful grammatical and textual study.

Question words are by nature focused and typically appear fronted in focus position, e.g.,

{mènē nè̀} yāròn ya sāmù?
    What did the boy get?

{yàushè} zā kà dāwō?

{kudī nawà} akà bā tà

When will you come back?

How much money did they give her?

With all constituents except the subject, the movement of the focused element to the beginning of the sentence is obvious. With subjects, the movement is not immediately evident, because on the surface the NP appears to be in the same position, but with the STAB added. Nevertheless, even with subjects it is important to recognize that movement into the focus position has taken place, e.g., {Focus} [**Audù**]subj **yā tàfī kàsuwā** ⇒ {**Audù nē**} [Ø]subj **ya tàfī kàsuwā** 'It is Audu who went to the market.' Compare the following tree diagrams (fig. 2). (Note: PAC is the inflectional person-aspect-complex.)

Figure 2: Focus movement

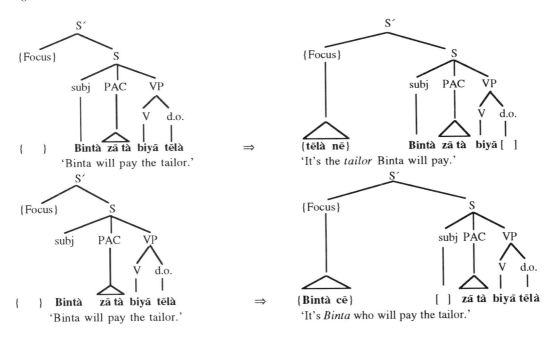

Unlike the case with topicalization, where constituents that are coreferential with the topic are usually pronominalized, with focus, deletion is the norm, with the exception of focused genitives and indirect objects, which allow pronominalization as an alternative. Examples:

{ɓàrāwòn nan nē} sukà ganī Ø à kàntī

cf. «ɓàrāwòn nan», sun gan shì à kàntī

{Lawàl nē} mukè ta kirà

cf. «Lawàl kùwa», munà ta kirànsà

{rìgā cè} zân sàyā

{mōtàtā cè} ya gōgà wà mâi

{ita cè} na gayà wà Ø (= matà) làbārì

     It was her I told the news to.

{Bàrau nè} ya kàmātà Asshà tà kai wà Ø (= masà) àbincîn

     It is Barau who it is fitting that Assha should take the food to him.

It was that thief they saw at the store.

As for that thief, they saw him at the store.

It's Lawal we're calling.

As for Lawal, we have been calling him.

It's a gown I'm going to buy.

It was my car he rubbed polish on.

As a general rule of the language, underlying subject pronouns that are identical to the weak subject pronoun (wsp) in the PAC are obligatorily deleted. They can, however, be focused, in which case they appear on the surface as independent pronouns in focus position, e.g.,

[3f]_{subj} tā dāwō jiyà ⇒ [Ø]_{subj} tā dāwō jiyà   She returned yesterday.
{ } [3f]_{subj} tā dāwō jiyà ⇒ {ita cè} [Ø]_{subj} ta dāwō jiyà
       She was the one who returned yesterday. (focus)
[1p]_{subj} munà nēman aikì ⇒ [Ø]_{subj} munà nēman aikì   We are looking for work.
{ } [1p]_{subj} munà nēman aikì ⇒ {mū nè} [Ø]_{subj} mukè nēman aikì
       We are looking for work. (focus)

In the continuous TAMs, one commonly gets surface sentences with a dynamic noun immediately following the PAC, e.g., tanà màganà 'She is talking', where màganà is a dynamic noun, not a verb. Such sentences are presumed to be derived from sentences containing the pro-verb yi 'do' (in its verbal noun form), e.g., tanà yîn màganà (lit. she is doing talking). These sentences are deemed grammatical, but actually are rarely used in practice. If, however, the object dynamic noun is focused, yî occurs commonly and naturally, e.g.,

màganà takè (yî)   It's talking that she is doing.
wàsā dà macìjī yakè (yî)   It's playing with a snake that he is doing.
kallon TV sukè (yî)   It's watching television that they are doing.

2.1. Focus with sai

Focused items are commonly preceded by the particle **sai** 'just, except, only, etc.'. (In Quirk et al. (1985: 604), such adverbial particles are termed *focusing subjuncts*.) The STAB is typically omitted. The clause following focused **sai** + X is generally in the affirmative, but semantically it tends to contrast with an implied/presupposed negative proposition. Examples:

sai kuɗī mukè sô   It is only money we want.
cf. bā mà sôn kōmē sai kuɗī   We don't want anything except money.
sai gwànī (nē) ya iyà yînsà   It is only an expert who could do it.
cf. bâ wândà ya iyà yînsà sai gwànī   There is no one who could do it except an expert.
sai ƙarfè ukù zân tāshì   It's not until three o'clock that I'm going to leave.
sai ƙàrà hàɓakà sukè (yî)   It was continual expansion that was happening.

Similarly, focused elements that are modified by a delimiter or by an intensifying adverb or ideophone usually occur without the STAB, e.g.,

Audù kaɗai ya ci jařřàbâwâr   Audu alone passed the exam.
fâm ɗaya tak akà bā nì   It was one pound only that I was given.
kàřùwai bìřjik sukà kūtsà cikin ɗākìn   A bevy of prostitutes barged into the room.
(lit. prostitutes in abundance...)

2.2. Equational sentences

Equational sentences (see chap. **23**) have the basic structure X Y STAB, where the STAB functions as a stabilizing/copular element rather than as a focus marker, e.g., [shī]_X [mālàmī]_Y [nè]_{STAB} 'He is a teacher.' If one focuses the X, one gets a sentence like shī nè mālàmī 'He is a teacher', which is normally thought of as having the structure X STAB Y, with the STAB having been moved immediately after the X. An alternative analysis, which is more consistent with the treatment adopted for verbal sentences, is to move the subject NP from the X slot into the focus position where it is marked by an obligatory STAB. In the presence of a STAB earlier in the sentence, the sentence-final equational STAB is then dropped. This is illustrated in fig. 3 and in the following examples.

Figure 3: Focus in equational sentences

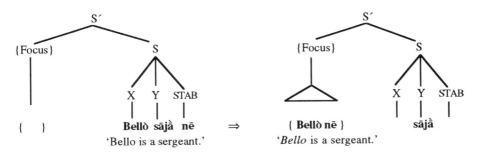

{ } [shī]$_X$ [mālàmī]$_Y$ [nè]$_{STAB}$ ⇒ {shī nè} [Ø]$_X$ [mālàmī]$_Y$ [Ø]$_{STAB}$ ⇒ **shī nè mālàmī**
    He is a teacher.

{ } [Bintà]$_X$ [ƙawàr̃tà]$_Y$ [cē]$_{STAB}$ ⇒ {Bintà cē} [Ø]$_X$ [ƙawàr̃tà]$_Y$ [Ø]$_{STAB}$ ⇒ **Bintà cē ƙawàr̃tà**
    It is *Binta* who is her friend.

This analysis of moving the focused item into the focus slot (with the STAB) and deleting the equational STAB works well in cases where it is the Y that is focused. (In the second examples, one also has topicalization.) Examples:

{ } [shī]$_X$ [mālàmī]$_Y$ [nè]$_{STAB}$ ⇒ {mālàmī nè} [shī]$_X$ [Ø]$_Y$ [Ø]$_{STAB}$ ⇒ **mālàmī nè shī**
    It's a *teacher* he is.

«Madonna», { } [ita]$_X$ [tàurār̃ùwā]$_Y$ [cè]$_{STAB}$ ⇒ «Madonna», {tàurār̃ùwā cè} [ita]$_X$ [Ø]$_Y$ [Ø]$_{STAB}$
    ⇒ **Madonna, tàurār̃ùwā cè ita**   As for Madonna, a *star* she is.

3. FOCUS FROM LOWER CLAUSE

As is the case with relativization and topicalization, a focused item does not have to be in the matrix sentences, but rather can be pulled out of a lower clause. Note that focus affects immediately following TAMs and not ones that occur later in the sentence, e.g

{**Jummai cè**} [mukè]$_{Rcont1}$ **tsàmmānì Mūsā** [yanà]$_{cont}$ **sô Ø**
    It's Jummai we think that Musa loves.

{**àbincin rāna nè**} [ya]$_{pret}$ **kàmātà Asshà tà kai wà mijìntà Ø**
    It is lunch that it is desirable for Assha to take to her husband.

{**màgên cē**} **Audù** [ya]$_{pret}$ **ƙaryàtà fàɗar̃ cêwā Ø tā kāmà ɓēr̃ā**
    It was the cat that Audu denied saying that it caught the rat.

{**wāyar̃ musù dà kâi**} **gwamnatì** [takè]$_{Rcont1}$ **sô tà yi Ø**
    It's enlightening them that the government wants to do.

{**àlhàzai nè**} [ya]$_{pret}$ **fi kyâu Ø sù tàfi dūtsèn Àr̃fā**
    It is the pilgrims that it is much better for them to go to Mount Arafat.

{sàraunìyā cè} [ya]_pret yìwu Maȓyàm tà zama Ø
    It is queen that is possible that Maryam might become.
{gà Bintà nē} [yakè]_Rcont2 dà muhimmancî mù bā dà kuɗîn Ø
    It is to Binta that it is important for us to give the money.

°AN: In the preceding example, note that the STAB **nē** agrees with the prepositional phrase (which is masculine) and not with the feminine proper noun **Bintà**.

4. ROLE OF THE FOCUSED ELEMENT

Essentially any thematic role in the sentence can undergo focus, i.e., subject, direct object, locative, prepositional phrase, etc. Selected examples:

{Bellò nē} yakè kàȓàtū	It's Bello who is reading.
{wànnē (nè) dàgà cikinsù} kukà zàɓā?	Which one among them did you choose?
{ìnā nè} ka gan shì? {à Kanò nē}	Where did you see him? At Kano.
{dàgà Kanò} nē sukà tāsō	It was from Kano they started.
{à zàune nè} mukè	Seated we were.
{gyàɗā cè} àkwai	Peanuts there are.
{maza-maza} nè sukà gamà aikìn	Very quickly they finished the work.
{à cikin nàtsuwā} nè ya shìga rījìyâȓ	It was very carefully that he entered the well.
{jiyà} nē sukà zō	It was yesterday that they came.
cf. jiyà sun zō (= sun zō jiyà)	Yesterday they came. (= They came yesterday.)

(with the optionally fronted, but nonfocused, temporal adverb)

Underlying prepositional phrases permit focus of the full pp itself (which is masculine) or the object of the preposition. In the latter case, one either has to insert a resumptive pronoun or, with genitive prepositions, one has to replace the preposition by a related adverb, e.g.,

(a) dà wuƙā (nè) ya sòkē shì	It was with a knife that he stabbed him.
cf. wuƙā (cè) ya sòkē shì dà ita	It was a knife he stabbed him with. (lit. …with it)
gà sàbàbbin-shìgā (nè) ya bā dà laccà	It was to the recruits that he gave the lecture.
sàbàbbin-shìgā (nè) ya bā dà laccà gàrē sù	It was the recruits he gave the lecture to.
(b) cikin kwālîn (nē) mukè sâ yādì	It is in the carton that we are put the cloth.
cf. kwālîn (nē) mukè sâ yādì à cikinsà = kwālîn (nē) mukè sâ yādì à ciki	
It is the carton that we are put the cloth in(side).	
gàban àlƙālī (nè) ya durƙùsā	It was before the judge he kneeled.
cf. àlƙālī (nè) ya durƙùsā gàbansà = ??àlƙālī (nè) ya durƙùsā à gàba	
It was the judge he knelt before.	

Phrases formed with the viative preposition **ta**, on the other hand, have to be focused in their entirety, i.e., it is not possible to focus the object alone. Examples:

ta ƙōfàȓ kudù sukà shìga	It was via the south gate that they entered.
cf. sun shìga ta ƙōfàȓ kudù	They entered via the south gate.
ta wata dàbāȓà dàbam zā mù cī sù	It by a different stratagem that we will defeat them.
cf. zā mù cī sù ta wata dàbāȓà dàbam	We will defeat them by means of a different stratagem.

The indirect object phrase in Hausa, which consists of **ma** plus a personal pronoun or **wà** plus anything else (including zero), does not constitute a prepositional phrase and cannot be focused as such. Rather one can only focus the indirect object NP leaving the i.o. marker in its original position. Use of a resumptive pronoun in place of the focused NP is sometimes possible, but stranding of the i.o. marker is the norm. Examples:

Hàlīmà (cē) na sayō wà Ø zōbè
not ****wà Hàlīmà na sayō zōbè**
nī nè sukà dafà wà Ø àbinci
cf. **sun dafà minì àbinci**

It was *Halima* I bought a ring for.

It was *me* they cooked the food for.
They cooked me the food.

°AN: By contrast, phrases with **gàrē** + pn / **gà** + NP *are* prepositional phrases, even though they semantically may represent indirect objects, and thus they can be focused in their entirety, e.g., **Bàlā nè sukà faɗà wà làbārì** 'It was Bala they told the news to' (< **sun faɗà wà Bàlā làbārì** 'They told Bala the news') vs. **gà Bàlā sukà fàɗi wannàn mùmmūnan làbārì** 'It was to Bala they told this terrible story' = **Bàlā sukà fàɗi wannàn mùmmūnan làbārì gàrē shì** 'It was Bala they told this terrible story to (him)' (< **sun fàɗi wannàn mùmmūnan làbārì gà Bàlā** 'They told this terrible story to Bala').

Finite verbs and verb phrases cannot be focused as such. Instead, one has to focus the corresponding verbal noun (phrase) or infinitive phrase, leaving the pro-verb **yi** 'do' (or its corresponding verbal noun **yî**, which can optionally be deleted) in the original position. Examples:

(a) **biyàn hàrājìn (nē) Tankò ya yi**
cf. **Tankò yā biyā hàrājìn**
tàimakon jūnā zā mù yi
cf. **zā mù tàimàki jūnā**
bàzamà sukà yi
cf. **sun bàzamà**
càncantà ya yi mù zìyàrci maràsā lāfiyà
cf. **yā càncantà mù zìyàrci maràsā lāfiyà**
ajìyař kuɗī nè ya kàmātà Sulè yà yi à bankì
    It is *depositing money* that it is right for Sule to do in the bank.
cf. **yā kàmātà Sulè yà ajìyè kuɗī à bankì**
    It is right for Sule to deposit money in the bank.

It is *paying the taxes* that Tanko did.
Tanko paid the taxes.
It is *helping one another* that we are going to do.
We are going to help one another.
They *bolted away*.
They bolted away.
It is *desirable* that we visit sick people.
It is desirable that we visit sick people.

In the following examples, the focused phrase translates best into English as a participial/gerundive form, but in Hausa it has the structure of an infinitive phrase.

faɗà manà gaskiyā takè (yî)
(lit. tell to.us truth she.Rcont1 (doing))
cf. **tanà faɗà manà gaskiyā**
ɗaurè ɓàrāwò (nē) sukà yi
(lit. tie thief (STAB) they.pret do)
cf. **sun ɗaurè ɓàrāwò**
shārè ɗākìn takè (yî)
(lit. sweep room.the she.Rcont1 (doing))
cf. **tanà shārè ɗākìn**

It was *telling us the truth* she was doing.

She was telling us the truth.
It was *jailing the thief* they did.

They jailed the thief.
It is *sweeping the room* that she is doing.

She is sweeping the room.

ginà masallācī (nè) sukè sô sù yi	It is *building a mosque* that they want to do.
cf. sunà sô sù ginà masallācī	They want to build a mosque.
rūsà gidân nē tīlàs Lawàn yà yi	It is *demolishing the house* that Lawan must do.
cf. tīlàs nē Lawàn yà rūsà gidân	It is necessary that Lawan demolish the house.
karàntà Kùr'ānì yârā sukè	It is *reading the Koran* that the children are doing.
cf. yârā sunà karàntà Kùr'ānì	The children are reading the Koran.

°AN: Tuller (1989) suggests that the use of the resumptive pro-verb **yi** is optional in the continuous. I would prefer to say that **yi** (or its verbal noun) is syntactically required in this structure but that in the continuous it can optionally be deleted in accordance with a more generally applicable deletion rule (see §58:3). Thus an example like **karàntà Kùr'ānì yârā sukè** 'It is *reading the Koran* that the children are doing' would be understood to be derived from **karàntà Kùr'ānì yârā sukè yî**.

Instead of focusing an entire VP as such, one can focus the verb alone, which is replaced by a corresponding verbal noun. The underlying direct object is then demoted to indirect object.

gyārā nè ya yi wà mōtà	It was repairing he did to the car.
cf. yā gyārà mōtà	He repaired the car.
zāgì nē ta yi wà mijìntà	It was insulting she did to her husband.
cf. tā zàgi mijìntà	She insulted her husband.

5. NEGATION AND FOCUS

It is very common to combine negation and focus. There are two means of doing this. The first means, which I think is the more common, although the matter needs to be investigated, is to negate the entire sentence that includes the focused constituent. This involves putting the entire sentence within the scope of the discontinuous negative **bà...ba**. Examples:

bà Audù (nē) ya tàfi kàsuwā ba	It is not Audu who went to the market.
bà Lawàn (nē) Mūsā ya faɗà wà màganà ba	It is not Lawan that Musa told something to.
bà makarantā cè zâ ta ba	It's not school she's going to.
bà sòsai takè ganī ba	It is not clearly that she sees.
bà dà sāfe Tankò ya tàfi kàsuwā ba	It is not in the morning that Tanko went to the market.
bà à zàune zā kà karàntà wākàr ba	It is not in a sitting posture that you will read the song.

The second alternative is to negate the focused element directly by enclosing it in **bà...ba**. If this is done, the stab is strongly preferred. Examples:

bà Audù ba nè ya tàfi kàsuwā	It is not Audu who went to the market.
bà Lawàn ba nè Mūsā ya faɗà wà màganà	It is not Lawan that Musa told something to.
bà sòsai ba takè ganī	It is not clearly that she sees.
bà dòmin shī gwànī nè ba mukà bā shì hēlùmà	
It is not because he is an expert that we made him headman.	

6. PSEUDO-CLEFT SENTENCES

The normal focus formation, namely, X + STAB, can be thought of as a cleft construction, e.g., **àlāwà cē nakè sô** 'It's halvah I like.' The corresponding pseudo-cleft sentence has a normal, nonfocused equational structure, e.g., [abîn dà nakè sô]ₓ [àlāwà]ᵧ cē 'The thing that I like is halvah.' In pseudo-cleft sentences the subject X is typically a relative clause headed by **abîn dà** 'what' (lit. the thing that) or **wândà/wâddà/waɗàndà** 'who' (m./f./pl.). Examples:

[àbîn dà sukà kāwō] nāmàn ràgō nè	[The thing that they brought] is mutton.
[wândà ya ci zàɓēn] Mūsā nè	[The one who won the election] is Musa.

Pseudo-cleft sentences can be and are often focused. This is accomplished by use of an independent pronoun following the relative formation accompanied by the STAB, e.g.,

àbîn dà nakè sô [shī nè] sābon gidā	*What I want* [it is] a new house.
wândà ya ci zàɓē [shī nè] Mūsā	*The one who won the election* [he is] Musa.
waɗàndà sukà tàimàkē mù [sū nè] bàƙī	*The ones who helped us* [they were] strangers.
àbîn dà ya càncantà [shī nè] Dèlu tà yi aurē	*What is proper* [it is] that Delu should get married.
àbîn dà ya dācè [shī nè] yârân sù kōmà gidā	

    What is appropriate [it is] that the children return home.

[References: Junaidu (1987); McConvell (1973)]

29. Frequentatives

1. FORM

THE term *frequentative* is used for pseudoplural deverbal nouns that have the fully reduplicated structure Base + -e)^{LH} x 2, i.e., a lexical base (usually deverbal) plus a short final /e/ with an associated L-H tone pattern, all of which is fully reduplicated. Monosyllabic CV words insert an epenthetic glide /y/ before the suffixal vowel, e.g.,

gyàre-gyàre	corrections (e.g., on written work) < **gyārà** repair
tàmbàye-tàmbàye	repeated questioning < **tàmbayà** ask
sàssàɓe-sàssàɓe	repeated carving < **sàssaɓà** carve
gàishe-gàishe	greetings < **gaisà** greet
cf. **gàisuwā**	greeting (with the feminative ending)
shìrye-shìrye	repeated preparations, radio/TV programs < **shiryà** prepare
cf. **shirì**	preparation (without the **-yà** verbal suffix)
sòke-sòke	criticisms, criticizing < **sòkā** pierce, criticize
cf. **sūkà**	piercing, criticism
cìye-cìye	constant eating < **ci** eat
shàye-shàye	drinks, repeated drinking < **shā** drink

> °AN/◊HN: If one ignores the reduplication, statives (see §67:1), such as **rùfe** 'closed', **sàssàɓe** 'carved', and **zàune** 'seated', have the same canonical shape as frequentatives, i.e., short final **-e** and L-H tone. This formal identity notwithstanding, I have doubts on functional and semantic grounds whether the two classes are derivationally related synchronically. Whether they have a *historical* connection to one another and/or to L-H verbal nouns ending in -ē is an open question.

With few exceptions, the frequentative is built on a verbal base. In cases where the frequentative is derived from a lexical noun, it is formed morphologically on a base containing the verbalizer **-TA**, whether the verb actually occurs or not, e.g.,

gùlmàce-gùlmàce	backbiting/badmouthing (< verbal base //**gulmat-**//), cf. **gulma** mischief
wàhàlce-wàhàlce	troubles, difficulties (< verbal base //**wahalt-**//), cf. **wàhalà** trouble
zàmbàce-zàmbàce	frauds (< verbal base //**zambat-**//), cf. **zàmba** swindling, deceit

Some nouns that presumably were verbal nouns in origin but that synchronically lack the corresponding verb build frequentatives directly on the base without use of the verbalizer, e.g.,

tàɗe-tàɗe	conversations, continual chatting < **tāɗì** conversation (in origin probably an H-L ì-final verbal noun from a now nonexistent verb)

gǔɗe-gǔɗe   repeated ululation < **gūɗà** ululation (in origin probably an H-L ā-final verbal noun from a now nonexistent verb)

Apart from the erstwhile verbal nouns, a few simple common nouns (including some loanwords) also allow the direct formation of the frequentative on a nominal base, e.g.,

àshàr̃e-àshàr̃e   repeated obscenities < **àshâr̃** obscene or abusive language (< Ar.)
màfar̃ke-màfar̃ke   dreams < **mafar̃kī** dream
tàr̃ìhe-tàr̃ìhe   histories < **tār̃īhì** history (< Ar.)

2. FUNCTION

One can distinguish two groups of frequentatives in terms of their syntactic function: (1) plurals of common nouns (including deverbal nouns), and (2) repeated action verbal nouns. Semantically the connection between the two is clear.

2.1. *Plurals of common nouns*
A small number of deverbal nouns, including those that now denote things rather than actions, form their plurals by means of the frequentative. This formation is used also as a plural of some nouns that are not verb derived. Examples:

camfì / càmfe-càmfe	superstition(s)	**canjì / cànje-cànje**	change(s)
cīwò / cìwàce-cìwàce	illness(es)	**dàbār̃à / dàbàr̃ce-dàbàr̃ce**	trick(s), plan(s)
shūkà / shùke-shùke	plant(s)	**sūkà / sòke-sòke**	criticism(s)
tàfìyà / tàfìye-tàfìye	journey(s)	**yāwò / yàwàce-yàwàce**	walk(s), stroll(s)
tàllà / tàllàce-tàllàce	hawking goods for sale, advertisement(s)		
wàhalà / wàhàlce-wàhàlce	trouble(s) (cf. alternative plurals **wahalōlī** and **wàhàlhàlū**)		

Being nominal plurals, these frequentatives take regular plural concord, e.g.,

wàhàlce-wàhàlce [màsu]$_{pl}$ yawà   many troubles
[bùsàssun]$_{pl}$ shùke-shùke   dried plants
tàllàce-tàllàcen gidan r̃ēdiyò [sun]$_{pl}$ fi shìgā jìkī   Radio advertisements are more effective.
(lit. advertisements.of house.of radio they exceed entering body)

2.2. *Repeated action verbal nouns*
Most frequentative nouns function as dynamic nouns indicating repeated actions, e.g.,

bùshe-bùshe   blowing (making music) < **būsà** blow
tàɓe-tàɓe   repeated pilfering, handling < **taɓà** touch
jèfe-jèfe   throwing < **jèfā** throw at
kàɗe-kàɗe   drummings < **kaɗà** beat (drum)
sàssàƙe-sàssàƙe   repeated carving < **sassàƙā** carve

These frequentatives occur in the same nonfinite environments as nonverbal dynamic nouns like **màganà** 'talking, conversation' or **barcī** 'sleep(ing)', i.e., after continuous TAMs, aspectual verbs, or the pro-verb **yi** 'do', e.g.,

yanǎ gùje-gùje dà tsàlle-tsàlle	He was running and jumping.
(also means 'He is a track and field athlete.')	
sunǎ kàɗe-kàɗe dà bùshe-bùshe	They are making music (lit. drummings and blowings).
(also means 'They are musicians.')	
yā sākè yàwàce-yàwàce	He again went wandering about.
cf. tā sākè màganǎ	She talked again. (lit. she.comp repeat talking)

A frequentative can be followed by a thematic object in a genitive-type linking construction, e.g.,

munǎ jèfe-jèfen duwàtsū	We were continually throwing stones (or stone-throwing).
yā riƙà sàssàƙe-sàssàƙen gumàkā	He kept on carving idols.
sunǎ ta tìƙe-tìƙen jūnā	They are hitting each other with fists.
yā fayè nème-nèmen mātā	He goes overboard chasing women (i.e., womanizing).

Sentences like the above are structurally different, however, from sentences with syntactic verbs or verbal nouns followed by direct objects. Sentences with real objects, for example, allow the object to be fronted or questioned, whereas this is not possible with the complement of the frequentative, e.g.,

a. sunǎ [kařkàɗà]$_V$ gangunǎ	They are beating drums.
More or less = a′ sunǎ kàɗe-kàɗen gangunǎ	
b. mè sukè kařkàɗâwā?	What are they beating?
but *not* b′ **mè sukè kàɗe-kàɗe?	
a. mātā sunǎ daddàfà àbinci	The women are cooking up a lot of food.
More or less = a′ mātā sunǎ dàfe-dàfen àbinci	
b. àbinci mātā sukè daddàfâwā	It is food that the women are cooking up.
but *not* b′ **àbinci mātā sukè dàfe-dàfe	

The dynamic frequentative nouns may be syntactically plural if they are treated as count nouns indicating multiple actions, but they can also be masculine singular if the focus is on the ongoing action as a whole, e.g.,

gùlmàce-gùlmàcenkù yā/sun yi yawà	Your backbiting/badmouthings was/were too much.
dàbàřce-dàbàřcensà bâ [shi]$_{sg}$ dà kyâu	His continual scheming is not good.
dàbàřce-dàbàřcensà bâ [su]$_{pl}$ dà kyâu	His schemes are not good.
kàɗe-kàɗen nàn [yanǎ]$_{sg}$ dāmùnā	This continual drumming is bothering me.
kàɗe-kàɗen mawàƙan nàn [sun]$_{pl}$ bàmbantà	

The drummings (rhythms) of these musicians were different (from one another).

30. Games and Activities (Nominal Derivation)

MANY names of games contain a tone-integrating suffix -e)[H] that is added to verbal roots, e.g. sunà wàsan ƙwāce 'They are playing snatching', cf. ƙwācè 'to grab, snatch'. These words, all of which are masculine, end in short -e and have an all H tone pattern. In a few cases, words with the requisite canonical shape exist without a corresponding verb. The derivation is not productive at the synchronic level although there is a good-sized list of such words (see Amfani 1984). Examples:

cake a game similar to darts < cakà stab; dambe boxing < ?; ɗalle a game with buttons < ɗallà strike with a finger; fashe egg-breaking game < fasà break/shatter; gare rolling a hoop or tire < garà roll a wheel, etc.; ƙirge game of counting < ƙirgà count; lale shuffling cards in a game < lālè shuffle cards; tsallake jumping game < tsallàkā jump/cross over; tsere racing < tsērè run away; zire a game of trickery < zirà lower sth into a hole, overcharge s.o.; zungure type of gambling < zungùrā poke
Irregular: carafke throwing and catching (pebbles) < càfkā catch in the air

In addition to games per se, which constitute a semantically coherent class, other miscellaneous (often antisocial) activities are also expressed using the same suffix, e.g.

dangwale	pretending to give sth to s.o. and then refusing	< dangwàlā dip into
gōge	deliberate contact with s.o. (esp. with a girl)	< gōgè rub
gwaje	measuring, testing	< gwadà test
jāgule	making a mess (esp. of food by children)	< jāgùlā spoil, mess up
kōre	setting up dupes for a con man	< kōrà drive (animals) in front
kwamɓale	making an ink blot (when writing with a fountain pen)	< kwamɓàlā splatter
ƙāƙale	being finicky	< ?
lālube	groping someone's body (or pockets by pickpockets)	< làlubà grope at
lēƙe	cheating by looking at s.o.'s work in a sneaky way	< lēƙà peek
wuřge	throwing things from one place to another	< wuřgà throw
yanke	a lie, lying	< yankà ƙaryā to lie (lit. cut a lie)

These activity forms can be contrasted with regular L-H verbal nouns ending in long -ē. Whereas the L-H verbal nouns preserve the general sense of the source verb, the derived activity forms typically have a specialized meaning. Compare the following:

(a) lèƙē	act of peeking (esp. by married women) (VN)	
(b) lēƙe	peeking at at someone's work in a sneaky way (derived noun)	
(a) làlùbē	act of groping (VN)	
(b) lālube	groping s.o.'s body or picking s.o.'s pocket (derived noun)	

199

31. Gender

GENDER in Hausa is a two-term system: masculine and feminine. It is operative only in the singular. There is no gender distinction in the plural, e.g.,

yārò m.	boy	yārinyà f.	girl	yârā pl.	children
farī m.	white	farā f.	white	faràrē pl.	white
tēbùr m.	table			tēburōrī pl.	tables
		tāgà f.	window	tāgōgī pl.	windows

°AN: The oft-repeated statements found in Hausa grammars going back over half a century that "plural nouns are always masculine" (Taylor 1923), or "all plurals are Masculine grammatically, no matter what the logical sex may be" (Abraham 1959b) are incorrect. There are a few morphemes, like the stabilizer nē/cē/nē (m./f./pl.) where the masculine and the plural markers are phonologically the same; but generally speaking masculine singular and gender-unmarked plural are grammatically distinct categories.

ΔDN: In most dialects of Hausa, gender is an essential, fully functioning part of the grammatical system. Some dialects of the south and southeast, however, such as Zaria and Bauchi, constitute an exception to this statement. Here one finds that grammatical gender has been lost to a great extent, being preserved inconsistently and in only some parts of the grammar, e.g., the pronouns. The loss of gender has progressed even further in dialects outside of Hausaland proper, such as Hausa spoken in Ghana.

Gender can be described from two points of view: the intrinsic gender of individual lexical items or classes of items, and concord phenomena (see chap. **32**).

1. INTRINSIC GENDER

All singular NPs have gender. Out of a list of just over 5,000 common nouns, some 3,000 are masculine, 2,000 are feminine, and approximately 75 are epicene (i.e., masculine or feminine depending on the sex of the referent).

°AN: These numbers are derived from a count of the first 8,000 lexemes entered in a Hausa dictionary database in progress, which includes all the words in Newman and Newman (1977) plus further additions. The numbers of course are crude because they depend among other things on how many derivative words are or are not given separate head entries; still, they give a rough indication of the percentage of masculine as opposed to feminine words in the language.

Nouns (or pronouns) denoting people or large animals that are biologically male have masculine gender. Similarly, nouns (or pronouns) denoting people or large animals that are biologically female have feminine gender. Examples:

Masculine: **mijì** husband; **angò** groom; **yārò** boy; **sauràyī** male youth; **sarkī** emir, king; **ùbā** father; **kāwù** uncle; **wâ** elder brother; **zākì** (male) lion; **ìngaȓmà** stallion; **bìjimī** large bull; **rāgō** ram; **bùnsurū** he-goat; **zàkarà** cock; **Mūsā** Musa (Moses); **Yūsufù** Yusufu (Joseph); **Hasàn** Hassan; **kai** you (m.); **shī** he

Feminine: **màtā** wife; **amaryā** bride; **yārinyà** girl; **bùdurwā** female youth; **sàraunìyā** queen; **uwā** mother; **gwaggò** aunt; **yâ** elder sister; **kànàȓī-bâ-kējì** prostitute (lit. canary without a cage); **zākanyà** lioness; **gōɗìyā** mare; **sānìyā** cow; **tunkìyā** sheep (ewe); **àkuyà** she-goat; **kàzā** hen; **Sāȓatù** Saratu (Sarah); **Maȓyàm** Maryam (Mary); **Hasànā** Hassana; **kē** you (f.); **ita** she

A small number of nouns are epicene, i.e., have a single invariant form but differ in gender depending upon the sex of the referent, e.g.,

agòlà m./f. stepchild; **àutā** m./f. last-born, youngest child; **bàȓē** m./f. outsider, s.o. not a blood relative; **bùtùlu** m./f. an ingrate; **fāsinjà** m./f. passenger; **jīkà** m./f. grandchild (f. = **jīkanyà**); **kàkā** m./f. grandparent; **kùmāmà** m./f. feeble person; **kurmā** m./f. deaf psn; **likità** m./f. doctor; **membà** m./f. member; **nâs** m./f. nurse; **sa'à** m./f. age-mate, peer; **shāshàshā** m./f. foolish, unreliable psn; **talàkà** m./f. commoner, poor psn; **wàdā** m./f. dwarf (psn or animal); **wāwā** m./f. fool (f. = **wāwanyà**); **zàbiyā** m./f. albino

1.1. Lexically specific
Gender assignment with most nonderived nouns is unpredictable and not determined on semantic grounds. (Derivational formations, like abstracts or instruments, tend to come with a set gender attached.) In some cases, described below in §1.2, classes of words share a common gender; but generally speaking, gender is "arbitrary" and lexically specific. (The matter of phonological marking of the two genders is discussed later in §2.) Examples:

Masculine: **awò** weighing; **dàbīnò** date (tree); **faȓjì** vagina; **hancì** nose; **kùmurcī** cobra; **làbāȓì** story; **māshì** spear; **shāyì** tea; **turmī** mortar; **watà** moon
Feminine: **bùrā** penis; **fuskà** face; **kūkà** baobab tree; **ƙīrà** smithing, manufacturing; **màganà** talk, matter; **mēsà** python; **miyà** soup, sauce; **rānā** sun; **taɓaryā** pestle; **wuƙā** knife

1.1.1. Variation
Generally speaking, the gender of words is rigid and quite consistent throughout the Hausa-speaking area. There are small numbers of cases, however, where (a) specific words exhibit variation in gender within the same dialect, or (b) where dialects differ in the gender of individual lexical items. Examples:

(a) m. or f.: **kàmā** likeness, like; **sàndā** stick; **tufà** garment, clothing; **yātsà** finger; **tèku** ocean, sea; **zumà** honey(comb), bee
(b) **iskà** wind, spirit, f. in Kano, m. in Katsina; **kèke** bicycle, m. in Kano, f. in Sokoto; **kyât** cake, m. in Kano, f. in Sokoto; **takòbī** sword, m. in Kano, f. in Katsina

> °AN: Some people make a distinction between **zumà** 'bee' (= **kuɗan zumà** (lit. fly.of honey)), which is masculine, and **zumà** 'honey', which is feminine. Other people treat **zumà** 'honey' as masculine, perhaps treating it as elliptical from **ruwan zumà** 'honey' (lit. liquid.of honey(comb)).

Within SH, a few words occur either as masculine (unmarked) or as feminine (marked by means to be described below) with essentially the same meaning. Preferences are idiolectal or subdialectal, e.g.,

tallē m. = talliyā f. (uncommon)   small soup pot;   tàurārɔ̀ m. = tàurārùwā f.   star;
tsuntsū m. = tsuntsuwā f.   bird;   zīnārè̃ m. = zīnārìyā f.   gold;   zōbè̃ m. = zōbanyà̃ f.   ring

°AN: When the terms tàurārɔ̀ m. and tàurārùwā f. are used to refer to people like movie stars, then the choice of gender is semantically assigned.

Verbal (and deverbal) nouns having alternative formations (see §77:3) and location words with ma- that have different endings (see §7:2) coexist as semantically equivalent words with different genders, e.g.,

(a) jērì̃ m. = jēriyā f.   row;   nācì̃ m. = nāciyā f.   persistence;   nānì̃ m. = nāniyā f.   sealing or mending; mɔ̀rō m. = mɔ̀riyā f.   benefit
(b) macēcī m. = macētā f.   place of refuge;   magangarī m. = magangarā f.   place of descent; makuɽɗī m. = makuɽɗā f.   pass or waterway through hills or mountains;   masukwānī m. = masukwānā f.   place for galloping, race track

In a small number of cases, the masculine and feminine variants of the same lexeme differ in meaning. Examples:

cībì̃ m.   swollen/raised navel vs. cībìyā f.   navel, center
duhù̃ m.   darkness, denseness (of forest) vs. duhuwà̃ f.   thickly wooded place in open country
ɗōrì̃ m.   setting bones vs. ɗōriyā f.   addition (both < ɗōrà put sth on sth)
kaɗē m.   used in mân kaɗē shea-nut oil vs. kaɗanyà̃ f.   shea-nut tree
kīshì̃ m.   jealousy vs. kīshìyā f.   co-wife
maɗācī m.   mahogany tree vs. maɗācìyā f.   gall bladder (both < ɗācī bitter)
nūnì̃ m.   showing, pointing vs. nūniyā f.   showing off (both < nūnà̃ show)
sakì̃   divorce, release vs. sakiyà̃ f.   releasing pus from an abscess (both < sàkā release, let go)
tōshì̃ m.   gift to girlfriend vs. tōshiyā f.   bribe (both < tōshè̃ stop up)

◊HN: Members of pairs like duhù̃ m. / duhuwà̃ f. and kīshì̃ m. / kīshìyā f. would originally have been identical in form, the meaning difference relating solely to the gender distinction, i.e., *[kīshì]$_m$ 'jealousy' vs. *[kīshì]$_f$ 'co-wife'. The difference in shape resulted later from a process of "overt characterization" described below in §4.

There are also a few cases (including compounds) where there is no difference in form but where there is a difference in meaning depending on the gender:

bâ-hayà̃ (lit. there is no renting) *m.*   excrement (euphemism), public toilet vs. *f.*   "Black Maria" van used to transport prisoners or those awaiting trial
hànà-sallà *m.* (archaic)   type of coiffure used by Fulani women (with wisp of hair on forehead) (cf. gɔ̀shī m. forehead) vs. *f.*   baseball cap (cf. hùlā f. cap)
ƙūsà̃ *m.*   a big shot (slang) vs. *f.*   a nail
ƙwallō *m.*   pit, nut, e.g., of palm tree vs. *f.*   ball (cf. tamaulā f. rag ball)
kūrā *m.*   hand cart vs. *f.*   hyena

°AN: For most people, kūrā is f. regardless of its meaning; some people, however, do distinguish 'cart' from 'hyena' by gender.

1.2. Set gender classes

Some semantic classes have a fixed gender regardless of the phonological or morphological shape of the members of the class. In most cases, the individual items get their gender as a result of their being hyponyms of some superordinate term with that gender; but this is not always so.

1.2.1. Geographical locations

Terms for most geographical locations are feminine.

(a) Names of countries are feminine (cf. **ƙasā** f. 'country'), as are continents (cf. **nāhiyà** f. 'continent'), e.g.,

Afìřkà f. Africa; **Amùřkà** f. America; **Indìyà** f. India; **Jāmùs** f. Germany; **Màřōkò** f. Morocco; **Masàř** f. Egypt; **Nàjēřiyà/Nìjēřiyà** f. Nigeria; **Tūřai** f. Europe

(b) Names of states are feminine (cf. **jihà** f. state), e.g., (states within Nigeria):

Bàřno f. Borno; **Bendèl** f. Bendel; **Fìlàtô** f. Plateau; **Kabì** f. Kebbi; **Nējà** f. Niger; **Sakkwato** f. Sokoto

(c) Names of cities and towns are feminine. This is true even if they are plural in form, e.g., **Tsanyāwā** f. 'Tsanyawa', or have a phrasal structure where the head word is masculine, e.g., **Dūtsèn Mā** (lit. mountain.of Ma) f. 'Dutsen Ma'. Examples:

Bàgàdāzà f. Baghdad; **Bàiřûl = Bàiřût** f. Beirut; **Dawākin Kudù** f. Dawakin Kudu; **Fàtàkwâl** f. Port Harcourt; **Kanò** f. Kano; **Kàtsinà** f. Katsina; **Marādi** f. Maradi; **Mūsāwā** f. Musawa; **Sakkwato** f. Sokoto; **Tsaunìn Kūrā** (lit. rock.of hyena) f. Tsaunin Kura

The words for 'city/town' (**gàrī**) and 'large city' (**biřnī**) are both masculine. This is thus a case where the feminine gender of the class members is not explicable in terms of the gender of the superordinate terms. If the city/town names are used in a phrase with **gàrī** or **biřnī** (plus a linker), they take masculine concord, e.g.,

Kanò [cē]f It's Kano; but biřnin Kanò [nē]m	It's Kano city.
Tsanyāwā [tanà]f dà kàsuwā mài kyâu	Tsanyawa has a good market.
but gàrin Tsanyāwā [yanà]m dà kàsuwā mài kyâu	Tsanyawa town has a good market.

(d) Names of quarters in a city or town are feminine (cf. **ùnguwā** f. 'quarter'). As was the case with names of towns, the feminine assignment generally overrides the gender/number that the words would have if they were not functioning as names of quarters. Examples (quarters in Kano city):

Dàmbàzau f.; **Daurāwā** f.; **Dōgon Nāmà** f. (lit. tall animal, where **dōgon** 'tall' and **nāmà** 'meat/animal' are masculine); **Fage** f. (cf. **fagē** m. open area); **Gìgìnyu** f. (cf. **gìgìnyū** pl. deleb-palm); **Lìmancì** f.; **Nasařāwa** f.; **Tudùn Wàdā** f.; **Yàlwa** f.

In a few cases, the internal structure creates interference such that one gets masculine gender as an alternative to the "correct" feminine assignment, e.g.,

Dan Àgundi m./f. (lit. son.of Agundi); **Sābon Gàri** m./f. (lit. new town, where **gàrī** is m.); **Sābon Lāyì** m./f. (lit. new line/street, where **lāyì** is m.)

(e) Names of rivers are feminine, e.g.,

Bàdumè f., **Cālāwā** f., **Haɗējà** f., **Kwārà** f., **Wàtàri** f., **Wùdil** f.
e.g., **Binuwài tā fārō dàgà ƙasaɽ Kàmaɽu**   The Benue begins in Cameroon.

The word for 'river' **kògī**—like the word for city—is masculine. When the river names are expressed as **kògin** X 'river.of X', which is common, they take masculine concord, e.g.,

Haɗējà [tā]ꜰ **yi ambàliyà** = **Kògin Haɗējà** [yā]ₘ **yi ambàliyà**   The Hadeija River is in flood.
Kwārà [tā]ꜰ **jânyē yànzu bà kàmaɽ dâ ba** = **Kògin Kwārà** [yā]ₘ **jânyē yànzu bà kàmaɽ dâ ba**
        The Niger has receded now, it not like before.
Kògin Nîl [sànannē]ₘ **nè**   The River Nile is well known.

1.2.2. Months and days of the week
Months, whether of the Islamic or Western calendar, are masculine (cf. **watà** m. 'month'), e.g.,

Maɽìs m. March; **Yūlì** m. July; **Sàtumbà** m. September; **Dìsambà** m. December;
Mùhaɽɽàm m. first Islamic month; **Shà'àbân** m. eighth Islamic month; **Zùlƙīdà** m. eleventh Islamic
month

Days of the week are feminine (cf. **rānā** f. 'day'), with the exception of (**ran**) **sātī** m. Saturday:

Àsabàɽ f. (= (**ran**) **sātī** m.) Saturday; **Lahàdì** f. Sunday; **Lìtìnîn** f. Monday; **Tàlātà** f. Tuesday; etc.

1.2.3. Prayer times
The times of day for the five Islamic prayers are all feminine (cf. **sallà** f. 'prayer'):

àsùbāhì f. (= **àsùbâ** f.) first prayer (early morning); **àzahàɽ** f. (= **àzàhàɽiyyà** f.) second prayer (early
afternoon); **là'asàɽ** f. (= **là'àsaɽiyyà** f.) third prayer (late afternoon); **màgàɽibà** f. fourth prayer
(sunset); **lìshā** f. fifth prayer (evening)

> °AN: The statement by Wolff (1993: 139) that times of day are feminine is inexact. Times of day
> other than prayer times have variable gender, some being masculine, others being feminine, e.g.,
> **àlfijìɽ** m. 'dawn'; **màràicē** m. 'afternoon', **darē** m. 'night', **sāfiyā** f. 'morning', **tsakaɽ rānā** f.
> 'noon'.

1.2.4. Temporal and other adverbial nouns
When used nominally, i.e., as clause subjects, temporal-adverbial terms like **yâu** f. 'today', **gòbe** f.
'tomorrow', **jiyà** f. 'yesterday'; **bana** f. 'this year', **bàɗi** f. 'next year'; **bàra** f. 'last year' are feminine
(but see below). Phrases indicating the time of day, e.g., **ƙarfè biyu** 'two o'clock' are feminine even
though the headword **ƙarfè** 'o'clock' (lit. metal) is masculine. Feminine gender is also the pattern with
locative-adverbial terms for the cardinal points of the compass, e.g., **kudù** f. 'south'. Examples:

[**jìbi**]ꜰ **ta Allàh cē**   The day after tomorrow belongs to God. (i.e., the future is up to God)
[**shēkaranjiyà**]ꜰ **tā yi kyâu**   The day before yesterday was good.
[**bàɗi**]ꜰ **wàccan**   the year after next (lit. next year that (distant))
[**gabàs**]ꜰ **tā fi** [**yâmma**]ꜰ, [**arèwa**]ꜰ **tā fi** [**kudù**]ꜰ
        East is better than west, north is better than south.

[sànnu]f bā tǎ hanà zuwà   (Going) slowly doesn't prevent getting there.

[(ƙarfè) gōmà dà rabì]f tā yi   It is 10:30. (lit. (o'clock) ten and half it did)

Strangely, when clock times are followed by a freestanding linker plus an adverb phrase specifying morning or evening, the linker, which one would expect to have the feminine form **ta**, appears as **na**. For example, one gets [(ƙarfè) gōmà dà rabì]f [na]m sāfe '10:30 in the morning', not ****(ƙarfè) gōmà dà rabì ta sāfe; [(ƙarfè) shâ biyu]f [na]m dare 'twelve midnight', not **(ƙarfè) shâ biyu ta dare. A sentence like 'It is twelve midnight' ought to be [(ƙarfè) shâ biyu na dare]f tā yi. This is indeed allowed, but the nearby phrase with the masculine linker provides a surface gender conflict with the result that [(ƙarfè) shâ biyu na dare] yā yi, with the 3m weak subject pronoun **yā**, ends up sounding better than the "correct" structure with the corresponding feminine pronoun **tā** (cf. (ƙarfè) shâ biyu tā yi 'It's twelve o'clock.'

1.2.5. Adverbs and prepositional phrases

Adverb phrases—which may consist of as few as one word!—and prepositional phrases are masculine. The gender is apparent when, for example, the adverb or prepositional phrase is followed by a gender-sensitive stabilizer for the purpose of focus, e.g.,

[jiyà]m nē sukà zō   It was yesterday that they came.

cf. [jiyà]f tā fi shēkaranjiyà ruwā   Yesterday was rainier than the day before yesterday.

[à zàune]m nè mukè   Seated we were.

[dà saurī]m nè zā kù yi wannàn mùhimmìn aikì

     It's quickly that you will do this important work.

[dà wuƙā]m nè ya sòkē shì   It was with a knife that he stabbed him.

cf. [wuƙā]f cè ya sòkē shì dà ita   It was a knife he stabbed him with.

[dàgà Kanò]m nē sukà tāsō   It was from Kano they started.

[à cikin nàtsuwā]m nè ya shìga rījìyâr   It was very carefully that he entered the well.

[maza-maza]m nè sukà gamà aikìn   Very quickly they finished the work.

[gà Bintà]m nē yakè dà muhimmancì mù bā dà kuɗin

     It is to Binta that it is important for us to give the money.

[à kàsuwā]m nè kakàn sàmē shì   It's at the market you always find him.

[ìnā]m nè ka gan shì? [à Kanò]m nē   Where did you see him? At Kano.

cf. [Kanò]f tā fi Kàtsinà yawàn mutànē   Kano has a larger popoulation than Katsina.

°AN: Because the preposition **à** can often be deleted, a phrase like [à [makaɽantā]f]m 'at school' with a feminine noun may appear as simply [makaɽantā]f]m. In this case, some speakers still allow masculine concord with the bare nominal form, e.g., [[makaɽantā]] nè sukà tàfi 'It was school they went to (cf. [makaɽantā]f cè sukà ginà 'It was a school they built' (Schachter 1966). With other speakers, however, the feminine gender of the bare nominal form is too dominant and thus it is the gender of the noun qua noun (and not as a one-word adverb phrase) that determines the agreement, e.g., [makaɽantā]f cè sukà tàfi 'It was school they went to.'

1.2.6. Numerals

When used nominally, numerals are feminine, e.g.,

gōmà tā fi takwàs   Ten is more than eight.

bakwài ita cè lambàr dà ta ɗarà shidà dà ɗaya   Seven is the number that exceeds six by one.

ɗaya / àshìrin bâ biyu / hàmsin / mètan / dubū cè   It's one / 18 / 50 / 200 / 1,000.

Terms for fractions and the word for zero (which are mostly loanwords from Arabic) are masculine, e.g., **rabî** '1/2'; **sulùsī** '1/3'; **sùlùsānī** '2/3', **ŕubù'ī** '1/4', **sifîŕī** 'zero'. Examples:

rabî yā fi sulùsī   Half is more than a third.   **sifîŕī nè na sanī**   Zero I know.

When used anaphorically, **ɗaya** 'one, the other' is either masculine or feminine depending on the referent; the numbers above 'one' are plural, e.g.,

gà 'yammātā biyu, ɗaya dōguwā cè, ɗayâŕ (kuma) gàjērìyā (cè)
>   Here are two young women; one (f.) is tall, the other one (f.) is short.

gà sàmārī biyu, ɗaya dōgō nè, ɗayân (kuma) gàjērē (nè)
>   Here are two young men, one (m.) is tall, the other one (m.) is short.

à gàrin nàn àkwai dubū waɗànda sukà ƙi biyàn hàŕājī
>   In this town there are a thousand who (pl.) refused to pay their taxes.

ukùnsù sun tsērè manà   Three of them (pl.) escaped from us.

1.2.7. Letters of the alphabet

The names of letters of the Roman alphabet are all feminine, e.g., **â**, **bâ**, **ɓâ**, **câ**, **dâ**, etc. The letters of the *ajami* (Arabic script) alphabet (see chap. **80**), on the other hand, vary in gender from letter to letter, and with individual differences among speakers. For some speakers, the majority are feminine with a small number masculine, e.g.,

feminine: **bā, tā, jâ, hâ, kâ, lâ, ŕā, sin, shin, yā, zal, ɗâ**
masculine: **àlû = àlîn** ('alif'); **dal, lan-jàyē** (medial /l/), **min-jàyē** (medial /m/), **ŕadī, wau**

Other speakers treat most of the letters as masculine, with just a few feminine, e.g., **kâ nē, sin nè** 'It's ka, it's sin', but **bā cè** 'It's ba.'

1.2.8. Abbreviations and acronyms

Abbreviations and acronyms are not gender specific in and of themselves. Rather, they take their gender from the gender of the full form. Thus NPC (the political party Northern Peoples Congress), is f. because **jàm'iyyà** 'party' is feminine; BUK (Bayero University Kano) is f. because **kwalējì** 'college' and **jāmi'à** 'university' are f.; and OPEC is f. because **ƙungìyā** 'organization' is f., etc. Conversely, UBA (United Bank of Africa) is m. because **bankī** 'bank' is masculine'. UNICEF is either m. because **asūsùn tàimakō** 'funds, financial aid' is m. or is f. because **ƙungìyā** 'organization' is f.

1.2.9. Infinitives, verbal noun phrases, and whole sentences

Infinitive phrases composed of a finite verb plus an object are masculine. The gender shows up most clearly when the infinitive NP functions as a noun subject controlling a weak subject pronoun. It can also be seen, when, for example, an infinitive phrase is followed by the stabilizer for purposes of focus or when it is topicalized and requires use of a resumptive pronoun. These phrases often translate best as English gerunds or present participles, but in Hausa they have an infinitival structure, e.g.,

[ƙērà kèkè]$_m$ [yanà]$_m$ dà wùyā	To manufacture bicycles is difficult.
[sayaŕ dà mōtàŕ wàje]$_m$ [yanà]$_m$ dà saukī	Selling foreign cars is easy.
[tūrō sù nân]$_m$ [zâi]$_m$ yi kyâu	Sending them here will be good.
[būɗè tāgàŕ]$_m$ [yā]$_m$ gàgarà	Opening/to open the window is impossible.

[jẽfà cêk]ₘ [nẽ]ₘ ta yi à kwàndon shằrā
> It was throwing the check she did in the trash can.

[tunằ masà kōmē dà kōmē]ₘ [yā]ₘ zama aikĩnā nề
> Reminding him of everything has become my job.

[durƙùsā wà mālàm]ₘ dai, Zàinabù tā yĩ [shì]ₘ
> As for kneeling down before the teacher, Zainabu did it.

Phrases composed of a verbal noun followed by an object are treated in two ways. For some (most?) speakers, the focus is on the N.L + N structure with the gender of the phrase being provided by the gender of the head verbal noun. If the verbal noun is feminine, the phrase is treated as feminine, e.g.,

[[ƙĩràr̃]f kèkè]f tanằ dà wùyā   Manufacturing bicycles is difficult.
[[sātàr̃]f gwaibằ]f ita cè àbîn dà bā mằ sô   Stealing guavas is the thing that we don't like.

Some speakers, however, treat verbal noun phrases like infinitival phrases and make them masculine regardless of the gender of the verbal noun itself, e.g.,

[[ƙĩràr̃]f kèkè]ₘ yanằ dà wùyā   Manufacturing bicycles is difficult.
[[sātàr̃]f gwaibằ]ₘ shĩ nề àbîn dà bā mằ sô   Stealing guavas is the thing that we don't like.

°AN: The alternative gender assignment of verbal noun phrases can even be extended to structurally similar dynamic noun phrases, e.g., [[jiyyàr̃]f maràsā lāfiyằ] yanằ/tanằ dà kyâu 'Looking after the infirmed is good', where jiyyằ 'tend the sick' is a dynamic noun and not a verbal noun, cf. tā yi musù jiyyằ 'She tended them' (lit. she did to.them tending). Historically, jiyyằ could possibly be an old verbal noun, but synchronically it is a simple noun, from which one can form a verb using the verbalizer -TA, e.g., jìyyatằ 'tend sick person'.

If the verbal noun itself is masculine, the problem does not arise because the phrase will be masculine regardless of which approach is employed, e.g.,

[[gyāran]ₘ mōtằ]ₘ nē ya yi   Repairing the car he did.
[[har̃bìn]ₘ-sù]ₘ zâi yi wùyā   Shooting them will be difficult.

Whole sentences are also masculine. This can be seen when, for example, the sentence as such takes the masculine stabilizer nē, or when it functions as a subject NP and thereby controls the gender of the weak subject pronoun, e.g.,

[sun taɓà zuwằ nân]ₛ nē, shĩ ya sâ...
> They had indeed previously come here, that (m.) is why...

[à sằmi gōr̃ò à Landàn]ₛ yanằ dà wùyā
> Getting kolanuts in London is difficult. (lit. one.sub get kolanut in London it (m.) is with difficulty)

°AN: Examples with the sentence functioning as a subject are considered clumsy and by some people even ungrammatical. The sentence is better if preceded by the complementizer cêwā 'that', e.g., cêwā à sằmi gōr̃ò à Landàn yanằ dà wùyā. Better still is the following with the subjunctive sentence as a complement: yanằ dà wùyā [à sằmi gōr̃ò à Landàn] 'It is difficult to get kolanuts in London.' In any case, there is no disagreement that *if* the sentence is allowed at the beginning, it definitely carries masculine gender.

2. PHONOLOGICAL MARKING

As a result of historical developments (see §4 below), most native Hausa words that are feminine end in the vowel -ā, e.g., **àkuyā̀** f. 'goat', **bùrā** f. 'penis', **fuskà̀** f. 'face', **gùguwā̀** f. 'whirlwind', **kibiyā̀** f. 'arrow', **kujèrā** f. 'chair', **rìgā** f. 'gown', **tsanyā̀** f. 'cricket'. There are, however, many more exceptions to this oft-stated generalization than one might expect. There are some hundred feminine words that end in a consonant or in a vowel other than -ā and another twenty-five non-ā-final epicene nouns that can be feminine. Most of the non-ā feminines are fairly recent loanwords, primarily from English (or French in Niger), but some come from Arabic and Fulani. In some cases, the gender assignment has been made on the basis of real-world sex, e.g., **kìlākì** f. 'modern prostitute' (< English 'clerk'), **gwaggò** f. 'aunt' (< Fulani); in others the gender assignment results from semantic analogy or association with some other words already in the language (e.g., **banatì** f. 'bayonet', cf. **wuƙā** f. 'knife'; **mòngwamaṛàn** f. 'beret' (< (General) Montgomery), cf. **hùlā** f. 'cap'). Selected examples of non-ā feminine words:

ambùlàs = ambùlan ambulance (cf. **mōtà̀** car); **bàlàm-balam** balloon (cf. **ṛōbà̀** rubber); **bâs** bus (cf. **mōtà̀** car); **en'è̀** native authority (N.A.) (cf. **hùkūmà̀** governing authority); **fìṛāmàṛè̀** primary school (cf. **makaṛantā** school), **gàzêt** gazette (cf. **takàṛdā** paper); **gwamnatì** government (cf. **hùkūmà̀** governing authority); **hàyâs** type of Toyota minivan (cf. **mōtà̀** car); **kōtù** court (cf. **shàṛi'à̀** court); **kwalējì** college (cf. **makaṛantā** school); **naggè** cow (< Fulani) (cf. **sānìyā** cow); **sìgāṛì** cigarette (cf. **tābà̀** tobacco, cigarette); **singìlētì** undershirt, singlet (cf. **taguwā** shirt); **tàsî** taxi (cf. **mōtà̀** car); **tōcìlàn** flashlight (cf. **fìtilā** lamp); **walàt** wallet (cf. **jàkā** leather sack); **wan-wề** one-way street (cf. **hanyà̀** road)

Other non-ā feminines are much older loanwords whose source is often not identifiable. These words are assumed to be loanwords on the basis of distinctive phonological features, most notably, non-final rolled ṛ and short final vowels, e.g., **màge** f. cat (= **kyânwā** f.). Examples (non-ā feminine words):

àṛādù thunder clap (cf. **tsāwā** thunder); **bàngyal** type of short gown (cf. **rìgā** gown); **bēnu** Senegal fire finch (= **tsàda**); **bùrƙùtù** a type of locally brewed beer (cf. **giyà̀** alcoholic beverage), **gàṛè** type of small gown without embroidery (cf. **rìgā** gown); **kulè** cat (cf. **kyânwā** cat); **ƙūbè̀** hand-embroidered cap (cf. **hùlā** cap); **mōɗì** gambling game involving tossing a coin for heads or tails (cf. **cāca** gambling); **ùngùlu** vulture

> ◊HN: [i] The word **màcè** 'woman' has always stood out because it would appear to be a very basic old Hausa word and yet it does not end in -ā as expected. My guess is that it has its aberrant shape—a final short vowel other than /a/ and L-L tone—because it originally was a derived form meaning 'female' (< **màtā** 'woman, wife'), which only later came to be used as a common noun (cf. **na-mijì** 'male' with **mijì** 'husband').
> [ii] Across the Chadic family, the words for 'vulture' are seldom cognate; nevertheless, they are usually feminine. A question that comes to mind about Hausa **ùngùlu = àngulu** (where the initial **Vn** is clearly a replacement for a syllabic nasal in the donor language) is why should the term for such a common bird be a loanword? The hypothesis (perhaps speculation is more accurate) that I would offer is the following: such words as **ùngùlu** 'vulture' and **nāmà̀** 'meat' (a masculine loanword ending in -ā, which replaced the original masculine word *****Luw-**) were associated with butchers, who, at the very early period when these words were borrowed, were not Hausas, but rather members of some Niger-Congo speaking group.

The essentially correct statement that feminine words normally end in -ā is often accompanied by a related statement (overt or implied) that masculine words do not end in -a(a). This does not logically follow and it is not in fact true. There are actually quite a number of ā-final masculine words (over 250 out of some 3,000 masculine (or epicene) nouns). Some are loanwords, primarily from English, in which the masculine gender has been assigned semantically, either by direct reference to the real world, e.g., fàdā 'Catholic father, priest', biřkìlà m. 'bricklayer' (although presumably one could have female bricklayers), or by analogy or semantic association with some pre-existing masculine word, e.g., fànjāmà m. 'loose-fitting trousers', cf. wàndō m. 'trousers'. Some are erstwhile plurals that have been reinterpreted as singulars, e.g., dumā m. 'gourd, calabash', originally the plural of dumè m. (still used in some dialects), and some are deverbal nouns, e.g., rawā m. 'dancing' (< *ràwa 'shake (intr.)', cf. rawař dà 'shake sth'). Many ā-final masculine words, however (e.g., gàbā m. 'front', kadà m. 'crocodile'), are native stems that simply reflect the earlier period in Hausa when gender was not phonologically marked and words of either gender could end in all five final vowels (as well as in consonants). Examples of ā-final masculines:

(a) Native: bābā indigo; bàbā eunuch; bāwà slave; bāyā back; bidà thatching needle; bìkā baboon; ɓēřā mouse; cìnnākà small black biting ant; dilà jackal; fā flat rock; gātā pampering, special privileges; gàurākà crownbird; gòrā large gourd; guzà water monitor; hànkākà crow; kadà crocodile; màrāyà orphan; nīsā distance; shilà young pigeon; sūnā name; ùbā father; wâ elder brother; wàsā game, sport; watà moon, month; wuyà neck (of body or of thing); zàkarà rooster

(b) Loanwords: basfà motor scooter (< the brand name Vespa) (cf. kèkè m. bicycle); faskìlà first class (e.g., on a plane or train); indìpendà independence (cf. mulkìn kâi m. self government); kūkà modern stove (cf. murhù m. cooking place); màntàlētà mentholatum (cf. mâi m. oil, balm); Nùwambà November (cf. watà m. month); ōzà ounce; silìfà slippers, slip-on shoes, sandals (cf. tàkàlmī m. shoe(s)); sūfà premium (super) grade gasoline; tùřōzà trousers (western style) (cf. wàndō m. trousers)

(c) Erstwhile plurals: dumā gourd, calabash; gidā house, compound; karā cornstalk; ƙudā housefly; ruwā water

ΔDN: The last three words above, karā, ƙudā, and ruwā, are still plurals in Sokoto and related dialects.

(d) Deverbal nouns: dūbā fortune-telling (< dùbā look at); jīfà a throw (< jèfā throw at / jēfà throw sth); kāyā goods, loads (< kai take (< *//kāyà//)); ƙūnā a burn on skin or burnt hole in clothing (< ƙōnè burn); kiɗà drumming, plucking, music (< kaɗà hit (drum)); sūkà criticism (< sòkā slash, criticize)

◊HN: Many of the words listed in (a) above derive directly from ā-final words. Some, however, historically ended in a nasal, which was subsequently dropped, the result being an ā-final masculine word, e.g., guzà m. < *guzàn 'water monitor', kadà m. < *kadàm 'crocodile' (see Schuh 1976).

3. GENDER MARKING: DERIVATION AND INFLECTION

Because many nouns (where gender is intrinsic) also function as adjectives (where gender is determined) a rigid distinction between derivation and inflection is not useful in describing gender marking. What is more significant is the form of the marking. Here one can distinguish three different feminine marking morphemes, the first two being etymologically related: (1) a suffix that one can indicate as {-ā}, (2) a suffix -ìyā; and (3) a suffix that one can indicate as {-nyā}.

3.1. The feminine suffix {-ā}

Synchronically, the suffix {-ā} has two overlapping functions. With adjectives, it forms the grammatically required feminine counterparts of masculine words, e.g., **farī** m. 'white' (e.g., **[farin]**$_m$ **[zanè]**$_m$ 'white cloth'), **farā** f. 'white' (e.g., **[farař]**$_f$ **[tagùwā]**$_f$ 'white shirt'), **dōgō** m 'tall', **dōguwā** f. 'tall'. With nouns, it usually serves to indicate the female counterpart of words denoting male persons or animals, e.g., **jàkī** m. 'donkey', **jàkā** f. 'she-ass', **kuturū** m. leper', **kuturwā** 'female leper'. With some inanimate nouns, it forms the grammatically feminine counterpart of the masculine form with little if any difference in meaning, e.g., **tàurārò** m. star' = **tàurārùwā** f. 'star'.

> °AN: Some speakers feel that **tàurārùwā** can be used only to refer to 'a large star'. Similarly, **kīfanyà** (with the feminine suffix {-nyā} is restricted by some speakers to 'a large fish' as opposed to the normal masculine form **kīfī**. The use of feminine suffixes to connote largeness exists in various Chadic languages alongside its use as a singulative marker.

The ending -ā is a toneless suffix that is added to full stems including the final vowel and tone. It is thus unlike most suffixes in Hausa, which are tone-integrating affixes added to morphological bases devoid of final vowel and tone. It appears on the surface as -ā, -(i)yā, and -(u)wā depending on the final vowel and syllabic structure of the word to which it is attached. The variant forms are accounted for by the following set of rules. Note that the rules are the same whether the m./f. pairs are adjectival or nominal and whether the function of the feminine addition could be viewed as inflection, derivation, or overt characterization.

Rule 1: H-tone -i(i) + {-ā} → -ā

If the -ā suffix is added to a word with final H tone -i (long or short), the -i drops and the feminine form appears with final H tone -ā. Note that palatalized alveolars generally "depalatalize" when the front vowel is replaced by -ā. Examples:

algàshī / algàsā   green (m./f.); **àlmùbazzàřī / àlmùbazzàřā**   extravagant, spendthrift (m./f.); **dùgùzunzùmī / dùgùzunzùmā**   shaggy-haired, unkempt (m./f.); **ɗālìbī / ɗālìbā**   student (m./f.); **fatsī / fatsā**   light red, esp. complexion (m./f.); **jāhìlī / jāhìlā**   ignorant, illiterate psn (m./f.); **jàkī / jàkā**   donkey/she-ass (m./f.); **ƙàramī / ƙàramā**   small (m./f.); **mùnāfùkī / mùnāfùkā**   hypocrite (m./f.)

Rule 2: H-tone -e(e) + {-ā} → -(i)yā; L-tone -ì(i) or -è(e) + {-ā} → -ìyā

If the suffix -ā is added to a word ending in a front vowel other than H-tone -ī, it appears as -(i)yā. (That is, the suffix is added to the full masculine stem *including* the final vowel rather than to a pre-affixal base minus the final vowel.) The transitional /i/ is present except when the penultimate syllable of the stem is light and the final consonant is a sonorant. The tone of the suffix depends on the final tone of the stem. If it is H, then the suffix appears as H-H; If it is L, then the suffix appears as L-H. Examples:

(a) **bēbē / bēbiyā**   deaf mute (m./f.); **bùgaggē / bùgaggiyā**   beaten, drunk (m./f.); **fàsasshē / fàsasshiyā**   smashed (m./f.); **kàrē / kàryā**   dog/bitch (m./f.)
(b) **mìtsītsì / mìtsītsìyā**   tiny (m./f.); **shàkiyyì / shàkiyyìyā**   rascal (m./f.); **shàƙīƙì / shàƙīƙìyā**   full brother/sister (m./f.); **shūɗì / shūɗìyā**   blue (m./f.); **Bàkatsinè / Bàkatsinìyā**   man/woman from Katsina (m./f.); **kōřè / kōřìyā**   green (m./f.); **shēgè / shēgìyā**   bastard(ly), rascally (m./f.); **zungurērè / zungurērìyā**   very long, tall (m./f.)
Irregular: **àlhajì / hajìyā**   psn who has made the hadj to Mecca (m./f.)

ɗanye / ɗanyā (< *ɗanyiyā)   raw, fresh (m./f.)

māyè̀ / mâyyā (< *māyìyā)   sorcerer, wizard, witch (m./f.)

Exceptions: gàjērē / gàjērìyā = gàjērùwā = gàjērā   short (m./f.);

Ƙàdangarè̀ / Ƙàdangarùwā   lizard (m./f.);

Ƙanè̀ / Ƙanwà̀   younger brother/sister; ƘànƘanè̀ / Ƙànƙanùwā)   small (m./f.)

◊HN: A reasonable hypothesis to explain the irregular alternation seen, for example, in Ƙanè̀ / Ƙanwà̀ m./f. 'younger sibling' is that historically the masculine form ended in -ō, i.e., *Ƙanò̀. Subsequently the final vowel underwent a sporadic shift to -ē, but the original vowel quality was still reflected in the feminine form.

ΔDN: In SH, the feminines of past participles and ethnonyms, which in the masculine end in -ē, are formed by adding -ā to the stem and applying the rules above, the surface output being final -iyā (tone depending on the previous tone). In WH, the -ā suffix is added to the base excluding the final vowel; thus, one gets such examples as bùgaggā f. 'beaten' (cf. SH bùgaggiyā) and Bàkatsinà̀ f. 'woman from Katsina' (cf. SH Bàkatsinìyā).

Rule 3: H-tone -u(u) or -o(o) + {-ā} → -(u)wā ; L-tone -ù(u) or -ò(o) + {-ā} → -ùwā

If the suffix -ā is added to a word ending in a back-rounded vowel it appears as -(u)wā. The conditions for the omission of the transitional vowel and for the assignment of tone are the same as in Rule 2. Examples:

(a) guntū / guntuwā   stub(by) (m./f.);   hūtsū / hūtsuwā   cantankerous (m./f.);   kuturū / kuturwā   leper (m./f.)

(b) bà̀Ƙō / bà̀Ƙuwā   strange(r), foreign(er) (m./f.);   dōgō / dōguwā   tall (m./f.);   sābō / sābuwā   new (m./f.)

(c) gurgù̀ / gurgùwā   lame, a cripple (m./f.);   Ƙūrù̀ / Ƙūrùwā   pony (m./f.);   sùllūtù̀ / sùllūtùwā   lazy, slatternly (m./f.)

 (d) bàhagò̀ / bàhagùwā   left-handed (m./f.);   gāɓò̀ / gāɓùwā   fool (m./f.);   tsòlōlò̀ / tsòlōlùwā   tall and skinny (m./f.)

Exception: mà̀dugū / mà̀dugā   caravan leader (m./f.)

◊HN: At an abstract/historical level the -ā suffix and the preceding reduced vowel, if any, copied the final tone of the stem, e.g., bēbē H-H + -ā > bēbiyā H-H-H 'deaf mute'; dōgō H-H + -ā > dōguwā H-H-H 'tall'. The same would have been true for words with final L tone. The output would then have fed a low-tone raising rule (see §34:3.2) that changed final L-L sequences to L-H when the final vowel was long (Leben 1971), the result being the forms we find today, e.g., shēgè̀ H-L + -ā > *shēgìyà̀ H-L-L > shēgìyā H-L-H 'bastard'; gāɓò̀ H-L + -ā > *gāɓùwà̀ H-L-L > gāɓùwā H-L-H 'fool'. (Whether this historical rule still has validity as an active rule in current-day Hausa, as proposed by Leben, is very questionable.)

With few exceptions, e.g., bāwà̀ / bâiwā (= [dv] bâuyā) 'slave' (m./f.), nouns and adjectives ending in -ā do not have distinct feminine forms, e.g., wà̀dā 'dwarf' (m./f.)', jā 'red (m./f.)'. The gender in these cases is shown not by the form of the words as such, but by concord, e.g.,

fāsinjà̀ nē m. / fāsinjà̀ cē f.   He / She is a passenger.

wani membà̀ m. / wata membà̀ f.   a certain male / female member

bàbban bà̀būr̃ m. / bàbbar̃ mōtà̀ f.   a large motorcycle / car

jan zanè̀ m. / jar̃ tagùwā f.   a red wrapper / shirt

mùmmūnan sarkī m. / **mùmmūnař sàraunìyā** f   an evil king / queen
zùzzurfan rāmì m. / **zùzzurfař rījìyā** f.   a very deep hole / well

°AN/◊HN: Parsons (1963) specifies that the feminine suffix for L-tone nouns and adjectives ending in -**à** is -**ìyā**, e.g., **ìngařmà** m. (f. **ìngařmìyā**) 'large and strong (horse)'. He treats such examples as **ràwayà** m. (f. **ràwayà**) 'yellow' as exceptions. He has it backward. The regular feminine ending for underlying stems with final L tone -**à** is (or at least historically was) -**à**. The -**ìyā** suffix as a distinct morphological element is a grammatically new innovation reflecting a process of overt characterization. (For example, for most speakers **ìngařmà** 'large and strong (horse)' is epicene, the grammatical gender depending on the sex of the referent, e.g., **ìngařmà nē/cē** 'It's a large stallion/mare.' The feminine form **ìngařmìyā** is a new creation, which for some speakers is marginal at best.) There are in fact very few adjectives ending in L-tone -**à(a)** and, as far as I am aware, no one has done a systematic study about what corresponding feminine forms people nowadays actually use.

Instead of treating words ending in -**ā** as being epicene, one might consider postulating an additional rule whose surface result would be vacuous, i.e.,

Rule 4:   H-tone -**a(a)** + {-**ā**} → -**ā**, e.g., **kurmā** m. 'deaf man' + {-**ā**} → **kurmā** f. 'deaf woman'
     L-tone -**à(a)** + {-**ā**} → -**à**, e.g., **jīkà** m. 'grandson' + {-**ā**} → **jīkà** f. 'granddaughter'

Although this rule feels right, it runs up against the problem that words with final short -**a** do not lengthen in the feminine, e.g., **bàbba nè** 'It's big (m.)', **bàbba cè** 'It's big (f.)', not ****bàbbā cè**.

3.2. The feminine suffix {-ìyā}

Originally, the suffix {-**ìyā**} was simply the surface result of adding the feminine ending -**ā** to a noun stem ending in L tone -**ī** or -**ē** as described above, e.g., ***shēgè** + -**à** > ***shēgìyà** > **shēgìyā** bastard (f.). Synchronically, however, the surface form has developed into an independent feminine suffix that can be added to masculine words with other endings, i.e., with H-tone -**ī** or -**ē** or with nonfront vowels, e.g.,

àbōkī / àbōkìyā	friend (m./f.)	**bàdādī / bàdādìyā**	close friend (m./f.)
gàjērē / gàjērìyā	short (m./f.)	**gàurākà / gàurākìyā**	crownbird (m./f.)
gògarmà / gògarmìyā	dauntless(m./f.)	**jàkādà / jàkādìyā**	ambassador, emissary (m./f.)

The suffix -**ìyā** as a distinct feminine formative (in this case with an unexplained H-H-L-H overall tone pattern) is also used in forming feminine agent nouns (see §7:1.1) e.g.,

mahàifī / mahaifīyā	parent (m./f.)	**maƙàryàcī / maƙaryacìyā**	liar (m./f.)
masòyī / masōyìyā	lover (m./f.)		

3.3. The feminine suffix {-nyā}

The ending {-**nyā**} is an essentially nonproductive suffix. It occurs in only a small number of words (which includes some archaic or dialectal items (indicated [dv]) that are cited in the dictionaries but are not used nowadays in SH). The suffix mainly indicates the female counterpart of a word denoting a male person or (large) animal, e.g., **màrāyà / màrainìyā** 'orphan m./f.', **zākì / zākanyà** 'lion/lioness'. When used with words other than for people or animals, the suffix creates items that, although grammatically feminine, differ only slightly in meaning (if at all) as compared with the grammatically masculine forms. Examples of inanimates (complete):

id̀ǒ m.	eye	= **idānìyā** f. [dv] (originally singulative?)
zṓbè̀ m.	ring	= **zōbanyà̀** f.
kaɗē m. (esp. **mân kaɗē**) shea-nut oil		**kaɗanyà̀** f.	shea-nut tree
kīfī m.	fish	**kīfanyà̀** f. [dv]	(large) fish
ɗācī m.	bitterness	**ɗātanyà̀** f.	a bitter grass

The suffix has essentially two variants: (a) With disyllabic (diconsonantal) words the suffix has the form -**anyā**)^{HL} (which I take to be tone integrating), e.g., **zākī̀ / zākanyà̀** 'lion/lioness'. (In a few cases, one gets a copy of the preceding vowel rather than -**a**.) (b) With trisyllabic (including CVCVC) words, the suffix has the form (-**nìyā**)^{LH} (which is clearly noninintegrating), e.g., **màrāyà̀ / màrainìyā** 'orphan m./f.'. Examples (complete):

(a) **barà̀ / baranyà̀** servant (m./f.); **birì̀ / birinyà̀** monkey (m./f.); **bōkā / bōkanyà̀** [dv] (= **bōkā**) native doctor, herbalist (m./f.); **darì̀ / daranyà̀** hartebeest (m./f.); **gwāmì̀ / gwāmanyà̀** [dv] (= **gwāmìyā**) knock-kneed psn. (m./f.); **gyādō / gyādanyà̀** [dv] boar (m./f.); **jīkà̀ / jīkanyà̀** (= **jīkà̀**) grandchild (m./f.); **kaɓò̀ / kaɓanyà̀** young gazelle (m./f.); **kūsù̀ / kūsanyà̀** [dv] mouse (m./f.); **mà̀zō / māzanyà̀** [dv] (= **mà̀zuwā**) harnessed antelope (m./f.); **mūgù̀** (base // **mug-**// / **mugunyà̀** [dv] (= **mūgùwā**) evil, ugly psn. (m./f.); **wāwā / wāwanyà̀** [dv] (= **wāwā**) fool (m./f.); **zākī̀ / zākanyà̀** lion/lioness
Exception: **yārò̀ / yārinyà̀** (< *yārunyà̀) (*not* **yāranyà̀**) boy/girl
(b) **ɓarāwò̀ / ɓaraunìyā** thief (m./f.); **jinjìri / jinjir̃nìyā** = **jinjinnìyā** infant (m./f.); **màkāhò̀** (base //**màkāf-**//) **/ màkaunìyā** blind psn. (m./f.); **màrāyà̀ / màrainìyā** orphan (m./f.); **mùtûm / mùtūnìyā** (< **mùtumnìyā**) man/woman; **zumù̀ / zūnìyā** (< *zumnìyā) age-mate, kinsman (m./f.)
Exceptions: **dòdō** (base //**dòdōn-**//) **/ dòdannìyā** monster, goblin (m./f.)
sarkī (base //**sàrāk-**//) **/ sàraunìyā** king/queen

◊HN: The derivatiom of **màkaunìyā** is *màkafnìyā > màkamnìyā (by assimilation), and then > **màkaunìyā** (by Klingenheben's Law). The weakening of syllable-final /m/ to /u/ before /n/ is also evidenced in **mùtūnìyā**. In WH, the syllabic-final /m/ is still retained.

4. OVERT CHARACTERIZATION (HISTORICAL)

Hausa has a large number of nonderived/noninflected feminine words ending in -**ā**, -**(i)yā**, and -**(u)wā**. Although the explanation is historical, one needs to be aware of it in order to have a proper understanding of the synchronic grammar of the language. Historically, feminine nouns were not restricted in terms of their phonological shape, i.e., they did not all end in -**a(a)**. Like masculine nouns, they could end in all five vowels and presumably in consonants as well (to the extent that there were consonant-final words). Feminine words like the following thus would have existed: *tumkì f. 'sheep', *mūɗù f. 'python', *bēgo f. 'porcupine', etc. (These hypothetical examples are transcribed with a short final vowel because the language probably did not have distinctive vowel length in final position at the time.)
Although adjectives would have carried feminine inflection, nouns themselves would have been phonologically unmarked from the point of view of gender. Subsequently, feminine nouns underwent a process of "overt characterization" (see Newman 1979a) by which they all added the overt feminine suffix {-**ā**}. The essence of "overt characterization" is that the feminine inflectional ending was added not to masculine forms but rather to words that were already feminine. For example, the feminine word **gàrkuwā** 'shield', which synchronically has a plural **gàrkī**, clearly comes from a base *gàrko. This original base was not, however, masculine (as most scholars have assumed) but rather was already

feminine. That is, the function of the suffixation process was not to turn masculine nouns into their feminine counterparts, but rather involved providing overt phonological marking to nouns that were already feminine.

When the {-ā} suffix was added, surface forms were produced in accordance with the still-active rules described above in §3.1. Note that with words now ending in -(i)yā and -(u)wā, it is sometimes possible to determine the height of the original final vowel, but sometimes not. Where there is doubt about the height of the final vowel of the postulated earlier form, it is represented as E or O. Examples:

*cinì f. + -ā > cinyà f. thigh
*gàye f. + -ā > gàyyā f. cooperative work
*mag(a)re f. + -ā > magaryā f. jujube tree
*tsire f. + -ā > tsiryā f. parakeet
*bēgo f. + -ā > bēguwā f. porcupine
*guyÒ f. + -ā > *guywà > gwīwà f. knee
*makw(a)rO f. +-ā > makwarwā f. bush fowl
*tsakÒ f. +-ā > tsakuwà f. gravel
*duhù f. + -ā > duhuwà f. thickly wooded place in open country (cf. duhù m. darkness)

*gafì f. + -ā > gafiyà f. bandicoot
*ƙūgì f. + -ā > ƙūgìyā f. hook
*tsāme f. + -ā > tsāmiyā f. tamarind tree
*zārÈ f. + -ā > zārìyā f. trouser string
*būtù f. + -ā > būtùwā f. poor tobacco
*kùrO f. + -ā > kùrwā f. soul
*shàmO f. + -ā > shàmuwā f. stork
*yēkò f. + -ā > yēkùwā f. proclamation

In addition to the general rules described above, there are further details regarding the epenthetic vowel and the tone of the -(i)yā / -(u)wā allomorphs that need to be spelled out to account for the overtly characterized forms. The full endings -iyā and -uwā with the transitional vowel appear if the preceding syllable was heavy. The tone of the suffix is H-H if the final tone was H, L-H if the final tone was L, e.g., *tsāme + -ā > tsāmiyā H-H-H 'tamarind tree'; *yēkò + -ā > yēkùwā H-L-H 'proclamation'.

The suffix also surfaces as -iyā / - uwā when added to CVCV light-syllable stems where the C₂ is an obstruent. In this case, the tone of the suffix surfaces as H-L if the final tone was L and H-H if the final tone was H, e.g., *kibì + -ā > kibiyà 'arrow'; *shaƙÒ f. + -ā > shaƙuwà f. 'hiccough', *tsage + -ā > tsagiyā 'tail hairs'; *wàze + -ā > wàjiyā 'fat in meat'. With CVCV light-syllable stems with a sonorant as C₂, the suffix appeared as -yā / -wā, along with the original final tone, e.g., *cinì + -ā > cinyà 'thigh', *kùrO +-ā > kùrwā 'soul'. The endings without the transitional vowel also characterize CVC(V)CV words with an epenthetic medial vowel, e.g., taɓ(a)re + -ā > taɓaryā 'pestle'.

Because H-tone -ī + -ā is/was realized as -ā, overtly characterized feminine words originally ending in -i and feminine words originally ending in -a would have ended up with the same indistinguishable final vowel, e.g., wutā 'fire' < *wuti + -ā, cf. kàzā 'hen' < *kàza + -ā. Synchronically these two classes have merged and cannot be told apart. Thus there is no way to know whether rùmfā 'shed', for example, came from *rùmfi + -ā or from *rùmfa + -ā. In a very few cases, the true etymology can be determined from comparative evidence (as with the word for 'fire'); but synchronically the original difference has been totally lost and has no functional significance.

Generally speaking, the "feminative" suffixes constitute frozen, intrinsic parts of the stems. (I call the endings resulting from overt characterization "feminatives" to distinguish them from the active derivational and inflectional "feminine" suffixes.) In two areas of the grammar, however, their status as separate formatives still shows up. First, some (but not all) words drop the feminative ending in forming plurals, e.g.,

amaryā   bride, pl. amàrē   cinyà   thigh, pl. cinai
daƙwalwā   hen, pl. daƙwàlē   gōɗìyā   mare, pl. gwàɗɗī (= gōɗiyōyī)
tunkìyā   sheep, pl. tumākī   zangaȓnìyā   stubble of corn, pl. zàngàȓnū
(cf. giginyà   deleb-palm, pl. gìgìnyū with the feminative -y- retained)

Second, adverbial forms of nouns containing feminative suffixes often drop the ending as part of the derivation, e.g.,

gàskiyā (now = **gaskiyā**)	truth, cf. **gàske** truly	**sāfiyā**	morning, cf. **sāfe** in the morning
wutsiyà	tail, cf. **wutsi** on the tail	**zūcìyā**	heart, cf. **zūci** in/on the heart

[References: Newman (1979a); Parsons (1960a, 1961, 1963)]

32. Grammatical Agreement

CONCORDIAL agreement is maximally a three-term system. Head words or phrases are either (1) masculine singular, henceforth "masculine" (m.); (2) feminine singular, henceforth "feminine" (f.); or (3) plural (gender unspecified), henceforth "plural" (pl.). With some morphemes, e.g., the stabilizer, the masculine and the plural agreement markers fall together, and with some, e.g., derived adjectives of sensory quality, the masculine and the feminine fall together. In most cases, however, the three categories are distinct. (The morphology of feminine nouns and adjectives is described in chap. **31**; the morphology of plurals is described in chap. **56**.)

The following are the major grammatical categories that reflect gender/number agreement.

1. STABILIZER

The stabilizer, which occurs in equational sentences and elsewhere (see chap. **66**), has the forms **nē** (m.), **cē** (f.), and **nē** (pl.), all with polar tone.

ràgō nè	It's a ram. (m.)	d̃ākì nē	It's a room. (m.)
tunkìyā cè	It's a sheep. (f.)	tāgà cē	It's a window. (f.)
dabbōbī nè	They're animals. (pl.)	tūlunà nē	They're water pots. (pl.)

2. LINKER

The genitive linker agrees with the head noun (or NP) to its left. Thus in a phrase like **d̃ākìn na yārinyàr̃** 'the girl's room' (lit. room.the of girl.the), the linker **na** 'of' agrees with the masculine word 'room' and not with the feminine word 'girl'. Like the stabilizer, the masculine and plural linker forms are identical. The basic full forms of the linker are **na** (m.), **ta** (f.), **na** (pl.), with the common short variants -**n** / -**r̃** / -**n**, respectively, e.g.,

zanì na Hàdīzà	a cloth (m.) of Hadiza's
mōtà̀ ta biyu	the second car (f.) (lit. car of two)
wàsànnī na yârā	children's games (pl.) (lit. games of children)

The gender of independent possessives (which are formed with a long-vowel variant of the linker) is determined by the gender of the referent in the discourse, whether it is actually present in the sentence or not.

mōtàr̃sà tā fi tāmù tsà̀dā	His car (f.) is more expensive than ours (f.).
gà littāfīnā; ìnā nākà?	Here is my book (m.); where is yours (m.)?
wad̃ànnân nātà nē	These (pl.) are hers (pl.).

| nàwa yā mutù | Mine (m.) (referring to some masculine thing) died. |
| ta Mūsā tā lālàcē | Musa's (f.) (referring to some feminine thing) has broken down. |

3. DEFINITE ARTICLE

The definite article (d.a.) uses the same basic morpheme as the stabilizer and the linker. It has the form `n (m.), `r̃ (f.), `n (pl.), consisting of a consonant preceded by a floating L tone. (If the d.a. is attached to a word ending in H tone, it appears on the surface as a fall.) The form of the d.a. depends, inter alia, on the gender/number of the word to which it is attached. Examples:

yāròn	the boy (m.) previously referred to
tunkìyâr̃	the sheep (f.) previously referred to
dabbōbîn	the animals (pl.) previously referred to

4. PERSONAL PRONOUNS

In the second and third persons, personal pronouns reflect the three-term m./f./pl. distinction. (They are illustrated here by pronouns belonging to the independent set and the weak direct object set.) In the first person, singular and plural are distinguished, but the m./f. contrast is not marked. The impersonal weak subject pronoun //a//, the so-called fourth person, shows no overt distinction in gender or number, e.g., **zā à kāwō ruwā** 'Someone (m. or f.) or some people (unspecified) will bring water.' Examples:

Independent pronouns

	m.		f.		pl.	
1st	nī	I	nī	I	mū	we
2nd	kai	you (m.)	kē	you (f.)	kū	you (pl.)
3rd	shī	he	ita	she	sū	they

Weak direct object pronouns

	m.		f.		pl.	
1st	nì	me	nì	me	mù	us
2nd	kà	you (m.)	kì	you (f.)	kù	you (pl.)
3rd	shì	him	tà	her	sù	them

Pronouns obligatorily exhibit gender/number agreement whatever their syntactic function. The commonly occurring weak subject pronouns are typical, e.g.,

tùlū [yā] fashè	The water pot (m.) [it (m.)] broke.
tukunyā [tā] fashè	The pot (f.) [it (f.)] broke.
tūlunà̀ / tukwầnē [sun] fashè	The water pots / pots (pl.) [they (pl.)] broke.

5. DEMONSTRATIVES AND NONPERSONAL PRONOUNS

Demonstratives, indefinite determiners, and identical or phonologically related nonpersonal pronouns indicating 'this (one)', 'that (one)', 'which (one)', etc., show three-term agreement (except for "accidental" cases where the m. and f. forms have phonologically fallen together). Examples:

1.a.**wannàn** (< *wa-n-nàn) **dōkì nằwa nề**	This horse (m.) is mine.
b. **wannàn** (< *wa-t-nàn) **gōɗìyā tầwa cề**	This mare (f.) is mine.
c. **waɗànnân dawākī nằwa nề**	These horses are mine.
2a. **wancàn nằwa nề**	That (referring to m. thing) is mine.
b. **waccàn tầwa cề**	That (referring to f. thing) is mine.
c. **waɗàncân nằwa nề**	Those (referring to pl. things) are mine.
3a. **yārồ wandà na ganī**	a boy (m.) whom I saw
b. **yārinyầ waddà na ganī**	a girl (f.) whom I saw
c. **yârā waɗàndà na ganī**	children (pl.) whom I saw
4a. **wani tsōhō yā zō**	Some old man (m.) came.
b. **wata tsōhuwā tā zō**	Some old woman (f.) came.
c. **wasu sun zō**	Some (pl.) came.
5a. **wànnē ka fi sô?**	Which (referring to m. thing) do you prefer?
b. **wàccē ka fi sô?**	Which (referring to f. thing) do you prefer?
c. **wàɗànnē ka fi sô?**	Which (referring to pl. things) do you prefer?

The question word **wằ** 'who', which in its monosyllabic form controls default masculine agreement (e.g., **wằ yakề wāk̃ằ?** 'Who (m.) is singing?') can mark gender in the singular by using a longer form built by adding the stabilizer, e.g., **wằnē nề** / **wằcē cề** 'who (m./f.)'. Similarly, **mề** 'what' = **mềnē nề** (cf. **mề(nē nề) ya fāɗì?** 'What (m.) fell?), has an overtly marked feminine long form **mề(cē cề)** although its use is much less common. The word 'who', whether in the long or short form, also has a distinct plural indicated by prefixing the 3rd person pl. pronoun **su** to the Q-word, e.g.,

wằnē nề ya zō?	Who (m.) came?	**wằcē cề ta zō?**	Who (f.) came?
su wằ(nē nề) sukà bar̃ aikìn?	Who (pl.) left the work?		
mềnē nề wancàn?	What (m.) is that?	**mềcē cề waccàn?**	What (f.) is that?

6. ADJECTIVES

Adjectives, whether basic or derived, have three-term agreement (except in those cases where the masculine and the feminine have phonologically fallen together). Concord is obligatory whether the adjective is used prenominally or postnominally. The feminine form is built on the masculine stem using the inflectional suffix {-ā}. (With masculine stems ending in -ā, the feminine form will be phonologically identical.) The plural form is lexically specific in the case of basic adjectives and determined by the morphological class of the word in the case of derived adjectives. Examples:

farin yādì white cloth (m.) / **farar̃ r̃ìgā** white gown (f.) / **farāren r̃īgunằ** white gowns (pl.)
tēbùr̃ k̃aramī small table (m.) / **kujềrā k̃aramā** small chair (f.) / **tēbur̃ōr̃ī k̃anānằ** small tables (pl.)
mahàukàcin kàrē a mad dog (m.); **mahaukacìyar̃ gīwā** a crazed elephant (f.) / **mahàukàtan birai** crazy monkeys (pl.)
rāmì zùzzurfā a very deep hole (m.); **r̃ījìyā zùzzurfā** a very deep well (f.) / **r̃ījiyōyī zurfằfā** very deep wells (pl.)

> °AN: Adjectival agreement is usually locally determined, i.e., the adjective takes its form from the nearby head noun. In some instances, however, masculine adjectives occur with feminine head nouns when the semantic referent is masculine, e.g., **sābon** (m.) **fitôwā** (f.) 'new moon' (lit. new coming out), not ****sābuwar̃** (f.) **fitôwā** (f.), cf. **watầ** 'moon' (m.).

7. DIMINUTIVE

The diminutive markers **ɗan / 'yaȓ / 'yan** (m./f./pl.), which are related to the nouns **ɗā / 'yā / 'yā'yā** 'son/daughter/children', exhibit three-term agreement with the NP that follows, e.g.,

ɗan rằgō   a little ram, **'yaȓ tunkìyā**   little ewe, **'yan tumākī**   little sheep
ɗan gàjēren yārồ   a wee short boy, **'yaȓ gàjērìyaȓ yārinyằ**   a wee short girl, **'yan gàjàjjềrun yârā** wee short children

By contrast, in *-er/-or* type compounds, the formatives **ɗan / 'yaȓ / 'yan** serve as the head and thus the assignment of gender and number is determined by meaning rather than by concord, e.g.,

ɗan-kallō / 'yaȓ-kallō / 'yan-kallō   male spectator / female spectator / spectators   (**kallō** 'looking' is m., but this is irrelevant)
ɗan-ƙwằyā / 'yaȓ-ƙwằyā / 'yan-ƙwằyā   male drug user / female drug user / drug users   (**ƙwằyā** 'pill' is f., but this is irrelevant)

8. DEPENDENT HEADS

In NP of NP phrases, the first NP is usually the head and thus controls gender/number concord. There are, however, a few exceptions where the syntactic head is semantically weak and it is the second item that is dominant and constitutes the head for agreement purposes. I shall here describe two common *dependent heads*, but there are probably others as well.
One is the word **irìn** 'kind of' (composed of **irì** 'kind/type' plus the linker **-n**), which is usually invariant for gender and number, e.g.,

[wànè]ₘ irìn zanè	what kind of wrapper (m.)?
[wàcè]f irìn mōtà	what kind of car (f.)?
[wàɗànnè]pl irìn wàsànnin shāƙàtâwā	what kinds of recreations (pl.)?
[wani]ₘ irìn mùtûm	a certain kind of person (m.)
[waccàn]f irìn bishiyằ (= irìn waccàn bishiyằ)	that kind of tree (f.)
[kōwàɗànnè]pl irìn atamfōfī	all kinds of printed cloths (pl.)

°AN: Although **irìn** is usually invariant, it does have two related plural forms, e.g., **ìre-ìren mutằnē** 'kinds of people' (with a frequentative-type plural), and **rawā irì-irì** 'different kinds of dances' (with a fully reduplicated plural).

There are two possible ways to analyze gender/number assignment with **irìn**. First, one could treat **irìn** as being transparent (or permeable) for gender, so that in **wàcè irìn mōtà**, for example, **wàcè** would pass through **irìn** unaffected and agree with **mōtà**. Alternatively, one could treat **irìn** as being invariant in form but nevertheless picking up number/gender features from its controlling noun, e.g., **irìn [mōtà]f** ⇒ **[irìn]f [mōtà]f**, whereupon **wàcè**, for example, would agree with **[irìn]f**. (Note that **-n** would be used regardless of the gender of **irì** since the **-ȓ** allomorph of the linker is added only to feminine words ending in **-ā**.) The advantage of the second analysis is that it permits one to account for phrases where **irì** appears without or separated from its head noun, e.g.,

wàcè irì ka fi sô?	Which kind [f.] (e.g., car) do you prefer?,
cf. **wànè irì ka fi sô?**	Which kind [m.] (e.g., bicycle) do you prefer?

rìgařsù kuma wata irì cē dàbam	In addition their gowns are a different kind [f.].
gidansù kuma wani irì nē dàbam	In addition their houses are a different kind [m.].

Another dependent head whose agreement is determined by the second N is **rashìn** 'lack of', e.g.,

yā yi [wani]$_m$ rashìn [ladàbī]$_m$	He showed a certain lack of obedience.
yā ràsu bāyan [wata]$_f$ dōguwař rashìn [lāfiyà]$_f$	He died after a long illness. (lit. lack.of health)
rashìn [kunyàřsà]$_f$ [tanà]$_f$ bā nì màmākì	His lack of shame (f.) amazes me.
[wannàn]$_m$ dōgon rashìn [ruwā]$_m$ yā dàmē mù ainùn	
This long drought (lit. lack.of water (m.)) is bothering us a lot.	

Interestingly, a phrase composed of **rashìn** plus a pronoun takes masculine concord even if the pronoun is feminine, representing an understood feminine noun, e.g.,

[kunyà]$_f$, rashìntà [yakàn]$_m$ (not ****takàn**) **jāwō wàhalà**
   Shame (f.), lack of it (f.) it (m.) brings on trouble.
[bìyayyà]$_f$, rashìntà [yanà]$_m$ (not ****tanà**) **dāmùnā**
   Obedience (f.), lack of it (f.) it (m.) annoys me.
cf. **rashìn bìyayyà, bā nà sôntà** (not ****sônsà**)   Lack of obedience, I don't like it (f.)

9. MAI AND RELATED ITEMS

The function words **mài/màsu** 'possessing, having', which form modifier phrases with a following noun (see chap. **45**), agree with their head nouns in number but not in gender. Examples:

bàbûř / mōtà mài amincì	a durable motorcycle (m.) / car (f.)
(lit. motorcycle/car possessing soundness)	
bābuřà / mōtōcī màsu amincì	durable motorcycles / cars (pl.)
dòdō / mâyyā mài ban tsòrō	a frightening goblin (m.) / witch (f.)
dòdànnī / māyū màsu ban tsòrō	frightening goblins / witches (pl.)

The negative counterparts of **mài/màsu** are **maràř/maràsā** 'lacking'. These are also marked for number but not gender, e.g.,

ɓàrāwò / ɓàraunìyā maràř īmānì	a merciless thief (m./f.)
ɓàràyī maràsā īmānì	merciless thieves (pl.)
yārò / yārinyà maràř kunyà	a shameless boy / girl
yârā maràsā kunyà	shameless children (pl.)

The superlative markers **mafì / mafìyā**, which are grammaticalized agentive nouns derived from the verb **fi** 'exceed', also exhibit number, but not gender, agreement. Examples:

gidan àbinci mafì tsabtà	the cleanest restaurant (m.)
mōtà mafì tsàdā	the most expensive car (f.)
'yan ƙwallon rāgā mafìyā kyâu	the best basketball players (pl.)

10. ABSENCE OF GENDER CONCORD

To contrast Hausa with common patterns in other languages, it is worth mentioning explicitly a few areas where gender concord does *not* apply.

To begin with, there is no gender (or number) marking on verbs themselves, e.g., in **yā/tā/sun shìga** 'He/She/They entered', the verb **shìga** has the same form regardless of the nature of the subject, and in **yā kashè birì / kūrā / tsuntsầyē** 'He killed a monkey (m.) / a hyena (f.) / birds (pl.)', the verb **kashè** has the same form regardless of the gender or number of the object.

◊HN: In some Chadic languages (e.g., Bole), one does get three-way m./f./pl. agreement between the verb and the subject, but this is extremely rare. More common is number agreement or semantic compatibility between the verb and the direct object (or other patient); see Newman (1990b).

Attributive cardinal numbers are also invariant, e.g., **zākì / zākanyầ ɗaya** 'one lion/lioness', **mîl ukù** 'three miles', **dawākī gōmà** 'ten horses'. The ordinals, on the other hand, are built with a preceding linker and thus reflect gender/number, e.g., **zākì na ukù** 'the third lion'; **zākanyầ ta biyu** 'the second lioness', **màsu gudù na huɗu** 'the fourth runners'.

Unlike the long-form relative pronouns **wandà/waddà/waɗàndà** (with tonal variants) 'who, which, that' (m./f./pl.)', the bare relative marker **dà** 'that' is invariant, e.g., **yārồ wandà na ganī / yārinyầ waddà na ganī / yārā waɗàndà na ganī = yāròn/yārinyàr̃/yârân dà na ganī** 'the boy/girl/children that I saw'.

[Reference: Rufa'i (1977)]

33. HAVE Sentences

1. FORMATION (AFFIRMATIVE)

AFFIRMATIVE "HAVE" sentences are formed with a continuous TAM plus a predicate headed by the preposition **dà** 'with' (see table 3 with the accompanying examples).

Table 3: HAVE

1 s	inà dà	1 p	munà dà
2m	kanà dà	2 p	kunà dà
2f	kinà dà		
3m	yanà dà	3 p	sunà dà
3f	tanà dà		
		4p	anà dà

yārinyà tanà [dà zōbè]	The girl has a ring. (lit. girl she.cont with ring)
yārò yanà [dà fensìř]	The boy has a pencil. (lit. boy he.cont with pencil)
sunà [dà kuɗī]	They have money. (lit. they.cont with money)

Pronoun objects of **dà** use the independent set.

Bellò yanà dà <u>ita</u> Bello has it (f.).   **kunà dà <u>sū</u>?** Do you (pl.) have them?

As is normal in the continuous, the wsp in HAVE sentences can be deleted if there is an expressed subject, e.g., **àbōkīn Gařbà nà dà sàbuwař mōtà** 'Garba's friend has a new car.' HAVE sentences with quality predicates are unusual in that they allow deletion of both the wsp and the continuous marker, e.g.,

aikìn nân dà saukī (< **aikìn nân yanà dà saukī**)	This work is easy. (lit. …with ease)
wurîn dà 'yař tazarā (< **wurîn yanà dà 'yař tazarā**)	The place is a short distance away.

°AN: A plausible alternative analysis would be to treat sentences without the wsp and the continuous marker as being formed not with the preposition **dà** but rather with the homophonous existential marker, i.e., **aikìn nân dà saukī** would literally mean 'work this, there is ease'.

In Rel environments, the continuous is replaced by the Rcont2 form, which, when attached to a weak subject pronoun, has the form **-kè** with a short vowel. (If the wsp is omitted then the bare **kè** automatically appears with a long vowel.) Examples:

yāròn dà yakè dà fensìr̃	the boy who has a pencil (= yāròn dà kè̃ dà fensìr̃)
Kànde cě takè dà jàn-bàki	*Kande* has lipstick.
wǎ yakè dà bīr̃ò?	Who has a ballpoint pen?
gàr̃mâr̃ dà mutǎnē kè̃ dà ita	the plow that the men have

As illustrated in the previous example, if the object of **dà** is displaced, its must be replaced by a resumptive pronoun, e.g.,

àshānā cě yakè dà ita	It's matches he has. (lit. matches STAB he.Rcont2 with it (f.))
mě kikè dà shī?	What do you have? (lit. what you (f).Rcont2 with it (m.))
farǎren r̃īgunǎ kàm, munǎ dà sū	As for white gowns, we have them.

2. NEGATIVE-HAVE

The corresponding negative sentences make use of a special negative-HAVE paradigm (table 4) consisting of a falling-tone negative marker **bâ** (identical in shape with the negative existential marker) plus a CV pronoun with H tone. In the 1s and 3m persons, there are optional contracted forms: **bâ ni → bân; bâ ya → bâi.**

Table 4: Negative-HAVE

1s	bâ ni / bân	1p	bâ mu
2m	bâ ka	2p	bâ ku
2f	bâ ki		
3m	bâ shi / bâ ya / bâi	3p	bâ su
3f	bâ ta		
		4p	bâ a

The negative paradigm is followed by a **dà** + NP phrase as with the corresponding affirmative sentences, e.g.,

bâ mu dà ruwā	We don't have water. (lit. neg we with water)
bân dà làsīsì	I don't have a license.

An alternative means of negating HAVE sentences is to use a normal negative-continuous PAC rather than **bâ** plus a CV pronoun, e.g.,

bā yǎ dà fensìr̃ =	bâ shi dà fensìr̃	He doesn't have a pencil.
bā tǎ dà kōmē =	bâ ta dà kōmē	She doesn't have anything.

3. MEANING AND FUNCTION

3.1. Possession
HAVE sentences are so called because they indicate simple possession in a manner comparable to English constructions with the verb 'have', e.g.,

àbōkīnā yanǎ dà sābuwar̃ hùlā mài kyâu	My friend has a new good cap.

sunằ dà 'yā'yā bìyař	They have five children.
munằ dà dàbāřằ	We have a scheme.
Tàlātù bâ ta dà zōbẽ	Talatu doesn't have a ring.

3.2. Predicative qualities

HAVE sentences with complements consisting of abstract nouns indicate predicative qualities, e.g.,

munằ dà ƙarfī	We are strong. (lit. we.cont with strength)
yanằ dà ban-màmākī	It is amazing.
(lit. it.cont with giving.of-amazement)	
ƙauyènmù wàndà yakè dà nīsā	our village which is far away
(lit. village.of.our which it.Rcont2 with distance)	
rĩjìyâř nan (ta)nằ dà zurfī	That well is deep. (lit.well.of that 3f.cont with depth)
cf. rĩjìyâř nan zùzzurfā cẽ	That well is very deep. (lit.well.of that very deep STAB)
(equational sentence with the adjective zùzzurfā instead of the noun zurfī] (see §23:1)	

3.3. "Tough" and "quick" constructions
3.3.1. "Tough construction"

An English "tough construction" of the type 'The book is tough to read' is expressed in Hausa by a HAVE sentence in which the predicate consists of wùyā 'difficulty' or sauƙī 'ease' plus a linker (L) plus a verbal noun (VN). Examples:

tāgàř tanằ dà wùyař būɗằwā	The window is hard to open.
(lit. window.the 3f.cont with difficulty.L opening)	
igiyâř nân bâ ta dà wùyař tsinkềwā	This cord is not hard to snap.
madařā tanằ dà sauƙin shâ	Milk is easy to drink.
mōtàř nan bâ ta dà sauƙin gyārằwā (= gyārā)	That car is not easy to repair.

°AN: For a discussion of this construction in Hausa from a more theoretical perspective, see Bature (1991) and Yalwa (1995).

Verbs that have both weak and strong VNs, e.g., gyārằwā (weak) = gyārā (strong) 'repairing' (both < gyārằ 'repair'), normally allow either one to be used in a tough construction without any difference in meaning.

A thematic subject can be expressed by means of a prepositional phrase (à) wurin X 'at the place of X', e.g.,

mōtōcin wàje sunằ dà wùyař sàyē (à) wurin Gàmbo	Foreign cars are hard for Gambo to buy.
(lit. cars.of ourside 3p.cont with difficulty.L buying (at) place.of Gambo)	

Sentences semantically comparable to those with the tough construction (and from which the tough sentences are presumably derived via extraposition) exist that have an infinitive phrase or VN (phrase) as subject. Unlike tough sentences, which are restricted to transitive verbs, this structure is also found with intransitive verbs.

[rufềwā] tanằ dà wùyā	Closing (it) is difficult. (lit. closing 3f.cont with difficulty) (VN)
[tsinkè igiyâř nân] bâ shi dà wùyā	Snapping this cord is not hard. (IP)
[kařàntà littāfìn] yanằ dà wùyā	Reading (lit. read) the book is difficult. (IP)

ɓallèwā dàgà wannàn kûr̃kukù tanà̀ dà wùyā   Breaking out of this jail is difficult. (VN)
[sàyen mōtōcin wàje] yanà̀ dà wùyā à wurin Gàmbo   Buying foreign cars is hard for Gambo.
cf. [sàyen mōtōcin wàje] à wurin Gàmbo yanà̀ dà wùyā, which can either mean the same as the preceding or 'Buying foreign cars at Gambo's (dealership) is difficult.'

An alternative paraphrase is to have an 'It is hard/It is easy' HAVE clause at the front of the sentence followed by a tensed complement in the subjunctive, e.g.,

yanà̀ dà saukī [à kar̃àntà littāfìn]   It is easy to read (lit. that one read) the book.
bâ shi dà wùyā [à tsinkè igiyar̃ nân]   It is not difficult to break this cord.
yanà̀ dà saukī [Tankò yà gyārà halinsà]   It is easy for Tanko to improve his behavior.
yanà̀ dà wùyā [Gàmbo yà sàyi mōtōcin wàje]   It is difficult for Gambo to buy foreign cars.

Alternative paraphrases are also possible using a simple intransitive verb like fàskarà 'be impossible', e.g.,

yā fàskarà à kāmà ɓàrāwòn nan   It is impossible to catch that thief.
cf. ɓàrāwòn nan yā fàskarà kàmuwā   That thief is impossible to catch.

3.3.2. "Quick construction"

Sentences of the type 'The butter is quick/slow to melt' parallel the "tough construction" but use different qualitative nouns, namely, saurī 'quickness' and nàwā 'slowness', e.g.,

mân shānū yanà̀ dà saurin narkèwā   The butter is quick to melt.
gyàmbôn yanà̀ dà nàwar̃ warkèwā   The abscess is slow to heal.
zàrên yanà̀ dà saurin tsinkèwā   The thread is quick to snap.

Unlike "tough" sentences, the verbal noun in "quick construction" is built on an intransitive form of the verb, e.g.,

gìlāshìn yanà̀ dà saurin fashèwā   The glass is quick to break. (< fashè̀ v4-intr.)
cf. gìlāshìn yanà̀ dà wùyar̃ fasàwā   The glass is difficult to break. (< fasà v1-tr.)

The quick sentences semantically correspond to simple intransitive sentences containing a prepositional phrase or other adverb of manner, e.g.,

mân shānū yanà̀ narkèwā dà saurī   Butter melts quickly.
gyàmbôn yanà̀ warkèwā sànnu sànnu   The abscess is healing little by little.

4. OTHER MEANS OF EXPRESSING 'HAVE'

In place of normal HAVE sentences with abstract qualitative objects, it is possible to use an existential structure made up of àkwai plus a weak object pronoun followed by a dà + NP phrase. This alternative, which requires àkwai itself and not dà or dà àkwai, is semantically more marked and expressive than the normal HAVE construction. Examples:

àkwai shì dà wàyō ƙwar̃ai   He is very clever.
(lit there is him with cleverness very) = the normal yanà̀ dà wàyō ƙwar̃ai

mutằnen nàn, àkwai sù dà rōwằ   These men, they are misers.
(lit. men these, there is them with miserliness)

àkwai shì dà ban haushī   He's really aggravating.
(lit. there is him with giving.of annoyance)

◊HN: This construction helps explain the nonparallelism in SH between the affirmative HAVE sentences (e.g., **tanằ dà...**) and their normal SH negative counterparts (**bâ ta dà...**). Originally, the negative-HAVE forms (1b) would have been the negative counterpart of existential sentences (1a), whereas the tensed HAVE sentences in the continuous (2a) would have been negated by using the negative-continuous forms (2b), e.g.,

Affirmative | Negative
(1a) **àkwai tà dà...** | (1b) **bâ ta dà...**
(2a) **tanằ dà...** | (2b) **bā tằ dà...**

What happened historically is that the affirmative existential-type construction essentially dropped out as a normal means of expressing possession, whereas the corresponding negative remained and, for many speakers, tended to drive out the negative-continuous forms. The result was the skewed pairing of (2a) and (1b) that one finds in SH today.

34. Historical Sound Laws

COMPARATIVE studies of Hausa and other Chadic languages and internal reconstruction within Hausa have led to the discovery of a number of historical sound changes that the language has undergone. Some of these changes, e.g., *r > y, would appear to be quite old, as evidenced by the fact that they apply fully to all dialects, they feed other phonological developments, and they do not appear in synchronically active alternations. Others, e.g., *B > u, which only apply in some dialects, are historically recent and give evidence of still being ongoing. Some of the changes, e.g., Klingenheben's Law, are well established and well known. Others, e.g., final *ū > ō, still need to be verified. Some eleven sets of changes are described here.

1. CHANGES AFFECTING CONSONANTS

1.1. *r > y/i

Non-initial *r regularly changed to y/i. (In modern Hausa, the resultant glide appears as y in syllable onset position and i elsewhere.) This is clearly a very early change. Here are some selected examples. (The Proto-Chadic [PC] citations, which are not marked for tone, are drawn from Newman (1977a, and unpublished notes), supplemented by data from Jungraithmayr and Ibriszimow (1994). These all represent cognates widely attested throughout the Chadic family. The exact form of the PC citations, especially the vocalization, is not relevant here.)

àiki (< *arki) send (C-form) < PC *rəkə   kīfī fish < PC *kirfi
mâi oil < PC *mar   sōyằ fry < PC *surə
wuyằ neck < PC *wura
bùƙwī (< *bùƙuy) in a bare, exposed state < *buƙur?

Throughout Chadic, initial r tends to be a relatively uncommon phoneme, something also true of modern-day Hausa. It does, however, occur in a number of seemingly basic words, suggesting that the initial *r's that originally existed remained as such and did not undergo the change to /y/.

Assuming that all (or most) non-initial *r's changed to y/i, one needs to account for the fact that non-initial /r/ is extremely common in modern-day Hausa. A good hypothesis is that the source was *l, i.e., there was probably a regular change of *l > r. Suggestive cognates are yārò̀ 'child', PC *wulo; ɗārī 'cold', cf. Kanakuru ɗwal; cirè̀ 'extract', cf. Kanakuru tole; rufè̀ 'cover, close', cf. Kanakuru lipe.

The present-day l's probably have two sources, one internal and one external. The internal source in syllable-final position is the dialectally and idiolectally specific change from r̃, which itself represents rhotacism of an originally coronal obstruent, e.g., bìyar̃ 'five' (< bìyat < *bìyaɗ) (>) bìyal; far̃kè̀ 'become ripped' (>) falkè̀; gar̃mā 'large hoe' (>) gàlmā. The external source is the influx of loanwords from Arabic, many of which contain /l/, e.g., àlāmằ 'sign', àlbasằ 'onion', jāhìlī 'ignorant', fi'ìlī 'verb', làdân 'muezzin', lìnzāmì̀ 'bridle, bit'.

227

1.2. Initial *Ø > ' and **h**

In Old Hausa, neither / ' / nor /h/ existed as distinctive phonemes. (The lack of these phonemes was also true of Proto-Chadic (Newman 1977a, 1984b).) Before back-rounded vowels, phonetic [h] occurred, but this functioned only as an allophone of /f/, e.g., [màkāhò̃] = /màkāfò̃/ 'blind man'; [hūtà̃] = /fūtà̃/ 'rest'. The present-day / ' / and /h/ represent fairly recent phonemes, with language-external and language-internal sources (Newman 1976a). Externally, they represent borrowed phonemes that were introduced in initial and medial position along with Arabic loanwords that contained them (or phonetically related guttural consonants), e.g., **himmà̃** 'zeal, determination', **'àddu'à̃** 'prayer'. Internally, they resulted from the creation of an onset for vowel-initial words.

Modern Hausa has a rigid phonotactic constraint specifying that all syllables, and thus all words, must begin with a consonant. (Orthographically one finds vowel-initial words, but this is because initial glottal stop is not written, thus orthographic **aro** 'borrowing, a loan' is really / **'arō**/.) This was not always the case. At an earlier period, it was normal for words to begin with vowels, the occurring vowels being **a** and **i** (and possibly **u** as well). These word-initial vowels were probably pronounced with a glottal or breathy attack, but this was at a phonetic, subphonemic level. As some point in time a change occurred, possibly stimulated by the influx of Arabic loanwords, all of which are consonant-initial. This change involved the reanalysis and upgrading of the phonetic onsets as the phonemes / ' / and /h/.

°AN: This historical analysis, which was first presented in Newman (1976), was presaged by Parsons (1955: 388) some twenty years earlier when he wrote: "h and ' (the glottal stop) [are] the realizations of zero consonant with voiceless and glottalized prosodies respectively."

The nature of the word-initial phonetic attack (whether aspirated or glottal), which became the basis of the phonemicized consonantal onset, was determined essentially as follows. If the root already contained a glottalized consonant, then it was the nonglottal [h] that was added. This was in keeping with a general phonotactic aversion in Hausa to having two different glottal(ized) consonants in the same word (see §54:5.2). Examples:

haɓà̃	chin < *Øaɓa		**hatsī**	grain < *Øatsi
haɗè̃	swallow < *Øaɗe		**haƙà̃**	dig < *Øaƙa

°AN: In all of the examples, /h/ is followed by /a/. It is not clear what happened to words, assuming that they existed, that originally had the shape *ØiC$_{[+glot]}$V.

If the vowel-initial word did not contain a glottalized consonant, then ['] served as the phonetic onset. Examples:

'idò̃	eye < *Øido		**'ita**	she < *Øita
'aduwà̃	desert date < *Øado + f. suffix)		**'askì**	shaving < *Øaski (< *səki)
'àiki	send (C-form) < *Øaiki (< *Øarki < *rəkə)			

ΔDN: In some eastern dialects (like Guddiri) there is an additional source for initial glottal stop, namely the change of initial /ƙ/ to /'/, e.g., **'ōfà̃** = SH ƙōfà̃ 'doorway', **'ōtà̃** = SH ƙōtà̃ 'tool handle'.

Because there is no restriction against /h/ co-occurring with nonglottalized consonants, it is not surprising that some originally vowel-initial words have dialect variants using the two different initial consonants, e.g.,

'aihù /'aifù = haihù / haifù give birth (< *Øaifu)
'antà = hantà   liver (< *Øanta)

Terms for body parts present a particular puzzle. Many such words begin with /ha/, e.g.,

haɓà chin; haƙàrƙarī ribs; haƙōrī teeth; hamàtā / hammàtā armpit; hancì nose; hanjì
intestines; hannū arm, hand (cf. Ngizim **amai**); hantsà udder; harshè tongue (cf. PC *alse)

Leslau (1962) suggested that the initial /h/ in these Hausa words could reflect an old Afroasiatic body part
prefix. Because we now know that Old Hausa did not have /h/ as a phoneme, the /h/ that one sees could
not represent a direct reflex of such a prefix. On the other hand, Hausa could have had an **a**- prefix, for
which there is evidence elsewhere in Chadic, e.g., *alse 'tongue', *anji 'intestines', etc. Given our
general rule regarding the choice of glottal vs. aspirated onsets, the question here is why do these words
not begin with glottal stop? We would naturally expect the words containing a glottalized consonant to
have initial /h/, e.g., *Øaɓa > haɓà 'chin', but not the words without a glottalized consonant, which
should have become **/'alsè/, **/'anjì/, etc. The only plausible explanation that I can offer is that
morphological factors, i.e., the patterning of body part terms as a class, overrode or regularized the
output of the historical sound rules per se.

1.3. The sequence ɗiy > 'y
The Hausa phoneme /'y/, a laryngealized palatal semivowel, has an unusual status in the language.
Although it has a high frequency of occurrence, it is found only in what could be considered variants of
one root, namely, 'yā 'daughter' (cf. ɗā 'son, freeborn child'), 'yā'yā 'children', 'yaȓ 'diminutive
marker (f.)', 'yan 'diminutive marker (pl.)', 'yam + indirect object 'give a little (food)', 'yântā
'manumit', and 'yancì 'freedom'. (It is also used by some speakers in the place name 'Yōlà 'Yola' (<
Fulani).) This historically recent phoneme was created by the reduction of the morphemes ɗìyā
'daughter' and ɗiyā 'children', which are still extant in some WH dialects, to 'yā, both the LH and HH
tones on the resulting monosyllabic words being realized as H. The developmental sequence (ignoring
the tone) was *ɗiy > *ɗy > 'y.

> °AN: [i] Instead of viewing ['y] as a glottalized /y/, which is what is normally done by Hausaists,
> there is no reason why one couldn't treat it synchronically (in SH at least) as a palatalized /ɗ/, i.e.,
> /ɗy/, notwithstanding its phonetic realization as a semivowel. Note that phonetic [ɗy] doesn't
> occur in the language any more than [ty], for example, does, in the latter case, the palatalized /t/
> being realized as [č].
> [ii] As correctly emphasized by Gouffé (1969), although it is obvious how 'y historically came
> about, we still cannot deny it synchronic phonemic status, as was done by Parsons (1955: 388n). It
> is true that 'y represents a newly developed phoneme in the language, but a distinct phoneme it is.
> Interestingly, in the dialect of Filinge, in far northwest Hausa, 'y has separated even further from
> its *ɗiy source and is now pronounced as /ƙy/ (Malka 1978).

What is particularly informative about the *ɗiy > 'y change is that one can see how it developed. It
began with vowel loss and consonant fusion in a specific morpheme, the feminine diminutive marker,
and only later spread to other *ɗiy sequences. In WH dialects, the words for 'daughter'and 'children' still
preserve the original form, i.e., ɗìyā 'daughter' and ɗiyā 'children', and similarly in the words ɗiyàutā
'manumit', and ɗiyaucì 'freedom'. The diminutive markers, on the other hand, contain 'y as in SH,
e.g., 'yak kàssuwā 'small market'; 'yan tumākī 'small lambs'. Interestingly, in this latter example
with the plural diminutive (but not with the feminine diminutive) the unchanged form is still possible,

i.e., **ɗiyan tumākī** 'small lambs'. In short, it seems that the phoneme first emerged as a contracted pronunciation ['yar̃] of the grammaticalized morpheme **ɗîyar̃** 'diminutive (f.)' (< **ɗîyā** 'daughter of'). This pronunciation subsequently spread to the corresponding plural form **ɗiyan** > **'yan** 'diminutive (pl.)'; and only then, in SH, was the change generalized to all ***ɗiy** sequences.

1.4. Word-final *N > Ø

Although many Chadic languages dislike word-final obstruents, word-final sonorants are quite common. Old Hausa clearly allowed both of its nasals, /m/ and /n/, in word-final position. At some early historical period, both of these nasals (**N**) were both lost by a general ***N > Ø** rule (Schuh 1976). Examples:

kadà	crocodile < PC ***kadam**		**kūsù**	rat < PC ***kusum**
gīwā	elephant < PC ***giwan**		**guzà**	Nile monitor < PC ***guzan**
ukù	three < PC ***kun(u)**		**zàbō**	guinea fowl < PC ***zaban**

Subsequent to the loss of final nasals, word-final /m/ and /n/ have been reintroduced through sporadic apocope, e.g., **mùtûm** 'man' < **mùtumî**, **gidân** 'the house' < ***gidā-nì**, and through the addition of loanwords, e.g., **mālàm** 'teacher' < Arabic, **kwastàn** 'customs' < English, **dùbbân** 'wine' < French (dù vin). In modern-day SH, both /m/ and /n/ are usually pronounced [ŋ] in final position. It is possible that this change is recapitulating the first step in the old nasal-loss rule, i.e., final ***m / *n > ŋ**, whereupon ***ŋ > Ø**.

1.5. Klingenheben's Law

The designation "Klingenheben's Law" refers to a set of three historical changes resulting in the weakening of syllable-final (coda) consonants. As used here the term "Klingenheben's Law" has a very limited and specific sense, which does not comprise all of the phonological changes discussed in Klingenheben's (1927/28) own study. The changes originally applied to word-internal codas followed by an abutting consonant. Application of the rule in word-final position, which is also evident, probably represents rule extensions at a later date. Geminates were not affected, nor normally were ideophones, which by their nature are phonologically aberrant. The first two of these changes are essentially dormant—they do not, for example, apply to recent loanwords—the third is still operative (Schuh 1974b).

1.5.1. Syllable-final velars

Syllable-final velars historically weakened to /u/, e.g.,

talaucî	poverty < ***talak-cî**, cf. **talàkà** common man
sàraunìyā	queen < ***sàrak-nìyā**, cf. **sarkī** king
hauni	left < ***hagni**, cf. the doublet **hagu(n)**
haurè	tooth < ***haƙrè**, cf. **haƙōrī** tooth/teeth (originally a plural form)
zauɗà	move aside < ***zakɗà**, cf. the doublet **zākùɗā**
wàtàu	that is to say < ***wàtàk**, cf. WH **wàtàkà**

°AN: According to the phonological analysis adopted here, /w/ in syllable-final position does not function as a coda consonant but rather constitutes a vowel /u/ that automatically attaches to the nucleus as the second part of a diphthong (or long vowel). Note, for example, that the word **ɓaunā** (<***ɓaknā**) 'buffalo' forms its plural either as **ɓakànē**, building an internal plural utilizing the historical C_2—this plural formation requiring three consonants—or else as **ɓaunàyē**, using the formation typical of other CVVCVV singulars. What one does not get is ****ɓawànē**, which would be the expected plural form if the correct phonemicization were truly /ɓawnā/ with a /w/ coda. Regarding the formulation of the historical change, one could still describe it as *velar > /w/, as traditionally done, i.e., as a change from one consonant to a weaker consonant, as long as one understands that the output is immediately subject to the /w/ → /u/ change. Whether there is any justification for the postulated /w/ between the velar starting point and the /u/ endpoint is still debatable. (The analytical issue discussed here applies equally to the *labial > /u/ component of Klingenheben's Law.)

If the vowel preceding the affected velar was /u/, the surface output was a long monophthongal vowel, thereby hiding the erstwhile consonantal coda, e.g.,

nǜna	ripen (naturally) < *nùk-na (with frozen suffix), cf. nùka	ripen (with assistance)
tūshìyā	stubble of corn < *tuk^Wsìyā (with fem. suffix), cf. alt. pl. tuk(w)āsū (= tūshiyōyī)	
zūcìyā	heart < *zuktìyā (with fem. suffix), cf. pl. zukā̀tā	

◊HN: Disyllabic words with a long /ū/ in the first syllable are fairly common. It is possible that many of these derive historically from CVCCV words, where the C_2 was a velar. Synchronically, there is no way to determine which of these words were originally CVVCV in shape and which were CVCCV. Words that could be suspected of hiding an original syllable-final velar (which one would need to examine comparatively) would include such examples as būɗè̖ 'open', cūnà̖ 'set psn or animal to catch or attack s.o.', cūsà̖ 'stuff sth into sth', hūɗà̖ 'bank up ridges in a farm with a plow', kūjè̖ 'abrade, scratch', tūɓè̖ 'take off (clothing)', ūfè̖ 'run away quickly, disappear'.

1.5.2. Syllable-final labials
Syllable-final labial consonants also weakened to /u/. The law affecting labials, which is the historically most shallow of the three, applied in SH only. In WH, labials in coda position remained as such, e.g.,

Audù	proper name	= Abdù [WH]
audùgā	cotton	= abdùgā [WH]
kaurī	thickness	= kabrī [WH]
sàuka	get down	= sàfka [spelled sabka] [WH]

ΔDN: Interestingly, such names as Àbdùllāhì, Àbdùlsàlâm, and Àbdùlmālìk are typically pronounced with /b/ rather than /u/ even by SH speakers who normally say Audù rather than Abdù.

The change also affected syllable-final /m/, but only when abutting with a following /r/ or /n/. When followed by other consonants, m remained a nasal and generally assimilated to the position of the abutting consonant, e.g., gàmzākì > gànzākì 'morning star'. Examples:

aurē	marriage (cf. amaryā bride)	= amrē [WH]
gàurākà̖	crownbird	= gàmrākà̖ [WH]
ɗaurè̖	tie (cf. ɗàmarà̖ amulet belt)	= ɗamrè̖ [WH]
màkaunìyā	blind woman	= màkamnìyā [WH]
zaunà̖	sit (cf. zamā being)	= zamnà̖ [WH]

◊HN: The SH form màkaunìyā 'blind woman' is usually described as being derived from the stem màkāfò̖ 'blind man' (with the final vowel dropped) + a feminine suffix -nìyā, thereby instantiating the */f/ > /u/ change. This is probably incorrect. More likely, the obstruent */f/ did not change directly into /u/, i.e., there was no *màkafnìyā > màkaunìyā change. Rather */f/ (and */b/) regularly assimilated to /m/ before nasal consonants in all dialects and only then did one get the SH change of */m/ followed by /n/ going to /u/. Other likely examples of the obstruent to nasal rule are **gwamnà** 'governor' < *gwabnà and **sàmmakō** 'getting an early start in the morning' < *sàfmakō (cf. **sāfe** 'morning').

ΔDN: Some northern dialects that preserved /m.r/ abutting sequences have undergone systematic metathesis to /r.m/, e.g., **amrē > armē** 'marriage'; **ɗamrè > ɗarmè** 'tie'; **gàmrākà > gàrmākà** 'crownbird'.

The labial to /u/ change fed a monophthongization rule *iu > ū (described below in §2.3), e.g.,

shūkà	sow (< *shiukà)	= shifkà [spelled **shibka**] [WH]
jūdà	musk (< *jiudà)	= j ibdà [WH]
jūrè	endure (< *jiurè)	= jimrè [WH]

It has long been known that the labial component of Klingenheben's Law was dialect-limited, Scholars have not, however, noticed the extent to which the weakening of labial obstruents was phonologically conditioned and lexically restricted. (This lack of regularity is what one would expect with a historical sound law that is so recent it has not had time to work its way systematically throughout the language.) For example, when abutting with /r/ or /sh/, the change was fully operative (see (a)); when abutting with /t/ (or /c/) or /g/, the weakening did not occur (see (b)); and when followed by /d/, or /k/, the law was lexically specific and unpredictable (see (c)). Examples:

(a) **taurè**	castrated goat	= tabrè [WH]
shūrà	kick (< *shiurà)	= shibrà [WH]
haushì	barking	= hafshì [spelled **habshì**] [WH]
taushī	type of drum (pl. **tafàshē**)	= tafshī [spelled **tabshi**] [WH]
(b) **kaftà**	dig ground for planting (no change)	
ƙìfcē	winking, blinking (no change)	
dàbgē	a stew with a lot of meat (no change)	
jibgà	pile loads on one another (no change)	
(c) **yauɗō**	an herb	= yabɗō [WH]
cf. **rìbɗā**	demolish (no change)	
àuku	happen, occur	= àfku [WH]
cf. **tafkì**	lake (no change)	

The weakening rule has generally not affected labial obstruents occupying coda position as a result of morphological suffixation, e.g.,

ɗālìbcē	become a student (not **ɗālùcē) < ɗālìbī student
hasàftā	give a small present to s.o. < hasàfī gift
màƙwàbtakà	neighborliness < //maƙwàb-// (cf. maƙwàbcī neighbor)
la'ifcì	impotence < là'ìfì impotent
zubshē	pour out (gr5 B-form) < zubà pour in (gr1)

Doublets with some Arabic loanwords indicate that the tendency to weaken syllable-final labial obstruents has spilled over into word-final position, e.g., àlû = àlîf the letter aleph; shàr̃û = shàr̃îf holy man tracing descent from the Prophet

1.5.3. Syllable-final coronals

Syllable-final coronal obstruents (**t**, **ɗ**, and **d**) changed to rolled /r̃/. (The phonemic opposition between the flap /r/ and the rolled /r̃/ is to a great extent due to this rhotacism rule.)

far̃kà	wake up = fàɗakà		ɓàr̃nā	damage (n.)	< ɓàtà to damage (vb.)
'yar̃sà	his daughter = 'yātasà		far̃kē	itinerant trader	(< *fatkē), cf. pl. fatàkē

ΔDN: In various, mostly WH, dialects, syllable final /r̃/ has altered into /l/. Although SH has not undergone this change as a regular rule, the word for 'trader' often appears as **falkē** rather than as **far̃kē**.

In Klingenheben's original formulation, the syllable-final change to rolled r̃ was described as also applying to /s/ and /z/. This is incorrect, as evidenced by the numerous examples of syllable-final /s/ and /z/ that remained unaltered, e.g.,

kaskō	earthen bowl		ƙyastà	strike flint
fìzgā	grab, snatch		ƙyàzbī	skin disease on face, neck
kwàsfā	shell, pod		ƙazwā	scabies

Some examples of the sibilants /s/ and /z/ undergoing rhotacism do exist, but like the labial codas, (a) the weakening is limited to SH only; (b) it is phonological conditioned (occurring primarily when folllowed by a nasal, esp. /n/); and (c) it is lexically sporadic. Examples:

binnè (< *bir̃nè)	bury		= biznè	[WH] (cf. bisò burying)
ar̃nā (= annā)	pagans		= aznā	[WH]
gàr̃mā	a large hoe		= gàsmā	[WH]
gur̃ɗè	sprain		= gusɗè	[WH]

°AN: Contrary to Klingenheben's assertion, which has been repeated by many Hausa scholars, syllable-final /r/ does not automatically change into rolled r̃, cf. **sarkī** 'chief', **farcè** 'fingernail', **fùrfurtà** 'go gray', **sartsè** 'splinter'. Rather, it does so only under specific phonological conditions, which still apply synchronically (see §54:1.1.1).

Although the rhotacism rule continues to operate in the language as an active process, it appears to be historically quite old. As a result it is much more difficult to find good examples of morphophonemic alternations involving a coronal obstruent and /r̃/ than it is between a velar obstruent and /u/. In modern Hausa, there are numerous examples of CVCCV words with syllable-final r̃. We can assume that in most cases the r̃ came historically from *t, *ɗ, or *d, even when there is no extant internal evidence. Such examples include the following:

bur̃gà (< *budga ?) whisk with swizzle stick; **bur̃gū** (< *budgu ?) giant male rat or bandicoot; **ɓar̃kè** (< *ɓatke ?) break out; **càr̃kī** (< *catki or *caɗki ?) ox-pecker bird; **màr̃gā** (< *madga ?) cassia tree; **màr̃kā** (< *matka or maɗka ?) heavy rainy days; **wur̃gà** (< *wudga ?) throw hard

The rhotacism applies also (or has historically applied) to some instances of coronal obstruents in word-final position. This, however, is *not* an automatic process, e.g., kâř < *kâd (< kadà) don't! kyař = kyat difficult; bìyař = [WH] bìyat (< *bìyaɗ) five

Some words ending in /s/ allow final ř as an alternative pronunciation, but most such words (especially loanwords from Arabic and English) do not, e.g.,

maràř = maràs lacking (cf. pl. maràsā); mâř = mâs (< masà) to him; fitař = fitas [WH] take out; takwàř = (but less common than) takwàs eight; wàřwař = wàřwas ideophone describing falling flat on ones back
cf. ìbìlîs devil (Ar.), mùřābùs resignation (Ar.), àlhàmîs Thursday (Ar.), ōfìs office (Eng.), dùřôs underpants (Eng.), kařàs carrots (Eng.)

1.6. Law of Codas in Reduplication

Most descriptions of Hausa (including Klingenheben's own study) cite reduplicated words to illustrate the operation of Klingenheben's Law, e.g., mařmàtsā (< *mats-màtsā) 'push, pester repeatedly', cf. matsà 'push, pester'; mařmaza (< *maz-maza) 'very quickly', cf. maza 'quickly'. This is a serious error. Properly speaking, these observed changes should not be lumped together with Klingenheben's Law but rather need to be accounted for by a distinct set of rules applying to codas in reduplicated forms. (I have designated these rules as the *Law of Codas in Reduplication*.) In the case of syllable-final **t, ɗ** and **d**, the Law of Codas in Reduplication and Klingenheben's Law coincide; otherwise they do not. The Law of Codas in Reduplication applied historically *and* is still operative. (In the description that follows, I shall thus conveniently use the historical present.)

1.6.1. Gemination

In reduplicative forms (both historically frozen and morphologically active), syllable-final "grave" obstruents (i.e., velars and labials) form a geminate with the following abutting consonant rather than weakening to /u/ as happens with Klingenheben's Law. Examples:

(a) Velar: fiffikè̌ < *fik-fikè̌ wing; hàɓàɓɓakà < *hàɓak-ɓakà expand significantly < hàɓakà swell; sassàɓ̂ā < *saɓ-sàɓ̂ā carve; kàfaffagō < *kàfag-fagō figlike tree; bubbùgā < *bug-bùgā beat repeatedly < bugà beat
(b) Labial: dûddufà̌ < *dûf-dufà̌ sacred white ibis; daddàfā < *daf-dàfā cook repeatedly < dafà cook; cicciɓā < *ciɓ-ciɓā big girl, big hen; lallàɓē < *laɓ-làɓē crouch repeatedly or by many < laɓè̌ crouch; sassàbē < *sab-sàbē clear land to make farm

ΔDN: Unlike the labial > /u/ component of Klingenheben's Law, which is restricted to SH, this rule applies to all dialects.

In simple words, syllable-final /w/, which phonologically counts as a velar, remains as such and is realized as the /u/ component of the vocalic nucleus, e.g., bàutā 'slavery' (< *bàwtā < bāwà̌ 'slave'). In reduplicated words, syllable-final /w/ commonly undergoes gemination. With certain items the gemination has become fixed; with others it is optional, e.g.,

dàddawā = dàudawā < *dàw-dawā   locust bean cake
shâsshāwà̌ = shâushāwà̌ < *shâw-shāwà̌   tribal marks
tsâttsēwà̌ < *tsêw-tsēwà̌   a swift, swallow
hàhhawà̌ = hàuhawà̌ < *hàw-hawà̌   rising (of river in flood or of blood pressure)
cf. **hau** climb up

By contrast, the palatal glide /y/ does not exhibit gemination in frozen reduplicated forms, although gemination is possible in some active reduplications, e.g.,

kwĩkwiyŏ < *kwiy-kwiyŏ < *kuy-kuyŏ   puppy
ràiràyī < *rày-ràyī   fine sand
zaizàyē < *zay-zàyē   erode
cf. sàisàyē = sàssàyē < *sày-sàyē   repeated buying, cf. **sàyē** buying

1.6.2. Rhotacism

In reduplication, all syllable-final obstruents change to r̃. Unlike the case with Klingenheben's Law, this change also affects the sibilants /s/ and /z/ (and their palatalized counterparts /sh/ and /j/). As with the reduplicated gemination rule, this change manifests itself in historically frozen forms (a) and continues to apply in active reduplicative formations (b). Examples:

(a) **kwâr̃kwatã** < *kwât-kwatã lice; **war̃wàɗā** < *waɗ-wàɗā write quickly; **gwàr̃gwadō** < *gwàd-gwadō proportion, moderation; **kwar̃kwàsā** < *kwas-kwàsā driver ant; **kwàr̃kwàshī** < *kwàs-kwàshī dandruff; **gir̃gìzā** < *giz-gìzā shake; **r̃agar̃gàjē** < *r̃agaz-gàzē be shattered
(b) **fir̃fìta** (= fiffìta) < //fìt-fìta// go out (many or often), cf. **fìta** go out; **mar̃màtsā** < //mats-màtsā// push, pester repeatedly, cf. **màtsà** push, pester; **hur̃huɗu** < //huɗ-huɗu// four each, cf. **huɗu** four; **kar̃kàshē** (= kakkàshē) < // kas-kàsē// kill many, cf. **kàshè** kill; **mar̃maza** < //maz-maza // very quickly, cf. **maza** quickly

It should be pointed out that the putative syllable-final **r** to r̃ change (see note above) is just as inapplicable in reduplicated as in nonreduplicated words, e.g.,

furfurã *not* ****fur̃furã** gray hair; **gùrgurà** *not* ****gùr̃gurà** gnaw ; **kirkirã** (= kikkirã) *not* ****kir̃kirã** call many, often

> ◊HN: In a small (but not inconsequential) number of frozen reduplicated words, one finds an anomalous nasal appearing in coda position in place of the expected /l/ or /r/ or other coronal consonant (see §62:3.1.1.3), e.g., **janjalō** 'pebble'< *jal-jalo, **kankarè** 'food scrapings from pot' < *kar-karè, **kyànkyasŏ** 'roach' < *kyàs-kyasŏ, **gyangyàɗā** 'nod from drowsiness' < *gyaɗ-gyàɗā. This change does not appear to be due to a phonologically regular sound law; on the other hand, the instances are too numerous to allow one to ignore them as insignificant exceptions. The matter needs and deserves a careful historical investigation.

2. CHANGES AFFECTING VOWELS

2.1. Medial *ī > ē and *ū > ō

Old Hausa most likely had a skewed 2-3-5 vowel system. That is, it had two short vowels, /i/ and /a/, in word-initial position; five short vowels, /i/, /e/, /a/, /o/, /u/, in word-final position (the lengthening of final vowels historically occurring later); and three vowels, /i(i)/, /a(a)/, /u(u)/, in medial position, all of which could be either long or short. (The language presumably also had two diphthongs, /ai/, and /au/, which need not concern us here.) Present-day Hausa also has /ē/ and /ō/—always long (apart from a few loanwords)—as commonly occurring medial vowels. These vowels historically resulted from a conditioned sound change, whereby long /ī/ and long /ū/ lowered to the corresponding mid vowels when followed in the next syllable by a mid vowel, i.e., $*V_{[+high, +long]} > V_{[+mid, +long]} / \underline{\quad} \cdots V_{[+mid]}$.

As best as one can determine, this anticipatory assimilation rule was exceptionless. Presumed examples of words having undergone this change are:

*bībe > bēbē mute; ***kīsò > kēsò̀** mat; ***tūzo > tōzō** hump, ***zūbè > zōbè̀** ring

The rule did not apply to short /i/ and /u/, which explains the absence of short /e/ and /o/ in medial position.

Originally the long high vowels and the long mid vowels would have been in complementary distribution, the phonetic distinction caused by the assimilation being subphonemic. Subsequent changes resulted in long high vowels being followed by a mid vowel and by long mid vowels being followed by a non-mid vowel, thus throwing the two sets of vowels into contrast. The following represent the major processes that resulted in the vowel split.

(1) When the feminative suffix -ā was added to words ending in /e/ and /o/, these vowels raised on the surface to /i/ and /u/, e.g.,

tōliyā tuft < ***tōle-ā** < ***tūle**; **tōtùwā** pulp < ***tōtò-ā** < ***tūtò**
cf. **dūdùwā** a song < ***dūdù-ā** < ***dūdù**

(2) Sporadic raising of /ā/ when preceded by a palatal(ized) or labialized consonant resulted in long mid vowels before /ā/, e.g ,

cēř̄ā crowing of cock < **cāř̄ā** (still extant in WH); **gōnā** farm < ***gwānā**

(3) Sporadic monophthongization of /ai/ (and less often /au/) resulted in examples of /ē/ and /ō/ before non-mid vowels, e.g.,

sēmā container < **saimā**; **lōmà̀** morsel of food < **laumà̀**; **dōkì̀** horse < ***daukì̀** (< ***dawkì**, cf. pl. **dawākī**)

(4) The operation of Klingenheben's Law weakening syllable-final consonants resulted in the creation of new long /ū/'s before mid-vowels. (The fact that Klingenheben's Law did not feed the mid-vowel rule indicates that it (KL) is historically more recent.) Examples:

tūshè̀ (not ****tōshè̀**)   base < ***tukwsè** (cf. pl. **tukwāsū**)
jūrè̀ (not ****jōrè̀**)   endure < **jimrè̀** (still found in WH)

(5) With the establishment of /ē/ and /ō/ as distinct phonemes in medial position, they were available for use in recent loanwords in nonconditioned environments, e.g.,

tēlà̀ tailor; **fēgì** peg; **mōtà̀** automobile; **jōjì** judge

2.1.1. Synchronic alternations

Because the vowel lowering is a historically old rule, the medial *ī/*ū > ē/ō change has left few active alternations in the language. It does manifest itself, however, in the small, lexically frozen set of "ablauted verbal nouns." A number of disyllabic verbs with /ē/ or /ō/ in the first syllable have corresponding verbal nouns with the pattern ī...ā)^{HL} or ū...ā)^{HL}, e.g.,

	Verb	*VN*		*Verb*	*VN*
pare	fērè	fīrà	rub	gōgè	gūgà
tan	jēmà	jīmà	scratch	sōsà	sūsà
comb	tsēfè	tsīfà	burn	tōyà	tūyà

Synchronically, it seems reasonable to derive the verbal noun from the corresponding verb by specifying the change in the initial vowel from mid to high. Viewed historically, however, the verbal noun formative probably consisted solely in the suffix -ā)^{HL}, the high vowel in the first syllable being the original, underlying vowel. What changed in these words was the initial vowel in the *verb*, e.g., *fīrè to pare > fērè; *gūgè to rub > gōgè. The exact details of the conditioning are not understood, i.e., we do not know what final vowel in what form of the verb caused the lowering of the medial high vowel, but the direction of the change and the class of words affected seems clear.

◊HN: The irregular alternation found in the gr2 verb 'to dip out', namely dībà (A-form, no object), dèbē (B-form, pre-pronoun object), dèbi (C-form, pre-noun object), is due to this vowel lowering followed by a redeployment of the originally H-L ā-final verbal noun dībà as a finite verb form.

The high/mid alternation appears also with certain irregular H-H verbs. Again, we can be sure that the high vowel was original and that the mid vowel was due to phonologically conditioned vowel lowering, e.g.,

tsīra (gr3a) escape, cf. tsērè (gr4) escape from; ɓūya (gr3a) hide, cf. ɓōyè (gr4) hide (from); kūkā (n.m.) crying, cf. kōkà (gr1) cry, complain

2.2 Lowering of final *ū > ō

Based on the method of internal reconstruction, one can postulate a historical lowering of word-final */u(u)/ to /o(o)/ when the preceding syllable contained long /ā/ (Newman 1990a). (Note: At present, all of the words that presumably underwent this change end in long /ō/. There is no way to know whether the vowel lowering took place before or after final vowels underwent lengthening.) Examples:

sābō < *sābū new, cf. sàbùntā freshness, newness; bàkō < *bàkū guest, stranger, cf. bākuncì hospitality, being a stranger; yārò < *yārù boy, cf. yàrìntā (< *yàrùntā) childhood, childishness; zàbō < *zàbū guinea-fowl, pl. zàbī; kwàɗō < *kwàɗū frog, pl. kwàɗī; tsàkō < *tsàkū chick, pl. tsàkī

The evidence for the proposed change is provided by various internal factors. These consist of phonotactic gaps, irregular morphophonemic alternations, and morphological asymmetries.

The phonotactic gap is the unexpected rarity in the language of words of the shape CāCū, as opposed to the very common CāCō pattern. Most of the examples of CāCū words that do exist are plurals, e.g., shānū 'cattle'; rāmū 'holes' (plural of rāmì), etc.

The irregular morphophonemic alternation involves the appearance of /u/ rather than /a/ in the formation of some abstract nouns. For example, sābō 'new' + -ntā is realized as sàbùntā 'newness' (which is what would be expected if the stem were *sābū) and not **sàbàntā (which is what would be expected if the stem were *sābō).

The morphological pattern asymmetry shows up with plurals formed by final vowel change, e.g., rāmì / rāmū 'holes', cf. zàbō / zàbī 'guinea-fowl'. Synchronically, one has to describe these plurals with totally ad hoc rules specifying that -ì ⇒ -ū and -ō ⇒ -ī (see §56:10). The original morphological rule, however, was probably a symmetrical one in which high vowels switched on a front/back dimension, i.e., -ī ⇒ -ū and -ū ⇒ -ī. Assuming that this was the nature of the morphological rule, then words like **zàbō** would have had to have come from words of the form **zàbū*, etc.

2.3. *Monophthongization of* *iu *and* *ui

Synchronically Hausa only has two phonemic diphthongs /ai/ and /au/, these two being the norm in Chadic languages. At a historically shallow period, it also had two more diphthongs, namely, *iu and *ui. These were eliminated by two monophthongization rules.

> °AN: A few scholars, e.g., Abubakar (1983/85), even ascribe synchronic status to these diphthongs, a position with which I am sympathetic, although not totally in agreement. Significantly, in Mischlich's (1911) dictionary, which dates back to the beginning of this century, words are written with the **iu** and **ui** diphthongs in both Roman and Arabic transcriptions.

Rule 1. *iu > ū. The *iu diphthong, which arose primarily as a result of Klingenheben's Law changing syllable-final velars and labials to /u/, e.g., *shifka > *shiuka 'to plant', monophthongized to /ū/. Conditioned palatalization of preceding obstruents was preserved. Examples:

*shiukà > shūkà   plant; *shiurà (< shibrà) > shūrà   kick; *shiu (short form of shirū) > shū silence; *jiujī (< jibjī) > jūjī   refuse heap; *jiudà (< jibdà) > jūdā   musk; *jiurè (< jimrè) > jūrè endure; *ciushè (< *cikshè) > cūshè   stuff in (< cikà fill?); *jiunā (< *jiknā) > jūnā   each other (< jìkī body); *kikiu-kikiu (< *kikiw-kikiw) > *kikyū-kikyū   describes standing alert; *riushè (< *rip-shè?) > rūshè   demolish, cave in; *biudè (< *bik-dè?) > būdè   open

Note the significant manner in which this *iu > ū vowel change had an impact on the consonantal system. Before the operation of the vowel change, palatal consonants occurred only preceding front vowels and a(a), e.g., /shī/, /shē/, and /shā/ were possible, but **/shū/ and **/shō/ were not. The monophthongization rule resulted in examples (as illustrated above) of /sh/, /j/, and /c/ before /ū/.

Rule 2. *ui > ī. The *ui diphthong probably arose earlier than *iu as a result of the old *r > y/i change, e.g., *mar > mâi 'oil'. It monophthongized to long /ī/, preserving conditioned labialization of preceding velar consonants. Examples:

*bù$\mathrm{ƙ}^W$ui (< *buƙui < *buƙuy < *buƙur) > bùƙwī   in a bare, exposed state
*g^{W}uiwà (< *guiwa < *gurwa ?) > gwīwà   knee
*k^{W}uiɓì > kwīɓì   flesh on side of body
*ƙ^{W}uita(a) > ƙwīta(a)   fart
*lug^{W}uigùitā > lugwīgwìtā   knead in order to soften
*luƙ^{W}ui (< *luƙui < *luƙuy < *luƙur) > luƙwī   emphasizing finely ground or pounded
*tuk^{W}uicì > tukwīcì   small gift, tip

> ΔDN: The change has not completely affected the Sokoto dialect; thus words like **tukuicì** are pronounced as such without the long ī.

Like the corresponding /iu/ to /ū/ change, the /ui/ to /ī/ change resulted in the appearance of previously non-occurring consonant vowel sequences. Originally, labialized velars, e.g., /kw/, occurred only preceding back-rounded vowels (where the labial element is normally not represented orthographically) or before /a(a)/, i.e., kwū, kwō, and kwā were possible but **/kwī/ and **/kwē/ were not. The change resulted in the appearance of /kw/, /gw/, and /ƙw/ before /ī/, as illustrated above.

Related to the historical */ui/ to /ī/ rule is a synchronic pronunciation rule that alters short /u/ into [i], when the /u/ is followed by /y/ in the next syllable. The rule is accompanied by preservation of labialization on the preceding consonant. In the examples that follow, the form on the left is the synchronically underlying form, normally found in spelling (apart from tone and vowel length); the form on the right is the colloquial pronunciation, e.g., **àkuyằ** → [àkwiyằ] 'goat'; **dằguyằ** → [dằgwiyằ] 'gnaw at, eat much of (meat)'; **kùyangā** → [kwìyangā] 'slave girl'; **tùnkùyau** → [tùnkwìyau] 'flea(s)'; **wuyằ** → [wiyằ] 'neck'.

ΔDN: SH does not have labialized labials, like /mw/, as part of the phonological inventory. In WH dialects, where they occur, the /u.y/ to /i.y/ results in such examples as **dùlmuyà** → [dùlmwiyà] 'sink deeply into a liquid', **sùlmuyà** → [sùlmwiyà] 'fall or slip into', etc.

Reduplicated words illustrate the change of /u/ to /i/ conditioned by /y/ in the same as well as in the following syllable, e.g.,

*cikwuykwùyā → cukwīkwìyā crumple; *gwùygwuyằ → gwĩgwiyằ gnaw; *kwuykwuyồ → kwīkwiyồ puppy, hyena pup, lion cub; *lukwuykwùyā → lukwīkwìyā grind or pound finely

3. CHANGES AFFECTING TONE

3.1. Monosyllabic H > F by tone bending

Falling tone in Hausa normally represents HL derived from a disyllabic sequence being realized on a single syllable, e.g., **kâř** 'don't' < **kadà**; **dâbgī** = **dābùgī** 'anteater'; **bêlbēlà** < *bēlàbēlà 'cattle egret', **zân** (= **zā nì**) 'I.future'. There are, however, a certain number of monosyllabic nouns with falling tone for which one has no reason, synchronically or diachronically, to postulate a lost syllable. All of these nouns have a heavy syllable. The historical explanation seems to be the following (Newman 1992a). In Old Hausa, monosyllabic nouns, which were either CVV or CVC, were all monotonal with H tone. (There were thus like present-day monosyllabic verbs, which do not contrast for tone.) Subsequently, they underwent a rule of "tone bending" whereby H > F. Possible examples would include:

mâi oil (cf. PC *mar); **sâ** bovine (cf. PC *hla); **kâi** head (cf. PC *kā or *kan); **wâ** elder brother; **gû** place (= **gurī** H-H)

This historical change may account for the tonal alternation found synchronically between monosyllabic grade 0 verbs, which have H tone, and their corresponding verbal nouns, which have falling tone. Note that all of the verbal nouns have a long vowel regardless of the vowel length of the verb. Examples:

ci to eat / **cî** eating (< *cī)   **jā** to pull / **jâ** pulling (< *jā)
sō to want, to love / **sô** wanting, love (< *sō)

The synchronic alternation may be due to the following historical scenario. Verbs with a short final vowel were altered into verbal nouns by vowel lengthening (a feature still found in other verb grades). The verbal nouns now being monosyllabic *nouns* with a long vowel were thus subject to the H > F tone bending rule. Postulated examples:

[ci]$_V$ ⇒ *[cī]$_N$ (category shift and vowel lengthening) > **cî** (phonological tone bending)
[jā]$_V$ ⇒ *[jā]$_N$ (category shift) > **jâ** (phonological tone bending)

3.2. Low-tone raising (LTR)

In the Chadic family, vowel-length contrasts, where they occur, tend to be restricted to word-medial position. Final vowels are typically all short (with the possible exception of monosyllabic **Cā** words). Presumably, this was also the case in Old Hausa. Due to various morphological processes, final vowels were lengthened. The result was that final long vowels are now the norm (at least in the case of common nouns). This vowel lengthening had major tonal consequences. Before the change, words could presumably have ended in all four ditonal patterns, i.e., H-H, H-L, L-H, and L-L. Subsequent to the change, there was a conditioned tone shift (low-tone raising (LTR)), namely, *L-L > L-H if the final vowel was long. (Ideophones, which by their nature are phonologically aberrant, were not subject to the rule.)

> °AN: Low-tone raising (LTR), which was first formulated by Leben (1971), is treated by him and others as a phonologically active rule in modern Hausa. While this may have been so until fairly recent historical times, there is no convincing evidence that LTR still has any synchronic viability; see Newman and Jaggar (1989a, 1989b); Schuh (1989c).

One can cite three phenomena as evidence for the historical operation of LTR.

(1) Phonotactic gap. Focusing on the final two syllables of polysyllabic words, one finds that H-L, L-H, and H-H occur but that L-L is conspicuously absent, except in the case of words with a short final vowel, like **màcè** 'woman', **dàgà** 'from', or with recent loanwords from English, like **sakandàrè** 'secondary school', **rēlùwè** 'railway'. (Ideophones, as would be expected, constitute an exception, e.g., **zòròrò** 'exceedingly tall', **buzū-bùzù** 'very hairy'.) Because L-L is not uncommon in related Chadic languages, and because there is no reason to believe that it was absent in Hausa at an earlier period, it is reasonable to postulate that its loss in Hausa was due to a phonological change, the most likely being the proposed *L-L > L-H change.

(2) Reduplicated nouns. In frozen reduplicated nouns of the form CVC(V)-CVCV (the (V) being deleted), the tone can be seen to have been copied exactly along with the segmentals. (Note: At the time of the reduplication, final vowels were probably still all short.) Examples:

bâlbēlà   cattle egret (< *bēl(à)-bēlà H-L – H-L)
marmarā   laterite (< *mar(a)-mara H-H – H-H)

A number of reduplicated nouns now appear with the tone pattern L-L-H (but none with L-L-L), e.g.,

gàngàmō turmeric; **shànshànī** flat centipede; **wàlwàlā** cheerful disposition

The simplest explanation to account for the occurring tones is that the reduplicative process was L-L x 2 ⇒ L-(L) – L-L, whereupon the final L automatically raised to H when the final vowel became long, e.g.,

*wàlà L-L x 2 ⇒ wàl(à)-wàlà L-L – L-L > wàlwàlà L-L-L > wàlwàlā L-L-H cheerful disposition
*shànì L-L x 2 ⇒ shàn(ì)-shànì L-L – L-L > *shànshànì L-L-L > *shànshànī > shànshànī L-L-H
flat centipede

Note that one cannot postulate underlying L-H on the stem in such examples as the above in order to get the L-H on the last two syllables because LH (= R) on a single syllable becomes realized as high, i.e., *wàl(a)-wàla LH–L-H would give the non-occurring **walwàlā** H-L-H (< R-L-H). Consider the following example, where this *is* the correct derivation: *bàmi L-H x 2 ⟹ bǎm(i)-bàmi L-H – L-H > bǎmbǎmī R-L-H > bambǎmī H-L-H 'upper part of deleb-palm'.

(3) Feminine/feminative formation. Feminine inflection and historical overt characterization (see §31:3.1) make use of a suffix -ā, which is often connected to the stem by an epenthetic glide. The suffix is underlyingly toneless; its tone is assigned by spreading the underlying tone of the immediately preceding syllable, e.g.,

jàkī + -ā ⟹ jàkā female donkey; bēbē + -ā ⟹ bēbiyā female mute; tsōhō + -ā ⟹ tsōhuwā old (f.); *shàmo f. + -ā > shàmuwā stork; *kùro f. + -ā > kùrwā soul; *cinì f. + -ā > cinyà̄ thigh

Many feminine words with final -iyā and -uwā (whether frozen or inflectional) end in L-H tone, e.g.,

Bàkatsinìyā	woman from Katsina	būtùwā	poor tobacco
gōɗìyā	mare	shūɗìyā	blue (f.) (cf. shūɗì m.)
tunkìyā	sheep	yēkùwā	proclamation

The best explanation for the tone of these words is that the suffixal -ā historically copied the low tone of the stem, whereupon final L-L raised to L-H, e.g.,

*gōɗè + -ā > *gōɗìyà̄ (...L-L) > gōɗìyā (...L-H)   mare
*yēkò + -ā > *yēkùwà̄ (...L-L) > yēkùwā (...L-H)   proclamation
Bàkatsinè + -ā > *Bàkatsinìyà̄ (...L-L) > Bàkatsinìyā (...L-H)   woman from Katsina

Regarding the last example, it is instructive to note that in western dialects that do not insert a transitional glide (-iy-) between the stem and the -ā suffix, a final L-L sequence is not generated and thus the -ā suffix surfaces with low tone, e.g., Bàkatsinè + -ā → Bàkatsinà̄ 'woman from Katsina'.

It should be emphasized that the examples of feminine and feminative formation cited here are intended to provide evidence for the *former* operation of LTR. Synchronically, words with frozen feminative suffixes like gōɗìyā 'mare' and yēkùwā 'proclamation' are underlyingly H-L-H; there is no reason to believe that native speakers underlying have H-L-L plus an active rule that recapitulates the historical rule. Similarly, with active feminine formation, there is evidence that -ìyā is emerging as a distinct suffix complete with intrinsic L-H tone, and thus it can now appear in contexts where it would not have been produced by the addition of -ā, e.g.,

gàjērìyā short (f.) < gàjērē (which with -ā added should have given **gàjēriyā with final H-H tone)
jàkādìyā emissary (f.) < jàkādà̄ (which with -ā added should have given **jàkādà̄, without the glide formation)

[Reference: Newman (1977a)]

35. Ideophones

IDEOPHONES constitute a class of phonaesthetic words that, using Cole's semantic characterization, are "descriptive of sound, colour, smell, manner, appearance, state, action or intensity...[that is, they are words that are] vivid vocal images or representations of visual, auditory and other sensory or mental experiences" (Cole 1955: 370). Phonologically they are marked by distinct phonotactics and special intonational features. Semantically they differ from "prosaic", i.e., non-ideophonic, vocabulary in the high degree of expressiveness and specificity of meaning and restricted collocations of these words. In Hausa, ideophones are numerous and many of them are very commonly used, in part making up for the paucity of simple adjectives and adverbs. Syntactically, they function primarily as adjectives and adverbs, but one also finds ideophonic nouns.

°AN: This section is based on a database of over 500 ideophones that I have been able to verify with native speakers of standard Hausa. There are obviously many more in the language, some of which are less commonly used, others of which are restricted to particular dialects. Ideophones have a much more significant role in the language than do English onomatopoeic words, with which they should not be compared.

1. PHONOLOGY

1.1. Distinctiveness
Ideophones generally employ the same inventory of consonants and vowels as non-ideophonic words, i.e., while they are phonologically aberrant in some respects, they are not wildly so. As a class, they do, however, display distinctive phonological properties, of which the following are the most prevalent.

1.1.1. Consonant-final
Ideophones are commonly consonant-final, whereas prosaic words, exclusive of recent loanwords, are almost entirely vowel-final. The final consonants include obstruents as well as sonorants. Unlike prosaic words, which, apart from pronouns and other function words, are rarely monosyllabic, many of the consonant-final ideophones are CVC. (Note: The glosses are intended only to give an approximation of the meaning. It is not possible out of context and without elaborate description to capture the full essence of these words.) Examples:

ɗùngum	entirely, completely	hàm-hàm	describes eating greedily
tàtul	be full with a drink, overdrink	tiƙis	shows intensity of tiredness
tuɓuř-tùɓùř	large and round (e.g., buttocks)	tukuf	very old
tsaf	neatly, completely	tsit	in complete silence,
hushtsan-tsan	cautiously, firmly, securely (tied)	wulik	shiny black or deep blue
zìgìdiř	stark naked		

°AN/ΔDN: When /f/ appears in final position in ideophones, it is usually pronounced as [p], e.g., **tukuf** 'very old' = [tukup]. By contrast, final /f/ in prosaic loanwords is typically pronounced [f], e.g., **kwâf** 'tournament cup' = [kwâf]. I have no information about the pronunciation of ideophone-final /f/ in western dialects where prevocalic /f/ is normally pronounced as [h] or [hw].

1.1.2. Diphthongs

In the prosaic vocabulary, the diphthongs [ai] and [au] generally behave as complex nuclei and pattern with monophthongal long vowels; in ideophones, they usually pattern with VC sequences where the C functions as a consonantal coda. Note, moreover, that in ideophones, **au/aw** is much more common than **ai/ay**, as compared with prosaic vocabulary where the opposite is the case.

dàu (i.e., /dàw/)   emphasizes deepness of hue; **zau** (i.e., /zaw/)   very hot; very sweet; **tsai** (i.e., /tsay/) still, pensively; cf. **fat**   emphasizes whiteness, **ƙal**   sparkling clean

řaɗau (i.e., /řaɗaw/)   very well, clearly; **wàlàu** (i.e., /wàlàw/)   indicates showing open palm; **wasai** (i.e., /wasay/)   emphasizes brightness of sky; cf. **ƙirin**   emphasizes blackness, darkness (but without shininess), turbid; **nùkùs**   damp and mushy (of cloth, carpet, or soil)

hànhai (i.e., /hànhay/)   wide open (of mouth, door, etc.); cf. **ƙàrƙaf**   completely, being used up

1.1.3. L-L long

Ideophones occur with final L-L tone and a long final vowel, a phonotactically aberrant sequence in the prosaic lexicon (see §71:5.2.1), e.g.,

butsū-bùtsù̀	untidy (hair, clothes, arrangement of teeth)
ɓalō-ɓàlò̀	large and round (of fruits, pimples) (sth with liquid in it)
dòsòsò̀	emphasizes ugliness of face or dullness of psn
shèƙèƙè̀	contemptuously

1.1.4. Vowel peculiarities

A few ideophones have /e/ and /o/ in closed syllables. One also finds an otherwise nonexistent /oi/ diphthong, e.g.,

fes very clean; **sol** emphasizes whiteness; **coi** (= **cwai**) very sweet

1.1.5. Tone in reduplication

In prosaic words, reduplication normally copies tone along with the segmentals. Some classes of ideophones appear with a reduplicative pattern X^t-$X^{\sim t}$ where the tone specification on the two segmentally identical components is not the same, e.g.,

ɓagā-ɓàgà̀ (H-L)	chunky; in large chunks (usu. of solid foods or fruits)
raɓē-ràɓè̀ (H-L)	pendulous (breasts), hanging and dangling (e.g., cloth)
shařtaɓā-shàřtàɓà̀ (H-L)	extremely long and sharp (pl.)
zungurā-zùngùrà̀ (H-L)	extremely long or tall (pl.)
kàzàř-kazař (L-H)	energetic nature (of a person or animal), vigor, restlessness
màƙò-maƙō (L-H)	miserliness
wùnì̀-wunī (L-H)	behaving or speaking in a shifty, suspicious manner

1.2. Canonical shapes

Ideophones can be grouped into regular phonological classes. Here are the most common.

1.2.1. CVC

Monosyllabic ideophones [approx. eighty items] typically consist of a CVC closed syllable (including **CVy** and **CVw**). These most commonly have H tone. A lesser number have L or F tone.

°AN: Out of a sample of some eighty CVC ideophones, seven have F tone, all of which describe a sound, eleven have L tone (in three cases with H as an alternative variant), and the rest have H tone.

H: **fau** (i.e., /**faw**/) emphasizes extremeness of thing or action; **kaf** emphasizes stealing all; **shař** emphasizes greenness, freshness; **tsai** (i.e., /**tsay**/)   still, pensively
L: **ɗîm** huge, of large volume; **gùm** (= **sùm**) emphasizes unpleasant odor; **wàl** describes a sudden flash/movement of light; **wùl** pass by very quickly (like a flash)
F: **cîř** sound made to drive away birds or children; **ɗîm** sound of hitting with a thud; **tîk** (= **bîf** = **tîm** = **řîm**?) sound of heavy object falling

Some of these CVC forms allow optional repetition, whereas with others the repetition/reduplication has become fixed.

(a) **cif** (**cif**) complete (of numbers or money); **kam** (**kam**) (pronounced [kaŋkam]) firmly, tightly; being adamant, insistent
(b) **ɓàl-ɓàl** sound of sth thick boiling; **ɗàř-ɗàř** palpitation of the heart (due to fear or anxiety); **ƙwal-ƙwal** smooth shaving of head.; **řàf-řàf** describes the sound of applauding; **tsan-tsan** cautiously, meticulously

One item—and there may be more—occurs optionally conjoined with itself, e.g.,

ƙut dà ƙut, e.g., **dàngàntakà̀ ƙut dà ƙut** an intimate relationship, cf. **àbōkī ƙut** a very close friend

There are also a few monosyllabic ideophones with the shape CVV, all of which describe some kind of movement or sound. Examples (complete):

ɗù describes a grouping of people moving along in a line; **lû** describes a swinging motion (vertically or horizontally); **řì** describes people or animals moving together as a group; **sù** sound of slithering or sliding; **cā** (or **câ**) sound of splattering of boiling fat

°AN: Abraham (1962: 129) lists a CV ideophone **ca** with a short vowel used in such sentences as **sun yi masà ca** 'They thronged around him.' I have been unable to verify this.

1.2.2. CV$_i$CV$_i$C

In this disyllabic, consonant-final pattern [approx. seventy items], the first vowel is always short (**i**, **a**, or **u**) and the two vowels are identical. Four tone patterns occur: H-H (the most common), L-L (about eight instances), H-L (three instances), and L-H (four instances). Examples:

H-H: **fatau** emphasizes greenness (completely green or deep green); **ƙuƙut** (= **ƙut**) emphasizes closeness of relationship; **sarai** excellent; **sumul** very well (of health); washed clean, smooth; **tiƙis** intensity of tiredness
L-L: **gùnùs** describes an outburst of stench; **shìrìm** shady (of shrub or tree)
H-L: **rirìs** indicates intensity of crying; **kwatsàm** (= **kwaràm**) suddenly
L-H: **gàlau** vacantly, with mouth wide open; **jùgum** being sad, dejected, despondent

°AN: The word **wulik** (= **wul**) 'shiny jet black or dark blue' is an exception to the rule that the two vowels have to be identical. The earlier dictionaries of Abraham and Bargery both list the word as **wuluk**. The front vowel pronunciation in the second syllable is possibly due to the phonological influence of the coronal /l/, and possibly due to rhyming with the semantically almost identical ideophone **sid̃ik**.

At first sight, the words **bùɓwī** 'in a bare, exposed state' and **luɓwī** 'emphasizing finely ground or pounded' would not seem to belong to this class because they end in a vowel rather than a consonant. Since, however, we know that all **C^{W}I** sequences historically derive from **Cui < *Cuy* (see §34:2.3), it is clear that **bùɓwī** and **luɓwī** comes from CV$_i$CV$_i$C forms with a final glide consonant, namely **bùɓuy* and **luɓuy*, respectively (which at a deeper historical level probably came from **bùɓur* and **luɓur*).

1.2.3. CV$_i$CCV$_i$C

This class [about twenty-five items] is similar to the preceding in being composed of consonant-final, disyllabic words with identical vowels. It differs in having a closed (heavy) initial syllable. With few exceptions, the tone pattern is L-H. Examples:

L-H: **bìr̃jik** in large numbers (scattered), plentifully, abundantly; **hànhai** (< /hànhay/) wide open (of mouth, door, etc.); **kìrtif** describes thickness of a fluid, or liquid (esp. of food); **ɓàr̃ɓaf** completely, being exhausted, being used up; **mùr̃tuk** dark, turbid; **sàmɓal** straight (e.g., lines, paths, roads); very tall; **wàr̃war̃** (= **wàr̃was** = **wànwar̃**) fall flat on one's back; **zùndum** (= **tsùndum**) describes being full of water (e.g., well, pond)
H-H: **ɓandas** lacking in moisture or oil
L-L: **tsùndùm** sound of a medium-sized object falling into water (e.g., a stone)

1.2.4. CVVCVC

There is a small set of disyllabic consonant-final ideophones that is prosodically similar to the preceding class in having an initial heavy syllable and L-H tone (L-L in one example). In this class, the initial syllable is open and the two vowels are always different. Examples (complete):

fètal indicates openness of a space; **jàwur̃** bright red; **jàzur̃** emphasizes redness/lightness of complexion (for Europeans or light-skinned Africans); **màɓil** very full (of people, water); **r̃èr̃as** well arranged; **tàtul** be full with a drink, overdrink; **ɓìɓàm** standing stiffly, motionless

°AN: The ideophones **jàwur̃** and **jàzur̃·** are sometimes analyzed as monosyllabic forms **wur̃** and **zur̃** preceded by the color term **jā** 'red', but with tone lowering. Note, however, that **jā** can be used along with the disyllabic ideophones, e.g., **tā sàyi mōtà jā jàwur̃** 'She bought a bright red car.' My guess is that **jàwur̃** and **jàzur̃** represent the original ideophones and that the monosyllabic forms **wur̃** and **zur̃** are the result of backformations.

1.2.5. CV$_i$C$_j$V$_i$C$_j$V$_i$

This group [approx. thirty items] consists of monotonal trisyllabic words containing identical short vowels and identical second and third consonants, i.e. the last two syllables are exact copies of one another. The vowels are either /a/ or /u/, never /i/. About two-thirds of the words have all H tone; the others have all L tone. Examples:

H: **danana** covered with oil; **fururu** white from dust; **r̃ututu** in large numbers; **tsalala** very thin or watery (esp. food)

L: **dùkùkù**   state of being ugly, dejected, or clumsy; **sàràrà**   walking aimlessly; **sùkùkù**   in a sad, despondent mood; **zàʀàʀà**   appearance of sth very long (esp. snakes or worms)

1.2.6. $CVV_iC_jVV_iC_jVV_i$

This small class of trisyllabic words is similar to the preceding in having identical vowels and matching second and third consonants. It is different in that the vowels are all long, typically the mid vowels /ē/ and /ō/ (with one example of /ā/). The tone pattern is all L. Examples (complete):

bòɗòɗò   in an exposing manner; **bònònò**   action thought to be secure but that turned out to be not secure; **ɓèlèlè**   with mouth wide open (in laughter); **dòsòsò**   emphasizes ugliness of face or dullness of psn; **gàlàlà**   unguarded, loosely, out in the open; **ʀèrèrè**   standing disrespectfully before one's superior; **zòlòlò** (= **tsòlòlò**)   long necked, tall and thin looking

1.2.7. $CV_iCC_jV_iC_kC_jV_iC_k$

This class [approx. 20 items] includes trisyllabic words consisting of three closed syllables, the last two of which are identical, i.e., these words are formed by reduplication of the final syllable of the (usually) disyllabic base. The vowels are all identical (usually /a/, less often /u/, rarely /i/) but the consonants are distinct. The words have an all L tone pattern. These ideophones are derived from corresponding augmentative adjectives (see §11:1). Examples:

bùrɗùnɗùn	emphasizes swellings (e.g., insect bites, whip marks)
ɓàngwàlgwàl	describes the appearance of a solid, round, and fleshy thing
jìmɓìrɓìr	heavy (from wetness)
ʀùrsùnsùn	describes the touch of hard objects (e.g., stones, kolanuts)
ràmɓàsɓàs	describes bare and huge appearance (e.g., of a head)
sàmɓàlɓàl	emphasizes the straight figure of tall and slender person

Although most of these words are trisyllabic, quadrisyllabic forms do occur, where, again, the final syllable of the base is reduplicated, e.g.,

bùgùzùnzùm   big, fat, untidy, ungainly (esp. woman), or animals (e.g., very hairy)

1.2.8. $CVCCVC \times 2)^{H-L}$

Plural counterparts to the above ideophones are formed by full reduplication of the base plus an H-L tone melody, e.g., (with glosses as above),

burɗun-bùrɗùn; ɓangwal-ɓàngwàl; jimɓir-jìmɓìr; buguzum-bùgùzùm, etc.

1.2.9. $CV_iCV_i \times 2$

These are fully reduplicated words built on a CVCV base containing identical short vowels [approx. twenty items]. (In two words the vowels do not match.) The repeated vowel is most often /a/, less often /u/, and never /i/ (except in the one **u**...**i** example). The tone is all H. Examples:

fata-fata   helter-skelter; destroying, breaking up; **kwata-kwata**   lack something completely; **rugu-rugu**   shattered into pieces (e.g., glass, window, etc.); **wara-wara**   spaced apartIrregular: **dushi-dushi**   hazy, dim, not bright, semiblind (of eyes); **sako-sako**   loosely

In two cases, ideophones of this class have equivalents belonging to the $CV_iC_jV_iC_jV_i$ class (§1.2.5):

buɗu-buɗu = buɗuɗu   be covered all over with powdery substance; having poor sight
caɓa-caɓa = caɓaɓa   in profusion

1.2.10. Base x 2)$^{L-H}$

Four classes of semantically similar ideophones are characterized by a fully reduplicated structure and L-H tone [approx. thirty-five items]. They differ in terms of the segmental canonical shape. (The use of these ideophones is described below in §6.)

1.2.10.1. (CVCVV x 2). The largest subclass has a short vowel in the first syllable and a long vowel in the second (producing an iambic rhythm), with the two vowels usually identical, e.g.,

fàcǎ-facā   reckless spending; getting deeply involved in trading; playing with (or in) water
cùkǔ-cukū   trying to obtain something in an underhanded way
gìɗǐ-giɗī   being a busybody, fidgeting

When the final vowel is /ē/ or /ō/, the first vowel is /a/, which at an abstract level could be thought of as /e/ or /o/ respectively, since Hausa does not allow short mid vowels in nonfinal position, e.g.,

jàlě-jalē (< //jèlě-jelē//)   going hither and thither
màƙǒ-maƙō (< //mòƙǒ-moƙō//)   miserliness

The other two examples of non-identical vowels involve **u**...**ī** sequences, where the /u/ is preceded by /w/. Here one can view the formation in abstract terms as having /i/ in the first syllable, where the /i/ to /u/ change is due to the absence of the sequence /wi/ in the Hausa phonological system, e.g.,

wùƙǐ-wuƙī (< //wìƙǐ-wiƙī//)   fidgeting by children
wùnǐ-wunī (< //wìnǐ-winī//)   behaving or speaking in a shifty, suspicious manner

1.2.10.2. (CVCVC x 2). This class [approx. ten items] also has an iambic light-heavy rhythm, the heavy syllable in this case having a syllable-final coda consonant rather than a long vowel. The two vowels in the word are always identical, /a/ in all cases except one, which contains /u/. Examples:

kàzàř-kazař   energetic nature (of a person or animal), vigor, restlessness.
wàtsàl-watsal   wriggling, squirming movement (of fish, snake, or boiling water)
bùdùm-budum   floundering about in water or work

A small number of ideophones with this same segmental shape uses a different tone pattern, namely H-L. Examples (complete):

baram-bàràm   parting with animosity/disagreement; **cukun-cùkùn**   be in a state of confusion about what to do; **gatsal-gàtsàl**   chunks (of food) poorly cut; careless/indecent talk; **tuɓuř-tùɓùř**   describes (shaking of) large and round buttocks

The following example appears on the surface with a long vowel rather than with a consonant. From an abstract/historical perspective, however, one can view it as having an underlying structure CiCiw, where the diphthong *Ciu < *Ciw becomes /Cyū/ (see §34:2.3):

kikyū-kìkyù (< *kikiu-kìkìu < *kikiw-kìkìw)   stand alert

°AN: The process reflected in **kikyū** < ***kikiw** is a counterpart to the one described earlier of **luɓwī** < ***luɓuy**.

1.2.10.3. (CVCCVC x 2). In these few words, both syllables are closed, i.e., one has a heavy-heavy pattern. The vowels in the two syllables are identical. Examples (complete):

ɓàngwàl-ɓangwal
  describes walking in an insecure way
wàndàr̃-wandar̃
  zigzagging, swaying from side to side
tìnjìm-tinjim
  moving around in water with a splashing sound
bùndùm-bundum (more or less = **fùnjùm-funjum**)
  floundering about noisily in water; floundering about attempting to do sth

1.2.10.4. (CVCCVV x 2). There are two words with a heavy-heavy pattern ending in long /ā/. In both cases, the initial vowel is nonmatching /i/:

ìndà̀-indā   talking indecisively, having disagreement about what decision to take
zìr̃gà̀-zir̃gā   constantly going to and fro

1.2.11. CVCVV x 2)^H-L

This large class [approx. seventy items] has an iambic light-heavy structure with an H-L tone pattern. The two vowels differ in length—the first is short and the second is long—but typically are segmentally identical, most often with /a/ or /u/, much rarer with /i/. Many of the ideophones in this class function as adjectives, a considerable number of which are intrinsically plural. Examples:

ɓagā-ɓàgà̀ chunky; in large chunks (usu. of solid foods or fruits); **darā-dàr̀à** bold and beautiful (of eyes or writing); **falā-fàlà̀** broad and thin (e.g., leaves, paper, ears); **gajā-gàjà̀** messily, in a disgusting manner; **tsalā-tsàlà̀** (pl.) long and skinny (esp. legs); **buɓū-bùɓù̀** large and round (e.g., buttocks, fruits, onions); **buzū-bùzù̀** long, unkempt hair; **durū-dùrù̀** in a confused manner, unable to make a decision quickly; **hulū-hùlù̀** swollen, puffed up (e.g., eyelids, cheeks, pimples); **sumū-sùmù̀** (pl.) despondent-looking, with protruding lips; **kikī-kìkì̀** manner of response of a cornered psn; **ɓirī-ɓìrì̀** openly, in broad daylight

ΔDN: In the Sokoto dialect, these words all have an HH-LF tone pattern, e.g., **tsalā-tsàlâ, sumū-sùmû**, etc.

As with the words of the same pattern with L-H tone described above in §1.2.10.1, the main exceptions to the rule that the vowels be identical are words with final /ē/ and /ō/, where the expected (but not allowed) short /e/ and /o/ in the first syllable appears as /a/, e.g.,

ɗagē-ɗàgè̀ skimpy, too short (e.g., miniskirt); **kanē-kànè̀** being well established in a place, monopolizing or controlling others; **raɓē-ràɓè̀** pendulous (breasts), hanging and dangling (cloth or other things); **zaɓē-zàɓè̀** unsuitably long, out of proportion
batsō-bàtsò̀ (pl.) poorly made, ugly looking; **ɓalō-ɓàlò̀** (pl.) large and round (e.g., fruits, pimples, or other things with liquid in them); **cakō-càkò̀** sharp and pointed (e.g., nails); unaligned teeth; **zagō-zàgò̀** dense and rich (of eyebrows)

The word **horō-hòrŏ̀** 'unusually large opening' (esp. nostril) is morphologically regular, because the two vowels match, but is phonologically aberrant because one normally does not get nonfinal short /o/. This H-L class includes one example of a **u**...**ī** sequence, where the **u** is preceded by /w/, e.g., **wuƙī-wùƙī̀** 'describes guilty look'. For inexplicable reasons, the word **butsū-bùtsŭ̀** 'sth that appears as disorganized or unkempt, esp. hair or grasses; sth done in haste just for the sake of finishing it' also appears as **butsā-bùtsā̀** with non-identical vowels. The non-matching initial /i/ in **jinā-jìnà̀** 'bloody' (of person or animal) can be understood on etymological grounds, cf. **jinī** 'blood'.

Two words, with easily identifiable prosaic cognates, have the H-L pattern of this class but a heavy first syllable:

gēmai-gèmài   old and bearded (cf. **gēmŭ** beard)   **tsōfai-tsòfài**   very old (cf. **tsōhō** old)

1.2.12. Polysyllabic all L
There exists a small group of trisyllabic (in one case quadrisyllabic) words with all L tone ending in **ai** or in **a** plus a nasal consonant. Examples (complete):

bàmbàràkwài   something unusual or unexpected state of thing(s); **bàr̃kàtài**   in a disorderly mess; **ɓàkàtàn**   idly, doing nothing; **r̃àkwàcàm**   in a littered, disarranged manner; **tàntàr̃wài** (= [Kts] **tàntàr̃kwài**)   being at a total loss (e.g., at a crossroad); **wùlà̀ƙ̀ài**   staring at s.o. rudely or contemptuously

1.2.13. Miscellaneous
Finally, one has an assortment of ideophones of different shapes that do not fall into any of the regular patterns, e.g.,

ayyur̃ur̃ûi   the sound of ululating; **dindìndin**   perpetually, permanently; **fìr̃gigit** (= **fìr̃gigi**) with a startled or frightened movement in most cases due to being awakened unexpectedly, or due to a frightening sleep; **gàr̃andàn** (= **gar̃andàn**)   emphasizes newness (esp. the quality of a shiny new vehicle); **kàshangararai**   have a tired and dejected appearance; **r̃ātātā**   being talkative; **r̃ìgìjà̀** describes the falling of a bulky person or tree; **tìjà̀**   seeing clearly; being glossy or bright; **tàntàr̃wai** describes the falling down of a big and clumsy person or object; **wujigā-wùjìgà̀** (= **wur̃gā-wùr̃gà̀**)   in a disheveled state; **wur̃jànjàn**   doing something relentlessly

2. FUNCTION AND USE
Ideophones are defined as a class primarily on the basis of their phonological and semantic properties. They do not constitute a distinct part of speech on a par with the other major word classes. Rather, some ideophones function to modify verbal actions or adjectives (and thus pattern syntactically with adverbs), others modify nouns (and thus function adjectivally), and others constitute nouns. (One even has some ideophonic verbs.) As with prosaic vocabulary, individual ideophones can function as more than one part of speech.

2.1. Adverbials
Many ideophones are essentially adverbial in function in that they serve to describe a manner, intensity, or quantity of an action or state or quality. They invariably follow the word or phrase that they modify. These ideophones can be separated into a considerable number of subcategories; but for convenience one can divide them into two main groups, namely, (a) those that modify the VP, and (b) those that intensify or specify a numeral or an adjective (or a semantically equivalent noun of quality).

2.1.1. VP modifiers

Included here is a mixed collection of ideophones describing manner, sound, etc. Examples (with the ideophone underlined):

Audù yā tāshì <u>farat</u>	Audu got up suddenly.
nā gan sù sunà yāwò <u>gàràrà</u>	I saw them roaming aimlessly.
sìnīmàr̃ El-Dūniyà tā ƙōnè <u>ƙùrmus</u>	The El-Duniya cinema burned down to the ground.
kòg̃ī yā cìka <u>màƙil</u>	The river is filled to its banks.
tā zaunà <u>r̃asha-r̃asha</u>	She sat all sprawled out.
yā rufè ƙōfar̃ <u>r̃uf</u>	He closed the door tight.
an d'aurè jàkîn <u>sako-sako</u> don yà wālà	They tied the donkey loosely so it could be at ease.
wani kùrēgē yā wucè <u>sùmùmù</u>	A squirrel passed by silently.
nā gàji <u>tiƙis</u>	I'm completely exhausted.
sun tsayà <u>tsai</u> sunà kallō	They stood still watching.
jàkatā tā cìka <u>tsàmbam</u> dà kud'ī	My bag is stacked full with money.
fàr̃āshì yā fād'ì <u>wànwar̃</u>	The price has tumbled. (lit. fallen flat on its back)

Ideophones most often occur at the end of the VP. They can however be moved to the front of a sentence for focus (where they occur without the use of the stabilizer). Examples:

<u>càncak</u> Audù ya d'âukè àkwàtìn	It is completely that Audu took away the box.
<u>farat</u> ya tāshì	Suddenly he stood up.
<u>màƙil</u> kòg̃în ya cìka	It is very full that the river is.

The general rule that answers to questions are in focus also applies to ideophones, e.g.,

<u>wànwar̃</u> ya fād'ì	Flat on his back he fell down.
cf. yā fād'ì <u>wànwar̃</u>?	Did he fall down flat on his back?
<u>sumul</u> mukà sàmē sù	It's very well we found them.
cf. yàyà kukà sàmē sù?	How did you find them?

A few ideophones that are often used in narratives are found in a restricted context as far as fronting is concerned. These almost always occur at the beginning of a sentence (or clause) followed by **sai** '(and) then' plus a clause in the preterite. The semantic import is to emphasize the immediacy of the ensuing action. Examples:

<u>kwatsàm</u> sai mukà hàd'u dà shī	Then suddenly we ran into him.
<u>wàlàu</u> sai mukà ga haskē	Flash then suddenly we saw a flash of light.
munà zàune <u>kwaràm</u> sai ya fitō	We were sitting there then suddenly he emerged.

2.1.2. Specifiers / Intensifiers

Certain ideophones serve to specify numerals or to intensify adjectives or nouns of quality, esp. ANSQs (see chap. **2**). The word order is invariably quality word + ideophone. The semantic collocation is often quite fixed as in English 'snow white' = Hausa **far̃ī fat** or 'brand new' = **sābō ful**. Examples:

gùdā d'aya tak	exactly one	kwānā bìyar̃ cur̃	exactly five days
gàjērē duƙus	very short	sābō gàr̃andàn	brand new (esp. a vehicle)
zāf̃ī zau	red hot	kaur̃ī kìrtif	very thick (e.g., gruel)

lāfiyà (ƙa)lau	very well, healthy	kōr̃è shar̃	bright green
baƙī wulik	shiny black		

The qualitative nouns that are intensified can be common nouns used in an adjectival/adverbial sense, e.g.,

yā yi sukàr̃ī coi	It is extremely sweet. (where sukàr̃ī = sugar)
mīyàr̃ tā yi gishirī fau	The soup is overly salty. (where gishirī = salt)

The ideophone and its head do not need to be adjacent. There are two common constructions where this is not so. First, in equational or identificational sentences, the stabilizer (**nē/cē**) usually appears immediately after the adjective and before the ideophone, e.g.,

Audù gàjērē nè <u>duƙus</u>	Audu is very short.
mōtàr̃sà baƙā cè wulik	His car is jet black.
ɗan yārò nē <u>tsir̃it</u>	He's a tiny little boy.

Second, with prenominal adjectives, the adjective occurs before the noun but the ideophone follows, e.g.,

sābon kèkè <u>ful</u>	a brand new bicycle (= kèkè sābō ful, but not **sābon ful kèkè)
ɗan ƙàramin yārò <u>tsir̃it</u>	a very small boy = yārò ɗan ƙàramī <u>tsir̃it</u>

In appropriate circumstances the head word can be deleted, leaving the ideophone to carry the full meaning, e.g.,

gàrī yā yi (haskē) <u>wasai</u>	The sky is very bright.
kō (ɗaya) <u>tak</u> bài bā nì ba	Even one he didn't give me.
bābù kō (ɗaya) <u>tak</u>	There isn't any, not even one.
tukunyâr̃ tā yi (zāfī) <u>zau</u>	The pot is burning hot.
ī, <u>sol</u> nè	Yes, very white (light complexioned).
e.g., in answer to shī nè far̃ī <u>sol</u>?	Is he very white?

Because the ideophones serve to emphasize a semantic sense and are not defined narrowly by traditional part of speech categories, one often finds that the same ideophone can be used to emphasize a noun or an adjective or a verb, e.g.,

tsōhō <u>tukuf</u>	a very old person,
cf. yā tsūfa <u>tukuf</u>	He has become very old. (lit. he has aged **tukuf**)
gàrī yā yi duhù <u>duɗum</u>	The town is very dark.
cf. gàrī duk yā rufè <u>duɗum</u> dà hadar̃ī	
The town is enveloped in darkness by the storm clouds.	

2.2. *Adjectivals*

Many ideophones and ideophonic adjectives pattern with normal adjectives in functioning to modify nouns. When used attributively, all (or almost all) occur postnominally. They are often expanded by a **dà** plus pronoun construction. Examples:

sun kāmà wani mahàukàcī <u>zìgìdiř</u> dà shī	They caught a stark-naked madman.
wasu haƙòrankà <u>gatsō-gàtsò</u> dà sū	teeth disproportionate as yours
yârā 'yan <u>dìɓī-dìɓī</u> dà sū	plump little children
nā ga yārinyàřsà <u>sàmɓàlɓàl</u> dà ita	I saw his tall and slender girl.
Ābù tā zubà minì nāmà <u>duƙū-dùƙù</u> à àbincīnā	

Abu poured large and round chunks of meat in my food.

Audù yā dāwō gidā <u>fururu</u> dà shī

Audu returned home white with dust. (e.g., during the harmattan)

One normally does not get ideophonic adjectives as predicates in equational sentences. Instead one tends to use a verbal sentence with the pro-verb **yi** 'do' or with some other verb like **zama** 'become'. Examples:

gēron gōnař Bàlā yā yi <u>gaɓā-gàɓà</u>	The millet of Bello's farm is large, thick, and strong.
kunnuwànsà sun yi <u>fatō-fàtò</u>	His ears are large and broad.
rìgā tā zama <u>dususu</u>	The gown has become faded
kwāɓìn fulāwàř yā yi <u>digiřgiř</u>	The balls of dough are firm.
kân Bàlā yā yi <u>řàmɓàsɓàs</u>	Bala's bare head is huge and shiny.

2.3. *Nominals*

A good number of ideophones function as nouns, most often dynamic nouns denoting an action.

> °AN: For scholars who are accustomed to thinking of ideophones as adverbial, one can liken Hausa ideophonic nouns to English words like mumbo-jumbo or hocus-pocus or ping-pong, which are clearly nouns, but which are phonologically and, to some extent, semantically distinctive.

These ideophonic nouns commonly occur in syntactic environments where one normally would find a verbal noun, e.g., after a continuous TAM or as object of a verb like **fiyà** or **cikà** 'do or be characterized by too much of' or the pro-verb **yi** 'do'; but they can fill other nominal roles as well. Those ending in /a(a)/ tend to be feminine (and thus take an -ř linker where appropriate); those with other terminations are masculine. Examples:

ɓàlli-ɓàlli yanà dāmùnsà	Palpitations of the heart are troubling him.
yā yi <u>cùkù-cukū</u> yā sàmi aikì	He got a job through the back door.
(lit. he did **cùkù-cukū** he got the job)	
yanà ta <u>kìcì-kicin</u> yà sàmi kuɗin yîn aurē	He is striving to get money to get married.
wannàn màtâř tā cikà <u>kwàlò-kwalō</u>	This woman is a difficult, unreliable customer.
gwamnà yanà ta yi manà <u>ƙùmbìyà-ƙumbiyā</u>	The governor was doing underhanded dealings with us.
bā nà sôn <u>wàndàř-wandař</u>	I dislike zigzagging.
an san shì kân <u>fàcà-facařsà</u>	He is well known for his reckless spending.
anà ta <u>ìndà-indař</u> kō wà zā à bâ sakatařè	

They were wishy-washy about whom to make secretary.

yanà wani <u>wùnì-wunì</u> sai kà cê marař gaskiyā

He was behaving in a certain shifty manner such that you would say he was dishonest.

In the following examples with the ideophone **bàmbàràkwài** 'something unusual or unexpected', one finds that the gender is not intrinsic but rather is determined by the referent, the gender being indicated by the form of the indefinite determiner **wani** (m.) / **wata** (f.):

nā ji wani <u>bàmbàràkwài</u> à jìkīnā   I felt a very strange feeling.

màganàr̃sà wata <u>bàmbàràkwài</u> cē   His talk was something unexpected.

2.3.1. Pseudonominals

Many adverbial ideophones of manner can optionally occur following the pro-verb **yi**, e.g., **yā yi <u>far̃at</u> yā tāshì** 'He went zoom and got up', cf. **yā tāshì <u>far̃at</u>** 'He got up in a flash.' Because they fill what syntactically seems to be the direct object nominal slot, they would appear to be nouns (and in fact are listed as such in some dictionaries), but they are only marginally so since they do not display other nominal properties. Here are typical examples, showing the same ideophones following **yi** and functioning in a normal adverbial position. (In the examples the = indicates more or less equivalent, there presumably being semantic, pragmatic, and stylistic differences.)

janàr̃ yā yi <u>ƙēmēmē</u> yā ƙi jîn màganàr̃ = janàr̃ yā ƙi jîn màganàr̃ <u>ƙēmēmē</u>
> The general flatly refused to listen to the matter.

yā yi <u>fùnjum</u> yā fāɗà ruwa = yā fāɗà ruwa <u>fùnjum</u>
> He fell in the water with a splash.

tā kwântā tā yi <u>r̃asha-r̃asha</u> dà ita (à kân gadō) = tā kwântā <u>r̃asha-r̃asha</u>
> She lay down sprawled out (on the bed).

Audù yā yi <u>ɓèlèlè</u> dà bàkinsà = Audù yā būɗè bàkinsà <u>ɓèlèlè</u>
> Audu is laughing with his mouth drooping open like a fool.

an yi musù <u>lilis</u>   They were given a severe beating. (lit. one.comp do to.them <u>lilis</u>)

cf. sun dàku <u>lilis</u>   They were beaten thoroughly.

yā yi <u>tàtul</u> dà giyà   He is intoxicated, cf. **cikìnā yā cìka <u>tàtul</u>** I'm bloated.

sātī yā yi <u>cur̃</u>   It's been a week exactly, cf. **sātī biyu cur̃**   exactly two weeks

2.3.2. Ideophones in other nominal slots

Ideophones that normally function as adverbs indicating manner or sound can appear as head nouns, in which case they allow genitive possessors (formed with **ɗin**), e.g.,

<u>bûm</u> ɗin fāɗùwar̃sà yā bā nì tsòr̃ō   The sound of its falling frightened me.

<u>dàs-dàs-dàs</u> ɗin tàfiyàr̃sà yā tàshē nì   His heavy walking woke me up.

<u>ɗis-ɗis-ɗis</u> ɗinsà   its dripping sound

<u>sùlùlù</u> ɗin shigôwar̃sà   the silence of his entering

cf. **yā shigō <u>sùlùlù</u>**   He entered silently.

3. FIXED COLLOCATIONS

Many ideophones are restricted in usage to co-occurrence with a single word or a very limited number of semantically related words. The presence of fixed collocational restrictions appears to be independent of the phonological or grammatical class of the ideophone. The ideophone **fat**, for example, occurs only with **far̃ī** 'white' (or its feminine and plural counterparts) and nothing else, e.g., **far̃ā fat** 'snow white' (ref. to feminine thing). Similarly, **ƙùrmus** occurs only with, and emphasizes, **ƙōnè** 'burn', e.g., **yā ƙōnè ƙùrmus** 'It burnt to ashes.' Because the collocation is semantic in nature, the gender/number of a noun or the grade of a verb is irrelevant. Here are some typical examples (where the double colon :: indicates "goes with"):

bada-bada :: màganà speech,
> e.g., **màganà bada-bada àlāmàr̃ rashìn lāfiyà cē**   Incomprehensible speech is a sign of an illness.

ɓèlèlè :: bàkī   mouth

e.g., **Audù yā yi ɓèlèlè dà bàkinsà**   Audu is laughing with his mouth drooping like a fool. (lit. Audu did ɓèlèlè with his mouth)

caɽ ::   tsayà   stand, or **mīƙè**   stretch out

e.g., **sàndân yā tsayà caɽ**   The stick stood straight.

caraf :: **cafè/cafkè**   catch

e.g., **yā cafkè bīɽò caraf**   He caught the pen adroitly.

(ɗa)ɗaf :: **ɗafè** or **maƙàlē**   both meaning cling to, stick to

e.g., **yāròn yā maƙàlē wà uwaɽsà (ɗa)ɗaf**   The boy clung to his mother's apron strings.

ɗau :: zāfī   heat

e.g., **wutā mài zāfī ɗau**   a blazing hot fire

daƙau :: **niƙà**   grind or **dakà**   pound

e.g., **gàrîn yā nìƙu daƙau**   The flour is finely ground.

duƙus :: gàjērē   short

e.g., **Mūsā gàjērē nè duƙus**   Musa is very short.

fatau :: kōɽè   green

e.g., **mōtà kōɽìyā fatau**   a deep-green car

ful :: sābō   new

e.g., **kèkè sābō ful**   a brand-new bicycle

gadā-gàdà :: idò   eyes

e.g., **kâi! wannàn yārinyàɽ tanà dà kyāwàwan idānuwà gadā-gàdà dà sū**   Wow! This girl has bold and beautiful eyes. (lit. ...she has beautiful eyes bold-and-beautiful with them)

ƙat :: ƙārè   finish up

e.g., **àbincîn yā ƙārè ƙat, kō laumà ɗaya bà zā à sāmù ba**   The food was finished up completely, even one mouthful one couldn't get.

ƙìƙàm :: tsayà   stand

e.g., **kanàɽ yā tsayà ƙìƙàm**   The colonel stood there tall and motionless.

kìrtif :: kaurī   thickness

e.g., **kùnûn yā yi kaurī kìrtif**   The gruel is made very thick.

màƙil :: cìka   fill

e.g., **kàsuwā tā cìka màƙil dà mutànē**   The market is crammed with people.

ɽaƙau :: būshè   dry up

e.g., **ɓāwon gyàɗā yā būshè ɽaƙau**   The peanut shells have dried up completely.

ɽèɽas :: jèru   be well lined up

e.g., **'yan makaɽantā sun jèru ɽèɽas à bàkin tītì sunà jiràn zuwàn fìɽīmiyà**   The schoolchildren lined up in an orderly manner along the street waiting for the premier.

ɽuf :: rufè   close

e.g., **yā rufè ƙōfàɽ ɽuf**   He closed the door tightly.

shaf :: mântā   forget or **shà'afà**   slip one's mind

e.g., **nā mântā shaf cêwā yâu zân aikà dà sàƙôn nan**   I completely forgot that I was going to send that message today.

tukuf :: tsōhō   old

e.g., **mùtumîn tsōhō nè tukuf**   The man is very old; **yā tsūfa tukuf**   He has aged strikingly.

yalā-yàlà :: gāshì   hair or **cìyāwà**   grass

e.g., **wata yārinyà mài gāshì yalā-yàlà**   a girl with long, soft, smooth hair

zau :: zāfī   heat or **zāƙī**   sweetness

e.g., **dūtsèn gūgà yā yi zāfī zau**   The iron is red hot.

4. SYNCHRONIC COGNATE FORMS

Even though ideophones are to some extent external to the regular prosaic lexicon, some of them do have "cognate" items elsewhere in the language. For example, ɗaʀ 'emphasizing leaping on and clinging to sth in a nimble fashion' can be related to the verb ɗarè 'leap on', e.g., sun ɗarè bishiyàʀ ɗaʀ 'They jumped up on the tree (like a monkey)'. That is, some ideophones can be morphologically identified with extant non-ideophonic words (mostly verbs) even though they cannot be related by any regular derivational process.

°AN: Although it is impossible to derive ideophones from their cognates by rule, there are some recurring processes, the most common of which are (a) dropping of final vowels (resulting in consonant-final ideophones), (b) perturbation of vowel length and tone, and (c) (usually full) reduplication.

In some instances the relation is fairly evident; in others, it is remote and strictly historical. Here are some examples (where <> indicates that the ideophone on the left is morphologically related to the non-ideophone on the right):

bàɗàɗà	years hence <> bàɗi next year
baja-baja	scattered around, disorganized <> bazà/bajè spread out
ɓus, ɓùs	describes breaking through of sth <> ɓusà break through
buɗu-buɗu	be all covered with powdery substance <> buɗà/baɗà spread powder, dust
buzū-bùzù	long, unkempt hair <> buzurwā long-haired goat
cakō-càkò	sharp and pointed (e.g., nails) <> càkā stab
cukun-cùkùn	be in a state of confusion <> cukunkùnē be(come) entangled
cùnkus	full of people or things <> cùnkùshē be crowded into, cùnkōsō congestion
dàlàlà	emphasizes sliminess (e.g., saliva, okra) <> dàlàlī sliminess, viscosity
dandan	firmly pressed <> dannè press down
dòɓòɓò	stooping slightly and awkwardly <> dūɓà stoop down
dushi-dushi	hazy, dim, not bright, semiblind (of eyes) <> dushè become dim
(ɗa)ɗaf	emphasizes clinging <> ɗafè (cling to)
ɗagē-ɗàgē	skimpy <> ɗagè shrink
ɗis	sound of sth dripping <> ɗîsa drip
fururu	white from dust <> furfurā gray hair (related to farī white?)
kam-(kam)	held firmly, tightly; being adamant, insistent <> kāmà catch, hold
ɓalɓal	glittering clean <> ɓalɓalē shave close, sweep clean
malā-màlà	describes minor flooding <> màlālā flow out, flow over
mùʀtuk	dark, turbid <> muʀtùkē stir up dust, etc.
ʀuf (rolled [ʀ])	well closed or covered (e.g., door, bowl) <> rufè (flap [r]) close
saɗaɗa	stealthily <> saɗàɗā sneak in
sako-sako	loosely <> sakì let go, release
taltal	smooth shaving of head <> taltàlē shave head clean, tàllī sheen
tsaf	neatly, completely clean <> tsaftà cleanliness
tsai	still, pensively <> tsayà stop, stand
wara-wara	spaced apart <> wārè separate, secede
wujigā-wùjìgà	in a disheveled state <> wujijjìgā swing thing about
zau	very hot or sweet <> zāfī heat, zāɓī sweetness

In a few instances of onomatopoeic words it appears that the ideophone is basic and that the verb is derived, i.e., the output could be considered an ideophonic verb, e.g.,

zùndùm	sound of heavy object falling into a body of water (e.g., well or pond)
<> **zundùmā**	fall into water
tsùndùm	sound of a medium-sized object falling into water (e.g., a stone)
<> **tsundùmā**	fall into water with a plop.

°AN: Note that these ideophones and their cognate verbs cannot normally be used together, thus **yā fāɗà ruwa tsùndùm** 'He fell in the water with a splash' and **yā tsundùmā ruwa** 'He plopped into the water' are OK, but ****yā tsundùmā ruwa tsùndùm** is not. This restriction is relaxed in the case of fixed expressions, e.g., **kōmī ta fànjamà fànjam** 'Let's do it regardless of the consequences!' (example provided by Malami Buba).

5. INTONATION (KEY RAISING, REGISTER SHIFT)

Ideophones are generally characterized by expressive pronunciation. This includes extra forcefulness or loudness and often an intonational break (indicated here by a comma before the ideophone). Examples:

àbîn dà ya bā nì ɗanyē nè, *shataf*	The thing that he gave me was fresh, *really so.*
yā fāɗà ruwa, *fùnjum*	He fell in the water, *splash.*

Perhaps the most striking characteristic of ideophones, which has commonly been noted from very early in Hausa studies, e.g., Prietze (1908), is their extra-high pitch.

°AN: Scholars have not, on the other hand, paid much attention to the pitch of L tones. Based on my observations, I would contend that the L tones are also pronounced distinctively, i.e., with an extra-low pitch. Nevertheless, because, as far as I am aware, this matter has not yet been studied systematically, I shall reluctantly ignore L tone for the rest of this discussion.

Moore (1968: 13), for example, says: "The ideophone occurring utterance finally is likely to have an extra high pitch which ignores the downward drift of the rest of the utterance...." This extra high tone can be described in terms of "register shift" or "key raising", indicated here by ↑. Examples (with the ideophone underlined):

farī ↑ <u>**fat**</u> snow white, **kōr̃è** ↑ <u>**shar̃**</u> very green, **tā tāshì** ↑ <u>**far̃at**</u>	She got up suddenly.
yā gàji ↑ <u>**tuɓus**</u> He became very tired; **tā sàmi kar̃ā ɗaya** ↑ <u>**tak**</u>	She got exactly one stalk.

°AN: Inkelas, Leben, and Cobler (1987) incorrectly equate the key raising in ideophones with the key raising in Yes/No questions. With ideophones, the extra H tone affects the entire word, i.e., applies at the *beginning*; in yes/no questions, the key raising applies only to the *last* H tone, the first syllable of an H-H word, for example, being unaffected.

Whereas ideophones in phrases and in short sentences typically display key raising, this is not an absolute requirement. Rather, it is more accurate to say that ideophones may undergo key raising in situations where they are candidates for "expressive prominence." One can illustrate a number of environments where ideophones occur without key raising.

In Yes/No questions, where the final H tone undergoes key raising, this intonational marker overrides any possible register shift on the ideophone as such, e.g.,

yā sàyi rìgā baƙā wu ↑ ^{lik} ?   Did he buy a very black gown?
cf. yā sàyi rìgā ba ↑ ^{ƙā} ?   Did he buy a black gown?
not ** yā sàyi rìgā baƙā ↑ ^{wu} ↑ ^{lik} ?   Did he buy a very black gown?
cf. yā sàyi rìgā baƙā ↑ ^{wulik}   He bought a very black gown.

°AN: For pragmatic reasons ideophones tend to be a bit odd in negative sentences or in questions. When they are produced in questions, however, the intonational realization is as indicated above.

Answers to questions often lack key raising on the ideophone, i.e., with the focus having switched to the truth value of the proposition, the ideophone no longer qualifies for expressive prominence, e.g.,

ē, kāyân sun wànku fes   Yes, the loads were washed spanking clean.
ē, nā ga ɗan tsàkō tsigil   Yes, I saw a wee small chick.

The following examples illustrate the difference between sentences with ideophones having expressive prominence, Yes/No questions with obligatory key raising, and answers to questions in which the ideophone is out of focus and does not carry expressive prominence.

cīwòn yā hanà ta ↑ ^{sakat}   The illness prevented her completely.
cīwòn yā hanà ta sa ↑ ^{kat} ?   Did the illness prevent her completely?
ē, cīwòn yā hanà ta sakat   Yes, the illness prevented her completely.

In sentences containing focus (including Q-words) the ideophone does not qualify for expressive prominence and thus occurs with its normal tone.

rashìn ilìmī nè ya hanà ta sakat   It was lack of knowledge that prevented her totally.
wà ya bā kà ɗanyē shatâf?   Who gave you a real fresh one?

In the preceding example, note that the floating L tone q-morpheme (see §60:1.2) has attached to the H-H ideophone **shataf** resulting in a final falling tone.

As mentioned in the note above, ideophones are not common in negative sentences. When they do occur in them, however, they generally lack expressive prominence and are pronounced without the extra high produced by key raising, e.g.,

bài sàyi bàbûr sābō fil ba   He didn't buy a brand new motorcycle.
Sulè dà Bellò bà sù gàji tuɓus ba   Sule and Bello didn't become exhausted.
bài zama tsōhō tukuf ba   He hasn't become very old.

Finally, with long, more complex sentences, it appears that the potential expressive energy of ideophones is dissipated with the result that they may be pronounced with normal nonraised intonation characteristic of end of sentences. Similarly, ideophones imbedded in the midst of a normal sentence may be pronounced without special prominence, e.g.,

yāròn dà ya kùɓutà dàgà hannun 'yan sàndā gàjērē nè <u>duƙus</u>
    The boy who escaped from the hands of the police was very short.
mùtumìn dà ya zō ƙōfàr fādà yanà sànye dà hùlā baƙā <u>wulik</u>
    The man who came to the palace entrance was wearing a very black cap.
wani tsōhō <u>tukuf</u> yā shigè nân   A very old man passed by here.

6. IDEOPHONIC NOUNS (SOUNDS AND MOVEMENTS)

In addition to the ideophones per se, Hausa has a class of words that are clearly nouns, but that phonologically and semantically are sound symbolic in nature. These expressive ideophonic nouns primarily denote sounds, movements, and related activities. They are formed by means of a suffix -niyā)^{LLHH} with a set L-L-H-H tone pattern, e.g., **fàcàlniyā** 'splashing around in water'. (There are some seventy-five or so nouns of this class, all of which are feminine.) These words are mostly dynamic action nouns that occur as the predicate in a continuous TAM or as the object of the pro-verb **yi** 'do' or some other function verb, e.g., **miyà̀ tanà̀ fàlfàlniyā** 'The soup is boiling/bubbling', **sunà̀ ta hàtsà̀niyā** 'They keep on wrangling', **mun shā ɗàwàiniyā dà shī** 'We suffered putting up with him', cf. **hàyà̀niyā tā yi yawà̀** 'The hubbub is too much.' All of the words in this class are quadrisyllabic. The syllable preceding the suffix is always heavy, either CVC or CVV. The initial syllable is usually light, thereby producing an iambic rhythm. In most cases, the lexical base does not occur independently of the suffix, although some of these words do have cognate forms, typically ideophones. Examples:

fàlfàlniyā   boiling rapidly, cf. id. **fàlfàl** palpitations; **dìdìmniyā**   noise of beating on a calabash, roof, etc. = id. **dìdim-dìdim**; **ɗàwàiniyā**   being busy struggling with one's tasks; **gàgà̀niyā** struggling with s.o. or sth; **hàtsà̀niyā**   wrangling, quarreling; **ƙàràuniyā**   rattling = **ƙàràmniyā**, cf. **ƙarau**   glass bangle, glassware, **ƙàrarrawā** bell); **mùtsù̀niyā**   giggling, fidgeting by children = id. **mùtsù̀-mutsū**; **rùgù̀mniyā**   heavy rumbling (e.g., of thunder); confused babble and drumming, cf. id. **rùgùm**; **wàtsàlniyā**   wriggling, squirming = id. **wàtsàl-watsal**

°AN: Many words in this class contain an abutting /m.n/ sequence, e.g., **kwàràmniyā** 'noise, din'. This is phonologically aberrant because in SH /m/ followed by a coronal sonorant has regularly changed into /u/, e.g., **zamnà̀** > **zaunà̀** 'sit', **ɗamrè̀** > **ɗaurè̀** 'tie'.

◊HN: Originally the suffix was most likely just -**ne**)^{LH}, the resulting words all being feminine. The second syllable of the now-occurring -**niyā** suffix resulted from the addition of the feminative ending {-**a**} in accordance with the general historical process of overt characterization (see §31:4), e.g., *****fàcàl-ne** + **a** > **fàcàlniyā** 'splashing in water'.

ΔDN: In WH, -**niyā** words with a nasal-final base commonly occur in reduplicated form with a suffix -**tū** and a fixed LL-LHH tone pattern. (Some of these words are also found in SH, but without the reduplication.) Descriptions suggest that the meaning of the -**niyā** and -**tū** formations are essentially the same. Examples include the following:

   fàgàm-fàgamtū = **fàgàmniyā** 'searching wildly and ineffectively'
   gwàlàn-gwàlantū (= SH **gwàlantū**) = **gwàlàmniyā** 'speaking unintelligibly'
   kàtsàm-kàtsamtū = **kàtsà̀mniyā** 'being scattered, disheveled'
   kwàràm-kwàramtū (= SH **kwàrantū**) = **kwàràmniyā** 'din'
   sàgàm-sàgamtū = **sàgà̀mniyā** 'brusque gait'
   sùgùm-sùgumtū = **sùgù̀mniyā** 'gait (coming and going) of a heavy psn'

6.1. Related reduplicated ideophones with the shape Base x 2)$^{L-H}$

Many of the -**niyā** words have semantically equivalent ideophones with the shape Base x 2)$^{L-H}$ (where the disyllabic base has an iambic (light-heavy) rhythm) (see §1.2.10.1–2 above), e.g., **bùdùm-budum** (= **bùdù̀mniyā**) 'floundering about in water or work'. The choice as to whether the -**niyā** derivative noun or the ideophone is preferred is lexically specific (examples in (a)). There are also semantically related reduplicated L-H ideophones that do not have corresponding -**niyā** forms (examples in (b)). In some of these, the initial syllable is closed (heavy) (see §1.2.10.3–4 above). Like the -**niyā** derivatives, all of the ideophones can function as dynamic action nouns, e.g.,

(a) fàcàl-facal (= fàcàlniyā) playing with, or splashing water all over

e.g., yârân sunà ta fàcàl-facal à gēfèn kùduddufī

The children were splashing around in the pond.

gìdì-gidī busybody, fidgeting; officiousness

e.g., wannàn yāròn yā cikà gìdì-gidī This boy is so fidgety.

(= gìdùniyā, with /ù/, but only with the meaning of 'officiousness')

gwàlàn-gwalan (= gwàlàmniyā) speaking unintelligibly, babbling by toddlers

e.g., ɗan-yàyē yanà gwàlàn-gwalan The toddler is babbling.

jàlè-jalē (= jàlèniyā) going hither and thither

e.g., 'yan kàsuwân sunà ta jàlè-jalē à hùkūmàr ̧ilìmī wajen nēman kwangilar ginà màkàràntun fìrāmàrèn

The businessmen are going here and there to the ministry of education trying to get contracts to build the primary schools.

kìcì-kicī (= kìcìniyā) struggling,

e.g., inà kìcì-kicī ìn ciyar dà ìyālìnā I am struggling to provide for my family.

wàcà-wacā (= wàcàniyā) squandering, extravagance

e.g., yanà ta wàcà-wacā dà kuɗī sai kà cê bài san martabàrsù ba

He squanders his money such that you would say he doesn't know the value of it.

(b) bàzàr-bazar going about attempting sth in a disorganized way

e.g., kà dainà bàzàr-bazar Stop going around like that.

cùkù-cukū trying to obtain sth in an underhand way

e.g., yā yi cùkù-cukū yā sàmi aikī He got the job through the back door.

dùrù-durū looking here and there searching for sth

e.g., yîn dùrù-durū dab dà lōkàcin tàfiyà makaràntā bâ shi dà àmfànī

Madly searching around just when it's time to go to school has no use.

wàndàr-wandar zigzagging, swaying from side to side

e.g., bā nà sôn wàndàr-wandar I hate zigzagging.

zìrgà-zirgā constantly going to and fro

e.g., Audù yā fayè zìrgà-zirgā dà yawà Audu is constantly moving back and forth.

[References: Galadanci (1971); Inkelas and Leben (1990); Inkelas, Leben, and Cobler (1987); Moore (1968); Newman (1968, 1989b, 1995); Prietze (1908); Williams (1970)]

36. Idiomatic Phrasal Verbs

IDIOMATIC phrasal verbs are fixed verb-object collocations that have a special idiomatic meaning that is not immediately deducible from its parts. (In a few cases the item following the verb is something other than an object.) Here are a few illustrative examples from the hundred or so common idioms that exist:

bā dà bàkī coax, sweet-talk (lit. give mouth); **bā dà fuskà** be receptive (by showing a smile) (lit. give face); **ɓad dà kàmā** disguise oneself (lit. lose appearance); **ɓātà râi** frown, have a grim face, be upset (lit. spoil life/mind); **ci àmānà** breach trust (lit. eat trust); **ci gàba** proceed, progress (lit. eat front); **ci wākē** become pregnant (lit. eat black-eyed peas); **haɗà bàkī** conspire (lit. combine mouth); **jā kûnnē** warn or reprimand (lit. pull ear); **kai takàrdā** die (humorous, provocative) (lit. take paper); **kāmà ƙafà** lobby (lit. catch foot); **kāwō hancì** approach, get close (lit. bring nose); **ƙurè àdakà** dress in one's best clothes (lit. constrict trunk/crate); **làshi takòbī** pledge (lit. lick sword); **rainà ƙurar̃ X** be contemptuous of someone (lit. despise dust.of X); **sâ râi** expect, anticipate (lit. put life/mind); **sàci jìkī** sneak out (lit. steal body); **shā kùnū** frown (lit. drink porridge); **shìga ukù** be in a difficult situation, suffer (lit. enter three); **yankè ƙàunā** lose hope, give up (lit. cut love); **zubà idò** wait in great anticipation (lit. pour eye)

Many phrasal verbs commonly occur with an indirect object that serves as the semantic object, e.g.,

làbār̃ìn yā ɓātà minì râi	The news upset me. (lit. ...spoil to.me life)
kadà kà cī masà fuskà!	Don't humiliate him! (lit. ...eat to.him face)
mun gamè masà kâi	We conspired against him. (lit. ...combine to.him head)
yā ƙurà wà wàdà idò	He stared at the dwarf. (lit. ...constrict to dwarf eye)
nā shā musù kâi	I pestered them. (lit. ...drink to.them head)

gwamnatì tā shāfà wà àbòkan hàmayyà miyà à bàkī

  The government falsely accused the opposition. (lit. ...smear to opposition soup on mouth)

gìlāshìn mōtà yanà kashè wà fāsinjà idò

  The windshield is dazzling the eyes of the passengers. (lit. ... kill to passengers eye)

Because of their noncompositional meaning and the fact that in some cases, one cannot replace either of the components by a synonym—both characteristics of compounds—these idiomatic expressions have been described by some scholars, e.g., Grabna and Pawlak (1989), as compound verbs. Morphosyntactically, however, they behave like ordinary verb phrases and *not* like compounds, i.e., they do not create new, invariant *words*. To begin with, the verb in an idiomatic phrase is not invariant. It can, for example, undergo pluractional (plurac.) derivation and it can alter into another grade. In addition, in nonfinite contexts, a verb that would ordinarily be replaced by a corresponding verbal noun does so in idiomatic phrases as well, e.g., plurac: **mun jajjā kûnnen 'yā'yanmù**

plurac: **tā ciccī masà mutuncī̀**

grade shift: **shùgàbā yā ciyar̃ dà shī gàba**

(gr5 < **ci gàba** proceed, progress)

grade shift: **kù karyō kùmallō!**

(gr6 < **karyà kùmallō** have breakfast)

grade shift: **sun lāsō takòbī**

(gr6 < **làshi takòbī** make a pledge)

VN: **yanà cîn àmānà**

(where **cîn** is the VN **cî** plus the **-n** linker) (< **ci àmānà** breach trust)

(cf. **yanà cîn àbinci** He is eating food. vs. **yā ci àbinci** He ate food.)

VN: **sunà sātàr̃ jìkī**

We reprimanded our children. (< **jā kûnnē** reprimand)

She humiliated him repeatedly. (< **ci mutuncī̀** humiliate)

The leader promoted him.

Have breakfast (and then come)!

They make a pledge (for some benefit here).

He is breaching trust.

They were sneaking out. (< **sàci jìkī** sneak out)

Second, one can separate the components of the phrasal verbs by inserting elements between them such as indirect objects (as illustrated earlier) or modal particles, e.g.,

yā sâ <u>masà</u> hannū à takàr̃dâr̃

kà iyà <u>fa</u> bàkinkà!

(< **iyà bàkī** watch one's speech (lit. be able mouth))

yā ƙurè <u>kò̀</u> àdakàr̃sà

(< **ƙurè àdakà** dress up in one's best clothes)

He signed the paper for him. (< **sâ hannū** sign)

Watch your mouth! (i.e., be careful in your speech)

He is very well dressed.

Third, the object can be separated from its verb by fronting, whether for the purpose of focus, topicalization, or relativization, e.g.,

ƙùrar̃kà ya rainà

(< **rainà ƙùrar̃** X be contemptuous of)

mutuncìn jàma'à̀ yakè cî

(< **ci mutuncī̀** humiliate)

àmānà kùwa, yā cī tà

(< **ci àmānà** breach trust)

dantsè kàm, dōlè nē mù zāgè shi

(< **zāgè dantsè** work might and main)

bàkîn dà ya bāyar̃ bài yi aikī̀ ba

(lit. mouth.the that he gave away didn't work) (< **bā dà bàkī** coax, sweet-talk)

inà nufîn darē dà kakè rabàwā kullum

(< **rabà darē** burn the midnight oil)

He is *contemptuous* of you. (lit. dust.of.your he despise)

It's *people* he is humiliating.

Trust, he has breached it.

We must really work hard.

His sweet-talk didn't work.

I am referring to your constantly burning the midnight oil.

Fourth, a sentence with a phrasal verb can be reformulated into an equivalent or related sentence with the erstwhile object as subject, e.g.,

yā ɓātà r̃ai (lit. he spoiled life)

= **r̃ânsà yā ɓācì** (lit. his life spoiled)

yanà bugà wayà

cf. **wayà nà bugàwā**

He became upset.

He is making a phone call. (lit. he.cont beat wire)

The phone is ringing. (lit. wire cont beating)

[References: Ahmad (1994); Dikko and Maccido (1991)]

37. Imperative

1. INTRODUCTION

COMMANDS in Hausa are expressed by means of two different constructions: the imperative, described in this chapter, and the subjunctive (sub), see §70:17. The imperative exists as a special verb formation for affirmative commands. This imperative form is not overtly marked for gender or number, e.g.,

tàshi!	Get up!	kàr̃àntā!	Read (it)!
kàwō ruwā!	Bring water!	tàmbàyè-shi!	Ask him!

Although the imperative verb form is itself unmarked for number, it is understood to be in the singular. This can be seen in such items as reflexives and anaphoric pronouns that reflect the number of the understood subject, e.g.,

tàfi àbinkà! (You (m.)) go on your way! (lit. go thing.of.2m), tàfi àbinkì! (You (f.)) go on your way! (lit. go thing.of.2f)
not **tàfi àbinkù**, for which one must say kù tàfi àbinkù! You (pl.) (sub) go on your way!
tàshi ìn tàimàkē kà / kì Get up (m./f.) and let me help you (m./f)! (i.e., you've got to earn your own living)
not **tàshi ìn tàimàkē kù** **Get up (pl.) and let me help you (pl.), for which one must say kù tāshì ìn tàimàkē kù You (pl.) (sub) get up and let me help you (pl.)!
rùfē ta dà kânkà / kânkì Open (m./f.) it by yourself (m./f)!
not **rùfē ta dà kânkù** Open (pl.) it by yourselves (pl.)! for which one must say kù rufè ta dà kânkù You (pl.) (sub) open it by yourselves (pl.)!

The special imperative form is restricted to the second person. Commands in other persons necessarily use the subjunctive, e.g.,

ìn hau wannàn dōkìn	Let me mount this horse!	mù jē-mu	Let's go!
kadà fa mù ɓatà	Let's not get lost!	kadà tà tsayà̀	She shouldn't stay!
dōlè sù tàimàki jūnā	They must help one another!		
Allàh yà bā mù àlhēr̃ì	May God be kind to us! (lit. give us kindness)		

In the second person singular, the subjunctive serves as a somewhat less abrupt, softer alternative to the imperative for expressing commands. Subjunctive commands are commonly preceded by expressions like dōlè or tīlàs 'perforce, must' or don Allàh 'please' (lit. for the sake of God). If the intention is to express the gender and number of the addressee, then one has to use the subjunctive, e.g.,

kà tāshì!	Get up (2m)!	dōlè kà yi masà tàimakō!	You (2m) must help him!
kì kāwō ruwā!	Bring water (2f)!	don Allàh kì matsā̀!	Please move aside (2f)!
kù hàr̄bē sù!	Shoot them (2p)!	tīlàs kù biyā mù!	You (2p) must pay us!

In sequences of commands, the first may be in the imperative but the others will typically make use of the subjunctive, e.g.,

kầwō kujèrā <u>kì</u> zaunầ!	Bring a chair and sit down!
fìta <u>kà</u> tàfi cân <u>kà</u> dūbầ cikin gār̄ējì!	Go out and go there and look in the garage!

The special imperative form is used only in the affirmative. Negative commands are expressed by the negative subjunctive. This is formed with the prohibitive particle **kadà** (= **kâr̄**) plus a subjunctive wsp plus a normal finite form of the verb. This subjunctive construction allows for the expression of gender and number, e.g.,

kadà kà tāshì!	Don't (you m.) get up! (cf. **tầshi!** Get up!)
kadà kì kāwō ruwā!	Don't (you f.) bring water!
kadà kù tàmbàyē shì!	Don't (you pl.) ask him!

2. THE FORM OF THE IMPERATIVE

The essential feature of the imperative is the absence of the PAC (person-aspect-complex), i.e., there is no weak subject pronoun before the verb and no overt TAM. The verb itself has a distinctive tone pattern (usually L-H) that overrides the tone of the verb found in normal non-imperative sentences. With verbs that already have L-H tone the imperative tone is superimposed vacuously, e.g., **fìta!** 'Go out!' cf. **yā fìta** 'He went out'; **wầtsu!** 'Clear off!' cf. **sun wầtsu** 'They dispersed'; **sàyi nāmầ!** 'Buy meat!' cf. **zā tà sàyi nāmầ!** 'She will buy meat.' This imperative tone is subject to some variation depending on the grade and the syntactic form of the verb. Segmentally, the imperative in most grades is identical to the non-imperative verb form. However, grade 2 verbs without an object expressed and some grade 3 verbs manifest a change affecting the final vowel.

2.1. Basic L-H pattern
Verbs belonging to grades 2, 3 (disyllabic only), 3a, 3b, 4 (long-vowel variant), 5 (final -**ar̄** form), 6, 7, the irregular verb **zama**, and all verbs with the -**aC** pre-dative suffix (pds) manifest L-H in all positions in which they occur (subject to certain adjustments and alternatives to be described below), e.g.,

tàimàki 'yan'uwankà! Help your relatives! < **tàimakầ** v2; **sàuka!** Get down! < **sàuka** v3; **kwầna à nân!** Spend the night here! < **kwāna** v3a; **tùba ga Allàh!** Repent to God! < **tūba** v3a; **ɓùya!** Hide! < **ɓūya** v3a; **tầshi!** Get up! < **tāshì** v3b; **rùfē!** Close (it)! < **rufē** v4; **kàr̄kàshē su / màcìzân!** Keep killing them / the snakes! < **kar̄kàshē** v4; **wùlầkàntar̄ dà sū!** Treat them contemptuously! < **wulầkantar̄** v5; **màyar̄ minì dà shī!** Return it to/for me! < **mayar̄** v5; **gàishē shì!** Greet him! < **gaishē** v5 (pre-pronoun form); **kòmō!** Return here! < **kōmō** v6; **nànnèmō!** Seek (them) repeatedly! < **nannēmō** v6; **kầwō shì / bàr̄gō!** Bring it / a blanket! < **kāwō** v6; **nànnèmō manà àljànnū!** Seek the jinns for us! **sòyu!** Get fried! < **sòyu** v7; **ràbu dà shī!** Ignore him, leave him alone! < **ràbu** v7; **zàma mahàukàcī!** Become a madman! **ìnā ruwānā?** What do I care? < **zama** v*; **gìrbam manà dāwầ!** Reap the corn for us! < **girbam** v2+pds; **fìtam minì gidā!** Get out of my house! < **fitam** v3+pds; **tùbar̄ wà iyầyenkì!** Repent to (i.e., seek the pardon of) your parents! < **tūbar̄** v3a+pds

The verb **barì** 'let, allow, leave (off)' behaves like a regular gr2 verb with final -i when followed by no object or, sometimes, when followed by a dynamic noun (phrase), e.g., **bàri!** 'Leave (it)!' **bàri zuwà can!** 'Stop going there!' **bàri kūkā!** 'Quit crying!' When followed by a simple NP direct object, it behaves like a clipped irregular verb, e.g., **bař kuɗîn!** 'Leave the money!'

2.2. Grade 2 verbs
2.2.1. A-form with final -i
In declarative sentences, the A-form (i.e., non-object form) of gr2 verbs ends in -ā, e.g., **yā sàyā** 'He bought it', **nī nè ya tàimakà** 'It was me he helped.' In the imperative, however, the A-form appears with final short -i. (The final -i is also used with the irregular verbs **barì** 'let, allow' and **ganī** 'see, look'.) This vowel replacement is in addition to the L-H tone pattern, e.g.,

sàyi!	Buy (it)!	**ɗèbi!**	Dip out (sth)!
tàimàki!	Help!	**tàttàmbàyi!**	Ask (many/often)!
zàɓi!	Choose!	**bàri!**	Leave (it)!
kàrɓi!	Take (it)!	**gàni!**	Look! (= the more common **ga**!)

◊HN: Historically, the underlying base form of gr2 verbs was (and probably still is!) identical to the present-day pre-object C-form, i.e., it ends in -i and has L-H tone (e.g., //zàɓi// 'choose', //càkùmi// 'nab'). (The A-form, e.g., zàɓā, càkumà, which is the standard dictionary citation form, is *not* the analytical underlying form.) It is also the case that *-i is a common imperative suffix in Chadic, and there is evidence that this suffix did exist in Hausa at some point in the past. Consider, for example, the following imperative-based compounds: **kwànci-tàshi** 'slowly, day by day'; **shìgi-dà-fìci** 'restlessness, going in and out, immigration' (cf. **shìga** 'enter' and **fìta** 'go out'). (It is of course well known that old linguistic forms tend to fossilize in compounds, idioms, and such.) The question then is what does the gr2 imperative with final -i reflect? Does an imperative like **kàrɓi!** 'Take (it)!' contain the archaic imperative suffix *-i, i.e., //karɓ-// + -i)^{LH}, or is it simply the bare stem //kàrɓi//, which, for unknown reasons, has been retained in the imperative when no object is expressed even though it otherwise has been replaced synchronically by the A-form with final ā? In Newman (1973: 302), I opted for the first explanation, a position also adopted by Jaggar (1992a: 94n.). My present inclination, however, is toward the second choice, although I am not aware of any evidence that unequivocally supports one answer as opposed to the other.

2.2.2. B-form with pronoun objects
With gr2 verbs, the weak object pronoun attaches itself to the verb as an enclitic. When the L-H imperative tone pattern is assigned, it applies to the entire verb + pn complex rather than just to the verb stem per se, e.g.,

sàyè-shi!	Buy it!	**tàimàkè-mu!**	Help us!
sàcè-ta!	Steal it!	**tàttàmbàyè-su!**	Keep asking them!
hàřbè-su!	Shoot them!		

ΔDN: In Sokoto, the verbs **jìrāyà** 'wait for' (= **jirā**) and **kìrāyà** 'call' (= **kirā**) reduce the final syllable /-yē/ in the imperative to /-y/, which forms a diphthong with the preceding syllable, e.g., **jìrài-mu** (< *jìrày-mu) 'Wait for us!' **kìrài-ta** (< *kìrày-ta) 'Call her!'

When occurring with pronoun objects in the imperative, gr2 verbs have a minimal tone contrast with gr4 verbs. The former manifest the L-H imperative tone melody over the entire word including the pronoun clitic, whereas the latter manifest L-H on the verb only while the strong object pronouns keep their inherent H tone, e.g.,

gr2 **sàyè̀-shi!**   Buy it!   gr4 **sàyē shi!**   Buy it up!

gr2 **hàr̃bè̀-su!**   Shoot (at) them!   gr4 **hàr̃bē su!**   Execute them!

ΔDN: The cliticization of the pronoun and the L-H melody are common features of pre-pronominal gr2 verbs in the imperative. The verb ending itself, however, displays considerable dialectal and idiolectal variation. Some speakers (esp. in some WH dialects) allow gr2 verbs to appear with final -aG (or, less commonly, with -ar̃) instead of the usual -ē, e.g., **sàyàs-su!** 'Buy them!'; **sàtàt-ta!** 'Steal her!'; **tàimàkàm-mu!** (= **tàimàkàr̃-mu!**) 'Help us!'; etc. This geminate option is also found with H-H gr0 verbs, e.g., **bìyàt-ta!** 'Pay her!' < **biyā** 'pay'; **rìgàm-mu!** 'Precede us!' < **rigā** 'precede'. (In the dialect of Ader (Caron 1991), this gr2 B-form variant is also found in non-imperative sentences, e.g., **yā bùgàt-ta** 'He hit her.')

Some speakers (provenience?) have long -ā before the pronoun rather than -aC (Jaggar 1992a: 94n.), e.g., **ɗàukà-ta!** 'Take it!'; **sàkà-ni!** 'Release me!'; **tàmbàyà̀-su!** 'Ask them!'

Another morphological alternative, which is found in Kano, is to use a short -e before the pronoun, e.g., **sàyè-shi!** 'Buy it!'; **hàrbè-ta!** 'Shoot it!'; **aìkè-su!** 'Send them!'; **tàimàkè-mu!** 'Help us!' This variant, the existence of which is well confirmed, is very surprising because it runs counter to the otherwise exceptionless generalization in the language that syllables immediately preceding direct object pronouns (whether in the imperative or in any other construction) are always heavy.

2.3. Monosyllabic and H-H gr0 verbs

Monosyllabic verbs—whether underlyingly gr0 monoverbs (e.g., **ci** 'eat', **shā** 'drink'), irregular verbs (e.g., **kai** 'take', **hau** 'mount'), or clipped forms of disyllabic verbs (e.g., **sau** < **sakì** 'let loose, release', **bar̃** < **barì** 'leave, let'), have special characteristics in the imperative. Although **sâ** 'put' must normally be viewed as a segmentally reduced disyllabic gr1 verb, in the imperative, it patterns with other surface monosyllabic verbs. The same is true for **cê** 'say', a reduced, irregular gr4 verb. The disyllabic H-H ā-final verbs (such as **kirā** 'call'), which constitute a special subclass of gr0, generally pattern with the monoverbs for purposes of imperative rules. They exhibit alternative tonal shapes depending on whether they are treated as constituting one or two tonal domains.

2.3.1. A-form

In the A-context, without an object, monosyllabic verbs display H tone. (The disyllabic gr0 verbs normally display the full L-H imperative pattern, i.e., they treat their two syllables as two tonal domains for purposes of tone assignment. They may also appear in the imperative with all H tone, i.e., they may behave as if they were monosyllabic with one tonal domain). Examples:

ƙi! Refuse!   **jā!** Pull!   **jē!** Go!   **hau!** Mount!   **ga!** See! (< **ganī**)   **sā!** Put! (< **sâ**)

bìyā! = **biyā!** Pay!   **jìrā!** = **jirā!** Wait!

°AN: There are two alternative strategies for deriving the surface H tone on monosyllabic verbs from the underlying imperative L-H pattern. The first analysis assigns the L-H tone syllable by syllable from right to left. The H goes on the one available syllable and the L is discarded for lack of anything to dock onto, e.g., ci)^{LH} → ci)^{H} → /ci/ 'eat'. This is the analysis that I find most appropriate. The other analysis assigns the full L-H to the one available syllable, the LH rising tone automatically simplifying to H in accordance with the general LH to H rule (§71:1.2), e.g., ci)^{LH} → ci)^{R} → ci)^{H} → /ci/ 'eat'. This is the analysis adopted by Jaggar (1982). My main objection to this analysis is that it requires the postulation of two tones on a light monomoraic syllable, e.g., ***ga**)^{LH}, ***ci**)^{LH}, something that is completely out of line with the overall workings of tone in Hausa.

Pluractional reduplicated monoverbs have H-H tone in the imperative, i.e., the imperative tone has to be assigned *before* the reduplication, e.g.,

jajjā! Pull many, often! < **jā!** Pull!   **cicci!** Eat many, often! < **ci!** Eat!

°AN: The implication of this ordering is that inflection (i.e., imperative formation) applies before derivation (pluractional formation), i.e., //jā// + imp)^{LH} → **jā** + plurac. → **jajjā**. If the order were reversed, one would get **jā** + plurac → **jajjā** + imp)^{LH} → ****jàjjā**, which is the wrong output.

2.3.2. C-form
In the C-context before direct objects (or before a locative goal, in the case of the verbs 'come' and go'), monosyllabic verbs normally have H tone. Again the H-H disyllabic ā-verbs have either L-H tone, the norm (if treated as consisting of two tone-bearing units), or H (if treated as consisting of one tone-bearing unit like a monoverb), e.g.,

(a) **ci kaɽàs!** Eat the carrots!; **yi aikì!** Do work!; **shā ruwā!** Drink water!; **sō maɽwàbcinkà!** Love your neighbor!; **san àbōkin gàbankà!** Know your enemy!; **hau dōkìn!** Mount the horse!; **ɗau kwālī!** Take the carton!; **sā rìgāɽ!** Put on the gown!; **zō wurin nàn!** Come to this place!; **jē bàkin kàsuwā!** Go to the edge of the market!; **ga mōtàtā!** (= **gàni mōtàtā!** with gr2-like pattern) See my car!
(b) **bìyā manajà!** = **biyā manajà!** Pay the manager!; **kìrā yāròn!** = **kirā yāròn!** Call the boy!; **jìrā mālàm!** = **jirā mālàm!** Wait for the teacher!

2.3.3. B-form
In the B-context before a weak object pronoun, one normally gets cliticization of the pronoun, as happens with gr2 verbs. The L-H imperative tone pattern then applies to the resulting word, e.g.,

(a) **bì-mu!** Follow us! **yì-shi!** Do it! **jà-ta!** Pull it! **bà-ni!** Give me! **jàjjà-ta!** Keep on pulling it! **bìbbì-su!** Follow them!
bàɽ-mu! Leave us! **gàn-ta!** See (i.e., look at) her! **sàn-su!** Know them!
(b) **ɗàu-su!** Lift them! **sàu-ta!** Let her go!
(c) **hàu-shi!** Mount it! **kài-ta cân** Take it there! **sà-ta** Put it on!
(d) **kìrà-ta!** Call her! **bìyà-shi!** Pay him! **jìrà-mu!** Wait for us!

The verbs in rows (c) and (d) exhibit an alternative pattern in which they are treated as verbs with a strong object pronoun without cliticization. The verb itself carries the (L)-H imperative tone and the following pronoun shows up with its inherent H tone.

hau shi! kai ta cân! sā ta!
kìrā ta! bìyā shi! jìrā mu!
rìgā mu zuwà can! Please precede us there! (but *not* ****rìgà-mu zuwà can!**)

As a third alternative, the H-H ā-verbs build imperatives on the model of H-H gr6 verbs, i.e., L-H on the verb itself and L on the object pronoun, i.e., **bìyā shì lādan aikìnsà!** 'Pay him his wages!' cf. **kàwō shì nân!** 'Bring him here!'

°AN: According to Jaggar (1982), the nonfused variant (e.g., **hau shi** 'Mount it!') is unmarked and the L-H variant (e.g., **hàu-shi**) has a special softening, hypothetical nuance. Speakers agree that the alternative forms are not semantically identical, but they do not all accept Jaggar's interpretation. The general consensus is that it is the fused variant (e.g., **hàu-shi**) that is the normal, unmarked case and it is the nonfused form (e.g., **hau shi**) that is semantically and pragmatically marked as having a stronger illocutionary force.

ΔDN: Some speakers are reported by Jaggar (1982) as also allowing an L-tone monosyllabic verb imperative with a softening nuance before a noun object (or locative goal), e.g., **shà ruwā**! 'Drink water! ' (please, it will be good for you); **bàr̃ kuɗîn**! 'Leave the money!' (if you don't mind); **ɗàu kwālī**! 'Take the carton!' (if you want); **zò wurin nàn**! 'Come to this place!' (if/when it suits you). Other speakers feel that only the H-tone imperative can be used in this context.

2.3.4. D-form

In the D-context preceding an indirect object, one also gets both L and H tone on the verb. As with the verb in the B-form, many speakers feel that the L-tone variant is the unmarked form whereas the H-tone variant indicates an imperative that is semantically more insistent, e.g.,

bì masà Bintà / bī masà Bintà Follow Binta for him! **jà manà kūrā / jā manà kūrā** Pull the cart for us! **jàjjà wà mutànên igiyàr̃ / jajjā wà mutànên igiyàr̃** Pull the rope for the men! **sà minì r̃ìgâr̃ / sā minì r̃ìgâr̃** Put on the gown for me! **kài musù kāyân / kai musù kāyân** Take the loads for them! **bàr̃ matà kuɗîn / bar̃ matà kuɗîn** Leave the money for her! **sàm minì nāmā̀ / sam minì nāmā̀** Get me some meat! **sài wà mālàm tùmātìr̃ / sai wà mālàm tùmātìr̃** Buy tomatoes for the teacher! **kìrā̀ masà likità / kìrā masà likità** (= kira masà likità!) Call a doctor for him!

2.4. Grade 1 and grade 4 verbs
2.4.1. A-form and B-form

In the A and B contexts, i.e., when followed by no object or by a pronoun d.o., gr1 and gr4 verbs manifest the general L-H imperative tone, e.g.,

kà̄mā!	Catch (it)! (< **kāmā̀** v1)	**kà̄mā su**!	Catch them!
kàr̃àntā!	Read! (< **kar̃àntā** v1)	**kàr̃àntā shi**!	Read it!
rùfē!	Close (it)! (< **rufè** v4)	**rùfē ta**!	Close (it)!
bìncìkē!	Investigate! (< **bìncìkē** v4)	**bìncìkē su**!	Search them!

°AN: Note that the strong direct object pronouns always appear with their inherent H tone even though the immediately preceding tone of the verb is H, i.e., these pronouns do *not* have polar tone as scholars mistakenly thought for a long period of time (see §59:1.1.2).

2.4.2. D-form

In the D context, the imperative tone of gr1 and gr4 verbs depends on whether the indirect object is a personal pronoun or not (i.e., anything other than a personal pronoun). If the i.o. is represented by the paradigm consisting of **ma-** plus a low-tone pronoun, the verb is L-H. If the i.o. is a noun, in which case the i.o. marker is low-tone **wà**, the verb normally has L-L tone, although L-H is also possible with a somewhat stronger connotation. Note that the L-H / L-L variants are also used with gr6 verbs, e.g.,

kàr̃àntā manà littāfì!	Read the book for us!
rùfē minì tāgà̀!	Close the window for me!
bìncìkē musù màganàr̃!	Investigate the matter for them!
nèmō masà aikì̀!	Seek work for him!

ràbằ wà mutằnên kuɗîn! / ràbā wà mutằnên kuɗîn!   Distribute the money to the people!
mìmmìƙằ wà bàƙī mintî! / mìmmìƙā wà bàƙī mintî!   Offer the guests mints!
kàshè wà yârā fìtilằ! / kàshē wà yârā fìtilằ!   Put the light out for the children!
gùtsùrồ wà mālàm tuwō! / gùtsùrō wà mālàm tuwō!   Break off some *tuwo* for the teacher!

2.4.3. C-form

In the C position before a nonpronoun direct object, gr1 verbs and the short final-vowel variant of gr4 have L-L tone. (The long final-vowel variant of gr4 appears with L-H tone.) Examples:

kằmà ɓàrāwồ!   Catch the thief!   dàfà ruwā!   Boil some water!   kà̀rànta bābìn nan!   Read that chapter!
rìƙè wannàn!   Grab this!   (cf. rìƙē wannàn!);   bìncìkè màganàȓ!   Investigate the matter! (cf. bìncìkē màganàȓ!);   kàȓkàɗè bàȓgō!   Shake out the blanket!   rùfè tāgằ!   Close the window!

2.5. Short-form grade 5 verbs

In the imperative, short-form gr5 verbs (see §74:9.1.1), e.g., sai dà 'sell' (= sayaȓ dà), generally have L tone both on the verb and on the L-tone pseudoclitic dà, i.e., they behave in some sense like disyllabic gr1 verbs. Examples:

sài dà nāmằ!   Sell the meat! (cf. gr1 sồyà nāmằ!   Fry the meat!)   ɓằ dà kuɗîn!   Give away the money!
fìd dà kāyā!   Take out the loads!   zùb dà ruwân!   Pour out the water!   kằ dà sū!   Knock them down!
kàu dà sū dàgà nân!   Move them away from here!   tsài dà ita!   Stop it!

Alternatively, the short-form gr5's can be treated as discrete H-tone monosyllabic verbs followed by the particle dà, e.g.,

sai dà nāmằ!   Sell the meat!   kā dà sū   Knock them down!

This variant with the H tone has a secondary status, by some speakers being rejected entirely. When it is allowed, it tends to add special emphasis and force to the imperative.

> °AN: Jaggar (1982), who documents both the fused L-L and nonfused H-L variants, interprets the H-L form as basic and ascribes a weakening feature to the L-L variant. Again, I would suggest that he has reversed what is marked and what is unmarked. From what I have been able to determine, the L-L variant is the neutral, preferred form. Significantly, compounds containing short-form gr5 verbs in the imperative invariably appear with L-L tone, e.g., ɓàd-dà-kàma 'disguise, camouflage' (lit. lose appearance); fìd-dà-kâi 'tithe given out at the end of Ramadan' (lit. take out head); gài-dà-yằya 'small basin or basket for presents' (lit. greet elder sibling).

The few short form gr5's with /ī/ behave differently from the above. With these verbs, the variant with H on the verb was fully accepted as equivalent to the L-L form. Examples:

bī dà yârân! = bǐ-dà yârân!   Control the children!
cī dà sū! = cǐ-dà sū!   Feed them! (both considered inferior to the full cìyaȓ dà sū!)

2.6. Polysyllabic grade 3 verbs

Disyllabic gr3 verbs appear with final -a and the expected L-H tone, e.g., fìta 'go out!' The situation with polysyllabic gr3's is more complicated. In the literature, one finds reference to an imperative hàƙùri! 'Be patient!' < hàƙurà, containing what appears to be the same -i imperative marker one finds with gr2 verbs. (Significantly, examples of this formation are found *only* with this verb or occasionally with the verb zàbùr̃i! 'Jump up!' < zàbur̃à.) Alternatively, one finds examples of polysyllabic gr3's with L-H tone, but with final -a, e.g., mùsùlùnta! 'Become a Muslim!' dùlmùya 'Sink down!' The SH norm, as far as I have been able to determine, is to use the base form of the verb as is *without* the L-H imperative pattern (although expressing the command by use of the subjunctive was always the preferred option). The imperative is thus marked simply by the absence of the weak subject pronoun without any segmental or tonal marking, e.g.,

hàƙurà! Be patient! cf. yā hàƙurà He was patient; kìshìngiɗà! Rest on your elbow!; mùsùluntà! Become a Muslim!; dògarà gà Allàh! Depend on God!; dùƙufà sòsai à aikìn nân nākà! Get down seriously on this work of yours!

°AN: There is a natural analogical explanation for the polysyllabic gr3 tone. If one interprets disyllabic gr3 imperatives like fìta! 'Go out!' as having the L-H imperative tone, one would expect to get polysyllabic forms such as dùlmùya 'Sink down!' (which is sometimes found). If, on the other hand, one interprets gr3 imperatives like fìta! 'Go out!' as reflecting the base form without the special imperative tone—whether this is or is not *correct*, analytically or historically—then by extension one should get polysyllabic imperatives like dùlmuyà, which is what is now becoming the norm.

2.7. *Verbs* go *and* come
The verbs *go* and *come* have special imperative forms:

jè-ka, jè-ki, jè-ku Go (m./f./pl.)! / Get going!   yā-kà, yā-kì, yā-kù Come here (m./f./pl.)!

Most previous descriptions limit the use of the special forms to the singular, which is consistent with the fact that imperatives in general occur only in the singular. Many modern-day speakers consider the plural forms (which probably represent an analogical extension) to be fully acceptable.

The jè-ka forms are easily analyzable synchronically as the verb jē 'go' + an ICP (intransitive copy pronoun), with the imposition of the regular L-H imperative tone pattern. (Cf. the completive mun jē-mu 'We went', where the verb and the following ICP manifest H-H tone.) The yā-kà forms with H-L tone, on the other hand, are anomalous archaisms whose structure and etymology are still unknown.

[References: Abraham (1959b); Jaggar (1982)]

38. Impersonal

1. FORM

IN addition to the eight pronominal categories found in most personal pronoun paradigms, the weak subject pronouns (wsp) include an impersonal 'one, they' that is unspecified for person and gender features, e.g., **an kāwō ruwā** 'One/They brought water' (i.e., water was brought by someone unknown or not worth mentioning); **bà zā à̠ tàimàkē kà ba** 'One/They won't help you' (i.e., you won't get any help). This impersonal is found in all TAMs (see chap. **70**). The impersonal has the form **an** (i.e., /'an/) in the heavy-syllable paradigm (used in the completive) and **a** (with variable tone) in the light-syllable paradigm (used in SH in all other TAMs), e.g., **anā̀** (continuous); **akàn** (habitual), **zā à** (future) **zâ a** (allative), **â** (< **a** + **à̠**) (potential), **akà** (preterite), **akā̀** (rhetorical), **bà à...ba** (negative-completive), etc.

The impersonal—which for ease of reference is labeled as fourth person plural (4p)—can be grouped with the plural pronouns on both morphological and syntactic grounds. For example, apart from the second person feminine, the singular completive pronouns all have the shape CVV whereas the plural pronouns are all **CVn**, cf. **nā** 'I', **yā** 'he', **kun** 'you (pl.)', **sun** 'they', etc. The impersonal 'an 'one/they' patterns with the **CVn** forms. Similarly, in the preterite, the impersonal appears with a marker -**kà** that is not found with the singular pronouns (again apart from the second person feminine), e.g., **mukà** 'we', **sukà** 'they', **akà** 'one/they', cf. **na** 'I', **ka** 'you (m.)', **ta** 'she'.

Perhaps even more significant in indicating the plurality of the impersonal pronouns is their behavior with reciprocals. In Hausa, as is probably the case in most languages, a reciprocal construction necessarily requires that the referent/antecedent be plural, e.g., **mun yàudàri jūnā** 'We deceived each other', **Bellò dà Mūsā zā sù yàudàri jūnā** 'Bello and Musa will deceive one another', but not ****yā yàudàri jūnā** 'He deceived each other.' Sentences with an impersonal pronoun pattern with the plurals in permitting a reciprocal, e.g., **an yàudàri jūnā** 'They (impersonal) deceived each other.'

2. FUNCTION

2.1. Normal uses of the impersonal

The impersonal wsp normally occurs in sentences without an underlying subject. It thus differs from all the other wsp's, which get their person/number/gender from the underlying subject, whether it is present in the surface sentence or not, e.g.,

[Mūsā]₃ₘ [yā]₃ₘ kāwō ruwā	Musa brought water.
[sun]₃ₚ kāwō ruwā	They brought water.

(where the underlying subject **sū** 'they' is not expressed)

[yārinyàr̃]₃f dà [ta]₃f kāwō ruwā   the girl who brought water

(where the coreferential subject of the relative clause has been deleted)

cf. **[an]₄ₚ kāwō ruwā**   One brought water. (where the subject slot is empty)

270

The impersonal occurs in three main environments.

First it serves as an unspecified subject corresponding to English 'one/they'. Generally speaking, it is restricted to human referents, e.g., **an zaunà bâ màganà** 'One just sat without talking' (not ****an narkè** 'One/they (inanimate) melted'); **anà gyārà mōtàtā** 'They (unspecified) are repairing my car', cf. **sunà gyārà mōtàtā** 'They (anaphoric 3pl.) are repairing my car.' These sentences with the impersonal wsp semantically correspond to English agentless passives, e.g., **an kāmà ɓàrāwòn** 'One has caught the thief', i.e., 'The thief has been caught.'

Second, the impersonal is used as the dummy subject of "weather" sentences, e.g., **an sōmà (yîn) ruwā** 'It began to rain'; **anà yayyafī tun sāfe** 'It has been drizzling since morning', and of certain temporal clauses, e.g., **an yi watà bìyař tun dà mukà gan shì** 'It's been five months since we saw him', **anà nan, anà nan** 'Time passed' (lit. one is there, one is there) (used in narratives to indicate the passage of time).

Third, the impersonal commonly shows up (usually with the neutral zero TAM) in compound nouns, e.g., **à-ci-bàlbàl** 'an oil-burning lamp' (lit. one-eats-flickering), **à-ji-garau** 'type of antidepressant pill' (lit. one-feels-fine), **à-kòri-kūrā** 'delivery truck' (lit. one-drives out-carts), **à-ƙwammàtā** 'old, ineffective vehicle/equipment' (lit. one-contents oneself with sth inferior).

2.2. Oblique Impersonal Construction

In addition to its normal use in sentences without a subject, the impersonal is also used in a special construction that I have termed the "oblique impersonal construction" (OIC).

°AN: Abdoulaye (1992: 90ff), one of the few scholars to discuss the existence of this construction, terms it the *empathic impersonal construction*. I have purposely chosen a fuzzier, less descriptive term because empathy is only one of the attitudes that this construction connotes, others being sarcasm, indirectness, and deference. (The description of the OIC presented here is a summary of unpublished work carried out by Mustapha Ahmad Isa and myself.)

The striking feature of this construction is the use of an impersonal wsp in sentences *that have* an underlying subject and that would therefore be expected to have an appropriate thirrd (or second) person wsp. In the OIC, the impersonal wsp serves to avoid direct reference to someone out of politeness or deference or for other stylistic purposes (see below §2.2.8). Examples:

Daudà <u>anà</u> shân wàhalà   Poor Dauda is having trouble.
(Emotionally more marked than the normal sentence,
Daudà [yanà]3m shân wàhalà   Dauda is having trouble.)
lallē, yârā zā <u>à</u> fārà kàřātū yâu   Surely, today is the children's first day at school.
(lit. well, children fut 4p begin reading today) (More empathetic than the normal statement of fact,
lallē, yârā [zā sù]3pl fārà kàřātū yâu   Yes, children will begin school today.)
<u>an</u> dāwō lāfiyà?   Did you have a nice trip? (lit. 4p.comp return healthy)
(Less direct and more deferential than the equivalent normal sentence, [kā]2m dāwō lāfiyà?)
mūgùn àlƙālin nàn <u>anà</u> zāluncì   This cruel judge is really a tyrant.
(lit. cruel judge.of this 4p.cont tyranny)
dagacìn ƙauyènmù sai tàƙamā <u>akè</u>!   How pretentious our village head is!
(lit. head.of village.of.us only swaggering 4p.Rcont)
gwamnatìn Amùřkà <u>anà</u> fāmā dà laifuffukà   The U.S. government is overwhelmed by crime.
(lit. government.of America 4p.cont struggling with crimes)
Audù hař <u>an</u> ci àbincîn?   Audu did you eat already?

2.2.1. Anomalous plurality

Prefixing the third person plural pronoun **su** to a noun or noun phrase normally creates *pseudoplurals*, i.e., the **su** indicates etc. or et al., e.g., **su Bàlā sunà shân lèmō** 'Bala and the others are drinking cola', **yanà sô yà kashè su dàmisà** 'He wants to kill leopards, etc.' In the OIC, however, one can prefix **su** to a subject noun *without* adding the normally expected semantic plurality, e.g.,

àshē <u>su</u> Mālàm bà <u>à</u> sàmu tàfiyà hajì ba	Sorry to hear that Teacher couldn't go on the hadj.
cf. **àshē <u>su</u> Mālàm bà <u>sù</u> sàmu tàfiyà hajì ba**	Oh, Teacher and the others couldn't go on the hadj.
<u>su</u> Lādì dà Kànde <u>anà</u> kūkā	Poor Ladi and Kande are crying.
(not **Ladi and Kande et al. are crying.)	
<u>su</u> wancè <u>an</u> sàmu jūnā biyu	So-and-so is pregnant.
(lit. 3p so-and-so 4p.comp get self two)	

2.2.2. Persons

The OIC is allowed with second and third person subjects, masculine and feminine and singular and plural. It is not possible in the first person whether singular or plural. Examples:

Mūsā / Lādì / yârā kadà <u>à</u> kàrayà dai!   Musa / Ladi / children, don't give up yet!

cf. **Mūsā kadà [kà]$_{2m}$ kàrayà dai / Lādì kadà [kì]$_{2f}$ kàrayà dai / yârā kadà [kù]$_{2pl}$ kàrayà dai**

àshē (su) Mūsā / Lādì / Mūsā dà Lādì <u>anà</u> fāmā dà cīwò

  Sorry to hear that Musa / Ladi / Musa and Ladi are chronically ill.

cf. **àshē Mūsā [yanà]$_{2m}$ fāmā dà cīwò / àshē Lādì [tanà]$_{2f}$ fāmā dà cīwò / àshē Mūsā dà Lādì [sunà]$_{3p}$ fāmā dà cīwò**

not **nī / mū sai gòbe zā <u>à</u> zō**   I / we will come but not until tomorrow.

cf. **nī sai gòbe [zân]$_{1s}$ zō**   I will come but not until tomorrow.

cf. **mū sai gòbe [zā mù]$_{1p}$ zō**   We will come but not until tomorrow.

2.2.3. Animacy

Generally speaking, the subjects of an OIC are animate (both human and, less often, nonhuman). Inanimate subjects are also possible, although they are less common. When the subject is nonhuman, the OIC always carries a humorous/poking fun connotation, e.g.,

(su) **Lādì <u>an</u> yi sābon kitsò**	Wow, Ladi has a new hairdo.
ɓērā <u>an</u> sàmu sakèwā	The mouse is relaxed. (perhaps the cat is not around anymore)
ràgō <u>an</u> shā wuƙā	Poor ram, it has been slaughtered. (lit. ram 4p.comp suffer knife)
wai, kàtīfà <u>an</u> fatattàkē!	What a wretched-looking mattress!
(lit. well, mattress 4p.comp has become shredded)	

2.2.4. Tense/aspect, negation, questions

With one exception, the OIC can be used in all TAMs, positive or negative, and declarative or interrogative, e.g.,

su Audù <u>an</u> dāwō gidā	Audu is back home. (comp)
su likità hař yànzu bà <u>à</u> isō asìbitì ba?	Has the doctor not reached the hospital yet? (Ncomp)
ɗan kōlì bā <u>à</u> sôn rānā	The petty trader abhors the hot sun. (Ncont)
Bàlā kuma zā <u>à</u> shā fāmā dà sanyī	Poor Bala is going to have a hard time with the cold. (fut)
àshē Mūsā <u>akàn</u> fitō shân iskà?	So Musa you often come out for a stroll?
	(or, So Musa often comes out for a stroll?) (hab)

tô Mūsâ, <u>à</u> matsō <u>à</u> kàrɓā!   All right Musa, come and get it! (sub)

habà Làdīdi kadà <u>à</u> tàfi <u>à</u> baɾ mù mànà!   Oh come on Ladidi, don't leave us! (neg sub)

For inexplicable reasons, the OIC does not occur in the potential unless the impersonal wsp has already been used earlier in the sentence. Thus, one cannot say ****Mūsā <u>â</u> ji dāɗī** 'Musa might enjoy himself', but one can say **Mūsā <u>an</u> sayō mōtằ kō <u>â</u> ji dāɗī** 'Musa bought (comp) a car so that he (pot) might enjoy himself.'

2.2.5. Sequence of clauses

In a sequence of clauses with the same subject, the person/number/gender of the wsp's have to be the same. Thus, if one uses the OIC in one clause, one has to use it in all (cf. the example above with the potential). Similarly, if one uses a regular wsp in one clause, this also has to be used in all, e.g.,

Lawàn <u>an</u> ci <u>an</u> shā <u>an</u> yi gòdiyā   Poor Lawan ate, drank, and said thanks. (OIC)

cf. Lawàn yā ci yā shā yā yi gòdiyā   Lawan ate, drank, and said thanks. (3m wsp's)

not **Lawàn yā ci <u>an</u> sha <u>an</u> yi gòdiyā, nor **Lawàn <u>an</u> ci yā sha yā yi gòdiyā

Mālàm, <u>à</u> ci àbinci mànà kō <u>â</u> ƙòshi!   Come on Teacher, eat, so that you may be replete! (OIC),

cf. Mālàm, <u>kà</u> ci àbinci mànà kō kâ ƙòshi!   Teacher, eat, so that you may be replete! (2m wsp's)

su ɗàlìbai <u>anà</u> sô <u>à</u> ji dāɗī   So the students want to have a good time. (OIC)

cf. su ɗàlìbai sunà sô sù ji dāɗī   The students et al. want to have a good time. (3p wsp's)

2.2.6. Topic, focus, and relativization

The OIC operates easily with a topicalized subject, e.g.,

Mūsā kàm, <u>an</u> shā dòke-dòke   As for Musa, he received a beating.

(more or less = **Mūsā kàm, yā shā dòke-dòke**)

However, given the oblique nature of this construction, which tries to divert attention (and responsibility) from the subject noun, the OIC cannot be used when the subject is in focus or is modified by a specifier pronoun.

su Abdù bà <u>à</u> ci jaɾɾàbâwā ba   Poor Abdu didn't pass the exam.

but not **shī Abdù bà <u>à</u> ci jaɾɾàbâwā ba

cf. shī Abdù bài ci jaɾɾàbâwā ba   He Abdu didn't pass the exam.

wai Mūsā <u>an</u> ci zàɓē   It is said that Musa won the election.

but not **Mūsā nè <u>akà</u> ci zàɓē   Amazingly it was *Musa* who won the election.

cf. Mūsā nè ya ci zàɓē   It was *Musa* who won the election.

su bòyi <u>anà</u> wankè mōtằ cikin rānā   The poor house boy is washing the car in the sun.

but not **bòyi nè <u>akè</u> wankè mōtằ cikin rānā

    It is the poor house boy who is washing the car in the sun.

cf. bòyi nè (ya)kè wankè mōtằ cikin rānā

    It is the house boy who is washing the car in the sun.

Interestingly, the incompatibility of the OIC and focus usually holds even if some noun other than the subject is focused, e.g.,

**lèmō nè yârā <u>akè</u> shâ   It is an orange that the children are eating.

Required is **lèmō nè yârā sukè shâ**

**littāfî nē Lādì <u>akà</u> sàyā	It is a book that Ladi bought.
Required is **littāfî nē Lādì ta sàyā**	

Since relativization puts the head in focus, it follows that the OIC is not allowed in relative clauses, e.g.,

**Bàlân dà <u>akà</u> sàmu kuɗī	the Bala who got some money
**jar̃r̃àbâwâr̃ dà yār̃ò <u>akà</u> ci	the exam that the boy passed

On the other hand, although question words are inherently focused, they are not incompatible with the OIC—at least with second person addressees, e.g.,

Bellò, mḕ <u>akḕ</u> ɓōyḕ manà nē?	Oh Bello, what is it that you are hiding from us?
Jummai, yàushē <u>akà</u> dāwō nḕ?	Oh Jummai, when did you return?

2.2.7. Reflexives

In an OIC sentence that contains a reflexive, the reflexive agrees with the impersonal wsp and not with the subject per se. Thus it appears as **kâi** 'self' rather than as **kânsà** 'himself', **kântà** 'herself', etc., e.g.,

'yan yârā, <u>à</u> nèmi àbin kâi!	Kids, get your own!
(lit. young children, 4p get thing.of self)	
more or less = **'yan yârā, kù nèmi àbin kânkù** (lit. young children, 2p get thing.of yourselves)	
su Audù <u>an</u> cùci kâi	Poor Audu cheated himself.
not ****su Audù an cùci kânsà**	
su Lādì da Bintà an cùci kâi	Poor Ladi and Binta cheated themselves.
not ****su Lādì da Bintà an cùci kânsù**	
(su) Sulè an sayà wà kâi tàkàlmī	So poor Sule bought shoes for himself.
cf. **Sulè yā sayà wà kânsà tàkàlmī**	Sule bought shoes for himself.

2.2.8. Semantics and pragmatics of the OIC

The exact meaning and function of the OIC is not fully understood. However, compared with a normal, neutral sentence, a sentence with the OIC tends to connote empathy, sympathy, amazement, derision, or a light-hearted jocular attitude towards the referent. One context in which OIC is used is when referring to a new event, especially one that a person experiences for the first time, e.g.,

(su) bēr̃à <u>an</u> jē zàncē!	Wow, the young girl went out on a date!

[Note: The word **bēr̃à** refers to a young girl whose breasts have not yet developed. The jocular connotation in this remark can be seen in the fact that girls of that age do not have any experience in dating, thus are very likely to be excited on their first time out.]

(su) Lādì <u>an</u> yi sābon kitsò	Wow, Ladi has a new hairdo.
(su) Audù an shìga jirgī, sai būɗè bàkī <u>akḕ</u>!	

Oh, Audu has got on a plane (for the first time), see his gaping mouth!

A second situation where an OIC is used is in the context of an undesired or malefactive event. The function of the OIC is to refer indirectly and sympathetically to that event or to the person involved. In this way, the event is portrayed as something unimportant, ephemeral, and not worth being bothered by. Intonation expressing sympathy can accompany OIC sentences portraying this meaning. Examples:

àshē (su) Lādì fāmā <u>akḕ</u> dà cīwò	Sorry to hear that Ladi is ill.

su ō'ò <u>an</u> fāɗ<u>à</u> rĩjìyā	So-and-so fell in the well (i.e., what a dummy!).
àshē (su) Mālàm bà <u>à</u> s<u>à</u>mu tàfiy<u>à</u> hajì ba	Sorry to hear that Teacher could not go on the hadj.
ɗàlìbai bā <u>à</u> sôn cîn wùyā	Students hate hard work.

A third function of the OIC is to avoid direct reference to a person when talking about sex, death, body functions, and other delicate or taboo matters. Thus a woman referring to a newly circumcised boy, or a man referring to a newly pregnant young woman might use the OIC, e.g.,

àshē (su) Audù <u>an</u> girma	So, Audu was circumcised. (lit. has grown up)
Less direct than àshē Audù yā girma	
àshē (su) Lādì <u>an</u> s<u>à</u>mu jūnā biyu	So Ladi is pregnant.
Politer than àshē Lādì tā s<u>à</u>mu jūnā biyu	

A fourth reason for the use of the OIC is the avoidance of a direct second person pronoun out of deference and respect. (This would seem to be one of the closest things there is to a pragmatic universal.) This avoidance is expected, for example, between a wife and her husband or when a person who is subordinate in rank or age addresses his or her superior. Examples:

mālàm, <u>à</u> tūrō mîn yārò à wàje!	Husband, send in the kid when you go outside!
tô Mūsâ, kadà <u>à</u> matsō nân dai!	All right Musa, don't move any closer!
Lādì, mènē nè bā <u>à</u> sô nē?	Ladi, what is it that that you don't like?
bābà, <u>an</u> gamà àbinci?	Mother, have you finished cooking?
<u>à</u> dāwō lāfiy<u>à</u>!	Come back safely!

39. Indirect Objects

THE term *indirect object* (i.o.) is used for a specific morphosyntactic structure that employs the indirect object marker (IOM). In SH this marker is underlyingly **ma-** before personal pronouns and **wà** elsewhere. In sentences with both direct and indirect objects, the word order is i.o. and then d.o., e.g., **yā gayà [wà mālàm]**i.o. **[làbāřì]**d.o. 'He told the teacher the news.' (Note: Although the IOM often translates in English as 'to' or 'for', etc., it is not classified as a preposition.) The Hausa indirect object does not exactly match the English indirect object, i.e., Hausa has sentences with the IOM that correspond to English sentences without an indirect object, e.g., **tâ tunà [manà]**i.o. 'She will remind us.' Conversely, Hausa has sentences without the IOM that correspond to sentences that in English have an indirect object, e.g., **yā bā mù dalà biyu** 'He gave us two dollars' (where **mù** is a d.o. pronoun). In addition, Hausa, like English, can express thematic roles like benefactive and recipient by use of various prepositional phrases (formed, for example, with **gà(rē)** 'to, at' or **don** 'for') rather than by means of an i.o. construction, e.g., **yā yi kirà [gà]**prep **mutànē sù biyā hàřàjì** 'He called on the people to pay their taxes' (lit. he.comp did calling to people they.sub pay taxes); **yā yankà nāmà don kânsà** 'He cut the meat for himself' = **yā yankà wà kânsà nāmà** (lit. he.comp cut for himself meat).

1. FORM: NONPRONOMINAL INDIRECT OBJECTS

1.1. Usual SH forms

In SH, the form of the IOM that is used when followed by anything other than a personal pronoun (or when it is followed by nothing) is **wà**. In most of Hausaland it has the form **mà**, which can substitute for **wà** in all the examples below. Examples:

sun sayō wà Mūsā wàndō	They bought trousers for Musa. (= [WH] **sun sayō mà Mūsā wàndō**)
zân kai wà mālàm littāfìn	I will take the book to the teacher.
nā řubùtā wà kâinā wàsīkà	I wrote myself a letter.
an yabà wà shī àlkālìn	They praised him the judge.
Amìřkà dà Rāshà sun yi wà jūnā kālūbàlē	
	America and Russia challenged each other. (lit. ...did to each other challenge)

◊HN: [i] The **wà** variant is probably derived historically from the preposition **gà**, the lenition to /w/ coming about as a result of the move from the strong position following the direct object—the typical position in Chadic for noun indirect objects—to a weak position immediately after the verb. The scenario would have been something like this: **an rarràbà gōřò gà mutànē** > *****an rarràbā gà mutànē gōřò** > **an rarràbā wà mutànē gōřò** 'They distributed kolanuts to the people.' The expression of a nominal dative object by a **gà** plus noun phrase to the right of the d.o. is still grammatical. Examples from older sources suggest that it was even more prevalent at an earlier date. In Westermann (1911), for example, which in other respects looks like normal modern Hausa (phonologically of the Katsina variety), the IOM before nouns is always **gà** (never **wà**) whereas the

276

pre-pronoun form is **ma**. If the d.o. is expressed, then it follows the pronoun i.o. but precedes the noun i.o. Examples (with original transcription): **ya nuna mini iyakan gōnansa** 'He showed me the boundary of his farm'; **ya kao kurɗi ga bature** 'He brought money to the European.'

[ii] The **mà** variant has two possible sources. (a) It may be derived historically from **wà** (which itself goes back to *gà), the change from **wà** to **mà** being due to analogic pressure from the indirect object pronoun forms, all of which contain the marker **ma-** (e.g., **masà** 'to him', etc.). (The suggestion by Eulenberg (1974) that the direction of change was **mà** > **wà**, representing a process of lenition, is without foundation.) (b) Alternatively, **mà**, like the pronominal forms, might go back directly to a possessive marker *ma that originally had two tonal variants, H before pronouns and L before nouns (see Newman 1982). Given this second analysis, the phonological similarity between **wà** and **mà** is accidental because there would be no historical relation between the two forms. My inclination is to favor alternative (b), but the matter is far from settled.

Unlike true prepositions, **wà** can be stranded without a following object, e.g.,

gà yârân dà mukà kōyà wà	Here are the children whom we taught.
wànē nè zā kà nūnā̀ wà hồtôn?	Whom are you going to show the picture to?

An innovation characteristic of some Kano speakers is the lengthening of **wà** to **wā̀** when it is stranded, e.g.,

shī nè mùtumìn dà na gayā̀ <u>wā̀</u>	He is the man I told it to.
= **shī nè mùtumìn dà na gayā̀ <u>wā̀</u>**	
wā̀ ka jī <u>wā̀</u> cīwò?	Whom did you injure? = **wā̀ ka jī <u>wā̀</u> cīwò?**
cf. **yā jī <u>wà</u> yārò cīwò**	He injured the boy. (lit. he.comp feel to boy injury)

°AN: A possible explanation would be that the dangling **wà** cliticizes to the verb, which then takes a long final vowel as is typical of the A-form of most transitive verbs (i.e., the form used when no object is expressed), i.e., **gayà wà → gayà-wā̀**. Note, interestingly, that the resulting "word" **gayà-wā̀**, which ends in L-L tone and a long final vowel, does not raise to L-H as one would have expected if LTR (the rule of low-tone raising) were still an active synchronic rule (see §34:3.2).

Even though the nonpronominal IOM in Standard Hausa is normally **wà**, in a few fixed verbal collocations, it takes the form **mà**, e.g.,

cim mà	achieve, overtake
e.g., **yā cim mà būrìnsà**	He achieved his desires.
im mà	control, overcome
e.g., **dà ƙyař na im mà dōkìnā**	It was with difficulty that I controlled my horse.
tāsam mà	attack, set for, approach
e.g., **mun tāsam mà ƙasā̀ř nan**	We headed toward that country.

1.2. Dialectal forms

The IOM displays considerable dialectal variation.

(a) In addition to **mà** (= SH **wà**), some WH dialects also have a long vowel falling-tone form **mâ** or **wâ**. (These forms optionally simplify to L-tone **mā̀** or **wā̀**, respectively, when preceded by a verb with final H tone, see §71:6.2.2). If the indirect object is not expressed, i.e., if the IOM is stranded, then this long-vowel form is required. Examples (where the choice of an IOM with initial /w/ or /m/ is as recorded in my notes):

Bintà cē ya gayầ mâ	It was Binta he told (it) to.
yāròn dà ka aikō mâ / mầ	the boy whom you sent (it) to

If the indirect object is expressed, the long-vowel form appears to be allowed only when preceded by a verb ending in an L tone or when there is no verb, i.e., when the pro-verb **yi** 'do' has been deleted, e.g.,

yā nēmầ mâ Bukàr̃ aikĩ	He sought work for Bukar. = **yā nēmầ mà Bukàr̃ aikĩ**
yā mâ / wâ Mūsā kyàutā	He did a good deed for Musa (or gave Musa a present).
= yā yī wà Mūsā kyàutā	

If the verb ends in an H tone, the use of the long vowel form is either rejected outright or considered clumsy and not preferred, e.g.,

tā kāwō mà sarkĩ zōbè	She brought the emir a ring. *not* ****tā kāwō mâ sarkĩ zōbè**
yā sōkam mà Sāni àkuyầ	He stabbed Sani's goat. (lit he.comp stab to Sani goat)
not **yā sōkam mâ Sāni àkuyầ	

(b) In Sokoto, the normal non-pre-pronoun IOM is **mà** with a short vowel and L tone. If, however, the pro-verb **yi** is dropped then one has to use **wâ** (which lowers to **wầ** when preceded by a high tone), e.g.,

mun / munkà yi mà Abdù aikĩ	We (comp/pret) did the work for Abdu.
(⇒) mun wầ Abdù aikĩ / munkà wâ Abdù aikĩ	
sun / sunkà yi mà mak̃wàbcīnā ɓàr̃nā	They did damage to my neighbor.
(⇒) sun wầ mak̃wàbcīnā ɓàr̃nā / sunkà wâ mak̃wàbcīnā ɓàr̃nā	

°AN/◊HN: Although I spoke above of **yi** 'deletion', this falling tone variant is perhaps better described in terms of a fusion of **yi + wà** → **wâ**, in which the segmentals are reduced and altered, but the underlying H-L tone sequence and the two moras are preserved. If one thinks of **yi** historically as a palatalized manifestation of ***wi**, then the derivation ***wi + wà** → **wâ** is even more straightforward and parallels the fusion that occurs with the verb **ɓā** 'give' (see below).

(c) In the dialect area of Katsina and Maradi, a common form used if the i.o. is not overtly expressed is **mà wā** (incorrectly transcribed **mà wà** by Abraham (1962)). Examples:

gà yârân dà mukè kōyầ mà wā	Here are the children that we are teaching.
ita bầ yārinyàr̃ dà na gayầ mà wā ba cè	She is not the girl I told (it) to.
dà wầ dà wầ ka r̃ubūtō mà wā?	Who (pl.) (lit and who and who) did you write to?
nī ka r̃ubūtō mà wā nè?	Is it me you wrote to?

°AN: Although we cannot be certain, **mà wā** most likely represents a redundant use of two IOMs in succession, i.e., **mà + wâ**, with an idiosyncratic tone adjustment. I see nothing to support the proposal by Abdoulaye (1991) that **mà wā** consists of the IOM **mà** plus the verbal noun suffix ˋ-wā.

1.3. The verb 'give'

The irregular verb **ɓā** 'give' requires a thematic recipient. This verb and the marker **wà** normally fuse into a single word **ɓâ** with falling tone (i.e., **ɓā + wà** → **ɓâ**). By contrast, when the object of **ɓā** is a pronoun, it appears as a d.o. (with a weak object pronoun) rather than as an i.o., e.g.,

kù bâ tsōhuwā lềmō!	(You pl.) give the old woman a soft drink!
cf. kù bā tà lềmō!	Give her a soft drink!
bài bâ àbòkansà kōmē ba	He didn't give his friends anything.
cf. bài bā sù kōmē ba	He didn't give them anything.
nī nề zā à bâ lambầ	I am the one they are going to give the medal to.

The **bâ** form with falling tone exists alongside a number of alternative variants. The first two are common in SH, the latter two less so: **bai wà, bā wà, bâ wà, bâi**, e.g.,

kù bâ = bai wà = bā wà = bâ wà = bâi tsōhuwā lềmō! (You pl.) give the old woman a soft drink!

2. FORM: PERSONAL PRONOUN INDIRECT OBJECTS

So-called indirect object pronouns consist of an IOM with the base form **ma-** plus a bound L-tone pronoun, e.g.,

1s	minì / mîn (= [mn̂]) / manì		1p	manà / \<mamù> / \<mumù> / \<munà>
2m	makà / mā / \<mâ>		2p	mukù / makù
2f	mikì / makì			
3m	masà / mishì /mâs / mâř / \<mai>		3p	musù / masù
3f	matà			

The first form in each row, with the /a/ of **ma-** undergoing anticipatory assimilation to the following vowel, is the everyday SH norm. The other variants, however, are all quite common, apart from the dialectal forms indicated in angle brackets (< >). Note that the vowel deletion in the first person singular takes place only after the vowel assimilation has affected the initial vowel. Examples:

sun sayō manà wàndō	They bought trousers for us.
zân kai masà littāfìn	I will take the book to him.
nā řubùtā mā wàsīkầ	I wrote you a letter.
bài kōyầ mîn ba	He didn't teach me.
'yan Amìřkà sun yi musù lềřen-àsīřī	The Americans spied on them.

◊HN: Apart from the i.o., the first person plural pronoun has the shape **mu(n)**, with variable tone. The allomorph /**na**/ in the i.o. paradigm is matched by a first person plural pronoun with the shape /**nV**/ in Angas, a related West Chadic language, but found in the possessive paradigm. It is this comparison that strongly suggests the historical derivation of the Hausa i.o. pronouns from erstwhile possessives (see Newman 1982).

ΔDN: [i] The WH form **mai** 'to him', where the /i/ comes from the /y/ of the 3m pronoun **ya**, has H tone rather than falling tone as one might expect. The 2m form **mâ** optionally (but usually) changes to **mà** when preceded by a verb with final H tone in accordance with a general WH tone absorption rule, e.g., **tā sayō mà kīfì?** 'Did she buy you fish?'

[ii] In the Guddiri dialect, the vowel (but not the H tone!) of the i.o. marker **má-** is dropped. The /m/ assimilates to the position of the following abutting consonant and the tone is preserved as a floating H tone (or H tone on the nasal consonant). One thus ends up with the following forms, which cliticize to the preceding verb: **´nnì, ´nkà, ´nkì, ´nsà, ´ntà, ´mmù, ´nkù, ´nsù**, for example, **yā kařàntansù** 'He read (it) to them.' If the verb ends in an L tone, the attachment of the suffix with the floating H produces a surface form that has a rising tone (!)—something totally atypical of Hausa, because, as a rule, rising tones automatically simplify to level H or L tones depending on the

tonal context. This rising tone results from the low tone on the long final vowel of the verb being followed by a high-tone syllabic nasal, e.g., **sún gáyằńsà** [gáyằnsà] 'They told it to him.' (Information on Guddiri indirect objects was obtained during a brief working session with Dauda Bagari, to whom I express my thanks. A fuller study is needed to verify and expand on the facts just presented.)

The category "indirect object pronoun" is restricted to the bound personal pronoun forms given in the paradigm above. If the i.o. is any other type of pronominal element, the **wà** marker is required, e.g., **yā gōgằ wà [wannàn] mâi** 'He rubbed oil on this one', **tā ƙauràcē wà [kōwā]** 'She avoids everyone', cf. **tā ƙauràcē masà** 'She avoids him.'

3. CLOSE BONDING OF VERB AND IOM

An IOM cannot be separated from the preceding verb by movement from its basic location, i.e., unlike a prepositional phrase, an entire i.o. phrase cannot be fronted under conditions of focus or relativization. Rather, any displacement affects only the indirect object noun, the bare marker **wà** or **ma-** plus a resumptive pronoun being left in situ, e.g.,

Daudà nē mukà yabằ wà = **Daudà nē mukà yabằ masà**   It was Dauda we praised.
not ****wà Daudà mukà yabằ**
nī (nè) takàn ƙauràcē wà   It's me she avoids. *not* ****minì takàn ƙauràcē**
wằnē nè zā sù shaidằ wà?   Whom will they inform? *not* ****wà wằnē nè zā sù shaidằ?**
yārinyằ waddà ya gayằ wà = **yārinyằ waddà ya gayằ matà**   a girl whom he told it to
not ****yārinyằ wà waddà ya gayằ**   a girl to whom he told it

The bonding between a verb and a following IOM is very tight. Not only can the IOM not be separated from the verb by movement, but it normally resists all insertions, including that of syntactically fairly free elements such as modal particles. The bonding is not absolute, however, Whereas native speakers tend to reject the insertion of disyllabic modal particles, some individuals do allow insertion of the light-syllable particle **fa** 'well, indeed' and, less readily, the monosyllabic heavy-syllable particles. Examples (with the modal particle underlined):

nā gayằ fa makà	I indeed told you.
yā yi fa wà Audù aikì	He did indeed do the work for Audu.
mun gōdè fa wà Allàh	We indeed thank God.
kà zubař fa minì dà mâi!	Do pour out the oil for me!
sun sayař fa wà Mūsā dōkì	They indeed sold the horse to Musa.
tā kāwō kò musù àbinci	She moreover brought them food.
nā gayằ kàm wà Hàbībù	I told (to) Habibu.
Bintà ya nūnằ fa wà hòtō	It was Binta he showed the picture to.
but not ****Bintà ya nūnằ fa wà**	It was Binta he showed (it) to.

°AN: [i] Because **fa** is phonologically so light—it consists of a single CV syllable with a short vowel—it causes the least disruption in the linguistic flow, which would explain why this modal particle is the one that is accepted most readily between a verb and the i.o.
[ii] Various scholars have suggested that **wà** is underlyingly a bound inflectional suffix. (Proponents of this view are notoriously silent about the status of pronominal i.o.'s with **ma-**.) As explained fully in Newman (1991b), there are many problems with this analysis, the most obvious of which is the fact that the supposed clitic **wà** can appear alone without a verb stem host as a result

of the deletion of **yi** 'to do', e.g., **yanà yi wà bàbansà màganà** (⇒) **yanà wà bàbansà màganà** 'He is talking to his father.' Rather than treat **wà** and **ma-** as verb suffixes, I would suggest that it is preferable to assume that indirect object phrases (with **wà** + NP or **ma**-pn) underlyingly constitute free formatives (comparable to, but not identical to, prepositions), i.e., one has structures like **yā gayà** [**wà yàrò**]ᵢ.ₒ. 'He told the boy' and **yā gayà** [**masà**]ᵢ.ₒ. 'He told him', *not* ****yā gayàwà** [**yàrò**] nor ****yā gayàma** [**sà**]. If the marker **wà**—but *not* **ma-**, which invariably attaches to the following pronoun—finds itself adjacent to the verb after all movement rules, the addition of resumptive pronouns, and the insertion of modal particles have taken place, then it will *phonologically* cliticize, i.e., **yā gayà wà yàrò** → /**yā gayà-wà yàrò**/. Note that this phonological attachment of **wà** is a late rule and thus cannot be cited as evidence to bolster the mistaken claim that its fundamental morphosyntactic status is that of an affix.

4. THE STRICT VERB REQUIREMENT

Only verbs can appear before an i.o. This includes verbs in tensed clauses as well as finite verbs in infinitive phrases. Verbal nouns, on the other hand, cannot be followed by an i.o. This is disallowed even in syntactic environments where a VN would normally be required in a verbal slot, e.g.,

tanà tsēfè (vb) **wà ƙawartà gāshì**	She is combing out the hair for her friend.
cf. **tanà tsīfàr̃** (VN) **gāshì**	She is combing out the hair.
(*not* ****tanà tsīfàr̃** (VN) **wà ƙawartà gāshì**)	
kà dingà kirā (vb) **minì shī!**	Keep on calling him for me!
cf. **kà dingà kirànsà!** (VN)	Keep on calling him!
an hanà mu hūɗà (vb) **masà gwāzā**	One prevented us from banking up the cocoyams for him.
cf. **an hanà mu hùɗar̃** (VN) **gwāzā**	We were prevented from banking up the cocoyams.
munà yi (vb) **wà mālàm aikì**	We are working for the teacher.
(*not* ****munà yî** (VN) **wà mālàm aikì**)	
cf. **aikì mukè yî** (VN)	It's work we're doing.

4.1. **yi** *deletion*

An exception to the rule that an i.o. must follow a verb results from deletion of the pro-verb **yi** 'do'. In the continuous TAMs, where **yi** is regularly deleted, the i.o. commonly ends up on the surface immediately following the PAC, e.g.,

munà yi masà aikì (⇒) **munà masà aikì**	We are working for him.
cf. **munà yîn aikì** (⇒) **munà aikì**	We are working.
bā sà yi mukù gaskiyā (⇒) **bā sà mukù gaskiyā**	
They are not being honest with you (pl.).	
gà yārinyàr̃ dà kè yi manà wāƙà (⇒) **gà yārinyàr̃ dà kè manà wāƙà**	
Here is the girl who sings for us.	

In noncontinuous TAMs, deletion of **yi** is normally not possible, i.e., **mun yi màganà** 'We talked' (lit. we did talk) cannot be altered into ****mun màganà**. The deletion *is* possible, however, if there is an i.o. present. Examples:

mukàn yi masà aikì (⇒) **mukàn masà aikì**	We work for him. (habitual)
sun yi wà maƙwàbcīnā ɓar̃nā (⇒) **sun wà maƙwàbcīnā ɓar̃nā**	
They did damage to my neighbor. (completive)	

5. PRE-I.O. VERB FORMS (THE D-FORM)

As described in the chapter on grades (chap. **74**), verbs have four possible forms depending on the syntactic context: A with no following object; B with a personal pronoun d.o; C with any other d.o., and D with an immediately following i.o. With one or two exceptions, to be discussed, the D-form is always the same whether the i.o. is a noun or a personal pronoun.

5.1. The D-form: Most verbs
Verbs belonging to grades 1, 4, 5, 5d, 6, and the ā-final gr0 verbs have pre-i.o. D-forms that are identical to the A-forms, e.g.,

tā <u>dafà</u> masà àbinci	She cooked him food. (v1), cf. **mè ta <u>dafà</u>?** What did she cook?
kà <u>rufè</u> manà ƙōfà!	Close the door for us! (v4), cf. **bài <u>rufè</u> ba** He didn't close (it).
kà <u>gayar</u> minì dà shī!	Greet him for me! (v5) (A-form = **gayar**)
mun <u>zubdà</u> mukù shàrā	We threw out the trash for you. (v5d) (A-form = **zubdà**)
zâi <u>kāwō</u> mikì bàrgō	He will bring you (f.) a blanket. (v6) (A-form = **kāwō**)
nā <u>shā</u> musù kâi	I pestered them. (lit. I drank to.them head) (v0) (A-form = **shā**)
yā <u>biyā</u> minì bāshìnā	He paid my debt for me. (v0) (A-form = **biyā**)

5.2. The D-form: Grade 0 **Ci** verbs
Grade 0 verbs with final /-i/ differ from other verbs in having a D-form that is not always identical to the A-form. This class is also unusual in treating individual verbs differently and in exhibiting dialectal and idiolectal variation. One common system is for the pro-verb **yi** 'do' to keep its short vowel in the D-form, but for the verbs **bi** 'follow', **ci** 'eat', and **ji** 'feel', which have a short vowel in the A-form, to have a long vowel in the D-form.

yā yi masà aikì	He worked for him. (lit. did for.him work)
yā yi wà mālàm aikì	He worked for the teacher.
tā jī matà cīwò	She injured her. (lit. she.comp feel to.her injury)
tā jī wà Lādì cīwò	She injured Ladi.
yanà bī minì sōjà	He is following the soldier for me.
kadà kà cī wà àmīnìnkà mutuncì!	Don't humiliate your best friend!

(lit. don't you eat to friend.of.you manhood) = the following preferred sentence without an i.o.:
kadà kà ci mutuncìn àmīnìnkà! (lit. don't you eat manhood.of friend.of.you)

> ΔDN: Some Hausa speakers have regularized the system and now use a long vowel in the D-form for all **Ci** verbs including **yi**, e.g., **yā yī masà aikì** 'He worked for him.' Some speakers (e.g., in the Maradi area) do have **yi** with a short vowel but only before a pronoun, e.g., **yā yī wà Mūsā kyàutā** 'He did a good deed for Musa' vs. **yā yi mishì kyàutā** 'He did him a good deed.' Some speakers (dialect uncertain) have a long vowel with all the **Ci** verbs with the exception of the verb **ci** when it occurs before a noun i.o., e.g., **yā ci mà mùtumìn mutuncì** 'He humiliated the man' (lit. he.comp eat to man.the manhood).

The Ci verb **ƙi** 'hate, refuse' switches to the gr4 form **ƙiyè** before an i.o., e.g., **yâu kàsuwā tā ƙiyè minì** 'Today the market is not looking good' (lit. today market 3f.comp refuse to.me).

5.3. Clipped forms
A few verbs have idiosyncratic clipped forms that are used as an alternative to the normal grade form in

specific environments, e.g., **nā sai àbinci = nā sàyi àbinci** 'I bought food.' This short form has the shape CVC or CVV (where the VV is a diphthong derived from CV plus a glide). A common use of the clipped form—and for some verbs, the only use—is as a pre-dative D-form, e.g.,

nā ɗař masà shèkàrū (= **nā ɗarà shi shèkàrū** with a d.o. rather than an i.o.)	
	I am slightly older than him. (< **ɗarà** v1 exceed slightly)
kù ɗau wà lēbùřà kāyân!	Lift the load for the laborer! (< **ɗaukà** v2 lift)
Tankò yā fař matà dà faɗà	Tanko ranted at her. (< **fāɗà** v1 fall on)
(lit. Tanko he.comp fell on.her with fighting)	
yā sai wà Mūsā hùlā	He bought a cap for Musa. (< **sàyā** v2 buy)
nâ sam masà lèmō	I'll give him a small amount of cola. (< **sāmù** v2 get)
sàu minì àkuyàtā!	Let go of my goat! (< **sàkā** v2 release)

5.4. The pre-dative suffix (pds)

Verbs belonging to grades 2, 3, and 7 (as well as certain dialectal forms) do not have a D-form as such. When used with an i.o., they either switch to another grade containing a derivational extension (see below §6) or else they add the pre-dative suffix $-aC)^H$ (= pds), the choice depending on the intended meaning. The final consonant of the pds generally appears as /-**m**/ before the IOM **ma-** (with H or L tone) and -**ř** before **wà**, e.g.,

sun girbam manà dāwà	They reaped the guinea-corn for us.
cf. **sun gìrbi dāwà**	They reaped the corn. (v2)
sun girbař wà manòmī dāwà	They reaped the guinea-corn for the farmer.
wà ya sōkam makà řàƙumī?	Who slaughtered your camel?
(lit. who he.pret stab+pds to.you camel) (< **sòkā** v2 stab)	
kunà nēmař wà yārònā aikì?	Are you seeking work for my boy? (< **nèmā** v2 seek)
kà fitam minì gidā!	Get out of my house! (< **fìta** v3 go out)
zākì yā zābuřař wà dìlā	The lion sprang up at the jackal. (< **zàbuřà** v3 jump up)
yā aukam masà	It happened to him (< **àuku** v7 happen)
yaɓ ɓassam min tuhwà [dv]	He lost my clothes. (lit. he lost from.me clothes)
cf. **yaɓ ɓassà tuhwàn Àbdū** [dv]	He lost Abdu's clothes.
(Ader dialect variant corresponding to SH gr.5)	

◊HN/°AN: Pilszczikowa (1969) and Parsons (1971/72) identified the pre-i.o. verb form containing the pds with the gr5 "causative" (i.e. efferential), an analysis still adhered to by many scholars, e.g. Frajzyngier (1985). As indicated in Newman (1977b, 1983), with fuller discussion by Jaggar and Munkaila (1995), phonological, morphological, dialectal, semantic, and comparative evidence all indicate that the identification of the pds and the efferential suffix is incorrect. Unlike the gr5 -**ař**, which we know derives historically from *-**as**, we have no solid indication of what was the original final consonant of the -**aC** ending used as the pds; but there is nothing to suggest that it was /s/. In Newman (1977b), I proposed that the original form of the pds was *-**an**, based on similar-looking benefactive extensions found elsewhere in West Chadic. Jaggar and Munkaila propose that the surface /-ř/) represents /t/, being a pleonastic use of the 3f object pronoun. Neither of these proposals is convincing. In short, we can be pretty sure what the pre-dative -**aC** suffix is *not*, namely, it is not the gr5 extension; but we still have no clear evidence indicating what it historically derives from.

◊HN/ΔDN: There is good evidence that gr2 verbs formerly had a D-form ending in -**i(i)**, i.e. a form identical to the C-form (the underlying lexical form of the verb) with perhaps a long rather than a short vowel. This is in fact attested in early grammars, for example (tone and vowel length unmarked): **ya fadi ma bature** 'He said to the white man' Migeod (1914: 47); **ya seyi ma wannan zobe** 'He bought for this one a ring', **ya seyi mata munduwa** 'He bought for her a bracelet' (Taylor 1923: 59). This D-form (with regular A-form tone but with a long final -ī) is amply documented in Pilszczikowa (1969: 20-22, and elsewhere). Here are some examples (tone and vowel length are hers): **yā màrī masà yārò** 'He slapped his son' (lit he.comp slap to.him boy), **yā sàrī min itàcē** 'He cut off my tree' (lit. he.comp cut off to.me tree). The provenance of the examples, however, is puzzling. They are not normal Kano forms nor are they normal in Sokoto or in Niger (where they were said to have been found). Swets (1989), who did a careful study of the dialect of Dogondoutchi, the home of one of Pilszczikowa's assistants, found people who would reluctantly accept such forms (with a long final -ī) but concluded that they were not natural parts of the grammar of that dialect. Munkaila (1990) accepts such forms more readily, but he is from Potiskum, a town to the east that is outside the limits of true Hausaland. The most reasonable interpretation of the evidence, then, is that Hausa *used* to allow gr2 verbs to operate a D-form, but that synchronically this has been lost in most dialects, apart from a few archaic retentions. Instead, gr2 verbs now adhere to a widespread Chadic pattern in requiring some derivational extension on pre-i.o. verbs. In Hausa, this verbal extension can be the pds, the applicative (now = gr1), the totality/separative/deprivative (= gr4), or the ventive (gr6), the choice depending primarily on the meaning intended and on dialectal preferences.

6. GRADE SHIFT

One strategy employed, especially by gr2 and gr3 verbs, is to switch grades before an i.o., that is, a verb that normally operates some grade, e.g., **mutù** gr3b 'die', appears before an i.o. in another grade, e.g., **macè** gr4. Sometimes this grade shift is obligatory, in other cases it is optional. Examples:

rānā tā fàɗè masù à dājì (v4)   The sun set while they were still in the bush.
(lit. sun it fell.malefactive gr4 to.them at woods) < **fāɗì** v3b fall
ƙwan fìtilà yā macè manà (v4)   The light bulb died on us. < **mutù** v3b die
àbîn yā zamō (= zamè) masà alàƙaƙài (v6 = v4)   It has become a thorn in his flesh.
< **zama** v* become (= **àbîn yā zamam masà alàƙaƙài** (v* with pds)
sun ƙauràcē minì (v4)   They avoided me. (lit. migrated from.me) < **ƙaura** v3a migrate
zā sù faɗà masà làbārì (v1)   They will tell him the news. < **fàɗà** v2 tell
nā zāɓà makà dōkì (v1) = **nā zāɓam makà dōkì** (v2+pds)   I chose a horse for you.
cf. **nā zāɓè makà dōkì** (v4)   I chose the horse that you wanted to choose.
mù nēmà masà aikì kō? (v1) = **mù nēmam masà aikì kō?** (v2+pds)
    Should we look for work for him?

In some instances, the grade shift before the i.o. has no direct semantic consequences. In many instances, however, sentences differ in meaning depending on whether there has been a grade shift or whether the verb appears with the pds. (Note: There is speaker variation in the interpretation of the following sentence pairs, but on the whole these can be taken as representative of the meaning differences.) Examples:

1.a. **nā ambàtā wà Bàlā màganàr** (v1)   I mentioned the matter to Bala.
1.b. **nā ambatar wà Bàlā màganàr** (v2+pds)   I mentioned the matter for Bala.
2.a. **nā arà masà gàrmā** (v1)   I lent him a plough.
2.b. **nā aram masà gàrmā** (v2+pds)   I borrowed a plough for him.
3.a. **tā haifà mîn 'yā'yā bìyar** (v1)   She bore five children for me.
3.b. **tā haifam minì 'yā'yā bìyar** (v2+pds)   She bore my five children for me.

4.a. **nā sōkà masà wuƙā** (v1)
(lit. I stabbed to.him the knife)

I stabbed him with the knife.

4.b. **nā sōkam masà dōkì** (v2+pds)

I stabbed his horse.

5.a. **zā mù yarjè mukù kù shìga gidanmù** (v4)

We will allow you to enter our house.

5.b. **zā mù yardam mukù** (v2+pds)

We will trust you.

7. INTRANSITIVE VERBS

Intransitive verbs by definition do not have direct objects. As has been shown in various examples, they may, however, take indirect objects, with the range of formatives and meanings found with transitive verbs, e.g.,

yā tsērè musù	He escaped from them. (v4), cf. **yā tsīra** He escaped. (v3a)
yā shigam minì gidā	He entered my house. (v3+pds) (lit. he.comp enter to me the house)
yā kōmà wà aikìnsà	He returned to his work.
gàrī yā wāyè manà à Kanò	The day dawned on us in Kano.
nā tūbam musù	I sought their pardon. (v3a+pds) (lit. I repented to.them)
kadà kà kwântā wà mùtûm!	Don't prostrate yourself before a human being!

durƙùsā wà wàdā bà gajìyâwā ba cè
    Kneeling down before a dwarf is not falling short. (i.e., one does what one has to do)
sukà ɓullō wà gàrîn ta fuskà biyu, gabàs dà yâmma
    They appeared in the town from two directions, east and west.

8. WORD ORDER

The basic word order in sentences with i.o.'s is V + i.o. + (d.o.), i.e., verb followed immediately by the indirect object followed by the direct object (if present). This word order is the same whether the i.o. is a noun or a pronoun, e.g.,

Mūsā yā kāwō [wà tsōhuwā]$_{i.o.}$ **ruwā**	Musa brought the old woman water.
Mūsā yā kāwō [matà]$_{i.o.}$ **ruwā**	Musa brought her water.
kadà kà gayà [wà ƙanènkà]$_{i.o.}$**!**	Don't tell your younger brother!
kù gayar [minì]$_{i.o.}$ **dà shī!**	Greet him for me!

ΔDN: In the Bauchi dialect, spoken in the far southeastern extent of the Hausa-speaking area, noun indirect objects (marked by **wà** or **mà**) occur *after* the d.o. (Gital 1987), e.g., **Zainàb tā kai àbinci wà/mà Mūsā** 'Zainab took food to Musa'; **Bàlā yā aikà wàsīƙà wà/mà Lādì** 'Bala sent a letter to Ladi'; **Gàmbo yā yi tsīwà wà/mà sarkī** 'Gambo was rude to the emir.' (Pronoun indirect objects occur immediately after the verb and before the direct object as in all other dialects.) This word order is undoubtedly an innovation due to interference from Chadic languages in the region, where noun i.o. phrases typically occur after the d.o. (see Newman 1982). It is very unlikely that this represents a retention of an old Chadic word-order pattern.

With grade 5 verbs, thematic direct objects are normally expressed as oblique object phrases with **dà**, e.g., **yā tsayar dà mōtà** 'He stopped the car.' Pronoun indirect objects occur immediately after the verb and before the **dà** phrase, e.g.,

yā tsayar [manà]$_{i.o.}$ **dà mōtà**	He stopped the car for us.

sunằ zubař [matà]_{i.o.} dà mâi   They are pouring out the oil for her (or spilling her oil).

When occurring with nonpronominal i.o.'s, gr5 verbs use four different structures. These are illustrated by the following sentences, all of which mean 'He stopped the car for the teacher.'

1. **yā tsayař wà dà mālàm mōtằ**   2. **yā tsayař wà dà mālàm dà mōtằ**
3. **yā tsayař wà mālàm mōtằ**   4. **yā tsayař wà mālàm dà mōta̍**

In the first structure, the indirect object marker **wà** and the particle **dà** are "stacked" one after the other, followed by their respective objects. In SH, this is the preferred option. In the second structure, one gets **wà** and **dà** stacked after the verb followed by an oblique **dà** phrase after the i.o. noun. In the third option, **dà** is deleted, resulting in a structure that parallels normal transitive V + i.o. + d.o. sentences. Finally, the fourth structure exactly parallels the pronoun i.o. construction, i.e., one gets V + i.o. + the **dà** + NP phrase. Surprisingly, in SH this "straightforward" structure is the least preferred option. (These four alternatives are further exemplified in the section on grades (see §74:9.3.1).)

9. MEANING AND USE

Indirect objects in Hausa express a wide range of meanings, which in English are often marked by the use of different prepositions. The exact semantic interpretation in Hausa depends on the verb grade, the nature of the individual verb, and the general context, e.g.,

sun nēmam masà aikî̀   They sought work for him. (benefactive / for)
zâi sayō mîn yādì̀   He's going to buy me some cloth. (benefactive / for)
yakàn arà wà yârā kèkè   He lends the kids bicycles. (dative (recipient) / to)
sun ƙwācè manà kāyā   They stole the goods from us. (malefactive (deprivative) / from)
tā sōmè minì   She fainted on me. (malefactive / on)
an shiřɓùnā masà mâi   They applied/rubbed oil on him. (affected / on)
nā sōkà matà māshì̀   I stabbed a spear into her. (affected / into)
sun yi musù dàriyā   They laughed at them. (goal / at)

The i.o. commonly serves to express a possessive, especially, but not exclusively, when the verb contains the pds, e.g.,

yā bugam minì ɗā   He beat my son. (lit. he.comp beat.pds to.me son)
kadà kà shigam matà ɗākì̀!   Don't barge into her room! (lit. don't you enter.pds to.her room)
yā māƙālē masà à màƙōgwàrō   It stuck in his throat. (lit. it.comp stuck.gr4 to.him in throat)
wằ ya sācè minì zōɓè?   Who stole my ring? (lit. who 3m.pret stole.gr4 from.me ring)

With a particular lexical class of verbs, termed dative verbs, the thematic object that semantically corresponds to and translates best as an English direct object is expressed syntactically by an indirect object. Examples:

nā amìncē mukù   I trust you.
sōjà sun bijìrē masà   The soldiers betrayed him.
sun ƙauràcē wà jūnā   They avoided each other.
Allàh yà tsīnè wà ɓàràyī!   God damn the thieves!
sunằ ƙuntàtā minì   They are harassing me.

tā sā6à wà mijìntà   She disobeyed her husband.
mālàm yā tsāwàtā wà àlmàjìr̃ai   The teacher scolded the pupils.
wannàn gwamnatìn tanà gallàzā wà mutầnē   This government is persecuting people.
yanà bâutā wà r̃asar̃sà tsàkānī dà Allàh   He serves his country well.

Very common in Hausa are sentences consisting of the pro-verb **yi** 'do' plus an i.o. (which represents the semantic object) plus a dynamic noun (which represents the action as such). Examples:

zân yi musù màganà   I'll talk to them. (lit. fut.I do to.them conversation)
sōjà yā yi wà mâtâr̃ fyàɗē   The soldier raped the woman.
(lit. soldier he.comp do to woman rape)
don Allàh kà yi minì tàimakō!   Please help me! (lit. for God you.sub do to.me aid)

The pattern verb + i.o. + dynamic noun, where the action in question is indicated by the direct object noun and not the verb, also applies to verbs indicating 'do a lot of sth' or 'do sth profusely', e.g.,

an gallà masà mār̃ì   They slapped him hard. (**mār̃ì** slap(ping))
zā mù shirgà wà yār̃ò dūkà   We are going to beat the boy severely. (**dūkà** a beating)
yā shirgà minì r̃aryā   He told me a whopping lie. (**r̃aryā** lie, lying)

With idiomatic phrasal verbs, the i.o. again serves as the semantic object, e.g.,

yā cī minì àmānà   He betrayed me. (**ci…àmānà** lit. eat…trust)
yā dakà manà tsāwā   He scolded us. (**dakà…tsāwā** lit. pound…thunder)
dōlè mù wāyar̃ wà dà talakāwā kâi   We must enlighten the masses.
(**wāyar̃…dà kâi** lit. lighten…head)

With gr1 applicative verbs, the semantic goal (or recipient) appears as a syntactic i.o. and the semantic instrument, which elsewhere might be expressed by a prepositional phrase, appears syntactically as the d.o., e.g.,

an sōkà (v1) masà wur̃ā   One stabbed a knife in him. (lit. …stab to.him knife)
= an sòkē (v2) shì dà wur̃ā (lit. …stab him with knife)
yā gōgà (v1) wà mōtà mâi   He rubbed oil on the car. (lit. …rub to car oil)
= yā gōgè (v4) mōtà dà mâi (lit. …rub car with oil)
nā tsōkànā (v1) masà tsinkē à ido   I poked him in the eye with a sliver.
(lit. …poke to him sliver at eye)
an ɗāɗàr̃ā (v1) wà sānìyā wutā   The cow has been branded. (lit. …brand to cow fire)
an lullù6à matà mayāfī   They covered her with a shawl. (lit. …cover to her shawl)
(cf. tā lùllu6à (v3) dà mayāfī   She covered herself (intransitive) with a shawl.)

[References: Munkaila (1990); Newman (1982)]

40. Infinitives and Gerundives

1. INFINITIVE PHRASES

THE term *infinitive* is used to refer to a nonfinite verb phrase containing a finite verb stem. The structure of an infinitive phrase (IP) is [V OBJ]$_N$ (e.g., **sōyà kīfī** 'to fry fish'), where V is a finite verb stem and OBJ is a direct and/or indirect object. In a sentence like **yā fārà gyārà mōtà** 'He began to repair the car', [[gyārà]$_V$ [mōtà]$_N$]$_N$, which follows the aspectual verb **fārà** 'begin', is an infinitive phrase. This sentence can be contrasted with a tensed sentence like **yā [gyārà]$_V$ [mōtà]$_N$** 'He repaired the car', in which the finite verb phrase is preceded by the third person masculine completive PAC. Note that as far as the surface makeup is concerned, IPs and normal VPs are identical—as is also true of infinitives without 'to' in English; *syntactically*, however, they have to be distinguished.

A sentence with an infinitive can also be contrasted with a semantically similar sentence with a verbal noun, e.g., **yā fārà [[kòyon]$_{VN}$ [Hausa]$_N$]$_N$** 'He began learning Hausa', where the aspectual verb **fārà** is followed by a nonfinite verbal noun phrase.

Because the verb in an infinitive phrase (unlike the verbal noun) is a finite verb form, it behaves just like a tensed finite verb in a normal verbal context. That is, it exhibits regular vowel length alternations depending on the nature of the following object (final vowel long before pronoun objects, short (for certain verb grades) before non-pronoun objects); it is followed immediately by a direct object (noun or pronoun) without use of a genitive linker; and it can be followed by an indirect object (which verbal nouns cannot), e.g.,

yā fārà gyārà mōtà	He began to repair the car. (IP with C-form of verb)
cf. yā gyārà mōtà	He repaired the car. (C-form of verb)
cf. yā fārà gyāran mōtà	He began repairing the car. (VN with linker -**n**)
yā fārà gyārà ta	He began to repair it. (IP with B-form of verb)
cf. yā gyārà ta	He repaired it. (B-form of verb)
yā fārà gyārà manà mōtà	He began to repair the car for us. (IP with D-form of verb)
cf. yā gyārà manà mōtà	He repaired the car for us. (D-form of verb)
not **yā fārà gyārā manà mōtà	He began repairing the car for us. (**VN before i.o.)

Semantically, IPs include constructions that in English would be expressed by gerunds or present participles as well as by infinitives. Many of these in fact have semantically equivalent gerundive/verbal noun structures. Notwithstanding the closeness in their semantics, infinitive phrases and verbal noun phrases are syntactically very different.

From an *external* point of view, infinitive phrases constitute NPs; thus they are able to occupy most syntactic roles that can be filled by normal NPs, like subject, direct object, complement, etc. Examples:

[kāmà ɓàrāwòn] yanà dà wùyā	To catch the thief is difficult. [IP]
cf. wà ya kāmà ɓàrāwòn?	Who caught the thief? [finite verb]
cf. munà sô mù kāmà ɓàrāwòn	We want to catch the thief.
(lit. we.cont want we.sub catch thief.the)	[finite verb in subjunctive]
bà tà iyà [gayà manà] ba	She wasn't able to tell us. [IP]
cf. bà tà gayà manà ba	She didn't tell us. [finite verb]
yā sàyi àlƙalàmī don [ɽubùtà wàsīƙà]	He bought a pen in order to write a letter. [IP]
cf. yā ɽubùtà wàsīƙà	He wrote a letter. [finite verb]

[zubaɽ dà ruwā à kân hanyà] yanà dà ban haushī
  Pouring water on the road is annoying. [IP]

sun fārà [būɗè ƙōfà] bà tàre dà izìnī ba
  They began to open the door without permission. [IP]

[wāyaɽ musù dà kâi] gwamnatì takè sô tà yi
  It's enlightening them the government wants to do. [IP]

inà tàimakon bàbānā wajen [wankè mōtà]
  I am helping my father in connection with washing the car. [IP]

lìttàttàfai màsu [gundumaɽ dà mutànē]
  books that bore people (lit. books having bore people) [IP]

cf. lìttàttàfai màsu kyâu   good books (lit. books having goodness)

°AN: The standard, almost universally accepted, view is that Hausa does not have an infinitive. (The statement by Tuller (1986: 174) that "there are no infinitives in Hausa, as we have already had occasion to mention" represents the received viewpoint about Hausa.) It is not clear how this idea became so established, but it is incorrect. The analysis leads, for example, to the totally untenable position that a normal verb like **dafà** 'cook' in a sentence like **tā iyà dafà àbinci** 'She is able to cook food' is a verbal noun, even though it has no nominal features and behaves in all respects just like a verb. By contrast, **dàfuwā** in the sentence **tanà tàimakon innàɽtà wajen dàfuwaɽ àbinci** 'She is helping her mother with cooking the food' is a verbal noun and thus requires a genitive linker before its object. The analysis adopted by Tuller and others also requires, for example, that the verb **gayà** 'tell' in **yā ƙi gayà musù làbāɽī** 'He refused to tell them the news' be interpreted as a verbal noun even though indirect objects are never preceded by verbal nouns. The phrases **dafà àbinci** and **gayà musù** are indeed nonfinite *phrases*, but the verb itself is not a verbal noun. Rather, it is a "bare infinitive," comparable to bare infinitives without 'to' in English, e.g., 'What she likes to do is cook food'; 'He had better tell them' (see Quirk et al. 1985).

Like other NPs, infinitive phrases can be focused or topicalized, e.g.,

[ɓōyè kāyan màsàɽūfì]IP sukà yi   It was hoarding basic foodstuffs that they did.
[shāfà hōdà]IP nē takè yî   It was putting on powder that she was doing.
[rufè tāgà]IP, bâ shakkà yanà dà kyâu   As for closing the window, no doubt it's good.
[ɓōyè kāyan màsàɽūfì]IP kàm, gwamnatì zā tà hanà shi
  As for hoarding staple foods, the government is going to stop it.
[sakà yārònkà à makaɽantā]IP dai, àbù nē dà ya wàjabà
  As for enrolling your boy in school, it is something that is obligatory.

Unlike simple NPs, infinitive phrases do not permit premodification. They can, however, be followed by a relative clause modifier, e.g., [[sāmař dà wutař làntařkì]]ₚ dà gwamnatì ta yi] yā yi àmfànī

    Providing (lit. provide) electricity that the government did was helpful.

[[mayař musù dà mařtànîn]]ₚ dà ka yi] nè ya bā sù haushī

    It was your retaliation on them that made them angry.

    (lit. [[return to.them retaliation] that you did])

sun yi zàngà-zangà sabòdà [[sōkè zàɓên]]ₚ dà akà yi]

    They had a demonstration because the elections were cancelled.

    (lit. [[cancel election] that one did])

1.1. Object requirement for infinitives

Infinitives occur only in phrases with an expressed object, either direct or indirect, i.e., in the infinitive structure [V OBJ]ₙ the OBJ *must* be present. If the OBJ is not overtly expressed, because it was either deleted or fronted, the N feature on the phrase attaches to the finite verb, thereby altering it into a corresponding weak verbal noun (formed with the suffix ⸌wā). This can be shown schematically as follows: [V OBJ]ₙ ⇒ [V Ø]ₙ ⇒ [V]ₙ. Examples:

yā iyà [[kařàntà]ᵥ littāfìn]ₙ	He is able to read the book. [IP]
cf. littāfìn dà ya iyà [kařàntâwā]ₙ	the book that he is able to read [VN]
yā hau katangā don [[jēfà]ᵥ duwàtsū]ₙ	He climbed on the fence to throw stones. [IP]
cf. yā hau katangā don [jēfàwā]ᵥₙ	He climbed on the fence to throw (them). [VN]
[[tsinkè]ᵥ igiyàř nân]ₙ bâ shi dà wùyā	Snapping this cord is not hard. [IP]
cf. igiyàř nân bâ ta dà wùyař [tsinkèwā]ₙ	This cord is not hard to snap. [VN]
tā hanà ni [[gayà]ᵥ musù]ₙ	She forbade me to tell (it) to them. [IP]
cf. tā hanà ni [gayàwā]ₙ	She forbade me to tell (it). [VN]

    °AN: Scholars have long been puzzled why it is that in nonfinite environments, verbs in certain grades sometimes appear with the VN suffix ⸌wā and sometimes without, e.g., sunà cikà tùlū 'They are filling a water pot', but mè sukè cikàwā? 'What are they filling?' The simple rule that alters infinitives into verbal nouns, i.e., [V Ø]ₙ ⇒ [V]ₙ, provides the solution. In an infinite phrase with an overt object, e.g., [cikà tùlū]ₙ, the syntactic noun feature governs the phrase as a whole, but it does not dominate the verb per se, which thus remains a verb. If there is no object, on the other hand, e.g., [[cikà]ᵥ Ø]ₙ ⇒ [cikà]ᵥₙ, one ends up with a verb that is immediately dominated by N, which is the structural definition of a verbal noun. The finite verb is thus obligatorily altered into a verbal noun by means of the suffix ⸌wā. Note that the ⸌wā suffix is added only to *verbs*. If the sentence already contains a verbal noun, then the absence of an object doesn't affect it and it still appears without ⸌wā. For example, sunà [[sàyen]ₙ tùlū]ₙ 'They are buying a water pot' (with the verbal noun sàyē plus the linker -n), cf. mè sukè [[sàyē]ₙ]ₙ 'What are they buying?'; yā dainà [[shân]ₙ giyà]ₙ 'He quit drinking beer' (with the verbal noun shâ plus the linker -n), cf. giyà ya dainà [[shâ]ₙ]ₙ 'It's beer he quit drinking' (*not* **giyà ya dainà shâwà).

Note that whereas infinitive phrases are masculine (see discussion of gender below), weak verbal nouns with ⸌wā are all feminine:

[[rufè]ᵥ tāgà]ₘ shīₘ nèₘ aikìnkà	Closing the window is your job. [IP]
cf. [rufèwā]f itaf cèf aikìnkà	Closing (it) is your job. [VN]
[[tsinkè]ᵥ igiyàř nân]ₘ bâ shi dà wùyā	Snapping this cord is not hard. [IP]
igiyàř nân bâ ta dà wùyař [tsinkèwā]f	This cord is not hard to snap. [VN]

Because infinitive phrases require objects, if follows that intransitive verbs in nonfinite constructions will necessarily appear as verbal nouns unless followed by an indirect object, e.g.,

kā iyà [dāwôwā]_{VN} dà yâmma?	Can you return in the evening? [VN]
not **kā iyà [dāwō]_V dà yâmma?	
yā hanà mu [zaunàwā]_{VN}	He prevented us from sitting down. [VN]
not **yā hanà mu [zaunà]_V	
cf. yā yi ƙòƙarin [[gujè]_V manà]_N	He made an effort to run from us. [IP]

1.2. The continuous TAMs

Syntactically the tense/aspect/mood categories (the TAMs) divide into two major classes with regard to the nature of the predicate. The "noncontinuous" TAMs, which include the completive, preterite, subjunctive, future, etc., occur with a finite VP, e.g., **sai tà dafà ruwā** 'She ought to boil water'. The other TAMs, namely, the continuous TAMs (general, relative, and negative), plus, in some WH dialects, the allative, are obligatorily followed by a nonfinite verb phrase. In some verb grades (like gr0 and gr2), this nonfinite VP must be a verbal noun (which necessarily takes a linker before objects). In other verb grades (like gr6), it is the infinitive phrase that constitutes the nonfinite VP. As indicated above, infinitive phrases require an overt object (direct or indirect), otherwise the underlying verb in a nonfinite environment is altered into a verbal noun. Examples:

tanà cîn àbinci	She is eating food. (VN)
cf. tā ci àbinci	She ate food. (completive with finite verb)
sunà sātàr̃ wākē	They steal beans. (VN)
cf. sunà sātō wākē	They steal and bring back beans. [IP]
cf. zā sù sàci wākē	They will steal beans. (future with finite verb)
bā nà r̃ubùtā masà	I am not writing (it) to him. [IP]
cf. bā nà r̃ubùtâwā	I am not writing (it). (VN because no object follows)
wà yakè kōyar̃ dà Lar̃abcī?	Who is teaching Arabic? [IP]
cf. shī nè yakè kōyâr̃wā	He is teaching (it). (VN because no object follows)
shī nè wândà kè kāwō ruwā	He is the one who brings water. [IP]
cf. shī nè wândà kè kāwôwā	He is the one who brings (it). (VN because no object follows)

2. GERUNDIVES

Gerundives (= present participials = "-ing" forms) are verbal nouns functioning as dynamic constituents in nonfinite environments. Unlike infinitives, a gerundive can stand on its own, i.e., it does not need an overt object (and in the case of weak verbal nouns may not be followed by an object). Examples:

zā sù sākè r̃ubùtū?	Will they be writing again? (lit. will they repeat writing) [VN]
ƙīràr̃ dà ya yi tā yi kyâu	The smithing that he did was good. [VN]
yā ƙi shāfàwā	He refused to wipe it. (lit. he.comp refuse wiping (it)) [VN]
mutànē sun cikà kàsuwā don <u>sàyē</u> dà <u>sayâr̃wā</u>	
	People filled the market for buying and selling. [VNs]
cf. mutànē sun cikà kàsuwā don [sayar̃ dà kāyansù]	
	People filled the market to sell their goods. [IP]

If the gerundive is used in a phrase with an object, it requires a linker (which agrees with the VN in gender), e.g.,

[shân tābằ] bâ shi dà kyâu	Smoking (lit. drinking tobacco) is bad. (with the VN **shâ**)
cf. kadà kà shā tābằ!	Don't smoke! (with the finite gr0 verb **shā**)
sun gamà [awòn hatsī]	They finished weighing the grain. (with the VN **awò**)
cf. sun aunà hatsī	They weighed the grain (with the finite gr1 verb **aunà**)
[gyāran mōtằ] zā sù yi	It's repairing the car they will do. (with the VN **gyārā**)
cf. gyārà mōtà zā sù yi	It's repairing the car they will do. (with the finite gr1 verb **gyārà**)
yā shìga don sātàr̃ zōbèn	He came in to steal (lit. for stealing) the ring. (with the VN **sātằ**)
cf. yā sàci zōbèn	He stole the ring. (with the finite gr2 verb **sàci**)

Because gerundives are verbal nouns, they may not be followed by an indirect object. (Indirect objects are only allowed after finite verb stems.) Thus one cannot, for example, say, ****sun gamà [awòn minì hatsī]** (nor [****…awò minì hatsī**]) 'They finished weighing the grain for me', with the verbal noun **awò**). Instead one has to use an infinitive phrase with a finite verb, e.g., **sun gamà aunà minì hatsī** 'They finished weighing the grain for me' (lit. they.comp finish weigh for.me grain).

3. GENDER

Infinitive phrases are masculine. (The gender can be seen in sentences in which the infinitive phrase functions as a subject or is focused or takes a resumptive pronoun, etc.) Examples:

[sayar̃ dà mōtàr̃]$_m$ [yā]$_m$ fi sātàr̃ kuɗī don à gyārà ta
    Selling (lit. sell) the car is better than stealing money to repair it.
[ƙauràcē manà]$_m$ [shī]$_m$ [nḕ]$_m$ àbîn dà sukà yi
    It is avoiding us that they did. (lit. migrate from.us it (3m) is thing that they did)
[ɓōyè kāyan màsàr̃ūf̃ī]$_m$ fa, gwamnatì zā tà hanà [shi]$_m$
    As for hoarding staple goods, the government is going to stop it.
[ƙḕrà mōtōcī]$_m$ [zâi]$_m$ ingàntà tattalin ar̃zìkī
    Manufacturing cars will help the economy.

By contrast, the gender situation with gerundives is more complex. If the gerundive verbal noun occurs without an object, it will manifest its intrinsic gender, e.g.,

[ɗinkì]$_m$ [yā]$_m$ fi sāƙà wùyā	Embroidering is more difficult that weaving.
[sātằ]$_f$ bâ [ta]$_f$ dà kyâu	Stealing is not good.
[zubâr̃wā]$_f$ [cḕ]$_f$ ya yi	It was pouring (it) away he did.

When the verbal noun is used in a phrase with an object, one finds some variation. If the head verbal noun is itself masculine, then the entire phrase will always be masculine.

[[r̃ùbùtun]$_m$ [wàsīƙằ]]$_m$ [yanà]$_m$ dà àmfằnī   Writing letters is useful.

If, on the other hand, the verbal noun is feminine, some speakers treat the phrase as feminine in keeping with the gender of the head word, whereas others treat the phrase as masculine so that it patterns with the masculine gender of infinitive phrases.

[[ƙīràr̃]$_f$ [mōtōcī]]$_f$ zā [tà]$_f$ ingàntà tattalin ar̃zìkī   Manufacturing cars will help the economy.
= [[ƙīràr̃]$_f$ [mōtōcī]]$_m$ [zâi]$_m$ ingàntà tattalin ar̃zìkī

41. Languages and Attributes

1. FORM

DERIVED nouns with the suffix -**ancī**)[H] indicate the language, style, behavior, or other attributes associated with a people or a place. What is apparently the same suffix is used also to indicate parts of cardinal directions. The suffix typically has the form -**ancī** with all H tone, e.g., **Bōlancī** 'Bole language', although with a few words -**cī** is added directly to the base-final consonant without the initial -**an**-, e.g., **Lāṟabcī** 'Arabic'.

> °AN: There is a similar-looking suffix of the form -(**VN**)**cī** with an H-L tone pattern that is used in forming abstract nouns, e.g., **zumù** 'close friend' / **zumuncī** 'friendship, solidarity' (see §1:2.1). Whether the language suffix and the abstract suffix are related, etymologically or synchronically, is an open question. For purposes of this grammar, I have opted in favor of treating them as independent formatives rather than as tonal variants of a single morpheme.

2. MEANING

The essential meaning of this derivation (apart from the cardinal directions described below) is "essential characteristics of some peoples or groups." For reasons of convention and exposition, it is convenient to separate out two partially overlapping submeanings, with the understanding that there is really no clear-cut distinction between the two categories. I will label these meanings as (1) languages and (2) attributes.

2.1. Languages
The "language" formation includes distinct languages as well as dialects and sociolects, e.g.,

Ādaṟancī	Ader dialect
Barbarcī	Kanuri language (cf. **bàbarbarè** a Kanuri psn)
Bausancī	Bauchi dialect
Bībīsancī	language and delivery style associated with BBC radio broadcasts in Hausa
Faṟansancī	French (< **Fàransà** France)
Fillancī	Fulani language (< **Fulànī** = **Filànī** Fulani people)
Filātancī	Fulani language (< **Filātànī** Fulani psn)
Gōbiṟancī	Gobir dialect (< **Gòbiṟ** an emirate)
Jāmusancī	German (< **Jāmùs** Germany)
Kanancī	Kano dialect
Lāṟabcī	Arabic (cf. **Bàlāṟabè** an Arab)
Tūṟancī	English (< **Tūṟai** Europe)
Yūnānancī	Greek (< **Yùnân** Greece)

°AN/ΔDN: In SH, the town and state name Bauchi is pronounced /**bauci**/. In the Bauchi area, on the other hand, it is generally pronounced /**baushi**/, from which the dialect name /**bausancī**/ is derived by depalatalization of the /**sh**/.

°HN/ΔDN: The terms **Tūřai** (place), **bàtūřè** (person), and **Tūřancī** (language) originally referred to non-Africans in general, at first to Arabs and later to Europeans. In Nigeria, **Tūřancī** has come to mean the English language. In Niger it means French.

Although the -**ancī** language suffix is quite productive, there are, nevertheless, many language names that do not use it. A few use the bare noun without a suffix whereas some Arabic loanwords occur with a frozen suffix that was borrowed along with the words. Examples:

Hausa	Hausa language (*not* ****hausancī**)
Ingìlīshì	English
bùřōkà	Pidgin English (< Eng. 'broken')
Àřàbiyyà	Arabic (language or culture)
gàřgàliyyà (= **gàlgàliyyà**)	colloquial Arabic

Other language names are indicated by means of a phrase of the form **harshèn** X 'language of X' or **harshèn mutànen** X 'language of the people of X', e.g.,

harshèn Gwāri	Gwari language (not **gwārancī** 'unintelligible speech')
harshèn Efìk	Efik language
harshèn Ibò	Igbo language
harshèn Tibi	Tiv language
harshèn mutànen Habashà	Amharic
harshèn mutànen Rûm	Latin
harshèn mutànen Sin	Chinese

2.2. Attributes

Derived words with -**ancī** indicating manner, style, characteristics, and attributes include the following:

bìřnancī	sophistication, being a city slicker (< **bìřnī** city)
dūniyancī	secular, nonreligious, worldly lifestyle (< **dūniyà** world)
fādancī	sycophancy, obsequiousness (< **fādà** palace)
fìř'aunancī	despotism, ruthless and cruel behavior (< **fìř'aunà** Pharaoh)
Filātancī	modesty, shyness [also Fulani language] (< **Filàtànī** Fulani psn)
gangancī	recklessness (< **gàngan** on purpose)
gwārancī	unintelligible speech (gibberish) (< **Gwāri** Gwari psn)
Kanancī	Kano style (of fashion, speech, etc.) [also Kano dialect] (< **Kanò** Kano)
ƙādiřancī	the tenets of the Qadiriyya (**ƙàdìřiyyà**) sect
ƙabīlancī	tribalism (< **ƙàbīlà** tribe)
mālamancī	language and/or mannerisms of traditional teachers (< **mālàmī** teacher)
marāyancī	the cocksureness of urban people (< **marāyā** urban area)
sāɓulancī	wearing trousers in a way exposing part of the buttocks (< **sāɓùlē** slip off)

In two examples, the derivative is built on a plural rather than a singular stem:

gidādancī	stupidity, naiveté, being a dimwit < **gìdàdàwā** homebodies

kaṙnukancī   quarrelsomeness, naughtiness < **kaṙnukằ** dogs

The following derivatives indicate a quantity rather than a characteristic quality:

ƙarancī   shortage (< **ƙàramī** small)
yawancī   majority, most (of) (< **yawằ** quantity, many, much)

2.3. *Adjectival directionals*

The words for the four cardinal directions, which are adverbial in nature, have adjectival derivatives with -a(n)cī)^{H}, e.g., **kudancī** 'southern' < **kudù** 'south'. This suffix is like the attributive suffix in that it ends in -cī and has an all H tone melody, but it differs in that the /n/ shows up only in one case. (It is thus not entirely clear whether these forms should be grouped here or not.) These directionals are normally used as prenominal adjectives, in which case they require a linker, but they can stand alone in citation form or in the case of ellipsis, e.g., **yammacī ya kōmằ** (< **yammacin Kanồ ya kōmằ**) 'It was the western part (of Kano) he returned to.' With the word **gabashī** (< **gabàs** 'east'), the suffix is reduced to the final vowel and the tone melody. Examples (complete):

arēwacī   northern (< **arèwa** northern), e.g., **arēwacin Rāshà** northern Russia
gabashī   eastern (< **gabàs** east), e.g., **gabashin Kanồ** eastern Kano
kudancī   southern (< **kudù** south), e.g., **kudancin Zāriyà** southern Zaria area
yammacī   western (< **yâmma** west), e.g., **yammacin Tūṙai** western Europe

The use of these adjectives can be contrasted with phrases of the form Noun L cardinal-direction, e.g., **kudancin Afìṙkà** 'southern Africa' vs. **Afìṙkà ta Kudù** 'South Africa' (lit. Africa of south).

42. Linguistic Play

THE term "linguistic play" is used as a cover term for manipulation of language for playful effect. There are two main categories: (1) play on words, and (2) language games.

1. PLAY ON WORDS

This process involves the juxtaposition of two phonologically similar words or phrases so as to create a humorous effect.

°AN: The account here is based entirely on unpublished work carried out at Indiana University by Mustapha Ahmad Isa.

In most cases, the real meaning of one word differs significantly from that of the other, but they are treated as oppositional. That is to say, one term, which constitutes the standard, and whose meaning portrays an element of genuineness, is contrasted with the other term, which is imbued with meanings that are either negative or have pejorative connotations. The play on words is thus expressed as an opposition between two items, one viewed as genuine and the other as bogus. For example, **makaṙantā** 'school', whose connotations are positive, is contrasted with **makaṙkatā** 'a place where one goes astray', a word with the same **ma-** prefix, the same **-ā** suffix and the same tone pattern, but which has negative connotations. Thus, if a very traditional person wanted to make an unfavorable comparison between **makaṙantaṙ àllō** 'Koranic school' and **makaṙantaṙ bōkò** 'modern Western school', he could say something like **wannàn bà makaṙantā ba cè, makaṙkatā cè** 'This is not a school but a deviant place (i.e., a place of going astray)'.

Sometimes the "genuine" word does not have a readily available, straightforward phonological counterpart. In these cases, people sometimes create phrases that semantically relate to the genuine word and also phonologically (and tonally) rhyme with it. Thus **injìniyà** 'engineer' is contrasted with **injìn-miyà**, lit. engine.of-soup, as a means of mocking an engineer. Another source for the pejorative term is a dialect variety of the standard term that is used by uneducated, (usually) rural Hausa speakers and that therefore is stigmatized. An example of this is **mātò**, a rustic pronunciation of **mōtà** 'car, vehicle'. Examples:

Standard		*Pejorative*	
makaṙantā	school	**makaṙkatā**	place where one goes astray
injìniyà	engineer	**injìn-miyà**	soup-making machine
daktà	doctor	**daftàn**	quack doctor
mōtà	car, automobile	**mātò**	an old (broken down) automobile
sakandìṙè	secondary school	**sàkàn-ni-ìn-dirè**	drop me
		(lit. let go of me so that I drop)	

hajì	hadj; **hajìyā** pilgrim (f.)	**hàjījiyà**	turning round and round to become dizzy, messing about

The typical sentence structure for expressing the opposition is X is a Y, not a Z; or X is not a Y, but rather a Z, where Y refers to the genuine and Z to the nongenuine item, e.g.,

mōtà nakè sô ìn sàyā, bà mātò ba	It is a (good) car that I want to buy, not a crummy one.
àbōkîn nākà daktà nē kō kùwa daftàn?	Is that friend of yours a (true) doctor or just a quack?
bà hajì ya jē ba, hàjījiyà ya jē	It is not the hadj that he did, just going and messing around.
bà hajìyā ba cè, hàjījiyà cē	She's not a real *hajiya*, just s.o. who went and messed around.

2. LANGUAGE GAMES

Hausa has a considerable number of language games. Like English pig Latin, with which they can be compared, they tend to be utilized for fun and amusement, primarily by young people.

°AN: This section is based on the thesis by Ousseina Alidou (1997), which provides a comparative description of language games in Hausa (northern and western dialects) and five other languages of Niger, namely Fulani, Gurmance, Kanuri, Tuareg, and Zarma-Songhai. In the examples, the two R's are not distinguished because the contrast does not exist in the dialects that were studied.)

The games can be grouped into three different categories depending on the basic principle of the formation.

2.1. Suffixation

The most common game pattern is to suffix a syllable (or polysyllabic sequence) after each CV (or each syllable) of the normal word except the last, e.g., **ràgō** 'ram' ⇒ **rabàgo** 'game form'. (Whether the "suffix" is added to a whole syllable or to a CV sequence varies from game to game. From the perspective of the resultant game form, the added element looks like an infix; however, since the affix is appended to the right of some specified constituent rather than being inserted within it, it is preferable to describe the process as suffixation.) In all suffixal games, the consonant of the suffix is fully specified whereas the vowel is a copy of the preceding vowel. Here are examples illustrating the straightforward -**bV** game:

	Normal word	*Game form*
house	**gidā**	**gibìda**
grain	**hatsī**	**habàtsi**
mat	**tàbarmā**	**tabàbabàrma**
Maimuna (name)	**Màimunà**	**Maibàimubùna**
oily	**maskī**	**mabàski**

In the -**bV** game, monosyllabic words are reduplicated to provide a nonfinal syllable to which the -**bV** can be attached, e.g.,

son	**ɗā** (⇒ //ɗāɗā//)	**ɗabàɗa**
life	**râi** (⇒ //rairai//)	**raibàirai**

°AN: In this game, diphthongs behave as complex vowels subject to copying. In some other games, they behave as sequences of a vowel plus a /y/ or /w/ coda.

This game is typical of Hausa affixation games in that vowel length and tone tend to be assigned by rule and thereby override underlying lexical specification. Thus, in the -**bV** game, (i) all monophthongal vowels become short, and (ii) an alternating H-L tone pattern (with H at the end) is imposed on the output game form, e.g., **hùlā** 'cap', with long-long and L-H ⇒ **hubùla** 'game form', with short-short-short and H-L-H.

Other suffixes that are used include (a) -**sV**, (b) -**grV** (with a normally unallowable consonant cluster!), (c) -**gVdV**, (d) **'VsrV**, and (e) **'VsVdV**. There are individual differences depending on whether the suffix is added to CV or to a syllable, whether final vowels are shortened, and in how tone is handled. The -**sV** game is unusual in allowing the suffix to be added to the final syllable of the word; but essentially, the overall principles of game formation are the same as with the -**bV** game. Examples:

	Normal word	*Game form*
(a) milk	**nōnò**	**nosònosò**
stick	**sàndā**	**sansàdasà**
calabash	**ƙwaryā**	**ƙwarsàyasà**
Bingel (name)	**bingèl**	**binsìgelsè**
(b) grain	**hatsī**	**hagràtsi**
word	**kalmà**	**kalgràma**
hand	**hannū**	**hangrànu**
camel	**ràƙumī**	**ragràƙugrùmi**
(c) bird	**tsuntsū**	**tsùgùdùntsū**
small hoe	**kalmè**	**kagadalmè**
whip	**būlālà**	**bùgùdùlagadalà**
bull	**sâ**	**sàgàdàsâ**
(d) house	**gidā**	**gi'isridā**
small bowl	**kaskō**	**ka'asraskō**
Huseina (name)	**Husènā**	**Hu'usrusè'èsrènā**
egg	**ƙwai**	**ƙwai'àsràiƙwai**
(e) prayer	**sallà**	**sa'asadallà**
blanket	**bàrgō**	**bà'àsàdàrgō**
kindness	**mutuncì**	**mu'usudutu'usuncì**
head	**kâi**	**kai'asadakài**

2.2. Prefixation

One game prefixes **da**- to each syllable of the regular word. The **da**- + the following syllable form an iambic foot with L-H tone. If the normal syllable to which **da**- is prefixed is light (i.e., contains a simple short vowel), then it undergoes lengthening. Examples:

	Normal word	*Game form*
grain	**hatsī**	**dàhādàtsī**
hand	**hannū**	**dàhandànū**
camel	**ràƙumī**	**dàrādàƙūdàmī**
egg	**ƙwai**	**dàƙwai**

2.3. Syllable permutation

One game (of which there are various subvariants) transposes syllables, e.g., **zaurè** 'entrance room' becomes **rēzàu**. What is striking about this game is that the original tone melody (in this case H-L) is preserved even though the segmental components of the syllable are switched. With disyllabic words, the application of the game is straightforward, i.e., $S_1 S_2 \Rightarrow S_2 S_1$. With trisyllabic words, the most common deformation is to move the initial syllable to final position, the next common alternative being to move the final syllable to initial position. With quadrisyllabic and longer words, the rules get more complicated and the options more varied. Examples:

	Normal word	*Game form*
(a) bowl	tāsà̰	sātà̰
hoe	kalmḛ̀	mēkàl
Sallau (name)	sàllau	làusal
(b) camel	rà̰ƙumī	ƙùmīrā
greeting	gaisuwā	suwāgai
shoes	tà̰kàlmī	kàlmĩtā
(c) help	tàimakō	kòtaimā
double-reed instrument	'àlgaità̰	tà̰'algài
(d) pupil, beggar	'àlmājìrī	jìrī'àlmā
workplace	ma'aikatā	tāma'aikā

[Reference: Alidou (1997)]

43. Linker

THE genitive linker, henceforth referred to simply as the linker (L), is one of the most widely used, most important grammatical markers in the language. It serves, for example, to connect an NP with a following NP or adverb in an X of Y construction, where X is the possessed and Y is the possessor, e.g., **gidā na Sulè** 'Sule's house' (lit. house of Sule); and it also serves to connect an adjective with a following NP, e.g., **sābon gidā** 'new house' (lit. new.of house). (For consistency, the linker will be glossed as 'of' regardless of its syntactic or semantic function.) Like the stabilizer (see chap. **66**) and the definite article (see chap. **20**), the linker reflects a widespread Afroasiatic **n / t / n** pattern in which the masculine singular and the plural go together as opposed to the feminine singular.

The linker has two main variants, a free particle **na(a) / ta(a)**, which has two grammatically conditioned allomorphs differing in vowel length, and a bound clitic **-n / -r̃** (which is written connected to its host).

1. FREE LINKER

1.1. Form
The free linker normally has the form **Ca**, with a short vowel. When prefixed to a personal pronoun, however, it appears as **Cā**, with a long vowel.

1.1.1. Free linker with short vowel
The basic freestanding linker has the shape **na / ta / na** (m./f./pl.) with a short vowel and H tone. The **ta** allomorph is used if the head NP that governs agreement is feminine singular; the **na** allomorph is used if the head NP is masculine singular or is plural. The governing NP is the X in the X L Y construction. The gender and number of the Y item to the right are irrelevant in determining the form of the linker, e.g.,

[bàkā]ₘ **na mahàr̃bī**	the hunter's bow
[kibiyà̃]f **ta mahàr̃bī**	the hunter's arrow

[bakunkunà̃]pl **na mahàr̃bī**	the hunter's bows
[kibiyōyī]pl **na mahàr̃bī**	the hunter's arrows

1.1.2. Prefixal linker with long vowel (independent possessive pronouns)
When the linker combines with a personal pronoun to produce a self-standing independent possessive, e.g., **nāmù** 'ours', **tākù** 'yours (pl.)', it has the shape **nā / tā / nā** (m./f./pl.) with a long vowel. The tone is high except in the case of the first person singular possessive, where it is low, i.e., **nàwa / tàwa** 'mine' (m. or pl. / f.). (see §**59**:1.1.5 for full paradigm).

°AN: Unlike the other pronouns, all of which have low tone, the first person singular pronoun **-wa** has inherent high tone. The normally high-tone prefixes **nā-** and **tā-** thereupon dissimilate and become low. Strictly speaking, it is inexact to speak of the linker that is attached to the following pronoun as being "free". I do so only to distinguish this allomorph of the linker from the one that occurs as a clitic attached to the preceding word.

As with the corresponding short-vowel linkers, **tā** is used if the referent is feminine singular; **nā** is used if the referent is masculine (sg.) or plural, e.g.,

fensìr̃in nàn nàwa nè	This pencil (m.) is mine.
tāsà tā fi tātà kyâu	His (ref. to some f. thing) is better than hers (ref. to some f. thing).
ìnā nākù sukè?	Where are yours (ref. to some pl. things)?

1.2. Use
1.2.1. Non-adjacent possessor
The free linker is required in possessive constructions whenever the possessor is separated from the noun possessed by some constituent such as an adjective, numeral, demonstrative, or even bound definite article, e.g.,

littāfì gùdā <u>nà</u>wa	one book of mine
gidan nàn <u>na</u> Mūsā	this house of Musa's
makar̃antâr̃ <u>tā</u>sù	the school of theirs
tantēbùr̃ ɗîn <u>ta</u> wannàn ɗan kwangilā	the large truck (in question) of this contractor
àl'àdū irìn <u>na</u> Hàusàwā	customs like those of the Hausa people
rìgā baƙā <u>ta</u> Lawàn	Lawan's black gown (lit. gown black of Lawan)

cf. **rìgar̃ Lawàn baƙā**, a semantically equivalent phrase with the bound clitic

1.2.2. Headless possessor
The free linker is required whenever the genitive phrase does not contain an overt host, e.g.,

zanèn Kànde dà <u>na</u> Hàdīzà	Kande's cloth and Hadiza's
làbàr̃un dâ dà <u>na</u> yànzu	tales of old and of the present
<u>ta</u> Mūsā tā lālàcē, <u>ta</u> Bellò fà?	Musa's has broken down, how about Bello's?

In the case of pronouns, the forms that occur without hosts are the independent possessives, e.g.,

gà dōkìnsà, ìnā <u>nākà</u>?	Here is his horse (m.), where is yours?
ta Daudà tā fi <u>tākù</u> kyâu	Dauda's (f. thing) is better than yours.
nā ajìyè <u>nāmù</u> cikin ɗākì	I put ours (m. or pl. thing(s)) away in the room.
wannàn <u>tāsà</u> cē	This is his (f. thing).

Possessives normally follow the head noun. With pronoun possessors, the independent possessive pronoun can stand in front of the (normally definite) noun in an appositional relationship. This structure serves to emphasize the possessor.

yā sācè <u>tàwa</u> mōtàr̃	He stole *my* car. (lit. he stole mine the car)
ìnā <u>nākà</u> kuɗîn? (= ìnā kuɗîn <u>nākà</u>?)	Where is *your* money?
cf. the neutral ìnā kuɗinkà?	Where is your money? (with the bound linker)
gà <u>nàwa</u> littāfìn gùdā	Here is *my* one book.

1.2.3. Ordinal numerals
The free linker is used in forming ordinal numerals, e.g.,

yār̃ò <u>na</u> ukù	the third boy

yārinyằ <u>ta</u> farkō	the first girl
<u>na</u> huɗu yā fi <u>na</u> biyu gudù	The fourth (man) can run faster than the second.

1.2.4. Alternative to the clitic

The nonpronominal free linker is used as an optional alternative to the bound linker in possessive and other N of N expressions. With simple possessives, one normally gets the bound form. Where the possessed noun is complex, e.g., a compound, or where the "of" relationship is not possessive in the narrow sense, the free form is more common. Examples:

dōkì na Daudằ = dōkìn Daudằ Dauda's horse; gidan-saurō na Mařyàm = gidan-sauron Mařyàm Maryam's mosquito net; hùkūmằ ta Bicì = hùkūmằř Bicì the governing authority of Bichi; wani àbù na mùgùntā = wani àbin mùgùntā an evil thing (lit. some thing of evil); zōbè na azùřfā = zōbèn azùřfā a silver ring

1.2.5. Loanwords

The free linker (with nouns) or the independent possessive pronouns may be used after loanwords (especially those that are not fully integrated). It is also normal with foreign words, as in the case of language mixing by bilinguals. Examples:

(a) lāsìn nāsà (= lāsìn ɗinsà = lāsìnsà) his license; cêk na bankì a bank check
(b) *vice-chancellor* nāmù our vice-chancellor; *Madonna* ta gàrinmù the Madonna of our town; wani *friend* nằwa (= ɗīnā) yā zō dàgà Landàn A friend of mine came from London.

2. BOUND LINKER WITH ZERO VOWEL

2.1. Allomorphs (-n / -ř)

When the linker attaches to the preceding word as an enclitic, it has the toneless forms -ř and -n, e.g., hùla-ř Gařbà 'Garba's cap'; mōtà-ř Bàlā 'Bala's car'; wàndo-n Yūsufù 'Yusufu's trousers', bīřò-n Sāni 'Sani's ballpoint pen'. (In orthography, the bound enclitic linker is written together with its head noun; the hyphen has been added here for descriptive clarity.) The -ř is (historically) a rhotacized syllable-final manifestation of the /t/ of the feminine linker t(a). The enclitic form can be used when followed either by NPs or adverbs or by pronouns, e.g., hùla-ř Gařbà 'Garba's cap', jirgi-n ƙasà 'train' (lit. ship-of on the ground), hùla-ř-sà 'his cap'.

The choice of -ř as opposed to -n has both grammatical and phonological conditioning. The -ř form is used only if the preceding word is feminine *and* ends in the vowel -a (whether long or short). Otherwise, -n is used. That is, -n is used with all masculine and plural words, regardless of the final vowel, and with all words ending in vowels other than -a, regardless of the gender and number, e.g.,

kibiyà-ř yārò	the boy's arrow (kibiyằ is f. and ends in -a)
màta-ř Bellò	Bello's wife (màtā is f. and ends in -a)
kwàmìtî-n ɗàlìbai	the students' committee (kwàmìtî is m.)
bàka-n gizò	rainbow (lit. bow-of Gizo (trickster)) (bàkā is m.)
watà-n Yūlì	month of July (watằ is m.)
takubbàn azùřfā	swords of silver (takubbằ is pl.)
gwamnatì-n Ingilà	the government of England (gwamnatì is f. but ends in /i/)
gwaggò-n-mù	our aunt (gwaggò is f. but ends in /o/)
màge-n-sà	his cat (màge is f. but ends in /e/)

°AN: Apart from tone, the rules describing the required allomorph of the bound enclitic linker also apply to the definite article, e.g., **hùlâr̃** 'the cap', **bàkân** 'the bow', **gwamnatìn** 'the government'.

By contrast, in the case of the free linker, the form is determined by gender/number only without regard to phonological shape, i.e., all feminine nouns take **ta** (whether they end in -a(a) or not) and all masculine and plural nouns take **na**, e.g.,

f: **gwamnatì** ta **Ingilà** the government of England; **gwaggòn nân tāmù** this aunt of ours; **màge ta biyu** the second cat

m/pl: **kwàmìtîn nân nāsù** this committee of theirs; **watà na ukù** the third month; **takubbà na azùr̃fā** swords of silver

The surface forms of the zero-vowel linkers are determined partially by the general phonological rules governing -n and -r̃ in coda position and partially by morpheme-specific rules. Thus -n automatically assimilates to the position of the following consonant, whether in the same word or across a word boundary, e.g., **dōkìn-kà** [dōkìŋkà] 'your horse', **dōkìn kanàr̃** [dōkìŋkanàr̃] 'the colonel's horse'. When followed by /m/, the assimilation produces a surface geminate, e.g., **gidan-mù** [gidammù] 'our house'. The -n also tends to assimilate completely to following liquids, depending on speech tempo, e.g., **kāwùn Lādì** [kāwùllādì] 'Ladi's uncle'.

Although syllable-final rolled /r̃/ sporadically assimilates fully to following coronal consonants (thereby producing surface geminates, e.g., **sayar̃-dà** = **sayad-dà** 'sell'), this change is far from being automatic. With the zero-vowel linker -r̃, on the other hand, assimilation to the following abutting consonant is very common, whether that consonant is a coronal or not, e.g., **madatsa-r̃-ruwā** → [madatsarruwā] 'dam' (lit. blocking place-of-water); **'ya-r̃-sà** (→) ['yassà] 'his daughter'; **rìga-r̃ Daudà** (→) [rìgaddaudà] 'Dauda's gown'; **ƙawa-r̃-tà** (→) [ƙawattà] 'her female friend'; **makar̃anta-r̃-mù** (→) [makar̃antammù] 'our school', **hùla-r̃-kà** (→) [hùlakkà] 'your cap'. Before the demonstratives **nân/nan** 'this/that near you', the assimilation is obligatory and in earlier orthographic practice was always written as such, i.e., //bishiyà-r̃ nân// → **bishiyàn nân** 'this tree', **tāgà-r̃ nan** → **tāgàn nan** 'that window'.

°AN: In the lexicalized demonstratives, **wannan** (tone variable) 'this one/that one (f.)', and **waccan** (tone variable) 'that one (f.)', the first member of the geminate pair represents the zero-vowel form of the feminine linker (cf. the corresponding masculine forms **wannan** and **wancan**). In these cases, it probably makes sense to bypass the -r̃ stage and derive the surface forms by direct assimilation of the original //t//, i.e., **wannan** < //wa-t-nan// (not ****war̃nan**), and **waccan** < //wa-t-can// (not ****war̃can**), contrast **bishiyà-c cân** = **bishiyà-r̃ cân** 'that tree', with the /r̃/ not undergoing gemination allowed.

ΔDN: In many WH dialects, the zero-vowel feminine linker *always* becomes a geminate with the following consonant, e.g., **hùlak-kà** 'your cap', not ****hùlar̃-kà**, **mōtà-m Mūsā** 'Musa's car', not ****mōtà-r̃ Mūsā**. In these dialects, one has to analyze the feminine linker as having become morphologized as -G (= geminate), i.e., the linker consists of a completely unspecified consonant that copies its features fully from the following consonant. In these dialects, there is no justification synchronically in postulating an underlying -t or -r̃ that is then subject to an automatic and exceptionless complete assimilation rule.

2.1.1. Gender conflict in the form of the linker with compounds

In compounds having the internal structure N + L + N, the internal linker naturally agrees with the gender of the word to its left (see §16:2.1), i.e., /-r̃/ for feminine words ending in -a, and /-n/ for masculine and plural referents and for all words not ending in -a, e.g., [gida-n]$_m$ **saurō** 'mosquito net' (lit. house-of mosquito); [ƙafà-r̃]f kàzā 'type of facial marks' (lit. foot-of chicken). Problems arise, however, when a linker is added to the end of a compound. If both the last word of the compound and the compound as a whole have the same gender, then the assignment is straightforward: the linker simply takes the required concordial form, e.g.,

[gida-n [saurō]m]m + L + NP ⇒ gida-n-sauro-n yāròn   the boy's mosquito net (with the linker -**n**)
[ƙafà-r̃ [kàzā]f]f + L + NP ⇒ ƙafàr̃-kàza-r̃ yāròn   the boy's facial marks (with the linker -r̃)

If, however, the gender of the final word and the gender and number of the compound as such do not match, one gets gender conflict. When this occurs, some speakers opt for local agreement of the linker with the final word, e.g., in [[dūtsè-n]m [gūgà-r̃]f]m Bàlā 'Bala's pressing iron' (lit. stone-of pressing-of Bala), the linker before **Bàlā** agrees with the feminine word **gūgà** rather than with the masculine compound **dūtsèn-gūgà**. (The gender of the compound can be seen when, for example, it functions as a subject controlling a weak subject pronoun, e.g., **dūtsèn-gūgàr̃ Bàlā** <u>yā</u> (not ****tā**) **làlàcē** 'Bala's iron (3m) quit working.') Other examples:

[[àbōki-n]m [gàba-r̃]f]m -sà   his enemy (lit. friend-of enmity-of-him)
[[aikì-n]m [gàyya-r̃]f]m ùnguwa-r̃-mù   the communal work of our neighborhood
(lit. work-of crowd-of neighborhood-of-us)
[[bàki-n]m [fàra-r̃]f]m kàkā-nā   my grandfather's turban
(lit. mouth-of grasshopper-of grandfather-of.me)
[[haɓà-r̃]f [kadà-n]m]f Lādì   Ladi's hat (that resembles a crocodile's mouth)
(lit. chin-of crocodile-of Ladi)

With other speakers, however, the form of the linker is determined by the gender of the compound as such, the result being that one commonly finds an -**n** linker attached on the surface to a compound-final feminine word, e.g.,

[[dūtsè-n]m [gūgà]f]m -n Bàlā   Bala's pressing iron
[[àbōki-n]m [gàba]f]m -n-sà   his enemy
[[aikì-n]m [gàyya]f]m -n ùnguwa-r̃-mù   the communal work of our neighborhood
[[bàki-n]m [fàra]f]m -n kàkā-nā   my grandfather's turban

With feminine compounds, the problem of adding an -r̃ to a final masculine noun seldom arises because -**n** is usually required on phonological grounds anyway, e.g., in the phrase [audùga-r̃-rīmi-n]f nàn 'this kapok', the linker has to be -**n** whether agreement is determined locally or not because **rīmī** ends in a vowel other than /a/. If the final word ends in -**a**, on the other hand, it is possible to get -r̃ attached to a masculine noun, although this is much less common than the use of -**n** attached to a feminine word, e.g.,

??[[haɓà-r̃]f [kadà]m]f -r̃ Lādì   Ladi's hat

The variation in the form of the linker resulting from gender conflict in compounds occurs only with the enclitic zero-vowel linkers -**n** / -r̃. If the **na** / **ta** free form is used, agreement is with the compound as a whole, the gender of the final word not normally having any influence on the choice of the linker, e.g.,

[dūtsè-n-gūgà]m na Bàlā   Bala's pressing iron
[àbōki-n-gàbā]m na dâ   former enemy (lit. enemy of formerly
[bàki-n-fàrā]m na biyu   second turban (i.e., turban of two)

[ɓaɓà-r̃-kadà]f ta Lādì   Ladi's hat

[audùga-r̃-rīmī]f ta zāmànī   modern kapok (i.e., kapok of modern times)

2.1.2. Enclitic short vowel linkers

There are two exceptions to the general rule that the enclitic bound linker has a zero vowel. First, the linker takes the short vowel-form (**ta** / **na**) when it occurs with the first person singular pronoun /**a**/ (which is unique among the pronouns in being vowel-initial), e.g.,

kibiyà̀-ta-a (= /**kibiyà̀tā**/)	my arrow (cf. **kibiyà̀-r̃-sù** their arrow)
hùlā-ta-a	my cap, cf. **hùla-r̃ yār̃ò** the boy's cap
bàkā-na-a	my bow, cf. **bàka-n-sà** his bow
mijì̀-na-a	my husband, cf. **mijì̀-n-tà** her husband
màgē-na-a	my cat, cf. **màge-n-sù** their cat (cf. **màge tà̀wa cè** The cat is mine.)
takubbà̀-na-a	my swords, cf. **takubbà̀-n-kù** your (pl.) swords
talàbijì̀n ɗī-na-a	my television, cf. **talàbijì̀n ɗi-n-kà** your television

°AN: I am convinced that the internal analysis presented here is the correct one, i.e., /**kibiyà̀tā**/, for example, has the structure **kibiyà̀-ta-a**, and /**mijì̀nā**/ has the structure **mijì̀-na-a**. Two other analyses are commonly found in the literature, the first not being as bad as the second. First, the linker is interpreted as /**t**/ or /**n**/ and the first person pronoun is represented with a long vowel /**ā**/, i.e., **kibiyà̀-t-ā** and **mijì̀-n-ā**. This analysis sets the first person apart as the only possessive pronoun with a long vowel and ignores the fact that in the independent pronouns, the first person /**wa**/ does have a short vowel, i.e., **tà̀-wa** / **nà̀-wa** 'mine' (f. / m. and pl.). Second—this is the old Abraham analysis (1959b: 20)—the linker is interpreted as /**ta**/ and /**na**/ and the pronoun is assumed to be Ø, i.e., understood/unexpressed. The main problem here, apart from the fact that the first person possessives normally have a long -**ā**, is that the linker is left stranded, which is totally inconsistent with the way it functions throughout the language.

ΔDN: [i] In SH, the short-vowel linker forms **na** / **ta** are essentially limited to the first person, where the pronoun consists solely of the vowel /**a**/. (All the other personal pronouns are CV.) In WH one also gets the **na** / **ta** forms in the third person masculine because this pronoun also consists of a single vocalic element /**i**/ (< *****y**), e.g., **dōkì̀-na-i** 'his horse'; **màtā-ta-i** 'his wife'.
[ii] In SH, the rules governing the choice of **ta** vs. **na** in the first person are the same as those applying to the choice of -**r̃** vs. -**n**, i.e., **ta** is used only with feminine nouns ending in -**a**, e.g., **sānìyā-tā** 'my cow', but **gwaggò̀-nā** 'my aunt', **màgē-nā** 'my cat'. Some WH speakers, on the other hand, optionally treat these first person forms (as well as the third person possessives -**nai** and -**tai**) like the free nonclitic linkers in that they allow **ta** with feminine nouns not ending in -**a**, e.g., **màgē-tā** 'my cat', (but **màge-n-kà** 'your cat'), **gwamnatì̀-tai** 'his government' (but **gwamnatì̀-nkù** 'your government'). Use of -**ta** is allowed also when the feminine noun is connected to the possessor by the particle **ki** (= SH **ɗi**), e.g., [Maradi] **kâr̃ kī-tā** 'my bus' (= [Skt] **bâs ɗī-tā**, cf. [SH] **bâs ɗī-nā**), but **kâr̃ ki-n-sù** 'their bus'; **làkkwâl kī-tai** 'his school', but **làkkwâl ki-n-tà** 'her school'.

Second, the short-vowel form -**ta**- is optionally used with **a**-final feminine nouns when followed by a third person singular pronoun, e.g.,

màtā-ta-sà = **màta-r̃-sà** his wife; **'yā-ta-sà** = **'ya-r̃-sà** his daughter; **k̃awā-ta-tà** = **k̃awa-r̃-tà** her friend

°AN: In standard orthography, such items as **màta-r̃-sà** 'his wife' are written as one word (**matarsa**) whereas the variant **màtā-ta-sà** is represented as two words (**mata tasa**). Analytically there is no difference: in both cases the linker and following pronoun are phonologically attached to the head noun.

This archaic usage is quite common with a few high-frequency nouns referring to closely related persons; otherwise the zero-vowel linker is preferred or required, e.g., **hùla-r̃-sà** 'his cap', not ****hùlā-ta-sà**. One normally cannot use the corresponding masculine linker -na- in place of the zero-vowel -n, i.e., **mijì-n-tà** 'her husband' would not be expressed as ****mijì-na-tà**. One does, however, run across examples of nonreduced -na- scattered here and there in written sources (literary license?), e.g., **àkū-na-sà** 'his parrot', cf. the more normal **àku-n-sà**.

2.1.3. Form of the noun to which the linker is attached

The enclitic bound linkers attach directly to vowel-final words. Changes in the vowel, e.g., vowel shortening, centralization of mid vowels, and diphthong simplification, follow automatically from the application of general phonological rules affecting vowels in closed syllables, e.g.,

rìgā + -r̃ → rìgar̃	gown of	dōkì + -n → dōkìn	horse of
màge + -n → màgen [màgyan]	cat of	zōmō + n → zōmon [zōmən]	hare of
mâi + -n → mân	oil of		

The vowel changes affecting underlying final /e(e)/ and /o(o)/ are not indicated in standard orthography, e.g., **magensa** 'his cat' (not ****magyansa**), whereas the diphthong reductions are indicated, e.g., **man shanu** 'butter' (lit. oil of cattle) (not ****main shanu**).

Whenever the syllable preceding the enclitic linker is open, as in the first person (or in the third person in some WH dialects), it always has a long vowel. If the final vowel of the head word is underlyingly short, it is lengthened, e.g.,

kàrē + -na + -a →	kàrēnā	my dog	hùlā + -ta + -a →	hùlātā	my gown
àku + -na + a →	àkūnā	my parrot	àyàbà + -ta- + -a →	àyàbàtā	my banana
gōr̃ò + -na + i →	gōr̃ònai	his kolanuts	hwādà + -ta + i →	hwādàtai	his palace

The vowel length rule also applies before the enclitic short-vowel linkers found in the third person feminine forms -tasà / -tatà 'his / her' and the less common masculine counterparts, e.g.,

màtā + -tasà → màtā-tasà his wife; **hausa + -tatà → hausā-tatà** her language / her Hausa; **à tsakà + -tasà → à tsakà-tasà** in its center (= **à tsakà-r̃sà**); **àku + -nasà → àkū-nasà** his parrot

Note that the lengthening applies only to the enclitic linker and not to the free form, e.g., **gwàdò** 'blanket', **gwàdònā** 'my blanket', but **gwàdò na Mūsā** 'Musa's blanket'.

°AN: Following Carnochan's (1951) discovery that words with a short final vowel lengthened in the first person, e.g., **cuku** 'cheese', but **cukū-nā** 'my cheese', it has generally been accepted that there was a special *morphological* rule limited to first person possessive pronouns. In a brief note, which has been overlooked by most Hausaists, Schuh (1977a: 74) proposed a better analysis. Without specifying the first person, one could postulate a general morphological rule requiring that final vowels before an enclitic linker be long/lengthened in all cases. If a zero-vowel form of the linker was used *and* it was followed by a consonant-initial pronoun, i.e., the -n or -r̃ occupied the coda position, the preceding vowel automatically shortened by the phonologically regular rule affecting vowels in closed syllables, e.g., **cuku + -L + -sà ⇒ *cukū-n-sà → /cukunsà /** 'his cheese'; **hausa + -L + -sà ⇒ *hausā-r̃-sà → hausar̃sà** 'his language'. In *phonological* environments where the long vowel can appear on the surface (such as in the first person), it does, e.g., **cuku** + **-L** + **-a** ⇒ **cukū-na-a** → /**cukūnā**/. The cases of lengthening described above in the third person follow naturally from this analysis, e.g., **hwādà** 'palace' + **-L** + **-i** ⇒ **hwādà̂-ta-i** → /**hwādàtai**/ 'his palace' (WH); **hausa** + **-L** + **-tà** ⇒ **hausā-ta-tà** → /**hausātatà**/ 'her language'.

2.1.4. Consonant-final words before the linker: Insertion of an epenthetic vowel

Some consonant-final words insert an epenthetic /i(i)/ before the linker, the surface length being determined as for lexical-final vowels. (Word-final coronals palatalize when /i(i)/ is inserted.) A couple of words insert /u(u)/ rather than /i(i)/. Words that do not add the vowel use a connector **ɗi** (described in the next section). The usual grammatical descriptions give the impression that use of the epenthetic vowel is standard with consonant-final words. In fact, it is uncommon, being restricted to the examples given below plus probably a few more words that have been overlooked. The inserted vowel is never used with monosyllabic words. Examples:

àlhàmîs	Thursday	**àlhàmīshì-n nan**	that Thursday (= **àlhàmîs ɗî-n nan**)
àlhànzîr̃	wart hog	**àlhànzir̃ì-n-sà**	his wart hog (= the preferred **àlhànzîr̃ ɗ'insà**)
gìlâs	glass	**gìlāshì-n mōtà̂**	the car glass (windshield)
ìbìlîs	Satan	**ìbìlīshì-n yār̃ò̂**	a devil of a boy
kànànzîr̃	kerosene	**kànànzir̃ì-nā**	my kerosene
lìmâm	imam	**lìmāmì-n kir̃istà**	bishop (Christian)
mùtûm	man	**mùtumì-n nân**	this man
ōfis	office	**ōfìshi-n-mù**	our office
r̃àsît (< //r̃àsîɗ//)	receipt	**r̃àsīɗì-n nan**	that receipt
samfùr̃	sample(s)	**samfùr̃i-n ɗan tir̃ēdà**	the trader's sample(s)
shàiɗ'ân	Satan, rogue	**shàiɗ'ānì-n nan**	that rogue
shēbùr̃	shovel	**shēbùr̃i-n lēbùr̃à**	the worker's shovel
takwàs	eight	**takwàshi-n-sù**	eight of them (= the preferred **takwàs ɗin-sù**)
tēbùr̃	table	**tēbùr̃ī-nā**	my table
tùmātìr̃	tomato	**tùmātìr̃i-n nàn**	these tomatoes
hàr̃âm	prohibition	**hàr̃āmù-n nan**	that prohibition
ƙāmùs	dictionary	**ƙāmūsù-n mālàm**	the teacher's dictionary (= **ƙāmùshi-n mālàm**)

If the base word ends in a falling tone, the HL spreads over the last two syllables. The length of the penultimate vowel, which is now open, remains short in a few cases, e.g., **mùtûm** / **mùtumì-n** 'man (of)'. However, it generally becomes long e.g., **gìlâs** /**gìlāshì-n** 'glass (of)'; **hàr̃âm** / **hàr̃āmù-n** 'prohibition (of)'. If the base word ends in low tone, the inserted vowel has high tone and the penultimate vowel is invariably short, e.g., **ōfis** / **ōfìshi-n** 'office (of)'. The word **ƙāmùs**, gen. **ƙāmūsùn** 'dictionary (of)' is tonally exceptional.

°AN: Although one can speak of the inserted vowel as an epenthetic element, it is preferable to analyze it as a "latent" vowel that underlyingly belongs to the lexical stem. This latent vowel is preserved when the zero-vowel linker (or definite article) is attached, otherwise it is optionally (and for some words, usually) dropped. Words such as **tēbùr̃** 'table' and **r̃àsît** 'receipt', which were described as C-final, would thus have the underlying lexical forms **tēbùr̃(ī)** and **r̃àsîɗ(ì)**, respectively. This analysis explains why such a small number of C-final words actually add a vowel in the genitive—namely, there is no such rule! Words that are truly C final (over 250 items) do not add /ī/; rather they employ the connector **ɗi**. The only words that add /ī/, i.e., appear to do so, are the dozen or so words that already have a lexical final vowel, albeit a latent one. Thus, a true consonant-final word like **màshîn** 'motorcycle' does not allow use of the presumed epenthetic

vowel, i.e., to express 'his 'motorcycle', one must say **màshîn ɗinsà** (or **màshîn nàsà**) not
**màshînìnsà. Note, moreover, that this latent vowel analysis allows us to account for the length
of the penultimate vowel when the syllable is opened. (In closed syllables all vowels are
necessarily short.) The contrast between **mùtûm** / **mùtumìn** 'man (of)', with a short vowel, and
gìlâs / **gìlāshìn** 'glass', with a long vowel, is due to the difference in vowel length in the presumed
lexical entries **mùtumì** vs. **gìlās(h)ì** and is not an artifact of the putative vowel-insertion rule.

The word **àbù** 'thing' has an irregular genitive form **àbi-n** (e.g., **àbi-nsà** 'his thing'. (There is also a
corresponding feminine form **àba-ř**, which is much less commonly used.) In the genitive, the consonant
final word **àshâř** 'obscene language; curse' either uses the connective **ɗi** (see below), e.g., **àshâř ɗin
nàn** 'this curse', or else switches to its equivalent feminine counterpart, e.g., **àshāřiyà-ř nân**. The word
màcè 'woman, wife', can take a linker, e.g., **màcèn Sulè** 'Sule's wife', but it is usually replaced in the
genitive by **mâtā**, e.g., **mâtař Sulè**.

> °AN: Some speakers totally reject phrases like **màcèn Sulè** 'Sule's wife', or, if they accept them,
> they view them as insulting and derogatory.
> ◊HN: Originally the only nominal form for 'woman/wife' was probably **mâtā**. The word **màcè** at
> that time would have been a derived adverbial-like form meaning 'female', cf. **'yā màcè** 'female
> child'. (The derivational process would have been something akin to the one found in the pair **bàkī**
> 'mouth' vs. **bakà** 'in the mouth', where one also finds shortening of both the final and the internal
> vowel.) Later the use of **màcè** would have spread into the nominal domain with the general meaning
> of 'woman'.

The word **rāna-ř** 'day of' is standardly clipped to **ran** (e.g., **ran kàsuwā** 'market day'). Other clipped
genitives are generally restricted to compounds, e.g.,

ban-ɗākì toilet < **bāya-n ɗākì** back-of room; **kan-sallà** gifts given at Sallah time < **kāya-n sallà**
goods-of holiday; **san-kurmì** the head of the prison < **sarki-n kurmì** chief-of wooded district;
gajen-hàkurī impatience < **gàjēre-n hàkurī** short-of patience

2.1.5. The connector ɗi-

Most consonant-final words do not attach the linker by means of a transitional vowel. Instead they
employ a connector **ɗi-** (= **ki-** in some northwestern Hausa dialects). The **-n** linker is always used (i.e.,
one gets **ɗin** (or **kin**)) regardless of the gender of the head word because the connectors end in a vowel
other than **-a**. C-final words that form the genitive with the inserted vowel (i.e., words with the latent
final vowel described above) may allow use of the connector as an alternative depending on dialectal and
idiolectal preference.

inifàm ɗin yârā children's uniforms; **têf ɗin Kànde** Kande's tape; **sandàl ɗin-sà** his sandals (=
sandàli-n-sà); **tsit ɗin-tà** her reticence; **bôm ɗin nàn** this bomb; *sweetheart* **ɗin-kà** your
sweetheart; **tantēbùř ɗin-sà** his semitrailer truck, cf. **tēbùři-n-sà** his table (preferred over ?**tēbùř
ɗin-sà**)

In open syllables, the vowel of **ɗī-** (or **kī-**) is always long (as is true of all vowels before the linker), i.e.,
bêl ɗī-nā 'my belt'. In closed syllables, one gets **ɗin** with a short vowel. This often reduces
phonetically to /ɗ/ followed by a syllabic nasal, i.e., /ɗn/. When **ɗi** occurs with the low-tone definite
article, one gets **ɗîn** (or **ɗn̂**) with a falling tone, e.g., **daimòn ɗîn** 'the diamond in question'.

> °AN: [i] Although I cite the connector as **ɗi-** with a short vowel, there is in fact no way to determine

the length of the underlying vowel. As indicated earlier, all vowels in open syllables followed by the linker are long, e.g., **dīnā**, cf. **àkūnā** 'my parrot' (< **àku**), and all vowels in a closed syllable are automatically short, e.g., **dinsà**, cf. **jàkinsà** 'his donkey' (< **jàkī**); so if one applies the rules properly, one always ends up with the right result whether one starts out with an underlying long vowel or an underlying short vowel.

[ii] My impression is that native Hausa speakers consider **din** to be an unanalyzable monomorphemic word, i.e., a variant form of the linker (or definite article) rather than as a bimorphemic word containing the -**n** linker. In standard orthography it is written as a single word **din**. For a detailed study of this connector, see Buba (1997b).

The connector **di** is also used (in some cases optionally, in others obligatorily) with certain vowel-final words like numerals, temporal adverbs, proper names, recent loanwords, compound nouns, and independent pronouns, e.g.,

biyu-n-mù = **biyu din-mù** two of us; **dùbba-n-sù** = **dùbbai din-sù** thousands of them; **yâu din nàn** this very day; **Bellò-n-tà** = **Bellò din-tà** her Bello; **Jànairu din-mù** our January; **fàsfô-n-sà** = **fàsfô din-sà** his passport; **furōfàgandà-r̃-sù** = **furōfàgandà din-sù** their propaganda; **kòmfyūtà-r̃ nân** = **kòmfyūtà din nàn** this computer; **'yan-sàri-kà-nōk̃è din-sù** their guerrillas (lit. sons.of-strike-you-withdraw); **fàdi-kà-mutù din-tà** her chinaware (lit. fall-you-die); **ita din nan** *she* (that psn we were referring to) (lit. she **di**.of that)

°AN: Normally the formation rules for the zero-vowel linkers -**n** / -**r̃** and the segmentally identical low tone definite articles ˋ**n** / ˋ**r̃** are the same. However, the use of **di** is much more prevalent with the latter than with the former and in fact can be used with almost any noun or NP. Thus **r̃àgō dî-n** (= **r̃àgô-n**) 'the ram in question' is possible whereas ****r̃àgō din-sà** is not an appropriate substitute for **r̃àgo-n-sà** 'his ram'.

2.1.6. Word-final /n/

With **n**-final loanwords, some speakers allow the final /**n**/ to serve doubly as the linker as well as the lexical final consonant. (Alternatively, one could say that **n**-final words allow a zero linker.) This is a new development; whether it will catch on is yet to be determined. Examples:

lāsìn nē It is a license.	**lāsì-n-sà** = **lāsìn din-sà** = **lāsìn nāsà**	his license
lilìmàn nē It is liniment.	**lilìmà-n-tà** = **lilìmàn din-tà** = **lilìmàn nātà**	her liniment
mishàn nē It is a mission.	**mishà-n-sù** = **mishàn din-sù**	their mission
mòngwamar̃àn cē It is a beret.	**mòngwamar̃à-n-sà** = **mòngwamar̃àn din-sà**	
= **mòngwamar̃àn tāsà** his beret		

°AN: In **mòngwamar̃à-n-sà** the interpretation of /**n**/ as a linker creates an anomaly because **mòngwamar̃àn**, a loanword derived from (Field Marshall) Montgomery, has feminine gender.

2.2. Use

The enclitic linker has a wide range of uses, comparable to, but probably even more extensive than, the uses of 'of' in English. Here are a number of its major functions.

2.2.1. Possessives

The linker is used to form possessives. (Noun possessors allow the free form as an alternative, subject to certain constraints.) There is no formal distinction between normal possession of things and inalienable possession having to do with kin terms or body parts, e.g., dōkì-n Daudā̀ (= dōkì̄ na Daudā̀)   Dauda'a horse;   mā̀ta-r̃ Sulè   Sule's wife;   dōgon hancì-n Bàtūr̃è the European's long nose;   'yā-ta-sà   his daughter;   gidā̀je-n-sù   their house;   gwamnatì-n-mù   our government;   fuskā̀-tā   my face;   gidan-sauro-n Mar̃yàm (= gidan-saurō na Mar̃yàm)   Maryam's mosquito net

2.2.2. Miscellaneous N of N

The linker serves to connect nouns in a range of N of N or N of Adverb constructions in which the genitive phrase modifies the head noun in some way, e.g.,

àmfā̀ni-n gōnā   agricultural products (lit. produce of farm);   d̃ākì-n hayà̄   apartment, rented room   (lit. room-of renting);   fīli-n wā̀sā   playground (lit. field-of play);   gida-n sìmintì̄   cement house (lit. house-of cement);   gōga-n d̃àzu   the hero of the moment;   hùkūmà̄-r̃ Bicì (= hùkūmā̀ ta Bicì)   the governing authority of Bichi;   lèmo-n tànjàr̃în   tangerine (lit. orange-of tangerine);   nauyi-n yâu-dà-kullum everyday responsibilities (lit. weight-of today-and-always);   ruwa-n zāfī   hot water (lit. water-of heat);   tāshà̄-r̃ jirgī   train station (lit. station-of vehicle);   wani àbi-n mùgùntā = wani àbù na mùgùntā   an evil thing (lit. some thing-of evil)

Semantically, the linker sometimes indicates 'for, toward, etc.' and sometimes 'from, against'; sometimes it indicates the goal or object, and sometimes the possessor, e.g.,

māgàni-n k̃arfī   medicine to give strength, cf. māgàni-n zàzzàɓī   medicine against fever
gida-n saurō   mosquito net (lit. house-from/against mosquitoes)
gudù-n gyāra-n dāgā   a strategic retreat (lit. running-from fixing-of battle)
gudù-n màsīfà̄   running from the tragedy
(also 'a hell of a lot of running', with màsīfà̄ functioning as a modifier of gudù̄)
làbā̀r̃ì-n-sà   story about him or his story (that he was telling)

2.2.3. Part of

The linker is used to indicate 'part of' relationships, e.g.,

hannu-n r̃ìgā   the sleeve of the gown;   bāya-n gàrī   the back of the town (or behind the town); ba-n-d̃ākì̄   toilet (< bāya-n d̃ākì̄   back of hut);   k̃afà̄-r̃ tēbùr̃   the leg of the table;   k̃ōli-n dūtsè the top of the mountain

2.2.4. Quantity of

The linker is used with numerals and other quantifiers to indicate 'X of them'. (The words dukkàni-n and d̃àukaci-n 'all of, the entirety of' invariably occur with the linker attached.) Examples:

biyu-n-kù   two of you;   takwàs d̃in-sù   eight of them;   d̃aya-r̃-mù   one (f.) of us ;   dùbban bāyī thousands of slaves;   dukkà̄-n-mù   all of us;   d̃àukaci-n d̃à̀lìbai   all of the students

2.2.5. Genitive prepositions

The use of the linker with body-part terms and some locative adverbs has become fixed in the formation of "genitive prepositions" (see §57:2), e.g.,

bāyan   behind, after, cf. bāyā̄ = bâi   back;   gàban   in front of, cf. gàbā̄   front, chest;   kân   on (top of), cf. kâi   head;   samàn   above, on top of, cf. samà̄   sky;   wurin (= gûn)   at, cf. wurī (= gû)   place

2.2.6. Diminutives, persons of

The use of the linker has become fixed and frozen in the diminutive and occupational/ethnonymic morphemes ɗan / 'yaɍ / 'yan (m./f./pl.), which are built on the words for son/daughter/children, namely, ɗā /'yā / ('yā)'yā, e.g.,

ɗan râgō   a small ram; 'yaɍ tunkìyā   a small lamb; 'yan tumākī   small lambs/sheep; ɗan ƙàramin zōmō   a wee small rabbit; 'yaɍ kàsuwā   a small market (or a market women) ɗan kàsuwā   a trader; 'yaɍ Kanò   a Kano woman; 'yan amshì   chorus/backup singers (< amshì 'answering'); 'yan kazagī   yes-men (lit. children of the small drum kazagī); 'yan Bosniyà   Bosnians

2.2.7. Compounds

The enclitic linker (but not the free form) serves to connect nouns in the very common N of N compounds (including those with ɗan / 'yaɍ / 'yan), e.g.,

tàwadà-ɍ-Allàh   birthmark, dark pigmentation on skin. (lit. ink-of-God) (not **tàwadà-ta-Allàh); kara-n-hancì   bridge of the nose (lit. cornstalk-of-nose); kwānò-n-sarkī   head-pan (lit. pan-of-chief); ƙuda-n-zumà   bee (lit. fly-of-honey); mâ-n-shānū   butter (lit. oil-of-cattle); rìga-ɍ-nōnò   brassiere (lit. gown-of-breast); ɗan-adàm   human being (lit. son.of-Adam); 'yaɍ-yâu   cake made of cassava flour (lit. daughter.of-today); 'yan-biyu   twins (lit. children.of-two)

2.2.8. Prenominal adjectives

The enclitic linker connects prenominal adjectives with a following noun. (By contrast, postnominal adjectives are juxtaposed to the noun without a linker.) Examples:

gàjēre-n yārò (not **gàjērē na yārò	short boy (= yārò gàjērē)
fara-ɍ mōtà	white car (= mōtà farā)
sàbàbbi-n gidàjē	new houses (= gidàjē sàbàbbī)

2.2.9. Object genitives

The enclitic linker connects a verbal noun with its thematic object. Because of the linker, one gets genitive pronouns rather than direct object pronouns. (Semantically one has what can be translated as a verb plus object; syntactically one has a genitive construction.) With third person pronouns attached to feminine VNs, it is possible to use the short-vowel enclitic linker -ta- instead of the zero-vowel -ɍ form. Examples:

tanà sàye-n nāmà	She is buying meat.
sun dainà shâ-n giyà	They quit drinking beer.
tanà ta zāgì-n-sà	She keeps on insulting him.
Bellò yanà kirà-nā (< //kirà-na-a//)	Bello is calling me. (cf. Bellò yā kirā nì Bello called me.)
munà kàrɓa-ɍ-tà (= munà kàrɓā-ta-tà)	We are receiving it.

The linker can also introduce semantic objects of nonverbal dynamic nouns, e.g.,

kadà kà ji tsòro-n dòdôn!	Don't be afraid of the goblin!
(lit. don't you feel fear.of goblin.the)	

2.2.10. Subject genitives

Because verbal nouns are nouns, it follows that an enclitic genitive linker phrase following a verbal noun can also be a semantic possessor or agent, e.g.,

har̃bì-n wàzīr̃ì yā bur̃gè ni	The vizier's shooting impressed me.
(cf. **har̃bì-n wàzīr̃ì àbin kunyà nē**	The shooting (assassination) of the vizier was shameful.
r̃ùbùtu-n-sà yā fi kyâu	His writing is best.

◊HN: The ambiguity found in 'his shooting' (i.e., he was shot) and 'his shooting' (i.e., he did shooting) is due to the fact that Hausa has lost the formal distinction between a short genitive (inalienable possession), which would have been used for thematic objects of verbal nouns, and a long genitive (alienable possession), which would have been used for semantic agents. This distinction is alive and well in related West Chadic languages like Kanakuru (Newman1974) and Miya (Schuh1989a).

[Reference: Parsons (1961)]

44. Loanwords

1. SOURCE OF LOANWORDS

THE Standard Hausa lexicon contains a large number of loanwords. Of these, something over a half come from English and just under a half come from Arabic. Loanwords from other languages probably make up no more than five percent of the identifiable loanwords.

°AN: The figures above refer to Hausa as spoken in Nigeria. The percentages represent the number of loanwords found in a list of some 8,800 words in a lexical database assembled for the grammar project.

1.1. English

The introduction of English loanwords began with the British takeover of northern Nigeria at the beginning of the twentieth century. By the time of Bargery's dictionary (1934), there was already a sizable number of fully integrated English loanwords. Since then, their number has increased at a rapid rate, such that the number of English loanwords (over 600) now exceeds that of Arabic loanwords. Almost all of the loanwords are nouns, mostly denoting material objects, governmental/military positions, items connected with Western education, calendar months, etc. Selected examples:

bankì bank; bīzà visa; danjà brakelight on car, danger; Dìsambà December; fàřfēsà = fùřòfēsà professor; fensìř pencil; hamà hammer; hōdà powder; kanàř colonel; laità cigarette lighter; māsinjà messenger; mòngwamařàn beret (< (General) Montgomery); ōzà ounce (< abbreviation oz.); řēzà razorblade; sakandàřè secondary school; tikitì ticket

There are a few borrowed verbs, but these are in reality internal creations backformed from borrowed verbal nouns (which, fortuitously, are phonologically similar in Hausa and English), e.g.,

càjā	to charge (s.o. of a crime)	< cājì	charging, a charge
canzà	to change	< canjì	changing, change
fācè	to patch	< fācì	patching, a patch
hàyā	to rent	< hayà	renting (British Eng. hiring)
jōnà	to splice	< jōnì	splicing (joining)
wānà	to wind (e.g., a clock)	< wānì	winding

There is one numeral in common use borrowed from English, namely miliyàn 'million' (although biliyàn 'billion' can be expected) and one adjective, namely the color term yalò 'yellow'.

313

1.2. French

In Niger, which was a French colony, many French loans have been adopted instead of the English loanwords that one has in standard Nigerian Hausa. As with the English loanwords, most of the words borrowed from French are nouns denoting objects and occupations that were introduced during the colonial period. Examples:

àbòkâ lawyer (Fr. avocat); bìyêr̃ beer (Fr. bière); dìmāshì Sunday (Fr. dimanche); dùbbân wine (Fr. du vin); gâs butane gas (Fr. gaz); gàtô cake (Fr. gateau); kàdô gift for children (Fr. cadeau); kàr̃ê quarter of a town (Fr. carré); kàmyô truck (Fr. camion); kasò prison (Fr. cachot); làkìlê key (Fr. la clé); lùlētì eyeglasses (Fr. lunettes); luwùl motor oil (Fr. l'huile); màtàlâ mattress (Fr. matelas); mùshê Mr., educated man (Fr. monsieur); pàr̃mî driver's license (Fr. permis); pàsàjê passenger (Fr. passager); pîl flashlight battery (Fr. pile); shàpô hat (Fr. chapeau); tambùr̃ postage stamp (Fr. timbre(-poste))

> °AN: Hausa does not have /p/ as a distinct phoneme. English words with /p/ tend to be borrowed into SH with /f/, which is the closest sound, e.g., pencil > fensìr̃. In WH dialects spoken in Niger, which have /hw/ or /h/ in place of SH /f/, the /f/ is not available to represent /p/ in loanwords. The dialectal /hw/ and /h/, on the other hand, are phonetically too distant from /p/ to serve as reasonable substitutes. As a result, such words as pàr̃mî, pîl, etc. are borrowed with the foreign /p/ phoneme.

1.3. Arabic

Arabic loanwords have entered the language over a long period of time beginning with the introduction of Islam over five hundred years ago and continuing to the present day. Semantically, the loanwords cover the areas of religion, warfare and horsemanship, government and law, mathematics (including numerals from twenty up), calendrical periods, science, business and trading (including trade goods), abstract ideas, etc. Examples:

àlbàr̃ūshì gunpowder; gahawà̀ (Turkish) coffee; har̃àfì letter of the alphabet; làdân muezzin; Làr̃àbā Wednesday; lìnzāmì bridle; lìshā = ìshā fifth prayer of the day; Mùhar̃r̃àm first month of the year in the Muslim calendar; mulkì rule, government, control, power; r̃ìba bank interest, usury; r̃idda apostasy; rejection of one's religious beliefs; safar̃à̀ itinerant trading; sulhù̀ reconciliation, arbitration; peace; sūr̃à̀ a chapter of the Koran; tàmànin eighty; wàsiyyà̀ will, last testament

Most of the loans are nouns or numerals but the list also includes some verbs and some function words, e.g.,

(a) bayyànā explain; reveal, display, expose (cf. bàyyanà appear (of sth stolen), be revealed); fassàr̃ā translate, explain; k̃addàr̃ā predestine, determine, estimate; tà'àzzar̃à become serious or difficult
(b) àmmā but; hàttā including, even (cf. har̃ probably from same Ar. source via Kanuri); illā except; làbuddà definitely, for sure; muddìn so long as, provided that; wàtàk̃ìlà perhaps

1.4. Fulani

In spite of the political domination of Hausaland by Fulani rulers since early in the nineteenth century, the Fulani language has contributed only a small number of loanwords, some twenty or so. (These are often phonologically recognizable by geminate consonants and a short final vowel.) These loanwords have to do with kinship relations and with cattle. Surprisingly, there is an absence of Fulani loans dealing with government and administration. Examples:

baffà paternal uncle (usu. pronounced and sometimes even spelled **bappà**); **bonè** serious difficulty; **dattījò** gentleman, a respected older person; **gwaggò** paternal aunt; **hāɓè** persons of Hausa as opposed to Fulani ancestry; **haɓɓōjè** hay fever; **hubbāřè** tomb of religious leader (esp. that of Shehu Usman dan Fodio); **kāɗò** pejorative term referring to a non-Fulani indigenous person or more generally to a pagan; **kìndìřmō** sour milk with curd and cream, yogurt; **naggè** cow (= nonloan **sānìyā**); **shařò** ritual test of manhood among Fulani youths in which they must endure flogging without showing pain; **yallàɓâi** respectful term of address for a superior

> °AN: In Fulani, **kāɗò** and **hāɓè** are singular and plural counterparts of the same word. In Hausa, they have semantically diverged, the former being pejorative, the latter being neutral.

1.5. Kanuri

Kanuri loanwords date from the period of Kanuri political influence on Hausaland prior to, but continuing into, the period of Fulani domination. The loanwords, which are relatively few, include a number of traditional titles and occupations formed with the suffix -**mà(a)**. (The number of words borrowed from Kanuri is undoubtedly underestimated because many words of Arabic origin that are included in lists of Arabic loanwords in fact came into Hausa via Kanuri.) Examples:

alàřammà psn who has memorized the Koran (may serve as a teacher in a Koranic school); **biřnī** city, large town; **ciřòmà** traditional title (usu. held by son of an emir); **dandalī** open area in a town center, generally in front of the chief's residence; **ìngařmà** large stallion; **kaigamà** a traditional title; **kāřùwà** prostitute; **kàsuwā** market; **màngúl** type of salt; **mainà** prince; **řùbùtū** writing; **siřdì** saddle; **ùngōzòmà** midwife; **yàřīmà** a traditional title (usu. held by younger brother or son of an emir)

> ◊HN: The etymology of the word **kàsuwā** 'market' provides a lovely illustration of the vagaries of diachronic processes. (I shall ignore tone for purposes of the discussion.) The Arabic root *suq was borrowed into Kanuri with a replacement of /g/ for /q/ and the addition of a final vowel, i.e., *sugu. The root was then given a Kanuri prefix, i.e., *kāsugu. Intervocalic /g/ in many Kanuri dialects is mute, so that what Hausas heard and borrowed was *kāsū. Subsequently Hausa underwent a process of overt characterization whereby feminine words added -ā, which, with the insertion of an epenthetic glide, resulted in the now-occurring form **kàsuwā**.

1.6. Tuareg

Tuareg loanwords are the result of intermittent contracts of an essentially commercial and social nature extending over the past few centuries. Semantically the words tend to group around animals and elements of material cultures characteristic of Tuareg desert life. Examples:

akàlà lead-rope of camel; **àlabè** leather purse or wallet; **amālè** large, strong male camel; **amāwàlī** end of turban cloth used as mouth veil; **azùřfā** silver; **cōkàlī** spoon; **takòbī** sword; **talàkà** common man; **tàttabařā** pigeon; **tōzàlī** antimony

1.7. Other

A small number of recent loanwords have come in from Yoruba (or Nupe or other languages to the south), e.g., **àdìře** 'tie-dyed cloth'; **àdùdù** 'large lidded wicker basket'; **àgàdè** 'plantain(s)'; **àgushī** 'melon seeds used for making soup'; **àkàwu** 'clerk'; **àladè** 'pig'. These loanwords include a number of items that themselves were borrowed from English, e.g., **kwānò** 'pan'; **likità** 'doctor'; **tashà** 'station'; **tītì** 'street'. At an earlier period, there were probably also linguistic influences from Mande languages to the west; and even further back, there is evidence of borrowings from unidentified Niger-Congo languages (see Hoffmann 1970), the most striking being the word **nāmā̀** 'meat' (cf. Proto-Chadic ***Luw**-).

2. INCORPORATION OF LOANWORDS

2.1. *Phonological adjustment of loanwords*

Words that were borrowed into Hausa were generally modified to fit into the pre-existing phonological system of the language. The adjustments involved such changes as segmental replacements, avoidance of some word-final consonants, elimination of consonant clusters by reduction, addition of epenthetic or final vowels, and reinterpretation of stress as tone. The following description is intended to be illustrative rather than exhaustive. It deals only with loanwords from English, although the same processes are applicable to loanwords from other languages as well.

°AN: The incorporation of Arabic loanwords into Hausa has been studied extensively by many scholars over a long period of time (see references at end of this chapter). Among the more regular changes were the interpretation of Arabic emphatic consonants as glottalized (with emphatic T sometimes being represented by **ts** and sometimes by **ɗ**) and the following replacements: **q** by **ƙ**, **th** and **dh** by **s** and **z** (or **d**) respectively, **x**, **H** (voiceless pharyngeal fricative), and **h** by /**h**/, and **ʔ** (glottal stop) and **ʕ** (ayn, i.e., voiced pharyngeal fricative) by / '/.

2.1.1. Segmental replacement of consonant phonemes

English words that contained consonants that were not part of the Hausa phonemic inventory (e.g., /**v**/ or /**th**/) were borrowed with the "closest" comparable native phoneme. Examples:

visa > **bīzà**; television > **talàbijìn**
throttle > **tōtùr̃**; operation (< (operating) theater) > **tìyātà̀**; (Catholic) father > **fàdā**

English /**p**/ and /**f**/ were both borrowed as Hausa /**f**/, which is typically pronounced as a bilabial fricative, as compared with the English labio-dental /**f**/. Examples:

fridge > **fir̃(i)jì**; foul (sports) > **fāwùl**
paint > **fentì**; plank > **filankì̀**

Because the phoneme /**f**/ has the allophone [**h**] before back-rounded vowels, the result is loanwords that look quite different from their English sources, e.g.,

photo > **hòtō** (< /**fòtō**/); foreman > **hōmàn** (< /**fōmàn**/); powder > **hōdà̀** (< /**fōdà̀**/); polo > **hōlò̀** (< /**fōlò̀**/)

Hausa has two rhotics, a retroflex flap, indicated /**r**/, historically the native sound, and a tap or roll, indicated /**r̃**/. The English /**r**/, which is a retroflex approximant, would appear to be phonetically closer to the Hausa flap; nevertheless, it is (almost) always borrowed with the tap/roll /**r̃**/. Examples:

carrots > **kar̃às**; report > **r̃àhōtò̀**; cholera > **kwalar̃à̀**; grease > **gìr̃îs**; ruler (measuring device) > **r̃ūlà̀**; insurance > **ìnshōr̃à̀**; razor (blade) > **r̃ēzà̀**

°AN: One possible explanation is that Hausas were first exposed to British dialects like Scottish English in which the R's are rolled.

At the time that English words began to be borrowed, Hausa already had a phonotactic requirement that all words begin with a consonant. Vowel-initial English words were thus phonemicized with a prothetic glottal stop / '/ (which is not represented in standard orthography). Examples:

accountant > **'àkantà**; acre > **'ēkằ**; engine > **'injî**; hour > **'awằ**; office > **'ōfìs**

2.1.2. Avoidance of word-final consonants

With minor exceptions, words in the indigenous Hausa vocabulary all end in a vowel. By contrast English words are typically consonant-final, thereby presenting a phonotactic conflict between the two systems. In the case of words ending in a nasal, in /f/ (whether from original /f/ or /p/), or in /s/, the words were generally borrowed with the final consonant preserved, e.g.,

mason > **mēsìn**; (Christian) mission > **mishàn**; frame > **fìřâm**; neem (tree) > **nîm**; (tournament) cup > **kwâf**; a safe > **sêf**; canvas (tennis shoes) > **kambàs**; compass > **kamfàs** (cf. price > **fàřāshî**)

In early English loanwords, final /l/ was replaced by /ř/. More recent loanwords, however, retain the /l/, e.g.,

candle > **kyandìř**; level > **lēbùř**; pencil > **fensìř**; throttle > **tōtùř**
appeal (legal) > **àfîl**; buckle > **bōkùl**

Words with final /sh/, /c/, /j/, /g/, and /d/ invariably added an unstressed postthetic vowel, usually /i(ì)/. (The rules for determining the length of the final vowel are unclear.) Examples:

brush > **bùřōshî**; church > **cōcì**; clutch > **kulōcì**; college > **kwalējì**; judge > **jōjì**; peg > **fēgì**; bread > **buřōdì**; railway shed > **shēdì**; yard > **yādì**

> °AN: In a few instances, English final /d/ appears in Hausa as /t/, e.g., parade > **fařātì** = **fàřētì**; grenade > **gùřnêt**. In one strange case, final /d/ appears as /k/, namely salad > **sàlâk**.

Some early loanwords with final /t/ and /k/ also were incorporated with a postthetic vowel. More recent words, however, appear with the consonant preserved in final position, e.g.,

(a) bayonet > **banatì**; court > **kōtù**; packet > **fākitì**; plot (of land) > **fulōtì**
barrack > **bāřikì**; clerk > **kìlākì** (modern) prostitute
(b) certificate > **sàtifikèt**; cricket (the sport) > **kuřkèt**; jacket > **jākèt**
(bank) check > **cêk** (= **cakì**); jack > **jâk** jack, bicycle stand

English words spelled with final *r* appear in Hausa without the consonant, e.g., motor > **mōtà** 'automobile'; (windshield) wiper > **waifà**, etc. This however, is not due to a phonological deletion in Hausa, but rather reflects the final r-less British English pronunciation that served as the source of the loanwords.

2.1.3. Elimination of consonant clusters

Hausa does not have true consonant clusters, i.e., sequences of two or more consonants functioning as a syllable onset or coda. (It does, however, have abutting consonants where the consonantal coda of one syllable is followed by the onset consonant of the next, e.g., **han.tằ** 'liver'.) Syllable-initial clusters in the source word were usually broken up by the insertion of a short epenthetic vowel, e.g.,

bread > **buřōdì**;   plot (of land) > **fulōtì**;   (motor) scooter > **sùkūtằ**;   spanner (American English 'wrench') > **sùfānằ**;   store > **sìtô**;   sweater > **sùwaitằ**;   tractor > **tàřaktằ**

Two different processes operated to eliminate syllable-final clusters. With clusters composed of a nasal plus a stop (or affricate), a postthetic vowel was usually added, thereby splitting the cluster between two syllables. Examples:

bank > **bankì** (i.e., /ban.kì/);   bench > **bencì**;   cement > **sìmintì**;   inch > **incì**;   paint > **fentì**; regiment > **řajimantì**;   (piston) ring > **řingì**;   syringe > **sìřinjì**;   tank > **tankì**;   (arrest) warrant > **wařantì**

> °AN: Interestingly, the final *ng* in English 'ring', which phonetically ends in a single consonant [ŋ], is interpreted as a cluster.

Other final clusters underwent simplification to a single consonant, e.g.,

communist > **kwamìnìs**;   (thermos) flask > **fìlâs**;   kiosk > **kyâs**;   yeast > **yîs**;   (bank) draft > **dìřâf**; belt > **bêl**;   diamond > **daimòn**;   stamp > **sìtâm** = **sìtampì**;   an advance > **àdìbâs**;   balance (financial) > **balàs**;   ambulance > **ambùlàs** = **ambùlàn**;   carrots > **kařàs**

2.1.4. Tone assignment

Source words with initial stress generally appear with H-L-(L) tone, e.g.,

bank > **bankì**;   office > **ōfìs**;   petrol > **fētùř**;   shovel > **shēbùř**;   visa > **bīzà** aspirin > **asfìřìn**;   bricklayer > **bìřkìlà**;   communist > **kwamìnìs**;   estimate > **istìmàn**

Three - (and four-) syllable words with stress on the second syllable appear with L-H-(H)-L tone, e.g.,

accountant > **àkantằ**;   allowance > **àlāwùs**;   December > **Dìsambà**;   insurance > **ìnshōřà**;   pajamas > **fànjāmằ**;   verandah **bàřandà**;   battalion > **bàtāliyằ**;   commissioner > **kwàmishinằ**

Originally disyllabic words that became trisyllabic because of the breakup of an initial consonant cluster by means of an epenthetic vowel usually appear with this L-H-L pattern, although H-H-L is also attested, e.g.,

(a) blotter > **bùlōtằ**;   clinic > **kìlīnìk**;   slippers > **sìlīfằ** = **silīfằ**;   sweater > **sùwaitằ**
(b) driver > **dìřēbà**;   flour > **fulāwằ**

Words with final stress typically take a falling tone on the last syllable, with all previous tones L. (The F is also found on all monosyllabic words and is typical of disyllabic words formed by epenthesis from monosyllabic sources with an initial consonant cluster.) Examples:

advance (down payment) > **àdìbâs**;   appeal (legal) > **àfîl**;   (cement) block > **bùlô**;   grenade > **gùřnêt**;   paper clip > **kìlîf**;   reverse (esp. of a car) > **řìbâs**;   (university) degree > **dìgìřî** belt > **bêl**;   bus > **bâs**;   (tournament) cup > **kwâf**

Words with final *-ine* in English, which are pronounced /ɪn/ or /aɪn/, have an F on the last syllable with the preceding syllables all L, i.e., the final English syllable is treated as if it carried stress whether it actually does so or not, e.g.,

iodine > **àidîn**; tangerine > **tànjàřîn**; Vaseline > **bàsìlîn**

2.2. *Phonological impact of loanwords*
To a great extent loanwords from whatever source were made to fit into the then pre-existing phonology. The loanwords did, however, alter the phonology of the language in a number of significant ways.

°AN: A major early study on this topic is Greenberg (1941). The issue is taken up again in Newman (1976, 1980b).

Perhaps the major change resulting from the introduction of Arabic loanwords was the phonemicization of / '/ and /h/. Prior to the loanwords, ['] existed as a phonetic feature of word onset. Loanwords like **'àddu'à** 'prayer', **'uzùřî** 'excuse', and **jàm'iyyà** 'society, association', helped upgrade the initial ['] into a fully fledged phoneme / '/ and also introduced / '/ in word medial position. Similarly, phonetic [h] predated the loanwords, but it existed only as an allophone of /f/ before rounded vowels and also as an alternative manner of word onset. The introduction of Arabic loanwords with initial and medial /ha/ resulted in the upgrading of [h] to a distinct phoneme /h/. A major consequence of the emergence of / '/ and /h/ as phonemes is that words that formerly began with a vowel were now consonant initial, this now being the required canonical shape of all syllables. Another important development was the phonemicization of /ř/. Originally, [ř] existed in syllable-final position as a realization of coronal obstruents, e.g., **fařkà** 'wake up' < ***fadkà**, or as a conditioned allophone of /r/, e.g., **kařnukà** 'dogs', plural of **kàrē**, **bař** 'let, leave', pre-object form of **barì**. It also occurred in initial position as a strengthened, expressive pronunciation of /r/, e.g., **řafkà** 'hit, do a lot of', **řamas** 'emphasizing being dry and crunchy' (ideophone). Arabic words were all borrowed with the rolled /ř/, in word initial and in intervocalic position, e.g., **řa'àyî** 'opinion, attitude, point of view', **hàřàjî** 'tax(es)'. This resulted in a clear contrast between the two rhotics and strengthened the incipient phonemicization of /ř/ as opposed to /r/. Finally, the introduction of Arabic loanwords with /s/ and /z/ before front vowels, e.g., **sifîřî** 'zero, null' (not ****shifîřî); **zìnā** 'adultery' (not ****jìnā**), has served to undermine the originally allophonic relation between coronals and their corresponding palatals. (Coronals, both fricatives and stops, that have not undergone palatalization before front vowels are also characteristic of English loanwords, e.g., **fentî** 'paint' (not ****fencî**); **gàřàntî** 'warranty, guarantee' (not ****gàřàncî**); **gādì** 'guarding' (not ****gājì**); **làsîsî** 'license' (not ****làshîshì**); **zîk** 'zipper' (not ****jîk**).
  English has had a major impact on the phonological system by introducing large numbers of words with final consonants. Previously, almost all lexical items ended in a vowel, with the exception of ideophones and a few apocopated or clipped forms (e.g., **mùtûm** 'man' < **mùtumì**). The nasal /n/ and the rolled /ř/ occurred word finally in their function as gender-sensitive articles, so although word-final sonorants were not common lexically they were not ruled out by the phonological system and were thus allowed in loanwords. Word-final obstruents, on the other hand, were prohibited. English loanwords containing them added a postthetic vowel in keeping with the phonotactic rules of the language, e.g., **gējì** 'gauge', **facì** 'patch'. New loanwords from English that have come in over the past thirty years or so, however, have kept the final consonants, e.g.,

mishàn Christian mission; **(h)òtâl** hotel, bar; **řēhùl** raffle; **gwâl** goal (e.g., in soccer); **tîf** inner tube; **shât** shirt; **fàmît** a permit; **cêk** check; **kìlìnìk** clinic

In terms of canonical word form, Hausa previously had just a handful of monosyllabic words, these being mostly verbs and function words. English loanwords have increased the number of monosyllabic nouns in the language (all of which have come in with falling tone). Examples:

bâm bomb; **dîm** low-beam headlight, **fîm** film; **jâk** bicycle stand; **kwâf** cup; **nâs** nurse; **nîm** neem tree; **têf** tape; **tî** tea, **tôn** ton; **yîs** yeast

The introduction of numerous words with syllable-final codas has also affected the vowel system. In native lexical items, the vowels /ē/ and /ō/ occur only in open syllables and, unless word finally, only long. When closed by a coda as a result of morphological formations, /ē/ and /ō/ automatically shorten and centralize to /a/ (sometimes to [ə]), e.g., [kàransà] 'his dog' < **kàrē + n + sà** lit. dog of his; [tantònā] 'dig up many or often' < **tōn-tònā** pluractional of **tōnā** 'dig up'; **kwâs** 'course' < **kôs** (early Eng. loanword). In recent times, English loanwords have been coming in with short /e/ and /o/ in closed syllables. (Whether they will stay as such with a resultant change in the phonological system or whether they will eventually be integrated with centralized /a/ or schwa remains to be seen.) Examples:

bêl belt ; **bencì** bench ; **cêk** check ; **jākèt = jākêt** jacket ; **membà** member; **sêf** safe (for valuables); **têf** tape (measuring or recording)
fôm a form; **tàmfôl** tarpaulin; **tôn** ton

There are a few loanwords that have been borrowed with short /e/ and /o/ in open syllables, namely **elemantàr̃è** 'elementary school'; **ogànēzà** 'organizer'; cf. **bonè** 'trouble' [dv] (< Fulani).

English loanwords have also served to increase the number of common nouns with short final vowels. In the indigenous system, the major function of final vowel length was grammatical, e.g., distinguishing nouns from adverbs (e.g., **bāyā** 'back' vs. **bāya** 'on the back'; distinguishing common from proper nouns (e.g., **sarkī** 'emir' vs. **Sarki** 'proper name'); marking syntactically determined allomorphs of verb forms, e.g., **yā bī tà** 'he followed her' vs. **yā bi yār̃inyà** 'he followed the girl'), etc. Many common noun loanwords, e.g., **àyàbà** 'banana' (< Yoruba), **gwaggò** 'aunt' (< Fulani), **cir̃òmà** 'prince' (< Kanuri), and presumed loanwords, e.g., **màge** 'cat' (< ?) end in a short final vowel. English loanwords have added significantly to the number of such items, e.g.,

dir̃ēbà driver, chauffeur; **būzāyè** bull's-eye; **shànshàn-bālè** gentian violet; **bandējì** bandage; **tikitì** ticket ; **daffò** depot, warehouse; **kōtù** court ; **Jànair̃ù** January

The borrowed words with a short final vowel plus those with a final consonant have also resulted in an increase in the number of nouns with final L-L tone, a previously very atypical class, e.g.,

asfir̃ìn aspirin; **faskìlà** first class (e.g., on a plane or train); **lēbùr̃à** laborer; **mangwàr̃ò** mango (fruit or tree); **ōdàlè** orderly (military), **sigìnà** signal, sign; **tōcìlàn** flashlight

Historically, words with a long final vowel that ended in L-L tone raised the final vowel to H, e.g., *Cà(a)Cà > Cà(a)Cā (where /a/ represents any vowel).

°AN: Leben (1971) has described this as a synchronic rule in the language, a position rejected by Newman and Jaggar (1989a).

The result of the tone change was a phonotactic gap in the language, i.e., whereas final L-L was possible if the final vowel was short, there were no words left with L-L and a long final vowel. Recent English loanwords borrowed with L-L and a long final vowel have started to fill the vacuum (which is also attracting items from internal sources as well), but there is also evidence of a tone shift away from this "undesired" pattern, e.g.,

asambùlḕ   assembly (at school) (sometimes → **àsambulḕ**); **elemantàr̃ḕ**   elementary school (sometimes → **elèmantar̃ḕ**); **fìr̃āmàr̃ḕ**   primary school (sometimes → **fìr̃āmar̃ḕ**); **lōtàr̃ḕ**   lottery; **mājistàr̃ḕ**   magistrate; **r̃ēlùwḕ**   railroad (< **r̃ēlùwài**); **sakandàr̃ḕ**   secondary school

2.3. *Gender of loanwords*
Nouns borrowed into Hausa from other languages necessarily have to be assigned grammatical gender. Three criteria have been employed in making this assignment. (For purposes of the description here, I shall limit my discussion to English loanwords. The same principles can be applied to loanwords from other languages as well.)

2.3.1. Natural gender
The first criterion is natural gender. Loanwords denoting males are assigned masculine gender; those denoting females are assigned feminine gender. Words denoting people belonging to groups or having occupations that might likely be filled by either men or women are epicene. Examples:

(a) Masculine: **bìr̃gēdiyà** m.   brigadier; **bìr̃kìlà** m.   bricklayer; **bòyi** m.   house boy, cook steward; **fàdā** m.   Catholic father, priest; **fastò** m.   pastor; **hafsà** m.   army officer; **hēlùmà** m.   headman, foreman; **janàr̃** m.   general (military); **làftanàn** m.   lieutenant; **sùfētò** m.   inspector of police
(b) Feminine: **hedìgêl** f.   head girl (in school); **kìlākì** f.   modern prostitute (< Eng. clerk); **sistà** f. nursing sister
(c) Epicene: **ēdità** m./f.   editor; **Kir̃istà** m./f.   Christian; **lauyà** m./f.   lawyer; **likità** m./f.   doctor; **mìlōniyà** m./f.   millionaire; **nâs** m./f.   nurse

2.3.2. Analogy
The second approach is gender assignment by association with some previously existing word or class of words in the language. Examples:

(a) Masculine: **āyàn** m.   a pressing iron (cf. **dūtsèn gūgà** m.   iron, lit. stone.of rubbing); **basfà** (< Vespa) m.   motor scooter (cf. **kèkè** m. bicycle); **fànjāmà** m.   loose-fitting trousers, pajamas (cf. **wàndō** m.   trousers); **gâm** m. or **gùlú** m.   glue, paste (cf. **līkì** m.   gluing substance); **indìpendà** m. independence (cf. **mulkìn kâi** m.   self-government); **kējì** m.   birdcage (cf. **gidā** m.   house, enclosure); **kūkà** m.   modern stove (cf. **mur̃hù** m.   cooking place); **màntàlētà** m.   Mentholatum (cf. **mâi** m.   oil, balm); **Mār̃ìs** m.   March (and all other names of months) (cf. **watà** m.   month); **silìfà** m.   slippers, slip-on shoes, sandals (cf. **tàkàlmī** m.   shoe(s)); **sūfà** m.   premium grade (super) gasoline (cf. **mân fētùr̃** m.   gasoline); **tùr̃ōzà** m.   trousers (Western style) (cf. **wàndō** m.   trousers)
(b) Feminine: **ambùlàs** f.   ambulance (cf. **mōtà** f.   car); **āyìs** f.   ice (cf. **k̃ank̃ar̃ā** f.   sleet, hail); **bâl** f. ball (cf. **tamaulā** f.   rag-ball); **banatì**   bayonet (cf. **wuk̃à** f.   knife); **bâs** f.   bus (cf. **mōtà** f.   car); **fankèkè** f.   face powder (cf. **hōdà** f.   powder); **fìr̃āmàr̃ḕ**   primary school (cf. **makar̃antā** f.   school), **gàzêt** f.   gazette (cf. **takàr̃dā** f.   paper); **gwamnatì** f.   government (cf. **hùkūmà** f.   governing authority); **kōtù** f.   court (cf. **shàr̃i'à** f.   court); **kwalējì** f.   college (cf. **makar̃antā** f.   school); **sìgār̃ì** f.   cigarette (cf. **tābà** f.   tobacco, cigarette); **singìlētì** f.   undershirt, singlet (cf. **taguwā** f.   shirt); **tàr̃hô** f.   telephone (cf. **wayà** f.   wire, telephone); **tàsî** f.   taxi (cf. **mōtà** f.   car); **tōcìlàn** f.   flashlight

(cf. **fìtìlā̀** f. lamp); **walàt** f. wallet (cf. **jàkā** f. leather sack); **wan-wê** f. one-way street (cf. **hanyā̀** f. road)

2.3.3. Phonological patterning

In the absence of semantic criteria for assignment, either direct or by analogy/association, the default assignment of gender seems to have been on the basis of phonological shape. Words ending in -ā̀ were treated as feminine, whereas all others were treated as masculine. Examples:

(a) Masculine: **àdìrēshì** m. address; **àidîn** m. iodine; **bāwùl** m. valve; **bìrkì** m. brakes; **cìngâm** m. chewing gum; **daffò** m. depot, warehouse; **dùrô** m. storage drum (for water, gasoline, etc.); **famfò** m. water faucet, pump, **fàrfèsū** m. pepper stew (cf. **miyà** f. soup, sauce); **fenshò** m. pension; **hòtō** m. photograph, picture; **jâk** m. bicycle stand; **kābējì** m. cabbage; **karàs** m. carrot(s); **sīlì** m. ceiling; **tāyè** m. necktie; **tikitì** m. ticket; **ūlù** or **wûl** m. wool, wool thread

(b) Feminine: **bàrandā̀** f. balcony, verandah; **bàtāliyā̀** f. battalion; **bulā̀** f. washing blue; **dastā̀** f. blackboard eraser, rag for cleaning car; **ēkà̀** f. acre; **fàrfēlā̀** f. propeller, car engine fan, blade of a fan; **gwaibā̀** f. guava; **kalà̀** f. color (cf. the nonloanword **launī** m. color); **kwalarā̀** f. cholera; **mītà̀** f. electric meter; **mōtà̀** f. automobile; **rìtāyà̀** f. retirement; **shakàsōbà̀** f. shock absorber; **tābà̀** f. tobacco, cigarette; **waifà̀** f. windshield wiper

[References: [Arabic]: Baldi (1988, 1995); El-Shazly (1987); Goerner, Salman, and Armitage (1966); Greenberg (1947); Hiskett (1965); [English]: Ikara (1975); Leben (1996); L. Muhammad (1968); Salim (1981); [French]: Gouffé (1971); [Kanuri]: Greenberg (1960b); [Tuareg]: Gouffé (1974)]

45. MAI and MARAS

1. MAI

THIS formative, for which I shall use MAI with capital letters to stand for both the singular (**mài**) and the plural (**màsu**), is an extremely common, high-frequency word in the language. It always occurs with a following NP. In the dictionary of Bargery (1934: 748) it is glossed as "the owner or possessor of; the doer or embodiment of", e.g., **kèkè mài kyâu** 'a good bicycle' (lit. bicycle characterized by goodness); **àkuyà mài ƙàhō ɗaya** 'a one-horned goat' (lit. goat having horn one); **mài gyārā** 'repairman' (lit. doer of repairing); **sōjōjī màsu ban tsòrō** 'frightening soldiers' (lit. soldiers characterized by giving fright). (There is no simple English word that serves conveniently to translate **mài**. In literal glosses, I will, therefore, indicate it conventionally as either 'charac. by', 'having', or 'doer of'.)

◊HN: The plural form **màsu** is presumably composed of a marker **mà**- plus the third person plural pronoun -**su**. This suggests that the singular **mài** etymologically consists of the same formative **mà**- (whatever its origin) plus a clipped allomorph -**y** of the third person masculine pronoun -**ya**, i.e., **mà + y(a) > *mày > mài*. Assuming that this is correct, **mài** originally would have been a distinctly masculine marker and it ought to have had a feminine counterpart. Synchronically, however, **mài** is neutral with regard to gender, being used with both masculine singular and feminine singular NPs.

An alternative possibility would be to derive **mài** historically from a short-form agentive of the verb **yi** 'do' (see §7:1.6.3), i.e., **ma-** + **yi** > **mayì** 'doer of' > **mày > mài*. The attraction of this analysis is that it treats MAI in a parallel fashion to its negative counterpart MARAS (see below), which morphologically is clearly an agentive form. Its major drawback, apart from the low rather than expected falling tone—which could be explained by its grammaticalization into a distinctly functional morpheme—is that it fails to capture the relation between the singular **mài** and its plural counterpart **màsu**.

MAI has two main functions: (1) to form adjectival modifier phrases, which occur in post-nominal position, and (2) to derive nominal expressions. It also has a third, poorly understood, function in continuous verbal sentences.

1.1. Modifiers

The formative MAI combines with nouns of quality (especially abstract nouns) or other NPs (including gerundives and infinitive phrases) to produce modifier expressions. The exact translation varies depending on the construction, but the function of MAI is to associate the qualities or attributes of the following word or phrase to the head noun. These expressions compensate for the paucity of true adjectives in Hausa. Note that MAI agrees with the head noun in number but not in gender. Examples:

àl̃kālī mài rōwầ   a stingy judge (lit. judge charac.by stinginess) (= mar̃òwàcin àl̃kālī with the adj. mar̃òwàcī stingy); dōkī̀ mài faɗầ   a vicious horse (lit. horse charac.by fighting) (= mafàɗàcin dōkī̀ with the adj. mafàɗàcī vicious); yār̃ò mài hankàlī   a sensible boy; jàr̃īdầ mài farin jinī   popular newspaper; kwālī mài ɗan nauyī   a somewhat heavy carton; Janàr̃ Gar̃bà mài r̃ìtāyầ   retired General Garba (lit. General Garba charac. by retirement); wani mùtûm mài sūnā Bellò   a man called Bello (lit. ...having name Bello); yārinyầ mài k̃īrar̃ kàlàngū   a slender girl with good hips (lit. ...having construction of an hourglass drum); lìttàttàfai màsu gundumar̃ dà mutầnē   boring books (lit. ...charac.by bore people); k̃ōfà mài kallon kudù   door that faces south; tēbur̃ōr̃ī màsu k̃warī   strong tables; sānìyā mài shèkar̃à bīyu   a two-year-old cow (lit. ...having year two); mōtầ mài bōdìn kātākō   a truck with a wooden body; watầ mài zuwầ   next month (lit. ...charac. by coming); k̃ābā mài kùmburī   rheumatism accompanied by swelling; àbinci mài yawầ   a lot of food (lit. food having abundance)

In addition to serving as attributive modifiers, MAI phrases can be used also as predicate adjectives, e.g.,

shī mài fàr̃a'ầ nē	He is cheerful.
kàren nàn bầ mài cīzò ba nē	This dog doesn't bite. (lit. ...neg doer of biting neg)
bàk̃în màsu gàskiyā nè	The strangers are honest. (lit. ...charac. by truth)

1.2. Derivative noun phrases

MAI formations without a preceding noun constitute semantically close-knit NPs. The constructions sometimes translate as English '-er' or '-man' words, sometimes as 'one who...' phrases. Examples:

mài tàfīyầ   traveler, passerby; mài màganầ   speaker; mài sàna'ầ   tradesman; mài gyārā repairman; mài idò ɗaya   one-eyed man; mài shī   one who has it; mài yìwuwā   it is possible (lit. doable); mài kulầ dà mânyan màkàr̃àntū   one who looks after secondary schools; mài kàmā dà nī one who looks like me (lit. one having similarity with me); mài sūnānā   my namesake (lit. one having my name); mài kōyar̃ manà dà Hausa   the one who teaches us Hausa; mài bàkin kīfī   Citroën car (lit. having mouth of a fish); màsu gōyon bāyan shùgàban k̃asā   supporters of the president; màsu r̃a'àyin rìk̃au   conservatives, reactionaries (lit. ones having ideas of well held); màsu hannū dà shūnī rich people (lit. ones having hands with indigo dye)

Some MAI phrases have become so fixed that they now must be considered as noun compounds or near compounds. These often do not have plural counterparts. Included in this category are some personal names. Examples:

mài gādì   watchman; mài gàrī   chief of a town; mài ɗākì   wife; màigidā (usu. spelled as one word) householder, Mr.; bindigà mài ruwā   machine gun (lit. gun charac.by (spraying) water); mài girmā his excellency; Màir̃ìga   traditional name for a child born in a caul (lit. having gown/covering); Màitamā   nickname for any person named Yūsufù (lit. doer of ore)

1.3. Continuity in past

In written Hausa, and in the language of broadcasters, such as from the BBC, one comes across examples of MAI in third person singular continuous sentences occurring after the TAM and before the verb or verbal noun. It is not clear exactly when the MAI is appropriate and exactly what it means, but it tends to be used for past events prior to some other event or to conceptualize the event as a state rather than as an action. All of the following examples would remain grammatical if mài were omitted.

yanà mài ɗaukō kāyan làmbū	He was carrying the garden produce here.
tanà mài kūkā lōkàcîn dà takè shigôwā	She was crying as she was entering.
yanà mài gòdiyā gà dukkàn waɗàndà sukà bā shì haɗîn kâi	

    He was grateful to all who had given him support.

°AN: This construction, which is found scattered throughout written sources, still awaits a detailed description by Hausa grammarians. It is mentioned here, even though I have little to say about it, for purposes of documentation and as a stimulus for further research.

2. MARAS

The semantic opposite of MAI is MARAS (sg. **maràs**, pl. **maràsā**), which indicates 'the one(s) lacking in…', e.g.,

sōjà maràs lāfiyà	an unhealthy soldier (lit. soldier lacking health)
yārinyà maràs kunyà	a shameless girl (lit. girl lacking shame)
yârā maràsā hankàlī	boys without sense (lit. boys lacking sense)

The singular **maràs** has a number of phonological variants depending on dialect and idiolect, all of which are quite common. These are: **maràs, maràr̃, maràG** (where G indicates a geminate with the following consonant), and **marà**, e.g., **yārinyà maràs kunyà** = **yārinyà maràr̃ kunyà** = **yārinyà maràk kunyà** = **yārinyà marà kunyà** 'a shameless girl'. The plural has the one form **maràsā**.

    Etymologically, **maràs** and **maràsā** are grammaticalized agentive nouns (§7:1.6.3) formed with the prefix ma- and the verb **rasà** 'to lack'. The plural still has the regular form of an agentive. The singular, however, has become phonologically reduced and does not appear with the regular morphological shape, which would be ****maràshi(n)**. Note also that **maràs** (and equivalent variants) is invariant for gender whereas regular agentives have distinct feminine variants.

    MARAS functions to produce modifier phrases, either attributive or predicative, e.g.,

ɗākì maràt tāgà	a room without (lit. lacking) windows
kèken-ɗinkì marà àmfànī	a useless sewing machine (lit. sewing machine lacking use)
àbinci maràr̃ kyâu	bad food (lit. food lacking goodness)
sōjōjin nàn maràsā īmānì nē	These soldiers are merciless. (lit. …lacking mercy)

If the head noun is clearly understood from the context, it can be left unexpressed, e.g.,

| kà ƙauràcē wà Ø maràsā tàusàyī | You should avoid unsympathetic people. |

(where **mutànē** 'people' is not expressed).

46. Modal Particles

1. INTRODUCTION

THE term *modal particle* (MP) encompasses a small, closed set of intensifying, specifying, restricting, focusing, connecting particles which indicate 'well, indeed, in fact, also, however, on the other hand, etc.' They serve to express a personal attitude, state of mind, emphasis or contrast, corrective, conversational flow, or other pragmatic or discourse functions. They are often essentially untranslatable, their linguistic contribution being expressed in English by stress, intonation, or non-verbal gestures. (Their pragmatic significance in sprucing up a sentence is reflected in the Hausa term for these words, namely **gishirin Hausa**, lit. 'salt of the language'.) Except in cases where they function as conjuncts (see below), the MPs appear after the word, phrase, or clause to which they apply, e.g., **nī fa̱, bā nà sônsà** 'As for me, I don't like him'; **kadà kà mântā fa̱!** 'Don't forget now!'

°AN: The term *modal particles* as applied to Hausa goes back at least to 1972, when it was used in a London seminar paper presented by Parsons. (This is included in Parsons 1981: 15–20.) The term was already familiar to Hausa linguists by 1976 when Parsons presented a lecture at Hamburg University (never published) entitled "Modal particles in Hausa". For lack of a better term, Kraft (1963, vol. 2, pp. 29ff.) had earlier called them simply "inserts".

2. INVENTORY

There are six phonologically small words that are generally recognized as constituting the class of modal particles, namely **fa, dai, kùwa, kuma, mā**, and **kàm**.

2.1. **fa**

The MP **fa**, which one could conventionally gloss as 'indeed', has a very broad, nonspecific emphatic function, serving to focus attention on the constituent in question. As with some of the other MPs, **fa** is a conversational marker that is used more commonly in direct speech than in narratives. Examples:

nī fa̱, nā gàji	I indeed, I'm worn out.
dà ganìn hakà fa̱, sai tsòrō ya kāmà shi	On seeing that, well, he became afraid.
(lit. ...fear caught him)	
yā fa̱ shìga jaR̄àbà mùtumìn nân	He really set about testing this man.

°AN: Because tone is not marked in standard orthography, there is a potential confusion between the high-tone modal particle **fa** and the common low-tone question marker **fà** 'how about?'; e.g., **kai fà, kā gàji?** 'How about you, are you tired?'; **tā fa̱ sàmi tikìtì, shī fà?** 'She indeed got a ticket, how about him?'

2.2. dai

The MP **dai** 'just, only' serves as a limiter/restricter or as a contrastive or corrective marker. It can also be used to soften the abruptness of a statement. Examples:

nī <u>dai</u> bā nà̀ sônsà	I (for one) don't like him (but others might).
àmmā <u>dai</u> bà kà kyâutā masà ba	But really you haven't been kind to him.
tsàyā <u>dai</u>!	Hang on just a moment!
bà̀ Yūsī ba <u>dai</u>, wânsà̀ <u>dai</u> yā mutù	

It wasn't Yusi, but rather his elder brother who died.

Don Allàh kà bā nì dalà̀ hàmsin. Ai, â bā kà àshìr̃in <u>dai</u>

Please give me fifty dollars. Well, you'll be given just twenty.

The MP **dai** commonly accompanies the conditional **in** 'if' and the conjunction/preposition **sai** 'except, but, only', e.g.,

in <u>dai</u> kun kasà kûnnē, kwâ ji	If you would only listen, you would hear.
kuɗī gàr̃ē shì sai <u>dai</u> mūnì	He's rich but ugly.

2.3. kuma

The word **kuma** '(and) also, too, likewise' is conventionally grouped with the other MPs because it patterns with them to some extent both syntactically and semantically. It differs from the others, however, in having one fairly well defined adverbial meaning 'also', and in its straightforward function as a connecting element (where it compensates for the lack of a conjunction 'and' between sentences and full clauses). Examples:

shī bā yà̀ sônā, nī <u>kuma</u> bā nà̀ sônsà	He doesn't like me and I also don't like him.
yā <u>kuma</u> cê, bâ wandà zâi fìta à r̃àye	He also said, no one is going to get out alive.
gà shi <u>kuma</u>	Here it is furthermore.
nā yi mur̃nà̀ <u>kuma</u> nā gōdè mukù	I am happy and also I thank you.
yā jē Kanò <u>kuma</u> yā jē Sakkwato	He went to Kano and also to Sokoto.
uwar̃gidā ta yi matà kyàutā, sarkī <u>kuma</u> ya ƙār̃à yi wà Hasàn kyàutā	

The senior wife gave her presents, and the emir likewise gave Hassan more presents.

ɗākìn nân nākà yā fayè ƙuncī <u>kuma</u> iskà bā tà̀ shèƙuwā

This room of yours is too small and also the air isn't breathable.

yā bā tà àbinci dà sùtur̃à̀ dà <u>kuma</u> kuɗī mài yawà̀

He gave her food and clothing and also a lot of money.

2.4. ma

The high-frequency MP **mā** 'too, also, even, still' semantically partially overlaps with **kuma**, but is more particlelike in its assertive nature, its sometimes semantic vagueness, and in its range of syntactic usage.

nī <u>mā</u> nā gan shì	I also saw him.
shin yàyà <u>mā</u> zân zānà hòtôn?	How did you say I should draw the diagram?
wannàn shī <u>mā</u> yanà dà ban dà̀r̃iyā	This one's funny too.
wata r̃ānā, zâi tàfi dà kū <u>mā</u>	One of these days, he will take you away too.
yànzu <u>mā</u> anà̀ yî	It is still being done.
yā bā nì àgōgo, gà <u>mā</u> àgōgôn	He gave me a watch, and here is the watch.

à cikin yârân m̲ā̲, àkwai 'yā'yan sarkī huɗu

    And among the children there were four children of the king.

tā yī minì 'yaȓ màganà̀, bà̀ m̲ā̲ ta tāshìn hankàlī ba

    She made a small remark to me, and not an offensive one either.

The MP **m̲ā̲** commonly follows the counterfactual conditional marker **dà̀**, especially when the consequent clause is not expressed, e.g.,

dà̀ m̲ā̲ inà̀ dà mōtà̀	If only I had a car.
cf. dà̀ inà̀ dà mōtà̀, dà̀ zân tàimàkē kà	If I had a car I would help you.
dà̀ m̲ā̲ kun zō jiyà	If only you had come here yesterday.

It also occurs frequently in 'especially' phrases formed with the discontinuous marker **tun bà̀...bâ**, where its meaning or pragmatic function is difficult to discern.

yârā sunà̀ dà ban shà̀'awà̀, tun bà̀ (mā) k̓anānà̀ bâ

    Children are enjoyable, especially young ones.

inà̀ sô ìn zìyàrci garūruwà̀ dà yawà̀ tun bà̀ (mā) Kanò̀ bâ

    I want to visit many towns, especially Kano.

An important use of **mā** is with the time adverb **dâ** 'formerly, in olden times'. In this case, however, the addition of **mā** affects the meaning to the point where one could almost think of **dâ mā** as a fixed adverbial compound meaning 'previously, from the start, all along, etc.' Examples:

dâ m̲ā̲ inà̀ sônsà	I have always liked him. (i.e., from the start)
cf. dâ inà̀ sônsà	Formerly I liked him. (but now I don't)
dâ m̲ā̲ zân zō makaȓantā	Even before [some event] I was coming to school.
cf. dâ can zân zō makaȓantā, àmmā bâ kuɗī	
	A long time ago, I was going to go to school, but there was no money.
dâ m̲ā̲ Hàusàwā sun iyà kāsuwancì	From way back Hausas were good at trading.
dâ m̲ā̲ nā san hakà zā à yi	I knew all along that this would happen.
dâ m̲ā̲ an cê ganī gà wani yā ìsa tsòron Allàh	
	It has been said, seeing another's fate is enough to evoke the fear of God.

Another fixed combination is **cê mā** (with the verb **cê** 'say'), which connotes 'suppose, imagine, let's say, etc.', e.g.,

cê mā munà̀ iyà̀wā...   Suppose we could do it...

cê mā kyâ iyà shìgā, tô, ìnā àmfà̀ninsà?

    Let's say that you (f.) could get in, OK, what use would it be?

2.5. kùwa

The MP **kùwa** is used to affirm or contrast something, and thus it sometimes corresponds to English 'moreover' or 'however'. It is perhaps the most commonly used MP. In speech and in writing, it is often shortened to **kò̀** (sometimes pronounced **kò**). (In the examples I shall regularize usage and transcribe all occurrences of the short form as **kò̀**.) Examples:

yāròn nan k̲ù̲w̲a̲ yā iyà   That boy, however, can do it.

Mūsā k<u>ùwa</u> yā zō	Musa has certainly come.
ita cè ta yĭ shì k<u>ùwa</u>	It was she who did it in fact.
zā sù zō k<u>ò̀</u> gòbe	They will really come tomorrow.

'yā ɗaya kaɗai gàrē shì, an k<u>ùwa</u> yi matà aurē

He had only one daughter, and she moreover was married. (lit. ...one moreover did to.her marriage)

Bàlā tun watàn jiyà yā kōmǎ gidā; nī k<u>ò̀</u>, sai watàn gòbe

Bala returned home last month; me, however, not until next month.

ìnā àmfǎnin wannàn? àkwai k<u>ùwa</u>!

This is of no use. (lit. where (is) value.of this?) But it is! (lit. there is however)

◊HN: The change k<u>ùwa</u> > *k<u>ùw</u> > k<u>ò̀</u> is not historically systematic, but there is a parallel in the language in the case of verbal nouns of grade 7 verbs, e.g., **ɗinkuwā** (→) ***ɗinkuw** → **ɗinkō** 'be sewable'; **shàwuwā** (→) ***shàwuw** → **shàwō** 'be drinkable'. An alternative analysis would be to derive **k<u>ò̀</u>** from **kàu** by simple monophthongization, where **kàu** would represent a clipped form of ***kàwa**. Both **kàu** and **kàwa** are reported to occur as dialect variants equivalent to **kùwa** but they are not widely attested.

The variant **kò** with the short vowel, which some SH speakers now use to the exclusion of **k<u>ò̀</u>**, appears to be a recent innovation, formed by analogy with the short vowel found with other monosyllabic function words, e.g., **fa** (MP), **fà** (question marker), **dà** 'with', **wà** (i.o marker). Although **k<u>ò̀</u>** and **kò** are etymologically short forms of **kùwa**, there is some indication that the two variants are beginning to split, i.e., it appears that they are no longer totally interchangeable in all environments. This is a matter that needs further study.

The MP **kùwa** (= **k<u>ò̀</u>**) is used following the word **kō** 'or' to form alternative questions. (Due to the influence of question formation, the vowel /a/ in sentence final position undergoes lengthening and, for some speakers, the addition of a falling tone.) Examples:

Tùřàwā nǎ cîn ɗanyen ƙwai, kō k<u>ùwā</u>?	Do Europeans eat raw eggs, or not?
wannàn kakè sô kō k<u>ò̀</u> wannàn?	Do you want this one or that one?
wannàn māgànîn banzā nè kō k<u>ò̀</u>?	Is this medicine useless or what?

2.6. kàm

The status of the particle **kàm** is far from clear. Some scholars contend that it is a dialect variant essentially equivalent to **kùwa**; others equate it with **dai**; others view it as a separate topic restricter. In extensive texts analyzed by Kraft (1963), which included both written and tape-recorded sources, **kàm** appears only three times (compared with over a hundred occurrences of **kùwa** and **dai**). On the other hand, when questioned, native speakers of SH seem comfortable with **kàm** and do not view it as aberrant in any way. Examples:

nī zân tàfi k<u>àm</u>	I will definitely go.
shī k<u>àm</u> bài yàřda ba	He for one doesn't agree.
mōtā k<u>àm</u>, wàccan tā fi tằwa kyâu	On the subject of cars, that one is prettier than mine.
wannàn yārŏ k<u>àm</u> bā yằ jî	This boy is really naughty. (lit. doesn't listen)

3. MULTIPLE MODAL PARTICLES

Sentences readily occur with more than one modal particle, e.g.,

in kò̱ sarkī mā̱ yā ci, duk ɗaya nè̱	If however the king wins, it's all the same.
kai fa, zā kà biyā kō kùwā?	Hey you, are you going to pay or not?
Bellò yā dai sàci ƙwai kuma	Bello in fact stole eggs again.
wâutā nè̱ kàm wai kà ƙi biyàn hàr̃ājìn dà wuri fa	
It is foolish that you would refuse to pay the taxes early.	
àmmā nī dai, sai ìn cê wàtàkīlà̱ mā̱ sunà̱ dà māgànin sàndan nàn	
But as for me, then I said perhaps they have a solution for this stick (i.e., this beating).	
zân nūnà̱ fa matà kùwa takàr̃dâr̃ wani lōkàcī	
I will indeed show her the letter moreover sometime.	

It is even possible to string a number of modal particles in succession one after the other, e.g.,

sū dai kàm, sunà̱ mārìnā	As for them, they were slapping me.
nī mā̱ fa, dâ kàmar̃ hakà na ganī	I too had earlier got essentially the same impression.
dâ mā̱ dai, bà̱ kyânwā tā cī kà ba	In fact, it was never the case that the cat ate you
Audù fa dai kàm, yakàn màkarà	As for Audu, yes indeed he comes late.
kō kùwa mā̱ dai, kà bâ Audù wuƙâr̃ yà yankè̱ àbîn dà kânsà	
Or else, why not simply give Audu the knife so that he can cut off the thing himself.	

The following sentence, though clearly a tour de force, is considered to be grammatical:

nī kò̱ kàm dai mā̱ fa, zân tàfi kùwā?	Do I really feel like going though?

4. SYNTACTIC POSITION OF OCCURRENCE

What characterizes MPs as opposed to items belonging to other word classes is the considerable syntactic freedom regarding where they can be used, and the fact that in many (but not all) cases, the exact placement of the particle has very little effect on the meaning. Consider the following:

Sulè mā̱ bài faɗà̱ wà mầtar̃sà ba	Sule too didn't tell his wife.
Sulè bài mā̱ faɗà̱ wà mầtar̃sà ba	Sule didn't even tell his wife.
Sulè bài faɗà̱ wà mā̱ mầtar̃sà ba	Sule didn't even tell his wife.
Sulè bài faɗà̱ wà mầtar̃sà mā̱ ba	Sule didn't tell even his wife.
Sulè bài faɗà̱ wà mầtar̃sà ba mā̱	Sule didn't tell his wife even.

MPs cannot, however, occur just anywhere. There are some syntactic positions where MPs typically occur and others where they may not occur. (The following outline is intended to be illustrative, not exhaustive.)

4.1. *Verbal sentences*

In verbal sentences, MPs commonly occur (a) between the subject and the person-aspect-complex (PAC), and (b) between the PAC (with optional diminutive ɗan 'a little') and the VERB (where the VERB can be a finite verb or a verbal noun), e.g.,

(a) Mūsā dai yā san Abdù	Musa indeed knows Abdu.
àbò̱kansù mā̱ sunà̱ sàurāren r̃ēdiyò̱	Their friends too are listening to the radio.
(b) Mūsā yā dai san Abdù	Musa truly knows Abdu.
àbò̱kansù sunà̱ mā̱ sàurāren r̃ēdiyò̱	Their friends too are listening to the radio.

yanà <u>fa</u> sôntà	He does love her.
kù ɗan <u>dai</u> jūrè kàɗan, kù ga tàwa dàbāràř	Be patient a little bit more and hear my plan.
(lit. you (pl.) little MP forbear a little...)	

In HAVE sentences, the MP occurs naturally between the PAC and the **dà** + NP phrase, e.g.,

yanà <u>kuma</u> dà wani àku	He also had another parrot.
inà <u>kùwa</u> dà râi	I am moreover still alive. (lit. ...with life)
bâ ta <u>kò̃</u> dà niyyàř fìtā	She had no intention of going out.

Whether an MP can or cannot be inserted between the components of the PAC depends on how tightly they are bonded. Insertion is allowed with the future and allative markers and, for some speakers, with the habitual, but not with the other TAMs, including formations with the initial negative marker, e.g.,

wani mùtûm zā <u>fa</u> yà sàyi dōkìn	Some man will indeed buy the horse. (fut)
(cf. **wani mùtûm zâi sàyi dōkìn** with the common contraction of **zā** 'fut' + **yà** 'he')	
zâ <u>dai</u> ta gidā	She going home. (allat)
mùtumìn yā <u>kò̃</u> kàn sàyi àlbasà	The man buys onions. (hab)
not ** su <u>kuma</u> -nà̃ sàyensù	They are buying them. (cont)
not **yāròn dà su <u>fa</u> -kà kāmà̃	the boy that they caught (pret)
not **Hàdīzà bà <u>kò̃</u> tà fìta ba	Hadiza did not however go out. (Ncomp)
not **Mùsùlmī bā <u>mā</u> sà̃ cîn nāmàn àladè	Muslims don't eat pork. (Ncont)

The prohibitive marker **kadà**, which serves inter alia to form negative imperatives, is structurally a separate word that readily welcomes an MP, e.g.,

kadà <u>fa</u> kà taɓà shi!	Don't dare touch it!
...kadà <u>dai</u> ìn sâ musù cùtā	...lest I actually cause them harm
tàmbàyi duk àbîn dà kakè bùkātà̃, (don) kadà <u>kùwa</u> kù rūɗè!	
Ask whatever you need, lest you get confused!	

°AN: The marker **kadà** is commonly shortened to **kâř**, e.g., **kadà kà taɓà shi** 'Don't touch it' = **kâř kà taɓà shi**. My impression is that the short form is less preferred when followed by an MP; but this needs to be verified.

MPs can also be inserted between a transitive (or efferential) verb and its NP d.o. (even when they have an idiomatic meaning). The verb appears in its pre-noun d.o. C-form. Examples:

sun shā <u>mā</u> giyà̃	They even drank beer.
mun kāwō <u>fa</u> màkàmai	We indeed brought weapons.
yā jā <u>kò̃</u> kûnnentà, àmmā bà tà yàřda ba	He really warned her but to no avail.
(< **jā kûnnē** warn (lit. pull ear))	
yā ga <u>kuma</u> irìn kāyàyyākîn dà kè ciki	He saw also the kind of goods that were inside.
tā tàmbàyi <u>kùwa</u> mà̃tâř	She moreover asked the woman.

Because direct object pronouns are clitics, they cannot be separated from the verb by an MP. Sentences like ****yā tàmbàyē <u>kùwa</u> tà** 'He asked her' or ****mun kāwō fa sù** 'We brought them' are thus totally ruled out.

The MP is allowed only between a finite verb and its NP d.o. It cannot be inserted between a verbal noun and its object (which structurally form a genitive relationship). Such sentences as **yanà shân mā̀ giyà** 'He is even drinking beer' or **tā dingà tàmbayàr̃ kùwa mātā̀** 'She moreover kept on asking the woman' are ungrammatical.

Grade 5 verbs, which require the particle **dà** before an object, and sociative verbs, which also use **dà** (either the same particle or a homophonous preposition) permit insertion of the MP either before or after the **dà**, although the position after is preferred, e.g.,

yā saya r̃ dà <u>dai</u> mōtà̀	He sold the car. (gr5)
tā kōya r̃ <u>fa</u> dà ɗàlibai	She taught the students. (gr5)
sun sàdu dà <u>dai</u> sarkī	They met the chief. (soc)
sun gaisà̀ <u>kuma</u> dà jūnā	They also greeted each other. (soc)
kì lùr̃a <u>fa</u> dà ƙawar̃kì	Look after your friend. (soc)

°AN: True prepositions other than **dà** also allow insertion of an MP between the preposition and its object, e.g., **à <u>dai</u> wannàn hālī dà takè ciki** 'in this situation that she is in'.

4.2. Indirect objects

MPs are allowed between the i.o. marker **wà** and its object (although examples are not frequent), e.g.,

Sulè bài faɗà̀ wà <u>mā̀</u> màtar̃sà ba	Sule didn't even tell his wife.
yā r̃ubùtā wà <u>kuma</u> Audù wàsīƙà	He also wrote a letter to Audu.
kà kaucè wà <u>dai</u> mahàukàcin nàn!	Avoid this madman!

An MP cannot, however, be inserted between the i.o. marker **ma-** and its pronoun object, e.g., **matà** 'to her', because they constitute indivisible words.

It has been claimed, e.g., by Parsons (1963: 172) and many people following him, that absolutely nothing can separate a verb from a following indirect object, including an MP. This assertion turns out to be inexact (Newman 1991b; Jaggar and Munkaila 1995) (see discussion in §39:3). Whereas MPs do not normally occur between a verb and an i.o., a variety of native speakers do accept some instances of monosyllabic MPs (particularly **fa**) in the position between a verb and an i.o., e.g.,

ya zābur̃ō <u>fa</u> masà	He jumped up on him.
nā mayar̃ <u>fa</u> masà kuɗinsà	I really did return the money to him.
Har̃ū yā nūnà̀ <u>fa</u> wà yārinyà̀ hòtō	Haru showed the girl the picture.
yā r̃ubùtā <u>dai</u> wà Mammàn wàsīƙà̀	He did write a letter to Mamman.

4.3. Question words

Sentence-initial Q-words occur comfortably with MPs, e.g.,

wànē nè <u>kùwa</u> ya fi ƙarfī?	Who is the strongest?
wàcè màtā <u>kàm</u> kukà zō dà ita?	Which woman did you come with?
yà̀yà̀ <u>kuma</u> zā kà biyā kuɗin makar̃antā?	How also are you going to pay the school fees?
yàushè <u>fa</u> sukà tāshì?	When in fact did they leave?
don mè <u>dai</u> sukà rufè hanyà̀?	How is it that they closed the road?
ìnā <u>fa</u> zân yàr̃da?	There's no way I would agree to that!
(lit. where **fa** fut.I agree)	

4.4. Existential and presentational sentences

Existential and presentational sentences allow an MP before or after the predicate, e.g.,

àkwai <u>dai</u> shìnkāfā = àkwai shìnkāfā <u>dai</u>	There is rice.
àkwai tà dai There is some. (lit. it) (but not **àkwai dai tà, because tà is a clitic pronoun)	
bābù <u>kùwa</u> wata dàbārà	There is no other solution.
àkwai fa	There is.
bābù fa	There is not.
gằ <u>kuma</u> zāfī	Here is also heat.
gằ shi nân <u>kùwa</u>	Here he is however.

4.5. Topicalization

One important function of MPs is to set off topicalized NPs (§72:2), e.g.,

Bellò <u>kùwa</u>, gằ dai àlāmằ zā à zằɓē shì
       As for Bello, there is indeed indication that they will choose him.

Bintà <u>dai</u>, nā jī tà tanà minshārī à ɗākì	As for Binta, I heard her snoring in the room.
nī <u>mā</u>, zân shìga takařā	I too, I will enter the competition.
kyàutā dai, 'yam-mātā sun fi sôn 'yan-kunne	As for presents, young women prefer earrings.
mū fa, bà zā mù sàmi kōmē ba	As for us, we're not going to get anything.

     °AN: When occurring with topics, the exclamation **ai** patterns with the MPs, e.g., **Kànde ai, inà tàusàyintà** 'Oh Kande, I feel sorry for her.'

4.6. Complementation

Another function of MPs is to set off and qualify a complement-taking expression, e.g.,

dōlè nē fa mù gyārà halinmù
       It is necessary that we better ourselves.

wâutā nề kàm wai kà ƙi biyàn hàřājìn dà wuri fa
       It is foolish that you refuse to pay the taxes early.

yā kàmātā kùwa yâran nàn sù yi aurē bana
       It is desirable really that these children get married this year.

yanà dà muhimmancì kùwa mù gamà aikìn ban dà daɗèwā
       It is important that we finish the work without delay.

4.7. Within an NP

MPs are permitted within an NP after the head noun and before modifiers, e.g.,

rìgā <u>fa</u> farā <u>kùwa</u> kyàkkyāwař gàske	a white and moreover very beautiful gown
abūbuwà <u>dai</u> na adō	things for adornment

One position where MPs occur naturally is between a head noun and a relative clause, e.g.,

lōkàcîn <u>kùwa</u> dà sukà zō	the time moreover that they came
būlālàř <u>mā</u> dà mukè tsòrō	a whip also that we are fearing
rìgâř <u>fa</u> dà yakè dà ita	the gown that he indeed has
àku <u>dai</u> dà sarkī ya naɗà wàzīřì	a parrot that the chief appointed as vizier

Another place where MPs occur readily is after the conjunction in a phrase with conjoined NPs or modifiers, e.g.,

gērō dà <u>kuma</u> dāwằ	millet and also guinea corn
Bàlā dà <u>dai</u> Mūsā	Bala and Musa
gàjērē àmmā <u>kồ</u> dà ƙarfī	short but however strong (lit. with strength)

A few prehead specifiers like the isolator ɗaya (lit. 'one') and independent possessive pronouns can be separated from the head by an MP, e.g.,

ɗaya <u>dai</u> yāròn zâi zō gòbe	The other boy will come tomorrow.
duk <u>dai</u> cikin wannàn hālī	all (people) in this situation
tằwa <u>fa</u> bùdurwâr tā tàfi ƙauyè	My sweetheart (lit. mine **fa** friend) went to the village.

Within an NP one cannot, however, insert an MP between a determiner and the head. Nor can one use an MP between a prenominal adjective or diminutive (both of which contain a linker) and the head. Thus, such phrases as the following are all unacceptable: ****wani fa mùtûm** 'some **fa** man'; ****kōwàcè dai yārinyằ** 'every **dai** girl'; ****wannàn kuma mōtằ** 'this **kuma** car'; **** 'yař dai rìgā** 'small **dai** gown'; ****ɗan kàm zākì** 'small **kàm** lion'; ****dōgon fa mùtumìn** 'tall **fa** man'.

> °AN: Inkelas (1988) contends that it is possible to insert **fa** between an adjective and a head noun under certain circumstances. She claims (p. 381) that the following sentence, for example (given in standard orthography), is acceptable: **sabon fa littafi ya yi tsada** 'The new book is expensive.' I have not been able to find a native Hausa speaker whose judgments coincide with the claims of this paper. The general rule seems to be that MPs are disallowed inside genitive X.L N constructions whether the X is an adjective, e.g., **sābo.n** (**MP) **littāfì** 'new book', a verbal noun, e.g., **nēma.n** (**MP) **aikì** 'seeking work', or a common noun, e.g., **màta.ř** (**MP) **mālàm** 'teacher's wife'.

4.8. Adverbials and exclamations
MPs occur comfortably after sentence initial adverbials, exclamations, and such, e.g.,

wàshègàrī <u>dai</u> yā jē fādà	The next day he went to the palace.
lallē <u>kùwa</u> yanằ dà àbin hannū	Definitely he is rich.
dà farkō <u>dai</u> inằ sô kù shārè ɗākìn	To begin with I want you to sweep the room.
ā'ằ, ai <u>kồ</u> gàskiyařsà	No, well however he's right.
hakà <u>kuma</u> shùgàbā yā yi màganằ à kântà	Thus also the president spoke about it.
wàllāhì <u>kùwa</u> kā yi lâifī	By God you have made a mistake.

[Reference: The definitive study of modal particles, on which this chapter has drawn heavily, is the master's thesis of Schmaling (1991).]

47. Mutuality

THERE are two suffixes that are used to form nouns indicating mutuality or reciprocity: -ayyā)^{LHL} and -ēCēniyā)^{LHHLH}, e.g., sàrayyà 'mutual slashing, accusing' (< sārè 'slash'); màrērēnìyā 'mutual slapping' (< màrā 'slap'). With a few exceptions, the derivatives are formed from verbal stems. The derived nouns are all feminine. The two suffixes have overlapping, but not identical, meanings and lexical membership.

1. MUTUALITY-1: -ayyā)^{LHL}

This semiproductive derivational class is formed by adding a tone-integrating suffix -ayyā)^{LHL} to the base. (In terms of pronunciation the short /a/ is phonetically raised in the environment of the following /yy/, i.e., bùgayyà 'exchange of blows', for example, sounds something like [bùgeyyà], or [bùgeiyà] rather than [bùgayyà].) Monoverbs insert an epenthetic /y/ before the suffix, e.g.,

àikayyà	mutual sending of messages < àikā send
bàyayyà	mutual giving < bā give
dàuràtayyà	being side by side, close to each other < dàuratà be close by
gàbzayyà	struggle or fight that involves hitting < gàbzā hit
hùjjàtayyà	laying down mutual conditions < hujjàtā set conditions
jàyayyà	controversy, dispute, discord < jā pull
kàrɓayyà	mutual relieving (e.g., two carriers of a load) < kàrɓā receive
ƙìyayyà	hatred < ƙi refuse, hate
rìbɗayyà	severely hitting each other < ribɗà hit
Irregular: zàntàkayyà	mutual conversation (< base *//zantak-// < zântā converse)

The form àuràtayyà 'marriage relationship, intermarriage' (= àurayyà) is built on an abstract verbal base //aurat-// containing the verbalizing suffix -TA derived from aurē 'marriage', which itself is a verbal noun from the verb àurā 'marry'. Similarly, bàřkàtayyà 'mutual congratulations' is built on a generally nonoccurring verbal base //bařkat-//, derived from the Arabic loanword bařkà 'blessing'.

A few mutuality forms are built directly on nouns rather than verbs. These are clearly recent analogical creations as indicated by the fact that they are not cited in the major dictionaries.

hàlayyà living conditions, behavior or attitude (of people) < **halī** character, condition
cìnìkayyà mutual trading < **cìnikī** trade
(e.g., **àkwai cìnìkayyà tsàkānin Amìřkà dà Jàpân** There is trade between America and Japan.)

Although -ayyā typically connotes mutuality or reciprocity, in some words it has become lexically frozen with a set meaning where the interactive element is minimal or nonexistent. The word **bìyayyà** 'obedience, loyalty' (< **bi** 'follow'), for instance, denotes something that is always unidirectional, from a subordinate to a superior. Similarly, **sàyayyà** 'a purchase' (< **sàyá** 'buy') does not mean mutual buying by two or more persons, but rather an individual's unidirectional purchase. Other examples of mutuality forms with essentially fixed meanings include **fìyayyà** (less common than the equivalent **fìfìkò**) 'superiority' (< **fì** 'exceed'); **tàrayyà** 'federation, confederation, partnership' (< **tārà** 'collect together'); **sàkayyà** 'reward or punishment' (< **sākà** 'pay back in kind'); **tsàyayyà** 'perseverance' (< **tsayà** 'stop, stand').

2. MUTUALITY-2: -ēCēniyā)^{LHHLH}

This variant is formed by adding the suffix -ēCēniyā)^{LHHLH}, with a fixed L-H-H-L-H tone pattern, where the C represents a copy of the base-final consonant. The -ē of the suffix conditions automatic palatalization. Examples:

gàjējēnìyā	several persons alternately inheriting from each other collaterally < **gàdā** inherit
gùrmùjējēnìyā (= **gùrmùzayyà**)	struggling together (e.g., wrestling) < **gùrmuzà** overpower
jìbgēgēnìyā (= **jìbgayyà**)	beating of one another by two or more persons < **jìbgā** beat
màrērēnìyā	mutual slapping < **màrā** slap
rùngùmēmēnìyā	mutual embracing < **rùngumà** embrace
yàřjējēnìyā	mutual consent, agreement < **yàřda** agree

◊HN: Originally, the suffix probably had the shape -ēCēne)^{LHHL} although the derived words were all grammatically feminine. The -ìyā ending would have appeared later when grammatically feminine words in the language underwent overt characterization (see §31:4), e.g., *[**jìbgēgēnè**]$_f$ + -ā 'feminative marker' > **jìbgēgēnìyā** 'mutual beating'.

2.1. Variant with gemination

The -ēCēniyā suffix has a variant form -aCCēniyā (with a geminate consonant). This is preferred in some dialects. (The exact geographical distribution is not known.) The tone and prosodic structure of the two variants are identical, e.g.,

bùgaggēnìyā = **bùgēgēnìyā**	exchanging blows
màrarrēnìyā = **màrērēnìyā**	mutual slapping of one another
ràntsattsēnìyā = **ràntsētsēnìyā**	competing in swearing

The surface form -aCCēniyā comes from -eCCēniyā (< -ēCēniyā) with centralization of the short /e/ to /a/ in closed syllables. This is shown by the fact that in the geminate variant, the stem-final consonant that occurs before the surface /a/ still shows the effects of the conditioned palatalization rule, e.g.,

gàbjajjēnìyā (< **gàbjejjēnìyā**) (not ****gàbzajjēnìyā**) = **gàbjējēnìyā**
        struggle or fight that involves hitting (cf. **gàbzayyà**)
tùrmùshasshēnìyā (not ****tùrmùsasshēnìyā**) = **tùrmùshēshēnìyā**
        struggling on ground by two or more persons

3. COMPARISON OF MUTUALITY-1 AND MUTUALITY-2

Some stems occur with both suffixes with essentially identical meanings, e.g.,

bùgayyà	= bùgēgēnìyā	hitting each other
jìbgayyà	= jìbgēgēnìyā	hitting each other
kàrɓayyà	= kàrɓēɓēnìyā	taking turns in work or carrying load
kìrɓayyà	= kìrɓēɓēnìyā	pounding on one another
yàƙayyà	= yàƙēƙēnìyā	battling each other, mutual warfare

Some words occur with only one suffix or the other. Monoverbs, for example, occur only with the -ayyā suffix. (The only exception, if it in fact is one, is bàyēyēnìyā (?) = bàyayyà (< bā 'give'), which the dictionaries give with the meaning of 'bickering, mutual recriminations', but which is now not known.) Similarly, denominal verb stems with the -TA suffix appear to be limited to -ayyā. Other restrictions would appear to be lexically or semantically determined, e.g.,

(a) -ayyā only:

sòyayyà	love, mutual affection (*not* = **sòyēyēnìyā)
àuràtayyà	intermarriage
cìnìkayyà	mutual trading
sànayyà	mutual acquaintance

(b) -ēCēniyā (= -aCCēniyā) only:

ɗàukēkēnìyā	carrying one another competitively (*not* = **ɗàukayyà)
ràntsētsēnìyā	competing in swearing to testify to one's truthfulness
tùnkùɗēɗēnìyā	repeated pushing away of each other

Semantically, the two mutuality derivations differ somewhat. In the first place, it is only with -ayyā forms that one finds such words as bìyayyà 'obedience' and sàyayyà 'purchase(s)' without the mutuality connotation. With -ēCēniyā forms, the mutual, interactive meaning is always prominent. Moreover, words with the -ēCēniyā suffix often entail the notion of competition, i.e., they connote mutual activity in a competitive mood. A word like tàrayyà 'federation', which implies mutual cooperation, would thus not be expected to have a corresponding **tàrērēnìyā form. Consider the following, as well as the examples in (b) above:

cùɗayyà	mutual interraction, intimacy, washing one another's backs
cf. cùɗēɗēnìyā	rubbing up against and pushing one other
gìlmayyà	constantly passing across something
cf. gìlmēmēnìyā	passing each other competitively
àikayyà	mutual commissioning
cf. àikēkēnìyā	sending one another repetitively

48. Names (Proper Nouns)

TO quote Quirk et al. (1985: 288): "Proper nouns are basically names of specific people…, places…, months…, days…, festivals…, magazines…, and so forth." This section focuses on personal names and place names, with a brief listing of names for days of the week and months of the year.

In Hausa, proper nouns differ from common nouns not only semantically/lexically but also phonologically, particularly with regard to final vowel length. Whereas common nouns (apart from many loanwords) normally end in a long final vowel, proper nouns very often have a short final vowel, the pattern varying from one subclass of proper nouns to another. (Transcription note: The tap/rolled rhotic is normally transcribed in this grammar with a tilde, i.e., ř. With proper names, initial ř is transcribed as simply capital **R** without the diacritic, e.g., **Rāshà** = /řāshà/ 'Russia'.)

1. PERSONAL NAMES

Personal names can be classified into two main categories, which one can call (1) birth names (**sūnan yankā**), i.e., primary given names, and (2) everyday names (**sūnan rānā**), i.e., descriptive names, titles, nicknames, etc.

1.1. Birth names (**sūnan yankā**)

A week after a child is born he/she is given an "Islamic name" (derived from Arabic) at an official naming ceremony. At the ceremony, prayers are offered and a ram is slaughtered, thus the designation **sūnan yankā**, lit. name of slaughtering.

> °AN: This description applies to the overwhelming major of Hausas who are Muslim. As far as I am aware, the naming pattern for Hausas who are Christian or adherents of traditional religion has not been studied in detail.

The label "Islamic name" includes **Mùhammadù** (Muhammad), the names of members of the Prophet Muhammad's family, e.g., **Hàdīzatù** (one of the Prophet's wives) or **Zàinabù** (one of the Prophet's daughters), and other people involved in the emergence of Islam. It also includes the names of major figures in the Old and New Testaments like **Sāřatù** (Sarah) and **Īsā** (Jesus).

A number of male Islamic names are derived from the ninety-nine names and epithets of God preceded by the formative **Àbdùl** 'servant of' (where the final /l/ often forms a geminate with the following consonant). Examples include: **Àbdùllāhì, Àbdùlhàmîd, Àbdùlkādìř, Àbdùřřàhîm, Àbdùssàlāmù**.

The most common Islamic male name is **Mùhammadù**, often used in combination with other names serving to extol attributes of the Prophet, e.g., **Mùhammadù Kàbīřù** (Muhammad the Great), **Mùhammadù Àmīnù** (Muhammad the Faithful), etc. The name **Mùhammadù** is also commonly accompanied by a second name indicating a chronological order of the children in a family named Muhammad, e.g.,

Mùhammadù Àuwalù	Muhammad the first
Mùhammadù Sāni	Muhammad the second
Mùhammadù Sālisù	Muhammad the third
Mùhammadù Rābi'ù	Muhammad the fourth
Mùhammadù Hāmisù	Muhammad the fifth
Mùhammadù Sādisù	Muhammad the sixth
Mùhammadù Sābi'ù	Muhammad the seventh
Mùhammadù Sāminù	Muhammad the eighth
Mùhammadù Tāsi'ù	Muhammad the ninth
Mùhammadù Ashiřù	Muhammad the tenth

Persons with two names, like **Mùhammadù Àmīnù** or **Mùhammadù Sāni**, may be known (a) by both names, (b) by **Mùhammadù** (or one of its variants), or (c) by the second name.

Other common male names are **Àli** (son in law of the Prophet) and **Ìbřāhìm** (Abraham). Common female names include **Ā'ìshatù** (one of the Prophet's wives) and **Hàuwa** (Eve).

As a general rule, proper names ending in L tone have a short final vowel. (The name **Daudà** 'David' is an exception). Names ending in H tone have a long vowel if the vowel is -/ā/; otherwise the final vowel is usually short. (The name **Hàuwa** 'Eve' is an exception). (The correlation between tone and final vowel length is illustrated in the doublet **Amīnà = Amìnā**.) Examples: (Where the name has a common English equivalent, this is provided.)

Male names: **Àdàmu** (Adam); **Fàřuɓù = Fàřukù**; **Hāfizù**; **Hàlīlù**; **Hasàn** (first-born twin); **Hùsainì** (second-born twin); **Īsā** (Jesus); **Isiyākù** (Isaac); **Ìsmā'īlù**; **Jìbìřīlù** (Gabriel); **Mùhammadù** (Muhammad); **Mūsā** (Moses); **Nuhù** (Noah); **Sulèmānù** (Solomon); **Tànīmù**; **Yàɓubù = Yàkubù** (Jacob); **Yūsufù** (Joseph); **Zùbairù**

Female names: **Ā'ìshatù**; **Fādîmatù**; **Hàdīzatù**; **Hàfsatù**; **Hàlīmà**; **Hànsatù**; **Hàuwa** (Eve); **Mařyamù** (Mary); **Ràhīlā** (Rachael); **Rakìyā**; **Ruɓàyyatù**; **Sāřatù** (Sarah); **Zàinabù**

°AN: Hausa spelling is normally narrowly phonemic. Some proper names, however, have special orthographic forms that deviate from the phonology, e.g., Mustapha = /Mustàfā/, Ahmad = /Āmàd/, Mahmudu = /Màmūdù/, Mohammed = /Mùhammàd/, Muhtari = /Mùktāři/. The spelling of names with medial /auwa/ varies according to individual preference, e.g., Hauwa = Hawwa, Auwal = Awwal, etc.

1.2. Gender

Some names are limited to one sex. For example, **Daudà**, **Hařūnà**, and **Yūsufù** are strictly male names whereas **Bintà**, **Hàdīzà**, and **Mařyàm** are names for females. Generally speaking the sex referent of the name is not immediately evident from the form, cf. **Mùhammadù** m. and **Zàinabù** f., both of which end in low-tone /ù/. The major exceptions are Arabic-derived names with overt feminine suffixes, specifically (a) the well-recognized optional suffix **-atù** and (b) the lexically more restricted frozen suffix **-iyyā** (with an associated L-H-H melody). Examples:

(a) **Fādîmatù, Hàdīzatù, Hànnatù, Ruɓàyyatù, Sà'ādatù, Sàlāmatù, Wàsīlatù, Zàhàřatù**

(b) **Fàuziyyā** (< Ar. *fauz* success, victory, achievement, triumph), **Hàbàsiyyā** (= **Hàbàshiyyā**) (probably < Abyssinia (*Habasha*)), **Màřaɓìsiyyā** (probably < Marakesh), **Màřàliyyā** (< Ar. *Maradhiyyah* (< *ridha* fidelity), **Sà'àdiyyā** (< Ar. *Sa'adiyyah* wet nurse of the Prophet Muhammad (< Sa'ad place name), **Shàmsiyyā** (< Ar. *shams* sun(light))

Some names, on the other hand (whether **sūnan yankā** or **sūnan rānā**), have distinct masculine and feminine counterparts. Most often the masculine form can be taken as basic and the corresponding feminine name suffixes -**ā** (which in some cases replaces the original vowel and in other cases is added to it). Occasionally the counterparts have unsystematic tonal differences as well. Examples:

Male	*Female*
Àlhajì	Hajìyā
Àmīnù	Amīnà = Amìnā
Bàlāřabè	Bàlāřabà
Bàtūřè	Bàtūřìyā
Hàlīřù	Hàlīřā
Hasàn (= Àlhasàn)	Hasànā (not = **Àlhasànā)
Jàmīlù	Jamīlā
Shèkàrau	Shēkārā

In other cases, the masculine still can be taken as basic (whether morphologically simple or not) but the feminine is formed not by a simple addition of -**ā** but by some other kind of morphological process, e.g.,

Male	*Female*
Jàtau	'Yař-ja
Màntau	Àmânta (lit. one should forget) (both from **mântā** forget)
Bàrau	Bàraukà
Àbařshì (lit. leave him)	Àbařtà (lit. leave her)
Masàllàcī (lit. one who prays)	Tasallà (lit. of prayer)
Sīdì	Tasīdì (lit. of Sidi)

With some names, primarily names based on days of the week or other time periods, the feminine form is the one that is basic and the corresponding masculine is built using the formative **Dan** (lit. son of). These names are sometimes spelled as two words, sometimes as one, but the convention is not fixed. Examples:

Female	*Male*
Àsàbe	Dan Àsàbe (cf. Àsabař Saturday)
Azùmi	Dan Azùmi (cf. **azùmī** fasting (during the month of Ramadan))
Jummai	Danjūmà (cf. **Jumma'à** Friday)
Làdì	Danlādì (pronounced [ɗallādì]) (cf. **Lahàdì** Sunday)
Màřka	Dan Màřka (cf. **màřkā** wettest part of rainy season)

Finally, there are names, mostly descriptive **sūnan rānā**, which are gender neutral, e.g.,

Cì-tumù m./f.	name for child born at the end of the rainy season
Cindò m./f.	name for child born with a sixth finger
Gàmbo m./f. (usu. m.)	name for child born after twins
Kòsau m./f.	name for child born at harvest time
Shànōnò m./f.	name for child born at same time as a new calf
Yauci m./f.	name for child born after parents have been planning to divorce

1.3. Short forms

In English, many names have short variants, e.g., Jonathan ⇒ John, Frederick ⇒ Fred, Montgomery ⇒ Monty, Rebecca ⇒ Reba or Beck, Elizabeth ⇒ Liz or Beth, Catherine ⇒ Cathy, etc. This is also the case in Hausa. As in English, many short-form names are created by chopping off the end of the word. Two shortening processes are more or less systematic; the others are idiosyncratic and unpredictable. The first regular process is the dropping of the suffix **-atù** in feminine names. The high-tone /a/ of the suffix is sometimes retained, sometimes replaced by a vowel different in tone, length, or quality, e.g.,

Ā'ìshatù ⇒	Ā'ìshā	Hàdīzatù ⇒	Hàdīzà
Hànnatù ⇒	Hànne	Rukàyyatù ⇒	Rukàyyā
Sār̀atù ⇒	Sār̀ai	Zàhàratù ⇒	Zàhàrā

The second general process is the dropping of final L tone **-ù**, which is primarily found with masculine names. When the vowel is deleted, the L tone remains and attaches to the preceding syllable, which produces a falling tone, except where the result would be H-F in which case the tone simplifies to H-L. (There are also other sporadic tone adjustments.) When the **-u** drops, the final syllable becomes closed, thereby causing automatic shortening of long vowels. Examples:

Àbdùlsàlāmù ⇒	Àbdùlsàlâm	Àmīnù ⇒	Àmîn
Fàrukù ⇒	Fàrûk	Kàbīrù ⇒	Kàbîr
Mùhammadù ⇒	Mùhammàd	Nāsirù ⇒	Nāsir̀
Ùsùmānù ⇒	Ùsmân	Yūsufù ⇒	Yūsùf
Àwwalù ⇒	Awwàl	Zàinabù ⇒	Zainàb

◊HN: At a synchronic level, the relation between pairs like **Nāsirù** and **Nāsir̀** is best viewed as final vowel dropping. At a deeper historical level, one could possibly argue that the form without the final vowel was original and that Hausa added the final **-ù** to avoid consonant final words.

If the consonant preceding the **-ù** is / '/ or /**h**/, it is dropped along with the vowel because these phonemes do not occur in word-final position e.g.,

Hàuwa'ù (f.) ⇒	Hàuwa	Sālihù ⇒	Sālè

°AN: Phonemically, final /'/ doesn't occur, although phonetically, short final vowels before pause are pronounced with a glottal closure, e.g., [nā ga hàuwa?] 'I saw Hauwa', cf. [hàuwa cè] 'It's Hauwa', [bà hàuwa ba cè] 'It's not Hàuwa'.

Sporadic dropping of nonfinal /'/ and /**h**/ is also found in short forms of names, e.g.,

Zàhàrā ⇒	Zàra	Ā'ìshā ⇒	Aishà (= Asshà)

In many cases, the relation between the full name and the short form is more idiosyncratic and involves greater deformation than just dropping a vowel or a suffix. (One can think here of Robert ⇒ Bob or Rebecca ⇒ Beck.) Here one commonly finds chopping of the beginning of the full name. The resulting short forms with final H tone often manifest a long final vowel even in the case of vowels other than /ā/ (cf. the pattern noted above with full names). Note that as with English names (e.g., Elizabeth ⇒ Liz or Beth) many names allow alternative short forms. Examples:

Ā'ìshatù ⇒   Ā'ì = Aishà (= Asshà) = Shatù (= Shàtu)
Àbdùllāhì ⇒   Abdù (= Audù)
Àbūbakàř ⇒   Àbū = Hàbū = Būbà = Bukàř
Bàlāřabè ⇒   Bàlā (but Bàlā is not used as short for the corresponding feminine name
           Bàlāřabà̀, whose short form is Lāřai)

Bìlƙīsù = Bìlkīsù (f.) ⇒ Bìlƙi   Fādîmatù ⇒   Fātimà = Fàtī
Hàdīzà ⇒   Dìje = Dīzà (= Dījà̀)   Hařūnà ⇒   Hařū
Hùsainì ⇒   Sàinō   Inūsà and Inuwà ⇒ Inū
Jìbìřīlù = Jìbìřîn ⇒ Jibò   Mařyàm = Mařyamà (f.) ⇒ Màiřo
Mùhammadù ⇒   Mùhammàn = Mammàn   Màmūdù ⇒   Mūdī
Mustàfā ⇒   Àlmu = Mùɗɗe   Sulèmānù ⇒   Sulè = Mānù
Ùsùmānù ⇒   Mānī = Mānù   Yūsufù ⇒   Yūsī
Zàinabù ⇒   Ābù (with long initial ā)

The commonly occurring names **Abdù** and **Audù** (with H-L tone) serve as short forms for all names beginning with **Àbdùl** (lit. servant of…), e.g., **Àbdùlƙādìř**, **Àbdùlsàlāmù**, etc.

°AN: The **Audù** pronunciation reflects the operation in some dialects of Klingenheben's Law, which changes syllable-final labials to /u/. Interestingly, even people who say **Audù** preserve the syllable-final /b/ in the longer **Àbdùl** names like **Àbdùllāhì**.

1.4. Plurals of names

One often thinks of names as referring to unique individuals. In appropriate contexts, however, proper names can be pluralized, like in English "There are five Tamaras in my class." Only three plural markers are employed. By far the most common plural formative used with proper names is -ōCī. The -ai suffix comes in a distant second (mainly with longer names), and the -unà̀ suffix (limited to disyllabic names) is the least common. (Many of the names forming plurals with -ai or -unà̀ allowed -ōCī as an alternative.) Examples:

Àlmu pl. Almōmī   Àsàbe pl. Asabōbī
Hamīdù pl. Hamīdōdī   Kumbula pl. Kumbulōlī
Mù'āzù pl. Mu'āzōjī   Shēkàrā pl. Shēkarōrī
Bàlāřabè pl. Bàlā̀řàbai   Bàshîř pl. Bàshîřai
Hàbîbà pl. Hàbîbai   Mùhammadù pl. Mùhàmmàdai
Ɗàlhā pl. Ɗalhunà̀   Kànde pl. Kandunà̀
Làmî pl. Lāmunà̀

°AN: I have seen no mention of plurals of proper nouns in the Hausa linguistic literature, so the description here is based strictly on my own preliminary investigations with a small number of speakers. What I am reporting is probably accurate in general, but one needs to keep in mind that the details have not been verified by careful checking in the field.

1.5. Everyday names: Morphophonological shape

All names apart from the true Islamic names can be grouped together as "everyday names" or "additional names". In Hausa these are called **sūnan rānā** (lit. name.of day) or **laƙàbī**. (The term **laƙàbī** is sometimes translated as 'nickname'; but these names are less casual and ephemeral than the term 'nickname' connotes.)

These everyday names are based on a variety of factors such as the time or occasion of a birth, the appearance of the baby, or some conventional connection between the additional name and the Islamic name. They can be described both in terms of their morphophonological makeup and in terms of the circumstances prompting their use.

Some everyday names are morphologically simple and basic, e.g., **Dèlu** (f.), **Gàmbo**, **Kànde** (f.) **Lēkò**, **Sambò**, **Tankò**; but most are morphologically derived in one way or another. Here are some of the more common processes.

1.5.1. Vowel shortening of common nouns

Many names are derived from common nouns by shortening the final vowel. Examples (with feminine names indicated as such):

Angò (cf. **angṑ**   groom)
Azùmi (f.) (cf. **azùmī**   (month of) fasting)
Bàƙo (cf. **bàƙō**   stranger, guest)
Dōgo (cf. **dōgō**   tall)
Gàjēre (cf. **gàjērē**   short)

Kàka (usu. f.) (cf. **kàkā**   harvest season)
Magàji (cf. **magàjī**   heir)
Màsōro (f.) (cf. **màsōrō**   small peppercorn)
Sābo (cf. **sābō**   new)
Yàlwa (usu. f.) (cf. **yàlwā**   abundance)

◊HN: At an earlier period, final vowels in Hausa were intrinsically short. Subsequently the final vowel of common nouns (and adjectives) underwent morphologically conditioned lengthening (see Greenberg 1978). This lengthening did not, however, apply to certain word classes like proper nouns or adverbs. Thus, from a historical perspective, such proper nouns as **Sābo** represent words that failed to undergo lengthening rather than words that actively undergo a process of shortening. Synchronically, however, the shortening rule is probably fully operative.

A few names preserve the long final vowel of the common noun, e.g., **Wàdā** (cf. **wàdā** 'wealth'), **Màimakō** (cf. **màimakō** 'substitution'), and in one case the proper name has a long vowel whereas the corresponding item (in this case an adjective) has a short vowel, e.g., **Bàbbā** (cf. **bàbba** 'big').

1.5.2. Suffix -au

Some names contain the derivational suffix -au)^{LH} (see chap. **10**), a suffix that is semantically hard to pin down but that generally indicates being characterized by properties or qualities or attributes of the underlying verb (or, rarely, noun). These are mostly masculine names, e.g.,

Gàgàrau (cf. **gàgarà**   be difficult)
Hàƙùrau (cf. **hàƙurà**   be patient)
Kòsau (cf. **ƙōsà**   be well fed)
Màntau (cf. **mântā**   forget)

Sàdau (m./f.) (cf. **sàdu**   get together)
Sàllau (cf. **sallà**   prayer, festival)
Shèkàrau (cf. **shèkarà**   spend the year)
Tùnau (cf. **tunà**   remember)

1.5.3. The genitive na/ta + N

A small number of phrasal names are built using the independent forms of the linker: **na** for male names and **ta** for female names. (As names, these phrases are sometimes written as one word, sometimes not.) Examples:

Na-Allàh m. / **Ta-Allàh** f. (lit. of God)
Namakà m. (lit. of Mecca)
Tasallà f. (lit. of the festival), cf. the corresponding masculine names **Sàllau** and **Masàllàci**
Tasīdì f. (lit. of **Sīdì**, where **Sīdì** is a masculine name)

1.5.4. The formative **mài** + N

Some names have the form of phrases consisting of **mài** 'possessor of, being characterized by' plus a common noun (see chap. **45**). These names are mostly masculine. A few names with final H tone -**a** and a light penultimate syllable have a long final vowel; all other names of this type have a short final vowel. As proper names, these phrases are usually written as one word. Examples:

Màiɗākì f. (cf. **ɗākì** room)	**Màigado** f. (cf. **gadō** throne)
Màigàri (cf. **gàrī** town)	**Màikuɗi** (cf. **kuɗī** money)
Màirìga (cf. **rìgā** gown, caul)	**Màitamā** (cf. **tamā** iron ore)
Màiwàdā (cf. **wàdā** wealth)	

1.5.5. Compounds with **ɗan**

As indicated above in §1.2, a number of feminine names, especially day names, have masculine counterparts built with the formative **ɗan** 'lit. son of', e.g.,

Danjūmà (cf. **Jummai** f.); **Danlādì** (cf. **Lādì** f.); **Dantàlā** (cf. **Tàlātù** f.)

The feminine counterpart of **ɗan**, namely **'yař**, occurs much less frequently in proper names; however, there are a few examples:

'Yař Fulàni f. (cf. **Fulànī** Fulani); **'Yař Sakkwato** f. (cf. **Sakkwato** Sokoto); **'Yař Ja** (with short final vowel) f. (cf. **Jàtau** name for a light-skinned male < **jā** red)

In addition to the compounds with **ɗan** and **'yař** illustrated above, one also finds names with **ɗan** and **'yař** operating in their role as diminutive markers, e.g.,

Dan Àutā	Little **àutā** 'youngest child'	**Danyàrò**	Little **yàrò** 'boy'
'Yař Bàtūřìyā	Little **Bàtūřìyā** 'European female'	**'Yař Gwaggò**	Little **gwaggò** 'aunt'

The feminine **'yař** may accompany a birth name, especially in the short form, e.g.,

'Yař Husè	Little **Husè** (< **Husàinā**)	**'Yař Sà'àde**	Little **Sà'àde** (< **Sà'ādatù**)

1.5.6. Verb-based compounds

Some names are compounds of the form V + NP (where the V is a monoverb that appears with low tone and a long vowel) or **à** (impersonal subjunctive wsp) + VP. Examples:

Bìsallà	lit. follow prayer	**Cìgàri**	lit. conquer town
Cìtumù m./f.	lit. eat roasted millet head	**Kìgijì** m./f.	lit. refuse home
Shàgàri	lit. drink flour	**Sògijì** m./f.	lit. love home
Àbařtà f.	lit. one should leave her (alone)	**Àjēfas**	lit. one should throw (it) out
Àmânta f.	lit. one should forget		

1.6. Everyday names: Semantic/pragmatic characteristics

Birth names (**sūnan yankā**), like first names in English, are typically given in honor of and in remembrance of a deceased relative. The everyday names, on the other hand, normally relate to real-world phenomena like the time or circumstances of a birth or the physical appearance of the baby. Some of these are given to a baby shortly after birth, whereas others are acquired at some later time in an individual's life. Here are selected categories.

1.6.1. Day names

There are specific names associated with the day of the week on which someone is born. Most of these names occur in feminine / masculine pairs. (Optional short forms for many of these names have been illustrated earlier.) Examples (f. / m):

Jummai / Ɗanjūmà	child born on Friday	(cf. **Jumma'à**	Friday)
Àsàbe / Dan Àsàbe	child born on Saturday	(cf. **Àsabàr̃**	Saturday)
Lādì / Ɗanlādì	child born on Sunday	(cf. **Lahàdì**	Sunday)
Àltìne / Dan Àltìne	child born on Monday	(cf. **Lìtìnîn**	Monday)
Tàlātù / Ɗantàlā	child born on Tuesday	(cf. **Tàlātà**	Tuesday)
Bàlār̃abà / Bàlār̃abè	child born on Wednesday	(cf. **Làr̃abā**	Wednesday)
Làmî / Ɗanlàmî	child born on Thursday	(cf. **Àlhàmîs**	Thursday)

In addition to the names built on the words for the days of the week, there are other names associated with particular days for semantic reasons. For example, a child born on Friday could be named **Àdàmu** 'Adam' or **Hàuwa** 'Eve' because this is the first day of the week. Or, a girl born on Tuesday could be named **Bàtūrìyā**, indicating that she is to be wealthy like a European girl. (This is based on the fact that the word **tàlātà** also means '3,000 cowries', which in olden days represented a large sum.)

1.6.2. Names relating to other times

Names may also be associated with other temporal periods. Examples (f. / m.):

Azùmi / Ɗan Azùmi (= Làbàr̃an)	child born during the month of Ramadan
Gànau m. (< **ganī** see)	child born at new moon
(= **Magàwatà** lit. one who sees moon)	
Kàka / Dan Kàka	child born at harvesttime
Kòsau m. (< **ƙōsà** be well-fed)	child born at harvesttime
Màr̃ka / Ɗan Màr̃ka	child born at height of the rainy season
(= **Anà-ruwa** lit. it is raining)	
Sàllau m.	child born during a festival
Shànōnò (f./m.) (lit. drink milk)	child (usually Fulani) born when a calf was being delivered
Yàlwa (f./m.)	child born during a bumper harvest

1.6.3. Names relating to birth sequence and related events

Names may refer to the sequence of a birth in relation to previous births (or miscarriages) that the mother has had or to other events associated with the birth, e.g.,

Bàrau (< **barì** leave)	name for boy born after many of mother's babies have died in infancy
Ɓōyì (< **ɓōyè** hide)	child born late after mother had given up hope of conceiving
Gàmbo	boy born after twins
Kyàuta	child born after years of childlessness (cf. **kyàutā** gift (from God))
Màyau (< **màyā** replace)	child born after death of father
Sambò	a second son
Talle / Ɗantalle	child being brought up by s.o. else because the mother has died
Tankò	son born after a succession of girls

A child born after a number of previous children have died young or who has been born to parents who have been childless for some time, due to miscarriage or the inability to conceive, may be given names like the following with hope that the child will survive. The purpose of such a name as **Àjēfas** m. (lit. one should throw (him) out), for example, is to indicate that it is not a good child and thus God should not want to take him. Examples:

Àbařshì m. / **Àbařtà** f.	(lit. one should leave him /her)
Àjūji f.	(lit. in the rubbish heap)
Bāwà m. / **Bâiwa** f.	(lit. slave (of God)
Dànganà m./f.	(lit. resignation)
Dògarà m./f.	(lit. dependence (on God))
Màntau m. (lit. forgetfulness) / **Àmânta** f. (lit. one should forget (her))	

In the case of twins, special birth names are assigned:

Hasàn m. / **Hasànā** f.	first-born twin
Hùsainì m. / **Husàinā** (= **Usàinā**) f.	second-born twin

1.6.4. Names relating to physical features

Names may refer to physical or other characteristics of a child (cf. the English nicknames Red and Shorty), e.g.,

Gàjēre	name for a short boy (cf. **gàjērē** short)
Hàƙùrau	name for a patient psn (cf. **hàƙùrī** patience)
Jàtau	name for light-skinned boy (cf. **jā** red)
Màsōro f.	name for a small woman (cf. **màsōrō** small peppercorn)
Samɓali m. / **Samɓalā** f.	name for a tall and good looking psn (cf. **samɓalī** tall, well formed)

1.6.5. Names derived from titles, occupations, kin terms, etc.

Titles, occupations, and kin terms may be employed as proper names, usually with shortening of the final vowel of the corresponding common noun, e.g.,

Angò	groom	**Dìllālì**	broker
Magàji m. / **Magājìyā** f.	heir	**Mainà**	prince
Sarki	chief	**Tēlà**	tailor
Wāli	head judge	**Zābìyā** f.	singer
Abbà	father	**Gwaggò** f.	aunt
Kāwù	uncle	**Uwa** f.	mother

°AN/ΔDN: In some, especially WH, areas, the word **magājìyā** is used for a madam who is the head of the prostitutes. As a result, the feminine name **Magājìyā** is avoided, although the masculine counterpart is still fully acceptable.

1.6.6. Names indicating ethnicity or place of origin

Ethnonyms formed with the prefix **bà-** or the proclitic **ɗan** / **'yař** function as everyday names, e.g.,

Bàgòbiřī m. / **Bàgòbiřā** f.	psn from Gobir (or of Gobir ancestry)
Ɗanfage m. / **'Yařfage** f.	psn from Fage quarter (in Kano)

| Ɗanfìlằni m. / 'Yaɽfìlằni f. | Fulani psn |
| Ɗanbàɽno m. / 'Yaɽbàɽno f. | psn from Borno (or of Borno ancestry) |

1.6.7. Names with fixed associations

Some names are regularly connected with specific Islamic names because of historical associations with certain renowned persons, e.g.,

Everyday name	*Associated birth name*
Gàgàrau (lit. unconquerable)	Àbūbakàɽ
Gìnsau (lit. abundance)	Haɽūnà
Mài-Kanò (lit. possessing Kano)	Àbdùllāhì
Mài-tùrằre (lit. possessing perfume)	Àbūbakàɽ
Mài-gado f. (lit. possessing throne/bed)	Bìlkīsù
Mālàmi (lit. scholar)	(Shēhù) Ùsùmānù
Sandà	Ùmmaɽù

1.7. Nicknames

Young, generally urban, males sometimes acquire nicknames (or "guy names") based on Western movie characters or sports stars or other English-related words or activities. These guy names usually accompany a person's real name(s). Examples:

Àmīnù Dìjangò <	Django (character in earlier Westerns)
Kàbīɽù Fēlè <	Pele (a soccer star)
Àmīnù Kīlằ <	killer
Bellò Chansin <	Chang Seng (a Chinese actor)

°AN: The names that young men adopt clearly reflect the dominant icons of the time. Notice that in spite of the religious disapproval of guy names they are still prevalent.

Other nicknames are joking names or playful names used among close friends or members of a club or group. These names are often facetious or sarcastic in nature. Interestingly, although they are based on common nouns, they have a long final vowel, e.g.,

Ɓàrāwò thief; Jāhìlī ignoramus; Ministằ (government) minister; Māyè witch; Sūfằ super

Although guy names and joking names are usually acquired by men and boys when they are young, they sometimes persist throughout life and thus one finds some older people (including a number of well-known individuals) who have retained these names as surnames. Examples:

Alh. Mūdī Sìpīkìn (a famous Hausa poet) < spic and span
Alh. Hālī Tàzân (a well-known advocate in Sokoto for children's (beggars') rights) < Tarzan
Audù Sìkāwùt < scout
Alh. Gaɽbà Tāgèt < Target brand cigarettes
Alh. Bùhāɽi Zōɽò < Zorro

1.8. Hypocoristics

Hypocoristic (henceforth HC) formation involves modification of a given name by affixation or reduplication in order to indicate attitudinal information about the affection of the speaker toward the person referred to. (In other languages, HC forms are referred to variously as pet names, terms of fondness and endearment, diminutives, effeminate diminutives, and familiarity markers.) Hypocoristics are used mainly by adults or older children in addressing or referring to younger children. The HC form may portray both the affection of the speaker as well as the diminutive nature of the referent. For example, **Sàlēle** connotes 'my dear little Sale'. (Although we have a fairly good understanding of the morphology of HC formation (Newman and Ahmad 1992), the pragmatic use of Hausa HCs in their cultural context remains to be studied.)

There are some seven different HC formations of greater or lesser productivity. Most apply to male as well as female names. Where names have short forms, the hypocoristics are usually built on these rather than on the full variants.

1.8.1. Suffixal reduplication -:CV)^{LHH}

In these HCs, the final syllable is copied, a long-short pattern is imposed on the identical vowels in the last two syllables, and a L-H-H melody is assigned to the resulting HC form. Examples:

Regular name	HC variant	Regular name	HC variant
Àlhajì	Àlhàjīji	Mùďďe	Mùďďēďe
Àmadù	Àmàdūdu	Sàlè	Sàlēle
Bintù f.	Bìntūtu f.	Ùbàlè	Ùbàlēle
Lādì f.	Làdīdi f.	Yārò	Yàrōro

If the final vowel of the regular name is -a(a), it reduplicates as -ēCe rather than -āCa, e.g.,

Regular name	HC variant	Regular name	HC variant
Bàlā	Bàlēle	Īlà	Ìlēle

These forms normally have a fixed L-H-H tone melody. Two names, both of which are disyllabic with a light initial syllable, do not use the melody but rather simply add an H-tone reduplicative suffix while preserving the base tone:

Regular name	HC variant	Regular name	HC variant
Inū	Inūnu	Kulù f.	Kulùlu f.

1.8.2. Suffix -:tī)^{LHH}

This formation involves addition of a tone-integrating suffix -:tī with a L-H-H melody. As with the previous class, the penultimate vowel (in all cases /a/) undergoes lengthening. Note that the suffixal /t/ preceding the high front vowel does not palatalize to /c/. Examples:

Regular name	HC variant	Regular name	HC variant
Abbà	Àbbātī	Ummà f.	Ùmmātī f.
Bàba	Bàbātī	Yàlwa m./f.	Yàlwātī (f. only)
Garɓà	Gàrɓātī		

1.8.3. Suffix -alō)^H = -alā)^H

This formation involves the addition of an all H suffix -alō or, less often, -alā. With the one i-final name, the suffix appears as -ilō. With the noun **Mammadù**, the stem-final consonant serves as part of the suffix in place of the /l/. Examples:

Regular name	HC variant	Regular name	HC variant
Bìntà f.	Bìntalō f.	**Mammàn**	**Mammalō**
Kànde f.	Kandalā f.	**Ā'ì** f.	**Ā'ilō** f.
Mammadù	Mammadō = Mammadā		
Jummai f.	Jummalō (= Jummàlā) f. (with aberrant tone)		

1.8.4. Suffix (-lle)^H

This formation involves the addition of an H-tone suffix -lle whose tone does not override the basic tones of the regular names. Two examples are slightly irregular.

Regular name	HC variant	Regular name	HC variant
Bàba	Bàballe	Hajìyā f.	Hajìyalle f.
Yā'ù	Yā'ùlle		
Àli	Àlilli	Kàbîr	Kàbille

1.8.5. Suffix -(:)le

This formation involves the suffixation of -le with an assortment of unpredictable tones. The length of the vowel preceding -le is generally determined by weight polarity, i.e., long if the preceding syllable is light and short if the preceding syllable is heavy; but there are a few exceptions. Examples:

Regular name	HC variant	Regular name	HC variant
Bàba	Bàbalè	Kàka m./f.	Kàkalè m.
Bāwà	Bāwale	Uwa f.	Uwàle f.
Gàmbo	Gambalè	Baffà	Baffàle

The HC form of the name **Àli** is **Alèle** with the stem-final vowel assimilating to the /ē/ of the suffix. Curiously, this is exactly the opposite of what happens with the -lle formation (namely, **Àli / Àlilli**) where the suffixal vowel assimilates to the stem-final vowel.

1.8.6. Suffix -ndi

Some three names have HC variants with a suffix -ndi. (With the n-final name, //nndi// simplifies to ndi). Although the sample is too small to be sure, it appears that there is an associated tone melody, which is L-H if the first syllable is heavy and all H if the first syllable is light. Examples (complete):

Regular name	HC variant	Regular name	HC variant
Bàba	Bàbàndi	Lawàn	Lawandi
Kàka m./f.	Kàkàndi (m. only)		

1.8.7. Suffix (-ùwā)^{LH}

This HC class consists almost exclusively of feminine names ending in -u. The L-H suffix -ùwā can be identified with the feminine suffix used elsewhere in the language, e.g., Bàkanò m. / Bàkanùwā f. 'a Kano man/Kano woman'; dùkūkù m. / dùkūkùwā f. 'glum, hesitant'.

Regular name	HC variant	Regular name	HC variant
Bìntūtu f.	Bìntūtùwā f.	Kulù	Kulùwā f.
Dūdù f	Dūdùwā f.	Shatù f	Shatùwā f.
Hànsatù f.	Hànsatùwā f.	Ùmmàr̄ūru m.	Ùmmàr̄ūrùwā m.

Two regular names with final L-H tone employ a suffix -**uwà** with H-L tone and a *short* final vowel, e.g.,

Regular name	*HC variant*	*Regular name*	*HC variant*
Kulùlu f.	**Kulùluwà** f.	**Kyàllu** f.	**Kyàlluwà** f.

A variant of the same suffix (-**iyà(a)**) appears with three names ending in -**le** (with variable tone):

Regular name	*HC variant*	*Regular name*	*HC variant*
Alèle (< //**Alìle**//) m.	**Alìliyà** m.	**Uwàle** f.	**Uwàliyà** f.
Ùbālè m.	**Ùbāliyà** m.		

1.8.8. Double hypocoristics

In a certain number of cases (some already illustrated), hypocoristics are built on names that are themselves already HC forms. The tone pattern of the doubly marked forms is determined by the rightmost formative. Examples:

Regular name	*HC variant-1*	*HC variant-2*
Iyà f.	**Ìyàle** f.	**Ìyàlēle** f.
Ùbā	**Ùbālè**	**Ùbàlēle**
Bintù f.	**Bìntūtu** f.	**Bìntūtùwā** f.
Kulù f.	**Kulùlu** f.	**Kulùluwà** f.
Ùmmarù	**Ùmmàrūru**	**Ùmmàrūrùwā**
Uwa f.	**Uwàle** f.	**Uwàliyà** f.

1.9. Surnames

Traditionally, Hausas did not have surnames comparable to English family names. A person would be known by his birth name plus his everyday name (e.g., **Hasàn Danlàmî**) or some other descriptor like an occupation, e.g., **Hasàn Mài Tùrārē** (Hassan the perfume seller); **Àlhajì Mūsā Mài Tāyà** (Alhaji Musa the tire dealer); **Audù Makèrī** (Audu the blacksmith—cf. all the Smiths in English!). Alternatively a man could be indicated as X (son) of Y, e.g., **Abdùn Bāwà** (Abdu (son) of Bawa); and a woman as X (wife) of Y, e.g., **Kulùn Shēkarè** (Kulu (wife) of Shekare).

Under English (and French) influence, especially as applied in Western-style schools, Hausas have adopted a first-name last-name system. In some cases, the additional name or the occupation has become set as the person's last name, e.g., **Yūsùf Dūnà** (Yusuf the swarthy); **Audù Màkānikè** (Audu the mechanic); **Hajìyā Lādì Mài Shìnkāfā** (Hajiya Ladi the rice seller). In other cases, boys have taken their father's first name as their last name, without the genitive linker, e.g., **Abdù Bāwà** or **Ismàil Jùnaidù**. Alternatively—and this was particularly prevalent when the system was first introduced—a person's hometown or district serves as a last name, e.g., **Àmīnù Kanò**, **Īsā Kaita**, **Àbūbakàr Tafāwà Balēwà**. Modern women tend to take one of their husband's names as a last name, e.g., a woman named **Hàdīzà** who is the wife of someone named **Mūsā Dantàlā Gòbir**, could be called **Hàdīzà Mūsā** or **Hàdīzà Dantàlā** or **Hàdīzà Gòbir**, or she might keep the last name she had acquired earlier, like one of her father's names, e.g., **Hàdīzà Jùnaidù**.

1.10. Titles

Titles are used to designate professions, military ranks, religious and political positions, social roles (including kinship relationships), etc. Titles occur in front of the names, e.g., **Cîf Joseph Johnson** (Chief Joseph Johnson), **Janàr Yākubù Gowon** (General Yakubu Gowon); **Yàya Jummai** (elder sister Jummai), **Fùròfēsà Mùhammadù Jinjù** (Professor Muhammadu Jinju). A person who has done the hadj has the title **Àlhajì** (f. **Hajìyā**). This title precedes all other titles, e.g., **Àlhajì Dr. Àbūbakàr̃ Imâm** (Alhaji Dr. Abubakar Imam). (In written Hausa, Alhaji is commonly abbreviated as Alh.) An adult person without any other title will normally be addressed as **Mālàm** (m.) / **Mālàmā** (f.), which corresponds to Mr./Mrs.

A personal name, with or without a title, can be preceded by an honorific or other descriptor, e.g., **mài girmā Gwàmnà Audù Bàk̃o** (His excellency Governor Audu Bako); **matàimàkin shùgàbā Àlhajì Shēhù Galàdancì** (Vice-Chancellor Alhaji Shehu Galadanci); **marìgàyī Àmīnù Kanò** (the late Aminu Kano).

As a general rule, only young people may be called or referred to by name without using a title. Otherwise, an appropriate title normally accompanies a name, even among people of the same social level.

Because of the questionable status of the surname, it is not normal to use a title with the surname alone as we do in English (e.g., Mr. Smith, Dr. Jones). Rather, a first name—either the birth name and/or the everyday name, whichever the person is known by—will accompany the surname, e.g., **Dr. Lawàn Ɗanlādì Yàlwa, Malàm Àmīnù Kanò**. In a familiar context, the title can accompany one name only, but it will be the person's customary name, not the surname, e.g., **Dr. Lawàn** or **Malàm Àmīnù**. A common alternative means of addressing someone is simply to use the title alone without a name, e.g., **Àlhajì/Hajìyā, Mālàm/Mālàmā, Fùr̃òfēsà** (Professor), **Sājà** (Sergeant), **Kāwù** (Uncle), etc.

When used as titles, some words are phonologically marked as compared with their use as simple common nouns.

1.10.1. Tone change H-L → L-L
Some words, esp. disyllabic words, typically lower the tone to L-L when functioning as titles. These words are all English loanwords, e.g.,

Kànàr̃ Sāni Bellò	Colonel Sani Bello (< **kanàr̃**, e.g., **shī kanàr̃ nē** He's a colonel.)
Mànjà Hasàn	Major Hassan (< **manjà** = **manjò** major)
Sànàtà Sālisù Bicì	Senator Salisu Bichi (< **sanatà** senator)

°AN: Initial (L)-L is also a common feature of compounds. The question is whether the lowering in titles is an indigenous process related to compound lowering or whether it is a reflection of English de-stressing.

Here is a list of common words that undergo the tone change to all L when functioning as titles:

bìr̃gēdiyà brigadier; **doktà** doctor; **janàr̃** general (but *not* **manjò-janàr̃** 'major general', which does not change); **kanàr̃** colonel; **kōfùr̃** corporal (but *not* **lâskōfùr̃** 'lance corporal', which does not change); **kyaftìn** captain, **manjà / manjò** major (but *not* **sàmanjà** 'sergeant major'); **mistà** Mr. (which occurs only as a title); **sājà** sergeant; **sanatà** senator; **sistà** nursing sister

°AN: When used as a title, either for M.D.s or for Ph.D.s, the word for 'doctor' is the loanword **doktà**. The common noun for 'medical doctor', on the other hand, is the much older loanword **likità**.

1.10.2. Vowel shortening
Some titles, again mostly loanwords, shorten the final vowel, with or without the tone change, e.g.,

Wàzīr̃ì Bellò Jùnaidù	Vizier Bello Junaidu (< **wàzīr̃ì** a vizier)
Gwàmnà Frederick Luggà	Governor Frederick Luggard (< **gwamnà** a governor)

Sìstà Màiřo Gùsau	Nursing Sister Mairo Gusau (< **sìstà** nursing sister)
Shēhù Ùsùmānù	Sheikh Usuman Dan Fodio (< **shēhù** sheik, pious person)
Ànnabì Mūsā	The Prophet Moses (< **ànnabì** a prophet)

(The form **Ànnabì** by itself is a proper name referring to the Prophet Muhammad.)

1.10.3. Lack of final vowel

A few early Arabic loanwords have a latent final vowel, which may or may not be expressed. When these common nouns are used as titles, they invariably occur without the final vowel, e.g.,

Làdân Sāni Ɗanbàřno < **làdān(ì)**	muezzin
Lìmân Rābi'ù Bàtūřè < **lìmām(ì)**	imam
Mālàm Yāƙubù Mūsā < **mālàm(ī)**	teacher
Shàřû Àmīnù Dàurā (= **Shàřîf Àmīnù Dàurā**) < **shàřîfì**	a holy man, psn who traces his descent from the Prophet Muhammad

1.10.4. No change

Such words as the following retain the same shape whether used as simple common nouns or as titles:

àlƙālī judge; **fàřfēsà** = **fùřòfēsà** professor; **gimbìyā** princess; **gwaggò** aunt; **hajìyā** woman who has done the hadj; **kāwù** = **kàwu** maternal uncle; **mâdākī** traditional Kano title (e.g., **Mâdākī Kwaiřangà**); **mālàmā** woman teacher, Mrs.; **manajà** manager; **sarkī** king, emir (e.g., **Sarkī Sànūsi** Emir Sanusi); **sàraunìyā** queen; **shùgàbā** president

> °AN: As a title **Sarkī** 'king, emir', has restricted usage. In most cases one indicates king or emir of some place with the name in apposition, e.g., **Sarkin Gwàmbè, Mālàm Àbūbakàř** 'The Emir of Gombe, Malam Abubakar'. Similarly **shùgàbā** 'president' functions less readily as a title than it does, for example, in English, thus **shùgàban ƙasā, Àlhajì Shēhù Shàgàri** 'The head of state, Alhaji Shehu Shagari' would be more common than simply **Shùgàbā (Shēhù) Shàgàri** 'President (Shehu) Shagari'.

1.10.5. Titles vs. compounds

Although titles and their accompanying names form a unit, semantically and phonologically, they are not as closely bound as lexical compounds. This is shown by the fact that unlike compounds, titles plus names can be broken up by the insertion of a modal particle, e.g.,

Gwaggò <u>kò</u> Àsàbe tā zō nēmankà	Indeed Aunt Asabe (**Gwaggò Àsàbe**) came looking for you.
Mālàm <u>fa</u> Audù nē ya àikē shì	It was Mr. Audu, mind you, who commissioned him.

Interestingly, the modal particle insertion blocks the tone-lowering rule but allows the vowel shortening, e.g.,

Gwamnà fa Audù Bàƙo nè yakè jàwābì Governor Audu Baƙo indeed is giving a speech.
< **gwamnà** (H-L with long final vowel) a governor, cf. **Gwàmnà Audù Bàƙo**

2. PLACE NAMES

In describing names of countries, states, emirates, cities and towns, quarters within towns, rivers, oceans, etc., one needs to distinguish between places within Hausaland (or places long familiar to Hausa people), which one can refer to as native place names, versus foreign places outside Hausaland, where the designation is historically recent. Regardless of the etymological nature of the place name, they all tend to be feminine. The major exception is when a proper noun is used in a phrase along with a masculine common noun indicating 'town of' or 'river of'. Thus the town **Tsanyāwā**, for example, is feminine, but **gàrin Tsanyāwā** (lit. town.of Tsanyawa), is masculine; similarly, **Bàdumè**, the name of a river, is feminine, but **kògin Bàdumè** (lit. river.of Badume) is masculine.

Place names within Hausaland are of two types. Some are morphologically unanalyzable (as far as we know); others are morphologically complex and often overtly descriptive.

2.1. Unanalyzable names

Many of the old, historically traditional places in Hausaland like **Kàtsinà** and **Mārù** have unanalyzable names. Most of these end in a short final vowel, **Kanò** and **Dàurā** being striking exceptions. A number of the unanalyzable names also end in consonants, an additional characteristic that sets them apart from common nouns.

> ◊HN: Names with final consonants, such as **Jāhùn, Katāgùm, Gòbir̃**, and **Gumàl** could possibly reflect pre-Hausa (Niger-Congo?) names that were already in existence when the Hausa people moved into their present area a millennium ago. Alternatively, they could be due to sporadic internal phonological developments resulting in the loss of final short (low-tone?) vowels, e.g., **Jāhùn** < *__Jāhùnì__, **Katāgùm** < *__Katāgùmù__, and **Gumàl** < *__Gumàlì__, etc.

Here are examples of some native towns and emirates (unglossed) and geographical features (glossed). (Interestingly, the place names with an initial rhotic have the flap /**r**/.)

Bicì; Bìr̃òm; Ɓāɓùrà; Dàmagàr̃am; Fùntuwà; Gòbir̃; Gùsau; Gwandu; Jèga; Jibiyà; Kàzaure; Kaita; Marāɗi; Mārù; Miryà; Rano; Ringìm; Sakkwato; Sòba; Tākùm; Tàwa; Zazzàu (< *__Zagzàg__) = **Zāriyà**
Bàdumè Badume River; **Dàla** Dala Hill; **Wàtàri** Watari River; **Wùdil** Wudil River (and town)

2.2. Analyzable names

Many place names are related to and or built on personal names or common nouns. These include anthroponyms (e.g., **Mūsāwā** 'Musa's community'), ethnonyms (e.g., **Zangòn Barèbarī** 'the Kanuri camp'), physical or qualitative characteristics of a place (e.g., **Yàshi** 'river sand'), flora (e.g., **Rīmi** 'silk cotton tree'), fauna (e.g., **Tsaunìn Kūrā** 'the hyena's mountain'), occupation or other activities associated with the place (e.g., **Majēmā** 'tannery'), and positional or directional description (e.g., **Bir̃nin Kudù** 'south city'), etc. These places are derived from non-place names by means of a number of different formations, of which the following are the most prevalent.

2.2.1. Common noun names

Some place names are identical to a common noun representing a physical feature or thing associated with the place (at present not always evident), but with a short final vowel, e.g., **Rōgò** (name of a town), cf. **rōgò** 'cassava'. Note that names of towns and town quarters are all feminine regardless of the gender of the related common noun, e.g., **Rōgò tā yi kyâu** 'Rogo town (3f) is good', cf. **rōgò yā yi kyâu** 'The cassava (3m) is good'. Examples: (The gloss represents the meaning of the related common noun, which is identical to the place name except that it has a long final vowel.)

Dùtsè stone, mountain; **Gamjì** gutta percha tree; **Gēzà** shrub; **Gwadabè** road; **Kanyà** ebony tree; **Kibiyà** a bow; **Kūra** hyena; **Lāfiyà** health; **Yàlwa** abundance; **Yàshi** river sand

The place name is most often built on a singular common noun, but names built on plurals also exist, e.g.,

Dògàrai (a quarter in Kano) emir's bodyguards (pl. of **dògarì**); **Gàrki** (a town) shields (pl. of **gàrkuwā**); **Gìgìnyu** (a quarter in Kano) deleb palms (pl. of **giginyà**)

Note that these place names are also feminine singular in spite of their plural form, e.g., **Gìgìnyu cḕ** 'It's Giginyu quarter', cf. **gìgìnyū nḕ** 'They're deleb-palms.'

2.2.2. Derivatives with the suffix -āwā

The suffix -āwā forms plural of ethnonyms built from ethnic, occupational, or place names (see §24:3), e.g., **Hàusāwā** 'Hausa people' (cf. **Bàhaushḕ** 'a Hausa person'), **Katsināwā** 'Katsina people', (cf. **Bàkatsinḕ** 'a Katsina person'). It can also be used with personal names to indicate someone's followers or adherents, e.g., **Sanūsāwā** 'supporters of Sanusi'. This same suffix, with the long final vowel retained, also occurs commonly with a variety of common and proper nouns in forming place names, e.g., **Mālamāwā**, lit. community of teachers, **Tākalmāwā**, lit. community of shoe(maker)s. Again we find that when these words are used as place names referring to towns or quarters, they are feminine singular even though the suffix as an ethnonymic formative is always plural, e.g., **Kanāwā cḕ** 'It's the town Kanawa', cf. **Kanāwā nḕ** 'They're Kano people'. Examples:

Amaryāwā	cf. **amaryā**	bride	**Manōmāwā**	cf. **manòmī**	farmer
Gabasāwā	cf. **gabàs**	east	**Nā'ibāwā**	cf. **nā'ibī**	deputy
Gāgarāwā	cf. **gàgarà**	be difficult	**Tamburāwā**	cf. **tamburà**	ceremonial drums
Gōbiřāwā	cf. **Gòbiř**	Gobir emirate	**Tsanyāwā**	cf. **tsanyà**	cricket
Hařūnāwā	cf. **Hařūnà**	Haruna	**Yařīmāwā**	cf. **Yàřīmà**	prince, emir's son

2.2.3. Derivatives with locational ma-

Common locational nouns are formed productively from verbs by means of a prefix **ma-** plus a suffix -ā)[H] or less ofter -ī)[H] , e.g., **makařantā** 'school' (< **kařàntā** 'read'); **masaukī** 'lodging place' (< **sàuka** 'alight, stop for the night') (see §7:2). Not surprisingly, one finds a number of place names (of towns and quarters) having the **ma-** locational form. What is surprising is that the length of the final vowel is unpredictable. Whereas most such place names end in a long final vowel, some have a short final vowel. Examples:

Mahūta	cf. **hūtà**	rest	**Malumfāshi**	cf. **lumfàsā**	take a breath
Malaɓā	cf. **laɓè**	hide in waiting	**Makwaråřī**	cf. **kwàrārà**	flow swiftly

2.2.4. Compounds with ɗan / 'yan

A number of place names have the form **ɗan** 'man of' or **'yan** 'people of' plus a noun. In some cases this noun is a personal name, in others it is a common noun that typically serves to indicate a professional activity. The compound generally ends in a short final vowel regardless of the normal vowel length of the noun. Note that the place names are all feminine in spite of the masculine and plural formatives. Examples:

Ɗan Hasàn	cf. **Hasàn**	personal name	**'Yan Àlēwà**	cf. **àlēwà**	halvah
'Yan Mammàn	cf. **Mammàn**	personal name	**Ɗan Sūrì**	cf. **sūrì**	termite hill
Ɗan Amarya	cf. **amaryā**	bride	**'Yan Tumāki**	cf. **tumākī**	sheep

2.2.5. Adjective + noun compounds

Some place names are overtly descriptive, having the form adjective + linker + noun. Most preserve the long final vowel of the common noun, but in a few cases, the place name is treated as a unitary name and is marked by a short final vowel, e.g.,

Dōgon Tafkì lit. long lake
Sābon Gidā lit. new home
Dōgon Dūtsì (indicated as Dogondoutchi on maps) lit. high outcrop/mountain

Jař Kasā lit. red soil
Bàbban Dòdo lit. big bogeyman

2.2.6. Noun of noun compounds

Place names that have the structure noun + linker + noun (or adverb) also tend to be overtly descriptive. Most preserve the underlying vowel length of the second noun, e.g.,

Bāřikìn Lādì lit. barracks.of Ladi
Biřnin Kudù lit. city.of the south
Dūtsèn Mā lit. mountain.of Ma
Gàřun Gabàs lit. town wall.of east
Gidan Àlƙālī lit. house.of judge
Kafìn Hausa lit. stockade.of Hausa
Kurmìn Gōřò lit. plantation.of kolanut

Mararrabař Jòs lit. junction.of Jos
Rījìyař Giginyà lit. well.of deleb-palm
Sōron 'Dinkì (quarters) lit. hall.of sewing
Tudùn Wàdā (quarters) lit. hill.of wealth
Ùnguwař Filànī lit. quarter.of Fulani
Zangòn Barèbarī (quarters) lit. camp.of Kanuri

2.3. Foreign names

Names of places outside of Hausaland (e.g., in southern Nigeria or elsewhere in the world) are normally loanwords that have been adjusted to Hausa phonology in one way or the other. Names of some places in the Islamic world are old loanwords from Arabic that are now fully integrated as Hausa words, e.g.,

Alƙāhìřa (=**Àlƙāhiřà**) (now usu. **Kaiřò**) Cairo; **Bàgàdāzà** Baghdad; **Bàhàř Māliyà** Red Sea; **Bàhàř Rûm** Mediterranean Sea, lit. sea of Rome; **Dūtsèn Àřfā** Mount Arafat; **Habashà** Ethiopia; **Ìsƙandàřiyà** Alexandria; **Lùbayyà** El Obeid (Sudan); **Masař / Misiřà** Egypt; **Pàlàsɗìnù** Palestine; **Shâm** (= **Sīřiyà**) Syria; **Tařābulùs** Tripoli

Other place names are more recent borrowings from English, having been nativized to a greater or lesser extent. Some of these modern names are spelled using the letter *p*, which normally is not part of the Hausa alphabet, e.g., **Jàpân, Pāshà** (Persia), **Pākistàn**. With some English-based names, even including the name Nigeria (!), the form of the Hausa name is still in flux. Place names that do not end in a consonant typically have a short final vowel, but, interestingly, not **Nàjēřiyà = Nìjēřiyà = Nàijēřiyà**, which has a long final vowel. Examples:

Afiřkà Africa; **Amiřkà / Amùřkà** America; **Ànàcà** Onitsha; **Bàdùn** Ibadan; **Bàřno** Borno; **Bosniyà** Bosnia; **Cādì** Chad; **Fàřansà** France; **Fàtàkwâl** Port Harcourt; **Filàtô** Plateau State; **Ìkko** (= **Lēgàs**) Lagos; **Ingìlà** England; **Ìsřā'ìlà** Israel; **Jāmùs** Germany; **Kàmàřu** Cameroon; **Kyanadà** Canada; **Lakwajà** Lokoja; **Landàn** London; **Màidugùři** Maiduguri; **Màřōkò** Morocco; **Nèjà** Niger State (but cf. **Kògin Kwàrà** Niger River); **Pāřis** Paris; **Rāshà** Russia; **Sàlìyô** Sierra Leone; **Wàgàdugù** Ouagadougou; **Yàmài** Niamey; **Yùgandà** Uganda

3. TEMPORAL NAMES

The days of the week are borrowed from Arabic (with one alternative name from English).

Sunday	**Lahàdì**	Thursday	**Àlhàmîs**
Monday	**Lìttìnîn / Lìtìnîn**	Friday	**Jumma'à**
Tuesday	**Tàlātà**	Saturday	**Àsabàr̃ (= Sātī)**
Wednesday	**Làr̃àbā**		

The months of the Islamic calendar are borrowed from Arabic:

1st month	**Mùhar̃r̃àm**	7th month	**Rajàb**
2nd month	**Safàr̃**	8th month	**Shà'àbân**
3rd month	**Ràbī'ù Lawwàl**	9th month	**Ràmàlân / Ràmàdân**
4th month	**Ràbī'ù Lāhìr̃**	10th month	**Shàwwâl**
5th month	**Jìmādā Lawwàl**	11th month	**Zùlk̃īdà**
6th month	**Jìmādā Lāhìr̃**	12th month	**Zulhajjì**

The months of the Western calendar are borrowed from English:

January	**Jànair̃ù**	July	**Yūlì**
February	**Fàbr̃air̃ù**	August	**Àgustà**
March	**Mār̃ìs**	September	**Sàtumbà**
April	**Àfr̃īlù**	October	**Òktōbà**
May	**Māyù**	November	**Nùwambà**
June	**Yūnì**	December	**Dìsambà**

[References: [Personal names] Abraham (1959b); Daba (1987); Newman and Ahmad (1992); Salim (1981); Yahaya and Sani (1979); [Place names] Bross (1995); Gouffé (1967); Kirk-Greene (1964); [Both] R. M. Newman (1990)]

49. Negation

HAUSA effects negation by the employment of five overt negative (neg) markers. Four of the negs (the "**BA** negs") make use of variants of the same marker. The other neg (**kadà**) uses a totally different marker. Two of the **BA** negs are discontinuous in structure. See table 5.

Table 5: Negative markers

Marker	Goes with
(1) bà(a)...ba	TAMs other than the continuous and subjunctive
(2) bā	negative continuous TAM
(3) bābù / bâ	existential; HAVE sentences, etc.
(4) bà̀...ba	equational (nonverbal) sentences, NPs, etc.
(5) kadà / kâř	subjunctive

1. NEGATIVE WITH TAMS OTHER THAN THE CONTINUOUS AND SUBJUNCTIVE (bà(a)...ba)

Verb phrases of tensed sentences in TAMs other than the continuous and subjunctive are negated by use of the discontinuous marker **bà(a)...ba**. The initial neg marker occurs immediately before the PAC, the person-aspect-complex that consists of the weak subject pronoun and the TAM. If there is an overt subject, this occurs before the neg marker, e.g.,

yārinyà bà tà dāwō ba	The girl didn't return. (lit. girl neg she return neg)
màlàmai bà sù ji kōmē ba	The teachers didn't hear anything.
bà zā mù biyā sù ba	We will not pay them.
bà zâ ka kàsuwā ba?	Will you not go to the market?
dà nī dà kai bà mâ zaunà tàre cikin àmānà̀ ba	You and I will not live together peacefully.

The length of the vowel in the initial **bà(a)** is subject to variation. In SH, the following would seem to represent current-day usage. The neg **bà(a)** is (1) always short in the negative completive, e.g., **bà sù dāwō ba** 'They didn't return'; (2) usually short in the potential and the allative, e.g., **bà sâ dāwō ba** 'They will likely not return', **bà zâ ka kàsùwā ba?** 'Will you not go to the market?'; (3) normally short but also long in the future, e.g., **bà zā mù biyā sù ba = bầ zā mù biyā sù ba** 'We will not pay them'; and (4) sometimes short but usually long in the habitual, e.g., **bầ sukàn yi azùmī ba** 'They don't normally fast.' (In examples in this entry and elsewhere, I transcribe the length of **bà(a)** as it is recorded in my notes.)

In the neg completive, the first and third person masculine wsp's generally drop their final vowels and contract with the initial **bà**, e.g., **bà + nì → bàn** 'I didn't', **bà + yà → bài** 'he didn't'.

357

°AN: The length of the **bà(a)** can be accounted for in terms of a difference between free forms and clitics. (This linguistic factor is generally not recognized because of the orthographic rules (generally adhered to in this grammar) that specify that the initial **bà(a)** be written as a separate word except in the case of the CVC fused forms, e.g., **bà sù...ba** 'neg they...neg', cf. **bàn...ba** 'neg.I...neg'.) If the **bà(a)** phonologically attaches itself to the following element, then it is short; if it is a free-standing item, it is long, e.g., **bàtà zō ba** 'She didn't come', **bằ takàn zō ba** 'She doesn't normally come', **bàzātà zō ba** = **bằ zātà zō ba** 'She won't come' (orthographically **ba za ta zo ba**). Support for this analysis comes from the fact that if an element, like **kuma** 'also', is inserted between the neg and the following PAC, **bằ** is necessarily long even in TAMs where it is commonly short, e.g., **bằ zā tà hàɗu dà ƙawằyên ba**, **bằ kuma zā tà tằfi sìnīmằ ba** 'She is not going to meet her friends, (and) she is also not going to go to the movies', cf. **bằ zā tà tằfi sìnīmằ ba** 'She is not going to go to the movies.' This analysis also explains why the initial nonclitic **bằ** in equational/identificational sentences is invariably long, e.g., **bằ ràgō ba nề** 'It's not a ram.'

The second **ba** typically occurs at the end of the basic VP, i.e., after such core arguments as locative goals and direct and indirect objects, but before adverbial clauses, e.g.,

mằtā tasà bà tâ shiryằ manà kằlằcī dà rùɓaɓɓen nāmằ <u>ba</u>
      His wife wouldn't prepare us a meal with rotten meat.
bằ zā mù ƙārằ masà àbinci <u>ba</u> sabồdà shī malằlằcī nề
      We will not bring him more food because he is a slacker.
bằ nakàn jē hồtâl-hồtâl <u>ba</u> sai dai sìnīmằ   I don't usually go to bars, only to the movies.

Simple adverbs (e.g., of time, place, or instrument) usually fall within the scope of the second **ba**, e.g.,

bằ mukàn fìta dà tsakař rāna <u>ba</u>   We don't normally go out at midday.
Lằmî bà tà ci àbinci à kằsuwā <u>ba</u>   Lami didn't eat food at the market.
bà yâ yankà ràgō dà wuƙā irìn wannàn <u>ba</u>
      He's not likely to slaughter a ram with a knife such as this.

ΔDN: In some northern dialects, the second neg occurs earlier in the sentence before direct objects, e.g., **bà mù kāmà ba ɓàrāwòn** = [SH] **bà mù kāmà ɓàrāwòn ba** 'We didn't catch the thief.'

Some temporal adverbs or adverb phrases like **gồbe** 'tomorrow', **jiyà dà yâmma** 'yesterday afternoon', or **ran kằsuwā** 'market day' can occur either before or after the **ba** with essentially the same meaning. The inherently negative adverb **tùkùna** 'not yet', on the other hand, occurs more frequently after the **ba**. Examples:

bàn jē makařantā jiyà <u>ba</u> = **bàn jē makařantā <u>ba</u> jiyà**   I didn't go to school yesterday.
màkānikề bà zâi gyārà mōtàř gồbe <u>ba</u> = **màkānikề bà zâi gyārà mōtàř <u>ba</u> gồbe**
      The mechanic won't repair the car tomorrow.
bằƙîn bà sù dāwō <u>ba</u> tùkùna, cf. ?**bằƙîn bà sù dāwō tùkùna <u>ba</u>**
      The guests haven't returned yet.

°AN: The word **tùkùna** 'not yet' has variant forms, which for some speakers are syntactically limited to final position after **ba**, e.g., 'Ladi hasn't sat down yet' = (1) **Lādì bà tà zaunằ <u>ba</u> tùkùn**, not ****Lādì bà tà zaunằ tùkùn <u>ba</u>**; (2) **Lādì bà tà zaunằ <u>ba</u> tùkùnna**, not ****Lādì bà tà zaunằ tùkùnna <u>ba</u>**, cf. (3) **Lādì bà tà zaunằ <u>ba</u> tùkùna** = ?**Lādì bà tà zaunằ tùkùna <u>ba</u>**.

In a sentence containing an indirect question, the second **ba** may occur at the end of the entire sentence, although some speakers, especially of WH dialects, prefer to have the **ba** earlier, right after the matrix clause. Examples:

bàn san kō wằ ya yi hakà <u>**ba**</u> = **bàn sanì** <u>**ba**</u> **kō wằ ya yi hakà**
　　I don't know who did that.
bài gayằ minì kō nawà zân biyā <u>**ba**</u> = **bài gayằ minì** <u>**ba**</u> **kō nawà zân biyā**
　　He didn't tell me how much I should pay.

A complement clause typically occurs after the **ba**, although sentences with the **ba** at the very end are possible, depending, inter alia, on the length of the complement, e.g.,

bàn ji dādī <u>**ba**</u> **dà kukà shā giyằ** = **bàn ji dādī dà kukà shā giyằ** <u>**ba**</u>
　　I am not happy that you (pl.) drank beer.
bài yi kirằ gà mutằnē <u>**ba**</u> **dà sù zō dandàlī** = ?**bài yi kirằ gà mutằnē dà sù zō dandàlī** <u>**ba**</u>
　　He didn't call upon the people to come to the town square.
bài kàmātà <u>**ba**</u> **Tankò yà biyā hàřājì** = **bài kàmātà Tankò yà biyā hàřājì** <u>**ba**</u>
　　It's not appropriate that Tanko pay taxes.
bằ dōlè <u>**ba**</u> **nề mù jē fīlin wằsā** = **bằ dōlè nē mù jē fīlin wằsā** <u>**ba**</u>
　　It's not required that we go to the playground.

The negated VP does not have to be in a main clause; it can also be in an embedded or subordinate clause, e.g.,

ìdan bà mù yi saurī ba, sai mù kwântā cikin jējì
　　If we don't hurry we're going to have to spend the night in the forest.
inằ nēman yàròn dà bài cikà fôm ba
　　I am looking for the boy who didn't fill out the form.
kōwànè kuřtù dà bài ji ùmàřnī ba zâi shìga ukù
　　Any recruit who doesn't take orders is going to be in a jam.

If two negative sentences co-occur in such a way that the second **ba** should occur twice in succession, one of them is dropped by a process of morphological haplology, i.e., the one **ba** does double duty, e.g.,

<u>**bàn**</u> **ga yàròn dà** <u>**bài**</u> **tàimàki Lādì** <u>**ba**</u>　　I didn't see the boy who didn't help Ladi.
(< *[<u>**bàn**</u> **ga yàròn dà** [<u>**bài**</u> **tàimàki Lādì** <u>**ba**</u>] **ba**])
<u>**bà**</u> **sù biyā yàròn dà** <u>**bài**</u> **gamà aikìn ba**　　They didn't pay the boy who didn't finish the work.

◊HN: In Tera, on the other hand, a distantly related Chadic language (Newman 1970), two juxtaposed instances of the final neg marker (**ɓa**) are perfectly acceptable, e.g., [**nə gwa njib nəke** [**nə vi nə dam ɓa**] **ɓa**] 'He didn't find the man who didn't come out' (lit. he.neg find man who is he.neg enter to out neg neg).

There is no problem, however, with a final **ba** being immediately followed by an initial **bà(a)** in the next clause, nor of the final **ba** being followed by the morpheme **ba** functioning as a question marker, e.g.,

[**yārinyàř dà** <u>**bà**</u> **tà hanằ mu barcī** <u>**ba**</u>] [<u>**bà**</u> **tà zō** <u>**ba**</u>]
　　The girl who did not prevent us from sleeping did not come.

[yāròn dà b̲à̲i̲ tàimàki Lādì b̲a̲] [b̲à̲ zâi sầmi lādā b̲a̲]

    The boy who didn't help Ladi will not get a reward.

[ìdan b̲à̲ kù kasà kûnnē b̲a̲] [b̲à̲ zā kù ji lābārī̲ b̲a̲]

    If you (pl.) don't pay attention, you won't hear the news.

shī nè [dirēbàn dà b̲à̲i̲ zō b̲a̲] [b̲â̲]?   Is he (not) the driver that didn't come?

If two negative sentences are conjoined, each comes with its own neg marking, e.g.,

b̲à̲i̲ kàrɓā b̲a̲ (kuma) b̲à̲i̲ kařàntā b̲a̲

    He didn't accept it (and) he didn't read it.

b̲à̲ tà shārè ɗākì b̲a̲, b̲à̲ tà yi wankā b̲a̲, (kuma) b̲à̲ tà tàfi makařantā b̲a̲

    She didn't sweep the room, she didn't bathe, (and) she didn't go to school.

b̲à̲ zā sù shā giyà̲ b̲a̲ (kuma) b̲à̲ zā sù yi rawā b̲a̲

    They are not going to drink beer and they are not going to dance.

If, on the other hand, two VPs are negated, there is only one neg marker, which encompasses the entire sentence. The first TAM will take the neg form whereas a subsequent TAM will take the corresponding affirmative TAM or the default neutral form, e.g.,

b̲à̲ mù ci mun shā b̲a̲	We didn't eat and drink.
b̲à̲i̲ kàrɓā yā kařàntā b̲a̲	He did not accept it and read it.

b̲à̲ tà shārè ɗākì tā yi wankā tā tàfi makařantā b̲a̲

    She didn't sweep the room, bathe, (and) go to school.

b̲à̲ sù kō tsayà̲ sun haɗà shāwařà̲ b̲a̲

    They didn't even stop and consult one another. (lit....combine advice)

b̲à̲ zā sù shā giyà̲ sù yi rawā b̲a̲	They are not going to drink beer and dance.
b̲à̲ yâ zō yà biyā bāshìn dà akè bînsà b̲a̲	He will probably not come and pay the loan.

    ΔDN: An alternative for dialects that tend to have the second **ba** earlier in the sentence is to place the **ba** after the first of the conjoined VPs, i.e., **b̲à̲ mù ci b̲a̲ mun shā** 'We didn't eat and drink.'

In sentences with the aspectual verb **rìgā** (= **rigā** = **rìgāyà**) 'have already done', which requires a subsequent clause with the same TAM, one negates only the TAM in the matrix clause, e.g.,

b̲à̲n rìgā nā gan shì b̲a̲	I haven't already seen him.
(cf. nā rìgā nā gan shì	I have already seen him.)

2. NEGATIVE IN THE CONTINUOUS (bā)

The single negative **bā** accompanies the long-vowel, L-tone pronouns in the negative-continuous paradigm (see §70:10), e.g., **bā nà̲** 'I am not...', **bā mà̲** 'we are not...', etc. These forms negate continuous verbal sentences as well as locative and stative sentences. Examples:

bā tà̲ sōyà̲ kàzā	She is not frying chicken.
Bellò bā yà̲ dāwôwā	Bello is not returning.
bankì bā yà̲ nân à wannàn tītì	The bank is not here on this street.
sōjōjī bā sà̲ rìƙe dà bindigōginsù	The soldiers are not holding their guns.

ΔDN: [i] In some WH dialects, the single negative **bā** occurs in the continuous with the light wsp paradigm (with short vowel and L tone), e.g., **bā nì** (= **bân**), **bā kà**, **bā kì**, **bā shì** (= **bā yà** = **bâi**), **bā tà**, **bā mù**, **bā kù**, **bā sù**, **bā à**.

[ii] The neg continuous serves in many dialects as an alternative means of expressing negative HAVE sentences, e.g., **bā tằ dà bīzằ** (= **bâ ta dà bīzằ**) 'She doesn't have a visa.'

◊HN: Caron (1990a) has suggested that the single initial **bā** represents the historically original situation and that the discontinuous neg **bà(a)...ba** resulted from reinforcement of the single **bā** by an adverbial element, i.e., the development was parallel to what happened in French, where the neg *ne* was strengthened to *ne...pas*. From a comparative Chadic perspective, this hypothesis seems extremely unlikely. The typical pattern in Chadic is to have the negative at the end of the sentence, with or without a preverbal neg marker, and Proto-Chadic can almost certainly be reconstructed with a single neg marker at the end (Newman n.d.). The initial neg markers that are found in various Chadic languages have derived independently from a number of different sources, like the prohibitive, negative existential, etc.

3. NEGATIVE OF EXISTENTIAL AND HAVE SENTENCES (**bābù** / **bâ**)

The neg form **bābù** '(no) there isn't, there aren't' negates existential sentences. It is the negative counterpart of **àkwai** 'there is/are' (and related forms). The short variant **bâ** has two functions. It (a) serves as an alternative neg marker (= **bābù**) for existential sentences with a complement expressed, and (b) it serves as a negative formative for HAVE sentences. In this latter usage, it is the negative counterpart to affirmative sentences in the continuous, e.g.,

(a) **bābù**   There isn't any. (not ****bâ**), cf. **àkwai (ruwā)**?   Is there any (water)?

bābù mâi = **bâ mâi**   There isn't any oil.

bābù 'yan tāwāyè à ƙauyèn nân = **bâ 'yan tāwāyè à ƙauyèn nân**

    There aren't any rebels in this village.

(b) **Lādì bâ ta dà lāfiyằ**   Ladi is not well. (lit. Ladi neg she with health)

cf. **Lādì tanằ dà lāfiyằ**   Ladi is well.

bâ ni dà lāsìn   I don't have a license, cf. **inằ dà lāsìn**   I have a license.

> ΔDN: In spoken Hausa, **bābù** is sometimes used as an alternative to **à'ằ** 'no' as an answer to interrogative verbal sentences, e.g., **yā isō**? 'Has he arrived?' **bābù** 'No.' This is colloquial speech that not all speakers accept.
>
> ◊HN: A historical note on the etymology of **bābù** is presented in §26:1.2.

If the object of the negative existential is a pronoun, **bābù** is strongly preferred. The pronoun will be an independent form. Object pronouns after **bâ** are attested but are not liked by SH speakers. If they are used, however, an independent pronoun is strongly preferred, although the H-tone strong object pronoun set is also attested, e.g.,

bābù sū cikin kàsuwā   There aren't any of them in the market.

= ?**bâ sū cikin kàsuwā** = ??**bâ su cikin kàsuwā**

àkwai mōtằ dà zā mù shìga? bābù ita   Is there a car we can enter? No there isn't (it).

> ΔDN: In the Sokoto dialect, the short form **bâ** is not used. The pronouns that occur after **bābù** belong to the strong object paradigm, e.g., **bābù ta** 'There isn't it.'

When, however, **bâ** functions as the negative of HAVE constructions, it requires a pronoun belonging to the H-tone short-vowel paradigm, e.g.,

mutânên nan bâ su dà hankàlī   Those men don't have any sense.
bâ ta dà mōtầ   She doesn't have a car.

4. NEGATIVE OF EQUATIONAL SENTENCES, NPs, ADVERBS (bầ...ba)

The discontinuous neg **bầ...ba** serves to negate items other than those in the PAC found in tensed sentences, e.g., equational predicates, NPs, adjectives, adverbs, prepositional phrases, and full sentences. This allomorph is also used for negative focus.

4.1. Predicate negation

Equational and identificational sentences with the structure (X) Y stabilizer (where the STAB is **nē** or **cē** (with polar tone)), negate the predicate (Y) by enveloping it in **bầ...ba**, e.g.,

Bàlā <u>bầ</u> **àlƙālī** <u>ba</u> <u>nề</u>   Bala is not a judge.
kuɗinsà <u>bầ</u> **dalầ gōmà** <u>ba</u> **nề**   Its price is not ten dollars.
ita <u>bầ</u> **'yātā** <u>ba</u> **cề**   She is not my daughter.
<u>bầ</u> **kāsā** <u>ba</u> **cề**   It is not a puff adder.

The second **ba** and the stabilizer may optionally be inverted. Some dialects and some speakers like this option better than others.

Bàlā bầ àlƙālī nề ba   Bala is not a judge.   **ita bầ 'yātā cề ba**   She is not my daughter.

Complement-taking expressions like **tīlàs** 'perforce' allow the second **ba** either after the CTE or after the complement, e.g.,

<u>bầ</u> **tabbàs** <u>ba</u> **nề Audù yà zō dà yâmma** = <u>bầ</u> **tabbàs nē Audù yà zō dà yâmma** <u>ba</u>
        It is not certain that Audu will come in the evening.
<u>bầ</u> **dōlè** <u>ba</u> **nề à gàrē shì dà yà kammàlà aikìn yâu**
= <u>bầ</u> **dōlè nē à gàrē shì dà yà kammàlà aikìn yâu** <u>ba</u>
        It is not required that he finish the work today.

4.2. Adverbs, prepositional phrases, NPs

The **bầ...ba** formative serves to negate adverbs and prepositional phrases in situ. The implication is often a contrastive 'but not' although the conjunction **àmmā** 'but' is not required. Examples:

tanầ ganī (àmmā) <u>bầ</u> **sòsai** <u>ba</u>   She sees (but) not clearly.
Audù yā tàfi kàsuwā (àmmā) <u>bầ</u> **dà sāfe** <u>ba</u>
        Audu went to the market (but) not in the morning.
zā kà karầntà wāƙầr̃ (àmmā) <u>bầ</u> **à zàune** <u>ba</u>
        You will read the song (but) not in a sitting position.
nā san shùgàban ƙasā sanìn-shānū, <u>bầ</u> **na hàƙīƙầ** <u>ba</u>
        I know the president casually (lit. knowledge of cattle), not very well.
zân kammàlà aikìn nân <u>bầ</u> **dà jumầwā** <u>ba</u>
        I'll finish the work soon. (lit. not with passing time)

yā tāshì **b̀** tàre dà sanīnā **ba**
> He left without my knowledge. (lit. neg together with knowledge.my neg)

ta yàyà zā kà iyà hayèwā dà sū **b̀** tàre dà wani yā ci wani **ba**?
> How would you be able to take them across (the river) without one (of them) eating the other?

Contrastive '(but) not' phrases enveloped in **b̀...ba** can also consist of NPs and adjectives, e.g.,

Mūsā nè zā sù zàɓā, **b̀** Harūnà **ba**	It is Musa they are going to elect, not Haruna.
bàrēwā cè ka kashè, **b̀** gàdā **ba**	It was an antelope you killed, not a duiker.
ƙwai nē yârā sukè sàyē, **b̀** gōr̃ò **ba**	It's eggs the children are buying, not kolanuts.
Hàdīzà cē ta ci lambà, **b̀** Kànde **ba**	It's Hadiza who won the prize, not Kande.
tā fi sôn baƙar̃ mōtā, **b̀** farā **ba**	She prefers black cars, not white.
yârā nàgàr̃tàttū zā sù sāmù, **b̀** malàlàtā **ba**	The good children will get (it), not the lazy.

°AN: Semantically contrastive 'especially' phrases are formed using the discontinuous **b̀...bâ** formative (with final falling tone) even though we do not think of these in English as negatives, e.g., **tanā sôn lèmō tun b̀ mā Fanta bâ** 'She likes soft drinks, especially Fanta' (see §5:11).

4.3. Sentence negation

A sentence as a whole can be negated by **b̀...ba**. The semantic interpretation is that it is the truth value of the entire sentence that is being negated, i.e., 'It is not (the case) that ...'. A full range of sentences can be negated. Examples:

b̀ wai mutànen nàn sun bā tà dàriyā ba nè; ā'à, tunzùrā ta sukà yi
> It is not the case that these men made her laugh; no, irritating her they did.

cf. **mutànen nàn b̀ sù bā tà dàriyā ba**	These men didn't make her laugh. (VP negation)
b̀ rashìn nāmà (nē) zâi kashè mùtûm ba	It is not that lack of meat will kill a person.
cf. **rashìn nāmà b̀ zâi kashè mùtûm ba**	Lack of meat will not kill a person. (VP negation)
b̀ Lādì tanà dà kuɗī ba nè	It is not that Ladi has money.
cf. **Lādì bâ ta dà kuɗī**	Ladi doesn't have money. (predicate negation)
b̀ àkwai làbār̃ī ba nè	It is not that there is news.
b̀ ita cè 'yātā ba	It is not that she is my daughter.

In sentence negation, one commonly uses a "commentary" phrase after the first **b̀** (introduced by the reportive particle **wai**), a strategy that some speakers strongly prefer, e.g.,

b̀ (wai nā cê) Lādì tanà dà kuɗī ba nè	It is not (hearsay that I said) that Ladi has money.
b̀ (wai) ita cè 'yātā ba	It is not (hearsay) that she is my daughter.
cf. **bâ wai ita cè 'yātā**	There is no doubt (but that) she is my daughter.

The full sentence that is negated can itself be in the negative. In this case any repeated //ba ba// at the end is reduced to a single **ba**, e.g.,

b̀ (wai) Lādì bâ ta dà kuɗī ba (nè)	It is not that Ladi has no money.
b̀ (wai) bābù làbār̃ī ba (nè)	It is not that there is no news.
b̀ (wai nā cê) b̀ zā mù tàfi ba nè	It is not that we are not going.
< *[**b̀**...[**b̀** zā mù tàfi **ba**] **ba**] **nè**	

4.4. Negation and focus

In tensed affirmative sentences, a focused item is fronted, optionally followed by the stabilizer (STAB). Completive and continuous TAMs are replaced by the corresponding Rel forms (pret and Rcont), e.g.,

a. **Audù yā tàfi kàsuwā**	Audu has gone to the market. (neutral)
b. **Audù (nē) ya tàfi kàsuwā**	It is *Audu* who went to the market. (focused)
a. **sunà gyārà mōtàr̃mù**	They are repairing our car. (neutral)
b. **mōtàr̃mù (cē) sukè gyār̃àwā**	It is *our car* they are repairing. (focused)

"Negative focus" (i.e., focus of a negative constituent) can be achieved by surrounding the entire affirmative sentence by **bà̀...ba**. Although in this structure the second **ba** does not occur until the end of the sentence as a whole, semantically the negative focus is on the fronted item. Examples:

bà̀ Tàlātù (cē) ta zàgē shì ba	It is *not Talatu* who insulted him.
bà̀ 'yan'uwānā (nè̀) sukè bā dà tàimakō ba	It is *not my brothers* who are helping.
bà̀ ɓàrāwò sukà kāmà ba	It's *not a thief* they caught.
bà̀ dà saurī sukà tahō ba	It is *not fast* that they came.
bà̀ kàsuwā Audù ya tàfi ba	It is *not to market* that Audu went.
bà̀ dà sāfe Aishà ta tàfi kàsuwā ba	It is *not in the morning* that Aisha went to the market.
bà̀ kèkè Bàlā ya sayà wà 'yā'yansà ba	It is *not a bicycle* that Bala bought for his children.

Alternatively, one can move the second **ba** up immediately after the focused constituent. If this is done, the stabilizer is strongly preferred, e.g.,

bà̀ Tàlātù ba cè ta zàgē shì	It is *not Talatu* who insulted him.
bà̀ ɓàrāwò ba nè sukà kāmà	It's *not a thief* they caught.
bà̀ kèkè ba nè Bàlā ya sayà wà 'yā'yansà	It is *not a bicycle* that Bala bought for his children.

5. PROHIBITIVE MARKER USED IN THE SUBJUNCTIVE (**kadà/kâr̃**)

The prohibitive marker **kadà** (= **kâr̃**) serves to negate sentences with a subjunctive TAM. When serving to form negative commands, the prohibitive generally translates as 'don't'. In other contexts it often translates as 'should not' or, if it occurs with **don** 'in order to' (whether overt or implied), as 'lest'.

> °AN/◊HN: Strictly speaking, **kadà** is not a true negative marker on a par with the BA forms. Rather it is an adverbial that is semantically negative, i.e., one should think of it as the counterpart to such adverbs as **dōlè** 'must', **tīlàs** 'perforce', etc. In other Chadic languages, like Bole, **kadà**-type words commonly co-occur with a true negative marker, e.g., (with tone not marked), (kobo) **ka pete sa!** 'Don't go out!' (lit. (prohibitive) you go out neg).

The very common form short form **kâr̃** is the result of final vowel apocopation accompanied by rhotacism of the resulting syllable-final /d/. The original L tone on the second syllable of **kadà** is preserved and combines with the preceding H to produce a fall, i.e., **kádà** → *kád` → **kâr̃**.

kadà kì bā shì kōmē! = **kâr̃ kì bā shì kōmē!**	Don't (you (f.)) give him anything!
kadà / kâr̃ mù tàimàkē sù!	Let's not help them!
tàfi dà laimà don kadà / kâr̃ ruwā yà bā kà kāshī!	Take an umbrella lest you get soaked!

When occurring immediately before the wsp, the F-tone **kâɍ** and the L-tone pronoun often combine and simplify to H-L. (In standard orthography, the two elements are written as separate words; for clarity of exposition, I shall transcribe the fused forms here with a hyphen.) Examples:

kâɍ kà dāwō = kaɍ-kà dāwō	Don't return!
…ɓàràyī kâɍ sù shìga = …ɓàràyī kaɍ-sù shìga	…lest thieves enter
kâɍ mù zaunà hakà = kaɍ-mù zaunà hakà	We shouldn't just sit like this.

If something intervenes between **kâɍ** and the pronoun, like a noun subject or a modal particle, the fusion is blocked and the tone simplification does not take place, e.g.,

kâɍ fa kà dāwō!	Now don't you return! (*not* ****kaɍ fa kà dāwō**)
…kâɍ ɓàràyī sù shìga	…lest thieves enter (*not* ****…kaɍ ɓàràyī sù shìga**)

The final -ɍ of **kâɍ** (with F or H tone) commonly assimilates fully to the initial consonant of the abutting weak subject pronoun, e.g.,

kaɍ-kà dāwō! = kak-kà dāwō!	Don't return!
an rufè ƙōfà kaɍ-tà fita = …kat-tà fita	They closed the door so she wouldn't go out.

> ΔDN: In some WH dialects this assimilation has become obligatory, such that one has to represent the morpheme with underlying final **-G** (= geminate) rather than with a **-d** or **-ɍ** that assimilates, e.g., //**kaG kà dāwō**// → **kak-kà dāwō** 'Don't return!' In some (all?) dialects with the **kaG** representation, the gemination takes place whether the following item is a pronoun or not. In these dialects, one also commonly finds that the H tone on the **kaG/kaɍ** morpheme (which in SH derives from a fall by tonal simplification) has become lexicalized and always appears as such, e.g., **kaɓ ɓàràyī sù shìga** 'lest thieves enter'; **kah hwa kà dāwō!** (= [SH] **kâɍ fa kà dāwō!**) 'Now don't you return!'

Syntactically the prohibitive differs strikingly from the various **BA** formatives in being allowed (sometimes even required) before the subject rather than immediately before the PAC. Examples: (In all sentences **kadà** can be replaced by **kâɍ**.)

[kadà] [yârā] sù cikà sùɍūtù	The children shouldn't chatter so.
(= **yârā kadà sù…**), cf. **[yârā] [bà] sù yi sùɍūtù̀ ba**	The children didn't chatter excessively.
nā rōƙē kà [kadà] [Lādì] tà sābà̀ masà	I implore you not to let Ladi disobey him.
(= **nā rōƙē kà Lādì kadà tà…**)	
kadà Audù mālàmin makaɍantaɍmù yà tàfi	Audu our school teacher shouldn't leave.
mun rufè ƙōfà (don) kadà màge tà fita	We closed the door lest the cat go out.
nā ɓōyè kuɗīnā (don) kadà ɓàrāwò̀ yà sācè mîn	I hid my money lest a thief steal it from me.
kadà mùtumìn nan dà ya sācè mîn rìgā shēkaranjiyà yà zō	
That man who stole my robe two days ago shouldn't come.	

[References: Bature (1985); Caron (1990b); Hill (1976); Newman (1971a)]

50. Noun Derivation by Affixation: An Overview

HAUSA has a rich system of nominal derivation. Some derivations are endocentric, e.g., nouns derived from other nouns, others are exocentric, e.g., nouns derived from verbs. Most of the derivations employ suffixes, some employ prefixes, some employ both. The derivations are used to express such categories as abstracts, agentives, language names, activities, resultatives, etc. A full discussion of each formation is given in the separate chapter provided for that construction. Presented here is an inventory of the derivational formations, along with a few illustrative examples, for the purpose of providing a general overview.

1. ABSTRACT NOUNS

Abstract nouns (chap. 1) are derived from common nouns by means of a set of related suffixes -(n)cī^{HL}, -(n)tā (variable tone), and -(n)takā)^{LHL}.

ādalcì fairness, justice (< ādàlī just, honest (psn)); kāsuwancì trading (< kàsuwā market)
kuturtà leprosy (< kuturū leper); sàbùntā newness (< sābō new)
tàgwàitakà̀ twinship (< tagwai twins); dàngàntakà̀ relationship (< dangì kin, relatives)

2. LANGUAGES/ATTRIBUTES

Names of languages or dialects are formed by adding a suffix -(an)cī^{H} (with all H tone) to a noun typically indicating a place or ethnic group (chap. 41). The same suffix is used to indicate attributes associated with the base noun. What is probably the same suffix also serves to form nouns indicating a directional part.

(a) Lārabcī Arabic; Gōbiřancī Gobir dialect; Bìbīsancī Hausa language and delivery style associated with BBC broadcasts
(b) fādancī sycophancy, obsequiousness (< fādà palace); mālamancī language and/or mannerisms of traditional teachers (< mālàm teacher); kudancī southern part (< kudù south)

3. AGENT/LOCATION/INSTRUMENT

Nouns indicating agents, locations, or instruments are formed from verbs using a common prefix ma- (chap. 7). The three derivations make use of distinct final vowels and tone.

3.1. Agent: ma-...-ī

These derivatives potentially have three different forms for number and gender. The masculine forms end in -ī with an H-(L)-L-H tone pattern; the feminine forms end in -ìyā with an H-H-L-H tone pattern; and the plural forms end in -ā with the same H-(L)-L-H tone pattern found in the masculine singular.

mahàifī / mahaifìyā / mahàifā	parent (< **hàifā** give birth to)
marôƙī / marōƙìyā / marôƙā	praise-singer, beggar (< **rôƙā** beg for)
matsôràcī / matsōracìyā / matsôràtā	coward (< **tsôratà** be afraid)

3.2. Location: **ma-...-ā / ma-...-ī**

Most nouns of location end in -ā; a lesser number end in -ī. They have an all H tone pattern.

majēmā	tannery; **makařantā** school
masaukī	lodging place, overnight quarters, guest room/house

3.3. Instrument: **ma-...-ī**

Nouns of instrument all end in -ī. They have an all H tone pattern.

magirbī   harvesting tool; **masassaƙī**   adze, carpenter's tool; **murfī** (< **marufī**)   bottle top, cover

4. ETHNONYMS

Ethnonyms (chap. **24**), which include some occupational groups, are formed from place names by means of a prefix **bà-**, commonly, but not obligatorily, accompanied by a masculine singular suffix **-ē**)[HL]. The suffix **-āwā** (with variable tone, L-H or all H) serves to form (a) plural ethnonyms and related terms indicating a community of people, and (b) names of towns and quarters.

(a) **Bàkatsinè / Katsināwā**   psn / people from Katsina; **Bàhaushè / Hàusàwā**   Hausa(s); **bàdūkù / dùkàwā**   leather worker(s); **ànnabì / annabāwā**   prophet(s); **talàkà / talakāwā**   commoner(s), poor people

(b) **Gōbiřāwā**   a quarter in Kano (< **Gòbiř**   an emirate); **Tamburāwā**   name of town/village (< **tamburà**   ceremonial drums); **Tsanyāwā**   name of town/village (< **tsanyā**   cricket)

5. ABSTRACT NOUNS OF SENSORY QUALITY (ANSQ)

This is a nonproductive derivation built by adding a suffix -ī)[H] to bases (all of which have the form CVVC- or CVCC-) that do not normally occur in nonderived words. The words of this class are all abstract nouns denoting sensory qualities (chap. **2**).

ɗācī   bitterness, e.g., medicine, neem bark, quinine; **fāɗī**   breadth, width (diameter, surface area, extent); **kaifī**   sharpness (of an edge); **santsī**   slipperiness, glossiness (e.g., silk cloth)

6. MUTUALITY

Nouns indicating mutuality (chap. **47**) are derived from verbs by means of two fairly productive suffixes with overlapping meaning.

6.1. Subtype mutuality-1: **-ayyā**)[LHL]

This formation utilizes a suffix **-ayyā** with a set L-H-L tone pattern.

rìbɗayyà	severely hitting one other (< **ribɗà** beat)
hùjjàtayyà	laying down mutual conditions (< **hujjàtà** lay down conditions)
ƙìyayyà	hatred (< **ƙi** hate)

6.2. *Subtype mutuality-2: -ēCēniyā*)LHHLH

This formation utilizes a suffix -**ēCēniyā** (where C is a copy of the base-final consonant) with an associated L-H-H-L-H tone pattern. (There is a variant in which the copied C is geminated.)

bùgēgēnìyā (= bùgaggēnìyā)	exchanging blows (< **bugà** hit)
cùɗēɗēnìyā	rubbing up against and pushing one other (< **cùɗā** knead)
kàrɓēɓēnìyā (= kàrɓayyà)	taking turns in work or carrying load (< **kàrɓā** receive)
rùngùmēmēnìyā	mutual embracing (< **rùngumà** embrace)

7. SOUNDS AND MOVEMENT

Ideophonic nouns indicating sounds and movement are formed by means of a suffix -**niyā**)LLHH with a fixed L-L-H-H tone pattern (see §**35**:6). The words of this class are typically quadrisyllabic with an alternating light-heavy prosodic structure. This is a nonproductive derivation in that many of the words are frozen, i.e., the bases are not found as independently occurring words. Examples:

ɗàwàiniyā	being busy struggling with one's tasks
hàtsàniyā	wrangling, quarrelling
mùtsùniyā	giggling, fidgeting by children
wàtsàlniyā	wriggling, squirming

7.1. *Related ideophones*

Semantically similar words—in some cases alternative variants—are formed by full reduplication with an associated L-H tone pattern (see §**35**:6.1).

fàcàl-facal (= fàcàlniyā)	playing with, or splashing water all over
wàndař-wandař	zigzagging, swaying from side to side
zìřgà-zìřgā	constantly going to and fro

8. SYSTEMS/ERAS

A number of Arabic loanwords indicating political systems, eras, and such (chap. **68**) contain a frozen suffix -**iyyā**)LHL .

fàtìmiyyà	the Fatimid dynasty
ìslàmiyyà	Islamic tenets or calendar
mùlùkiyyà	monarchical system of government

9. ASSOCIATED CHARACTERISTICS

There are numerous nouns derived from verbs by means of the suffix -**au**)LH with a fixed L-H tone pattern (chap. **10**). It is impossible to give a consistent meaning for the suffix; about all that one can say is that nouns with -**au**)^LH denote people or things that have characteristics associated in one way or another with the semantic properties of the source verb. This suffix is commonly found with proper names.

àikàtau   verb (< **aikàtā** to work); **cầsau**   threshing grain for payment (< **cầsā** thresh); **màntau** very forgetful psn (< **mântā** forget); **tùnkùyau**   flea (< **tùnkuyầ** butt, gore); **Bàrau**   proper name (< **barì** leave); **Hàƙùrau**   proper name (< **hàƙurà** be patient)

10. GAMES AND ACTIVITIES

A limited number of nouns indicating games and activities are derived from verbs by means of a suffix -**e**)^H with a fixed all H tone pattern (chap. **30**). The derivation does not appear to operate productively at a synchronic level.

cake   a game similar to darts (< **cakầ** stab); **lēƙe**   cheating by looking at s.o.'s work in a sneaky way (< **lēƙầ** peek); **jāgule**   making a mess of sth (esp. by children) (< **jāgùlā** spoil, mess up); **tsallake** jumping game (< **tsallàkā** jump/cross over); **wur̃ge**   throwing things from one place to another (< **wur̃gầ** throw)

51. Noun Phrase: Structure and Word Order

NOUN phrases (NP) consist of a head noun with optional prenominal and/or postnominal elements, e.g., [wani sābon]_{pre} [littāfî]_{Head} [mài kyâu]_{post} 'a new good book', lit. [some new] [book] [possessing goodness].

1. THE HEAD

The head of an NP typically consists of a simple noun (singular or plural), conjoined nouns, nouns in a genitive X of Y relationship, compound nouns, etc. (For purposes of this chapter, we will essentially ignore NPs with pronoun heads.) Examples:

tēbùr	table	**tēbuřōřī**	tables
cōkàlī dà wuƙā	spoon and knife	**mazā dà mātā**	men and women
fallen tākàřdā	sheet of paper	**gìndin bishiyà**	base of the tree
mashà-ruwā	rainbow (lit. drinker of water)		
bàř-ni-dà-mūgù	pimples/acne in adolescents (lit. leave-me-with-ugliness)		

The head is optionally accompanied by specifying or modifying elements. Some of these, e.g., the demonstratives (excluding the deictics indicating 'this, that', etc.) and the personal pronouns functioning as determiners, occur only before the head; a larger number of elements, like the definite article and relative clauses, occur only after the head. A few items, namely, the deictic demonstratives and simple adjectives, occur both in prenominal and postnominal position.

2. PRENOMINAL ELEMENTS

There are two primary constituents that occur in pre-head position, namely, (1) specifiers, and (2) adjectival modifiers, which occur in that order.

wani mahàukàcin kàrē	some crazy dog (specifier + adj + N)
wânnan bàbbař ƙasā	that large country (specifier + adj + N)

2.1. Specifiers

The category specifier includes determiners, pronouns, and the quantifier **duk** 'all, every' (see §53:2). A determiner can co-occur with the other two categories. Examples:

wannàn dōkì	this horse (det + N)
wàcè hanyà	which road? (det + N)
kōwànè mùtûm	every man (det + N)

mū Hàusàwā	we Hausas (pn + N)
ita sàraunìyā	she the queen (pn + N)
sū àbòkanmù	they our friends (pn + N)
duk talakāwā	all common people (all + N)
shī wannàn mālàmī	he this teacher (pn + det + N)
duk waɗànnân ɗàlìbai	all these students (all + det + N)

There are three other elements (apart from adjectives) that can precede the head. The first is the third person plural pronoun **su** used to form pseudoplurals indicating 'et al.' or 'etc.', e.g.,

su Tankò Tanko and the others; **su bàrēwā** gazelles and similar animals

The second is the "isolator" **ɗaya**, which is the numeral 'one' used in the sense of 'the other'. The head noun necessarily contains a definite article, e.g.,

ɗaya littāfìn	the other book (cf. **littāfì ɗaya** one book)
ɗaya hùlâr̃	the other cap (cf. **hùlā ɗaya** one cap)

The third pre-head element that occurs readily in surface structure is a long-form independent possessive. Again we find that the head must have a definite article, e.g.,

nàwa dōkìn	the horse of mine (lit. mine horse.the), cf. **dōkìnā** my horse
tāsà rìgâr̃	the gown of his (lit. his gown.the), cf. **rìgar̃sà** his gown
nāmù gidàjên	the houses of ours (lit. ours houses.the), cf. **gidàjenmù** our houses

°AN: Although the above examples could be viewed at a shallow level as prenominal modifiers, it is probably preferable to analyze them syntactically as appositional structures with an independent possessive pronoun juxtaposed to a noun, e.g., **nàwa dōkìn** would be interpreted as 'mine, the horse', **tāsà, rìgâr̃** as 'his, the gown', etc.

2.2. Adjectives

The prenominal modifier is typically a simple attributive adjective. It obligatorily contains a linker and obligatorily agrees in number and gender with the head noun. This adjective may be preceded by the diminutive marker **ɗan / 'yar̃ / 'yan** (m./f./pl.). In principle any number of adjectives can be strung together, although in practice, three seems to be the maximum.

shùɗɗan rīgunà	blue gowns (adj + N)
duk dōgwàyen ƙarfàfan sōjōjī	all the tall, strong soldiers (all + adj + adj + N)
zungurēr̃ìyar̃ tsōhuwar̃ farar̃ mōtà	a very long old white car (adj + adj + adj + N)
ɗan ƙàramin yārò	a wee small boy (dim + adj + N)
'yar̃ gàjēr̃ìyar̃ àkuyà	a little short goat (dim + adj + N)

3. POSTNOMINAL ELEMENTS

Most NP specification and modification occur after the head noun. The noun can be followed by a number of specifiers/determiners as well as by a range of modifiers, e.g.,

dawākin nàn biyu nāmù	these two horses of ours (lit. horses.of this two ours)

mōtàr̃kà sābuwā dà akà sācè   your new car that was stolen (lit. car.of.you new that one.pret steal)

3.1. Postnominal specifiers

The postnominal specifiers/determiners include the following: (1) definite article, (2) demonstrative determiner, (3) possessive, and (4) numeral (or other quantifier).

3.1.1. Definite article

Hausa has no indefinite article corresponding to English 'a/an'; thus the word yārò, for example, means 'boy' or 'a boy'. The so-called definite article (chap. **20**), which indicates an item previously referred to in the discourse (or context inferable), normally occurs right after the head. It has the form ˋn / ˋr̃ / ˋn (m./f./pl.), which either attaches directly to the noun or to the connector d'i-, e.g.,

tùlûn	the water pot (< tùlū + ˋn)	r̃ìgâr̃	the gown (< r̃ìgā + ˋr̃)
ƙasàshên	the countries (< ƙasàshē + ˋn)	cêk d'în	the check (< cêk d'i- + ˋn)

The definite article can also occur at the end of the entire NP as well, e.g.,

dōgwàyen yârân dà mukà gayà musùn   the tall boys that we told
(lit. tall.of boys.the that we.pret tell to.them.the)

3.1.2. Demonstrative determiners

All determiners can occur in pre-head position. The demonstrative determiners 'this/that/those, etc.' have variant forms that occur in postnominal position. These postnominal forms, namely, nân 'this', nan 'that near you', cân 'that there', and can 'that yonder' (which etymologically were adverbs meaning 'here/there/etc.') attach directly to a noun plus a linker or, in appropriate contexts, to a noun plus the connective d'i- plus a linker. (The orthographic convention is to write nân and the other forms as separate words, even though they cliticize to their hosts.) The demonstratives themselves are invariant for gender and number, these features bring reflected in the form of the linker, e.g.,

dōkìn nân   this horse; r̃ìgâr̃ nan   that gown (near you); gidàjen càn   those houses (there); cêk d'in nàn   this check

A noun can be specified by both a prenominal determiner and a postnominal definite article, e.g.,

wancàn gidân	that very house (lit. that house.the)
wad'ànnân b̃àrảyîn	these very thieves (lit. these thieves.the)
kōwàcè yārinyàr̃	every girl (known from the discourse) (lit. every girl.the)
wani yāròn	another boy (lit. some boy.the)

3.1.3. Possessives

Apart from the special formation with the prenominal independent possessives (see §2.1 above), possession is indicated by a post-head noun or clitic pronoun preceded by the linker, e.g.,

dōkìnsà   his horse; ƙasàshenmù   our countries; cêk d'intà   her check; r̃ìgar̃ Sulè   Sule's gown

Possessives can occur with a postnominal definite article or demonstrative. If the possessive is not attached to the head noun, it appears as a long form, i.e., nā-/tā- plus pronoun or na/ta plus noun, e.g.,

dōkìn nân nāsà this his horse (i.e., this horse of his); **rìgâř ta Sulè** the gown of Sule's

If the definite article (with **d'i-**) follows the possessive, it is generally interpreted as applying to the possessor rather than to the possessed head noun, e.g., **rìgař Sulè d'în** 'the gown of the very Sule in question'.

3.1.4. Numerals and other quantifiers
Cardinal numbers and other quantifiers (including ideophones) directly follow the head noun, with optional use of various unit measure terms (see §53:1.7), e.g.,

naiřà dubū 1,000 nairas; **'yan makařantā tàlàtin** thirty students; **fensìř (gùdā) d'aya** one (unit) pencil; **sōjōjī dà yawà** lots of soldiers; **mangwàřò nawà?** how many mangoes? **mutànē tìnjim** oodles of people; **'yammātā dukà** all the girls (= **duk 'yammātā**)

With possessed nouns, the typical order is N + possessor + numeral, e.g.,

mātansà hud'u his four wives (lit. wives.his four); **mōtōcinmù shidà** our six cars (lit. cars.our six)

One can reverse the order and have the numeral before the possessive (in which case one has to use an independent possessive). This is less common and is more highly marked than the possessive plus numeral order. Examples:

mātā hud'u nāsà his four wives (lit. wives four his)
mōtōcī shidà nāmù our six cars (lit. cars six ours)

Nouns with a numeral and a definite article occur in that order (with the d.a. requiring the connector **d'i-** as its host), e.g., **mōtōcī shidà d'în** 'the six cars (in question)'.

If the NP contains both a numeral and a postnominal demonstrative, both alternative orders are equally acceptable, e.g.,

mātā hud'u d'in nàn = mātan nàn (gùdā) hud'u these four women

Ordinal numbers connect to the head noun by means of a free linker, e.g.,

bābì na ukù the third chapter; **bàbban yāk̃ìn dūniyà na biyu** Second World War

If the NP with an ordinal number contains other determiners, the ordinal phrase usually occurs last, e.g.,

d'ākìn nân na d'aya this first room; **mātātā ta ukù** my third wife

By contrast, the definite article form **d'în** typically occurs at the end of the entire NP rather than immediately after the head, e.g., **sukùwā ta hud'u d'în** 'the fourth race'.

3.2. Postnominal modifiers
Nouns allow a large number of postnominal modifiers of different types, most of which can co-occur, subject to semantic appropriateness and length limitations. The modifiers include the following: (1) adjectives, (2) the words indicating 'different (kinds)', (3) genitival nouns, (4) the MAI construction

(and its negative counterparts), (5) the **mafî** construction, (6) prepositional phrases, (7) stative phrases, (8) relative clauses, (9) the construction with **wai**.

3.2.1. Adjectives

Postnominal adjectives are immediately juxtaposed to the head without the use of a linker or other particle, e.g., **yārò ƙaramī** 'a small boy' (lit. boy small). They nevertheless must agree with the head in gender and number. All adjectives that can occur in pre-head position can also occur following the head. (Where semantically appropriate, they can be preceded by the diminutive marker **ɗan / 'yaȓ / 'yan**.) In addition, there are some phonologically heavy adjectives (i.e., those that are fully reduplicated, multi-word, etc.) that occur only in post-head position, e.g.,

kwālī bàbba = bàbban kwālī	large carton
nāmà sòyayyē = sòyayyen nāmà	fried meat
tumākī 'yan ƙanānà = 'yan ƙanānàn tumākī	wee small lambs
haƙòrā gatsō-gàtsò	disproportionately large teeth
'yammātā santalā-sàntàlà	shapely girls
rìgā ruwan-hōdà	a pink gown (lit. gown color.of-powder)

Postnominal adjectives typically follow the various specifiers, e.g.,

kwālin nàn bàbba	this large carton
haƙòrankà gatsō-gàtsò	your disproportionately large teeth
birai biyu ƙâttā	two huge monkeys

3.2.2. The words indicating 'different (kinds)'

The expressions **dàbam (dàbam)** 'different' and **irì irì** 'different kinds' (< **irì** 'kind' (lit. seed)) serve as exclusively postnominal modifiers. Although their English equivalents are generally labeled as adjectives, these words do not pattern neatly with Hausa adjectives and are better set apart as a special class on their own. Examples:

littāfì dàbam	a different book	**wuràrē dàbam dàbam**	different places
àbinci irì irì	different kinds of food	**mōtōcī irì irì**	different kinds of cars

3.2.3. Genitival nouns

In N of N constructions, the second N typically serves as a possessor, e.g., **gidan Mūsā** 'Musa's house'. However, if the second noun is an inanimate noun indicating a quality or activity, it can serve as a modifier, corresponding semantically, though not syntactically, to an adjective, e.g.,

ruwan zāfī	hot water (lit. water of heat)
maròƙan banzā	stupid beggars (lit. beggars.of uselessness)
mahàjjàtan wòfī	foolish pilgrims (lit. pilgrims.of foolishness)
ɗākìn kàȓàtū	reading room (lit. room.of reading)
māgànin tàrī	cough medicine (lit. medicine of cough)

3.2.4. The MAI construction (and its negative counterparts)

In lieu of true adjectives, one commonly uses a postnominal modifier phrase of the form **mài** (pl. **màsu**) 'having' or **maràs** (pl. **maràsā**) 'lacking' plus a noun (often, but not exclusively, signifying a quality) (see chap. **4**), e.g.,

àlƙālī mài rōwằ	a stingy judge (lit. judge having stinginess)
rījìyā mài zurfī	a deep well (lit. well having depth)
mōtằ mài tsằdā	an expensive car (lit. car having expensiveness)
tēbur̄ōr̄ī màsu ƙwārī	strong tables (lit. tables having strength of construction)
kar̄às maràs dāɗī	bad-tasting carrots (lit. carrots lacking pleasantness)
yârā maràsā hankàlī	senseless children (lit. children lacking sense)

The MAI phrase can accompany a simple adjective. If the adjective is used postnominally, the order is usually N + adj + MAI phrase, e.g.,

sābuwar̄ mōtằ mài tsằdā = mōtằ sābuwā mài tsằdā	an expensive new car
ɗanyen kar̄às maràs dāɗī = kar̄às ɗanyē maràs dāɗī	raw bad-tasting carrots

3.2.5. The comparative modifier construction

Corresponding to the MAI phrases is a postnominal phrase having the structure of a short-form agentive (see §7:1.6.3), namely, **mafī** (pl. **mafīyā**) 'lit. the one exceeding' plus an object. This forms a comparative (or superlative) modifier, e.g.,

gidan àbinci mafī tsabtằ	the cleanest restaurant
mōtằ mafī tsằdā	the most expense car
'yan ƙwallon rāgā mafīyā kyâu	the best basketball players

As with the MAI phrases, these phrases typically follow simple postnominal adjectives, e.g.,

mōtằ farā mafī tsằdā	the most expensive white car

3.2.6. Prepositional phrases

Nouns may be modified by a post-head prepositional phrase. Examples:

wani tēbùr̄ à ɗākīnā	a table in my room
kùjērū don mânya-mânya	chairs for important people
bàƙōn dàgà Kanò	the visitor from Kano
ɗālìbī à jāmi'à	a university student (lit. student at university)
hafsằ gàba dà nī	an officer ahead of me (in rank)

3.2.7. Stative phrases

Stative phrases of the form stative + **dà** 'with' + NP', which sometimes translate as English adjectival past particles, can function as postnominal modifiers, e.g.,

yārinyà ɗaure dà zanī	a girl dressed in a wrapper
bangō shàfe dà fentī	a wall covered with paint
sōjà rìƙe dà bindigằ	a soldier armed with a gun

If another modifier occurs immediately after the head, the phrase is often expressed as a relative clause introduced by **dà kè** 'that is', e.g.,

yārinyà kyàkkyāwā (dà kè) ɗaure dà zanī	a beautiful girl (who is) dressed in a wrapper
bangō mài tsawō (dà kè) shàfe dà fentī	a tall wall (that is) covered with paint

3.2.8. Relative clauses

All relative clauses (RCs) occurs postnominally (see chap. **64**), e.g.,

mùtumìn [dà mukà sằmi làbằr̃ìnsà jiyằ]   the man [whom we heard the news of yesterday]

A relative clause typically follows all other modifiers, e.g.,

yār̃ồ gàjēr̃ē mài dàbār̃ằ [dà na sanì]	a short clever boy that I know (N adj **mài**-phrase RC)
jìminā mafî tsawō [dà na taɓà ganì]	the tallest ostrich I have ever seen (N **mafî**-phrase RC)
wuƙā cikin kwabàd [wâddà nakề bùƙātằ]	a knife in the cupboard that I need (N pp RC)

3.2.9. The **wai** construction

There are alternative means in Hausa of expressing a phrase like 'a boy named/called Musa'. One is to use a relative clause, e.g., **yār̃ồ dà akề kir̃ằ Mūsā** (lit. boy that one.Rcont1 calling Musa). Another is to modify the common noun by a phrase of the form **wai** 'it is said' + an independent pronoun + the name, e.g., **yār̃ồ wai shī Mūsā**. In colloquial speech, the pronoun can be omitted. Examples:

wata màcè wai (ita) Lādì	a woman named Ladi
tsōhon gwamnằ wai (shī) Audù Bằƙo	a former governor named Audu Baƙo
ƙasā wai (ita) Bosniyà	a country called Bosnia

> °AN: The word **wai** (pronounced [wei]), which, in the reduplicated form **waiwai** exists as a common noun meaning 'rumor or hearsay', also serves as a function word optionally introducing complement clauses, e.g., **yā kàmātà (wai) Tankồ yà biyā hàr̃ājî** 'It is fitting that Tanko pay taxes.'

The **wai** phrase is a late modifier that typically follows all other modifiers other than RCs, where the order can sometimes be reversed, e.g.,

yārinyằ kyàkkāwā wai ita Hàdīzà	a beautiful girl named Hadiza
littāfî mài farin jinī wai (shī) Shaihù Umàr̃	a popular book called *Shaihu Umar*
mālàmī à makar̃antar̃sù wai shī Dr. Nuhù	a teacher at their school named Dr. Nuhu
wani wằsā dà mukề sô wai shī mar̃wằ	a game that we like called *marwa*
wata ɗālìbā dà ta sằmi lambằ wai ita Bintà	a student who won the prize named Binta
= wata ɗālìbā wai ita Bintà wâddà ta sằmi lambằ	a student named Binta who won the prize

[References: Furniss (1991); Galadanci (1969)]

52. Noun Subcategorization

FOR syntactic purposes, a major division in nouns (whether derived or nonderived) is between non-dynamic and dynamic.

1. NONDYNAMIC

The term *nondynamic* is defined negatively to apply to all nouns other than the dynamic nouns. These nouns indicate persons, places, things, qualities, ideas, etc., e.g., **yārinyằ** 'girl', **makaṛantā** 'school', **zōbề** 'ring', **zurfī** 'depth', **àddīnì** 'religion'. Nondynamic nouns can be subdivided into (1) concrete nouns, e.g., **takồbī** 'sword', and (2) abstract nouns, e.g., **kaifī** 'sharpness'.

1.1. Concrete nouns

The concrete nouns are defined as nondynamic, not abstract nouns. They can be further divided into (a) proper nouns, which includes both personal names, e.g., **Mūsā** 'Musa' and place names, e.g., **Jāmùs** 'Germany', and (b) common nouns, e.g., **kềkề** 'bicycle', **ruwā** 'water'.

The concrete nouns can also be classified as to whether they are (1) count nouns, (2) collectives, or (3) noncount nouns.

Count nouns are characterized by the potentiality for pluralization and enumeration, e.g., **àkuyằ ɗaya** 'one goat', **dawākī (ukù)** '(three) horses', **mùtûm na ukù** 'the third man'.

Collectives are nouns referring to a group or assemblage. They allow either singular or plural concord depending on whether the focus is on the group as a whole or on the individual members, e.g., **[jàma'aṛ]**$_{sg}$ **tanằ nēman tàimakō** 'The populace is seeking aid'; **[jàma'aṛ]**$_{pl}$ **sunằ gaṛdamằ à kân sìyāsằ** 'The people are arguing about politics'; **tằrō [yā]**$_{sg}$ / **[sun]**$_{pl}$ **wātsề** 'The crowd dispersed.'

Noncount nouns include various masses and liquids, e.g., **mâi** 'oil', **yằshī** 'sand'. Most of these take singular concord, although **ruwā** 'water' is sometimes treated as a plural—a common Chadic and Afroasiatic feature—as is the word **kuɗī** 'money'. Some noncount nouns have plural forms, which are used in the sense of "kinds of", e.g., **kuɗằɗē** 'monies of different kinds'. To specify quantities of noncount nouns, one has to use an appropriate measure term, e.g., **mâi galàn biyu** 'two gallons of oil' (lit. oil gallon two) (not ****mâi biyu**); **shìnkāfā mūdù ɗaya** 'one bowl of rice'. On the whole, what is or is not a noncount noun is essentially the same as in English. There are, however, a few culturally determined differences, e.g., **sukàrī** 'sugar' is usually a count noun because the unmarked reading of the term is 'a cube of sugar'; similarly **buṛōdì** 'bread' can be a count noun meaning 'a loaf of bread'.

1.2. Abstract nouns

Abstract nouns signify static, usually inherent or permanent qualities or attributes. Morphologically, they fall into three major categories: (a) simple, e.g., **rōwằ** 'miserliness', **farī** 'whiteness'; (b) derived nouns with the suffixes {-CI}, {-TA}, and {-TAKA} (see chap. 1), e.g., **talaucì** 'poverty', **wâutā** 'foolishness', **màṛwàbtakằ** 'neighborliness'; and (c) abstract nouns of sensory quality (see chap. 2),

377

e.g., **zurfî** 'depth', **tsāmī** 'sourness'. Note that when color terms function as abstract nouns, they take the unmarked masculine form, whereas when they function as adjectives they reflect the gender of the head noun, e.g., [**tūtà**]$_f$ [**shūdîyā**]$_f$ 'blue flag' (lit. flag blue), but [**tūtà**]$_f$ **mài launìn** [**shūdî**]$_m$ 'blue flag' (lit. flag having color.of blueness). Instead of using adjectives, attributive and predicative descriptions are often expressed employing abstract nouns of quality, e.g., **àlƙālī mài rōwà** 'a miserly judge' (lit. judge possessing miserliness); **rījìyā tanà dà zurfî** 'The well is deep' (lit. the well is with depth). The expression of comparatives and superlatives, which has the structure X exceeds Y (with regard to) Z requires that Z be an abstract noun, e.g., **Mūsā yā fi Daudà ƙarfî** 'Musa is stronger than Dauda' (lit. Musa exceeds Dauda strength); **mōtàtā tā fi tākà sàbùntā** 'My car is newer than yours' (lit. car.my exceeds yours newness), cf. the noncomparative, which uses the related true adjective, **mōtàtā sābuwā cè** 'My car is new.' One should note that the same word can belong to more than one category, thus **baƙī**, for example, is an abstract noun when it denotes 'blackness' but a concrete common noun when it denotes 'consonant'. This is in addition to its role as an adjective meaning 'black' (in which case it has a corresponding feminine form **baƙā**).

2. DYNAMIC

Dynamic nouns serve to indicate actions or activities, e.g., **aikî** 'work', **ɗàwàiniyā** 'suffering with', **kàɗe-kàɗe** 'drumming', **màganà** 'talk(ing)', **rùbùtū** 'writing', **wàsā** 'play(ing)'. They commonly function in phrasal VPs as the object of the pro-verb **yi** 'do' to express what in English would be indicated by a simple intransitive verb, e.g., **yā yi màganà** 'He talked' (lit. he did talking), **zā sù yi wàsā** 'They will play' (lit. will do playing). They also occur readily as the object of aspectual verbs, another environment in which they commute with nonfinite verb phrases, e.g., **yā fārà rùbùtū** 'He began writing', **kù yi ta aikî!** 'You (pl.) keep on working!' **mun shā ɗàwàiniyā dà shī** 'We suffered putting up with him / we suffered together in doing sth.' In the continuous TAM s, where **yî(n)**, the verbal noun corresponding to **yi**, is commonly deleted, dynamic nouns often occur immediately after the TAM, e.g., **sunà kàɗe-kàɗe** 'They are drumming' (< **sunà yîn kàɗe-kàɗe**), **bā sà kūkā** 'They are not crying' (< **bā sà yîn kūkā**).

Some dynamic nouns are simple nonderived words, e.g., **sū** 'fishing', **màganà** 'talking', **wàsā** 'playing'; others are gerundivelike verbal nouns, e.g., **sàyē** 'buying' (< **sàyā** 'buy'), **gaisuwā** 'greetings' (< **gaisà** 'greet'), **gòdiyā** 'thanks' (< **gōdè** 'thank'), **gyārā** 'repairing' (< **gyàrà** 'repair'), **yàbō** 'praise/praising' (< **yàbā** 'praise'), **bùshe-bùshe** 'playing music' (< **būsà** 'blow').

It is important to stress that not all verb-derived nouns are dynamic, i.e., the dynamic/nondynamic distinction applies to verb-derived nouns as well as to basic nouns. Here are examples of some concrete nondynamic verb-derived nouns, which are referred to as "deverbal nouns" (see chap. **22**): **gutsurè** 'fragment, piece broken off' (< **gutsùrē** 'break a piece off'), **mulmulè** 'a kneaded ball' (< **mulmùlā** 'knead'), **ràiràyī** 'fine sand' (< **ràirayà** 'sift'), **wankî** 'the wash/laundry' (< **wankè** 'wash, launder').

As would be expected, many verb-derived nouns exist as both dynamic and nondynamic nouns, e.g., **ginî** 'a building or the activity of building' (< **ginà** 'build'); **ɗaurî** 'a knot, an arrest, or the action of tying up' (< **ɗaurè** 'tie'); **sanî** 'knowledge or knowing' (< **sanì** 'know'); **aurē** 'a marriage or marrying' (< **àurā** 'marry'); **shìgā** 'an outfit or entering' (< **shìga** 'enter'); **yàɓē** 'plaster or plastering' (< **yāɓà** 'to plaster').

ΔDN: According to Malami Buba (personal communication), the Sokoto dialect makes a distinction between **ginî** 'a building' and **gīnî** 'the activity of building', both from **ginà** 'build'. If this represents a general pattern—which needs to be investigated—it would be quite unusual, because Hausa (unlike some other Chadic languages) does not normally make use of word-internal vowel lengthening for derivational purposes.

53. Numerals and Other Quantifiers

1. NUMERALS

1.1. Cardinal numbers

The basic cardinal numbers from one to ten are as follows. (Items in < > indicate common dialect variants.):

1 ɗaya, 2 biyu, 3 ukù <ukkù>, 4 huɗu, 5 bìyař < bìyat , bìyal>,
6 shidà <shiddà>, 7 bakwài, 8 takwàs <takwàř>, 9 tařà, 10 gōmà

As contrasted with common nouns, note that these numerals do not end in a long vowel. Most end in a short vowel; two end in a consonant, and one ends in a diphthong /ai/, presumably derived from *ay.

Cardinal numbers are optionally preceded by the word gùdā 'unit' (originally meaning 'lump'), e.g., mangwàřò (gùdā) biyu 'two mangoes'. Note that gùdā by itself often serves in place of ɗaya to indicate 'one', e.g., bīřȍ gùdā = bīřȍ gùdā ɗaya = bīřȍ ɗaya 'one ballpoint pen'.

The numbers from eleven to nineteen are made up of gōmà 'ten'+ the connecting particle shâ + a basic numeral from one to nine. (Etymologically, shâ is probably related to the verbal noun shâ 'drinking'.) The word gōmà is optionally omitted, e.g.,

11 (gōmà) shâ ɗaya, 12 (gōmà) shâ biyu, 13 (gōmà) shâ ukù, 14 (gōmà) shâ huɗu, etc.

The numbers eighteen and nineteen have an alternative expression built on twenty (àshìřin) less two and one, respectively. The 'less' phrase, which makes use of the negative existential marker bābù / bâ, has two alternative word orders, with bâ before and bābù after the lower numerals, e.g.,

18 àshìřin bâ biyu = àshìřin biyu bābù (= (gōmà) shâ takwàs)
19 àshìřin bâ ɗaya = àshìřin ɗaya bābù (= (gōmà) shâ tařa)

The numbers twenty through ninety are loanwords from Arabic:

20 àshìřin, 30 tàlàtin, 40 àřbà'in, 50 hàmsin,
60 sìttin, 70 sàbà'in, 80 tàmànin, 90 càsà'in (= tìs'in)

◊HN: Before the introduction of the Arabic loanwords, twenty through ninety were expressed by multiples of ten using the form gòmiyā (related to the current form gōmà 'ten'), e.g., gòmiyā biyu 'twenty', gòmiyā huɗu 'forty', etc. At the time of Bargery (1934), over half a century ago, this formation was reported to still be used in some dialects; whether this is still so, I cannot say.

Another archaic system, now essentially defunct, used the word hâuyā 'score (i.e., twenty)' as a base, e.g., hauyā ukù dà gōmà 'seventy' (i.e., three score and ten). (According to Bargery

(1934), from whom this information is taken, the initial syllable of **hâuyā** was falling when used alone, but high when used in multiples.)

Numbers between the decades are indicated by a decade numeral + **dà** 'and/with' + a basic numeral, e.g.,

29 **àshìr̃in dà tar̃à**, 38 **tàlâtin dà takwàs**, 43 **àr̃bà'in dà ukù**, 56 **hàmsin dà shidà**

A hundred is **d̃àr̃ī** (pl. **d̃àrūruwâ**), a thousand is **dubū** (pl. **dùbbai**), and a million is **miliyàn** (borrowed from English) (pl. **miliyōyī**). Multiples are indicated by immediately juxtaposing a following lower number, e.g.,

200   **d̃àr̃ī biyu**, 500 **d̃àr̃ī bìyar̃**, 7,000 **dubū bakwài**, 20,000 **dubū àshìr̃in**,
600,000 **dubū d̃àr̃ī shidà**, 3,000,000 **miliyàn ukù**

Intermediate numbers are formed using the connector **dà**, e.g.,

238   **d̃àr̃ī biyu dà tàlâtin dà takwàs**
515   **d̃àr̃ī bìyar̃ dà (gōmà) shâ bìyar̃**
7,482   **dubū bakwài dà d̃àr̃ī hud̃u dà tàmânin dà biyu**
3,001,250   **miliyàn ukù dà dubū d̃aya dà d̃àr̃ī biyu dà hàmsin**

Note the possibility of ambiguity as seen in the following example:

23,000 or 20,003 **dubū àshìr̃in dà ukù** (= **dubū àshìr̃in dà gùdā ukù** in the second meaning only)

Apart from **dubū**, there are two other words for 'thousand': **zambàr̃**, an equivalent, but less common equivalent of **dubū** used only in multiples, and **alìf** (borrowed from Arabic), the normal substitute for **dubū** in calendar dates. Examples:

7,400   **zambàr̃ bakwài dà d̃àr̃ī hud̃u** = **dubū bakwài dà d̃àr̃ī hud̃u**
20,000   **zambàr̃ àshìr̃in** = **dubū àshìr̃in**
1960 (the year) **(shèkar̃àr̃) alìf dà d̃àr̃ī tar̃à dà sìttin**

In addition to the multiples of a hundred and a thousand formed according to the above patterns, there are equivalent lexical items borrowed from Arabic (esp. found in written sources). These "esoteric/prestige" forms are also used in the spoken language with greater or lesser frequency depending on the background and degree of Islamic education of the speaker and on the individual item. Examples:

100 (in combinations only) **minyà** (= **miyyà**), 200 **mètan**, 400 **àr̃bàminyà**,
500 **hàmsà(a)minyà**
2,000 **àlfyan**, 3,000 **tàlātà**, 4,000 **ar̃bà**, 5,000 **hamsà**, 6,000 **sittà**, 7,000 **saba'à**,
8,000 **tàmāniyà**

When forming combinations with these numerals, one tends to use **alìf** (instead of **dubū**) for 1,000 and the connective **wà** 'and' instead of **dà**.

1,100 **alìf wà minyà**, 1,200 **alìf wà mètan**, 1,400 **alìf wà àr̃bàminyà**
but 1,300 **alìf dà d̃àr̃ī ukù**, 2,500 **àlfyan dà d̃àr̃ī bìyar̃**, 6,600 **sittà dà d̃àr̃ī shidà**

The numbers 1,800 and 1,900 can be expressed either in an additive manner using **dà** or in a subtractive manner using **gaiřà** 'minus', e.g.,

1,800	**alìf dà ɗàrī takwàs** =	**àlfyan gaiřà mètan**	(lit. 2,000 minus 200)
1,900	**alìf dà ɗàrī tařà** =	**àlfyan gaiřà minyà̀**	(lit. 2,000 minus 100)

Numbers less than one are indicated by nominal forms (mostly Arabic loanwords), e.g., **sifìřī** 'zero', **ushìřī** 'a tenth', **humùsī** 'a fifth', **řubù'ī** (= **kwatà̀** 'a fourth' (< Eng. 'quarter')), **sulùsī** 'a third', **rabī̀** 'a half', e.g., **rabìn awà̀** 'a half hour' (lit. half.of an hour)' cf. **awà̀ biyu** 'two hours' (lit. hour two).

Other fractions are usually expressed using the preposition **bisà** 'on, over', e.g., **ukù bisà huɗu** 'three-fourths (lit. three over four), **bakwài bisà gōmà** 'seven-tenths', **ɗàrī bisà ɗàrī** 'a perfect score' (lit. 100 over 100). This formation is especially common in modern-day mathematics.

Percentages are formed with the preposition **cikin** 'in', e.g., **gōma cikin ɗàrī** '10%' (lit. 10 in 100), **sìttin dà bìyař cikin ɗàrī** '65%' (lit. 65 in 100).

1.2. Enumerators

Attributive numerals (and the question word **nawà** 'how many') are optionally preceded by the word **gùdā** 'unit', especially if anything intervenes between the noun and the quantifier, e.g.,

kujèrā gùdā ɗaya one chair; **gidan-àshānā gùdā hàmsin** fifty matchboxes; **màkàřàntun càn gùdā biyu** those two schools; **mōtōcin nàn na Mūsā gùdā bìyař** these five cars of Musa (lit. cars.of this of Musa unit five); **gidàjē řùsàssū gùdā nawà?** how many demolished houses?

With nouns referring to humans, independent pronouns may serve as optional enumerators. They add a degree of definiteness and extra specificity to the phrase, e.g.,

ɗàlìbai sū bìyař five students (exactly); **'yan tāwāyè̀ sū gōmà** (the) ten rebels

1.3. Distributives

Repetition of numerals, quantifiers, and unit/measure terms expresses the notion of 'X each', e.g.,

bìyař bìyař five each, e.g., **zā sù bā kù fensìř bìyař bìyař** They will give you five pencils each.
cf. **zā sù bā kù fensìř bìyař** They will give you five pencils (in toto).
nawà nawà? how many/much each?
e.g., **bàřgō nawà nawà zā à bā sù?** How many blankets each should one give them?
gōmà gōmà ten each; **hàmsin hàmsin** fifty each; **dubū dubū** a thousand each
naiřà naiřà a naira each; **dalà̀ dalà̀** a dollar each,
e.g., **kuɗin wannàn dalà̀ dalà̀** These cost a dollar each.

The repeated form **kàɗan kàɗan** (< **kàɗan** 'few') does not indicate 'a few each' but rather 'just a few, just a little bit', e.g., **kà bā sù shāyì̄ kàɗan kàɗan** 'Give them just a little bit of tea!'

When they undergo repetition, the numbers 'one', 'two', and 'four' have optional, but commonly used, reduced forms, e.g.,

ɗai ɗai = **ɗaiɗaya** = [less common] **ɗaya ɗaya**)	one each
bībiyu (<**bibbiyu**>) = **biyu biyu**	two each
huřhuɗu = **huɗu huɗu**	four each

With phrasal numbers, only the last element is repeated, e.g.,

tàlàtin dà bìyař bìyař 35 each (< **tàlàtin dà bìyař** 35); **dubū dà ɗàrī ukù ukù** 1,300 each

1.4. Nouns with numerals (and other quantifiers)

With many nouns, it is normal to use the singular form with numerals and other quantifiers even when the noun has a corresponding plural form, e.g.,

[kàtīfà]$_{sg}$ **huɗu** four mattresses (cf. pl. **kàtīfū**); [bâm]$_{sg}$ **ɗàrī** 100 bombs (cf. pl. **bàmàbàmai**); [kīfī]$_{sg}$ **mètan** 200 fish (cf. pl. **kīfàyē**); [naiřà]$_{sg}$ **dubū** 1,000 nairas (cf. pl. **naiřōřī**); [hùlà]$_{sg}$ **nawà?** how many caps? (cf. pl. **hūlunà**); [kadà]$_{sg}$ **dà yawà** many crocodiles (cf. pl. **kadàndanī**)

> °AN: Jaggar (personal communication) points out that the use of the individuating unit term **gùdā** normally requires that the head noun be plural, e.g., [akāwunà]$_{pl}$ **gùdā huɗu** 'four clerks' = [àkàwu]$_{sg}$ **huɗu**, but *not* ??**àkàwu gùdā huɗu**. An interesting question is whether this restriction applies to nouns that do not have overt morphological plurals. As indicated below in §1.7, **gùdā** is allowed with singular nouns functioning as unit measure terms.

Common words with phonologically simple plural forms, on the other hand, tend to use the plural with numerals, as do compounds built with **ɗan- /'yař- /'yan-** (m./f./pl.) 'psn of' and certain derived nouns (such as agentives), e.g.,

[mātā]$_{pl}$ **gōmà** 10 women (cf. sg. **màcè**); [àbòkai]$_{pl}$ (**gùdā**) **ukù** 3 friends (cf. sg. **àbōkī**); [birai]$_{pl}$ **kàɗan** a few moneys (cf. sg. **birī**); ['yan-sàndā]$_{pl}$ **hàmsin** 50 policemen (cf. sg. **ɗan-sàndā**); [masànā]$_{pl}$ **bakwài** 7 scholars (cf. sg. **masànī**)

> ◊ HN: My impression is that modern SH speakers use plural nouns with numerals more than was apparently the case half a century ago when such scholars as Abraham were describing the language. This may be a natural drift or it may be due to the influence of English.

1.5. Numerals with pronouns

Plural personal pronouns can occur with numerals, e.g., **mū ukù** 'we 3, the 3 of us'. Singular pronouns occur with **kaɗai** 'only, alone', e.g., **kai kaɗai** 'you only', but not normally with **ɗaya** itself. In such examples as **mū ukù** 'we 3', it is not clear whether the numeral is functioning as a modifier of the pronoun or whether the numeral is functioning in a pronominal manner preceded by a personal pronoun specifier. Examples:

kū bakwài ɗin nàn, bà zā à kàrɓē kù ba   You these seven, they're not going to take you.
mū shidà mukà ci jařřabâwā   It was we six who passed the exam.
tā gayà musù sū huɗu   She told the four of them. (lit. she told them they four)

1.6. Word order with attributive quantifiers

The basic word order with quantifiers (apart from **duk** 'all') is noun (with associated definite article or demonstrative) + quantifier, e.g.,

naiřà dubū 1,000 nairas; **'yan-makařantā tàlàtin** 30 students; **sōjàn gwamnatì mètan dà hàmsin** 250 government soldiers; **mutànē nawà?** how many people?; **ɓērā** (= **ɓēřàyē**) **dà yawàn gàske**

a real lot of rats; **awākîn gùdā gōmà shâ biyu** the 12 goats (cf. **awākī shâ biyu** 12 goats); **kūkōkin nàn gùdā bìyař = wad̀ànnân kūkōkī (gùdā) bìyař** these five baobab trees

The numeral **d̀aya** 'one' can occur before the head noun (plus definite article), in which case it indicates 'the other', e.g.,

d̀aya yāròn the other boy, cf. **yārò̂ d̀aya** one boy; **d̀aya yārinyàř** the other girl

With normal postnominal possessives, the basic order is N + possessor + quantifier, e.g.,

mātansà (gùdā) hud̀u	his four wives (lit. wives.his (unit) four)
yâran sarkī (gùdā) gōmà	the chief's ten followers (lit. children.of chief (unit) ten)

One can reverse the order and have the numeral before the possessive, in which case one has to use an independent possessive. This is less common and more highly marked than the order shown above, e.g.,

mātā hud̀u nāsà	his four wives (lit. wives four his)
yârā gōmà na sarkī	the chief's ten followers (lit. children ten of chief)

With prenominal adjectives, the word order is adj N + num, e.g.,

mahàukàtan kařnukà̂ hud̀u	four mad dogs (lit. mad dogs four)
jājàyen motōcī bìyař	five red cars
kyāwà̀wan 'yammātā gùdā ukù	three attractive girls

With postnominal adjectives (or adjectival phrases), the order is N + num followed by the adjective, e.g.,

kařnukà̂ hud̀u mahàukàtā	four mad dogs (lit. dogs four mad)
mōtōcī bìyař jājàyē	five red cars
'yammātā ukù màsu kyân ganī	three good-looking girls

Similarly, numerals precede relative clauses, which are postnominal, e.g.,

mōtōcī ukùn dà mukè̂ sô	the three cars that we want
awākī bìyař d̀in nàn dà wānè ya bā mù	these five goats that so-and-so gave us
mutànē takwàs dà sukà rasà rāyukànsù	eight men who lost their lives

1.7. Unit measures with non-count nouns

Non-count nouns like water, grain, sand, etc., denote an undifferentiated mass and thus cannot be modified directly by a numeral. To express quantity one must use a "unit measure" noun, in the singular, like **bùhū** 'sack', **damī** 'bundle', **kwalabā** 'bottle', **tàfī** 'handful'. There are two alternative formations. One structure is noun + unit measure + numeral, e.g. **mâi galàn hud̀u** 'four gallons of oil' (lit. oil gallon four). Here are some selected examples of unit measure nouns in this structure:

bùhū :	**dāwà̀ bùhū gōmà**	ten sacks of guinea-corn (lit. guinea-corn sack ten)
damī :	**gērō damī bìyař**	five bundles of millet
dùř ô :	**kànànzîř dùř ô gōmà**	ten drums of kerosene
gwangwanī :	**farař-ƙasā gwangwanī biyu**	two cans of whitewash

kâi :	itằcē kâi huɗu	four bundles of firewood (lit. wood head four)
kwalabā :	mân-jā kwalabā shidà	six bottles of palm oil
lūdàyī :	furā lūdàyī biyu	two scoops (ladlefuls) of fura
mōtằ :	itằcē mōtằ bìyař	five truckfuls of firewood
mūdừ :	masằřā mūdừ tařà	nine measuring bowls of sweet corn
turmī :	shaddằ turmī ukừ	three rolls of brocade cloth

In some cases the association between the non-count noun and the unit measure noun has become so fixed that the former can be deleted, e.g.

fallē :	takàřdā fallē ɗaya =	fallē ɗaya	a single sheet of paper
jařkằ :	fētừř jařkằ huɗu =	jařkằ huɗu	four jerry-cans of gasoline
tīfằ :	yằshī tīfằ takwàs =	tīfằ takwàs	eight dump truck loads of sand

A few older unit measure terms have acquired a specialized meaning, e.g. ƙwaryā 'calabash' = 100 kolanuts (e.g. gōřò ƙwaryā biyu '200 kolanuts'); jàkā 'bag' = 100 pounds in the old Nigerian currency.

Another means of expressing quantities with noncount nouns is to connect the measure term plus the noncount noun in a linking construction followed by the numeral, e.g.,

bùhun dāwằ gōmà   ten sacks of guinea-corn (lit. sack.of guinea-corn ten) = dāwằ bùhū gōmà (lit. guinea-corn sack ten); kân itằcē gùdā huɗu   four bundles of firewood ; fallen takàřdā ɗaya   one sheet of paper; gwangwanī na farař-ƙasā biyu   two cans of whitewash; kwalabař mân-jā gùdā shidà six bottles of palm-oil; mūdừn masằřā tařà   nine measuring bowls of sweet corn

With this structure, the phrases are often ambiguous. For example, in addition to meaning 'six bottles of palm-oil', kwalabař mân-jā gùdā shidà could also mean 'six palm-oil bottles'. Similarly, tīfař yằshī takwàs can mean either 'eight dump-truck-loads of sand' or 'eight sand trucks'.

An additional means of expressing quantities with non-count nouns is by a structure of the form unit-measure + numeral + linker + noncount N. In this case, the unit-measure noun may be in the plural, which indicates that what is being quantified is the container and not the content, e.g.,

bùhū tàlằtin na shìnkāfā	thirty sacks of rice (lit. sack 30 of rice)
galàn shidà na mân gyàɗā	six gallons of peanut oil
jařkằ huɗu (= jařèkanī huɗu) na fētừř	four jerry-cans of gasoline
lūdàyī biyu (= lūdayằ biyu) na furā	two ladlefuls of *fura*

1.8. Numerals as equational predicates

In addition to their common use as noun modifiers in an NP, numerals also function as predicates in equational sentences (normally with the stabilizer omitted), e.g. [mātansà] [huɗu] 'His wives (are) four' (i.e. he has four wives). (The same surface form could mean 'his four wives' in a sentence like [mātansà huɗu] sun yi yājì 'His four wives have gone off in a huff.') The equational construction with numerals is especially common with the word ɗaya 'one' (usually with a stabilizer), characterized by an extended meaning, e.g.,

[sōjōjinmừ] [gùdā hàmsin]	Our soldiers are fifty. (i.e., we have fifty soldiers)
duk ɗaya nề	It's all the same. (lit. all one STAB)
kânsừ ɗaya nề gà yînsà	They are unanimous that it should be done.
(lit. themselves one STAB at doing.of.it)	

1.9. Coordination and numerals

Two (or more) NPs containing a numeral can be conjoined, e.g.,

àyàbà shā biyu dà mangwàr̃ò huɗu	twelve bananas and four mangoes
littāfì shidà dà bīr̃ò shidà	six books and six ballpoint pens
màge dà kar̃nukà bìyar̃	a cat and five dogs
màge bìyar̃ dà wasu kar̃nukà	five cats and some dogs
jàjàyen awākī ukù dà baƙāƙen jākunà	three red goats and (some) black donkeys

Conjoined nouns can be modified by a single numeral, thereby indicating the total number of the two nouns, e.g.,

[awākī dà tumākī] gōmà	ten goats and sheep
[warwarō dà zōbè] àshìr̃in	twenty bracelets and rings
[māsū dà takubbà] hàmsin dà biyu	fifty-two spears and swords
[àlmàjìr̃ai dà yâran makar̃antā] ɗàrī	hundred pupils and students

To get a reading of the number in toto, the two nouns have to be semantically related, they have to match morphologically in terms of singularity/plurality, and neither can contain a determiner or definite article. The following conjoined nouns thus do not qualify for a combined number reading, e.g.,

wuƙāƙē dà [dawākī takwàs]	knives and eight horses (not ** eight knives and horses)
warwarō dà [zôbbā àshìr̃in]	a bracelet (or some bracelets) and twenty rings
awākī dà [tumākîn gōmà	goats and the ten sheep
awākîn dà tumākī gōmà	the goats and ten sheep

When the appropriate conditions are met for a total sum reading, a surface sentence may be ambiguous, e.g.,

ɗan-kunne dà ɗan-wuyà huɗu
(a) four earrings and necklaces, i.e., **[ɗan-kunne dà ɗan-wuyà huɗu**
(b) an earring and 4 necklaces, i.e., **ɗan-kunne dà [ɗan-wuyà huɗu]**
tūlunà dà tukwànē shidà
(a) six water pots and cooking pots, i.e., **[tūlunà dà tukwànē] shidà**
(b) (some) water pots and six cooking pots, i.e., **tūlunà dà tukwànē shidà**

The ambiguity can be avoided by inserting **kuma** 'also' before the second conjunct or by having the two nouns disagree in plurality, e.g.,

ɗan-kunne dà kuma ɗan-wuyà huɗu	an earring and also four necklaces
tùlū dà tukwànē shidà	a water pot and six cooking pots

If the intention is to have the number refer individually to the two nouns, the distributive form with the repeated numeral must be used, e.g.,

awākī dà tumākī gōmà gōmà	ten goats and ten sheep
'yan-kunne dà 'yan-wuyà hur̃huɗu	four earrings and four necklaces

With nouns that semantically occur together as a paired set, the numeral is understood to specify the number of pairs rather than the number of individual objects, e.g.,

turmī dà taɓaryā takwàs	eight mortar and pestle sets (not **a mortar and eight pestles)
shakwarā dà jamfā̀ gùdā shidà	six gown and jumper sets
kwàrī dà bàkā tàlā̀tin	thirty bow and arrow sets

If the numeral occurs after the first conjunct, then normally only one reading is possible, e.g., **awākī ukù dà tumākī** 'three goats and (some) sheep'. In very clear contexts, however, an elliptical reading is possible, i.e., 'three goats and (three) sheep' where the assumed underlying **ukù** after **tumākī** 'sheep' has been deleted. This ellipsis is more normal in disjoined clauses with **kō** 'or', e.g.,

yā cê zâi bā nì faifai bìyař kō kāsèt (< **yā cê zâi bā nì faifai bìyař kō kāsèt bìyař**)
   He said he would give me five records or (five) cassettes

1.10. Ordinals
Ordinal numbers are indicated by means of the short-vowel linker (na or ta depending on the gender and number of the preceding (or understood) noun) plus a cardinal number, e.g.,

dōkì na bìyař   the fifth horse; **na gōmà**   the tenth (e.g., a bank, which is m.); **mōtā̀ ta ukù**   the third car;   **ta shidà**   the sixth (e.g., an owl, which is f.)

'First' can be expressed either as **na̋ ta ɗaya** (lit. 'of one') or more commonly as **na / ta farkō** (= **na / ta fārì**) (lit. of beginning from **fārā̀** 'begin'). 'Last' is expressed as **na / ta ƙàrshē** (< **ƙāràsā** 'end, finish'.) 'Middle' is **na / ta tsakiyā̀**. Examples:

shirìnmù na farkō   our first (radio or TV) program; **ɗā̀lìbai na fārì**   the first students; **laccà ta ƙàrshē** the last lecture; **yārinyā̀ ta tsakiyā̀**   the middle girl

> °AN: The nouns **farkō** 'beginning' and **ƙàrshē** 'end' are not limited to use as ordinal modifiers, e.g., **farkon wā̀sā** 'the beginning of the game', **farkontà** 'its beginning', **dà farkon zuwànsà** 'when he first arrived' (lit. with beginning.of coming.of.him); **ƙàrshen watà** 'the end of the month', **dàgà ƙàrshē** 'in the end'. When serving as modifiers, these words are sometimes connected to the preceding noun by a zero-vowel bound linker rather than **na / ta**, e.g., **karòn farkō** 'the first incident', **ƙòƙarin ƙàrshē** 'the last attempt' (cf. **ƙòƙarinmù na ƙàrshē** 'our last attempt').

With dates, one normally uses the zero-vowel linker instead of the short vowel form, e.g.,

rānař gōmà gà watàn Māřìs   March 10th (lit. day.of ten at month.of March) (= **rānā ta gōmà...**)
shèkařař alìf dà ɗàrī tařà   1900 (lit. year.of thousand and hundred nine)

Hausa uses ordinal numbers in some constructions where English might uses a cardinal, e.g.,

shāfī na tàlā̀tin   page 30 (lit. thirtieth page); **bābì na farkō**   volume 1 (i.e., first volume); **ɗākì na hàmsin dà biyu**   room 52 (lit. fifty-second room)

The examples above could also have an ordinal reading, e.g., 'the 52nd room', but this would not be the normal interpretation.

1.11. Times/multiples

The notion of times, as in 'once', 'twice', 'three times', etc. is expressed by **sàu** 'time(s)' immediately followed by a numeral or other quantifier, e.g.,

sàu ɗaya once; **sàu huɗu** four times; **sàu dubū** a thousand times; **sàu nawà?** how many times? **sàu dà yawà** many times

> ◊HN: The word **sàu** is etymologically the same as the word **sau/sāwū** 'foot(print)'. The grammaticalization process is indicated by the semantic and functional properties of **sàu** 'times' and by its phonological distinctiveness vis-à-vis its source noun, namely, its low tone and its clipped shape, i.e., it is always **sàu** and never ****sàwù** (but see below). (Skinner (1996: 230–31) notes the connection between 'foot' and 'times' in other Chadic languages as well.)

An alternative, but less common, way of expressing 'times' is by means of a cognate accusative construction (see §13:1.2), e.g.,

tā zàgē shì zāgì ukù   She insulted him three times. (lit. she insulted him insulting three)
jirgin samà yā tāshì tāshì shidà   The plane took off six times. (lit. ...arose rising six)

To express 'the second time, fourth time, etc.', as opposed to 'twice, four times, etc.', one uses a normal ordinal construction with the H-tone nominal form **sau/sāwū**, e.g.,

sau (= sāwū) na biyu second time; **sau (= sāwū) na huɗu** fourth time

1.12. Modifying/emphasizing numerals

Numerals can be modified in two ways. First, the quantity term can be specified by a following adverb or ideophone, e.g.,

lèmō ɗaya <u>tak</u> akà bā nì   They gave me precisely one orange.
awà biyu <u>cur</u>   exactly two hours
yànzu (gōmà) shâ biyu <u>daidai</u>   It is now exactly twelve o'clock.

Second, the numeral or the NP containing the numeral can be preceded by a prepositional qualifier, like **wajen = kàmar** 'about, approximately', **kusan** 'close to, almost', **har** 'as much as, to the extent of', 'more than', e.g.,

yanà nan wajeñkàmar mîl gōmà dàgà gàrinmù   It's there about ten miles from our town.
sōjōjī kusan ɗàrī sukà ɓullō   Nearly a hundred soldiers appeared.
an kashè mutànē har gùdā tàlàtin   They killed up to thirty people.
sun kāmà ɓàràyī fiye dà hàmsin   They caught more than fifty thieves.

1.13. Numerals as nouns

When numerals function as nouns naming a particular number, they have intrinsic gender and are all feminine, e.g.,

hàmsin cè   It's fifty.
gōmà tā fi takwàs   Ten is more than eight.
ɗaya bà tà kai biyu ba   One is not as much as two.

Terms for fractions and for zero, on the other hand, function only as nouns and do not qualify as numerals. They are all masculine, e.g.,

sìfìřì nè	It's zero.
rabì yā fi bābù	Half is better than none.
sùlùsānì yā fi sulùsì	Two-thirds is more than one third.

1.14. Numerals as pro-forms

Numerals can function as anaphoric pro-forms, i.e., as surface heads, e.g., **ukù sun jē Kanò** 'Three (men, women, whatever is understood) went to Kano'; **bà ni biyu** 'Give me two (mats, caps, whatever is understood)'. When so used, **ɗaya** 'one' is masculine or feminine depending on the gender of the referent; the numbers from two on up are plural, e.g.,

ɗaya tā fi sôn kòfî, ɗayâř tā fi sôn shāyì
    One (woman) prefers coffee, the other one (f.) prefers tea.

gà ɗayân dà zân ɗaukà	Here is the one (m. psn or thing) that I'll take.
gōmà <u>sun</u> ƙi tāshì	Ten (persons) refused to get up.
cf. gōmà <u>tā</u> fi takwàs	(The number) 10 is more than 8. (where **gōmà** is feminine)

Instead of standing alone, one can have the anaphoric numerals extended by a phrase consisting of a genitive linker (sometimes attached to the connector **ɗi-**) plus a pronoun, e.g.,

ɗayankù 1 of you; **bìyař ɗinsù** 5 of them; **ukùnmù** 3 of us
àkwai sōjōjì dà dāma à tàrô; ukù (= ukùnsù) kō mōtsì bā sà̀ yî   There were a lot of soldiers at the
        meeting; three (of them) were absolutely still. (lit. even budging they weren't doing)

2. ALL

The universal quantifier DUK 'all' functions as a determiner, as a pronoun, and as an adverb.

2.1. Determiner

As a determiner, 'all' has two equivalent allomorphs: **dukà** and **duk**. In some dialects, the variant **duk** appears with the surface forms **dū** or **duG** (where G forms a geminate with the following abutting consonant). Examples: **dukà/duk/dum màlàmân = màlàmân dukà/dū** 'all the teachers'. (When I want to refer to this morpheme without regard to its specific phonological shape, I shall indicate it as DUK in capital letters.)

DUK can generally occur either before or after the head NP with, as far as one can determine, essentially identical meaning. In pre-head position, **duk** without the final vowel is the more common variant, although **dukà** is also allowed. In post-head position, **dukà** is more common, and for some speakers actually required, **duk** being rejected altogether. Like other quantifiers, and unlike demonstratives, DUK is grammatically invariant, i.e., there is no difference in the form used as far as plurality or gender is concerned, e.g.,

duk fāsinjōjìn =	fāsinjōjìn dukà	all the passengers
duk(à) Hàusàwā =	Hàusàwā dukà	all Hausas
duk jàma'àř Kanò =	jàma'àř Kanò dukà	all the people of Kano
duk tsawon rānā =	tsawon rānā dukà	all day (lit. all the length of the day)
duk àbinci =	àbinci dukà	all the food

When modifying a numeral, DUK always goes in front, e.g.,

duk(à) gōmà   all ten;   **duk(à) biyu**   both (lit. all two);   **duk biyunsù**   both of them

The phrase **duk ɗaya** ('all one') means 'all the same', e.g., **duk ɗaya gàrē nì** 'It's all the same to me.'

With a noun modified by a relative clause, DUK in post-head position occurs at the end of the noun phrase, e.g.,

mutànên dà na sanì dukà	all the people I know (= **duk mutànên dà na sanì**)
wuràrên dà zā mù tàfi dukà	all the places that we will go to (= **duk wuràrên dà zā mù tàfi**)

When a relative clause modifies a noun used in a generic sense (which in Hausa takes a singular rather than a plural form), DUK goes in pre-head position. (Semantically these sentences are very similar to sentences using the universals **kōwànè / kōwàcè** (m./f.) 'every'.) The pre-head **duk** is also commonly used in such phrases as **duk àbîn dà** 'everything that (= whatever)' (lit. all thing.the that), **duk lōkàcîn dà** 'whenever' (lit. all time.the that), **duk wani X** 'whatever' (lit. all some X). Examples:

zā sù ƙwācè duk mōtàr̃ dà akà shigō dà ita	They will confiscate all cars that are imported.
cf. **zā sù ƙwācè kōwàcè mōtàr̃ dà akà shigō dà ita**	They will confiscate every car that is imported.
dilā yā ga duk àbîn dà hànkākà ya yi	Jackal watched everything that Crow did.
duk lōkàcîn dà kūrā ta kāwō àbinci...	Whenever the hyena brought food...
duk wani aikì (dà) mùtûm ya yi...	Whatever work a man does...

2.2. Pronoun

In addition to modifying an NP, DUK can stand on its own as a pronominal element.

dukà sun mutù	All (of them) died.
duk zā sù shìga jirgī	All (e.g., the pilgrims) are going to enter the plane.
duk kun ci jar̃r̃àbâwâr̃	All (of you) passed the exam.
yā sayar̃ dà dukà	He sold all (of them).

The phrase **duk dà hakà** lit. 'all with thus' means 'nevertheless' or 'all the same', e.g.,

duk dà hakà nā fi sôn wannàn   All the same, I prefer this one.

sun yi iyā ƙōƙarinsù, àmmā duk dà hakà bà sù ci ba
    They did their best but nevertheless they failed.

As is the case with numerals, DUK can co-occur with plural personal pronouns, e.g.,

mū dukà mun yàr̃da We all agree;   **kū dukà sai kù yi hàƙurī** You all should be patient;   **zân hàr̃bē sù (sū) dukà** I will shoot them all.

When used in a genitive phrase of the type 'all of Y', DUK is most often represented by **dukkà** (with geminate **kk**) plus the linker **-n**. With pronouns, a possible, but less common, alternative is **duk** plus **ɗin** plus the pronoun, e.g.,

dukkàn birai all of the monkeys;   **dukkànsù = duk ɗinsù** all of them

°AN: [i] The standard grammars and dictionaries all give **dukàn** as an equivalent (and often a first) alternative to **dukkàn** with the geminate /kk/. Modern-day SH speakers tend to reject **dukàn**. It is not clear whether the early sources were in error in ascribing a preference for **dukàn**, whether that form reflects dialectal or sociolectal usage, or whether the language has undergone change over time.

[ii] In many cases there is very little semantic difference between an NP consisting of the determiner 'all' plus a noun and an 'all' (pronoun)-of-noun phrase, e.g., **yā kashè duk birai** 'He killed all the monkeys' = **yā kashè dukkàn birai** 'He killed all of the monkeys'. (For me, the difference in English is equally unclear.)

An alternative to using DUK is to use the full nominal form **dukkànin** 'the totality of', a form that is semantically more emphatic/specific, e.g.,

dukkànin fāsinjōjī all of the passengers; **dukkàninmù** all of us

°AN: Instead of viewing **dukkàn** as an emphatic, geminated form of the quantifier **dukàn**, as done, for example, by Abraham (1962: 230), it might be more appropriate to analyze it as a clipped form of the noun **dukkànin**.

These phrases are comparable to similar X of Y (pl.) structures with other quantity nouns, e.g.,

ɗàukacin mōtōcîn	the entirety of the cars	**ìlāhìřin jàma'à**	all (the whole) of the people
gālìbin mutànē	the greater number of the men	**akasàřin sōjōjī**	the majority of the soldiers
yawancinsù	most of them	**rabìn 'yan jàřìdū**	half of the reporters

2.3. Adverbial

The allomorph **duk** (with its variants **dū** and **duG**) functions in verbal sentences as an adverb indicating 'entirely, completely'. It normally appears after the subject but before the PAC (person-aspect-complex); but it can also be used at the beginning of the sentence, e.g.,

duk yā lālàcē	It spoiled entirely.
cf. **duk sun lālàcē**	They all spoiled. = They spoiled entirely.
duk bàn dàmu ba	I'm not bothered at all.
duk nā gàji (= **dū nā gàji** = **dun nā gàji**)	I'm tired out completely. = **nā gàji duk**
dukkàninmù duk mun gàji	All of us are tired completely.
wurîn duk yā harmùtsē	The place became completely muddled .
(lit. the place completely it became muddled)	
ɓēřan dājì, duk tsòrō yā kāmà shi	As for the field mouse, he became entirely frightened.
(lit. ...entirely fear it caught him)	
nā ga Audù, kânsà duk yā yi furfurā	I saw Audu with his hair turned.completely gray.
(lit. ...his head completely it did gray), cf. the following with the determiner 'all':	
nā ga Audù, duk kânsà yā yi furfurā	I saw Audu with his hair all gray
(lit. ...all his head it did gray)	

3. OTHER QUANTIFIERS

Whereas numerals are restricted to count nouns, other quantifiers and quantifier phrases can be used both with count nouns and with noncount nouns, e.g., **yawà** means 'many' or 'much', e.g., **mutànē dà yawà** 'many people', **gishirī dà yawà** 'a lot of salt'. Syntactically the quantifiers fall into two main groups: adverbial and nominal. Adverbial quantifiers, e.g., **kaɗai** 'only'; **kàɗan** 'few, a little amount', **ƙalīlàn** 'few, a trivial amount', **nawà (nawà)**? 'how many, how much (each)', directly follow the head noun. Examples:

kai kaɗai you only; **māgànī kàɗan** a little bit of medicine; **ɗàlìbai ƙalīlàn** just a few students; **mōtōcī nawà?** how many cars? **kuɗī nawà nawà?** how much money each?

Nominal quantifiers, e.g., **dāmā** 'quite a lot, many', **dāma dāma** 'a moderate amount'; **yawà** 'many, much', modify nouns by means of phrases formed with **dà** 'with' or **mài** (sg.) / **màsu** (pl.) 'having', or **mafì** 'exceeding'. Examples:

mutànē dà dāmā a lot of people; **ruwan samà dà dāma dāma** a moderate amount of rain; **sàu dà yawà** many times; **mātā dà yawà** = **mātā màsu yawà** many women; **sōjōjī mafì yawà** the largest number of soldiers

Both **dāmā** and **yawà** can be strengthened by means of a phrase consisting of a bound linker + **gàske** 'in truth', e.g., **kuɗī dà yawàn gàske** 'a truly large amount of money'; **kuɗī dà dāman gàske** 'a truly moderate/adequate amount of money'. One can also use **yawà** in the phrase **màsu ɗimbin yawà** 'a hell of a lot' (lit. a superabundance of quantity), e.g., **mutànē màsu ɗimbin yawà** 'oodles of people'.
As with numerals, other quantifiers can be used pronominally, e.g.,

yanà nēman [dà yawà]   He is seeking lots.
[mafì yawàn] mutànē sunà gōyon bāyansà   Most of the people are supporting him.
[dà yawà] dàgà cikin ɗàlìbai mātā sun ci jařřabâwā
     Many of the female students passed the exam.
['yan kàɗan] (dàgà cikinsù) sun zaunà hař tsakař darē
     A few among them remained until midnight.

54. Phonology

1. PHONOLOGICAL INVENTORY

1.1. Consonants

The thirty-two consonant phonemes of Standard Hausa (SH) are presented in table 6, with illustrative examples in table 7. The consonants are indicated in standard orthography, with a few exceptions to be mentioned below.

Table 6: Hausa consonants

		lab.	cor.	pal.	vel.	lab-vel.	pal-vel.	laryn.
obst	vl	(f, fy)	t	c	k	kw	ky	
	vd	b	d	j	g	gw	gy	
	gl	ɓ	ɗ	'y	ƙ	ƙw	ƙy	'
	vl	f, fy	s	sh				h
	vd		z	(j)				
	gl		ts					
son		m	n					
			l					
			r					
			r̃					
				y		w		

Table 7: Examples of consonants

': 'àbù	thing	b: bàkī	mouth
ɓ: ɓērā	rat	c: cāca	gambling
d: dafī	poison	ɗ: ɗākì	room
f: farī	white	fy: fyàɗē	rape
g: gàdā	duiker	gw: gwànī	expert
gy: gyàlè	shawl	h: haɓà	chin
j: jā	red	k: kadà	crocodile
kw: kwàɗō	frog	ky: kyaurō	arrow shaft
ƙ: ƙafà	foot	ƙw: ƙwai	egg
ƙy: ƙyàllī	shininess	l: lākā	mud

392

m: mâi	oil	n: nàsō	dampness
r: rānā	sun, day	ř: řahà	chatting
s: samà	sky	sh: shānū	cattle
t: tāgà	window	ts: tsakā	gecko
w: watà	moon, month	y: yàbō	praise
'y: 'yā'yā	children	z: zāfī	heat

The letters **c** and **j** represent the affricates [tʃ] (as in Eng. 'church') and [dʒ] (as in Eng. 'judge') respectively. The digraph **sh** represents the palatal fricative [ʃ] (as in Eng. 'shush').

ΔDN/°AN: In Niger, the phoneme /**j**/ is pronounced [ʒ] as in French 'Jacques' [ʒak]. This is probably the original pronunciation of this phoneme, i.e., historically it was a fricative and only later developed into an affricate in some dialects. Apparently the correlation of the [dʒ] vs. [ʒ] pronunciation with the distinction between anglophone Nigeria and francophone Niger is a very remarkable coincidence but nothing more. (Nineteenth-century descriptions of Hausa speakers from what is now Niger indicated the [ʒ] pronunciation at a time that predated French presence and influence in the area.) It should be pointed out that although the SH pronunciation of /**j**/ approximates the corresponding English phoneme, the stop component is much weaker, i.e., the phonetic difference between /**j**/ in the two dialects is much less than our discrete transcriptions imply.

Hausa has no contrast between /**f**/ and /**p**/. The phoneme indicated as /**f**/ is pronounced variably as [ɸ] (the norm), [f], [p], or [h], depending on dialect/idiolect and phonological environment. The orthographic /**f**/ represents an approximation of the usual SH fricative pronunciation. In this regard, the speech of Kano city, which normally is taken to be SH, is not typical. In Kano, /**f**/ before unrounded vowels is commonly pronounced as [p], e.g., /**fìta**/ [pìta] 'go out', /**fāwà̀**/ [pāwà̀] 'butchery', /**faifai**/ [peipei] or [pēpē] 'phonograph record', **lōfè** [lōpè̀] 'smoking pipe', /**lafà̀**/ [lapà̀] 'die down (e.g., of fire)'; but there is considerable idiolectal and lexical variation. Before the back-rounded vowels **u(u)** and **o(o)**, the phoneme /**f**/ is often pronounced (and, if so, written) as [h], e.g., **dàfuwā = dàhuwā** 'cooking', cf. **dafà̀** 'cook'; WH **fuɗu** = SH **huɗu** 'four'; **tahō** 'come this way', cf. **tàfi** 'go'.

°AN: For reasons of pattern symmetry, I personally would prefer to place /**f**/ in the row with /**t**/ and /**k**/, i.e., treat it structurally as the voiceless counterpart of the bilabial stop /**b**/. On phonetic grounds, however, it is customary to include it along with the other fricatives.
ΔDN: The preference for [p] is certainly a Kano City phenomenon (Salim 1980). How widely this extends throughout Kano State and beyond is yet to be determined. In WH dialects spoken in Niger, /**f**/ is generally pronounced (and written) as **hw** before /**a(a)**/ and **h** before other vowels, e.g., **hwādî** 'fall' (= SH **fādî**), **tàhi** 'go' (= SH **tàfi**). In these **hw/h** dialects, /**f**/ in syllable-final position is pronounced as a voiceless bilabial stop [p], although it is spelled with **b** because **p** is not part of the phonological/orthographic system, e.g., **shibka** 'plant, sow' (= SH **shūkà̀** < *shifkà̀).

The glottalized series includes both laryngealized stops and ejectives. The "hooked" letters **ɓ** and **ɗ** are laryngealized, sometimes implosive, stops and the hooked letter **ƙ** is an ejective stop. The digraph **ts** is generally pronounced as an ejective sibilant [s']. The symbol /**'y**/ represents a glottalized palatal semivowel, which is limited to a few very high frequency words like **'yā'yā** 'children'. It is a historically very recent phoneme, having developed from the sequence /ɗiy/ via /ɗy/, cf. SH **'yā** with WH **ɗîyā** 'daughter'.

°AN: For details on the phonetics of the glottalized consonants, see Carnochan (1952), Lindau (1984), and Lindsey, Hayward, and Haruna (1992).

ΔDN: WH (including the Katsina dialect) also has an ejective [c'] as part of its glottalized consonant series. This affricate exists as an allophone of /ts/ before front vowels, e.g., WH **dūc'ì** 'stone' = SH **dūtsè**, and also as a contrastive phoneme before /a(a)/, e.g., **c'àda** 'expensiveness' = SH **tsàdā**, cf. WH and SH **tsayà** 'stop'.

◊HN: Synchronically, the ejective **ts** can be viewed as the glottalized member of the **s, z, ts** triad in the same way that **ƙ** is the glottalized member of the **k, g, ƙ** triad. Although we lack solid information about the history of this phoneme, my hunch is that it will not turn out to be a glottalized /s/, but rather will be found to be derived from an ejective /t/ or /c/ or from a possibly nonglottalized alveolar affricate /ts/.

The palatalized labial /fy/ is lexically infrequent and is often replaced by its plain counterpart, e.g., **fyācè** = **fācè** 'blow one's nose'. The palatalized and labialized velars, on the other hand, are quite common. Before the vowel /a(a)/, they contrast with their plain counterparts, e.g., **gàdā** 'duiker', **gwàdā** 'test, try!' **gyàɗā** 'peanuts'. Before the back-rounded vowels, the velars are all redundantly labialized; before front vowels they are redundantly palatalized. These features are not shown in standard orthography, i.e., **dōgō** 'tall' = [dōgwō], cf. the pl. **dōgwàyē**, **gēfè** 'side' = [gyēfè], cf. the pl. **gyâffā**. There are also examples of labialized velars followed by /i(i)/, e.g., **gwībà** 'sediment', **kwīkwiyò** 'puppy'. Their appearance is due to the historically recent change of /u/ to /i/, especially in connection with the assimilation of /u/ to /i/ before /y/, plus the monophthongization of the */ui/ diphthong to /ī/, i.e., **gwībà** < *gwuiɓà, **kwīkwiyò** < *kwuikwuyò.

ΔDN: Some WH dialects also have labialized coronals and labials as part of their consonant inventory, the number and extent depending on the particular dialect. These additional labialized consonants are sometimes lexically specified, e.g., SH **tàrī** = [dv] **twàrī** 'cough'; and sometimes due to phonological processes, e.g., SH **mâ** = [dv] **mwâ** 'we (potential future)' (< **mu** + **à**), SH **ɗòyī** = [dv] **ɗwai** (< *ɗōy) 'stench'.

In word-final position /n/ is pronounced [ŋ], e.g., **cân** 'there' = [câŋ]. SH speakers also normally pronounce final /m/ as [ŋ], thereby resulting in a merger of the two phonemic nasals, e.g., **mālàm** 'teacher' = [mālàm] or [mālàŋ]. This merger does not however, extend to ideophones, where the contrast between word-final /m/ and /n/ is preserved, e.g., **yā ɗaurè tam** [tam] 'He tied (it) very tight' vs. **baƙī ƙirin** [ƙiriŋ] 'jet black'.

1.1.1. The two R's

The symbol **ř** is used to distinguish the apical tap or roll from the retroflex flap **r**. (Proper names are written with initial capital R without the tilde, e.g., **Ràhīlā** 'Rachel' = /řàhīlā/.) This distinction is *not* indicated in standard orthography. The two rhotics contrast in initial, intervocalic, and (with restrictions) syllable-final position within a word, e.g., **řahà** 'pleasant chatting', **rānī** 'dry season'; **tařà** 'nine', **tārà** 'collect'; **màrkā** 'height of the rainy season', **sarkī** 'emir'. There are very few minimal pairs, but some do exist, e.g., **bařà** 'begging', **barà** 'servant'; **kōřè** 'dark green', **kōrè** 'drive away'; **fařkō** 'recover, revive', **farkō** 'beginning'. There is no contrast in word-final position: in that environment one gets only **ř**, e.g., **àshâř** 'obscene language', **tēbùř** 'table'. In syllable-initial position, flap **r** is the norm, except with loanwords. In syllable-final position within a word, the flap **r** is the norm when the following abutting consonant is **ts**, e.g., **sartsè** 'splinter'. By contrast, in syllable-final position preceding the coronals **d, ɗ,** and **n**, only **ř** occurs, e.g., **ƙařdàjī** 'a thorny mimosa', **murɗè** 'twist', **dàřnī** 'cornstalk fence'. Occasionally, rules implementing the restrictions result in morphophonemic alternations between the two rhotics, e.g., **barì** 'leave, let' (citation form), but **bař** pre-object form; **jinjìrī** 'infant', but **jinjiřnìyā** 'female infant'; **kàrē** 'dog', but **kařnukà** 'dogs'. In syllable-final position, many speakers, especially in WH dialects, commonly substitute /l/ for both the flap and the roll.

ΔDN: In WH dialects, /l/ is regularly found in place of the rhotics in syllable-final position within a word. This applies both to ř and, less commonly, to **r**, e.g., **gàřmā** = WH **gàlmā** 'hoe'; **fařkà** = WH **falkà** 'wake up'; **zaɓè** = WH **zalɓè** 'heron'. The substitution of /l/ for ř does not take place, however, when the abutting consonant is **d**, **ɗ**, or **n**, e.g., **muřnà** = WH **muřnà**, not ****mulnà**.

◊HN: The flap /r/ is the native Hausa R. The rolled /ř/ has come into the language (a) through rhotacism of alveolar obstruents in syllable-final position, e.g., **fařkà** 'wake up' (< *faɗkà < *fàɗakà), cf. **fàrkā** 'paramour'; (b) from the rolled allophone of /r/ required in certain positions, e.g., **jinjiřnìyā** 'female infant' < **jinjìrī** 'infant'; (c) via loanwords, primarily from Arabic, Kanuri, and English, e.g., **řù'ùyā** 'vision, dream', **řàfàlî** 'referee', and (d) from the phonemicization of expressive pronunciation used with ideophones and intensive forms, e.g., **řagařgàzā** 'shatter', **řamas** 'emphasizes dryness' (Newman 1980b). In some dialects, e.g., that of Ader, the contrast between the two rhotics has been lost, only /ř/ being retained.

The apostrophe / ' / is used in standard orthography to indicate glottal stop, e.g., **sā'à** 'luck, **jam'ì** 'plural'. It is not employed orthographically in word-initial position (a convention followed in this work), i.e., orthographic **abu** 'thing' = [ʔàbù], orthographic **amma** 'but' = [ʔàmmā].

Orthographic **h** is used both for the independent phoneme /h/, e.g., /hatsī/ grain' and for the pseudo-allophone of /f/, e.g., **tahō** 'come here' (< **tàfi** 'go' + -ō 'ventive marker').

◊HN: Glottal stop and /h/ are historically recent phonemes in Hausa, having developed in a similar manner (Newman 1976a). Phonetically, they both probably existed in the language for a long time, in the case of [ʔ] as a phonetic marker of vowel-initial words and, with short vowels, of prepausal position, and in the case of [h] as an allophone of /f/ as well as being an alternative means of attack for vowel-initial words. The phonemicization of / ' / and /h/ resulted from a combination of language internal sound changes that were reinforced and stimulated by their introduction in medial and initial position in Arabic loanwords (see §44:2.2), e.g., **'àddu'à** 'prayer', **sàbà'in** 'seventy', **'azùmī** 'fasting', **hàjà** 'merchandise', **hàmsin** 'fifty', **jāhìlī** 'ignorant psn', **shàhādà** 'martyrdom'.

1.1.2. Glides/semivowels
The semivowels /y/ and /w/ occur only in syllable onset position (or when they form the first part of a geminate sequence, e.g., **niyyà** 'intention', **kuwwà** 'shouting').

°AN: The sequence **awwa** (which is much less common than the corresponding **ayya** sequence) is often treated by native speakers as /auwa/, as reflected in their orthographic preference, e.g., **Hauwa** 'proper name', **yauwa** 'bravo', **sauwaƙa** 'bring relief'. (Note that these same people often prefer the spelling **gayya** 'communal work', **sakayya** 'recompense', etc.) It is not clear whether this practice reflects real phonological intuition or whether it is a question of orthographic aesthetics.

If the glides are shifted into the coda because of vowel apocope or morphological processes, they automatically alter into their corresponding vowels /i/ and /u/ and attach to the nucleus along with the preceding vowel. (See discussion of diphthongs in §1.2.3 below.) This is illustrated in the diagrams in fig. 4. (Long vowels here are indicated by double letters; tone is not marked.)

Figure 4: Glides and their corresponding vowels

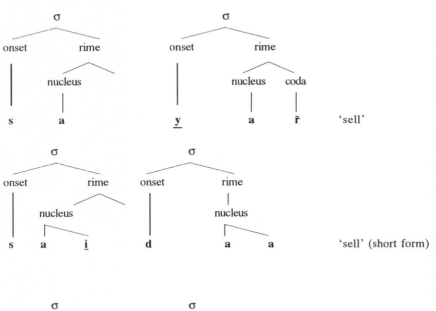

'sell'

'sell' (short form)

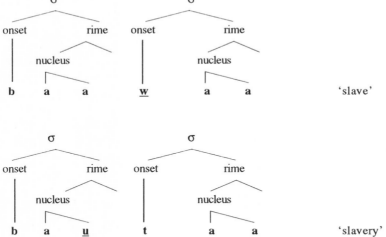

'slave'

'slavery'

Examples (with syllable division indicated by .):

mà.rā.yà	orphan	**mà.rai.nì.yā**	female orphan (< //**mà.ray.nì.yā**//)
ga.yà	tell	**gai.su.wā**	greeting
sà.yi	buy (pre-noun form)	**sai**	buy (optional clipped form)
bā.wà	slave	**bàu.tā**	slavery
ɓà.rā.wò	thief	**ɓà.rau.nì.yā**	female thief
a.wò	weighing	**au.nà**	weigh

1.1.3. Geminates

Geminates in Hausa, which occur only in medial position, are extremely prevalent. All consonants can be geminated. (With consonants represented by a digraph, only the first letter is written doubled, e.g., [gàsaššee] 'roasted' is indicated **gàsasshē**, [kwakwkwàfā] 'tamp' is indicated **kwakkwàfā**.) Geminate flap /r/ does occur, e.g., **kùrurrùmī** 'broken-necked' (< historically reduplicated word ***kùrumrùmī**); [madatsarruwā] < **madatsař-ruwā** 'dam' (lit. blocking place.of-water); [sârrâi] < **sôn râi** 'selfishness' (lit. love.of life); but its absence in some common plural forms where it would be morphologically expected suggests that at an earlier stage it was probably disallowed, e.g., **yârā** (not ****yârrā**) pl. of **yārò** 'boy'; **tâurā** (not ****târrā**) pl. of **taurè** 'castrated goat', cf. **kwârřā** pl. of **kōřè** 'green' and **nônnā** pl. of **nōnò** 'breast', which belong to the same plural class. Phonetically, the geminate flap **rr** is quite distinct from the tap/roll **řř**. The latter increases the number of taps, i.e., it becomes a discernible trill, whereas the former simply increases the temporal period of the retroflex flap gesture.

In morphologically derived forms, geminates of all consonants are extremely common, e.g., **zôbbā** 'rings', pl. of **zōbè**, **hahhau** 'mount many or often', pluractional verb stem of **hau**; **fàffāɗā** 'broad', derived adjective from **fāɗī** 'breadth'; **zàɓaɓɓē** 'chosen', adjectival past participle of **zàɓā** 'choose'. Geminates also commonly arise from complete assimilation of abutting consonants, e.g., **gidan-mù** → **gidammù** 'our house', **mōtàř-sà** → **mōtàssà** 'his car'.

Lexically, however, geminates are not so common. In underived native words, one tends to find only geminate nasals, liquids, and /yy/, e.g., **kunnà** 'light (lamp or fire)', **gammō** 'head pad', **tallē** 'small soup pot', **gàyyā** 'communal work'. Others, however, do occur, e.g., **tukkū** 'bird's crop', **città** 'four days hence', **shaddà** 'brocade', **râggā** 'rags', **ƙâbbā** 'syphilis', **câssā** 'bow-leggedness'.

◊HN: One can often identify the geminates as being secondary even in the so-called underived native words, Thus **gammō** 'head pad' comes from **ganwō** (still extant in some WH dialects); **kunnà** 'light (lamp or fire)' contains a suffix -**nà**; and **râggā** 'rags' (like similar words with initial falling tone) probably comes from an old reduplicated plural (i.e., < * **rāgàgā**) (cf. the extant **zôbbā** 'rings', plural of **zōbè**). This suggests that at an earlier period there were probably no geminates in monomorphemic words. All geminates now in the language would thus have come from internal morphological or phonological (assimilatory) processes or from loanwords (for some of which the source is not identifiable). If this is so, it would set Hausa apart from its sister Chadic languages, like Bole, where gemination is quite common. At the same time, the re-acquisition of geminates in Hausa could be taken as indication of a Chadic drift/predisposition favoring geminates.

Nonsonorant geminates do, however, occur readily in loanwords, especially from Arabic and Fulani, e.g., **hajjì** 'the hadj' (< Ar.), **jabbà** 'sleeveless robe' (< Ar.), **baffà** (usually pronounced [bappà]) 'uncle' < Ful.), **naggè** 'cow' (< Ful.).

At an analytical level, geminates can be viewed as a sequence of identical consonants abutting across a syllable boundary, i.e., **jabbà** 'sleeveless robe', for example, has the canonical form $C_1VC_2.C_3VV$, where C_2 and C_3 happen to be identical. (Phonetically, however, geminates tend to appear as long "hefty" consonants (Carnochan 1957).) Nouns using the -ōCī plural suffix, for example—where the C is a copy of the preceding consonant— copy only one segment of the identical abutting pair and not the whole geminate as a unit, e.g., **jabbà** / **jabbōbī** 'robe(s)' (not ****jabbōbbī**); **bukkà** / **bukkōkī** 'grass hut(s)', cf. **hařkà** / **hařkōkī** 'business affair(s)', **kafà** / **kafōfī** 'hole(s)'. In language games involving insertions or permutations, geminates behave exactly like non-identical abutting consonants, e.g.,

| **Sàllau** / **Salgràlau** | proper name / *game form* | cf. **kalmà** / **kalgràma** | word / *game form* |
| **hannū** / **dàhandànū** | hand / *game form* | cf. **'armē** / **dà'ardàmē** | marriage / *game form* |

kissằ / dàkisdàsā	intrigue / *game form*	cf. **Màngū** / **dàmandàgū**	proper name / *game form*
sallằ / lāsàl	prayer / *game form*	cf. **tafkì** / **kītàf**	lake / *game form*
bukkằ / kābùk	hut / *game form*	cf. **kalmè** / **mēkàl**	hoe / *game form*

Note, however, that various instances of geminate $C_x.C_x$ exist where C_x otherwise does not occur as a coda, i.e., where abutting sequences of $C_x.C_y$ are not possible. As indicated above, all consonants occur as geminates. This includes **hh**, ” (glottal stop), **cc**, and **ƙƙ**, for example, even though **h**, ’, **c**, and **ƙ** do not occur as the first member of a non-identical abutting pair.

1.2. Vowels

Hausa has twelve vowels (which appear to be the same for all dialects): five monophthongal short vowels, five monophthongal long vowels, and two dipththongs. These are presented in table 8 and exemplified in table 9.

Table 8: Hausa vowels

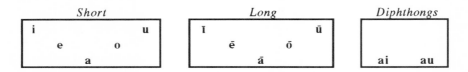

Table 9: Examples of vowels

a: kadà	don’t	ā: fātā	hoping
e: màcè	woman	ē: bēbē	deaf mute
i: minì	to me	ī: kīshì	jealousy
o: gwàdò	heavy blanket	ō: zōmō	rabbit
u: mutù	die	ū: tūrù	stocks
		ai: faifai	mat, record
		au: tautàu	spider

Long /ā/, as in **fātū** 'skins', is similar to the vowel in Eng. 'father'. Short /a/, on the other hand, is difficult to specify precisely because it ranges over the entire phonetic vowel space below and between [e] and [o]. The allophones of /a/ show considerable variability depending on the speaker and the tempo and are subject to strong influence from neighboring phonemes. For example, when followed by /y/ or when preceded by /'y/, /y/, or a palatalized consonant, /a/ raises and is pronounced as [ɛ], e.g. sàyā [sèyā] 'buy'; gyàɗā [gyèɗā] 'peanuts'; 'yan-sàndā ['yɛnsàndā] or ['ɛnsàndā] 'policemen'; yàbō [yèbō] 'praise'. In some cases, the /a/ following /y/ raises all the way to [i], e.g. yanằ [yɛnằ] or [yinằ] 'he.continuous'. When followed by /n/ + /y/, the /a/ fronts and/or adds an anticipatory glide, e.g. tsanyằ [s'ɛnyằ] 'cricket'; kanyằ [kaⁱnyằ] 'ebony tree'. In other closed syllables, /a/ is pronounced as a low vowel similar to that in American English 'box' or 'taco', e.g. fařkằ [fařkằ] 'wake up'. In open syllables, /a/ often raises to the schwalike sound in English 'cut', e.g. kàrē [kòrē] 'dog', dafằ [dofằ] 'cook'. The schwa pronunciation does not usually apply if the /a/ is preceded by / ' / or /h/, e.g. afằ [ʔafằ] 'throw in the mouth'; hanằ [hanằ] 'prevent' (but **habà** 'now there!' is usually [həbà]).

The vowels /e(e)/ and /o(o)/, are normally pronounced like the vowels in Eng. 'bait' and 'boat', but without the offglide. In final position, they occur both long and short, e.g., **shàfē** 'wiping', **shàfe** 'wiped' (stative), **dōgō** 'tall', **Dōgo** (nickname for a tall person). In word-medial position they are underlyingly always long and occur only in open syllables. If the syllable becomes closed, due to any number of morphophonological processes, the vowels /ē/ and /ō/ automatically shorten to /e/ and /o/, respectively, and centralize toward [a] (or [ə]). For most SH speakers, the short mid vowels thereby merge with short /a/, e.g., kàrē 'dog', cf. [kə̀ransà] 'his dog' (< *kàre-nsà < kàrē-nsà); gēfè [gyēfè] 'side', pl. gyâffā (with preservation of the conditioned palatalization on the /gy/) (< *gyêffā < *gēfàfā); tōnà 'dig up', plurac. tantònā (< *tontònā < *tōntònā); sābō 'new', cf. [sābən sōjà] 'new soldier' (< sābon... < *sābōn...); dòmin 'for sake of' = don [dən] (optional short form). When preceded by /h/, short /o/ in a closed syllable shifts toward [ɔ] but does not become [a], e.g., tsōhō 'old', cf. [tsōhɔn sōjà] 'a former soldier' < tsōhon.... Standard orthography is not totally consistent in how it represents short /e/ and /o/. On the whole, it follows pronunciation in representing the vowels in word-medial position, e.g., tantònā (< *tōn-tònā) 'dig up many', but follows underlying form in representing word-final vowels with a linker attached, e.g., kàrensà (< *kàrē-nsà) 'his dog'. CVC words appear with various spellings. For example, the word pronounced [dən] 'for sake of' (< dòmin) is usually spelled don in Nigeria but dan in Niger. Recent loanwords from English with short /e/ and /o/ in closed syllables generally preserve the front and back qualities of the vowels and do not shift all the way to [a] or [ə] e.g., fensìr̃ [fɛnsìr̃] 'pencil', bôs [bôs] = [bâs] 'bus'. Depending upon speech tempo, word-final short /e/ and /o/ in open syllables also tend to centralize when not phrase final, e.g., gòbe [gòbe] 'tomorrow', but gòbe nè [gòbə nè] 'It's tomorrow'; mangwàr̃ò 'mango', bà mangwàr̃ò ba [bà maŋgwàr̃ə ba] 'not a mango'. Note the pronunciation of reduplicated frequentatives: kàɗe-kàɗe [kàɗəkàɗe] 'drummings', càmfe-càmfe [càmfəcàmfe] 'superstitions'.Long /ī/, as in fītò 'whistling', is similar to the vowel in English 'feet' (but without the offglide) whereas short /i/, as in fìtò 'ferrying', is similar to the initial vowel in Eng. 'fitting'. Long /ū/, as in kūkà 'baobab', is similar to the vowel in Eng. 'boot', whereas short /u/, in kukà 'you (pl.) preterite', is similar to the vowel in Eng. 'cook'.

Phonemically, the two short high vowels do contrast with one another, both word medially and word finally, e.g., gidā 'house', vs. gùdā 'lump, unit', bisà 'on' vs. ɓusà 'haft', kì 'you (f.)' vs. kù 'you (pl.)'; but there are restrictions on their occurrence and considerable phonetic variability. For example, when preceded by a coronal consonant—and even more so when also followed by a coronal—the vowel /u/ tends to be pronounced toward the front, even overlapping with allophones of /i/, e.g., tunkìyā [tɪnkìyā] 'sheep' (cf. pl. [tumākī]; tsullùmā [tsɪllùmā] 'fall in water'; zurà [zɪr̃à] 'lower bucket in a well'; akwàtunà [ˈakwātɪnà] 'boxes' (with the plural suffix -unà), cf. rīgunà [rīgunà] 'gowns', with the back-rounded [u] surfacing because of the preceding /g/. In some cases, the only way one knows that the vowel is underlyingly (historically?) /u/ and not /i/ is the fact that it does not condition palatalization, e.g., //tunyà// phonetically [tɪnyà] 'cactus', cf. //tinyà//, phonetically (and spelled) with /c/) [cɪnyà] 'thigh'. Not surprisingly, a number of words now appear with alternative pronunciations, e.g., dùddùk̃e = dìddìk̃e 'crouched', dunshè = dinshè 'single bunch of bananas', sullē = sillē 'top section of cornstalk', aibù = aibì 'fault, blemish' (but àbù 'thing' requires the final /ù/).

The realization of /u/ as a front vowel is strongly conditioned by an immediately following /y/ glide, whether in the same syllable (i.e., constituting a uy (= ui) diphthong) or not, e.g., wuyà [wiyà] neck, *gùiguyà [gwìgwiyà] 'gnaw'. The underlying /u/ conditions labialization on the preceding consonant, with the result that a sequence such as //kuya// appears as [kwiya], e.g., àkuyà [ˈàkwiyà] 'goat'; dàguyà [dàgwiyà] 'gnaw'; tùnkùyau [tùnkwìyau] 'flea'; tsùnguyà [tsùngwiyà] 'pinch off sth'; *//zuguigùitā// [zugwīgwìtā] 'exaggerate' (cf. zùgūgù 'exaggeration'); //dùlmuyà// [dùlmwiyà] 'sink'; *//cimuimùyā// [cumwīmwìyā] [dv] 'crumple'; *//dùmùimuyà// [dùmwìmwiyà] [dv] 'eat in a clumsy manner'. In a number of cases, the surface Cwī has achieved phonemic status and the underlying //Cuy// sequence no longer exists synchronically. This change in status is reflected in orthographic representation, e.g., kwīɓì 'side' (< *kuiɓì), gwīwà 'knee' (< *guiwà).

Fronting of /u/ also results from optional anticipatory assimilation to a high front vowel in the following syllable, e.g., /bùkī/ (→) [bìkī] 'celebration', **fushī** (→) [fìshī] 'anger'. The matter of the short high vowels is further complicated by the fact that /i/ sometimes phonetically moves toward [u] if followed by a labialized consonant or by /u/ in the following syllable, e.g., //**cikwīkwìyē**// 'entangle' → [cukwīkwìyē]; //**cikunkùnē**// → [cukunkùnē] 'entangle'.

°AN/◊HN: Parsons (1970) proposed that medial **i** and **u** are synchronically not in contrast and Schuh (1984) went further and extended this idea historically. I think that they are both mistaken. I would suggest that (a) although the contrast is in the process of being lost (i.e., much of the original contrast has been shifted to the preceding consonant), it still exists synchronically, and (b) it certainly was there at an earlier period (Newman 1979b).

◊HN: In many cases, the /u/ → [i] shift has become lexicalized, e.g., ***buyu** > /biyu/ 'two', cf. the cognate form **bolu** found in Bole and related languages.

1.2.1. Vowel length

All five basic vowels have long and short counterparts. The long vowels generally have typical IPA values whereas the corresponding short vowels are more lax and centralized. The vowel length distinction is not noted in standard orthography, e.g., /**dagā**/ 'charm bangle' and /**dāgā**/ 'battle line' are both written as **daga**. The length contrast is only found in open syllables; in closed syllables all vowels are short. In nonfinal position, vowel length functions lexically, e.g., **fītò** 'whistling' vs. **fitò** 'ferrying'; **fāsà̀** 'postpone' vs. **fasà** 'smash'; **ɗānà̀** 'borrow temporarily' vs. **ɗanà** 'set bow, cock trigger'; **dūkà̀** 'beating' vs. **dukà** 'all'. Medial vowel length is generally stable (apart from automatic shortening in closed syllables) and not subject to morphological alternations. The exceptions consist of a few loanwords from Arabic, e.g., **wājìbī** 'necessity' vs. **wàjabà** 'be incumbent on', **bàyānì̀** 'explanation' vs. **bayyànà** 'explain', and a few noun/adverb pairs, e.g., **bàkī** 'mouth' vs. **bakà** 'in/on the mouth'; **ɗākì̀** 'room' vs. **ɗakà** 'in the room'; **mātā** 'wife' vs. **màcè** 'woman, female'.

In final position, the function of vowel length is to a great extent morphological and grammatical, e.g., **hannū** 'hand' vs. **à hannu** 'in the hand'; **sarkī** 'emir' vs. **Sarki** (proper name); **fìtā** 'going out' vs. **fìta** 'go out'; **bugà̄** 'beat (pre-pronoun form)' vs. **bugà** 'beat (pre-noun form)'; **shi** 'him (direct object pn)' vs. **shī** 'he, him (independent pn). Excluding loanwords, common nouns tend to end in a long final vowel whereas the length of the final vowel of verbs depends on the verb's grade and its syntactic position (see chap. **74**).

◊HN: The present balanced vowel system derives historically from a skewed 2–3/3–5 system in which the number of contrasts varied depending on the position within the word. In final position, all five vowels occurred, but, probably, without a length contrast. The rule seems to have been that all final vowels were short, apart from monosyllabic nouns and verbs ending in /ā/, which had a long vowel. On the whole, the old Hausa final vowels have carried over into the present-day language in their original form. In word-initial position—and pre-Hausa did have vowel-initial words—only short /a/ and /i/ were used. (If [u] occurred, it would have been a conditioned variant of /i/.) In word-medial position, the language had three vowels (/i(i)/, /a(a)/, and /u(u)/, all of which could occur long or short. Medial /ē/ and /ō/, which are now quite common, historically resulted from the lowering of /ī/ and /ū/, respectively, generally due to assimilation to the height of a mid vowel in the following syllable (Newman 1979b).

Before the phonemicization of initial / ' / and /h/, Hausa had vowel-initial words beginning with /a/ and /i/, and to a lesser extent /u/. (It did not have /e(e)/ or /o(o)/ in word-initial position.) All these initial vowels were short only. As a result, words that now begin with / ' / are invariably followed by a short vowel (excluding recent loanwords), e.g., **'àrā** (< **àrā*) 'borrow', **'idò̀** (< **idò̀*) 'eye', **'ùbā** (< **ùbā*) 'father' (cf. **'āyà** 'verse of the Koran' and **'Ïdî** 'Muslim religious festival' < Ar.). Similarly, words with initial /h/, again apart from loanwords, are invariably followed by short /a/, e.g., **haɓà** (< **aɓà*) 'chin' (cf. **hātìmī** 'seal, official stamp' < Ar.). Apart from those dialects where /f/ is pronounced as [h], there are no native words beginning with **hi(i)**. One does get native words with initial **h** followed by /u(u)/, but in these cases the [h] is an allophone of /f/ and not a reflex of an originally vowel-initial word, e.g., **hùlā** (< **fùlā*) 'cap', **huɗu** (< *fuɗu*) 'four'.

In prepausal position, the qualitative difference between the vowels is much less clear, the short vowels being pronounced essentially like their long counterparts. There are two phonetic cues that distinguish the long and short vowels in prepausal position. First, there is a difference (albeit small) in the duration of the two phonemic lengths. Second, and probably more important from a perceptual point of view, there is a phonetic glottal closure after short vowels, but not after long vowels e.g., /gàba/ [gàbaʔ] 'in front', cf. /gàbā/ [gàbā] 'chest'; Sàbo (proper name) [sāboʔ], cf. **sābō** [sābō] 'new', /gudù/ [gudùʔ] 'run' vs. /gudū̀/ [gudū̀] 'running'.

1.2.2. Half-long vowels with glottal stop

As just indicated, the general rule in the language is that short vowels in prepausal position have phonetic glottal closure whereas long vowels do not. There is, however, a third contrast in prepausal position (R. M. Newman and van Heuven 1981), namely "half-long" vowels. Some specified sets of words and morphemes with long final vowels (including diphthongs!) are characterized by prepausal glottal closure, contrary to the general expectation. Examples (where [a·] represents a half-long vowel and [a:] represents a regular long vowel):

tā jā [ta: ja·ʔ] She pulled (it). cf. **bà tà jā ba** [bà tà ja: baʔ] She didn't pull (it).
tābà sukà sātō [ta:bà: sukà sa:to·ʔ] It was cigarettes they stole. cf. **sun sātō tābà** [sun sa:to: ta:bà:] They stole cigarettes.
zōbènā [zo:bè:na·ʔ] my ring, cf. **zōbènā nè** [zo:bè:na: nè:] It's my ring.
yā fāɗì à kā [ya: fāɗì à ka·ʔ] He fell headlong. cf. **yā fāɗì à kā cikin rāmì** [ya: fāɗì à ka: cikin ra:mì:] He fell headlong in the hole.

These underlyingly long vowels with prepausal glottal closure have been termed "indeterminate vowels" because phonetically they are identical neither to long vowels nor to short vowels. They are found in the following classes of words, all of which have level high tone(s) only:
1. Monoverbs (i.e., CVV verbs), e.g., **jā** 'pull', **shā** 'drink', **zō** 'come', **sō** 'want', **jē** 'go', **kai** 'take', **hau** 'mount', **kau** 'move aside'
2. Pseudomonoverbs (i.e., monotonal **CVCā** verbs), e.g., **biyā** 'pay', **kirā** 'call', **jirā** 'wait for'
3. Grade 6 verbs (which contain the H tone -(w)ō ventive suffix), e.g., **kōmō** 'return here', **sātō** 'steal and bring', **jāwō** 'pull here', etc.
4. Expressives of contempt (which contain the H tone -ō suffix), e.g., **mātō** 'the hell with the car!'; **hūlō** 'the hell with the cap!'; etc.
5. The bound first person possessive forms **-nā** (< **na + a**) and **-tā** (< **ta + a**) 'my' (m./f.)
6. The adverbial form **kā** 'on the head' (< **kâi** 'head')

°AN: [i] With some speakers the prepausal half-long vowels seem to be merging with the short vowels. (Hausa assistants from Kano consistently transcribed these half-long prepausal vowels as short, even though they transcribed them as long in nonfinal position.) Even where the contrast exists, it does so only in a statistical sense, i.e., when large numbers of examples are taken into account, shortened vowels as a class can be differentiated from an equivalent number of short vowels. If one looks at any particular token, on the other hand, the half-long vowel may be indistinguishable from a short vowel.

[ii] That **kai** and **hau**, for example, pattern with monovocalic verbs like **shā** and **jē** in adding a final glottal stop is further evidence in support of the analysis of Hausa [ai] and [au] as true vocalic diphthongs (/ai/ and /au/) rather than as VC /ay/ and /au/ sequences.

◊HN: Voigt (1983) proposed that the prepausal glottal closure with indeterminate vowels derived from an etymological word-final consonant (such as glottal stop), i.e., **jā**, for example, would have come from *jāC, kōmō < *kōmōC, etc. There are at least three things wrong with this analysis. (1) It requires postulating overheavy CVVC syllables, which synchronically are excluded in Hausa and which historically probably weren't allowed either. (2) It ignores the fact that /ē/ and /ō/, which regularly centralize in closed syllables, do not centralize before the prepausal glottal stop. (3) There is no comparative evidence to support the idea that the etymons of the items in question ever had a final consonant (Newman 1975; Schuh 1977). A more plausible analysis is that the prepausal glottal closure is simply an intonational/prosodic phenomenon—why found in this restricted set of words still being a mystery—and that this glottal stop is no more indicative of a lost consonant than the prepausal glottal stop found at the end of short vowels.

To summarize, in open, but not prepausal, syllables, Hausa has a two-way length contrast: short vs. long. In closed syllable, there is only one length: all vowels are short. In open syllables in prepausal position, there is a three-way length contrast: short /a/ (with glottal closure), long /ā/ (without glottal closure), and (in restricted contexts) half-long /a·/ (with glottal closure).

1.2.3. Diphthongs

Synchronically there are two diphthongs /ai/ and /au/, which function as long vocalic nuclei, e.g., **mâi** 'oil', **kaifī** 'sharpness', **sàu** 'times', **ɓaunā** 'buffalo'. ("Nasal diphthongs" as a special category are discussed belowed in §2.1.1.) The /ai/ diphthong is pronounced [ai] (or sometimes [əi]) when occurring in a monosyllabic word with a falling tone or when preceded by / ' / or /h/, e.g., **mâi** [mâi] 'oil', **aikà** [ʔaikà] 'send'. Elsewhere it is pronounced as [ei] or even monophthongizes to [ē], thereby phonetically merging with long /ē/, e.g., /naiřà/ [neiřà] = [nēřà] 'naira', **mài-gidā** [mèigidā] = [mègidā] 'householder'. In the English loanwords **diřēbà** 'driver' and **ogànēzà** 'organizer' the /ai/ in the source has been lexicalized as /ē/ and does not normally have a diphthongal pronunciation. The back diphthong /au/ varies in the [au] to [ao] to [ou] range. It usually remains distinct from /ō/, e.g., **zaunà** [zaonà] 'sit' (not **[zōnà]), although there are some exceptions where the monophthongization takes place, e.g., **wàtàu** = **wàtò** 'that is to say', **sàu** = **sò** 'times', **bōcà** 'voucher', **hōdà** (< //fōdà//) 'powder', **tùřōzà** 'trousers'. With both diphthongs, the transition glides are phonetically shorter in duration and cover a narrower range than comparable diphthongs in many other languages.

°AN: The traditional phonological analysis has been to treat the .diphthongs as vowel-consonant sequences, e.g., [ai] = /ay/ and [au] = /aw/, where the glide occupies the coda position in the syllable, see Klingenheben (1927/28) and Greenberg (1941). This interpretation is still widely accepted among Hausa linguists. This earlier analysis allows easy representation of alternations resulting from (morpho)phonological processes, especially apocopation, e.g., **ɗaya** 'one', cf. **ɗay-ɗay** [ɗeiɗei] 'one by one'; **sàyi** 'buy', cf. **say** [sei] (clipped form of same word); **rawā** 'dancing', cf. **raw-dà** [rau-dà] 'shake'; **nàwa** 'mine' = **naw** [nau] (dialect variant). (In some instances, however, the /ay/ analysis adds an unnecessary complication, cf. the proper name **Ā'ìshā** with the short form **Aishà**, which appears with an /ai/ diphthong resulting from the loss of the intervocalic glottal stop.) The approach adopted here, i.e., diphthongs as complex nuclei, is one I have proposed earlier (Newman and Salim 1981) and that has been supported on comparative grounds by Schuh (1989b). Its advantage is that it accounts for the fact that the diphthongs in Hausa most often pattern with monophthongal long vowel rather than with -VC sequences. For example, the rule shortening a long VV in syllables closed by a coda consonant applies to diphthongs as well as to monophthongs, e.g., **sâa** 'bull', vs. **sân** 'the bull', cf. **mâi** 'oil' vs. **mân** 'the oil'. Similarly, the phonetic rule that adds a glottal closure to certain high tone long vowels in prepausal position also applies to diphthongs, e.g., [yā ja·ʔ] 'He pulled', cf. [yā hauʔ] 'He ascended.' Regarding the alternations illustrated above, note that the transformation of the glide into a component of a vocalic nucleus implicit in this analysis follows automatically from the shift of the syllable-initial glide into the rime of the preceding syllable (which would be required under either approach) and thus does not require any complicated rule changing one phoneme into another.

◊HN: In the not so distant past, there were two other diphthongs: */ui/ (probably derived at a deeper historical depth from */ur/), which monophthongized to /ī/, e.g., *gwuiwà̀ > gwīwà̀ 'knee', *kwuiɓì̀ (< *kwurɓì̀?) > kwīɓì̀ 'side of the body, trunk'; and */iu/ (normally derived from *i + a velar or labial obstruent), which monophthongized to /ū/, e.g., *ciurà̀ (< *tibrà̀) > cūrà̀ 'knead', *shiukà̀ (< *sifkà̀) > shūkà̀ 'to sow'. In one example that we know of, */iu/ appears to have monophthongized to /ī/, e.g., *riujìyā (< *rigzi + the feminative suffix) > rījìyā 'well' (cf. the archaic plural rigōjī).

1.3. Tone

Hausa has two contrastive level tones, H(igh) (unmarked in transcription) and L(ow) (indicated by a grave accent), e.g., **rānā** 'sun, day', **dàgà** 'from', **tāgà̀** 'window', **bàra** 'last year', **gōrà̀** 'bamboo', **gòrā** 'large gourd'. It also has a F(alling) contour (indicated by a circumflex), which occurs only on heavy (bimoraic) syllables, e.g., **mântā** 'forget', **kōmôwā** 'returning'. (In the transcription convention adopted here, the circumflex on an open vowel indicates falling tone *and* length.) The language has no rising tone.

For a full discussion of tonal phenomena, see the separate chapter on tone (chap. **71**).

2. SYLLABLE STRUCTURE AND PHONOTACTIC CONSTRAINTS

Three syllable types occur in the language: CV, CVV, and CVC. A CV syllable is made up of a consonantal onset plus a simple nucleus consisting of a short vowel, e.g., **wa**.**tà̀** 'moon'. A CVV syllable is made up of a consonantal onset plus a long nucleus consisting of a long monophthongal vowel or a diphthong, e.g., **nā**.**mā** 'meat', **kai**.**fī** 'sharpness'. A CVC syllable is made up of a consonantal onset plus a simple short vowel nucleus plus a consonantal coda, e.g., **fus**.**kà̀** 'face'. In a few instances, a syllabic nasal serves as the vocalic nucleus in place of a vowel, e.g., **'ṇ**.**gùlu** = **'ùngùlu** 'vulture'; **ɗṇ̀** = **dîn** 'the one in question'; **'ṇ**.**nà̀** [orthographically **ina**] 'I.cont', e.g., **'ṇ**.**nà̀ zuwà̀** 'I am coming.'

All syllables begin with a consonant. Words that appear orthographically with an initial vowel begin phonemically with a glottal stop, e.g., orthographic **aure** 'marriage' = /ʔaurē/; **aske** 'shave' = /ʔaskè/. The existence of the glottal stop shows up when, for example, a word like **askè̀** undergoes CVG-prefixation to form a related pluractional verb, e.g., /ʔaʔʔàskē/ 'shave many or repeatedly'.

◊HN: This restriction against vowel-initial words is *not* an inherited Afroasiatic feature. Unlike many Afroasiatic languages, which require that all syllables (and thus all words) begin with a consonant, Hausa originally had true vowel-initial words. The phonotactic requirement that now applies in the language is due to a historically shallow change whereby a prothetic, originally sub-phonemic, consonant, /ʼ/ or /h/, was added to vowel-initial words, e.g., *askì̀ > 'askì̀ 'shaving', *aɓà̀ > haɓà̀ 'chin' (see §**34**:1.2).

True consonant clusters are not allowed, i.e., there are no complex onsets or codas. The consonants written with digraphs, e.g., /ts/, /kw/, /gy/, are unit phonemes and do not run counter to the generalization. A sequence of two consonants may, however, abut across a syllable boundary, e.g., **fus.kà** 'face', **sar.kī** 'chief'.

2.1. Coda consonants

All consonants occur as onsets. With the exception of the rare phoneme /fy/, which occurs only word initially, there is no restriction as to whether the onset is word initial or word medial (i.e., intervocalic). Excluding geminates, which are permissible with a full range of consonants, only a small number of consonants occur in coda position. (Apart from ideophones and recent loans, very few words end in consonants, thus the specification of possible codas refers only to word-internal consonants.) Words of the shape CVC.CV(V) with a medial coda followed by an abutting consonant are quite common, e.g., **gàm.su** 'be satisfied', **gwan.kī** 'roan antelope', **fař.kà** 'wake up', **sar.kī** 'emir', **kal.mà** 'word', **fus.kà** 'face', **fiz.gè** 'snatch'. The inventory of consonants that can serve as a coda, however, is limited. The consonants /h/ and /'/ and the velars and palatals do not occur as codas, nor do any of the palatalized or labialized consonants. With the exception of word-final /t/, found primarily in loanwords and ideophones, the coronal stops (**t, ɗ, d**) do not constitute possible codas. The fricatives /s/ and /z/, on the other hand, do occupy coda position. (See below for a discussion of the /s/ vs. /z/ contrast.) All of the sonorants (/m/, /n/, /r/, /ř/, and /l/) function comfortably as codas. The glides /y/ and /w/ may enter coda position, but when they do so they automatically attach to the nucleus and alter into /i/ and /u/, respectively.

In WH, the labial obstruents occur frequently in coda position, e.g., **àfku** 'happen', **abdùgā** 'cotton'. In SH, on the other hand, labials historically weakened to /u/ by Klingenheben's Law (see §34:1.5), thereby eliminating many of these codas, e.g., **àuku** 'happen', **audùgā** 'cotton'. SH does, however, still have /f/ and /b/ codas for a number of reasons. First, the sound law appears to have been phonologicaly conditioned and lexically irregular, e.g., **kaftà** 'dig up ground', **gabjējè** 'huge'. Second, new labial codas have been created as a result of vowel syncope, e.g., **kubcè** 'excape' (= **kuɓùcē**), **dàbgī** 'anteater' (= **dābùgī**). Third, there continues to be dialect borrowing from WH, not to mention borrowings from other languages, especially Arabic, e.g., **Abdù** = **Audù** (proper name), **kàftānì** 'caftan'. Fourth, base-final labial obstruents are preserved in codas when certain morphological suffixes are added, e.g., **ɗālìbcē** 'become a student' < **ɗālìbī** 'student', **hasàftā** 'give a small present to s.o.' < **hasàfī** 'gift', **la'ifcì** 'impotence' < **là'īfì** 'impotent'. Note that the labial codas in the preceding words are generally pronounced [p] and that any contrast between the fricative /f/ and the stop /b/ is marginal at best. Standard spelling is inconsistent, but, where possible, it follows etymology, i.e., [ɗālìpcē] 'become a student' is spelled **ɗalibce** because of **ɗālìbī** 'student', whereas [hasàptā] 'give a small present' is spelled **hasafta** because of **hasàfī** 'gift'. By contrast [tsaptà] 'cleanliness', whose etymology is unknown, sometimes appears spelled as **tsafta** and sometimes as **tsabta**.

In general there is no phonation contrast in coda position, i.e., the opposition between voiced, voiceless, and glottalized is neutralized. In word-final position, where obstruents are uncommon apart from ideophones and recent loanwords, they are all voiceless, e.g., **bìyat** 'five' [dv] (< *bìyaɗ); **řàsît** = **řàsīɗì** 'receipt'; **tîf** 'tube', **kamas** (< //kamaz//) = **kazam** 'emphasizes rising suddenly'; **dùřôs** 'drawers/underpants'. A few words, e.g., **bìřgêd** [bìřgêt] 'brigade'; the name of a quarter in Kano', **gùlôb** [gùlôp] 'bulb for a flashlight or car light' (< Eng. 'globe') are spelled with a final **d** or **b**; but this is essentially orthographic and does not reflect pronunciation except in the case of people who are bilingual in English.

Word-medial obstruents in coda position take the same phonation feature as the following abutting consonant, e.g., **fuskà** 'face' (both voiceless) (not ****fusgà** nor ****fuzkà**), **càzbī** 'prayer beads' (both voiced), **abdùgā** 'cotton' [WH] (both voiced). A word like /caɓdî/ 'expression of great surprise' is spelled **cabɗì** because **ɓ** is never written in coda position, but the glottalization extends across both consonants. The spelling of words like [tsaptà] 'cleanliness' (both voiceless) poses a problem because /p/ is not part of the Hausa alphabet. As a result one finds both **tsafta**, reflecting the fact that both consonants are voiceless, and **tsabta**, capturing the fact that they are both stops.

°AN: Possible exceptions to the rule that the phonation feature extends phonetically across both abutting obstruents are provided by derived words with the suffixes -**tā** and -**cī**, e.g., **annabtà** = **annabcì** 'prophethood; divine message revealed to a prophet' (cf. **ànnabì** 'prophet'); **Lārabcī** 'Arabic language' (cf. **Lārabāwā** 'Arabs'). Careful instrumental work is necessary to confirm that the /b/ is indeed voiced or whether this is just an etymological spelling.

◊HN: The synchronic rule that two abutting obstruents must both be voiceless or both be voiced is easiest to express by making the first consonant dependent on the second, assimilation in Hausa normally being anticipatory. Historically, however, there may be some cases where the opposite was the case. Many verbs contain a remnant suffix that appears as -**kà** or -**gà** (see §76:3). It is possible—although far from certain—that they originally were variants of the same suffix. If the preceding abutting consonant was voiced, then -**gà** would appear, e.g., **fizgà** 'tug', otherwise the suffix would surface as -**kà**, e.g., **haskà** 'light', **fařkà** (< **faɗkà** < **fàɗakà**) 'wake up'.

2.1.1. Nasal diphthongs

The nasal /n/ commonly occurs in syllable-final position, where it is always homorganic with the following abutting consonant (i.e., it could be represented as an unspecified nasal N), e.g., **mântā** [mântā] 'forget', **ɗinkì** [ɗiŋkì] 'sewing', **fùnfùnā** [fùmfùnā] 'food mold', [bàkansà] 'his bow', [bàkammù] 'our bow', [bàkaŋkà] 'your bow' all from **bàkā** 'bow' + **n** linker + pronoun. At first sight, a CVN syllable would appear to have the structure CVC, where the /n/ would be the coda consonant, i.e., **kundì** 'notebook, thesis', for example, could be considered parallel to **maskō** 'mallet'. However, the /n/ behaves in many respects as if it were part of a complex nucleus, i.e., /an/ and /in/ and /un/ could be considered to constitute "nasal diphthongs" comparable to the oral diphthong /ai/ and /au/. The presumed structural contrast between nasal diphthongs and CVC syllables, and their similarity to oral diphthongs, is shown in the initial syllable of the examples in fig. 5 (next page) (where long vowels are indicated by double letters).

The motivation for treating /VN/ sequences as nasal diphthongs is provided by their morphophonological behavior in such constructions as the following:

(1) Disyllabic H-H nouns with a long/complex nucleus in the initial syllable form plurals with the suffix -**āyē**)^{HLH}. Those with an initial CVC syllable with a coda use the affix -**ā–ē**)^{HLH}, the internal -**ā**- being inserted after the coda consonant. Words with CVN in the initial syllable pattern with those having the long nucleus (CVV) rather than those with the coda consonant (CVC), e.g.,

long monophthong: **kīfī / kīfàyē** fish; **sūnā / sūnàyē** name
(long) diphthong: **maisō / maisàyē** fallow field; **gaulā / gaulàyē** simpleton
nasal diphthong: **shingē / shingàyē** fence; **tandū / tandàyē** small hide vessel
cf. vowel plus coda: **biřnī / biřânē** city; **kaskō / kasàkē** small earthen bowl

(2) In almost all morphological processes, vowel-initial suffixes replace the final nucleus (monophthong or diphthong) of the stem, e.g., **tāgà** 'window', pl. **tāg-ōgī**; **kamfai** 'underpants', **kamf-ō (matà)**! 'the hell with the underpants!'; **Sànusi** (name), **Sanùs-āwā** 'adherents of Sanusi'; **Jummai** (name), **Jummalō** 'dear little Jummai'. Final consonants, on the other hand, are preserved, e.g., **tēbùř** 'table', pl. **tēbuř-ōřī**; **Jāmùs** 'Germany', **Jāmus-āwā** 'Germans'. Words with final -VN typically treat the ending as a complex vocalic nucleus and drop it when suffixes are added, e.g.,

tangaɍan   chinaware, dishes, pl. **tangaɍ-àyē**   (not ****tangaɍanàyē**); **tambùlàn**   drinking glass, pl. **tambul-à**; **miliyàn**   million, pl. **miliy-ōyī**; **Àlāsàn**   (name), **Alās-āwā**   clan members of Alhasan Dantata; **ambùlàn**   envelope, **ambul-ō (matà)**   Who gives a hoot about the envelope!; **hàmsin**   fifty, **hams-ō (matà)**   So what about fifty!; **Mammàn**   (name), **Mamm-alō**   dear little Mamman

(3) In some lexically specific instances, earlier existing consonants that have changed into vocalic elements are "recovered" in plural formations, e.g., **ɓaunā** 'buffalo' < historical ***ɓaknā**, pl. **ɓakànē** (now usually **ɓaunàyē**); **jūjī** 'refuse heap' < historical ***jibjī** (still extant in WH), pl. **jibàjē** (now usu. **jūjàyē**). Not surprisingly, this same process occurs also with nasal diphthongs, i.e., words with nasal diphthongs sometimes recover a historically prior full consonant /**m**/ in plural formations, e.g.,

kuncì (< *kumtì)   cheek, pl. **kumàtū** (now usually **kuncunà**)
gwankī (< gwamkī)   roan antelope, pl. [WH] **gwamàkkā** (SH now **gwankàyē**)

Figure 5: Nasal diphthongs

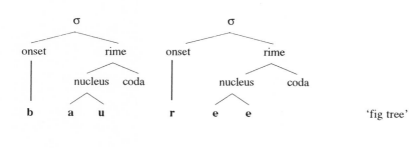

'fig tree'

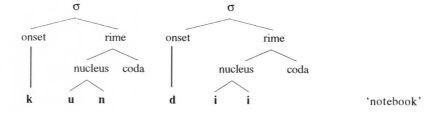

'notebook'

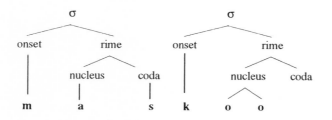

'mallet'

°AN: In his analysis of an early twentith-century Hausa text written in Arabic script, Piłaszewicz (1992: 26) noted the common omission of syllable-final /n/ . Consistent with (and independent of) my structural notion of nasal diphthongs, he suggests that in syllable-final position "the nasalization of the preceding vowel may have [phonetically] taken place. In such a case the consonant **n** might be pronounced very lightly and, therefore, it could be left unmarked or leave its trace in a lengthened vowel in the writing."

3. SYLLABLE WEIGHT

The basic division in a syllable is between the onset and everything else (= the rime). The CV syllable type with a simple rime consisting of a short vowel is light. The CVV and CVC syllable types with a complex rime (i.e., have a rime that contains either a long nucleus or a nucleus plus a coda) are heavy. Syllables may not contain both a long nucleus (whether monophthongal or diphthongal) and a final coda consonant. Such over-heavy CVVC syllables, which commonly result from morphological processes, are automatically pared down by nucleus reduction rules that delete the second component of a complex nucleus, i.e., CV_1V_2C (where V_1 and V_2 may be identical) $\rightarrow CV_1C$, e.g., //râi-n-sà// (lit. life-of-him) $\rightarrow$ **rânsà** 'his life'; //fâr-kō// $\rightarrow$ **farkō** 'beginning' (cf. **fārà** 'begin'); //cūs-cùsā// $\rightarrow$ **cuccùsā** 'stuff repeatedly'.

Syllable weight plays an essential role in a number of different areas of phonology and morphology.

3.1. Falling tone
Only heavy syllables can carry falling tones, which require that the host consist of two tone-bearing units, e.g., **yârā** 'children', **mâi** 'oil', **jânyē** 'pull away'. There are no falling tones on light syllables. Note that the restriction refers to syllable weight and not to vowel length; thus falling tones are allowed not only in CVV syllables but also in CVC syllables, including those with an obstruent coda, e.g., **ƙâttā** 'huge (pl.) ', **zîk** 'zipper'.

3.2. Canonical shape
(a) Different pronoun paradigms are generally marked by a fixed weight pattern. For example, direct object pronouns, indirect object pronouns, and the weak subject pronouns in most TAMs are characterized by a light syllable, whereas the completive wsp's and the disjunctive (independent) pronouns are characterized by a heavy syllable. Examples (1, 2m, 2f, 3m, 3f, 1p, 2p, 3p, (4p)):

d.o. (strong H tone set):	**ni, ka, ki, shì, ta, mu, ku, su**
i.o.	**nì, kà, kì, sà, tà, nà, kù, sù**
subjunctive:	**nà, kà, kì, yà, tà, mù, kù, sù, à**
completive:	**nā, kā, kin, yā, tā, mun, kun, sun, an**
disjunctive:	**nī, kai, kē, shī, ita, mū, kū, sū**

°AN: The feminine disjunctive pronoun **ita** 'she' illustrates the metrical equivalence of a heavy syllable to two light syllables, an equivalence commonly found in languages with distinctive syllable weight (Newman 1972b).

(b) Abstract nouns of sensory quality (chap. **2**), a group of semantically related nouns ending in -ī, all have a heavy first syllable, e.g., **zāfī** 'heat', **nauyī** 'heaviness', **ƙarfī** 'strength'.

(c) Verb + noun compounds in which the first element is monosyllabic invariably have a heavy first syllable, even if the verb would normally have a short vowel, e.g., **shà-zumāmì** 'sugar ant' (lit. drink-honey); **cì-rāni** 'dry-season work' (lit. eat-dry season < **ci** 'to eat'); **bì-bango** 'water dripping along the wall' (lit. follow-wall < **bi** 'to follow'); **kàs-dafī** 'a poison antidote' (lit. kill-poison).

3.3. Rhythmic weight polarity

In certain morphological constructions, the length of a vowel formative is determined by the weight of the preceding syllable to produce either a heavy–light or a light–heavy rhythmic pattern.

(a) With the verbalizing suffix -a(a)ta, the /a(a)/ is short if the preceding syllable is heavy, and long if the preceding syllable is light, e.g., **tsōràtā** 'frighten' < **tsŏrō** 'fear'; **ƙàunatà** 'love s.o.' < **ƙàunā** 'love'; **ɗanyàtā** 'moisten' < **ɗanyē** 'fresh, moist'; cf. **fùsātà** 'be angry' < **fushī** 'anger'; **wàdātà** 'be enriched, contented' < **wàdā** 'wealth, contentment'. (The length of the final vowel of these verbs also varies, but this is determined grammatically by grade assignment and not phonologically by weight polarity.)

(b) The length of the vowel -a(a) in the reduplicative -a(a)Ca suffix that derives verbs from sensory quality nouns is fully determined by weight polarity, e.g., **zāfàfā** 'make hot' < **zāfī** 'heat', **kaifàfā** 'sharpen' < **kaifī** 'sharpness'; cf. **ɗumàmā** 'warm up' < **ɗùmī** 'warmth'.

(c) The length of the final vowel (usually -a(a)) of each component of reduplicated LL-HL nouns is determined by weight polarity, i.e., it is short if the preceding syllable is heavy and long if the preceding syllable is light, e.g., **bòkò-bōkò** 'fraud' < **bōkŏ** 'fraud'; **kàusà-kausà** 'a small plant with coarse leaves like sandpaper' < **kaushī** 'roughness'; **hàntà-hantà** 'talking through one's nose' < **hancī** 'nose'; cf. **ràmà-ramà** 'jute' < **ramǎ** 'hemp'.

3.4. Syllable weight and tone

In various morphological constructions, one finds a correlation, albeit imperfect, between syllable weight and tone.

(a) Basic disyllabic intransitive verbs ending in -a (the grade 3 verbs) typically have L-H tone and a light first syllable, e.g., **tùma** 'jump', **shìga** 'enter', **tsìra** 'germinate, sprout'. Grade 3a verbs, which have a heavy first syllable, have H-H tone, e.g., **girma** 'grow up', **ƙaura** 'migrate', **tsīra** 'escape'.

(b) Plurals of ethnonyms are formed by means of a suffix -āwā. Those that are built on disyllabic stems with a heavy first syllable often have an L-L-H tone pattern (although in some cases all H is possible). Ethnonyms with a light first syllable invariably have all H tones, e.g., **Hàusàwā** 'Hausa people', **Gwàràwā** 'Gwari people', **dùkàwā** 'leather workers'; cf. **Badāwā** 'Bade people', **Kanāwā** 'Kano people'.

(c) Hypocoristic names formed by reduplication of the final syllable have L-H-H tone if the initial syllable is heavy. If the initial syllable is light, the word has an initial H tone, the other tones being unpredictable, e.g., **Àudūdu** 'Little Audu' < **Audù** (masc. name); **Làdīdi** 'Little Ladi' < **Lādì** (fem. name); **Mùɗɗeɗe** 'Little Mustapha' < **Mùɗɗe** (masc. name, short for Mustapha); cf. **Inūnu** 'Little Inusa' < **Inū** (masc. name, short for Inusa); **Kulùlu** 'Little Kulu' < **Kulù** (fem. name).

4. WORD STRUCTURE

Because all syllables begin with a consonant, it follows that all Hausa words necessarily begin with a consonant. Although CVC is a normal syllable type in the language, it is very uncommon at the end of a word, i.e., most words end in a vowel. Even sonorants, which naturally occur in word-medial position as codas, are lexically uncommon in word-final position. Consonants do, however, occur word finally. They are found, for example, in (a) ideophones, ideophonic adjectives, and exclamations, which by nature are extrasystemic, e.g. **wulik** 'emphasizing blackness', **jùgum** 'indicating silence, **santal-sàntàl** 'svelte, handsome (pl.)', **kas** 'expression of annoyance'; (b) some adverbs and function words, e.g., **ainùn** 'very much', **tun** 'since'; (c) grade 5 "efferential" verbs with the suffix -as/-ař, e.g., **zubař** 'pour out' (< **zubà** 'pour'); and (d) allomorph resulting from clipping or vowel apocope, e.g., **baȓ** pre-object form of **barì** 'let, allow', **kâȓ** = **kadà** 'don't, lest', **mîn** = **minì** 'to me', **mùtûm** < **mùtumì** 'man', **mālàm** 'teacher, Mr.', cf. **mālàmī** 'teacher'. Most consonant-final nouns are recent loanwords from Arabic or English (or French in Niger), e.g., **hàȓâm** 'forbidden according to Islamic laws and precepts' (< Ar.), **ƙāmùs** 'dictionary' (< Ar.), **kaȓàs** 'carrot(s)' (< Eng.), **kōfùȓ** 'corporal' (< Eng.), **bêl** 'belt' (< Eng.), **têf** 'tape' (< Eng.), **bîk** 'ball-point pen' (< Fr.), **kâȓ** 'bus' (< Fr.), **làkwâl** 'school' (< Fr.). It should be emphasized that because of the massive influx of loanwords in this century, C-final words are now far from negligible in Hausa, a fact that is bound to have an impact on the future phonological development of the language.

◊HN: The restriction against word-final obstruents seems to be very old. The near absence of word-final nasals is due to a historically more recent phonological loss affecting both final /n/ and /m/ (Schuh 1976), e.g., ***guzan** > **guzà** 'water monitor', ***kadam** > **kadà** 'crocodile'.

4.1. Number of syllables

Most words in the language (excluding recent loanwords from English (or French)) tend to be disyllabic, trisyllabic, or even quadrisyllabic. The norm for basic monomorphemic words is disyllabic. Longer words tend to be derived or inflected forms or else loanwords from Arabic.

Hausa does have some monosyllabic words, but these tend to be restricted to particular lexical classes. They are typical, for example, in the case of personal pronouns, connectors, modal particles, and other function words, e.g., **mū** 'we', **dà** 'and/with', **fa** 'indeed', **mὲ** 'what?' They are also common with ideophones, where they tend to contain a final consonant or a diphthong, e.g., **fat** 'very white', **zau** 'very hot, very tasty'. On the other hand, there are only some twelve or so monosyllabic verbs. Some of these belong to the class of H-tone gr0 monoverbs, which have mostly the shape **Ci** or **Cā**, e.g., **bi** 'follow', **jā** 'pull'. Some are clipped or apocopated verbs, e.g., **sau** 'release' (< //sàki//), **ga** 'see' (pre noun form of **ganī**), **kàs** 'kill' (compound form of **kashè**). Finally, there are a few defective disyllabic verbs, e.g., **sâ** 'put, cause', **cê** 'say'.

There are very few native monosyllabic nouns and only one monosyllabic adjective in the language. These all have a heavy syllable, usually containing a coda consonant or a diphthong. They have either falling (most common) or high tone, e.g., **sû** 'fishing'; **yâu** 'today', **yau** 'saliva', **ƙwai** 'egg', **fā** 'rock slab'. Some of these historically derived from monosyllabic words, e.g., **mâi** 'oil' (< ***mar**); others are the result of word shortening, e.g., **sau** 'foot' (< **sāwū**), **jā** 'red' (< ***jāja**), **kyâu** 'goodness' (< //kyāwò// = //kyāwù//). In recent times, loanwords have added greatly to the inventory of monosyllabic words. Like native words, these typically have a heavy syllable and falling tone, e.g., **bâm** 'bomb', **tî** 'tea', **shât** 'shirt', **pîl** 'battery' (Fr.), **shû** 'cabbage' (Fr.).

4.2. Final vowel length

Most native common nouns and adjectives have a long final vowel, e.g., **watā** 'month', **kàrē** 'dog', **gafiyà** 'bandicoot', **durùmī** 'fig tree', **farī** 'white', as do most loanwords from Arabic, e.g., **hātìmī** 'seal', **bàyānì** 'explanation'. Loanwords from other languages (e.g., English, Yoruba, Fulani, Kanuri), on the other hand, often end in a short final vowel, e.g., **faskìlà** 'first class' (Eng.), **gwamnatì** 'government' (Eng.), **àgàdè** 'plantain(s)' (Yor.), **gwaggò** 'paternal aunt' (Ful.), **ciȓòmà** 'traditional title' (Kan.). Noun plurals invariably have a long final vowel regardless of the final vowel length of the singular, e.g., **wàtànnī** 'months', **gwamnatōcī** 'governments'. Two exceptions to this generalization are reduplicated frequentatives, which function sometimes as plurals, e.g., **càmfe-càmfe** 'superstitions' (< sg. **camfì**) and fully reduplicated plurals of loanwords, e.g., **jōjì-jōjì** 'judges' (< sg. **jōjì**).

Islamic or Biblical personal names generally have a short final vowel unless they end in H-tone /ā/, in which case the vowel is long, e.g., **Àdàmu** m., **Hàlīmà** f., **Haȓūnà** m., **Maȓyamà** f., **Mùhammadù** m., **Mùhtāri** m., **Rùfā'i** m., **Sāȓatù** f., cf. **Hasànà** f., **Īsā** m., **Jamīlà** f., **Muȓtàlā** m., **Mūsā** m., **Ràhīlā** f., **Yàhàyā** m., **Yàhūzā** m. The name **Daudǎ** m., with L-tone long /ā/, is an exception. Short forms of names typically end in a short vowel if the tone is L. If the tone is H, one often gets a long vowel (unless the vowel is /e/); but this length is individually determined and not predictable, e.g., **Jibò** short for **Jìbìřílù** m., **Sulè** short for **Sulèmānù** m., **Ābù** short for **Zàinabù** f., **Àdō** short for **Àdàmu** m., **Bàlā** short for **Bàlāřabè**, **Fàtī** short for **Fātimà**, **Hàbū** short for **Àbūbakàř**, **Hànne** short for **Hànnatù** f., **Hàusu** short for **Hàfsatù** f., **Ìdī** short for **Ìdìřìsù** m., **Màiřo** short for **Màiřamù** f., **Mùɗɗe** short for **Mustàfa** m., **Zàřa** short for **Zàhàřá'ù** f. With proper names derived from common nouns, the final vowel is almost always short, regardless of the tone, e.g., **Sābo** / **Sābuwa** m./f., cf. **sābō** /**sābuwā** 'new' m./f.; **Gòshi** f., cf. **gòshī** 'forehead'; **Bāwà** m., cf. **bāwǎ** 'slave'. An exception is **Wàdā** m., cf. **wàdā** 'wealth'. An even more striking exception is the pair **Bàbbā** m., cf. **bàbba** 'big', where the name has a long vowel as opposed to the underlying form (an adjective) that has a short vowel.

Adverbs as a class have short final vowels, e.g., **jiyà** 'yesterday', **nēsà** 'far', **zàune** 'seated'. Numerals, apart from **ɗàrī** 'hundred' and **dubū** 'thousand', end either in a short final vowel or, in the case of higher numbers borrowed from Arabic, in a consonant, e.g., **huɗu** 'four', **àřbà'in** 'forty'.

As would be expected with a highly marked phonaesthetic class, ideophones display a range of shapes, ending in long vowels and short vowels as well as consonants, e.g., **zòřòřò** 'exceedingly tall', **kaca-kaca** 'in disarray', **tsiřit** 'very tiny'.

With verbs, the length of the final vowel is not an inherent lexical property of the root but rather depends on the grade and the specific syntactic use. The only significant generalizations that hold are that the exclusively intransitive grades (3 and 7) end in a short final vowel (e.g., **fìta** gr3 'go out', **fāɗì** gr3b 'fall', **gyàru** gr7 'be well repaired') and that verb forms before a personal pronoun direct object have a long final vowel (e.g., **yā kāmà ta** 'He caught her', **yā bī tà** 'He followed her', **yā nēmē tà** 'He sought her.').

5. PHONOTACTIC CO-OCCURRENCE RESTRICTIONS

5.1. *Sonorants*
In normal CVCV sequences, /l/ and /n/, and /l/ and /r/ cannot co-occur. The restriction does not, however, apply to the plural suffix -**unà**, or to the -**n** linker, e.g., **tùlū** 'water pot', pl. **tūlunà**, **tùluntà** 'her water pot' (lit. water pot.of.her). The l/r restriction applies only to the flap /r/. It does not affect the rolled **ř**, i.e., words with the sequence /ř/ – /l/ and /l/ – /ř/ occur, e.g., **lùřa** 'look after', **řūlà** 'ruler (for measuring length)'. In the case of flap /r/ and /n/, there is a unidirectional restriction: /r/ – /n/ occurs readily, e.g., **rinà** 'dye', **rānī** 'dry season', but /n/ – /r/ does not, the word **narkè** 'melt' being an exception.

5.2. *Glottalized consonants*
There are two main restrictions that affect the glottalized consonants.

(a) One cannot have two different glottalized consonants in the same word, i.e., /ɓ/, /ɗ/, /ts/, /ƙ/, and /'y/ (and dialectal (/c'/) do not co-occur in the same word, whether in immediate sequence or separated by other elements. (The Arabic loanword **ɗàřīƙà** 'religious sect' is an exception.) (Remember that the digraph **ts** represents an ejective consonant and belongs in the same class with the "hooked" letters.) One can, however, have successive instances of the same glottalized consonant, e.g., **ɓàɓè** 'quarrel', **ɗàɗumà** 'drive away', **tsātsà** 'rust', **ƙūƙùtā** 'try hard', **'yā'yā** 'sons and daughters'.

(b) Generally speaking, glottalized consonants and their nonglottalized counterparts cannot co-occur in the same word, i.e., sequences of /b/ – /ɓ/ or /k/ – /ƙ/ do not occur in either order. On the other hand, whereas the sequence /ɗ/ – /d/ does not occur, /d/ – /ɗ/ is quite normal, e.g., **dāɗī** 'pleasantness', **daɗè** 'last long'. Similarly, /ts/ – /s/ does not occur, although there are a few examples of /s/ – /ts/ with an intervening consonant, e.g., **santsī**, 'slipperiness', **sartsè** 'splinter'.

°AN/◊HN: It is not entirely clear what qualifies as the true counterpart of /ts/. Synchronically, reasons of pattern symmetry suggest that /ts/ is the glottalized member of the /s, /z/, /ts/ fricative triad (voiceless, voiced, glottalized). Historically, however, /ts/ could just as likely be viewed as the ejective counterpart of the palatal /c/. (This would avoid having to postulate a contrast between an implosive (ɗ) and an ejective (ts) at the same position of articulation, something that i s uncommon in the languages of the world.) Alternatively, /ts/ could be viewed as having developed from an ejective */t'/ or from a non-ejective affricate */ts/, neither of which has been preserved in the modern language.

Words do occur that contain both /ƙ/ and /k/ when the /k/ is part of a suffix, e.g., ƙauyukà 'villages' (< ƙauyè sg.), ƙàràrrakī 'complaints' (< ƙārā sg.), ƙarkō 'durability' (< *ƙar- '?' + suffix -kō), cf. ƙwārī 'strength'). These examples suggest that the phonotactic restriction regarding the co-occurrence of glottalized segments may be a property of lexical roots rather than full words.*5.3. High vowels*The vowels /i/ and /u/ exhibit special phonotactic restrictions in relation to one another and to their semivowel counterparts. The first is that /i/ before /y/ and /u/ before /w/ are always short; thus, words like bìyař 'five' and zuwà 'coming' are normal whereas **bìyař and **zūwà are impossible.

> °AN: [i] As pointed out by Gouffé (1965: 195n), the usually reliable dictionary of Abraham (1962) is systematically wrong in this regard: Abraham invariably transcribes long /ī/ before /y/ and /ū/ before /w/.
> [ii] The syllable-final glide in words like niyyà 'intention', kuwwà 'shouting', and tsuwwà 'rumbling of stomach' has to be interpreted as the first part of a geminate. If the glide were analyzed as a vowel, i.e., **/nīyà/, **/kūwà/, and **/tsūwà/, one would get a violation of the length restriction. Note that what is involved here is a question of phonological analysis. Phonetically, a word like /tsuwwà/ could possibly be pronounced sometimes as [tsūwà] with a long vowel rather than with a geminate [ww].

The second restriction is that in nonfinal position /i/ after /y/ and /u/ after /w/ are also necessarily short, e.g., yifà 'cover temporarily', wutā 'fire'. In final position, the long vowels occur, e.g., nauyī 'heaviness', sāwū 'foot(print)'.

The third restriction, which runs counter to universal tendencies, is the fact that whereas the sequences /yi/ and /wu/ occur, **/yu/ and **/wi/ normally do not, apart from a few loanwords, e.g., Māyù 'May', Yūnì 'June', tàswīrà 'map', ɗāwīsù 'peacock', wīlì 'wheel'. The restriction, however, is not the same for the two glides. Whereas it holds fully in the case of /w/, the situation with regard to /y/ is more complicated. Although /yu/ is lexically uncommon, it does occur in a small number of native words, e.g., biyu 'two', yumɓū 'pottery clay', yunkùrā 'strain, make an effort', yunwà 'hunger'. Because the latter three all have /u/ or /w/ in the next syllable, they could historically represent assimilation from *yi, but synchronically one can hardly treat the initial syllable as anything but /yu/. When one turns to derived words, however, the phonotactic restriction breaks down because /y/ is permitted before u-initial suffixes, e.g., lāyukà, pl. of lāyì 'line, lane'; māyū, pl. of māyè 'sorcerer'; sàyu 'be bought', gr7 of sàyā 'buy'; bìyuwā 'traversable, can be followed', gr7 verbal noun of bi / biyà 'follow'.

The fourth restriction relates to vowel sequences. In trisyllabic words with a short high vowel in the first syllable, a high vowel in the next syllable will necessarily be identical, i.e., CiCiCV and CuCuCV are possible, but **CiCuCV and **CuCiCV are not, e.g., bincìkē 'investigate', jìminā 'ostrich', rìgimà 'dispute'; durùmī 'fig tree', gùndurà 'become fed up', tùkùna '(not) yet'. The only exceptions are verbal nouns of gr7 verbs with the ending -uwā, e.g., nìtsuwā 'reflection', nìƙuwā (sometimes pronounced [nùƙuwā]) 'grindable'.

6. (MORPHO)PHONOLOGICAL PROCESSES AND ALTERNATIONS

Hausa morphology reflects a number of phonological processes. Some of these processes are essentially historical in nature, although their existence is still evident in morphological alternations, whereas others still function as synchronic rules, although not necessarily in a totally productive, exceptionless manner. Some of the changes concern syllable-final coda consonants, others relate to the influence of vowels on syllable-initial consonants.

6.1. Syllable-final nasals
6.1.1. Assimilation to position

In prevocalic position, there are two distinct nasals: the bilabial /m/ and the coronal /n/. When occurring in syllable-final position followed immediately by another consonant, whether within the same word or across word boundaries, /n/ always undergoes anticipatory assimilation to the position of articulation of that abutting consonant. (As indicated above in §2.1.1, this weak, unspecified /N/ behaves in many respects as if it were attached to the nucleus, thereby creating a "nasal diphthong," rather than occupying the coda slot.) For determining the homorganic nasal rule, note that /w/ counts as a velar and not as a bilabial, e.g., **/kanwā/** 'potash' → [kaŋwā] not **[kamwā]. Similarly, glottal stop and /h/ also condition the velar [ŋ].

gidankù	your (pl.) house →	[gidaŋkù], cf. [gidansù] their house, [gidammù] our house
gingìnā	build many →	[giŋgìnā], cf. **ginà** build
hanyà	road →	[haɲyà] road

nā san Audù I know Audu → [nā saŋ 'audù], cf. [nā sam bellò]   I know Bello.
sun bi They followed → [sum bi]
cf. [sun tayà]   They made an offer.
cf. [suŋ ƙàru]   They benefited.

Note that the nasal assimilation is a late rule that follows other processes, such as the rule changing /f/ to /h/ before back rounded vowels, e.g., **lanfō** → [lamfō] = **lanhō** → [laŋhō] 'new foliage on lopped trees', **fùnfùnā** → [fùmfùnā] = **hùnhùnā** → [hùŋhùnā] 'food mold'.

In SH, but not in WH dialects, /m/ codas also undergo place assimilation. (This is reflected orthographically by the use of **n** rather than **m**.) Examples:

//**kamkàmā**// [kaŋkàmā], orthographically **kankama**   catch many, cf. **kāmà**   catch
//**ƙàzâmtā**// [ƙàzântā]   filthiness, cf. **ƙàzāmī**   filthy
yā sam [saŋ] **wà Kànde nāmà**   He gave Kande a piece of meat. cf. **sāmà**   provide for

Although syllable-final /m/ in SH normally becomes homorganic with the following consonant, in derivations, some speakers preserve etymological /m/ in specific lexical items, e.g., **jàrùmtakà** (= **jàrùntakà**) 'bravery' < **jārùmī** 'brave man'; **hàramtà** (= **hàrantà**) 'be unlawful' < **hàrâm** 'unlawful according to Islam'.

> °AN: In SH some people have a contrast between **gamjì** (epithet for the Sardauna of Sokoto) (a dialect borrowing from WH) with the /m/ preserved, and **ganjì** 'gutta percha [hardwood] tree', which reflects the normal assimilation rule. Both are pronounced **gamjì** in WH, where the connection between the epithet emphasizing the Sardauna's strength and the tree with its very hard wood is transparent.

6.1.2. Full assimilation of /n/ to liquids

When followed immediately by /l/, /r/, or /r̃/, the nasal /n/ undergoes full anticipatory assimilation to that abutting consonant. Examples:

Ɗan Lādì proper name (lit. son of Sunday) → [ɗallādì]
watàn Ràmàlân the month of Ramadan → [watàr̃r̃àmàlâŋ]
***kùrumrumī > *kùrunrumī → kùrurrumī** broken-necked pot (frozen reduplicated noun)
sôn râi selfishness (lit. loving.of life) → [sôrrâi] → [sârrâi] (vowel adjustment)

◊HN: This assimilation rule is probably the historical explanation for at least some of the geminate /ll/'s found in the lexicon (e.g., **tallē** 'small soup pot' < ***tanlē**?), although the presumed original nasal can be verified only by comparative evidence. The change */nl/ to /ll/ can, however, be identified in the case of recent loanwords, e.g., **sallāyè** (< ***sanlāyè**) 'Sunlight (brand of soap)', **Hwàndà bellè** (< ***benlè**) 'Honda Bentley' (type of car).

Generally speaking the geminate pronunciation across a word boundary is not reflected in orthography, i.e., the final /n/ is written as such. An exception is the clipped form /kwal/ < **kwāna** 'spend the night', used in such phrases as //**kwan lāfiyà**// → **kwal lāfiyà** 'Rest well!'

6.2. Rhotacism

Historically, syllable-final coronal obstruents changed to rolled /r̃/ (see §34:1.5.3). (In some dialects, the resulting /r̃/ now appears as /l/.) This rule continues to operate in the language as an active process. Examples:

kar̃kàɗā beat repeatedly < ***kaɗkàɗā**, cf. **kaɗà** beat; **mar̃màtsā** push, pester repeatedly, cf. **matsà** push, pester; **kar̃kàshē** kill many < **kashè** kill; **hur̃huɗu** four each, cf. **huɗu** four; **'yar̃sà** = **'yātasà** his daughter; **far̃kà** wake up = **fàɗakà**; **ɓar̃nā** damage, destruction < **ɓātà** to damage; **far̃kē** trader (< ***fatkē**), cf. pl. **fatàkē**; **gir̃gijè** (< ***gizgizè**) raincloud, cf. pl. **gìzàgìzai**; **mar̃maza** very quickly, cf. **maza** quickly

The rhotacism also applies (or has historically applied) to some instances of coronal obstruents in word-final position. This, however, is *not* an automatic process, the surface realization depending on the dialect and the lexical item in question, e.g.,

kâr̃ = **kad**(à) do not! **kyar̃** = **kyat** difficulty; **bìyar̃** = [dv] **bìyat** five; **mâr̃** = **mâs** to him < **masà**; **zubar̃** = [dv] **zubas** pour out; **maràr̃** = **maràs** lacking (cf. pl. **maràsā**) < **rasà** to lack

6.3. Gemination

Surface gemination is the output of both phonological processes of assimilation (described here) and morphologically conditioned gemination (described along with the relevant morphological categories). (Note: With digraphs the orthographic convention is to represent geminates by doubling the first letter only, e.g., geminate **ts** is written **tts**, not ****tsts**.)

As a phonological process, gemination is simply the result of total assimilation affecting abutting consonants (sometimes obligatory, sometimes optional), e.g.,

//**fit-shē**// → **fisshē**   take out (gr5 B-form)
//**fit dà**// → **fiddà**   take out (gr5 short-form)
//**kwan lāfiyà**// → **kwal lāfiyà**   Rest well!

//gidanmù// → **gidammù**   our house
duk dà hakà (→) **dud dà hakà**   nevertheless (lit. all with thus)

The rolled /ř/ is particularly prone to full assimilation (i.e., geminate formation), especially when abutting with a coronal consonant, e.g.,

ařzìkī (→) [azzìkī]	wealth		**sayař dà** (→) [sayaddà]	sell
hař zuwà (→) [hazzuwà]	up until		**hař Lahàdì** (→) [hallahàdì]	until Sunday
fuskàřkà (→) [fuskàkkà]	your face		**rìgař Sāni** (→) [rìgassāni]	Sani's gown
rawař-dājì (→) [rawaddājì]	military maneuvers		**madatsař-ruwā** → [madatsarruwā]	dam

Gemination is extremely common in reduplicative constructions, as found, for example, in pluractional verbs or adjectives derived from sensory quality nouns. With coda coronals, gemination and rhotacism occur as alternative options.

daddàkā (< //dakdàkā//) plurac. of **dakà** pound; **kakkàfā** (< //kafkàfā//) plurac. of **kafà** affix; **fiřfìta** (= **fìřfìta**) (< //fìtfìta//) plurac. of **fìta** go out; **mammàtsā** (= **mařmàtsā**) (< //matsmàtsā//) plurac. of **matsà** push aside, pester; **gwàggwāɓā** very thick, adj. < **gwāɓī** thickness; **zàzzāfā** very hot, adj. < **zāfī** heat; **kàkkausā** very rough, adj. < **kaushī** roughness

6.4. Palatalization
Palatalization is significant both as an active process and as the historical result of the process.

6.4.1. Palatalization as an active process
6.4.1.1. When followed by a front vowel, either **i(i)** or **e(e)**, the alveolars **s**, **z**, and **t** palatalize to **sh**, **j**, and **c**, respectively, e.g.,

gàshe stative form of **gasà** roast; **Bàhaushè** Hausa person < **Hausa** Hausa; **fàsasshē** adj. past participle of **fāsà** break (with -aCCē suffix); **kàjī** pl. of **kàzā** hen; **cìji** imperative of **cìzā** bite; **sàcē** pre-pronoun B-form of gr2 verb **sàtā** steal; **mōtōcī** pl. of **mōtà** car (with -ōCī suffix)

At a historically earlier period, the palatalization was probably an automatic phonological rule. Now, however, although palatalization regularly accompanies morphological formations involving the addition of a front vowel, it does not apply across the board. Nonpalatalizing alveolars (**s**, **z**, and **t**) followed by a front vowel are in fact quite common in the language. One reason is the heavy influx of loanwords from English and Arabic, e.g.,

sìtātì starch (Eng.); **lāsīsì** license (Eng.); **tēbùř** table (Eng.); **tēlà** tailor (Eng.); **gàzêt** gazette (Eng.); **zîk** zipper (Eng.); **Sīdì** proper name (Ar.); **sìyāsà** politics (Ar.); **zaitì** eucalyptus oil (Ar.); **lafàzī** pronunciation, speech (Ar.); **zīnāřì** gold (Ar.), **zìndīkì** heretic, apostate, blasphemer (Ar.)

Another reason is the occurrence of vowel changes that have taken place subsequent to the operation of the palatalization rule, namely the sporadic monophthongization of /ai/ to /ē/, and the ongoing shift of short /u/ to /i/ in various environments, e.g., between coronals or when there is a front vowel in the following syllable. Examples:

ƙōsē < **ƙōsai**	fried beancake	**tèbà** < **tàibà**	cooked cassava flour
sillē < **sullē**	top section of cornstalk	**tikàtikī** < *****tukàtukī**	calf, shin

tinyằ < tunyằ   poisonous cactus-like plant   tirjè̀ < turjè̀   refuse to budge, balk
Zènabù < Zàinabù   proper name   zirằ < zurằ   lower bucket into well

Short /e/ normally changes to /a/ in closed syllables. The palatalization rule takes place before the /e/ → /a/ change, resulting in surface palatals followed by /a/, e.g.,

shasshè̀ƙā (< //shēsshè̀ƙā//< //sēssè̀ƙā//) (not **sasshè̀ƙā) winnow repeatedly < shēƙằ winnow
jânnā [dv] (not **zânnā)   rows of reaped corn < sg. jēnè̀ (//zēnè̀//)
sàtaccân   the stolen one (< //sàtattē ˋn//), cf. pl. sàtàttûn (< //sàtàttū ˋn//)

The sonorants **n**, **l**, **r**, and **r̄** do not undergo palatalization, nor does **ɗ**. The ejective sibilant **ts** palatalizes to **c'** (an ejective affricate) in WH dialects, but not in SH, e.g., SH **dūtsè̀** = WH **dūc'ì̀** 'stone', SH **tsīlā** = WH **c'īlā** 'tapeworm'.

6.4.1.2. The voiced stop **d** also palatalizes to **j**, with resultant neutralization of the **z/d** contrast, but less regularly than in the case of /s/, /z/, and /t/. Examples:

gadàjē   pl. of gadō bed
hūjī̀   hole (noun from hūdằ bore)
yar̄jè̀   agree to, gr4 of yàr̄da agree

In fact, one could argue that *nonpalatalization* is the norm for /**d**/ and the words that undergo palatalization are the exception. The non-automatic /**d**/ → /**j**/ change thus should not be grouped with the rule affecting the other alveolar obstruents as is normally done.

◊HN: The /**d**/ → /**j**/ rule is historically more recent than the /**z**/ → /**j**/ rule, i.e., the neutralization of the contrast is a recent phenomenon. At an earlier period, /**z**/ and /**d**/ before front vowels would have been distinct, the former appearing phonetically as [ž] or [j], the latter as [d] or [dy].

The /**d**/ → /**j**/ change is systematically blocked by a preceding /**n**/, e.g.,

gìndī (not **gìnjī)   base   kundī   pad of paper, thesis
landè̀   type of cloth;   yandì̀   type of fig tree
cf. hanjī (< *hanzī)   intestines

°AN: Many scholars, including Parsons, considered non-palatalizing forms like **gìndī** 'base' to be "exceptions" to the presumed palatalization rule. These forms are in fact quite regular as long as one recognizes the conditioning effect of the preceding nasal.

Even when not preceded by a nasal, many nonderived words still preserve nonpalatalized /**d**/ before a front vowel, e.g., **càdī** miser; **dilā** jackal; **dīmùn** undoubtedly; **gìdī-gidī** being a busybody; **gōdè̀** thank, **gòdiyā** thanks; **kudī** black-bordered, red, cotton fabric; **tānàdī** thrift, foresight; **tar̄dè̀** head-pad.

Morphologically derived/inflected forms can be divided into two classes, with a few words falling in-between. In the first group (a), the /**d**/ does not (or normally does not) palatalize; in the second group (b), which contains a number of common, high frequency words, the palatalization normally takes place, e.g.,

(a) **bàfādè** courtier, ethnonym from **fādà** chief's residence; **barȧdē** (= **barȧjē** ?), pl. of **bardē** mounted attendant of chief; **bidōdī**, pl. of **bidȧ** thatching needle; **Hamīdōdī**, pl. of **Hamīdù** (proper name); **jàkādìyā** female emissary, f. of **jàkādȧ** emissary; **jìdē** / **jìdi**, B and C forms of gr2 verb **jìdā** transport; **marȉdī** snatcher, agentive of **rȉdā** snatch at; **rēdè** grind all, gr4 of **rȅdā** grind, separate grain from bran; **shaddōdī**, pl. of both **shȃddā** cesspit and **shaddȧ** brocade fabric; **yàrdaddē** trustworthy, adjectival past participle of **yàrda** agree (but **yarjȅ** agree to, gr4 of **yàrda**)

(b) **gadōjī**, pl. of **gadȧ** bridge; **gȧjē**/ **gȧji**, B and C forms of gr2 verb **gȧdā** inherit; **gidȧjē**, pl. of **gidā** home; **gùdȧjī**, pl. of **gùdā** unit; **gùdajjē** a runaway, adjectival past participle of **gudù** run; **gwajȉ** experiment, test, deverbal noun of **gwadȧ** measure, test; **kadōjī** = **kadōdī**, pl. of **kadȧ** crocodile; **ƙudȧjē**, pl. of **ƙudā** a fly (itself originally a plural of **ƙujȅ**)

6.4.1.3. The semivowel **w** regularly palatalizes to **y**, e.g.,

ɓàrāwȍ thief, pl. **ɓàrȁyī** (with -ī suffix); **kȧsuwā** market, pl. **kāsuwōyī** (with -ōCī suffix); **ƙawā** woman's female friend, pl. **ƙawȧyē** (with -āCē suffix.); **rawā** dancing, pl. **ràye-ràye** (with -e suffix and reduplication)

The only exceptions in which /w/ remains before a front vowel are recent loanwords like **wējȉ** 'wedge' and **wīlȉ** 'wheel', and the ideophonic word **wî-wî** 'marijuana'. The word **wuyȧ** 'neck' is pronounced [wiyȧ], but the phonetic fronting of the high vowel (conditioned by the neighboring /y/) does not affect the initial /w/.

6.4.1.4. Viewed in the context of the palatalization rule affecting alveolar obstruents, the **w** → **y** change seems totally ad hoc, but this is not so. The fact is that the velars **k**, **g**, **ƙ** also undergo regular palatalization before front vowels. (Remember that /w/ in Hausa constitutes a velar rather than a bilabial.) Although scholars have known this for some time, the change has tended to be neglected because the palatalization of velars, unlike the palatalization of alveolars, is not reflected in orthography or in standard linguistic transcription. Examples:

kīfī [kyīfī] fish; **gēmù** [gyēmù] beard; **baƙī** [baƙyī] black, cf. pl. **baƙȧƙē** [baƙȧ̀ƙyē]; **dàkē** [dàkyē] type of ink; **bȅgē** [bȅgyē] yearning, longing; **hànkȧkī** [hàŋkȧ̀kyī] crows, pl. of **hànkākȧ**

As is the case with palatalized alveolars, palatalization of velars applies before the change of /e/ to /a/ that takes place in closed syllables, e.g.,

ràkē + nsà → [ràkyēnsà] → [ràkyansà]   his sugar cane
gêffā → [gyêffā] → [gyâffā]   sides (pl. of **gēfè** [gyēfè])
baƙȧ̀ƙē-n mōtōcī → [baƙȧ̀ƙyen]... → [baƙȧ̀ƙyan]   black cars

The palatalization is not retained, however, when a final front vowel is replaced by a morphological suffix beginning with /a/. In this respect, palatalization does not behave identically with labialization (see below §6.5), e.g.,

gwankī [gwaŋkyī]   roan antelope, pl. **gwankȧyē** (not **[gwaŋkyȧyē])
shingē [shiŋgyē]   fence, pl. **shingȧyē** (not **[shingyȧyē])
cf. **bangō** [baŋgwō]   wall, pl. **bangwȧyē**

The palatalization also applies to labialized velars (whether distinctive/phonemic or redundant). Thus

gw, for example, becomes /**gy**/ (orthographic **g**), e.g.,

àgwàgwā	duck, pl. **àgwàgī** [àgwàgyī] (< //**àgwàgwī**//)
ìgwā	cannon, pl. **igōgī** [igwōgyī] (< //**igwōgwī**//)
ɗan tsàkō [tsàkwō]	baby chick, pl. **'yan tsàkī** [tsàkyī]
bàƙō [bàƙwō]	stranger, guest, pl. **bàƙī** [bàƙyī]

The palatalization rule does not apply to **Cwī** sequences representing underlying (historical, if not synchronic) /**Cui**/ syllables, e.g., **gwīɓī** 'viscousness' (< //**guiɓī**//) does not palatalize to ****g**ʸ**īɓī**; nor does **luƙwīƙwìyā** 'ground or pound finely' (< //**luƙwuiƙùyā**//) palatalize to ****luƙ**ʸ**īƙ**ʸ**ìyā**.

6.4.2. Sporadic anticipatory palatalization

In a few cases, an alveolar consonant occurring before a nonfront vowel assimilates to its derived palatal counterpart in the following syllable, e.g.,

gùjajjē = gùdajjē	a runaway (past participle of **gudù** run away)
màcaccē = màtacce	dead (past participle of verb base //**mat**-//) die (cf. **mutù** die))

6.4.3. Depalatalization

Because the palatalization rule was presumably fully regular at an earlier historical stage, one now finds words with the palatalized consonant in the underlying lexical form and the nonpalatalized counterpart in the derived form representing the earlier lexical base, e.g.,

gāshì (< //**gāsì**//)	hair, cf. **gàr̃gāsà** (< ***gàsgāsà**) hairy
dùƙushī (< //**dùƙusī**//)	colt, cf. **dùƙusā** female colt
mijì (< //**mizì**//)	husband, cf. pl. **mazā** males
ƙuncī (< //**ƙuntī**//)	constriction, cf. **ƙuntàtā** restrict, pester

The depalatalization also shows up in words backformed from loanwords that have an etymological palatal, e.g.,

canzà change < **canjì** changing (Eng.); **fàtu** be patched < **fācì** a patch, patching (Eng.); **àlhàzai** pilgrims < **àlhajì** a pilgrim (Ar.)

The plural **hankitōcī** from **hankicì** 'handkerchiefs' is interesting in that the stem-final /**c**/ backforms into /**t**/, but then undergoes palatalization as part of the -**ōCī** plural formative.

With the breakdown in the originally allophonic relationship between alveolars and corresponding palatals, derived forms are now being created without the "depalatalization" before non-front vowels, e.g.,

ajì	class, pl. **ajūjūwà̀** = **azūzuwà̀**; **hancì** nose, pl. **hancunà̀** = **hantunà̀**
kuncì	cheek, side of face, pl. **kuncunà̀** (cf. the archaic pl. **kumàtū**)

6.5. *Labialization*

Velar consonants are automatically labialized when followed by a back-rounded vowel. (In some WH dialects, labials and alveolars undergo labialization as well.) This redundant labialization is not indicated in orthography, e.g., the word for 'ram' is spelled **ràgō**, not ****ragwo**. The labialization takes place whether the conditioning vowel is lexical or morphological. Examples:

kūrā [kwūrā] hyena; gòrā [gwòrā] large calabash; ƙōfà [ƙwōfà] doorway; dōgō [dōgwō] tall; danƙò [daŋƙwò] stickiness (< dànƙā grip); tāgōgī [tāgwōgyī] windows (< tāgà window); saukō [saukwō] come down toward here (< sàuka alight, descend)

If the final back-rounded vowel is morphologically replaced by a suffix beginning with /a(a)/, the labialization is sometimes retained, sometimes not, depending on dialect or idiolect or on the individual word, e.g.,

[dōgwō] tall, pl. dōgàyē = dōgwàyē; [zugwū] roll of native cloth, pl. zugàgē
[zaŋkwō] bird's crest, roof corner point, pl. zankàyē = zankwàyē

⁻The weak subject pronoun ku (phonetically [kwu]) 'you (pl.)' appears with initial /kw/ when it is attached to the TAM marker /-à/ used in the negative continuous and in the potential, e.g., bā kwà tàfiyà 'You are not going'; kwâ tàfî? 'Will you possibly go?' (cf. kunà tàfiyà 'You are going.').

In closed syllables, /ō/ automatically shortens to /o/ and usually centralizes to /a/ as well. When this happens, the labialization is invariably retained, e.g.,

bàƙō `-n [bàƙwân]   the stranger (not **[bàƙân])
dōgō-n mùtûm [dōgwan mùtûm]   tall man (not **[dōgan mùtûm])
ƙòƙō-n gwīwà [ƙwòƙwaŋ gwīwà]   kneecap (lit. small calabash-of knee)
sunà cikò-n [cikwàn] rāmì   They're filling up the hole.

6.6. Alternation of /f/ and /h/
Historically the phoneme /f/ was pronounced [h] when followed by the back-rounded vowels /ū/ and /ō/, e.g., /tsōfō/ 'old' = [tsōhō]; /fòrā/ 'discipline' = [hòrā]; /fūtà/ 'rest' = [hūtà]; /mafūcī/ 'fan' = [mahūcī] (cf. the alternative form [mafīcī] with the [f] intact). When followed by short /u/, the /f/ to [h] rule was less general and subject to greater individual and dialectal variation, e.g., /fuɗu/ 'four' = [fuɗu] or [huɗu]; /fùmfùnā/ 'food mold' = [fùmfùnā] or [hùnhùnā]; /haifù/ 'give birth' = [haifù] or [haihù] (cf. hàifā 'give birth to'); but /furā/ 'millet balls' = [furā] only. This realization rule was clearly operative until very recently as evidenced by its application to English loanwords, e.g., 'photo' > hòtō; 'polo' > hōlò (with p first replaced by f, which then altered into h); 'powder' > hōdà; 'raffle' > ṙēhùl. There is one example of the change applying before /au/ (the pronunciation of which tends toward [ou]), namely, mahàucī / mahautā 'butcher / butchering place' < fāwà 'butchery'. The present orthographic (and transcription) convention is to use the symbol h whenever it is pronounced as such whether it represents a conditioned variant of /f/ (historical or synchronic) or not.

◊HN: As mentioned earlier, old Hausa did not have a distinct /h/ phoneme. This entered the language as a development from word-initial zero (e.g., *aɓà > haɓà 'chin'), from the adoption of loanwords, especially from Arabic (e.g., hùsūfì 'eclipse'), and from the phonemicization of the [h] that previously existed as an allophone of /f/.)

Vestiges of the originally /f/ → [h] allophonic rule show up in the alternation between /f/ and /h/ in morphological processes. These processes work in two directions.

6.6.1. f → h
With a few specific lexical items, f → h functions as a synchronically active morphophonemic rule. (The rule does not affect /f/ if it has been strengthened by gemination.) Consider the following examples in which a nonrounded vowel in the stem is replaced by a rounded vowel in the derived form.

tàfī	go + -ō ventive →		tahō	come here
jèfā	throw + -ō ventive →		jēhō	throw this way
mafè	to patch + -ō VN formative →		mahò̀	a patch on a cloth
dafà	cook + -u sustentative →		dàhu	be well cooked

(cf. **dàfaffē** cooked + -ū plural → **dàfàffū** (not ****dàfàhhū**))

Although Hausaists tend to think of **f** → **h** as an active, productive rule because of its occurrence in high-frequency pairs like **tàfī/tahō** 'go/come', it turns out that it is actually quite limited. With the exception of the few examples above, modern SH speakers do *not* change /f/ to /h/ in derived forms beginning with a back-rounded vowel. Rather, the /f/ remains as such. The following are typical examples taken from a list of over fifty words with base-final /f/:

dāfà	lean on, press on + -ō ventive →		dāfō	lean on for
nùfā	head toward + -ō ventive →		nufō	head toward this way
tsāfà	squeeze + -u sustentative →		tsàfu	be squeezed
kafà	set up + -u sustentative + -wā verbal noun →		kàfuwā	establishment
gaggāfā	bateleur eagle + -ū pl. →		gàggàfū	eagles
kafā	small hole + -ōCī pl. →		kafōfī	holes
ƙafà	foot, leg + -àCū/-āCuwà pl. →		ƙafàfū / ƙafāfuwà	feet, legs
samfò̀ [dv] grass basket + -unà pl. →			samfunà	grass baskets

(cf. [SH] **sanhò̀** + -unà → **sanhunà**)

6.6.2. Recovered /f/
In a few examples, the original /f/ in words now ending in /hō/ or /hū/ is recovered in derived forms. (This process is comparable to the depalatalization described earlier in §6.4.3.) Examples:

īhù	yelling, shout, pl. ìfàce-ìfàce	màkāhò̀	blind man, pl. màkàfī
tsōhō	old, pl. tsòfàffī	murhù	hearth, fireplace, pl. muràfā = muràfū (!)

The alternative plural form **muràfū** is remarkable in that the switch back to the etymological /f/ takes place even though it is followed by /ū/. With some modern SH speakers, the [h] in the singular has now become lexicalized as /h/ with **murhunà** as the preferred plural.

6.7. *Vowel assimilation*
Anticipatory assimilation of /a/ to the vowel in a following syllable is a property of a few specific grammatical morphemes. It is not a general phonological process.

The pre-pronominal indirect object marker **ma-** usually assimilates to the vowel of the following pronoun, e.g.,

manì (→) **minì** to me, **makì** (→) **mikì** to you (f.), **mashì** → **mishì** to him (= **masà**), **makù** (→) **mukù** to you (pl.), **masù** (→) **musù** to them

The **ma-** instrument prefix is commonly pronounced /mu/ if the following syllable contains /u/ (especially short /u/). The assimilation is, however, lexically specific and does not apply in all cases, e.g.,

magurjī (→) **mugurjī** stone for rubbing/scraping off; **mahūjī** (→) **muhūjī** boring tool; **mazurārī** (→) **muzurārī** funnel cf. **mabūd̃ī** *no*t → ****mubūd̃ī** opener; **matūƙī** *no*t → ****mutūƙī** stirring stick

Short /**u**/ sometimes assimilates to /**i**/ if there is a front vowel in a following syllable. Again the changes are word specific and do not constitute general phonological processes. Examples:

bùkī (→) **bìkī** celebration (pl. **bukūkuwằ**); **dudduge̖** (→) **diddige̖** heel (pl. **dùgằdùgai**)
*guddùgī → **giddìgī** a cripple (pl. **gùddùgai**); ***tukầtukī** → **tikầtikī** calf, shin (pl. **tùkầtùkai**)

°AN: Note that the vowel fronting does not feed the palatalization rule, even in cases where /**i**/ synchronically has effectively replaced /**u**/, e.g., the word for 'calf' is **tikầtikī**, not ****cikầcikī**.

6.8. Metathesis

Metathesis does not function as an active process in any synchronic phonological or morphological rules. It does, however, show up lexically in a number of idiolectal variants and in one regular historical change affecting some non-SH dialects.

(a) Switch of consonants in adjacent syllables, e.g.,

bincìkē = [dv] **binkìcē** investigate; **dằƙumằ** = **dằmuƙằ** clutch at, grab; **gàbằruwā** = **bàgằruwā** Egyptian mimosa; **nauyī** = [dv] **yaunī** heaviness; **tàwadằ** = [dv] **tàdawằ** ink

In one case the metathesis affects the onset and coda consonants in the same syllable: **àwàr̃takì** = **àr̃àutakì** 'tongs, pincers, pliers'.

(b) Metathesis of abutting consonants (with automatic adjustment of the glides /**y**/ and /**w**/ and their vocalic counterparts /**i**/ and /**u**/ depending upon their position in the syllable), e.g.,

kwàsfā = **kwàfsā** eggshell; **Bà'azbinè** = [dv] **Bà'abzinè** psn from Asben; **bâiwā** = [dv] **bâuyā** (= **bồyā**) female slave; **gauràyā** = [dv] **garwàyā** mix up, stir; **sâiwā** = [dv] **sâuyā** root

(c) Systematic historical metathesis of abutting */**m.r**/ to /**r.m**/ in certain WH dialects. (The metathesis is not immediately evident if one looks at Standard Hausa because SH has undergone a subsequent weakening of syllable-final /**m**/ to /**u**/ when followed by /**n**/ and /**r**/). Examples:

amrē (= SH aurē) >	armē	marriage
d̃amrè (= SH d̃aurè) >	d̃armè	tie
kyamrō (= SH kyaurō) >	kyarmō	arrow shaft
gàmrākằ (= SH gàurākằ) >	gàrmākằ	crownbird
samrī (= SH saurī) >	sarmī	speed

(d) Switch from **a**...**i** to **i**...**a** in adjacent syllables, e.g.,

barì = **birằ** let, leave; **sakì** = **shikằ** let loose; **sanì** = **shinằ** know

Note that the tone *and* vowel length remain in place and do not accompany the transposition in vowel quality, i.e., **barì** → **birằ**, not ****bīrà** or ****bìra**. Note also that palatalization of the coronal /**s**/ applies to the occurring surface structure after the metathesis has taken place.

The deverbal noun **kisằ** 'killing, murder', which is synchronically related to **kashè** 'to kill', is a metathesized form of a final -**i** H-L verbal noun form ***kas(h)ì**, which still exists in Sokoto, e.g., **kashìn kâi** = **kisàn kâi** 'murder'.

The word **kiɗà** 'drumming' is a metathesized variant of the verbal noun form **kaɗî** 'spinning', which is derived from the verb **kaɗà** 'spin, drum, churn, etc.' Unlike the case of **barî = birà**, etc., the metathesized variants here are not semantically equivalent, but rather have lexically diverged, each taking on a special, narrow meaning from the range of meanings covered by the source verb.

6.9. *Clipping, apocopation, contraction*
There are three partially overlapping processes of word shortening. I use the following terminology to keep the three processes distinct.

6.9.1. Clipping
The term *clipping* is used to describe lexicalized, sometimes grammatically conditioned, short forms where the shortening cannot be considered as simply a fast-speech variant. Generally speaking, clipping results in the deletion of the tone along with the deleted segment(s), e.g., **ƙasà** 'on the ground' (⇒) **ƙas**, not ****ƙâs**; **sanî** 'know' ⇒ **san** pre-object form, not ****sân**; cf. **ìdan** 'if'(⇒) **in**. Examples:

(a) clipped verbs: **ɗaɍ < ɗarà** exceed slightly; **ɗau < ɗaukà** lift, take; **faɍ < fāɗà** fall on; **ga** (pre-object form) **< ganī** see; **kas < kashè** kill; **kwan < kwāna** spend the night; **sam** give a little to **< sāmà** provide for; **sau < sàkā** release; **zam < zama** become
(b) clipped adverbs: [WH] **bis < bisà** up above; **ƙas < ƙasà** on the ground; **tùkùn < tùkùna** (not) yet
(c) clipped N + linker: **ran < rānaɍ** day of, e.g.,.**ran kàsuwā** market day; **bân** (esp. in compounds) **< bāyan** back of, e.g., **bân-ɗākì** toilet (lit. back.of-room); **san** (esp. in compounds) **< sarkin** chief.of, e.g., **san kurmì** title for head of the Kano city market and prison
(d) clipped conjunctions/prepositions: **don < dòmin** in order to; **ì < yà** like; **in < ìdan** if; **kàn < kàfin** or **kàmìn** before
(e) others: **jìm < jimàwā** used in **jìm** (= **jimàwā**) **kàɗan** after a little while; **mā / mâ < makà** to you (m.); **sau < sāwū** foot(print); **yau < yāwū** saliva; **yō < yiwō** do and come

Clipping is particularly common in creating short forms of proper names, e.g., **Haɍū < Haɍūnà**; **Inū < Inūsà**; **Dìje < Hàdīzà**

6.9.2. Apocopation
The term *apocopation* is used for the optional dropping of final vowels where the tone is retained, e.g., **kadà** (→) **kâɍ** 'don't', **Hàlīlù** (→) **Hàlîl** (proper name). The consonant in the last syllable, which after the vowel dropping becomes word final, is typically a sonorant or a glide (although obstruents do occur, especially with some proper names). With some of the items, the apocopation is so common that the words are in the process of becoming established as lexically clipped forms. Examples of apocopation include the following:

kâɍ < kadà don't, lest
[WH] **nau / tau < nàwa / tàwa** mine (m. or pl. / f.)
    (Note that LH on a single syllable becomes H.)
tàusai < tàusàyī mercy; **gwàigwai < gwàigwàyī** evil spirit; **kàbûs < kàbūshì** large white squash; **wànzâm < wànzāmì** barber; **gawài < gawàyī** charcoal

> ΔDN: WH has monosyllabic third person masculine possessive pronoun forms, namely, **-nai /-tai** (m. or pl. / f.), e.g., **dōkìnai** 'his horse', **rìgātai** 'his gown' (cf. SH **dōkìnsà** and **rìgaɍsà**, respectively). These are presumably derived from the linker **na- / ta-** plus the pronoun **yà**. Note, however, that the L tone is not preserved, i.e., the forms have high rather than falling tone.

6.9.3. Contraction

The term *contraction* is used for apocopation that accompanies the cliticization or phonological attachment of specific items across underlying word (or morpheme) boundaries. The reduced item is either a light-syllable CV pronoun or else the verb **yi** 'do'. When the contraction takes place, the tones are usually (but not always) preserved. Examples:

zân < **zā nì** future I; **zâi** < **zā yà** future he (cf. **zā tà** future she)
e.g., **zân rufè ta** I'm going to close it.
bàn < **bà nì** neg I; **bài** < **bà yà** neg he (cf. **bà tà** neg she)
mîn < **mi.nì** to me, **mâs / mâř** < **ma.sà** to him
rânkài daɗè < **rânkà yà daɗè** May your life be lengthened. (greeting to a superior)
sun dòkâs < **dòkē shì** They beat him; **sun màrân** < **màrē nì** They slapped me.
yai < **ya yi** he did; **tai** < **ta yi** she did; etc.
mukài < **mukà yi** we did, **sukài** < **sukà yi** they did; etc.
e.g., **gà àbîn dà mukài** Here is what we did.

[References: Abraham (1959a); Gouffé (1965); Greenberg (1941); Klingenheben (1927/28); Lindau, Norlin, and Svantesson (1990); Newman (1972b, 1992b); Newman and Salim (1981); Parsons (1970); Salim (1981); Sani (1983)]

55. Pluractional Verbs

VERBS connoting plurality of action, for which I have adopted the term *pluractional*, are derived from corresponding nonpluractional verb stems by reduplication, e.g., **tuntùnā** 'remind many or often' < **tunà** 'remind'. In traditional Hausa grammars, this derivation was called *intensive*, a label that misses the semantic essence of these verb forms.

> °AN: The term *intensive* was used, for example, by Abraham (1934: 98ff.) and by most scholars after him. The term *pluractional* was first used in Newman (1980a: 13n; 1989a) and has since gained widespread acceptance by Hausaists as well as by linguists working on other Chadic languages, where this feature is also very common. Interestingly, earlier scholars had already recognized that the essential semantic component of these forms was plurality and not intensification, thus Westermann (1911: 36), for example, labeled this class the "Pluralform des Verbum" [the plural form of the verb].

The pluractional formation functions as a very productive synchronic derivation applying to simple as well as derived verbs, and to verbs in all grades. One also finds many verbs that historically were pluractionals but that have become frozen as lexically reduplicative forms, i.e., the original simple stem has now been lost, e.g., **gùrgurà** 'gnaw' < presumed earlier, but unattested ***gùrā**.

1. ACTIVE PLURACTIONALS

Pluractional verbs (abbreviated as plurac.) indicate multiple, iterative, frequentative, distributive, or extensive action. They often occur with plural NPs functioning as subjects of intransitive verbs or as objects of transitive verbs. Note, however, that the co-occurrence between the plural noun and the pluractional verb is semantic and/or pragmatic in nature and is not grammatically determined, i.e., this is not a case of ergative-type agreement. Examples:

mutằnē sun fìr̃fìta	The men went out (one by one or going in and out).
cf. the simple sentence **mutằnē sun fìta**	The men went out.
sun ɓuɓɓullō	They suddenly appeared (in numbers or all over the place).
ai yanà karairàyâwā	Oh he is breaking (them) up into many pieces.
yanà mìmmìƙe à kân gadō	He is sprawled out all over the bed.
tā hàhhàifi 'yā'yā	She gave birth (repeatedly or to numerous children).
yā kar̃kàshē birai	He killed (lots of) monkeys (all over the place or one after the other).

Occasionally, the pluractional verb takes on a semantically specialized meaning as compared with the simple stem, e.g.,

ninnìnkā multiply, cf. **ninkằ** fold; **rarràbē** differentiate, distinguish, cf. **rabằ** divide; **taitàyā** encourage along a tired or sick psn or animal, cf. **tayằ** [WH] assist; **tattàunā** discuss, talk over, cf. **taunằ** chew

Pluractional verbs have corresponding verbal nouns belonging to the same inflectional and derivational classes that one finds with simple stems (see §77:3), e.g.,

sunằ ɓuɓɓullôwā	They were appearing. (in numbers or all over the place)
cf. **sunằ ɓullôwā**	They were appearing.
munằ ta nannēmansù	We kept on looking for them.
cf. **munằ ta nēmansù**	We were looking for them. (cf. the verb **nềmā / nànnēmằ** look for)
yanằ sàssàyen (= **sàsassayàř**) **abūbuwằ dà yawằ**	
	He was scurrying around buying lots of things.
cf. **yā sàssàyi abūbuwằ dà yawằ**	
	He scurried around and bought a lot of things. (finite plurac. verb)
cf. **yanằ sàyen abūbuwằ dà yawằ**	
	He was buying lots of things. (non-plurac. VN)
sun fārà ciccîn làshe-làshe dà tànɗe-tànɗe	
	They started eating the (many) snacks.
cf. **munằ sô sù cicci làshe-làshe dà tànɗe-tànɗe**	
	We want them to eat the snacks. (finite plurac. verb)
cf. **sun fārà cîn àbinci**	They started eating the food. (non-plurac. VN)

Pluractional stems can also serve as the input to other derivations, such as statives and adjectival past participles, e.g.,

mìmmìƙe	be all stretched out (plurac. stative) (< **mimmìƙē** stretch out (by many people or all over the place)); cf. **mìƙe** be stretched out (stative) (< **mìƙề** stretch out)
nìnnìnkakkē	multiplied (plurac. adj. past participle) < **ninnìnkā** multiply
cf. **nìnkakkē**	folded (adj. past participle) < **ninkằ** fold

1.1. Basic form: Prefixal reduplication
Synchronically, most pluractionals are formed by a reduplicative prefix, of which there are two variants, C_1VG- and C_1VC_2-.

1.1.1. C_1VG-
The most common variant is C_1VG-, where G forms a geminate with the following consonant. If the reduplicated vowel is underlyingly long, it automatically undergoes the shortening and adjustment rules that affect closed syllables. Examples: (The plurac. verb is to the right of the slash mark. The gloss is given only for the simple verb unless the plurac. verb has a special reading. Note that with geminates of consonants transcribed with digraphs, only the first letter is repeated, i.e., **ssh** represents the geminate /shsh/.)

bugà / bubbùgā beat; **dannề / daddànnē** press down, oppress; **dařnàcē** (< **dàřnī** fence) / **daddařnàcē** fence in; **gyằru / gyàggyằru** be well repaired; **kirā / kikkirā** call; **jềfā / jàjjềfà** throw at; **kāwō / kakkāwō** bring; **kařàntā / kakkařàntā** read; **sayař / sassayař** sell; **tākằ** step on / **tattằkā** trample; **tōkàrē / tattōkàrē** prop against, block; **wàgề / wawwằgề** open mouth widely

°AN: Historically, the C_1VG- prefix undoubtedly derived from C_1VC_2- plus complete assimilation. Synchronically, however, the C_1VG- variant has full and direct morphological status, i.e., one does not replicate the historical development and utilize an assimilation rule. The pluractional **kakkāwō**, for example, comes directly from C_1VG- + **kāwō**, not from an intermediate ****kawkāwō**; similarly **kakkàmā** 'catch many' comes from C_1VG- + **kàmà**, not from the coexisting **kankàmā**. Note that /nk/ → /kk/, for example, does not exist as a synchronically active assimilation rule in the language, which would be required if one were to postulate C_1VC_2- as the synchronic formative for all pluractional verbs.

The normal orthographic convention in Hausa, which is employed in the transcription system adopted here, is not to write word-initial glottal stop. The phonological status of the glottal stop shows up clearly in plurac. formation, e.g., the plurac. verb corresponding to **àikā** 'send' (actually / 'àikā/) is **'à''aikà** with the C_1VG- prefix.

Monoverbs, i.e., CV(V) verbs, form pluractionals by C_1VG- prefixation. With these verbs, one clearly could not postulate C_1VC_2- prefixation with assimilation since these verbs do not contain a C_2. Examples:

bi / bibbi follow; **ci / cicci** eat; **shā / shasshā** drink; **jē / jajjē** (< /jejjē/) go

1.1.2. C_1VC_2-
If the second consonant of the stem is a sonorant (nasal, liquid, or /y/) or any coronal, one may attach a C_1VC_2- prefix as an alternative to C_1VG-. Reduplicated C_2 nasals automatically assimilate to the position of the following consonant. (This change is shown orthographically in the case of /n/ and /m/; it is not shown in the case of [ŋ].) The syllable-final glide /y/ alters into the corresponding high vowel /i/. Coronal obstruents undergo rhotacism and appear as rolled /r̄/. Examples:

ɓalgàtā / ɓalɓalgàtā chip off; **fizgè / fīr̄fizgē** snatch; **gàdā / gàr̄gādà** inherit; **kàɗu / kàr̄kàɗu** be spun, beaten, frightened; **kāmà / kankàmā** [kaŋkàmā] catch; **kashè** (base //kas-//) / **kar̄kàshē** kill; **kirā / kirkirā** call; **mutù / mur̄mutù** die; **ninkà** fold / **ninnìnkā** multiply; **sōmà / sansòmā** begin; **tayà / taitàyā** offer, help; **tunà / tuntùnā** remind

All verbs that form pluractionals by C_1VC_2- reduplication also allow the C_1VG- formation, but not vice versa, e.g.,

fita / fīr̄fīta = fīffīta go out; **gasà / gar̄gàsā = gaggàsā** roast; **kāmà / kankàmā = kakkàmā** catch; **kirā / kirkirā = kikkirā** call; **sàyā / sàiṣayà = sàssayà** buy; **tàmbayà / tàntàmbayà = tàttàmbayà** ask

1.1.3. Tone
Pluractional formation does not affect tone per se, i.e., it is not part of the derivational process. Instead, one builds a pluractional stem by reduplication at the segmental level and then one assigns the tone that is required for verbs of that grade and syllabic shape, e.g.,

C_1VG- + **bi**)^H	follow ⇒	**bibbi**)^H	(v0)
C_1VG- + **tsōràtā**)^{HLH}	frighten ⇒	**tsattsōràtā**)^{HLH}	(v1)
C_1VG- + **dàgurà**)^{LHL}	gnaw at ⇒	**dàddàgurà**)^{LHL}	(v2)
C_1VG- + **tsòratà**)^{LHL}	be afraid ⇒	**tsàttsòratà**)^{LHL}	(v3)
C_1VG- + **girma**)^H	grow up ⇒	**giggrma**)^H	(v3a)

C_1VC_2- + **mutù**$)^{HL}$ die $\Rightarrow$ **muřmutù**$)^{HL}$ (v3b)
C_1VG- + **dařnàcē**$)^{HLH}$ fence in $\Rightarrow$ **daddařnàcē**$)^{HLH}$ (v4)
C_1VG- + **sayař**$)^{H}$ sell $\Rightarrow$ **sassayař**$)^{H}$ (v5)
C_1VG- + **kāwō**$)^{H}$ bring $\Rightarrow$ **kakkāwō**$)^{H}$ (v6)
C_1VC_2- + **kàɗu**$)^{LH}$ be spun, beaten $\Rightarrow$ **kàřkàɗu**$)^{LH}$ (v7)

Disyllabic gr1, gr2, and gr4 verbs at first sight look as if they change tone when they go from two syllable simple stems to three syllable pluractional stems. In fact there is no tone change; rather, it is just a question of tone assignment, which does not happen until after the pluractional formation (like other derivational formations) has determined the number of syllables in the stem, e.g.,

C_1VG- + **bugà̰** beat $\Rightarrow$ **bubbùgā** (v1) because H-L-(H) is the tone assigned to the citation form (the A-form) of all gr1 verbs, whether derived or basic (cf. **kařàntā** v1 read)
C_1VG- + **sàyā** buy $\Rightarrow$ **sàssayà̰** (v2) because L-H-(L) is the tone assigned to the citation form (the A-form) of all gr2 verbs, whether derived or basic (cf. **tàmbayà̰** v2 ask)
C_1VC_2- + **kashḛ̀** kill $\Rightarrow$ **kařkàshē** (v4) because H-L-(H) is the tone assigned to the citation form (the A-form) of all gr4 verbs, whether derived or basic (cf. **bincìkē** v4 investigate)

The pluractionals of the special **nyē**-final gr4 verbs built on monoverbs, e.g., **shânyē** 'drink up' (< **shā** 'drink') exhibit two different tone patterns. In one pattern, the pluractional output is interpreted as a straightforward trisyllabic verb and thus is assigned H-L-H tone like any other trisyllabic gr4 verb, i.e., **shasshanyē**$)^{HLH}$ $\rightarrow$ **shasshànyē**. In the other pattern, the nonpluractional verb with the falling tone is treated as if it were trisyllabic and the corresponding pluractional is then assigned the regular quadrisyllabic H-H-L-H tone, i.e., **shasshanyē**$)^{HHLH}$ $\rightarrow$ **shasshânyē**. Further examples:

C_1VG- + **jânyē**$)^{HLH}$ pull away (< **jā** pull) $\Rightarrow$ **jajjànyē**$)^{HLH}$ or **jajjânyē**$)^{HHLH}$
C_1VG- + **cînyē**$)^{HLH}$ eat up (< **ci** eat) $\Rightarrow$ **ciccìnyē**$)^{HLH}$ or **ciccînyē**$)^{HHLH}$

Grade 3 verbs are an exception to the general rule that pluractional formation does not require its own tone specification. Normal trisyllabic gr3 verbs have L-H-L tone, e.g., **zàburà** 'jump up', **dùlmuyà** 'sink'. The quadrisyllabic pluractionals based on these trisyllabic gr3 stems are tonally regular, e.g., **zàzzàburà**$)^{LHL}$, **dùddùlmuyà**$)^{LHL}$. Trisyllabic pluractionals derived from disyllabic gr3 verbs, however, do not always appear with L-H-L tone, as one might expect, but rather with L-L-H tone, e.g.,

cìka / cìccìka get filled; **ɗìga / ɗìɗɗìga** drip; **sàuka / sàssàuka** get down

Trisyllabic gr3 pluractionals with the expected L-H-L tone (e.g., **fìřfìtà**) are cited in the literature and are recognized as an alternative pronunciation, but they do not constitute the norm in modern-day SH.

> ◊HN: Historically, intransitive verbs ending in -**a** (= gr3) were all disyllabic with a light initial syllable. They all had an L-H tone pattern. The present-day trisyllabic gr3 verbs with L-H-L were originally not members of the same class. (They probably ended in the vowel schwa rather than -**a**.) Although all grade 3 verbs, whether disyllabic or polysyllabic, can be treated synchronically as belonging to the same grade on the basis of their shared intransitivity and final short -**a**, historically they were distinct. That is, the specification of a single L-H-(L) tone pattern for all grade 3 verbs (identical to the tone pattern for gr2 (A form)) is a strictly synchronic phenomenon that masks the fact that historically there were two tonally distinct classes: the "true" gr3, which

was L-H, whether simple or pluractional (e.g., **fìta** 'go out', plurac. **fìřfìta**), and another verb class, which was L-H-L (e.g., **dùlmuyà** 'sink', plurac. **dùddùlmuyà**).

1.2. Alternative archaic form: Antepenultimate reduplication

Instead of attaching the C_1VC_2- (or C_1VG-) word-initially, some trisyllabic verbs derive pluractionals by infixing a reduplicative -CVC- in antepenultimate position. (This is an archaic method that is restricted to specific lexemes.) What is copied in this infixal formation is the second syllable plus the initial C of the third syllable, e.g., **dà.gu.rà** 'gnaw' ⇒ **dà.gùr.gu.rà**. In this formation, the choice of VC (where the C is a copy of the final consonant of the stem) vs. VG (where G forms a geminate with the following abutting consonant) is not free; rather CVC- is employed if it is phonologically allowed. Tone assignment is the same as for prefixal reduplication, i.e., it is fully determined by the tone pattern of the grade in question. Verbs that allow this formation almost all allow, and often prefer, the synchronically now productive prefixal form as well (illustrated in the first two examples), e.g.,

maƙàlē ⇒	m**aƙa**lƙàlē (= **mam**maƙàlē)	get lodged
rikìɗā ⇒	ri**kiř**kìɗā (= **rir**rikìɗā)	metamorphose
fàrautà ⇒	fa**rau**ràutā	hunt
hàɓakà ⇒	hà**ɓa**ɓɓakà	swell
haɗìyā ⇒	ha**ɗìɗ**îyā (< //haɗiyɗîyā//)	swallow
haƙurař dà ⇒	ha**ƙur**ƙurař dà	enjoin patience on
rikìtā ⇒	ri**kiř**kìtā	tangle, confuse someone
tafàsā ⇒	ta**fař**fàsā	boil sth (tr.)

◊HN: Although I am describing the prefixal and infixal reduplications as being distinct processes—and synchronically I believe that this is true—historically the rule was basically the same, namely, antepenultimate reduplication. With disyllabic verbs, antepenultimate attachment would have turned out to be prefixal and with trisyllabic verbs antepenultimate attachment would have turned out to be infixal, but the rule was really the same, compare the formation **gasà** 'roast' ⇒ **gař.gàsā** with **tafàsā** 'boil' ⇒ **ta.fař.fàsā**.

In Newman (1989a), the formation of pluractionals was described, not as -CVC- infixation but rather as suffixal -CVCV reduplication (with dropping of the base-final vowel as is normal with suffixation), i.e., **dà.gu.rà** 'gnaw' ⇒ **dàgùrgurà**. I now believe that the earlier analysis was erroneous and that the one adopted here is correct.

The trisyllabic stems that allow infixal reduplication generally have an open initial syllable. There are, however, a few verbs—borrowed from Arabic—in which the initial syllable is closed by the first part of a geminate consonant. In the corresponding pluractional, the initial syllable occurs without the geminate, e.g.,

hallàkā ⇒	ha**lal**làkā	destroy	**hàllařà** ⇒	hà**làl**lařà	appear, attend
kallàmē ⇒	ka**lal**làmē	sweet-talk s.o.	**sawwàřā** ⇒	sa**wař**wàřā	ponder

The most likely explanation for the loss of the initial geminate is metrical/rhythmic. The favored foot structure for quadrisyllabic infixal pluractionals is iambic, i.e., light-heavy, e.g., **tafař.fàsā** 'boil much, often'. The geminate reduction achieves this favored pattern by altering what would be a heavy initial syllable into a light one. It also avoids a sequence of geminates. Examples:

kallàmē ⇒ *kal.**lam**.làmē → *//kal**lal**làmē// → kalallàmē
sawwàřā ⇒ *saw.**wař**.wàřā → *//saw**wař**wàřā// → sawařwàřā

Historically, pluractional formation by antepenultimate -CVC- infixation was the norm for polysyllabic verbs. Nowadays, most polysyllabic verbs use the CVC- prefix, generally in the CVG- form. Note that a geminate normally appears rather than a copied C₂ even when the C₂ of the stem is a nasal or liquid, which would easily allow C_1VC_2- prefixation, i.e., the choice of the form is morphologically rather than phonologically determined. Examples:

markaɗō ⇒	mammarkaɗō	grind into puree or pulp
(not **marmarkaɗō by C_1VC_2- prefixation nor **markaȓkaɗō by CVC infixation)		
bangàjē ⇒	babbangàjē	push aside rudely (not **bambangàjē)
danƙàrā ⇒	daddanƙàrā	compress (not **dandanƙàrā)
fandàrē ⇒	faffandàrē	deviate (not **famfandàrē)
naƙàltā ⇒	nannaƙàltā	explain
ràtàyu ⇒	ràrràtàyu	be hung up well
ȓubùtā ⇒	ȓuȓȓubùtā	write

Some CVCCV verbs with a syllable-final rhotic or glide also form pluractionals by the antepenultimate infixation method. What they do is build on a trisyllabic base created by inserting an epenthetic vowel between the abutting consonants, e.g.,

girma (base //girima//) ⇒	girirrima	grow up
hàifā (base //hayafa//) ⇒	hàyàyyafà	give birth
karyà (base //karaya//) ⇒	karairàyā	break
sarƙè (base //saraƙe//) ⇒	sararràƙē	intertwine
tartsè (base //taratse//) ⇒	tararràtse	smash

1.3. Difference in meaning between the two formations

The alternative pluractionals formed by the prefixal and infixal methods are usually equivalent in meaning. In a few cases, however, the two variants have semantically diverged:

hàifā give birth: (a) hàhhaifà give birth many times or to many children (e.g., màtan wàzīȓī sun hàhhàifi yârā dà yawà The vizier's wives bore many children.) (b) hàyàyyafà engender, proliferate (e.g., [with gr5] tàȓzòmaȓ ɗàlìbai tā hayayyafaȓ dà zàngà-zangà dà dāma à wuràȓē dàban-dàban The student rebellion precipitated demonstrations all over.)
ƙirgà (< *ƙidgà) count: (a) ƙiƙƙìrgà count several times (b) ƙididdìgà calculate

°AN: Normally *ƙidgà would be expected to be realized as **ƙiȓgà with the rolled/tap ȓ. The occurring form ƙirgà with the flap is inexplicable.

Prefixal pluractional reduplication is synchronically very productive and potentially available to all verbs. As such, it can be used even with pluractionals formed by infixal reduplication, thereby producing semantically strengthened *hyperpluractionals*, e.g.,

maƙàlā ⇒	maƙalƙàlā ⇒	mammaƙalƙàlā	lodge, stick in
zaɓàkā ⇒	zaɓaɓɓàkā ⇒	zazzaɓaɓɓàkā	boil, cook
girɗà ⇒	giriȓȓìɗā ⇒	giggiȓiȓȓìɗā	uproot
tartsè ⇒	tararràtse ⇒	tattararràtse	smash

2. FROZEN PLURACTIONALS

The term *frozen pluractional* is used for reduplicated verbs that historically must have been active pluractionals but now lack the nonreduplicated counterparts and generally have undergone bleaching of the pluractional semantics. These are described in detail in the section on lexically frozen reduplicated verbs (see §62:4.1). Here are a few examples:

babbàkā	grill, burn (< *bakà̀)	**ƙwanƙwàsā**	tap with knuckles (< *ƙwasà̀)
famfàrē	fall out (tooth) (< *farè̀)	**làllāsà̀**	soothe, coax (< *làsā)
kanannàɗē	coil up (< *kanàɗē)	**yagalgàlā**	tear to pieces (< *yagàlā)

[References: Al-Hassan (1983); Frajzyngier (1965); Gouffé (1975b); Newman (1989a, 1990b); Pawlak (1975)]

56. Plurals

HAUSA is well known for the complexity of its plural formation. This is a morphological feature shared with many other Chadic languages (see Newman 1990b). Plurals of nouns and adjectives are generally formed by means of a suffix or an infix-suffix combination, e.g., **jàkī / jāk-unà** 'donkey(s)', **fìffìkè / fìk-à-fìk-ai** 'wing(s)'. They are indicated less commonly, by full reduplication, e.g., **jōjì / jōjì-jōjì** 'judge(s)'. In this chapter, the slash / serves to separate singulars and their corresponding plurals. The English gloss will normally be given in the singular only. (Plural pronouns and demonstratives are presented elsewhere (chaps. **54** and **21**), as are "pluractional" verbs (chap. **55**).)

Almost all of the plural suffixes are vowel initial (generally -V or -VCV) and almost all are tone-integrating, i.e., they have an associated tone melody that overrides the tone of the singular stem. These suffixes are added to the lexical base rather than to the full stem. In most cases this base is the singular word minus its final vowel and tone (sometimes with minor adjustments affecting epenthetic vowels), e.g., **rìgā** 'gown', base //**rīg**-//, pl. **rīgunà**. There are, however, deviations from the straightforward pattern of forming bases from stems by simple subtraction. In some cases the segmental shape of the base used in the plural reflects a historically earlier shape of the word rather than the synchronically occurring form, e.g., **kyaurō** 'tall reed', base //**kyamr-**//, pl. **kyamàrē**. In some cases the base is formed by removing the feminative suffix (see §31:4), e.g., **tufānìyā** 'screen on doorway', base //**tufān**-//, pl. **tùfànū**. The alternation between palatal consonants and their nonpalatal counterparts commonly appears in plural formation, showing up either in the singular or in the plural, e.g., **mōtà / mōtōcī** 'car' (where the /c/ in the plural is a palatalized copy of the /t/ in the singular); **algàshī / àlgàsai** 'green' (where the /sh/ in the singular and the /s/ in the plural are variants of the "same" consonant).

Affixes are sometimes accompanied by internal "expansion" achieved sometimes by vowel insertion (see later) and sometimes by gemination or partial reduplication, e.g., the plural of **cikì** 'belly', which uses the **-unà**)[HL] plural suffix, is **ci-k̲-kunà** or **ci-kun̲-kunà**. With particular words or particular constructions, the expansion is optional; in other cases it is obligatory. The gemination found in plurals affects either the penultimate or the last consonant of the word depending on the specific formation and on dialectal preferences. The partial reduplication copies the CVC of the last two syllables of the plural stem (i.e., the base plus the suffix), e.g., //**kwān-**// 'pan' + **-ukà** → **kwānukà** ⇒ ****kwānuk̲nukà**, which, after assimilation of the abutting /kn/ sequence, is realized as **kwānunnukà**. The resulting syllable-internal vowel automatically shortens and, where appropriate, centralizes, and the resulting syllable-final consonant undergoes various phonological deformations, e.g., **gàjērē** 'short' ⇒ ****gà-j̲èr̲-jèrū** → **gàjàjjèrū** 'short'.

°AN: My former view (as reflected in earlier writings) was that such reduplicated plurals as **cikunkunà** 'bellies' and **kwānunnukà** 'pans' should be analyzed in terms of two-syllable reduplication to the right, with dropping of the stem-final vowel, as is normal in Hausa derivation and inflection, i.e., ****cikun(à)k̲unà** and ****kwānuk(à)n̲ukà**, respectively. I am now convinced that infixal -CVC- reduplication in antepenultimate position, i.e., **ci-k̲un̲-kunà** is indeed the right analysis, both for plural nouns and for pluractional verbs (see §55:1.2). Although internal reduplication is less common universally than prefixal or suffixal reduplication, it is not unknown and in fact is attested in West Chadic languages. Let me just mention two inadequacies in the earlier suffixal analysis. First, tone in Hausa is very stable and tends to be preserved when vowels are dropped. Thus, a structure of the type *cikun(à)**kunà** would be expected to surface with a falling tone on the antepenultimate syllable, i.e., ****cikúnkunà**, which is not what one finds. Second, there are plurals with internal -CVC- reduplication that parallel plurals with vowel insertion. These latter plurals allow one to see clearly that the expansion is in antepenultimate position; compare **kāyàyyakī** (< *kāyakī), pl. of **kāyā** 'load' + -akī, with **garèmanī** (< *garmanī), pl. of **gàrmā** 'large hoe' + -anī.

There are numerous different plural formations. Although the particular plural type used is not completely predictable from the form of any particular singular word, there are significant regularities. For examples, plurals of the form -āCē)^{HLH}, e.g., **wurī / wurārē** 'place', are found exclusively with nouns having the canonical shape CVCVV and all H tone, whereas plurals using the affix -ā–ā)^{HLH}, e.g., **sirdì / sirādā** 'saddle' generally correlate with triconsonantal singulars of the form CVCCVV and H-L tone. One also finds plural types accompanying particular derivational formations, e.g., ethnonymic nouns formed with the prefix **bà-** generally form their plurals by suffixing -āwā to the base (which does not include the prefix), e.g., **Bàkatsinè / Katsināwā** 'Katsina person'.

Plural formation is an area where there appears to be a great amount of dialectal and idiolectal variation. As documented in the major dictionaries, many words allow a number of alternative plurals, e.g., **kwabò / kwàbbai** or **kwabbunā** 'penny, kobo', **idò / idànū** or **idandunā** 'eye', **wàhalà / wàhàlce-wàhàlce** or **wahalōlī** or **wàhàlhàlū** 'trouble', etc. Salim (1981) has reported that individual speakers manifest uncertainty and day-to-day variation in the forms of plurals they use with specific words. The plural formation rules provided here are thus designed to describe the operation of the basic SH rules as such. The accompanying examples are intended simply to exemplify the rules; they are not intended to be inclusive (unless it is explicitly stated that the lexical membership constitutes a closed set), nor do they exclude the possibility that the words cited might take other, perhaps even more common, plurals.

The major plural classes, each accompanied by one illustrative example, are outlined in table 10.

Table 10: Plurals

Major Class	Example (sg.)	Example (pl.)	gloss
1: -OXI)^H	tāgà	tāgōgī	window
2: -ai)^{LH}	dàlīlì	dàlīlai	reason
3: -aXe)^{HLH}	damō	damàmē	land monitor
4: -(a)Xa)^{HLH}	sirdì	sirādā	saddle
5: -aXu)^{HLH}	gurgù	gurāgū	cripple
6: -uXa)^{HL}	hùlā	hūlunà	cap
7: -aXI)^{LH}	fùrē	fùrànnī	flower
8: (...)-aXi)^{HLHH}	guntū	guntàttakī	stub
9: -U/-I)^{LH}	kujèrā	kùjèrū	chair
10: -V$_\alpha$ ⇒ -V$_\beta$	kwàɗō	kwàɗī	frog
11: -āwā)^{LLH} ~ ^{HHH}	bàdūkù	dùkàwā	leather worker
12: x 2 (Redup.)	jōjì	jōjì-jōjì	judge
13: -e)^{LH} x 2 (Redup)	tsirò	tsìre-tsìre	a shoot, sprout
14: x 2)$^{H-L}$ (Redup)	mākēkè	mākā-màkà	expansive
15: -ī x 2)$^{H-H}$ (Redup)	mìnīnì	minī-minī	tiny

The plural formations are organized into fifteen major classes, which encompass major types, which in turn include various subtypes. In the descriptions, the symbol X represents a consonantal "slot" that may be filled inter alia by a specific suffixal consonant or a base final consonant. The symbol C represents a copy of the preceding consonant. Affixes with a single parenthesis mark on the right followed by a superscript tone are tone-integrating, i.e., the specified tone spreads across the entire word from right to left. For example, the suffix -ai)^{LH} added to the singular form **madōgarī** 'prop, support' gives the plural form **màdôgàrai** with an L-H tone pattern.

1. CLASS 1: -OXI)^H

This class contains two types: the highly productive -ōCī suffix and the archaic -ō–ī and -ā–ī affixes. The base is always simple without any expansion.

1.1. Plural type -ōCī)^H

Form: This plural type, often noted in the literature simply as -oCi without the vowel length indicated, consists of a suffix -ōCī (where C represents a copy of the base-final consonant) and an all high tone pattern. The copied C automatically undergoes palatalization rules because of the following -ī, e.g., **tāsà̃ / tāsōshī** 'bowl'. In the case of geminates, which behave as identical abutting consonants across a syllable boundary, only a single consonant is copied, e.g., **fannì̃ / fannōnī** (not ****fannonnī**) 'category'. Words with a feminative suffix (e.g., -**iyā** or -**uwā**), which commonly occur with this plural type, preserve the suffix in the lexical base, e.g., **tàtsūnìyā / tātsūniyōyī** 'folktale'.

Comment: This is the largest, most productive plural type in the language. Originally it seems to have been limited to disyllabic feminine nouns with H-L tone and then was extended to longer feminine words containing the feminative suffix. Nowadays it occurs with words of both genders and words having a variety of shapes. It is not, however, used with adjectives. It is the typical plural type found with Arabic loanwords ending in -ā. (Arabic loanwords ending in -ī, on the other hand, generally employ the -**ai** plural suffix.) It is the most common plural formative employed with recent loanwords from English. (Out of a list of some 175 common nouns borrowed from English, about 100 words, both masculine and feminine, use the -ōCī plural whereas the remaining 75 nouns were scattered among all the other plural forms.) Examples:

gulà̃ f. / **gulōlī** drum stick; **tāgà̃** f. / **tāgōgī** window; **gēzà̃** / f. **gēzōjī** shrub with white flowers; **battà̃** / f. **battōcī** small receptacle; **ƙāguwā** f. / **ƙāguwōyī** crab; tongs, pincers; **rāgā** f. / **rāgōgī** net; **gyàlè** m. / **gyalōlī** shawl, head veil; **dilā** m. / **dilōlī** jackal; **dàmisà̃** m. or f. / **dāmisōshī** leopard; **sànā'à̃** f. / **sanā'ō'ī** occupation; **bindigà̃** f. / **bindigōgī** gun; **tàmbayà̃** f. / **tambayōyī** question; **àlmàr̃à̃** f. / **almār̃ōr̃ī** fable, fantasy, fiction; **fassar̃à̃** f. / **fassar̃ōr̃ī** translation, explanation; **hùkūmà̃** f. / **hukūmōmī** governmental body, agency, authority; **fensìr̃** m. / **fensir̃ōr̃ī** pencil; **ōfìs** m. / **ōfisōshī** office; **kamfànī** m. / **kamfanōnī** company, business; **kwàmìtî** m. / **kwamitōcī** committee

1.2. Plural type -ō–ī)^H / -ā–ī)^H

A small number of old native words have archaic plurals that are formed not by copying the final consonant but rather by using the base-final consonant in the C slot. That is, instead of suffixing -ōCī with a copied C, they add -ō–ī with the base-final consonant between the two vowels. The canonical shape for words utilizing this formation was originally CVCCVV. The surface forms of the now-occurring singulars deviate markedly from this ideal form because of the addition of feminative suffixes and various phonological deformations. These plurals are rare in modern SH and coexist alongside plurals with the productive -ōCī suffix. Examples (complete):

jījìyā f. (base //ziyz-//) /	jiyōjī	vein, blood vessel (= jījiyōyī)
rījìyā f. (base //riyz-//) /	riyōjī	well (= rījiyōyī)
tsarkìyā f. (base //tsark-//) /	tsarōkī	bow string (= tsarkiyōyī)
zūcìyā f. (base //zukt-//) /	zukōcī	heart (= zūciyōyī)

◊HN: The words jījìyā and rījìyā also have plural variants jigōjī and rigōjī, respectively, suggesting that the historically earlier forms of these words were *zigzì and *rigzì. If so, the forms jiyōjī and riyōjī are neologisms built on reinterpreted underlying bases and not reflexes of the true ancestor form of the words. The plural zukōcī given above is cited in the dictionaries, but is rare. More usual is zukàtā, with an alternative internal formation, or the straightforward zūciyōyī.

The following three words take plurals with -ā–ī. In all cases the consonant preceding the /ā/ is a bilabial.

àkuyà f (base //'awk-//) /	awākī	goat
dōkì m. (base //dawk-//) /	dawākī	horse
tunkìyā f (base //tumk-//) /	tumākī	sheep

The word àkuyà 'goat' (pronounced and sometimes spelled àkwiyà) has undergone irregular metathesis and tone change. It derives from a Chadic root *awki. In the word dōkì the /ō/ comes from the /au/ diphthong, which itself came from an /aw/ rime. The replacement of the original syllable-final /m/ by /n/ in the singular tunkìyā is due to a historically recent nasal assimilation rule in SH.

◊HN: Parsons (1970) has suggested that the -ā–ī vowel pattern was the historically original form and that the -ō–ī pattern (which includes the now productive -ōCī suffix) resulted from a phonological change. This seems right, but I have yet to identify the phonological and/or morphological factor(s) responsible for such a change.

Although the -ō–ī and -ā–ī plurals are now limited to the examples provided above, there is indication that at one time, they were not so restricted. The evidence is provided by the existence of words that are now singular but that have the shape of -ō–ī and -ā–ī plurals, e.g.,

hayāƙī m.	smoke
haƙōrī m.	tooth (cf. haurè tusk)
karōfī m.	dye-pit area (< *karfè?)
kiyāshī m./pl.	type of small ant (pl. now -ai or -ū)
zabōrī m.	strings at top of bucket [dv] (< *zabrè?)

◊HN: At an earlier stage, the -ōCī and -ō–ī / -ā–ī plurals probably had a corresponding suffix with a fully specified consonant, i.e., *-ōkī. This is reflected in some archaic plurals given in older dictionaries and grammars, e.g., yārò / yārōkī 'child' (pl. now yârā); tsûmmā / tsummōkī 'rag'; zākì / zākōkī 'lion'. (Note: zākōkī is now interpreted as an -ōCī plural because of the accidental identity of the base-final and suffixal consonants; but historically this analysis is probably wrong, becausse -ōCī plurals were originally restricted to feminine nouns.)

2. CLASS 2: -ai)^LH

This class includes the major plural formative -ai with L-H tone and a few minor subclasses employing the same suffix in other formations.

◊HN: The -**ai** suffix possibly derives from a longer suffix of the form *-**ay**E)^{LH} (where E represents either /i/ or /e/ and vowel length is not indicated). Synchronically the phonological element indicated as /ai/ functions as a vocalic diphthong; diachronically, however, the /ai/ diphthong probably derived from /a/ plus a consonantal glide /y/. This would make -**ai** the only -VC plural suffix in the language, which is hardly likely. Because -VCV is the typical shape of plural suffixes—and in fact is the favored shape for most suffixes in the language—the derivational sequence -**ai** < *ay < *ayE seems highly likely. Given this reconstruction, the suffix can be compared with the now-occurring -**āyē**)^{HLH} suffix, e.g., kĩfĩ / kĩfâyē 'fish'. Significantly, the -**āyē**)^{HLH} suffix is restricted almost exclusively to disyllabic singular stems whereas the -**ai** suffix typically occurs with polysyllabic stems.

2.1. Plural type -**ai**)^{LH}

Form: This plural type consists of a suffix -**ai** and an overall L-H tone pattern. Many of the singulars taking this plural suffix end in -ĩ, which conditions palatalization of preceding coronal consonants. One normally undoes the palatalization in the plural form, e.g., àlmakàshĩ / àlmàkàsai 'scissors'.

ΔDN: In WH, polysyllabic plurals with -**ai** generally geminate the final consonant before the suffix, e.g., SH **màlàmai** = [WH] **màlàmmai** 'teachers'.

Comment: This is the standard plural formation for polysyllabic words, especially those ending in vowels other than -ā. The suffix -**ai** is the second most common plural formation in the language (following -o**Ci**). It is the standard plural choice for the many Arabic loanwords that end in -ĩ.

àlhajĩ m. / **àlhàzai** psn who has done the hadj; **àlmùbazzàrĩ** m. / **àlmùbàzzàrai** spendthrift; **dàlĩlĩ** m. / **dàlĩlai** reason; **ďàlĩbĩ** m. / **ďàlĩbai** student; **bōkitĩ** m. / **bôkìtai** bucket; **kāfĩrĩ** m. / **kâfĩrai** infidel; **kànàrĩ** m. / **kànàrai** canary; **kyarkĕcĩ** m. / **kyàrkètai** wild dog; **wàkĩlĩ** m. / **wàkĩlai** representative; **bùnsurū** m. / **bùnsùrai** he-goat; **dùkūkù** m./adj. / **dùkùkai** glumly hesitant; **màdugū** m. / **màdùgai** caravan leader; **àlabĕ** m. / **àlàbai** leather purse or wallet; **màkānikĕ** m. / **màkànìkai** mechanic; **sankacĕ** m. / **sànkàtai** reaped corn laid down in a row so that the heads can be cut off; **kàdarkò** m. / **kàdàrkai** small bridge; **kòfatò** m. / **kòfàtai** hoof; **kwàzazzabò** m. / **kwàzàzzàbai** gorge; **tsòlōlò** m./adj / **tsòlòlai** tall and skinny

The following items, which take -**ai** plurals, are slightly irregular in that their singulars are disyllabic:

dâbgĩ m. (< dābùgĩ) /	**dàbùgai**	anteater
jàkĩ m. /	**jàkai** (= jākunà)	donkey
ràsĩt m. (< ràsĩdĩ) /	**ràsĩďai**	receipt
mālàm m. (< màlàmĩ) /	**màlàmai**	teacher

Plurals formed with the -**ai** do not normally undergo stem expansion by internal reduplication. The word **littāfĩ** m. / **lìttàttàfai** 'book' is at exception. (The penultimate short /à/ in the plural is anomalous.)

The -**ai** suffix also occurs with some polysyllabic **a**-final singulars. Apart from nouns of location formed with **ma...ā**, these are mostly words that are either identifiable as loanwords or else can be presumed to be loanwords because of phonologically marked characteristics (such as final L-L tone), e.g.,

àdàdà m. / **àdàdai** rectangular house or shed; **àllūrà** f. / **àllùrai** needle; **fàrillà** f. / **fàrìllai** obligatory religious duty; **kārùwà** f. / **kàrùwai** prostitute; **tàntabàrā** f. / **tàntàbàrai** pigeon; **màkatà** f. / **màkàtai** hooked stick

The -ai plural suffix is used with a number of derived noun classes. Nouns of instrument derived using the **ma…ī** affix form their plurals regularly by means of this suffix, as do those locational nouns that appear with **ma…ī**. (Locational nouns formed with **ma…ā** use either this suffix or the plural suffix -ū, or, with some words, allow both alternatives.) Quadrisyllabic (and quinquisyllabic) type C augmentative adjectives (see §11:1.2) regularly use this plural. Most ethnonyms, which are derived by means of a prefix **bà-**, form plurals by dropping the prefix and adding a suffix -**āwā**. The few that preserve the prefix in the plural generally add the suffix -**ai**. Examples:

magōgī m. / **màgôgai** grater; brush; eraser; **masassabī** m. / **màsàssàbai** harvesting tool; **murfī** m. (< *marufī) / **mùrfai** cover, lid; **masaukī** m. / **màsàukai** lodging place, overnight quarters, guest room/house; **masallācī** m. / **màsàllâtai** mosque; **mafakā** f. / **màfàkai** shelter; **madatsā** f. / **màdàtsai** a dam, a place for a dam; **maɓuɓɓugā** f. / **màɓùɓɓùgai** spring of water
cằkuřkùřī m / **cằkùřkùřai** short and slight (psn or animal); **dùgùzunzùmī** m. / **dùgùzùnzùmai** shaggy-haired, disheveled (psn or animal); **wàngangàmī** m. / **wàngàngàmai** extensive or broad (e.g., container, pond)
bàdūkŭ m. / **bàdŭkai** leather worker; **bàhagô** m. / **bàhàgwai** left-handed person

2.1.1. Gemination
The -**ai** plural suffix is found with about twelve disyllabic words (apart from the pseudodisyllabic words illustrated above), in almost all cases as an alternative to some other plural formation. These words all have a light first syllable and almost all have H-L tone. In forming plurals with -**ai**, the base-final consonants undergoes gemination. This ensures that one has a minimum of two moras in the base to which the suffix is added. Examples (complete):

damì m. /**dàmmai**	bundle	**dubū** f. / **dùbbai**	thousand
gaɓằ f. / **gàɓɓai**	joint, limb	**kwabô** m. / **kwàbbai**	penny
ƙyamì m. / **ƙyàmmai**	fan-palm beam	**rabì** m. / **ràbbai**	half
ràbô m. / **ràbbai**	share, division	**samà** f. / **sàmmai**	sky, heavens
tabô m. / **tàbbai**	scar	**tsirô** m. / **tsìrrai**	sprout, shoot
tudŭ m. / **tùddai**	hill		

2.1.2. Nasal insertion
The following words are exceptional in adding /**n**/ (in one case, /**nn**/) to the base before adding the suffix. The resulting plural is either disyllabic with a heavy initial syllable or polysyllabic. Examples:

àbōkī m. / **àbôkànai** (= **àbôkai**)	friend
fā m. / **fànnai**	flat rock
kàrē m. / **kàřnai**	dog

(The change of **r** to **ř** preceding /**n**/ is automatic.)
kằwu = **kāwù** m. / **kằwùnai** ([WH] **kằwùnnai**)   maternal uncle
shaihì = **shaihù** m. / **shàihìnai** or **shàihùnai** ([WH] **shàihùnnai**) learned pious psn

°AN/◊HN: In some of the above cases, the added /**n**/ is probably an original root consonant that has been lost in the singular, e.g., **kàrē** < *kàrnē (a dialectal form attested in older sources), **fā** < *fan (?). In other cases, however, the /**n**/ is probably a plural formative. We know, for example, that the loanwords **kāwù** and **shaihù** did not have a final /**n**/ in the source languages, and we have no reason to believe that **àbōkī** ever contained an additional nasal consonant either.

2.2. Plural type -ā-...-ai)^{LH}

Form: This plural pattern has a reduplicated quadrisyllabic structure C$_1$VC$_2$āC$_1$VCai and an iambic light-heavy light-heavy rhythmic pattern. The plurals contain an internal -ā- in addition to the suffix -ai. The associated L-H tone melody spreads across the entire word, e.g., **birbirī / bìràbìrai** 'type of bat'. The plural is built on a CVC base that can be found by looking at the -CVC(V) at the end of the singular stem. Again one finds final consonants undergoing "depalatalization" when the affixes with the low vowels are added.

Comments: Three groups of singular nouns employ this plural type. The first two typically have a reduplicative CVC-CVCV structure; the third is made up of CVC loanwords.

(a) The first groups consists of reduplicated trisyllabic nouns that have the set shape CVC-CVCè with H-L tone. (One example has final -ò instead of -è.) A few are deverbal nouns; most are frozen reduplicated nouns (see §62:3.3). (In many cases, the C at the end of the first syllable has undergone gemination or other syllable-final adjustments that disguise the originally reduplicated nature of the word, e.g., **tsittsigè** 'tree stump, root of tooth' (< ***tsig-tsigè**), pl. **tsìgàtsìgai**.) Examples:

gir̃gijè m.	(base //giz-//) /	**gìzàgìzai**	rain cloud
gungumè m.	(base //gum-//) /	**gùmàgùmai**	log
kwīkwiyò m.	(base //kwiy-//) /	**kwìyàkwìyai**	puppy
shisshikè m.	(base //shik-//) /	**shìkàshìkai**	forked post, pillar
Irregular: **kankarè** m. (base //kar-//) /		**kàràkàrai**	a scraping
kuskurè m.	(base //kur-//) /	**kùràkùrai**	mistake

°AN: [i] The /s/ in the first syllable of **kuskurè** 'mistake' is totally inexplicable. Given the pl. **kùràkùrai**, one would have expected the corresponding singular to be **kurkurè**. This form is in fact cited by Bargery as equivalent to **kuskurè**, but it is not current in SH. (The nonreduplicated form **kurè**, on the other hand, *is* still encountered, although **kuskurè** is more common.)[ii] The plural noun **ɓùràgùzai** 'fragments, crumbs' appears to employ this plural formative even though the CVCCVCè singular from which it is derived, namely, **ɓurgujè** (used in WH only), does not have a reduplicated structure.

CVCCVCè words indicating objects that occur in pairs, which have alternative singulars of the form CVCàCVCī, regularly use this plural type, e.g., **fiffikè** = **fikàfikī** 'wing', pl. **fìkàfìkai**. (In some cases, the CVCCVCè variant is no longer used.) Examples:

diddigè = **digàdigī** m. (base //dug-//) /	**dùgàdùgai**	heel
(***kumkumè**) > **kumàkumī** m. /	**kùmàkùmai**	type of corset (made in two halves)
mummuƙè = **muƙàmuƙī** m. /	**mùƙàmùƙai**	jaw, mandible
(***tiktikè**) > **tikàtikī** m. /	**tìkàtìkai**	calf of leg
zuzzugè = **zugàzugī** m. /	**zùgàzùgai**	bellows

(b) The second group consists in reduplicated words of the form CVC-CVCV other than those cited above. Most of these have all H tone. A number of these words appear in the singular with a nasal consonant at the end of the first syllable in place of the expected reduplicated C$_2$ (a phenomenon found with other nouns and verbs with a frozen reduplicated structure), e.g., **janjalō** 'pebble' (< ***jaljalō**), pl. **jàlàjàlai** (not ****jànàjàlai** nor ****jànàjànai**). Examples:

faifai m. (< ***faifayi**)	(base //fay-//) /	**fàyàfàyai**	round mat, phonograph record

janjalō m.	(base //jal-//) /	jàlå̀jàlai	pebble
jinjìrī m.	(base //jir-//) /	jìrå̀jìrai	baby
kwalkwalī m.	(base //kwal-//) /	kwàlå̀kwàlai	battle helmet
kwaŕkwaɗā f.	(base //kwaɗ-//) /	kwàɗå̀kwàɗai	top of horse's head
kwaŕkwaŕō m.	(base //kwaŕ-//) /	kwàŕå̀kwàŕai	spindle
ƙwâŕƙwaŕå̀ f.	(base //ƙwaŕ-//) /	ƙwàŕå̀ƙwàŕai	concubine, slave girl
Irregular: jaujē m.	(base //jaw-//) /	jàwå̀jàwai	type of drum
ƙùlūlù̀ m.	(base //ƙul-//) /	ƙùlå̀ƙùlai (= ƙùlùlai)	cyst; locust bean bobbles

(c) Some monosyllabic CVC words recently borrowed from English, all of which have falling tone, also use this plural type, e.g.,

bâl f. / bàlå̀bàlai ball; bâm m. / bàmå̀bàmai bomb; fâm m. / fàmå̀fàmai = fàmfàmai pound (money unit); kwâs m. / kwàså̀kwàsai course; mîl m. / mìlå̀mìlai mile
Irregular: fîm m. / fìlå̀fìlai = fìnå̀fìnai film, movie

°AN: The plural fìlå̀fìlai would presumably be derived from a putative singular *fìlìm. The plural fìnå̀fìnai is anomalous. Although both of these plural forms are attested, it is not clear how common either of them is nowadays.

2.3. Plural type -aiCai)^HLH

Form: This plural type consists of a suffix -aiCai and an H-L-H tone pattern.

Comments: This plural formation is rarely used by modern-day SH speakers. (Historically, it is probably related to the -āCē)^HLH plural type described below (§3.1).) Scattered examples are found in older dictionaries and grammars and written texts. It is not clear the extent to which this formation is still used in other dialects. The words reported as forming plurals in this manner are primarily disyllabic items with all H tone plus a few H-L bases with a feminative ending (which is dropped in this formation). Examples:

hatsī m. / hatsàitsai	grain/guinea-corn	kumfā m. / kumfàifai	foam
shingē m. / shingàigai	fence	wākē m. / wākàikai	black-eyed peas
bisā f. / bisàisai	pack animal	ƙasā f. / ƙasàisai	country, province
wutsiyå̀ f. (base //wutsì//) / wutsàitsai tail			

3. CLASS 3: -AXE)^HLH

This class contains three related plural formations that are characterized by the vowel sequence ā...ē and an H-L-H tone melody. With a few exceptions, the resulting plural forms are always trisyllabic.

◊HN: Apart from this class, there are no plural suffixes in the language ending in the vowel /ē/. Moreover, there are no plurals at all ending in the corresponding mid vowel /ō/. Rather, one finds that plurals end either in one of the "primary" vowels /ī/, /ā/, /ū/ or in the diphthong /ai/ (but not /au/!). This suggests that the final /ē/ of this plural class is historically secondary, most likely resulting from monophthongization of /ai/, e.g.,, gulbī 'stream', pl. gulå̀bē < *gulå̀bai, etc.

3.1. Plural type -āCē)^HLH

Form: This type consists of a tone-integrating suffix -āCē)^HLH, where C is a copy of the preceding consonant, the copied C, of course, being subject to palatalization before the final ē.

Comments: This is a very large plural class. It includes most disyllabic words (adjectives as well as nouns) whose singular form has H-H tone and a light first syllable, e.g.,

damō m. / **damǎmē** land monitor   farī m. / **farǎrē** white
gidā m. / **gidǎjē** house   Ƙasā f. / **Ƙasǎshē** country, nation, province
Irregular: **uwā** f. mother / **iyǎyē** parents (= [dv] **uwǎyē**)

◊HN: The dialectal form **uwǎyē** is regular. The SH form **iyǎyē** possibly has the following derivation: **uwā** ⇒ **uwǎyē** → **uyǎyē** (by anticipatory assimilation of w to y in the next syllable → **iyǎyē** (by a change of u to i before y). Alternatively, **iyǎyē** could be the morphological plural not of **uwā** but rather of **iyà**, another term for 'mother', which is usually used as a term of address.
°AN: In Newman (1972b), I proposed that this plural formative did not involve partial suffixal reduplication, as it appears but rather involves the imposition of the vocalization pattern -ā–ē)^{HLH} on a prepared stem in which the second consonant had been doubled, i.e., **damō** ⇒ //**damm**-// ⇒ **damǎmē** 'land monitor'. Having led people astray for a quarter of a century—this analysis proved to be popular—I now feel compelled to offer a retraction: there is no evidence, synchronic nor diachronic, to indicate that this plural formative is anything other than a reduplicative -āCē suffix.

Older dictionaries include a few exceptions where the singular has the "wrong" tone or syllable weight. Only the first of these, where the erstwhile plural is now treated as a singular, is accepted comfortably by modern SH speakers.

icè m./   **itǎcē** (now treated as a singular)   tree, (fire)wood
bìkā m. /   **bikǎkē**   baboon
tàfā f. /   **tafǎfē**   grass armlet
wāgā f. /   **wāgǎgē**   basket with handle

3.2. Plural type -āyē)^{HLH}

Form: In this type the suffix contains a fixed /y/ consonant instead of a copy of the preceding consonant, e.g., **rīmī / rīmǎyē** 'silk cotton tree'. Words with a feminative suffix use a base without the ending in forming the plural, e.g., **munduwā** f. (base //**mund**-//), pl. **mundǎyē** 'brass bracelet, anklet'.
Comments: This is also a large plural class. Most of the singulars using this variant have the following characteristics: they are disyllabic, have H-H tone, and have a heavy first syllable. The rime of the heavy syllable consists of (a) a long vowel or a diphthong, (b) a vowel plus a nasal consonant (where the nasal consonant can be considered to be part of a "nasal diphthong" belonging to the nucleus (see §54:2.1.1)), or (c) a vowel plus the first part of a geminate (the occurring geminates being /ll/, /nn/, /mm/, and, one case, /kk/.) In a few cases, one finds a vowel plus /r̃/. The class does not include singulars of the form CāCā, with the exception of the reduplicated word **wāwā** m. / **wāwǎyē** 'fool'.

(a) **bāmī** m. / **bāmǎyē** novice; **dūlū** m. /**dūlǎyē** type of basket; **kīfī** m. / **kīfǎyē** fish; **sūnā** m. / **sūnǎyē** name; **ɓaurē** m. / **ɓaurǎyē** fig tree; **maisō** m. / **maisǎyē** unworked farm
(b) **dumɓū** m. / **dumɓǎyē** worn-out hoe; dimwit; **gwankī** m. / **gwankǎyē** roan antelope; **shingē** m. / **shingǎyē** fence; **wundī** m. / **wundǎyē** large grass mat; **gwangwan** m. (base //**gwangw**-// with the nasal diphthong dropped) / **gwangwǎyē** tin can
(c) **Ƙyallē** m. / **Ƙyallǎyē** piece of cloth; **sulluwā** f. (base //**sull**-//) / **sullǎyē** type of bangle; **gammō** m. / **gammǎyē** head pad (for carrying loads); **hannū** m. / **hannǎyē** hand; **tukkū** m. / **tukk(w)ǎyē** braid of hair; bird's crest
(d) **bur̃tū** m. / **bur̃tǎyē** ground hornbill; **gwar̃zō** m. / **gwar̃zǎyē** psn of great energy

Exception (with light first syllable): **ragō** m. / **ragwàyē** coward, slacker

◊HN: The word **ragō** historically derives from ***raggō** with a geminate consonant, a form still found in WH with the corresponding plural **ragg(w)àyē**, i.e., the SH singular did originally have the proper canonical shape for this plural type.

Three apocopated monosyllabic words with H tone use this plural formation:

ƙwai m. (base //ƙwāy-//) /	**ƙwāyàyē** (= [dv] **ƙwayàƙwai**)	egg
sau (= **sāwū**) m. /	**sāwàyē**	foot(print)
jā adj. (base //jāj-//) /	**jājàyē**	red

Five trisyllabic words use this plural formation. Three of them have the expected all H tone pattern; two of them do not, e.g.,

ƙūlumī m. /	**ƙūlumàyē** (= **ƙūlùmai**)	stingy (psn)
gwangwanī m. /	**gwangwanàyē** (= **gwangwàyē** < alternative sg. **gwangwan**)	tin can
tangaṛan m. (base //tangaṛ-//) /	**tangaṛàyē**	chinaware, dishes
kùnkurū m. /	**kunkuràyē**	tortoise
ùngùlu f. /	**ungulàyē**	vulture

ΔDN: Not surprisingly, because -**āyē**)^HLH plurals as a rule have a fixed trisyllabic shape, these longer forms exhibit variation in the assignment of the tone melody. For example, some speakers allow an H-L-L-H tone pattern for the plural forms **gwangwànàyē** and **tangàṛàyē**. In addition, some people pronounce the plurals of 'tortoise' and 'vulture' with an L-H tone melody, i.e., **kùnkùràyē** and **ùngùlàyē**, respectively.

In addition to the five trisyllabic words just indicated, some dozen disyllabic words using the -**āyē** plural have singulars with a "wrong" canonical shape. Most have H-L tone instead of being all H; two have initial L tone, one of which, in addition, has a light first syllable. Examples:

angò m. / **angwàyē** bridegroom; **gwāmì** m. / **gwāmàyē** knock-kneed; **kōṛè** m. / **kōṛàyē** green; **mūdù** m. / **mūdàyē** measuring bowl of a standard size used in selling grain; **mūgù** m. / **mūgàyē** wicked; **nōnò** m. / **nōnàyē** breast; **shūɗì** m. / **shūɗàyē** blue; **sōkò** m. / **sōkàyē** dimwitted psn; **sūrì** m. / **sūràyē** anthill; **wundì** m. / **wundàyē** type of gown; **wòṛì** m. / **wōṛàyē** silly psn; **gwànī** m. / **gwanàyē** expert

◊HN: Many of the above words have alternative plurals formed according to the class 4 pattern, e.g., **nōnàyē** = **nônnā** 'breast', **shūɗàyē** = **shūɗɗā** 'blue'. The historical question is the following: Do these -**āyē** plurals with phonologically "wrong" singulars represent an earlier stage when the -**āyē** plural was more general and phonologically not as restricted as it is today, or do they represent an expansion of the -**āyē** plural into new domains? My guess is that the answer is the former, but I have no solid evidence to support this hypothesis.

3.3. Plural type -**ā**–**ē**)^HLH

Form: In this type the consonantal slot of the suffix is filled by the final (i.e., third) consonant of the base, i.e., -**ā**- is inserted between the second and third consonants and /ē/ is attached at the end. The regular H-L-H tone pattern is used, e.g., **gulbī** / **gulàbē** 'stream'. Feminative suffixes are dropped in forming this plural type.

Comments: The canonical shape for singular employing this plural type is CVCCVV with all H tone, i.e., disyllabic with a closed first syllable (see examples in (a)). Excluded from this type are words where the C$_2$ is a nasal or the first part of a geminate because these append the suffix -**àyē**. A few singulars of this class are trisyllabic (CVCVCVV), but the short vowel in the second syllable is clearly epenthetic in nature (see (b)). Trisyllabic words with a feminative suffix, which also contain an epenthetic medial vowel, drop the suffix in forming the plural (see (c)). Examples: (Notes: [i] In standard orthography, initial /'/ is not represented. It is transcribed here to reflect the canonical shape. [ii] Palatalized and labialized consonants, e.g., **ky** and **kw**, are written as such in standard orthography. They are indicated here by raised letters, e.g., **k^y** and **k^w**, to make it clear thay they fit into the canonical shape as unit phonemes.

(a) **'askā** f. / **'asàkē** straight razor; **bir̃nī** m. / **bir̃àne** city, large town; **ɓurmā** f. / **ɓuràmē** rat trap; **kulkī** m. / **kulàkē** club, cudgel; **kurfō** m. / **kuràfē** whip, lash
(b) **gishirī** m. / **gishàrē** salt (archaic plural); **guzumā** f. / **guzàmē** old cow or old woman; **kuturū** m. / **kutàrē** leper; **k^{w}al(a)bā** f. / **k^{w}alàbē** bottle
(c) **'amaryā** f. (base //'amr-//) / **'amàrē** bride; **buzurwā** f. (base //buzr-//) / **buzàrē** long-haired goat; **daɓ^{w}alwā** f. (base //daɓ^{w}l-//) / **daɓ^{w}àlē** large hen; beautiful, well-built girl; **magaryā** f. (base //magr-//) / **magàrē** jujube tree; **taɓaryā** f. (base //taɓr-//) / **taɓàrē** pestle; **tukunyā** f. (base //tuk^{w}n-//) / **tuk^{w}àne** cooking pot

Some singulars taking this plural type synchronically have the shape CVVCVV, where the vowel in the first syllable is either a long monophthong or a diphthong, i.e., they look as if they ought to form their plurals with -**āyē**, e.g., **ɓaunā** / **ɓakàne** 'buffalo'. This morphological aberration is due to the historical weakening in syllable-final position of the original C$_2$ (according to Klingenheben's Law), which is recovered in the base used in the plural. Nowadays, many of these words use the more transparent -**āyē** plural suffix formation.

ɓaunā f. (base //ɓak$^{(w)}$n-//) /	**ɓak$^{(w)}$àne** (= **ɓaunàyē**)	buffalo
būzū m. (base //bugz-//) /	**bugàje** (= **būzàyē**)	Tuareg
far̃kē/falkē m. (base //fatk-//) /	**fatàkē**	itinerant trader
jūjī m. (base //zibz-//) /	**jibàje** (= **jūjàyē**)	refuse heap
k^{y}aurō m. (base //k^{y}amr-//) /	**k^{y}amàrē**	tall grass, arrow shaft
ƙaimī m. (base //ƙaym-//) /	**ƙayàmē**	spur
ƙ^{y}aurē m. (base //ƙ^{y}amr-//) /	**ƙ^{y}amàrē** (= **ƙ^{y}auràyē**)	door
taushī m. (base //tafs-//) /	**tafàshē**	type of drum
g^{w}aurō m. (base //g^{w}ag^{w}r-// or //g^{w}abr-//) / **g^{w}ag^{w}àrē** = **g^{w}abàrē** (= **g^{w}auràyē**) unmarried man		

◊HN: The historically original form of the singular for 'unmarried man' was probably **g^{w}ag^{w}rō*. The syllable final /g^w/ changed to /b/, resulting in the form **g^{w}abrō**, still present in WH. In SH, /b/ in coda position followed by an abutting coronal sonorant weakened to /u/, resulting in the now-occurring form **g^{w}aurō**. The alternative plural forms illustrate synchronic uncertainty on the part of native speakers as to which consonant to recover in constructing the plural base. The now most common SH strategy is to avoid the problem altogether by suffixing -**āyē** to the surface CVVCVV singular form, i.e., **g^{w}auràyē**.

The pair **mùtûm** m. / **mutàne** 'person/people' is irregular and represents an old suppletion. The word **mutàne** appears to be a normal plural of this subtype, but its corresponding singular lacks the requisite shape.

4. CLASS 4: -(A)XA)^{HLH}

This class contains four related plural formations characterized by final -ā and an H-L-H tone melody.

4.1. *Plural type* -Gā)^{HLH}

Form: These plurals are built by geminating the base-final consonant and adding the suffix -ā. The H-L-H tone pattern is assigned to the disyllabic plural form resulting in a falling-high sequence, e.g., **gāgò** / **gâggā** 'pagan chief'. Base forms ending in a palatalized consonant preceding a front vowel depalatalize before the suffixal -ā, e.g., **sāshè** m. / **sâssā** 'section, part, segment'. Because the initial syllable of the plural is always closed, long vowels in the base automatically shorten in according with general phonological rules, and, in the case of /e/ and /o/, normally centralize to /a/. As a result, redundant palatalization or labialization of initial consonants often comes to the fore, e.g., **gēfè** [gʸēfè] / pl. **gyâffā** 'side' (< **gyêffā** < **gyêeffā**; **kōřè** [kʷōřè] / pl. **kwâřřā** 'green'. Plurals with initial coronal consonants are usually written (and sometimes pronounced) with the /o/ retained e.g., **zōbè** / **zôbbā** = **zábbā**.

Comments: The words that take this plural all end in a vowel other than /a/ and are masculine nouns or adjectives. The typical shape of the singular is CVVCVV)^{HL}, i.e., disyllabic with a long monophthongal vowel in the first syllable and H-L tone. Many of these words allow alternative suffixal plurals, e.g., **kēsò** / **kyâssā** = **kēsunà** 'old worn-out mat', **ƙātò** / **ƙâttā** = **ƙàttī** 'huge'. Examples:

bābè m. / **bâbbā**	locust	**gāgò** m. / **gâggā**	pagan chief
gēbè m. / **gyâbbā**	water channel	**gīɓì** m. / **gîɓɓā** (or **gyâɓɓā**))	tooth gap
gōřò m. / **gwâřřā**	kolanut	**kōřè** m. / **kwâřřā** (= **kôřřā**)	green
ƙūrù m. / **ƙûrrā**	pony	**mūdù** m. / **mûddā**	corn measure
nōnò m. / **nônnā** (= **nânnā**)	breast	**rēshè** m. / **râssā**	branch
shūɗì m. / **shûɗɗā**	blue	**tūshè** m. / **tûssā**	base
tsāwò m. / **tsâwwā**	doorway covering	**zōbè** m. / **zôbbā** (= **zâbbā**)	ring

◊HN: Historically this plural formation involved -aCā)^{HLH} reduplication, i.e., originally this suffix was vowel initial as is the case with all other plural suffixes. The present forms are due to syncope of the short medial /a/, i.e., **zōbè** 'ring' ⇒ *zōbàbā → **zôbbā**. In an earlier work (Newman 1972b), I suggested that the reduplicated suffix was *-āCā)^{HLH}, with a long penultimate vowel. This has to be wrong. The principle of syllable-weight polarity and the phonetic naturalness of the syncope rule indicate clearly that the historically lost vowel had to have been short.
ΔDN: In some WH dialects where a falling-high tonal sequence simplifies to L-H (see §71:6.2.1), this plural class appears as L-H, e.g., **ràssā** 'branches', **shùɗɗā** 'blue' (pl.), etc.

Two words with medial flap /r/ have slightly irregular plurals without the gemination, i.e.,

taurè m. / **tâurā**   castrated he-goat; **yārò** m. / **yârā**   boy

ΔDN: Abraham's (1962) dictionary contains a few more examples, with which current SH speakers are not familiar, e.g., **mōrì** / **môrā** 'stable', **ƙūrù** / **ƙûrā** (= **ƙûrrā**) 'pony'.

There are a few words with a light first syllable listed in the dictionaries as utilizing this plural type. Modern SH speakers generally prefer other plural types, if any, with these words, e.g., **tudù** m. / **tûddā** = **tùddai** 'hill'. Attested examples (complete):

dajè m. / **dâzzā**	handsome	**dakè** m. / **dâkkā**	bullock
damì m. / **dâmmā**	bundle of grain or grass	**kagò** m. / **kâggā**	round thatched house
tabò m. / **tâbbā**	scar	**tudù** m. / **tûddā**	hill

Irregular: **gabò** m. / **gûbbā**   tooth

°AN/◊HN: These words with light syllable roots attach the geminate suffix -Gā directly, i.e., they form plurals by analogy with the more usual forms like **ƙàtò** /**ƙàttā**. They do not go through the historical reduplication followed by syncope processes, i.e., they never would have added the original *-aCā suffix with the short penultimate vowel.

4.2. Plural Type -āCā)HLH

Form: This plural type consists of a suffix -āCā (where C is a copy of the preceding consonant) and an H-L-H tone pattern. The suffix is added to the base, which does not include the CVC- prefix found on the corresponding singular forms. The plurals are all trisyllabic with all three syllables heavy.

Comments: This form is essentially restricted to plurals of the derived class of adjectives known as DASQ (derived adjectives of sensory quality) (see §2:2). Examples:

kàkkausā adj. (base //**kaus-**//) / **kausàsā**	very rough
mùmmūnā adj. (base //**mūn-**//) /**mūnànā**	ugly, evil
zùzzurfā adj. (base //**zurf-**//) / **zurfàfā**	very deep

The diminutive word **sīřīřī** (= sīřīřī) 'thin' uses this DASQ plural form as one of its plurals even though it does not have a corresponding singular DASQ, i.e., **sìřīřī** (= sīřīřī) adj. (base //**sīř-**//) / **sīřàřā** (= siřī-sìřī = sìřìřai) 'thin'. The very common irregular word **àbù** 'thing' has an archaic plural form built on this pattern in addition to its more usual plurals: **àbù** / **abàbā** (= abūbuwà) 'thing'.

4.3. Plural type -ā–ā)HLH

Form: In this type, the consonantal slot of the suffix is filled by the third consonant of the base, i.e., /ā/ is inserted between the second and third consonants and /ā/ is added at the end. The regular H-L-H tone pattern of this class is used, e.g., **garkè** / **garàkā** 'herd, flock'. (In WH, the final consonant is usually geminated, e.g., **garàkkā**.) In the single example that occurs with a feminative suffix, it is dropped in forming the plural. Base forms ending in a palatalized consonant preceding a front vowel depalatalize before the -ā, e.g., **ƙurshè** / **ƙuràsā** 'bundle of grass'. As with the -āC3ē plurals (§3.3 above), some bases recover a C2 that was historically present, but which in the singular form has undergone syllable-final weakening or assimilation, e.g., **dantsè** (base //**damts-**//) / **damàtsā** 'forearm'.

Comments: The canonical shape for singulars employing this plural type is CVCCVV with H-L tone. Some singulars are CVVCVV, where the vowel in the first syllable is either a long monophthong or a diphthong. This is invariably due to the weakening of the historically original C2. Almost all of the words taking this plural are masculine. Examples:

(a) **burjì** m. / **buràzā**	gravel, hillock	**farcè** m. / **faràtā**	fingernail
garkè m. / **garàkā**	herd, flock	**harshè** m. / **haràsā**	tongue, language
kuřtù m. / **kuřàtā**	recruit (in police or army)	**sìřdì** m. / **siřàdā**	saddle
turkè m. / **turàkā**	tethering post	**zařtò** m. / **zařàtā**	saw, file
ƙìrjī m. / **ƙiràzā**	chest (exceptional singular with L-H tone)		
(b) **dantsè** m. (base //**damts-**//) / **damàtsā**	forearm		
gunkì m. (base //**gumk-**//) / **gumàkā**	idol, statue		
kwībì m. (base //**kuyɓ-**//) / **kwiyàɓā**	side of the body		

Ɓauyè m. (base //Ɓawy-//) /	Ɓawàyyā [dv]	rural area
runjì m. (base //rumd-//) /	rumàdā	slave settlement
taikì m. (base //tayk-//)	tayàkā	hide bag used on pack animals
zūcìyā f. (base //zukt-//) /	zukàtā	heart, mind
Irregular: gèzā f. (base //girz-//) /	giràzā	mane

4.4. Plural type -ā)^HLH

Form: In this plural type, all that is left of the suffix is the vowel -ā and the H-L-H tone pattern.

Comments: This is the regular plural formation for agent nouns and adjectives formed with ma...ī, or the corresponding feminine ma...ìyā.

mahàr̃bī / mahàr̃bā   hunter; mahàukàcī / mahàukàtā   crazy, madman, idiot; makitsìyā f. / makìtsā hairdresser; manòmī / manòmā   farmer; matsōracìyā f. / matsòràtā   coward(ly)

This plural formation is also used with the word haƙōrī 'tooth' / haƙòrā. Note that the singular was originally a plural itself (type 1.2), built on a form *haƙ(ʷ)rè 'tooth'.

5. CLASS 5: -AXU)^HLH

This class contains two subtypes. They are both characterized by the vowel sequence -ā–ū and (usually) an H-L-H tone melody.

5.1. Plural type -ā–ū)^HLH

Form: This plural type is similar to the -āC₃ā)^HLH type except that the final vowel is -ū rather than -ā. For many present-day SH speakers, the tone for all plural words of this type is regularly H-L-H. The dictionaries and older grammars give H-H-H as a lexically determined alternative for some, but not all, of the words. These are listed in the examples by (= HHH). (In a few cases, H-H-H is the only tone listed.)

Comments: As with the -āC₃ā)^HLH type, the singulars taking this plural type are typically H-L disyllabic words that synchronically have the shape CVCCVV or else they are CVVCVV forms where the base recovers the erstwhile coda of the initial syllable. The base for words that take this -ū suffix generally either have /u/ as the initial vowel or else have //y// as the coda of the first syllable (the //y// surfacing as part of the long vowel /ī/). Words using this plural type are almost all masculine. Examples:

(a) gurbì m. /	guràbū (= HHH)	hollow place
gurgù m. /	guràgū	lame (psn)
kurmì m. /	kuràmū	copse, jungle
murhù m. /	muràfū (= HHH)	cooking place;
turkè m. /	turàkū (= HHH)	tethering post
kùr̃fī m. /	kur̃àfū	lair (singular with L-H tone!)
(b) dūtsè m. (base //duwts-//) /	duwàtsū	stone, rock
gībī m. (base //giyɓ-//) /	giyàɓū (= HHH)	tooth gap
kuncì m. (base //kumt-//) /	kumàtū	cheek
kwībī m. (base //kuyɓ-//) /	kwiyàɓū (= HHH)	side of the body
mīkì m. (base //miyk-//) /	miyàkū (= HHH)	ulcer
mūgù m./adj. (base //muyg-//) /	miyàgū (< mʷiyàgū)	evil (psn or thing)
tūshìyā f. (base //tukws-//) / /	tukwāsū [dv]	stubble of corn (= SH tūshiyōyī)
kuràdā f. (base //kurd-//) /	kuràdū	small axe
Irregular: lūdàyī m. (base //luwd-//) / luwàdū		ladle

°AN/◊HN: Some scholars, notably Jungraithmayr and Ibriszimow (1994), have proposed that **idò** 'eye' derives from a stem containing /**n**/ as a third consonant, i.e., // '-d-n //. The plural **idànū** would then be a straightforward instantiation of the -āC₃ū)^{HLH} formative. Although this analysis seems reasonable at first sight and perhaps *could* be right, it is not really very likely. It is questionable on internal grounds—the proposed singular does not fit the canonical shape of this plural class—as well as externally—it is not supported by comparative Chadic evidence. A more likely interpretation is that **idò** is a reflex of a monoconsonantal root *(**i**)**dV** and that the -**nū** in **idànū** is an archaic plural suffix still evidenced in such forms as **kānū** 'headlines', pl. of **kai** 'head' and **hannū** 'hand', now a singular but originally a plural consisting of *(**h**)**am** + -**nū**.

5.2. Plural type -āCū)^{HLH}

Form: This plural subtype is formed by adding the suffix -āCū)^{HLH}, where the C is a copy of the final consonant of the base. One word, which contains a feminative suffix that is dropped, has all H tone in the plural.

Comment: This archaic formation is only used with a small number of basic body part terms. The singulars are all CVCVV with a light initial syllable and H-L tone. Examples (complete):

gaɓà f. /	**gaɓàɓū** (= **gaɓɓunà**)	joint, limb
ƙafà f. /	**ƙafàfū**	foot
tsuwè m. /	**tsuwàwū**	testicle
gwīwà f. (base //**guy-**// /	**gwiyāyū** (with all H tone) (= **gwīwōyī**)	knee

The now masculine singular word **ɗuwàwū** 'buttocks' originally must have been a plural of this class.

6. CLASS 6: -UXA)^{HL}

Grouped here are five related plural formations including -**unà** and -**ukà**, among others, which contain a number of different subtypes and various surface manifestations. (Curiously, there are no adjectives in this class.) The common characteristics of the class are the vowel sequence **u...ā** and the set H-L tone melody. Words with base-final palatals generally depalatalize before the plural suffix, e.g., **zàncē** m. / **zantukā** 'conversation'. The specific plural types in the class have a number of subvariants that make use of identical processes of gemination and internal reduplication.

6.1. Plural type -unā)^{HL}

Form: This plural type takes the suffix -**unà** with the H-L tone pattern, e.g., **hùlā** / **hūlunà** 'cap'.
Comments: The singulars are typically disyllabic words with a heavy first syllable and L-H or H-L tone. The choice of -**unà** vs. the -**ukà** suffix is partially predictable depending on the nature of the stem-final consonant (see discussion in §6.2). Both masculine and feminine L-H words use this plural type. With few exceptions, the H-L words are all masculine, because singular feminine words normally use the class 1 -ōCī plural. A few trisyllabic words, mostly recent loans, also use this plural type.

gàngā f. / **gangunà** drum; **kògī** m. / **kōgunà** river; **ràgō** m. / **rāgunà** ram; **kwàndō** m. / **kwandunà** basket; **gòrā** f. / **gōrunà** gourd; **tùlū** m. / **tūlunà** water pot; **bencī** m. / **bencunà** bench; **famfò** m. / **famfunà** faucet; **kēsò** m. / **kēsunà** worn-out mat; **lar̃dì** m. / **lar̃dunà** province; **yankì** m. / **yankunà** piece of sth., section; **hantà** f. / **hantunà** liver (= **hantōcī**); **àgōgo** m. / **agōgunà** clock, watch; **àkàwu** m. / **akāwunà** clerk; **àkwàtì** m. / **akwātunà** box; **kàlàngū** m. / **kalangunà** hourglass drum
Irregular: **kâi** m. (base //**kāw-**// < *kāy-) / **kāwunà** head; **sarkī** m. (base //**sarāk-**//) / **sarākunà** chief, emir

◊HN: The H-H word **sarkī** appears to have the "wrong" tone to take this suffix. The historical explanation is that it is derived from a stem *sàrāki. (The change of L-H to H, with the collapse of the first two syllables into one, is totally regular.) The initial L tone is preserved in the feminine form **sàraunìyā** 'queen', and the lost medial /ā/ can be seen in such forms as **bàsarākè** 'office holder under an emir'. The singular form **sàrākī** does in fact still exist, although not in the literal sense of 'king' or 'emir', e.g., **kâi, Lawàn sàrākī** 'Hey, Lawan big shot!'

ΔDN: In the Tibiri dialect (Gouffé 1967/68: 42n), as well as in the dialect of Sokoto (Malami Buba, personal communication), this plural type appears with an H-L-H tone pattern rather than the standard H-L pattern, i.e., **rāgùnā** = [SH] **rāgunà** 'rams', **tūlùnā** = [SH] **tūlunà** 'waterpots', **akwātùnā** = [SH] **akwātunà** 'boxes', **dammùnā** = [SH] **dammunà** 'bundles'. This pronunciation has also been noted by McIntyre (1992) for the speaker on the tape accompanying the *Spoken Hausa* course (Cowan and Schuh 1976), who is supposed to be—but in fact may not be—an SH speaker. Surprisingly the H-L-H tone pattern occurs only with plurals formed with the **-unā** suffix and not with those formed with the closely related **-ukā** suffix.

Disyllabic words taking the **-unā** suffix that have a light first syllable generally undergo expansion of the stem in antepenultimate position, either by gemination or by internal -CVC- reduplication , e.g., **cikì / cikkunà** = **cikunkunà** 'belly'. The choice of gemination as opposed to reduplication seems to be lexically specific and variable depending on dialectal or idiolectal preference. Some words allow both as alternatives.

The formation rule works on an intermediate plural stem made up of the lexical base plus the suffix, e.g., **cikì** ⇒ //cikunà//. One then either geminates the C_2 or else inserts a copy in antepenultimate position of the CVC of the final two syllables. (Note, interestingly, that what is reduplicated is not a morphological constituent: the reduplicated CVC copies the final C of the base plus the **-un** portion of the plural suffix.) Examples:

bàkā m. / **bakunkunà**	bow
bùhū m. / **buhunhunà**	sack
cikì m. / **cikkunà** = **cikunkunà**	belly
damì m. / **dammunà**	bundle
gwàdò m. / **gwaddunà**	type of blanket
jìkī m. / **jikunkunà** (= **jikunà**)	body
kwabò m. / **kwabbunà**	penny, plastic chip

ΔDN: The gemination of the C_2 in the plural produces syllable weight polarity (heavy-light) between the first two syllables. In some WH dialects, the /n/ of the suffix is geminated instead, thereby producing a light-heavy alternation, e.g., [SH] **cikkunà** = [WH] **cikunnà**.

6.2. Plural type -ukā)^{HL}

The plural suffix **-ukā** has a close relation to the suffix **-uwā** (§6.3). Historically the /w/ in the **-uwā** variant is probably derived from /k/ by intervocalic lenition. Synchronically, the choice between the variants is partially predictable and partially lexically or dialectally determined.

Form: This plural type takes the suffix **-ukā** with the H-L tone pattern, e.g., **zaurè / zaurukà** 'entrance room'. (In WH, the suffix **-ukkà** with a geminate /kk/ is common.)

Comments: The singulars are typically disyllabic words with H-L or L-H tone and a heavy first syllable (most often an open syllable). Most of the words are masculine. Words with base-final **y, n, r̃,** and **f** (but see note) use **-ukā** exclusively as opposed to the related **-unā** suffix, whereas words with base-final velars do not use **-ukā**, a dissimilatory process apparently being operative. Words with other base-final consonants take either **-ukā** or **-unā**, the choice being lexically specific. Examples:

Ƙauyè m. / Ƙauyukà   village; râi m. (base //rāy-//) / rāyukà   life, soul; tsānì m. / tsānukà   ladder; dàřnī m. / dařnukà   cornstalk fence; gàřè f. / gāřukà   type of gown; ràfī m. / rāfukà   stream Ƙwàurī m. / Ƙwaurukà   shin, calf; rāmì m. / rāmukà   pit, trench; wīlī m. / wīlukà   wheel

°AN: Although there are some words with base-final /f/ that use the -unā suffix, e.g., màl(à)fā / malfunà (= malèfanī [older form]) 'brimmed hat', fàsfô / fasfunà [< Eng.] 'passport', kôfī / kôfunà [< Eng.] 'cup', originally they all probably required the -ukà suffix. One can understand on phonological grounds why there might be an incompatibility between, for example, base-final /n/ and the -unā suffix; but there seems to be no reason why /f/ should belong to this curious, unnatural class.

Many plurals using the -ukā suffix require or allow internal -CVC- reduplication. The /k/ of the internal -CVC- automatically geminates with the following consonant, e.g., kwānô / kwānukà ⇒ /kwānuknukà/ → kwānunnukà 'pan'. Examples:

bāshì m. / bāsussukà   loan, credit   cùtā f. / cūtuttukà   ailment, disease
dājì m. / dāzuzzukà   bush, forest   lâifī m. / laifuffukà   crime, wrongdoing
tsaunì m. / tsaununnukà   mountain   zàncē m. / zantuktukà (= zantukà) conversation
Irregular (singular with light first syllable): sulè m. / sulullukà shilling

The -ukā suffix with internal reduplication also occurs with a few trisyllabic words as well (all of which are loanwords from Arabic), e.g.,

haɗàřī m. /   haɗařuřřukà   danger; accident
kabàřī m. /   kabařuřřukà   grave
sha'ànī m. /   sha'anunnukà   matter, affair

6.3. Plural type -uwā)^HL

Form: This plural type takes the suffix -uwā with the H-L tone pattern. In simple inflections, it is always accompanied either by internal -CVC- reduplication—the most usual case—or by gemination. The reduplicated -Cuw- element appears phonologically as /Cū/, e.g., hakūkuwà < /hakuwkuwà/ 'grasses'.
Comments: The singulars are typically disyllabic words with a light first syllable and H-L or L-H tone. This contrasts with the -ukā plurals, which typically go with singulars with a heavy first syllable. Examples:

ajì m. / azūzuwà (= ajūjuwà) class, section   bàtū m. / batūtuwà   conversation, matter
faƙô m. / faƙūƙuwà   hard ground   gàrī m. / garūruwà   town, city
hakì m. / hakūkuwà   grass   Ƙàshī m. / Ƙasūsuwà   bone

ΔDN: In WH, -ukā with internal reduplication is commonly used instead of -uwā, especially with roots ending in a liquid or other coronal consonant, e.g., gàrī / garurrukà 'town'. This dialectal formation appears to be spreading into SH.

Four words, all with base-final /n/, add the -uwā suffix without reduplication. In two of them, the /n/ undergoes gemination; in the other two, the /n/ is already geminate in the synchronically occurring singular form. Examples (complete):

Ƙanè m. / Ƙannuwà   younger brother   zanè m. / zannuwà   wrapper, body cloth hannū m. / **hannuwà**   hand   kûnnē m. / **kunnuwà**   ear

The other instances of the **-uwā** suffix being used without reduplication are "plurals of plurals." In these cases, the base to which the suffix is added is already a plural form (which may or may not be treated as a plural synchronically). (Note that this was probably also the case with the latter two examples listed above.) Examples:

itàcē m. (originally pl. of **icè**) / **itātuwà**   tree, wood
ƙafàfū (plural of **ƙafà** f.) / **ƙafāfuwà**   foot
ƙiràrē m. or pl. / **ƙirāruwà**   twigs, kindling

6.4. Plural type -u–ā)^HL

Form: In this type the consonantal slot of the suffix is filled by the final consonant of the base rather than by a set consonant /n/ or /k/ or /w/, i.e., /u/ simply replaces the penultimate vowel of the singular (sometimes vacuously) and /ā/ is added at the end. The regular H-L tone pattern is used, e.g., **gàtarī / gāturà** 'axe'.

> ◊HN: Wolff (1992) has proposed that the **-u–ā** vocalization pattern constitutes the essence of this plural class (and certain others) and that the /n/ and /k/ that one finds in the **-unā** and **-ukā** suffixes, for example, were originally demonstratives. Although the hypothesis deserves some consideration, I am far from convinced that it accurately describes what historically was the case. Given the comparative Chadic evidence, I think that the straightforward identification of /n/ and /k/ as plural markers is much more likely (see Newman 1990b).

When the resulting plural contains a sequence of light syllables (excluding the final syllable), the final consonant is often geminated, especially in WH, e.g., **haràfī / haɽuffà** 'letter of alphabet'. The goal here is to create a two-syllable foot structure with syllable weight polarity, contrast **gāturà**, in which the word evidences a heavy-light rhythm, with **haɽuffà**, which has a light-heavy rhythm.

Comments: The typical singular is polysyllabic ending in -ī. All are masculine. Examples:

(a) **cōkàlī** m. / **cōkulà**   spoon; **dāgùmī** m./ **dāgumà**   charm; **dàmfamī** m./ **damfumà**   temporary fence; **fuɽtùmī** m. / **fuɽtumà**   bullock; **kallàbī** m. / **kallubà**   woman's head-tie; **tambùlàn** m. (base //tambul-//) / **tambulà** (= **tambulōlī**)   drinking glass; **amāwàlī** m. / **amāwulà**   part of turban for covering face

(b) **daràsī** m. / **daɽussà**   lesson; **haràfī** m. / **haɽuffà**   letter of alphabet; **shaɽàɗī** m. / **shaɽuɗɗà** (= **shaɽuɗà**)   agreement, condition; **takòbī** m. / **takubbà** (= **takubà**)   sword; **agalàmī** m. / **agalummà**   sheepskin; **àl'amàɽī** m. / **al'amuɽɽà** (= **al'amuɽà**)   matter, issue

This plural formation is used also with a few disyllabic English loanwords of the shape CVVCVC, some of which have a "latent" final -ī. Examples:

bātìɽ (= **bātìɽī**) m. / **bātur̀à** (= **bātiɽōɽī**)   battery; **bàbûɽ** m. / **bāburà**   motorcycle; **bāwùl** m. / **bāwulà**   valve; **tēbùɽ** (= **tēbùɽī**) m. / **tēbur̀à** (= **tēbuɽōɽī**)   table

A few words using the **-u–ā** affix obligatorily undergo internal -CVC- reduplication. The reduplication is effected *after* the vowel replacement. Plurals that are characterized by this reduplication never geminate the base-final consonant. Examples:

kabàrī m. / **ka̱bu̱r̄bu̱r̀à** grave; **māgànī** m. / **māgu̱ngu̱nà** medicine, remedy; **nak̄àlī** m. / **naḵulḵulà** instruction; **shagàlī** m. / **shagu̱lgu̱là** celebration

In one example using this plural formation, the singular noun, which in fact is an erstwhile plural, is already reduplicated. Nevertheless, one has to redo the -CVC- reduplication in order to get the correct /u/ vowel in the antepenultimate syllable: **hak̄àrk̄arī** m. / **hak̄urk̄urà** (not **hak̄àrk̄urà) 'rib(s)'.

There are a small number of disyllabic native words that use the -u–ā affix rather than -unā or -ukā. These are H-L nouns with the shape CVCCVV. With one exception, they are all masculine. In the plural, one usually geminates the base-final consonant, e.g.,

garkè m. / **garukkà** herd, flock; **hargì** m. / **haruggà** sword fastener; **harshè** m. / **harussà** tongue, language; **sartsè** m. / **saruttsà** splinter; **tafkì** m. / **tafukà** lake; **cūnà** f. (base //ciwn-//) / **ciwunnà** gusset joining sleeve to gown

In SH, the plural of the word **aikì** (base //'ayk-//) geminates the /y/ rather than the final /k/, i.e., **aikì** m. / **ayyukà** (= WH **ayukkà**) 'work'.

6.5. Plural type -uCCā)^HL

Form: This type consists of a suffix -uCCà, where CC is a geminated copy of the preceding consonant.
Comments: This is an archaic plural type recorded in the dictionaries and attested in written sources and in other dialects. In SH, the examples listed below generally take other plural forms:

àbù m. /	**abubbà** (usu. **abūbuwà**)	thing
ɗàrī /	**ɗarurrà** (usu. **ɗarūruwà**)	hundred
gaɓà̀ f. /	**gaɓuɓɓà** (usu. **gaɓōɓī**)	limb
k̄àshī m. /	**k̄asussà** (usu. **k̄asūsuwà**)	bone

6.6. Plural type -ā)^HL

Some five polysyllabic words utilize the final -ā vowel and the H-L tone pattern of this class, but without inserting the /u/. These are all masculine.

dàbaibàyī m. / **dabaibayà**	hobbling rope		**lifìdī** m. / **lifidà̀**	cavalry quilting
lūdàyī m. / **lūdayà̀**	ladle		**tàkàlmī** m. / **tākalmà̀**	shoe
tūbàlī m. / **tūbalà**	brick			

7. CLASS 7: -AXI)^LH

Grouped here are four different plural types with varied surface manifestations. The common shared characteristics are the final vowel sequence a–I (where I represents a high vowel, usually -ī, but in one case -ū) and the set L-H tone melody.

7.1. Plural type -annī)^LH

Form: These plurals make use of a suffix -annī and an L-H tone pattern.
Comments: The singulars are typically disyllabic nouns ending in a nonhigh vowel, generally /a(a)/ or /o(o)/ and a tone pattern other than all H. The large majority of the words are masculine. There is one monosyllabic word that takes this plural and four polysyllabic words. The latter include a compound noun, a loanword from English, and two older loans with a feminative suffix.

baffà m. / **bàffànnī** paternal uncle; **dòdō** m. / **dòdànnī** monster, goblin; **fùrē** m. / **fùrànnī** flower; **gwàdò** m. / **gwàdànnī** type of blanket; **gwàfā** f. / **gwàfànnī** forked end of a stick; **màkò** m. / **màkwànnī** week; **ùbā** / **ùbànnī** father; **wàsā** m. / **wàsànnī** play, game, joke; **watà** m. / **wàtànnī** month, moon; **fā** m. / **fànnī** flat rock; **kàsuwā** f. / **kàsùwànnī** (usu. **kāsuwōyī**) market; **r̃àhōtò** m. / **r̃àhòtànnī** report; **shùgàbā** m. / **shùgàbànnī** leader, head; **ùnguwā** f. / **ùngùwànnī** hamlet, neighborhood, quarter
Irregular: **kàkā** m./f. / **kàkànī** (= **kàkànnī**) grandparent; **k̃àhō** m. / **k̃àhōnī** (= less common **k̃àhwànnī**) horn

> ΔDN: In some WH dialects there is a plural suffix reported variously as **-innē**, **-innai**, or **-innī**. The choice of the final vowel depends on the specific subdialect. The tone pattern in all cases is L-H-L. Here are some xamples (illustrating the **-innē** variant): **àgōgo** m. / **àgògìnnè** 'clock'; **fàr̃antì** m. / **fàr̃àntìnnè** 'plate, tray'; **kàlàngū** m. / **kàlàngìnnè** 'hourglass drum'; **kàragà** f. / **kàràgìnnè** 'couch, throne'; **makar̃antā** f. / **màkàr̃àntìnnè** (not ****màkàr̃àncìnnè**) 'school', **takàr̃dā** f. / **tàkàr̃dìnnè** 'paper'.

7.2. Plural type -aCCī.)^{LH}

Form: The suffix in this type contains a geminated copy of the preceding consonant rather than a fully specified consonant. Some speakers, esp. in WH dialects, have truncated variants of these plurals formed by deleting the medial **Ca** syllable.

Comments: This type is restricted to two very common adjectives (= adjectival nouns) with H-H tone. (The plural of **tsōhō** is built on a base containing /f/ instead of the surface **h**.)

sābō m. /	**sàbàbbī** =	**sàbbī**	new
tsōhō m. /	**tsòfàffī** =	**tsòffī** (= [WH] **tswahhī** (with H-H tone))	old (psn)

7.3. Plural Type -a(i)kU)^{LH}

Form: This plural type employs an L-H suffix ending in /k/ plus a high vowel. The suffix has three surface variants: (a) **-àikū** or-**àkū**, and (b) **-àkī**. Eight words use the suffix **-kū**. The vowel preceding the **-kū** appears as /ai/ in some words and /a/ in others. (Some speakers monophthongize the /ai/ to /ē/.) Some words allow both /ai/ or /a/, others seem to be fixed with one or the other. The choice seems to be lexically/idiolectically specific and not synchronically predictable. In the examples below, I give the forms as listed in the dictionaries and as preferred by my assistants. The variant **-àkī** is used with two common words, both of which have (or had) an initial labialized consonant. (The final **-ī** thus seems to be conditioned by some kind of dissimilatory principle.)

Comments: The singulars taking this plural are typically feminine words of the shape **CāCā** with all H tone. Three of the words contain a feminative ending **-iyā**, which is dropped when the plural suffix is added. Examples (complete):

(a) **mārā** f. / **màràkū** calabash scoop; **rānā** f. / **rànàikū** (= **rànàkū**) day; **tsārā** m./f. / **tsàràikū** age-mate; **zānā** f. / **zànàkū** reed mat; **zāzā** f. / **zàzàikū** low-lying grassy land; **cēd̃iyā** f. / **cèd̃àkū** fig tree; **rāriyā** f. / **ràràikū** under-wall drainage hole, sieve; **tsāmiyā** f. / **tsàmàikū** tamarind
(b) **gōnā** f. (< ***gwānā**) / **gònàkī** farm; **kwānā** m. / **kwànàkī** day (24-hour period)

7.4. Plural Type -ā–ī)^{LH}

Form: In this type the consonantal slot of the suffix is filled by the final consonant of the base, i.e., the vowel **-ā-** is inserted between the second and third consonants and /ī/ is attached at the end.

Comments: This is a frozen one-member class consisting of the word **sauràyī** 'youth', pl. **sàmā̀rī**. Synchronically, it is probably best treated as an irregular suppletive plural. Viewed historically, the formation pattern can be seen if one assumes a base without the -àyī singular suffix but including the former syllable-final /m/, which has changed into /u/ in accordance with Klingenheben's Law, i.e., **sauràyī** m. (base //samr-//) + -ā–ī)^{LH} ⇒ **sàmā̀rī** 'youth, young man'.

8. CLASS 8: (…)-AXI)^{HLHH}

Four related plural types are characterized by internal expansion (vowel insertion or internal reduplication) and the imposition of an H-L-H-H tone pattern. The resulting plurals are always quadrisyllabic.

8.1. Plural type -èC₃anī)^{HLHH}

Form: This type is formed by inserting /ē/ after the second consonant of the base and suffixing -anī after the third (base-final) consonant, e.g., **garkā / garèkanī** 'fenced in garden'.
Comments: This is a small class of some ten words consisting of mostly feminine triconsonantal nouns of the form CaCCV. (The middle -a- in **màlàfā** is epenthetic.) The C₂ is always a liquid. With the exception of **farcè** 'fingernail', whose more usual plural is **farā̀tā**, and the loanword **jaȓkà̀** 'jerry-can', the singulars all end in H-tone /-ā/. Most of the words displaying this plural have alternative plurals in other classes. Examples:

farcè m. / **farètanī**	fingernail	**fàrkā** m./f. / **farèkanī**	illicit sexual partner
farsā f. / **farèsanī**	split kolanut	**garkā** f. / **garèkanī**	fenced in garden
gàȓmā f. / **garèmanī**	large hoe	**garwā** f. / **garèwanī**	four-gallon can
jaȓkà̀ f. / **jaȓèkanī**	jerry-can	**karma(a)** m./f. / **karèmanī**	foot soldier
kwàrgā f. / **kwarèganī**	hole in rock [Kts]	**sàlkā** f. / **salèkanī** (= **salkunà̀**)	hide water bag
màlàfā f. (base //malf-//) / **malèfānī** (= **màlàfū** = **malfunà̀**)		wide-brimmed straw hat	

8.2. Plural type   -èC₃aC₄ī)^{HLHH}

Form: This type is formed by inserting /ē/ after the second consonant of the base and adding -a–ī, after the third consonant, with the fourth consonant of the base serving in the suffixal slot between the vowels, e.g., **malmalā / malèmalī** 'mound of *tuwo*'.
Comments: This is a small class of some eight items. The base on which the plural is built has to have four consonants. Some of the singulars are reduplicated words having the structure CaC-CaCV. A few are CaCVV stems that create reduplicated bases to acquire the requisite number of consonants. A couple are nonreduplicated words with four consonants (one of which has a feminative suffix that is dropped). Examples (complete):

Bàbadè m. (base //badbad-//) /	**Badèbadī** (= **Badāwā**)	Bade psn
Bàbarbarè m. (base //barbar-//) /	**Barèbarī**	Kanuri psn
Bàzazzàgī m. (base //zagzag-//) /	**Zagèzagī**	Zaria psn
malmalā f. (base //malmal-//) /	**malèmalī**	mound of *tuwo*
marmarā f. (base //marmar-//) /	**marèmarī**	laterite [Kts]
raɗā̀ f. (base //raɗraɗ-//) /	**raɗèraɗī**	whispering, rumor
faȓtanyà̀ f. (base **faȓtan-**//) /	**faȓètanī**	hoe
taȓwaɗā f (base //taȓwaɗ-//) /	**taȓèwaɗī**	mudfish

8.2.1. Dual type -**à**C_3VC_4**ī**)^{HLHH}

Reduplicated CVCCVCè words denoting items that occur in pairs (see §**62**:3.3), have alternative forms that are structurally the same as the above plurals but with internal -ā- rather than -ē-, e.g., **fìkàfikī** = **fiffikè** (pl. **fikàfikai**) 'wing'. Although such words as **fikàfikī** are plural in shape (and refer to a pair of items), synchronically they are generally treated as singular—Hausa does not have a dual category—and thus control singular concord.

8.3. Plural type -CVC-...-**akī**)^{HLHH}

Form: These words add the suffix -**akī** plus undergo internal -CVC- reduplication. The H-L-H-H tone melody extends over the resulting quadrisyllabic plural form. The **k.C** abutting sequence that results from the antepenultimate reduplication invariably produces a surface geminate, e.g., **guntū** ⇒ ***guntakī** ⇒ ***guntaktakī** → **guntàttakī** 'fragment'.

Comments: The singulars are (almost) all disyllabic with level H tone and a heavy initial syllable. (One word, which contains the feminative ending, is trisyllabic in the citation form.) The words taking this formation include a number of deverbal nouns. Examples:

aurē m. / **auràrrakī** marriage; **ɓēr̃ā** m. / **ɓēr̃àr̃r̃akī** mouse; **ganyē** m. / **ganyàyyakī** leaf; **gāwā** f. / **gāwàwwakī** corpse; **gōyō** m. / **gōyàyyakī** baby on the back; **guntū** m. / **guntàttakī** stub, fragment; **kāyā** m. / **kāyàyyakī** goods, load, thing; **kurciyā** f. (base //**kurt**-//) / **kurtàttakī** dove; **ƙārā** f. / **ƙāràrrakī** screaming, complaint, legal suit; **mārā** f. / **māràrrakī** (= **màràkū**) calabash scoop; **sūnā** m. / **sūnànnakī** naming ceremony; **tsārā** m./f. / **tsāràrrakī** (= **tsàràikū**) age-mate, thing of same size

°AN: [i] In plurals of the type **garkā** / **garèkanī** 'fenced-in garden', it seems evident that in addition to the -**anī** suffix, there has been an insertion—in this case a long vowel—in antepenultimate position. The formation of the above plurals with the -**akī** suffix, e.g., **sūnā** / **sūnànnakī** 'naming ceremony' is clearly parallel (including the tone), the only difference being that there is reduplicative -CVC- insertion in place of -ē insertion. Once one accepts the analysis of **sūnànnakī** as involving internal -CVC- reduplication, which to me is very compelling, then it becomes natural to analyze such plurals as **cikunkunà** 'bellies' as also involving antepenultimate -CVC- reduplication.

[ii] Examples like **sūnànnakī** obviously use the same -**akī** suffix found in such plurals as **gònàkī** 'farms' (type 7.3). They are grouped here under class 8 on the basis of the quadrisyllabic shape and the distinctive tone pattern.

8.4. Plural type -CVC-...-**a–ī**)^{HLHH}

Form: These words add the affix -**a–ī** plus undergo internal -CVC- reduplication. The C slot between the suffixal vowels is provided by the final consonant of the base. The H-L-H-H tone melody extends over the resulting quadrisyllabic plural form, e.g., **gutsurè** ⇒ ***gutsarī** ⇒ ***gutsartsarī** → **/gutsàttsarī/** 'small fragment'. The syllable-final C resulting from the reduplication undergoes phonologically required rhotacism, assimilation, and gemination rules. If the stem-final C preceding the suffixal -**ī** is a coronal obstruent, it undergoes regular palatalization.

Comments: The singulars taking this suffix are either polysyllabic or disyllabic with at least three base consonants. The feminative ending is dropped before the plural affix is added. Examples:

amaryā f. (base //'**amr**-//) /	**amàrmarī**	bride
gar̃damà f. /	**gar̃dàndamī**	dispute, argument
gutsurè m. /	**gutsàttsarī**	small fragment
kaɗanyà f. (base // **kaɗan**-//) /	**kaɗànɗanī**	shea tree or nut

kuncì m. (base //kumt-//) /	kumàr̃macī (< //kumàtmatī//) (now usu. kuncunà)	cheek
k̃aryā f. /	k̃aràirayī (= [k̃ar̃erayī])	lie
k̃urjī m. /	k̃uràrrajī	pimple, rash
numfāshī m. /	numfàr̃fashī	breath
shāwar̃à f. /	shāwàr̃war̃ī	advice, counsel
tukunyā f. (base //tukwn-//) /	tukwànkwanī	pot
Irregular: nāfilà f. /	nāfìlfilī	supererogatory prayer
sàfā f. (base *//sāfam-//) /	sāfàmfamī	socks, gloves
tsakuwà f. (base *//tsakwn-//) /	tsakwànkwanī	small stone, gravel
dūtsè m. (base //duwts-//) /	duwàr̃watsū	stone

9. CLASS 9: -U/-I)^LH

Grouped together here are two plural types characterized by a suffix consisting simply of a high vowel (-ū or -ī) and an accompanying L-H tone melody.

9.1. Plural type -ū)^LH

Form: This plural type consists of a suffix -ū and an L-H melody spread over the word. Quadrisyllabic singulars containing the -iyā feminative suffix drop the suffix before the -ū is added, e.g., tufānìyā / tùfànū 'screen on doorway'. Trisyllabic singulars with final -yā, on the other hand, retained the suffix as part of the base to which the -ū is added, e.g., kaɗanyà f./ kàɗànyū 'shea-nut tree or fruit'.

Comments: The singulars in this class are typically polysyllabic words ending in /ā/ or, less often, /ē/. This class is much larger than the one taking the sister -ī suffix and the singular forms are phonologically less restricted in terms of tone and syllable weight. A number of words that take the -ī plural also allow -ū as an alternative.

(a) àl'ādà f. / àl'àdū custom, habit, tradition; àwazà f. / àwàzū rib cage; bùkātà f. / bùkàtū need; cìnnākà m / cìnnàkū (= cìnnàkī) black biting ant ; fatalà f. / fàtàlū woman's head-tie; kàtangà f. / kàtàngū (= kàtàngī) large potsherd; katangā f. / kàtàngū wall; kujèrā f. / kùjèrū chair, stool; tàttabàrā f. / tàttàbàrū pigeon

(b) giginyà f. / gìgìnyū deleb-palm; fatanyà f. / fàtànyū hoe; k̃awanyà f. / k̃àwànyū metal ring; tsumangìyā f. / tsùmàngū stick, cane; zangar̃ìyā f. / zàngàr̃nū head of corn

In addition to its use with nonderived words, this plural type is commonly used with nouns of location formed with ma...ā (see §7:2). (Some words of this class form plurals with the -ai suffix; some allow either -ū or -ai as equal alternatives.) Examples:

ma'aikatā f. / mà'àikàtū factory, place of work; mafarautā f. / màfàràutū hunting ground; mak̃ērā f. / màk̃ērū blacksmith shop, smithy, forge; marinā f. / màrìnū dyeing place, dye-pit

In SH, -ū is the regular plural formative with adjectival past participles.

bùɗaɗɗē / bùɗàɗɗū opened; càkùɗaɗɗē / càkùɗàɗɗū entangled, mixed, confused; dàkakkē / dàkàkkū pounded; ɗaurarrē / ɗauràrrū tied, imprisoned; gàsasshē / gàsàssū roasted

> ΔDN: In WH dialects, plurals of adjectival past particles make use of the suffix -ī (§9.2) instead of -ū, e.g., bùɗaɗɗē / bùɗàɗɗī 'opened'; ɗaurarrē / ɗauràrrī 'tied'; gàsasshē / gàsàsshī 'grilled'; zàmnannē / zàmnànnī 'settled'.

A few words with the -ū suffix undergo internal antepenultimate -CVC- reduplication as well, e.g.,

gàjērē adj. (m.) /	gàjàjjḕrū = gàjàrjḕrū	short (= gàjḕrū)
màganā̀ f. /	màgàngànū	speech
nagàri adj. (m.) /	nàgàrgàrū	good
rìgimā̀ f. /	rìgìngìmū	quarrel, dispute
wàhalā̀ f. /	wàhàlhàlū	trouble

There are a just few disyllabic words that take the -ū suffix, all of which have a heavy initial syllable, e.g.,

d̃anyē m. / d̃ànyū   raw, unripe; shaidā̀ m./f. / shàidū   witness, evidence; shēgè m. / shḕgū   bastard; tsabgā̀ f. / tsàbgū (usu. tsabgōgī)   cane, rod

9.2. *Plural type* -ī)^{LH}

Form: This plural type consists of a suffix -ī and an L-H melody spread over the word. In most cases, the feminative suffix is dropped before the -ī is added.

Comment: The singulars are typically polysyllabic words that have an initial L tone, a heavy penultimate syllable, and final /ā/ or /ō/, e.g., kàbēwā̀ / kàbèyī 'pumpkin'. Some singulars with a feminative suffix, which is dropped in the plural, have a base-final front vowel. The base-final consonant of words taking this plural type tends to be either a velar, a nasal, /r/, /f/, or /w/ (again a strange and unnatural class of consonants). (Note that /w/ automatically palatalizes to /y/ when followed by /ī/.) There are some thirty words attested with this plural type. Examples:

(a) ɓarāwò m. / ɓàrày ī   thief; cìnnākā̀ m. / cìnnàkī (= cìnnàkū)   black biting ant; gàyaunā f. / gàyàunī   small farm; kàtangā f. / kàtàngī (= kàtàngū)   large potsherd; màkāhò (base //màkāf-//) m. / màkàfī   blind psn; tàbarmā f. / tàbàrmī   mat; tàurārò m. = tàurārùwā f. / tàurārī   star
(b) gàbàruwā f. / gàbàrī   acacia tree; gàràmbuwā f. / gàràmbī   children's grass armlet; ràhōnìyā f. / ràhònī   small clay corn bin; tùfānìyā f. / tùfànī   mat doorway screen (= tùfànū); tùmfāfìyā f. / tùmfàfī   milkseed shrub

The plurals ƙàttī 'huge' and gwàɗɗī 'mares' are formed by adding the suffix -ī to a plural stem of the -Gā)^{HLH} type (§4.1). In the former case this -Gā plural is synchronically attested; in the latter, it is historically postulated.

ƙātò (pl. ƙàttā) / ƙàttī (not **ƙàccī)	huge
gōɗìyā (base //gōɗ-//) (presumed pl. *gwàɗɗā) / gwàɗɗī	mare

10. CLASS 10: -V_α ⇒ -V_β

Grouped together here are four small plural types characterized by final vowel replacement or ablaut. These four types have been treated as variants of a single class partially on the basis of the canonical shape of their singulars, partially on the basis of tone, partially on the basis of presumed historical factors, partially on the basis of convention, and partially on the basis of linguistic intuition.

10.1. *Plural type* -V ⇒ (-ū)^{H}

Ten disyllabic H-L words with the shape CāCV (where the underlying final vowel is /ī/, /ē/, or /ā/) replace the final nonback, nonrounded vowel of the stem by the high back-rounded vowel -ū. The singulars generally have H-L tone—one word has L-H as an alternative. The plurals all have H-H tone. Examples (complete):

fātà f. /	fātū	skin, hide		lāyà f. /	lāyū	amulet
māshì m. /	māsū	spear		māyè m. /	māyū	witch
nāmà m.	nāmū	animal		rāmì m. /	rāmū	hole
sāyè m. /	sāyū	root [WH]		yātsà m./	yātsū	finger
yàyà (usu. yàya) m. or f. /	yāyū	older sibling				

◊HN: [i] The singulars were originally restricted to words ending in /ā/ or /ì/. The final /ē/ in **māyè** and **sāyè** is a reflex of an earlier *-**ì**, the vowel lowering probably being due to dissimilation to the preceding /y/ semivowel.

[ii] The irregular surface pair **sānìyā** f. (base //**sānì**-// + the feminine suffix) / **shānū** (with inexplicable initial **sh** instead of **s**) 'cow / cattle' *could* reflect this plural type, but this is not certain.

Two singular words with a different canonical shape, namely with a light first syllable and all H tone, undergo CVC- reduplication in addition to the suffix:

farī m. / **farfarū** (1) vowel in Arabic script, (2) used in **maƙèrin farī** / **maƙèran farfarū** silversmith (cf. **farī** / **faràrē** white (with the -āCē)^{HLH} suffix)

baƙī m. /**babbaƙū** (1) consonant in Arabic script, (2) used in **maƙèrin baƙī** / **maƙèran babbaƙū** blacksmith (cf. **baƙī** / **baƙàƙē** black (with the -āCē)^{HLH} suffix)

°AN: Although these two examples have been included here on the basis of the final -**ū** and H-H tone, it is not certain that they truly belong (or historically belonged?) to this plural class.

10.2. Plural type -V ⇒ (-ī)^{H}

These plurals are formed by replacing stem-final /ō/ or, less often, /ā/, i.e., a non-front vowel, by the high front vowel -**ī**, which has H tone. Because these plurals make use of a suffix -**ī**, they look on the surface as if they could be grouped with those in class 9, which consists primarily of trisyllabic words, e.g., **tàurārò** / **tàurārī** 'star'. Such a grouping has the disadvantage of separating these -**ī** plurals from what I feel are its sister plurals, namely the disyllabic plurals that end in -**ū**, -**ai**, and -**ā** and which also seem to reflect a vowel ablaut process. I have thus included these -**ī** plurals in class 10. Since, apart from one problematic case, the singulars all have L-H tone, the plurals also appear with L-H. With one exception (which may not properly belong to this class), all of the singulars have the canonical shape CāCā or CāCō. In two cases, alternative singulars exist with and without the feminine suffix, and in one case only the stem with the feminine suffix occurs. This plural type is limited to some ten basic disyllabic words. Examples (complete):

bàƙō m. /	bàƙī	stranger, guest	fàrā f. /	fàrī	locust, grasshopper
kwàɗō m. /kwàɗī		frog	kàzā f./	kàjī	hen
ƙwàrō m./ ƙwàrī		insect, bug	bāwà m. /	bāyī	slave (sg. irregular tone)
màzō m. / màjī		antelope			
tsàkō m. = tsàkuwā f. / tsàkī		chick			
zàbō m. = zàbuwā f. / zàbī		guinea-fowl			
Irregular: gàrkuwā (< *gàrkō) / gàrkī		shield			

°AN: [i]It is hard to determine whether the suffixes in class 10 should be treated as tone non-integrating (as I have done) or as tone-integrating. This is because the plurals with H-H surface tone (type 10.1) all derive from singulars with initial H-tone, whereas the plurals with L-H tone (type 10.2) derive from singulars with initial L-tone, e.g., (**rām-**)^H + (-**ū**)^H ⇒ **rāmū** (H-H) 'holes', *or* (**rām-**) + -**ū**)^H ⇒ **rāmū** (all H); (**kwàɗ-**)^L + (- ɪ)^H ⇒ **kwàɗî** (L-H) 'frog', *or* (**kwàɗ-**) + - ɪ)^{LH} ⇒ **kwàɗî** (L-H). The example **bāwà** m. / **bāyī** 'slave' (not * **bàyī** with an L-H tone melody) does, however, support the analysis of the tone as being non-integrating.

[ii] I have included **bāwà** m. / **bāyī** 'slave' as a tonally irregular member of this plural type 10.2. Another possibility would be to assign this example to type 10.1 on the basis of the tone and treat the final -ɪ instead of the expected -**ū** as the unexplained deviance.

The words that now end in -ō originally ended in *-**ū**, the vowel lowering being conditioned by the preceding long /ā/ (Newman 1990a). The original *-**ū** ⇒ -ɪ plural formation (now -ō ⇒ -ɪ) is the mirror image of the -ɪ ⇒ -**ū** ablaut change.

10.3. Plural type -V ⇒ (-**ai**)^H

In this type, the final vowel of the stem, which is (or was) a high vowel, is replaced by the diphthong -**ai**. The plurals all have H-H tone. This is an archaic plural formation that synchronically applies only to a small number of basic disyllabic nouns, all of which have a light first syllable and H-L tone. The feminative suffix on these words is dropped when the plural is added. Examples (complete):

birì m. / **birai**	monkey	**cinyà** f. (< *cinì) / **cinai**	thigh
wutsiyà f. (< *wutsì) / **wutsai**	tail	**zumù** m. / **zumai**	close friend, relation

◊HN: This is an archaic plural formation that many modern Hausa speakers no longer use. Instead of the plural forms given above, one generally finds **cinyōyī** and **wutsiyōyī**, with the productive -**ōCī** formative, or **bìrai** and **zùmai** with the tone pattern of the common -**ai**)^{LH} suffix. Historically the very common -**ai**)^{LH} plural formative and the (-**ai**)^H ablaut ending could possibly be related, but they may very well have distinct origins.

The plural of the word **kibiyà** 'arrow' (< *kibì) is **kibau**. (The regular **kibiyōyī** is also very common.) Because this is the only example in the entire language of -**au** appearing as a plural suffix, it is reasonable to hypothesize that the original plural was **kibai**, a form that is in fact attested as a dialectal variant, and that the change from **kibai** to **kibau** was the result of a sporadic (and unexplained) change in the form of the final diphthong. Present-day SH speakers tend to pronounce the word as **kìbau**, with L-H tone, parallel to **bìrai** and **zùmai**.

10.4. Plural type -V ⇒ -**ā**)^H

These plurals replace the final vowel of the stem by -**ā** and impose an all H tone pattern. In the cases in which the singular already ends in -**ā**, the tone pattern serves as the distinctive marker of plurality. Like the accompanying plural types in this class, this is an archaic plural formation that synchronically is restricted to a small number of basic disyllabic nouns. Examples:

ařnè m. /	**ařnā**	pagan	**ɗîyā** f. daughter / **ɗiya**	children [WH]
kūsù m. /	**kūsā** (= **kūsàyē**)	rat	**màtā** f. / **mātā**	wife
mijì m. /	**mazā**	husband /men, males		

◊HN: [i] Although the plural **mātā**, synchronically serves as the plural of **màcè** 'woman', morphologically it derives from **màtā** by the application of this formation rule.

[ii] The **i/a** alternation reflected in the initial vowel of **mijì** / **mazā** could be a retention of an old morphological feature found elsewhere in Chadic; but it is probably just a case of **mijì** being derived from ***mazì** by a sporadic vowel assimilation rule.

Additional examples of this formation are found in WH. In SH, these plural forms have been reinterpreted as singulars, which now have their own plurals. Examples:

dumè m. [WH] /	**dumā**	gourd (sg. in SH, with pl. **dumằmē**)
gijì m. [WH] /	**gidā**	house (sg. in SH, with pl. **gidằjē**)
karè m. [WH] /	**karā**	cornstalk (sg. in SH, with pl. **karằrē**)
ƙujè m. [WH] /	**ƙudā**	fly (sg. in SH, with pl. **ƙudằjē**)

The word **ruwā** 'water', which is usually treated as a singular in SH, also reflects this H-H **ā**-final plural form.

◊HN: On the basis of comparative evidence, one can hypothesize that the original plural suffix may have been ***-an)^H**, i.e., one would have had singular/plural pairs like **dumè** / ***duman**. (Note that the historical loss of final nasals in Hausa was regular (Schuh 1976).) The existence of plural suffixes of the form **-Vn** is well attested in related Chadic languages, cf., for example, the following citations from Kanakuru (Newman 1974: 83–84), where one also finds a fixed H-H tone melody: **ɓili** / **ɓilan** 'horn', **miyò** / **mishan** 'co-wife', **kom** / **komen** 'mouse', **dawà** / **dawin** 'granary'. If this analysis is correct, then from a historical perspective, this plural type with the tone-integrating suffix ***-an)^H** should not be grouped with H-tone **-ū**, **-ī**, and **-ai** ablaut-type suffixes.

11. CLASS 11: -āwā)$^{LH \sim HH}$

Form: These plurals use a suffix -**āwā** with two different tone melodies. There is an L-H pattern that only occurs with lexically specific trisyllabic plurals having a heavy initial syllable. (There is also one reduplicated quadrisyllabic form.) All other plurals with the -**āwā** suffix, namely, quadrisyllabic (or longer) words, trisyllabic words with a light initial syllable, or trisyllabic words with a heavy initial syllable but not lexically specified for the L-H pattern, have all H tone.

Comments: This is the standard plural formation for ethnonymic nouns formed with the prefix **bà-** (examples in (a)). (Note that the **bà-** prefix is dropped before the suffix is added.) It is also used with a small number of non-ethnonymic nouns referring to categories of people, some of which have other plurals (examples in (b)). Examples:

(a) [i] **Bàhaushè** / **Hàusàwā**	Hausa
Bàtūrè / **Tūrằwā** = **Tūrāwā**	European
bàdūkù / **dùkằwā**	leather worker
bàgidājè / **gìdằdằwā**	rustic, homebody
[ii] **bà'askarè** / **askarāwā**	soldier
Bàbōlè / **Bōlāwā**	Bole psn
Bàkanò / **Kanāwā**	Kano psn
Bàyaɾabè / **Yaɾabāwā**	Yoruba psn
bàzawàrā / **zawarāwā**	widow, divorcee
(b) [i] **dattījò** m. / **dàttằwā** (= **dàttìjai**)	gentleman
kūrì m. / **kùrằwā**	young pupil
gaɾdì m. / **gàɾdằwā**	advanced Koranic student, snake charmer
Gwāri (= **Bàgwārī**) m. / **Gwàɾằwā**	Gwari psn

[ii] **ànnabì** m. / **annabāwā**   prophet
dògarì m. / **dōgarāwā**   emir's bodyguard
kìlākì f. / **kilākāwā**   modern-day prostitute
Mūsā m . / **Mūsāwā**   followers of Musa
talàkà m. / **talakāwā**   poor psn, commoner
yārì m. / **yārāwā**   chief jailer

°AN: Although -āwā can be described synchronically as a plural inflectional suffix, it is essentially a derivational suffix indicating a community or a class of people belonging to a common group. It is found commonly, for example, in the names of towns or quarters, e.g., **Amaryāwā** (a village name) (< **amaryā** 'bride'), **Yařīmāwā** (a town name) (< **yàřīmà** 'prince'), **Tsanyāwā** (name of a village) (< **tsanyà** 'cricket'), **Daurāwā** (name of a quarter in Kano) (< the town **Dàurā**). Note that toponyms with -āwā are feminine singular rather then plural, cf. **Mūsāwā** f. (a town name) vs. **Mūsāwā** pl. 'supporters/followers of Musa'.

12. CLASS 12: x 2 (REDUP)

Form: These plurals are formed by complete reduplication of the full singular form, including the tone and final vowel.

Comments: This is not a traditional plural formation pattern in Hausa. Full reduplication as a native device is used for distributives, e.g., **gàrī gàrī** 'from town to town', and for pluralization of ideophones, e.g., **shafal / shafal-shafal** 'weightless, very light'. With common nouns, however, this formation is not commonplace, being used only with quite recent loanwords from English, and only a small number of these. Many words listed in earlier works as forming plurals by full reduplication now use some other, more native, plural formation, e.g., **àkàwu / àkàwu-àkàwu** 'clerk', now usually **akāwunà**; **kwâs / kwâs-kwâs** 'course', now commonly **kwàsàkwàsai**. Examples:

bòyi m. / **bòyi-bòyi**   houseboy, cook-steward
cōcì m. / **cōcì-cōcì**   church
en'è f. / **en'è-en'è**   native authority (N.A.)
jōjì m. / **jōjì-jōjì**   judge
kanàř m. / **kanàř-kanàř**   colonel
nâs m. or f. / **nâs-nâs**   nurse
sìkêt m. / **sìkêt-sìkêt**   skirt

ΔDN: Pluralization by full reduplication is apparently not used in the francophone Hausa areas with loanwords from French. To the extent that plurals are used at all for recently borrowed words, one gets other forms, e.g., **bîk / bikkōkī** (not ****bîk-bîk**) 'ballpoint pen', **pîl / pillunà** (not ****pîl-pîl**) 'battery'. It is possible that the fully reduplicated plurals found in SH came into Nigerian Hausa along with English loanwords borrowed via Yoruba or Pidgin English.

The only native word that looks to be a fully reduplicated plural is **'yā'yā** 'children', pl. of **ɗā** 'son' and **'yā** 'daughter'. This in fact is not a reduplicated form of the singular word **'yā** 'daughter', as it appears on the surface, but rather is a doubling (serving an overt characterization function) of the homophonous plural form **'yā** 'children'. (The nonreduplicated plural form **'yā** is still used in certain constructions such as compounds and diminutives.) Historically the singular and plural words were tonally distinct as they still are in WH, i.e., **ɗìyā** 'daughter' had L-H tone whereas the plural **ɗiyā** had H-H tone. With the contraction of the **ɗiy**- sequence into /'y/, the tonal contrast was lost, thereby stimulating the secondary reduplication.

13. CLASS 13: -e)^{LH} x 2 (REDUP)

Form: These plurals (sometimes termed "pseudoplurals of diversity") add short -e to the base, impose an L-H tone melody, and then undergo full reduplication, e.g., tādî̀ / tàɗe-tàɗe 'conversation/chatting'. (Note that the tone is assigned to the stem before the reduplication.) In many cases one uses an expanded base made up of the nominal root plus -(a)c- or -anc-, which is the same as the -ant verbalizer suffix (with the palatal /c/ conditioned by the front vowel), e.g., zàmba / zàmbàce-zàmbàce 'fraud, swindling'.

Comments: This morphological construction is the same as that used in forming frequentatives from verbs (see chap. **29**), i.e., most words of this shape function as noncount dynamic nouns, e.g., sunā̀ bù̀she-bù̀she 'They are playing music' (< bū̀sà 'to blow'). A few, however, constitute plurals of nondynamic common nouns, e.g., tār̂ihî̀ / tàr̂ihe-tàr̂ihe 'history'. When functioning as frequentatives, these reduplicated forms are often treated syntactically as singulars. In the examples below, however, the forms constitute normal plural nouns with plural concord just like common nouns containing any of the other plural affixes (including suffixes that occur as alternative forms with these same words). Examples:

cîwò̀ m. / cîwàce-cîwàce illness; dàbār̂à̀ f. / dàbàr̂ce-dàbàr̂ce (= dàbàr̂ū) trick, plan; dàshē / dàshe-dàshe seedling; ginî̀ m. / gìne-gìne building; habaicî̀ m. / hàbàice-hàbàice innuendo; ir̂î̀ m. / ìre-ìre kind, type; kwanā̀ f. / kwàne-kwàne corner, curve; shirî̀ m. / shìrye-shìrye radio/TV program (cf. shiryà̀ 'prepare'); tàllà m. / tàllàce-tàllàce hawking goods for sale, advertisement; tsir̂ò̀ m. / tsìre-tsìre (= tsìrrai) a sprout; wàhalà̀ f. / wàhàlce-wàhàlce (= wahalōlī) trouble

14. CLASS 14: x 2)$^{H\text{-}L}$ (REDUP)

This class consists of fully reduplicated ideophonic plurals in which the tone specification of the two segmentally identical halves is not the same. There are two subtypes.

14.1. Plural type -ā̀ x 2)$^{H\text{-}L}$ (Redup)

Form: This plural type suffixes the vowel -ā̀ to the base and then undergoes full reduplication and the imposition of an H-L tone melody, e.g., fir̂ɗî̀ = fir̂ɗēɗè (base //fir̂ɗ-//) / fir̂ɗā̀-fîr̂ɗà̀ 'huge' (e.g., a horse).

Comments: This is the regular plural formation for "type A" and "type B" augmentative adjectives (see §**11**:1), i.e., those formed by -I)^H or -ēCē)^{HL}, respectively. Examples:

bundumī = bundumēmè / bundumā̀-bùndùmà̀	fat-bellied
ɓangwalī = ɓangwalēlè / ɓangwalā̀-ɓàngwàlà̀	large and round (e.g., kolanut)
mākēkè / mākā̀-màkà̀	expansive
tabɗēɗè / tabɗā̀-tàbɗà̀	huge
tankamēmè / tankamā̀-tànkàmà̀	massive (e.g., mountain)

14.2. Plural type x 2)$^{H\text{-}L}$ (Redup)

Form: This plural type is marked by a fully reduplicated stem over which an H-L tone melody is imposed. The canonical shape for the stem is CVCVV, where the vowels in both syllables are often, but not always, identical in quality.

Comments: This form characterizes a phonologically fixed class of ideophonic adjectives (see §**35**:1.2.11), most of which are inherently plural and do not have corresponding singular counterparts. (What we really have here is a canonical shape characteristic of a specific class of plural words rather than a plural formative as such.) The syntactic plurality of these forms is shown by the fact that they normally occur with plural nouns. When they occur with singular nouns, as is possible, semantic plurality/multiplicity is still connoted. Examples:

dìɓī-dìɓī adj.	plump (of small things)	**fàtō-fàtò̃** adj.	large and broad (e.g., leaves, ears)
ƙwadā-ƙwàdā̀ adj.	large (esp. kolanuts)	**tsàlā-tsàlà̀** adj.	long and skinny (esp. legs)
zàƙē-zàƙè̃ adj.	unsuitably long, out of proportion		

15. CLASS 15: CiCī x 2)$^{H\text{-}H}$

Form: These plural forms consist of **CiCī** light-heavy stems that are completely reduplicated. The overall tone pattern is H-H.

Comment: These plurals correspond to partially reduplicated diminutive adjectives (see §11:3) characterized by three long vowels. Some of these items occur only in the plural without corresponding singulars. Examples:

(a) **mìnīnì̃** adj. /	**mìnī-mìnī**	small (of food items)
sìrīrì̃ adj. /	**sìrī-sìrī**	very thin, skinny
	gìɗī-gìɗī	narrow, skimpy (pl. only)
	yìsī-yìsī	tiny, of teeth (pl. only)

16. MISCELLANEOUS

The following are plurals that have not been assigned to any of the general classes described, either because the formations are lexically restricted to the occasional word, because there are small irregularities involved, because suppletion is involved, or because the morphological analysis is problematic. Examples:

idò̃ m.	**idằnū**	eye
kâi m. head	**kānū**	headlines (cf. **kāwunà̀** heads)
sâ m. ox, **sānìyā** f. cow	**shānū**	bovines

◊HN: The plural **shānū** 'bovines' could represent **sâ** plus an archaic plural suffix **-nū** (with unexplained palatalization of the initial /s/); but it could equally reflect the operation of the **ī** ⟹ **ū** ablaut plural (type 10.1) on a stem *sānì (synchronically occurring with the feminative ending) in which /n/ is indeed part of the lexical item. (In either analysis, the palatalization of the initial consonant remains unexplained.)

ƙàramī, ƙànƙanè̃ adj.	**ƙanānà̀** (= **ƙânƙanà̀** = **ƙânƙanānà̀**)	little, small
ƙwaryā f.	**ƙôrai**	calabash
lēɓè m.	**lèɓằtū** (usu. **lâɓɓā**)	lip
tsûmmā m.	**tsummōkarà̀**	rag
tufà̀ f.	**tufāfì̃**	clothes
bàbba adj.	**mânyā** (= **mânya-mânya**)	big, adult

◊HN: [i] The plural suffix **-tū** in **lèɓằtū** is totally inexplicable. The plural **ƙôrai** probably derives from *ƙôràyē from a base *//ƙōr-// without the **-yā** feminative suffix. The only other word that appears to reflect the plural pattern seen in **tufāfì̃** is **kìrārì̃** 'praise epithet', now a masculine singular word, presumably derived from **kìrà̀** 'calling' (Russell Schuh, personal communication).

[ii] In the suppletive pair **bàbba / mânyā**, it is not the plural form that is strange. The F-H final-ā shape is plural-like (cf. class 4) and the word has likely cognates in other Chadic languages, cf. Kanakuru **manjò** 'old', Karekare **mayuwa** 'big'. It is the singular with its geminate obstruent and its short final vowel that is out of place and in need of a proper historical explanation.

wâ m. elder brother, **yâ** f. elder sister, **yàya = yāyà** elder sibling / **yayyē** (= **yāyū**) elder siblings **yārinyà** f. / **'yammātā** girl

The word **yârà** 'children' can refer either to boys (sg. **yárò**) or to boys and girls (sg. **yārinyà**). The word **'yammātā** refers strictly to girls (lit. little women). It is a fused form made up of the diminutive marker **'yan** plus **mātā** 'women'.

The plural of the kinship terms **ɗā** 'son' and **'yā** 'daughter' is **'yā'yā**. When used with a linker as a diminutive marker or an '-er/-man' compound formative, **ɗan** and **'yar** employ a nonreduplicated plural form **'yan**.

ɗā m. son, **'yā** f. daughter / **'yā'yā** children
ɗan m., **'yar** f. / **'yan** small (diminutive)
e.g., **'yar gàjèrìyar yārinyà** a wee short girl / **'yan gàjàjjèrun yârā** wee short children
cf. **'yā'yan kanàr** the colonel's children
ɗā m., **'yā** f. / **'yan** compound formative
e.g., **ɗan sàndā** policeman / **'yan sàndā** policemen

ΔDN: In WH, the feminine and plural words for 'daughter/children' have the forms **ɗìyā** and **ɗiyā**, respectively. The diminutive forms, on the other hand, are identical to those in SH. Thus in WH one can contrast **ɗiyā mātā** 'female children' vs. **'yammātā** 'girls' (lit. little women).

17. ASSOCIATIVE PLURAL su

The pronominals 'who?' and 'so-and-so' prepose a clitic **su** to indicate plurality. This **su** is identical to the third person plural pronoun, e.g., **tā kāmà su** 'She caught them.' (In the following examples, I have followed standard orthography in writing **su** as a separate word; from a linguistic perspective it would be preferable to attach it to the following word by means of a hyphen.) Examples:

wà(nē nè)	who?	**su wà(nē nè)**	who? (pl.)
wàyê	who?	**su wàyê**	who? (pl.)
wānè	so-and-so (m.)	**su wānè**	so-and-sos (pl.)
wancè	so-and-so (f.)	**su wancè**	so-and-sos (pl.)

°AN: Semantically, there is a distinction between **su wānè** 'so-and-sos' (= John Does) and **su wancè** 'so-and-sos' (= Jane Does). Grammatically however, they both take normal plural concord because Hausa does not distinguish gender in the plural.

Another use of the associative plural **su** is to indicate 'and others of the same ilk' (i.e., 'et al.' and 'etc.'), e.g.,

su Mūsā sun dāwō dà sāfe	Musa and the others returned in the morning.
su Maryàm dà Jummai sunà sôn rawā	Maryam and Jummai et al. like to dance.
munà nēman su bàrēwā	We are looking for gazelles, etc.

18. HOMOPHONOUS PLURALS

Plural affixes are added to a lexical base, which in most cases is the singular word minus its final vowel and tone. Because distinct words with different tones and different final vowels may have the same segmental bases, resulting plural forms are sometimes homophonous, e.g.,

singular			*plural (of both singulars)*
dāgì	digger,	dằgī feline paw	dāgunằ
kàntī	store,	kantù block of salt or sesame	kantunằ
kwarì	valley,	kwàrī quiver	kwarūruwằ
kògī	river,	kògō a cavity	kōgunằ
kōmī	dugout canoe,	kōmā small fishing net	kōmằyē
kàtangằ	large potsherd,	katangā wall	kàtàngū

Although the form of the plural overrides distinctions in the singular, the *choice* of the plural type is based on phonological properties of the singular word as such, and thus one often gets distinct plurals of minimally distinct words even though the intermediate base forms are identical, e.g.,

a. gōrằ	cane (base //gōr-//)	gōrōrī
b. gòrā	large gourd (base //gōr-//)	gōrunằ
a. tūrū	a drum (base //tūr-//)	tūrằyē
b. tūrù	log/stocks (base //tūr-//)	tūrunằ
a. hantằ	liver (base //hant-//)	hantōcī
b. hancì	nose (base //hant-//)	hantunằ (= hancunằ)

19. ALTERNATIVE PLURALS

The choice of the plural type to be used is only partially predictable from the form and class of the singular. Words of the form CVCVV with H-H tone and a light first syllable almost all have corresponding -āCē plurals; similarly, disyllabic feminine words ending in -ā with H-L tone can be expected to have -ōCī plurals. In other cases, however, the form of the singular is consistent with two or more plural types. As a result, individual lexical items are attested with alternative plurals, the choice being dialectally, idiolectally, or idiosyncratically determined. The alternative plurals can be separated into three groups. The first group includes those that could be considered essentially equivalent alternatives.

dilā	dilằlē = dilōlī	jackal
ɓēřā	ɓēřằyē = ɓēřàřřakī	rat
dāgùmī	dāgumằ = dằgùmai	leather amulet
guntū	guntāyē = guntàttakī	stub
hannū	hannằyē = hannuwằ	arm
kōřè	kōřằyē = kôřřā	green
kwabò	kwabbunằ = kwàbbai	penny, kobo
kwâs	kwâs-kwâs = kwàsằkwàsai	course
ƙawanyā	ƙawanyōyī = ƙàwànyū	small ring
harshè	harussằ = harsunằ	tongue, language
jìgāwā	jìgằyī = jìgằwū	sandy soil
lēɓè	lâɓɓā = lēɓunằ	lip

shìgifà	shìgìfū = shìgìfai = shigifōfī	room with arched roof
taṝdè	taṝàdā = taṝdunà	head ring for carrying loads
tàwadà	tàwàdū = tawadōjī	ink
tēbùṝ	tēbuṝà = tēbuṝōṝī	table
tsabgà	tsàbgū = tsabgōgī	cane, switch
tudù	tûddā = tùddai = tuddunà	hill
wàhalà	wàhàlhàlū = wàhalce-wàhalce = wahalōlī	trouble

In the following examples, the alternative plurals relate to alternative forms of the singular:

hoe (i) **faṝtanyà** / **faṝètanī** (= **fàṝtànyū**)   (ii) **fatanyà** / **fàtànyū**
pot (i) **tukunyà** (H-H-L) / **tukwànkwanī**   (ii) **tukunyā** (H-H-H) / **tukwànē**

The second group includes alternatives where one of the choices (given first below) is "archaic" in relation to a newer plural belonging to a more productive, overt class. (The dividing line between this group and the previous is not clear-cut and discrete.) These alternatives are particularly common in the case of words having undergone Klingenheben's Law, such that the archaic plural requires that one recover a historically lost consonant.

būzū	bugàjē = būzàyē	sheepskin mat; Tuareg
ɓaunā	ɓakằnē = ɓaunằyē	buffalo
cūnà	ciwunnà [Kts] = cūnōnī	gusset
gōɗìyā	gwàɗɗī = gōɗiyōyī	mare
gwaurō	gwagwằrē = gwaurằyē	unmarried psn
kwībī̀	kwiyàɓā = kwībunà	fat on side of body
rījìyā	riyōjī (= rigōjī) = rījiyōyī	well
zūcìyā	zukằtā = zūciyōyī	heart

The third group includes a small number of cases where different plurals of the same singular item have different (but related) meanings.

baƙī black / [i] **baƙằƙē** black (pl.); [ii] **babbaƙū** (a) consonants in Arabic script; (b) used in **maƙèrin babbaƙū** blacksmiths (pl. of **maƙèrin baƙī**)
dūtsè stone, mountain / [i] **duwàtsū** stones, mountains; [ii] **duwàṝwatsū** small stones, gravel
farī white / [i] **farằrē** white (pl.); [ii] **farfarū** (a) vowels in Arabic script; (b) used in **maƙèran farfarū** silversmiths (pl. of **maƙèrin farī**)
kuncì cheek / [i] **kuncunà** cheeks, sides of the face; [ii] **kumằtū** fleshy part of the cheek (sg. or pl.)
ƙafà foot, leg / [i] **ƙafằfū** one's own feet/legs; [ii] **ƙafāfuwà** feet of an animal when used as food
magājìyā (a) female heir (counterpart of **magàjī** m.); (b) head of the prostitutes; (c) [Skt] elder sister / [i] **magàdā** heirs (m. or f.), but not the other two meanings; [ii] **magàjiyōyī** pl. of all three meanings
sūnā name; naming ceremony / [i] **sūnằyē** names; [ii] **sūnànnakī** naming ceremonies

20. DOUBLE PLURALS

A common feature of Hausa is to have "double plurals," i.e., plurals built not on the singular but on a plural stem. Sometimes, the double plurals simply constitute alternative plural forms and do not differ in meaning from the morphologically simpler plurals; but in many cases people feel that the double plurals are more marked and connote extra plurality. Examples:

dàwầkai	horses < **dawākī** pl. of **dōkì** m.
ɗuwaiwayầ	buttocks < **ɗuwàiwai** pl. of **ɗuwai** m. [dv]
ƙafāfuwầ	feet < **ƙafầfū** pl. of **ƙafầ** f.
ƙàttī	huge < **ƙâttā** pl. of **ƙātồ** m.
ƙirāruwầ	twigs, kindling < **ƙirầrē** pl. (sg. not attested)
mazầjē	men < **mazā** pl. of **mijì** m.
mātầyē	women < **mātā** pl of **mầtā** f. wife (also pl. of **màcè** f. woman, female)
shānànnakī	bovines < **shānū** pl. of **sâ** m. ox, bull and/or **sānìyā** f. cow

21. ERSTWHILE PLURALS

There has been a historical drift in Hausa whereby plural forms have come to be treated as singulars. In some cases, the original singular has to be postulated on internal or comparative grounds. In these instances we are not always sure that the form in question was originally a plural. In other cases, the singular is still attested as an alternative form or as a dialect variant. Most of the reinterpreted singulars, including a number of words ending in -ā, are masculine. With certain items, there is some degree of indeterminacy whether they are grammatically sg. or pl. Once these erstwhile plurals are indeed reinterpreted as singulars, they are available for pluralization using the full range of plural formatives. Examples:

dumā m.	gourd, formerly pl. of **dumè** (still used in [WH]) (current SH pl. **dumầmē**)
gidā m.	house, home, formerly pl. of **gijì** (still used in [WH]) (current SH pl. **gidầjē**)
haƙarƙarī m.	rib(s) < ? (current SH pl. **hàƙarƙàrai**)
haƙōrī m.	tooth, formerly pl. of *haƙrè, cf. **haurè** tusk (current SH pl. **haƙồrā**)
hannū m.	arm < *ham-nu? (current SH pl. **hannuwầ**)
hayāƙī m.	smoke < ?
itàcē m.	tree, wood, formerly pl. of **icè** wood (current SH pl. **itātuwầ**)
karā m.	cornstalk, formerly pl. of **karè** (still used in [WH] (current SH pl. **karầrē**)
kầraukī m.	slender post for fence < ?
karōfī m.	dye-pit area < *karfè ?
kirārì m.	praise epithet, formerly pl. of **kirầ** calling ?
kiyāshī m./pl.	type of small ant < ? (current SH pl. **kìyầsai**)
kûnnē m.	ear, formerly pl. of *kum- ? (current SH pl. **kunnuwầ**)
kurầdā f.	chopper, small axe < ? (current SH pl. **kurầdū**)
ƙudā m.	fly, formerly pl. of **ƙujè** (still used in [WH]) (current SH pl. **ƙudầjē**)
Mùsùlmī m./pl.	a Muslim (current SH pl. **Mùsùlmai**)
ruwā m./pl.	water, rain (current (restricted) SH pl. **ruwầyē**)
tàkàlmī m	shoe, formerly pl. of **tàkalmè** (still used. in [WH]) (current SH pl. **tākalmầ**)
tàttầsai m./pl.	pepper(s) < ?
tsûmmā m.	rag < ? (current (rare) SH pl. **tsummōkarầ**)
tufàfī m.	clothing, formerly pl. of **tufầ** garment
washèwashī m.	cracks on bottom of cooking pot < ?
zabōrī m.	string(s) at top of bucket < *zabrè ?

A few feminine singulars have the shape CâGGā (where the GG represents geminate consonants). Because this canonical pattern is extremely rare except in the case of plurals formed with the -Gā)^{HLH} suffix (see §4.1), it is likely that these words are erstwhile plurals, although there may be some other historical explanation. Examples (complete):

câssā f.   bow-leggedness; ƙâbbā f.   syphilis; ƙwâllā f.   tears; râggā f.   rags, ragged garment
(current SH pl. raggōgī); shâddā f.   pit latrine   (current SH pl. shaddōdī)

22. SINGULAR FORMS WITH PLURAL MEANING AND CONCORD

22.1. *Words without morphological plurals*

In spite of the large number of plural formations available, many nouns do not have an overt
morphological plural form. (In some cases, the dictionaries list a plural, but it is seldom used.) Rather,
like the English word *sheep*, the plurality is indicated by plural concord, e.g., **mangwàr̃ò gōmà ɗîn sun
ruɓè** 'The ten mangoes (they) have become rotten'; cf. **mangwàr̃ò yā ruɓè** 'The mango (it) has become
rotten' or 'The mangoes (as a collection) have become rotten.' Nouns without corresponding
morphological plurals include, but are not restricted to, the following. (The gloss is given in the
singular only but is to be read as 'pineapple(s)', etc.)

àbàr̃bā f.   pineapple; àgàdè f.   plantain; àlbasà̃ f.   onion; almìnjîr̃ m.   mousetrap; amālè m.
large, strong male camel; awarwarō m.   bracelet; ɓar̃wà̃ f.   quail; bāhò̃ m.   bathtub, large basin;
badò̃ m.   water lily; bìkā m.   baboon; būlālà̃ f.   a whip; dànda m.   piebald horse; dinyā f.   goose;
fatsa f.   fishhook; gāɓà̃ f.   (river) bank; gàwō m.   winterthorn; gàdā f.   duiker; gìzàgō m.   adze;
hazbiyā f.   stye; jàllō m.   gourd water bottle; kà̀mē m.   arrests; kàrkarā f.   rural area; kìlīshī m.
soft oriental rug/bedspread; kwàlekwàle m.   canoe; làbulē m.   curtain; làgwànī m.   wick; lōfè̃ m.
smoking pipe; màkàrā f.   bier; sāfī m.   thimble; sāfiyā f.   morning; sàrēwà̃ f.   flute; shà̃-rā̃ɓa f.
calf of leg, shin; sīlī̃ m.   ceiling; sumbā f.   a kiss; tōshiyā f.   bribe; tsēre m.   race, contest; yālō
m.   native yellow tomato; zàitûn m.   olive; olive tree

22.2. *Singulars with numerals*

Even if a word has a distinct plural, the singular form is often preferred if the word is modified by a
numeral or other quantifier, e.g.,

gidā (= gidàjē) biyu	two houses
mōtà̃ (= mōtōcī) dà yawà̃	a lot of cars
incì (not **incunà̃) gōmà	ten inches
lābà̃ nawà nawà nē?	how many pounds each?

Some common words, on the other hand, primarily with human referents, generally prefer the plural form
even with a numeral, e.g., **yârā** (not **yārò̃) tàlàtin 'thirty children', mātā** (not **màtā) huɗu 'four
wives'.

22.3. *Collectives*

Collectives and certain noncount nouns allow the use of the singular form with both singular and plural
concord. If such words have overt morphological plurals, they usually connote individuated members of
a group. Examples:

sōjà yā/sun dāwō	The army returned. (cf. pl. sōjōjī soldiers)
ruwā yā/sun ɗâukē	The rain has let up.
jàma'à̃ tanà/sunà sàurà̃rē	The people are listening.
kāyā yā/sun yi minì nauyī	The loads are too heavy for me. (cf. pl. kāyàyyakī)

22.4. *Generic nouns*

When nouns are used in a generic sense, they typically occur in the singular with singular concord, although plurals are sometimes allowed (except, of course, in the case of noncount nouns that do not have morphological plurals). This is unlike the situation in English, where generic nouns are normally in the plural. Examples:

ilìmin bōkò dà [Bàtūr̃è]$_{sg}$ **ya kai ƙasar̃ Hausa**   (=...**dà [Tùr̃àwā]**$_{pl}$ **sukà kai...**)
> Western knowledge which Europeans (lit. a European) brought to Hausaland

à lōkàcin dàmunā [manòmī]$_{sg}$ **yanà shân wàhalà sabòdà kullum yanà gōnā yanà aikì**
> During the wet season farmers (lit. a farmer) suffer because everyday they are in the farm working.

[Hondà]$_{sg}$ **tanà dà sauƙin tūƙàwā**	Hondas (lit. Honda) are easy to drive.
[ƙudā]$_{sg}$ **yanà kāwō cùtā**	Flies (lit. a fly) bring disease.
yā sābà wàsā dà [macìjī]$_{sg}$	He is accustomed to playing with snakes (lit. snake).
yā iyà sāƙar̃ [tàbarmā]$_{sg}$	He is an expert at weaving mats.
(lit. he is able to weave mat)	= He is an expert at mat weaving.
	= He is able to weave the mats.)

ita dai [gyàɗā]$_{sg}$, **Hàusàwā sunà nōmà ta sòsai**
> As for peanuts (lit. peanut), Hausas really farm them (lit. it).

[References: Newman (1972b); Parsons (1981); Wolff (1992)]

57. Prepositions

PREPOSITIONAL phrases (pp) consist of a preposition (prep.) plus an NP or an adverb, e.g., **dà wuƙā mài kaifī** 'with a sharp knife', **ƙàrƙashin tēbùřinsà** 'under his table', **dàgà nân** 'from here'. The so-called prepositions in Hausa fall into two main groups: basic (e.g., **à** 'at') and genitive (e.g., **gàban** 'in front of' < **gàba** 'front'). A few words, e.g., **don** 'for', and **kàmař** 'like', which are described below with the genitive prepositions, are transitional between the two categories. Two important morphemes that correspond to prepositions in English are not classified as prepositions in Hausa but rather are treated as grammatical particles. These are (1) the indirect object marker (IOM) 'to, for, from', which has the pre-pronoun form **ma-** and the pre-noun form **wà** (with the alternative variants **mà, wâ**, etc.) (see chap. 39), and (2) the linker 'of', which has the nonbound form **ta** with feminine head nouns and **na** with non-feminine head nouns (see chap. 43).

1. BASIC PREPOSITIONS

Hausa has a small set of basic, unitary prepositions, many of which also function as conjunctions. Phonologically, many of these are distinctive in terms of the short final vowel and L tone. With the exception of **gàrē**, which is followed by an L-tone weak object pronoun (e.g., **gàrē tà** 'by her'), basic prepositions that allow pronoun objects require the independent set (e.g., **dàgà ita** 'from her', **illā kai** 'except you'). Morphologically/lexically the basic prepositions are a heterogeneous lot. Here is a list of the most common ones:

à at, in, on; **dà** with; **dàgà** from; **bisà** on, about; **fâcē** except; **gà/gàrē** by, in, near, in connection with, in relation to; **hař** up to, until; **hàttā** including; **iyā** as far as; **illā** except; **kàfin** (= **kàfin**) before; **sabòdà** because of, on account of; **sai** except, until; **ta** via, by means of, by way of; **tun** since; **wàř** like; **yà** (= **ì**) like, among; **zuwà** to

One can identify **à, dà, dàgà, gà, yà** as the 'true' prepositions par excellence; otherwise, the prepositions do not lend themselves to a useful subclassification.

The prep. **à** 'at, in, on' is a very high frequency, semantically varied word that is used in a wide range of contexts. Its complement is normally a locational noun or noun phrase, a temporal noun (phrase), or an adverb of location or state, e.g., **zā à sāmù à kàsuwař Kanò** 'One will find (it) at Kano market'; **à lōkàcîn bā mà̀ nân** 'At that time we weren't here'; **sun yi wannàn à àsìřce** 'They did this in secret' (where **àsìřce** is an adverbial stative derived from the noun **àsìřī** 'secret'). It is commonly used along with a genitive prep. (see below), e.g., **kù sâ su (à) cikin àkwàtì!** 'Put them in the box!' (lit. you (pl.) put them (at) inside.of box). (In general, when prepositions of the two types co-occur, the order is always basic prep. plus genitive prep.) The prep. **à** translates as 'by' in such sentences as **nā zō à mōtà̀/ƙafà** 'I came by car /by foot.' With body-part terms, Hausa commonly uses an intransitive verb followed by a prepositional phrase with **à** where English would use a transitive verb, e.g., **nā guřɗè à** wuyàn-hannū 'I sprained my wrist' (lit. I sprained (intr.) at wrist). When following a continuous TAM, **à** is usually (and for some speakers, obligatorily) deleted, e.g., **yanà makaṟantā** 'He's at school', cf. **à makaṟantā yakè** 'It's at school he is.'

The prep. **bisà** 'on top of, regarding' is often preceded by **à** 'at' and/or followed by **kân** 'on', e.g., **yā hau bisà kân dōkì** 'He climbed up on the horse'; **ṟa'àyin Bintà bisà kântà** 'Binta's opinion of herself'; **à Rānaṟ Kìyāmà kōwā yà ji hukuncìn dà akà yankè masà à bisà abūbuwàn dà ya yi à ṟàyuwaṟsà ta dūniyà** 'On Judgment Day, everyone should hear the sentence that is passed on him regarding the things that he did during his life on earth.'

There is a related form **bìsà** 'regarding, according to', with L-L tone and a long final vowel, that normally occurs in sentence-initial phrases, e.g., **bìsà dòkā ta biyu an hanà X** 'According to decree number 2, one may not do X'; **bìsà àl'ādàṟmù mātā sunà lullubì** 'According to our custom women cover their heads.'

The prep. **dà** 'with', which is the same as the conjunction **dà** 'and', is a heavily worked item. It is one of the most common words in the language, serving to form phrases of accompaniment, instrument, manner, etc., e.g., **mun yi gàddamà dà shī** 'I had a quarrel with him', **yā yankà dà wuƙā** 'He slaughtered (it) with a knife', **kà bugà shi dà ƙarfī** 'Hit it with force.' The **dà** morpheme is commonly used as the second member of complex prepositions formed with locative, stative, or other adverbs, e.g., **bāya dà** 'behind (in rank or social position)', **ban dà** 'apart from; besides, without' (cf. **shā bamban dà** 'be different from'), **dab dà** (= **gab dà**) 'right near to', **danganè dà** (= **dàngàne dà**) 'regarding, relating to', **daurà dà** 'right next to, adjacent to', **duk dà** 'in spite of, despite', **kusa dà** 'close to', **ƙasà dà** 'below, junior to', **gàba dà** 'ahead of (in rank or social position)', **gàme dà** 'concerning', **nēsà dà** 'far from', **sàbīlì dà** 'on account of, because of', **samà dà** 'above (in rank or social position)'.

> °AN: [i] In Abraham's dictionary (1962), the extensive entry for **dà** goes on for three pages, see also Kraft (1970).
> [ii] In the word **sabòdà** 'because' (= [Skt] **sabàddà**), which is historically derived from *sabàb dà < *sabàbī dà 'the reason that', the **dà** has become fused synchronically with the stem.

Whereas 'with' is indicated by the true prep. **dà**, the corresponding negative 'without' is expressed either by means of the negative existential marker **bâ** 'there is not', e.g., **yā yi tàfiyà bâ gùzurī** 'He left on his journey without provisions', or else by means of the phrase **ban dà**, e.g., **kì bā nì kòfī ban dà madaṟā!** 'Give me coffee without milk!'

The prep. **dàgà** denotes 'from' both in locative and temporal senses, e.g., **dàgà Kanò** 'from Kano', **dàgà yâu** 'from today onward', **dàgà bāya** 'afterward' (lit. from back). As with **à**, **dàgà** commonly occurs preceding another prep., e.g., **dàgà cikin ɗākì** 'from in the room'. A special use of **dàgà** is in constructions with **sai** to indicate 'in addition to, only, apart from', e.g., **bâ wandà ya san màganaṟ dàgà nī sai kai (kawai)** 'No one knows about it except (only) you and I.'

The presumably native word **fàcē**, like the Arabic loanword **illā**, means 'except', e.g., **duk yârân sun shigō fàcē shī** 'All the children entered except him'; **bâ àbîn dà yakè sô illā wannàn** 'There is nothing he wants except this.' In everyday language, 'except' is usually expressed by **sai** (see below), e.g., **bâ wandà ya iyà sai mū** 'There is no one who can do it except us.'

The prep. **gà/gàrē** 'by, in relation to, etc.' is unique in that it is the only preposition that has grammatically conditioned allomorphs: **gàrē** when followed by a personal pronoun and **gà** elsewhere, e.g., **yā wàjabà (à) gàrē shì / gà Mùsùlmī yà yi sallà** 'It is incumbent on him / on a Muslim to do his prayers'; **yā yi kirà gàrē sù / gà sōjōjī...** 'He called on them / on the soldiers ...'; **mōtàṟ bā tà gyàruwā gàrē shì / gà Bellò** 'This car cannot be repaired (i.e., is not repairable) by him / by Bello'; **Mūsā ƙarfī gàrē shì** 'Musa is strong' (lit. Musa strength in relation to him). One difference between **gà** and **gàrē** (in addition to the type of object they take) is that **gàrē** commonly co-occurs with a basic prep.

like à but **gà** does not, e.g., **yanằ dà muhimmancì à gàrē mù Audù yà bar̃ nân** 'It is important for us that Audu leave here'; **nā sàmi làbār̃ì dàgà gàrē tà** 'I got the news from her', not ****nā sàmi làbār̃ì dàgà gà Hàdīzà** 'I got the news from Hadiza.'

An important function of **gà/gàrē** is to express semantic indirect objects *after* a direct object, especially when the object of the prep. is heavy and thus an i.o. construction before the d.o. would be clumsy, e.g., **yā fàɗi làbār̃ì gà mutằnên dà sukè gōyon bāyansà** 'He told the news to the men who were supporting him', cf. **yā faɗằ wà mutằnên làbār̃ì** 'He told the men news.' Like other prepositions, **gà/gàrē** covers an extremely wide semantic range and thus its core meaning is extremely difficult to characterize. (In general, because the basic prepositions are so few in number, they all are semantically broad and far reaching.) Here are a few additional examples to illustrate its use:

mēnē nè àmfằnin kògin Kwār̃à gà Nàjēr̃iyà?	What is the value of the River Niger for Nigeria?
àkwai ilìmī gà Sāni	Sani has knowledge. (lit. there is knowledge at Sani)
yâu rānar̃ gōmà gà watà	Today is the tenth of the month.
Bàrau, r̃āriyar̃-hannu gàrē shì	Barau, money slips through his fingers.
(lit. Barau, sieve.of-hand at him)	

The word **har̃** 'up to, including', which is extremely common both as a conjunction and as a preposition, connotes action moving forward toward something or some time or some place, e.g., **an yi hanyằ dàgà Kanò har̃ Dàurā** 'A road has been built all the way from Kano to Daura'; **tun jiyà akè yîn ruwā har̃ yâu dà sāfe** 'Since yesterday it has been raining going into this morning'; **ɗàlìbai dà yawà sun ci jar̃r̃abâwā har̃ mū mā** 'Many students passed the exam, including us also.' It commonly occurs followed by another basic prep., e.g., **àbîn yā kai mù har̃ gà sarkī** 'The affair has led us right up to the chief'; **Audù yā zō har̃ dà ɗan'uwansà** 'Audu has come with his brother as well' (lit. Audu has come including with his brother); **tā iyà harsunằ dà dāmā har̃ dà Japanancī** 'She speaks a lot of languages even including Japanese'; **sun yi tàfiyằ har̃ zuwằ Masàr̃** 'They traveled (to many places) including to Egypt.'

The word **iyā** (= **iyākā**) 'up to, as far as', which etymologically is presumably related to **iyàkā** 'frontier, limit', is used in such sentences as **ruwā yā kāwō masà iyā wuyà** 'Water came up all the way to his neck', or **yā yi aikìn iyā yînsà** 'He did the work to the extent of his ability.'

The temporal prep. 'before' has the tonally variant forms **kằfìn = kàfìn**, both of which are quite common, e.g., **kằfìn ƙarfè biyu** 'before two o'clock'. (Some dialects use **kằmìn = kàmin**.) When followed by the phrase **nân dà...** 'here/now and...', it indicates 'between' in a temporal sense, e.g., **kằfìn nân dà ƙarfè biyu** 'between now and two o'clock'. (When used as a subordinating conjunction, in which case the following TAM must be the subjunctive, it also has a contracted form **kàn**, e.g., **kằfìn / kàn kà dāwō** 'before you return'.)

The word **sabòdà** 'because of' (with dialect variants **sabàddà** and **sàbīlì dà**) functions as a preposition as well as a conjunction, e.g., **sabòdà rashìn ruwā** 'because of lack of water' (prep.), **sabòdà zuwànkà nakè yîn wannàn** 'because of your coming, I am doing this' (prep.), cf. **sabòdà shī mài kuɗī nè** 'because he is rich' (conj.). Etymologically it represents a fusion of the Arabic loanword **sabab** 'reason' plus the common prep. **dà**. In standard orthography, it is now written as one word.

The word **sai** 'except, not until', which functions both as a preposition and as a conjunction, is another extremely common, versatile lexeme. In its basic meaning, it usually occurs with an explicit or implied negative, e.g., **bâ wandà zâi hau dōkìn nân sai shī** 'There is no one who can ride this horse except him'; **an hanà mu fìtā sai bāyan àzahàr̃** 'They prevented us from going out until the afternoon' (lit. ...until after the ± 2 p.m. prayer). By contrast, **fàcē**, which also translates as 'except', occurs readily in the affirmative, e.g., **kōwā yanằ sôn rōgò fàcē Bellò** 'Everyone likes cassava except Bello.' A striking feature of **sai** is its common usage in elliptical constructions (both in writing and in speaking), e.g.,

dà sukà wucè [...] **sai Kàdūna**   When they passed by [they kept on going] until Kaduna.
tsàkānin mutằnen nàn [...] **sai zùmùntā**
       Between these men [nothing existed] except friendship.
gyāran iyằkwàndishàn [...] **sai gòbe**
       Repairing the air conditioning [won't get done] until tomorrow.
kōmē akà bā kà [...] **sai gòdiyā**
       Whatever you get you should be thankful. (lit. anything one.pret gives you [don't do anything]
       except thanks)

°AN: The multifunctional word **sai**, which occupies some four pages in Abraham's dictionary (1962), has been the subject of a number of specialized studies, e.g., Lukas (1955), Kraft (1970), Meyers (1974).

The word **ta** 'via, by means of' is the only preposition in the language that consists of a single H tone light syllable, e.g., **yā fitō ta tāgàr** 'He came out through the window', **mun biyō ta bāyan ganuwằr** 'We followed via behind the city wall.' In addition to its basic prepositional usage, **ta** also occurs with the pro-verb **yi** to form a phrasal aspectual verb indicating 'keep on doing', e.g., **sun yi ta zāgìnsà** 'They kept on insulting him.'

As a preposition, **tun** denotes 'since' in a temporal sense, e.g., **tun yàushè?** 'since when?'; **tun mākòn dà ya wucè** 'since last week'; **yanằ nân tun jiyà** 'He has been here since yesterday.' It commonly occurs followed by another prep. e.g., **tun kằfin Bàbbar Sallằ** 'since before Id el Kabir'. Sometimes **tun** connotes a beginning reference point in a locative sense, e.g., **nā ga jērìn mutānē tun dàgà Bātà har (zuwằ) Daulà** 'I saw a line of people (beginning) from Bata [shoe store] (all the way) to Daula'; **tun à Kanò na bā shì shāwarằ yà gyārà birkìn mōtằr** 'Back in Kano (lit. since at Kano) I advised him that he should repair the car brakes.'

The prep. **wař** 'like' is limited to the fixed phrase **wằr hakà** (lit. like thus), which accompanies temporal terms to indicate 'at the same time', e.g., **gòbe wằr hakà** 'tomorrow at this time', **bằra wằr hakà** 'last year at this time', etc.

The basic prep. **yà** (= **ì** = <**yì**> = <**wà**>) indicates 'like, among', e.g., **mutằnē yà mū** 'people like us'; **kujèrā ì wannàn** 'a chair like this one'. In an expression formed with identical pronouns, the preposition often takes the form **yè**, e.g., **kū yè kū** 'people of your status', **mū yè mū** 'people of our class' (= **yà mū yà mū**). This prep. (usually in the /ì/ form) is commonly used in such temporal expressions as **rānā ì ta yâu** 'a week from today' (lit. day like of today). It is also used (usually in the /yà/ form) in such phrases as **yà zuwằ yànzu** (or **yà zuwằ yâu**) 'up till now', e.g., **dàgà watàn Mārìs yà zuwằ yànzu** 'from March to the present'.

Finally, **zuwằ**, which is the verbal noun of the verb **zō** 'come', e.g., **inằ zuwằ** 'I'm coming, I'm on the way', functions as a preposition meaning 'to, toward' in both locative and temporal senses, e.g., **kògin nàn yā biyō zuwằ Kanò** 'This river flows toward Kano' (lit. river.of here it.comp follow toward Kano); **dàgà sāfiyā zuwằ darē** 'from morning to night'. It is commonly accompanied by the basic prep. **gà/gàrē**, e.g., **zuwằ gà edità** 'to the Editor' (a common opening salutation in a letter); **yā tàfī zuwằ gàrē sù** 'He went to them.'

A locative goal of a motion verb does not require an overt prep. because the notion of 'to' is included in the meaning of the verb, e.g., **sun zō Ø ōfìs** 'They came to the office', cf. **sun zō dàgà ōfìs** 'They came from the office'; **zā tà kōmằ Ø makaṟantā** 'She will return to school.'

1.1. Complex prepositions

There are a number of two-word prepositions comparable to English 'together with', 'close to', 'far from', etc. These are typically composed of an adverb (or occasionally a noun) plus the basic prep. **dà** 'with' (sometimes = **gà** in other dialects). The adverb is commonly an adverbial derived from a noun, e.g., **nēsà** 'far' < **nīsā** 'distance', or a stative derived from a verb, e.g., **hàɗe** 'combined' < **haɗà** 'combine'. In a few cases, the adverb does not exist except when used as part of the complex prep., e.g., **dab dà** 'right next to'. Here are some common examples:

ařèwa dà   north of; **ban dà**   apart from; **dab dà** = **gab dà**   right next to; **danganè dà** = **dàngàne dà** regarding, relating to (cf. **dangì** kin, relatives, **dàngantà** be related to); **daurà(a) dà**   right next to, adjacent to (cf. **daurà(a) dà daurà(a)**   side by side, right next to one another); **duk dà**   in spite of, despite (cf. **duk** all); **fìye dà**   more than (cf. **fi** exceed); **gàme dà**   concerning, having to do with (cf. **gamà** join, connect); **hagu dà**   left of; **kusa dà** (= **kusa gà**)   close to; **ƙasà dà**   below (cf. **ƙasà** on the ground < **ƙasā** earth, ground); **nēsà dà**   far from (cf. **nēsà** far < **nīsā** distance); **samà dà**   above in rank or position (cf. **samà** sky); **tàre dà**   together with, [in negative] without (cf. **tàru** meet, assemble)

2. GENITIVE PREPOSITIONS

What I am calling genitive prepositions are words composed of a noun or adverb plus a zero-vowel linker -n /-ř (usually -n). These are quite numerous in the language. The genitive prepositions are commonly preceded by a basic prep. like **à** 'at', **dàgà** 'from', or **ta** 'via', e.g., **à/dàgà/ta cikin gàrī** '(at)/from/via in the town'. Many of the genitive prepositions are built on body part terms, but other nouns and adverbs also serve as the source. Examples:

bàkin   at the edge/side of, in exchange for, as equivalent to (< **bàkī** mouth)
e.g., **nā gan shì à bàkin hanyà**   I saw him on the side of the road.
e.g., **nā bā dà sàbulù à bàkin madařā**   I gave some soap in exchange for some milk.
bāyan   after, behind (< **bāya** at the back) (= **bân** with inexplicable falling tone))
cikin   inside of (< **cikī** the inside, cf. **cikì** belly)
dòmin   for the sake of, because of (< *dòmī (?)) (= **don**)
gàrin   while, in the process of (< **gàrī** town (?))
gòshin   just prior to (< **gòshī** forehead),
e.g., **gòshin àzahàř**   just before the afternoon prayer
gurin   variant of **wurin** (see below) (< **gurī** = **gû** place) (= **gûn**)
jìkin   against, embedded in (< **jìkī** body)
kàmař   like (< **kàmā** similarity, likeness)
kân   on top of (< **kâi** head)
ƙarƙashin   under (< **ƙarƙashī** the underneath)
ƙasàn   below, at the bottom of (< **ƙasà** on the ground < **ƙasā** ground, earth)
e.g., **ƙasàn shāfì**   at the bottom of the page
madàdin   in place of/instead of (< Ar. loanword **madàdī** representative)
e.g., **Mūsā yā zō à madàdin Audù**   Musa came instead of Audu.
màimakon   instead of (< **màimakō** replacement)
samàn   above, over (< **samà** above, sky)
tàmkař   like (= **kàmař**) (< *tàmkā, which does not normally occur as an independent noun)
e.g., **kàrē tàmkař wannàn**   a dog like this one
tsàkānin   between (< **tsàkānī** in between)

e.g., **yā shìga tsàkānin ɗā dà mahàifī**   He came between the father and his son.

wajen   in relation to (space, time, or action); to, toward; about, approximately; at, with respect to, with, at (< **wajē** place)

e.g., **yā yi wajen Bicì**   He went towards Bichi.

e.g., **yā gōgè wajen kìɗe-kìɗe**   He is an expert at drumming.

e.g., **dàgà nan dařajář wàzīřī ta ràgu wajen Sarkī**   From then on the vizier lost the Emir's favor.

(lit. the value of the vizier decreased with the Emir)

wàjen   outside of (< **wàje** outside)

wurin   in relation to; around, near, at place of (< **wurī** place)

e.g., **yanà̀ wurin mālàm**   It is with the teacher.

e.g., **sunà̀ wurin aik̀ì**   They are at work.

Irregular: **gèfin**   on the eve of (presumably < **gēfè** edge)

Genitive prepositions that allow pronoun objects normally use the bound possessive set, e.g., **gàbānā** 'in front of me', **kânsù** 'on them', **cikintà** 'in it'. The prepositions **kàmař** 'like' and **dòmin** 'for, on account of' can be followed either by a bound possessive or by an independent pronoun, the latter being considered somewhat stronger, e.g., **kàmātā = kàmař nī** 'like me', **kàmařmù = kàmař mū** 'like us'; **dòminkù = dòmin kū** 'on account of you (pl.)', **dòmintà = dòmin ita** 'on account of her'. The commonly used short form **don** (< **dòmin**) only allows an independent pronoun, e.g., **kā yi hakà nē don nī** (not ****dōnā**) **kō don sū** (not ****donsù**)? 'Did you do it for me or for them?'

> ∆DN: [i] In Skt, **don** is followed by a weak object pronoun, e.g., **don nì, don kà, don shì**, etc. 'for me, for you, for him', etc.
>
> [ii] In the Guddiri dialect, **don** has developed another idiosyncratic property as compared with the source word **dòmin**—namely, it has polar tone (i.e., its tone is opposite that of the following word), e.g., **don bàba** 'for father', but **dòn Allàh** 'for God's sake'.

Because most genitive prepositions are identical in shape to the genitive of the source word, the same surface sequence can often have two readings, e.g., **jìkinsà** = 'against, embedded in him' or 'his body'; **kântà** = 'on her/it' or 'her/its head', etc. (The latter is also the reflexive pronoun 'herself'.) When the prep. is built on an adverbial form, its surface output may be distinct from a nominal genitive construction, e.g., **ƙasànsù** 'below them', but **ƙasařsù** 'their country, earth'.

Some of the adverb-based genitive prepositions have corresponding phrasal prepositions with **dà**. The two preposition types are semantically close in meaning but usually not identical, e.g.,

gàban	in front of, before, cf.	**gàba dà**	senior to, in front of in rank or position
kusan	close, almost, cf.	**kusa dà**	close to (physically)
ƙasàn	below, at the bottom of, cf.	**ƙasà dà**	junior to, below in rank or position
samàn	above, over, cf.	**samà dà**	senior to, above in rank or position

3. PREPOSITION STRANDING

Basic prepositions (and complex prepositions containing a basic prep.) may not be stranded, i.e., one cannot end a phrase with **à** or **gà** or **sai**, etc. In questions, focus, relative clauses, etc., either the entire prepositional phrase is moved or else a resumptive pronoun is required, e.g.,

yā cikà bùhū dà gyàɗā   He filled the sack with peanuts.

⇒ **dà mè ya cikà bùhū?**   With what did he fill the sack?

not ****mḛ̀ ya cikà bùhū dà**	What did he fill the sack with?
zā mù kùɓutà ta wata dàbār̃à̰	We will escape by means of a certain stratagem.
⇒ **ta yày̰à̰ zā mù kùɓutà?**	How (lit. via how) can we escape?
sunà̰ màganà̰ dà yār̰ò̰	They are talking with the boy.
⇒ **yār̀òn dà sukḛ̀ màganà̰ dà shī**	the boy that they are talking with (lit. ...with him)
not ****yār̀òn dà sukḛ̀ màganà̰ dà**	the boy that they are talking with
sun tāsō dàgà gabàs	They started out from the east.
⇒ **dàgà gabàs sukà tāsō**	It was from the east they started out.
not ****gabàs sukà tāsō dàgà**	It was the east they started out from.

By contrast, the indirect object marker **wà**, which is not classified as a preposition, readily allows stranding, e.g., **nā gayà̰ wà Mūsā** 'I told it to Musa' ⇒ **Mūsā nḛ̀ na gayà̰ wà** 'It was Musa I told (it) to.'

Exceptions to the general rule are colloquial expressions with **dà** like the following:

bar̃kà̰ dà   Greetings! (elliptical for such greetings as **bar̃kà̰ dà hūtà̰wā**   Greetings on resting, **bar̃kà̰ dà zuwà̰**   Greetings on arriving, **bar̃kà̰ dà yâmma**   Good afternoon, etc.)
kō kwabò̰ bân dà   Even a penny I don't have. (i.e., I am flat broke.) (colloquial for **kō kwabò̰ bân dà shī** with the resumptive pronoun **shī** 'him/it')

ΔDN: In some dialects—and even for some SH speakers—stranding of the preposition **dà** in HAVE sentences is becoming the norm in casual speech, e.g., **kanà̰ dà hùlā̰? ī, inà̰ dà** 'Do you have a cap? Yes I do' (lit. I.cont with).

Genitive prepositions, on the other hand, behave differently. They can make use of a resumptive genitive pronoun, but it is not required, i.e., gapping is allowed. If the erstwhile preposition (e.g., **kân** 'on') is stranded, it will appear in its nominal or adverbial form without the linker (e.g., **kâi** 'top' or **kā** 'atop'). Examples:

gà̰ tēbùr̃in dà ya sâ kuɗī à kânsà	Here is the table that he put the money on. (lit. ...on it)
= **gà̰ tēbùr̃in dà ya sâ kuɗī à kâi (= à kā)**	Here is the table that he put the money atop.
Bellò̰ nē sukà zàɓā à màimakonsà = Bellò̰ nē sukà zàɓā à màimakō	
It was Bello they chose instead (of him).	

[Reference: Parsons (1961)]

58. Pro-Verb yi

1. MAIN VERB

THE grade 0 monoverb **yi** is a main verb meaning 'do' or 'make' (or some semantic extension thereof), e.g.,

gà àbîn dà ya yi	Here is the thing that he did.
sun yi kùjèrā	They made a chair.
zā mù yi shèkarà biyu à Kanò	We will stay (lit. do) two years in Kano.
āyàrī yā yi arèwa	The caravan headed (lit. did) north.

The verb also operates a gr6 form **yiwō** (sometimes contracted to **yō** or **wō**) and a gr7 form **yìwu**, e.g.,

yā yiwō itàcē	He collected (lit. did) firewood and brought it back.
yâ yìwu	It is doable/possible.

In nonfinite environments, **yi** is automatically replaced by the VN **yî** (except when followed by an indirect object). If there is a direct object immediately after **yî**, the VN obligatorily attaches the linker **-n** (but see below for **yîn** deletion), e.g.,

mè yakè̀ yî?	What is he doing?
yā fārà yînsà	He began doing it.
bā yà̀ yîn kōmē	He isn't doing anything.

2. PRO-VERB

This high-frequency lexical item also functions widely and commonly as a "pro-verb" in two important constructions—namely, as a dummy 'do' verb, and as an anaphoric replacement verb.

2.1. Dummy verb 'do'

As a dummy verb, **yi** occurs as a more or less semantically empty carrier with direct objects belonging to such categories as dynamic noun, abstract quality noun, adverb, and ideophone. Sentences with a dynamic noun indicate what in English would be expressed by an intransitive action verb, e.g.,

sun yi màganà̀	They talked. (lit. do talking)
bà tà yi barcī ba	She didn't sleep. (lit. not do sleep)
sun fārà yîn dàriyā	They began to laugh. (lit. begin doing laughter)
sun dainà yîn sùrūtù	They have stopped chattering. (lit. cease doing chattering)

Sentences with qualitative nouns as objects sometimes translate as simple copular sentences, e.g.,

àbinci yā yi kyâu	The food was good. (lit. do goodness)
mun yi muřnà	We are pleased. (lit. do pleasure)
nāmà yā yi wārī	The meat reeks. (lit. do stench)
yā yi manà zāfī	It was tough going for us. (lit. do to.us heat)

Sometimes, especially with indirect objects, the connotation is not just 'is' but 'is too much', e.g.,

ɗākìn nân yā yi sanyī	This room is too cold. (lit. do coldness)
kyât ɗîn yā yi mikì zāk̃ī?	Is the cake too sweet for you? (lit. do to.you (f.) sweetness)
bùhûn yā yi minì nauyī	The sack is too heavy for me. (lit. do to.me heaviness)
ìdan hùlâř tā yi makà kàɗan, zân kāwō wata	
	If the cap is too small (lit. do to.you (m.) little), I'll bring another.

The dummy **yi** plus an adverb or ideophone of manner often occurs in conjoined sentences where the core semantics is expressed in the second clause, e.g.,

kù yi maza kù dāwō!	Return quickly! (lit. you (pl.) do quickly you return)
yā yi fařat yā tāshì	He got up suddenly. (lit. he did *rush* he got up)
tā yi wup tā kāmà shi	She grabbed him in a flash. (lit. she did *wup* she caught him)

2.2. Anaphoric replacement verb

When a verb or VP is fronted for purposes of topicalization or focus—in which case it appears as a corresponding infinitive phrase (IP) or verbal noun (VN)—the original verb slot is filled by the pro-verb **yi**. This function of **yi** is similar to that of English 'do', e.g.,

shārè ɗākìn, yā kàmātà sù yi	As for sweeping the room (IP), they ought to do (it).
sàyē dà sayâřwā, bâ shakkà zā sù yi	Buying and selling (VN), no doubt they will do (it).
sāk̃ař tàbarmā ta yi	It was weaving a mat (VN) she did.
g̃yārà mōtàř mukà yi	Repairing the car (IP) we did.

The pro-verb **yi** combines with the deictic pro-form **hakà** 'thus' as a replacement for an entire VP or clause, e.g.,

Kànde tā zaunà à kân kujèrā, Tàlātù mā tā yi hakà	Kande sat on a chair, and so also did Talatu.
Bellò yā taɓà kûnnensà, Daudà kuma yā yi hakà	Bello touched his ear, and Dauda also did so.

3. yi DELETION

A general feature of the language is the optional (but usual) deletion of **yi** in nonfinite predicates, e.g., **yanà yîn aik̃ì** (⟹) **yanà aik̃ì** 'He is working' (lit. he is (doing) work), **nā ga mazàjē sunà yîn wànnan himmà** (⟹) **nā ga mazàjē sunà wànnan himmà** 'I saw men making that effort.'

°AN: [i] A convention that is followed here is to speak of **yi** deletion. As the above examples show, if **yi** is not deleted, it undergoes nominalization and, if an object follows, adds the linker **-n**. Viewing things at a very surface level, one thus might speak of **yîn** deletion. Because the deletion affects **yi**, **yî**, and **yîn**, however, there are analytical advantages in treating **yi** deletion as happening at a deeper, more abstract level before the nominalization takes place.

[ii] Generally speaking, sentences with and without the **yi** deletion mean the same thing. According to Jaggar (1992a: 103n), however, some speakers do make a distinction such that the presence of **yi** implies habitual action.

This deletion rule occurs with all continuous TAMs and when **yi** is preceded by an aspectual verb, e.g.,

ɗàlìbai kullum sunà (yîn) màganàr̃ kuɗī	The students are always talking about money.
tanà (yi) musù tsāwā?	Is she scolding them? (lit. do to.them scolding)
su wà sukè (yîn) kòkawà?	Who are wrestling?
bā yà (yîn) barcī	He doesn't sleep.
kàfin kù ƙàrè (yîn) tùnànin wannàn...	Before you finish thinking about this...
yā ƙi (yi) minì tàimakō	He refused to help me. (lit. do to.me help)
aikì nē yakè (yî)	It's work he is doing.

There are some nonfinite environments, however, where the deletion cannot take place. First, deletion is not allowed if the continuous or the negative continuous PACs would be left stranded, e.g.,

tanà yî	She is doing (it). *not* ⇒ ****tanà**
cf. tanà (yîn) kitsò	She is doing hairdressing. (deletion allowed)
bā sà̀ yî	They aren't doing (it). *not* ⇒ ****bā sà̀**
cf. bā sà̀ (yîn) gaddamà	They aren't arguing. (deletion allowed)

By contrast, the relative continuous TAM, formed with the marker **kè**, can be stranded in final position and thus permits **yi** deletion. The deletion is not allowed, however, if the sentence lacks an underlying object, e.g.,

ɗinkì (nē) takè yî	It's embroidery she is doing. ⇒ **ɗinkì (nē) takè**
mènē nè yakè yî?	What is he doing? ⇒ **mènē nè yakè?**
cf. Jummai (cè) takè yî	Jummai is doing (it). *not* ⇒ ****Jummai (cè) takè**
wànē nè yakè yî?	Who is doing (it)? *not* ⇒ ****wànē nè yakè?**

In finite environments, i.e., when following a TAM other than the continuous, deletion of **yi** is normally not allowed, e.g., **sun yi màganà** 'They spoke' (lit. did talk) cannot be changed into ****sun màganà**. When followed by an indirect object, on the other hand, **yi** can be deleted, although this is less common than the deletion in nonfinite environments, e.g.,

sun (yi) masà màganà	They talked to him.
sū nè mutànên dà sukà (yi) wà Mūsā aikì	They are the men who worked for Musa.

59. Pronouns

PRONOUNS are of two main types: (1) personal pronouns, and (2) non-personal pronouns. The former are marked for person, number, and—in the singular only—gender, e.g., **ita** 'she' (3 sg. f.), **mū** 'we' (1 pl.). The latter may be marked for number and gender, but not for person; like nouns they are inherently third person. These non-personal pronouns include, inter alia, demonstratives, e.g., **wannàn** (m.) 'this one'; interrogatives, e.g., **mè̀**? 'what?'; and universals, e.g., **kōmē** 'everything'.

1. PERSONAL PRONOUNS

The personal pronouns fall into two distinct classes: (a) non-subject pronouns, i.e., all pronouns other than the "weak subject pronouns", and (b) the weak subject pronouns (wsp's). (These latter occur in the person-aspect-complex (PAC) that functions in the tense-aspect system (see §70:1).)

1.1. Non-subject pronouns
The non-subject pronoun sets contain eight pronouns, with gender distinguished only in the second and third persons singular. The gender feature does not apply to the plural pronouns. The first person singular may be specified semantically for gender but the form itself is invariant, e.g., **nī nè̀** 'It's me' (a male speaking), **nī cè̀** 'It's me' (a female speaking). The pronoun categories are: 1st person sg. (1s), 2nd person sg. masculine (2m), 2nd person sg. feminine (2f), 3rd person sg. masculine (3m), 3rd person sg. feminine (3f), 1st person pl. (1p), 2nd person pl. (2p), and 3rd person pl. (3p).

There are some eight different pronoun sets, the members of each set having a common tone and syllable weight. Paradigms for all of the sets are presented in table 11. The following conventions have been adopted: Alternative forms current in SH are separated by /. The variant listed first can be considered the norm. Variants generally used outside the core SH area but that are familiar to SH speakers are given in angle brackets < >. Other dialect forms are presented in notes and discussion.

Table 11: Non-subject pronouns

	independent	*strong object*	*weak object*	*indirect object*
1 s	nī	ni	nì	minì / mîn / manì
2m	kai	ka	kà	makà / mā / mâ
2f	kē	ki	kì	mikì
3m	shī	shi	shì	masà / mishì / mâs / mâr̃
3f	ita	ta	tà	matà
1 p	mū	mu	mù	manà <mamù> <munà>
2 p	kū	ku	kù	mukù
3 p	sū	su	sù	musù

476

	free possessive		bound genitive	
	m./pl.	*f.*	*m./pl.*	*f.*
1 s	nàwa	tàwa	-nā	-tā
2m	nākà	nākà	-nkà	-r̃kà
2f	nākì	tākì	-nkì	-r̃kì
3m	nāsà / nāshì	tāsà / tāshì	-nsà / -nshì / (-nasà) <-nai>	-r̃sà / -r̃shì / -tāsà <-tai>
3f	nātà	tātà	-ntà / (-natà)	-r̃tà / -tātà
1p	nāmù	tāmù	-nmù	-r̃mù
2p	nākù	tākù	-nkù	-r̃kù
3p	nāsù	tāsù	-nsù	-r̃sù

	reflexive	reciprocal
1 s	kâinā	
2m	kânkà	
2f	kânkì	
3m	kânsà / kânshì	
3f	kântā	
1p	kânmù	jūnanmù
2p	kânkù	jūnankù
3p	kânsù	jūnansù

Each individual paradigm will now be repeated and discussed in turn.

1.1.1. Independent pronouns

1 s	nī	1p	mū
2m	kai	2p	kū
2f	kē		
3m	shī	3p	sū
3f	ita		

The syntactically nounlike independent pronouns have H tone and are bimoraic. Except for the 3f pronoun **ita**, which is unique in being disyllabic—but still having two moras—the independent pronouns are monosyllabic with a long vowel. In the 2m pronoun **kai**, this long vowel is diphthongal. Uses of these pronouns include the following:

1. Subject or predicate of nonverbal equational sentences, e.g., **nī mālàmī nè** 'I am a teacher', **kē cè màtar̃sà?** 'Are you his wife?'; **àlkālī nè shī** 'A judge he is', **dà nī kai nè** 'If I were you.' They occur also as complements of the quasi-rhetorical interrogative **wànē?** 'who?' used in such expressions as **wànē ita?** 'Of what account is she?' (or 'She's not up to it').

2. Member of a conjoined phrase, e.g., **(dà) nī dà yārò** 'I and the boy', **(dà) mū dà sū** 'we and they'.

3. Focused or topicalized element, e.g., **mū nè mukà ɓōyè zōbèn** '*We* are the ones who hid the ring'; **kai dai, bà zā mù mântā dà kai ba** 'As for you, we will not forget you'; **nī kâinā inà sô ìn bar̃ wurîn** 'I myself want to leave the place.'

4. Direct object when not immediately following the verb, e.g., **mù shiryà matà sū** 'Let's prepare them for her' (**matà** is an i.o.), cf. **mù shiryà su** 'Let's prepare them'; **yā nèmi kò ita** 'He moreover sought her' (**kò** is a modal particle meaning 'moreover'), cf. **yā nèmē tà** 'He sought her.'

5. Object of "basic prepositions" (see §57:1) like **dà** 'with, **dàgà** 'from', **sai** 'except, but only', and **yà** 'like', e.g., **yanà d'àuke dà sū** 'He is laden with them'; **dàgà nī sai kai** 'After me it's your turn' (lit. from me except/only you), **mùtûm yà shī** 'a man like him'.

6. Object of the gr5 particle **dà**, which is homophonous with the preposition **dà**, e.g., **zā sù tsōratař dà kū** 'They will frighten you away.'

7. Complements of certain function words like **gāra/gwàmmà** 'It would be better', the existential marker **dà** 'there is/are' (probably the same as the preposition **dà** 'with'), and the negative existential markers **bābù** and **bâ** 'there is/are not', e.g., **gāra ita** 'Better her (than s.o. else)'; **ī, dà shī** 'Yes, there is it/one'; **bābù sū** 'There aren't any of them'; **bâ mū cikin 'yan tākařā** 'We aren't among the candidates' (lit. There isn't we...).

°AN: According to some descriptions (e.g., Furniss 1991a), the pronoun set following the monosyllabic variant **bâ** is the strong H-tone d.o. set, e.g., **bâ su** 'There aren't any of them.' While this may be the case for some speakers, the norm—as was already noted by Abraham (1962: 47) a half-century ago—is to use an independent pronoun after **bâ**. Even more preferable, however, is to avoid the problem of which pronoun to choose after **bâ** by using the long form **bābù**, where only the independent pronoun is allowed.

8. Determiner/specifier of a following animate noun, e.g., **shī Mūsā zâi tàimàkē nì dà mōtà** 'He Musa will give me ride'; **sū Hàusàwā sunà dà ìyālì màsu yawà** 'They the Hausa have large families'; **an yabà wà shī àlƙālîn** 'They praised him the judge.'

1.1.2. Strong object pronouns

1 s	ni	1 p	mu
2m	ka	2p	ku
2f	ki		
3m	shi	3 p	su
3f	ta		

There are two different sets of object pronoun distinguished only by tone. The pronouns share the same segmental shapes (all being inherently CV) and the rule that requires that they must be preceded by a heavy syllable. The set labeled strong object pronoun is characterized by a fixed H tone. Following conventional usage, it is referred to as an "object" set, although it actually has other functions as well. Here are its main uses:

1. It occurs as the direct object of gr1, gr4, and gr5d verbs when immediately following the verb, e.g., **sun dakà shi** 'They pounded it'; **kàmā ni!** 'Catch me!'; **tā gajàrtā shi** 'She shortened it'; **kadà kà kashè mu** 'Don't kill us'; **mù jânyē su** 'Let's pull them away'; **mun kařàncē su** 'We read them all; **yā hiddà ta** [WH] 'He took it/her out.' (As indicated above, if the object is separated from the verb, an independent pronoun is required.) It occurs also as the d.o. of gr5 verbs in the infrequent usage without the **dà** particle, e.g., **yā ciyař su** 'He fed them' (cf. the more usual **yā ciyař dà sū**, with the independent pronoun following **dà**, or **yā cīshē sù**, with the weak object pronoun following the verbal suffix -shē).

°AN/◊HN: Most descriptions of Hausa postulate a single set of direct object pronouns with polar tone, i.e., H after L and L after H. The H-tone pronoun seen in **kadà kà kashè mu** 'Don't kill us!'

(gr4), for example, is assumed to have the same underlying tone as the surface L-tone pronoun in **yā harbē mù** 'He shot us' (gr2). This long-accepted analysis is wrong, as clearly shown, inter alia, by the many constructions (seen in some of the examples above) in which the H-tone set occurs after a preceding H tone. Historically, the two sets probably differed in their vowels as well as in their tone, e.g., (strong) *tá '3f' vs. (weak) *tò '3f' (Newman 1979b).

2. It occurs as the object of the presentational particle **gà**, e.g., **gà ta cân zàune à kân kujèrā** 'There she is seated on a chair'; **yā kàmàtà mù yi mùhāwarà dà sū gà mu, gà su** 'We ought to have a discussion with them face to face' (lit. here we are, here they are).
3. It functions as an optional "intransitive copy pronoun" (ICP) after the verbs 'come' and 'go', e.g., **nā zō ni** 'I came', **mù jē mu gidā** 'Let's go home.' (Note that the pronoun appears with its inherent H tone even though the preceding verb has H tone and not with L tone as would be expected from the polarity analysis.)

◊HN: In many Chadic languages, intransitive verbs may (or must) be followed by a pronoun that copies the person, gender, and number of the subject, the pronoun now generally referred to as an "intransitive copy pronoun" (ICP) (Frajzyngier 1977; Newman 1971b, 1974; Tuller 1997). Here are a few typical examples from Kanakuru, where the construction is obligatory with all intransitive verbs: **nà pòrò-no** 'I went out' (lit I go out-I), **wù gòmò-wu** 'They met.' Hausa has preserved just a vestige of this construction, this being stylistically restricted and limited only to the two verbs **zō** and **jē**.

4. It serves as a pre-head pluralizing marker (3p only), e.g., **su Bellò** 'Bello and the others', **su wānè** 'so-and-sos', **su wà sukà ki tāshì?** 'Who (pl.) refused to get up?'

1.1.3. Weak object pronouns

1s	nì	1p	mù
2m	kà	2p	kù
2f	kì		
3m	shì	3p	sù
3f	tà		

The weak object pronoun set consists of clitic pronouns. In standard orthography, these pronouns are written as separate words, a practice followed in this grammar. In the examples below, however, they will be connected by means of a hyphen to emphasize their bound nature. This set differs from the strong object set in not having inherent H tone. (With certain verb classes, the weak object pronouns fuse with the verb *before* the L-H imperative tone pattern is imposed (see §37:2) and thus the pronouns appear on the surface with H tone, e.g., **màrè-shi!** (gr2) 'Slap him!'; **bì-ni!** (gr0) 'Follow me!') Following customary usage, the weak object pronouns are presented in the paradigm with L tone and they will be referred to throughout as L-tone pronouns. Analytically, however, the set could possibly be treated as underlyingly toneless, with the surface low being assigned either by default, by incorporation, or perhaps even by tonal polarity.

°AN: Previous scholars were not necessarily wrong in appealing to polarity to account for the surface tone of the weak object pronouns that one finds after gr2 verbs. The mistake was in thinking that this same principle could be applied to the H-tone strong object pronouns that one finds, for example, after gr1 verbs.

This set has the following uses:

1. It occurs as the direct object of all verb forms other than those using the strong object pronouns. These verb classes include gr0, gr2, gr5 (final -ē form), gr6, and certain irregular verbs, e.g., **yakàn bī-mù** (gr0) 'He habitually follows us'; **bà mù kirā-kù ba** (gr0) 'We didn't call you'; **tâ màrē-shì** (gr2) 'She will slap him'; **à gaishē-tà** (gr5) 'Greet her!'; **kàwō-sù!** (gr6) 'Bring them!'; **nā gan-kà** (irreg.) 'I saw you.'

2. It occurs as the object of the existential morpheme **àkwai** 'there is/are', the preposition **gàrē** 'to, in connection with', and the particle **ungo** 'here it is, take it', e.g., **àkwai-sù cikin kwālī** 'There are some (lit. them) in the carton', **sunà gàrē-nì** 'They are by/with me'; **ungō-tà!** 'Take it!' (Notice that the final vowel of **ungo** automatically lengthens before the object pronoun.)

Unlike the phonologically similar indirect object pronouns (see following), which have common apocopated variants, the direct object pronouns normally retain the final vowels in all persons. In casual speech, however, the 1s and 3m pronouns **nì** and **shì** can be reduced to **-n̄** and **-s̄** respectively when occurring as the object of a gr2 verb. If the final /i/ is apocopated, the underlying /s/ of the 3m form does not palatalize to /sh/. It either is pronounced as /s/ or else undergoes rhotacism and appears as /r̃/. The L tone of the pronoun is realized as a fall on the preceding syllable. The final -ē characteristic of the gr2 pre-pronoun form reduces to /a/ in the resulting closed syllable, e.g.,

yā bùgân < **yā bùgē-nì**	He beat me.
nā bùgâs (= **nā bùgâr̃**) < **nā bùgē-shì**	I beat him.
yā gàr̃gàɗân < **yā gàr̃gàɗē-nì**	He warned me.
sun tàmbàyâs (= **sun tàmbàyâr̃**) < **sun tàmbàyē-shì**	They asked him.

ΔDN: Abraham (1959b: 104) describes this construction with the reduced object pronoun as being a Sokoto dialect form. Whether it was or was not dialectally limited in Abraham's time, nowadays it is a well-established variant in SH, including the final -s/-r̃ alternation.

In modern-day Sokoto speech, this construction differs from the cited examples in two respects (Malami Buba, personal communication). First, the tone of the pronoun is deleted along with the vowel, so that one ends up with a final H rather than falling tone. Second, the 3m pronoun normally appears as /i/ (< /y/) rather than /s/, e.g., **yā bùgan** 'He beat me'; **nā bùgai** 'I beat him'; **yā gàr̃gàɗan** 'He warned me', **yā gàr̃gàɗai** 'He warned him.'

1.1.4. Indirect objects

1s	**minì / mîn / manì**	1p	**manà** <mamù> <munà>
2m	**makà / mā / mâ**	2p	**mukù**
2f	**mikì**		
3m	**masà / mishì /mâs / mâr̃**	3p	**musù**
3f	**matà**		

The so-called i.o. pronouns that immediately follow the verb are made up of an indirect object marker //ma-// and a set of bound L-tone pronouns, e.g., **mun gayà matà làbār̃ì** 'We told her the news.' In SH the vowel of **ma-** usually assimilates to that of the attached pronoun, although in careful speech it can be pronounced as such, e.g., //manì// (→) **minì**, //makù// (→) **mukù**. The 3m pronoun appears either as -sà (the usual written form) or as -shì, this latter variant almost always conditioning assimilation of the preceding **ma-**, i.e., //mashì// → **mishì**. In the 1s (**minì**) and 3m (**masà**) forms, the final vowel is commonly deleted. Note that the vowel assimilation in the first person has to be ordered before the vowel apocope, i.e., **manì** → **minì** and only then to **mîn**. (The form ****mân** does not normally occur.) In rapid speech, **mîn** reduces even further to [mн̀], i.e., **m** followed by a syllabic nasal with falling tone. The final /s/ resulting from the change **masà** → **mâs** commonly undergoes rhotacism to /r̄/, i.e., **mâr̄**. All four 3m variants are extremely common, the choice being a matter of subdialectal, ideolectal, and free variation. The **kà**-less variants of the 2m pronoun with high and the falling tone suggest two different possible derivations: (a) **makà** → *ma (by dropping the **kà**) followed by compensatory lengthening to **mā** to preserve the needed second mora; or (b) **makà** → **maØà** → **mâ** by weakening and loss of the intervocalic /k/ followed by fusion of the two short vowels to a long vowel with falling tone. Details on the use of these pronouns is found in §39:9.

°AN/◊HN: The i.o. forms with **ma**- derive historically from possessive pronouns (Newman 1982). The original i.o. pronouns were most likely identical to the present-day weak object pronouns, i.e., CV with (default) L tone. The presumably original situation is still found with the verb **bā** 'give to', whose thematic recipient is indicated synchronically by what looks like a d.o. rather than an i.o. pronoun, e.g., **tā bā nì zōbè̀** 'She gave me a ring', not ****tā bā minì zōbè̀**.

Another possible example of the expression of an indirect object by an immediately following weak object pronoun is a rare construction used only with first person indirect objects, only with a few specific verbs, and only (primarily?) in the imperative, e.g., **tùrô-n yāròn!** (= **tùrō minì yāròn**) 'Send the boy to me!'; **rìk̄yâ-n wannàn!** 'Hold this for me!' (= **rìk̄ē minì wannàn**). Wolff (1993: 116) suggests that the final **-n̄** (< **nì**) represents an extreme phonological reduction of **minì**. This may be right. However, one has to consider the possibility that the **-n̄** found here is an erstwhile weak object pronoun that is suffixed directly to the verb in an archaic fashion.

ΔDN/◊HN: The SH first person plural variant **manà** is the original archaic (possessive) pronoun form. The two WH dialect variants, namely, **mamù** and **munà**, result from processes of analogical regularization working in two different ways. In **mamù**, the archaic (and synchronically anomalous) pronoun **-nà** is replaced by the usual first person plural form **-mù**. (Interestingly, the vowel of the marker **ma**- normally fails to assimilate to the following /u/.) In the case of **munà**, the /mu-/ in **mukù** and **musù** is taken to be the underlying form of the indirect object marker used with plural pronouns (rather than being due to low-level assimilation) and thus it has been extended to the first person plural by a process of paradigmatic regularization so that all of the plural i.o. forms share the same marker.

1.1.5. Free possessives

	m./pl. reference	*f. reference*
1 s	nàwa	tàwa
2m	nākà	tākà
2f	nākì	tākì
3m	nāsà / nāshì	tāsà / tāshì
3f	nātà	tātà
1p	nāmù	tāmù
2p	nākù	tākù
3p	nāsù	tāsù

The free-standing possessive pronouns 'mine', 'yours', 'ours', etc., are composed of a genitive linker with a long vowel plus a genitive personal pronoun. These pronouns are essentially the same as the weak object pronouns with the exception of the first person **-wa**. This first person pronoun is like the others in having the shape CV with a short vowel but unlike the others in having H tone. The linker is **nā** with masculine and plural referents and **tā** with feminine referents. The tone of **nā/tā** is polar to that of the following pronoun, e.g., **nàwa yā fi nākà gudù** 'Mine (e.g., a horse (m.)) is faster than yours'; **gà̀** hùlā ɗaya, ìnā tāsà? 'Here is one cap (f.), where is his?'; mōtōcîn nan nāmù nē 'Those cars (pl.) are ours.'

ΔDN: In WH the first person pronouns are **nau** and **tau**. These are derived by (a) apocopation of the final vowel, (b) automatic shortening of the over-heavy syllable, (c) incorporation of the coda /w/ into the nucleus, and (d) change of LH tone on the single syllable to H, e.g. nằwá → nằw̓ → nàw̓ → nàú → náu.

In addition to the "independent" uses of these pronouns, they are also used as attributive post-head possessors when another modifier, like a demonstrative, definite article, ideophone, or numeral, intervenes between the possessed noun and the possessor, e.g., **mōtàr̃ nân tāmù** 'This car of ours' (lit. car.of this ours), cf. **mōtà-r̃mù** 'our car'; **àmīnìn nằwa** 'the confidant (m.) of mine' (lit. confidant.the mine); **ƙawâr̃ tằwa** 'the friend (f.) of mine' (lit. friend.the mine); **màge 'yar̃ tsirit tằwa** 'my very tiny cat' (lit. cat small wee mine), cf. **màgē-nā** 'my cat'; **yârā biyu nātà** 'her two children' (= yâra-ntà biyu). The free possessives are sometimes used attributively with loanwords or with foreign words, e.g., **ambùlàn nātà** 'her envelope'; **fur̃ōfàgandằ tāsù** 'their propaganda'; *dissertation* **nằwa** 'my dissertation'.

The free possessives are also used prenominally in an appositional structure for contrastive emphasis or greater specificity, e.g., **tāmù rījìyâr̃** 'the well of ours' (lit. ours well.the); **nằwa dōkìn** *'my* horse in question' (lit. mine horse.the), **nāsù tằrôn** *'their* meeting' (lit. theirs meeting.the). Note that when the free possessive is used prenominally, the noun usually takes the definite article.

1.1.6. Bound genitive pronouns

	m./pl.	*f.*
1 s	-nā	-tā
2 m	-nkà	-r̃kà
2 f	-nkì	-r̃kì
3 m	-nsà / -nshì / (-nasà) <-nai>	-r̃sà / -r̃shì / -tasà <-tai>
3 f	-ntà / (-natà)	-r̃tà / -tatà
1 p	-nmù	-r̃mù
2 p	-nkù	-r̃kù
3 p	-nsù	-r̃sù

1.1.6.1. The bound genitives are composed of a usually vowel-less genitive linker, /n/ or /r̃/ plus a genitive pronoun, e.g., **jàkar̃mù** 'our sack' (< //jàkā// 'sack' + r̃mù//. (Underlying long final vowels naturally shorten when the genitive forms are attached because of the phonological rule that automatically shortens vowels in closed syllables.) In Parsons' terminology, these bound genitive pronouns are referred to as "zero form possessives." In standard orthography, the head noun (or other head) and the linker plus the pronoun are written as one word—at least when the genitive is functioning as a possessive, e.g., **ɗàkì-nsà** room-of.his = orthographic **ɗakinsa** 'his room'. In this section I shall insert a hyphen before the linker for purposes of clarity; elsewhere in the grammar I follow the accepted orthographic word division.

The genitive pronouns with the feminine linker /r̃/, which represents rhotacized //t//, are used only when suffixed to feminine words ending in -a(a). That is to say, the choice has both grammatical and phonological requirements, e.g., **mōtà-r̃mù** 'our car' (f.), **'ya-r̃kà** 'your daughter' (f.), cf. **kìlākì-nsà** 'his harlot' (f.), **bàka-nsù** 'their bow' (m.). The choice of the linker depends on the gender and number of the head to which it is attached and not on the gender or number of the following genitive pronoun, e.g., **mōtà-r̄sà** 'his car', **mōtà-r̄tà** 'her car', **ɓàka-nkà** 'your (m.) bow', **ɓàka-nkì** 'your (f.) bow'. In normal speech, the /r̄/ usually assimilates to an abutting coronal consonant, e.g., **mōtà-r̄sù** = [mōtàssù] 'their car', **ƙawa-r̄tà** = [ƙawattà] 'her friend', and commonly to other consonants as well, e.g., **tāgà-r̄mù** = [tāgàmmù] 'our window'.

ΔDN: In WH dialects, the feminine linker always assimilates to and becomes a geminate with the initial consonant of the following possessor, noun or pronoun, e.g., **hừla-kkà** 'your (m.) cap', **mōtà-mmù** 'our car', **àkuyà-ttà** 'her goat', **r̀gas Sāni** 'Sani's gown'. Thus the linker has to be interpreted morphologically as having the form **-G**, where the **G** indicates an underspecified consonant that is realized as a geminate with the following consonant.

Many WH dialects have a fairly strict phonotactic aversion to word-final L-L. As a result, words like **àkuyà-ttà** 'her goat' appear as **àkuyà-tta** with final L-H. Where this occurs, it is a general phonological feature and not a property of possessive pronouns per se.

The genitive pronouns with the linker /n/ are used in all other environments, i.e., with masculine and plural words, and with all words ending in vowels other than -a(a), including feminine words, e.g., **mijì-ntà** 'her husband (m.)', **gida-nmù** [gidammù] 'our house (m.)', **shānu-nkà** [shānuŋkà] 'your cattle (pl.)', **gwaggò-nsà** 'his aunt (f.)', **gwamnatì-nmù** [gwamnatìmmù] 'our government (f.)', **zîk ɗi-ntà** 'her zipper (m.)', **bâl ɗi-nkù** [ɗiŋkù] 'your ball (f.)'. (As illustrated, the syllable-final /n/ automatically assimilates to the position of the following abutting consonant. In the case of [m], but not [ŋ], this is often reflected in writing, especially in older works).

The third person bound possessive has an alternative (archaic?) form in which the linker appears with its vowel intact, e.g., **màtā-tasà** (= **màta-r̄sà**) 'his wife' (normally spelled **mata tasa** vs. **matarsa**). This variant is generally restricted to feminine nouns with a third person singular possessor. It is most commonly used with phonologically short (mono- or disyllabic), high-frequency words, e.g., **'yā-tasà** 'his daughter', **fuskà-tatà** 'her face', **r̀gā-tatà** 'her blouse', **jīmằ-tasà** 'his tanning (or tanning of it)'. Some speakers consider a phrase like **mōtà-tasù** 'their car' as grammatical but it is seldom encountered in normal usage. Similarly, masculine nouns with -nasà and -natà (e.g., **àkū-nasà** 'his parrot', **mijì-natà** 'her husband' are deemed grammatical and examples are occasionally found in written sources, but they are far from common.

With the exception of the first person singular, the pronouns per se are identical to those used in the absolute possessives, e.g., **jàkar̄-sà cē** 'It is his sack', **tā-sà cē** 'It is his'; but **jàkātā cè** (where **tā** = //ta-a//) 'It is my sack', **tằ-wa cè** 'It is mine.'

ΔDN: In WH, one also gets a difference between the bound pronoun and the free possessive in the third person masculine singular. The bound 3m pronoun is normally -i attached to the na/ta form of the linker, e.g., **dōkìnai** 'his horse', **àkūnai** 'his parrot', **màtātai** 'his wife', **kujèrātai** 'his chair', whereas the pronoun used with the absolute possessives is -shì, e.g., **nāshì / tāshì** 'his (m./f.)'.

In the first person singular, the linker takes the form **na-/ta-** (rather than -n/-r̄). The pronoun itself is H-tone -a, which combines with the linker to produce the genitive forms -nā/-tā, e.g., **hừlā-tā** 'my cap', **'yā-tā** 'my daughter', **mijì-nā** 'my husband', **shānū-nā** 'my cattle', **gwaggò-nā** 'my aunt', **bâl ɗī-nā** 'my ball'.

For reasons that we do not understand, the first person bound genitive pronouns end in an "indeterminate vowel" (see §54:1.2.2), i.e., a vowel that normally appears as long, but that adds a glottal closure and becomes half-long in prepausal position, e.g., [**wannàn gidānā nè**] 'This is my house' vs. [**gà gidāna·ʔ**] 'Here is my house'; [**bài gyārà mōtàtā ba**] 'He didn't repair my car' vs. [**yā gyārà mōtàta·ʔ**] 'He repaired my car.'

ΔDN: According to Malami Buba (personal communication), this prepausal rule does not apply in the Sokoto dialect. Rather, the first person genitive pronoun remains long in all positions.

For many speakers, prepausal half-long vowels remain distinct from short vowels; for other speakers, however, the half-long vowel vowels are in the process of merging with the short vowels. For the speakers with the phonological merger, the language will have added a new morphophonemic rule to produce the alternation between the long and short vowel allomorphs of the first person pronouns, e.g., **gidānā nè** 'It's my house' (with long /nā/) vs. **gà gidāna** 'Here's my house' (with short /na/). In this grammar, the vowel of the -**nā**/-**tā** endings (as well as that of all other items with "indeterminate vowels") are transcribed as long, regardless of the position in the sentence, with the understanding that the vowel of these morphemes is subject to a prepausal phonetic implementation rule requiring glottal closure accompanied by reduction in duration.

Such forms as **gidānā** 'my house' have been segmented in various ways by different scholars: (1) **gidā** + ∅ + **nā** {house + first psn pn, with linker absent}. (This analysis requires that there be a distinct first person feminine pronoun -**tā**, a form that exists nowhere else in the language.) (2) **gidā** + **nā** + ∅ {house + linker containing a long vowel, with missing pronoun understood}. (This analysis requires that the bound linker, which has a short vowel or no vowel in all other persons, be long in the first person.) (3) **gidā** + **n** + **ā** {house + linker + first psn pn with a long vowel}. (This analysis requires that the vowel of the first person pronoun be long, unlike that of all the other persons and unlike the first person free possessive, where it is short.) The correct segmentation—at least from a historical perspective—is (4) **gidā** + **na** + **a** {house + short-vowel linker + short-vowel first psn pn}, with a morpheme break falling in the middle of the long vowel. The first person singular pronoun /a/ probably represents a historical reduction of *wa when preceded by a short vowel, i.e., *gidā-na-wa > gidā-na-a (= gidānā) 'my house', *rìgā-ta-wa > rìgā-ta-a (= rìgātā) 'my robe', cf. **tàwa** 'mine', where the /w/ after the long vowel has been retained.

1.1.6.2. As a general morphophonological rule, the bound possessives require that the preceding vowel be long. If the final vowel of a noun is lexically short, it necessarily undergoes lengthening in a possessive construction, e.g., **àkū-nā** 'my parrot' < //àku//; **à tsakà-tasà** 'in its center' < //tsakà//; **fādà-tai** [dv] 'his palace' < //fādà//.

1.1.6.3. The bound genitive pronouns have the following uses:
1. Attributive possessives, e.g., **gida-nmù** 'our house', **hùlā-tā** 'my cap', **māgàni-ntà** 'its medicine' (i.e., medicine against it)', **hařbì-nsà** 'his shooting (that he did)', **ìsa-řmù** 'our arrival'; **kâ-ntà** 'her head, herself'.

°AN: Hausa does not have the formal distinction between alienable and inalienable possession that is so common throughout Chadic. (Schuh (1974a) has suggested, probably correctly, that the insult phrase **uwākà!** 'Screw you!' (lit. mother.your), with the linker absent, is a historical reflex of an old inalienable possessive formation.) With body parts, the inalienable relation is often expressed by means of an oblique prepositional/adverbial phrase rather than with a direct possessive, e.g., **nā kūjè à hannu** 'I scraped my hand' (lit. I was scraped at hand), rather than **nā kūjè hannūnā**; **tā karyè à ƙafà** 'She broke her leg' (lit. she broke at leg), cf. **tā karyà gōràřtà** 'She (purposely) broke her staff', **gōràřtà tā karyè** 'Her staff broke.'

2. Objects of verbal nouns, e.g., **tanà zāgì-nā** 'She is insulting me', **bà sù fàrà yî-nsà ba** 'They didn't start to do it', **munà hařbì-nsà** 'We are shooting it.' Note that genitive pronouns with verbal nouns (apart from weak verbal nouns) can function either as thematic objects or as (possessive) subjects. Thus

hařbì-nsà, for example, could mean either 'shooting him' or 'his shooting' (i.e., the shooting that he did).

3. Objects of "genitive prepositions," e.g., **kâ-ntà** 'on her', **bāyā-nā** 'behind me', **ciki-nsù** 'in them'.

4. Partitive possessives, e.g., **biyu-nsù** 'two of them', **bìyař ɗi-nkù** 'five of you', **dukkà-nmù** 'all of us'.

1.1.7. Reflexives

1 s	kâinā	1 p	kânmù
2 m	kânkà	2 p	kânkù
2 f	kânkì		
3 m	kânsà / kânshì	3 p	kânsù
3 f	kântà		

The reflexive pronouns are composed of the word **kâi** 'head' plus a bound genitive pronoun, e.g., **kâinā** 'myself' = 'my head'; **kânkì** 'yourself (f.)' = 'your (f.) head'. (In closed syllables, the /ai/ diphthong automatically reduces to /a/.) The singular form of the word **kâi** 'head' is used with all reflexives, whether singular or plural. Reflexive pronouns have two functions, which we can call "basic" and "emphatic," e.g., (basic) **mun cûci kâ-nmù** 'We harmed ourselves'; (emphatic) **nī kâi-nā nā gamà aikìn** 'I *myself* finished the work.' For a full discussion of reflexives, see §**63**:1.

1.1.8. Reciprocals

1 p	jūnanmù	(= jūnā)
2 p	jūnankù	(= jūnā)
3 p	jūnansù	(= jūnā)

The reciprocal pronouns are composed of the word **jūnā** 'self' plus a bound possessive pronoun. Whereas English uses the same phrase, e.g., 'each other' or 'one another', regardless of the person of the antecedent, Hausa has different forms that can be used in the first, second, and third persons, e.g., **mun tsallàkē jūnanmù** 'We jumped over each other'; **kù tàimàki jūnankù** 'You (pl.) should help one another', **Bellò dà Tankò bà zā sù cûci jūnansù ba** 'Bello and Tanko will not cheat one another.' The grammatical use of the reciprocals is described in §**63**:2.

1.2. Weak subject pronouns
1.2.1. Introduction

The so-called subject pronouns of traditional Hausa grammars, which are referred to variously as "tense/aspect pronouns," "person-aspect pronouns," "subject agreement markers," or "preverbal pronouns," are made up of a pronominal element plus a marker of tense/aspect/mood (TAM). The tradition in Hausa studies has been to refer to the entire person + TAM complex as a "pronoun" even though in many (but not all) cases the two elements are clearly segmentable. For example, the form **tanà** 'she [continuous]' (as in **tanà fìtā** 'She is leaving') is composed of the 3f pronoun **ta** + the continuous marker -**nà**. To be able to refer when needed either to the entire element or to its constituent parts, I have adopted the following terminology. The pronominal element per se (e.g., **ta** 'she' or **mu** 'we') is called a "weak subject pronoun" (wsp). (It is called "weak" because phonologically it tends to attach itself to the TAM marker and because syntactically it functions not as the subject per se but rather as an agreement marker, often accompanying an overt noun subject.) The marker of tense, aspect, and mood (e.g., **nà** 'continuous' or **zā** 'future') is called a TAM. The combination of the wsp and the TAM is called the "person-aspect-complex" (PAC). This PAC, which corresponds to INFL in theoretical syntax, is required in tensed sentences even when a noun subject is present, e.g., **yārinyằ [zā tà] sōyà nāmằ** 'The girl will fry the meat' (lit. girl [fut she] fry meat), not ****yārinyằ sōyà nāmằ**.

1.2.2. The impersonal

In addition to the eight person/number/gender categories found in the non-subject pronouns, the weak subject pronouns include an impersonal 'one, they' (//a// or //an// depending on the TAM), which is unspecified for person and gender features, e.g., **an kāwō ruwā** 'One/they brought water' (i.e., water was brought by someone unknown or not worth mentioning). The impersonal can be grouped with the plural pronouns on both morphological and syntactic grounds. It is listed in the paradigms under the plural pronouns and, for ease of reference, is indicated as fourth person plural (4p). (Detailed discussion of the use of the impersonal is provided in a separate unit, see chap. **38**.)

1.2.3. Heavy and light wsp paradigms

The pronouns in the various PACs appear on the surface in a number of different guises; but fundamentally there are only two major wsp paradigms: (1) First, there is a set of heavy-syllable pronouns with inherent H tone (sometimes referred to as the **sun** pronouns). In SH, this set occurs only in the completive, where it constitutes a portmanteau form incorporating both person and TAM features, e.g., **sun** 'they (completive)', **tā** 'she (completive)'. (In other dialects, these pronouns are also used in the preterite and in the potential.) (2) All of the other PACs make use of a set of inherently toneless, light-syllable pronouns, which in most (but not all) cases occur attached to an overt TAM, e.g., **su-kàn** 'they (habitual)', **ta-nằ** 'she (continuous)', **zā kì** 'you (2f) (future)', **mù** 'we (subjunctive)'.

	(1) *"heavy" wsp's*	(2) *"light" wsp's*
1s	nā	ni / in [ⁿ] / na
2m	kā	ka
2f	kin	ki
3m	yā	ya <shi>
3f	tā	ta
1p	mun	mu
2p	kun	ku
3p	sun	su
4p	an	a

The pronouns in the light set can be grouped into (a) a subset used when the TAM is phonologically zero (occurring in the subjunctive, the neutral, and negative completive), e.g., **tà Ø** 'she.subjunctive'; (b) a subset used after the TAM (occurring in the future, allative, and negative-HAVE), e.g., **zā tà** 'she future', and (c) a subset prefixed to the TAM (occurring everywhere else), e.g., **tanằ** 'she.continuous'. When occurring without an overt TAM or with a phonologically zero TAM, the light wsp's have default L tone. The post-TAM wsp's all manifest polar tone, i.e., L after H and H after L. The pre-TAM wsp's, all of which have H tone, were also polar originally, although synchronically, the singular preterite pronouns (apart from 2f) no longer preserve polarity on the surface, e.g., **ta** 'she.preterite' < ***ta-(kà)**, cf. **mukà** 'we.preterite'.

The full paradigms for the various PACs are presented in the unit on tense/aspect/mood (TAM) along with a detailed discussion of their meaning and use (see chap. **70**).

2. NON-PERSONAL PRONOUNS

The personal pronouns, like **kà** 'you, your, **mù** 'us, our', **shi** 'him', have special morphological and syntactic properties that set them apart as a morphosyntactic class. By contrast, the non-personal pronouns pattern syntactically with ordinary nouns. For example, the form of the verb within a particular grade is determined by whether a direct object is a personal pronoun or not (see §74:1). Here, the non-personal pronouns group with the nouns, e.g.,

bàn gan shì ba	I didn't see him/it. (personal pronoun)
bàn ga kōmē ba	I didn't see anything. (non-personal pronoun)
cf. **bàn ga hòtō ba**	I didn't see the picture. (noun)
yā zàɓē tà	He chose her/it. (personal pronoun)
yā zàɓi wancàn	He chose that one. (non-personal pronoun)
cf. **yā zàɓi mōtà**	He chose a car. (noun)

Similarly, the form of the indirect object marker (whether **ma-** (+ pronoun) or **wà** (+ noun)) differs depending upon whether it is followed by a personal pronoun or not. Again, the non-personal pronouns pattern with the nouns, e.g.,

yā gayà manà	He told us. (personal pronoun)
yā gayà wà kōwā dà kōwā	He told everyone. (lit. everyone and everyone) (non-personal pronoun)
yā gayà wà wândà ya biyā shì	He told the one who paid him. (non-personal pronoun)
cf. **yā gayà wà àlƙālī**	He told the judge. (noun)

The non-personal pronouns can be divided roughly into three categories: (1) demonstratives and relatives (see chap. 21), e.g., **wannàn** 'this one', **waɗàndà** 'the ones who'; (2) interrogatives (see §60:1), e.g., **wà** 'who?'; and (3) universals (see chap. 73), e.g., **kōmē** 'everything', **duk(à)** 'all'.

[References: Gouffé (1978); Kraft (1974)]

60. Questions

QUESTIONS are of two types: direct and indirect. The direct questions subdivide into (1) Q-word questions and (2) Yes/No questions.

1. Q-WORD QUESTIONS

1.1. Inventory

Q-word questions make use of the following interrogative words: **wằ** 'who?'; **mḕ** 'what?'; **wànè** 'which?'; **wànnē** 'which one?'; **ìnā** 'where?'; **yàushè/yàushē** 'when?'; **yằyằ** 'how?'; **nawà** 'how many, how much?'; **don mḕ** (= **sabồdà mḕ**) 'why?'. The Q-words are not marked for case, thus **wằ**, for example, also indicates 'whom?' and 'whose?' in addition to 'who?' The 'who', 'what', and 'which' interrogatives have distinct forms for masculine, feminine, and plural referents (see below).

1.1.1. Who?

wằ (= **wằnē nḕ**) m., **wằcē cḕ** f., **su wằ** (= **su wằnē nḕ**) pl.
wằyê m., **su wằyê** pl.

The simple form **wằ** is used if the gender and number of the person questioned is either masculine singular or unknown/unspecified/unimportant, e.g., **wằ ya tsayằ?** 'Who stopped?' To specifically indicate that the referent is plural one uses **su wằ** (with the third person plural pronoun **su**), e.g., **su wằ sukà tsayằ?** 'Who (pl.) stopped?' The plural, with individuating connotations, is sometimes indicated by conjoining **wằ** with itself, e.g., **(dà) wằ dà wằ** '(and) who and who?' Examples:

wằ dà wằ sukà zō?	Who (pl.) (i.e., who and who else) came?
dà wằ dà wằ akà kāmằ?	Whom (pl.) did they catch?
su wằ dà wằ zā kù zằɓā?	Whom (pl.) are you going to choose?

> °AN: In SH, sentences with a Q-word typically have a sentence final L-tone q-morpheme (see §1.2). When added to a word with final H tone, the result is a sentence-final fall, e.g., **wằ ya zō +`** = [wằ ya zô] 'Who came?' In keeping with standard practice among Hausaists, this final fall is not represented in the transcription of examples like the above although from a linguistic point of view it ought to be.

The long forms **wằnē nḕ**, **wằcē cḕ**, and **su wằnē nḕ** consist of **wằ** (or **su wằ**) plus a repetition of the stabilizer. (The orthographic convention is to write the first occurrence of the stabilizer attached to **wằ** and the second separate.) If the gender of the questioned referent is explicitly known to be feminine, one must use the long form **wằcē cḕ** (with f. concord), e.g., **wằcē cḕ ta tsayằ?** 'Who (i.e., which female) stopped?'; **kē wằcē cḕ?** 'Who (f.) are you (f.)?' With masculine and plural referents, the long forms are

488

optional in verbal sentences. They are generally required in equational sentences and when the interrogative stands alone, e.g.,

wǎ(nē nề) ka zǎɓā?	Whom did you choose?
su wǎ(nē nề) sukà jē har̃bǐ?	Who (pl.) went hunting?
wǎnē nề mālàmîn?	Who is the teacher?
wǎnē nề?	Who (is it)?

The variant wǎyê, like its equivalent wǎ, takes masculine singular concord and is used if the gender and number of the person questioned is either masculine singular or is unknown or unspecified, e.g., wǎyê nē dǎr̃ektà? 'Who is the director?' It can be pluralized (i.e., su wǎyê), but it does not have a corresponding feminine form.

ΔDN: The form wǎyê, which has generally been neglected in pedagogical grammars and practical dictionaries, is a common alternative among Kano speakers. There is no information available regarding its dialectal distribution.

The word wǎ (like its alternative forms) is syntactically invariant, i.e., it can represent a subject, direct object, indirect object, object of preposition, possessive, etc., e.g.,

wǎ ya sācè mîn awarwarō?	Who (subject) stole my bracelet from me?
wǎnē nề sukà har̃bề?	Whom (d.o.) did they execute?
su wǎ kakề gyārà wà?	Whom (pl.) (i.o) are you repairing (it) for?
dà wǎ ka yi tàfiyà?	With whom (obj. of prep.) did you travel?
màtar̃ wǎ ta haihù?	Whose (possessive) wife gave birth?
na wǎnē nề ya gujề makà?	Whose [m. referent understood] (possessive) ran away from you?

Questioned indirect objects optionally employ a resumptive pronoun in the original position. Objects of prepositions that cannot be stranded obligatorily use a resumptive pronoun, e.g.,

wǎcē cè kikà gayǎ wà (= …gayǎ matà)?	Whom did you tell (it) to?
su wǎnē nề ka yi aikǐ dà sū?	Whom (pl.) did you do the work with?
wǎ ta kàrɓi rancen kuɗǐ dàgà gàrē shì?	Whom did she get a loan from?

1.1.1.1. The interrogative form wǎnē (with a single bound stabilizer) followed by an NP or independent pronoun is used in a special contemptuous rhetorical expression whose best translation varies depending on the context. In this special usage, wǎnē is invariant for gender and number, e.g.,

wǎnē Daudà?	Who the hell is Dauda?
wǎnē mùtûm?	Of what account is a human being?
	(i.e., this is beyond human ability; only God could do this)
wǎnē màtā mài zaman kântà?	Of what worth is an unattached, unmarried woman?
wǎnē sàraunìyar̃ kyâu?	Of what account is the beauty queen?
wǎnē 'yan-sàndā?	This is beyond the expertise of policemen.
wǎnē fàdàwan sarkǐ?	Who do the chief's courtiers think they are?
wǎnē nī?	Who am I (to attempt such a thing)?
wǎnē ita?	Of what account is she? (i.e., she is not up to it)
wǎnē kai / kē?	Who the hell do you (m./f.) think you are (to try this)?

Note that with the final L-tone question marker added (see below §1.2), words with final high tone are normally pronounced with falling tone, e.g., [wǎnē kâi], [wǎnē kê], [wǎnē itâ], etc.

1.1.2. What?

mè̀ (= **mènē nè̀**) m., **mècē cè̀** f. (rare), **su mènē nè̀** pl.
mèyê m.

The variants for the neutral/masculine word for 'what?' **mè̀** (= **mènē nè̀**) = **mèyê** parallel the 'who?' forms **wǎ** (= **wǎnē nè̀**) = **wǎyê**, e.g., **mè̀** (= **mènē nè̀**) = **mèyê ya fādì** 'What fell?' The corresponding feminine form exists but is rarely used except in idiomatic or figurative constructions. The overt plural formed with **su** is much less common than in the exzpression **su wǎ(nē nè̀)** 'who?'; instead one normally uses the conjoint phrase (**dà**) **mè̀ dà mè̀** (lit. (and) what and what?). Examples:

mè̀(nē nè̀) ka zàɓā?	What did you choose?
mè̀(nē nè̀) ya fashè̀?	What broke?
mènē nè̀ wannàn?	What is this?
dà mè̀ dà mè̀ sukà ƙwācè̀?	
What (things) did they confiscate?	
mècē cè̀ ita dà zā tà hanà ka tàfiyà gidā?	
Who (lit. what) the hell is she that she will prevent you from going home?	

◊HN: The historically original form of 'what?' was **mì̀**, which is still used in WH but with variable tone. The change to **mè̀** probably began as anticipatory assimilation to a following mid vowel, presumably that of the stabilizer, i.e., **mìnēnè̀ → mènēnè̀. Subsequently, the pronunciation **mè̀** was extended to all environments. Note that the original form of the stabilizer was **nā/tā**, which is also still found in WH. The change from **mì̀** to **mè̀** thus must have been subsequent to the **nā/tā** to **nē/cē** change. Using the masculine form for illustration, the derivational sequence can be presented as **mìnānā̀ > *mìnēnè̀ > mènēnè̀* (and thence, by back formation, to **mè̀**).

1.1.3. Which? / Which one?

which?: **wànè̀** m., **wàcè̀** f., **wàɗànnè̀** pl.
which one(s)?: **wànnē** m., **wàccē** f., **wàɗànnē** pl.

The interrogative determiners immediately precede their head nouns (with which they agree in number/gender). If the stabilizer is used, which is possible, it occurs after the NP, e.g.,

wànè̀ yārò̀ nē ya ci gàsā?	Which boy won the competition?
wànè̀ irìn lèmō ka fi sô?	Which type of soft drink do you prefer?
wàcè̀ mōtà̀ cē ta fi tsàdā?	Which car is more expensive?
wàɗànnè̀ hūlunà̀ kakè̀ sayârwā?	Which caps are you selling?

The interrogative pronominal forms optionally occur with the stabilizer **nē/cē**. They often appear followed by a prepositional phrase indicating 'among them', etc., or by a genitive pronoun. They can also appear as sentences by themselves, in which case they will end in falling tone because of the addition of the L-tone q-morpheme. Examples:

wànnē/wàɗànnē (nè) ya/sukà fi kyâu?	Which one/ones is/are best?
wàccē (cè) zā kà zàɓā?	Which one are you going to choose?
wàɗànnē cikinsù bà malàlàtā ba nè?	Which ones among them are not slackers?
wànnensù ya yi sātàr̃ kuɗîn?	Which one of them stole the money?
wànnê / wàccê / wàɗànnê?	Which one(s)?

1.1.4. Where?

The general word for 'where?' is **ìnā**, e.g.,

ìnā yār̃òn? Where is the boy? **ìnā ta tàfi?** Where did she go? **ìnā ka gan sù?** Where did you see them?

In addition to its general meaning of 'where?' **ìnā** also functions as a Q-word in a few other contexts.

First, **ìnā** is used in asking someone's name, e.g., **ìnā sūnan yār̃òn?** 'What (lit. where) is the boy's name?' (= **yàyà sūnan yār̃òn?** lit. how is the boy's name).

Second, it is used in standard greetings, e.g., **ìnā làbār̃ì?** 'How are things?' (lit. where is news); **ìnā gàjiyà?** 'How are you?' (lit. where is tiredness); **ìnā kwānā** 'Good morning' (lit. where is sleeping); **ìnā wunì** 'Good afternoon' (lit. where is spending day); **ìnā gidā** 'How's the family?' (lit. where is house(hold)). It is also used in the expression **ìnā ruwankà?** 'What business is it of yours?' (lit. where is your water)

Third, it is used—with intonational prominence—as an exclamatory question **ìnâ?!** (= **ànâ?!**) 'Who could do that? No way! Impossible!'

Fourth, it appears in a special construction having the form **ìnā X ìnā Y**, which semantically indicates incompatibility between the X and the Y, e.g.,

ìnā nī ìnā Bàlā?	Bala is not my equal / I have no business with Bala.
(lit. where am I where is Bala?)	
ìnā kū ìnā gidan giyà?	What business do you (pl.) have going to a bar?
(i.e., it is not fitting for you (e.g., as a Muslim nondrinker) to go to a bar)	
ìnā mātā ìnā cîn àbinci à hanyà?	It is not fitting for women to eat on the street.
ìnā kai ìnā bōlà-gajà?	A wooden truck is not your type of vehicle.

°AN: This **ìnā X ìnā Y** construction has been described in detail by Attouman (1987). There is another essentially equivalent construction indicating incompatibility that has the structure **bâ X bâ Y** (lit. there is not X there is not Y), e.g., **bâ nī bâ Bàlā** 'I have no business with Bala' (see §26:1.2.3).

1.1.5. When?

The general word for 'when?' is **yàushè** or **yàushē**. The two different pronunciations—**yàushè** with a short final vowel and L-L tone and **yàushē** with a long final vowel and L-H tone—are both common in SH, but the latter appears to be in the ascendancy. (In examples, the two different variants are used indiscriminately.) Examples:

yàushē (nè) sukà dāwō?	When did they return?
yàushè (nē) zā à sākè būɗè makar̃antā?	When will school open again?

Common paraphrases for **yàushè** are **wànè lōkàcī?** 'what (lit. which) time?' and **ƙarfè nawà?** 'what clock time?' (lit. o'clock how many), e.g., wànè lōkàcī (nè) yârā sukè yîn kàr̃àtunsù?

    When (lit. what time) do the children do their studies?

ƙarfè nawà zā kà jē bankì?   When (i.e., at what time) are you going to go to the bank?

1.1.6. How?

The general word for 'how?' is **yàyà**. It is often preceded by the preposition **ta** 'via' to indicate 'how?' in the sense of 'by what means?', e.g.,

yàyà likità ya bar̃ shì yà shā tābà?	How is it that the doctor let him smoke?
yàyà kikè jî?	How are you feeling?
ta yàyà kukà sàmi wurin shìgā?	How did you find a way to get in?

Like the word **ìnā** 'where?' **yàyà** can be used when asking about someone's name and in greetings, e.g., **yàyà sūnankà?** 'What's your name?' (= **ìnā sūnankà?**); **yàyà gidā?** 'How's the family?' (= **ìnā gidā?**); **yàyà làbār̃ì?** 'How's news?' (= **ìnā làbār̃ì?**) (but *not* ****yàyà kwānā?** 'Good morning', for which one must use **ìnā kwānā?**).

    In spoken Hausa, **ƙàƙà** 'how?' is sometimes used in place of **yàyà**. In the written language, **yàyà** is the more common variant.

1.1.7. How many? How much?

The general word for 'how many, how much?' is the interrogative quantifier **nawà**, which follows the head noun, e.g.,

(mutànē) nawà akà kāmà?	How many (men) did they arrest?
kuɗī nawà zā kà sāmù?	How much money are you going to get?
sàu nawà ìn tàfi ìn dāwō?	How many times should I go and come back?

The repeated form **nawà nawà** indicates the distributive 'how many or how much each?', e.g.,

ƙwai nawà nawà nē?	How much are the eggs each?
dalà nawà nawà nē zā kà bā sù?	How many dollars each are you going to give them?

1.1.8. Why?

The interrogative 'why?' is expressed not by a single Q-word but rather by a prepositional phrase with **mè** 'what?'; either **don mè** (pronounced [dommè]) (= **dòmin mè**) 'for what?' or **sabòdà mè** 'because of what?'; e.g.,

don mè kakè ƙauràcē manà?	Why are you avoiding us?
bà kà zō ba; sabòdà mè?	You didn't come; why not?

    °AN: The orthographic convention is to write **don me** as two words with an unassimilated /n/, thereby reflecting the etymology. Synchronically, it would probably make more sense to write it as a single word **domme**.

Another way to express 'why?' is by means of the phrasal expression **mè ya sà** lit. 'what caused?'; e.g.,

mè ya sà sōjà sukà wāshè gàrîn?	Why did the soldiers sack the town?

1.2 The q-morpheme

Sentences containing a Q-word add a "q-morpheme" / `:/ at the end. The morpheme, which consists of length and L tone, attaches itself to the immediately preceding syllable. The morpheme serves (a) to lengthen short final vowels, and (b) to add a low tone to words ending in a high tone (thereby producing a fall). If the last word in the sentence is consonant-final or if it ends in a vowel that is already long, then adding the length component has no surface consequences. Similarly, if the preceding syllable already ends in an L tone or in a fall (= HL on a single syllable), then the L-tone component of the morpheme attaches vacuously and has no effect on the surface tone. Examples:

wầ zâi fìta + `: → wầ zâi fìtâ?   Who will go out? (length and tone added)
yàushè ta haihù + `: → yàushè ta haihǔ?   When did she give birth? (length added)
mè sukà sayar̃ + `: → mè sukà sayâr̃?   What did they sell? (tone added)
kuɗin wannàn nawà nē + `: → kuɗin wannàn nawà nê?   How much does it cost? (tone added)
ìnā ka ga yāròn + `: → ìnā ka ga yāròn?   Where did you see the boy? (vacuous addition)

The q-morpheme attaches to the last word in the sentence, whatever that word might be, e.g.,

wầ yakè rawā + `: → wầ yakè rawâ?   Who is dancing?
wầ yakè rawā yànzu + `: → wầ yakè rawā yànzû?   Who is dancing now?

°AN: It should be emphasized that the falling tone that is found at the end of Q-word sentences is due to the q-morpheme and not to intonational effects (Newman and Newman 1981). (Unlike Yes/No sentences, which utilize special question intonation, Q-word sentences use what is essentially declarative sentence intonation.) Because there are other recognized morphemes in the language, like the verbal noun formative with monoverbs, which consist only of length and/or tone, e.g., **bi** 'follow', but **bî** 'following', there seems to be no reason not to recognize the q-morpheme at the morphemic level. Nevertheless, most scholars treat the final vowel lengthening and falling tone found in questions as being intonational features associated with the question mark and thus fail to indicate them in normal transcriptions. Thus **wầ ya fìta?** 'Who went out?' for example, is normally transcribed with a short final vowel and H tone (cf. **Bellò nē ya fìta** 'It was Bello who went out') rather than as **wầ ya fìtâ?** with the occurring long final vowel and falling tone. A practical reason for sticking with the standard convention is that dialects differ as to when (and if) they add the L tone. Therefore, throughout the grammar as a whole, I have gone ahead and followed the usual transcription convention, i.e., I have not indicated the length and L tone associated with the q-morpheme. In this chapter, however, I have done so when it seemed necessary to illustrate the nature of question formation.

◊HN: Historically, the q-morpheme (or morphemes?) had segmental shape, of which the tone and vowel length are the only vestiges in modern-day Hausa. The most probable shape for the morpheme was *à, which is still preserved in some Chadic languages.

1.3. Word order

In tensed sentences, a Q-word or an NP containing a Q-word normally moves to the front of the sentence into focus position. The general TAMs are obligatorily replaced by the corresponding Rel forms, e.g.,

wầ sukà kāmà?   Whom did they catch? (preterite)
cf. **sun kāmà janàr̃**   They captured the general. (completive)
mè Jummai takè dakàwā?   What is Jummai pounding? (Rel-continuous1)
cf. **Jummai tanà dakàwā**   Jummai is pounding (it). (continuous)
su wầnē nè ya gayà wà?   Whom (pl.) did he tell it to?

<u>wànnē</u> dàgà cikinsù ya mutù?	Which among them died?
<u>yàushè</u> yāròn zâi dāwō dàgà bankì?	When will the boy return from the bank?
<u>wàcè</u> irìn mōtà̄ ka fi sô?	Which kind of car do you prefer?
<u>ìnā</u> likità zâi sàmē tà?	Where will the doctor find her?
<u>ìnā</u> ɗàlìbai sukè à lōkàcîn?	Where were the students at the time?
mutànē <u>nawà</u> sukè wàr̄wàtse cikin jējì̄?	How many men are scattered in the bush?
littā̄fī <u>nawà</u> zā kà bāyar̄?	How many books are you going to give away?

Instead of fronting a questioned direct object and leaving the verb in its original position, it is possible in some circumstances to front an infinitival VP consisting of the a verb plus a Q-word or a verbal noun (participial/gerundive) phrase including the Q-word. (All of my examples involve complementation.) The original position of the VP is then filled by the pro-verb **yi** 'do' (occasionally followed by a resumptive pronoun).

rūsà <u>mènē</u> nè tīlàs (nē) Audù yà yi?
> Demolishing what is it necessary for Audu do?

kāmà <u>mènē</u> nè ya kàmātà Tankò yà yi à wannàn kòg̣ī?
> Catching what does it behoove Tanko to do in this river?

ɗaurè <u>wànē</u> nè mài yìwuwā (nè) sarkī yà yi?
> Imprisoning whom is it possible/likely that the emir might do?

A Q-word can be left in situ, but if so it is generally interpreted as a semantically marked echo question, e.g.,

an kashè wà̄?	They killed *who*?
tā sàyi mè̀?	*What* did you say she bought? (lit. she bought what?)
à cê mè̀?	One should say *what* ?

> °AN: The marked nature of the Q-word in situ even applies to double questions. For example, **wà̀ ya sàyi mè̀?** 'Who bought what?' is not semantically comparable to the corresponding English sentence, but rather carries the connotation, 'What did you say who bought?' with echo focus on 'What?'

A Q-word functioning as the object of **dà**, whether functioning in HAVE sentences or as a sociative marker, must leave a resumptive pronoun in its place. A questioned i.o. may (and commonly does) use a resumptive pronoun, but it is not obligatory since the i.o. marker **wà** can occur without an overt object, e.g.,

mè̀ kukè dà shī?	What do you have?
(cf. kunà dà mè̀? You have *what*?)	
mènē nè yārò yakè dà shī à jàkâr̄?	What does the boy have in the sack?
cf. yārò yanà̀ dà kwàɗo à jàkâr̄	The boy has a frog in the sack.
su wànē nè kikè kulàwā dà sū?	Whom (pl.) are you (f.) looking after?
cf. munà̀ kulàwā dà sū˙	We are looking after them.
wàcē cè zâi kōyà̀ wà Tūr̄ancī? (= wàcē cè zâi kōyà̀ matà Tūr̄ancī?)	Whom (f.) is he going to teach English to?
wà̀ sukà nūnà̀ wà takàr̄dâr̄? (= wà̀ sukà nūnà̀ masà takàr̄dâr̄?)	To whom did they show the letter?

Grade 5 efferential verbs do not normally require a resumptive pronoun. Because the particle **dà** that accompanies gr5 verbs is inserted only if the verb is followed on the surface by a thematic direct object, i.e., it is inserted by a late rule, it does not appear when the d.o. is questioned except in the uncommon cases where a pronoun is left behind, e.g.,

wằ dà wằ kukà tsōrataȓ?	Whom did you (pl.) frighten off?
mề zā tà sayaȓ?	What is she going to sell?
cf. **zā tà sayaȓ dà awarwarō**	She is going to sell a bracelet.
cf. **mềnē nề zā tà sayaȓ dà shī dà ȓàhūsā?**	What is she going to sell at a bargain price?

A Q-word in subject position carries focus and thus conditions the switch from a general to a Rel TAM, e.g.,

wằyê ya cînyē minì kyât?	Who ate up all my cake? (pret)
cf. **yā cînyē minì kyât**	He ate up my cake. (comp)
wàccē cề (ta)kề sàurằren ȓēdiyồ?	Which one (f.) is listening to the radio? (Rcont1)
cf. **tanà sàurằren ȓēdiyồ**	She is listening to the radio. (cont)
wàɗànnè ɗàlìbai zā sù tàimàki mālàminsù?	Which students are going to help their teacher? (fut)
cf. **ɗàlìban nàn sâ tàimàki mālàminsù**	These students will likely help their teacher. (pot)

Because Q-words are in focus, they may optionally be followed by the stabilizer **nē/cē** (with polar tone), e.g.,

ìnā nề likità zâi sằmē tà?	Where will the doctor find her?
wàcè mōtằ cē zā kằ gyārằ?	Which car are you going to repair?
wàccē cề dàgà cikinsù ta mutù?	Which among them died?
wằyê nē ya cînyē minì kyât?	Who ate up all my cake?
wàɗànnè ɗàlìbai nề zā sù tàimàki mālàminsù?	
Which students are going to help their teacher?	

If the nominal object of a preposition is (or contains) a Q-word, one can front either the entire phrase or else just the object. If the preposition left behind is a basic preposition that does not allow stranding, then a resumptive pronoun has to be inserted, e.g.,

dà wằ kukà jē sìnīmằ? = **wằcē cề kukà jē sìnīmằ dà ita?**
   With whom did you go to the movies? (= Whom did you go to the movies with her?)
dà mề akề cikà kushìn irìn wannàn? = **mề akề cikà kushìn irìn wannàn dà shī?**
   With what does one stuff this kind of cushion?
à cikin wànè kồgō ɓàrāwòn ya ɓōyè kuɗîn? = **wànè kồgō ɓàrāwòn ya ɓōyè kuɗîn à ciki?**
   Which hollow did the thief hide the money in?

As illustrated in the examples above, normal prepositional phrases with **dà** can be fronted. However, when functioning in the predicate of HAVE sentences or when serving as a component of a sociative verb (indicated here with a hyphen), the prepositional particle **dà** cannot be moved from its original location, e.g.,

mề kakè dà shī? (lit. what you.are with it) = **kanằ dà mề?** (lit. you.are with what)   What do you have?
   but *not* ****dà mề kakè?** (lit. with what you.are)

mề ka tunằ-dà shī? = (?) kā tunằ-dà mề?   What did you remember?
   but normally *not* **dà mề ka tunằ?

Although fronting is the norm, adverbial Q-words can remain in regular declarative sentence position with only a slightly strengthened nuance. With normal word order, the general rather than the Rel TAM is used). Examples:

yanằ ìnā? (= ìnā yakề?)   Where is he?
sunằ fitôwā dàgà ìnā? (= dàgà ìnā sukề fitôwā?)   They are coming out from where?
yā tàfi yàushē? (= yàushē ya tàfī?)   When did he go?
an bā kà dalằ nawà? (= dalằ nawà akà bā kằ?   How many dollars did they give you?

Q-words in simple equational sentences normally occur in initial subject position. When, however, the other argument in the sentence is an independent pronoun, the Q-word usually occurs in the predicate. The interrogative **nawà (nawà)** 'how many/much (each)?' is equally allowed at the front or at the end of the sentence. Examples:

wầyê nē mālàmîn nan nākù?   Who is that teacher of yours?
wầcē cề sàraunìyař kyâu?   Who is the beauty queen?
wàɗànnè dawākîn nē nākà?   Which of the horses are yours?
wànnē nề àlƙālîn?   Which one is the judge?
mềnē nề wannàn?   What is this?
kē wầcē cề?   Who are you (f.)?
sū ɗin nàn su wầnē nề?   Who are they?
nawà nē kuɗin kềkên? = kuɗin kềkên nawà nề?
   How much is the bicycle? (= The price of the bicycle is how much?)
nawà nawà nē gōřòn? = gōřòn nawà nawà nề?
   How much are the kolanuts each? (= The kolanuts are how much each?)

A personal pronoun in a questioned equational sentence can be repeated at the end for emphasis. In this position, it will appear with falling tone because of the q-morpheme, e.g.,

kai wầnē nề kâi?   Who are *you* (m.)?
kū su wầnē nề kû?   Who are *you* (pl.)?
shī wầyê shî?   Who is *he*?

In existential sentences, Q-words commonly occur in predicate position. Fronting is possible but it is marked, e.g.,

dà sōjà nawà?   How many soldiers are there?
àkwai mề? = mềnē nề kề àkwai?   What is there?

2. YES/NO QUESTIONS

Yes/No (Y/N) questions preserve normal word order, e.g., **Bintà tā tàfi kằsuwā?** 'Did Binta go to the market?'; cf. **Bintà tā tàfi kằsuwā** 'Binta went to the market'; **manajà bài biyā kù bā?** 'Did the manager not pay you?'; cf. **manajà bài biyā kù ba** 'The manager didn't pay you.' (Note that negative questions are answered "logically," i.e., the answer to the previous question is either 'Yes, he didn't pay us' or 'No, he paid us.') The question, as opposed to the declarative statement, is overtly marked in one or more of four ways: (1) by addition of the q-morpheme; (2) by question intonation; (3) by a sentence-final interrogative tag; and (4) by a sentence-initial interrogative word.

2.1. The q-morpheme

As indicated earlier (§1.2), the q-morpheme has two component parts: final vowel lengthening and a floating low tone. Y/N questions, like Q-word questions, invariably employ the first part, i.e., final vowel lengthening. Whether the L tone is added or not is subject to dialectal and idiolectal variation. The SH norm nowadays, as far as I can determine, is *not* to have the L tone (i.e., not to have the surface fall) unless some special expressiveness is intended, e.g.,

zâi fìta	He will go out.
zâi fìtā?	Will he go out? (= for some speakers **zâi fìtâ?**)
sun ga Sābo	They saw Sabo.
sun ga Sābō?	Did they see Sabo? (= for some speakers **sun ga Sābô?**)

°AN: Because of the final vowel lengthening of the q-morpheme, the distinction between such pairs as sābō 'new' and Sābo (proper name) is neutralized in final position in questions. Compare the declarative sentences **sun ga sābō** 'They saw a new one' and **sun ga Sābo** 'They saw Sabo (proper name)' with the question **sun ga sābō?** (= **sun ga sābô?**) 'Did they see a new one / Sabo?'

2.2. Question intonation

There is a considerable amount of variability regarding the nature of the intonation used in Y/N questions. Although the matter is yet to be investigated in detail the variation seems to be dialectal, sociolectal, and even idiolectal. All speakers replace the downward slope (downdrift) characteristic of declarative sentences by an essentially level, somewhat raised grid, but there are numerous differences that appear at the end of the sentence.

Here I shall limit myself to a description of two intonational patterns for Y/N questions, what I call the "classic" pattern and the "final raising" pattern.

2.2.1. The "classic" pattern

The main feature of the "classic" pattern (described in standard grammars) is key raising (= register shift) before the last H tone of the sentence (indicated in the examples by ↑). The key raising raises the pitch of the H tone and also of any succeeding L tones. (A final H-L sequence, for examples, surfaces as something that sounds like an extra high pitch followed by a high or mid.) If the final syllable has falling tone (= HL), either lexically or because of the addition of the L tone component of the q-morpheme (for those speakers who have it), one gets a raised H with a small fall to the raised L level. This is shown schematically in the following examples:

```
7 _____nā_____
6 _____
5 _____sun_____yi_____mà_____
4 _____sà_____
3 _____
```

sun sàyi ↑ nāmà?   Did they buy meat?

```
7 _____
6 _____ bē _____
5 ____ zā _____ dā ____ wō _____
4 _____ gồ _____
3 ____ sù _____
```

zā sù dāwō gồ ↑ bē?   Will they return tomorrow?

```
7 _____ bô _____╲_____
6 _____ ╲_____
5 _____ bi ____ yā ____ Sā _____
4 _____
3 ___ mù _____
```

mù biyā Sā ↑ bô?   Should we pay Sabo? (with L tone of q-morpheme)

```
7 _____ bâ ___╲_____
6 _____ ╲_____
5 _____ zō _____
4 ___ bà tà _____
3 _____
```

bà tà zō ↑ bâ?   Did she not come? (with L tone of q-morpheme)

```
7 _____ nâřr ___╲____
6 _____ ╲_
5 ___ bi ____ rai ____ sun _____ ga ____ gō _____
4 _____ shì _____
3 _____
```

birai sun shìga gō ↑ nâřr?   Did monkeys enter the farm?

2.2.2. The final raising pattern

In the raising pattern, the tone of the last syllable is raised to a level higher than that of the immediately preceding syllable. (The L tone of the q-morpheme is not added. If the final syllable has L or F tone (= HL), that tone becomes H. If the preceding syllable was H, the new H will be even higher, e.g.,

```
7 _____
6 _____ bā _____
5 ____ zā _____ kā ____ wō _____
4 _____ à ____ yà _____
3 _____ kà _____
```

zā kà kāwō àyà ↑ bā? (< **àyàbà**)   Are you going to bring bananas?

7				mā	
6					
5	sun		yi	nā	
4		sà			
3					

sun sàyi nā ↑ mā? (< nāmà̠)?   Did they buy meat?

7				mai	
6					
5	tā	zu	bō		
4					
3					

tā zubō ↑ mai? (< mâi) ?   Did she pour in oil?

7					nař	
6						
5	birai	sun		ga	gō	
4			shì			
3						

birai sun shìga gō ↑ nař? (< gōnâř) Did the monkeys enter the farm?

2.3. Sentence-final interrogative tags

Various grammatical morphemes can be used as sentence-final interrogative tags in Yes/No sentences. These all have a slightly difference nuance. To begin with, one has the negative marker **ba** and the conjunction **kō** 'or'. Because of the addition of the q-morpheme, **ba** necessarily appears with a long final vowel and, for many speakers, also a falling tone; **kō**, on the other hand, usually remains H, although a fall is possible. They are both preceded by key raising (↑), i.e., they are pronounced on a pitch higher than that of a preceding H tone. Examples:

kā ji bâ?	So you've understood?
yā àuri Aishà bā?	He married Aisha did he not?
zā kà dāwō dà wuri kō?	Are you going to return soon?
an naɗà shi sarkī kô?	Did they install him as chief?
shân giyà̠ hàřāmùn nē kō?	Drinking of alcohol is forbidden isn't it?

The tag **kō** can be thought of as a grammaticalized reduction from an elliptical negative sentence or from the clausal tag **kō bà hakà bâ?** 'or is it not thus?' (This clausal tag marks a question where the expectation is that there will be an affirmative answer.) Examples:

gòbe zā kà gyārà mōtàř kō?	Are you going to repair the car tomorrow?

cf. gòbe zā kà gyārà mōtàr̃ <u>kō</u> bà zā kà gyārà mōtàr̃ bā?

> Are you going to repair the car tomorrow or are you not going to repair the car?

gòbe zā kà gyārà mōtàr̃ <u>kō</u> bằ hakà bâ?   Are you going to repair the car tomorrow or not?

As described in §66:2.3, the stabilizer **nē** can be used as a reinforcement marker at the end of a sentence. In an interrogative sentence, it takes on the function of a question tag. When preceded by an H tone, **nē**, which underlyingly has polar tone, will appear with L tone. When preceded by a L tone, **nē** will either appear as H (without the q-morpheme L) or as falling (with the q-morpheme L), e.g.,

zā kà kāwō lèmō nè?   Are you going to bring a soft drink?
zā kà kāwō Fantằ nē? (= ... nê?)   Are you going to bring Fanta?
yā àuri Aishà nē? (= ... nê?)   Did he marry Aisha?

The modal particle **kùwa** 'indeed' also functions as an interrogative tag, in which case it appears with a long final vowel and optional falling tone, e.g.,

yā tàfi kùwā?   Has he in fact already gone?
kā sằmi Audù à gidā kùwâ?   Did you in fact find Audu at home?

The same particle **kùwa** (or its variant **kò**) commonly follows **kō** 'or' in forming alternative questions, e.g.,

yā kāwō sù, kō kùwâ?   Did he bring them or not?
wannàn māgànin banzā nè, kō kò?   Is this useless medicine or what?

The particle **fà** 'how about?' functions exclusively as a question tag. It serves in place of the q-morpheme and thus does not normally undergo vowel lengthening. It commonly occurs with NPs rather than full sentences, e.g.,

zân bā kà naiṟằ dubū. Mūsā fà?   I'll give you 1,000 nairas. How about Musa?
kanà sôn mangwàr̃ò? Ī. gwaibằ fà?   Do you like mangoes? Yes. How about guavas?
mālàm zâi zō. kai fà?   The teacher will come. How about you?

2.4. Sentence-initial interrogative words
2.4.1. kō

A common interrogative marker used in sentence-initial position in Yes/No sentences is **kō** 'or', e.g.,

kō zuwàn gwamnằ gidānā zâi bā kù mằmākì? (= zuwàn gwamnằ gidānā zâi bā kù mằmākì kō?)

> Will the governor's coming to my house surprise you?

kō Mūsā nằ nan?   Is Musa there?
kō yā sâ ku kun shārè duk ɗākìn?   Did he make you sweep the entire room?

This usage as an interrogative marker is obviously an extension of the use of **kō** as a disjunctive 'or' in alternative questions, e.g.,

kō kin yàr̃da kō bà kì yàr̃da bā?   Do you agree or do you not agree?
kō zā kà tāshì kō (kò) zā kà zaunằ à gidā?

> Are you going to get up or are you going to stay at home?

A sentence with a propositional complement can be questioned with the help of **kō**, e.g.,

kō yā kàmātà (wai) Tànî tà biyā hàr̃ājì?   Is it fitting that Tani should pay taxes?
kō wājìbī nè Mùsùlmī sù yi aikìn hajì?   Is it obligatory for Muslims to do the hadj?

Alternatively, it is possible to treat the sentence as consisting of two clauses both subject to questioning in which case one can add a question mark after the complement-taking expression (CTE) and also insert **kō** before the complement. (Note: The question mark at the end of the CTE will be realized as vowel lengthening, intonational raising, and, for people who use the L-tone of the q-morpheme, a final fall on H-final words.)

yā kàmātà̀? kō tà biyā hàr̃ājìn?   Is it fitting that Tani should pay taxes?
tīlàs nê? kō yà yi azùmī?   Is it necessary that he should fast?
bà̀ àbin kunyà̀ ba nè̀? kō (wai) à kwāna à gidan sùrùkai?
    Is it not shameful that a person should sleep overnight at one's in-laws?

2.4.2. anyà̀

The particle **anyà̀** (which can be followed by a modal particle) introduces questions where there is a serious doubt, e.g.,

anyà̀ kò̀ bài yi wà yāròn nauyī bâ?   Is it not too heavy for that youth?
anyà̀ hakà nê?   Is that really so?

2.4.3. shîn

The particle **shîn** with questions seeks confirmation. It can be used with Q-words or preceding the initial question marker **kō** in Yes/No questions, e.g.,

shîn yà̀yà̀ mā zân zānà hòtôn?   How did you say I should draw the diagram?
shîn kō kā sàmi Audù à gidā kùwâ?   (By the way) did you in fact find Audu at home?
shîn kō kā san an k̃ār̃à̀ manà̀ àlbâshī watàn nân?
    Did you know that our salary was raised this month?

3. INDIRECT QUESTIONS

Indirect questions are normally formed by **kō** plus a clause with a Q-word. The Q-word clause requires a Rel TAM, e.g.,

bàn san kō mè (= kō mènē nè̀) ya dàmē shì ba   I don't know what bothered him.
anā̀ ta ìndà-indar̃ kō wā̃ zā à bâ sakatar̃è   They were arguing about whom to pick as secretary.
bàn san kō wā̀ ya yi hakà ba   I don't know who did it.
kàdà kà tàmbàyē nì kō don mè na k̃i zìyar̃tàr̃sà   Don't asked me why I refused to visit him.
bài gayà̀ minì kō nawà̀ zân biyā ba   He didn't tell me how much I should pay.
bài kùla dà kō nawà̀ sukà mutù ba   He didn't care how many died.
yā tàmbàyē sù kō ta yà̀yà̀ zâi sàmi izìnī yà̀ shigō
    He asked them how he could get permission to come in.

Indirect questions do not themselves have the essential phonological features associated with direct questions, namely, final vowel lengthening and final L tone, e.g.,

tàmbàyè̀ shi kō wằ ya fìta!	Ask him who went out!
cf. wằ ya fìtâ?	Who went out?

If indirect questions appear with normal question intonation features, it is only because they are embedded in direct questions, e.g.,

shîn kā san kō wằ ya fìtā?	Do you know who went out?

In some instances an indirect question is possible without the **kō**, although some speakers find examples like the following without **kō** to be only marginally acceptable.

Audù fa, mun san wằ zâi àurā	As for Audu, we know who he will marry.
cf. the more usual **Audù fa, mun san kō wằ zâi àurā**	
bà à san dàgà wànè wurī ya zō ba	One didn't know from which direction he came.

One can express the semantic equivalent (more or less) of an indirect question by means of a relative clause construction headed by a noun or a relative pronoun, e.g.,

bàn san <u>wândà</u> ya yi hakà ba	I don't know who (i.e., the one who) did it.
= bàn san kō wằ ya yi hakà ba	
kā gànè <u>yâddà</u> 'yan-lèƙen-àsīrī sukè yî?	Do you understand how spies operate?
= kā gànè kō ta yàyầ 'yan-lèƙen-àsīrī sukè yî?	
bàn san <u>àbîn dà</u> ya dằmē shì ba	I don't know what (lit. the thing that) bothered him.
kà nūnằ manà <u>indà</u> ka sằmē shì!	Show us where you found it!
bà sù tabbataȓ dà <u>lōkàcîn dà</u> haḍàrîn ya fằru ba	
They weren't sure when (lit. the time that) the accident occurred.	

An indirect question introduced by **kō** that does not contain a Q-word constitutes a 'whether' clause, e.g.,

nā tàmbayằ kō sun yi aikìn	I asked whether they did the work.
bàn san kō zâi zō ba	I don't know whether he will come.
kā san kō dà saurā?	Do you know whether there is any left?
wàḍànnè yârā Hàlīmà ta tàmbayằ kō sun sằci kuḍîn?	
Which children did Halima ask whether they stole the money?	

[References: D. Muhammad (1968); Newman and Newman (1981)]

61. Reason and Purpose

1. REASON ('BECAUSE')

BECAUSE clauses and phrases are indicated by **sabòdà** (= **sàbīlì dà**) or **dòmin/don** plus a full sentence or an NP. Tensed sentences take a general TAM (like the completive or continuous) rather than a Rel TAM counterpart (e.g., preterite or Rel-continuous). The 'because' clauses and phrases are allowed either before or after the main sentence, e.g.,

bàn amìncē dà shī ba dòmin kùwa nā san hālinsà
    I don't trust him because I know what he is like.
sunà nēmansà sabòdà shī mālàminsù nē
    They were looking for him because he was their teacher.

tā yi fushī sabòdà bài bā tà kōmē ba	She was angry because he didn't give her anything.
dòmin tanà kūkā bàn ji dādī ba	Because she was crying I was unhappy.
zân bā shì kyàutā sabòdà yā tàimàkē nì	I'm going to give him a gift because he helped me.
= sabòdà yā tàimàkē nì zân bā shì kyàutā	Because he helped me I'll give him a gift.
munà mur̃nà sabòdà mun sàmi aikì	We were happy because we got the job.
= sabòdà mun sàmi aikì munà mur̃nà	Because we got the job we were happy.
mun shā wàhalà sabòdà rashìn ruwā	We suffered because of lack of water.
an bā shì aikì sabòdà (= don) k̃arfinsà	He was given the job because of his strength.

°AN: As far as I am aware **sabòdà** and **dòmin/don** generally mean the same thing. I suspect, however, that there are pragmatic/stylistic differences in their use, but this remains to be studied.

Reason clauses and phrases are negated by means of the discontinuous marker **bà...ba**. This normally connotes negative contrastive focus.

b̲à̲ dòmin gwànī nè b̲a̲ mukà bā shì hēlùmà...
    It wasn't because he is an expert that we made him headman (but for some other reason).
munà gōyon bāyankà b̲à̲ sabòdà kanà dà kuɗī b̲a̲ nè...
We are supporting you not because you're rich (but for some other reason).
yā yi hakà b̲à̲ don k̃ètā b̲a̲ sai don rashìn tùnànī
He did that not because of maliciousness but rather because of lack of forethought.

°AN: Because **don** is simply a short form of **dòmin**, one might expect them to be interchangeable. This, however, is not always the case. In the above example, for instance, it would be considered clumsy to say ...****sai dòmin rashìn tùnànī**.

2. REASON ('SINCE')

The function word **tun** 'since' serves to indicate both time and reason, e.g., **munȁ nân zàune tun jiyà / tun dà ya shìga bankȉ** 'We have been sitting here since yesterday / since he went into the bank'; **tun dà yakè yā bā nì cêk, sai ìn tàfi bankȉ** 'Since/because he gave me a check, I should go to the bank.' The temporal uses of **tun** are treated in §69:7; the various uses of **tun** in constructions indicating reason are described here.

2.1. Basic formation
Reason clauses indicating 'since', 'inasmuch as', 'given that', 'in view of the fact that', etc., are indicated by **tun dà yakè** (lit. since that 3m.Rcont2) plus a full clause. The reason clause usually occurs before the matrix sentence, but it can occur after. Both the subordinate clause and the main clause normally use a general rather than a Rel TAM. Examples:

tun dà yakè tanȁ barcī, zā mù zaunȁ à wàje haɽ sai tā tāshì
> Since she is sleeping we will sit outside until she gets up.

tun dà yakè sun sȁmi aikȉ à Bauci, zā sù tàfi can
> Given that they found work in Bauchi, they will go there.

tun dà yakè Lāɽai ùngōzȍmà cē, zā tà fàhìmci àbîn dà kȅ dāmùnā
> Since Larai is a midwife, she will understand what is troubling me.

tun dà yakè bài zō ba, bà zân ci gàba dà jirȁ ba
> Since he hasn't come I won't wait any longer.

tun dà yakè bà sù gamȁ dà saurī ba, mun yi fushī
> In view of the fact that they didn't finish quickly, we were angry.

an zȁɓi yārinyàɽ tun dà yakè (ita) kyàkkyāwā cȅ
> They chose the girl since she was pretty.

2.2. Reduction of **tun dà yakè**
The **tun dà yakè** phrase is typically reduced. This is done in one of two ways. First, the PAC **yakè** can be omitted, leaving **tun dà**, which is the same surface form as the temporal 'since'. The meanings of the clauses remain distinct, however, because the reason 'since' is followed by a general TAM whereas the temporal 'since' requires a Rel TAM, e.g.,

tun dà [an]$_{comp}$ kirā sù, sun baɽ aikìnsù
> Since (given that) they were called, they stopped their work.

cf. **tun dà [akà]$_{pret}$ kirā sù, sukà baɽ aikìnsù**
> Since (the time that) they were called, they stopped work.

tun dà yā yi wannàn, mun ji dāɗī
> Given that he did this, we were pleased.

cf. **tun dà ya yi wannàn, mukà ji dāɗī**
> Since (the time that) he did this, we were pleased.

tun dà tanȁ kūkā, mun bā ta àlēwȁ don tà dainȁ
> Since (in view of the fact that) she was crying we gave her candy so that she would stop.

tun dà bài gamà kàɽȁtū ba, bà zâi fìta wȁsā ba
> Inasmuch as he didn't finish his studies, he won't go out to play.

àlhamdù lìllāhì tun dà sun gānè
> Thank God that (i.e., since it is the case that) they have understood.

A second, very common, option is to omit the word **tun**, leaving just **dà yakè**. (This can have only a reason reading and not temporal one.) Examples:

dà yakè kanà nân, zân fita shân iskà
>Seeing that you are here, I'm going to go out for some fresh air.

dà yakè màkānikè̀ bài gamà dà saurī ba, sai mù kwāna à nân
>Since the mechanic didn't finish quickly, we will spend the night here.

dà yakè yārinyà̄r santalēlìyā cè̀, zā tà zama sàraunìyar̄ kyâu
>Since the girl is slim, she will become the beauty queen.

dà yakè zâ ka kàsuwā, don Allàh kà sayō mîn mân-jā
>Since you are going to the market, please buy me some palm oil.

2.3. *Subject fronting (topicalization)*

The normal word order in the adverbial phrase is **tun dà yakè** 'since' followed by the embedded sentence, e.g., [**tun dà yakè**] [**yārinyà̄r tanà̀ barcī**] '[since] [the girl is sleeping]'. One can, however, extract the subject from its regular position and move it to the front of the sentence as a topic or prementioned element. The topicalization is generally marked by a modal particle or by an intonational break (indicated in the examples by a comma), but it is also possible without. If the fronted item is the subject of an equational sentence, an independent pronoun is optionally left in its place, e.g.,

[yārinyà̄r] (dai) [(tun) dà yakè] tanà̀ barcī...   The girl, since she is sleeping...

[màkānikè̀] dîn, [(tun) dà yakè] bài gamà dà saurī ba, yā yàr̄da mù kwāna à nân
>The mechanic, since he didn't finish quickly, he agreed that we could spend the night here.

[yayyenmù], [(tun) dà yakè] (sū) likitōcī nè̀, sunà̀ jîn dādī
>Our senior brothers, since they are doctors, they are enjoying themselves.

[ɓàrāwòn], [(tun) dà yakè] (shī) tittiƙēƙè̀ nē yâ firgìtā ku
>The thief, given that he is huge, he'll likely startle you.

If **tun** is omitted *and* the sentence with the fronted subject flows without an intonational break *and* the subject is masculine singular, one ends up with a surface construction that is identical to (and usually interpreted as) a noun followed by a relative clause, e.g.,

Audù dà yakè kàren-mōtà̀ nē zâi fi mù sanī
>(1) Audu, who is a bus conductor, will know better than us.
>*or* (2) Audu, given that he is a bus conductor, will know better than us.

shī dà yakè dōgō nè̀ yā iyà wàsan ƙwallon-ƙwàndō
>(1) He who is tall is able to play basketball.
>*or* (2) He, since he is tall, is able to play basketball.

ɓàrāwòn dà yakè tittiƙēƙè̀ nē yâ firgìtā ku
>(1) The thief, who is huge, will likely startle you.
>*or* (2) The thief, given that he is huge, will likely startle you.

If the fronted noun is not third person masculine singular, there shouldn't be any interpretive confusion between a 'since' clause and a relative clause, insofar as **ya** in (**tun**) **dà yakè** is invariant whereas the weak subject pronoun in a relative clause agrees with the antecedent head noun, e.g.,

yārinyà̄r dà <u>yak</u>è tanà̀ barcī...   The girl, since she is sleeping...
cf. **yārinyà̄r dà <u>tak</u>è tanà̀ barcī...**   The girl who is sleeping...

kē dà y̲akè gwànā cè...   Since you (fem.) are an expert...
cf. kē dà k̲ikè gwànā...   You (fem.) who are an expert...
mū dà y̲akè munà̀ sàurà̀ron r̄ēdiyò̀...   Since we are listening to the radio...
yayyenmù dà y̲akè likitōcī nè̀, sunà̀ jîn dādī̀
     Since our senior brothers are doctors, they are enjoying themselves.

Instead of keeping the causal/reason **dà yakè** as a fixed form, some speakers produce sentences in which the wsp is inflected for person, gender, and number *as if* it were being controlled by the preceding NP. Note that these constructions with the gender/number agreement generally have the same surface form as relative clauses. Examples:

kē dà k̲ikè gwànā cè̀
     (1) Since you (fem.) are an expert...
     or (2) You who are an expert... (first interpretation)
yârân dà s̲ukè bà̀ fìtìnànnū ba nè̀, sun zō
     (1) Since the children are not troublesome, they came.
     or (2) The children who are not troublesome... (first interpretation)
Lār̄ai dà t̲akè ùngōzòmà cē, zā tà fàhìmci àbîn dà kè dāmù̀nā
     (1) Since Larai is a midwife, she will understand what is troubling me.
     or (2) Larai, who is a midwife... (first interpretation)
mū dà m̲ukè munà̀ sàurà̀ron r̄ēdiyò̀, bā mà̀ jîn kūkan kūr̄ā
     Since we were listening to the radio, we didn't hear the cry of the hyena.
cf. mū dà m̲ukè̀ sàurà̀ron r̄ēdiyò̀, bā mà̀ jîn kūkan kūr̄ā
     We who were listening to the radio...

The above examples illustrate surface proximity overriding constituency in concord assignment. When presented for inspection out of context, the first interpretation of the above sentences was invariably that of a relative clause; but in producing 'since' clauses, such "mistakes" with overt pronominal agreement were in fact made.

3. PURPOSE ('IN ORDER TO')

Purpose clauses are indicated by **dò̀min/don)** '(in order) to, so that' plus a clause in the subjunctive. (As with many contractions in English, in everyday language, the short form **don** is more common than **dò̀min**.) Examples:

tā zō don tà sàyi yādì̀   She came in order to buy cloth.
mun kirāwō shì don yà gyār̄à manà̀ fīr̄jì   We called him to (come) repair the fridge.

     °AN: According to Bagari (1987), **sabò̀dà** can serve in place of **dò̀min/don** in purpose clauses. This is probably very much less common than the use of **dò̀min/don** for **sabò̀dà** in reason clauses.

If the subject of the main clause and the purpose clause are the same, the conjunction can be deleted. This is sometimes also possible when they are not the same, but the exact rules governing the deletion are not clear, e.g.,

mun bazà kāyā à inuwà̀ (don) mù yi cìnikī
     We spread our wares in the shade (in order) to do business.

yā kāwō nāmằ (don) màtar̃sà tà yi masà miyằ

He brought food so that his wife could make stew for him.

yā fàɗā (don) yà tsōràtā mu — He said (that) to frighten us.

zā sù yi kàr̃ātū sòsai (dòmin) sù ci jar̃r̃àbâwā — They will study hard in order to pass the exam.

nā kāwō mukù àbinci (don) kù ji dāɗī — I brought you food so that you would be happy.

The purpose clause, usually with **don**, can be preceded by the adverbial particle **wai** to indicate 'merely, just', e.g.,

ƙòƙarī yakè yî wai (don) yà sāmằ — He's putting in an effort just so as to get it.

yā kafằ musù idồ wai (don) yà ga àbîn dà sukè nufī

He kept his eyes on them just to see what they were up to.

bài kyàutu ba kà wulāƙàntà talakāwā wai (don) kà nūnằ kā fī sù àbin-hannu

It is not nice to treat the poor so harshly just to show that you are wealthier than they are.

Negative purpose clauses are indicated by **dòmin** (= **don**), which may be deleted as indicated above, plus a negative subjunctive clause formed with the prohibitive marker **kadà** (= **kâr̃**). The clauses often correspond to English 'lest' clauses. Examples:

kà tàfi dà laimằ (don) kadà ruwā yà bā kà kāshī — Take an umbrella lest you get soaked.

mù yi saurī (don) kadà wani yà ƙwācè

Let's be quick so that no one grabs it. *or* Let's go quickly lest someone grabs (it).

Hajìyā tanằ kai tà makar̃antā wai don kâr̃ à bar̃ tà tà tàfi ita kaɗai tà hàɗu dà Gìde

Hajiya would take her to school so that she was not left to go alone to meet up with Gide.

Instead of using a subjunctive clause, it is possible to express 'purpose' by means of a phrase consisting of **don** plus a dynamic noun (which includes verbal nouns). Note that one normally uses **don** rather than the full-form **dòmin**. Examples:

sun shìga don màganằ — They entered in order to talk. (lit. they entered for speech)

yā hau bishiyằ don hàngen nēsà

He climbed the tree to look in the distance. (lit. he climbed tree for looking afar)

In certain constructions, especially when the main clause contains a motion verb, **don** can be omitted. The purposive expression that follows can be a verbal noun phrase, a dynamic noun resulting from the deletion of **yîn** or, if **don** is omitted, an infinitive phrase (IP), e.g.,

tā tàfi (don) cîn àbinci — She has gone to eat (food). (lit. she went (for) eating.of food)

sun zō nân (don) nēman zīnār̃ìyā — They came here to look for gold.

(lit. they came here (for) seeking.of gold)

sun fìta (don) (yîn) wàsā — They went out to play. (lit. they went out (for) (doing) playing)

nā zō gaishē kà — I've come to say hello to you. (lit. I came (to) greet you) (IP)

tā zō dūbà lāfiyàr̃kù — She's come to see how you (pl.) are.

(lit. she came (to) inspect health.of.you) (IP)

[References: Bagari (1987); Koops (1991)]

62. Reduplication

REDUPLICATION (redup) can be viewed from two perspectives: (1) function and degree of productivity, and (2) nature of the (morpho)phonological process.

1. FUNCTION AND DEGREE OF PRODUCTIVITY

The term *reduplication* serves to describe both (a) active functional processes (productive or partially productive) and (b) the results (synchronically frozen) of such reduplicative processes.

1.1. Active reduplication

Active reduplication refers to word formation rules in which reduplication functions as a synchronically recognizable derivational or inflectional process. The derivations/inflections themselves may be more or less productive, but the operation of the process as a process is evident. Reduplication as an active process is usually comparable in function to normal affixation processes, e.g., **àkàwu** 'clerk', pl. **àkàwu-àkàwu** (redup), cf. **àgōgo** 'clock', pl. **agōgunà** (suffix). Reduplication may serve as a derivational/inflectional formative in its own right, as in **àkàwu-àkàwu**. In other cases, however, it accompanies affixation, e.g., **littāfī** 'book', pl. **lìttàttàfai** (partial redup plus suffix -ai)^{LH}). Where reduplication is used for synchronically functional purposes, it has been described under the appropriate derivational or inflectional headings. Formations involving reduplication include the following:

(1) Pluralization of nouns (chap. **56**), e.g., **jōjì-jōjì** pl. < **jōjì** 'judge'; **damàmē** pl. < **damō** 'monitor'; **bàmàbàmai** pl. < **bâm** 'bomb'; **shāwàřwařī** pl. < **shāwařà** 'advice'.

(2) Attenuation of adjectives and adverbs (§4:2.3, §5:4.2), e.g., **fari-fari** 'whitish' < **farī** 'white'; **dà dāma-dāma** 'moderate quantity, fairly good' < **dà dāmā** 'quite a lot'.

(3) Intensification of adverbs (§5:4.1), e.g., **sassāfe** 'very early in the morning' < **sāfe** 'early in the morning'; **mařmaza** (= **maza maza**) 'very quickly' < **maza** 'quickly'.

(4) Formation of pluractional verbs (chap. **55**), e.g., **kirkirā** 'call many/often' < **kirā** 'call'; **maƙalƙàlē** (= **mammaƙàlē**) 'get all lodged in' < **maƙàlē** 'get lodged in'.

(5) Formation of sensory quality verbs and adjectives (chap. **2**), e.g., **zurfàfā** 'heat up', **zùzzurfā** / pl. **zurfàfā** 'very hot' < **zurfī** 'heat; **fāɗàɗā** 'widen', **fàffāɗā** / pl. **fāɗàɗā** 'very wide' < **fāɗī** 'breadth, width'.

(6) Formation of augmentative adjectives (chap. **11**), e.g., **gandamēmè** / pl. **gandamā-gàndàmà** 'long and strong' (e.g., knife, sword, horse), cf. **gandamī** 'essentially same meaning'; **samɓalēlè** / pl. **samɓalā-sàmɓàlà** 'tall and well-formed', cf. **samɓalī** 'essentially same meaning'.

(7) Formation of adjectival past participles (chap. **3**), e.g., **shàfaffē** 'wiped' < **shāfà** 'wipe'; **gàgàrarrē** 'rebellious' < **gàgarà** 'be impossible for'.

(8) Formation of frequentatives (chap. **29**), e.g., **bùshe-bùshe** 'blowing (of musical instruments)' < **būsà** 'blow'; **bùge-bùge** 'beatings' < **bugà** 'beat'.

(9) Formation of hypocoristic names (§48:1.8), e.g., **Làdīdi** 'Little Ladi' < **Làdì** (a female name); **Sàlēle** 'Little Sale' < **Sàlè** (a male name).
(10) Formation of distributives (§53:1.3), e.g., **bībiyu** 'two each' < **biyu** 'two'; **huřhuɗu** 'four each' < **huɗu** 'four'.

°AN: I am limiting the term *reduplication* to processes that apply within a word. I do not use the term for successive occurrences of the same word, as in English 'very very tall', which I am calling 'repetition'. I thus consider the specific examples of distributives indicated above to involve reduplication whereas such examples as **watà watà** 'monthly' < **watà** 'month' or **sulè sulè** 'a shilling each' < **sulè** 'shilling' are viewed as repetition. Even though there are obviously some borderline cases, I feel that the distinction between reduplication and repetition is a valid one.

1.2. Frozen (vestigial) reduplication
Frozen reduplication refers to words that phonologically have a reduplicated structure, but which from a synchronic point of view constitute essentially unanalyzable simple lexical items. These include:

(1) Reduplicated nouns and adjectives, e.g., **kwàlekwàle** 'canoe'; **bilbilō** 'swallow' (bird); **jàrīrì** 'infant'; **ƙìfìfiyà** 'turtle'; **fiffikè** (< *fik-fikè) 'wing'; **tsòlōlò** 'tall and skinny'; **zàngà-zàngà** 'riot, demonstration'.

°AN: Many reduplicated words with the LL-HL pattern, such as **jìnà-jìnà** 'a red-juiced weed' (cf. **jinī** 'blood') can be related to simple nonderived words in the language. However, because the semantic relationship between the reduplicated and nonreduplicated items is extremely tenuous and because the formation is (totally?) unproductive, I have chosen to include these items among the frozen reduplicated forms.

(2) Reduplicated verbs, e.g., **sansànā** 'smell'; **yagalgàlā** 'tear to pieces'; **gàgarà** 'be impossible for'; **saɗàɗā** 'go stealthily'.
(3) Reduplicated ideophones, e.g., **cakō-càkò** 'sharp and pointed'; **zòmòmò** 'describes pouting, protruding ones lip'; **wàndàř-wandař** 'zigzagging, swaying from side to side'; **kaca-kaca** 'in a mess'.

2. NATURE OF THE (MORPHO)PHONOLOGICAL PROCESS

From the point of view of form, reduplication covers a considerable variety of processes. At one extreme is total and exact reduplication of the simple stem including consonants, vowels, and tone. At the other extreme is partial reduplication in which the only element that is copied is a single consonant, everything else in the added material being fully specified. These various processes are described in turn. (Note the terminology adopted here: reduplicand = the constituent or string that is copied; duple = the copy.) (For purposes of clarity of exposition, I have inserted a hyphen between the reduplicated elements in examples. In standard orthography, reduplicated items are usually written either as two separate words (in the case of full reduplication) or as single words (in the case of partial reduplication).)

(1) Full redup (exact copy). In this process, the underlying stem is repeated twice exactly as is, i.e., the full stem serves as the reduplicand, e.g., **jōjì-jōjì** 'judges' < **jōjì** 'judge'; **sànnu-sànnu** 'very slowly and carefully' < **sànnu** 'slowly and carefully'.
(2) Full redup with morphologically specified vowel shortening. The basic process here is also full redup, including tone, but the final vowel of each component is shortened, e.g., **shūɗì-shūɗì** 'bluish' < **shūɗì** 'blue'; **dōgo-dōgo** 'medium height/not very tall' < **dōgō** 'tall'.

(3) Full redup with a prespecified tone pattern and final vowel. The process here is full redup operating on a prepared stem containing a tone-integrating suffix, e.g., **bùge-bùge** 'beatings' (< //**bug**-// + -**e**)^{LH} x 2) < **bugà** 'beat'; **càmfe-càmfe** 'superstitions' < **camfî** 'superstition'.

(4) Full redup with tone pattern imposed on the output. The process here is exact redup of the segmentals but not of the tone. A set tone pattern extends over the resulting reduplicated word, e.g., **santalā-sàntàlà** (H-L) 'svelte (pl.)'; **ruƙū-rùƙù** (H-L) 'large (pl.) of round things'; **bàdàm-badam** (L-H) 'floundering about'; **zàngà-zanga** (LL-HL) 'demonstration'; **dùrù-durù** 'dim-sighted person' (LL-HL).

(5) Full redup with loss of the final vowel in the first element. The basic process here is also full redup, but it is accompanied by a secondary (usually optional) loss of the stem-final vowel in the first element, resulting in surface partial redup (with adjustments in the syllable-final consonants), e.g., **huř-huɗu** (< **huɗu-huɗu**) 'four each' < **huɗu** 'four'; **wur-wuri** (< **wuri wuri**) 'very early' < **wuri** 'early'.

(6) Rightward redup of the final two syllables of the stem (including tone). The process is accompanied by loss of the final vowel in the reduplicand with concomitant adjustments in the resulting syllable-final consonant. This process is essentially limited to remnant/frozen reduplicated nouns. If the stem consists of two syllables only, then the process appears on the surface to be full redup, but the behavior of longer stems shows clearly that the redup applies at the level of the syllable (or foot) rather than at the level of the word. At the time the redup took place, all word-final vowels were short. Examples (with the duple being underlined): **awarwarō** 'bracelet' (< *awaro-<u>waro</u>); **gâggàfà** 'type of axe' (< *gāfà-<u>gāfà</u>); **bùduddùgī** 'type of edible frog' (< *bùdùg´-<u>dùgi</u> < *bùdùgi-<u>dùgi</u>). (Note: LH on a single syllable simplifies to H.)

(7) Rightward redup of the final syllable of the stem (not including tone). In this process, which is limited to remnant/frozen nouns or to ideophones, only the segmentals of the final syllable (CVV or CVC) are reduplicated. The tone appears to be a property of the resultant reduplicate as a whole, e.g., **jàrīrì** (L-H-L) 'infant'; **tsòlōlò** (L-H-L) 'tall and skinny'; **zòmòmò** (all L) 'describes pouting, protruding one's lip', **ɓàngwàlgwàl** (all L) 'describes the appearance of a solid, round, and fleshy thing'.

(8) -aCCe suffixal redup with tone specification on the output. This process, which is found only with adjectival past participles, involves the addition of a suffix -**aCCē** (in the masculine singular) where the CC represents a geminated copy of the stem-final consonant of the related verb. The resultant word appears with a set L-H-H tone pattern, e.g., **shàfaffē** 'wiped' < **shāfà** 'wipe'; **kòmàɗaɗɗē** 'buckled, bent' < **kōmàɗē** 'buckle'.

◊HN: Historically, this formative may have involved two-syllable redup to the right, including tone, of stems containing a tone-integrating suffix -ē)^{LH}. The present surface forms would be due to the subsequent loss of the penultimate vowel of the reduplicated word plus obligatory gemination of the thereby produced abutting consonants, e.g., **shàfaffē** < *shàfashfē < *shàfē-sh(à)fē; **kòmàɗaɗɗē** < *kòmàɗamɗē < *kòmàɗē-m(à)ɗē. Note that this historical derivation, while not unreasonable, is still clearly speculative and in need of confirmation.

(9) CVC or CVG antepenultimate redup (toneless). The basic process here is leftward copying of the CVC of the final two syllables of the stem that serves as the reduplicand. The second C is either copied or, more often, replaced by an unspecified consonant (G) that forms a geminate with the following abutting consonant. The duple, which is toneless, appears either as an infix or as a prefix depending on the number of syllables in the stem. The reduplicated word as a whole gets its tone by morphological assignment, e.g., **maƙalƙalē** 'become lodged' (plurac. of **maƙalē**) has H-H-L-H tone because this is the pattern for polysyllabic gr4 verbs; **babbàkā** 'roast' (< *baka) is H-L-H because this is the pattern for trisyllabic gr1 verbs; **cikunkunà** bellies' (pl. of **cikì**) (< *cikunà) and **sulullukà** 'shillings' (pl. of **sulè**) (< *suluklukà < *sulukà) are H-H-H-L because of the patterns produced by the H-L tone-integrating plural suffixes -**unā**)^{HL} and -**ukā**)^{HL}.

(10) CVC- or CVG- prefixal redup. The basic process here is leftward copying of the initial CVC of the stem excluding tone. (The coda C normally appears as a geminate G rather than as a fully copied consonant.) In the case of derived adjectives of sensory quality (DASQ), the CVC- comes with a preset L tone, e.g., **z̀ùzzurfā** 'very deep' (< **zurfī** 'heat'); **fàffāɗā = fàr̃fāɗā** 'very broad, wide' (< **fāɗī** 'breadth'); **sàssantsā = sànsantsā** very smooth, slippery' (< **santsī**'smoothness'). In the case of pluractional verbs, tone is assigned to the resultant word as a whole on the basis of the grade, e.g., **kakkar̃àntā** 'read many or often' (< **kar̃àntā** 'read'); **tàttàmbayà = tàntàmbayà** 'ask many or often' (< **tàmbayà** 'ask').
(11) **Cā-** prefixal redup (toneless). In this process, which is limited to verbs with frozen/remnant reduplication, the initial consonant of the verb stem is copied but the vowel /ā/ is fully specified. The duple itself is toneless; the tone of the reduplicated word as a whole is provided by the verb grade, e.g., **dādàrā** (gr1) 'cut with sth blunt'; **ràrumà** (gr2) 'grab, snatch'; **gàgarà** (gr3) 'be impossible'.

2.1. Pseudoreduplication

Hausa has a variety of "reduplicative" -VCV formatives, in which the C copies the consonant of the preceding syllable, e.g., **wurī** 'place', pl. **wuràrē**. In most studies, these are included as types of partial reduplication. It is probably more accurate, however, to describe them as being simply suffixes (rather than reduplicated elements), where the vowels (and usually the tone) are fully specified but the consonants are phonologically underspecified. Examples of these -VCV suffixes are the following:

$-\bar{a}C\bar{e})^{HLH}$ plural suffix: **dam-àmē** monitor lizards < **damō** sg. + suffix $-\bar{a}C\bar{e})^{HLH}$, cf. **zōmàyē**
rabbits < **zōmō** sg. + suffix $-\bar{a}y\bar{e})^{HLH}$
$-\bar{o}C\bar{i})^{H}$ plural suffix: **tāg-ōgī** windows < **tāgà** sg. + suffix $-\bar{o}C\bar{i})^{H}$, cf. **tsarōkī** bow strings < **tsarkìyā**
(base //tsark-//) sg. + affix $-\bar{o}-\bar{i})^{H}$
$-\bar{a}C\bar{a})^{HLH}$ plural suffix of DASQs [derived adjectives of sensory quality]: **zurfàfā** very deep (pl. of **z̀ùzzurfā**) < //zurf-// + $-\bar{a}C\bar{a})^{HLH}$, cf. **fusàkā** faces < **fuskà** sg. + affix $-\bar{a}-\bar{a})^{HLH}$
-aCa(a) verbalizing suffix for DVSQs [derived verbs of sensory quality]): **fāɗàɗā / fàɗaɗà**
widen/become wide < **fāɗī** width + suffix -aCa(a)
$-\bar{e}C\bar{e})^{HL}$ augmentative suffix: **fandamēmè** huge < **fandamī** huge + suffix $-\bar{e}C\bar{e})^{HL}$

3. REDUPLICATED NOUNS (LEXICALLY FROZEN)

Frozen reduplicated nouns are items that are reduplicated in form, but for which no simple stem now exists in the language, or if there is a simple stem, with which the relation is synchronically tenuous at best. These reduplicated nouns are the historical vestiges of presumed, but no longer active, derivational processes. With these items, one cannot associate any meaning to the formation as such (with the exception of the partially-frozen LL-HL class described below in §3.5). A description of these frozen reduplicated nouns thus tells us something important about the morphophonological structure of the lexicon, but not about its semantic structure.

The fully frozen reduplicated nouns divide into three subclasses depending on whether the present-day word is the result of (1) two-syllable reduplication, (2) CV reduplication, or (3) full reduplication. There are over 250 words resulting from two-syllable reduplication, some 50 words exhibiting CV reduplication, and a handful of nouns exhibiting full reduplication.

3.1. Two-syllable reduplication to the right

The typical frozen reduplicated noun reflecting two-syllable reduplication has the form $(\ )C_1V_1C_2-C_1V_1C_2V$ (where the length of the V is variable), e.g., **bâlbēlà** 'cattle egret'; **awar̃war̃ō** 'thin metal bracelet'. The fundamental process is rightward reduplication of the final two syllables of the stem (including the tone). This is followed by deletion of the original stem-final vowel. (Note that at the presumed time that the process took place, final vowels were all short—the word-final lengthening came later.) The essential point to keep in mind in looking at frozen reduplicated nouns is that the reduplicated syllables (i.e., the morphologically secondary syllables) are the ones that tend to reflect the original shape whereas the original source syllables are the ones that have undergone phonological reduction and deformation. Examples (with the duple underlined):

fura + <u>fura</u> ⇒ fura<u>fura</u> ⇒ fur<u>fura</u> → /furfurā/   gray hair
bēlà + <u>bēlà</u> ⇒ bēlà<u>bēlà</u> ⇒ bēl`<u>bēlà</u> → bêlbēlà → /bâlbēlà/   cattle egret
awařo + <u>wařo</u> ⇒ awařo<u>wařo</u> ⇒ awař<u>wařo</u> → /awařwařō/   thin metal bracelet

    ΔDN: In Sokoto the tone melody F-H-L has simplified in many cases to L-H-L, e.g., SH /bâlbēlà/ → [Skt] bàlbēlà.

3.1.1. Segmental adjustments

Because of the vowel deletion rule, e.g., *furafura ⇒ furfura, the two syllables that were originally true copies of one another do not appear identical on the surface. The original reduplication process is further disguised because of various phonological changes affecting the vowel and the coda consonant in the antepenultimate CVC closed syllable. Two sets of changes (§3.1.1.1 and §3.1.1.2) reflect general phonological processes that still operate synchronically in the language with greater or lesser regularity. The third (§3.1.1.3) is a strictly historical change.

3.1.1.1. All long vowels in closed syllables shorten and, if originally /ē/ or /ō/, centralize to /a/, e.g.,

kûkkūkì <   *kūk(ì)kūkì   gum tree
bâlbēlà <   *bēl(à)bēlà   cattle egret
dâddōkà <   *dōk(à)dōkà   waterbuck

3.1.1.2. The coda consonant in the closed syllable is subject to assimilation to point of articulation (in the case of nasals), rhotacism (in the case of coronal obstruents), or gemination (in the case of labials and velars, or in the case of /r/ before another coronal), e.g.,

gwângwāmà (= [gwâŋgwāmà]) < *gwâm<u>gwāmà</u>   canna plant
fùmfùnā (= [hùŋhùnā]) < *fùnfùna   mold on food
kwâřkwatà < *kwâtkwatà   lice   yařyàɗī < *yaɗyàɗi   a twiner
kwařkwàsā < *kwaskwàsa   driver ant   bâřbajè < *bâzbazè   biting ant
kàfaffagō < *kàfagfago   fig tree   shìninnikī < *sìniknikī   dilatoriness
dûddurù < *dûrdurù   small stream   ɗaɗɗòrī < *ɗarɗòri   a creeper

When the semivowel /w/ occurred in coda position, it either formed a geminate with the following consonant or else attached to the nucleus and was realized as the second part of the /au/ diphthong. The corresponding semivowel /y/, on the other hand, rarely was geminated. Examples:

tsâttsēwà = tsâutsēwà < *tsâwtsēwà   a swift, swallow
kàsassawā = kàsausawā < *kàsawsawa   type of long spear
cf. daidayā (*not* **daddayā) < *daydaya   large millipede

3.1.1.3. In some dozen cases where the stem-final consonant was /r/ or /l/ (or /s/ in two instances), the coda consonant dissimilated to a nasal, e.g., *jal-jalo > janjalō 'pebble'. (That this is in fact a reduplicated word can be seen from the form of the plural, e.g., **janjalō**, pl. **jàlàjàlai**.) This is a strictly historical change without a synchronic counterpart. Even historically it is not clear what conditioned the replacement by the nasal since this change was not automatic; contrast **janjalō** 'pebble' < ***jal-jalo** with **fàlfàlā** (*not* ****fànfàlā**) 'a type of basket' < ***fàl-fàla**. Examples (complete):

(a) **bàmbarō** (< ***bànbaro** < ***bàrbaro**) puffiness, swelling; **dàndarì** coccyx; **dandarī** bare; **famfarō** destitute land; **jinjìrī** baby (cf. pl. **jìràjìrai**); **kankarè** scrapings of *tuwo* from pot (cf. pl. **kàràkàrai**); **kijinjirī** type of palm tree; **kùdundurā** knife for women to cut meat, okra etc.; **kùdundurī** (1) = **kùdundurā** (2) type of tall grass; **kùnkurū** tortoise; **ɓanɓarà** flint; **ɓùnɓùrù** putting aside one of a hundred cowries; **shanshèrā** beans without pods, unhusked peanuts or rice; **zànzarō** dauber wasp
(b) **gwangwalā** midrib of a raffia palm branch; **gwangwalē** flower of custard apple tree; **janjalō** pebble (for breaking antimony); **ɓwanɓōlī** (< ***ɓōnɓōli** < ***ɓōlɓōli**) summit
(c) **kwànkwasò** rear lumbar region; **kyànkyasò** cockroach

3.1.2. Tone classes
Frozen reduplicated nouns fall into six main tone classes defined in terms of the tones of the final three syllables. (The initial tone of quadrisyllabic words can be either H or L.)

3.1.2.1. (H-H-H). Words with an H-H-H tone pattern derive directly from stems with final H-H, e.g., **marmarā** 'laterite' < ***mara-mara**. This is the most common tone pattern; there are a good hundred examples, e.g.,

birbirī	Bruce's fruit pigeon	**gaggāfā**	bateleur eagle
gwaɍgwādā	male lizard	**kankanā**	water-melon
kùduddufī	borrow-pit	**maɓwaɓɓwafī**	woodpecker

3.1.2.2. (F-H-L). Words with an F-H-L (falling-high-low) tone pattern derive from stems with final H-L. The HL on the CVC syllable, which results from the vowel syncope, is realized as a fall, e.g., **gwângwāmà** 'canna plant' < ***gwāmà-gwāmà**. There are approximately thirty examples, all of which are trisyllabic, e.g.,

bâɍbajè	biting ant	**gâggāfà**	type of axe
kwâɍkwāsà	driver ant	**ɓânɓanà**	measles
ɓyâɍɓyārì	starling	**tsâttsēwà**	swift, swallow

3.1.2.3. (H-L-H). Words with the H-L-H tone pattern derive from stems with final L-H. The LH on the CVC syllable, which resulted from the vowel syncope, is realized as H in accordance with the general LH to H rule (see §71:1.2), e.g., **tsattsàgī** 'a shrub' < ***tsăg-tsàgi** < ***tsàgi-tsàgi**. There are some fifty examples, over half of which are quadrisyllabic, e.g.,

bambàmī	upper part of deleb-palm	**bùduddùgī**	type of edible frog
jinjìrī	baby	**ɓyàfiɍfîtā**	sand fly
magaɍgàrā	self-sown guinea corn	**yaɍyàdī**	climbing vine

Because of the anomalous nasal replacement and the tone simplification, it is not immediately evident that the word **jinjìrī** 'baby', for example, reflects reduplication, but it does. The derivation is ***jìri-jìri** > ***jìɍjìri** > ***jìɲjìri** > **jinjìrī**.

3.1.2.4. (L-L-H). Words with the L-L-H tone pattern probably derive from stems that originally had final L-L. Subsequently, when final vowels were lengthened—originally they were all short—the word-final L-L changed to L-H in accordance with a historical rule of low-tone raising (*L-L > L-H) that applied to long final vowels (see §34:3.2). There are some fifty examples, e.g.,

fàřfètsī	a shrub	< *fètsfètsī	< *fètsì-fètsì)
fùmfùnā	food mold	< *fùmfùnà̀	< *fùnà-fùnà
gàngàmō	turmeric	< *gàngàmò̀	< *gàmò-gàmò
hàřàřřàmī	uproar	< *hàřàmřàmī	< *hàřàmì-řàmì
sàssàgō	small saw	< *sàssàgò̀	< *sàgò-sàgò
wàlwàlā	cheerful disposition	< *wàlwàlà̀	< *wàlà-wàlà

The tone patterns above appear to have been derived by a reduplication process in which the final two syllable of the stem were copied exactly including the tone. The next two tone classes, both of which have under twenty examples each, do not lend themselves easily to such an analysis. They derive either from two-syllable reduplication where the output received a set tone melody, or else (less likely) from prefixal CVC- reduplication where the CVC- had inherent L tone.

3.1.2.5. (L-H-L). Some fifteen frozen reduplicated nouns have the tone pattern L-H-L. (Two words also contain the feminative suffix.) A few seem to have come from F-H-L words that subsequently underwent tone simplification, e.g., ƙàrƙārà̀ = ƙàrƙārà̀ 'thorny acacia'. (As indicated in a note above, this F-L-H to L-H-L change is well attested in the Sokoto dialect.) The others may derive from words that originally had a set LL-HL melody similar to what one finds today in such reduplicative words as gòrà-gōrà 'type of grass' (cf. gōrà 'bamboo, cane') (see §3.5 below). A word like kàřkāzà̀ 'industrious psn', for example, would thus come from *kàz(à)-kāzà. Alternatively, these L-H-L nouns may derive from H-L stems to which an L-tone CVC- prefix was added, i.e., kàřkāzà̀ < *kàzkāzà. Examples:

bàbbāwà̀ pagan (cf. bāwà̀ slave); gwàřgwādà̀ male lizard; kyànkyasò̀ roach; ƙànƙanè̀ small; bùbbūƙùwā (< *bùƙbūƙù + (w)ā) white pelican; fàřfājìyā (< *fàzfāzì + (y)ā) open area in front of a compound

3.1.2.6. (L-H-H). A dozen frozen reduplicated nouns have the tone pattern L-H-H. All of these have a heavy first syllable in the stem. As with the preceding class, there are two possible sources. Either they come from reduplicated words with a set LL-HH melody, e.g., sànsanī war camp < *sànì-sani)$^{LL-HH}$, or else they come from H-H stems to which an L-tone CVC- prefix was added, i.e., sànsanī < *sàn-sani. Examples (complete):

bàmbarō	puffiness, swelling	dàddawā	locust bean cake
dìddigā	crumbs	dìndimī	night blindness
gàřgazā	cichlid perch	gwàřgwadō	proportion
kàkkařai	inflammation of finger or toe	kàrkarā	inhabited area near city
kùnkurū	tortoise	nànnahō	a weed
sànsanī	war camp	zànzarō	dauber wasp

3.2. One-syllable reduplication to the right
3.2.1. S₁-S₂-S₂)^{LHL}
Some fifty or so words have the reduplicated shape cv(v)CVVCVV, where the second and third syllables are segmentally identical. These words have a set L-H-L tone pattern, e.g., jàrīrì 'infant'. The copied

syllables all contain a long monophthongal vowel. Four of the five long vowels occur in these words; for inexplicable reasons, /ē/, which is normally a common vowel, does not. The initial vowel is typically either the same as the following vowel or else /a/. The initial vowel is usually long, like the vowels that follow, but it is sometimes short. In two instances there is an initial /ū/ followed by /ā/ and in one instance one finds /ai/ followed by /ā/.

This class of words includes an assortment of common nouns referring to plants, birds, and other items. It also includes a number of semantically expressive words describing appearance, most of which can function as adjectives as well as nouns.

Words of this class that can undergo pluralization use the -ai suffix, e.g., **jàrìrai** 'infants', **tsòlōlò** / **tsòlōlai** 'tall and skinny' (sg./pl.). Corresponding feminines are formed according the regular feminine inflectional rules (see §31:3.1), e.g., **jàrīrìyā** 'female infant', **tsòlōlùwā** 'tall and skinny' (f.). Examples (in the unmarked masculine form):

bòrōrò bird's crop; **bùshāshà** luxurious living, having a good time; **bùzūzù** dung beetle; **dàƙīƙì** stupid (psn) (n. or adj.); **dòsōsò** ugly looking (of psn's face) (usu. adj.); **dù(u)kūkù** glumly hesitant; **dùsūsù** bran from wetted ground corn (cf. **dùsā** bran), carbuncle; **dùzūzù** psn with unkempt body hair (n. or adj.); **gàɓūɓù** senseless psn (n. or adj.) (cf. **gāɓò** simpleton); **gàrārà** blind psn whose eyes look all right; psn with poor eyesight; **gàtūtù** slow-witted psn (n. or adj.); **gùrārà** hide pannier for pack animals; **hùlūlù** immoral (re. psn's behavior); **jàrīrì** infant; **jòlōlò** tall, lanky psn with blank/inexpressive face (e.g., psn with muscular dystrophy or other disability); **kàcācà** cheap type of beer; **kùrūrù** bird's crop; **kùtūtù** pulp of gourd; **kwàtsātsà** tactless; **ƙàfāfà** affectation; **ƙàzāzà** spinal deformity; **ƙàibābà** thorny leaf-stem of doum-palm; **ƙìrīrì** coccyx; **ƙùdūdù** internal lump in the body, tumor; **ƙùlūlù** cyst; bobbles of locust bean tree; **làɓūɓù** flabby, soggy; **màƙōƙò** goiter; **màrīrì** white oryx; **màrūrù** a boil on the buttocks or thigh; **sàrūrù** nincompoop; **sòfōfùwā** empty honeycomb; anything puffed out; **tsòlōlò** tall and skinny; **zòlōlò** tall with a long neck, e.g., a camel; **zùgūgù** exaggerating

3.2.2. S_1-S_1-S_1)^{HLH}

Two trisyllabic nouns/adjectives have all three syllables identical and H-L-H tone:

shāshàshā   foolish, stupid psn (n. or adj.)
sūsùsū   nincompoop, silly psn (n. or adj.)

3.2.3. One-syllable reduplication to the right plus feminative suffix -yà / -wà

There are a small number of quadrisyllabic feminine words with the second and third syllables identical and final -yà or -wà. The initial vowel is usually short. These words all have an L-H-H-L tone pattern. These words do not form plurals. Unlike the reduplicated words above, none of these items are adjectival. Examples (complete):

càkwaikwaiwà	starling; chatterbox	**dànīniyà**	dilly-dallying
hàgūguwà	experiencing difficulties	**hàjījiyà**	giddiness
hànīniyà	neighing	**ƙìfīfiyà**	turtle
kàlūluwà	swelling, esp. in the armpits	**kìcīciyà**	auger-beetle
kùrūruwà	shouting, calling loudly (esp. by women)		

3.3. CVC plus suffix -ē

Some fifteen nouns have the canonical shape C_1VC_2-C_1VC_2è with H-H-L tone. (Two end in -ò rather than -è.) (There is no way to know whether one historically added a CVC- prefix to a CVCè stem with the suffixal vowel already attached or whether one doubled the CVC to the right to create a reduplicated base to which one added the H-L -ē suffix.) Many of the members of this class are words for things that exist in pairs, most of which have an equivalent H-L-H-H form with final -ī. The standard plural for this class has the canonical shape C₁VC₂āC₁VC₂ai with L-H tone. One thus has three possible forms, e.g., **fîffîkè̖**, **fîkâfîkī**, pl. **fîkâfîkai** 'wing(s)'. Examples (complete):

filfilô̖	windmill toy	**gir̃gijè̖**	rain cloud
gungumè̖	log	**jijjigè̖**	forked post, beam
kankamè̖ [dv]	palm frond	**kwīkwiyô̖** (base //kuy-//)	puppy, cub
shisshikè̖	forked post, pillar	**tsittsigè̖**	stump (tree, tooth)
diddigè̖ = **digâdigī**	heel	(**filfîlè̖** [archaic]) > **filâfîlī**	paddle
(***kumkumè̖**) > **kumâkumī**	type of corset	**mummuk̃è̖** = **muk̃âmuk̃ī**	jaw, mandible
(***tiktikè̖**) > **tikâtikī**	calf of leg	**zuzzugè̖** = **zugâzugī**	bellows

◊HN: According to Parsons (1975: 427–28), words of the H-L-H-H I-final pattern were originally duals, i.e., **fîkâfîkī** would have denoted 'a pair of wings' as opposed to **fîffîkè̖**, which would have indicated 'a single wing'. For most speakers nowadays the two forms have fallen together and are essentially equivalent in meaning.

3.4. Full reduplication
3.4.1. x 2 with short final vowels
A small number of disyllabic words have the fully reduplicated structure CV(V)CV-CV(V)CV where the final vowels of both parts are short. The tone is reduplicated as well as the segmentals. (Some of these items are written as single words.) Many of these words denote small creatures. Examples:

dōlì-dōlì	a myriapod	**gizò-gizò**	spider
k̃ōk̃ì-k̃ōk̃ì	praying mantis	**kwàlekwàle**	canoe
mùnu-mùnu	large black scorpion	**tàlotàlo**	turkey
dage-dage (usu. **miyàr̃ dage-dage**)	stew with oil, tomatoes, peppers, and a lot of meat		

Some nouns of this shape are loanwords from Arabic. Interestingly, they too, are characterized by the short final vowel even though borrowings from Arabic normally end in a long final vowel. (In one case, the tones are not identical.) Examples:

(**àl)hudàhudà** Senegal hoopoe; **lu'ù-lu'ù** pearl; **na'à-na'à** mint (the plant or the flavoring)

3.4.2. x 2 (consonant final)
A few reduplicated words are consonant final. The tone of the two parts is sometimes an exact copy, sometimes heterotonic. Examples:

bàlàm-balam	balloon	**màlùm-mālum**	large gown with circular embroidery design
k̃ishin-k̃ishin	rumor	**nyàm-nyam**	cannibal
ɓel-ɓèl	milk that has been dishonestly watered down by the seller (< Fulani)		

3.5. Full (disyllabic) reduplication with LL-HL tone melody
There is a small set of fully reduplicated nouns whose meaning is related in a tangential way to some base word (usually a noun), e.g., **bàbà-bābà** 'a type of wild indigo' < **bābā** 'indigo'. Unlike the fully frozen vestiges, many of these reduplicated words do have corresponding nonreduplicated words extant in the

language. However, the derivation is not productive and the meanings of the individual items are lexically specific and unpredictable. The gender of the derived words, which is also lexically specific, is generally determined not by the gender of the source noun but rather by semantic association between the meaning of the derived word and some other word. For example, **jìnà-jìnà** 'a red-juiced weed', which is related to the masculine word **jinī** 'blood', is feminine because **cìyàwà**, the generic term for weed, is feminine. Similarly, **Ƙàsà-Ƙasà** 'grain sweepings' is normally masculine because **hatsī**, the generic term for grain, is masculine. If, however, **Ƙàsà-Ƙasà** were used to refer to a specific type of grain, like **dāwà** 'guinea-corn', which is feminine, then it too would be feminine.

The typical form of words of this class is CV(C)CA-CV(C)CA with an associated LL-HL tone melody. (There is one example with final /u/ and one with final /o/, in both cases this being a retention of the final vowel of the source stem.) In SH, the length of the final vowel of each component is determined by syllable weight polarity. If the initial syllable is light, then the vowel is long (examples in (a)); if the initial syllable is heavy, then the vowel is short (examples in (b)), e.g., **ràmà-ramà** 'type of jute', cf. **làngà-langà** 'baling wire'. Examples:

(a) **àyà-ayà** f.   type of wild tiger-nut grass and fruit, cf. **ayā** tiger-nut; **dùrù-durù** n./adj. dim-sighted person, cf. **duru-duru** id. seeing poorly; **jìnà-jìnà** f. a red-juiced weed, cf. **jinī** blood; **Ƙàsà-Ƙasà** m./f. corn sweepings (gender depending on grain referred to), cf. **Ƙasà** earth, soil; **màzà-mazà** m./f. tireless, energetic, dauntless person, cf. **mazā** males; **ràmà-ramà** f. jute, cf. **ramā** hemp; **rùwà-ruwà** f. partially ripe, soft, undried, tenderly cooked (e.g., corn or peanuts), cf. **ruwā** water; **wàsà-wasà** m. food made from coarse bean flour, cf. **wasa-wasa** id. emphasizes coarseness of sand or grain; **wùtà-wutà** f. a red-flowered weed, cf. **wutā** fire

(b) **àikà-aikà** f. a blunder, cf. **aikì** work; **bàbà-bābà** m type of wild indigo, cf. **bābā** indigo; **bàngà-bangà** f. blocking of a way (cf. **'yan bangà** thugs (originally guards for politicians)) (< **bangō** wall?); **bòkò-bōkò** m. fraud, cf. **bōkò** fraud, Western education; **dàgà-dāgà** f. iron band at end of spear (= **dàddāgà**); **dàmfà-damfà** adv. in profusion , cf. **dàmfam** id. emphasizes largeness of a crowd **ɗàtà-ɗātà** f. a bitter grass (= **ɗàtànniyā**), cf. **ɗācī** bitterness; **ɗàngà-ɗangà** adj. skimpy, cf. **ɗàngal** id. characterizes cloth or skirt that is skimpy and too short; **gòrà-gōrà** f. type of grass, cf. **gōrà** bamboo, cane; **hàntà-hantà** f. talking through one's nose, cf. **hancì** nose; **kàusà-kausà** f. a small plant with coarse leaves like sandpaper, cf. **kaushī** roughness; **rànà-rānà** m./f. sth done late in the morning, cf. **rānā** sun, day; **tàbà-tābà** f. a type of shrub, cf. **tābà** tobacco; **tàikà-taikà** m. four persons holding sth or s.o. with each one holding one side, cf. **taikì** large hide bag

ΔDN: In some dialects, the length of the vowel in the first component is determined by weight polarity, as in SH, but the word-final vowel is invariably long, as is typical of common nouns, e.g., [WH] **làngà-langå** = [SH] **làngà-langà** 'baling wire'; [WH] **zàngà-zangå** = [SH] **zàngà-zangà** 'demonstration, protest march'.

Some words of this pattern do not have synchronically extant source nouns, e.g.,

jìmfà-jimfà f. a strong grass used in making screens; **Ƙàzà-Ƙāzà** m./f. [Kts] energetic person (cf. **Ƙwàzō** energy, effort); **Ƙwìbà-Ƙwībà** f. pneumonia; **làngà-langà** m. long thin metal baling strips; **sàngà-sangà** f. a common shrub; **zàngà-zangà** f. demonstration, protest march

Although this derivation serves primarily to create common nouns, some words of this class can be used adjectivally or adverbially, e.g.,

Lādì tā bā nì wata gyàɗā rùwà-ruwà   Ladi gave me some fresh peanuts.

nā ga wani dùrù-durùn yārò	I saw a dim-sighted boy.
tā sâ wani sìkêt ɗàngà-ɗangà	She put on a skimpy skirt.
kâi, wà zâi àuri màzà-mazār̃ màcè?	Oh, who would marry a masculine woman?
yā yi hàntà-hantār̃ màganà̰	He has made a nasal utterance.
yanà̰ màganà̰ hàntà-hantà	He is talking through his nose.
aikì rà̰nà-rā̰nà bā yà̰ daɗèwā	Late morning work doesn't last.
nā zō rà̰nà-rā̰nà	I came late in the morning.
mutà̰nē sunà̰ fìtôwā dàmfà-damfà	People are coming out in profusion.

4. REDUPLICATED VERBS (LEXICALLY FROZEN)

Frozen reduplicated verbs are lexical items that are reduplicated in form, but for which no simple stem now exists in the language. There are two main classes of frozen reduplicates. The first class consists of erstwhile pluractional verbs, i.e., verbs that have the form (and often elements of the meaning) of synchronically produced pluractionals but without corresponding simple verb stems. The other class consists of reduplicated verbs that cannot be generated by a synchronically extant derivational process.

4.1. Frozen pluractionals

The term *frozen pluractional* is used for reduplicated verbs that historically were active pluractionals (see chap. 55) but that synchronically are not derived from a nonreduplicated counterpart, e.g., ɓaɓɓàkē 'uproot' (< reconstructed *ɓàkḛ̀, which no longer exists); gir̃gìzā 'shake' (< reconstructed *gizà̰); dabaibàyē 'hobble; tangle something up' (< reconstructed *dabàyē). With many verbs, the original pluractional (= plurac.) semantics is still recognizable in the meaning; in other cases, the verb has become semantically bleached and it is only the form that attests to its origin as a pluractional.

   In most cases, the simple stem from which the frozen pluractional was historically formed has been lost. In a few cases, however, the simple stem still exists, but the two forms have diverged (phonologically and/or semantically) such that their relation no longer could be considered to have any synchronic reality, e.g.,

far̃faɗō (< *faɗō) recover (e.g., from unconsciousness or illness) cf. far̃kà wake up (from the same base //faɗ-// plus a remnant suffix -kà)
sakwar̃kwàcē (< *sakwàtē) become slack, cf. sassàucē become loose, slack, which itself is a frozen pluractional
tak̃war̃k̃wàshē (< *tak̃wàsē) become weighed down by age, cf. taushḛ̀ (< *//tak̃ws-//?) press down on
gyangyàɗā (< *gyaɗà̰) nod from drowsiness, cf. gyaɗà̰ nod (head), take a nap (This latter has an active plurac. gyaggyàɗā or gyar̃gyàɗā.)
yayyàfā (< *yafà̰) sprinkle water, cf. yāfà̰ scatter seeds, sprinkle water; throw (e.g., cloth) over one's shoulder (This latter has an active plurac. yayyàfā.)

4.1.1. Basic formation

Frozen pluractionals all exhibit CVC reduplication in antepenultimate position, e.g., *ɗa.na ⇒ ɗan.ɗa.na 'taste', *ya.ga.la ⇒ ya.gal.ga.la 'tear to shreds'. The CVC is a copy of the CV of the penultimate syllable plus the initial C of the final syllable. Unlike active pluractionals (see §55:1.1), trisyllabic frozen pluractional stems do not exhibit prefixal reduplication. The frozen forms also differ from the active pluractionals in other ways. Synchronically, essentially all verbs allow C_1VG attachment (where the G forms a geminate with the following consonant), whatever the segmental shape of the stem, e.g., kāmà̰ ⇒ kakkà̰mā (= kankà̰mā) 'catch many', sàyā ⇒ sàssayà̰ (= sàisayà̰) 'buy many, often'. In the frozen form, on the other hand, the basic attachment is C_1VC_2 (e.g., mulmùlā 'knead') (examples in (a) below). The C_2 is subject to phonological deformations depending upon its nature and that of the following abutting consonant so that it sometimes may appear as a geminate, but the appearance of the geminate is phonologically conditioned rather than being part of the morphological process per se. If the copied C_2 is /y/, it automatically alters into /i/ and attaches itself to the nucleus, thereby partly disguising the essentially regular nature of the morphological formation, e.g., cukwı̄kwìyē (< *cikuikùyē < *cikuykùyē) 'entangle', sàisayà̰ 'shear wool' (not **sàssayà̰, which is an active plurac. of sàyā 'buy'). If the C_2 is a nasal, it assimilates to the position of the following consonant, e.g., [kìŋkimà̰] (< *kìmkimà̰) 'carry heavy thing with hands' (examples in (b) below). This nasal undergoes further full assimilation to a following liquid, e.g., làllāmà̰ (< *lànlāmà̰ < *làmlāmà̰) 'soothe, coax'. If the C_2 is a coronal obstruent it undergoes rhotacism to /ř/, e.g., bar̄bàɗā (< *baɗbàɗā) 'sprinkle (e.g., spices)' (examples in (c) below). The resulting /ř/ fully assimilates to an immediately following coronal consonant, e.g., lallàsā (< * lar̄làsā < * laslàsā) 'beat up'. (Full assimilation to coronal consonants also applies to flap /r/, e.g., tattàrā (< *tartàrā) 'collect', and, with some exceptions, /l/, e.g., duddùlā (< *duldùlā) 'fill bottle by immersion', cf. taltàlā = tattàlā 'speed off'.) If the C_2 is a labial or velar obstruent, one gets only a surface geminate, e.g., babbàkā (< *bakbàkā) 'grill, burn' (examples in (d) below). Examples:

(a) fùrfurà̰ barter; yagalgàlā tear to pieces; dabaibàyē hobble; tangle something up
(b) sansànā smell; tsantsàmē wash lightly; tagangànē [tagaŋgànē] sit with legs apart
(c) far̄faɗō recover (e.g., from unconsciousness or illness); gar̄gaɗà̰ warn, chastise; kanannàɗē coil up; gir̄gìzā shake; řagar̄gàzā smash up; sakwar̄kwàcē (< *sakwatkwàtē) become slack; tùmùr̄musà̰ wallow in the dirt
(d) ɓaɓɓàkē uproot; cìcciɓà̰ lift heavy load; fatattàkā tear into pieces; rout; kwakkwàfā tap, tamp; takwakkwàɓē become worn out; become too weak or old; tsàttsagà̰ peck (by fowl)

4.1.2. Anomalous nasal

A curious feature of frozen pluractionals that is not found in active pluractionals—but is found in frozen reduplicated nouns (§3.1.1)—is C_1Vn reduplication instead of the expected C_1VC_2, e.g., gangàrā 'flow/roll down' (not **gargàrā). There are some twenty or so words in this class, all trisyllabic words built on disyllabic bases. Some of the examples below may be fallacious, i.e., they may not be derived historically by derivational reduplication, but most of them probably are pluractionals in origin. There are a few examples where /ɓ/ is the stem-final consonant and one with /ʄ/. If one excludes these examples as not reflecting the same formation, then all of the examples have a coronal as the stem-final consonant. It is probably significant that the stem-final obstruents are either voiceless (namely /s/) or glottalized, but never voiced. Examples:

(a) ɓamɓàrē break off (e.g., maize grains from husk); dandàtsā beat, break into small fragments; ɗanɗàsā used in ɗanɗàsà adō be well dressed; famfàrā gallop, flee; famfàrē fall out (tooth); gangàrā descend, flow/roll down; gùngutsà̰ defame; gyangyàɗā nod from drowsiness (cf. gyaɗà̰ (kâi) nod (head), take a nap); gyangyàrē fall down unconscious, dead; ʄanʄàrā make sth very well; ʄwanʄwàsā knock at door, tap with knuckles; ʄyanʄyàshē hatch (eggs); kànkarā [= Kts kàrkarà̰] scrape lightly; kwànkwaɗà̰ drink a lot of liquid fast; kwankwàtsā smash into fragments; tantàlā take off, flee
(b) janjàɓā dump sth unpleasant on s.o.; tùntuɓà̰ ask (question); inquire of (psn); dandàʄā grind into sediment

4.1.3. Short vowel

The penultimate vowel of frozen pluractionals is invariably short, i.e., there is a metrical opposition between the heavy antepenultimate syllable and the light penultimate syllable, e.g., **giř.gì.zā** 'shake', **ya.gal.gà.lā** 'tear to pieces'. This is not the case with active pluractionals, which preserve the vowel length of the basic stem, e.g., **kan.kà.mā** 'catch many', **jaj.jè.fā** 'throw many or often'. As a result of the restriction, one finds a small number of frozen pluractionals with a short penultimate vowel that correspond to present-day simple stems with a long vowel, e.g.,

ɗàiɗayà	strip off epidermis	**ɗâyā**	strip off bark, fiber
diddìƙā (= **duddùƙā**)	crouch down	**dūƙà**	stoop
kwàikwayà	imitate	**kòyā** (< *kwàyā ?)	learn
ƙìrƙirà	invent, start	**ƙērà** (VN **ƙīrà**)	manufacture
tattàrā	collect things	**tàrà**	collect (plurac. **tattàrā**)
yayyàfā	sprinkle water	**yàfà**	scatter, sprinkle, throw cloth over one's shoulders (plurac. **yayyàfā**)

cf. also **caɓalɓàlē**   be(come) muddy, slushy = **càɓùlē**

4.1.4. Geminate /ll/

Excluding Arabic loanwords like **bayyànā** 'explain' and **zayyànā** 'adorn', trisyllabic verbs with medial geminates are rare. There are, however, some dozen or so verbs of the shape CVllVCVV with medial geminate /ll/, e.g., **fallàsā** 'disclose a secret'. A possible explanation is that they derived historically from frozen quadrisyllabic pluractionals by a process of haplology affecting the liquid in adjacent syllables, i.e., **fallàsā** < *fal_al_làsā (< *fa_l_as_làsā). Examples:

dallàřā   dazzle with bright light; **fallàsā**   disclose a secret to cause s.o. shame; **gàllabà**   worry, pester, harass; **gallàzā**   persecute, harass, torture; **kallàmē**   try to sweet-talk s.o.; **ƙallàfā**   be very keen about, obsessed with; (with i.o.) accuse falsely; **sullùɓē**   slip away, escape; **tàllabà**   support, help; **tàllafà**   provide for, give relief to; **tsallàkē**   jump over; **tsillùmā**   fall, jump, throw in water (cf. ideophone **tsilum**   sound of plopping in water)

4.2. Frozen reduplicates: C$_\alpha$-C$_\alpha$-C- and C-C$_\beta$-C$_\beta$-

There are a number of open syllable trisyllabic verbs in which either the first and second or the second and third consonants are identical.

4.2.1 Pattern 1: C$_\alpha$āC$_\alpha$VCV(V)

In pattern 1, the first two consonants are identical. The initial syllable has the shape Cā with a long /ā/. The examples with /ē/ and /ō/ probably come by sporadic change from Cyā and Cwā respectively, e.g., **ƙēƙàsā** (< *ƙyàƙàsā) 'dry sth (e.g., leaves)', **dōdànā** (< *dwàdànā) 'touch with stick, set fire to'. The second syllable, which has the same onset consonant as the first syllable, contains a short vowel (either /a/ or /u/, but seldom /i/), thereby producing a heavy-light rhythmic alternation. (The final vowel is variable and is determined by the verb grade and the syntactic environment.) There are some forty verbs of this type. Examples:

dādàrā	cut with sth blunt	**ɗāɗàřā**	brand with fire
fàfarà	chase, pursue, drive away	**gàgarà**	be impossible
gwàgwiyà (< *gwàg^{w}uyà//)	gnaw at	**ƙàƙabà**	pester
ƙwàƙulà	reach out for, scrape out	**lālùbā**	grope
màmayà	attack silently	**māmùlā**	eat (without teeth)
ràrumà	grab, snatch	**wàwurà**	snatch, grab

4.2.2. Pattern 2: CVCβāCβV(V)

In pattern 2, the second and third consonants are identical. The second syllable has the shape **Cā** (**Cū** in one case). The initial syllable, which begins with a different consonant, contains a short vowel, thereby producing a light-heavy rhythmic alternation. (The final vowel is variable and is determined by the verb grade and the syntactic environment.) There are some forty verbs of this type, many of which semantically relate in some way to flowing of a liquid. Examples:

dàlālà	dribble (saliva)	**fìyàyē**	become mildewed, moldy
hàrārà	give a disapproving side glance	**kwaràrā**	pour through a narrow channel
laɓàɓā	approach stealthily, sneak up	**màlālà**	flow or spread over
rìɓāɓà	drink large amount of	**sàdūdà**	give up, give in
sadɗàɗā	go stealthily	**sulàlā**	warm up (a liquid); sneak/slide into
taƙàƙē	establish mastery over	**tàrārà**	drip
tsiyàyā	pour out in a thin stream	**zùrārà**	trickle down

[References: Gouffé (1975b); Newman (1986a, 1989a, 1989b, 1990b]

63. Reflexives and Reciprocals

1. REFLEXIVES

REFLEXIVES are indicated by the word **kâi** 'head', normally accompanied by a bound genitive pronoun, which consists of the masculine linker **-n** plus a possessive pronoun; see table 12.

Table 12: Reflexive pronouns

1 s	**kâinā**	myself	1 p	**kânmù**	ourselves
2m	**kânkà**	yourself (m.)	2 p	**kânkù**	yourselves
2f	**kânkì**	yourself (f.)			
3m	**kânsà / kânshì**	himself	3 p	**kânsù**	themselves
3f	**kântà**	herself			
			4 p	**kâi**	oneself

Reflexive pronouns have two functions: "basic" and "emphatic."

1.1. Basic reflexives

In its basic function, a reflexive pronoun indicates an NP that is coreferential with the subject or other appropriate argument in the sentence. The reflexive can appear in most positions in which an ordinary NP can occur, e.g., as a thematic direct object (either a real d.o. of a transitive verb, a genitive object of a verbal noun, or an oblique object of **dà** used with a gr5 efferential verb), an indirect object, a genitive complement, or an object of a preposition. (The reflexive cannot, however, appear in subject position.) Examples:

mun$_i$ cùci kânmù$_i$	We harmed ourselves.
Bàlā$_i$ yā zàrgi kânsà$_i$	Bala accused himself.
cf. Bàlā$_i$ yā zàrgē shì$_j$	Bala accused him (s.o. else).
yârā sun sàuràri kânsù à r̃akōdà	The children listened to themselves on the recorder.
zā tà kulà dà kântà	She will take care of herself.
don mè kakè yàbon kânkà?	Why are you praising yourself?
nā jāwō wà kâinā wàhalà̀	I brought the trouble on myself.
sun ɓātà gidàjen kânsù	They ruined their own houses.
bà tà bā dà kyât gà kōwā ba sai kântà	She didn't give cake to anyone except herself.
sun bā dà màkì mài yawà̀ gà kânsù	They gave themselves high grades.
mun ji r̃a'àyin Fàtī bisà kântà	We heard Fati's opinion of herself.
mun ji r̃a'àyin Fàtī bisà kânmù	We heard Fati's opinion of ourselves.
kā yi fentì dà kânkà?	Did you do the painting by yourself?

522

mun sayar̃ wà kânmù dà mōtōcin gwànjôn	We sold the auction cars to ourselves.
Mūsā yā yi wà Audù màganà̃ gàme dà kânsà	Musa talked to Audu about himself.

(where 'himself' can refer to Musa or to Audu)

Like other NPs, reflexive pronouns and phrases can be focused by fronting, e.g.,

kânmù mukà cùtā	It was *ourselves* we harmed.
kântà nē ta jāwō wà wàhalà̃	It was *herself* she brought trouble on.
dà kânsù (nē) sukà yi aikì̃	They did the work *by themselves*.
dà kâinā (nè̀) zân gyārà̃ ta	I will repair it *by myself*.

Basic reflexives cannot, however, be topicalized, i.e., one cannot say **kânmù kàm mun cùtā 'As for ourselves we harmed.'

As is typical of languages in general, the reflexive must be in the same clause as its coreferential subject, e.g.,

bā nà̀ₐ sô Bintà tà màrē nì̀ₐ (not **...màri kâinā)   I don't want Binta to slap me.

Mar̃yàmₐ tā amìncē Bàlā yā dòkē tà̀ₐ (not **...dòki kântà)   Maryam believed Bala hit her.

cf. Mar̃yàm tā amìncē Lādì̀ₐ tā dòki kântà̀ₐ   Maryam believed Ladi hit herself (i.e., Ladi).

Bellò̀ₐ yā gānè Mūsā̀ⱼ yā gutsùrē tuwôn don kânsà̀ⱼ
    Bello understood that Musa got the *tuwo* for himself (i.e., Musa).

Zàinabù̀ₐ tā tabbàtā Bintà̀ⱼ tā ginà̃ wà kântà̀ⱼ gidā
    Zainabu is convinced that Binta built herself (i.e., Binta) a house.

cf. Zàinabù̀ₐ tā tabbàtā Bintà̀ⱼ tā ginà̃ matà̀ₐ gidā
    Zainabu is convinced that Binta built her (i.e., Zainabu) a house.

In addition to the eight categories of person/number/gender found in the non-subject pronouns, weak subject pronouns have a ninth category, the so-called fourth person impersonal pronoun /a/, e.g., **an kāwō ruwā** 'One brought water.' Reflexives of sentences with the impersonal wsp are expressed by using the bare **kâi** without a possessive pronoun attached, e.g.,

akàn cùci kâi à ƙasar̃ nàn	One habitually harms oneself in this country.
cf. mutàr̃nē sukàn cùci kânsù à ƙasar̃ nàn	People habitually harm themselves in this country.
yā kàmātà à tàimàki kâi	One should help oneself. (lit. it befits that one help self)
à nèmi àbin kâi	One should get one's own.

The bare **kâi** can also be used in other sentences, phrases, and compounds where the person/number features are irrelevant, e.g.,

Audù yā tàmbàyi Bintà hanyàr̃ kārè kâi	Audu asked Binta how to save oneself.
cf. Audù yā tàmbàyi Bintà hanyàr̃ kārè kânsà	Audu asked Binta how to save himself.
cf. Audù yā tàmbàyi Bintà hanyàr̃ kārè kântà	Audu asked Binta how to save herself.
kùlā dà kâi cikin tàrō yanà̃ dà kyâu	Behaving oneself in a meeting is good.
ƙungìyar̃ haɗà-kâi	a cooperative society
tàimakon kâi dà kâi	self-help (lit. helping oneself with oneself)
dògarō dà kâi	self-reliance
yàbon-kâi	self-praise, conceit
girman-kâi	pride

1.1.1. Inclusive reflexives

As a general rule, the reflexive pronoun and its antecedent must be coreferential. However, a singular subject can take a plural reflexive if the subject is included in the referential group. (I translate these examples with plural reflexives (in quotation marks) even though the English may be ungrammatical.) Examples:

Lādì$_i$ **tā sòki kânsù**$_{i+x}$ Ladi criticized "themselves".
(i.e., she criticized herself and the others in her group), cf. **Lādì tā sòkē sù**   Ladi criticized them.
à wannàn karò dai, kā$_i$ **tàimàki kânkù**$_{i+x}$ On this occasion, you (sg.) helped "yourselves".
à yâu dai, nā$_i$ **bā wà kânmù**$_{i+x}$ **kunyà**   Today I embarrassed "ourselves".
nā$_i$ **sō kânmù**$_{i+x}$ **cikin fîm ɗin nàn**   I like "ourselves" in this movie.

°AN: In English, the non-coreferential object in this last example would be expressed with an object pronoun, e.g., 'I like us in this movie.' Note that in certain circumstances, English can use an object pronoun even when the subject and object *are* coreferential, e.g., 'I like me in this movie.'

1.1.2. Nonreflexive coreferential pronouns

With mental/sensation verbs, object pronouns can optionally be used instead of reflexives even when the subject and object are coreferential. Verbs of this class include: **ganī** 'see', **kàllā** 'look at', **dùbā** 'look at', **hàngā** 'espy', **sō** 'want, like', **ɗaukā** 'consider', **sanì** 'know', **ji** 'feel, hear', **sàurārà** 'listen', **taɓà** 'touch', **sāmù** 'find', **zàtā** 'think, imagine', **gānè** 'recognize'. Examples:

Tàlā tā gan tà (= **ga kântà**) **à madūbîn**   Tala saw herself in the mirror.
(The sentence with **tà** can also mean 'Tala saw her (s.o. else) in the mirror.')
Sāni yā jī shì (= **ji kânsà**) **yanà màganà à ɍēdiyò**   Sani heard himself talking on the radio.
tā sàmē tà (= **sàmi kântà**) **à wani hālì**   She found herself in a certain situation.
in nā kàllē nì (= **kàlli kâinā**), **kūkā nakè** (**yî**)   When I look at me/myself, I cry.
(lit. if I observe me (observe myself) crying I.Rcont1 (doing))
yârân sun sō sù (= **sō kânsù**) **à wànnan hòtôn**   The children loved themselves in that photo.
cf. **yârân sunà sôn kânsù**   The children like themselves.
(*not* = **yârân sunà sônsù**, which means 'The children like them.')

ΔDN: Speakers differ considerably regarding how comfortable they are with coreferential non-reflexive pronouns. SH speakers do allow them whereas other speakers, e.g., Malami Buba, a native WH speaker, invariably interpreted such sentences as **Sāni yā jī shì yanà màganà à ɍēdiyò** as meaning 'Sani heard him (someone else) talking on the radio.'

In some sentences, the d.o. pronoun is required (or strongly preferred) over the reflexive, e.g.,

nā san nì (not ****san kâinā**) **dà shàunī**   I know myself with regard to procrastination.
dà Màrka ta faɍkà dàgà barcī, sai ta gan tà (not ****ga kântà**) **à ɗaure**
    When Marka woke up, she found (lit. saw) herself tied up.
don Allàh kun gan kù (not ****ga kânkù**) **dà wata màganà maràɍ dāɗī**
    For God's sake, (you (pl.)) look at you with this bad talk.
dùbè ka!   Look at yourself! (lit. look at you), cf. **dùbi kânkà!**   Look at your head!

With the preposition **don** 'for the benefit of' (and probably some others as well) a coreferential non-reflexive pronoun is allowed as an alternative to a reflexive form, e.g., nā sàyi mōtàr̃ don nī (= don kâinā)   I bought the car for me (for myself).

The normal semantic interpretation of a third person possessive pronoun is coreferential, i.e., **yā hau dōkìnsà** 'He rode his (not someone else's) horse.' Coreferential possessors may be expressed by reflexives but these are highly marked. They translate best into English as possessives with 'own', e.g., **dōkìn kânsà** 'his own horse' (lit. horse of himself). Examples:

mālàm yā kar̃àntà littāfìn kânsà   The teacher read his own book.
cf. mālàm yā kar̃àntà littāfìnsà   The teacher read his book.
(This is understood to be his own book unless someone else's book was the topic of the discourse.)
yâr̃ân sun ɗàuki hōtunàn kânsù (= hōtunànsù)   The children took their own pictures.
ɗàlìbân sun gyārà mōtōcin kânsù (= mōtōcinsù)   The students repaired their (own) cars.
nā$_i$ fār̃à ginà gidan kânmù$_{i+x}$ (= gidanmù) à bir̃nîn   I started building our own house in the city.

To indicate clearly that the possessor is not coreferential with the subject, one often uses an indirect object construction, e.g.,

ɗàlìbân sun gyārà musù mōtōci(nsù)
      The students repaired their (other people's) cars (for them).

With inalienably possessed nouns, i.e., kin terms, body parts, and such, the use of the reflexive possessor is generally disallowed. This restriction also extends to genitive prepositions built with body part terms, e.g.,

Bintà tā yànki ɗan-yātsàntà dà wuƙā (not **ɗan-yātsàn kântà)
      Binta cut her finger with a knife.
mātân sunà lùr̃ā dà 'yā'yansù (not **'yā'yan kânsù)
      The women are looking after their (own) children.
kā sòki ƙafàr̃kà? (not **ƙafàr̃ kânkà)   Did you stab your own foot?
Audù yā ga bābàr̃sà (not **bābàr̃ kânsà)   Audu saw his (own) mother.
nā sâ shi bāyānā   I put it behind me.
(not bāyan kâinā, which would mean 'behind my head')
tā sōkà àllūr̃à à jìkintà (not **jìkin kântà)   She stabbed the needle into herself.

A common means of emphasizing coreferential possession is by using a regular possessive phrase (or an independent possessive pronoun) along with a genitive phrase made up of the short vowel linker **na / ta** + a reflexive. Examples:

ɗàlìbân sun gyārà mōtōcinsù na kânsù   The students repaired their own cars.
(lit. ...cars.of.them of themselves)**Bintà tā ga hòtontà na kântà** Binta saw her own picture.
Audù yā ginà gidansà na kânsà   Audu built his very own house.
zā kà kāwō tākà ta kânkà?   Are you going to bring your very own?
nā sayar̃ masà dà kòmfyūtà ɗīnā ta kâinā   I sold him my own computer.
sai mù ajìyè nāmù na kânmù   We should put away our own.

This construction with a regular possessive followed by a possessive reflexive is also available with inalienably possessed nouns, e.g.,

Làmî tā hàifī ɗantà na kântà   Lami gave birth to her own son.
nā sòki ƙafàtā ta kâinā   I stabbed my own foot.
mun kāwō řa'àyinmù na kânmù   We brought our own opinion.

1.1.3. "Pseudoemphatic" reflexives

Pseudoemphatic reflexives consist of a prepositional phrase composed of **dà** 'with/by' plus a reflexive pronoun coreferential with the subject. (The construction is comparable to an English 'by' phrase like **nā yi aikì dà kâinā** 'I did the work (by) myself.') These phrases indicate that the person(s) referred to by the reflexive did the action in question and not someone else. These structures are labeled *pseudo-emphatic* because structurally they constitute basic coreferential reflexives functioning as the object of a preposition, whereas semantically they approach the meaning of emphatic reflexives, e.g., **nī kâinā nā yi aikì** 'I myself did work' (see below §1.2). The neutral position for pseudoemphatic reflexives is at the end of the VP after objects and locative goals.

ɗàlìbai sunà̄ shārè ɗākunàn dà kânsù   The students are sweeping the rooms by themselves.
Mūsā yā gyārà řēdiyòn dà kânsà   Musa repaired the radio by himself.
Shatù tâ dafà àbinci dà kântà   Shatu will likely cook the food by herself.
nā jē Kanò dà kâinā   I went to Kano by myself.
munà̄ sàurārō dà kânmù   We were listening by ourselves.
wannàn mahàukàcī yā shìga rījìyā dà kânsà
    This madman entered the well by himself.

Intransitive sentences with a non-agential subject also allow pseudoemphatic reflexive phrases, e.g.,

gìlāshìn yā fashè dà kânsà   The glass broke by by itself.
ginìn yā rūshè dà kânsà   The building collapsed by itself.
wutā tā mutù dà kântà   The fire died out on its own.

The pseudoemphatic reflexive phrase is not allowed with grade 7 passive sentences because they have an understood, but unexpressed, agent, e.g.,

**gìlāshìn yā fàsu dà kânsà   The glass was broken itself.
**mōtàř tā gyàru dà kântà   The car was repaired by itself.
cf. mōtàř tā gyàru   The car has been well repaired (by someone).

The 'by' phrase optionally can be (and often is) fronted to a position immediately following the subject. This adds extra emphasis. With the completive, continuous, and potential, this movement conditions a shift from a general to a corresponding Rel TAM, namely, preterite, Rel-continuous, and future, respectively, e.g.,

ɗàlìbai [dà kânsù] [sukè]$_{Rcont1}$ shārè ɗākunàn
    The students (by) themselves are sweeping the rooms.
cf. ɗàlìbai [sunà̄]$_{cont}$ shārè ɗākunàn [dà kânsù]
    The students are sweeping the rooms (by) themselves.
Mūsā [dà kânsà] [ya]$_{pret}$ gyārà řēdiyòn   Musa (by) himself repaired the radio.
cf. Mūsā [yā]$_{comp}$ gyārà řēdiyòn [dà kânsà] Musa repaired the radio (by) himself.
Shatù [dà kântà] [zā tà]$_{fut}$ dafà àbinci   Shatu (by) herself will cook the food.
Shatù [tâ]$_{pot}$ dafà àbinci [dà kântà]   Shatu will likely cook the food (by) herself.

°AN: In surface structure, the subject plus the **dà** phrase forms a constituent. The evidence for the movement is provided by two factors. First, Rel TAMs (which are required with the pseudoemphatic reflexive) are generally conditioned by focus movement to the left of the PAC. Second, sentences with pseudoemphatic reflexives after the subject invariably have corresponding sentences with the **dà** phrase after the VP; see examples above. By contrast, this is not the case with real emphatic reflexives (to be described below), e.g., **Bellò kânsà yā ràsu** 'Bello himself died', but not ****Bellò dà kânsà yā ràsu** nor ****Bellò yā ràsu dà kânsà**.

A pseudoemphatic reflexive can be strengthened by using an independent pronoun (in which case it looks just like a real emphatic pronoun), e.g.,

ɗàlìbai sunà̄ shārè ɗākunàn sū dà kânsù

> The students are sweeping the rooms themselves. (lit. ...they by themselves)

Mālàm Bàlā yā bā wà ɗàlìbai mākì̄ shī dà kânsà

> Malam Bala gave the grades to the students himself.

Jummai ita dà kântà zā tà yāgà takàr̃dâr̃

> Jummai herself will tear up the paper.

Shatù zā tà dafà àbinci ita dà kântà	Shatu will cook the food (by) herself.
gāra kà tū̃kà mōtàr̃ kai dà kânkà	It is better if you drive the car (you) yourself.
Bellò shī dà kânsà zâi taimàkā	Bello himself will help.

1.2. Emphatic reflexives

An emphatic reflexive serves to focus attention on the head NP (noun or pronoun) or to contrast it with some other person or thing, e.g., **Bellò shī kânsà yā ɗauki àkwàtì** 'Bello himself lifted up the box.' It sometimes connotes 'as well, also' as opposed to the pseudoemphatic reflexive, which tends to connote 'singly' or 'exclusively', e.g., **ita kântà tā yànki nāmà̄** 'She herself (as well as the others) cut off some meat', cf. **ita dà kântà ta yànki nāmà̄** 'She herself cut off some meat (on her own)'; **sunà̄ gayà̀ minì nī kâinā** 'They are telling me (as well)', cf. **sunà̄ gayà̀ minì nī kaɗai** 'They are telling me, me only.'

Emphatic reflexive pronouns are formed by an independent pronoun followed by an immediately juxtaposed reflexive pronoun, e.g., **kū kânkù** 'you yourselves'. Examples:

kàfin [shī kânsà] yà yàr̃da dōlè yà tàmbàyi wânsà

> Before he himself agrees he should ask his older brother.

[nī kâinā] bā nà̀ sô ìn bar̃ wurîn	I myself don't want to leave the place.
[ita kântà] tàurārùwā cè	She herself is a star.
tā jāwō wàhalà̀ gà [ita kântà]	She brought trouble on she herself.

°AN: All (or almost all) grammars, e.g., Abraham (1959b), Kraft and Kirk-Greene (1973), describe the emphatic reflexive as consisting of X + **dà** + the reflexive pronoun, e.g., **ita dà kântà** 'she herself' (lit. she with herself). This is not accurate. The direct juxtaposition, e.g., **ita kântà** 'she herself', is the means of expressing 'she herself', whereas the construction with **dà** (the pseudoemphatic reflexive described above) is restricted to action sentences in which a 'by' phrase is semantically appropriate.

Emphatic reflexives with nouns are indicated in two ways, with speakers differing as to which they prefer. One means is to follow a noun by an emphatic reflexive phrase consisting of an independent pronoun plus its corresponding reflexive pronoun, e.g., **Bellò shī kânsà** 'Bello himself' (lit. Bello he himself). The other means is simply to add a reflexive pronoun immediately after the noun, e.g., **Bellò kânsà** 'Bello himself'.

Jummai (ita) kântà zā tà yāgà takàr̃dā̃r̃   Jummai herself will tear up the paper.
d̃àlìbai (sū) kânsù sun san anǎ taimàkā musù
    The students themselves know that they are being helped.
'yan sàndā (sū) kânsù sukàn yi irìn wannàn ɓàr̃nā̃r̃
    Policemen themselves do this kind of damage.

Nouns followed by an emphatic reflexive phrase containing the independent pronoun often undergo transposition, e.g.,

[yārǒ] [shī kânsà] = [shī kânsà] [yāròn] yanǎ tàimakon iyàyensà
    The boy (he) himself is helping his parents. (lit. boy he himself = he himself the boy)
[gwamnatì] [ita kântà] = [ita kântà] [gwamnatì] zā tà ɓatar̃ dà kud̃ī dà yawǎ
    The government itself is going to spend a lot of money.
yā sâ [Kande] [ita kântà] tā kōmǎ gidā   He caused Kande herself to return home.
= yā sâ [ita kântà] [Kànde] tā kōmǎ gidā   He caused she herself Kande to return home.

Bound pronominal clitics cannot be modified directly by a reflexive pronoun. They thus use the nominal strategy of employing an emphatic reflexive phrase in apposition, e.g.,

mun hàr̃bē-shì [shī kânsà]   We shot him himself. (lit. him he himself)
sunǎ gayǎ minì [nī kâinā]   They are telling me myself. (lit. me I myself)
nâs tā yi jinyàr̃sù [sū kânsù]   The nurse took care of them themselves.

Pseudoemphatic reflexives with **dà** usually presuppose agential conrol, i.e., that some action has been done by the subject in question. They thus cannot be used to modify an object or the subject of a non-action sentence, such as an equational sentence. Emphatic reflexives, on the other hand, can modify an NP in almost any function, e.g.,

munǎ kallon wannàn yārinyǎ ita kântà   We were looking at this girl herself.
nī kâinā d̃an sarkī nè̀   I myself am a prince. (*not* ****nī dà kâinā d̃an sarkī nè̀**)
yā kàmātà à gàyyàci Mūsā shī kânsà   One should invite Musa himself.
not ****yā kàmātà à gàyyàci Mūsā shī dà kânsà**
Mālàm Bàlā yā bā wà d̃àlìbai [sū kânsù] mākì̃
    Malam Bala gave the grades to the students themselves.

An emphatic reflexive strengthens its head but does not automatically put it in focus. It thus does not create a Rel environment that requires a Rel as opposed to a general TAM. A fronted pseudo reflexive 'by' phrase, on the other hand, does condition a TAM shift. Examples:

sū kânsù [sun]$_{comp}$ zō   They themselves came.
cf. **sū dà kânsù [sukà]$_{pret}$ zō**   They came by themselves.
(lit. they by themselves came)
mū kânmù [munǎ]$_{cont}$ sàurār̃ō   We ourselves are listening.
cf. **mū dà kânmù [mukè̀]$_{Rcont 1}$ sàurār̃ō**   We are listening by ourselves.
d̃àlìbai sū kânsù [sunǎ]$_{cont}$ shārè d̃ākunàn
    The students themselves are sweeping the rooms.
cf. **d̃àlìbai sū dà kânsù [sukè̀]$_{Rcont1}$ shārè d̃ākunàn**
    The students are sweeping the rooms by themselves.

Mūsā shī kânsà [yā]_{comp} **gyārà r̃ēdiyòn**	Musa himself repaired the radio.
cf. **Mūsā dà kânsà** [ya]_{pret} **gyārà r̃ēdiyòn**	Musa repaired the radio by himself.

Although the use of an emphatic reflexive does not automatically entail focus, optional focus, which involves fronting plus the use of the stabilizer, is permitted (which then naturally conditions the switch to a Rel TAM), e.g.,

sū kânsù nē [sukà]_{pret} **gòyi bāyan màganàr̃sà**
   It was they themselves who supported his statement.
Mūsā kânsà nē [yakè]_{Rcont2} **ɓòye**   Musa himself (as well) is hidden.

Emphatic reflexive phrases can be topicalized, i.e., they can be set off intonationally or by the use of a modal particle, e.g.,

[**sū kânsù**] (**mā**), [**sun**]_{comp} **gòyi bāyan màganàr̃sà**
   As for themselves, they (as well) supported his statement.

Since basic reflexives and emphatic reflexives or pseudoemphatic reflexives serve quite different semantic functions, they can co-occur in the same sentence, e.g.,

yā bugar̃ dà [**kânsà**] [**dà kânsà**]	He himself got himself drunk.
(lit. he beat himself by himself)	
Shatù [**ita kântà**] **tā jāwō wà** [**kântà**] **wàhalà**	Shatu herself brought the trouble on herself.
yā gayà mîn [**tār̃īhìn kânsà**] [**dà kânsà**]	He himself told me his autobiography.
(lit. history of himself by himself)	
mutằnē sunà tàimakon [**kânsù**] [**dà kânsù**]	
The people are helping themselves by themselves.	

2. RECIPROCALS

Reciprocals are indicated by the word **jūnā** 'other', optionally including a bound genitive pronoun (i.e., linker -**n** plus a possessive pronoun).

1p	**jūnanmù**	each other (we)
2p	**jūnankù**	each other (you, pl.)
3p	**jūnansù**	each other (they)
4p	**jūnā**	each other (they, impersonal)

◊HN: The word **jūnā** etymologically comes from **jìkī** 'body' + a suffix -**nā** of unknown origin. (Jaggar, personal communication, has suggested that -**nā** may be an erstwhile plural marker, a proposal that is not unreasonable, but which I am not prepared to endorse.) The derivation is *//jìk´// + **nā** > ***jiúnā** (by Klingenheben's Law) > ***jùúnā** (by monophthongization) > **jūnā** (by LH to H tone simplification). The 'body' meaning of **jūnā** is still preserved in the phrase **jūnā biyu** 'pregnant', e.g., **tanà dà jūnā biyu** 'She is pregnant', lit. she has two bodies. The use of 'head' and 'body' for reflexives and reciprocals, respectively, is widespread throughout the Chadic family.

Whereas English uses 'each other' or 'one another' regardless of the person of the antecedent, Hausa has distinct forms in the first, second, and third persons, e.g., **mun tsallàkē jūnanmù** 'We jumped over each other'; **kù tàimàki jūnankù** 'You (pl.) should help one another'; **Bellò dà Tankò bà zā sù cùci jūnansù ba** 'Bello and Tanko will not cheat one another.'

The first, second, and third persons also allow use of the bare reciprocal **jūnā** instead of the **jūnan** + pronoun forms, i.e.,

mun tsallàkē jūnanmù = **mun tsallàkē jūnā**	We jumped over each other.
Bellò dà Tankò sun cùci jūnansù = **Bellò dà Tankò sun cùci jūnā**	
Bello and Tanko cheated one another.	

The alternative examples above are probably not exactly equivalent in meaning. Although the matter remains to be studied carefully, it appears that in some cases the **jūnan** + pronoun variants are more specific, i.e., they refer to identifiable groups or individuals, often limited to two, whereas the **jūnā** variant is more general. Thus **kù tàimàki jūnankù** might mean 'You (two) should help each other', whereas **kù tàimàki jūnā** might mean 'You people (number unspecified) should help one another.'

In all but the most simple sentences, the bare **jūnā** is either required or strongly preferred over the form with the possessive pronouns, which is considered clumsy if not unacceptable, e.g.,

Amìrkà dà Rāshà sun yi wà jūnā lèɓen-àsīřī hař na tsawon wajen shèkàrū hàmsin
America and Russia spied on each other for some fifty years.
Audù yā tàmbàyi Mūsā hanyàř tàimakon jūnā
Audu asked Musa about a means of helping each other.

Reciprocal possessives are usually, but not necessarily, expressed by the bare **jūnā**, e.g.,

mātân sun ga 'yā'yan jūnā	The women saw each other's children.
màlàmân sunà kařàntà lìttàttàfan jūnā	The teachers are reading each other's books.
yârân sun ɗauki hōtunàn jūnā	The children took pictures of one another.
cf. **Bellò dà Tankò sun ɗauki hōtunàn jūnansù**	Bello and Tanko took each other's picture (in turn).

The bare **jūnā** form is required with the impersonal 4p subject, which, although often glossed as 'one', behaves as a plural, e.g.,

an yàudàri jūnā	They (impersonal) deceived each other.
cf. **sun yàudàri jūnansù**	They (3p) deceived each other.
anà cùtař jūnā à nân ƙasâř	One (impersonal) cheats each other in this country.
an bā wà jūnā kunyà	They (impersonal) embarrassed each other.

°AN: The impersonal weak subject pronoun in the completive patterns morphologically with the plural pronouns in having a final **-n**. Compare **an** 'one' with **mun, kun, sun** 'we, you (pl.), they', as opposed to **yā/tā** 'he/she'. It is primarily on this basis that various scholars (including myself) have labeled the impersonal wsp as fourth person plural. Its behavior with reciprocals provides supporting syntactic evidence that it should be treated as a plural.

The reciprocal normally requires a plural subject. As in English, the Hausa reciprocal **jūnā** can be used with the universal pronoun **kōwā** 'everyone', even though grammatically it takes singular concord, e.g.,

kōwā [yā]3m san jūnā nân   Everyone knows each other here.

The bare **jūnā** form occurs also in other constructions, like nominalizations and modifier phrases, where the person feature is irrelevant, e.g.,

sôn jūnā	mutual love
duwầtsū mahàihàyan jūnā	stones superimposed on one another
abūbuwầ makùsàntā dà jūnā	things closely connected to each other

In a complex sentence, the reciprocal can refer only to an antecedent within its clause, e.g.,

mằlàmai sunằ sô yârā sù tàimàki jūnā
> The teachers want the children to help one another.

[Kànde dà Jummai]ᵢ sun san (cêwā) [Bàlā dà Tankò]ⱼ sun cùci jūnāⱼ
> Kande and Jummai know (that) Bala and Tanko cheated each other.

Contrast the following sentence with a d.o. pronoun (which has two possible readings, given in preferred order):

Kànde dà Jummai sun san (cêwā) Bàlā dà Tankò sun cùcē sù
1. [Kande and Jummai]ᵢ know (that) [Bala and Tanko]ⱼ cheated themᵢ (i.e., Kande and Jummai).
2. [Kande and Jummai]ᵢ know (that) [Bala and Tanko]ⱼ cheated themₖ (some other people).

ΔDN: In the dialect described by Alidou (1992), the full form **jūnansù** *can* have an antecedent that is outside of its clause. In this case the semantic interpretation is on 'each of' rather than 'each other', e.g.,
Kànde dà Jummai sun san (cêwā) Bàlā da Tankò sun cùci jūnansù
1. Kande and Jummai know (that) Bala and Tanko cheated each other. (normal reciprocal)
2. Kande and Jummai know (that) Bala and Tanko cheated each of them (i.e., Kande and Jummai individually). (long-distance reference)
     When the intended antecedent is outside the clause, the subject within the clause does not have to be in the plural, e.g., **Kànde dà Jummai sun san (cêwā) Bàlā yā cùci jūnansù** 'Kande and Jummai know that Bala cheated each of them.'

[References: Jaggar (1998); Yalwa (1992)]

64. Relative Clauses

1. BASIC FORMATION

RELATIVE clauses (= RCs) occur after the NP (noun or pronoun) that they modify. They have the structure **dà** 'relativizer' + an embedded S (which generally preserves normal word order). The TAM in the RC must be a Rel form (see below). In place of the bare relativizer, it is also possible to use a relative pronoun or adverb that contains **dà** as an integral constituent (see §3). Examples:

[yāròn] [dà [na ganī]]
    [the boy] [whom [I saw]]
[ɗākìn] [dà [àkwai yârā]]
    [a room] [where [there are children]]
[mùtumìn] [dà [mutằnē (su)kề gudù sabồdà tsananin jàfā'ìnsà]]
    [the man] [whom [people are avoiding because of his ill-will]]

The relativizer **dà**, which one can gloss as 'that' or 'who' or 'which', etc., depending on the context, is invariant, i.e., it is the same regardless of the head noun's number, gender, animacy, or syntactic function. Examples:

yārinyằr dà ta ràsu	the girl who died
tùlûn dà Jummai ta sàyā	the water pot that Jummai bought
gwamnàn dà akà yabằ masà	the governor whom they praised
yârā dà kề jàjjère à hanyằ	children who were lined up on the road
ɗằlìbân dà zā sù gamà aikìnsù	the students who will finish their work

It is possible to have a modal particle between the head noun and the RC, e.g.,

lōkàcîn (kùwa) dà sukà zō	the time (moreover) that they came
wàndôn (mā) dà na sàyā	the trousers (too) that I bought

A relative clause can contain an NP that itself is modified by an RC, e.g.,

yāròn [dà ya yi kūkā dà mālàmâr [dà ta kồrē shì dàgà makařantā]]
    the boy who complained about the teacher who suspended him from school
bishiyằr [dà Mūsā ya sārề dà gằtarîn [dà na bā shì arō]]
    the tree that Musa cut down with the axe that I lent him
màtâr [dà ta nūnằ mîn àlƙālîn [dà ya ɗaurè shēgèn [dà ya zằgi mijìntà]]]
    the woman who showed me the judge who sentenced the bastard who insulted her husband

2. DEFINITE ARTICLE

Semantically definite nouns modified by an RC typically contain the definite article (d.a.) ˋn / ˋř, e.g., **yārò-n dà na ganī** 'the boy whom I saw', **rīgunà-n dà mukè̀ sô** 'the gowns that we want', **àkuyà-ř dà ta gujè̀ manà** 'the goat that ran from us'. In normal speech, the feminine d.a. ˋř typically assimilates to the initial /d/ of the relativizer, e.g., **yārinyà-ř dà** 'the girl who' is pronounced [yārinyàddà], **tāgà-ř dà** 'the window that' is pronounced [tāgàddà]. When added to a word with final H tone, the addition of the L-tone article produces an F, e.g., **wàndō** 'trousers' + ˋn → **wàndôn** 'the trousers'. In RCs, the tonal phrase consisting of the word-final F and the L-tone **dà** usually simplifies to H-L, e.g.,

wàndôn dà ka sàyā =	**wàndon dà ka sàyā**	the trousers that you bought
tunkìyâř dà ta mutù =	**tunkìyař dà ta mutù**	the sheep that died
lōkàcîn dà sukà zō =	**lōkàcin dà sukà zō**	when (the time that) they came

    ΔDN: In SH, the tone simplification rule is optional for most speakers. It appears that in some WH dialects, at least, the rule has become obligatory.
    °AN: Note that the tone simplification rule depends on the immediate juxtaposition of the word-final F and the **dà**. If anything intervenes, for example, a modal particle, then the noun appears with its F tone intact, e.g., **wàndôn dai dà ka sàyā** 'the trousers really that you bought', not ****wàndon dai dà…**; **tunkìyâř kò̀ dà ta mutù** 'the sheep however that died', not ****tunkìyař kò̀ dà…**; **lōkàcîn fa dà sukà zō** 'when (the time that) indeed they came', not ****lōkàcin fa dà…**.

Instead of affixing the d.a. directly, some words make use of the connector **ɗl-**. These will thus appear before the relativizer **dà** as **ɗîn** (or **ɗin** with the tone simplification), e.g.,

mutằnē takwàs ɗin dà sukà rasà rāyukànsù	the eight men who perished
Audù ɗîn dà na sanì (= **Audùn dà na sanì**)	the Audu whom I know
software **ɗîn dà na sāmù**	the software that I got

The d.a. is not obligatory in RCs, i.e., it belongs to the head noun and is not part of the relativization process per se. The head noun can occur equally well with a possessive pronoun, with a demonstrative, with a prenominal specific-indefinite determiner, or with nothing, e.g.,

mālàminmù dà ya ci lambà	our teacher who won a prize
àbōkinsà dà ka sanì	his friend whom you know
mōtầtā dà akà ƙwācè	my car that they snatched
kàntin nàn dà mukà fi sô	this store that we prefer
dūtsèn cân dà zā mù hau	that mountain that we're going to climb
ɓàrāwòn nan dà ya tsērè̀ manà	that thief who escaped from us
wani yārò̀ dà ya ƙi tāshì	a boy who refused to get up
wata hanyằ dà sukè̀ bî	some road that they follow
tàimakō dà akà bā mù	help which they gave us
malằlàcī dà bā yằ yîn kōmē	a slacker who doesn't do anything

Because of their nature, certain heads, e.g., universals, nouns with postnominal adjectives, and pronouns, normally occur without the d.a., e.g.,

kōwā dà kukà ganī	everyone whom you saw

kōmē dà kikè sô	everything that you want
yārò̄ farī dà ya kirā kà	a/the light-skinned boy who called you
mōtà̄ baƙā dà ka sàyā	a/the black car that you bought
cf. baƙar̃ mōtàr̃ dà ka sàyā	the black car that you bought
mū dà mukè gòyon bāyansà	we who are backing him
ita dà mukà fi sô	she whom we prefer
cf. ita ɗîn dà kàkā ta sâ tà kōmà̄ wajen mijìntà	
she (the very one) whom grandmother caused to return to her husband	

In addition to suffixing the d.a. to the head noun, it can also appear at the end of the RC, i.e., at the end of the entire NP, e.g.,

yārò-n dà na gayà̄ masà-n	the boy I told it to
(= yārò-n dà na gayà̄ masà ɗî-n)	
ɓàrāwò-n dà ya sācè sû-n	the thief that stole them
mutànê-n dà sukà zaunà-n	the men who sat down
ɗàlìbâ-n dà sukà shigō ɗî-n	the students who came in
Hàlīmà-r̃ dà bà tà zō bâ-n	the Halima who didn't come

°AN: The `-r̃ variant of the d.a. is used only if it is attached to a feminine noun ending in -a(a). In the example above, although the final d.a. refers back to the feminine noun **Hàlīmà**, the `-n form is required because it is attached on the surface to the negative marker **ba**.

3. THE RELATIVIZER AND RELATIVE PRONOUNS/ADVERBS

Instead of using the simple relativizer **dà**, relative clauses can be introduced by a relative pronoun that agrees in number and gender with the head noun, namely, **wândà** (m.), **wâddà** (f.) **waɗàndà** (pl.). The singular forms commonly—and in some dialects, obligatorily—simplify tonally to H-L, i.e., **wandà** (m.), **waddà** (f.) (with a segmental variant **waccè**). Less common, although still quite normal, is a tonal change to all L, i.e., **wàndà**, **wàddà** (= **wàccè**), **wàɗàndà**. Examples (using the F-L variant):

[mùtûm]$_m$ [wândà]$_m$ na ganī	a/the man whom I saw
[tsōhon gwamnà̄]$_m$ [wândà]$_m$ ya jē Jāmùs	the former governor who went to Germany
[yārò farī]$_m$ [wândà]$_m$ ya kirā kà	the light-skinned boy who called you
[ɗākìn]$_m$ wândà [dōlè nē [kà]$_{sub}$ yi barcī à ciki	the room which you must sleep in
[yārinyà̄]$_f$ [wâddà]$_f$ ta fāɗī	the girl who fell
[zākanyà̄]$_f$ [wâddà]$_f$ sukà kāmà	a lioness that they caught
[birai] [waɗàndà]$_{pl}$ mukà kashè	monkeys that we killed
[wasu màlàmai]$_{pl}$ [waɗàndà]$_{pl}$ sukà ƙi yājìn aikī	some teachers who refused to go on strike

°AN: The relative pronouns are complex items composed of the morpheme **wa-** (probably related to **wằ** 'who') + the d.a. + the relativizer **dà**, e.g., **wa + `-n + dà → wândà** 'the one that', e.g., **wândà ya ci jar̃r̃àbâwā** 'the one who passed the exam' (see chap. 21). In a phrase like **yārò wândà na ganī** (= **yāròn dà na ganī**) 'the boy I saw', the **wândà** is strictly speaking in apposition with the head noun, i.e., 'boy the.one.that I saw'. One can speculate that originally this would have been relatively uncommon and that the normal relative clause would have had the structure N(d.a.) + **dà** + S. The relative "pronouns" are in the process of becoming grammaticalized as relative markers so that the structures noun **wândà**... and noun `-n **dà**... will soon be nothing more than long and short variants of the same thing. (Future linguists will probably analyze the structure {noun `-n **dà**} (e.g., yāròn dà) as a phonologically reduced form of the variant {noun **wândà**} (e.g., **yārồ wândà**), which etymologically it is not.)

In simple sentences, RCs with the structure NP + d.a. + **dà** (e.g., **mùtumìn dà**...) and NP + relative pronoun (e.g., **mùtûm wândà**...) are essentially equivalent. The further the relative clause is separated from the head noun, the more likely that the relative pronoun will be preferred over the simple **dà**, e.g., **yârā biyu sīr̃ār̃ā dà sū wad̃àndà mukà sanì** 'two very thin boys whom we know' (lit. boys two thin with them whom we know) (= the less preferred **yârā biyu sīr̃ār̃ā dà sū dà mukà sanì**). In the sentence **àkwai wani dūtsè à wata k̃asā wândà kō'ìnā anà jîn làbārìnsà** 'There is a stone in a country which everywhere one hears about it (the stone)', the masculine relative pronoun **wândà** is required. If one simply used **dà** instead, the interpretation would be that it was the adjacent noun **k̃asā** 'country' (fem.) that was being relativized and that the speaker had made a grammatical mistake by saying **làbārìn-sà**, with the masculine pronoun **sà**, instead of **làbārìn-tà** with the feminine pronoun **-tà** to agree with **k̃asā**.

Relative clauses can also be introduced by the relative adverbs **îndà** 'where, place that' (< **ìnā** 'where?') and **yâddà** 'how, manner that' (< **yàyà** 'how?'). (These relative adverbs also have H-L and L-L tonal variants.) Examples:

kàntī îndà zā kà sàmi kōmē dà kōmē	a store where you can get everything
nā san îndà sukà binnè shi	I know where they buried it.
(**îndà = wurîn dà** 'the place that')	
hanyà̀ yâddà sukà yi	the way they did it

If the RC lacks an overt noun head, then the use of a relative pronoun or relative adverb is obligatory, e.g.,

cikin wad̃àndà sukà yi jar̃r̃àbâwā bâ wândà ya ci
  Among those who took the exam, no one passed.

an d̃aurè wândà ya zàgi mijìntà	They imprisoned the one who insulted her husband.
sun kāmà wâddà ta tsērè masà	They captured the one (f.) who escaped from him.
mun dūbà îndà zā sù ginà bankì	We looked where they are going to build a bank.
bàn san yâddà sukà sācè kòmfyūtà̀ ba	I don't know how they stole the computer.

Hausa does not have a special relative pronoun for inanimates. Thus, whereas the question word **wà** 'who?' has the corresponding relative form **wândà** '(the one) who', a comparable form does not exist to match **mè** 'what?'—i.e., there is no comparable form ****mîndà** or some such. Instead, one may use **wândà** if the noun head is expressed, e.g., **d̃ākìnmù wândà sukà ginà** 'our room that they built', or else one can use the "pseudo -relative pronoun" **àbîn-dà** (= **àbin-dà**) 'what', lit. the thing that, e.g.,

àbîn dà ya fashè nàwa nè	What broke was mine.
kā sân àbîn dà zā sù yi?	Do you know what they are going to do?

In the absence of a relative adverb corresponding to **yàushè?** 'when?', one uses either the full noun **lōkàcī** (or **sā'à̀**) 'time', or else the "pseudo -relative adverb" **sân-dà** (= **san-dà**), e.g.,

bàn san lōkàcîn dà (= **sân-dà**) **ya isō ba**   I don't know when he arrived.

  °AN: The noun **sā'à̀** is normally feminine. When it functions in RCs, however, it is just as commonly masculine. One thus gets the following forms (ignoring tone variants): **sā'àn dà =**

sā'àd da = sân-dà = sâd-dà. In standard orthography the short forms are usually written as one word, i.e., **sanda** or **sadda**. This is also true of the expression **sannan** 'then' = /sàn nan/ (lit. time.of that) < **sā'àn nan**).

4. GENERIC RELATIVES

Generic relatives are formed with universal **kō**-forms (see chap. **73**) like **kōwā** 'whoever, anyone who', **kō'ìnā** 'wherever'. These occur without a relativizer, e.g.,

kōwā ya shìga rījìyā zân bā shì dalà dubū
> Whoever (= anyone who) enters the well, I'll give him $1,000.

kōmè akà bā kà sai gòdiyā   Whatever one gives you, you should be thankful.

kō'ìnā ka ɓūya banzā nè̀   Wherever you hide is useless.

> °AN: Quirk et al. (1985: 1056ff.) refer to these as "nominal relative clauses" (for reasons that escape me).

Paraphrases of generic relatives with the universal quantifier **duk** 'all' occur as regular relative clauses using a relative pronoun/adverb (including the pseudo-relative **àbîn dà**), e.g.,

duk wândà ya shìga rījìyā...   Everyone who enters the well...

duk àbîn dà akà bā kà...   Everything that one gives you...

duk îndà ka ɓūya...   Every place you hide...

5. REL TAMS (TENSE-ASPECT-MOOD MARKERS)

Relative clauses constitute one of the primary Rel environments that require the shift from a general TAM to a corresponding relative TAM (see §**70**:3), e.g., continuous to Rel-continuous, completive to preterite, potential to future. Examples:

a. [sunà̀]$_{cont}$ **gyārà kèkên**   They are repairing the car.

b. **kèkên dà sukè̀**]$_{Rcont1}$ **gyārà̀wā**   the car they are repairing

a. **Bintà** [tanà̀]$_{cont}$ **dà laimà̀**   Binta has an umbrella.

b. **laimàr̃ dà Bintà** [takè]$_{Rcont2}$ **dà ita** the umbrella that Binta has

a. **mālàm**[yanà̀]$_{cont}$ **sàne dà shī**   The teacher is aware of it.

b. **mālàmîn dà** [yakè]$_{Rcont2}$ **sàne dà shī** the teacher who is aware of it

a. [mun]$_{comp}$ **ga gāwâr̃**   We saw the corpse.

b. **mū dà** [mukà]$_{pret}$ **ga gāwâr̃**   we who saw the corpse

a. **mùtumìn** [yâ]$_{pot}$ **kāwō ruwā**   The man will probably bring water.

b. **mùtumìn dà** [zâi]$_{fut}$ **kāwō ruwā**   the man who will bring water

Because the rhetorical is an inherently Rel TAM, it occurs naturally in RCs, e.g.,

gāra à ragè rìkicîn dà [kà̀]$_{rhet}$ **iyà tāshì̀ nân gàba**
> One should lessen the disturbances that are likely to rise up in the near future.

duk mùtumìn dà [kà̀]$_{rhet}$ **ci wannàn àbinci yâ shā wàhalà̀**
> Whoever (lit. every man who) would dare to eat this food will be in trouble.

There is one unexplained exception to the general rule. In the following construction—and the examples of this type are very limited, although high frequency—the relative clause uses the general rather than the Rel TAM:

lōkàcin dà [inà]$_{cont}$ yārò...   when I was a child...
lōkàcin dà [yanà]$_{cont}$ sarkī   during his reign... (lit. time that he.cont king)

The subjunctive is not allowed in Rel environments and thus cannot occur in RCs, e.g., the following is ungrammatical: **mùtumìn dà [yà]$_{sub}$ kāwō ruwā 'the man who should bring water'. The restriction against having the subjunctive in RCs is overcome by various paraphrases. For example, one can embed ya kasàncē 'it is the case that' (with an invariable wsp) in the relative clause followed by a sentential complement, or else one can do the same with an identificational sentence plus a complement, e.g.,

yārinyàr̃ dà [ya kasàncē tīlàs [ìn]$_{sub}$ àurē tà]
  the girl whom I had to marry (lit. girl.the that it happens perforce I.sub marry her)
mùtumìn dà [ya kasàncē [dōlè [yà]$_{sub}$ kāwō ruwā]]
  the man who (it is the case that he) should bring water
à cikin ɗākìn wândà [dōlè nē [kà]$_{sub}$ yi barcī
  inside the room, which you must sleep in

All the remaining TAMs, positive and negative, are allowed in RCs, e.g.,

mùtumìn dà [zâi] kāwō ruwā   the man who will bring water [fut]
àbòkai dà [bà zā sù] r̃àbu dà jūnā ba   friends who won't separate from one another [neg fut]
sū dà [bà sù] yàrda ba   they who didn't agree [Ncomp]
irìn wàhalàr̃ dà [bā mà] sô   the kind of trouble that we don't like [Ncont]
yārinyàr̃ dà [zâ ta] kàsuwā   the girl who is off to the market [allative]

6. COREFERENTIAL NPS: DELETION OR RESUMPTIVE PRONOUN

If the NP in the embedded clause that is coreferential to the relativized NP is a subject, it is obligatorily deleted. The pronoun that one sees in tensed sentences is the weak subject pronoun (wsp), e.g.,

yārinyàr̃ dà Ø ta fāɗì   the girl who fell
cf. yārinyàr̃ tā fāɗì   The girl fell.wani
àbōkīnā wândà Ø yakè dà mōtà   a friend mine who has a car
cf. wani àbōkīnā yanà dà mōtà   A friend mine has a car.
mùtumìn dà Ø bâ shi dà kuɗī   the man who has no money
cf. mùtumìn bâ shi dà kuɗī   The man has no money.

Similarly, if the coreferential NP in the embedded clause is a direct object, it must be deleted, e.g.,

zōbèn dà ya ɓōyè Ø   the ring that he hid (cf. yā ɓōyè zōbèn   He hid the ring.)

If, however, the NP is an indirect object, the object of a genitive preposition, or the object of an existential marker (àkwai 'there is' or bâ/bābù 'there is not') then one has the option of either deleting it or leaving a resumptive pronoun in its place. Examples:

likitàn dà na gayà [wà Ø] = likitàn dà na gayà [masà]
    the doctor I told it to
kwālîn dà mukà sâ yādì à [ciki Ø] = kwālîn dà mukà sâ yādì à [cikinsà]
    the carton that we put the cloth in
yârân dà yakè zàune à [bāya Ø] = yârân dà yakè zàune à [bāyansù]
    the children that he was sitting behind
ɗālìbân dà sukè [àkwai Ø] à makaɽantā = ɗālìbân dà sukè [àkwai sù] à makaɽantā
    the students that there are at school
màsu bā dà tàimakon āgàjîn dà [bābù Ø] = màsu bā dà tàimakon āgàjîn dà [bābù sū]
    aid workers which there weren't

If the NP is a possessor or the object of a true preposition, then the resumptive pronoun is obligatory, e.g.,

mùtumìn dà ruwā ya rūshè gidansà   the man whose house the rain destroyed
(lit. man.the that rain it.pret destroyed house.his)
ilìmîn dà mātân sukè dà shī   the knowledge that the women have
(lit. knowledge.the that women.the they.Rcont2 with it)

    ΔDN: In very colloquial Hausa, some people allow the preposition dà to be stranded, e.g., ilìmîn dà mātân sukè dà Ø 'the knowledge that the women are with'. I have no solid evidence how widespread this practice is, but it appears to be quite prevalent in some WH dialects.

When objects of prepositions are relativized, the prepositions (like the similar i.o. marker) typically remain in their original position. Thus, unlike English, which allows both 'the knife he cut the rope with' and 'the knife with which he cut the rope', Hausa allows only the former, e.g., wuɓāɽ dà ya yankà igìyā dà ita (lit. knife.the that he cut rope with it). The prepositions ta 'via' and dàgà 'from', however, are different: they are necessarily fronted and accompany the relative adverb, e.g.,

wata hanyà ta yâddà mukà kāmà su   a means by which we caught them
tāgàɽ ta îndà sukà shìga   the window via (through) which they entered
gàrîn dàgà îndà ya tāsō   the town from which he started

7. DEEPLY EMBEDDED NPS

The underlying NP that is coreferential with the head of an RC need not be in the clause immediately following the relativizer dà, but rather can be more deeply imbedded. If the deeply imbedded NP is an object, there is a tendency to use a resumptive pronoun although it is not always required, e.g.,

jāɽùmîn dà mukà ji làbārì cêwā Ø yā yi ƙòƙarin kashè sarkī sabòdà ƙarfinsà
    the warrior that we heard had tried killing the king because of his might
mutànên dà kàkaɽmù ta faɗà manà cêwā àljanī yā sâ Ø sun haukàcē
    the people that our grandmother told us a spirit had made them go crazy
yàròn dà Lādì ta cè Ø yā dāɗàɗà matà râi sabòdà màganàɽ dà ya fàɗà
    the boy who Ladi said has made her happy because of what he said
sānìyâɽ dà mahàutā sukà cê Fulànī sun tātsaɽ wà Ø nōnò kàfin sù sayaɽ musù dà ita
    the cow that the butchers claimed the Fulani people milked before selling (it) to them

gàrîn dà mukà ji à cikin làbārìn dà kàkařmù ta fađằ manà cêwā ràiràyī yā binnè <u>shi</u>
>the town that we heard in the story told to us by our grandmother that (desert) sand had buried

kuđîn dà àlƘālī ya cè ɓàrāwòn dà ya sācè hòton gwamnàn dà Hāfīzù ya zānằ zâi biyā Ø
>the money (i.e., fine) that the judge said the thief who stole the portrait of the governor that
>Hafizu drew will pay

mùtumìn dà đàlìbai sukà san cêwā mālàmařsù tanằ sô Ø (= sônsằ)
>the man who(m) the students know that their teacher likes

If the relativized noun comes out of a propositional complement (see §15:2), one sometimes gets surface interference with the choice of the weak subject pronoun (wsp) that follows the relativizer. Intransitive complement-taking verbs like **kasàncē** 'happen that, be the case that' and **kàmātà** 'be fitting that, should' typically occur with a fixed third person masculine wsp; however, in casual speech, one sometimes finds agreement between the wsp and the nearby head noun (which strictly speaking shouldn't be allowed). Examples:

1a. **yārinyàř dà [ya]$_m$ kasàncē Ø 'yař mahàucī cè**
>the girl who it happens is the butcher's daughter

< **[yā]$_m$ kasàncē yārinyàř 'yař mahàucī cè**   It happens that the girl is the butcher's daughter.

= 1b. **yārinyàř dà [ta]$_f$ kasàncē Ø 'yař mahàucī cè**

2a. **abūbuwàn dà [ya]$_m$ kàmātà à yi Ø**   the things that it is right that one do

< **[yā]$_m$ kàmātà à yi abūbuwàn**   One ought to do the things.

= 2b. **abūbuwàn dà [sukà]$_{pl}$ kàmātà à yi**

> °AN: This "agreement by proximity" is similar to what happens in colloquial English in sentences like 'Everyone who attempted these exams have a chance of passing', cf. 'Everyone has (not **have) a chance of passing.'

8. CONJOINED RELATIVE CLAUSES

An NP can be modified by conjoined relative clauses. In the following examples, the underlying coreferential NP is subject of both clauses:

littāfìn dà ya bā nì shà'awằ àmmā (kuma) yakè dà tsằdā
>the book that interests me but is expensive

kàrên dà yakè yîn haushī kullum sàu ukù sànnan yà tsarè hanyằ
>the dog that barks everyday three times and then blocks the way

mùtumìn dà ya yi minì àlƘawàřī àmmā ya Ƙi cikàwā
>the man who made a promise to me but did not fulfill (it)

yārinyàř dà ta ɓātằ wà Audù râi àmmā ta kyautàtā wà Mūsā
>the girl that was rude to Audu but was nice to Musa

yāròn dà yakè jîn sanyī àmmā ya Ƙi tàfīyà gidā sabòdà Ƙin-jî
>the boy who was cold but refused to go home because of stubbornness

In the following examples, the underlying coreferential NP is object in both clauses:

yārinyàř dà Mūsā yakè sô kuma Audù yakè Ƙî   the girl whom Musa likes and Audu hates

àbōkīnā dà na zìyařtằ àmmā bàn sằmē shì à gidā ba
>my friend that I visited but did not find at home

tītìn dà gwamnatì ta ginằ bằra wàccan àmmā ruwan samà ya lālằtā bāyan shèkarằ ɗaya kawài

>the road that the government built two years ago but was destroyed by rain after only one year

In the following examples, the underlying coreferential NP is subject in one of the clauses and object in the other:

yāròn dà ya ƙi zuwằ ajì kuma mukà gujè wà à hanyằ

>the boy who refused to come to class and we avoided on the way

àgōgôn dà ya bā nì shà'awằ àmmā na kāsà sàyā sabồdà rashìn kuɗī

>the watch that appealed to me but I could not buy because of lack of money

kyàutằř dà ta faràntā wà Lādì râi àmmā Zàinabù ta kūshè ta

>the gift that made Ladi happy but which Zainabu belittled

mùtumìn dà na bā shì aron bàřgōnā àmmā duk dà hakà yakè jîn sanyī

>the man whom I lent my blanket to but who still felt cold

9. RELATIVE CLAUSE EXTRAPOSITION

Normally a relative clause immediately follows the NP that it is modifying. Extraposition to the right is, however, possible, although we lack a detailed understanding of the limitations on its occurrence. A few examples are presented here to document the phenomenon.

wata [wàsīƙằ] tā zō jiyà [wâddà àbōkīnā ya řubūtā]

>A letter came yesterday which my friend wrote.

cf. wata [wàsīƙằ] [wâddà àbōkīnā ya řubūtā] tā zō jiyà

>A letter which my friend wrote came yesterday.

[mangwàřò] yā ìsa Kanồ [wândà Audù ya aikō]

>The mangoes arrived in Kano which Audu sent.

marồƙī zâi yi wà [mùtûm] zàmbō [wândà ya bā shì kuɗī]?

>Would a professional beggar ridicule someone who gave him money?
>(lit. beggar fut.he do to man ridicule who he gave him money)

kâř kà yi wà [mahàifìnkà] rashìn kunyằ [wândà shī ya hàifē kà]!

>Don't show your father disrespect who he was the one who gave birth to you!

10. EXTENDED RELATIVE CLAUSES

The normal relative clause is a direct NP modifier with the structure [dà + (S)], e.g., ɗằlìbân [dà (sukà ci jařřàbâwā)] 'the students who passed the examination'. What I am calling an extended RC has the structure [dà {[(wsp) kè] S)}] where the S is syntactically a complement clause rather than a directly embedded sentence, e.g., ɗằlìbân [dà {yakè (sun ci jařřàbâwā)}] 'the students [who {it is the case that (they passed the examamination)}]'. The TAM after the relativizer dà is Rcont2, i.e., the Rel continuous form that occurs when the PAC is not followed by a VP. The TAM in the complement S takes the general rather that the Rel form because its clause is not controlled by the relativizer dà. Examples:

àlƙālîn dà <u>yakè</u> yā kàmātà yà rabà shi ràbon Allàh

>the judge who it is appropriate that he divide it fairly

cîn nāmàn àladè kàm shī nề àbîn dà <u>yakè</u> yā hàřamtà

>As for eating pork, it is what is forbidden.

irìn àbincîn dà <u>yakè</u> yârā bā sằ cî   the kind of food that (it is) children don't eat

This so-called extended RC structure is particularly common when what is embedded is a nontensed non-verbal sentence like a presentational or equational sentence. Examples:

tsōhuwâř dà <u>takè</u> gầ ta nan râi gà Allàh
        the old woman who is still here (but) really old
        (lit. woman.the that she.Rcont2 there is her here life with God)
Tankòn dà <u>yakè</u> gầ shi yanằ tầ̱kamā dà sābon kambàs mài tsầdā
        the Tanko who is there showing off his new expensive sneakers
        (lit. Tanko.the that it.Rcont2 here is he he.cont strutting with new.L sneakers having
        expensive)
ɗākìn dà <u>yakè</u> dōlè (nē) (wai) Lawàn yà yi barcī à cikinsà
        the room which it is necessary that Lawan sleep in it.

yârân dà <u>sukè</u> fìtìnànnū (nè) sun zō	The children that are troublesome came.
kē dà <u>kikè</u> gwanā (cè) kin fī mù sanī	You (f.) who are an expert know more than we do.
yārinyầř dà <u>takè</u> ’yařsà (cē)	the girl who was his daughter.
makarantâř dà <u>takè</u> àkwai ɗàlìbai dà yawà	the school where there are many students
Jòs dà <u>takè</u> bābù zāfī	Jos where there isn't any heat

Negative equational sentences can form direct RCs or can be expressed by means of an extended RC structure, e.g.,

shī [dà (<u>yakè</u>) bầ dagacī ba (nè)] yā sābầ   He who is not a district head is used to it.
àkwai mutầnē dà yawà [waɗàndà (<u>sukè</u>) bầ Hàusầwā ba]
        There are many people who are not Hausas.
Lāřai [dà (<u>takè</u>) bầ ùngōzòmà ba (cè)] bà tà fàhimtầ ba
        Larai who is not a midwife didn't understand.

RCs introduced by the complement-taking expression yā kasàncē 'it so happens that, it is the case that' are similar to extended RCs in serving to introduce clauses that do not embed easily as direct relative clauses. Examples:

yārinyầř dà ya kasàncē ’yař mahàucī cè   the girl who it happens is the butcher's daughter
mùtûm wândà ya kasàncē ɗan-fàsà-ƙwàuri nè   a man who it is the case that he is a smuggler
ruwân dà ya kasàncē dà àkwai à wurîn
        water which it happens that there is some at the place
wani mài māgànī wândà ya kasàncē bābù kàmařsà
        a doctor who it so happens there was no one like him

11. RESTRICTIVE VS. NONRESTRICTIVE

Relative clauses in Hausa are most commonly restrictive, e.g.,

ìnā sābuwař řìgâř dà kikà sàyā?   Where is the new gown that you bought?
an kāmà wani yārò dà yakè nēman jēfà bôm à kàsuwā
        They caught a boy who was about to throw a bomb in the market.
mālàmin dà (= mālàmī wândà) ya řubùtà tàkàřdū bìyař màshàhūřì nē
        The teacher who wrote five papers is famous.

One also, however, has nonrestrictive RCs. These nonrestrictive RCs are typically characterized by (a) a relative pronoun or adverb (often—for some speakers always—the L-L variant) rather than the bare relativizer **dà** and (b) an intonational pause between the head and the pronoun and, where appropriate, at the end of the RC as well.

°AN: Until recently, the distinction between restrictive and nonrestrictive RCs in Hausa has received very little explicit attention by linguists. It has generally been ignored in pedagogical grammars. The best treatment of the question is by Jaggar (1998), building, inter alia, on an earlier paper by Rufa'i (1983).

malàmîn, wàndà ya r̄ubùtà tàkàr̄dū bìyar̄, màshàhūr̄ì nē
: The teacher, who (it so happens) has written five papers, is famous.

hùlar̄ nàn, wàddà Bintà ta bā nì kyàutā, tā kēcè
: This cap, which Binta gave me as a present, has ripped.

sun tahō dà su gōr̄ò, dà àlēwà, dà bìskît, wàndà zā à rarràbā
: They brought kolanuts, candy, and biscuits, which will be handed out.

inà dà wasu dawākī fir̄ɗā-fir̄ɗà, wàɗànɗà bā nà sayâr̄wā kō nawà kuɗîn
: I have some super horses, which I wouldn't sell at any price.

[References: Jaggar (1998); McConvell (1977); Parsons (1981: esp. pp. 46–54); Schachter (1973); Tuller (1986)]

65. Sentence Types

IN Hausa, there are two major divisions in characterizing sentence types. The first is between tensed sentences and nontensed sentences. The second, which cross-cuts the first, is between verbal sentences and nonverbal sentences. The two variables produce four sentence types: (a) tensed verbal, (b) tensed nonverbal, (c) nontensed verbal, and (d) nontensed non-verbal. See table 13:

Table 13: Sentence types

	verbal	*nonverbal*
tensed	(a) **Bellò yā fāɗì** Bello fell down.	(b) **Mūsā yanà dà mōta** Musa has (lit. is with) a car.
nontensed	(c) **zàunā!** Sit down!	(d) **Bintà dōguwā cè** Binta is tall.

1. TENSED SENTENCES

Tensed sentences make use of a person-aspect-complex (PAC), consisting of a weak subject pronoun (wsp) and a marker of tense/aspect/mood (TAM), that occurs between the subject (if expressed) and the predicate, e.g., **yārinyà [takàn]**$_{PAC}$ **dafà àbinci** 'The girl cooks food' (lit. girl she.hab cook food). Tensed sentences can be divided into (1) verbal sentences and (2) nonverbal sentences.

1.1. Verbal sentences
Verbal sentences (see chap. **78**) contain an underlying VP with a VERB as the head, where the item functioning as VERB may appear on the surface either as a finite verb or else as a verbal noun, i.e., a nominalized verb, e.g., **sun [tàfi]**$_V$ **kàsuwā** 'They went to market' (lit they.comp go market), **munà [kòyon]**$_{VN}$ **Hausa** 'We are learning Hausa' (lit. we.cont learning.of Hausa).

1.2. Tensed nonverbal sentences
Nonverbal sentences are defined as those in which the predicate does not contain a VERB as its head. There are four main subtypes of tensed nonverbal sentences.

(a) HAVE sentences (see chap. **33**) are formed with a continuous or Neg-HAVE PAC plus a predicate composed of the preposition **dà** 'with' and an NP, e.g., **yārinyà tanà [dà zōbè]** 'The girl has a ring' (lit. girl she.cont with ring); **yāròn bâ shi [dà hankàlī]** 'The boy has no sense' (lit. boy.the neg he with sense).

(b) Locative sentences (see §**70**:7.2) are made up of a continuous PAC plus a predicate consisting of a locative adverb or prepositional phrase, e.g., **sunà [can bāyan gàrī]** 'They are there behind the town'; **bankìn yanà [kusa dà kàsuwā]** 'The bank is close to the market.'

(c) Stative sentences (see chap. **67**), which also require a continuous PAC, have a "stative" (= verb-derived adverb of state) as the head of the predicate, e.g., **wǎ yakè** [zàune]? 'Who is seated?'; **tanǎ [sànye dà zanè]** 'She is wearing a wrapper' (where 'wearing' refers to a state, not an action).

(d) Allative sentences are made up of an allative PAC (see §70:13) plus a predicate consisting of a locative adverb or NP, e.g., **zâ mu [kàsuwā]** 'We're going to market' (lit. allat we market); **[ìnā] zâ ka?** 'Where are you off to?' (lit. where allat you); **Lādì zâ ta [gidan Ràwaȓtà]** 'Ladi is going to her friend's house' (lit. Ladi allat she house.of friend.of.her).

◊HN: Historically, the present-day allative sentences were presumably verbal sentences with **zâ** 'go' as the main verb. The **zâ** plus the following pronoun—which was an ICP (intransitive copy pronoun) and not a postverbal subject pronoun—have been grammaticalized as a PAC, so that synchronically we are left with a special type of nonverbal sentence.

2. NONTENSED SENTENCES

Nontensed sentences are characterized by the absence of the PAC. These sentences can be divided into (1) imperative (verbal sentences) and (2) nonverbal sentences.

2.1. Imperative (verbal) sentences
The imperative (see chap. 37), which is only used in the singular affirmative, employs a bare verb (usually with a distinctive tone pattern) without a preceding subject or PAC, e.g., **kàwō minì ruwā!** 'Bring me water!'; **tàshi!** 'Get up!'; cf. the continuous tensed sentence **yârā sunà kāwō minì ruwā** 'The children are bringing me water' or the subjunctive tensed sentence **kù tāshì!** 'You (pl.) get up!'

2.2. Nonverbal sentences
In nontensed nonverbal sentences, the head of the predicate is something other than a VERB and there is no PAC. These sentences include (but are not limited to) the following subtypes:

(a) Equational and identificational sentences (see chap. 23) have the structure (X) Y STAB, where the stabilizer is a gender-sensitive particle, and *not* a verb, e.g., **Mūsā mālàmī nè** 'Musa is a teacher'; **wannàn bà kāsā ba cè** 'This is not a puff-adder'; **Bellò hāzìƙì nè** 'Bello is intelligent'; **bà jirgī ba nè** 'It's not a plane.'

(b) Existential sentences (see §26:1) have the structure **àkwai** 'there is/are' (or other equivalent forms) plus an NP (which can be omitted). The negative of **àkwai** is **bâ** or **bābù**, e.g., **àkwai kuɗī?** 'Is there any money?'; **bābù** 'There isn't any.'

(c) Presentational sentences (see §26:2) have the structure **gà** 'here is/are' plus an NP, e.g., **gà dōkì** 'Here is a horse'; **gà 'yan tākaȓā** 'Here are the candidates.'

◊HN: Historically, presentational sentences with **gà** were almost certainly verbal sentences with the pre-noun imperative verb form of **ganī** 'see', cf. **yā ga dōkì** 'He saw a horse'; **yā ganī** 'He saw (it).' The synchronic means of expressing the command 'See (i.e., look at) the horse!' would be **gàni dōkì!**

(d) Qualitative sentences (see §26:3) have the structure X Y **gàrē** + pronoun, where Y is an abstract quality noun, e.g., **Bellò hāziƙancì gàrē shì** 'Bello is intelligent', lit. Bello quick-intelligence at him.

(e) 'Rather' sentences (see §26:4) have the structure **gāra** (or an equivalent form) 'rather' plus an NP, often accompanied by a prepostional phrase formed with **dà** 'with, than', e.g., **gāra kai dà shī** 'Better you than him.'

(f) Exclamatory sentences (see chap. 25) are typically one-word sentences with an exclamation as the head, e.g., **shiȓgì!** 'What a huge thing!'; **wâyyō!** 'Oh mercy on me!'

66. Stabilizer nē / cē

1. FORM

THE stabilizer (STAB) takes the form **nē** when agreeing with items that are masculine singular or plural and **cē** when agreeing with items that are feminine singular. The tone is polar to that of the tone of the immediately preceding syllable:

dōkì nē	It's a horse.	**àkuyà cē**	It's a goat.	**awākī nè**	They're goats.
mâi nē	It's oil.	**bâs cē**	It's a bus.	**bâs-bâs nē**	They're buses.
jàkī nè	It's a donkey.	**rìgā cè**	It's a gown.	**jākunà nē**	They're donkeys.

◊HN: The **nē/cē/nē** 'masculine/feminine/plural' pattern, where the plural and the masculine singular forms are identical, is the same as that evidenced in the genitive linker (**na/ta/na**); see chap. **43**. (The /c/ is a palatalized manifestation of /t/.) This is presumably a retention of an old Afroasiatic pattern of gender and number, see Greenberg (1960a), Newman (1980a).

ΔDN: In WH, the stabilizer appears as **nā/tā/nā**, also with polar tone. The variant with the /ā/ vowel represents the historically original shape.

The tonal polarity shows up clearly with words that have alternative forms or with structures that have alternative word orders, e.g.,

tēbùrī nè̲ = **tēbùr̃ nē̲**	It's a table.
Audù bà̀ yār̃ò ba nè̲ = **Audù bà̀ yār̃ò nē̲ ba**	Audu is not a lad.

2. FUNCTION

The stabilizer has three main functions: (1) as an equational/identificational marker (see chap. **23**), (2) as a focus marker (see chap. **28**), and (3) as a clause-level reinforcement marker (see below, §2.3).

2.1. Equational sentences

Equational sentences, which translate as English copular sentences, do not contain a verb. Rather, they are nonverbal sentences with the basic structure X (neg) Y (neg) STAB, where X is the subject and Y is a predicate nominal or adjective.

Haladù wàkīlìnmù nē	Haladu is our representative.
yārinyàr̃ dà ta ɓatà ƙawar̃ Tàlātù cē	The girl who got lost is Talatu's friend.
màtar̃sà dōguwā cè	His wife is tall.
mōtōcîn ƙònànnū nè?	Are the cars burnt up?

545

shī bằ mahàukàcī ba nề	He is not crazy.
jàkaȓ nàn bằ tằwa ba cề	This bag is not mine.
mutằnen nàn bằ wāwằyē ba nề	These people are not stupid.
Mūsā dà Shēhù bằ àbòkai ba nề	Musa and Shehu are not friends.

If the subject is not expressed, then one gets an identificational sentence, which corresponds to English 'it's (a) / they're ...,' e.g.,

gwàdò nề It's a blanket. **Kanò cē** It's Kano. **nī nề** It's me (m.). **gàjērā cề** She's / it's short.
bằ lềmō ba nề It's not a soft drink. **bằ mū ba nề** It's not us.
àljànū nề They're spirits. **ƙònànnū nề** They're burnt.

2.2. Focus marker

Focus is accomplished by moving a focused constituent to the front of the sentence into the focus slot. The focused element is followed by the STAB, which can optionally be deleted. Question words inherently carry focus, e.g.,

Hàdīzà (cē) na ganī bằ Kànde ba	It was *Hadiza* I saw not Kande.
ìnā (nề) ka sằmē shì?	*Where* did you find him?
nawà (nē) zā kà biyā?	*How much* will you pay?
Bellò (nē) ya san wândà ya ɓōyề shi	*Bello* knows who hid it.

Equational sentences with focus require that the STAB appear immediately after the focused element, e.g.,

Audù nē mālàmī	It is *Audu* who is a teacher.
cf. **Audù mālàmī nề** Audu is a teacher.	
Bintà cề wùlàƙàntacciyā	It is *Binta* who is shameless.
mū nề màsu rawā	It is *we* who are the dancers.
wàccē cề gōɗìyaȓ lìmân?	*Which one* is the imam's mare?

2.3. Reinforcement marker

The stabilizer also functions as a sentence-level or clause-level reinforcing element. (In this function, it always appears as **nē** because sentences and clauses are intrinsically masculine.) The STAB sometimes occurs at the very end of the sentence, and sometimes at the end of the core sentence but before adverbial adjuncts or complements. The exact semantic contribution of the STAB is not clear. Sometimes it appears to add a degree of insistence to the truth value of the clause or sentence, e.g., **nā sanì nē** 'I *do* know (it)' (cf. **nā sanì** 'I know (it)'). Other times, it appears to demarcate the core sentence from subsequent modifiers or adjuncts. Finally, in some instances, it seems to be little more than a pragmatic pause filler comparable to 'you know' in colloquial English. In the following examples (mostly taken from Ahmad and Botne (1992), but with tone and vowel length added), I have noted the presence of the STAB, but I have made no attempt in the translation to represent its semantic import.

kàkànnin kàkànninsù sun zō <u>nề</u> dàgà arềwa	Their ancestors came STAB from the north.
maɗìnkin hannū yanā yîn ɗinkìnsà <u>nē</u> dà hannu	The hand tailor does his sewing STAB by hand.
an sằmi sūnan wannàn ƙasā nē dàgà sūnan Kògin Kwāȓà, wằtò Kògin Nējà	
	One got the name of this country STAB from the name of the River Kwara, that is to say, the River Niger.

inà sô nē nà faɗà mukù àbîn dà na yi à rānaṛ Sallà Bàbba dà ta wucè
> I want STAB to tell you what happened at the *Id* festival that just passed.

an shiryà wannàn ɗan littāfì nē mùsammàn don màsu kòyon Hausa
> One has prepared this little book STAB especially for those learning Hausa.

In interrogative sentences, a stabilizer at the end serves as a question tag. (It often has the surface form nê because of the addition of an L-tone q-morpheme (see §60:1.2). Examples:

zā kù zaunà <u>nê</u>?	Are you going to stay?
kanà sô kà hàṛbē shì <u>nê</u>?	Do you really want to shoot it?
af, yàushè ta sàuka <u>nê</u>?	Oh, when did she deliver?

3. kè nan

An alternative to the stabilizer is the fixed phrase kè nan (invariable for number and gender), which is made up of the relative continuous marker kè plus the locative nan 'there, in existence', e.g., àbîn dà nakè gayà mukù kè nan 'It's what I was telling you', bàbbaṛ màtsalà kè nan 'It's a big problem.' Sentences with the stabilizer and with kè nan are not identical in meaning, but the exact difference is difficult to describe. A simple sentence with the stabilizer is often a neutral factual identificational sentence 'It's a Y', whereas the sentence with kè nan generally connotes 'That's the way Y is', often in response to an assertion by some other participant in the discourse. When used at the end of a verbal sentence, kè nan commonly adds a notion of finality. Examples:

jì-ta-jì-ta kè nan	That's just a rumor. (referring back to sth discussed earlier)
rashìn àbinci kè nan	It's lack of food. (which caused the event).
mutànē maràsā īmànì kè nan	They're merciless people. (which explains their actions)
cf. mutànē nè maràsā īmànì	They're merciless people. (statement of fact)
àbincinmù kè nan	It's our (kind of) food. cf. àbincinmù nē It's our food.
hālin yârā kè nan	That's just the way kids are.
cf. hālin yârā nè	It's childish behavior.
yàushè zân dāwō kè nan?	When should I come back then?
wàtàu sun kōmà sun sākè wàsā kè nan	So, they returned and played some more.

The kè nan phrase is used to express temporal cleft sentences, often denoting time spans, e.g.,

shèkarà ukù kè nan yanà kīwò He has been herding animals for three years.
yâu watà gōmà kè nan anà tùhumaṛ wannàn mùtumìn dà lâifin kisàn kâi
> It's now ten months that they have been suspecting this man of murder.

yâu shèkaràṛsà àshìrin kè nan à wannàn wurī
> He's been at this place for twenty years. (lit. today year.of.his twenty kè nan at this place)

sàu huɗu kè nan inà ganin zàzzàɓin-rānā à ràyuwātā
> It's four times that I have seen an eclipse in my lifetime.

The kè nan phrase is used in expressing arithmetical calculations, e.g.,

ukù dà biyu bìyaṛ kè nan	3 and 2 is 5.
ukù à tārà dà bìyaṛ takwàs kè nan	3 and 5 (lit. 3 one adds with 5) is 8.

The sequence **shī kḕ nan** (lit. it is there) has become fixed as an essentially one-word expression meaning 'That's that!'; e.g.,

shī kḕ nan, sai na kōmā̀ gidā	That was that, then I left and went back home.
shī kḕ nan, an gamā̀	That's that, it's finished.
shī kḕ nan	OK.

[References: McConvell (1973); Parsons (1963); Schachter (1966)]

67. Statives

S UBJECT to semantic plausibility, all verbs have a related adverbial form that denotes the state resulting from the completion of an action, e.g., **yàɓe** 'plastered' [stative], cf. **yāɓà** 'to plaster'; **tsùgùne** 'kneeling (position, not action)' [stative], cf. **tsugùnā** 'kneel'. Use of these statives can be contrasted with use of cognate verbs, e.g., **yanà zàune à kân kujèrā** 'He is sitting (i.e., is seated) on the chair', vs. **yanà zaunàwā à kân kujèrā** 'He is (in the process of) sitting down on the chair'; **àkuyà tanà ɗàure** 'The goat is tied up', vs. **àkuyà tā ɗàuru** 'The goat has been well tied up.' Although statives commonly translate into English as past or present participles, in Hausa they pattern as adverbs of state, comparable to place or manner adverbs. Some stative forms are semantically more mannerlike than stativelike, e.g., **sàce** 'furtively', cf. **sàtā** 'steal'.

°AN: Parsons (1981: 30ff.) referred to statives by the acronym VANS ("verbal adverbial nouns of state"). He was right about the deverbal, adverbial, and stative features; however, there is little about these words that justifies labeling them as nouns.

1. FORM

Statives are formed in a totally regular fashion by adding the tone-integrating suffix -e)^{LH} to the lexical base.

°AN/◊HN: Synchronically, one has to treat statives as being formed by the addition of a distinct vocalic suffix. At a deeper level—historical or synchronic—it is possible that they reflect the adverbial counterpart with a short final-vowel to L-H verbal nouns ending in -ē (§77:3.3.3), e.g., **yàɓe** 'plastered' vs. **yàɓē** 'plastering', **bàkàce** 'winnowed' vs. **bàkàcē** 'winnowing', cf. noun-derived adverbs like **ruwa** 'in the water' vs. **ruwā** 'water', **gòshi** 'on the forehead' vs. **gòshī** 'forehead' (see §5:3.1).

In most cases the stative is derived from a synchronically extant verb. I call these "class 1 statives." The base may be simple or pluractional and it may be nonderived or may contain a suffix like the productive verbalizer -TA. Note that the suffix is added to the base and not to any specific grade form. The -e suffix is short, short final vowels being typical of adverbs. Like other suffixal front vowels, -e conditions palatalization of preceding consonants, e.g., **gasà** 'roast', **gàshe** 'roasted'. Monoverbs insert an epenthetic /y/ between the base and the final -e, e.g., **ji** 'hear', **jìye** 'heard'. The verb **tàfi** 'go' has two alternative stative forms, one built on the simple base, i.e., **tàfe**, the other on a base containing /iy/, i.e., **tàfìye**. The stative **màce** 'dead' does not derive directly from **mutù** 'die' but rather from a base //mat-//, which is found in the gr4 verb **macè** and other derived forms. The L-H tone pattern of the suffix spreads from right to left over the entire word regardless of the number of syllables. Examples: (Note: In citation form, statives are usually preceded by the optional preposition **à** 'at'.)

549

(à) cìke	filled, cf. **cikà** fill	
(à) gìccìye	cross-wise, cf. **gìccìyā** lay across	
(à) gòye	carried on the back cf. **gòyà** carry on the back	
(à) gùje	on the run, cf. **gudù** run	
(à) jàye	pulled back, cf. **jā** pull	
(à) jìye	listening, cf. **ji** hear	
(à) rìƙe	held, cf. **rìƙè** hold	
(à) sàne	aware, cf. **sanì** know	
(à) tàgàngàne	sitting with legs apart, cf. **tagangànē** sit with legs apart	
(à) tsàye	standing, cf. **tsayà** stand	
(à) wàr̃wàtse	scattered, cf. **war̃wàtsē** scatter	

Some statives, which I am calling "class 2 statives," are built on underlying noun rather than verb roots, e.g., **à kànànce** 'in the Kano style'. These generally occur with the preposition **à** and connote manner rather than state. When occurring with these nonverb roots, the stative suffix is commonly attached to an expanded base containing the formative -(**n**)**t**- (where the **t** appears as the palatal /c/), e.g., **kànànce** < //**kano-nt** + **e**//. Examples:

(à) àsìr̃ce	secretly, cf. **àsīr̃ī** secret
(à) fìllànce	in Fulani language; in a shy manner, cf. **Fillancī** Fulani language, shyness
	e.g., **yā yi màganà à fìllànce** = **yā yi màganà dà Fillancī** He spoke in Fulani.
(à) hàbàice	by innuendo, cf. **habaicì** innuendo
(à) hàgùnce	gauche, clumsy, cf. **hagu** left
(à) hàusànce	in Hausa; in a clear manner, cf. **Hausa** Hausa language
(à) sìyàsànce	politically, cf. **sìyāsà** politics
(à) tsànàke	carefully, cf. **tsànākī** care
(à) wàsànce	playfully, cf. **wàsā** play (n.), a game
(à) zàurànce	in code/pig Latin, cf. **zaurè** entrance room, cf. **zaurancī** pig Latin

> °AN: The -(**n**)**t**- formative is used productively as a verbalizer deriving verbs from nouns, e.g., **farī** 'whiteness', **faràntā** 'whiten, gladden' (see chap. **79**). It is thus reasonable to propose that the purpose of the -(**n**)**t**- formative seen in the above statives is to create verb bases—whether they actually occur as verbs or not. One would then be able to say that stative formation almost always involves the creation of an adverb from a verb.

2. FUNCTION

The stative has two primary functions: (a) nonverbal predicate in "stative sentences" and (b) adverbial modifier. It also enters into a few other constructions.

2.1. *Predicates in "stative sentences"*

Stative sentences, which are tensed, nonverbal sentences, consist of a continuous TAM followed by a class 1 stative (optionally preceded by the preposition **à**). As with verbal sentences in the continuous, the semantic reading can be present or past (or even future) depending on the context. Examples:

sunà tàfe shèkarà dà shèkàrū	They have been on the way for years.
malàlàcī yanà mìmmìƙe à kân gadò	The lazy guy is sprawled out on the bed.
tanà nànnàɗe cikin lēdà	It was wrapped in plastic.

bā mằ zàune	We were not seated.
kwālằyên bā sằ jère	The cardboard boxes are not lined up.
tanằ nan ɓòye bāyan katangā	She is there hidden behind the fence.
gidân yanằ (à) kàr̃kàce	The house is out of kilter.
(cf. kar̃kàtā twist out of shape)	

°AN: In informal speech, such sentences as the above normally appear without the preposition à. For some speakers, à can be included, thereby indicating a greater degree of specificity (see Jaggar 1992a: 59n).

When the stative occurs in a Rel environment (focus, relativization, etc.), some speakers use the Rel-continuous1 form -kề with the long vowel, whereas others use the Rel-continuous2 form -kè with the short vowel, e.g.,

wằ yakè(e) làɓe à d'ākì̃?	Who is crouched secretly in the room?
Jummai cề takè(e) kwànce	It is Jummai who is lying down.
kwālằyên dà sukè(e) jère	cardboard boxes that are in a row

If, however, the stative is preceded by à, then only the short vowel Rcont2 kè form can be used, e.g.,

wằ yakè à làɓe à d'ākì̃?	Who is crouched secretly in the room?
Jummai cề takè à kwànce	It is Jummai who is lying down.
kwālằyên dà sukè à jère	cardboard boxes that are in a row

◊HN: One can hypothesize that the required structure was originally *wsp.kè (with short kè) + à (obligatorily present) + stative, e.g., wằ yakè à làɓe..., and that the long kề represents a phonological fusion of *kè-à, e.g., *wằ yakè-à làɓe... > wằ yakề làɓe. This would explain why the long kề does not occur when à is present.

If the wsp is omitted, then the free form kề with the long vowel is required for all speakers whether the preposition à is there or not. (This is a general property of the Rel-continuous marker and has nothing specifically to do with the stative construction.) Examples:

wằ kề (à) làɓe à d'ākì̃?	Who is crouched secretly in the room?
Jummai cề kề (à) kwànce	It is Jummai who is lying down.
kwālằyên dà kề (à) jère	cardboard boxes that are in a row

Statives built on underlying intransitive verbs are necessarily "intransitive" and may not take a complement, e.g.,

yanằ gùje	He was on the run.
bā mằ zàune	We were not seated.
mutằnên dà kề ɓòye	The men who were hiding. (state, not action)

Statives of lexically transitive verbs may also be "inactive/intransitive," with the subject serving as the affected patient. In these sentences, there is no underlying agent overtly expressed nor is one understood. These statives often enter into corresponding sociative sentences with an experiencer as subject (see §2.1.1 following).

zanè yanằ ɗàure gà jìkintà	The wrapper is tied around her.
(lit. wrapper it.cont tied at body.of.her)	
cf. Hàdīzà tanằ ɗàure dà zanè	Hadiza has on a wrapper.
cf. zanè yā ɗàuru	The wrapper was tied on well (by someone). (passive gr7)
kāyā sunằ làbce à kân jàkī	The goods are loaded up on the donkey.
cf. jàkī yanằ làbce dà kāyā	The donkey is laden with goods.
jinjìrī yanằ gòye	The baby is being carried on its mother's back.
(lit. baby is in the state of being tied on)	
cf. Kànde tanằ gòye dà jinjìrī	Kande has a baby on her back.

2.1.1. Sociatives

Statives of some transitive verbs can be semantically "active/transitive" in the sense that they can take a sociative complement representing the thematic patient or objec. Syntactically, the complement appears as the object of the preposition **dà** 'with', Examples:

yanằ sànye dà rìgā mài kyâu	He is wearing a good gown.
(i.e., he is clothed (state) with a good gown)	(< sânyā put on)
cf. yanằ sâ rìgā mài kyâu	He is putting on a good gown.
(with the gr1 verb sâ (= sânyā))	
wàɗànnè askaṟāwā (nè) sukè rìƙe dà māsū?	
Which soldiers were holding (i.e., had in their grasp) spears?	
cf. sunằ rìƙe māsū	
They were grabbing spears. (with the gr4 verb rìƙè)	
sunằ bìye dà shī	They are following him.
(cf. the semantically similar verbal sentence sunằ bînsà)	
ukù tanằ fìye dà biyu	Three is more than two. (< fi exceed)
sunằ kằme dà hannun jūnā	They were holding hands.
(lit. they were held with hands.of each other)	
cf. sunằ kāmà hannun jūnā	They were grasping each other's hands.
(with the gr1 verb kāmà)	
bā mằ sàne dà sātàṟ	We were not aware of the theft.
cf. bà mù san àbîn dà ya fằru ba	We didn't know what happened. (with the gr* verb sanì)

2.1.2. Focus

Stative predicates can be moved to the front of the sentence for focus. In such cases, they optionally (and commonly) occur preceded by the preposition **à**. The required TAM is Rcont2 with the short vowel -**kè**, e.g.,

(à) zàune mukè	Seated we were.
(à) sànye dà bàbbaṟ rìgā yakè	Dressed in a big gown he is.
(à) gòye yakè	On the back he is.
(à) gòye dà jinjìrī takè	With a baby on the back she is.
(à) shìrye nakè	It's ready I am.

°AN: At an abstract formal level, the simplest analysis would be to postulate all stative constructions as containing an underlying preposition **à**, which is deleted in specific environments, sometimes obligatorily, sometimes optionally, e.g., **munằ zàune** 'We are seated' < **munằ à zàune**. A serious drawback to this analysis at the synchronic level is that it conflicts with the express intuition of native speakers, including those with linguistic training and sophistication who understand the linguistic attraction of the analysis.

If the stative is followed by a prepositional phrase with à, the initial à that normally occurs in the focus position is strongly disliked, e.g.,

mìmmĭƙe à kân gadō yakè	He is sprawled out on the bed

not **à mìmmĭƙe à kân gadō yakè; but à mìmmĭƙe kân gadō yakè with the second à deleted is fine.

Sentences with stative focus can contain a topicalized NP as well. This topic goes at the beginning of the sentence in the topic slot. When the focused stative is not sentence initial, the à preceding the stative is still optional but it tends to be preferred, e.g.,

màlàmai kàm, (à) zàune sukè	As for the teachers, *seated* they were.
cf. màlàmai kàm, sunà zàune	As for the teachers, they were seated.
cf. màlàmai nè sukè zàune	*The teachers* were seated.
Hàdīzà, à ɗàure dà zanè takè	As for Hadiza, *wearing a wrapper* she was.
ɓàrāwòn, làɓe à ɗākĭ yakè	As for the thief, *crouched/hidden in the room* he was.

With active/transitive statives, the object of dà can be focused instead of the stative phrase as a whole. This requires that a resumptive pronoun be left in its original place, e.g.,

hùlā nakè sànye dà ita	It is a *cap* that I am wearing. (lit. cap I.am wearing with it)
< inà sànye dà hùlā	I am wearing a cap.
sarkī nè sukè bìye dà shī	It was the *chief* they were following.
< sunà bìye dà sarkī	They were following the chief.

One cannot, however, separate dà from the stative and focus the dà + NP phrase. A sentence like the following, for example, is ungrammatical: **dà sarkī sukè bìye. In this respect, active statives do not behave identically with sociative verbs (see §75:4).

2.2. Modifiers
In addition to serving as the head of the predicate in nonverbal stative sentences, statives also function as modifiers. First, they act to modify verbs and VPs, e.g.,

yā fìta à gùje	He went out on the run.
gà shi cân yanà tàfiyà à dùddùƙe	There he is going along bent over in a crouching manner.
kù tāshì tsàye!	Get on with it! (lit. you (pl.) rise standing)
kù zō minì dà shī kō à ràye kō à màce	Bring him to me dead or alive. (lit. either alive or dead)
tùlū yā cìka cìke (dà ruwā)	The water pot filled full (with water).
kadà kà ɗaukē nì à hàgùnce	Don't get me wrong. (lit. don't you take me left-handedly)
yā gayà mîn à tàkàice	He told me briefly.
yā dùbē nì à kàikàice	He look at me askance.
bà zā mù tàfi à sàce ba, sai dà sanìnkà	We will not go on the sly, only with your knowledge.

Second, statives (usu. without the à) enter into postnominal modifying phrases, e.g.,

nā ga 'yan sàndā tsàitsàye bàkin tītì	I saw the police posted along the street.

mun zaunà kusa dà bangō shằfe dà fentǐ   We sat next to a wall covered with paint.
yanà kallon wata yārinyằ d'àure dà sābon zanè mài kyâu
     He was looking at a girl wearing (lit. tied with) a beautiful new wrapper.

The word **tàre** 'together' is in origin a stative form of the verb **tārà** 'collect'; synchronically, however, it has been lexicalized as a distinct word and does not behave like other statives. It does not, for example, allow the use of the preposition **à**, e.g., **mù tàfi tàre** 'Let's go together', not ****mù tàfi à tàre**. Similarly, the grammaticalized phrase **fìye dà** 'more than', which is derived from **fi** 'exceed', is normally used without the preposition **à**, e.g., **munà bùk̃ātar̃ bindigōgī fìye dà hakà** 'We need more guns than this' (lit. we.cont need.of guns exceeding thus).
    Statives without the **à** occur immediately after specific nouns in a number of fixed adverbial phrases, e.g.,

kâi tsàye	immediately, determinedly (lit. head standing),
e.g., **zâ ni wurin dằr̃aktà kâi tsàye**	I am going directly to the director.
idò rùfe	obliviously (lit. eyes closed),
e.g., **sunà d'agà muryà à ajī idò rùfe**	They were raising their voices in the class unawares.
râi ɓàce	in despair, angrily (lit. life ruined)
râi kwànce	contentedly (lit. life lying down)
bằkī bùd'e	mouth agape (lit. mouth opened)

Statives, like other adverbs, sometimes occur as the second member of a genitival compound or phrase, e.g.,

fitsārin-kwànce	bed wetting (lit. urine.of lying down)
ɓàrāwòn-zàune	a fence (i.e., dealer in stolen goods) (lit. thief.of sitting)
k̃auyukàn r̃àɓe dà bir̃nī	villages skirting the city

Some stative forms occur along with **dà** 'with' in morphologically complex prepositions (indicated here with a hyphen but written as two words in standard orthography). Examples:

tàre-dà	together with
e.g., **mun jē Landàn tàre-dà ita**	I went to London (together) with her.
cf. **nī dà ita mun jē Landàn tàre**	She and I went to London together.
gàme-dà	concerning
e.g., **mè akà yi gàme-dà màtsalàr̃?**	What has one done concerning the problem?
dàngàne-dà	regarding (= **danganè dà** with the deverbal noun **danganè**)

e.g., **gwamnatì tā kafà d'òkā dàngàne-dà shân k̃wằyā**
    The government has issued a decree regarding the use of drugs.

68. Systems and Eras (Suffix -iyyā)

THE Hausa ending **-iyyā**)^{LHL} (which has a set L-H-L tone pattern) is an Arabic-derived suffix (the feminine "nisba" suffix) indicating abstract notions relating to governmental or religious systems, temporal periods or reigns, ethnic or linguistic qualities, etc. The suffix, which is found with some forty or so words, is essentially (but not entirely) nonproductive, having come into Hausa along with the Arabic loanwords to which they were attached. Examples:

àr̃àbiyyà	Arabic language	kìmiyyà	science, chemistry
àzàhàr̃iyyà	the early afternoon prayer	k̃àdìr̃iyyà	Islamic mystical sect (Qadiriyya)
(= àzahàr̃)			founded by Sheik Abdulk̃adir Jilani
dìflòmàsiyyà	diplomacy (< Eng.?)	màlìkiyyà	Maliki school of Islamic law
dìmòkùr̃àɗiyyà	democracy	màsìhiyyà	Christian calendar/era
fàtìmiyyà	the Fatimid dynasty	mùlùkiyyà	monarchy
hìjìr̃iyyà	the Muslim calendar	sànàdiyyà	cause, reason
ìslàmiyyà	Islamic tenets or calendar	tà'àziyyà	condolences
jàhìliyyà	the pre-Islamic period	tàr̃biyyà	good upbringing, religious character
	("the period of ignorance")		training
jàm'iyyà	political party	tìjjàniyyà	Islamic mystical sect (Tijaniyya)
			founded by Ahmad Tijjani

°AN: [i] The Hausa word **kìmiyyà = kìmiyyà** appears to contain the **-iyyā** suffix even though it is not present in the source Arabic loanword **kimiya** 'chemistry'.
[ii] With a term like **tìjjàniyyà**, it is not clear whether the word was borrowed as such with the suffix attached or whether it is an internal creation built by adding the **-iyyā** suffix to the proper name **Tìjjāni**.

Although the suffix was (and still is) essentially frozen, it has been extended to names of recent Hausa political leaders to indicate reigns. It has also been used in the creation of new vocabulary for names of scientific fields.

jùgòr̃àfiyyà	geography [This recent neologism is a loan blend.]
Bùhàr̃iyyà	the period or the difficulties experienced during the regime of General Muhammad Buhari, a former Nigerian military head of state (1983–85)
Sànùsiyyà	the reign or the kind of government of Alhaji Muhammadu Sanusi, a former Emir of Kano (1953–63)

°AN: The example **Sànùsiyyà** was given to me as a neologism with the modern definition cited above. In fact, the term *Sanusiyya* predates this usage as an Arabic-derived name for the Sufi order founded in North Africa by Muhammad ibn Ali al-Sanusi (1787–1859).

69. Temporal Clauses

THIS chapter describes various means by which Hausa indicates what in English would be expressed by subordinate temporal clauses.

1. WHEN

1.1. Clause with dà 'when / (time) that'

'When' clauses are typically indicated by a restrictive relative clause in the preterite that has as its head a temporal noun meaning 'time' (generally lōkàcī or yàyī or sā'à̀). (When followed by a relative clause sā'àn dà commonly contracts to sândà (with tone simplification = sandà).)

> °AN: As a noun meaning 'time, hour', sā'à̀ is feminine. When used grammatically as a subordinating conjunction 'when', it either employs the masculine linker -n (see above) or it adds the feminine linker -r̃, which invariably forms a geminate with the following /d/, e.g., sā'àd dà = sâddà = saddà.

The temporal expression can occur before or after the matrix sentence. If it occurs before, a main sentence in the past will use the preterite (often preceded by sai) rather than the completive. Examples:

bā mà̀ gidā [lōkàcîn dà sukà zō]
> We weren't at home when they came. (lit. ...[time.the that they.pret come])

kīshìn Ābù yā fā̀rà̀ [lōkàcîn dà ta ga mijìntà tà̀re dà Rābi]
> Abu's jealousy began when she saw her husband with Rabi.

[yà̀yîn dà ta shigō ɗākìn], bà̀ tà ji kōmē ba
> When she entered the room, she didn't hear anything.

[sândà mukà̀ dāwō], (sai) [mukà̀]pret gayà̀ musù là̀bā̃r̃ì
> When we returned, we told them the news.

= [mun]comp gayà̀ musù là̀bā̃r̃ì [sândà mukà̀ dāwō]
> We told them the news when we returned.

The 'when' clause may be introduced simply by dà (presumably due to deletion of the head noun). With completed actions in the past, dà is followed by the preterite. Examples:

[dà kukà̀ ƙi gaisà̀wā dà jūnā], na yi mà̀māki̇̀
> When you refused to greet each other, I was surprised.

[dà ya ga zākì̇̀], bà̀i gudù ba, sai ya yi tsàye
> When he saw the lion, he didn't run away, (but) stood his ground.

[dà akà̀ hàifē nì], iyà̀yēnā bā sà̀ zamā tà̀re
> When I was born, my parents were not living together.

As is generally true in Hausa with regard to pronominal reference, if the thematic subject of a 'when' clause and the main clause are the same, the noun subject must appear first, e.g.,

[dà sarkī ya ji hakà], (sai) ya hàsalà   When the chief heard this, he flew into a rage.

≠ [dà ya ji hakà], sarkī ya hàsalà, which cannot mean **When he (the chief) heard this, the chief flew into a rage, but only 'When he (someone else) heard this, the chief flew into a rage.'

cf. Hàdīzà tā bar̃ makar̃antā kàfin tà yi aurē   Hadiza left school before she got married.

≠ tā bar̃ makar̃antā kàfin Hàdīzà tà yi aurē   She (*not* Hadiza) left school before Hadiza got married.

°AN: In an appropriate context the 'she' in **Hàdīzà tā bar̃ makar̃antā kàfin tà yi aurē** could refer to someone else, but the first reading would always be that it referred to Hadiza. In **tā bar̃ makar̃antā kàfin Hàdīzà tà yi aurē**, on the other hand, the 'she' who left school can only be someone other than Hadiza.

If a sentence contains more than two verbs, **sai** is almost always used to set off the verb in the main clause, e.g.,

[dà mukà dāwō gidā mukà ci àbinci], sai mukà kwântā
     When we got home and ate, we went to bed.

[dà mukà dāwō gidā] sai mukà ci àbinci (sā'àn nan) mukà kwântā
     When we got home, we ate (and then) went to bed.

To indicate 'only when' or 'only after' or '(not) until', one uses **sai** before the **dà** clause, e.g.,

sai [dà sukà ƙàràsà aikìn tùkùn] mukà biyā sù
     It was only after they finished the work that we paid them.

sai [dà akà bā nì àlbâshī] na fārà yîn cèfànē
     It was only after I had been paid that I started buying groceries.

bà sù mayar̃ masà dà mōtà ba sai [dà akà kai sù gàban àlƙālī]
     They didn't return the car to him until after they were taken before the judge.

If the 'time' noun is followed by a relative clause in the relative continuous (rather than the preterite), it may translate best as 'while' rather than 'when', e.g.,

[lōkàcîn dà nakè kàr̃àtū] yanà barcī   When/while I was reading, he was sleeping.
(lit. [time.the that I.Rcont1 reading]...)

1.2. Clause with **ìdan** *'if/when'*

The 'when' expressions above all refer to past events that already took place. To indicate temporal events that have not yet happened, Hausa uses a conditional construction with **ìdan** (= **in**) 'if/when' followed by the completive TAM (see §17:1). Examples:

in mun gamà cîn àbinci, sai mù fìta yāwò   When (lit. if) we finish eating, let's go for a walk.

ìdan kā zō gòbe, zân bā kà littāfìn   When you come tomorrow, I'll give you the book.

in mutànensà sun isō, kadà kà gayà musù kōmē   When his men arrive, don't tell them anything.

The conditional construction is also used to express habitual 'when(ever)' clauses, e.g.,

in nā ji ƙishirwā sai ìn tàfi ràfī   When I am thirsty, I go to a stream.
in sun yi tsallē bā sà̀ jîn zāfī   When they jump, it doesn't hurt them.
takàn gan shì in tā jē kầsuwā   She sees him whenever she goes to market.

2. CLOSE TEMPORAL SUCCESSION

There are a number of different ways of indicating that one event closely follows some other event.

2.1. *Clause formed with* dà (zārař)

The expression **dà zārař** (or **dà zārař cêwā** or **dà cêwā** (lit. with saying)) plus a clause in the completive denotes 'as soon as' referring to non-past events. If the temporal clause occurs first, (which is mostly commonly the case) it tends to be followed by **sai** plus a clause in the neutral TAM or by a clause in the future, e.g.,

dà zārař [kun]comp dāwō, zā mù tāshi   As soon as you return, we will leave.
dà zārař mālàm [yā]comp fita ɗākì, sai yârā [sù]pret shìga tādī
    As soon as the teacher leaves the room, the children start talking.
dà zārař cêwā [mun]comp yi màganà̀, sai [sù]neut ɓātà fuskà̀
    As soon as we speak, they frown.
dà cêwā [kin]comp ji kūkan yārò̀, maza kì jē kì dūbà àbîn dà ya sầmē shì
    As soon as you hear a child crying, you should hurry to see what's the matter with it.

The 'as soon as' clause can be (and often is) introduced by **dà** alone, e.g.,

d<u>à</u> rānā [tā]comp fāɗì dōlè nē kù shā ruwā nan dà nan
    As soon as the sun sets you must break your fast at once.
zâi fi kyâu kà biyā hàřājì dà lōkàcin biyà̀ [yā]comp isō
    It would be better to pay the taxes as soon as the time to pay has arrived.
d<u>à</u> an yi makà ɗan lâifī kàɗan, sai kà cê à kashè mùtûm
    As soon as one commits the slightest offense against you, you order his execution.

Note that when one uses the bare **dà** in (a) 'as soon as' or (b) 'when' clauses, the only thing that distinguishes them on the surface is the choice of the TAM, namely completive vs. preterite, e.g.,

(a) d<u>à</u> [yā]comp tsayà̀ sai sù yi ta bugùnsà   As soon as he stops they keep on beating him.
(b) d<u>à</u> [ya]pret tsayà̀ (sai) sukà yi ta bugùnsà   When he stopped they kept on beating him.
(a) d<u>à</u> hafsàn hafsōshī [yā]comp gayà̀ musù àbîn dà zā sù yi, bâ màganà̀ (*or* màganà̀ tā ƙārè)
    As soon as the chief of staff tells them what to do, there is no argument.
(b) d<u>à</u> hafsàn hafsōshī [ya]pret gayà̀ musù àbîn dà zā sù yi, bâ màganà̀ (*or* màganà̀ tā ƙārè)
    When the chief of staff told them what to do, there was no argument.

2.2. *Clause formed with* kō dà

To express 'as soon as' in the past, one uses **kō dà** plus a clause in the preterite. The main clause, often preceded by **sai**, also tends to be in the preterite, e.g.,

kō dà ta sầmi kuɗī, sai ta sàyi jàn-bầki   As soon as she got money, she bought lipstick.
kō dà akà lầlàbē shì dà bàtun sàrautà̀, nan dà nan sai ya yàřda
    As soon as he was approached about succeeding to the throne, he immediately accepted.

kō dà na gan shì, sai na ga yā dācè nà tausàyā masà

> As soon as I saw him, then I realized that it was appropriate that I should sympathize with him.

When followed by a clause in the future, **kō dà** indicates 'even when', e.g.,

kō dà zā tà zìyàřci gidā, sai dà ta nèmi izìnin mijìntà

> Even when she was going to visit home, she had to seek permission from her husband.

2.3. *Clause plus* **kè nan**

To indicate that an event had just happened or was in the process of happening when another event took place, one can use a construction consisting of a sequence of full clauses. The first clause is a simple statement (normally in the completive or the continuous) plus the particle **kè nan** (lit. 'is there'). The second clause is introduced by **sai**. If it is tensed, it will be in the preterite. Examples:

yā zō kè nan sai ya tārař tā tàfi	When he came he found that she had already gone.
tā shigō d'ākìn kè nan, sai akà fārà ruwā	She had just entered the room when it started to rain.
nā zō bàkin kògī kè nan sai sukà gan nì	As soon as I reached the riverbank, they saw me.
inà zuwà bàkin kògī kè nan sai sukà gan nì	I was just reaching the riverbank when they saw me.
munā fitôwā kè nan sai bôm ya fashè	We were just coming out when the bomb exploded.
sunā ràbuwā kè nan sai gà Abdù	They were about to separate when Abdu arrived.

(lit. they.cont separating **kè nan** until here was Abdu)

yanà shirìn fārà wāk̃à kè nan sai gà 'yan sàndā sunā nēmansà

> He was just getting ready to sing when here came the police looking for him.

Completive sentences with a **kè nan** clause are semantically similar to 'as soon as' sentences formed with **kō dà**, e.g.,

yā gamà cîn àbinci kè nan sai ya yi barcī	He finished eating and then immediately when to sleep.
cf. kō dà ya gamà cîn àbinci sai ya yi barcī	As soon as he finished eating he went to sleep.

2.4. *Clause plus* **kè dà wùyā**

Another means of expressing the idea of events immediately following one another is to have an initial clause with a nonfinite verb phrase + **kè dà wùyā** (lit. 'is with difficulty') followed by a preterite clause introduced by **sai**. The nonfinite verb can be either a verbal noun (VN), often accompanied by a subject possessor, or an infinitive phrase (IP), e.g.,

fìtařmù kè dà wùyā sai bôm ya fashè — We had barely got out when the bomb exploded.

(lit. exiting.of.us (VN) is with difficulty then bomb it exploded)

shìgā tasà kè dà wùyā sai ya gan mù — He had just entered when he saw us.

(lit. entering his (VN) is with difficulty then he saw us)

gamà gyārà wayōyin jànàřētòn kè dà wùyā sai injìn ya kāmà wutā

> One had just finished repairing the generator wires when the engine caught fire.

(lit. finish repair wires.of generator (IP) is with difficulty then engine it caught fire)

2.5. *Phrase formed with* **dà** *plus verbal noun or infinitive*

The notion of 'as soon as' can also be expressed by a prepositional phrase consisting of **dà** 'with' (or **dàgà** 'from') plus a nonfinite verb phrase, either a verbal noun phrase or an infinitive phrase. This is typically followed by a preterite clause introduced by **sai**, e.g.,

dà hangō shì sai àku ya būshḕ dà dàriyā	On catching sight of him the parrot burst out laughing. (IP)
dà jînsà sai mukà yi fushī	On hearing it we became angry. (VN)
dà isôwaṛsà sai sarkī ya yi tsallē	On his arrival the chief jumped up. (VN)
dà ajìyè kāyā sai ya gan sù	As soon as he put down his load he saw them. (IP)
dàgà gamà jaṛṛàbâwā sai ta tāshì	As soon she finished the exam, she got up and left. (IP)

3. WHILE, AS

3.1. Conjoined clauses

To indicate that one action happened while another one was ongoing, one can conjoin two full clauses, one of which is in the continuous. No conjunction is required between the clauses, although **sai** 'except, then' is commonly employed with past events. There are two possible orders, with somewhat different semantics: (a) a continuous clause plus a preterite clause (often with **sai**), and (b) a main clause (various types being allowed) plus a continuous clause. The best translation for the (b) construction is often that of an English subordinate participial phrase.

(a) **inā kàṛātū, mutànē sukà shigō**	As I was reading, people came in.
sunà cikin cîn àbinci, kūràyên sukà faṛ musù	
	While they were eating food, the hyenas attacked them.
Mūsā nà ta shùke-shùke, (sai) Bàlā ya shânyē furâṛ	
	While Musa was busy planting, Bala drank up the *fura*.
yanà nan kân aikìnsà, sai akà zō masà dà làbāṛìn ràsuwaṛ mahàifìnsà	
	While he was there working away at his job, the news of his father's death reached him.
(b) **nā gan shì yanà dūkàn dōkì**	I saw him beating a horse.
yanà wàsā Biṛnin Rûm yanà ƙōnèwā	He was fiddling while Rome was burning.
bā yà shân ruwā yanà cîn àbinci	He doesn't drink water while eating.
gà cùnkōson mutànē sunà jiràn kàntōmà	
	There was a crowd of people waiting for the government administrator.

3.2. Clause formed with **tun**

One can also express 'while' by using the subordinating conjunction **tun** 'since, while' followed by a (usually nonverbal) clause in the continuous. The implication is that the action or event is still going on. Examples:

kà faɗà musù tun sunà nân	Tell them while they're here.
tun tanà ƙàramā akà yi matà aurē	She married while she was still very young.
(lit. since she.cont small one.pret did to.her marriage)	
yanà kīwòn garkè tun yanà ɗan shèkarà gōmà	
	He has been tending flocks since he was ten years old.

4. UNTIL / NOT UNTIL / UP UNTIL

The conjunctions **haṛ** and **sai** followed by a tensed sentence form clauses that correspond to 'until' clauses in English. The difference between the two conjunctions is that **haṛ** pushes the action forward, sometimes with an implied causal relation between the events, whereas **sai**, which often occurs with an expressed or implied negative, focuses on the stopping point. The conjunction **haṛ** is usually followed by the completive or neutral TAM. When the event described is clearly in the past, the clause with **sai** (or sai dà) is usually in the preterite. The two conjunctions may be used together (the order being **hař sai**) with the sense of 'up until', e.g.,

sun ajìyè àbîn hař sun bùkằcē shì	They have put the thing away until they need it.
kù ci gàba hař kù kai ƙauyèn!	Keep on going until you reach the town!
bàn yi barcī ba sai dà gàrī ya wãyè	I didn't fall asleep until daybreak.
bà zân yàřda ba sai nā gwadằ tùkùna	I won't agree until I try it first.
zâi bař tà à gōnâř hař sai tā būshè	He will leave it in the farm up until it dries.
mun yi aikì hař mun gàji	We worked until (with the result that) we became tired.
mun yi aikì sai (dà) mukà gàji	We worked until we became tired (then we stopped).

5. AFTER

Clauses indicating 'after' are formed by either **bāyan** plus a sentence in the completive or **bāyân dà** (= bāyan dà (with tone simplification)) plus a sentence in the preterite. (The clause with **dà** is structurally parallel relative clause type 'when' expressions). Apparently the two formations are identical in meaning and equally acceptable. Examples:

bāyan sun tàfi mukà kwântā = bāyan dà sukà tàfi mukà kwântā
    After they left, we went to bed.
bāyan nā kařàntà takàřdā sai na dunƙùlē na jēfằ à kwàndon shằrā = bāyan dà na kařàntà takàřdā...
    After I read the letter I crumpled it up and threw it in the wastebasket.
an tāshì wằsā bāyan faɗằ yā ɓarkè à fīlîn = ...bāyan dà faɗằ ya ɓarkè à fīlîn
    The games ended after the fight broke out at the stadium.

If the first clause does not have a past reading, only **bāyan** plus the completive is allowed, e.g.,

bāyan kun gamằ kwâ iyà tàfiyằ gidā	After you finish you may go home.

not ****bāyan dà kukà gamằ kwâ iyà tàfiyằ gidā**

bāyan kun kōmằ ƙauyè mề zā kù yi?	After you return to the village, what will you do?

cf. **bāyan dà kukà kōmằ ƙauyè mề kukà yi?**
    After you returned to the village, what did you do?
Audù zâi shiryà kōmē dà kōmē bāyan mun ci àbinci
    Audu will straighten up everything after we eat.
cf. **Audù yā shiryà kōmē dà kōmē bāyan dà mukà ci àbinci**
    Audu straightened up everything after we ate.

6. BEFORE

6.1. The conjunction **kằfìn** 'before'

'Before' clauses are formed with the conjunction **kằfìn** 'before' plus a sentence in the subjunctive. The subjunctive is required regardless of the semantic/temporal reading of the clause. The conjunction itself has the following common variant pronunciations: **kằfìn = kằfìn = kằmìn = kằmin**. Examples:

kằfìn à hàifē kà nā fārà zuwằ Kàtsinà   Before you were born I had already started going to Katsina.
kằfìn sù cê àkul, hař mā mun aikō dà māsinjà
    Before they said a word, we had already dispatched a messenger.

zā kà iyà ƙàràsà aikìn kàfìn kà tāshì?   Will you be able to finish the work before you leave?

yā baỉ ƙasâỉ kàfìn 'yan sàndā sù kāmằ shi   He left the country before the police caught him.

kàfìn ìn gan kà nā ji làbāỉìnkà   Before I saw you I had heard of you.

kàfìn Hàdīzà tà yi aurē, tā baỉ makaỉantā

    Before Hadiza got married, she had already left school.

cf. kàfìn Hàdīzà tà yi aurē, sai tà baỉ makaỉantā

    Before Hadiza gets married, she should leave school.

Note that **kàfìn** (like **bāyan** 'after') also functions as a preposition that forms temporal phrases, e.g.,

kàfìn isôwaỉsà sai mukà shiryằ masà wurin zama

    Before his arrival we prepared him a place to stay.

cf. **kàfìn yà isō mukà shiryằ masà wurin zamā**   Before he arrived...

6.2. Construction with **tun** *'since'*

An alternative way of expressing 'before' is by means of a 'since' clause formed with the conjunction **tun** (optionally followed by the modal particle **mā**) plus a sentence in the negative completive. Sentences with this construction are essentially equivalent to corresponding sentences formed with **kàfìn**. The ones with **tun** are, however, a bit more insistent and perhaps could be better translated as 'even before', e.g.,

tun bài zō ba (sai) mukà gamà aikì (= kàfìn yà zō mun gamà aikì)

    Before he even came (lit. since he hadn't come) we had finished working.

tanằ tằre dà nī tun (mā) bà à yi yāƙì ba (= tanằ tằre dà nī kàfìn à yi yāƙì)

    She was with me before the war broke out.

tun bà à ginà gidân ba yakè ɗòkin shìga

    Even before the house was built, he has been anxious to enter it.

cf. kàfìn à ginà gidân yanằ ɗòkin shìga

    Before the house was built he was anxious to get in it (but perhaps not now).

In affirmative clauses, **tun** and **kàfìn** can be used together to express 'since/even before', e.g.,

tun kàfìn à hàifi Lādì nakè zuwà gidân   Even before Ladi was born, I had been going to the house.

7. SINCE (TEMPORAL)

As in English, 'since' (**tun**) in Hausa has both reason (see §61:2) and temporal readings (e.g., **tun jiyà** 'since yesterday'). Temporal 'since' (or 'ever since') clauses are indicated by **tun dà** plus an embedded sentence with a Rel TAM, usually the preterite, e.g.,

an yi watằ bìyaỉ tun dà mukà gan shì   It's been five months since we saw him.

tun dà mukà isō, bà mù gan shì ba   Since we arrived, we haven't seen him.

tun dà ya ci sàrautằ, ya riƙà yankan mutằnē

    Ever since he came to power, he has been steadily murdering people.

tun dà ɗarī ya wucè, sai sukà yi ta ƙèrà bindigōgī

    Ever since the cold season ended, they have been manufacturing weapons.

tun dà nakè, bàn taɓà yî ba

    I've never in all my life done so. (lit. since I was, I neg touch doing it neg)

°AN: Jaggar (personal communication) has suggested that **tun dà** is an elliptical reduction of **tun lōkàcîn dà** 'since the time that' (where **lōkàcîn** could be replaced by some other temporal noun). Historically, this strikes me as probably correct; but synchronically I would think that **tun-dà** has become grammaticalized as a fixed expression in its own right.

[References: Jaggar (1992a, esp. 73–75, 108–9); Parsons (1981, pp. 510–30)]

70. Tense/Aspect/Mood (TAM)

IN Hausa, tense, aspect, and mood (TAM) are components of a single conjugational system. They do not serve as independent cross-cutting categories. With a few TAMs, the corresponding negative constitutes a distinct conjugational category; with others, one simply negates the affirmative TAM as such. Two of the conjugational categories, namely, "allative" and "negative-HAVE", are borderline pseudo-TAMs that are usually not included in descriptions of the Hausa TAM system.

1. THE PERSON-ASPECT-COMPLEX (PAC)

Tense and aspect categories (excluding the imperative, which is not treated as a TAM) are indicated not by changes in the form of the verb per se, but rather by a preverbal pronoun-aspect-complex (PAC), e.g., **lēburōřī [sù]**$_{PAC}$ **ɗaukà** 'The laborers should lift (it)', cf. **lēburōřī nè [sukà]**$_{PAC}$ **ɗaukà** 'It was the laborers who lifted (it).' This PAC, which corresponds to INFL in modern theoretical formulations, is made up of two components: a weak subject pronoun (wsp), whose particular shape depends on the conjugational category, and a marker of tense/aspect/mood (TAM). (There are two sets of wsp's: one characterized by a heavy syllable and H tone, which in SH is used in the completive only, and one characterized by a light syllable and variable tone, which is used in all other TAMs.) In the future and the allative, the TAM marker occurs before the wsp. Elsewhere, the order is wsp + TAM, e.g., **Tàlātù [zā tà] dafà àbinci** 'Talatu [fut she] will cook food'; cf. **Tàlātù [tanà] dafà àbinci** 'Talatu [she.cont] is cooking food.' The accepted orthographic convention is to write wsp + TAM as one word (e.g., **tanà**) but TAM + wsp as two words (e.g., **zā ta**), unless they are phonologically contracted (e.g., **zâi** 'fut.3m' < **zā yà**). All conjugational categories require use of an overt PAC whether an NP subject is expressed or not, e.g., **lēburōřī zā sù zubà yàshī à wurîn** 'The laborers will dump sand at the place.' (lit. laborers fut they pour sand in place.the).

1.1. Optional omission of the wsp
Some PACs allow omission of the wsp in certain appropriate environments. Examples:

yārò [yanà]$_{cont}$ gyārà kèkè = yārò [Ø nà] gyārà kèkè	The boy is repairing a bicycle.
yārinyàř dà [takè]$_{Rcont1}$ rawā = yārinyàř dà [Ø kè] rawā	the girl who is dancing
wà [yakà]$_{rhet}$ iyà? = wà [Ø kà] iyà?	Who could possibly be able?
màtâř dà [takè]$_{Rcont2}$ dà 'yan-kunne = màtâř dà [Ø kè] dà 'yan-kunne	
the woman who has earrings	
mutànen nàn [sukàn]$_{hab}$ shārè tītì ran Lahàdì = mutànen nàn [Ø kàn] shārè tītì ran Lahàdì	
These men sweep the street every Sunday.	

The wsp drop depends on a number of intersecting factors with regard to what goes before and what goes after it.

(1) The omission is possible only in the affirmative and only with certain morphologically segmentable TAMs, namely, the continuous TAMs (general and relative), the rhetorical, and the habitual (this latter for some speakers in some dialects only). Examples:

yārinyà Ø nà dafà ruwā	The girl is boiling water. [cont]
yārinyař dà Ø kè dafà ruwā	the girl who is boiling water [Rcont1]
yāròn dà Ø kè dà bīřò	the boy who has a ballpoint pen [Rcont2]
wà Ø kà ganè makà?	Who in the world would spare you a glance? [rhet]
mài kitsò Ø kàn zō nân ran Lahàdì	The hairdresser comes here on Sundays. [hab]
cf. mài kitsò bà takàn zō nân ran Lahàdì ba	The hairdresser does not come here on Sundays.
not **mài kitsò bà Ø kàn zō nân ran Lahàdì ba	

The other TAMs require that the wsp always be present, i.e., one cannot, for example, say **Hàdīzà Ø dafà ruwā for Hàdīzà [tā]comp dafà ruwā 'Hadiza boiled water'; nor can one say **mùtumìn bā Ø dàriyā for mùtumìn [bā yà]Ncont dàriyā 'The man is not laughing.'

(2) The possibility of wsp drop (in the case of the above TAMs) is syntactically conditioned both by what goes before and what goes after the PAC.

First, wsp omission requires (a) that its subject NP be overtly expressed or (b) that it be in a relative clause with a reduced subject, e.g.,

(a) yārinyà Ø nà (= tanà) dafà ruwā	The girl is boiling water.
cf. tanà dafà ruwā She is boiling water. *not* **Ø nà dafà ruwā **is boiling water.	
shī Ø kè (= yakè) jīfař kàrē	*He* is throwing (sth) at the dog.
not **Ø kè jīfař kàrē	
su wà dà wà Ø kè (= sukè) sàuràron řēdiyò?	Who (pl.) are listening to the radio?
mùtumìn nan dà 'yam-mātā sukà fi sô Ø nà (= yanà) barìn ƙasâr	
That man whom the young women prefer is leaving the country.	
(ii) gwamnatìn dà Ø kè (= takè) cî yànzu	the government that is ruling now
(= yakè) dà bīřò	yāròn dà Ø kè the boy who has a pen

In appropriate environments, wsp omission is also possible in first and second persons, e.g.,

mū dà Ø kè (= mukè) nēman tàimakō	we who are seeking help
kai Ø kè (= kakè) dà wannàn?	Do *you* have this?

In some conjoined sentences where each has an overt subject, each can drop the wsp, e.g.,

Būbà (ya)nà can rùmfā Bàlkī (ta)nà masà askì
Buba is there in the shed and Balki is cutting his hair.

The subject needs to be overtly present in order to permit wsp drop, but it does not have to occur immediately before the PAC. It can, for example, be separated from the PAC by phonologically small elements like modal particles or the stabilizer, e.g.,

Būbà fa Ø nà (= yanà) wankè mōtàřsà	Buba is indeed washing his car.
àku dai Ø nà dà hàzāƙà	The parrot indeed is clever. (lit. has cleverness)
Mūsā nè Ø kè (= yakè) nēman mātā	It is Musa who is chasing women.

In conjoined sentences where the underlying subject of both clauses is the same, the subject is only expressed once in the first clause. Whether the scope of the subject is sufficient to allow wsp drop in the second clause depends on the length and complexity of the first clause. Examples:

Bellò (ya)kàn tāshì wajen ƙarfè bakwài yakàn yi wankā

> Bello gets up at seven o'clock and bathes.

not ****Bellò yakàn tāshì wajen ƙarfè bakwài Ø kàn yi wankā**

Gàmbo (ya)nà̀ awà̀ biyu à gidan Sābo, yanà̀ fāmā dà wāshìn wuƙā

> Gambo was two hours at Sabo's house struggling to sharpen the knife.

not ??**Gàmbo (ya)nà̀ awà̀ biyu à gidan Sābo, Ø nà̀ fāmā dà wāshìn wuƙā**

Gàmbo Ø nà̀ can Ø nà̀ (= yanà̀) fāmā dà wāshìn wuƙā

> Gambo is there struggling to sharpen the knife.

mōtà̀ Ø nà̀ nan Ø nà̀ (= tanà̀) bā nì wàhalà̀

> The car is there (i.e., exists) and is giving me trouble.

ɗà̀lìbai Ø nà̀ nan Ø nà̀ (= sunà̀) kà̀ṛà̀tū

> The students are there studying.

> °AN: Although I have not been able to check this out in detail, it appears that the wsp deletion in the second clause is possible only if it is deleted in the first clause, i.e., **Bintà̀ Ø nà̀ nan Ø nà̀ kà̀ṛà̀tū** 'Binta was there reading' = **Bintà̀ tanà̀ nan tanà̀ kà̀ṛà̀tū**, but not ****Bintà̀ tanà̀ nan Ø nà̀ kà̀ṛà̀tū**.

Complements do not allow wsp deletion unless they have their own overt subjects, e.g.,

mà̀làmai (su)nà̀ tsàmmānìn sunà̀ dà īkò̀ dà yawà̀

> The teachers think they have a lot of authority.

not ****mà̀làmai (su)nà̀ tsàmmānìn Ø nà̀ dà īkò̀ dà yawà̀**

cf. **ɗà̀lìbai (su)nà̀ tsàmmānìn mà̀làmai (su)nà̀ dà īkò̀ dà yawà̀**

> Students think that teachers have a lot of authority.

Although a focused subject strictly speaking occupies the focus slot rather than the subject slot, it still permits wsp drop, e.g., **Bellò nē Ø kè̀ shìgā sōjà** '*Bello* is entering the army.' By contrast, a topicalized NP is structurally outside the main sentence—it occupies what I like to think of as the "front porch"—and thus does not support wsp deletion, e.g.,

Bellò kuma lallē, yanà̀ sô mù yi tàfiyà̀ tà̀re

> As for Bello also in fact, he wants to travel with us.

not ****Bellò kuma lallē, Ø nà̀ sô mù yi tàfiyà̀ tà̀re**

Bintà̀, takàn tāshì dà wuri   As for Binta, she gets up early.

not ** **Bintà̀, Ø kàn tāshì dà wuri**

cf. **Bintà̀ (ta)kàn tāshì dà wuri**   Binta gets up early.

(c) As far as the morphosyntactic environment to the right is concerned, the rule is that wsp drop is possible only if the PAC is followed by an overt VP or locative predicate, e.g.,

ɗinkì̀ nē tēlà̀ Ø kè̀ (= yakè̀) yî = **ɗinkì̀ nē tēlà̀ yakè̀** (with optional deletion of the VN **yî**)

> It is sewing that the tailor is doing. *not* ****ɗinkì̀ nē tēlà̀ Ø kè̀**

Audù nē Ø kè̀ (= yakè̀) nân   Audu is here.

cf. **Audù à nân yakè** Audu it's here he is. *not* ****Audù à nân Ø kè**
ìnā mutằnên kè̀ (= sukè̀) zàune? Where are the men seated?
cf. **mutằnên à zàune sukè̀** The men, seated they are. *not* ****mutằnên à zàune Ø kè̀**

(3) A special case is the deletion of the subjunctive wsp **yà** in expressions with **Allàh**, e.g.,

Allàh Ø ji ƙansà! = Allàh yà ji ƙansà! May God have mercy on him!
Allàh (yà) bā dà sā'à̀! May God bring good luck!

2. THE GENERAL / RELATIVE / NEGATIVE TRICHOTOMY

The conjugational TAM categories of tense/aspect/mood that occur in the PAC can be classified in terms of three rubrics that cut across the continuous/noncontinuous dichotomy: (a) general, (b) relative, and (c) negative.

(a) The general category is defined as everything that is not relative and not negative, i.e., it is the category that occurs in normal affirmative clauses, e.g., **[sun]**comp **tàfi kàsuwā** 'They went to market'; **[tanā̀]**cont **shân tî** 'She is drinking tea'; **dōlè [kù]**sub **biyā kuɗin tikitì** 'You must pay for the ticket.' All TAM sets except the rhetorical have a general form.

(b) The (so-called) relative category covers the affirmative TAMs that are grammatically allowed and/or required in what will be referred to as Rel environments. Rel environments are defined as those in which the verb is preceded by (1) the relativizer **dà** 'that', (2) a question word or whoever-type expressions (which inherently carry focus), or (3) any other focused element.

°AN: In this grammar, I have followed the long-established convention in Hausa studies of using the label *relative* for this category. Jaggar (work in progress) has recently suggested switching to *focus*, an innovation that in my opinion does not provide sufficient analytical or mnemonic advantages to justify the change.

The rhetorical only occurs in Rel environments. The relative-continuous1 and relative-continuous2, which obligatorily replace the general continuous, also occur only in Rel environments. The completive does not occur in Rel environments: its Rel counterpart is the preterite (which is allowed both in Rel and in non-Rel environments). The potential also does not occur in Rel environments: its Rel counterpart is the general future. Finally, the subjunctive neither occurs in Rel environments nor does it have a Rel counterpart. Examples:

wà [yakà̀]rhet **iyà̀?** Who could possibly do it? (Rel)
mutằnên dà [sukè̀]Rcont1 **tàfiyà̀ kàsuwā** the men who are going to market (Rel)
cf. **mutằnên [sunà̀]**cont **tàfiyà̀ kàsuwā** The men are going to market. (Gen)
mōtà̀ dà [sukè̀]Rcont2 **dà ita** the car that they have (Rel)
bāyan dà [kukà̀]pret **tàfi...** after you left... (Rel)
= **bāyan [kun]**comp **tàfi...** after you left... (Gen)
su wà [sukà̀]pret **ganī?** Whom did they see? (Rel)
cf. **[sun]**comp **ga Yūsufù** They saw Yusuf. (Gen)
à nân nē mutằnē [kè̀]Rcont1 **tằruwā kullum** It is here people gather everyday. (Rel)
Hàdīzà ita cè̀ [mukè̀]Rcont1 **nēmā** It is *Hadiza* we are looking for. (Rel)
Sālè à zàune [yakè̀]Rcont2 Sale *is seated*. (lit. Sale at seated he-Rcont2) (Rel)
wândà [zâi]fut **bā kà tàimakō** the one who will help you (Rel)
cf. **mālàm [yâ]**pot **bā kà tàimakō** The teacher will probably help you. (Gen)

(c) The negative category covers all sentences in the negative, whether in general or in relative contexts, e.g., **bà sù tàfi kàsuwā ba** 'They didn't go to market'; **kumbòn dà bà sù ganī ba** 'the satellite they didn't see'. Some TAMs use the general form in the negative with an appropriate negative marker, e.g., **bà [zā tà]**$_{fut}$ **dāwō ba** 'She will not return', cf. **[zā tà]**$_{fut}$ **dāwō** 'She will return.' Others use a distinctive TAM that is not identical to the corresponding general form, e.g., **bà [sù]**$_{Neg-comp}$ **fāɗì ba** 'They didn't fall', cf. **[sun]**$_{comp}$ **fāɗì** 'They fell'; **[bâ shi]**$_{Neg-HAVE}$ **dà wuƙā** 'He doesn't have a knife', cf. **[yanà]**$_{cont}$ **dà wuƙā** 'He has a knife.'

In some TAMs, e.g., the future, the same form is used in all three categories. In others, e.g., the continuous, the general, relative and negative have three distinct forms. Some TAMs are restricted in that they only occur in some categories and not others. This is summarized in table 14, where each paradigm is represented by the third person plural, e.g., **sunà** 'they.cont'. Empty cells are left blank.

Table 14: TAM overview

	General	*Relative*	*Negative*
Completive	Completive **sun**		Neg-completive **bà sù...ba**
Preterite	Preterite **sukà**	Preterite **sukà**	Neg-completive **bà sù...ba**
Continuous *(verbal)*	Continuous **sunà**	Rel-continuous1 **sukè**	Neg-continuous **bā sà**
Continuous *(nonverbal)*	Continuous **sunà**	Rel-continuous2 **sukè**	Neg-continous **bā sà** *or* Neg-HAVE **bâ su**
Subjunctive	Subjunctive **sù**		Subjunctive **kadà sù**
Habitual	Habitual **sukàn**	Habitual **sukàn**	Habitual **bà sukàn...ba** *or* Neg-continuous **bā sà**
Future	Future **zā sù**	Future **zā sù**	Future **bà zā sù...ba**
Potential	Potential **s(w)â**		Potential **bà s(w)â...ba**
Rhetorical		Rhetorical **sukà**	
Allative	Allative **zâ su**	Allative **zâ su**	Allative **bà zâ su...ba**

3. THE CONTINUOUS / NONCONTINUOUS DICHOTOMY

Syntactically the TAM categories divide into two major classes with regard to the nature of the elements in the predicate: (a) the "continuous" tense/aspects, namely, the continuous TAMs (general, negative, and relative) plus, in some WH dialects, the allative; and (b) the "noncontinuous" tense/aspects, which include the completive, negative completive, preterite, subjunctive, neutral, habitual, future, potential, and rhetorical.

(a) The "continuous" TAMs occur in nonverbal HAVE sentences, in adverbial (locative or stative) sentences, and in verbal sentences with a nonfinite VP (either a verbal noun (VN) or an infinitive phrase (IP)) (see §40:1), e.g., [cont]: **munà dà kuɗī** 'We have money' (lit. we.cont with money); [Ncont] **gidansà bā yà nēsà dà masallācī** 'His house is not far from the mosque'; [cont]: **tanà [shân]**$_{VN}$ **tî** 'She is drinking tea'; [Rcont1]: **wằ yakè** [**rufè tāgàr̃**]ₗₚ 'Who is closing the window?'; [Ncont]: **bā kằ** [**dāwôwā**]ᵥₙ? Are you not returning?'

(b) The "noncontinuous" TAMs occur only in verbal sentences with a finite VP containing a finite V as head, e.g., [hab]: **takằn** [**shā**]ᵥ **tî** 'She drinks tea'; [fut]: **zā sù** [**aunà**]ᵥ **gyàɗā** 'They will weigh the peanuts'; [pret]: **mutằnên dà sukà** [**gyārà**]ᵥ **mōtằtā** 'the men who repaired my car'; [sub]: **kadà kà** [**dāwō**]ᵥ 'Don't return.' TAM-less PACs, which result from the deletion of a repeated TAM, pattern with the "noncontinuous" TAMs in requiring that they be followed by a finite verb, e.g., [yanằ]꜀ₒₙₜ [**gyāran**]ᵥₙ **fuskà** [**yà Ø**] **kuma** [**tsēfè**]ᵥ **gāshìn kâi** 'He is shaving and combing his hair.'

We now turn to a presentation of the individual TAMs.

4. COMPLETIVE

The general completive paradigm is presented in table 15. The completive (= perfective, past) consists of heavy-syllable, H-tone pronouns, which function as portmanteau wsp + TAM forms that incorporate person and tense/aspect marking into single items. Because of the morphological nature of this paradigm, i.e., the wsp and the TAM are fused items that cannot be separated from one another, the wsp's in the completive are always obligatory whether the sentence has an overt NP subject or not, e.g., **Mūsā** [**yā**] **tàfi Bicì** 'Musa went/has gone to Bichi' (not ****Mūsā tàfi Bicì**).

Table 15: Completive

1s	nā	1p	mun
2m	kā	2p	kun
2f	kin		
3m	yā	3p	sun
3f	tā		
		4p	an

◊HN/°AN: Some scholars, e.g., Gregersen (1967) and Schubert (1971–72), have analytically segmented the forms by treating the initial CV as the pronoun and the -n and -a (forming a long vowel) as allomorphs of the completive TAM, i.e., **sun** = su-n; **tā** = ta-a, etc. This is fallacious. Historically, the now-occurring completive paradigm was a noncliticized direct object set that was redeployed for use as a preverbal subject pronoun. In this set, the length and final nasal are intrinsic parts of the pronominal forms. The final -n in the plural pronouns was originally a plural marker, which is widespread in Chadic. The final -n in the feminine **kin** is not related to the plural ending but rather derives from ***m**, an archaic Afroasiatic marker found in the second person feminine. The impersonal **an**, which patterns with the plurals, was most likely a later analogical creation, being added to the paradigm after the erstwhile object pronouns—which would not have included an impersonal form—were shifted into the weak subject position (see Newman and Schuh 1974).

The completive, which is only used in non-Rel, affirmative sentences, primarily expresses actions that were completed or had achieved a resultative state prior to the time locus. To the extent that the time locus is the moment of speaking, then the completive corresponds to the English past tense or present perfect. Examples:

Mūsā yā kōmằ gidā   Musa returned/has returned home.
yârā sun ga macìjîn?   Did the children see the snake?
jiyà an yi ruwā sòsai   Yesterday it rained a lot.

kā dāwō?	So you have returned?
mun zō bàkin kồgī kề nan, sai sukà gan mù	As soon as we reached the riverbank, they saw us.

(lit. we [comp] came to the riverbank is-that, then they [pret] saw us)

If the time locus is in the past, then the completive translates as a past perfect, e.g.,

dà sāfe dà akà tarad dà sū, kōwànnē yā kùmburà

In the morning when they were assembled, every one of them had swollen up.

If the time locus is in the future, then the completive serves as a future perfect (or sometimes a future habitual).

bàɗi wàř hakà mun yi girbĭ	Next year at this time we will have harvested.
rānā yì ta yâu nā zama shùgàbā	A week from today I will have become president.

dà sun bā mù kuɗîn, sun fid dà hannū gàrē mù

As soon as they give us the money, then they will be out of our grasp. (i.e., we won't have any claim on them anymore)

kàfîn mù kai Kanồ mutằnē sun shìga ɗakà   Before we reach Kano, people will have gone to bed.

(lit. before we [sub] reach Kano people they [comp] enter in room)

> °AN: The subordinating conjunction **kàfîn** 'before' requires that the following clause be in the subjunctive regardless of the temporal semantics of the event. The same sentence could also mean 'Before we reached Kano, people had (already) gone to bed.'

The completive can also be used for an imminent/intended event in the future, particularly with motion verbs, e.g.,

tô, nā tàfi kề nan	Well, I'm going. / Well, I'm off now.

With expressions of sensation or state the completive often has a present reading, although the actual interpretation depends on the specific sentence and the overall context. Essentially timeless, generic events, such as expressed in proverbs, make use of the completive. Examples:

nā san sù	I know/knew them.
dà yakè mun san kinằ zuwằ...	Since we knew that you were coming...
kā ji kō?	Do you understand? / Did you hear?
miyàř tā yi gishirī	The sauce is too salty.
nā tūba	I repent.
kwālîn yā ɗauru	The package is/has been well tied up.
kồgin Binuwài yā fārō dàgà ƙasař Kàmàřu	The River Benue originates in Cameroon.

dâ yā fi nì ƙarfī, àmmā yànzu dai nā fi shì

Formerly he was stronger than me, but now I am stronger than him.

bā à yàbon gwànin rawā sai yā zaunằ

One doesn't praise the skill of a dancer until he has sat down. (proverb)

ganī yā kồri jî   Seeing is believing. (proverb)

(lit. seeing it.comp drive away hearing)

The present reading is also typical of various aspectual and complement-taking verbs, e.g.,

yā kyàutu mù tàimàkē sù	It is good that we help them.
yā kàmātà kà biyā hàřājì	It behooves you to pay the taxes.
yā hàřamtà gà Mùsùlmī sù ci nāmàn àladè	It is forbidden for Muslims to eat pork.
ma'àikàtā sun kusa gamàwā	The workers are close to finishing.
kā iyà gyāràwā?	Can you (do you know how to) repair (it)?

In conditional clauses (regular, counterfactual, or concessive), the semantic reading of the completive depends primarily on the TAM in the main clause, e.g.,

zā à bā shì lambà in yā ci jařřàbâwā	They will give him a medal if he passes the exam.
in sun zō, zā mù tàfi kàsuwā	If they come, we will go to market.
in Allàh yā yàřda	God willing. (lit. if God he.comp agree)
dà an tàmbàyē nì dà nā yàřda	If they had asked me I would have agreed.
dà nā tàfi jiyà dà kògîn yâ kètàru	

    If I had gone yesterday, the river would have been crossable.

kō Hasàn yā gàji, yâ kāràsà aikìnsà

    Even if Hassan is tired, he will (likely) finish the work.

| kō an yi mîn àzābà bà zân yàřda ba | Even if I were tortured, I would not agree. |

ìdan mayàkā sun kai wà gàrī harì, sai sù kāmà bāyī

    Whenever the warriors would attack the town, they would capture slaves.

5. PRETERITE (REL-COMPLETIVE)

The paradigm of the preterite is presented in table 16. Some of the forms consist of a light syllable (CV) H-tone pronoun plus the marker -**kà**; others have simply the H-tone pronoun by itself, e.g.,

Table 16: Preterite

1s	na	1p	mukà
2m	ka	2p	kukà
2f	kikà		
3m	ya	3p	sukà
3f	ta		
		4p	akà

◊HN: Historically this paradigm was used as the normal, unmarked completive set. (The marker *kà (or *kə̀) is reconstructible for Proto-Chadic (Newman and Schuh 1974: 7).) With the introduction of the new general completive (the heavy syllable set), this paradigm has been functionally restricted to narrative uses or to the marked Rel environments.

°AN/◊HN: Synchronically, the **Ca** pronouns have to be specified as H. Historically, however, they were high by polarity because they were also followed by **kà**, which underwent loss. The pathway (using the 3f as an example) was as follows: *takà > *tak > *taG (where G represents a geminate with the following consonant) > **ta**.

ΔDN: In a wide range of WH dialects, the singular pronouns (including the 2f) still have the final geminate, i.e., **naG/niG, kaG, kiG, yaG, taG**, e.g., **wàzīřì yak kashè** 'It was the vizier he killed'; **zanèn dà kis sàyā** 'the wrapper that you (f.) bought'. A geographically more restricted group of dialects (specifically in Sokoto, Dogondoutchi, etc.) have plural forms of the shape **CVnkà**, i.e., **munkà, kunkà, sunkà, ankà**, e.g., **wàzīřì sunkà kashè** 'It was the vizier they killed'; **zanèn dà** munkà ɗaukằ 'the wrapper that we took'. The geminate -G is also used with the interrogatives 'who?' and 'what?' without an overt wsp, e.g., **wa-b bi sarkī?** 'Who followed the chief?'; **mi-k karyề?** 'What broke?'

The label preterite (= relative perfective, relative completive, perfective-2, focus perfective, narrative, historicus, etc.) has been chosen as the designation for this TAM because it is a distinct TAM that semantically denotes discrete events in the past. The label is admittedly inadequate and infelicitous because one important function of the preterite is to replace the general completive in Rel environments—which is why it is referred to in most grammatical descriptions as the relative-completive or relative-perfective. Nevertheless, preterite seems preferable to "Rel-completive" because this TAM *can* occur in narratives and in other non-Rel environments. Here are some of its uses:

First, the preterite functions as a syntactically required Rel form that replaces the general completive in Rel environments (e.g., focus, relative clauses, etc.). Examples:

shī nề ɓàrāwòn dà mukà hàngā	He is the thief that we sighted.
birìn dà ya sācề manà gyàɗā	the monkey that stole peanuts from us
dà mukà gàbằcē sù sai sukà gudù	When we approached them, they fled.
kō'ìnā ka dūbằ bà zā kà sằmē shì ba	Wherever you look, you won't find it.
yàushē kukà gamằ?	When did you finish?
nằwa nề ya fi kyâu	*Mine* is best.
bāwàn Allàh akà kōrề	It was a simple person they chased away.
bằ bàrēwā cề ka kashề ba, gàdā cề	It wasn't a gazelle you killed, it was a duiker.

It needs to be emphasized that not all subordinate clauses constitute Rel environments. Some qualify as general environments and in these cases one gets the completive as opposed to the preterite, e.g.,

bāyan [mun]_{comp} gaisằ dà shī na bayyànā masà nufìnmù
   After we exchanged greetings I explained our intentions to him.

dà [kun]_{comp} gan sù, kù kāmằ su	As soon as you see them, arrest them.
dà [kin]_{comp} zō gòbe nâ gayằ mikì làbārì	As soon as you come tomorrow, I'll tell you the news.
dà zārař yârā [sun]_{comp} dāwō, zā sù kwântā	The moment the children return, they will lie down.

The alternation between the preterite and the completive shows up clearly in clauses preceded by subordinating conjunctions that occur both with and without the relativizer **dà**, sometimes with a difference in meaning, e.g.,

kō dà [mukà]_{pret} jē, bà mù gan shì ba	Even when we went, we didn't see him.
kō [mun]_{comp} jē, bà zā mù gan shì ba	Even if we went, we wouldn't see him.
bāyân dà [kukà]_{pret} gamằ zā kù iyà fìtā	After you (pl.) have finished you can go out.
= (more or less) bāyan [kun]_{comp} gamằ kwâ iyà fìtā	After you (pl.) finish you'll be able to go out.

Adverbs of time may occur at the front of the sentence without focus. In such cases, the choice of the completive or preterite may be the only overt indication of whether focus is intended or not, e.g.,

jiyà [sun]_{comp} sanař dà mū	Yesterday they informed us.
jiyà [sukà]_{pret} sanař dà mū	*Yesterday* they informed us.

The preterite rather than the completive is used in narratives, even in non-Rel environments, e.g.,

Mūsā ya tāshì ya shigè, bài cê masà kōmē ba

> Musa [the hero of the narrative] got up, went past, [and] didn't say anything to him.

wasu sàmârī sukà haɗà kâi sù yi ƙòƙarī sù ci r̃ībà kō ta yàyà

> Three young men combined to try and make profit by whatever means.

A series of simple conjoined (or paratactic) sentences tend to be all in the preterite or all in the completive. Examples:

pret: **nāmōmin dājī** <u>sukà</u> **gàji dà kisà,** <u>sukà</u> **kai ƙārā gùn zākī sarkinsù**

> The animals in the forest got tired of the killings (so) they complained to the lion, their king.

pret: <u>sukà</u> **yi shirī,** <u>sukà</u> **shìga masallācī,** <u>sukà</u> **dūƙà**

> They made their preparations, they entered the mosque and they stooped down.

pret: **sarkī** <u>ya</u> **aikà** <u>akà</u> **kirā shì**

> The emir had him called. (lit. chief he.pret send one.pret call him)

comp: **sarkī** <u>yā</u> **aikà** <u>an</u> **kirā shì**

> The emir had him called. (non-narrative)

comp: <u>yā</u> **ci àbinci yā wankè hannunsà** <u>yā</u> **gōgè à r̃ìgar̃sà** <u>yā</u> **kuma yi hamdalà dàgà ƙarshē**

> He ate food and washed his hands and wiped them on his gown and then expressed appreciation.

comp: <u>an</u> **ƙi cîn kàrē,** <u>an</u> **kōmō** <u>an</u> **ci kwīkwiyò**

> One refused to eat a dog, (but) one returned and ate a puppy. (proverb)

Semantically the preterite is temporally more punctual and specific than the completive, the difference being comparable, in some respects, to the difference between a simple past and a present perfect. The preterite is thus commonly used when one wants to indicate an action directly subsequent to, simultaneous with, or even prior to some other action. In semantically appropriate contexts, it is possible to find the preterite and the completive co-occurring in the same sentence. Examples:

[sun]$_{comp}$ **yi wata gaddamâr̃ gàske, dàgà nan sai wata tsōhuwā** [ta]$_{pret}$ **kir̃āwō 'yan-sàndā**

> They had a serious dispute whereupon an old woman called the police.

sai [ta]$_{pret}$ **ga mutànē** [sun]$_{comp}$ **ci adō** [sun]$_{comp}$ **hau dawākī**

> Then she saw that the people had gotten all dressed up and had mounted the horses.

wani màdugū [yanà]$_{cont}$ **dāwôwā dàgà Gwànjā** [ya]$_{pret}$ **isō Kwārà** [ya]$_{pret}$ **shìga jirgī**

> A trader was returning from Gonja and he reached the River Niger and entered a boat.

[tā]$_{comp}$ **zō kè nan, sai** [akà]$_{pret}$ **fàrà ruwā**

> As soon as she came, it began to rain.

[munà]$_{cont}$ **fitôwā kè nan sai bôm** [ya]$_{pret}$ **fashè**

> We had just come out (or we were just coming out) when the bomb exploded.

shìgar̃sù [kè]$_{Rcont2}$ **dà wùyā, sai** [sukà]$_{pret}$ **zaunà**

> They had barely entered when they sat down. (i.e., their entering was difficult, then they sat)

[sunà]$_{cont}$ **cikin cîn àbinci kūràyên** [sukà]$_{pret}$ **far̃ musù**

> As they were eating food, the hyenas attacked them.

dà [mukà]$_{pret}$ **tìnkàrē sù sai** [sukà]$_{pret}$ **gudù**   When we approached them, they fled.

wani mùtûm [zâi]$_{fut}$ **yi tàfiyà** [ya]$_{pret}$ **ɗaukō kuɗinsà** [ya]$_{pret}$ **cikà tukunyā**

> A man was about to travel and then he took his money and filled a pot.

The completive and the preterite both occur in the protasis of regular conditional sentences with essentially the same (but not identical) meanings (see note in §17:1.1), e.g.,

in yârā sun/sukà dāwō zân bā sù kwabô̄ kwabô̄
    If the children come back, I'll give them a penny each.
in an/akà fārà ruwā, zā mù shìga ɗākìn   If it starts to rain, we'll go in the room.

In counterfactual conditionals, only the completive is used; the preterite is not allowed, e.g.,

dằ [yā]comp **shìga tākaɍā dằ yā ci zàɓē** *not* ****dằ [ya]**pret **shìga…dằ ya ci…**
    If he had been a candidate, he would have won the election.
dằ [sun]comp **zō dằ [nā]**comp **biyā sù** *not* ****dằ [sukà]**pret **zō dằ [na]**pret **biyā sù**
    Had they come I would have paid them.

    °AN: The above counterfactual, unfulfilled examples support the idea that the preterite is temporally more punctual and event-factual than the completive.

6. NEGATIVE-COMPLETIVE

The negative-completive paradigm is presented in table 17. The forms consist of (a) the initial short **bà** of the discontinuous **bà…ba** negative marker, plus (b) a light syllable wsp with default L tone, plus (c) a neutral phonologically zero TAM, e.g., **bà tà Ø dāwō ba** 'She didn't return.' In the 1s and 3m persons, the final vowel of the pronoun normally drops and the consonant attaches to the vowel of the negative marker, e.g., **bà nì → bàn** 'I didn't', **bà yà → bày → bài** 'he didn't'. Except for these contractions, the negative marker and the wsp are represented orthographically as separate words; linguistically, however, they are phonologically fused and ideally should be written as single items, with or without a hyphen (e.g., **bà-tà** or **bàtà** 'she didn't').

Table 17: Negative-completive

1s	bàn…ba / (bà nì…ba)	1p	bà mù…ba
2m	bà kà…ba	2p	bà kù…ba
2f	bà kì…ba		
3m	bài…ba / (bà yà…ba)	3p	bà sù…ba
3f	bà tà…ba		
		4p	bà à…ba

The negative-completive serves as the negative counterpart both of the completive and of the preterite, e.g.,

Mūsā bài tàfi Bicì ba	Musa didn't go / hasn't gone to Bichi.
bà sù taɓà zuwằ Jāmùs ba	They have never been to Germany.
bà mù san sù ba	We don't know them.
bài kai nì ƙarfī ba	He is not as strong as I.
bài kyàutu kà ɓōyè su hakà ba	It is not good that you hide them like that.
in bà kà yi ƙòƙarī ba kâ fāɗì	If you don't try you are likely to fail.
dằ sun tàmbàyē nì dằ bàn yàrda ba	Had they asked me I wouldn't have agreed.
tsòfàffîn dà bà sù iyằ ba	the old people who aren't able
nằwa nè bài narkè ba	*Mine* didn't melt.
wằnē nè bài sằmi ràbonsà ba?	Who didn't get his share?

°AN: The term *negative-completive* leaves much to be desired because this TAM has no special relation with the completive (as opposed to the preterite), morphologically, grammatically, or semantically. From a linguistic point of view, a three-term system like *completive, preterite,* and *negative-aorist,* for example, would be preferable; but practically speaking, such a terminological innovation would be unlikely to catch on with Hausa linguists and would make the grammar unfamiliar and less easy to use for the general reader.

In sequences of conjoined negative sentences (as well as sequences forming the paratactic construction with **rigā/rìgāyà** 'do already'), the negative-completive appears only in the first clause. Subsequent clauses typically use the completive (or preterite, if called for). Both clauses, however, fall within the scope of the negation as shown by the fact that the second **ba** appears at the very end of the sentence. Examples:

[bà mù]_{Ncomp} fìta [mun]_{comp} ganī ba	We didn't go out and see.
[bài]_{Ncomp} rìgāyà [yā]_{comp} gan nì ba	He hasn't already seen me.
Làmî bà tà]_{Ncomp} kàrɓi littāfì [tā]_{comp} kaɽàntā ba	Lami didn't receive the book and read it.
su wà [bà sù]_{Ncomp} sàmi tikìtì [sukà]_{pret} ga wàsā ba?	
Who (pl.) didn't get a ticket and see the show?	

The completive TAM cannot be negated as such, i.e., one has to switch to the negative-completive. One can, however, have a negative equational sentence containing a sentence in the completive, e.g.,

bà [Mūsā [yā]_{comp} tàfi] ba (nè)	It is not the case that Musa went.
cf. Mūsā [bài]_{Neg-comp} tàfi ba	Musa didn't go.

The following example illustrates the use of the completive, the preterite, and the negative-completive (as well as the subjunctive) all in the same sentence.

[bài]_{Neg-comp} kō tsayà ba [yà]_{sub} ji kō làbāɽìn [yā]_{comp} ƙārè, sai [ya]_{pret} yi tsàkī [ya]_{pret} jūyà [ya]_{pret} shìga gidā

He didn't stop to hear whether the story had finished, he just went 'tsk' [a sucking noise], turned around, and went in the house.

7. CONTINUOUS

The paradigm of the continuous (= continuative, imperfect(ive), incompletive, progressive) is presented in table 18. It consists of a light-syllable wsp (which gets H tone by polarity) plus the TAM marker **-nà**.

Table 18: Continuous

1s	inà ['n̄nà]	1p	munà
2m	kanà	2p	kunà
2f	kinà		
3m	yanà <shinà>	3p	sunà
3f	tanà		
		4p	anà

The first person singular form is spelled **ina** in standard orthography, but it is actually pronounced [ˈńnà]with a high-tone syllabic [ń] in the first syllable (this being a phonological reduction of a historically fuller form *nínà). The third person masculine is typically pronounced [yɛnà] or [yɨnà] with raising and fronting of the initial vowel. The dialectal 3m form **shinà** is not the norm in SH, but it is well recognized. In sentences with an overt NP subject, the third person wsp is commonly deleted, e.g., **mutằnē [(su)nà] jirànmù** 'The men are waiting for us.' In conjoined sentences, the repeated **nà** is deleted and the bare wsp with default L tone appears, e.g., **[yanà] wankè fuskằ [yà Ø] gōgè haƙòrā [yà Ø] kuma tājè gāshì** 'He is washing his face, brushing his teeth, and combing his hair.'

The continuous and its Rel and negative counterparts occur in both verbal and nonverbal sentence types (see chap. **65**).

7.1. Verbal

Verbal sentences are defined as those in which the head of the predicate, which either is or is derived from a lexical verb, fills the verb slot. Note that a sentence is treated as "verbal" for syntactic classificatory purposes even if the VERB following the continuous TAM is actually a nominalized verb (= verbal noun). Verbal sentences that employ verbal nouns in the continuous generally have comparable sentences with finite verbs in noncontinuous TAMs or with a different verb grade or with an indirect object. Thus **[yanà]**$_{cont}$ **[gyāran]**$_{VN}$ **mōtằ** 'He is repairing the car' is treated here as a verbal sentence with **gyāran mōtằ** as the (nominalized) VP even though **gyāran** 'repairing' (with the linker **-n**) is strictly speaking a verbal noun and not a verb. One can compare this sentence to corresponding sentences with surface finite verbs such as **[yā]**$_{comp}$ **[gyārà]**$_V$ **mōtằ** 'He repaired the car' or **[yanà]**$_{cont}$ **[gyārà]**$_V$ **masà mōtằ** 'He is repairing the car for him.' In verbal sentences, the continuous generally indicates ongoing action or durativity, without specific reference to time. It thus commonly corresponds to the English present, past, and future progressives. Examples:

sunằ gyārà mōtàtā	They are repairing my car.
kunằ kòyon Hausa?	Are you (pl.) learning Hausa?
dà na gan shì yanằ fìtā dàgà wàncan ōfìs	When I saw him he was leaving that office.
in kā dāwō gòbe, zā kà sằmē mù munằ tattàunâwā	
If you return tomorrow, you will find us talking it over.	
inằ zuwằ! I'm coming! (i.e., I'm about to get up and come, or I'll be back in a few minutes)	
yanằ nēman mutuwằ	It's about to wear out. (lit. it is seeking dying)
tanằ sôn karyèwā	It's about to break. (lit. it is wanting breaking)
inằ mutuwàř sôn sauràyin nàn	I am crazy about this boy. (lit. dying.for love.of this youth)

The progressive reading is commonly strengthened by means of the iterative particle **ta**, e.g.,

mằtā tasà (ta)nà ta zāgìnsà	His wife keeps on insulting him.
sunằ ta kàɗe-kàɗe dà bùshe-bùshe	They kept on drumming and making music.

Continuous sentences with a (usually dynamic) noun as head of the predicate are treated syntactically as verbal sentences containing the pro-verb **yi** 'do', which, when it occurs, appears as the verbal noun **yî** plus the **-n** linker, e.g.,

sunằ màganằ	The are talking. (lit. they.cont conversation)
= (more or less) **sunằ yîn màganằ** (lit. they.cont doing.of conversation)	
cf. **sun yi màganằ** (*not* ****sun màganằ**)	They talked.
tanằ wằsā = tanằ yîn wằsā	She is playing.

bà nâ zō nà ga [kanà̃] (yîn) ìrìn wannàn àbù ba

> I don't want to come and see that you are doing this kind of thing. (lit. neg I.pot come I.neut see you.cont (doing.L) type.L this thing neg)

°AN: The presumed underlying **yi** (or **yî**), commonly shows up when the dynamic noun is fronted for purposes of focus or topicalization, e.g., **màganà sukè (yî)** 'It's talking they're doing'; **wàsā dai, tanà̃ yî** 'As for playing, she is doing (it).'

Sometimes the continuous indicates normal, customary action, in which case it is semantically overlaps with the habitual, e.g.,

'yā'yā sunà̃ gàdař iyà̃yensù	Children inherit from their parents.
rānā tanà̃ fitôwā dàgà gabàs nē	The sun rises in the east.
dà dàminā ruwā (ya)nà̃ ɓařnā dà yawà̃	During the wet season rain causes much damage.

Some sentences are ambiguous on the surface as to whether the semantic reading should be progressive or habitual, e.g.,

Bellò nà̃ gyāran àgōgo	(1) Bello is repairing the clock. *or* (2) Bello repairs clocks.
yâddà takè girkì bâ kyâu	(1) How she is cooking is not good. *or* (2) How she cooks is not good.

ΔDN: Some WH dialects optionally insert the preposition **gà** 'at' or **kân** 'on' after the continuous TAM to indicate progressive, ongoing action, e.g., **Bintà tanà̃ (gà) lùřā dà shī** 'Binta is looking after him'; **macìjī yanà̃ (gà) mōtsàwā** 'The snake is moving'; **shinà̃ (kân) sàuràràř řēdiyò̃** 'He is listening to the radio'; **dalmà̃ tanà̃ (kân) narkèwā** 'The lead is melting.' (The use of **gà** may be due to influence from Zarma, but this is not certain.)

Sequences of conjoined sentences in the continuous allow repetition of the full PAC each time. Alternatively, one can use the continuous marker **-nà̃** in the first clause only, deleting it from the PAC in subsequent clauses. If the second option is chosen, the neutral TAM with the bare wsp must be followed by a finite verb rather than a verbal noun or dynamic noun. Examples:

(a) [yanà̃]$_{cont}$ ɗinkìn hùlā [yanà̃]$_{cont}$ kâiwā kà̃suwā

> He embroiders caps and takes (them) to the market.

[tanà̃]$_{cont}$ wāǩà̃, [tanà̃]$_{cont}$ rawā, [tanà̃]$_{cont}$ kiɗà̃ duk à lōkàcī gùdā

> She was singing, she was dancing, she was drumming all at the same time.

(b) [yanà̃]$_{cont}$ ɗinkìn hùlā [yà Ø]$_{neut}$ (kuma) kai kà̃suwā

> He embroiders caps and (also) takes (them) to the market.

[tanà̃]$_{cont}$ wankè zanèntà [tà Ø]$_{neut}$ (kuma) gōgè shi

> She was washing her wrapper and (also) ironing it.

7.2. Nonverbal

The continuous is used in various nonverbal sentences in which the predicate is an adverb or a prepositional phrase. The three main predicate subtypes are HAVE (lit. 'with' X), locative, and stative. As with verbal sentences, the reading is often present, but it can equally be past or future depending on the context. Examples:

Tàlātù (ta)nà̃ dà zōbè Talatu has a ring. (lit. Talatu (she).cont with ring) [HAVE]

àbinci (ya)nằ dà dādĩ	The food is good. (lit. with pleasantness) [HAVE]
gidanmù yanằ kusa dà nākù	Our house is near yours. [locative]
munằ Kanồ à lōkàcîn	We were at Kano at the time. [locative]
gòbe wằr hakà sunằ nân	Tomorrow at this time they will be here. [locative]
sunằ zàune à gìndin bishiyằ	They are/were seated at the base of the tree. [stative]
kinằ sànye dà sābon zanè?	Are you wearing a new wrapper? [stative]
cf. kinằ sanyà sābon zanè?	Are you putting on a new wrapper? (where **sanyà** is a verb)

The continuous is also used with predicate nouns and adjectives in certain 'while/since/when' clauses, including some where one might expect a relative-continuous, e.g.,

kà kashè wutā tun <u>tanằ</u> ƙàramā!	Kill the fire while it is small!
tun <u>yanằ</u> jinjìrī yanằ ƙyằmař kyànkyasồ	Since he was a baby he has abhorred roaches.
(lit. he.cont abhorrence.of roaches)	
lōkàcîn dà <u>yanằ</u> yārồ iyàyensà sukà mutù	While he was a boy his parents died.

8. RELATIVE-CONTINUOUS1

The Rel(ative)-continuous1 paradigm is presented in table 19. It consists of a light-syllable wsp (which gets H tone by polarity) plus the TAM marker -kề.

Table 19: Rel-continuous1

1s	nakề <nikề>	1p	mukề
2m	kakề	2p	kukề
2f	kikề		
3m	yakề <shikề>	3p	sukề
3f	takề		
		4p	akề

There are two Rel-continuous paradigms that substitute for the general continuous in Rel environments. One contains **kề** with a long vowel, and one contains **kè** with a short vowel.

> °AN/ΔDN: Because the distinction between the two Rel-continuous paradigms is marked only by vowel length (in a morpheme with low tone where length is less noticeable), it was overlooked by Hausa scholars until the 1970s (see R. M. Newman 1976). Even now scholars tend to minimize the distinction by presenting a single Rel-continuous paradigm indicated **takề(e)**, **sukề(e)**, etc. In WH, on the other hand, the distinction is marked segmentally and thus is clearer (Gouffé 1966/67). The Rel-continuous1 paradigm uses a marker -kà, i.e., **nikà, kakà, kikà, shikà, takà, mukà, kukà, sukà, akà**, whereas the marker for the Rel-continuous2 is -kè (as in SH), i.e., **nikè, kakè, kikè, shikè, takè, mukè, kukè, sukè, akè**. Presumably, the WH contrast represents the original distinction and it is SH that has innovated by undergoing a vowel shift from *-kà to -kề, with inexplicable lengthening.

The Rel-continuous1, with the long vowel -kề, is used in two main environments. First it is used in Rel contexts as a replacement for the general continuous in "verbal sentences"—which are defined as those that contain an underlying lexical VERB whether the verb appears as such or not. As with the general continuous, the wsp with the Rel-continuous1 can be omitted in appropriate contexts. Examples:

hatsîn dà akè dakàwā	the corn that is being pounded
yāròn dà (ya)kè shìgā makaràntā	the boy who was entering school
mè kakè kaɍàntâwā?	What are you reading?
su wằ (su)kè jâ dà bāya?	Who (i.e., which people) are retreating?
Hondằ cē mukè sô	It's a Honda we want.
Lādì cē (ta)kè dafà dōyằ	It is Ladi who is cooking yams.
mū nè sukè nēmā	It is us they are looking for.
baccī sukè (yî)	It's sleeping they're doing.
kŏyằyằ kakè yî, shēgèn nân zâi bā kà wàhalằ	

However you are doing it, this bastard will give you a hard time.

Second, the Rel-continuous1 occurs in nonverbal sentences when it is immediately followed by a locative phrase headed by a genitive preposition. (Note: "Genitive prepositions" (§57:2) have the internal structure of a noun plus a linker, e.g., **kân** 'on' < **kâi** 'head' plus **-n** 'of', as opposed to basic prepositions such as **à** 'at'.) Examples:

wằ yakè cikin ɗākî?	Who is in the room?
don mè sōjōjī (su)kè bāyan gàrī?	Why are the soldiers behind the city?
mìɍō mîn àbîn dà yakè kân tēbùɍ!	Hand me the thing that is on the table!
nī nè nakè gàbankà	*I* am ahead of you.

In addition, the Rel-continuous1 is sometimes used, with considerable variation among speakers, when followed either by a locative other than one beginning with a genitive preposition or by a stative. In this environment the Rel-continuous1 functions as an alternative to the Rel-continuous2, e.g., **mùtumìn dà yakè(e) zàune** 'the man who is seated'. This is exemplified in fuller detail in the following section.

9. RELATIVE-CONTINUOUS2

The Rel(ative)-continuous2 paradigm is presented in table 20. It consists of a light-syllable wsp (which gets H tone by polarity) plus the short vowel TAM marker **-kè**, e.g., **yāròn dà <u>yakè</u> dà bīɍò** 'the boy who has a ballpoint pen'. If the wsp is omitted, then the vowel of **kè** is automatically lengthened, in keeping with the requirement that all self-standing TAMs must be bimoraic. The resulting /**kè**/ is phonologically identical to the Rel-continuous1 marker, e.g., **yāròn dà <u>kè</u> dà bīɍò** 'the boy who has a ballpoint pen', cf. **yāròn dà <u>kè</u> kāwō minì littāfìn** 'the boy who is bringing me the book'.

Table 20: Rel-continuous2

1 s	nakè \<nikè>	1 p	mukè
2m	kakè	2p	kukè
2f	kikè		
3m	yakè \<shikè>	3p	sukè
3f	takè		
		4p	akè

The Rel-continuous2 paradigm corresponds to the general continuous in certain nonverbal sentences. It, rather than the Rel-continuous1, occurs in Rel environments when the PAC is followed by a true basic preposition (such as the **dà** of HAVE predicates) or when it occurs phrase final. (The examples will be given mostly with the wsp present in order to show the contrast between the short vowel Rel-continuous2 **sukè** forms and the long-vowel Rel-continuous1 **sukè̀** forms, a contrast that is neutralized when **kè̀** stands by itself.)

zōbèn dà kikè dà shī	the ring that you have (lit. you are with it)
Sālè nē yakè dà zōbèn	*Sale* has the ring.
àku nè̀ yakè dà wà̀yō	It is the *parrot* that is clever.
mutằnên dà sukè gà Mūsā	the men who are with (i.e., backers of) Musa
'yam-mātā dà sukè dàgà can	girls who are from there (='yam-mātā dà kè̀ dàgà can)
mè̀ yakè à gìndin bishiyà̀?	What is at the base of the tree?
bằ à màce takè ba	It's not that she is dead.
à zàune sukè	They are seated.
dà mūgùn halī yakè	He is mean. (lit. with evil disposition he is)
à kân kè̀kè <u>yakè</u>	On the bicycle he is.
cf. shī nè̀ <u>yakè̀</u> kân kè̀kè	*He* was on the bicycle.

(Rcont1 before the genitive preposition)

Although the norm is to use the Rel-continuous2 before statives and locatives, some speakers use the Rel-continuous1 in these environments. If, however, the stative or locative is preceded by the optional preposition **à**, or if the stative or locative has been fronted leaving the PAC stranded, then only the Rel-continuous2 variant is allowed, e.g.,

littāfìn dà yakè(e) cân	the book that is there
but only littāfìn dà yakè à cân	
yârân dà sukè(e) gidansà	the children that are at his house
but only yârân dà sukè à gidansà	
màkaunìyâř dà takè(e) kwàncè	the blind woman who is lying down
but only màkaunìyâř dà takè à kwàncè	
kẁālằyên dà sukè(e) jè̀re	cardboard boxes that are lined up in a row
but only à jè̀re sukè	lined up they are

The Rel-continuous2 occurs in the fixed phrases (**tun**) **dà yakè** 'since' and **kō dà yakè** 'although'.

tun dà yakè shī bằ dīřēbà ba nè̀ bài sanī ba	Since he is not a driver, he doesn't know.
kō dà yakè inà̀ rashìn lāfiyà̀, àmmā nā jē tà̀rôn	Although I was sick, I still went to the meeting.

The Rel-continuous2 is used also in forming extended relative clauses with nontensed embedded sentences, i.e., equational, existential, and presentational sentences, e.g.,

mùtumìn dà yakè shī sarkī nè̀	the man who is chief
sanyîn dà yakè àkwai à Jòs	the cold that there is in Jos
tùlûn dà yakè nākà yā fashè̀	The water pot that is yours got smashed.
cf. tùlûn nan nākà nē	That water pot is yours.
ɗàlìbân dà sukè bâ sū à makařantā	the students who aren't there at school
(lit. student that 3pl.Rcont2 there is not them at school)	
yayyenmù dà sukè likitōcī sunà̀ jîn dāɗī	
Our older brothers who are doctors are enjoying themselves	

9.1. The WH *aG* form

In many WH dialects, a high-tone particle **aG** (where G forms a geminate with the following abutting consonant) serves as the Rel-continuous2 marker when there is no overt weak subject pronoun, e.g.,

sūnānai **am** Mūsā *His name* is Musa, cf. **Mūsā as** sūnānai	*Musa* is his name.
Bellò (nā) Ø **ad** dà ràgō = Bellò (nā) yakè dà ràgō	*Bello* has a ram.
rìgad dà Ø **ar** rìnannā = rìgad dà takè rìnannā	the gown that is dyed
shī (nà̀) Ø **ag** gàrī = shī (nà̀) shikè gàrī	*He* is in town.

◊HN: Information on **aG** is found in Gouffé (1966/67) and Matsushita (1995). Abraham (1962) enters the morpheme as /ad/, stating that it automatically assimilates to what follows, e.g., **nī ad dà shī** 'I have it.' There is no justification, analytical nor historical, for choosing /d/ as the underlying consonant. Synchronically, one has to represent the morpheme as **aG** with a totally unspecified consonant that acquires its features from the following abutting consonant. Historically it probably derived not from **ad** but rather from *ak, the syllable-final /k/ being subject to a general assimilation rule. (The development of final /k/ into a geminate /G/ has also taken place in WH in the preterite, e.g., niG < *ni-k < *ni-kà), e.g., **dōyàd dà ni̱c ci** 'the yam that I ate' vs. **dōyàd dà ni̱s sōyà** 'the yam that I fried', cf. **dōyàd dà muṉkà sōyà** 'the yam that we fried'.)

Syntactically, **aG** is used in essentially the same environments as the SH freestanding Rel-continuous2 marker **kè̀**, i.e., in relative clauses or when there is focus, e.g.,

shī ad dà pîl	He has (is with) a battery. (= SH **shī kè̀ dà bātùr̃**)
shī am mālàmī	He is a teacher.
wandà̀ ab baƙī	the one that is black

10. NEGATIVE-CONTINUOUS

The neg(ative)-continuous paradigm is presented in table 21. The forms consist of a single negative marker **bā** followed by a pronoun containing the TAM **-à̀**, e.g., [bā tà̀] zuwà̀ 'She is not coming.' (Again, standard orthography dictates that the negative marker and the pronoun should be written as separate words, even though, in my opinion, hyphenated forms like **bā-tà̀** would be preferable.) The complex made up of the negative marker plus the PAC exhibits a fixed H-L tone pattern. The palatalization and labialization on the 2f and 2p forms derive from their underlying high vowels, i.e., **ki** + -à̀ → kyà̀ and **ku** + -à̀ → kwà̀. The 1p and 3p pronouns lack the labialization on the initial consonant since /mw/ and /sw/ are not part of the SH phonological inventory, e.g., **mu** + -ā → //mwà̀// → **mà̀**, **su** + -ā → //swà̀// → **sà̀**. The 1s and 3m pronouns have contracted forms without the final vowel, i.e., **bân** < **bā nà̀**, **bâi** < **bā yà̀**. In SH, these contractions are less common than the comparable contractions in the negative-completive.

Table 21: Negative-continuous

1s	bā nà̀ <bân>	1p	bā mà̀ <bā mwà̀>
2m	bā kà̀	2p	bā kwà̀
2f	bā kyà̀		
3m	bā yà̀ <bâi>	3p	bā sà̀ <bā swà̀>
3f	bā tà̀		
		4p	bā à̀

In SH, the negative-continuous serves as the negative counterpart of the continuous (general or relative). The only exception is the HAVE construction, where a special negative-HAVE paradigm is used (see §11 below), e.g.,

bā sà gyāran mōtà	They are not repairing the car. / They do not repair cars.
bā m à màganàr̃ kuɗī	We were not talking about money.
rānā bā tà fìtôwā dàgà yâmma	The sun does not rise in the west.
bā kyà sànye dà sābon zanè?	Were you not dressed in a new wrapper?
gòbe wàr̃ hakà bā sà nân	Tomorrow at this time they won't be here.
Wùdil bā tà nēsà dà Kanò	Wudil is not far from Kano.
àlmājìr̃în dà bā yà kàr̃àtū	the pupil who is not reading
su wànē nè bā sà jâ dà bāya?	Who are not pulling back?
baccī bā nà yî sai gyàngyàɗī	I'm not sleeping, just nodding.
màkaunìyā wâddà bā tà r̃ìk̃e dà gōrà	a blind woman who is not holding a staff

In conjoined sentences with identical subjects expressing non-co-occurrence or nonsimultaneity of events, negation is overtly marked in one clause only. The other clauses will be in the affirmative continuous. Examples:

bā à màganà anà sallà	One doesn't talk and pray (at the same time).
Lādìn dà bā tà hīr̃a tanà kàr̃àtū	the Ladi who doesn't chat while she is studying

[bā à]Neg-cont gudù [anà]cont wàiwàyē
        One does not run and turn around (at the same time). (Proverb indicating 'Get on with it!')
don mè sukè būsà àlgaità bā sà kiɗàn kàlàngū?
        Why are they playing the *algaita* ('double-reed instrument') (but) not playing the drums?

◊HN: Synchronically the negative-continuous functions as the negative of the continuous (general or relative) and sometimes the habitual as well. Historically, however, it was probably the negative counterpart of the potential, which is also formed with a TAM marker -à. Assuming that the negative-continuous was historically the regular counterpart of the potential, the PAC originally would have had falling rather than L tone. The present L tone on the PAC is undoubtedly due to simplification of the whole tonal phrase *including* the preceding negative marker. Exactly what the original tone of the negative marker was, we do not know for certain. One hypothesis that appeals to me is that the single negative marker originally had falling tone; but whether it was H or F it seems clear that the change to the tone one finds at present involved contour simplification, i.e., (using 3f) *bâ tâ > bā-tà *or* bā tâ > bā-tà.
ΔDN: Some WH dialects have variant negative-continuous paradigms without the erstwhile -à TAM suffix but preserving the long vowel of the pronoun, e.g., bā nà, bā kà, bā kì, bā yà, bā tà, bā mù, bā kù, bā sù, bā à. Other WH dialects use the normal light-syllable wsp with default L tone, e.g., bā nì (= bân), bā kà, bā kì, bā yà (= bâi), bā tà, bā mù, bā kù, bā sù, bā à.

11. NEGATIVE-HAVE

Affirmative HAVE sentences make use of the continuous and Rel-continuous2 paradigms. The corresponding negative sentences have their own distinct paradigm, negative-HAVE, which serves in place of the normal negative-continuous. This paradigm is presented in table 22. The forms consist of the falling-tone negative marker **bâ** plus a H-tone CV pronoun, e.g., **bâ ta** 'not she'. In the 1st and 3m persons, there are optional contracted forms: **bâ ni** → **bân; bâ ya** → **bâi.** Note that in the contractions the underlying H tone on the pronoun is lost, i.e., the surface tone is falling (= HL), because it is not possible for a tone to dock onto a syllable that already contains two tones.

Table 22: Negative-HAVE

1 s	bâ ni / bân	1 p	bâ mu
2 m	bâ ka	2 p	bâ ku
2 f	bâ ki		
3 m	bâ shi / bâ ya / bâi	3 p	bâ su
3 f	bâ ta		
		4 p	bâ a

The negative-HAVE paradigm is followed by a **dà** + NP phrase, just like a corresponding affirmative sentence, e.g.,

bâ mu dà ruwā	We don't have water. (lit. neg we with water)
cf. **munà̄ dà ruwā**	We have water.
Tàlātù bâ ta dà zōbè̀	Talatu doesn't have a ring.
bân dà lāsìn	I don't have a license.
yâran nàn bâ su dà hankàlī	These boys have no sense. (lit. ...are not with sense)
àbinci bâ shi dà dāɗī	The food is not tasty. (lit. ...is not with niceness)
zōbèn dà bâ ki dà shī	the ring that you don't have
wà̄nē nè̀ bâ shi dà laimà̀?	Who doesn't have an umbrella?

°AN: The **bâ** in the negative-HAVE construction is commonly identified with the negative existential **bâ**, e.g., **bâ kuɗī** 'There is no money', **bâ mū à cikin 'yan tākaɍā** 'We are not (lit. there is not us) among the candidates.' This may be so etymologically, although it is far from certain. Synchronically, the two negatives need to be distinguished. First, the existential **bâ** is usually followed by an independent pronoun whereas the negative-HAVE paradigm uses the same light-vowel H-tone pronoun set found with the allative. Second, the negative-HAVE paradigm includes an alternative 3m form **bâ ya** (with the weak subject pronoun /ya/) that is never found as the object of the existential **bâ**, e.g., **bâ ya dà kōmē** 'He doesn't have anything' = **bâ shi dà kōmē** (but not ****bâ ya** 'There is not him', only **bâ shī**). In addition, the negative-HAVE paradigm includes the impersonal form **bâ a**, with the 4p weak subject pronoun. This pronoun cannot be interpreted as an object of the existential **bâ** because the impersonal never serves as an object pronoun of any type. ΔDN: In some WH dialects, the negative-HAVE paradigm is used as the negative counterpart of regular verbal sentences in the continuous, e.g., **bâ ta cîn nāmà̀** 'She is not eating the meat' (cf. SH **bā tà̀ cîn nāmà̀**). This is paralleled by the use of the allative (with the same F-H pattern) instead of the SH future, e.g., **zâ ta cîn nāmà̀** 'She will eat meat' (cf. SH **zā tà̀ ci nāmà̀**).

An alternative means of negating HAVE sentences is to use the normal Neg-continuous PAC rather than **bâ** plus the H tone CV pronoun. This alternative is quite widespread outside of the core Kano area, although exact details of its dialectal distribution are unknown. Examples:

[bā yà̀]_{Neg-cont} dà fensìɍ = bâ shi dà fensìɍ	He doesn't have a pencil.
Tàlātù [bā tà̀]_{Neg-cont} dà zōbè̀ = Tàlātù bâ ta dà zōbè̀	Talatu doesn't have a ring.
[bā mà̀]_{Neg-cont} dà ƙarfī = bâ mu dà ƙarfī	We are not strong.
yāròn dà [bā yà̀]_{Neg-cont} dà hankàlī = yāròn dà bâ shi dà hankàlī	
the boy who doesn't have sense	

ΔDN: Dialects with other negative-continuous forms (e.g., **bā mù** rather than **bā m̀à** 'neg we') may use these variants in negative constructions, e.g., [WH] **bā mù dà ƙarhī** 'We are not strong.'

12. FUTURE

The future PAC paradigm is presented in table 23. It is made up of a TAM **zā** (etymologically derived from a verb 'to go') followed by a wsp with default L tone. Note that the order TAM + wsp is the reverse of the order in other PACs. The 1s and 3m contracted forms **zân** and **zâi** are much more common than the non-contracted forms **zā nì** and **zā yà**. The standard orthography dictates that the **zā** + wsp sequences should be written as two words, except in the case of the contractions. The main reason given for this rule—which does not strike me as persuasive—is that the two elements of the PAC can be separated by a modal particle, e.g., **zā kò̃ sù dāwō** 'They however will return.' (lit. fut however they return), whereas this is not possible with other PACs, e.g., ****yàushè su kò̃ kà dāwō** (lit. when they however pret return). The future uses the same PAC paradigm in the affirmative and in the negative.

Table 23: Future

	Future	*Future (neg)*
1s	zân / zā nì	bà(a) zân…ba / bà(a) zā nì…ba
2m	zā kà	bà(a) zā kà…ba
2f	zā kì	bà(a) zā kì…ba
3m	zâi / zā yà	bà(a) zâi…ba / bà(a) zā yà…ba
3f	zā tà	bà(a) zā tà…ba
1p	zā mù	bà(a) zā mù…ba
2p	zā kù	bà(a) zā kù…ba
3p	zā sù	bà(a) zā sù…ba
4p	zā à	bà(a) zā à…ba

The future TAM expresses future and/or intentional actions or events. It occurs both in general as well as in Rel environments, and in the affirmative as well as in the negative. The negative marker used in the future is **bà(a)…ba**. Examples:

mutằnên zā sù dāwō nân gàba	The men will return before long.
ƙawařtà zā tà kōm̀à gidā ran Tàlātà	Her friend will return home on Tuesday.
wằ zâi shìga rījìyař nàn?	Who will enter this well?
zā kà ji màganằtā, kō kùwa?	Are you going to listen to me, or what?
in nā gam̀à zā sù biyā nì dalằ hàmsin	If I finish they will pay me $50.
bà zā mù yàřda ba kō kàɗan	We will not agree at all.

hař gòbe hanyàř bà zā tà bìyu ba

Even tomorrow the road won't be passable.

gằ gidân dà zân sàyā

Here is the house that I am going to buy.

jiyà zân tàfi ōfis sai zàzzàɓī ta kām̀à ni

Yesterday I was about to go to the office when I came down with a fever.

°AN: The length of the vowel in the initial **bà(a)** is in free variation. Most descriptions of Hausa specify the initial negative marker solely as **bà** with a short vowel. It is unclear whether the variant with the long vowel represents a recent innovation or whether it is an old feature missed by earlier scholars, and, if the former, how widespread (dialectally and sociolinguistically) the long-vowel variant has become.

In conjoined sentences with a tightly knit sequence of future tense clauses, the overt TAM **zā** normally appears in the PAC in the first clause only; in subsequent clauses one uses the neutral PAC that consists of the bare wsp with default L tone. Examples:

[zā tà]_{fut} **wankè kwānukằ** [Ø tà]_{neut} **ajè su** [Ø tà]_{neut} **(kuma) kōmằ ɗākì** [Ø tà]_{neut} **kwântā**
> She will wash the dishes, put them away, (then) return to her room, and lie down.

bà [zā mù]_{fut} **jē sìnìmằ** [Ø mù]_{neut} **ɓatař dà kuɗì ba**
> We are not going to go to the movies and waste our money.

[zân]_{fut} **gyārà fuskằ sànnan** [Ø ìn]_{neut} **sâ rìgā mài kyâu**
> I'm going to shave and then put on a good gown.

cf. [zân]_{fut} **gyārà fuskằ sànnan kuma** [zân]_{fut} **sâ rìgā mài kyâu**
> I'm going to shave and then I am also going put on a good gown.

13. ALLATIVE

The allative (allat) indicates imminent or future motion toward a place. It is not normally included in descriptions of Hausa TAMs. It is done so here both on formal grounds—the paradigm is comparable to the future, which is always included among the TAMs—and on functional grounds—in some WH dialects it functions as the normal future. In SH, the allative is restricted to sentences with a locative goal (expressed or implied). This is a structurally specific, but very high frequency formation. The allative is allowed in general, Rel, and negative contexts. The allative paradigm is presented in table 24. It contains a formative **zâ** (etymologically related to the future marker **zā**) followed by a CV pronoun with H tone, e.g., **zâ mu kằsuwā** 'We are going to market.' In the 1s and 3m persons, some dialects allow the optional contracted forms: **zân < zâ ni** and **zâi < zâ ya**. As with the parallel negative-HAVE forms, the underlying H tones on the pronoun are lost because a third tone cannot dock onto a syllable that already contains two tones, thus the contracted forms surface with falling (= HL) tone.

Table 24: Allative

	Allative	*Allative (Neg)*
1s	zâ ni <zân>	bà zâ ni...ba <...zân...>
2m	zâ ka	bà zâ ka...ba
2f	zâ ki	bà zâ ki...ba
3m	zâ shi <zâ ya> / <zâi>	bà zâ shi...ba <...zâ ya...> / <...zâi...>
3f	zâ ta	bà zâ ta...ba
1p	zâ mu	bà zâ mu...ba
2p	zâ ku	bà zâ ku...ba
3p	zâ su	bà zâ su...ba
4p	zâ a	bà zâ a...ba

The allative uses the same paradigm in the affirmative and in the negative (marked by **bà...ba**). Examples:

Bellò zâ shi bankì	Bello is going to the bank.
zâ ni gòbe	I'm going tomorrow (place understood).
ita cè zâ ta disfensàr̃è	*She* is the one who is going to the clinic.
zâ mu kàsuwā sai hadarì ya tāsō	We were heading off to the market when a storm arose.
ìnā zâ ka?	Where are you off to?
kàntîn dà zâ mu shī nè Kingsway	The shop that we're going to go to is Kingsway.
bà zâ su makar̃antā ba	They are not going to school.
zâi (< zâ ya) Kanò gòbe [dv]	He's going to Kano tomorrow.
(= [SH] zâ shi Kanò gòbe)	

ΔDN: In some WH dialects, one normally uses the allative in place of the future. The VP in such cases patterns with the continuous (rather than with the future) in obeying the nonfinite verb rules, i.e., it has to contain a verbal noun or an infinitive phrase, e.g.,

[zâ ta]_{allat} [shân]_{VN} shāyì She will drink tea. = [SH] [zā tà]_{fut} [shā]_V shāyì
[zâ ya]_{allat} [dāwòwā]_{VN} He will return. = [SH] [zâi]_{fut} [dāwō]_V
[zâ mu]_{allat} [cîn]_{VN} nāmà We will eat meat. = [SH] [zā mù]_{fut} [ci]_V nāmà
[zân]_{allat} (< zâ ni) [jiràn]_{VN} mālàm I will wait for the teacher.
= [SH] [zân]_{fut} (< zā nì) [jirā]_V mālàm I will wait for the teacher.

In the negative, however, the future rather than the allative is usually preferred, i.e., the normal negative of zâ ta shân shāyì would be bà zā tà shā shāyì ba 'She will drink tea', not **bà zâ ta shân shāyì ba.

There are surface examples that make it look as if WH dialects sometimes use a nonfinite verb with the future, e.g., [WH] zân [naɗèwā]_{VN} = zân [naɗè]_V 'I will coil up'; zâi [shân]_{VN} shāyì = zâi [shā]_V shāyì 'He will drink tea.' The explanation is that in the contracted forms, the allative and the future have phonologically fallen together, e.g., the allatives zâ ni and zâ ya (with the underlying HL-H sequence) contract to zân and zâi, respectively, as do the futures zā nì and zā yà (with the underlying H-L sequence). A sentence like [zân][naɗèwā] is thus *not* an example of a future followed by a verbal noun, which would be abnormal, but rather is a grammatically regular example (in this dialect) of an allative plus a verbal noun.

◊HN: The allative zâ like the future marker zā is clearly a variant of the verb zō (and its various forms) 'come/go'. The allative pronoun is probably an erstwhile intransitive copy pronoun (ICP) that has become grammaticalized, with obligatory deletion of the presumed original pre-TAM weak subject pronoun, e.g., zâ mu kàsuwā 'We will go to market' < *mù zâ-mu kàsuwā; cf. the still occurring mù jē-mu! 'Let's go!'). It is possible that the pronoun used in the future could also be an old ICP, but the identity here is less certain.

14. POTENTIAL

The potential (= future-2, predictive, ingressive, indefinite future, restricted future) consists of a light-syllable wsp (which gets H tone by polarity) plus the TAM -à, e.g., yâ shā wùyā 'He is likely to have trouble.' The vowel of the pronoun plus the long vowel of the TAM simplify to a single long /ā/ and the H + L sequence coalesces into a fall, e.g., ya + -à → /yâ/. (Reminder: The circumflex accent, e.g., â, indicates falling tone *and* length.) With the 2f and 2p pronouns, the underlying high vowels show up as palatalization and labialization of the preceding consonant respectively, i.e., ki + -à → /kyâ/; ku + -à → /kwâ/. SH does not have labialized consonants other than velars. With dialects that do, the 1p and 3p pronouns appear as mwâ and swâ respectively; in SH they appear as mâ and sâ. The potential is allowed in general and negative contexts (marked by bà...ba), but not in Rel environments.

Table 25: Potential

	Potential	Potential (neg)
1s	nâ	bà nâ...ba
2m	kâ	bà kâ...ba
2f	kyâ	bà kyâ...ba
3m	yâ	bà yâ...ba
3f	tâ	bà tâ...ba
1p	mâ <mwâ>	bà mâ...ba <mwâ>
2p	kwâ	bà kwâ...ba
3p	sâ <swâ>	bà sâ...ba <swâ>
4p	â	bà â...ba

ΔDN: In some WH dialects, the suffix -à as such has been eliminated and the falling tone (with length) has become the marker of the potential paradigm. (The impetus would presumably have been singular forms such as yâ and tâ, where the existence of -à as a distinct entity is hidden.) Different dialects add the falling tone to different pronoun sets. One pattern uses the heavy pronouns found in the completive as the input, e.g., **nâ, kâ, kyâ, yâ, tâ, mûn, kûn, sûn, ân**. The other pattern uses simple light syllable wsp's as the input, e.g., **nî, kâ, kî, yâ, tâ, mû, kû, sû, â**. (Note: Because Hausa does not have extra-long vowels, tā (from the heavy syllable wsp paradigm) plus -ˋ and ta (from the light-syllable wsp paradigm) plus -à̀ end up identically as tâ.)

The category termed here as the "potential", which is short for potential-future, indicates an action that will possibly take place in the future (God willing). On semantic grounds, it might better be called the "conditional future" or "modal future." I have adopted potential as a label of convenience. It differs from the normal future in having a lesser degree of certainty and a lesser element of intentionality or commitment, e.g.,

wàtàƙīlà makàɗā sâ dāwō	Perhaps the drummers will come back.
kògîn bà yâ ƙètàru ba	The river will probably not be passable.
kàfìn mù zō, yâ gamà̀	Before we come he'll probably have finished.
bà mâ kāmà ɓàrāwòn ba	We will probably not catch the thief.
ɗālìbā tâ kai makà	The student may bring (it) to you.
cf. ɗālìbā zā tà kai makà	The student will (intends to) bring it to you. (fut)

One often encounters the potential in proverbs, e.g.,

kō birì yā karyè̀ yâ hau rùmbū
    Even if a monkey breaks (his leg), he will climb up into the corn bin.
    (You can't stop the inevitable.)

kōmē nīsan darē, gàrī yâ wāyè̀
    However long the night, day will dawn. (Every cloud has a silver lining.)

kōwā ya haɗîyè̀ taɓaryā, yâ kwāna tsàye
    Whoever swallows a pestle will sleep standing up. (Evil recoils on the doer.)

The potential is commonly used in the consequence clause (apodosis) of conditional sentences, where it functions as an equivalent alternative to the future (in normal conditionals) or the completive or negative-completive (in counterfactual conditionals). Examples:

in sun zō, [mâ]₍pot₎ (= [zā mù]₍fut₎) tàfī kàsuwā	If they come we will go to the market.
dằ an tàmbàyē nì, dằ [nâ]₍pot₎ (= [nā]₍comp₎) yàr̃da	Had I been asked I would have agreed.
dằ an tàmbàyē nì, dằ bà [nâ]₍pot₎ (= [bàn]₍Ncomp₎) yàr̃da ba	
Had I been asked I would not have agreed.	

It is also used in the conditional clause (protasis) in future counterfactual conditionals, e.g.,

dằ [â]₍pot₎ (= [zā à]₍fut₎) tàmbàyē nì dằ [nâ]₍pot₎ (= [nā]₍comp₎) yàr̃da   Were I to be asked, I'd agree.

The potential also can function as a mixture of a conditional and a threat, i.e., it serves as an admonition to warn someone of the consequences of an action or event, e.g.,

mâ gàmu!	We shall meet! (i.e., you will pay the price)
kâ jiƙè	(If you go out in the rain) you'll get soaked.
kâ ga tsìyā	You shall see disrespect. (i.e., I will humiliate you.)
jar̃r̃àbâwā nằ zuwằ, kâ ganī	
Exams are coming up, you will see! (i.e., you will suffer if you don't study.)	

A common use of the potential is as a reply to a greeting to a third party, e.g., **à gayar̃ minì dà màigidā** 'Please greet your husband for me', to which the response is **yâ ji** 'I will convey the greeting to him' (lit. he will hear (it)).

As with the future, sequences of conjoined clauses in the potential express the TAM only once. Subsequent clauses appear with a neutral PAC consisting of the bare wsp.

jè-ka, [mâ]₍pot₎ zō [mù Ø]₍neut₎ gan shì	
Go, we may eventually come and see him.	
bà [nâ]₍pot₎ zō [nà Ø]₍neut₎ ga kanằ irìn wannàn àbù ba	
I should not like to come and see that you are doing this kind of thing.	

The potential does not occur in Rel environments; instead, one has to use the normal future (or some other alternative).

wằ [zâi]₍fut₎ tàimàkē mù?	Who will help us? not **wằ [yâ]₍pot₎ tàimàkē mù?
sābō (nè) [zân]₍fut₎ sāmù	It's a new one I'm going to get. not **sābō (nè) [nâ]₍pot₎ sāmù
lōkàcîn dà [zā mù]₍fut₎ ci àbinci	the time when we will eat
not **lōkàcîn dà [mâ]₍pot₎ ci àbinci	
bà nī nè [zân]₍fut₎ kāwō mā kuɗī ba	I'm not the one who is going to bring you money.
not **bà nī nè [nâ]₍pot₎ kāwō mā kuɗī ba	
(cêwar̃) Shatù tà àuri Bàlā (nè) [ya]₍pret₎ yìwu	That Shatu might marry Bala is possible.
cf. [yâ]₍pot₎ yìwu Shatù tà àuri Bàlā	It is possible that Shatu might marry Bala

15. RHETORICAL

The rhetorical (also referred to as rhetorical future or relative future) consists of a light-syllable wsp (which gets H tone by polarity) plus the TAM marker **-kằ**. If the subject is expressed, the wsp is typically deleted.

Table 26: Rhetorical

1s	nikằ	1p	mukằ
2m	kakằ	2p	kukằ
2f	kikằ		
3m	yakằ <shikằ>	3p	sukằ
3f	takằ		
		4p	akằ

The rhetorical is an infrequently encountered TAM that has not been adequately studied and about which we therefore know very little. It is used primarily in set expressions, idioms, epithets, proverbs, compounds, and such, but not exclusively so. As far as one can determine, the rhetorical is pan-dialectal and—our linguistic ignorance notwithstanding—still alive and well in the current language. Syntactically, it is restricted to Rel environments, i.e., questions, focus, and relative clauses. It occurs in the affirmative only.

◊HN: Historically, the rhetorical is almost certainly the Rel counterpart to the potential, which, as indicated above, is excluded from Rel environments. (This relation was suggested many years ago by Gregersen (1967: 50).) Over time, however, the two have diverged such that one cannot consider them synchronically as syntactic counterparts of one another comparable to the continuous/Rel-continuous pairing. Semantically/stylistically, the rhetorical is a highly marked TAM, whose relationship to the potential is probably not recognized by native speakers. Note, for example, that if a sentence in the potential is put into a Rel environment, native speakers automatically replace the potential with the regular future and not with the rhetorical.

The rhetorical implies doubt or even a dare with respect to the possibility of achieving some action. It is often best translated with such English modals as 'should' or 'could'. As the name indicates, it is commonly used in rhetorical questions or statements. It is also found in fixed expressions and compounds. The following examples illustrate the semantic range and content of this TAM.

ìnā nakằ sakằ?　　Where on earth could I put (it)?
nī kaɗai kằ iyà hakằ　　Only I could do this.
wằ kằ ganè makằ?
　　Who in the world would spare you a glance?
wằ kằ jā wằ kâi irìn wannàn wàhalằ?
　　Who would bring this kind of trouble on himself?
duk mùtumìn dà kằ ci wannàn àbinci yâ shā wàhalằ
　　Whoever would dare to eat this food will be in trouble.
gāra à ragè rìkicîn dà kằ iyà tāshì nân gàba
　　One should lessen the disturbances that are likely to rise up in the near future.
inuwằr giginyằ, na nēsà kằ shā tà　　You neglect your family and favor strangers.
(lit. shade.of deleb-palm, it's the one at some distance who will drink (i.e., enjoy) it) [fixed saying]
wằ kằ shāfà wằ tsūlìyā bàřkònō?　　Who would bring trouble on himself?
(lit. who will wipe on anus pepper?) [fixed saying]
na-bāya-kằ-shā-kallō　　type of embroidery on back of gown
(lit. that of back will undergo (lit. drink) looking) [compound noun]
hālin ƙàƙằ-nikằ-yi　　dilemma, hard times, in a catch-22 situation
(lit. condition of how-I could-do?) [compound expression]

Although the rhetorical is stylistically restricted and limited in usage, structurally it is quite regular. As the above examples show, it favors (almost requires) the deletion of the wsp when there is an overt subject in the sentence, i.e., ??**wằ yakằ iyằ?** = **wằ kằ iyằ?** 'Who could possibly do it?' As with other PACs with an overt TAM, conjoined rhetorical sentences delete the marker **kằ** in all clauses except the first. When the **kằ** is deleted, the bare wsp appears in the neutral form with default L tone.

wâddà [kằ]_{rhet} **iyà tāsôwa [tà Ø]**_{neut} **tāyař manà dà hankàlī**
    the one that could rise up and arouse us
wằ [kằ]_{rhet} **iyà tāshī [yà Ø]**_{neut} **bā dà jàwābī gà tàrôn?**
    Who would dare get up and give a speech to the crowd?

16. HABITUAL

The habitual consists of a light syllable wsp (which gets H tone by polarity) plus the TAM marker -**kàn**, e.g., **sukàn shā tî dà ƙarfè huɗu** 'They have their tea at four o'clock.' The habitual occurs in general and Rel environments. In principle, it is allowed in the negative, although many speakers switch to the negative-continuous. There is free variation in the length of the initial **bà(a)** of the negative, but in SH, the long vowel variant now seems to be the norm.

Table 27: Habitual

	Habitual	*Habitual (neg)*
1s	nakàn / nikàn	bằ nakàn…ba / bằ nikàn…ba
2m	kakàn	bằ kakàn…ba
2f	kikàn	bằ kikàn…ba
3m	yakàn	bằ yakàn…ba
3f	takàn	bằ takàn…ba
1p	mukàn	bằ mukàn…ba
2p	kukàn	bằ kukàn…ba
3p	sukàn	bằ sukàn…ba
4p	akàn	bằ akàn…ba

The habitual denotes customary action, without explicit reference to time. It often expresses an ongoing habit, where it is best translated by the English present tense, 'I do so and so.' It can, however, also refer to past time as indicated by English 'used to'. Examples:

à ƙasař Jàpân akàn ci ɗanyen kīfī   In Japan one eats raw fish.
akàn kashe fìtilàřmù dà ƙarfè tařà   One turns off our light at nine o'clock.
wằ yakàn shārè ɗākìn?   Who sweeps the room?
takàn jē cōcì lōkàcī lōkàcī   She goes to church from time to time.
gà mahàukàcîn dà yakàn yi fītò   Here is the madman who whistles.
dâ can, nakàn yi aikī na awà gōmà shā biyu kōwàcè rānā
    Back then, I used to work twelve hours a day.

The habitual, like other PACs with an overt TAM, allows omission of the wsp (in the affirmative).

mài kitsồ (ta)kàn zō nân ran Lahàdì   The hairdresser comes here on Sundays.

In sequences of clauses in conjoined sentences, the habitual marker is only expressed once, e.g.,

[nakàn]hab **tāshì wajen ƙarfè bakwài [nà Ø]**neut **gyārà fuskǎ [nà Ø]**neut **karyà kùmallō [nà Ø]**neut **shìga mōtǎ don tàfiyǎ ōfìs**
    I get up around seven o'clock, shave, have breakfast, and get in my car to go to the office.
(lit. I.hab arise about seven o'clock, I Ø repair face, I Ø break hunger, I Ø enter car for going office).
mài hàƙurī shī [(ya)kàn]hab **dafà dūtsè (haƙ) [yà Ø]**neut **shā rōmō**
    The patient man cooks a stone and drinks broth. (i.e., with patience you can do/get anything)

Although the habitual paradigm *can* be negated directly using **bà(a)...ba**, many SH speakers prefer to express negative habitual actions by use of the negative-continuous rather than with the habitual. Some dialects (e.g., Sokoto) go further and do not allow the habitual in the negative at all. Examples:

bà sukàn shā giyǎ ba = bā sà shân giyǎ   They don't drink beer.
shī yāròn bà yakàn zō makaƙantā ba = shī yāròn bā yà zuwà makaƙantā
    This boy doesn't attend school.

17. SUBJUNCTIVE

The subjunctive paradigm (table 28) consists of a set of bare light-syllable pronouns with default L tone.

Table 28: Subjunctive

	Subjunctive	*Negative Subjunctive*
1s	**ìn / nà**	**kadà ìn / kadà nà**
2m	**kà**	**kadà kà**
2f	**kì**	**kadà kì**
3m	**yà <shì>**	**kadà yà / kadà <shì>**
3f	**tà**	**kadà tà**
1p	**mù**	**kadà mù**
2p	**kù**	**kadà kù**
3p	**sù**	**kadà sù**
4p	**à**	**kadà à**

The subjunctive TAM itself is phonologically zero, e.g., **kù [Ø] yi hàƙurī** 'You (pl.) be patient.' The 1s pronoun is written orthographically as **in**, but it is pronounced [ǹ] with an L-tone syllabic nasal (derived historically from *nì). In Kano, **nà** is commonly used in place of **ìn**. In certain fixed expressions, the 3m pronoun **yà** elides with the preceding word, e.g., **rânkà yà daɗè = [rânkài daɗè]** 'May your life be extended!' (greeting to a superior). The subjunctive is negated by means of the prohibitive marker **kadà** (or an equivalent phonologically reduced form), e.g., **kadà sù [Ø] dāwō** 'They should not return.' The subjunctive does not occur in Rel environments. The subjunctive expresses wishes, desires, purpose, obligation, etc. In the second person, it serves as a somewhat softer alternative to the imperative for expressing commands. It also allows the speaker to specifically identify the number and gender of the addressee, which is impossible with the bare imperative, e.g., **kù tāshì** 'Get up! (you (pl.))'; cf. **[tàshi]**imp 'Get up!' In sequences of commands, the first one is often in the imperative with subsequent ones in the subjunctive. The subjunctive is frequently preceded by a modal adverbial indicating necessity, preference, etc., such as **sai** 'must', **gāra** 'ought', **dōlè** 'perforce'. Examples:

kì dāwō dà wuri!	You (f.) come back early!
fìta kà yi wằsā!	Go out and (you) play!
mù haɗà kânmù!	Let's cooperate!
Allàh yà bā mù hàɓurī!	My God give us patience!
nufìnsà yà kòɽē sù	His intention was to chase them away.
gāra à ɓārà kuɗin àlbâshîn	One ought to increase the salary.
dōlè ma'àikàtā sù kōmằ aikìn	The workers must return to work.

Subjunctive sentences commonly occur in purposive 'in order to' clauses (often following the conjunction **dòmin/don** 'in order to'), or as embedded objects or complements of sentences expressing volition or opinion (where the subjunctive often corresponds to an infinitive in English), e.g.,

bài kō tsayằ ba <u>yà</u> ji kō lằbāɽìn yā ɓarè	He didn't even stop to hear if the story was finished.
kadà fa <u>kà</u> mântā <u>kà</u> dāwō dà kwalabâɽ	Don't forget to return the bottle.
inằ sô <u>kū</u> yârā <u>kù</u> tàimàkē nì	I want you children to help me.
yā kàmātà <u>kà</u> sâ yârònkà à makaɽantā	It behooves you to put your child in school.
wằ zâi hanà <u>kàtòn</u> <u>yà</u> ɓwācè mafì kyâu?	Who will prevent the hulk from grabbing
	(lit. that he should grab) the best one?

tā bugằ mîn wayằ bằ don kōmē ba sai don <u>tà</u> dằmē nì

   She telephoned me for no reason except to bother me.

munằ fằfùtùkā <u>mù</u> gamà aikìnmù dà saurī

   We are straining every nerve to finish our work quickly.

yā tunằ musù <u>sù</u> yi shirì

   He reminded them to make preparations. (lit. he reminded to.them (that) they should do preparation)

bài kyàutu mùtûm <u>yà</u> zằgi na gàba dà shī ba

   It is not appropriate for a person to insult someone senior to him.

yā fi saukī <u>kà</u> bi waccàn hanyàɽ

   It is easier to follow that road. (lit. it exceeds ease (that) you follow that road)

Sentences introduced by the subordinating conjunction 'before' (**kằfin = kằmìn**, both of which have L-L or L-H tone depending on dialect or ideolect) require the subjunctive regardless of the specific temporal interpretation.

yā zaunằ hakà mintì gōmà kằfin <u>yà</u> bā dà amsằ

   He sat like that for ten minutes before he replied.

zā <u>kà</u> shā wàhalằ kằfin <u>kà</u> kai ɓauyèn

   You're going to suffer a lot before you reach the village.

The subjunctive is negated by means of a semantically negative prohibitive marker **kadà** 'don't/should not/lest'. Structurally, it behaves more like an adverb such as **dōlè** 'perforce' than a true negative marker, i.e., **kadà kù tàfi!** 'Don't go! You musn't go!' is structurally parallel to **dōlè kù tàfi** 'You must go.' The marker **kadà** is often followed by a model particle for emphasis, e.g., **kadà fa kù bar̃ mù!** 'Now don't you (pl.) leave us!' Unlike true negative markers, which occur after an overt subject and immediately preceding the PAC, e.g., **[Bintà]**$_{sbj}$ **[bà]**$_{neg}$ **[zā tà]**$_{PAC}$ **amsằ ba** 'Binta will not answer', **kadà** usually occurs before the subject, separated from the subjunctive PAC, e.g., **[kadà]**$_{neg}$ **[Bintà]**$_{sbj}$ **[tà]**$_{PAC}$ **amsằ** 'Binta should not answer.'

Subjunctive sentences with **kadà** express negative commands. (The imperative per se is restricted to the affirmative.) Examples:

kadà kà yi masà tsīwà̀!	Don't badger him!
kadà sù sàkē shì	They shouldn't release him.
kadà Kànde tà dāwō	Kande should not return.
kadà fa kà mântā kà dāwō dà kwalabâr̃	Now don't forget to return the bottle!
(lit. prohibit now you (sub) forget you (sub) return with bottle)	

The **kadà** construction also functions as the negative subjunctive in purposive 'in order to' clauses to express 'lest' and in other embedded or complement clauses that indicate prohibition or irrealis, e.g.,

an d'aurè shi tam (don) kadà yà tsērè	They tied him up tightly so he wouldn't escape.
bà sù kulà dà kō sù ci kō kadà sù ci ba	They didn't care whether they should win or not.
sai mù zubà bak̃in-mâi yànzu (don) kadà injì yà lālàcē	
We should put in some engine oil now lest the engine get ruined.	

The prohibitive marker **kadà** has a common apocopated form **kâr̃**, e.g., **mun ɓōyè kâr̃ ɓàrāwò yà sācè manà** 'We hid (it) lest the thief steal (it) from us.' (The form **kâr̃** derives from loss of the final vowel, rhotacism of the final /d/ to /r̃/, and fusion of the H + L tone sequence into a surface fall.) Many speakers now treat **kâr̃** + the following wsp as a phonological word that tonally simplifies to H-L, e.g., **kâr̃ kà zō = kar̃-kà zō** 'Don't come!' The final **-r̃** commonly assimilates fully to the following consonant, e.g., **kar̃-kà zō = kak-kà zō**. (This assimilation/gemination is independent of the tone rule.)

> ΔDN: In some WH dialects, the assimilation has become obligatory whether the following word is a pronoun or a noun, i.e., the underlying form of the marker for these speakers has to be considered **kaG** (with F or H tone), where **G** represents an unspecified geminate, e.g., **kâm/kam Mūsā yà dāwō** 'Musa should not return.'

18. NEUTRAL (UNMARKED FORM)

A pronoun paradigm identical to the one used in the subjunctive also serves as a neutral unmarked form (but in the affirmative only).

The subjunctive is a distinct TAM with clearly defined syntactic and semantic properties. Analytically speaking, it enters in the formation of the PAC just like any other TAM. For example, in **Mūsā [yà] dāwō** 'Musa should return', **yà** represents the PAC [3m + sub], in the same way that **yâ** in **Mūsā [yâ] dāwō** 'Musa will likely return', represents the PAC [3m + pot]. What makes the subjunctive PAC appear different on the surface from other TAMs—and which results in confusion with other constructions—is the fact that the subjunctive TAM *phonologically* has zero shape.

As a result, the subjunctive looks on the surface exactly the same as PACs with bare wsp's that occur *morphosyntactically* without a TAM, and which most scholars, incorrectly, have labeled as subjunctive. I am calling this functionally distinct TAM-less PAC the "neutral" form. The analytical contrast here is between (1) a PAC with a TAM that happens to be phonologically zero, e.g., {3f + sub} = **tà** + /∅/ → **tà** 'she (sub)' and (2) a PAC that lacks a TAM, e.g., {3f + ( )} = **tà** → **tà** 'she (neut)'.

> °AN: This contrast may at first sight seem like a sleight of hand, but it is very real, both synchronically and historically, and it is essential to a proper understanding of the Hausa TAM system. Wolff (1993: 416ff) deserves credit for the important observation that the so-called

subjunctive paradigm synchronically incorporates two grammatically distinct, although phonologically identical, categories. My treatment differs from his in that he treats the non-subjunctive category as a full-fledged TAM, the "aorist," on a par with the other TAMs, whereas I see it as an unmarked neutral pronoun form lacking a TAM.

◊HN: In many West Chadic languages, the subjunctive—but not the neutral form (sometimes termed "Grundaspekt")—is distinctively characterized by a change in the verb stem (Newman and Schuh 1974), and thus it is possible to keep the two apart, even though, on the surface, they both lack overt TAMs. In present-day Hausa, on the other hand, verb stems themselves are not inflected for tense/aspect/mood (with the exception of the imperative), and thus the true subjunctive and the neutral form have fallen together. They can, nevertheless, still be distinguished synchronically by their different meanings and functions and the fact that only the subjunctive and not the neutral form can be negated using **kadà**.

The neutral form is found in a number of different constructions in which grammatical specification of tense/aspect is not essential since it is deducible from the sentential or pragmatic context. Examples include the following:

(1) Neutral TAM-less PACs appear (as bare wsp's) in the consequent clause of conditional sentences as an alternative to the future or the potential (see §17:1). The bare pronouns are optionally, but commonly, preceded by **sai** 'then'.

in sun zō, (sai) <u>ìn</u> tàfi kàsuwā	If/when they come, I'll go to market.
cf. in sun zō, zân/nà tàfi kàsuwā	If they come, I intend to/will probably go to market.
in an sâ masà kāyā dà yawà, sai <u>yà</u> gàji	If he's given too heavy a load, he'll tire.
kō kā sàmi lāyì sai <u>kà</u> ga bâ shi dà kyâu	
Even if you get a [telephone] line, you find it is no good.	

Note that the order of clauses in conditional sentences cannot be reversed if the neutral form is used. That is, whereas **zân tàfi kàsuwā in sun zō** 'I will go to market if they come' is a grammatical alternative for the more common **in sun zō, zân tàfi kàsuwā**, the sentence **sai ìn tàfi kàsuwā (in sun zō)** 'I will go to market if they come' (with **sai** obligatorily present) can exist only as an alternative to **in sun zō, (sai) ìn tàfi kàsuwā** as the answer to a question like **mè zā kà yi in sun zō?** 'What will you do if they come?' Note, moreover, that since the TAM-less form (unlike the subjunctive) does not occur in the negative, negative apodosis clauses must use the future or some other suitable TAM, e.g., **in sun zō, sai mù gayà musù** 'When they come we will tell them', but not ****in sun zō, kadà mù gayà musù** 'When they come, we will not tell them.' Rather, one needs **in sun zō, bà zā mù gayà musù ba** 'If they come we will not tell them.' The sentence **in sun zō, kadà mù gayà musù** 'If they come, let's not tell them' is grammatical, but only when the second clause is understood to be in the subjunctive, which, unlike the TAM-less construction, *may* be negated.

(2) The expression of an action temporally dependent on and closely connected to the time indicated in another clause is commonly accomplished by means of a neutral PAC not carrying its own TAM, e.g.,

san dà sukà zō, sai <u>ìn</u> tàfi kàsuwā	When they come, I'll go to market.
kàfìn yà zō nân, sai <u>ìn</u> gamà	Before he comes here, I'll finish.
bāyan bà kà gamà aikìn ba sànnan <u>kà</u> cê zā kà tàfi?	
(How is that) after you haven't finished the work then you say you're going to go?	
dàgà wannàn zaurèn, sai <u>à</u> ìsa wata ƙātùwař bàřgā	
After this room, then one reaches a certain large stable.	

(3) As indicated in descriptions of the individual tense/aspect/mood categories, paradigms with overt separable TAMs allow (in some cases require) the deletion of the repeated TAM in conjoined sentences. When the TAM is deleted, all that remains in the PAC is the bare wsp, which automatically takes default L tone. (Note that when a repeated continuous TAM is omitted, the resulting neutral PAC is followed by a finite verb form rather than a verbal noun or infinitive.) Examples:

[tanà]$_{cont}$ ɗinkìn hùlā <u>tà</u> kai kàsuwā <u>tà</u> sayar̃ (don) tà yi cèfànē dà kuɗîn

    She sews caps and takes them to the market and sells them in order to do her grocery shopping with the money. (< [ta nà]$_{cont}$ ɗinkìn hùlā [ta n̰à]$_{cont}$ kai kàsuwā [ta n̰à]$_{cont}$ sayar̃ (don) [tà + /Ø/]$_{sub}$ yi cèfànē dà kuɗîn)

(cf. the following without the deletions: [tanà]$_{cont}$ ɗinkìn hùlā [tanà]$_{cont}$ kâiwā kàsuwā [tanà]$_{cont}$ sayâr̃wā (don) [tà + Ø]$_{sub}$ yi cèfànē dà kuɗîn)

[mâ]$_{pot}$ tàfi gidā <u>mù</u> kāwō littāfîn

    We will likely go home and bring the book.

[sunà]$_{cont}$ fāràwā dà wannàn <u>sù</u> yi wannàn <u>sù</u> k̃ar̃è dà wannàn

    They begin with this one and do this one and finish with this one.yārinyà [zā tà]$_{fut}$ wankè zanè <u>tà</u> kuma gōgè (shi)

    The girl is going to wash her wrapper and also iron it.

don mè yârā [sukè]$_{Rcont1}$ masà ba'à <u>sù</u> yi ta jīfànsà dà dūtsè?

    Why are the children mocking him and throwing stones at him?

wàcē cè [takè]$_{Rcont1}$ ɗinkìn hùlā <u>tà</u> kai kàsuwā?

    Who (f.) is sewing the caps and taking them to market?

ran Jumma'à mutànē [Ø kàn]$_{hab}$ jē masallācī [sù Ø]$_{neut}$ sàuràri huɗubà

    On Fridays people go to the mosque and listen to the sermon.

The preceding example illustrates deletion of the wsp from the first PAC and deletion of the TAM from the second. One or the other, however, must appear, i.e., one cannot delete both items, leaving a completely empty PAC.

°AN: Conjoined sentences in the future, habitual, etc., are usually described as involving a category shift to the subjunctive in clauses other than the first, e.g., [sukàn]$_{hab}$ tàru [sukàn]$_{hab}$ shā tî ⇒ [sukàn]$_{hab}$ tàru [sù]$_{sub}$ shā tî 'They meet and drink tea.' This is a mistaken analysis. There is, in fact, no such shift. Rather, the structure is [sukàn]$_{hab}$ tàru [sù ( )] shā tî where the empty ( ) shows where the habitual TAM has been deleted. According to the analysis adopted here, the pronoun sù is *not* in the subjunctive, i.e., there has been no tense/aspect shift, but rather is a bare wsp occurring in a TAM-less PAC (i.e., the neutral unmarked form). (The analysis presented here is similar to the one anticipated many years ago by Gregersen (1967) in that it views the derivation as involving *deletion* of a tense/aspect element. Gregersen's error was in equating the subjunctive with *all* clauses without an overt aspectual particle.) Previous scholars were misled by the fact that the bare pronoun has L tone as opposed to the H that one finds, for example, in the habitual, and thus were led to postulate a "tense/aspect shift." In fact, the surface tone on the pronoun is a minor low-level phenomenon and is not a property of the subjunctive per se. The general tone rule is that if a wsp belonging to the light-syllable CV paradigm is followed by an L-tone TAM, it takes H tone by polarity; if it is not, it takes L tone by default, e.g., su + kàn → /súkàn/, but su + Ø → /sù/.

    Note that one *can* have a true subjunctive after a matrix clause. Such a sentence, however, would have a different meaning—reflecting the semantic attributes of the subjunctive—from one with a sequence of underlying habituals. It would, moreover, allow the insertion of the purposive marker don 'so that', e.g., [sukàn]$_{hab}$ tàru (don) [sù]$_{sub}$ shā tî 'They meet in order to drink tea.'

(4) In a sequence of sentences with an essentially timeless sense, the neutral TAM, often preceded by **sai**, can optionally be used in place of the explicit habitual TAM, e.g.,

dalằ tằ hau tằ sàuka   (The value of) the dollar rises and falls.
(Less cumbersome than **dalằ [takàn]**ₕₐᵦ **hau [takàn]**ₕₐᵦ **sàuka)**
in an kāwō àbinci, ằ ci sânnan ằ shā   When food is brought one eats and then one drinks.
wani sā'ì sai yằ zō nân, wani sā'ì sai mù̱ jē gidansà
      Sometimes he comes here, sometimes we go to his place.

(5) One means of indicating reported speech is by use of the clause **ìn ji** X 'according to X' (lit. I hear X) after the statement, e.g.,

zā à rufè fïlin-jirgin-samà ìn ji kằkằkin gwamnatì
      According to the government's spokesman, one is going to close the airport.
      (lit. fut 4p close airport I hear spokesman.of government)
'yan tāwāyè̱ sunằ gudù̱ ìn ji *Gaskiya*
      Gaskiya (the newspaper) reports that the rebels are running away.
Bellò yā shìga sōjà ìn ji Mūsā   Bello has joined the army, says Musa.

(6) The neutral form with the bare TAM-less pronouns, especially the impersonal, is commonly used in compounds, where exact specification of tense/aspect/mood is not needed, e.g.,

à-ci-bàlbàl   oil lamp (lit. one burns **bàlbàl** ('sound/sight of flickering'))
à-kò̱ri-kūrā   delivery truck (lit. one banishes hand-pushed cart)
mù-hàďu-à-bankì   type of cap (lit. we meet at bank)

Finally, it needs to be pointed out that although the fundamental distinction between the subjunctive and the homophonous neutral form is essential to an understanding of the Hausa TAM system, there are individual cases where it is not immediately evident which form is being used. For example, the bare wsp's used in clauses introduced by **màimakon** 'instead of' could be instantiations of neutral TAM-less PACs, but they could also represent a required use of the subjunctive, such as one finds after the subordinating conjunction **kàfìn** 'before'. Examples:

yā kirā nì màimakon [yà]ₙₑᵤₜ *or* ₛᵤᵦ **barì [nà]**ₛᵤᵦ **kirā shì**
      He called me instead of letting me call him.

zā tà jē kàntī [tà]ₙₑᵤₜ **ɓataȓ dà kuďîn dukà màimakon [tà]**ₙₑᵤₜ *or* ₛᵤᵦ **ādànà wasu à bankì**
      She is off to the store and is going to spend all of the money instead of saving some in the bank.

[References: Gouffé (1963/66, 1966/67, 1967/68); Gregersen (1967); Mohammed (1991); Newman and Schuh (1974); Schubert (1971–72); Schuh (1993)]

71. Tone and Intonation

1. TONAL INVENTORY

HAUSA has three surface tones: high (H), which has no accent mark, e.g., **shā** 'drink', **maza** 'quickly', **makaṙantā** 'school'; low (L), which is marked by a grave accent, e.g., **dà** 'with, and', **màtā** 'wife'; **fuskà** 'face', **àkwàtì** 'box', **fìkàfìkai** 'wings'; and falling (F), which is marked by a circumflex accent, e.g., **dâ** 'formerly', **tî** 'tea', **mântā** 'forget', **lìmâm** 'imam', **kìlîf** 'paper clip', **kōmôwā** 'returning'. The language has no rising tone.

°AN: It has long been the transcription convention among Hausaists to leave high-tone vowels without tone marks rather than to use an accute accent, as is commonly done by Africanists working on other language groups. This convention does not entail any claim about which Hausa tone, if any, is unmarked from a theoretical phonological point of view.

1.1. Falling tone

Falling tone occurs only on heavy, bimoraic syllables. Light syllables, which consist of only one mora, carry only single level tones. (In the transcription convention adopted here, the circumflex on an open vowel indicates falling tone *and* length, i.e., /shâa/ 'drinking' is transcribed as **shâ**.) Note that the falling tone requirement is specified in terms of the need for a heavy *syllable*; a falling tone does not necessarily have to be on a long vowel, nor even on a syllable closed with a sonorant coda, e.g., **gyâffā** 'sides', **ƙâttā** 'huge (pl.)'.

The falling tone can be decomposed into a sequence of H + L on a single syllable, e.g., **yârā** (F-H = HL-H) 'children'. Three processes suffice to demonstrate the validity of this analysis.

°AN: The fact that the falling tone can be decomposed into H + L does not imply that it lacks the status of a distinct phonemic toneme. The situation is no different from that of languages that have complex prenasalized consonants like /**mb**/ or affricates like /**dz**/, all of which are phonetically decomposable, but which, nevertheless, may exist at some level as unit phonemes.

(a) In words shortened by the loss of a vowel, an original H-L tone sequence on two syllables becomes HL (= F) on a single syllable, e.g.,

kadà H-L =	**kâṙ** HL = F	don't
Kàbīrù L-H-L =	**Kàbîṙ** L-HL = L-F	proper name
mabiyìyā H-H-L-H =	**mabîyyā** H-HL-H = H-F-H	female follower
dābùgī [dv] H-L-H =	**dâbgī** HL-H = F-H	anteater

(b) When the L-tone definite article `ˋn` / `ˋṙ` is attached to a word ending in H tone, the result is a falling tone (i.e., H-L → HL = F), e.g.,

597

wàndō	trousers	+ `-n →	wàndôn L-F	the trousers
rìgā	gown	+ `-r̃ →	rìgâr̃ L-F	the gown
tāgōgī	windows	+ `-n →	tāgōgîn H-H-F	the windows

(c) In assigning tone to the stabilizer (**nē** (m. or pl.) / **cē** (f.)), whose tone is always polar to that of the preceding syllable, words with a final F tone behave as if they ended in L (i.e., F = HL), e.g.,

hàr̃âm nē L-F H It's prohibited; **nân nē** F H It's here; **gōnâr̃ cē** H-F H It's the farm.
cf. **zōbè nē** H-L H It's a ring; **mōtà cē** H-L H It's a car; **gwàdò nē** L-L H It's a blanket.
cf. **rìgā cè** L-H L It's a gown; **nan nè** H L It's there (by you); **kèke nè** L-H L
= **kèkè nē** L-L H It's a bicycle.

◊HN/°AN: Although the falling tone can structurally be analyzed as a combination of H + L on a single syllable, there are, nevertheless, areas in which one needs to think of it as a unitary contour. For example, the many intra- and interdialectal contour simplification rules (discussed elsewhere) are explicable only if one views falling tone psycholinguistically as a disfavored element in Hausa. Significantly, in drumming, a falling tone is always played as a single tone with a contour and not as a sequence of H + L (Ames, Gregersen, and Neugebauer 1971). Finally, it appears that at least some synchronic falling tones on monosyllabic words derive historically not from H-L sequences, but rather from original words with level H tone by a phonetic process of tone bending (Newman 1992a, 1995).

1.1.1. Falling tone simplification
With certain grammatical morphemes, a sequence involving a falling tone is simplified to a sequence of level (but opposite) tones.

The sequence F-L commonly changes to H-L when a noun with a definite article is followed by the relativizer **dà** 'that'. This change is optional in SH; it is obligatory in some other dialects, e.g.,

gidân dà mukà ganī (→) **gidan dà mukà ganī**   the house that we saw
(but **gidân** 'the house' by itself does not simplify to ****gidan**)
rìgâr̃ dà mukà sàyā (→) **rìgar̃ dà mukà sàyā**   the gown that we bought

This simplification is particularly common with the morphologically complex relative pronouns and adverbs in which the **dà** is an incorporated element.

wândà = wandà	the one (m.) who
wâddà = waddà	the one (f.) who
sândà (< sā'àn dà) = sandà	(the time) when
îndà = indà	where (e.g., **nā san îndà / indà yakè ɓòye** I know where it is hidden.)

Some speakers, especially outside the core SH area, apply the F-L → H-L simplification rule to the prohibitive marker **kâr̃** (< **kadà**) plus the following low-tone wsp, e.g.,

kâr̃ kà dāwō (→) **kar̃ kà dāwō!**   Don't return!
kâr̃ mù ɓatà (→) **kar̃ mù ɓatà**   Lest we get lost.

The change F-H → L-H is also found, but it is more limited (but see below for dialectal changes). In SH, it is essentially restricted to the definite demonstratives and to the lexicalized adverb 'then', e.g.,

wânnan (→) wànnan that, near you (m. or f.); wâncan (→) wàncan that yonder (m.)
wâccan (→) wàccan that yonder (f.); sânnan (< sā'àn nan that time) (→) sànnan then

1.2. Absence of rising tone

Hausa does not have a rising tone corresponding to its falling tone. LH tones on a single syllable, which sometimes develop in intermediate structure as a result of synchronic processes or historical changes, automatically simplify to H or to L depending on the context. There are two conditioned rules:

Rule 1: LH → L / H____ (i.e., LH on a single syllable simplifies to L if the preceding tone in the word is H). Examples: (Note: The change of syllable final /y/ to /i/ and the depalatalization of /sh/ to /s/ are phonologically automatic and have nothing to do with the tone rule per se.)

gawàyī H-L-H (→) *gawày′ H-LH → gawài H-L   charcoal
mukà yi H-L-H (→) *mukày′ H-LH → mukài H-L   we did
mùƙaddàshī L-H-L-H (→) *mùƙaddàs′ L-H-LH → mùƙaddàs L-H-L   deputy, regent

Rule 2: LH → H / elsewhere (i.e., LH on a single syllable simplifies to H except when meeting the conditions for Rule 1). Examples (with the resultant H tone marked for clarity):

tàusàyī L-L-H (→) *tàusày′ L-LH → tàusái L-H   pity [dv]
jìmillà L-H-L (→) *jìmlà LH-L → jímlà H-L   total
*kàwa L-H (→) *kàw′ LH → káu H   move away
kwàɗayī L-L-H = *kwàɗày′ L-LH → kwàɗái L-H   lust [dv]
ɗòyī L-H (→) *ɗòy′ LH → ɗwái H   stench [dv]
tàwa L-H (→) *tàw′ LH → táu H   mine [dv]
*ɗàwúkà > *ɗàúkà LH-L → ɗáukà H-L   take, carry
*nàn′ LH → nán H   there by you
cf. nân F (= HL)   here by me

°AN: [i] The LH to H rule (Rule 2 above) was discovered independently by Parsons (1955) and Leben (1971). Until recently it was thought that this was an unconditioned rule. The observation that the simplification of the LH contour was subject to phonological conditioning was first pointed out in Newman (1995).
[ii] For a long time, the verb ɗaukà 'take' puzzled Hausaists because it looked like a grade 1 verb with H-L tone in its citation form, but behaved like a grade 2 verb in its pre-object forms. The explanation is that ɗaukà derives from a regular *trisyllabic* gr2 verb with L-H-L tone and that the surface H-L is a phonological accident due to vowel syncope and the LH to H tonal simplification rule.

2. FUNCTION OF TONE

Tone functions both lexically and grammatically. Although tone does not have a functional load comparable to that of many West African languages like Igbo or Yoruba, it does serve to distinguish a number of lexical items from one another, e.g.,

kai you (m.), kâi head; sū they, sû fishing; kūkà baobab tree, kūkā crying; wuyà neck, wùyā trouble; gōrà staff, bamboo, gòrā large gourd; bàba dad, bābà mom, aunt; wārī stench; wārì separating, ràinā look after a baby, rainà despise, have contempt for

Grammatically, tone serves a number of important functions, for example, in inflecting nouns for plurality, in creating different verb grades, in forming verbal nouns (and deverbal nouns), in deriving adverbs from nouns, and in the marking of tense/aspect/mood. The grammatical use of tone is sometimes done by tone alone and sometimes in conjunction with changes in vowel length. Examples:

màtā wife, **mātā** wives, women; **dafà** to cook, **dàfā** cook! (imperative); **hàr̃bē** shoot (at) (gr2 pre-pronoun form), **har̃bè** shoot dead, execute (gr4 form); **shā** drink, **shâ** drinking; **ma'aikatā** workplace, factory, **ma'àikàtā** workers; **idò** eye, **ido** in the eye; **ƙasā** earth, ground, **ƙasà** on the ground; **tā** she (completive), **tâ** she (potential)

3. TONE DOMAIN, TONE MELODIES, TONE ASSIGNMENT

3.1. *Tone-bearing unit*

The primary tone-bearing unit is the syllable. Normally, there is one tone per syllable and one syllable per tone, e.g., **kujèrā** 'chair' has three syllables **ku.jè.rā** and three tones H-L-H, **santalēlìyā** 'svelte' has five syllables **san.ta.lē.li.yā** and five tones H-H-H-L-H. If a word has more tones than syllables, then two tones can dock on the same syllable if that syllable has the necessary weight (i.e., two moras) to carry the two tones, e.g., **shânyē** 'drink up', which has three tones (H-L-H) but only two syllables **shan.yē**, carries both the H and the L on the first syllable, which is realized as F. Similarly, the word **ɗaukà**, which has three tones (L-H-L) but only two syllables **ɗau.kà**, carries both the L and the H on the first syllable, the non-occurring rising tone being realized as H.

3.2. *Tone melodies*

Whereas syllables carry individual tones, morphemes and words have associated tone patterns or melodies, e.g., **sūnàyē**$)^{HLH}$ 'names' is realized as **sūnàyē** with H-L-H tone; **dulmuya**$)^{LHL}$ 'sink' is realized as **dùlmuyà** with L-H-L. The tones of the melody are assigned to the syllables from right to left. If there are more syllables than tones, one keeps on spreading the tone in a leftward fashion, e.g., **makar̃antū**$)^{LH}$ → **màkàr̃antū** 'schools'; **ƙididdigā**$)^{HLH}$ → **ƙididdìgā** 'calculate'. If there are more tones than syllables, then one assigns the tones from right to left until one has run out of syllables, whereupon one assigns the remaining tone to the initial syllable (assuming that it is a bimoraic syllable that can carry two tones), e.g.,

zobbā$)^{HLH}$ → **zôb.bā**	rings (with HL on the initial syllable)	
mantā$)^{HLH}$ → **mân.tā**	forget (with HL on the initial syllable)	
ci$)^{LH}$ → **ci**	eat! (with only the H assigned to **ci** since the L cannot also be attached to the light monomoraic syllable)	

°AN: Jaggar (1982) has suggested that at an intermediate level, both the L and the H be assigned to the imperative form **ci**, with LH being realized as H in accordance with the tone rules described above (§1.2). Although such an analysis would generate the right surface form in this particular case, it strikes me as counterintuitive. My objection to Jaggar's proposal is that it runs counter to the overall functioning of the tone system which supports the contention that a monomoraic tone-bearing unit in Hausa cannot carry more than one tone.

3.3. *Tone-integrating suffixes*

Most suffixes have an associated tone melody that overrides the tones of the base to which the suffix is attached, e.g., **rìgā** + **-unā**$)^{HL}$ → **rīgunà**$)^{HL}$ 'gowns', where the H-L melody spreads across the entire word. These are referred to as "tone-integrating" suffixes.

°AN: The distinction between suffixes that are tone-integrating and those that are not was first presented in Newman (1986b), where the concept is discussed in full.

A tone-integrating suffix is indicated by a single righthand parenthesis marker) with an attached tone melody T. For example the plural marker-**ai**)^{LH} is a tone-integrating suffix. The convention is that the rightmost)^T overrides any earlier instance of)^T and keeps spreading until it reaches a new tonal domain, like that found with a tonally specified prefix. This operation is shown in the following examples. (The replacement of the stem-final vowel, which regularly accompanies affixation, doesn't concern us here.)

fita)^{LH} go out + -**ō**)^H ventive ⇒ **fit-ō**)^H → **fitō** come out
ribɗa)^{HL} beat + -**ayyā**)^{LHL} mutuality ⇒ **ribɗ-ayyā**)^{LHL} → **rìbɗayyằ** severely hitting one another
(**ba-**)^L ethnonymic prefix + **Katsina**)^{LHL} Katsina + -**ē**)^{HL} ethnonymic suffix
⇒ (**ba-**)^L (**Katsin-ē**)^{HL} → **Bàkatsinè** a man from Katsina

If more than one suffix is added, the tone of the rightmost tone-integrating suffix will prevail, e.g.,

daka)^{HL} pound + -**akkē**)^{LHH} past participle + -**u**)^{LH} plural ⇒ **dakakkē**)^{LHH} + -**ū**)^{LH}
⇒ **dakakkū**)^{LH} → **dàkàkkū** pounded (pl.)

In one instance, the imperative, the tone-integrating suffix is sometimes segmentally zero, i.e., the L-H tone pattern alone serves as the grammatical marker, e.g.,

tāshi)^{HL} get up + Ø)^{LH} imperative ⇒ **tāshi**)^{LH} → **tằshi**! Get up!
haɽbà)^{HL} shoot + -**ō**)^H ventive ⇒ **haɽbō**)^H shoot (this way or for us) + Ø)^{LH} imperative ⇒
haɽbō)^{LH} → **hàɽbō**! Shoot (this way or for us)!

A few suffixes are not tone integrating. These are indicated by double parentheses ( )^T with an attached tone. The feminine suffix (-**iyā**)^{LH}, for example, manifests its intrinsic L-H tone when added to a stem, but it does not override the stem's original tone, e.g.,

gajērē)^{LHH} short + (-**iyā**)^{LH} ⇒ (**gàjērē**)(-**ìyā**) → **gàjērìyā**   short (f.)
jakādā)^{LHL} emissary + (-**iyā**)^{LH} ⇒ (**jàkādằ**)(-**ìyā**) → **jàkādìyā**   emissary (f.)

Similarly, the weak verbal noun formative (-**wā**)^{LH} is non-integrating, e.g.,

kaɽantā)^{HLH} read + (-**wā**)^{LH} ⇒ (**kaɽàntā**)(ˋwā) → **kaɽàntâwā** reading (where the L of the suffix phonologically docks onto the preceding syllable to produce a fall)**fitō**)^H come out (< **fita**)^{LH} go out + -**ō**)^H ventive) + (-**wā**)^{LH} ⇒ (**fitō**)(ˋwā) → **fitôwā** coming out

Some affixes by their nature are necessarily non-integrating. Prefixes, for example, cannot be tone integrating because tone assignment operates from right to left. (They either have their own tone or they fall within the domain of a tone-integrating suffix.) In addition, toneless elements (like the feminine suffix -**ā**) cannot be integrating because they lack an underlying tone specification, e.g.,

(**ba-**)^L ethnonymic prefix + **Kanō**)^{HL} ⇒ **Bàkanò**   man from Kano
(**CVG-**)^L sensory quality adjective prefix + **zurfā**)^H deep ⇒ **zùzzurfā**   very deep
(**jākī**)^{LH} donkey + -**ā**) feminine ⇒ (**jāk-ā**)^{LH} → **jàkā**   she-ass

◊HN: The non-integrating, but tonally specified, feminine suffix (-**iyā**)^LH derives historically from the toneless suffix -**ā** by morphologization of what were originally phonetic glide and surface tone variants. It is this origin as a toneless morpheme that explains why (-**iyā**)^LH, unlike most derivational and inflectional suffixes, is non-integrating.

3.4. Tonal polarity

A small number of morphemes are specified as having polar tone, i.e., their tones are always opposite that of an adjacent tone. Tonal polarity occurs both leftward and rightward depending on the individual morpheme. (The ÷ sign has been employed to indicate the direction of dependency.) The stabilizer ÷**nē** / ÷**cē**, for example, always has a tone that is opposite that of the preceding syllable. The possessive markers **nā**÷ / **tā**÷, on the other hand, take a tone opposite to that of a following pronoun. Weak subject pronouns belonging to the light paradigm (see §59:1.2.3) are polar to the adjacent TAM markers, whichever side they occur on, e.g.,

rìgā + (÷**cē**) → **rìgā cè**	It's a gown.
but **mōtà̀** + (÷**cē**) → **mōtà̀ cē**	It's a car.
(**nā**÷) + -**kà** → **nākà**	yours
but (**nā**÷) + -**wa** → **nà̀wa**	mine
(**ta**÷) + **kàn fìta** → **takàn fìta**	She goes out. (habitual)
but **zā** (÷**ta**) **fìta** → **zā tà fìta**	She will go out. (future)

°AN: The most commonly cited example of tonal polarity in Hausa turns out not to be so. On the basis of such examples as **sun kāmà̀ ta** 'They caught her' vs. **sun mà̀rē tà** 'They slapped her', scholars have traditionally described the direct object pronouns as having polar tone. This is incorrect. There is not one set with polar tone, but rather two distinct object sets, each with its own tone specification. The first is a strong direct object set, which always has high tone regardless of the tone of the preceding syllable, e.g., **sun kāmà̀ ta** 'They caught her', **kà̀mā ta!** 'Catch her!'; **sun bincìkē ta** 'They investigated her.' The other is a weak object clitic set, which normally appears with low tone (which one *could* argue is due to polarity, although I would think that default or tonal incorporation is a better analysis), but which in certain contexts has high tone, e.g., **sun mà̀rē tà** 'They slapped her', **mà̀rè-ta!** 'Slap her!'

ΔDN: The Guddiri dialect has a few morphemes with polar tone in addition to the ones found in SH (Bagari 1982). (In SH, these morphemes both have H tone.) These are (a) the diminutive marker **ɗan**÷ (m.) /ʼ**yaȓ**÷ (f.) /ʼ**yan**÷ (pl.), and the preposition **don**÷ 'for, for the sake of'. Examples:

(a) **ɗan rà̀gō** 'small ram'; ʼ**yaȓ kà̀zā** 'chick'; **ɗàn ƙauyè̀** 'small village'; **ɗàn yārò̀** 'small boy'; **yā ɗan mà̀rē shì** 'He slapped him a little'; **yā ɗàn mōtsà̀** 'He moved a little.'

(b) **don wà̀?** 'for whom?'; **don Kànde** 'for the sake of Kande'; **dòn kōwā** 'for everyone'; **dòn Allàh** 'for the sake of God'

It should be emphasized that polarity is understood to refer to a situation where a morpheme appears as H or L under fixed conditions and where there is no *synchronic* basis for choosing one tone rather than the other as basic. Polarity thus has to be distinguished from tonal dissimilation, which describes a synchronic state of affairs in which one of the two occurring tones can be specified as basic and the other derived by rule.

◊HN: Viewed diachronically, polarity (almost) always begins as dissimilation. Thus the L tone variant of the Guddiri diminutive (**ɗan**÷) (e.g., **ɗàn yārò̀** 'small boy'), described in the note above, certainly began as dissimilation of an underlying H-tone morpheme (which still exists as such in

SH). The synchronic question one always has to ask is whether native speakers still have some sense of what the "real" underlying tone is or whether that information has been lost with the result that polarity becomes the underlying representation (as must be the case with the SH stabilizer).

3.5. Toneless morphemes

Items without an inherent tone specification get their surface tone in one of three ways: spreading, incorporation, or default.

(a) Some inherently toneless morphemes and all epenthetic vowels get their tones by rightward spreading of the preceding tone, e.g.,

*adò)^{HL} + -ā) → ad(u)wằ → aduwằ   desert date tree
(where the H tone of the initial syllable spreads to the surface epenthetic /u/ of the second syllable)
*gishri)^{HH} → gish(i)rī → gishirī   salt
(where the H tone of the initial syllable spreads to the epenthetic /i/ of the surface second syllable)

(b) Some toneless morphemes are incorporated into the stem and get their tone from normal assignment of the tone melody after the fusion of the affix, e.g.,

duguzunzumī)^{LHLH} + -ā → duguzunzumā)^{LHLH} → dùgùzunzùmā
    shaggy-haired, unkempt (f.)
mārē)^{LH} + Ø)^{LH} 'imperative' + -ta → mārē-ta)^{LH} → mằrē-ta!   Slap her!
cf. kāmā)^{HL} + Ø)^{LH} 'imperative' + (ta)^{H} → (kāmā)^{LH} (ta)^{H} → kằmā ta!   Catch her!

(c) Weak subject pronouns that occur without an overt TAM marker (as in the subjunctive or the neutral zero form) are assigned L tone by default, e.g.,

kadà [kà Ø]$_{sub}$ fita!   Don't you go out!
ran jumma'ằ mutằnē sukàn jē masallācī [sù ()]$_{neut}$ sàurằri huɗubằ
    On Fridays people go to the mosque and listen to the sermon.

4. TONE PRESERVATION / FLOATING TONES

4.1. Creation and attachment of floating tones

If a vowel undergoes apocope or syncope (this latter being less common), the tone typically remains. (The apocope is common with specific morphemes and with certain contractions.) The resulting floating tone then attaches to the preceding syllable, subject to the proviso that two tones cannot be attached to a light syllable. The vowel dropping may be optional, but the attachment of the floating tone is required. If the floating tone is attached to an identical tone, the process operates vacuously, e.g., àljanī L-H-H 'jinn' (opt. apocope) → àljan L-HH (→ L-H) ; bà yà L-L 'neg 3m (he didn't)' → bài LL (→ L) . If a floating L attaches to a preceding H, it produces a surface F, i.e., HL → F, e.g., minì H-L 'to me' (→) min˺ HL → mîn F. A floating H attached to a preceding L cannot produce a rising tone because Hausa doesn't have a rising contour. As provided for in the rising tone elimination rules (§1.2 above), the intermediate LH will surface either as L (if preceded by an H in the same word) or, more often, as H. Examples:

kadà H-L = kâr̃ F   don't
masà H-L = mâs F   to him
mùtumì L-H-L = mùtûm L-F   man

shàr̃îfì L-H-L = shàr̃îf L-F   holy man tracing descent from the Prophet

zā yà H-L = zā-yʻHL → zâi F   he (future)

yā màrē nì H L-H-L = yā màrē-nʻ H L-HL → yā màrân H L-F He slapped me.

yā sàkē tà H L-H-L = yā sàuʻ tà H LH-L (where /k/ has weakened to /u/) → yā sau tà
     H H-L   He released her. (i.e., divorced her)

tā sàyi L-H nāmằ = tā sàyʻ LH nāmằ → tā sai H nāmằ   She bought meat.

In many cases the H-L underlying a surface F tone is synchronically recoverable (as illustrated above). In other cases, e.g., with the internal geminate plural formation, the F is the historical result of vowel deletion followed by tonal reattachment, but the presumed earlier form cannot be postulated to have any synchronic reality, e.g.,

zôbbā   rings F-H (< HL-H) < *zōbàbā H-L-H (reconstructed form), pl. of zōbè
râssā   branches F-H (< HL-H) < *rāsàsā H-L-H (reconstructed form), pl. of rēshè

4.2. Underlying floating tones

Floating tones in Hausa generally emerge in intermediate structure from the loss of a vowel. One can, however, cite three common grammatical morphemes that contain a floating L tone as part of the underlying representation. These are (a) the verbal noun marker ʻwā, (b) the definite article ʻn / ʻr̃ / ʻn (m./f./pl.), and (c) the postnominal demonstrative ʻnan 'that near you' (and its distal counterpart ʻcan). The markers -wā and nan/can have H tone, while the floating tone attaches to the immediately preceding syllable. If the stem to which these morphemes is added ends in L tone, then the floating tone attaches vacuously; if the stem-final tone is H, then the result of the attachment is a surface fall, e.g.,

(a) rufè close + ʻwā →	rufèwā	closing (vacuous L-tone attachment)
kar̃àntā read + ʻwā →	kar̃àntâwā	reading
dāwō return + ʻwā →	dāwôwā	returning
(b) watằ month + ʻn →	watàn	the month (vacuous L-tone attachment)
hùlā cap + ʻr̃ →	hùlâr̃	the cap
manòmā farmers + ʻn →	manòmân	the farmers
(c) jihàr̃ + ʻcan →	jihàr̃ can	that state far away (vacuous L-tone attachment)
hùlar̃ + ʻnan →	hùlâr̃ nan	that cap near you
zōmon + ʻnan →	zōmôn nan	that hare near you

ΔDN: In SH the potential TAM is formed by adding the suffix -à to a pronoun belonging to the light paradigm, e.g., ku + -à → kwâ 'you (pl.).pot'. In some WH dialects, it is indicated by adding a floating L tone to a heavy pronoun, e.g., kun + ʻ → kûn 'you (pl.).pot'.

4.3. Clipping vs. apocopation.

In a small number of words, the final vowel is morphologically *clipped* rather than phonologically apocopated. That is, the short form without the final vowel is grammatically required or lexically chosen, but not phonologically determined. In such cases, the tone is generally deleted along with the vowel, e.g.,

far̃ (not **fâr̃) = fāɗà   fall onto
e.g., yā far̃ matà dà faɗà   He fell upon her with fighting. (i.e., he attacked her)
ƙas (not **ƙâs) = ƙasà   on the ground
tùkùn (not **tùkun < **tùkùnʻ) = tùkùna   not yet

The deletion of whole syllables or syllable rimes, which applies to certain grammatical forms and which is common with short forms of proper names, also entails the deletion of the associated tone. (With certain tone patterns, the output is the same whether one views the process as clipping or apocopation.) Examples:

maràs (= **maràr̃**) < **maràshin**	lacking in	**ran** < **rānar̃**	the day of	
Har̃ū < **Har̃ūnà**	proper name	**Inū** < **Inūsà**	proper name	

5. CANONICAL PATTERNS

5.1. Monosyllabic words

The tone of nonderived monosyllabic words depends to a great extent on the word class. Function words occur both with L tone, e.g., **dà** 'with, and', **mè?** 'what?', **bà** (initial negative marker), and with H tone, e.g., **kō** 'or', **ta** 'via', **ba** (final negative marker). They rarely occur with F tone apart from **shîn** (introduces doubt questions), **bâ** (negative existential marker), and **zâ** (allative marker). Pronouns occur as H or as L depending on the syntactic category, e.g., possessive pronouns are L, e.g., **zanèn-tà** 'her body cloth', whereas the strong direct object pronouns are H, e.g., **yā kāmà ta** 'He caught her.' (The potential pronoun forms with F tone, e.g., **tâ dāwō** 'She will likely return', are bimorphemic, being composed of an H-tone wsp (e.g., **ta**) plus the L-tone TAM -**à**.) Monosyllabic ideophones most often have H tone, e.g., **fes** 'emphasizes cleanliness', **kam** 'emphasizes being tied tightly'; but some have L or, less often, F tone, e.g., **sùm** 'describes an outburst of a bad smell', **bîf** 'sound of heavy object falling'.

The gr0 monoverbs, i.e., CV(V) verbs, e.g., **ci** 'eat', **shā** 'drink', all have H tone. The verbs **sâ** 'put' and **cê** 'say', with F tone, are reduced disyllabic verbs (at least historically) that one can treat as irregular grade 1 and grade 4 verbs, respectively. Most monosyllabic nouns, all of which consist of a heavy syllable, have F tone, e.g., **wâ** 'elder brother', **kâi** 'head', **wûl** 'wool'. A few—about six out of sixty—have H tone, namely, **ɗā** / **'yā** 'son/daughter'; **fā** 'flat rock', **hus** 'lint at the bottom of the pocket' [dv]; **ƙwai** (< *ƙwāyī) 'egg', **nai** 'nine pence' (in old Nigerian currency), **sau** (= **sāwū**) 'foot(print)'; **yau** = **yāwū** 'saliva'. None have L tone except for two grammaticalized items, namely, **jìm**, which is used in **jìm kàɗan** = **jimàwā kàɗan** 'after a while, shortly', and **sàu** 'times' (presumably derived from **sau** 'foot'), e.g., **sàu gōmà** 'ten times'.

◊HN: Synchronically, F tone often derives from the loss of a vowel with L tone, where the tone is preserved, e.g., **zân** 'I will' < **zā nì**. Historically, on the other hand, the monosyllabic nouns with F tone appear to come either from (a) old monosyllabic H-tone words by a process of "tone bending" or "tone slippage" (Newman 1992a), i.e., **mâi** 'oil' < *mai (< Proto-Chadic *mar), or (b) monosyllabic loanwords—mostly from English—of which there are large numbers, e.g., **shât** 'shirt', **tôn** 'ton'. The occurring monosyllabic words with H tone appear to be recent developments from disyllabic H-H words, some of which still exist as alternatives, e.g., **yau** < **yāwū** 'saliva'.

5.2. Disyllabic and polysyllabic words

Nonderived disyllabic words have three normal tone patterns: H-L, L-H, and H-H, e.g., **hantà** 'liver', **jiyà** 'yesterday'; **gàrī** 'town', **sàndā** 'stick'; **zōmō** 'rabbit', **darē** 'night'.

The most common tone patterns for nonderived trisyllabic nouns are H-L-H, H-H-L, L-H-L, and L-H-H, e.g.,

durùmī	fig tree	**dūkìyā**	wealth
jēmāgè	bat	**kibiyà**	arrow

| màkāhò̀ | blind man | kàtangà̀ | large piece of broken pot |
| jìminā | ostrich | màrak̄ī | calf |

The tone pattern L-L-H is very common with noun plurals, e.g., gò̀nàkī 'farms', mà̀làmai 'teachers', and also with frozen reduplicated nouns, e.g., gàngàmō 'turmeric', kwàr̄kwàshī 'dandruff'. It is less common with basic lexical items, but it does occasionally occur, e.g., tàfàsā 'a senna plant', tà̀kàlmī 'shoe, pair of shoes' (originally a plural). Polysyllabic nouns with an all H pattern tend to be (a) plurals with the -ōCī suffix, e.g., tāgōgī 'windows' (< tāgà̀), iskōkī 'spirits' (< iskà̀); (b) basic disyllabic nouns with an epenthetic vowel, e.g., kuturū 'leper' (< *kutru), gishirī 'salt' (< *gishrī); (c) basic disyllabic nouns with a feminative suffix added, e.g., tsāmiyā 'tamarind' (< *tsāme + -iyā), bēguwā 'porcupine' (< *bēgo + -uwā); and (d) frozen reduplicated nouns, e.g., birbirī 'Bruce's fruit pigeon', gaggāfā 'bateleur eagle'.

5.2.1. L-L tone
Apart from ideophones, words ending in L-L tone, whether disyllabic L-L words or polysyllabic L-L-L or (H/L)-H-L-L words, are relatively uncommon and mostly represent identifiable or presumed loanwords. (There are approximately eighty such words.) Most L-L final nouns end in a short final vowel, or, less often, in the consonant /n/. Examples:

àdùdù	large lidded woven basket	kùzà	tin
asfìr̄ìn	aspirin	lilìmàn	liniment
cir̄ò̀mà	traditional title (prince)	mangwàr̄ò̀	mango (fruit or tree)
fur̄sùnà	prisoner	shè̀là	proclamation
gyàlè	shawl, veil	tambùlàn	drinking glass

> AN: It is possible to get a sentence consisting of all L-tone words, but this is clearly a tour de force: gà̀ àlàlà dà àyàbà à àkwà̀tì 'There's *alala* (a type of bean food) and bananas in the box.'

Ideophones, which often exhibit partial or full reduplication, commonly end in L-L tone. The final vowel, if there is one, can be long, e.g.,

cakō-càkò̀	sharp and pointed (e.g., nails); unaligned teeth
dàɓàs	heavily (e.g., of a fat person sitting on the floor)
dàlàlà	in a slimy manner, viscously (e.g., saliva, okra)
hulū-hùlù̀	swollen, puffed up (e.g., eyelids, cheeks, pimples)
k̄è̀r̄èr̄è	standing disrespectfully before one's superior

Apart from ideophones, there are only a very few lexical L-L words with a long final vowel. These are yà̀yà̀ = k̄ā̀k̄à̀? 'how?'; bìsà̀ 'in accordance with'; tà̀kwar̄ākwàr̄à̀ (= kwàr̄ā-kwàr̄ā) 'stilts'; and wà̀tò̀ (= wà̀tàu) 'that is to say'; plus the following polysyllabic English loanwords: asambù̀lè̀ 'assembly at school'; dìsfansà̀r̄è̀ 'dispensary'; elemantà̀r̄è̀ 'elementary school'; fir̄āmà̀r̄è̀ 'primary school'; lōtà̀r̄è̀ lottery; mājistà̀r̄è̀ magistrate; r̄ēlù̀wè̀ (= r̄ēlù̀wài) 'railroad'; and sakandà̀r̄è̀ 'secondary school'.

5.2.2. Falling tone
Falling tone in nonderived disyllabic and polysyllabic words typically occurs on the last syllable. (There are some hundred words with final F, mostly loanwords from English and Arabic.) Here the F represents either (a) a truncated H-L disyllabic sequence or (b) an approximation, especially in the case of English loanwords, of the stress/intonation in the source language, e.g.,

(a) bàmbûs (= bàmbūshì)	type of perfume	mùtûm (< mùtumì)	man, person
làdân (= làdānì)	muezzin	shàr̃îf (= shàr̃īfì)	holy man
lìmân (= lìmāmì)	imam	zàitûn (= zàitūnì)	olive (tree)
(b) àfîl	legal appeal	kar̃anshâf	crankshaft
bàsìlîn	vaseline	kùnî	quinine
cìngâm	chewing gum	r̃àfàlî	referee
fìlâs	thermos, flask	zà'àfàr̃ân	saffron

Falling tone in initial position is found in derived words such as noun plurals (e.g., sâssā 'sections'), abstract nouns (e.g., wâutā 'foolishness'), frozen reduplicated nouns (e.g., bêlbēlà 'cattle egret'), and grade 4 forms of certain monoverbs (e.g., shânyē 'drink up'). It is also found in a few exclamations (e.g., yâuwā 'bravo!') and in a dozen gr1 verbs, many of which contain the -TA verbalizing suffix (e.g., bâutā 'worship', mântā 'forget', shâidā 'testify'). (These verbs all behave *as if* they were trisyllabic.) A handful of nonderived nouns have F tone, where it probably signifies the historical loss of a low-tone vowel. The presumed lost segment is sometimes identifiable, but not aways. Examples (complete):

bâmmī	palm wine
dâbgī	anteater (< dābùgī [dv])
dûllū	wild fig tree
gâujī	fool, jester (< gāwùjī)
gyâbjī / gyâzbī	a rodent (< gyābùjī)
kûnnē	ear
mânyā	large (pl.)
yâmmā	afternoon, evening

6. DIALECT FEATURES OF WESTERN HAUSA

The following is a brief sketch of specific tonal properties of WH dialects that are not characteristic of SH. In the absence of careful dialectological studies that set out tonal isoglosses in detail, it is impossible to specify exactly where these features are found. I shall thus simply identify the differences by referring to the name of one major dialect center where it occurs, without any implication as to the extent of its spread. Thus the indication <Katsina>, for example, means that we know that the tonal feature in question is typical of Katsina, but we do not know if it extends throughout WH or whether it is a local peculiarity.

6.1. Replacement of final L-L
Word-final L-L is a disfavored tone sequence in Hausa. As a result of a historical L-tone change (see §34:3.2), ordinary words ending in L-L and a long final vowel are practically non-existent (but see below). Words ending in L-L and a short final vowel are also relatively uncommon—many of them are loanwords—but they are not inconsequential. One finds two different processes in WH for dealing with final L-L.

6.1.1. Final L-L (short) corresponds to L-H /____# <Katsina>
SH has a certain number of L-L words with a short final vowel, e.g., màcè 'woman', àyàbà 'banana(s)', bēgìlà 'bugle'. (For convenience, I refer to these items as L-L words regardless of the number of syllables.) In Katsina (and Sokoto) such L-L words normally appear as L-H, i.e., this is the tone pattern that they have in citation form, when occurring in sentence final position, or when followed by some other phrase boundary. Examples:

Kano	Kts	
gwàdò	gwàdo	blanket
àdùdù	àdùdu	basket
màcè	màce	woman (= [Skt] **màcce**)
kùzà	kùza	tin
kāṛùwà	kāṛùwa	prostitute
gòbe Lahàdì	gòbe Lahàdi	Tomorrow is Sunday.
bā nà̀ shân mangwàṛò	bā nà̀ shân mangwàṛo	I don't eat mangoes.
Bintà tā sàyi àdùdù	Bintà tā sàyi àdùdu	Binta bought a basket.
gyàlè wandà ta arō	gyàle wandà ta arō	a shawl that she borrowed
wata shèlà waddà akà yi	wata shèla waddà akà yi	an announcement that was made

The L-H pattern is found in place of L-L not only in simple stems but also in words containing a low-tone bound possessive pronoun, e.g.,

Kano	Kts	
dōkìntà	dōkìnta	her horse
mōtàṛkà	mōtàkka	your car
jìdālìnsù	jìdālìnsu	their struggle

When a linker is added to an erstwhile L-L word with a short final vowel, the tone invariably becomes L-H, e.g., //gwàdò// 'blanket', but gwàdon yārò̀ 'the boy's blanket'. Because this tone change precedes the general L-L to L-H substitution, possessive pronouns attached to these words appear on the surface with their underlying L tone, e.g., //gwàdò + nkà// → gwàdonkà (*not* **gwàdònka); //àdùdù + ntà// → àdùduntà 'her basket' (*not* **àdùdùnta).

In non sentence-final position, L–L words preserve the L-L pattern and do not change to L-H (subject to further specification provided below), e.g.,

<u>kùzà</u> tā fi dalmà̄ daṛajà̀	Tin is more valuable than lead.
bà tà sayō <u>gwàdò</u> ba	She didn't buy a blanket.
kà bā nì <u>àdùdù</u> kō tàbarmā	Give me a basket or a mat.

When followed by the stabilizer (**nē/cē**), L–L words appear both with L-H and with L-L. (The tone of the stabilizer itself is polar.) If the erstwhile L-L word and the stabilizer occur at the end of the sentence, then the L-H pattern surfaces. If, on the other hand, the L-L word preceding the stabilizer occurs earlier in the sentence, it normally keeps its L–L tone. The sequence L-H is also possible, but in that case some degree of prominence is added, e.g.,

<u>àdùdu</u> nè̀	It's a basket.
<u>màce</u> cè̀	It's a girl.
<u>màcè</u> cē ta hàifā	It's a girl she gave birth to.
wannàn <u>gyàlè</u> nē mài c'àda	This is an expensive shawl.
<u>kùzà</u> cē akè̀ sāmù a Jihàṛ Fìlàtô = <u>kùza</u> cè̀ akè̀ sāmù...	
One gets tin in Plateau State. = It is tin one gets in Plateau State.	

Trisyllabic nouns with a heavy penultimate syllable that in SH have H-L-L tone (and a short final vowel) are invariably H-L-H in Katsina regardless of the position in the sentence, i.e., the H-L-H output of the tone raising has become lexicalized as the underlying form, e.g.,

Kano	Kts	
akàlà	akàla	lead rope for camel, e.g., **bà akàla ba cè** It's not a lead rope.
fankèkè	fankèke	face powder, e.g., **fankèke dà tùràrē** face powder and perfume

6.1.2. Final L-L (heavy) > L-F / ____# <Sokoto>

SH has a half a dozen L-L English loanwords with a long final vowel and about ten common items with final L-L that end in a consonant. In Sokoto these words are pronounced with final L-F in all environments, e.g.,

Kano	Skt	
dìsfansàr̃è	dìsfansàr̃ê	dispensary, clinic
elemantàr̃è	elemantàr̃ê	elementary school
lōtàr̃è	lōtàr̃ê	lottery
sakandàr̃è	sakandàr̃ê	secondary school
ambùlàn	ambùlân	ambulance
tambùlàn	tambùlân	drinking glass

> ΔDN: [i] Another L-L avoidance strategy attested with a small group of words of four or more syllables ending in /ē/ is to use an (H-)L-H-H-L pattern, e.g., **dìsfansar̃è**, **elèmantar̃è**. I am unable to document in which regions this variant is spoken.
>
> [ii] In Katsina there is a set of three L-L words that appear with a short final vowel (as found in SH) when not in prepausal position, but with a long final vowel, and thus ...L-F tone, in prepausal position. These words are **fākìlà / fākìlâ** 'first class'; **sikinkìlà / sikinkìlâ** 'second class'; and **tākìlà / tākìlâ** 'third class' (referring to travel status). For example, **bà sikinkìlà ba nè** 'It's not second class', cf. **nā fi sôn sikinkìlâ** 'I prefer second class.'

Although final L-L with long final vowels is rare with prosaic words, it does appear commonly in ideophones (which by their nature are phonologically aberrant). For example, there is a large class of ideophonic adjectives (often plural) with the set reduplicated pattern CVCVV x 2 with H-H L-L tone, e.g., **batsō-bàtsò** (pl.) 'poorly made, ugly looking', **ɓagā-ɓàgà** 'chunky; in large chunks' (usu. of solid foods or fruits). In Sokoto, these words follow the tone rule and appear as H-H L-F, e.g.,

Kano	Skt	
buzū-bùzù	buzū-bùzû	long and unkempt (of hair)
darā-dàrà	darā-dàrâ	bold and beautiful (of eyes or writing)
falā-fàlà	hwalā-hwàlâ	broad and thin (e.g., leaves, paper, ears)
tsalā-tsàlà	tswalā-tswàlâ	long and skinny (esp. legs)

6.2. Falling tone simplification

Although falling tone in Hausa is actually quite common, there nevertheless seems to be an ongoing drift throughout the Hausa dialect continuum to eliminate the contour tone in favor of sequences of level tones. I shall describe two such cases.

> °AN: Actually, there are two contradictory tendencies constantly at work. One, which we are describing here, is the elimination of contours by tone simplification rules (comparable to monophthongization rules). The other is the creation of new instances of contours as a result of various morphophonological processes (such as the loss of segments with low tone or the attachment of morphemes containing or consisting of a floating tone) and through the introduction

of loanwords where the F corresponds to falling intonation in the source word. This phonological cycle of creation and loss followed by further creation and loss is comparable to the morpho-syntactic and lexical cycles described by Hodge (1970) and Newman (1991b).

6.2.1. F-H simplification <Sokoto>

The tone sequence F-H is rarely found in Sokoto. This has been eliminated in two different ways.

Nouns that contain an F-H tone sequence in SH appear in Sokoto with L-H, i.e., F-H → L-H, e.g.,

SH	Skt		SH	Skt	
mâitā	màitā	witchcraft	bâiwā	bòyā (< bàuyā)	female slave
râssā	ràssā	branches	yârā	yàrā	children
bâlbēlầ	bàlbēlầ	cattle egret	bâṛbajè	bàṛbajè	biting ant

This F-H → LH rule does *not* apply to F-H words consisting of a falling-tone monosyllabic stem plus a high-tone possessive pronoun, e.g.,

mâinā my oil; **kâinai** his head; **sânā** my bull; **râinai** his life; **sônā** loving me

Disyllabic verbs in SH with F-H tone, like **kwântā** 'lie down', pattern with trisyllabic H-L-H verbs (grades 1 and 4) such as **kaṛàntā** 'read' and **bincìkē** 'investigate'. In Sokoto, these have regularly simplified to H-L and behave as normal disyllabic gr1 and gr4 verbs, e.g.,

SH	Skt		SH	Skt	
kwântā	kwantà	lie down	shâidā	shaidầ	give evidence
cînyē	cinyè	eat up	shânyē	shanyè	drink up
ɗâukē	ɗaukè	let up (e.g., rain)	îskē	iskè	come upon, find

6.2.2 Monosyllabic F → L rule <Maradi>

In the dialect of Maradi, there is a simplification rule that operates on falling tones preceded by H, namely, F → L / H___ if and only if the F is on a monosyllabic word. The basic process is the change of ...H-F (= H-HL) into ...H-L, the initial component of the fall being subject to tonal absorption. The rule is optional but is generally applied. Here are selected examples showing the F-tone word in isolation, when preceded by L, and when preceded by H:

sâ	bull:	(a) yanầ bugùn sâ He is beating the bull.	(b) **ḳàramin sầ** small bull
mâi	oil:	(a) gishirī dà mâi salt and oil	(b) gishirī kō mài salt or oil
nân	here:	(a) kù tsayầ nân Stop here!	(b) kù zō nàn Come here!
yâu	today:	(a) yā gamầ yâu He finished today.	(b) yā dāwō yàu He returned today.
mâ	to you:	(a) nā gayầ mâ I told you.	(b) nā aikō mầ I sent (it) to you.
sâ	put:	(a) bà mù sâ su ba We didn't put them.	(b) mun sầ su We put them.
jâ	pulling:	(a) yanầ jâ He is pulling.	(b) yā zanki jầ He kept on pulling.
cê	say:	(a) sai kà cê As you say.	(b) kā cè You said.

°AN: In SH, the verb **cê** also becomes **cè**, but in a very restricted environment, namely, when preceded by an H-tone light-syllable weak subject pronoun, e.g., **wâddà ta cè** 'the one who said', cf. **zā tà cê** 'she will say', **tā cê** 'she said'. Other monosyllabic words with falling tone do not exhibit a tone change.

Two groups of monosyllabic words are not affected by the tone change: (a) relatively recent loanwords (from French) like **pîl** 'flashlight battery', **bîk** 'ballpoint pen', e.g., **yā kāwō pîl** 'He brought a battery' (not ****yā kāwō pìl**); (b) grammatical formatives in the person-aspect-complex, e.g., **wai sûn dāwō** 'It is said that they will likely return' (not ****wai sùn dāwō**).

7. THE RULE OF LOW-TONE RAISING (LTR)

Hausa has almost no lexical items ending in L-L tone where the final vowel is long. The likely explanation offered for this phonotactic gap is a rule of low-tone raising (LTR), namely L-L > L-H if the final vowel is long. This change was first proposed by Leben (1971) and accepted by many scholars following him as a synchronically active rule of the present-day language. The synchronic viability of the rule, however, is highly questionable; see Newman and Jaggar (1989a, 1989b) and Schuh (1989c), with a contrary view presented by Leben (1996). There is in fact no convincing evidence of LTR actually functioning in the language at the present time. There *is* good reason, on the other hand, to believe that such a rule operated in the past as a historical rule of considerable importance. Its operation is thus described not here, but in the chapter on historical sound changes (see §**34**:3.2).

8. TONE / SEGMENT INTERACTION

Cross-linguistically, one finds that segments commonly affect tone but that tone rarely affects segments (Hyman and Schuh 1974). Hausa displays an example of the rare case.

The Hausa diphthong /**ai**/ has two quite distinct pronunciations, a "high variant" and a "low variant," e.g.,

1. high variant: [ɛi], [ei], even [ē]   (I shall transcribe this variant as [ei].)
2. low variant: [əi], [ɔi], [ai]   (I shall transcribe this variant as [ai].)

To some extent the phonetic difference is conditioned by the preceding consonant, e.g., after coronal consonants, one normally gets [ei] whereas after glottal stop and /**h**/ one gets [ai], e.g.,

1. **laimà** = [leimà]   umbrella   **tsaikò̃** = [sˈeikò̃]   roof frame
2. **aikì̃** = [ˈaikì̃]   work   **haihù** = [haihù]   give birth

After labial consonants, however, both pronunciations of the diphthong occur, and here one finds that tone is the conditioning factor. If the /**Cai**/ syllable has level tone, either H or L, then one gets the high [ei] variant of the diphthong; If, on the other hand, the /**Cai**/ syllable has falling tone, then the dipththong is pronounced with the low [ai] variant. Examples:

	H		L		F	
/**mai**/	[mei]	return	[mèi]	owner of	[mâi]	oil
/**bai**/	[bei]	give	[bèi]	3m neg completive	[bâi]	back [dv]
/**fai**/	[feifei]	(music) record	[fèilû]	peppermint	[fâi]	openly

The following pair nicely illustrates the dependency of the diphthongal pronunciation on the tone: **mai dà yājì̃** [mei dà yājì̃] 'return the spices' vs. **mâi dà yājì̃** [mâi dà yājì̃] 'oil and spices'. Note also the reduplicated adverb **bàibâi** [bèibâi] 'inside out, back to front' (lit. back.back).

9. INTONATION

In addition to tone, which functions at the syllabic or morphemic or lexical level, Hausa also has a variety of intonational patterns that function at the phrasal or sentential level. These patterns can generally be described in terms of how they influence the pitch of the tones. (For intonational purposes, the falling tone can be treated as HL on a single syllable.) Unlike the tones, which constitute discrete phonemic units, the intonational patterns are continuous and variable, covering a wide phonetic range, the realization of which depends on dialectal characteristics, sex/age differences, style and register, and idiolectal preferences. Nevertheless, one can provide a rough outline of significant intonational features even if one understands that this is a very approximate picture of the actual speech situation. Four major intonation patterns will be described: (1) neutral/declarative, (2) interrogative, (3) sympathetic address, and (4) vocative.

9.1. *Neutral/declarative*

Neutral/declarative intonation is characterized by an overall downward slope that causes tones later in the sentence to have a lower pitch than equivalent tones earlier in the sentence. (For convenience I am using "sentence" as the intonational unit even though strictly speaking it is the "intonational phrase." A short sentence will normally consist of one intonational phrase, but a longer sentence could consist of more, each new phrase resetting the intonation grid.) The downward slope can be formulated as a basic downdrift rule that specifies that each H tone after an L is a step lower that the preceding H. Thus a tonal sequence H-L-H-L-H-L-H, for example, as in the sentence **Lādì tā tàfi kàntī** 'Ladi (she) went to the store', is realized (schematically) as 5-3-4-2-3-1-2 (with 5 representing the highest pitch), e.g.,

5	Lā					
4			tā			
3		dì		fi		
2				tà		tī
1					kàn	

A sequence of level tones has a slight declination, but this is minor except at the end of a sentence where a final L tends to fall off a bit. (Note that the final L in a sentence tends toward the 1 level even if there are not enough downsteps to get there.)

The overall declarative pattern is subject to an important modification at the beginning of the sentence. Initial H tones begin at pitch 4 (not 5). In a sequence of H-H-L... (where, in a tensed sentence, for example, the second H is either the weak subject pronoun or the initial syllable of the verb) the second H raises to 5, which then sets the intonational grid. Compare the sentences **Mūsā yā sàyi hùlā** 'Musa bought a cap' and **Mūsā yā arà masà fensìř** 'Musa lent him a pencil.'

5			yā				
4	Mū	sā			yi		
3				sà			
2							lā
1					hù		
	Musa		he	bought		cap	

```
5                                   a
4    Mū    sā    yā              ma
3                          rà              fen
2                                sà
1                                              sìr̃
     Musa         he    lent    to.him        pencil
```

9.2. Interrogative

Q-word questions use the basic declarative intonation contour, but, sometimes, with a slightly higher pitch. A sentence-final H tone is realized as a fall because of the addition of the L-tone q-morpheme (see §60:1.2). Example (**wà ya kashè kūrā?** 'Who killed the hyena?'):

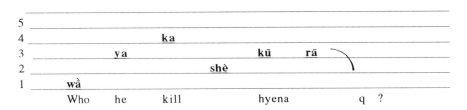

```
5
4                    ka
3           ya                   kū    rā  ⟍
2                          shè              ⟍
1      wà
       Who    he    kill    hyena        q   ?
```

Yes/No questions are characterized by suspension of downdrift (in longer sentences, only in the final intonational phrase) and an overall higher pitch. They are also characterized by key raising (indicated ↑), i.e., pitch raising that affects the last H tone of the sentence and any following lows. If the sentence ends in an H tone, it may or may not become a fall depending on whether the the q-morpheme carries L tone or not (this being subject to dialectal variation). (See §60:2.2 for fuller exemplification.) Examples (**Bellò yā ga zō↑mō?** 'Did Bello see a rabbit?'; **Bellò yā ga ↑ mōtàr̃?** 'Did Bello see the car?'):

```
7                               mō  ⟍
6                                   ⟍
5    Bel        yā    ga    zō
4
3         lò
     Bello      he    see   rabbit        q   ?
```

```
7                               mō
6                                    tàr̃
5    Bel        yā    ga
4
3         lò
     Bello      he    see   car           q   ?
```

9.3. Sympathetic address

What I am calling sympathetic address is an intonational contour that is used to address someone in a spirit either of sympathy or of exasperation. The name of the person addressed is often preceded by **tô** 'all right' or **habà** 'come on now'. The marker of sympathetic address is a floating L tone, which is realized as a falling tone on words with final H tone. (The falling tone results in phonetic lengthening of the vowel; words with final L tone do not normally lengthen the vowel.) There is also a slight pause (indicated by a comma) after the name. Examples:

tô Mūsâ, à matsō à kàrɓā	OK Musa (//**Mūsā**//), do come closer and get it.
habà Kàndê, kin san îndà yakè	Come on Kande (//**Kànde**//), you know where it is.
habà Bàlâ, bà kà kyâutā ba	Now now Bala (//**Bàlā**//), you weren't very nice.
tô Lādì, zân tàimàkē kì	That's all right Ladi (//**Lādì**//), I'll help you.

9.4. *Vocative*
The vocative used in calling someone is characterized by a raised pitch, lesser downdrift, if any, and lengthening of final short vowels. Examples:

Mūsā ! [5 5], cf. **Mūsā** [4 4]	**Mustàfā** ! [5 3 5], cf. **Mustàfā** [4 2 3]
Gàmbō ! [3 5], cf. **Gàmbo** [1 3]	**Bintà** ! [5 4], cf. **Bintà** [4 1]

[References: (Tone): Leben (1971); Newman (1986b, 1995); Wängler (1963); (Intonation): Hunter (1979); Inkelas, Leben, and Cobler (1987); Lindau (1986); Meyers (1976), Miller and Tench (1980, 1982); D. Muhammad (1968); Newman and Newman (1981)]

72. Topicalization

1. INTRODUCTION

TOPICALIZATION and focus (see chap. **28**) both involve fronting a constituent in order to give it prominence. They differ, however, in semantic characterization and in syntactic structure. The difference is shown in the following phrase structure representation and tree diagram (fig. 6).

SENTENCE → «Topic» S´ (where S´ is the "Comment")
S´ → {Focus} S (where S is the sentence from which the Focus is extracted)
S → Subject PAC Predicate (etc.)

Figure 6: Topicalization and focus

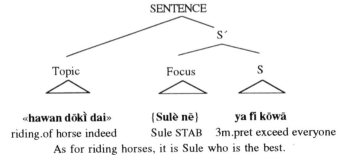

As for riding horses, it is Sule who is the best.

Topicalization involves the prementioning of some NP (usually discourse-old information) about which the main sentence makes a comment. The TAM utilizes a general form such as the completive. Examples:

«Bellò kàm»Topic [yā dāwō jiyà]Comment   As for Bello, he returned yesterday.
«waccàn kūrâř», Audù [yā]comp taɓà (ta)   That hyena, Audu touched (it).
cf. Audù yā taɓà waccàn kūrâř   Audu touched that hyena.
«Mūsā dai», ainìhin sōjà nē   As for Musa, he is a true soldier.

The topic stands outside the main sentence—it constitutes what I informally like to call a "front porch"—set off from the main sentence by a particle and/or by intonation (sometimes indicated here by a comma). It is thus unlike a focused element, which is also fronted but which remains in the main sentence and conditions the shift to a Rel TAM, e.g., **waccàn kūrâř (cē) Audù [ya]**pret **taɓà** 'It was that hyena that Audu touched.' Because the comment S´ is structurally distinct from the topic, it can be of almost any kind, e.g.,

Affirmative statement: «**yáròn kồ**», **Kànde tā màrē shì**   As for the boy, Kande slapped him.

Negative statement: «**Kàtsinà kùwa**», **ha ha ha, bà tà kai Kanồ yawàn mutầnē ba**

As for Katsina, (laughter), it isn't as populous as Kano.

Yes/No question: «**ɓàráwòn**», **yā kùɓutà?**   The thief, did he escape?

Q-word question: «**ƙwai ɗin nàn dai**», **yàushè akà dafà?**   These eggs, when did one cook them?

Imperative: «**àbồkankà fa**», **gàyyàcè su!**   Your friends, invite them!

Existential: «**kuɗī kàm**», **dà àkwai**   As for money, there is some.

Negative existential: «**ruwā**», **ai bābù à kồgī**   As for water, oh there isn't any in the river.

Negative equational: «**zõmõ dai**», **shī bà mālàminmù ba nề**

As for the hare, he is not our teacher.

It is important to note that topics, unlike focused elements, cannot be negated. Sentences like the following are thus ungrammatical:

«bà Sulè ba kàm», **yakàn sàyi ƙwai   **As for not Sule, he buys eggs.

cf. «**Sulè kàm**», **yakàn sàyi ƙwai   As for Sule, he buys eggs.

«bà sìnīmằ ba dai» **bā yằ sô   **As for not movies, he doesn't like them.

cf. «**sìnīmằ dai**» **bā yằ sô   As for the movies, he doesn't like them.

cf. «**rashìn lāfiyằ**», **bâ dāɗī   Lack of health, it's not pleasant.

2. FORM AND STRUCTURE

The topic appears in sentence-initial position. It is set off from the main sentence by either (a) intonation or (b) the insertion of a modal particle like **dai** 'indeed', **fa** 'well', **kàm** 'really', **kùwa** (= **kồ(o)**) 'moreover', etc. (or a succession of such particles).

Topic intonation, which is similar to that used in questions, consists of final vowel lengthening, a slight suspension of normal downdrift, and some degree of pause (indicated in the examples by ...), e.g.,

[**Audừ**...], **yanằ cîn nāmằ kullum**   As for Audu, he eats meat every day.

cf. **Audù yanằ cîn nāmằ kullum**   Audu eats meat every day.

[**Kàndē**...], **mun fi sôntà**   As for Kande, we like her the most.

cf. **mun fi sôn Kànde**   We like Kande the most.

[**gõřồ**...], **yā yi minì ɗācī**   As for kolanuts, they're too bitter for me.

cf. **bà nakàn ci gõřò ba**   I don't chew kolanuts.

°AN: This section has benefited greatly from ideas and materials contained in an unpublished paper by Mahamane L. Abdoulaye (1993).

If a modal particle is inserted, the topic appears without the vowel lengthening. A pause is allowed after the modal particle but it is not required, e.g.,

àku dai (...), **bàn yàřda dà shī ba** = **àkū** ..., **bàn yàřda dà shī ba**

As for the parrot, I don't agree with him.

Audù dai (...), **yanằ cîn nāmằ kullum**   As for Audu, he eats meat every day.

Kànde fa (...), **mun fi sôntà**   As for Kande, we like her the most.

gõřò kùwa (...), **yā yi minì ɗācī**   Kolanuts moreover, they're too bitter for me.

gwàdò mā (...), **zân sayằ makà** = **gwàdō**..., **zân sayằ makà**

The blanket also, I'll buy (it) for you.

tsuntsū kàm (...), mahàr̃bī yanā̀ kāmā̀ wà wàzīr̃ì
> The bird, well, the hunter is catching it for the vizier.

yằya fa ɗai kàm (...), bàn gayā̀ matà ba   My elder sister indeed certainly, I didn't tell her.

The topic can further be separated from the main sentence by exclamatory or expressive material, e.g.,

Audù dai, wàllāhì yanā̀ cîn nāmā̀ kullum   As for Audu, truly he eats meat every day.
Kànde, tô, mun fi sôntà   Kande, OK, we like her the most.
waccàn kūr̃âr̃, ìnâ! bà zân taɓā̀ ta ba   That hyena, no way! I wouldn't touch it.

3. MULTIPLE TOPICS

It is possible to have more than one topic in a single sentence, although out of context they seem clumsy, as are the English translations. Examples:

«Audù fa», «hùlā̀ kàm», yā sàyā   As for Audu, regarding this cap, he bought (it).
«àkuyàr̃ kùwa», «sanyī dai», yā gamā̀ dà ita   The goat, well the cold, it finished it off.

4. ROLE OF THE TOPIC

The topic can represent essentially any thematic role in the sentence, such as subject, direct object, object of preposition, etc. (In the discussion that follows, I shall refer to a topic that matches a subject in the main clause as a "topicalized subject," one that matches an indirect object as a "topicalized i.o.," etc., *as if* topicalization were accomplished by a movement transformation, even though one might well choose to analyze or generate such sentences in other ways.) Examples:

1. sbj.: **yàrònkà dai, yā shàr̃è gidân jiyà?**   Your boy, did he sweep the house yesterday?
2. d.o. (genitive): **nāmā̀, yàròn yanā̀ cî kullum**   Meat, the boy eats (it) every day.
3. d.o. (finite): **Mūsā dai, nā gan shì à sìnīmā̀**   Musa, I saw him at the movies.
   cf. {**Mūsā nè**} na ganī à sìnīmā̀   It was Musa I saw at the movies. (focus)
4. i.o.: **Audù, sai mù aikà masà gōr̃ò**   Audu, we should send him kolanuts.
5. obj. of preposition: **mōtà̀, bâ ni dà ita**   A car, I don't have one.
6. possessive: **Mūsā mā, Aishà tā ga ƙanìnsà jiyà**
   > Musa also, Aisha saw his younger brother yesterday.
7. possessive: **nàwa, littāfìn yā kēcè tùni**   Mine, the book got torn some time ago.
   cf. **littāfìnā, yā kēcè tùni**   As for my book, it got torn some time ago.
8. VP (infinitive): **kāmà̀ ɓēr̃ā, màgên tā yi**
   > As for catching the rat (lit. catch rat), the cat did (it).
9. VP (infinitive): **durƙùsā wà mālàm, Zàinabù tā yī shì**
   > As for kneeling down before the teacher, Zainabu did it.
10. locative: **Kanò, Mustàfā yanā̀ can**   As for Kano, Mustapha is there.
11. manner adverbial: **yaddà̀ akà kōyā̀ masà kàm, yàròn yanā̀ aikì (hakàn)**
    > As he was taught, the boy is working (thus).

4.1. Deletion or pronominalization of underlying topic

With animate topics, the underlying syntactic position is almost always filled by a resumptive pronoun; with inanimate topics, both pronominalization and deletion are allowed. (This situation is different from that of focus, where deletion is the norm.) Whether one gets pronominalization or deletion also depends on the specific syntactic role of the topicalized constituent.

With a subject topic, the original nominal is deleted, see ex. 1 above. The sentence will, of course, retain the weak subject pronoun (wsp) that is part of the PAC (person-aspect-complex). Complex non-personal subject topics can optionally be replaced by an anaphoric non-personal pronoun, like **wannàn** 'this', e.g., **yaddà Sulè yakè̄ zāgìn 'yā'yansà, (wannàn) yanà̄ bā nì màmākì** 'The way Sule insults his children, (this) surprises me'. With a d.o. topic (whether of a finite verb or of a verbal noun) one can either delete the main clause object or else replace it with a resumptive pronoun. The former is the norm if the noun is inanimate (see ex. 2), the latter is the norm if the noun is animate (see ex. 3). With an i.o. topic, one normally uses a resumptive pronoun (see ex. 4), although some speakers allow deletion, e.g., **Bintà kàm, Jummai tā shāfā̀ matà hōdà̄** 'Binta, Jummai applied powder on her.' Because there is a general rule that prepositions cannot be stranded, prepositional object topics require the use of a resumptive pronoun, e.g., **gōnā̄r, Audù yanà̄ kāwō zōmō dàgà ita** 'The farm, Audu is bringing a hare from it' (see also ex. 5). Similarly, possessor noun topics also require use of a resumptive pronoun (see ex. 6), although possessive pronoun topics do not (see ex. 7). When the topic represents the verb phrase (see below), the dummy pro-verb **yi** 'do' is left in its place, followed optionally by the 3m object pronoun (see ex. 8/9). A topicalized locative predicate is typically replaced by 'here' or 'there', etc. (see ex. 10). A manner adverbial allows deletion or replacement by the pro-adverb **hakà(n)** (see ex. 11).

An alternative, which is employed for extra emphasis or confirmation, is to repeat the topicalized element in its original position, e.g.,

mâi dai, yâu bâ mâi	As for gasoline, today there isn't any gasoline.
cf. **mâi dai, yâu bâ shī**	As for gasoline, today there isn't any.
Kanò, Mustàfā yanà̄ Kanò	As for Kano, Mustapha is in Kano.
cf. **Kanò, Mustàfā yanà̄ can**	As for Kano, Mustapha is there.
wuk̃ā fa, inà̄ dà wuk̃ā mài kaifī	As for a knife, I have a sharp knife.

gōr̃ò kàm, zân aikà̄ mā gōr̃ò har̃ Jàpân
   As for kolanuts, I will send you kolanuts all the way to Japan.
cār̃ā, yār̀òn bài yi barcī ba har̃ zàkar̀àn yā fār̀à cār̃ā
   As for crowing, the boy had not slept up to the time that the rooster began crowing.

Topicalized elements can come from the main sentence or they can be drawn out of a lower clause, e.g.,

«Mar̃yàm», munà̄ tsàmmānì Mūsā yanà̄ sôntà   As for Maryam, we think that Musa loves her.
«fensir̃ōr̃ì kàm», nā bā kà kuɗī don kà sàyā
   As for pencils, I gave you money in order to buy (some).
«àllūr̃àr̃», jàr̀ir̀ân sunà̄ kūkā tun dà akà yī musù
   As for the shot (injection), the babies have been crying since they were given (it).
«Mūsā», bà kà san kō wā̀cē cè̄ zâi àurā ba?
   As for Musa, do you not know who he will marry?
«àlhàzai dai», yā fi kyâu sù tàfi dūtsèn Àr̃f̃ā
   As for the pilgrims, it is much better for them to go to Mount Arafat.
«àbincin rāna fa», yā kàmātà̄ Asshà tà kai wà mijìntà
   As for lunch, it is fitting that Assha should take it to her husband.

Unlike the case with focused elements, it is possible in appropriate circumstances to have a topic that does not have a clear syntactic role in the sentence that follows. Examples (not all of which all speakers are comfortable with):

hājà kò, bà zā mù sàmi gàrī kàmař Kanò ba

As for merchandise, we won't find a town like Kano.

makařantā dai, Bellò bā yằ yîn kōmē sai wàsā

As for school, Bello doesn't do anything except play.

kāyan itātuwằ kàm, Lawàn yanằ shân mangwàřò kullum

As for fruit, Lawan eats mangoes every day.

kařtà kò, nā fi sôn wàsā irìn na *chess*

As far as cards are concerned, I prefer games like chess.

5. PART OF SPEECH

NPs or adverbials can serve as topics. The NP can be a simple noun (phrase), a pronoun, a verbal noun (phrase), or an infinitive phrase, e.g.,

màsu tàimakon āgàjī fa, zā kà sàmē sù à asìbitì

The relief workers, you'll find them at the hospital. (NP)

ita kàm, gwamma tà ci gàba	As for her, she ought to continue. (pn)
nằwa, littāfìn yā kēcè tùni	Mine, the book got torn some time ago. (pn)
hařbìnsà dai, yā buřgè mu	As for his shooting, it impressed us. (VP)
rufè tāgà, bâ shakkằ yanằ dà kyâu	As for closing the window, no doubt it's good. (IP)

Verbs qua verbs cannot function as topics. Rather, they have to be replaced by their corresponding verbal nouns (VN) or infinitive phrases (IP). The original verb slot is then filled by the pro-verb **yi** 'do' and the original direct object, if not fronted along with the verb, is altered into an indirect object, e.g.,

[gyārā]$_{VN}$, mutầnē sâ yi wà ɗākìn	Repairing, men will do it to the room.
cf. mutằnē sâ gyārà ɗākìn	Men will repair the room.
[tàlgē]$_{VN}$, Kànde takàn yi wà tuwō	Pouring in (flour), Kande does it to the *tuwo*.
cf. Kànde takàn talgà tuwō	Kande makes the *tuwo*.
[zubârwā]$_{VN}$, tanà (yi) wà shàrā	Throwing out, she was doing it to the trash.
cf. tanà zubař dà shàrā	She was throwing out the trash.
[gūgà]$_{VN}$, yā yi wà mōtàř	Polishing, he did it to the car.
cf. yā gōgè mōtàř dà mâi	He polished the car with oil.
[shāfà hōdằ]$_{IP}$, dâ mā mātā sunằ yî	

As for using powder, women have done so for a long time.

cf. dâ mā mātā sunằ shāfà hōdằ   Women have been using powder for a long time.

[yankè masà hukuncì]$_{IP}$ kùwa, àlƙālī yā rìgā yā yi

As far as sentencing him is concerned, the judge has already done (it).

cf. àlƙālī yā rìgā yā yankè masà hukuncì   The judge has already sentenced him.

Regarding topicalized verbs, it is possible to repeat the verb in its original position rather than replace it by **yi**. (In the examples below, I translate the sentences with and without **yi** differently, but in Hausa they are essentially equivalent.)

«kūkā», ai yakàn kōkà wani lōkàcī   As for crying, he cries sometimes.

cf. «kūkā», ai yakàn yi wani lōkàcī = kūkā, ai yakàn yī shì wani lōkàcī

As for crying, he does it sometimes.

«wāshì», maƙèrā sun wāsà wuƙàƙên

As for sharpening, the blacksmiths sharpened the knives.

cf. «wāshì», maƙèrā sun yi wà wuƙàƙên

As for sharpening, the blacksmiths did it to the knives.

«shìgā», wai yā shìga ban dà kō sàlāmù àlaikùm

Entering, well he entered without even (saying) *salamu alaikum*.

6. SPECIAL TOPIC CONSTRUCTIONS

There are two set constructions that occur as sentence-initial topics: (a) **àbinkà dà** NP, and (b) NP **dà** pn.

6.1. The construction **àbinkà dà** NP

This idiomatic but common topic construction consists of **àbinkà** 'your (m.) thing' plus **dà** 'with' plus an NP. The meaning of the construction is 'You know how it is with X....' Examples:

àbinkà dà kāyan zāluncì, anà cî àmmā bā à hamdalà

You know how it is with the fruits of oppression, one enjoys them but without gratitude.

àbinkà dà ɗan ƙauyè, dà shìgā biřnī sai fārà ƙwambò

You know how it is with villagers, no sooner do they get to the city than they start putting on airs.

àbinkà dà sàmàrtakà irìn ta dâ, sàmàrī bā sà sāmùn wàlwàlā

You know how it was with youth in the olden days, young people weren't able to enjoy themselves.

àbinkà dà zařàfin kàkā, mutànē sunà fāmā dà aikì

You know how it is in the harvest season, people are busy with work.

àbinkà dà ràyuwā irìn ta Kanò, kōwā nēman kuɗī ya sâ à gàba

You know how it is with life in Kano, everyone's first priority is getting money.

6.2. The construction NP (possessive) **dà** pronoun

This topic construction consists of a noun (usually plus a bound possessive pronoun) followed by **dà** 'with' plus a coreferential independent pronoun. (Some speakers prefer the construction in the form N **dà** pn without the possessive.) The meaning, which usually connotes criticism or disapproval, is illustrated in the following examples:

«yārònā dà nī» (= (?) «yārò dà nī») mè zân yi dà rawànī?

As young as I am (lit. my boy with me) what would I do with a turban?

«tsōhuwařtà dà ita» (= (?) «tsōhuwā dà ita») mè zā tà yi dà cōgè?

Old woman that she is (lit. her age with her) what would she do with high-heeled shoes?

(i.e., it is foolish for an old woman like her to think of wearing high-heeled shoes)

«bàbbankà dà kai» (= (?) «bàbba dà kai») bài dācè kà riƙà wàsā dà yârā ba

A grown up like you (lit. your adult with you) it is not fitting for you to play with kids.

7. TOPIC AND FOCUS

Because topicalization and focus are distinct processes with their own semantics and syntactic positions, it follows naturally that they can co-occur in the same sentence. The order is always topic then focus. Examples:

«ɓàrāwòn», {Audù (nē)} ya kashề shi

> As for the thief, it was *Audu* who killed him. (Topic and Focus)

cf. {ɓàrāwòn (nē)} Audù ya kashề

> It was a *thief* Audu killed. (without the resumptive pronoun) (Focus only)

cf. «ɓàrāwòn», Audù yā kashề shi

> As for the thief, Audu killed him. (Topic only)

«shừgàban sāshì», ɓầ {Dr. Smith} mukề sô ba

> As for chair of department, *it's not Dr. Smith* we want.

«sōjà», {bāyan gānuwā} sukề

> As for the soldiers, it's *behind the ramparts* they are.

«waɗànnân màràyū», {wầnē nề} zâi ciyař dà sū?

> These orphans, *who* will feed them?

«zīnāřìyā kàm», {wajen wani ɗan tiřēdầ} mukà sāmừ?

> As for the gold, *it was from a certain trader* that we got it.

«àbinkà dà mātā », {sừřūtừ} sukề ta yî

> You know how it is with women, they're always making a *racket*.

The topic and the focus can have the same referent, e.g.,

«ita kàm», {ita cề} ta mầrē nì

> As for her, *she* (was the one who) slapped me.

«sàyen sābon gidā (dai)», {shī nề} ya fī minì kyâu

> As for buying a new house, *that* is (what is) much better for me.

[References: Jaggar (1976, 1978); Junaidu (1987)]

73. Universals and Generic Relatives (kō- forms)

1. FORM

THE universals ('everyone', 'everything', etc.) and related generic relatives ('whoever', 'whatever', etc.) are formed by prefixing **kō-** to a question word (Q-word). (Although **dukà** 'all' semantically qualifies as a universal, it does not pattern with the universal **kō-** forms discussed here. It is described in the chapter on numerals and other quantifiers (see §53:2).) The full set of forms (with details and variants to be discussed below) is presented in table 29:

Table 29: Universals

Gloss	Universal Forms	Question Words
everyone, whoever	**kōwā**	**wằ** who?
everything, whatever	**kōmē**	**mè** what?
everywhere, wherever	**kō'ìnā**	**ìnā** where?
always, whenever	**kōyàushē = kōyàushè**	**yàushē = yàushè** when?
each, whichever one(s)	**kōwànnē, kōwàccē, kōwàɗànnē**	**wànnē, wàccē, wàɗànnē** whichever?
every, whichever	**kōwànè, kōwàcè, kōwàɗànnè**	**wànè, wàcè, wàɗànnè** which?
however much/many	**kō nawà**	**nawà** how much/many?
in every, whatever way	**kō(ta)yằyằ**	**yằyằ** how?

°AN: Orthographically, **ko nawa** and **ko yaya** (= kō ƙàƙà < ƙàƙà 'how?') are written as two words; all the others are written as single words.

The words **kōwā** 'everyone' and **kōmē** 'everything' are different from the other **kō-** forms in that they have a special tone pattern (H-H) that does not preserve the lexical L tone of the corresponding Q-words **wằ** and **mè** with which they are formed.

ΔDN/◊HN: In the dialect of Ader (Caron 1991), the words for 'who?' and 'what?' are **wā** and **mī** with H tone. These fossilized universal forms would suggest (but do not necessarily prove) that H is the original/archaic tone for these two Q-words and that the SH low tone represents an innovation.

Nowadays, some speakers pronounce—and write—**kōmē** as **kōmai**, with a final diphthong, even further distancing the lexicalized universal word from its Q-word source.

2. MEANING/FUNCTION

The kō- words have two main meanings/uses: universal pro-forms and universal generic relatives.

2.1. *Universal pro-forms*

The first use of the kō- words is as universal pro-forms or universal determiners indicating 'everyone', 'every (thing)', etc. The items that do not have distinct masculine/feminine/plural forms take masculine singular concord. Examples:

kōwā yà kāmà bàkinsà	Everyone should keep his mouth shut.
kōwā yā ci jařřàbâwā	Everyone passed the exam.
mun iskè kōmē à bàřkàtài	We found everything in a mess.
kōmē na dūniyà yanà dà iyàkā	Everything in the world (lit. of the world) has a limit.
yā dūbà kō'ìnā àmmā bài sàmē shì ba	He looked everywhere but he didn't find him.
wannàn yārò yanà kàřàtū kōyàushē	This boy studies all the time.
yā kàmātā kōwànnenkù yà jē Kanò	It is appropriate that each one of you should go to Kano.
yanà sô yà sàyi wannàn kuɗintà kō nawà	He wants to buy this at any price.

zân shìga makařantā ìn sàmi dìgìřî kō(ta)yàyà

      I will get into school and get a degree in whatever way (no matter how).

yanà dà kyâu kōwàcè ƙasā à Afìřkà tà sàmi 'yancìntà

      It is good that every country in Africa should get its independence.

2.1.1. Negation

Morphologically, these universal words do not have negative counterparts, i.e., Hausa does not have lexical items such as 'nothing', 'nowhere', etc. Rather, the universals occur in the positive form in various negative syntactic contexts, in which case they generally translate best as 'no one' or 'nothing' or 'nowhere', etc. Examples:

bàn ga kōwā ba	I didn't see anyone. *or* I saw no one.
(lit. 'I didn't see everyone', but this is not the semantic interpretation)	
bâ kōmē cikin tukunyā	There is nothing in the cooking pot.
(lit. there is not everything/anything...)	
bâ kōmē	It doesn't matter. (lit. there is not anything)
bā mā̀ bùƙātàř kōmē	We don't need anything.
bà zā mù jē kō'ìnā ba	We aren't going anywhere.
kadà kōwā yà fìta ɗākìn!	Nobody may leave the room!
kadà kōmē yà ɓatà!	Let nothing get lost!

Excluding prohibitive sentences (introduced by **kadà**), the universals cannot serve as subjects of sentences in the negative to express 'no one' or 'nothing'. Instead one must use a negative existential sentence with a relative clause headed by a relative pronoun or the pseudorelative non-personal pronoun **àbîn dà** 'the thing that', e.g.,

bâ wâddà ta san amsà	No one (f.) knows the answer.
(lit. there is not who 3f.pret know answer)	
bâ àbîn dà ya fàru	Nothing happened.
(lit. there is not thing.the that 3m.pret happen)	

cikin waɗàndà sukà yi jařřàbâwā bâ wândà ya ci
> Among those who took the exam, no one passed. (lit. ...there isn't who 3m.pret pass)

This structure can also be used as an alternative for negative sentences with the **kō-** form functioning in syntactic roles other than subject, e.g.,

bâ wândà na ganī	I didn't see anyone.
bâ àbîn dà mukè bùƙātà	There is nothing that we need.
bâ îndà zâ mu	There is nowhere that we will be going to.

To express the idea of 'not everyone,' etc., as opposed to 'no one,' etc., one uses the equational/sentential negative marker **bà̀...ba**, e.g.,

bà̀ kōwā kè̀ sôn wannàn jàrīdà̀ ba	Not everyone likes this newspaper.
sunà̀ gyāran tītì àmmā bà̀ kō'ìnā ba	They are fixing the streets, but not everywhere.

2.2. Generic relatives

The **kō-** words also function as universal generic relatives, where they correspond to English 'whoever, whatever', etc.

> °AN: Quirk et al. (1985: 1056ff.) refer to constructions with these types of forms as "nominal relative clauses." Bagari (1987: 77) labels them simply as "Wh-ever sentences."

In this usage, the universal forms typically occur in sentence-initial or clause-initial position. The **kō-** word is immediately followed by a sentence with a Rel TAM (like the preterite) without use of the relativizer **dà** 'that', e.g.,

kōwā ya yi hakà wāwā nè̀	Whoever (= anyone who) does this is a fool.
kōmē zā kà yi kà yī shì dà nìshāɗî	Whatever you are going to do, do it in good spirits.
kōwànnē ka bā nì zân kàrɓā	Whichever one you give me I'll accept.
kō'ìnā ka shūkà̀, sai kà tsarè wurîn	Wherever you plant, you must protect the place.
kō'ìnā ka ɓūya banzā nè̀	Wherever you hide is useless.
kō nawà ka tayà̀ bà zân kàrɓā ba	No matter how much you offer, I won't accept.
kōyàushè kikà ga dāmā, kì bugà̀ minì wayà̀	
Whenever (any time) you (f.) feel like it, give me a call.	

The generic relative **kōmē** 'whatever' can be followed by an NP rather than by a clause (in which case it often translates as 'however'). This is particularly common in proverbs, e.g.,

kōmē tsawon wuyà̀, kâi nē bisà
> Whatever the length of the neck, the head is on top.

kōmē dāɗin kiɗà̀, kurùm yā fī shì
> However pleasant the music, quiet is better. (i.e., silence is golden)

kōmē nīsan jīfà̀, ƙasà zâi fāɗō
> Whatever the distance of one's throw, it will fall to the ground.

When followed by a clause, the generic relatives 'whoever' and 'whatever' can be expressed in two ways. First, it is possible to use the universal pro-forms **kōwā** and **kōmē**. Alternatively, one can use **kō** plus

wằ 'who?' and **mề** 'what?' in the forms they have as Q-words. Examples: (To distinguish the two variants more clearly, I shall write **kō** plus the Q-word as separate words, even though this is not normally done in standard orthography.)

kōwā ya yi hakà wāwā nề = **kō wằ ya yi hakà wāwā nề**   Whoever does this is a fool.
kōmē sukề yī makà, kadà kà dằmu = **kō mề sukề yī makà, kadà kà dằmu**
   Whatever they are doing to you, don't worry.

The two alternatives are not entirely identical in meaning. The H-H universal variant tends to be totally nonspecified/generic, whereas the variant with the Q-word indicates indefiniteness from a subset of possibilities. Consider the following examples:

(a) **kōwā ya zō kà cê nā fìta**
   Whoever comes (i.e., if anyone comes), tell him I went out.
(b) **kō wằ ya zō kà cê nā fìta**
   No matter who comes (but I am assuming that someone will come), tell him I went out.
(a) **kōmē akà bā kà sai gòdiyā**
   Whatever you get (i.e., anything that you might get) you should be thankful.
(b) **kō mề akà bā kà sai gòdiyā**
   No matter what you get (but you expect to get something, and the choices may be known to you) you should be thankful.
kōwā ya rainà gàjērē bài tākà kùnāmằ ba   (*not* ****kō wằ ya rainà...**)
   Anyone who disparages small things/people has never stepped on a scorpion. (proverb)

The variant with the Q-word (as opposed to the set H-H forms) allows the question word in all of its manifestations, e.g., 'who?' = **wằ** or **wằnē nề** or **wằcē cē** or **wằyê**, etc. Examples:

kō wằyê mukà gàyyatằ zâi zō   Whoever we invite will come.
dōlè nē kō wằnē nề shī yà jirā sai nā gamằ dà wannàn aikìn
   It is necessary that whoever he is he should wait until I have finished with the work.
kō su wằnē nề sukề nēman shìnkāfā, à bā sù mūdù bībiyu
   Whoever (pl.) is seeking rice, give them two bowls each.
kō mềnē nề zā kà yi, kadà kà yī shì à gùr̃gùje
   Whatever you are going to do, don't do it in haste.

Hausa does not have a separate lexeme for 'why?'; rather, one uses a phrase containing **mề** 'what?'; either **don mề** (lit. for what?) = **sabòdà mề** (lit. because of what?) or **mề ya sâ** (lit. what caused?). This latter phrase can be used with **kō** to form a generic relative, e.g., **kō mề (nē nề) ya sâ ka shìga r̃ī]ìyā mahàukàcī nề kai** 'Whatever the reason you climbed in the well, you were crazy.'

3. PHRASAL NATURE OF kō- FORMS

The **kō**-forms are generally presented as morphologically complex *words*. However, apart from the fixed H-H words **kōwā** and **kōmē**, the **kō**-forms can be seen to be phrasal in nature in that it is possible to insert such items as modal particles between **kō** and the Q-word components, e.g.,

kō mā wằyê ya zō...   Whoever also comes...
kō fa nawà ka bā nì...   However much you give me...

Particularly interesting is that prepositions, which syntactically one would expect to occur before the kō- forms, are found inserted in the middle, e.g.,

kō <u>dà</u> wàcē cè	with whomever (f.)
kō <u>dà</u> mè	with whatever
kō <u>dà</u> yàushē (= kōyàushē)	anytime/always
kō <u>ta</u> yàyà	by whatever means
= kō <u>ta</u> hālin yàyà (lit. kō- via character.of how)	
kō <u>ta</u> wàcè = <u>ta</u> kōwàce	through whichever
e.g., kō <u>ta</u> wàcè ƙōfà̀ = <u>ta</u> kōwàcè ƙōfà̀	by whatever door
cf. ??kō <u>à</u> ìnā (= the more common <u>à</u> kō'ìnā)	at wherever

[References: Bagari (1987); Jaggar (1992a, esp. pp. 118–23); Parsons (1981, esp. pp. 589ff.)]

74. Verb Grades

1. GENERAL DISCUSSION

VERBS in Hausa occur in a number of morphological classes referred to as *grades*. (These are indicated throughout the grammar either as gr1, gr2, etc., or v1, v2, etc.) Each grade has a distinct phonological specification, defined in terms of tone pattern and "termination," which is either a final vowel, or, in a few cases, final -aC, e.g., **dafà** gr1 'cook', **zàgā** gr2 'insult', **kōmō** gr6 'return here', **gyàru** gr7 'be well repaired', **sayař** gr5 'sell'. Certain grades have an associated grammatical/semantic characterization; others do not.

Lexical verb bases occur in ("operate") numerous grades depending upon semantic and grammatical appropriateness. The verb **sàyā** gr2 'buy', for example, can also appear as **sayè** gr4 'buy up', **sayař** gr5 'sell', **sayō** gr6 'buy and bring', and **sàyu** gr7 'be well bought'. Similarly, the denominal verb **tsōratà** gr2 'be afraid of' (< **tsōrō** 'fright') also operates gr1 (**tsōràtā** 'frighten'), gr3 (**tsòratà** 'be afraid'), and gr5 (**tsōratař** 'frighten off'). Although different verb grades are normally mutually exclusive, because the derivational formation usually consists solely of a final vowel and an associated tone pattern, they are not semantically or syntactically incompatible. Thus, when morphophonologically feasible, combinations of grades do sometimes occur, e.g., **janyō** gr4 + gr6 'pull all this way' < **jā** gr0 'pull' (cf. **jânyē** gr4 'pull all/away', **jāwō** gr6 'pull this way'); **maidō** gr5d [dv] + gr6 'return something here', **bàdu** gr5d [dv] + gr7 'be given away', **halbìk(k)ē** (unnumbered ventive grade [dv]) + gr4 'shoot down and return'.

Within each grade, the verb form varies depending on the syntactic context. There are four recognized forms. The A-form is used if the verb occurs without a following object, either because the verb is intransitive and thus has no object, or because the verb is transitive but has had its object deleted or moved, e.g., **kwalabà tā fashè** (gr4-A) 'The bottle broke'; **sarkī yā hanà** (gr1-A) 'The chief forbade (it)'; **mōtà cē sukà sàyā** (gr2-A) 'It was a car they bought.' The B-form is used when immediately followed by a personal pronoun direct object, e.g., **kadà kà bī tà** (gr0-B) 'Don't follow her'; **tā tàmbàyē mù** (gr2-B) 'She asked us'; **mun fiddà su** (gr5d-B) 'We took them out.' The C-form is used before any other direct object, such as a simple noun or non-personal pronoun, e.g., **nā bincìkè màganàř** (gr4-C) 'I investigated the matter'; **zā sù kāwō wasu** 'They will bring some' (gr6-C). The D-form is used preceding an indirect object, e.g **tā gayà wà ƙawařtà làbāřì** (gr1-D) 'She told her friend the news'; **kadà kà cī minì àmānà** (gr0-D) 'Don't let me down' (lit. eat from.me trust). Unlike the A/B/C contexts, the pre-indirect object environment presents a number of complexities, including the fact that many verbs do not have D-forms. Rather, they either "borrow" a D-form from another grade or else add a pre-dative suffix (pds). This will be discussed in due course.

The accepted convention in Hausa dictionaries and grammars is to use the A-form as the citation form, a practice generally followed in this work. This citation form should *not*, however, be confused with the analytical underlying form, which, in the case of multiform verbs, is the C-form.

°AN: The analytical and historical justification for treating the C-form as the underlying base form is spelled out in Newman (1973).

In the scheme developed by Parsons (1960b), which serves as the point of reference for all treatments of the Hausa verbal system, there are seven grades, numbered and ordered 1 through 7. The grade labeled as grade 0 and the grades having letters added to the numbers (e.g., grade 3a) represent subsequent additions and modifications by other scholars. Table 30 presents the terminations and tone patterns for all grades. The grade tones given are those of finite verbs as they occur in non-imperative sentences: (As described in §37:2.1, the imperative imposes its own pattern that overrides normal tone assignments.) In the table, a notation like H-L-(H) indicates that a two-syllable verb has H-L tone whereas a three-syllable verb has H-L-H tone. Otherwise, tones are assigned and spread from right to left, e.g., the grade 6 verb **kakkařantō** 'read all and come' with an H-tone melody has H on each of the four syllables, whereas the grade 1 verb **řagařgàzā** 'shatter' with H-L-H tone surfaces as H-H-L-H. The indication (pds) in the D column means that the grade does not have a D-form as such but rather utilizes the pre-dative suffix before indirect objects. The [**dà**] included in the grade 5 row is a particle that accompanies these verbs; it is not a part of the verb per se. The H-tone pattern is a property of the verb only and not of the particle, which has inherent L tone. Alternatives noted with different grades will be explained later when that grade is discussed.

Table 30: Verb grade system

	A-Form	B-Form	C-Form	D-Form
Grade 0	-i H -ā/-ō H	-ī H -ā/-ō H	-i H -ā/-ō H	-i(i) H -ā/-ō H
Grade 1	-ā H-L-(H)	-ā H-L-(H)	-a H-L-(L)	-ā H-L-(H)
Grade 2	-ā L-H-(L)	-ē L-H	-i L-H	(pds)
Grade 3	-a L-H-(L)			(pds)
Grade 3a	-a H			(pds)
Grade 3b	-i/-u/-a H-L			(pds)
Grade 4	-ē H-L-(H) -nyē H-L-(H)	-ē H-L-(H) -nyē H-L-(H)	-e H-L-(L) -ē H-L-(H) -nye H-L-(L) -nyē H-L-(H)	-ē H-L-(H) -nyē H-L-(H)
Grade 5	-ař H	-ař [dà] H -shē H -Ø [dà] H	-ař [dà] H -Ø [dà] H	-ař [dà] H
Grade 5d	-dā H-L	-dā H-L	-dà H-L	-dā H-L
Grade 6	-ō H	-ō H	-ō H	-ō H
Grade 7	-u L-H			(pds)

We begin with a quick overview of the grade system as a whole, and then discuss each grade one by one in fuller detail.

1.1. Primary grades

The basic H-tone monosyllabic verbs, which typically end in /i/, e.g., **ci** 'eat' or /ā/, e.g., **jā** 'pull', and the small group of H-tone **CiCā** verbs, e.g., **kirā** 'call', have been incorporated into the grade system as the zero grade (gr0). Grade 1 contains basic **a(a)**-final verbs, e.g., **dafà** 'cook', as well as derived "applicatives" (often required with an indirect object), e.g., **faɗà** 'tell to'. This grade includes both transitive and intransitive verbs. Grade 2, an exclusively transitive grade, includes basic verbs, which historically were **i**-final, e.g., **sàyā** 'buy' (C-form **sàyi**), as well as derived verbs with a partitive sense. Before indirect objects, gr2 verbs, like those of grades 3 and 7, add the H-tone inflectional pds -aC)^H, e.g., **sun nēmam masà aikì** 'They sought work for him' (gr2+pds), cf. **sun nèmi aikì** (gr2-C) 'They sought work.' Grade 3 is an exclusively intransitive grade containing **a**-final basic verbs, e.g., **fita** 'go out'. Gr3a consists of a small number of disyllabic intransitive verbs that also have short final **-a**, but that have a heavy initial syllable and H-H tone, e.g., **ƙaura** 'migrate'. Gr3b consists of a small number of H-L disyllabic intransitive verbs ending in the short vowels **-i**, **-u**, and **-a**, e.g., **gudù** 'run away'. Grades 0, 1, 2, and 3 (including 3a and 3b) are primary grades. The other grades, which have a distinct semantic/grammatical characterization, are considered secondary. In principle, all verbs should operate (at least) one primary grade from which the secondary grades are derived. In fact, the system is defective in that some verbs only operate secondary grades, the presumed primary grade verb no longer being attested.

°AN: Parsons treats grades 1, 2, and 3 as primary, grades 4 and 5 as secondary, and grades 6 and 7 as tertiary. There are clear analytical advantages, however, in making a first cut between the primary and the nonprimary grades (all of which I call secondary) and then making whatever subdivisions of the secondary grades that are necessary.

1.2. Secondary grades

Grade 4 ("totality/finality"), which contains both transitive and intransitive verbs, indicates an action totally done or affecting all the objects, e.g., **sayè** 'buy up'. It sometimes also has a malefactive/deprivative sense, especially when used with an indirect object, e.g., **ƙwācè** 'take from'. The variant with /**nyē**/ is limited to a small number of monosyllabic gr0 stems, e.g., **shânyē** 'drink up'. Grade 5 ("efferential"), traditionally termed *causative*, is an exclusively (or almost exclusively?) transitive grade that indicates action directed away from the speaker, e.g., **zubař** 'pour out'. It also serves to transitivize inherently intransitive verbs with an actor subject, e.g., **fitař** 'take out' (cf. **fìta** gr3 'go out'). Semantic direct objects of gr5 verbs require the use of the oblique marker **dà**, e.g., **yā zubař dà giyà** 'He poured out the beer', **yā sayař dà ita** 'He sold it.' The B-form with -**shē**, followed by a direct object pronoun, occurs as an alternative to the citation form plus **dà**, e.g., **nā gaishē sù** = **nā gayař dà sū** 'I greeted them.' Some gr5 verbs have a short form used before a direct object, in which the grade termination is omitted, e.g., **yā zub dà ita** 'He poured it out' (= **yā zubař dà ita**). Grade 5d is a dialectal form, in which the oblique marker **dà** is fused to the verb stem, e.g., **yā zubɗà ta** 'He poured it out.' Grade 6 ("ventive") indicates action in the direction of or for the benefit of the speaker, e.g., **sayō** 'buy and bring back'. Grade 7 ("sustentative") indicates an agentless passive, middle voice, action well done, or the potentiality of sustaining action, e.g., **dàfu** 'be well cooked', **tàru** 'meet'. All secondary grades have corresponding weak verbal nouns formed with the suffix `-wā`.

1.3. Irregular verbs

In addition to the verbs that operate regular grade forms, there are some ten or so irregular verbs. These are verbs that, in their basic forms at least, do not appear to fall within any of the established grades, although some of them do operate secondary grades in a regular manner. (These verbs are all indicated as v*, even though some of them could be classified as gr2* or gr3*, i.e., irregular members of a normal grade.) Verbs in this group include **ganī** 'see', **sanì** 'know', **barì** 'leave, let', **kusa** 'draw near', **zama** 'become', **hau** 'mount', **kai** 'take', **bā/bai** 'give', **jē** 'go', and **zō** 'come'.

2. GRADE 0: BASIC MONOTONAL VERBS

2.1. Form

A-Form	B-Form	C-Form	D-Form
-i H-	-ī H	-i H	-i(i) H
-ā/-ō H	-ā/-ō H	-ā/-ō H	-ā/-ō H

Grade 0 is a small, very restricted class that includes some eight H-tone monosyllabic verbs (termed "monoverbs"), and four H-tone CiCā verbs. Six of the monoverbs end in -i (with variable vowel length), namely, **bi** 'follow', **ci** 'eat', **fi** 'exceed', **ji** 'hear, feel', **ƙi** 'hate', and **yi** 'do'; two end in -ā, namely, **jā** 'pull' and **shā** 'drink', and one ends in -ō, namely, **sō** 'want, love'. The four CiCā verbs are **biyā** 'pay', **jirā** 'wait', **kirā** 'call', and **rigā** 'precede'.

◊HN: Historically, some of the **Ci** verbs (e.g., **bi** and **ƙi**) probably derive from disyllabic verbs with a /y/ in the second syllable, e.g **bi** < **biyà*. Others (e.g., **ci** and **yi**) derive from true monoverbs reconstructable as such for Proto-Chadic, e.g., **ci** < **ti*. Eulenberg (1972) noted that the two ā-final monoverbs (**jā** 'pull' and **shā** 'drink') both contain a palatal consonant and on this basis made the reasonable suggestion that they derive from disyllabic stems belonging to the CiCā class, i.e., **jā** < **ziyā* and **shā** < **siyā*.

There is evidence in the language of the former existence of a few more **Cā** gr0 verbs. These are stems that now occur only in gr5, namely, **kā(yař)** [dà] 'knock down' < **kā*; **tā(yař)** [dà] 'raise' < **tā* (cf. **tāshì** 'get up', with an archaic **-sV* suffix); and **yā dà** 'throw out' < **yā* (cf. Bole **yā** 'throw').

The **CiCā** gr0 verbs all exist alongside equivalent gr2 verbs with final -yà, e.g., **kirā** 'call' = **kìrāyà**. This would suggest that the **CiCā** verbs might be apocopated forms of original trisyllabic verbs. Because, however, -yà exists (using the historical present) as a verb stem formative, it is not clear whether **kirā**, for example, is derived from **kìrāyà** or vice versa. Viewing -yà as a suffix allows one to spot another erstwhile **CiCā** verb now restricted to gr5, namely, **kiyā(yař)** [dà] 'protect' (more or less = **kìyāyà**).

As far as **sō** is concerned, we do not yet know whether it is an archaism, representing an earlier period when it was normal for monoverbs to end in vowels other than -i or -ā, or whether it is a relatively recent creation.

Not all monosyllabic verbs are classified as gr0. The falling-tone verbs **sâ** 'put' and **cê** 'say' are phonologically aberrant "disyllabic" verbs belonging to grades 1 and 4 respectively. The verb **yō** 'do and come back' is simply a shortened variant of the regular gr6 form **yiwō**. The irregular verbs **kau** 'move aside' (< **kàwa*) and **hau** 'mount, ride' (< **hàwa*) etymologically are phonologically reduced gr3 verbs. (In its transitive usage, **hau** is probably a clipped gr1 verb.) Synchronically **kai** 'take' is classified as v* (irregular verb) as is **bā/bai** 'give'. The high-frequency intransitive verbs **jē** 'go' and **zō** 'come' are also considered v* because they do not share the regular morphosyntactic features of the gr0 verbs.

The **Ci** verbs have an underlying short vowel, which is used in the A and C forms. The verb **yi** 'do' commonly drops the vowel and phonologically attaches to the final syllable of the preceding word, e.g., **àbîn dà mukà yi** → **àbîn dà mukà y** → **àbîn dà mukài** 'the thing that we did'. (This coalescence is reflected in the written language as well as in pronunciation.) In the pre-pronoun B-form, the vowel automatically lengthens. (Pronominal objects of gr0 verbs belong to the L-tone weak object set.) The D-form exhibits dialectal and lexically specific variation in the length of the vowel. The pattern for most

SH speakers is for **yi** to retain its short final vowel in the D-form and for the other **Ci** verbs to lengthen the vowel, e.g.,

A. **nāmà̠ nē sukà ci**	It was meat they ate.
B. **mun fī sù wày̠ō**	We are smarter than them. (lit. we.comp exceed them cleverness)
C. **sun ci nāmà̠**	They ate meat.
D. **kà yi masà aikìn!**	Do the work for him! (lit you.sub do for.him work.the)
D. **kadà kà cī masà àmānà̠!**	Don't let him down! (lit. don't you.sub eat to.him trust)

The verbs **yi** and **ji** also exhibit variation in the length of the /i/ when occurring in sociative constructions with the preposition **da**: for some speakers it is short, for others it is long, e.g.,

yà̠yà̠ ka ji dà mutà̠nên? = **yà̠yà̠ ka jī dà mutà̠nên?**	How do you feel about the people?
yā yi dà nī = **yā yī dà nī**	She slandered me.

°AN: If **yi/yī dà** 'slander, backbite' is not a semantically specialized use of the verb **yi** 'do', as I have tended to assume—but with little justification—then one has a homophonous verb **yi** to add to the list of **Ci** monoverbs.

Grade 0 verbs ending in -ā or -ō do not change the length of the final vowel in the different syntactic environments: phonologically the vowel is always long, whether in the A, B, C, or D environment. Like independent pronouns and certain other H-tone morphemes, however, the H-tone long-vowel gr0 verbs do undergo a phonetic change in prepausal position (see §54:1.2.2). Here they appear with final glottal closure and a half-long vowel, e.g., **yā jā** [jaˑʔ] 'He pulled (it)', **zā sù biyā** [biyaˑʔ] 'They will pay.'

Grade 0 verbs regularly form verbal nouns by means of a suffix -:)^HL, which consists of vowel lengthening (which affects only the short final vowel **Ci** verbs) and a set H-L tone melody. With the true monoverbs, the H-L is realized as a fall; with the disyllabic **CiCā** verbs, the H-L spreads over the two available syllables. These verbal nouns are all masculine, e.g., **bi** 'follow', **bî** 'following'; **shā** 'drink', **shâ** 'drinking'; **sō** 'want, love', **sô** 'wanting, loving, love (n.)'; **biyā** 'pay', **biyà̠** 'paying'; **kirā** 'call', **kirà̠** 'calling'.

2.2. Meaning and function

Grade 0 contains a small number of high-frequency, basic verbs. They do not have a common semantic characterization. What combines them as a class is the shared phonological shape and the use of the same verbal noun formative. All grade 0 verbs can function transitively. Some also function intransitively, e.g.,

sukàn shā tābà̠	They smoke. (lit. ...drink tobacco)
mù kirā tà	Let's call her.
zā sù yi aikìn	They will do the work.
lōkàcī yā yi	Time is up. (lit. time 3m.comp do)
kadà kà ci wannàn nāmà̠!	Don't eat this meat!
kàsuwā tanà̠ cî	The market is in full swing. (lit. market 3f.cont eating)
tā biyā mù	She paid us.
bùkātà̠r̃sà tā biyā	He achieved his wishes. (lit. need.of.his 3f.comp pay)

3. GRADE 1: BASIC VERBS, APPLICATIVES, ACTOR-INTRANSITIVES

3.1. Form

A-Form	B-Form	C-Form	D-Form
-ā H-L-(H)	-ā H-L-(H)	-a H-L- (L)	-ā H-L-(H)

Grade 1 verbs end in -a(a). In the A, B, and D contexts, the vowel is long and the tone pattern is H-L-(H), i.e., H-L if disyllabic, H-L-H if polysyllabic. (Gr1 verbs take strong object pronouns, which invariably have H tone regardless of the immediately preceding tone of the verb.) In the C-form, the final vowel is short and the tone pattern is H-L-(L). (Note: If there are more syllables than there are tones indicated, the tones spread to the left, thus a quadrisyllabic gr1 verb in the A-form will have surface H-H-L-H tone, whereas in the C-form it will have H-H-L-L tone.) Examples:

A. yā kāmà̀   He caught (it).
B. yā kāmà̀ ta   He caught her/it.
C. yā kāmà ɓàraunìyā   He caught the female thief.
D. yā kāmà̀ masà ɓàraunìyā He caught the female thief for him.
A. sun rāzànā   They terrorized (s.o.).
B. sun rāzànā su   They terrorized them.
C. sun rāzànà farar̃-hùlā They terrorized the civilians.
D. sun rāzànā manà farar̃-hùlā They terrorized the civilians for us.
A. zân tumur̃mùsā   I'll throw (him) to the ground. (e.g., in wrestling)
B. zân tumur̃mùsā shi   I'll throw him to the ground.
C. zân tumur̃mùsà yār̃ò   I'll throw the boy to the ground.
D. zân tumur̃mùsā mikì shī I'll throw him to the ground for you (f.).

> °AN/◊HN: [i] According to the usual descriptions of Hausa, the underlying final vowel of gr1 verbs (and of gr4 verbs) is long and there is a shortening rule in the C-form before noun direct objects. As explained in Newman (1973), there is/was no general shortening rule. Rather, the final vowel is underlyingly short (as seen in the C-form) and the long vowel found in the other forms is due to morphophonological processes, such as the general rule that lengthens vowels before personal pronoun objects.
> [ii] I am assuming that the underlying tone of polysyllabic gr1 verbs is H-L-H, e.g., **kar̃àntā** 'read'. The H-L-L tone found in the C-form is most probably a result of morphophonological lowering of the final H when occurring on a short vowel, e.g., *tā kar̃ànta littāfì → tā kar̃àntà littāfì 'She read a book.'

In the imperative, the A-, B-, and D-forms of gr1 verbs, which end in long -ā, have L-H tone, whereas the C-form with the short final-vowel has L-L tone, e.g.,

kàmā ta! Catch her! **kàmà ɓàraunìyā!** Catch the thief!
ràzànā manà farar̃-hùlā! Terrify the civilians for us! **ràzànà farar̃-hùlā!** Terrify the civilians!
tùmùr̃mùsā! Throw (s.o.) to the ground! **tùmùr̃mùsā shi!** Throw him to the ground! **tùmùr̃mùsà yār̃ò!** Throw the boy to the ground!

Gr1 verbs regularly take weak verbal nouns. These are formed by adding an L-H non-integrating suffix ˋ-wā to the A-form of the verb. With polysyllabic verbs, which end in an H tone, the L tone of the suffix attaches to the preceding H to produce a fall, e.g., **rāzànā** 'terrify' + **ˋwā** → **rāzànâwā** 'terrifying'. When added to a disyllabic word, which ends in an L tone, the L of the suffix is simply absorbed into the preceding syllable, e.g., **kāmà** 'catch' + **ˋwā** → **kāmàwā** 'catching'.

A handful of disyllabic verbs with the tone pattern falling-high behave as if they were trisyllabic, i.e., they have HL-H tone and a long final vowel in the A-, B-, and D-forms and HL-L and a short final vowel in the C-form. These verbs include **bâutā** 'worship', **gyârtā** 'repair' (= **gyārà**), **kwântā** 'lie down', **kyâutā** 'behave kindly toward, do a good deed to', **mântā** 'forget', **rântā** 'lend (money)', **sânyā** 'put' (= **sâ**), **shâidā** 'inform, testify', **shânyā** 'spread out to dry', **'yântā** 'manumit', **zântā** 'converse'. Examples:

A. **sun zântā**   They conversed. **sunà zântâwā** They are conversing.
B. **mun 'yântā su**   We redeemed them from slavery.
C. **nā mântà àdìrēshìnsà** I forgot his address.
D. **tā shâidā masà**   She informed him.

The verb **sâ** 'put, put on' is best analyzed as a phonologically reduced disyllabic gr1 verb with a zero second consonant, i.e., **sâ** < //saØà// (< *sakà?). Like other gr1 verbs, it forms regular verbal nouns with **ˋwā**, e.g., **mè yakè sâwā**? 'What is he putting on?'

3.2. *Meaning and function*

Grade 1 includes both transitive verbs, e.g., **dafà** 'cook', **sussùkā** 'thresh', **wāsà** 'sharpen' (e.g., a knife), and intransitive verbs, e.g., **tsayà** 'stop', **zaunà** 'sit'. Nevertheless, gr1 needs to be thought of as a fundamentally transitive grade. For example, when gr1 verbs pair with verbs of other grades to form transitive/intransitive pairs, the gr1 always serves as the transitive member, e.g., **zubà** gr1 'pour', cf. **zùba** gr3 'flow out', **fasà** gr1 'break' (e.g., a bottle), cf. **fashè** gr4 'become broken'. The use of gr1 as the transitive counterpart in verb pairs is particularly common with derived denominal verbs, e.g., **tājìrtā** gr1 'enrich', cf. **tàjìrtà** gr3 'become rich' (< **tājìrī** 'rich man'); **fāɗàɗā** gr1 'widen', cf. **fàɗàɗà** gr3 'become wide' (< **fāɗī** 'width'). The nature of gr1 intransitives will be discussed below.

Grade 1 includes some basic nonextended simple verb stems and some verbs where the ending is part of a derivational process, either active, as with the denominal verbs, or frozen, as in the case of historically remnant suffixes (see chap. **76**). It also includes many verbs with an applicative extensional suffix. Finally, it includes a number of verbs whose makeup is not clear.

3.2.1. Basic verbs

Many verbs belong to gr1 simply because they have the inherent lexical shape that puts them in that class, namely, final -ā and H-L(-H) tone. Some are morphologically simple; others are "complex," i.e., they contain synchronically productive or historically frozen morphological suffixes, or are/were pluractional variants of simple verbs. A certain number of loanwords are also found in gr1, the assignment to this grade presumably being on analogical or phonological grounds. The various non-extended verbs do not necessarily share common semantic characteristics. Examples:

a. (simple): **cikà** fill; **dafà** cook; **dasà** transplant; **daɓà** pound floor; **dakà** pound; **ɗagà** lift up; **ɗanà** set, adjust, cock (trigger, bow, etc.); **ɗasà** pour in drops; **gasà** roast; **ginà** build, make pottery; **gusà** (v.i.) move aside; **gwadà** measure; **hūtà** (v.i.) rest; **iyà** be able to; **jimà** (v.i.) wait, be a long time; **kafà** erect; **kaɗà** beat (e.g., drum), whisk; **kāmà** catch; **karà** (**dà**) (v.i.) clash (with); **kasà** put in separate heaps, classify; **kōmà** (v.i.) return; **matsà** pinch together, get nestled close to; **musà** deny, contradict; **niƙà** grind; **rakà** escort, accompany (s.o.); **rinà** dye (e.g., with indigo); **rumà** (= **rùmāmà** gr3) (v.i.) subside (e.g., of wind or crying); **sāƙà** weave; **sōyà** fry; **taɓà** touch; **tākà** tread on; **tayà** make an offer, help s.o.; **tunà** remember; **tsayà** (v.i.) stop; **turà** dye; **tisà** grind (condiments on millstone); **tsibà** heap up; **wāsà** sharpen (a blade); **zubà** pour in

b. (complex): **aunà** weigh; **biyà** go via, pass by; **babbàkā** roast, singe; **ɓallà** fasten, hook up; **ɓarkà** rip open; **dannà** press down; **duhùntā** darken; **ɗinkà** sew; **fāɗàɗā** broaden; **faràntā** whiten, gladden; **faɍkà** (v.i.) wake up; **fusàtā** anger s.o.; **gaisà** (v.i.) exchange greetings; **girmàmā** honor, show respect to; **jūyà** turn (sth) round or over; **ƙarfàfā** strengthen, encourage; **ƙididdìgā** calculate; **maimàitā** repeat; **sassàƙā** carve; **shiryà** prepare; **shūkà** plant; **sussùkā** thresh; **tallàtā** display goods for sale; **tsattsàgā** tap, shake down; **waiwàyā** (v.i.) turn one's head around; **zaunà** (v.i.) sit, settle, live; **zurfàfā** deepen

c. (loanwords): **bayyànā** (Ar.) explain, describe; reveal, display, expose; **canzà** (Eng.) change, exchange goods or money; **ɗabbà'ā** (Ar.) print, publish; **fassàɍā** (Ar.) translate, explain; **jōnà** (Eng.) splice, join together; **kaɍàntā** (Kanuri?) read, **ɍubùtā** (Kanuri) write; **wānà** (Eng.) wind

◊HN: From a comparative/historical point of view, basic verbs with final -a(a), which are reflected in Hausa in grades 1 and 3, are very restricted. The typical pattern in West Chadic is for "a-verbs" to be limited to disyllabic words with a light first syllable (Schuh 1977b). Disyllabic gr1 verbs with a heavy initial syllable and all polysyllabic gr1 verbs can thus be assumed to have some historical or analytical explanation, i.e., they are unlikely to be direct reflexes of basic a-verbs.

3.2.2. Applicatives
Many gr1 verbs that are identical in shape to basic a-verbs actually contain a hidden applicative derivational extension -a)$^{\text{HL(H)}}$. The applicative serves to direct the action of the verb onto the object (direct or indirect) or onto a location. This typically shows up in the argument structure of a sentence with an applicative as compared with a corresponding sentence without the applicative. Various functions of the applicative will be presented in turn.

3.2.2.1. The applicative is commonly used as a pre-i.o. D-form, either as a replacement for verbs that occur in other grades without the i.o., e.g., grades 2 and 3, or as the sole form for verbs that always take an i.o. In many cases, the applicative with the i.o. changes the orientation of the action. In some cases, a gr1 applicative followed by an i.o. means essentially the same as a corresponding gr2 verb with a direct object, e.g.,

tā **faɗà** masà **làbāɍì** (gr1)	She told him the news.
cf. tā **fàɗi làbāɍì** (gr2)	She told the news.
yā **fāɗà** matà dà **faɗà** (gr1)	He fell upon her with fighting,
cf. yā **fāɗì** (gr3b)	He fell down.
yā **gāfàɍtā minì** (gr1)	He forgave me. (lit. he.comp forgive to.me)
= yā **gàfaɍcē nì** (gr2)	
zā mù **nēmà** wà **àbōkinkà aikì** (gr1)	We will seek work for your friend.
cf. zā mù **nèmi aikì** (gr2)	We will seek work.
yārò yā **gātsà** minì **ɗan yātsà** (gr1)	The boy bit my finger. (lit. ...bit to.me finger)
cf. yā **gàtsi ràkē** (gr2)	He bit off a piece of sugar cane.
zân **arà** mukù wasu **lìttàttàfai** (gr1)	I'll lend you some books.
cf. zân **àri** wasu **lìttàttàfai** (gr2)	I'll borrow some books.
màsīfà tā **aukà** musù (gr1)	A calamity befell them, cf. yā **àuku** It happened. (gr7)
màtaɍ Audù tā **rufà** masà **àsīɍī** (gr1)	Audu's wife kept his secret. (lit. ...covered for.him secret)
yanà **kōyà** manà **Hausa** (gr1)	He is teaching us Hausa.
cf. munà **kòyon Hausa** (VN < gr2)	We are learning Hausa.

sun yaɾɓà masà lâifī (gr1)   They falsely accused him. (lit. ...smeared on.him blame)
gwamnatì tanà gallàzā wà mutằnē (gr1) The government is harassing/pestering people.
= gwamnatì tanà gàllazaɾ̃ mutằnē (VN < gr2)
nā taimàkā masà   I helped him. = nā tàimàkē shì (gr2)

Applicative gr1 verbs commonly take the thematic instrument as the syntactic d.o. and express the thematic object as an i.o., e.g.,

yā jēfà wà kàrē dūtsè (gr1)   He threw a stone at the dog. (lit. ...threw to dog stone)
= yā jèfi kàrē dà dūtsè (gr2) (lit. ...threw at dog with stone)
yā sōkà wà ràƙumī wuƙā (gr1)   He thrust a knife into the camel.
= yā sòki ràƙumī dà wuƙā (gr2)   He stabbed the camel with a knife.
yanà fyāɗà masà būlālà (gr1)   He is flogging him with a whip.
= yanà fyàɗaɾ̃sà dà būlālà (VN < gr2)
sun zungùrà wà gafiyà sàndā (gr1)   They poked the bandicoot rat with a stick.
(lit. poke to bandicoot stick)
zā tà shāfà wà jinjìrī mâi (gr1)   She will spread oil on the baby. (lit. ...wipe to baby oil)
yā līƙà matà cìngâm à lulluɓī (gr1)   He (maliciously) stuck chewing gum on her shawl.
(lit. ...stick to.her chewing gum on shawl)

With a few applicatives, the thematic instrument can serve as a direct object even in the absence of an indirect object, e.g.,

yā haɾ̃bà bindigà (gr1) He shot a gun, cf. yā hàɾ̃bi tsuntsū (gr2) He shot (at) a bird.
yā jēfà wàsīƙà (gr1) He mailed (lit. threw) a letter, cf. yā jèfē tà (gr2) He threw (sth) at her.

3.2.2.2. Applicatives commonly occur in sentences that require the expression of a locative.

yā fāɗà ruwa   He fell in the water. (*not* **yā fāɗà), cf. yā fāɗì (gr3b) He fell.
sun rūgà (cikin) ɗākì   They rushed into the room.
tā damfàrà tufāfìntà à tukunyā   She stuffed her clothes into the pot.
yā dankà fāyilōlī à hannūnā   He handed the files over to me.
nā ɗaurà sir̃dì gà dōkì   I saddled the horse. (lit. ...tie saddle to horse)
cf. nā ɗaurè dōkì I tied the horse. (gr4)
yā ɗōfànà gòshinsà à ƙasà   He lightly touched his forehead to the ground.
àkuyà tā dumà bàkintà à ƙwaryā   The goat put its mouth deep into the calabash food bowl.
nā tōkàrà sàndā gà tufānìyā   I propped a stick against the door screen.
yā kwaɓà gàtarī à ƙōtà   He hafted the axe onto the handle.
tā lullùɓà mayāfī à kântà   She covered her head with a cloth.
(lit. covered cloth at head.of.her)

In many cases, there exist pairs of related sentences in which an applicative verb with a locative phrase is matched by an applicative with an indirect object. Examples:

tā baɗà yājì [à nāmà] (lit. she.comp sprinkle spices [at meat])
= tā baɗà [wà nāmà] yājì (lit. she.comp sprinkle [to meat] spices)
        She sprinkled spices on the meat.
yā gōgà mân mōtà [à jìkin mōtà] (lit. he.comp rub oil.of car [at body.of car])

= yā gōgà [wà mōtà] mân mōtà (lit. he.comp rub [to ca]r oil.of car)
      He rubbed polish on the car.
yā dallàr̃à tōcìlàn [à idònā] (lit. he.comp dazzle flashlight [at eye.of.my])
= yā dallàr̃ā [minì] tōcìlàn (lit. he.comp dazzled [to.me] flashlight)
      He dazzled me with the flashlight.
tā dōdànà itàcē [à bāyansà] = tā dōdànā [masà] itàcē à bāya
      She touched him in the back with a stick.
tā zumbùd̃à gishir̃ī [à miyàr̃] = tā zumbùd̃ā [wà miyàr̃] gishir̃ī
      She put a lot of salt in the stew.
an shir̃6ùnà mâi [à jìkinsà] = an shir̃6ùnā [masà] mâi
      One applied a lot of oil on him.

3.2.3. Intransitives

Intransitive gr1 verbs can be divided into those that are "nonmotivated" as opposed to those that are "motivated."

The nonmotivated intransitive verbs are those that operate gr1 simply because their phonological shape threw them into gr1 and not because of any semantic or syntactic reason. Prime examples of this are far̃kà 'wake up' (< fàd̃akà gr3) and tafsà [dv] 'boil' (= tàfasà gr3), both of which became gr1 by accident when the syncope of the middle short vowel and an L-H to H tone simplification rule resulted in their having a surface shape with H-L tone and final -a(a). Some intransitive verbs acquired the canonical shape of gr1 verbs when they added a now frozen remnant suffix of the form -Cà(a), e.g., zaunà 'sit', waigà 'turn around', aukà 'collapse, cave in'. Finally, gr1 also contains a small number of what appear to be simple, basic intransitive verbs that just happen to be gr1 for no apparent reason, e.g., tsayà 'stop', jimà 'spend some time', lafà 'die down', nitsà 'settle down, calm down'.

Some intransitives, on the other hand, do have certain characteristics that indicate that their assignment to gr1 is motivated by lexical or grammatical factors. By "motivated", I mean simply that one can offer some reason why the particular verb operates gr1 rather than some other grade; it does not mean that the assignment had to have taken place or that all verbs with that property necessarily operate gr1. Generally speaking, intransitive counterparts of transitive verbs use the underlying patient as subject, e.g., yā cikà tùlū 'He filled the water pot' (v.t.) ⇒ tùlū yā cìka (v.i.) 'The water pot filled up.' Hausa tends to avoid intransitive sentences with actor subjects; in such cases, the activity may be expressed by means of the pro-verb yi 'do' plus an action noun or by some other paraphrase, e.g., yā har̃bi bàrēwā 'He shot an antelope' ⇒ yā yi har̃bì 'He hunted' (lit. he did shooting). The sentence yā har̃bā would mean 'He shot (it)', with object understood, and thus has to be considered a transitive sentence even though the object is not overtly expressed. Intransitives with actor subjects are not, however, impossible. In such constructions, the typical grade form is not the inherently intransitive gr3 nor the often intransitive gr4, but rather gr1. In other words, one function of gr1 verbs is to express intransitives with "actor subjects." Included here are "lexically reflexive" verbs requiring a plural subject. If the intransitive gr1 verb has a corresponding transitive counterpart, it may be in gr2 or, most often, in gr1 itself. Examples:

kin taimàkā (gr1)   You helped, cf. kin tàimàkē tà (gr2)   You helped her.
nā nēmà (gr1)   I tried, looked around, cf. nā nèmi aikì (gr2)   I sought work.
nā hangà àmmā bàn ga kōwā ba (gr1)   I looked (from a distance) but didn't see anyone.
cf. mun hàngi mayàk̃ā can nēsà (gr2)   We saw warriors there in the distance.
sun gwabzà (dà jūnā) (gr1)   They came to blows (with one another).
cf. sun gwàbji jūnā (gr2)   They beat one another.
sun dārà (gr1)   They laughed. = sun yi dàriyā (lit. they.comp did laughter)

kà dākàtā (gr1)	Wait, pause! cf. **kà dàkàci zuwànsù** (gr2)	Wait for their arrival!
iskà tā būsà (gr1)	The wind blew. cf. **yā būsà sàrēwà** (gr1)	He blew the flute.
lallè yā kāmà (gr1)	The henna took. (lit. caught hold)	
cf. **yā kāmà àku** (gr1)	He caught the parrot.	
yārò yā gařà à gùje à kân kèkensà (gr1)	The boy sped off on his bicycle.	
cf. **yārò yā gařà wīlì** (gr1)	The boy rolled the wheel (along the ground).	

3.2.4. Sociatives

Some gr1 verbs function syntactically not as transitives or intransitives but rather as sociatives, where the semantic object is expressed as the object of the preposition **dà** 'with' (see §75:4). These verbs include the following:

aikà dà	send sth		karà dà	clash with
ɓātà dà	no longer be friends with		kulà dà	attend to
ɗāsà dà	be on good terms with		mântā dà	forget (sth)
gānà dà	converse with		sābà dà	be acquainted with
gaisà dà	exchange greetings with		tunà dà	remember (sth)
gusà dà	move sth. away (from)		yabà dà	praise

4. GRADE 2: BASIC TRANSITIVE VERBS AND PARTITIVES

4.1. Form

A-Form	B-Form	C-Form	D-Form
-ā L-H-(L)	-ē L-H	-i L-H	(pds)

Grade 2 verbs, the infamous "changing verbs" of traditional Hausa grammars, are characterized by a change in the final vowel in the three syntactic environments A, B, C. (In the D context, gr2 verbs either switch to another grade or use the inflectional pre-dative suffix.)

The A-form (the conventional citation form) ends in -ā and has L-H-(L) tone, i.e., L-H if disyllabic, L-H-L if polysyllabic, e.g., **màrā** 'slap', **cìzā** 'bite', **shèƙā** 'sniff, smell', **jèfā** 'throw at', **tsòratà** 'fear sth/s.o.', **gàgarà** 'be difficult for', **tàttàmbayà** 'ask often'.

> °AN/◊HN: The common verb **ɗaukà** 'take, carry', which has the regular B- and C-forms **ɗaukē** and **ɗauki**, appears to have the wrong tones for a gr2 verb, i.e., H-L ā-final verbs are normally gr1. The explanation is that the now disyllabic A-form derives by shortening from a trisyllabic stem *ɗawukà* that *did* have the correct L-H-L tone pattern. (The LH to H simplification following the internal vowel syncope is fully regular (see §71:1.2).)

A few disyllabic verbs have irregular A-forms that are used in place of or as an alternative to the normal A-form. These A-forms are identical to corresponding verbal nouns and in fact represent the extension of a verbal noun into what is syntactically a finite verb environment. Examples:

faɗì (= fàɗā)	tell, e.g., **àbîn dà ta faɗì** what she said
dībà (verbal base //ɗēb-//)	dip out, take
sāmù (= sàmā)	get, e.g., **ī, nā sāmù** Yes, I got (it).
sakì (= sàkā)	let loose

There is also a systematic deviation from the standard A-form that occurs in the imperative. In the imperative, gr2 verbs manifest final -i in the A-form instead of the usual -ā (see §37:2.2.1 for fuller discussion). Examples:

hàr̄bi! Shoot (it)! (cf. **nā hàr̄bā** I shot (it)); **sàci!** Steal(it)!; **tàmbàyi!** Ask!

The pre-pronoun B-form has an L-H tone pattern and ends in long -ē. This vowel conditions palatalization of preceding coronal obstruents. The pronoun objects of gr2 verbs belong to the weak object set. These pronouns are underlying toneless clitics, which in non-imperative sentences are realized as L. In standard orthography, the pronoun is written as a separate word even though it is clearly a clitic bound tightly to the verb.

yā ɗàukē shì	He took it.
mun tàttàmbàyē sù	We questioned them a lot.
bà tâ cìjē kà ba	She probably won't bite you.
nā tsòràcē sù	I feared them.
kadà kà màrē nì!	Don't slap me!
(This is subjunctive, not imperative.)	

A few gr2 verbs have clipped forms that are used in the B (as well as C and D) environments, namely, **ɗau** < **ɗaukā̀** 'take', **sau** < **sàkā** 'let loose', **sai** < **sàyā** 'buy', e.g.,

zâi sau tà = zâi sàkē tà	He will divorce her. (lit. ...release her)
mù sai sù = mù sàyē sù	Let's buy them.

In fast speech, the 1s and 3m pronouns **nì** and **shì** (< //sì//) are sometimes reduced to `ⁿn and `ⁿs respectively, i.e., a consonant with an L tone. Note that if the final /i/ is omitted, the /s/ does not palatalize to /sh/; rather it is either pronounced as /s/ or else it rhotacizes to /r̄/. The floating L-tone of the pronoun is realized as a fall on the preceding syllable. The final -ē of the B-form shortens and alters into /a/ in the resulting closed syllable (i.e., ē → e → a /__C.), e.g.,

yā bùgân (< **bùgē nì**)	He beat me.
nā bùgâs (= **nā bùgâr̄**)	I beat him.
yā màrân	He slapped me.
yā sàuràrân	He listened to me.
yā ɗòkâs (= **yā ɗòkâr̄**)	He beat him.

An interesting question is what happens in this construction when the final consonant of the verb stem is one that normally palatalizes before -ē. Because the centralization of /ē/ to [a] appears to be a late, low-level phonological rule, one would expect the palatalization to remain. Surprisingly, this is not always the case. Verbs with underlying root-final /s/ and /z/ tend to appear before [a] without the palatalization, e.g.,

yā cîzân = yā cìjē nì	He bit me.
yā gàbzân = yā gàbjē nì	He whacked me.
yā ìsân = yā ìshē nì	It suffices me.
nā nàusâs = nā nàushē shì	I punched him.

Verbs that normally exhibit **d ~ j** alternation invariably appear with palatalization (giving further evidence that the **z → j** and **d → j** rules have a different status in the language), e.g.,

yā gùjân (not **gùdân) = yā gùjē nì	He ran from (is avoiding) me. (cf. gudù run)
yā gàjân = yā gàjē nì	He succeeded/inherited from me. (cf. gàdā inherit)

°AN: On first thought, the asymmetry of /z/ and /d/ is the opposite of what one might have expected given that phonologically z → j is a much more regular process in the language than is d → j. It makes sense, however, if one considers that d → j has a somewhat tenuous status as a phonological process rule and thus the /j/ one gets in verb forms like **gùjē** and **gàjē** is *morphologically* fixed and therefore impervious to the phonetics of the reduced vowel.

With stem-final /t/, speakers tried to sidestep the palatalization dilemma by avoiding the reduced pronoun form. When pressed to use the reduced pronoun form, however, the /t/ was generally retained without palatalization, e.g.,

yā gàyyàtân	He invited me. (better than yā gàyyàcân; but best is yā gàyyàcē nì)
mun sàtâs	We stole it. (= [Skt] mun sàtai), *not* **mun sàcâs, but best is mun sàcē shì)

The pre-non-pronoun direct object C-form has an L-H tone pattern and ends in short **-i**. This high front vowel also conditions palatalization. Examples:

'yan sàndā sun cåkùmi ɓàrāwò	The policemen nabbed the thief.
yakàn fàɗi gaskiyā	He tells the truth.
nā tsòràci dòdō	I was afraid of the goblin.
kàrên bà zâi cìji yāròn ba	The dog won't bite the boy.
kù tàimàki jūnā	You should help one another.
kù ɗàuki (= ɗau) wannàn!	Take this! [ɗau is an optional clipped form]
mutằnên sun nèmi sù bijìrē	The people tried to revolt. [sentence d.o.]
Irregular: yā såmu (= såmi) kuɗī	He got some money.

ΔDN/°AN: Unlike the B-form (of all grades), which must be followed *immediately* by a d.o. pronoun clitic, the C-form can be separated from its object. For example, any of the modal particles can be interposed between the verb and the d.o., e.g., **yā hàr̃bi mā gīwā** 'He even shot an elephant' (lit. he.comp shoot even elephant). Moreover, in certain northern dialects, the second **ba** of the discontinuous negative morpheme appears between the verb and a noun d.o., e.g., **bài hàr̃bi ba gīwā** 'He didn't shoot an elephant', but *not* **bài hàr̃bē ba tà** (lit. neg.he shoot neg it/her).

◊HN: The exact historical explanation for the final vowel alternation in gr2 verbs is still unknown. We can, however, say the following: The historically original lexical-final vowel was short **-i**, and not the **-ā** found in the conventional citation form used in dictionaries and such. Thus, the underlying form of a verb like 'choose' was originally *zàɓi, not zàɓā. This **-i** has been preserved in present-day Hausa in the C-form (and possibly in the imperative as well). The pre-pronoun vowel **-ē** undoubtedly represents a *phonological* deviation from long *-ī (for reasons still not clear), the lengthening of vowels before clitic pronoun objects being a regular morphological feature of the language, thus zàɓi + pn > zàɓī-pn > zàɓē-pn. (Suggestions that the -ē comes from the final -ā of the A-form plus the 3m pronoun -y or that it represents a distinct grammatical morpheme strike me as highly unlikely.) The final -ā of the A-form (the present-day "anaphora stem") was probably due to a *morphosyntactic* replacement of the lexical form by a related form with a distinct final vowel *and* tone pattern, namely, a stem-derived verbal noun, i.e., [zàɓi]$_V$ ⇒ [zàɓā]$_{VN}$. Note that the drift toward using verbal nouns in the finite A environment continues in Hausa, cf. the A-form **faɗì** 'tell', derived from an H-L -**ì** verbal noun), with the regular A-form **fàɗā**. (On this historical question, see the discussion in Newman (1973, 1979b), with an alternative viewpoint by Frajzyngier (1982).)

Grade 2 verbs in the D context makes use of the inflectional benefactive/dative marker that I have called the pre-dative suffix (pds). (This pds is also used in the D context with some gr3 and gr7 verbs.) The pds has the shape -**aC**)^H, i.e., it is a tone-integrating suffix with all H tone. The final consonant generally appears as /**m**/ before the **ma** allomorph of the i.o. marker (with H or L tone) and -**r̃** before **wà**. Examples:

sun girba̱m manà dāwà (gr2+pds)	They reaped the guinea-corn for us.
sun girba̱r̃ wà manòmī dāwà (gr2+pds)	They reaped the guinea-corn for the farmer.
	= They reaped the farmer's guinea-corn.
cf. **sun gìrbi dāwà** (gr2 C-form)	They reaped the guinea-corn.
kunà nēma̱m masà aikì? (gr2+pds)	Are you seeking work for him?
kunà nēma̱r̃ wà yārònā aikì?	Are you seeking work for my boy?
= [dv] **kunà nēma̱m mà yārònā aikì?** (gr2+pds)	
cf. **kunà nēman aikì?** (VN)	Are you seeking work?

A few clipped gr2 verbs occur without the suffix, e.g., **yā sam mini nāmà** 'He got meat for me', cf. **yā sàmu nāmà** 'He got meat'; **zō nân mù ɗau masà kāyân** 'Come here let's lift the load for him', cf. **zō nân mù ɗauki kāyân** 'Come here let's lift the load'; **yā sai matà / wà yārinyà zanè** 'He bought a wrapper for her / for the girl', cf. **yā sàyi zanè** (C-form) 'He bought a wrapper.'

4.2. Meaning and function

All grade 2 verbs are transitive and take direct objects, e.g., **yā sàci kèkè** 'He stole a bicycle', **nā tàmbàyē sù** 'I asked them.' With the non-object A-form, an underlying object is always understood, either from the sentence itself or from the discourse, e.g.,

mè ka hàr̃bā?	What did you shoot?
zân ɗaukà	I'll take (it).
yāròn dà na màrā	the boy that I slapped
Hondà cē ya sàyā	It was a Honda he bought.
mun fàhimtà	We understand (what you were talking about).

With indirect objects, some verbs add the pre-dative suffix (pds). Other verbs require or allow a switch to a gr1 applicative, often, but not always, with a difference in meaning as compared with the pds form. (Another option, especially when the indirect object is heavy, is to express the thematic beneficiary not by a syntactic indirect object phrase but rather by a prepositional phrase with **gà** 'to' that occurs after the d.o. (see §57:1). In this case, the verb will take its normal B-form or C-form depending on the nature of the d.o.) Examples:

tanà gamɓasar̃ wà yārò furā (gr2+pds)	She is breaking off a large chunk of *fura* for the boy.
mun zàɓar̃ wà ɗàlìbai littāfì (gr2+pds)	We chose a book for the students.
yā sātam minì dōkì (gr2+pds)	He stole the horse for me. / He stole my horse.
cf. **yā sācè minì dōkì** (gr4-D)	He stole the horse from me.
cf. **yā sātō minì dōkì** (gr6-D)	He stole the horse for me.

yā sōkam minì rā̀ƙumī (gr2+pds)   He stabbed my camel.

cf. yā sōkà̀ wà rā̀ƙumī wuƙā (gr1-D [applicative])   He thrust a knife into the camel.

kà rantam masà fâm gōmà (gr2+pds)   You should borrow ten pounds for him.

cf. kà rântā masà fâm gōmà (gr1-D [applicative])   You should lend him ten pounds.

zā sù nēmař wà yārònā aikī̀ (gr2+pds)   They will seek work for my boy.

= zā sù nēmà̀ wà yārònā aikī̀ (gr1-D [applicative])

yā faɗà̀ manà làbārī̀ (gr1-D [applicative])   He told us the news.

(< fàɗā tell) (no gr2+pds form allowed)

mun fàɗi làbārī̀ gà waɗànnân mutànē, mazā dà mātā (gr2-C)

     We told the news to these people, men and women.

tā ɗībam musù ruwā (gr2+pds)

     She dipped out some water for them. *or* She dipped out their water.

°AN: The verb 'dip out' has an irregular A-form (ɗībà̀) that is derived from the verbal noun. The B- and C-forms (ɗèbē, ɗèbi) are regular. In the D-form, there is variation among speakers as to whether they add the pds to the A-form stem or to the underlying lexical base, i.e., tā ɗībam musù ruwā = tā ɗēbam musù ruwā.

In nonfinite environments, the A, B, and C forms of gr2 verbs are obligatorily replaced by verbal nouns. By contrast, the form containing the pds in the D context, which is strictly a verbal stem, remains as is. Examples:

yā yi ta [hařbìn]ᵥₙ sù (not **yā yi ta hàřbē sù)   He kept on shooting at them.

sunà̀ [tàmbayàř]ᵥₙ sà (not **sunà̀ tàmbàyē shì)   They are asking him.

bā yà [kòyon]ᵥₙ Lāřabcī (not **bā yà kòyi Lāřabcī)   He is not learning Arabic.

sunà̀ [bugam]ᵥ minì ɗā   They are beating my son. (lit. …beat to.me son) (gr2+pds)

cf. sunà̀ [bugùn]ᵥₙ ɗānā   They are beating my son.

wà̀ yakè̀ [zāɓař]ᵥ wà ɗà̀lìbai littāfī̀?   Who is choosing a book for the students? (gr2+pds)

wà̀ yakè̀ [zāɓìn]ᵥₙ littāfī̀?   Who is choosing a book?

The grammatical replacement of gr2 finite verbs by verbal nouns also applies to A-forms, although here the verbs and verbal nouns are often (but not always) phonologically identical. (The reason for this is that A-forms are derived historically from verbal nouns.) Examples:

wà̀ kukè̀ tàmbayà̀? (VN)   Whom are you asking?

cf. wà̀ kukà tàmbayà̀? (gr2-A)   Whom did you ask?

mū nè̀ sukè̀ cùtā (VN)   It is us they are cheating.

cf. mū nè̀ sukà cùtā (gr2-A)   It is us they cheated.

yanà̀ sàyē (VN)   He is buying (it).

cf. yā sàyā (gr2-A)   He bought (it).

From the point of view of meaning, gr2 consists of two major classes: basic verbs not having a unified semantic component and derived partitives. Gr2 also includes a certain number of verbs that have various other characteristics.

4.2.1. Basic verbs

Many transitive verbs belong to gr2 because they happen to have the inherent lexical shape that puts them in that class. They do not necessarily share common semantic characteristics. The underlying lexical form (= the surface C-form) of a gr2 verb like as **fàɗi** 'tell sth', for example, is monomorphemic. It is *not* made up of a stem plus a semantically defined extensional affix, as is the case with the derived grades, e.g., **faɗō** gr6 'tell and come' < //faɗ-// 'tell' plus //-ō// 'hither'. As a semantically open, morphophonologically defined class, gr2 turns out to be the largest class of basic transitive verbs in the language. Examples include the following:

àikā send s.o.; **àmsā** receive, accept; **àrā** borrow sth; **àurā** marry s.o.; **bìɗā** look for, seek; **cètā** save, rescue; **cìzā** bite; **ɗaukà** take (up), carry; **dàgurà** gnaw at; **ɗìbà** dip out, scoop up; **dòkā** beat, hit; **fàfarà** chase, pursue furiously; **fàɗā** tell, say; **fànsā** redeem from slavery, manumit; **gàdā** inherit (from); **gàrgaɗà** warn, chastise; **hàrbā** shoot at, sting; **jèmā** tan (leather); **ƙwàrzanà** scratch; **kòyā** learn; **màmayà** attack by surprise; **mùsāyà** exchange; **nàusā** punch s.o.; **ràinā** care for a child; **rìgāyà** precede; **sàtā** steal; **sàurārà** listen; **tàtsā** milk an animal; **tàmbayà** ask; **tùnkuyà** butt, gore

> ◊HN: Historically basic gr2 verbs have two sources. Many gr2 verbs (e.g., **fàɗi** 'tell') are morphologically simple verbs that are direct reflexes of the Chadic "schwa class" (Newman 1973, 1975; Schuh 1977b), i.e., verbs with a lexically inherent non-low final vowel. Others, especially polysyllabic verbs (e.g **tàmbayà** 'ask'), contain a frozen suffix, the most common being *-yà (see §76:1). Because the resulting segmental and phonological shape was identical to that of the A-form of the simple gr2 verbs, these extended verbs fell into gr2. The behavior of synchronic doublets containing the not quite frozen -yà shows clearly that the grade assignment is a phonologically determined secondary phenomenon and not a deep grammatical/semantic one. For example, **rigā** gr0 'precede' + **-yà**$^{(L)HL}$ ⇒ **rìgāyà** gr2 (same meaning); **haɗè** gr4 'swallow' + **yà**$^{(L)HL}$ ⇒ **hàɗiyà** gr2 (same meaning); cf. **bi** gr0 'follow' + **yà**$^{(L)HL}$ ⇒ **biyà** gr1 (same meaning); **karè** gr4 'snap' + **yà**$^{(L)HL}$ ⇒ **karyà** gr1 'break sth' or **kàrayà** gr3 'lose hope'.

4.2.2. Partitive/displacive

In addition to the many semantically basic verbs, gr2 includes a number of derived partitive/displacive verbs, which can be analyzed as containing a tone-integrating extensional suffix **-i**$)^{LH}$.

> ◊HN: Partitive clearly was among the inventory of Proto-Chadic extensions. Given the regular Hausa sound change of non-initial *r > y (Newman 1977a), the gr2 partitive ending -i (< *-iyi? < *-iri?) could easily be cognate with the Margi partitive extension -ri (Hoffmann 1963).

Hausa partitives often have an associated separative meaning, i.e., not only do they indicate action affecting part of the object—in this sense being the opposite of the gr4 totality extension, to be discussed below—but they also tend to connote removal or displacement, e.g., **yànkā** gr2 'cut off a little piece of', cf. **yankà** gr1 'slice sth, slaughter'. In some cases the partitive verb can be contrasted directly with a synchronically co-occurring nonpartitive verb form; in other cases, only the presumed partitive form exists. (In these latter cases, one cannot be absolutely sure whether one is dealing with a basic i-verb or whether the verb really contains a derivational extension.) Examples:

àikatà v2	partially finish work, cf. **aikàtā** v1 do sth		**ɓallā** v2	unhook, cf. **ɓallà** v1 hook up
gàtsā v2	bite off a piece, cf. **gàtsà** v1 bite		**gùdā** v2	run from, cf. **gudù** gr3b run
hàƙā v2	dig up, cf. **haƙà** v1 dig		**jèmā** v2	tan part of, cf. **jèmà** v1 tan
kàryā v2	break off, cf. **karyà** v1 break		**ƙìrgā** v2	count out, cf. **ƙirgà** v1 count
sùssukā v2	thresh part of, cf. **sussùkā** v1 thresh		**yàɗā** v2	skim off, cf. **yāɗà** v1 spread
ɓàntarà v2	break a piece off		**fìzgā** v2	wrench out
tsàmā v2	pick out of a liquid		**tsìntā** v2	pick out one by one

4.2.3. Figurative/metaphorical

A few apparently derived gr2 verbs have a figurative meaning, usually with an animate object, in contrast to the literal meaning relating to an inanimate object. These verbs commonly have a negative connotation. Examples:

dàmā v2	bother, annoy s.o., cf. **dàmà̰** v1 stir
nìƙā v2	do a lot of sth (often unpleasant), cf. **nìƙà̰** v1 grind
sàrƙā v2	stick to a psn, be a regular at sth, cf. **sarƙà̰** interlace, intertwine
sôkā v2	criticize, cf. **sôkā/sōkà̰** v2/v1 stab
tùƙā v2	upset s.o., cf. **tūƙà̰** v1 stir, drive

5. GRADE 3: BASIC INTRANSITIVES

5.1. Form

A-Form	B-Form	C-Form	D-Form
-a L-H-(L)			(pds)

Grade 3 verbs end in short **-a**. (The related grades 3a and 3b are described in following sections.) Because all gr3 verbs are intransitive they do not have B-forms or C-forms. The corresponding verbal noun lengthens the final vowel, e.g., **shìga / shìgā** 'enter / entering'. In the D environment (i.e., when followed by an indirect object) gr3 verbs employ the same inflectional pds found with gr2 verbs, e.g., **yā shigam mìnì gidā** 'He entered my house' (lit. he.comp enter.pds to.me house). Disyllabic gr3 verbs all have L-H tone. Most have a light first syllable, although there are exceptions, which include some very common verbs such as **sàuka** 'get down'. Polysyllabic gr3 verbs have L-H-L tone (but see below). Examples:

(a) **bùra** ripen; **ɗìga** drip; **fìta** go out; **mùla** disappear; **rùɓa** rot, spoil; **shìga** enter; **tsìra** sprout, germinate; **nùka** become ripe by storing; **nṳ̀na** become ripe, mature; **yàrda** agree
(b) **dàgulà** become spoiled, disturbed; **màlālà** flow; **zàburà** jump up; **dùgùnzumà** become upset or confused

> ◊HN: [i] The syllable weight restriction on the disyllabic verbs is an old, inherited feature. In related West Chadic languages like Bole (e.g., Lukas 1970/71–1971/72; Schuh 1977b), it is common for basic nonderived verbs with lexical-final **-a** to be restricted to disyllabic verbs with a light initial syllable.
> [ii] In WH the word for 'ripen' is **nùna** with a short vowel in the first syllable. The SH form **nṳ̀na** probably derives from *nùk-na, built on the other 'ripen' root **nùka**.

Gr3 is an extremely large class because it contains a high number of intransitive polysyllabic verbs (trisyllabic and quadrisyllabic). Some of these (a) are monomorphemic as far as we can determine, but most (b) are morphologically complex, either containing derivational suffixes (frozen or active) or reflecting frozen reduplication (see §62:4). Examples:

(a) **bàlagà** reach puberty; **kùɓutà** escape; **màkarà** be late
(b) **dùlmuyà** sink in water; **fàɗakà** wake up; **gùdānà** flow, happen; **dùnānà** become mildewed; **gàgarà** be difficult; **kàlkalà** be(come) cleanly shaved or swept; **Mùsùluntà** become a Muslim; **tùmùrmusà** wallow in dirt; **zàfafà** become hot; **zàmanà** become

Although polysyllabic gr3 verbs typically have L-H-L tone, trisyllabic pluractional verbs derived from disyllabic gr3 forms normally have L-L-H tone, e.g., **fìřfítá** 'go out, many people' < **fíta** 'go out'; **shìsshìga** 'enter often' < **shìga** 'enter'. (The L-H-L pattern is also attested with the pluractional forms, i.e., **fìřfítá** = **fìřfìtà**, but with modern SH speakers, the L-L-H variant is clearly preferred.) The tonal distinction between pluractional and nonpluractional polysyllabic gr3 verbs is unique in the grade system, because elsewhere tone assignment depends simply on the number of syllables without regard to whether the verb is basic, derived by affixation, or derived by reduplication.

◊HN: Historically, the disyllabic gr3 verbs—all of which would have had a light first syllable—and the polysyllabic gr3 verbs, which synchronically constitute a single grade, belonged to different morphological classes. The former had a fixed L-H tone pattern, the initial L spreading to the left in the case of pluractional forms like **fìřfítá**. The attested L-H-L pluractional variant, as in **fìřfìtà**, represents an innovation by analogy with the tone of the very common L-H-L trisyllabic verbs. Intransitive polysyllabic verbs, such as **zàbuřà** 'jump up', had intrinsic L-H-L tone, and very possibly ended in schwa, not -a.

The irregular gr3* verbs **gàji** 'tire, **tàfi** 'go', and (also?) **ƙòshi** 'be replete' are presumably clipped forms of trisyllabic verbs containing the remnant **-yà** suffix, namely, *gàjiyà, *tàfiyà, and *ƙòshiyà, respectively. Note that these presumed fuller forms (evidenced in the verbal nouns **gàjiyà** and **tàfiyà**) serve as synchronic bases for various derivations, e.g., **gàjìyayyē** 'tired' (past participle) (< //gajiy-//) not **gàjajjē** (< //gaj-//), **tàfìyu** 'well traveled' (gr7) (< //tafiy-//) not **tàfu** (< //taf-//), but cf. **tàfe** 'on the go' (stative).

5.2. *Meaning and function*

Gr3 verbs are all intransitive (or sometimes sociative, accompanied by the preposition **dà** 'with'). This valency is the essential feature of gr3. The grade does not have any discrete semantic properties per se. The grade includes many of the most basic, inherently intransitive verbs in the language, such as **fíta** 'go out', **shìga** 'enter', **cìka** 'fill up', etc., which are mostly disyllabic. Some of these intransitive verbs take actor subjects, e.g., **yārò yā fíta** 'The boy went out'; others have patient subjects, e.g., **tùlū yā cìka** 'The waterpot filled.' Those with actor subjects can be transitivized by use of the gr5 efferential extension, e.g., **yārò yā fìtař dà kāyā** 'The boy took out the loads.' Those with patient subjects usually have corresponding gr1 transitive forms, e.g., **yārò yā cìka tùlū** 'The boy filled the waterpot'; **shìnkāfā tā sùlālà** 'The rice was parboiled' (gr3), **tā sulàlà shìnkāfā** 'She parboiled the rice' (gr1). With a few gr3 verbs (mostly polysyllabic), the semantic roles of the subject and object dictate that the corresponding transitive verb be gr2 rather than gr1, e.g., **nā gùndurà** (gr3) 'I have lost interest'; **hūtun nàn yā gùndurē nì** (gr2) 'This vacation bores me.'

Gr3 includes large numbers of derived polysyllabic verbs that operate gr1/gr3 transitive/intransitive pairs. For example, gr3 is the standard intransitive counterpart of gr1 for derived verbs of sensory quality (see §2:3), e.g., **fāɗaɗā** gr1 'broaden' / **fàɗaɗà** gr3 'become broad' < **fāɗī** 'breadth'; **zāfàfā** gr1 'heat up' / **zàfafà** gr3 'become hot' < **zāfī** 'heat'; and for denominal verbs with -TA (see chap. 79), e.g., **fusàtā** gr1 'anger s.o.' / **fùsātà** gr3 'be(come) angry' < **fushī** 'anger'; **tsawàitā** gr1 'lengthen' / **tsàwaità** gr3 'become long' < **tsawō** 'length'; **ƙaryàtā** gr1 'contradict, give lie to' / **ƙàryatà** gr3 'prove false' < **ƙaryā** 'a lie'; **tsōràtā** gr 1 'frighten' / **tsòratà** 'be(come) afraid' (cf. also **tsòratà** gr2 'be afraid of') < **tsòrō** 'fear'.

Gr3 is an important source of intransitive modal verbs with semantically empty subjects that take sentential complements, e.g., **yā kàmātà** (gr3) **kà tàimàkē shì** 'It is fitting that you help him'; **yā hàřamtà** (gr3) **gà Mùsùlmī sù ci nāmàn àladè** 'It is unlawful for Muslims to eat pork.' Other examples include **càncantà** 'be suitable/fitting/appropriate', **fàskarà** 'be impossible/difficult/hard to', **hàlattà** 'be legal/allowed/lawful to'. (For unexplained reasons, all of these complement-taking gr3 verbs are trisyllabic.)

A number of gr3 verbs enter into sociative constructions containing the preposition **dà**, e.g., **kà lùřa dà mōtōcī kàfìn kà ƙetàrè hanyà** 'Pay attention to the traffic before you cross the street.' These include **gàji dà** 'tire of', **hàƙurà dà** 'be patient with', **shàgalà dà** 'be occupied with', **yàřda dà** 'trust, accept', **zàƙwàiƙwatà dà** 'be eager to'. A few typically occur with the preposition **gà**, e.g., **dànganà gà** 'resign oneself to (God's will)', **dògarà gà** = **dògarà dà** 'rely on'.

Gr3 verbs before indirect objects normally make use of the pds. The exact semantic reading (benefactive/possessive/dative) depends on the verb in question, e.g.,

kà fitam minì gidā!	Get out of my house! (< **fita** go out)
zākì yā zābuřař wà dilā	The lion sprang up at the jackal. (< **zàburà** jump up)
cīwò yā ařalam masà à jējì	An illness came upon him in the bush.(< **àřalà** happen)
bàn yařdam mukù ba	I don't agree for you (to do it). (< **yàřda** agree)

6. GRADE 3A : BASIC INTRANSITIVES (H-H)

6.1. Form

A-Form	B-Form	C-Form	D-Form
-a H			(pds)

The designation gr3a is used for a small class of disyllabic intransitive verbs not accounted for in Parsons' original system. These are characterized by a final short -a, H-H tone, and a heavy first syllable. (Contrast the norm for regular gr3 disyllabic verbs, which is L-H with a light first syllable.) The mid vowels /ē/ and /ō/ are not included among the long vowels that occur in the initial syllable. The following is a full list of readily accepted gr3a verbs in SH:

ɓūya hide; **cāřa** crow; **fařga** realize, understand; **girma** grow up; **kwāna** spend the night, spend a 24-hour day; **ƙāra** cry out; **ƙaura** emigrate; **kūka** cry [in fixed expressions]; **saura/shaura** remain, be left over; **sūma** faint; **tsīra** escape; **tsūfa** become old; **tūba** repent

The verb **kwāna** has a clipped form **kwan**, the final /n/ being subject to anticipatory assimilation, e.g.,

kwan lāfiyà! = [kwallāfiyà] 'Sleep well!'

ΔDN: In WH, a few additional examples are attested, e.g., **ɗwāɗa** 'crackle' (referring to burning wood), **karya** (= SH **kàrayà** gr3) 'break, get discouraged', **nūtsa** 'sink under water', **shāfa** 'be forgetful'.

Simple gr3a verbs are all disyllabic; it is only their pluractional forms that are trisyllabic. These have the normal all H tone pattern, e.g., **ɓuɓɓūya** 'hide (many or often)', **giggirma** 'grow up (of various people)'.

Secondary grade forms derived from gr3a verbs often display an internal vowel change, e.g., **ɓūya** gr3a 'hide', **ɓōyè** gr4 'hide (sth)'; **tsīra** gr3a 'escape', **tsērè** gr4 'escape from'. (Corresponding Gr5 verbs sometimes have alternative forms with the two different vowels, e.g., **tsīrař** gr5 = **tsērař** gr5 'rescue'.) The gr3a form **ƙaura** 'emigrate' uses an extended -TA stem in other grades, e.g., **ƙauràcē** gr4 'emigrate from'.

6.2. Meaning and function

All grade 3a verbs are intransitive. However, as compared with regular gr3 verbs, they are thematically more restricted, i.e., the subject is never an affected patient. Moreover, they tend to enter into secondary grades less readily than simple gr3 verbs. Before indirect objects, gr3a verbs either use the inflectional pds or else switch to another grade, e.g.,

tā tūba gr3a	She repented.
cf. **tā tūbař wà iyàyentà** (gr3a+pds)	She repented (sought the pardon of) her parents.
sun kwāna à gidānā gr3a	They spent the night in my house.
cf. **sun kwānam minì gidā** (gr3a+pds)	They spent the night in my house (not to my liking).
yā tsīra gr3a	He escaped.
cf. **yā tsērè manà** (gr4-D)	He escaped from us. *or* He surpassed us.
sun ƙaura gr3a	They migrated.
cf. **sun ƙauràcē manà** (gr4-D)	They deserted/snubbed us.
tā sūma gr3a	She fainted.
cf. **tā sōmè masà** (gr4-D)	She fainted on him.

Like the regular gr3 class, gr3a verbs form their corresponding verbal nouns by lengthening the final vowel, e.g., **sunà ɓūyā** 'They are hiding', **bà zā sù iyà tsīrā ba** 'They will not be able to escape.' The major difference between the two classes is that the verbal nouns of gr3 verbs are all feminine whereas gr3a verbal nouns are mostly masculine. (Only **cāřā** 'crowing' and **fařgā** 'realizing, realization' are strictly feminine; all the others are either exclusively masculine, e.g., **girmā** 'size, importance', **kūka** 'crying', or variable in gender depending on dialect or idiolect, e.g., **tsīrā** m. or f. 'escaping'.)

◊HN: Synchronically, gr3a and gr3 can be viewed as phonologically partially determined subclasses of intransitive -**a** verbs, the former being disyllabic with a heavy first syllable (with accompanying H-H tone), the latter being either disyllabic with a light first syllable (with accompanying L-H tone) or polysyllabic (with L-H-L tone). Historically, however, gr3a verbs probably have a totally different origin, independent of the gr3 class. The usually masculine gender of the gr3a verbal nouns and the ablaut relation between gr3a verbs and other derivatives supports the suggestion, originally made by Parsons (personal communication), that these verbs were created by back-formation from the verbal nouns, i.e., **girma** 'grow up' and **tsīra** 'escape', for example, came from **girmā** 'size, importance' and **tsīrā** 'an escape/escaping', respectively, and not vice versa.

7. GRADE 3B: BASIC INTRANSITIVES (H-L)

7.1. Form

A-Form	B-Form	C-Form	D-Form
-**i** / -**u** / -**a** H-L			(pds)

Grade 3b verbs end in short -**i**, short -**u**, and short -**a**. The original/underlying final vowel is probably -**i** (or, at a more abstract level, *-**ə**). The surface -**u** is presumably due to assimilation to the /u/ in the preceding syllable or to the bilabial /f/, whereas the -**a** is due to assimilation to the /a/ in the preceding syllable. These verbs are all disyllabic and all have H-L tone. Examples (complete):

ɓācì become damaged, spoiled; **fāɗì** fall; **tāshì** stand up, get up; **wunì** (= **yinì**) spend the day; **gudù** run (away); **haifù** (= **haihù**) give birth, have a child; **mutù** die; **ɓatà** get lost

◊HN/ΔDN: The WH verb **zakà** 'come, go' (= SH **zō**) probably belongs to this class, i.e., it derives from a gr3b stem ***zakà**. Compare its verbal noun **zakùwā** with **fāɗùwā**, which corresponds to the gr3b verb **fāɗì** 'fall'.

The corresponding trisyllabic pluractional forms have H-H-L tone, e.g., **faffāɗì** 'fall (many people or times)', **hahhaifù** 'give birth often'.

7.2. Meaning and function

This is a lexically closed set of very basic intransitive verbs with a nonpatient subject. As with gr3 and gr3a, those gr3b verbs that allow an indirect object must either use the pds or switch to some other grade, the choice being lexically specific, e.g., **yā fāɗam minì** (gr3b+pds) 'It dropped on me', cf. **yā fāɗà** (= **faɼ**) **matà dà faɗà** (gr1) 'He ranted at her' (lit. fell upon her with fighting); **shēgèn nan yā gudam minì dà mōtà** (gr3b+pds) 'That bastard absconded with my car' (lit. ran from me with car), cf. **kadà kà gujè manà!** (gr4) 'Don't run away from us!'; **yanà tāsam matà da hàurāgìyā** (gr3b+pds) 'He is attacking her with wild talk'; **Bellò yā ɓacè minì** (g4) 'Bello escaped from my sight'; **tōcìlàn tā macè manà** (gr4) 'The flashlight died on us' (< **mutù**).

The corresponding verbal nouns of gr3b verbs are formed in two ways. Either they undergo final vowel lengthening, in which case they are masculine, e.g., **gudù** 'running', or else they add a suffix **-ā** (with insertion of epenthetic glides and tone adjustments), in which case they are feminine, e.g., **mutuwà** 'dying, death'.

◊HN: Historically gr3 and gr3b represent basic intransitive verb classes distinguished primarily by the final vowel. The former all ended in the low vowel **-a** (and had L-H tone), e.g., ***fìta** 'go out'. The latter ended in a high vowel (and had H-L tone), e.g., ***fāɗì** 'fall'. In Chadic, the exact quality of this non-low vowel (referred to loosely as "schwa") varies from language to language, appearing generally either as /i/, /u/, or /ə/. For the general distinction between Chadic a-verbs and schwa-verbs, see Newman (1975) and the discussion in §16.2 below.

8. GRADE 4: TOTALITY/FINALITY

8.1. Form

A-Form	B-Form	C-Form	D-Form
-ē H-L-(H)	-ē H-L-(H)	-e H-L- (L)	-ē H-L-(H)
		-ē H-L-(H)	
-nyē H-L-(H)	-nyē H-L-(H)	-nye H-L- (L)	-nyē H-L-(H)
		-nyē H-L-(H)	

Grade 4 verbs end in -e(e).The vowel is long in the A, B, and D forms. (Direct object pronouns use the strong H-tone set.) The pre-noun C-form has two variants, one with a short vowel (which patterns with gr1 verbs) and one with a long vowel. The long vowel variant is considered slightly more intensive than the short vowel variant, e.g., **yā kaɼkàɗè bàɼgō** 'He shook out (dirt from) the blanket'; **yā kaɼkàɗē bàɼgō** 'He shook out the blanket thoroughly.' Disyllabic gr4 verbs have H-L tone in all environments, e.g., **rufè** 'close', **fērè** 'pare', **narkè** 'melt'. The tone of polysyllabic verbs depends on the length of the final vowel. Verbs with long final -ē have H-L-H tone, e.g., **bincìkē** 'investigate', **kaɼkàshē** 'kill many', **ɼagaɼgàjē** 'be shattered, smashed up', **takaɼkàrē** 'strive hard, exert oneself'. Polysyllabic verbs with a short -e in the C-form have H-L-L tone, e.g., **tsōkànè** 'poke, prod s.o.'; **dabaibàyè** 'hobble an animal's forefeet'.

◊HN: A reasonable suggestion is that the original final vowel of verbs with the gr4 extension was invariably long (like that of the final -ō of gr6) and that the short vowel variant before noun objects was created by analogy with gr1. The slight semantic differences that now exist between the two forms would have ensued as a secondary development.

°AN: Underlyingly, polysyllabic gr4 verbs have H-L-H tone. The H-L-L tone on the short final vowel C-forms is due to the same morphophonological lowering rule that operates with gr1 verbs (see §3.1 above).

ΔDN: We do not know whether all Hausa dialects have the two vowel-length options in the C-form and if not which variant occurs. (According to Malami Buba, personal communication, the Sokoto dialect only has the short vowel gr4.) In SH, the short vowel C-form would seem to be the unmarked form. I would not, however, be surprised if the long-vowel form were found to be the norm in some other dialects.

A few gr0 monoverbs employ a suffix -**nye(e)**, instead of the bare final vowel. These behave as polysyllabic verbs with H-L-H tone (the initial HL surfacing as a fall), e.g., **jânyè** 'pull away' (= **jāyè** [dv]) < **jā** 'pull'; **shânyē** 'drink up' < **shā** 'drink'; **cînyē** (= **cânyè** [dv]) 'eat up' < **ci** 'eat'. The form **yînyē** 'complete' (= **wânyē** [dv]) < **yi** 'do' is given in the dictionaries, but is now considered archaic. The -**nyē** suffix is also attested with the disyllabic gr0 verb **kirā** 'call', but only in the specialized verbal noun form **kìrànyē** (= **kìràyē** [dv]) 'being summoned (often by magical means)'. Other monoverbs (ending in -**i**) add the regular -**ē** ending to an expanded base containing the suffix -**yà**, e.g., **ƙiyè** 'despise' (< **ƙi(yà)** 'hate'); **biyè** 'follow all' < **bi(yà)** 'follow'; **fiyè** 'exceed' (often pre-i.o.) < **fi(yà)** 'exceed'.

◊HN: The ending with -**nyē** is an archaism going back to a Proto-Chadic totality extension, which can be reconstructed, for West Chadic at least, as *-**àn(y)ē** (see Newman 1972a). The initial /a/ is reflected in the nonstandard forms **cânyē** (= **cînyē**) 'eat up' and **wânyē** (= **yînyē**) 'complete'.

The verb **cê** 'to say' can be treated as an irregular gr4 verb, probably derived from *can**è**. In SH, **cê** typically undergoes a morphotonemic change to **cè** when preceded by an H-tone CV (light-syllable) pronoun, e.g.,

wâddà ta cè "mādàllā"	the one who said "thank you"
nī nè na cè "mādàllā"	I was the one who said "thank you".
cf. yā/sun cê "mādàllā"	He/they said "thank you".
cf. sū nè sukà cê "mādàllā"	They were the ones who said "thank you".

All gr4 verbs form weak verbal nouns with -wā, e.g., **rufèwā** 'closing', **cêwā** 'saying', **shânyêwā** 'drinking up', **kařkàɗêwā** 'shaking out'.

8.2. *Meaning and function*

Grade 4, which includes both transitive and intransitive verbs, is an extremely common grade. Many of these verbs are derived from synchronically extant basic grade forms (gr0/1/2/3), but for others, gr4 has become the basic lexical item. Gr4 is a semantically heterogeneous grade whose verbs have a range of overlapping meanings and functions. The conventional label "totality" covers only one of these meanings and should not be interpreted too literally.

8.2.1. Totality/finality

Gr4 often indicates that the action of the verb has affected the totality or multiplicity of the object(s) or has affected them in such a way as to emphasize the intensity or finality of the action. With verbs indicating 'hitting' and such, gr4 generally adds the idea of 'knocking over'. If the verb is intransitive, use of the gr4 connotes totality of impact on the subject. (Note: In the examples, the length of the final vowel of the C-form, which can be long or short, will be given as found in my notes.)

sâ cikè buhunhunà	They will likely fill up the sacks. (< **cikà** v1 fill)
yā sayè audùgā	He bought up the cotton. (< **sàyà** v2 buy)
nā bugè shi	I hit him so that he fell. (< **bùgā** v2 hit)
sun haȓbè zākī	They shot dead the lion. (< **hàȓbā** v2 shoot)
kà shânyē madaȓā!	Drink up the milk! (< **shā** v0 drink)
nā ɓacè	I am completely lost. (< **ɓatà** v3b get lost)
mūgùn sarkī yanà dannè haȓȓìn talakāwā	
The evil king is oppressing the common people. (< **dannà** v1 press down)	
mōtàtā tā macè	
My car is kaput (i.e., died completely). (< **mutù** v3b die)	

Some verbs with "totality" semantics now operate gr4 to the exclusion of a basic verb, e.g.,

bindìgē gun down, execute (by firing squad); **binnè** bury; **garȓè** close tightly (a door); **kashè** kill; **kyankēnē** monopolize; **ȓārè** finish (tr.), be finished (intr.); **langàɓē** become soft, mushy from overcooking or being overripe; **lanȓwàmē** eat food greedily; **murȓùshē** knock down, subdue; **rāmè** become emaciated; **ȓatattàkē** shatter, disintegrate, deteriorate from age

8.2.2. Deprivative/separative

A second common meaning of gr4 (which may combine or overlap with the totality meaning) is action 'from' in a separative or deprivative (sometimes malefactive) sense. This shows up particularly when the sentence contains an indirect object. Examples:

yā jânyē kūrā	He dragged away the cart. (< **jā** v0 pull)
tā fizgè manà kuɗī	She snatched the money from us. (< **fìzgā** v2 snatch)
yâ naɗè tàbarmā?	Will he roll up the mat? (< **naɗà** v1 wind on (e.g., a turban))
zân yāgè yādìn nân	I'm going to tear off this cloth. (< **yāgà** v1 tear (up))
sun sācè mîn zōbè	They stole the ring from me. (< **sàtā** v2 steal)
cf. sun sātam mîn zōbè (gr2+pds)	They stole the ring for me. (*or* They stole my ring.)
kadà kà gujè manà!	Don't run away from us! (< **gudù** v3b run)
yā ɓōyè matà littāfì	He hid the/her book from her. (< **ɓūya** v3a hide)
sai kà ȓauràcē wà kàȓùwai	You should avoid prostitutes. (< **ȓaura** v3a migrate)
madaȓā tā zubè	The milk spilled away. (< **zùba** v3 leak)

Some verbs with separative/deprivative semantics also now operate gr4 to the exclusion of the basic verb, e.g.,

bauɗè	swerve aside	sālè	peel/scrape away
fīgè	pluck out hair, feathers	sullùɓē	slip from
kakkàɓē	shake dust off, shed leaves	tūɓè	take off (clothing), depose
kēɓè	set aside	wāgè	fly open (e.g., mouth)
kaucè	dodge, avoid	wārè	separate, set aside
kubcè	wrestle away from	yācè	wipe away perspiration
kwancè	untie (v.t.), become untied (v.i.)	yāyè	wean

8.2.3. Intransitive

In many cases, the grade 4 represents the intransitive (unaccusative) member of a transitive/intransitive verb pair without the addition of any extra semantic nuance. The transitive verb is usually gr1. Examples:

ɓalgàcē	become chipped (intr.)	ɓalgàtā	break off, chip off (tr.)
daɗḕ	be or last long (intr.)	daɗà̰	add, increase (tr.)
fashḕ	break, become smashed, explode (intr.)	fasà̰	break, smash (tr.)
hūjḕ	become pierced (intr.)	hūdà̰	pierce (tr.)
kafḕ	get stuck (intr.)	kafà̰	put up, erect (tr.)
karyḕ	break, snap (intr.)	karyà̰	break, snap (tr.)
lauyḕ	become bent, arched (intr.)	lauyà̰	bend (tr.)
narkḕ	melt (intr.)	narkà̰	melt (tr.)
r̃agar̃gàjē	fall apart, disintegrate (intr.)	r̃agar̃gàzā	break up (tr.)
yāmùtsē	crumble (intr.)	yāmùtsā	mix up (tr.)

◊HN: Furniss (1983) has suggested that the present gr4 might represent the merger of two historically distinct extensions: a totality extension and a detransitivizing extension. I have not been able to find any internal or comparative evidence to support this hypothesis. My guess is that we are dealing with one and the same extension and that the widespread use of the gr4 as a detransitivizer is due to a combination of semantic bleaching (weakening of the totality connotation) plus a natural association found in many languages between intransitive usage and finality/completeness.

A gr4 verb derived from a basic transitive verb can sometimes serve as a semantically fairly neutral intransitive or else as a transitive verb that is semantically marked (either as totality/finality or deprivative/separative), e.g.,

cījḕ	bite all (tr.), become jammed (intr.); cf. cìzā v2 bite
līɓḕ	seal up (tr.), be stuck (intr.); cf. līɓà̰ v1 stick on, attach to
tsāgḕ	split all (tr.), become split (intr.); cf. tsāgà̰ v1 split
yāgḕ	tear away (tr.), be torn (intr.); cf. yāgà̰ v1 tear (up)

Because of the development of grade 4 as a semantically neutral grade for intransitive verbs, one now finds doublets where an intransitive gr4 is semantically equivalent (more or less) to a basic gr3 intransitive, e.g.,

fìyà̰yē v4	become mildewed, moldy	= fìyāyà̰ v3
gìgìcē v4	be flustered	= gìgītà̰ (rare) v3
gumḕ v4	be filled with an odor	= gùma v3 (rare)
gurgùncē v4	become lame	= gùrguntà̰ v3 (less common)
ruɓḕ v4	rot	= rùɓa v3

8.2.4. Neutral/unmarked (semantic devaluation)

For large numbers of verbs, some transitive, some intransitive, and some both, gr4 has now become the basic form synchronically, i.e., these verbs no longer, or rarely, operate gr1, gr2, or gr3 forms. Originally these verbs must have carried distinctive gr4 extensional semantics—and in some cases, it is still recognizable—but nowadays the extra semantics has faded away and these verbs constitute semantically neutral forms. Note that the use of gr4 as the neutral form applies to derived verbs (such as those containing the verbalizing suffix -TA) as well as to simple stems. Here are some selected examples out of the hundreds that one could cite:

amằyē   vomit up; **cafề**   catch object that has been thrown; **cê** (irregular gr4)   say; **dabaibàyē** hobble an animal's forefeet, entangle (tr.), become entangled (intr.); **dāgùlē**   become spoiled, disturbed; **darjề**   slither, graze the skin; choose the best of; **daurề**   tolerate (tr.), be patient, persevere (intr.); **dunɗề**   be overcast; **dushề**   fade, become dim; **fācề**   patch sth (< Eng.); **fēɗề**   flay, skin an animal; **fēƙề**   sharpen to a point; **gōdề**   thank; **gurɗề**   twist, sprain (tr.), be twisted or sprained (intr.); **gwammàcē**   be preferable; **kasàncē**   become, happen, turn out that; **ƙōƙề**   fade (of colors); **ƙwarề**   become expert; **ƙyālề**   ignore; **mafề**   patch, mend (esp. clothing); **mōrề**   enjoy (tr.), enjoy oneself (intr.); **ragề**   reduce, decrease (tr.), remain left (intr.); **rantsề**   swear; **shantàkē**   dawdle, loll about; **tājề**   comb (cf. VN **tàzā** from original gr2 verb); **wallàcē** [WH]   swear; **warkề**   be cured, recover (tr. is gr5); **wāyề**   be enlightened, enlighten

9. GRADE 5: EFFERENTIAL

9.1. Form

A-Form	B-Form	C-Form	D-Form
-ař H	-ař [dà] H	-ař [dà] H	-ař [dà] H
	-shē H		
	-Ø [dà] H	-Ø [dà] H	

The gr5 ending -ař)[H], which is used in A, B, C, and D forms, is unique among the grade extensions (and most other Hausa suffixes) in that it ends in a consonant rather than a vowel, e.g., **fitař** 'take out', **sanař** 'inform', **kōyař** 'teach'. This suffix derives historically from //-as//, a shape that is still found in other dialects (and occasionally in SH) and still shows up synchronically in SH in the B-form allomorph -shē.

◊HN: The gr5 -as suffix has often been compared with the s-causative found throughout Afroasiatic (see, for example, Hodge 1971). There are two problems with this comparison. First, as will be discussed below, the description of the Hausa gr5 as a "causative" is inaccurate. Second, although good cognates exist throughout the Chadic family for many verbal extensions, /s/ as a causative-like affix in Chadic is barely attested, if at all. One thus has to entertain the possibility that the identity of the Hausa -s and other -s forms in Afroasiatic is simply a phonological accident without historical significance.

The tone pattern is all H, e.g., **tsōratař** 'frighten off', **wulākantař** 'treat contemptuously'. Gr0 monoverbs insert an epenthetic /y/ before the suffix, e.g., **bā-y-ař** 'give away', **ci-y-ař** 'feed'. (This glide is added by a phonological rule and is *not* evidence of a second root consonant in these words, as has been suggested by various scholars.) The verbs **tàfi** 'go' and **gàji** 'tire' build their gr5 stems on the extended bases //tafiy-// and //gajiy-// respectively, e.g., **tafiyař** 'administer, run' (not ***tafař**), **gajiyař** 'tire/bore s.o.' (not ***gazař**).

°AN: At an analytical level, there is reason to suggest that monoverbs require a heavy syllable as a host for the suffix, i.e., the base vowel must be lengthened if not already long. This morphophonological lengthening is then wiped out by a general phonological rule shortening long /ī/ before /y/, i.e., **ci** 'eat' + -ař ⇒ //cī-y-ař// → /ciyař/ 'feed'. (This seemingly inefficient sequence of morphophonemic lengthening followed by phonologically automatic shortening is also attested in the case of the genitive linker (see note in §43:2.1.3).)

Thematic objects of gr5 are typically expressed, not as syntactic direct objects, but rather as oblique objects of the particle **dà**, e.g., **yā shāyaȓ dà dōkì** 'He watered the horse', **tanà sayaȓ dà sū** 'She is selling them.' In normal speech, the /ȓ/ of the suffix assimilates fully to the /d/ of the particle, e.g., **yā sanaȓ dà gwamnà** → /**yā sanad dà gwamnà**/ 'He informed the governor', **kadà kì zubaȓ dà mâi** → **kadà kì zubad dà mâi** 'Don't pour out the oil.'

°AN: This assimilation is indicated, for example, in the entries in Abraham's dictionary (1962). According to the *Official Guide to Hausa Orthography* (1979), the assimilation is supposed to be ignored in writing; but in actual practice it is commonplace to find people writing **d** rather than **r** before **da**.

Gr5 verbs form weak verbal nouns with `-wā. The L tone of the suffix attaches to the preceding syllable to produce a fall, e.g., **fitaȓ** + `-wā → **fitâȓwā** 'taking out', **kaȓantaȓ** + `-wā → **kaȓantâȓwā** 'teaching'.

9.1.1. The short-form grade 5

Some twenty or so verbs—mostly gr0 verbs plus a few common disyllabic verbs with a light first syllable—have a short-form grade 5 without the -aȓ suffix. This form is always used along with the **dà** particle before an expressed direct object (noun or pronoun), e.g., **yā zub dà giyà** 'He poured out the beer' (= **yā zubaȓ dà giyà**); **yā zub dà ita** 'He poured it out/away.' The syllable preceding the **dà** is invariably heavy, either CVC or CVV, where the long vowel may be a monophthong or the dipththong /ai/ (derived from //ay//). In SH, **gajiyaȓ** 'tire, bore', **tafiyaȓ** 'run, administer', and **wahalaȓ** 'cause trouble' are about the only trisyllabic gr5 verbs to have corresponding short forms. Examples (complete):

bā dà	give away (= **bāyaȓ dà**) < **bā** / **bai** give to
bī dà	control (= **biyaȓ dà**) < **bi** follow
cī dà	feed (= **ciyaȓ dà**) < **ci** eat
kā dà	knock down (= **kāyaȓ dà**) < *kā
shā dà	give water to (= **shāyaȓ dà**) < **shā** drink
tā dà	raise (= **tāyaȓ dà**) < *tā (cf. **tāshì** get up)
yā dà	throw away (irreg. = **yar dà**) < *yā
ɓad dà (< //ɓat dà//)	lose, squander (= **ɓataȓ dà**) < **ɓatà** get lost
fid dà (< //fit dà//)	take out (= **fitaȓ dà**) < **fìta** go out
gai dà	greet (= **gayaȓ dà**) < **gayà** tell
ī dà (< //'iy dà//)	accomplish (= **iyaȓ dà**) < **iyà** be able
kau dà	move sth aside (= **kawaȓ dà**) < **kau** (< *kàwa) move aside
mai dà	return (= **mayaȓ dà**) < **màyā** replace
rau dà	shake sth (= **rawaȓ dà**) < *ràwa (cf. **rawā** dancing)
sai dà	sell (= **sayaȓ dà**) < **sàyā** buy
tsai dà	stop sth (= **tsayaȓ dà**) < **tsayà** stop, stand
zub dà	pour out/away (= **zubaȓ dà**) < **zubà** pour in
gajī dà	tire, bore (= **gajiyaȓ dà**) < **gàji** become tired
tafī dà	run, administer (= **tafiyaȓ dà**) < **tàfi** go
wahal dà	cause s.o. trouble (= **wahalaȓ dà**) < **wàhalà** have trouble

◊HN: [i] The variant **yař dà** (= **yā dà**) 'throw away' is probably derived by phonological haplology from an original long-form gr5 ***yāyař dà**. Note that unlike true short-form gr5 verbs, **yař** can be used without an immediately following direct object, e.g., **kadà kà yař**! 'Don't throw (it) away!' and forms a weak verbal noun with `-wā`, e.g., **àbîn dà sukè yâřwā** 'the thing that they were throwing away'.

[ii] The irregular verb **yī dà** (sometimes **yi dà**) 'slander', which does not have a corresponding long form, is sometimes included as a gr5 short form, but this is probably an error. More likely, it is a gr0 verb in a sociative construction with the preposition **dà**. As with other sociative verbs, the **yī** in **yī dà** alters into the corresponding verbal noun in nonfinite environments, e.g., **sunà yî dà mālàm** 'They are slandering the teacher', cf. a true gr5 short-form that retains its underlying H tone in the same environment, **sunà cī dà yârā** 'They are feeding the children.'

9.1.2. The -shē form

Gr5 verbs plus the particle **dà** are used before pronoun objects as well as before noun objects. The thematic object following **dà** is expressed by an independent pronoun, e.g., **nā kōyař dà ita** 'I taught her', **zā sù sanař dà mū** 'They will inform us', **kù cī dà sū** 'Feed them', **yâ kā dà nī** 'He will likely throw me down.'

Many verbs allow a true pre-pronominal B-form with what on the surface looks like a suffix **-shē**. With most verbs, especially those that have a short-form, the **-shē** appears as such directly after the base, e.g., **cīshē sù** 'feed them', **bāshē sù** 'give them away', **fisshē** (< //**fitshē**//) **sù** 'take them out', **tsarshē sù** 'protect them', **zubshē sù** 'pour them out/away', **wahalshē sù** 'cause trouble to them', **haƙurshē sù** 'enjoin patience on them'.

◊HN/°AN: Phonological differences notwithstanding, the so-called **-shē** suffix is really nothing but the gr5 final **-ř** followed by the pre-pronominal vowel **-ē**! That is, /sh/ is a palatalized manifestation of the //s// which is the historically and analytically underlying form of the gr5 suffix. In SH, the word-final -s is normally realized as /ř/, but in other dialects the /s/ is still preserved, i.e., //**zubas**// = **zubař** 'pour out'. When followed by the front vowel, the /s/ does not change to ř, but rather undergoes regular palatalization, i.e., //**zubsē**// → **zubshē**. The /ē/ in the **-shē** suffix is reminiscent of the /ē/ found in the B-form of gr2 verbs, compare **nā zubshē sù** 'I poured them away' (gr5) with **nā cìjē sù** 'I bit them' (gr2).

With some verbs, one finds a longer suffix, **-asshē** (with geminate /shsh/), e.g.,

ganasshē sù	show them	sanasshē sù	inform them
hūtasshē sù	put them at rest	kařantasshē sù	teach them

◊HN: The original shape of the gr5 suffix used in the B-form was probably ***-asē**, which, with palatalization, surfaced as **-ashē**. Thus one would have had such examples as ***zubashē** and ***sanashē**. In most cases, the medial short /a/ was dropped, e.g., ***zub(a)shē** → **zubshē**. In those instances where the vowel was retained, the **s** (= **sh**) was doubled for metrical purposes, e.g., ***sanashē** → **sanasshē**.

The object pronouns following **-shē** belong to the L-tone weak object set (which is also used with gr2 verbs), e.g., **mù gaishē shì** 'Let's greet him'; **zā sù sanasshē mù** 'They will inform us', **nā cīshē shì gàba** 'I promoted him.'

In SH (and in other dialects as well), the **-shē** form is becoming less and less common. Instead, the construction with **dà** is generally used, e.g., **zân fid dà sū** = **zân fitař dà sū** 'I will take them out' is preferred over **zân fisshē sù**. Exceptions are commonly used, lexicalized gr5 verbs such as **gaishē** 'greet', e.g., **mù gaishē shì**! 'Let's greet him!'

ΔDN: In recent times, the word **gaishē** has been reinterpreted in the Kano area as a fused form that is allowed to be used along with **dà**, e.g., **inà gaishē dà mijìnā** 'I am greeting my husband', **kà gaishē mîn dà ìyālî!** 'Greet your family for me!' I have no information as to how widely this innovation has spread.

◊HN: The -**shē** forms are well documented in the major dictionaries and clearly described in early grammars, e.g., Mischlich (1911: 57). What this indicates is that the loss of the -**shē** forms is a recent historical development. The explanation has to do with the phonological realization of the *-s suffix. The modern-day pronunciation of the /s/ is either /r̃/ in final position or /d/ before **dà**, e.g., **yā zubar̃** 'He poured (it) out', **yā zubad dà mâi** 'He poured out the oil.' In the case of the short-form gr5 verbs, which, when they exist, are commonly used, the /s/ is dropped entirely, e.g., **yā zub dà mâi.** Thus for native speakers—as has been the case for many linguists!—there is no immediately observable morphological relation between the ending -**shē** and the normal gr5 formation. Because it is easy to avoid the synchronically anomalous -**shē** form by using alternative constructions, speakers are increasingly avoiding its use.

9.1.3. Dialect variants:

Grade 5 is unusual among Hausa grades not only in its internal morphological complexity, but also in the considerable dialect variation that it exhibits, something that has still has been barely studied. Here, I shall simply present structures corresponding to the SH gr5 that have been reported in two dialects, one from the east, the Guddiri dialect of the Azare area (Katagum emirate) of Nigeria (Bagari 1982, [1984]), and one from the northwest, the Ader dialect of the Tawa area of Niger (Caron 1991). Note that in neither dialect is the **dà** particle used.

Guddiri "grade 5"

A-Form	B-Form	C-Form	D-Form
-sī H	-shē H	-si H	-sī H

A. **rìgā na saisī**   It's a gown I sold.
B. **nā saishē tà dà wuri**   I sold it early.
C. **yâu nā saisi kāyānā dà wuri**   Today I sold the goods early.
D. **wannàn nē rìgar̃ dà Audù ya saisī makà**   This is the gown that Audu sold to you.

All of the forms contain /s/, the essential pan-dialectal consonant in the gr5 morpheme. Interestingly, palatalization takes place only in the B-form before -**ē** and not in the C- or D-forms before -**i(i)**. (From the information available, it appears that the -**ī** in the D-form is long—which is what one would expect—however, this needs to be verified.)

Ader "grade 5"

A-Form	B-Form	C-Form	D-Form
-suwà H-L	-shē H	-sa H-L	-s (+pds) H

A. **tuhwànā yaɓ ɓassuwà** (< //ɓat-suwà//)   It was my clothes he lost.
B. **yaɓ ɓasshē sù**   He lost them.
C. **yaɓ ɓassà tuhwàn Àbdū**   He lost Abdu's clothes.
D. **yaɓ ɓassam min tuhwà**   He lost my clothes. (lit. he lost from.me clothes)

Verb bases with the shape CVV (plus some CVC and CVVC bases) add the suffix directly, e.g., **sai-suwà** 'sell' (< **sàyā** 'buy'), **his-suwà** 'take out' (< **hìta** 'go out'). Other verbs connect the base to the suffix by means of /a/ plus gemination (as found with some verbs in SH before the suffix -shē), e.g., **hirgitas-suwà** 'frighten s.o.' < **hìrgità** 'get frightened', or by means of long /ā/, e.g., **hirā-shē** 'make fly' (< **hìra** 'fly up'). The D-form uses both the gr5 suffix -s and the pds -aC)^H, which appears as -**am** because of the following /m/ initial indirect object marker, e.g., **his-s-am** 'take out for'.

°AN: Some scholars have erroneously equated the pds in SH, which has the shape -aC, with the gr5 -**ař** suffix. This confusion is due to the fact that in SH, they look alike on the surface, e.g., **yā nēmař** (gr2+pds) **wà Bàlā aikì** 'He sought work for Bala', vs. **yā sayař** (gr5) **dà mōtà** 'He sold a car.' The fact that these morphemes can co-occur in the Ader dialect, where they are phonologically distinct, e.g., **his-s-am** 'take out for' is strong evidence that they are fundamentally different from and independent of one another.

9.2. Meaning and function

In traditional works on Hausa, gr5 verbs were described as *causative*. This term, however, is semantically inaccurate at the descriptive level and is misleading for comparative and typological purposes. I have thus dropped the term. In its place, I have adopted the alternative *efferential*, a coinage that was proposed to capture the fact that the major feature of the gr5 extension is to indicate, not causation, but action directed out and away. (The true causative in Hausa is an analytical construction employing the verb **sâ** 'put, cause', see chap. 12.) The efferential has both semantic and syntactic functions. Semantically, it generally adds the notion of action directed away from the speaker. Syntactically, it serves to transitivize inherently intransitive verbs with an actor subject. The various semantic subclasses and the syntactic function of gr5 will be illustrated in turn.

°AN: The term *efferential* was first proposed in Newman (1983). Since then it has gained a considerable degree of acceptance among Hausaists and Chadicists although it has not entirely displaced the long established and familiar term *causative*. Some scholars have stuck with *causative* because they are convinced—wrongly in my opinion—that the syntactic/semantic properties of gr5 are such that *causative* is an appropriate label. Others, however, continue to use it, while acknowledging its descriptive inadequacies, either out of inertia or because they are not entirely happy with the alternative term *efferential*.

9.2.1. Action away in a fairly literal directional sense

With some verbs, the gr5 derivation adds the notion of action away, sometimes with an extra connotation of disposal or riddance, e.g.,

bāyař	give away, betray < **bā/bai** give to	**bugař**	knock over < **bùgā** hit
jēfař	throw away < **jèfā** throw at	**hařbař**	kick off < **hàřbā** shoot, kick
rabař	distribute < **rabà** divide, share	**tōfař**	spit out < **tōfà** spit
tūrař	push away < **tūrà** push	**zubař**	pour out, spill out < **zubà** pour (in)

e.g., **tā zubař dà madařā**   She poured out the milk. (gr5)
cf. **tā zubà madařā cikin ƙwaryā**   She poured the milk in the calabash. (gr1)

9.2.2. Action away in a conceptual sense

With many verbs, the gr5 extension serves to shift the locus of the action away from the speaker in a conceptual rather than a literally directional sense; compare, for example, the gr2 verb **sàyā** 'buy' with the gr5 **sayař** 'sell'. Other examples:

arař	lend < **àrā** borrow	**aunař**	weigh and sell off < **aunà** weigh
aurař	marry off < **àurā** marry	**gādař**	bequeath < **gàdā** inherit
kōyař	teach < **kòyā** learn	**kařantař**	teach < **kařàntā** read
sanař	inform < **sanì** know	**ganař**	show < **ganī** see
ciyař	feed, provide for < **ci** eat	**shāyař**	give water to < **shā** drink

Verbs such as the above that also operate gr1 applicatives (see §3.2.2 above) generally prefer the gr1 to the gr5 when used with an indirect object, e.g.,

sunà kōyař dà lìssāfì (v5)	They are teaching mathematics.
cf. **sunà kōyà manà lìssāfì** (v1)	They are teaching us mathematics.
bà zân arař dà kèkēnā ba (v5)	I won't lend my bicycle.
cf. **bà zân arà mā kèkēnā ba** (v1)	I won't lend you my bicycle.
yā aurař dà 'yā tasà (v5)	He married off his daughter.
cf. **yā aurà wà dattījò 'yā tasà** (v1)	He married his daughter to the gentleman.

Alternatively, one can sometimes express the thematic indirect object with a gr5 verb by means of a prepositional phrase with **gà(rē)** after the direct object, e.g.,

yā aurař dà 'yā tasà gà wani dattījò	He married off his daughter to some gentleman.
bà zân arař dà kèkēnā gàrē kà ba	I won't lend my bicycle to you.

The preference for the applicative gr1 over the efferential gr5 also applies in some cases where the added element is a locative rather than a dative, e.g.,

nā jūyař dà shī (v5)	I turned it around.
cf. **nā jūyà shi wajen ƙōfà** (v1)	I turned it toward the door.

9.2.3. Semantically empty, stylistic preference

With some verbs, especially denominatives formed with the verbalizing suffix -TA, gr5 is semantically equivalent (as far as one can determine) to the corresponding gr1 form. If gr5 adds anything, it is a little extra strength and stylistic nicety. Examples:

halakař = halàkā	destroy, wipe out	**ƙāwatař = ƙāwàtā**	beautify, adorn
rikitař = rikìtā	muddle up	**tsōratař = tsōràtā**	frighten (off)
wakiltař = wakìltā	appoint as representative	**wulākantař = wulākàntā**	treat contemptuously

9.2.4. Transitivizer

Intransitive unaccusative verbs with a patient subject usually appear in gr3 or gr4. The corresponding transitive verbs are normally gr1 (less often, gr2), e.g., **cìka** v3 'become full', **cikà** v1 'fill'; **karyè** 'break, become broken', **karyà** v1 'break sth'; **zàfafà** v3 'become hot', **zāfàfā** v1 'heat up'; **ƙàryatà** v3 'prove false', **ƙaryàtā** v1 'contradict'; **zùba** v3 'spill, leak', **zubà** v1 'pour (in)' (cf. **zubař** v5 'pour out'). Inherently intransitive verbs with a nonpatient subject, on the other hand, form their transitive counterparts by means of the gr5 derivation. This grammatical role of gr5 is part of the same overall efferential concept of having the action move away from the subject toward the patient. Examples:

ɓatař	lose, spend, squander < **ɓatà** v3b get lost
fāɗař	drop sth < **fāɗì** v3b fall

faɗakař	awaken s.o., enlighten < **fařkằ** v1 (= **fầɗakằ** v3) wake up
fitař	take out < **fìta** v3 go out
gajiyař	tire, bore s.o. < **gàji** v3* become tired
kawař	move sth to another place < **kau** (< *kàwa v3) move out of the way
saukař	lift sth down, unload < **sàukằ** v3 get down
tāsař	start (e.g., a car) < **tāshì** v3b get up
tafiyař	run, administer < **tàfi** v3* go
tsayař	stop sth < **tsayằ** v1 stop, stand
tsīrař / tserař	save, rescue < **tsīra** v3a escape, **tserè** v4 escape from
warkař	cure < **warkè** v4 get well

9.3. *Syntactic structure*

The grade 5 form with the suffix -**ař** is used in constructions corresponding to the A, B, C, and D syntactic environments, e.g.,

A. **mề sukà fitař?**	What did they take out?
B. **sun fitař dà ita**	They took it/her out.
C. **sun fitař dà mōtằ**	They took out the car.
D. **sun fitař manằ dà mōtằ**	They took out the car for us.

When followed by a semantic object, the particle **dà**, which phonologically is homophonous with the preposition **dà** 'with', is inserted between the -**ař** verb stem and the oblique object. The common inclusion of **dà** in the representation of gr5 verbs in grammatical tables and in dictionary entries is meant to show that although **dà** is not part of the verb, it obligatorily accompanies it when an object is expressed.

°AN/◊HN: Abraham (1959b: 68ff.) views the **dà** as an essential suffixal element on the verb, which is deleted in the A context. For him, one would get derivations such as **sun sayařdà nāmằ** 'They sold meat' ⇒ ***nāmằ sukà sayařdà** ⇒ **nāmằ sukà sayař** 'It was meat they sold.' I would view the matter in reverse fashion, i.e., treat the verb qua verb as *not* containing **dà**, the **dà** only being inserted by a late rule *if and only if* it is required by the surface syntactic structure. For example, *//**sun sayař nāmằ**// could be transformed directly into **nāmằ sukà sayař** (without requiring deletion of **dà**, which was never there); otherwise **dà** would be inserted, i.e., **sun sayař dà nāmằ**. This insertion rule approach can be illustrated well with topicalized structures, which allow either a resumptive pronoun or omission of the repeated noun: //**àkuyằ kàm, yā sayař Ø**// ⇒ **àkuyằ kàm, yā sayař** 'As for the goat, he sold (it)'; cf. //**àkuyằ kàm, yā sayař ta**// ⇒ **àkuyằ kàm, yā sayař dà ita** 'As for the goat he sold (it).' Viewed in this perspective, **dà** is neither a semantically specified preposition nor a grade formative, but rather an "empty morph" inserted by a late, morphophonological adjustment rule.

The introduction of **dà** into the verb system with gr5 verbs was undoubtedly due to the phonological "accident" that resulted in a consonant-final grade suffix (-**as** / -**ař**). (Originally, all verbs of whatever grade must have ended in a vowel.) The motivation for adding **dà** was clearly to avoid a consonant-final verb from being followed immediately by a direct object. (Note, for example, that in the Guddiri dialect, where the B-form and C-form of gr5 verbs end in -**shē** and -**si**, respectively, **dà** is not employed, nor is **dà** used in SH with the -**shē** form.) The details of the scenario obviously need to be worked out, but it would seem that what we have here is a straightforward instance of a syntactic change from direct object to oblique being put in motion by a morphophonological development.

Strictly speaking, the **-ař** form does not occur in B and C environments, because these environments are narrowly defined in terms of the verb being followed immediately by a direct object (personal pronoun or NP other than personal pronoun, respectively). With the gr5 **-ař** form, one does not have a true direct object; rather, the thematic object is expressed syntactically as an oblique object of the particle **dà**. The pronouns following **dà** are not direct object pronouns, but rather are independent pronouns, this also being the pronoun set used with true prepositions. By contrast, the so-called **-shē** suffix creates a true B-form, which takes enclitic weak object pronouns. Compare the following (where the hyphen marks clitics connected to the verb):

yā cī dà sū = yā cīshē-sù	He fed them.
sunà sanař dà shī = sunà sanasshē-shì	They are informing him.
kà zub(ař) dà ita = kà zubshē-tà	You should pour it out.

ΔDN: Another possibility, at least for some speakers, is to juxtapose a high-tone strong direct object pronoun immediately after the suffix -**ař** without using **dà**, for example, **an fitař ni** 'They sent me out' (= **an fitař dà nī**); **yā bāyař ta** 'He betrayed her' (= **yā bāyař dà ita**); **sun ciyař shi gàba** 'They promoted him' (= **sun ciyař dà shī gàba**); **sun azabtař mu** 'They tortured us' (= **sun azabtař dà mū**). (The final -**ř** normally assimilates fully to the following consonant, i.e., the examples above are pronounced [fitanni], [bāyatta], [ciyasshi], [azabtammu].) This variant is considered "archaic" by modern SH speakers and is rarely used, but it is still recognized and deemed grammatical.

Although **dà** is clearly a separable particle and not a verbal suffix—it occurs only with the verb in certain environments and not others—when it is found immediately next to the verb, it bonds to it as a clitic and phonologically often conditions full assimilation of the preceding ř. Contrary to the standard orthography, which puts a space between the verb and the **dà**, it would be preferable analytically to adopt a transcription involving a hyphen, i.e., **cī-dà**, **fid-dà**, **sanař-dà**, etc.

The difference between the synchronic status of the gr5 **-dà** and the homophonous preposition **dà** 'with', which occurs with sociative verbs (often gr1 or gr3), can be seen most clearly in how they affect the use of weak verbal nouns formed with ˋ-**wā**. With sociatives, where the **dà** functions as a separate word following the A-form of the verb, the verb in a nonfinite environment is necessarily replaced by the corresponding weak verbal noun, e.g.,

tanà kulàwā dà yârā	She is looking after the children.
cf. takàn kulà dà yârā	She looks after the children.
bā à sābàwā dà wàhalà	One doesn't become accustomed to trouble.
munà ta gaisàwā dà mutànē	We were greeting the men.

Grade 5 verbs, on the other hand, always use the finite verb form when followed by -**dà**, not the ˋ-**wā** verbal noun. The verbal noun is used only in an A environment where the -**dà** is absent. Examples (with a hyphen used to indicated the close bonding between the verb and **dà**):

tanà zubař-dà ruwā	She is pouring out the water. (*not* **tanà zubâřwā dà ruwā)
cf. ruwā nè takè zubâřwā	It is water she is pouring out.
bā mà tsōratař-dà sū	We are not frightening them off.
cf. wà kukè tsōratâřwā?	Who are you frightening off?
tsayař-dà injìn yanà dà wùyā	Stopping the engine is difficult.
cf. tsayâřwā tanà dà wùyā	Stopping (it) is difficult.

°AN: The gender distinction between **tsayař-dà injìn** (m.) and **tsayâřwā** (f.) is because infinitive phrases are masculine whereas weak verbal nouns with ꞌ-wā are feminine.

◊HN: Synchronically it seems evident that the preposition **dà** and the gr5 particle **dà** must be treated as distinct morphemes. What we don't know is whether historically they represent two separate morphemes that just happen to be phonologically homophonous, or whether they represent specialized uses of what originally was one and the same item—an alternative that I think is more likely.

9.3.1. Grade 5 with indirect objects

A peculiarity of gr5 verbs concerns the use and position of **dà** when the sentence contains an indirect object (i.o.). (For purposes of the exposition here, I shall refer to the thematic direct object as d.o. even when it syntactically consists of **dà** and an oblique object.) With pronoun i.o.'s, the situation is straightforward. The word order is V + i.o. + d.o.

zâi tsayař [mukù]$_{i.o.}$ **dà mōtà̃**	He will stop the car for you (pl.).
sōjà yā tsērař [manà]$_{i.o.}$ **dà 'yā'yanmù**	The soldier rescued our children for us.
sunà̃ zubař [matà]$_{i.o.}$ **dà mâi**	They are pouring out the oil for her.

With noun i.o.'s, on the other hand, the matter is much more complicated. Here one finds four different possibilities, all of which are considered to be fully grammatical: (1) In the first, the indirect object marker **wà** and the particle **dà** are "stacked" one after the other, followed by their respective objects, e.g., **zâi fitař wà dà Tankò àkwàtì** 'He will take out the box for Tanko.' This is the preferred option for many SH speakers. (2) The second option is to use **dà** twice, first immediately after **wà** and then also before the thematic d.o., e.g., **zâi fitař wà dà Tankò dà àkwàtì**. (3) The third option is to omit the **dà** and thus treat the thematic object as a true d.o. rather than an as an oblique object, e.g., **zâi fitař wà Tankò àkwàtì**. The preference with regard to the second and third options varies from speaker to speaker (and presumably from (sub)dialect to (sub)dialect). (4) The fourth option parallels the pronoun i.o. construction, i.e., one gets V i.o. (= **wà** + NP) d.o. (= **dà** + NP), e.g., **zâi fitař wà Tankò dà àkwàtì**. Surprisingly, for many speakers, this "straightforward" structure is the least preferred of the options. Examples:

1. **yā tsayař wà dà mālàm mōtà̃**	He stopped the car for the teacher.
= 2. **yā tsayař wà dà mālàm dà mōtà̃**	
= 3. **yā tsayař wà mālàm mōtà̃**	
= 4. **yā tsayař wà mālàm dà mōtà̃**	
1. **sunà̃ zubař wà dà tsōhuwā mâi**	They are pouring out oil for the old woman.
= 2. **sunà̃ zubař wà dà tsōhuwā dà mâi**	
= 3. **sunà̃ zubař wà tsōhuwā mâi**	
= 4. **sunà̃ zubař wà tsōhuwā dà mâi**	

Here are a few additional examples of the seemingly strange, but often preferred, structure with the two grammatical markers in succession:

yā lazumtař wà dà 'yā'yansà řùbùtū dà hannun dāma
> He made it compulsory for his children to write with the right hand.

wasu likitōcī sunà̃ zubař wà dà mātā cikì
> Some doctors perform abortions on women. (< **zubař dà cikì** 'abort', lit. pour away belly)

yā sayař wà dà Mūsā ita　　　　　　He sold it to/for Musa.

9.3.2. Grade 5 and double objects

Some gr5 verbs allow double direct objects, i.e., a sequence of two NPs, either of which can serve as the thematic direct object, e.g.,

tā kōyar̃ dà ɗàlìbai Tūr̃ancī	She taught the students English.
cf. tā kōyar̃ dà ɗàlìbai	She taught the students.
cf. tā kōyar̃ dà Tūr̃ancī	She taught English.

It is the first object that conditions the presence of the **dà**. If it is fronted, then the **dà** is omitted and the second object immediately follows the verb, e.g.,

ɗàlìbân dà ta kōyar̃ Tūr̃ancī	The students that she taught English to.

If the second object is fronted, on the other hand, the verb will take its normal form with **dà** before the thematic first object, e.g.,

Tūr̃ancī nè ta kōyar̃ dà ɗàlìbai	It is English she taught the students.

10. GRADE 5D: DECAUSATIVE

10.1. Form

A-Form	B-Form	C-Form	D-Form
-dā H-L	-dā H-L	-da H-L	-dā H-L

WH dialects have a variant gr5 form in which the **dà** particle is fused to the verb as a suffix. (This construction is well recognized in SH, even though it is not normally used.) This grade form, termed "décausative" by Gouffé (1962) and anglicized as "decausative," is especially prevalent with verbs that exhibit a short-form gr5 in SH (although there are others as well), e.g., **gaidà** 'greet', **maidà** 'return (sth)', **bādà** 'give away', **zubdà** 'pour out', **wahaldà** 'trouble (s.o.)', **kar̃antaddà** 'teach'. These **da**-stems form verbal nouns with ʾ-wā, e.g., **maidàwā** 'returning (sth)', **zubdàwā** 'pouring out (sth)'. In meaning, gr5d is equivalent to SH gr5.

Morphophonologically and syntactically, gr5d parallels gr1 in having A-, B-, and D-forms with final long /ā/ and a pre-noun C-form with final short /a/. Note, for example, that the pronoun object of the B-form is a true H-tone strong object pronoun and not an independent form. Note also that the indirect object, whether noun or pronoun, occurs between the verb stem and the direct object, just as is the case with any other verb grade, except the standard gr5. Finally, note that gr5d is similar to gr1 in its use of the weak verbal noun. Examples:

A. tā maidà	She returned (it).
B. tā maidà shi	She returned it.
C. tā maidà zōbè	She returned the ring.
D. tā maidà minì / mà sarkī zōbè	She returned the ring to me / to the chief.

Given the syntactic similarity between gr5d and gr1, many Hausaists have taken it for granted that with the fusion of **-dà** into the verb stem, these decausatives thereby became indistinguishable from gr1 verbs, i.e., **bādà** 'give away' could be classified as a gr1 verb like **kāmà** 'catch' or **ɗinkà** 'sew'.

Although this appears to be correct if one only looks at disyllabic verbs, the tone of polysyllablic gr5d verbs shows this proposal to be invalid. Whereas the tone pattern for polysyllabic gr1 verbs is H-L-H (or H-L-L for the C-form) the gr5d tone pattern is a fixed (H-)H-L. Contrast the following pairs: **haràmtā** gr1-A 'forbid' vs. **wahaldā̀** gr5d-A 'trouble s.o.'; **kakkaràntà** gr1-C 'read many' vs. **kařantaddà** gr5d-C 'teach'.

◊HN: It is not entirely clear whether the gr5d verbs historically underwent fusion, i.e., *zub dà > **zubdà** (thence to **zubdā̀** in the A- and B-forms) or whether the **dà** was originally a verb extension that was reanalyzed as a separate word through confusion with the preposition **dà** 'with', i.e., *zubdà > zub dà. In Newman (1971b) I proposed the latter analysis, i.e., that gr5d forms like **zubdā̀** exhibited an old extensional suffix *-da that is widespread in Chadic and probably reconstructable for the proto-language. According to this hypothesis, the now-occurring SH pattern, as seen in such sentences as **sun zub dà ita**, with the independent pronoun, would have been due to a mistaken identification of the suffix with the prepositional particle **dà** (used in sociative constructions and in full gr5 forms like **zubař dà**!). Although this hypothesis cannot be ruled out, it strikes me as less likely than the previously assumed fusion explanation. Wrong morpheme cuts and reanalyses of various sorts do, of course, happen in language change; but the overall drift in the history and development of the grade system in Hausa has been one of incorporation and fusion of grammatical items that originally had greater independence.

ΔDN: Some Kano speakers now have a mixed system that shares properties of both the SH short-form gr5 and the dialectal gr5d. In this system the **dà** before pronoun objects is treated as a particle as it is in SH, i.e., it has a short vowel followed by an independent pronoun, e.g., **yā mai dà ita** 'He returned it.' When no object follows, however, the short-form efferential behaves like a gr5d, i.e., it is allowed in the A environment (which short form gr5 verbs are not) and the **dà** behaves like a stem formative in undergoing vowel lengthening, e.g., **àbîn dà ya maidā̀** 'the thing that he returned'. In this incipient development, one sees a replication of the fusion process affecting verb + **dà** that presumably took place in WH dialects at an earlier period.

That the -**dà** in gr5d verbs is synchronically fused to the stem as a suffix is shown by the fact that this stem can serve as the input to other grade endings and other derivations. For example, from **tādà** 'raise', one can derive a gr6 verb **tādō** 'raise and come'; from **bādà** 'give away', one can derive a gr7 verb **bàdu** 'be given away'; from **fiddà** 'take out', one can create a nominal derivative **fìddau** 'a reject, sth taken out', etc. Some speakers even allow the formation of a redundant gr5 equivalent in meaning to the gr5d, e.g., **maidā̀** = **maidař** 'return sth'.

Dialects that have a gr5d form tend to use it to the exclusion of the SH gr5. The status of gr5d is thus unlike that of the short-form gr5, which is always an alternative to the full form (though frequently chosen). There are two modifications to this statement. First, some gr5d dialects do still use the pre-pronoun -**shē** form, at least with some verbs and set expressions, e.g., **à gaishē kà** 'One greets you.' Second, autonomous deverbal nouns consisting of a gr5 form plus ꜜwā exist alongside active gr5d inflectional verbal nouns with ꜜwā, e.g., **sanářwā** 'an announcement', but **sunà sanaddā̀wā** 'They are announcing (it)', **sayářwā** 'selling', as in **sàyē dà sayářwā** 'buy and selling', but **sunà saidā̀wā** 'They are selling (it).'

11. GRADE 6: VENTIVE

11.1. Form

A-Form	*B-Form*	*C-Form*	*D-Form*
-ō H	-ō H	-ō H	-ō H

Grade 6 verbs present a regular, morphologically homogeneous form with all H tone and long final -ō (the vowel being long even in the pre-noun C-form), e.g., **yā sātō jiyà** 'He stole (it) yesterday'; **yā sātō tà** 'He stole it'; **yā sātō mōtà̀** 'He stole a car'; **yā sātō minì mōtà̀** 'He stole me a car.' (Direct object pronouns of gr6 verbs belong to the L-tone weak object set.) In prepausal position in declarative or imperative sentences, the final vowel of gr6 verbs is closed by a glottal stop and becomes half-long (a peculiarity also characteristic of the H-tone, long-vowel gr0 verbs), e.g., **yā har̃bō** [har̃bo·ʔ] 'He shot (it)', cf. **bài har̃bō** [har̃bō] **ba** 'He didn't shoot (it)'; **sàukō** [sàuko·ʔ]! 'Get down!'; cf. **sàukō** [sàukō] **yànzun nàn!** 'Get down right now!'

Monosyllabic verbs ending in -ā and the H-H **CiCā** verbs insert /w/ between the stem-final vowel and the /ō/, e.g., **jāwō** 'pull here' (< **jā**), **sāwō** 'put here, put on and come' (< **sâ**), **kirāwō** 'call here' (< **kirā**). The gr6 of **yi** 'do' is **yiwō** 'do and come', which often shortens to **yō** (or **wō** in some dialects). The gr6 form corresponding to **kai** 'take', which is a clipped verb derived from *//kāy-//, is **kāwō** 'bring'. The monoverbs **ji** 'feel' and **bi** 'follow' appear with /y/ before the suffix, e.g., **jiyō** 'feel', **biyō** 'follow here'. The gr6 form of the verb **ci** 'eat', on the other hand, is typically **ciwō** 'eat and return', although **ciyō** is also common.

◊HN: Synchronically, it is not unreasonable to identify the gr6 suffix as -ō and to treat /w/ as an epenthetic glide. Historically, however, the /w/ was probably part of the originally CV ventive extension from which gr6 developed (Newman 1977b). Subsequently the language underwent a morphophonological change of *-wō > -ō that applied quite generally except in the case of the ā-final H(H) verbs.

°AN: The difference between the gr6 forms **yiwō** and **ciwō**, on the one hand, and **jiyō** and **biyō**, on the other, has a simple explanation. In **yiwō**, for example, one has a suffix -wō attached to the CV base of a monosyllabic verb, whereas in **jiyō**, one has a suffix -ō added to the CVC base (//jiy-//), which underlies the related disyllabic verb **jiyà**.

°AN/◊HN: The verb **zō** 'come' is often described as a gr6 form due to the final -ō and the 'hither' meaning. This is not necessarily so (see McIntyre 1990). To begin with, in analyzing **zō** as gr6, scholars have generally treated it as the counterpart of **jē** 'go', whereas it is possible that **zō** and **jē** relate etymologically to two different roots, the former with initial /z/ and the latter with initial /d/. If **jē** is indeed underlyingly *//dē// rather than *//zē//—both /d/ and /z/ palatalize to /j/—then its corresponding gr6 form can be identified as **dāwō** 'return here' rather than **zō**. Assuming for the moment that **zō** (and **jē**) derives from an irregular verb form ***zā** 'to go', it still would not follow that **zō** is a gr6 form containing the ventive -ō suffix. Note that the ventive forms of monosyllabic stems are normally disyllabic with an epenthetic glide and do not simply replace the lexical vowel, i.e., the gr6 corresponding to **zā** should be ****zāwō**. It is thus very possible that **zō** is etymologically not a ventive but rather is a clipped form of the dialect variant **zakà** (< ***zakà**) 'come' (i.e., ***zakà** > **zak** > **zau** (via Klingenheben's Law) > **zō**) and that the phonological identity of the final -ō and the gr6 -ō is fortuitous.

ΔDN: Unlike grades 1, 2, and 4, which have a short final vowel in the C-form but a long final vowel elsewhere, gr4 has an invariant long final vowel. Some WH speakers, however, have partially modified gr6 by analogy with the other grades and now shorten the final vowel before noun direct objects. This shortening is generally sensitive to syllable weight, i.e., one gets a short vowel if the penultimate syllable is heavy, but a long vowel if the penultimate syllable is light. For example, **yā kar̃anto làbār̃ì** 'He read the news'; **sun har̃bo zākì** 'They shot a lion'; but **mun barō yârā à gidā** 'We left the children at home.'

Gr6 verbs regularly use inflectional ˋ-wā weak verbal nouns, e.g., **bā sà̀ har̃bôwā** 'They are not shooting (at it) in this direction'; **aikì yakè̀ nēmôwā** 'It is work he is seeking', **sun yi ta shisshigôwā** 'They kept on entering.'

11.2. Meaning and function

Grade 6 is a very productive, commonly used grade, both with transitive and intransitive verbs. The ventive ending generally denotes action or movement in the direction of the speaker (or any other pragmatically established deictic center), sometimes emphasizing the distance of the occurrence from the speaker, e.g., **fitō** 'come out', cf. **fìta** 'go out'; **fāɗō** 'fall down this way', cf. **fāɗì** 'fall'; **gangarō** 'roll down here', cf. **gangàrā** 'roll down'; **kāwō** 'bring', cf. **kai** 'take'; **kirāwō** 'call to come here', cf. **kirā** 'call'; **janyō** 'drag in this direction' (gr6 built on a gr4), cf. **jânyē** 'drag away'; **fārō** 'begin at a distance', cf. **fārà** 'begin', e.g., **kògin Binuwài yā fārō dàgà ƙasaƙ Kàmàru** 'The River Benue begins (there) in Cameroon (and then comes this way)'; **haƙbō** 'shoot at in this direction', cf. **hàƙbā** 'shoot at', e.g., **yā haƙbō nì dà kibiyà̀** 'He shot me with an arrow', cf. **nā hàƙbē shì dà kibiyà̀** 'I shot him with an arrow.' With certain verbs, the gr6 form is commonly used even though the ventive reading is not evident, e.g., **ɓullō** 'appear suddenly', **bunkuɗō** 'come out in profusion' (of ants, pimples, etc.). The gr6 sometimes indicates 'do some action and come', e.g., **nā shāfō bangō** 'I whitewashed the wall and came back', **yā sayō nāmà̀** 'He bought some meat and brought it back here.' Because the locus/deictic center does not have to be the real-world position of the speaker, i.e., it can be transferred to someone or something else, the use or not of gr6 becomes flexible depending on how the situation is conceptualized by the speaker and what kind of semantic projection has taken place. For example, in the sentence **nā bugō masà wayà̀** 'I telephoned him' (lit. beat to.him wire) (more or less = **nā bugà̀ masà wayà̀**), the object 'him' is treated as the deictic locus toward which the action is directed. Similarly, if someone in London says **Audù yā kōmō Kanò̀** 'Audu returned to Kano', with the gr6 verb, instead of **Audù yā kōmà̀ Kanò̀**, it is because Kano rather than London is being treated as the deictic center or reference point.

Grade 6 commonly connotes association with, involvement by, or benefit for the speaker, e.g., **sun cīwō kwâf** 'They won the cup', **yā matō à kân yārinyàƙ nân** 'He is madly in love with this girl' (lit. he.comp die on girl.of this); **yā barō sù à gidā** 'He left them (e.g., children) at home (in good care)', cf. **yā baƙ sù à gidā**, which could imply that he left them there at home but they weren't happy about it or that he abandoned them at home. Indirect objects with the ventive gr6 invariably mean 'for' rather than 'from', e.g., **kà sayō manà àllō** 'Buy us a slate'; **yā ƙwātō makà kuɗîn** 'He seized the money for you' (cf. **yā ƙwācè̀ makà kuɗîn** 'He seized the money from you'); **zâi nēmō minì aikì̀** 'He's going to seek work for me.' Finally, there are a few verbs that for no obvious reason occur only in gr6 and not in one of the primary grades, namely, **faƙfaɗō** 'revive' (etymologically related to **faƙkà̀** 'wake up') and **zamantō** 'become, happen' (an extended verb essentially equivalent to **zama** or **zàmanà** 'become'). If the verb **dāwō** 'return here' is not viewed as the gr6 of **jē** 'go', then it constitutes a stem occurring exclusively in gr6, in this case, however, for obvious semantic reasons.

11.3. Ventive plus efferential

In addition to connoting action away in a directional sense (in which case it necessarily conflicts semantically with the ventive), the efferential (gr5) also changes the orientation of a verb (e.g., buy → sell) and to transitivize inherently transitive verbs with a nonpatient subject (e.g., go out → take out). In these latter functions, the efferential and the ventive are fully compatible and do in fact co-occur, although with only a restricted number of verbs.

In SH, one gets a combination of gr5 + gr6 in which the verb employs the gr6 morphology, i.e., displays the -ō suffix, but at the same time utilizes the particle **dà** and preserves the gr5 efferential semantics and syntax, e.g., with regard to the use of verbal nouns and indirect object formation. Examples:

yanà̀ fitō dà kāyā (gr5/6)	He is bringing out the loads.
cf. **yanà̀ fitôwā dà kāyā** (gr6)	He is coming out with the loads. (with the VN **fitôwā**)
sun dāwō dà shī Kanò̀ (gr5/6)	They returned him to Kano.

cf. **sun dāwō Kanȍ dà shī** (gr6)   They returned to Kano with him.

sun ɓullō wà dà Gwamnà sābuwař hanyȁ (gr5/6)
        They introduced a new plan for the Governor.

cf. **sun ɓullō wà Gwamnà dà tūtōcī** (gr6)
        They appeared before the Governor with banners.

munȁ jūyō dà hòtôn (gr5/6)   We were turning over the picture.

tanȁ kařkatō wà dà mijìntà fìtilař (gr5/6)   She is tilting the lamp for her husband.

(Note the use in sequence of the i.o. marker **wà** and the particle **dà** typical of gr5 verbs, as in **sun zubař wà dà mālàmī shȁrā** (gr5)   They threw out the trash for the teacher.)

> °AN: Semantically the distinction between a gr5/6 construction and a gr6 sociative construction is slight, for some speakers the two being essentially interchangeable (see Jaggar 1992a: 35n), e.g., **sunȁ shigō dà miyȁgun ƙwāyōyī** (gr5/6) = **sunȁ shigôwā dà miyȁgun ƙwāyōyī** (gr6 sociative) 'They are bringing in illicit drugs.'

In WH dialects that have gr5d, the efferential/ventive combination is morphologically straightforward because one can simply add -ō to the decausative form containing the fused -**dà**, e.g.,

fiddō   bring out < **fiddȁ** take out (cf. **fīta** go out)
saidō   sell and come back < **saidȁ** sell (cf. **sàyā** buy)
maidō   return sth here < **maidȁ** return sth (cf. **mayȁ** [WH] return)
bādō   give away money (there and come back) < **bādȁ** give away (cf. **bā** give to)

12. GRADE 7: SUSTENTATIVE

12.1. Form

A-Form	B-Form	C-Form	D-Form
-**u** L-H			(pds)

Grade 7 verbs contain a suffix -**u**)^{LH}, i.e., they end in the short vowel -**u** and have an L-H tone pattern. Gr0 verbs insert an epenthetic /**w**/ between the stem-final vowel and the suffix.

ɗàuru	be well tied	**gàmsu**	be pleased/satisfied
gyàru	be well repaired	**kàrkàru**	be scratched off
řàgàřgàzu	be fully smashed	**tàru**	have assembled
wàdàtu	have prospered, be contented	**kìrȁwu**	be called (< **kirā** call)
shȁwu	be drunk (< **shā** drink)	**yìwu**	be possible (< **yi** do)
jànyu	be completely pulled away (< **jânyē** gr4 pull away; cf. **jȁwu** be pulled < **jā** v0 pull)		

The irregular verbs **tàfi** 'go' (< *__tàfìyà__) and **gàji** 'tire' (< *__gàjìyà__), the monoverbs **bi** 'follow' (= **biyȁ**) and (optionally) **ji** 'feel' (= **jiyȁ**), and the H-H gr0 verb **rigā** 'precede' (= **rìgāyȁ**) use bases with final /**y**/ in forming gr7. Examples:

gàjìyu	be dog-tired	**tàfìyu**	travel far, be well traveled
bìyu	be followed, disciplined	**jìyu** = **jìwu**	be felt, heard
rìgàyu	be preceded [WH]		

Gr7 verbs form regular weak verbal nouns -**wā** (see discussion in §77:3.1.1), e.g.,

ɗinkuwā	be sewable	**gyằruwā**	be repairable
jằwuwā	be pullable	**nàtsuwā**	be reflecting
ȓàgàȓgàzuwā	be smashable	**tằruwā**	assembling

The -**uwā** sequence commonly simplifies to /ō/, e.g.,

wannàn hanyằ bā tằ bìyō (= **bìyuwā**)	This road cannot be followed.
bā sằ ràbō (= **ràbuwā**)	They are inseparable.
gērō yā fằrà dàkō (= **dàkuwā**)	The millet has begun to get pounded.
kīfīn bā yằ yànkō (= **yànkuwā**) **kō dàhō** (= **dàhuwā**)	The fish cannot be sliced or cooked.

The few gr7 verbs that allow indirect objects add the inflectional pds in the D-form, e.g., **yā aukaȓ wà manòmā** 'It befell the farmers' (< **àuku** 'happen'); **sun tāram masà** 'They assembled around him / they grouped together against him' (< **tằru** 'meet').

WH dialects with the gr5d decausative allow gr7 verbs to be built on the gr5d stems, e.g.,

fiddu v5d/7	be taken out <	**fiddằ** v5d	take out <	**fita** v3	go out
sàidu v5d/7	be sold <	**saidằ** v5d	sell <	**sàyā** v2	buy
bằduwa v5d/7	be giveable <	**bādằ** v5d	give away <	**bā** v*	give to

12.2. Meaning and function

Grade 7, which is strictly an intransitive (or sociative) grade, indicates that the subject of the verb has sustained or is capable of sustaining some action. In many cases, it thus corresponds to the English passive. There is usually an accompanying connotation that the action was done thoroughly. Gr7 is operable by a wide range of transitive stems (but not all) and many intransitives as well. With few exceptions, e.g., **jìtu** (**dà**) 'be on good terms with' and **wànzu** 'happen' (cf. **wanzaȓ** gr5 'make last long'), gr7 verbs all derive from extant lower-grade verbs.

> °AN: The verb **jìtu** is given in the dictionaries as **jìtu** with a short /i/. Present-day SH speakers pronounce the word as **jìtu** with a long /ī/, whereas for WH speakers, the word tends to be **jìttu** with a geminate /tt/.

Semantically gr7 verbs can be divided into two major classes, depending on whether the affected subject can be characterized as "patient" or "actor/experiencer."

12.2.1. Patient oriented gr7 ("Passive")

A major function of gr7 is to indicate an agentless passive in which the syntactic subject is the patient affected by the action of the verb. Consider the following pairs of sentences, the first being active/transitive, the second a gr7 passive.

a. **sun wāsà wuȓā**	They sharpened the knife. (gr1)
b. **dà wuȓā ta wằsu**...	When the knife was sharpened... (gr7)
a. **kà tsinkè igiyằ**	Snap the string. (gr4)
b. **igiyàȓ tā tsìnku**	The string was snapped. (gr7)
a. **sun fāsà tàfiyằ Marāɗi**	They postponed the travel to Maradi. (gr1)

b. **tàfìyầ Marāɗi tā fàsu**   The trip to Maradi was put off. (gr7)
a. **Abdù yā kḕɓè bùhū**   Abdu put away the sack. (gr4)
b. **bùhū yā kḕɓu**   The sack has been put away. (gr7)
a. **su Mūsā sun saidà shānū à Nìjēriyầ**   Musa et al. sold some cows in Nigeria. (gr5d)
b. **shānū sun sàidu à Nìjēriyầ**   The cows were sold in Nigeria. (gr7 < gr5d)

With the passive gr7 verbs, there is always an agent implied, though usually not expressed. These verbs thus differ from gr3 or gr4 intransitive unaccusative verbs, e.g.,

tùlū yā fàsu   The water pot was smashed up (by someone). (gr7)
tùlū yā fashḕ   The water pot broke. (gr4)
rāmì yā cìku   The hole was filled up (by someone). (gr7)
rāmì yā cìka   The hole filled. (gr3)
gērôn yā jìƙu dà gàngan   The millet was well soaked (by someone) on purpose. (gr7)
gērôn yā jìƙa (*not* **dà gàngan**)   The millet got wet. (**on purpose) (gr3)

Gr7 is semantically more heavily marked (connoting action thoroughly or well done) than a comparable passive sentence in English. The neutral translation of an English passive sentence would be by means of an active transitive sentence with an impersonal subject, e.g.,

an fasà tùlū   The water pot was smashed. (lit. one.comp break water pot)
zā à cikà rāmì   The hole will be filled. (lit. fut one fill hole)
an gyārà mōtàř   The car was repaired. (lit. one.comp repair car.the)
cf. **mōtàř tā gyằru**   The car was well repaired.

Stylistically, it is common to put a gr7 passive clause after a corresponding active clause in the same sentence to emphasize the thoroughness of an action, e.g.,

yā ɗaurè tunkìyā tā ɗàuru   He tied a sheep (such that) it was well tied up.
tā dafà àbinci yā dàfu   She cooked the food (so that) it was good and well cooked.

Related to the notion of 'thoroughly done', gr7 sometimes indicates that the action of the verb has come to fruition only after great effort, e.g.,

tuřƙầshi! Bintà tā kằmu   Yahoo! Binta has finally been caught.
duk dà hakà, gidanmù yā gìnu   Nevertheless, our house has been built at last.

In the continuous, gr7 verbs, which naturally appears as a verbal noun, normally indicate potentiality of action, i.e., they often correspond to English '-able' words. The semantic connotation is that the action in question is an inherent, generic, timeless quality of the subject. These sentences are particularly common in the negative.

wannàn mōtàř tanằ gyằruwā   This car is repairable. (by its nature)
kồgîn yanằ ƙètàruwā   The river is crossable.
zōbèn bā yằ sằtuwā   The ring can't be stolen.
kùnū mài zāfī bā yằ shằwuwā   A burning hot gruel is not drinkable.
màganàř bā tằ ɓòyuwā   The matter cannot be concealed.
wannàn bā yằ sàyuwā naiřằ ɗàrī   This cannot be bought for a hundred nairas.

One also finds the 'it is (not) possible to' reading in sentences in the negative potential future and for some speakers in the regular future as well. Here, however, there is sometimes a slight semantic difference as compared with the continuous sentences in that the action may be viewed as time delimited or specified, e.g.,

Abdù fa [yâ]$_\text{pot}$ gànu?	Can Abdu really be seen?
(i.e., Will it be possible to find Abdu?)	
Lēgàs bà [tâ]$_\text{pot}$ zàunu ba	Lagos won't be habitable. (in the future)
irìn yādìn nân bà [zâi]$_\text{fut}$ wànku ba	This kind of cloth isn't washable.
gòbe kàm kògîn [yâ]$_\text{pot}$ ƙètàru	Tomorrow the river will probably be crossable.

With verbs that operate gr1 and gr2 contrastively, the gr7 often incorporates both possible meanings.

1.a. (gr1) yā haȓbà bàbbaȓ bindigà̀	He shot a big gun.
b. (gr7) bàbbaȓ bindigà̀ tā haȓbu	The big gun has been shot off.
2.a (gr2) yā hàȓbi birì̀	He shot a monkey.
b. (gr7) birì̀ yā hàȓbu	The monkey has been shot.
1.a. (gr1) yā jēfà màge ruwa	He threw the cat into the water.
b. (gr7) màge tā jèfu cikin ruwa	The cat was thrown into the water.
2.a. (gr2) yā jēfi màge dà dūtsè̀	He threw a stone at the cat.
b. (gr7) màge tā jèfu	The cat was thrown at.
1 a. (gr1) Abdù yā yankà nāmà̀	Abdu cut the meat.
2.a (gr2) Abdù yā yànki nāmà̀	Abdu cut off the meat.
1/2b (gr7) nāmà̀ yā yànku	(1) The meat has been cut. *or* (2) ...has been cut off.
1.a. (gr1) yā jūyà takàȓdā	He turned the paper over.
2.a (gr2) yā jùyi takàȓdā	He copied the paper.
1/2b (gr7) takàȓdā tā jùyu	(1) The paper was turned over. *or* (2) ...was well copied.

Syntactically speaking, gr7 is an agentless passive. It does not take a straightforward 'by' phrase comparable to the one in English. A thematic agent can, however, be referred to in a less direct manner by using the relational preposition **gà**. (Some people use the preposition **wajen**. Some people use both, depending on the context.) This is most commonly done in negative continuous sentences. In positive sentences there is often an implication that the action relates *only* to an agent who is mentioned. Examples:

bindigaȓ nân bà zā tà haȓbu gà mùtûm ɗaya ba	This gun cannot be fired by one man.
wannàn hanyà̀ bā tà bìyuwā gà mânyan mōtōcī	This road is impassable for heavy lorries.
jàkī yā kàmu gà Abdù	The donkey was caught (only) by Abdu.
mōtaȓ tanà̀ gyàruwā gà Bellò	The car is repairable by Bello (only).
tsābaȓ Aishà bā tà ɗèbuwā gà su Bintà	Aisha's grain cannot be taken by the likes of Binta.
dàgà nan daȓajàȓ wàzīȓì̀ ta ràgu wajen sarkī	From then on the vizier lost the king's favor.

(lit. the value of the vizier was reduced with respect to the king)

ΔDN/°AN: According to Abdoulaye (1992), the **gà** phrase in the dialect of Maradi functions very much like the 'by' phrase in an English passive, i.e. it specifies the thematic agent. He gives such examples as the following: **tùlū yā fìddu gà Bìlki** 'The water pot was taken out by Bilki'; **gīwā tā yànku gà mahàlbā** 'The elephant was killed by the hunters'; **ɓāwā yanà̀ ɓàmɓàruwā gà Abdù** 'The bark can be torn off by Abdu.' In his thesis, Bature (1991) also gives gr7 passive sentences in which the prepositional phrase, consisting of **wajen** + NP, is treated as equivalent to a 'by' phrase in English, e.g., **mōtàř tā gyàru wajen Audù** 'The car was repaired by Audu.' All SH speakers with whom I have checked these examples find them to be strange and a bit forced. If the preceding example is accepted, it is invariably interpreted to mean 'The car got repaired but only by Audu' [Musa, for example, couldn't].

12.2.2. Actor/experiencer-oriented grade 7

With some gr7 verbs, the subject is not the thematic patient of a corresponding transitive verb but rather is an actor or experiencer affected by the verb. These verbs, which display a wide semantic range, can be divided roughly into a small number of groups. The first group includes "associative/lexical reflexive" verbs, namely verbs that require either a plural subject, if functioning as simple intransitives, or a sociative complement. Examples:

ɗùru	swarm, cf. **ɗūrà** v1 pour in
gàmu	meet, cf. **gamà** v1 join, mix
e.g., **mutằnē sun gàmu**	The men met.
e.g., **yārò yā gàmu dà Mūsā**	The boy met (with) Musa.
kàru	clash head-on, cf. **karà (dà)** v1 clash (with)
jìtu	be on good terms with
e.g., **mun jìtu dà jūnā**	We get along with each other.
kàsu	fall into classes, cf. **kasà** v1 divide
ràbu	part company, cf. **rabà** v1 divide
shàku	be close friends, be affectionate with, cf. **shàƙè** v4 choke, fill chock-full
e.g., **mun shàku**	We are close friends (with one another).
e.g., **nā shàku dà ita**	I am close friends with her (i.e., I love her very much), *not* **nā shàku
tàru	gather (crowd), cf. **tārà** v1 assemble, gather
wàtsu	scatter, cf. **wātsà** v1 spread sth

The second group consists of "happen" verbs, e.g.,

àuku	happen, cf. **aukà** v1 collapse, (with **dà**) encounter
fàru	happen, cf. **fārà** v1 begin
wànzu	happen, cf. **wanzař dà** v5 make last long

The next group consists of semantically strengthened forms of already intransitive verbs, e.g.,

dàidàitu	reach full agreement, cf. **dàidaità** v3 come to an agreement
gàjìyu	be dead tired, cf. **gàji** v3* be tired
hìmmàntu	strive one's utmost, cf. **hìmmantà** v3 strive
tàfìyu	travel a long way, cf. **tàfi** v3* go
tsàyu	stand a long time, cf. **tsayà** v1 stand, wait
wàdàtu	truly prosper, cf. **wàdātà** v3 prosper, be contented
tsòràtu	be very much afraid, cf. **tsòratà** v3 be afraid

°AN: The verb **tsòràtu** could perhaps also be analyzed as a passive from the gr1 **tsōràtā** 'frighten', e.g., **zākì yā tsōràtà yāròn** 'The lion frightened the boy' ⇒ **yāròn yā tsòràtu** 'The boy was frightened (by X).' However, speakers generally do not interpret the sentence with the gr7 form as having an implied agent.

Also derived from intransitives (generally motion verbs) are passivelike motion/action gr7 verbs, e.g.,

zàunu   be well lived in, cf. zaunằ v1 sit, live in, reside,

e.g., ɗākìn yā zàunu The room is (well) occupied. cf. yā zaunằ ɗākìn He lives in the room.

kòmu   be returned to, cf. kōmằ v1 return,

e.g., gidā bā yằ kòmuwā yànzu One cannot return home now.

(lit. home isn't returnable to now), cf. an kōmằ gidā One returned home.

The next group consists of "metaphorical" verbs that in gr7 have a semantically specific reading not found in the base verb. Some of these gr7 forms can also serve as the passive counterpart of the verb in its normal meaning, e.g.,

bùgu   be good and drunk, cf. bùgā v2 hit

e.g., Jằtau yā bùgu (dà giyằ)   Jatau was dead drunk (from beer).

cf. the literal passive rìgâr̃ tā bùgu   The gown was well and completely beaten.

ɗìgu   get on well in the world, cf. ɗìga v3 drip, ɗìgā v1 pour in drops

fàku   die (of prophets or saints), cf. fakè v4 hide

gògu   be experienced, polished, cf. gōgằ v1 rub, polish

e.g., mùtumìn nan yā gògu wajen ɗinkì   That man is an expert at embroidery.

cf. mōtàr̃ tā gògu dà mân mōtằ   The car has been well polished with car wax.

kàɗu   tremble/shake from fear, cf. kaɗằ v1 shake sth

kyàutu   be fitting, appropriate, cf. kyâutā v1 treat well

ƙàru   profit, benefit from, cf. ƙārằ v1 add

mòtsu   be upset, stirred up, crazy, cf. mōtsằ v1 stir

ràsu   die, cf. rasằ v1 lose, lack

ràyu   survive, prosper, cf. rāyằ v1 extend life

rùfu   close in on, cf. rufè v4 cover, close

shìryu   make up with / be well arranged, cf. shiryằ v1 prepare, arrange

tàɓu   be crazy, touched, cf. taɓằ v1 touch

tàmbàyu   take potions, be well questioned, cf. tàmbayằ v2 ask

yìwu   be possible, cf. yi v0 do

The semantic strength of gr7 verbs (indicating thoroughness or completeness) is shown by the fact that they may not be followed by contradictory weakening clauses or phrases, e.g.,

Abdù dà Tankò sun jìtu   Abdu and Tanko get along (well).

not **Abdù dà Tankò sun jìtu, àmmā bà sòsai ba

         Abdu and Tanko get along (well), but not very well.

Bàlā yā gògu   Bala is an experienced old hand.

not **Bàlā yā gògu, àmmā kīmằ

         Bala is an experienced old hand, but only moderately.

Some gr7s derived from transitive verbs function with subjects that are both (a) patient-affected and (b) actor/experiencer-affected. The semantic reading usually depends on the animacy of the subject, namely inanimate in the first case, animate in the second, e.g.,

(a) làbār̃ì yā wàtsu   The news was spread/was widely disseminated.

(b) mutằnē sun wàtsu   The people scattered.

(a) **tagùwař nàn bā tǎ gôguwā**   This shirt cannot be ironed.
(b) **yāròn yā gôgu gà sātǎ**   This boy is an expert at stealing.
(a) **ɓàrāwô yā kǎmu**   The thief was caught (by someone).
(b) **mùtumìn yā kǎmu dà wata mùmmūnař cùtā**   The man was infected by a serious disease.

Syntactically, gr7 verbs primarily function intransitively. As illustrated by examples found throughout this section, however, a few of them also enter into sociative constructions with the preposition **dà** 'with', where they sometimes translate into English as transitive sentences. Examples:

yā ràbu dà mǎtařsà   He divorced his wife. (cf. **rabǎ** v1   divide, separate)
ɓàn taɓà hàɗuwā dà shī ba   I have never met him. (cf. **haɗǎ** v1   combine, connect)
mun shâ ku dà mālàm   I'm close friends with the teacher.
Mūsā yā gàmsu dà jàwābìn   Musa was satisfied with the speech.
cf. **jàwābìn yā gàmshi Mūsā**   The speech satisfied Musa. (gr2)

13. THE -K- EXTENSION (DIALECTAL)

13.1. Form: -K- extension plus totality

In addition to the extensions that manifest themselves synchronically as distinct grade forms, some WH dialects also have an extension -K- that always occurs as an infix along with another grade stem, e.g., **gash-ìk-ē** gr4 'roast all and come' (< **gasǎ** 'roast'). In some areas (e.g., Maradi) this extension occurs only in combination with gr4; in the dialect of Ader, it is found with gr5 as well. The -K- extension combined with the gr4 ending appears as a suffix **-ik(k)ē**[HLH]. In some dialects (e.g., Ader) the /k/ appears as a single consonant, in others (e.g., Sokoto) it is normally a geminate. Monoverbs insert an epenthetic /y/ before the suffix, e.g., **jāyìkē** 'draw up this way' < **jā** 'pull, draw'. As with simple polysyllabic gr4 verbs, there are two variants for the pre-noun C-form, one with a long final vowel and H-L-H tone and one with a short final vowel and H-L-L tone. Verbal nouns are formed with `-wā (the tone being subject to dialectal variation not restricted to this grade). Examples:

	A-Form	B-Form	C-Form	D-Form
shoot	**halbìkē**	**halbìkē**	**halbìkē / halbìkè**	**halbìkē**
break off	**ɓalgacìkē**	**ɓalgacìkē**	**ɓalgacìkē / ɓalgacìkè**	**ɓalgacìkē**
uproot	**ciccirìkē**	**ciccirìkē**	**ciccirìkē / ciccirìkè**	**ciccirìkē**
enter/sneak in	**shigìkē**			**shigìkē**
roll all down here	**gangarìkē**			**gangarìkē**

°AN: From the surface appearance, the combination of (-**ik**-) and gr4 (-**ē**) would appear to occur morphologically in that order. On the other hand, a few examples suggest that the combined -**ikē** suffix is attached to a stem that is *already* a derivative gr4 rather than to a simple base. Thus **janyìkē** 'pull all here' clearly comes from **jânyē** gr4, not **jā** gr0, and **ficcìkē** 'escape out here' is derived from the secondary grade **ficcè** gr4, with irregular gemination, not from the basic verb **fìta** gr3, which has a single medial consonant.

13.2. Meaning and function

Semantically, verbs with -**ikē** carry the totality/finality meanings of normal gr4 verbs as well as some semblance of the meaning of gr6 ventive verbs ending in -**ō**. Thus they tend to indicate 'affect all and come here', e.g., **jēfìkē** 'throw at and come' (cf. **jèfā** 'throw at'); **gangarìkē** 'roll all down here' (cf. **gangàrā** 'roll'), **shanyìkē** 'drink up and come' (cf. **shā** 'drink').

ΔDN: Some speakers (e.g., Malami Buba from Sokoto), feel that the suffix forms semantically stronger gr4 verbs without adding a ventive component.

Semantically, verbs with -ikē are similar to the few gr4 + gr6 combinations allowed in SH with monoverbs, e.g., **janyō** 'pull all in this direction/and come', cf. **jânyē** gr4 'pull all', cf. **jāwō** gr6 'pull in this direction' (from basic gr0 verb **jā** 'pull'). As with simple gr4 verbs, gr4 verbs containing -ikē can be transitive or intransitive. The following examples, mostly taken from Abdoulaye (1992 and unpublished notes), illustrate the use of -ikē verbs.

tā kwāshìkè gàrîn	She took all the flour and came.
tā ciccìrìkè hakūkuwằ	She pulled out all the grass and came.
sun rātayìkē 6àrāwồ	They hanged the thief and came back.
sun gujìkē	They escaped (ran away) to here.
ɗan tsuntsū yā hwāɗîkē dàgà iccè	The little bird fell off here from the tree.
Bintà tā amshìkē mà Abdù zōbè	

    Binta wrestled away Abdu's ring and came.

kwānōnī takè wankìkēwằ (à) rwằhī

    It is dishes that she is washing at the river.

zōmō ya 6algacìkē 6āwā ya kāwō mà zākì

    The hare broke all the bark and brought it to the lion.

13.3. Form: -K- extension plus efferential

As illustrated earlier with combinations of gr5 + gr6 and gr5d + gr6, semantically, the efferential and the ventive are fully compatible. Thus we find that in the Ader dialect (Caron 1991), the -k- with ventive semantics combines readily with that dialect's efferential formation. (The entries in the D-form column have the pds attached.) Examples:

	A-Form	B-Form	C-Form	D-Form
feed and return	**cî-k-assuwằ**	**cî-k-asshē**	**cî-k-assằ**	**cî-k-ass-am**
assemble people	**târ-k-assuwằ**	**târ-k-asshē**	**târ-k-assằ**	**târ-k-ass-am**
make fly here	**hirằ-k-assuwằ**	**hirằ-k-asshē**	**hirằ-k-assằ**	**hirằ-k-ass-am**
anger s.o.	**hasàlằ-k-assuwằ**			
frighten s.o.	**hîrgitằ-k-assuwằ**			

(The missing B-, C-, and D-forms are not provided in the available source, but presumably they follow the regular pattern.) Note that the gr5 ending and the pds, which one would expect to be tone integrating and extend over the entire word, do not do so. Rather, these ventive-efferential forms consist of two discrete tonal domains. The first domain is that delimited by the -k- extension.

°AN: The ability of the -k- to create its own tonal domain supports Abdoulaye's contention that the -k- is a full extension and not just an infixal element.

The specifics of this tone pattern depend on the phonotactic structure of the verb, but the tone pattern associated with the -k- always contains initial H-L. The second domain is that of the Ader efferential extension, the tones of which are H-L in the A- and C-forms and all H in the B-form. The inflectional pds -aC found in the D-form also manifests all H tone. (These tone patterns without the -k- were presented above in §9.1.3.)

13.4. Meaning and function

As best as one can determine, Ader efferential verbs containing the ventive **-k-** semantically combine the meanings and functions of the two extensions. A form like **hîr-k-assuwà** 'bring out' (< **hìta** 'go out') is presumably comparable to the gr6 ventives built on gr5 and gr5d stems, e.g., [SH] **fitō dà** 'bring out' = [dv] **fiddō/hiddō** (< **fìta/hìta** 'go out'). The following examples are taken from Caron (1983) but adapted to the orthography employed here.

yā hirà-k-ass-am min tsuntsàyên nan
> He made the birds fly toward me.

sa'àn nan tat tàhi tab biɗō duƙ ƙwārin dāzhì tat târ-k-asshē sù
> Then she (the hyena) searched for all the animals of the bush and assembled them (back here).

14. IRREGULAR VERBS

After verbs have been assigned to their regular grade forms, there are some ten or so irregular verbs left over. These are noted v*. (From a historical perspective, some of these could be viewed as aberrant/irregular members of one of the basic grades.) The irregular verbs are: **ganī** 'see', **barì** 'leave, let', **sanì** 'know', **kusa** 'draw near', **zama** 'become', **hau** 'mount', **kau** 'move aside', **kai** 'take', **bā/bai** 'give', **jē** 'go', **zō** 'come', and **'yan/'yam** 'give a little to'.

(1) The irregular transitive verb **ganī** 'see' has distinct A-, B-, and C-forms. (The syllable-final /n/ in the B-form undergoes the normal assimilation typical of /n/ in coda position.) Before an indirect object the verb obligatorily switches to gr4.

	A-Form	B-Form	C-Form	D-Form
see	**ganī**	**gan**	**ga**	**ganè** (v4)

A. **wâddà na ganī**   the one I saw
B. **nā gan tà**   I saw her.
C. **nā ga yārinyà**   I saw the girl.
D. **kà ganè minì rìgā!**   Keep an eye on the gown for me!

Occasionally, the C-form **ga** can be used without an object, e.g., **kā ga?** 'Do you see?' Dialects other than SH have an alternative all H B-form with final **-ē**, e.g., **nā ganē tà** = [SH] **nā gan tà** 'I saw her.' (All of the irregular verbs use the weak direct object pronoun set.) The verbal noun is identical to the A-form, e.g., **munà ganin àbîn dà yakè yî** 'We were observing what he was doing.'

(2) The verbs **barì** and **sanì** drop the final vowel when followed by an object. (In final position, the /r/ of **barì** automatically becomes rolled /r̃/.) In the A-form, **barì** and **sanì** have the metathesized variants **birà** (uncommon) and **shinà** (quite common). Before an indirect object **sanì** obligatorily switches to gr4.

	A-Form	B-Form	C-Form	D-Form
leave, let, allow	**barì (birà)**	**bar̃**	**bar̃**	**bar̃**
know	**sanì (shinà)**	**san**	**san**	**sanè** (v4)

A. **wâddà na barì**   the one I left
B. **nā bar̃ tà**   I left her.

C. **nā baȓ yārinyàȓ**   I left the girl.
D. **nā baȓ makà kuɗī**   I left the money for you.
A. **wâddà na sanī** (= **shinà**)   the one I know
B. **nā san tà**   I know her.
C. **nā san yārinyàȓ**   I know the girl.
D. **wà zâi sanè makà?**   Who will take any notice of you? (lit. who fut.he know to.you)

The verbal nouns of these two verbs are identical to the standard A-forms:

barìnsà yā fi kyâu   Leaving it is best.
tanà sanìnsà   She is getting to know it.

At a shallow synchronic level, one can think of the verbal nouns **barī** and **sanī** as coming from their identical finite verb forms. Viewed historically, however, **barī** and **sanī** are probably H-L i-final verbal nouns belonging to the same class as **ginī** building' (< **ginà** 'build'), **haȓbī** 'shooting' (< **hàȓbā** 'shoot'), etc. Their use as A-forms is parallel to the use of other verbal nouns of this class as optional A-forms of gr2 verbs, e.g., **faɗī** (VN) = **fàɗā** gr2-A 'tell', **sakī** (VN) = **sàkā** gr2-A 'release'. One can push the parallelism further and suggest that **barī** and **sanī** are indeed (irregular) gr2 verbs that happen to require the use of a clipped form without the final -**ē** and -**i** in the B and C environments before direct objects. The sentence **nā san tà** 'I know her' (< **sanī**) is thus parallel to **nā sau tà** 'I released her' (< **sakī**), the only difference being that in the first case the clipping is obligatory while in the second case it is optional. Significantly, the imperative of **barī** with no object expressed is **bàri**! It thereby exhibits exactly the same L-H short final -**i** imperative pattern used with gr2 verbs, e.g., **sàki**! 'Let go, release!'; **nèmi**! 'Seek!'; **kàȓɓi**! 'Receive!' (The verb **sanī** doesn't occur in the imperative in the A-form.) Thus, strictly speaking, **barī** and **sanī** should not be grouped with the truly irregular verb **ganī** 'see', as they are always done, but rather should be viewed as aberrant gr2* verbs. (In this grammar I have, nevertheless, decided to stick with the traditional classification of **barī** and **sanī** as irregular v* verbs so as to avoid too many departures from standard practice.)

(3) The invariant verb **kusa** 'be near' (= the adverb **kusa** 'near') occurs most often as an aspectual verb followed by a nonfinite VP, e.g.,

yā kusa [ìsā Kanò]   He is about to reach Kano.
mun kusa [gamàwā]   We are almost finished. (i.e., we are close to finishing it)

It may also be used intransitively, e.g.,

[isôwaȓ Audù] tā kusa   Audu's arrival is near at hand.

(4) The usually invariant copular verb **zama** 'become' requires a following complement, e.g.,

màganàȓsà tā zama gaskiyā   What he said is true. (lit. his talk has become true)
yā zama sarkin tashà   He became head of the lorry park.

Some speakers, esp. in WH, use a clipped form **zam**, e.g., **yā zam màtsalà** 'It has become a problem.' Before an i.o., **zama** is replaced by the corresponding gr4 verb **zamè**, e.g.,

gàrîn yā zamè masà màsīfà The town has a hold on him. (lit. has become for.him calamity)

(5) The verb **hau** 'mount, climb up on', occurs in all four contexts, e.g., **dōkìn dà ya hau** (A-form) 'the horse that he rode', **yā hau shì** (B-form) 'He mounted it', **yā hau gadō** (C-form) 'He succeeded to the throne' (lit. he.comp mount bed), **yā hau masà dà bugù** (D-form) 'He thrashed him' (lit. he.comp mount to.him with beating). The verb may also be used intransitively, e.g., **fàrāshìn dōyà̀ yā hau** 'The price of yams has gone up.'

◊HN: The verb **hau** probably derives historically from a basic **a**-final verb by a process of final vowel clipping. When used transitively, it probably had the form of a gr1 verb (i.e., ***hawà̀**), whereas when used intransitively it patterned with gr3 verbs (i.e., ***hàwa**).

The corresponding verbal noun is **hawā** (m.), e.g., **yanà̀ hawan itàcē** 'He is climbing up a tree.' Although **hau** itself is irregular, it allows the regular formation of other grades and derived forms. (In the derivatives, the /**u**/ of the diphthong appears as /**w**/ or, when followed by a front vowel, as /**y**/.) Examples:

hawař dà = hau dà gr5	mount s.o. on sth
hawō gr6	mount and come
hàyayyē adj.pp	broken-in (of a horse)
mahàyī	a rider

°AN: There is a semantically and phonologically similar verb **hayà̀** 'cross over', whose etymological relation to **hau** is not clear. Synchronically, the palatalization rule before front vowels results in confusion between the two verbs, i.e., because of the /**w**/ → /**y**/ rule, their gr4 forms are identical, e.g., **hayà̀** + **-ē** → **hayè̀** 'cross beyond' and **hau** (base //**haw**//) + **-ē** → **hayè̀** 'climb onto'.

(6) The intransitive verb **kau** 'move away' probably derives historically from a gr3 verb ***kàwa**. (There is no corresponding verbal noun.) As with regular gr3 verbs with actor subjects, it transitivizes by means of gr5, e.g., **sun kau dàgà nân** v* 'They moved from here', cf. **mun kawař dà (= kau dà) sū dàgà nufìnsù** (gr5) 'We diverted them from their intentions.'

(7) The very common verb **kai** 'reach, take', which probably derives historically from a clipped gr1 verb ***kāyà̀**, occurs in all four contexts, e.g., **bâ indà bài kai ba** (A-form) 'There is no place he hasn't reached'; **yā kai tà kà̀suwā** (B-form) 'He took it to market'; **yā kai takàřdā** (C-form) 'He died' (slang, lit. he took the paper); **yā kai musù yāk̃ì̀** (D-form) 'He made war on them' (lit. he carried to.them war). The corresponding gr6 verb is **kāwō** 'bring, reach'. Among the irregular verbs, **kai** is unusual in using the weak ̀**-wā** verbal noun, e.g., **mè kukè̀ kâiwā?** 'What are you taking?' The masculine noun **kāyā** 'goods, loads' is probably an old deverbal noun derived from **kai**.

(8) The verb **bā** 'give' (or its dialectal variant **bai**) exhibits tonal variants in different syntactic contexts.

	A-Form	B-Form	C-Form	D-Form [pre-noun only]
give	bâ <bâi>	bā	bâ <bâi>	bā (wà) / bai (wà)

The normal object of the verb **bā** 'give' is the recipient, which must be expressed. This first object may optionally be followed by a second object specifying the thing that is given, e.g., **tā bā nì (kuɗī)** 'She gave me (money).' One cannot, however, simply say ****tā bā kuɗī** 'She gave money.' To express this one needs to use the gr5 form, i.e., **tā bā(yar̃) dà kuɗî**. The H-tone **bā** (the B-form) is used before a personal pronoun object, e.g., **zân bā kà (àbîn)** 'I'll give you (the thing).' (The pronoun belongs to the weak object set, which historically was used for both direct and indirect objects.) Before a noun object the verb has falling tone, e.g., **nā bâ Mūsā bīr̃ò** 'I gave Musa a ballpoint pen.' (The falling tone is a result of the historical incorporation of the i.o. marker **wà** into the verb, i.e., **bâ** < ***bā-wà**, i.e., what is listed above as a C-form is in reality a fused D-form.) Before non-pronoun recipients, some speakers use the H-tone verb stem (especially the **bai** variant) followed by the overt i.o. marker **wà**, rather than the fused falling-tone form, i.e., **nā bai wà Mūsā bīr̃ò** 'I gave Musa a ballpoint pen.' If the recipient is displaced, one uses either a falling-tone A-form (which in reality is also a fused D-form) or else the nonfused D-form, e.g., **wǎnē nè ka bâ Ø (= bai wà) bīr̃ò?** 'Whom did you give the ballpoint pen to?' Synchronically, **bā** does not have a corresponding verbal noun form, e.g., **munà [bā]$_V$ shì tàimakō** 'We are giving him assistance', not ** **munà [bân]$_{VN}$ sà tàimakō**.

> ◊HN: There are numerous compounds of the form **ban** + X, e.g., **ban tsòr̃ō** 'terrifying' (lit. giving of fear), **ban girmā** 'respect' (lit. giving of age), **ban màganà** 'coaxing' (lit. giving of speech). Note that **ban** has H tone, unlike normal gr0 verbal nouns that have falling tone, e.g., **shân ruwā** 'drinking water'. Primarily because of the tone, some scholars, e.g., Jaggar (1992a: 36), have proposed that **ban** comes from a contraction of **bà ni!** 'give me!' where the tone simplification of LH to H is regular. From a phonological point of view there is nothing wrong with this derivation, i.e., it *could* be correct, but no one has yet produced internal or comparative evidence to demonstrate that it is in fact correct. In my opinion, **ban** could just as easily represent an archaic verbal noun ***bā** plus the -**n** linker, notwithstanding the high rather than falling tone.

(9) The motion verbs **jē** 'go' and **zō** 'come' constitute a semantic pair, e.g., **yā jē wurin càn** 'He went to that place', **yā zō wurin nàn** 'He came to this place.' Whether they are morphological variants of one another, e.g., **jē** < ***zē**, or whether they are unrelated lexical items is another question. (As suggested in the historical note in §11.1, **jē** could possibly be derived from a root ***dā** whereas **zō** might go back to ***zakà**). The verbal noun of **zō** is **zuwà** (m.), e.g., **kā taɓà zuwà gàrin nàn?** 'Have you ever come (lit. coming) to this town?' The verb **jē** does not have its own verbal noun; instead one has to use either **zuwà** or else **tàfiyà**, the verbal noun of **tàfi** 'go', e.g., **mù jē kàsuwā!** Let's go to market!'; **munà zuwà/tàfiyà kàsuwā** 'We are going to market.'

(10) The verb **'yan/'yam** 'give a little to', which is more or less synonymous with the clipped verb **sam** (see §15 below), occurs only with an i.o. It is phonologically unusual in that it contains the glottalized semivowel **/'y/**, a consonant normally found only in variants of the morpheme **'yā** 'daughter'. Because this irregular verb is always followed by an i.o. marker, it is impossible to determine what its underlying lexical form is, i.e., we have no way to know whether the final nasal is underlyingly /**n**/, with the [m] resulting from assimilation to the following **ma**-, or whether it is underlyingly /**m**/, with the [ŋ] (orthographically represented by **n**) resulting from assimilation to **wà**. Examples:

tā 'yam minì	She gave me a little.
'yàm masà lèmō!	Give him some cola!
nā 'yan wà Audù nāmà	I gave Audu a little bit of meat.

> °AN: Although this verb is said to be commonplace in SH, it has been totally overlooked in standard pedagogical courses and abridged dictionaries of the language.
> ΔDN: According to Bargery (1934), **'yam** is a variant of the WH form **ɗam**, which is used only in the imperative, e.g., **ɗam mîn!** 'Give me (a little of something)!' Although this verb is often found

in commands, it is not restricted to the imperative in WH any more than it is in SH, e.g., [WH] **kai nè na ɗam mằ** 'It was you I gave a little to.'

15. CLIPPED VERBS

A few otherwise regular verbs have optional clipped forms that can be used when followed by an object. (These verbs are thus treated separately from the irregular verbs in the preceding section where historically clipped forms have now become frozen.) These clipped forms have the shape CVC or CVV (where the VV is a diphthong derived from V + a glide). The tone is H in all cases. (There is also one disyllabic clipped verb, namely, **kàrai** 'lose hope', which has L-H tone.) The clipped verb **ɗau** 'take' (< **ɗaukằ**) drops the final syllable; all the other clipped verbs simply leave off the final vowel. The form **sau** 'release' (< *sak < **sàkā**) reflects the operation of Klingenheben's Law changing syllable-final velars to /u/. The rolled /ř/ in **ɗař** 'exceed slightly' (< **ɗarằ**) is due to the fact that flap /r/ does not occur in word-final position. Synchronically, the clipped form **kas** 'kill' relates to the gr4 verb **kashè**. Historically, however, it probably derives from a gr2 form (***kàsi**), which is no longer used. With the clipped forms derived from gr1 verbs, the tone disappears along with the vowels, e.g., **ɗarằ** 'exceed slightly' (⇒) **ɗař**, not ****ɗâř**. The tone of the clipped gr2 verbs can be accounted for in one of two ways. One could preserve the tone and account for the surface H by the regular LH to H simplification rule, e.g., **tā sàyi nāmā** ⇒ **tā sày ´nāmằ** → **tā sai nāmằ** 'She bought meat.' Alternatively, one could delete the tone and propose H as a morphologically required property of all monosyllabic clipped verb forms regardless of the original grade and tone.

　　Some clipped verbs, given in (a) below, occur only before an i.o. Others, given in (b), can be used with a following d.o. (or complement). Some of these can also be used with an i.o. The d.o. of the verbs **sau** 'release' and **kas** 'kill' can be either a noun or a pronoun; the other verbs only allow noun d.o.'s. Some of the clipped forms, e.g., **sai** 'buy', are quite common; others, e.g., **kas** 'kill' tend to be restricted to compounds or set fixed expressions. There are also two intransitive clipped verbs, given in (c). The following is a complete list of clipped verbs (barring accidental omissions):

(a) **ɗař** < **ɗarằ** v1	exceed slightly
e.g., **nā ɗař masà shèkàrū**	I am slightly older than him.
fař < **fāɗằ** v1	fall on
e.g., **Tankò yā fař wà mằtařsà dà faɗằ**	Tanko attacked his wife. (lit. fell upon his wife with fighting)
sam < **sāmừ** v2 get	give a little to
e.g., **nâ sam masà lèmō**	I'll give him a small amount of cola / a few oranges.
(b) **ɗau** < **ɗaukằ** v2	lift
e.g., **zō nân mù ɗau (masà) kāyân!**	Come here let's lift the load (for him)!
cf. **zō nân mù ɗàuki kāyân!**	Come here let's lift the load!
cf. **zō nân mù ɗaukam/ɗaukằ masà kāyân!**	Come here let's lift the load for him!
kas < **kashè** v4	kill
e.g., **màganà tā kas bàkī**	The matter is settled. (lit. speech killed the mouth)
e.g., **kàs-kaifi**	charm to prevent being cut (lit. kill sharpness)
sai < **sàyā** v2	buy
e.g., **bà tà sai (wà kīshìyā) nāmằ ba**	She didn't buy food (for her co-wife).
sau < **sàkā** v2	release
e.g., **sàu ta!**	Release her!
e.g., **yā sau mằtā tasà**	He divorced his wife.
zam < **zama** v*	become
e.g., **yā zam màsīfà**	It has become a tragedy.

(c) kàrai < kàrayà v3   lose hope (e.g., **sun kàrai**   They lost hope.)
kwan < kwāna v3a   spend the night,
e.g., **kù kwan lāfiyà!**   Sleep well! (phonetically [kwallāfiyà])

Normally the clipped forms are identical in meaning to their corresponding full forms. The form **sam** ($\rightarrow$ [saŋ] when followed by **wà**), however, has developed the specialized meaning of 'give a little of something (especially food or drink)', as opposed to the full gr1 form **sāmà̀**, which has the general meaning of 'get for', e.g., **nā sam wà Lādì màzàrƙwailà̀** 'I gave Ladi a bit of sugarcane candy' vs. **nâ sāmà̀ wà Lādì aikì** 'I will get Ladi a job.'

16. THE ORIGIN OF THE GRADE SYSTEM: A HISTORICAL PERSPECTIVE

The grade system as developed by Parsons (1960b) serves as a reasonably sound synchronic basis for organizing the various morphological classes of verbs in Hausa. As such it has been adopted by most scholars around the world, for analytical as well as for pedagogical purposes. Nevertheless, if one considers Parsons' conceptualization of the system in a strict sense, one finds that it contains a number of major flaws. An alternative, historically based model, the vowel-class / extension (VCE) model, first proposed in somewhat different form by Newman (1973), allows one to understand the grade system better and to interpret it in a different light by seeing how it came about.

16.1. The grade system and its flaws

The essence of the classic grade system is that all verbs are bimorphemic, i.e., they are thought to consist of an abstract verb root, which has no tone or final vowel, plus one of seven mutually exclusive grade terminations. Thus **dafà̀** 'to cook', for example, is viewed as consisting of a root √**daf**-, which carries the general meaning of 'cook', plus a suffix -ā)$^{HL(H)}$, which is the gr1 termination; **shìga** 'enter' is viewed as consisting of a root √**shig**- plus the gr3 ending -a)$^{LH(L)}$, **haɾbō** 'shoot and come' is viewed as consisting of the root √**haɾb**- plus the gr6 ending -ō)^H, etc. While this system could be made to work most of the time, it runs up against a number of problems such as the following.

(1) In principle, all bases are supposed to be able to occur in all seven grades. In fact, although most verbs, subject to semantic appropriateness, can operate grades 4 and 5 (the secondary grades) and grades 6 and 7 (the tertiary grades), there are innumerable gaps when it comes to grades 1, 2, and 3 (the primary grades). The verb **dafà̀** 'cook', for example, occurs in gr1 only, to the exclusion of gr2 and gr3, whereas **fìta** 'go out' occurs only in gr3 but not in gr1 or gr2.

(2) If the basic meaning of a verb were provided exclusively by the root, with the grade endings adding only subsidiary semantic modification, one should not find verbs with the same segmental base having distinct meanings in different primary grades, but one does. Consider the following contrasts:

gamà̀ v1	finish, complete	vs.	**gàmā** v2	please, suit, satisfy
rainà̀ v1	despise, belittle	vs.	**ràinā** v2	tend, look after
zāgà̀ v1	go round	vs.	**zàgā** v2	insult
sakà̀ v1	put sth somewhere	vs.	**sàkā** v2	release, divorce
nūnà̀ v1	point at, show	vs.	**nùna** v3	ripen, be cooked

(3) Although all of the grade endings are supposed to be distinct morphemes in their own right, the primary grade formatives often have no identifiable meaning. In the gr6 verb **shigō** 'enter here', for example, one can specify the meaning of the ending -ō)^H as 'ventive' (= action in this direction), but in **shìga**, the supposed gr3 ending -**a** adds nothing to the basic meaning of 'enter'. Similarly, the gr7 -**u**)^{LH}

ending in **dàfu** 'be well cooked' can be identified as 'passive/well sustained', whereas the supposed gr1 morpheme -ā)$^{HL(H)}$ in **dafà** adds nothing to the general meaning of 'cook'.

(4) The grade system fails to incorporate very basic (H)H verbs such as **ci** 'eat', **shā** 'drink', **kirā** 'call', and other high-frequency "irregular" verbs like **fāɗì** 'fall' and **mutù** 'die'.

(5) Because a verb is supposed to consist of a root plus one of seven *mutually exclusive* grades, the system fails to account for the fact that grades can indeed co-occur, e.g., **janyō** gr4 *and* gr6 'pull all here' < **jā** 'pull'; **fìddu** gr5d [dv] *and* gr7 'have been taken out' < **fìta** 'go out'.

16.2. Historical vowel-class / extension (VCE) model

Throughout the Chadic family, it is common for basic verbs to fall into two (and only two) lexically arbitrary classes defined in terms of the final vowel, which is a morphologically integral part of the verb.

> °AN: For a general discussion of phonologically-defined verb classes in Chadic as a whole, see Newman (1975); for a description with specific reference to the West Chadic group to which Hausa belongs, see Schuh (1977).

Some verbs end in -**a** (usually the smaller class), whereas other verbs end in a non-low vowel (-**i**, -**u**, or -**ə**) or in no vowel. These are conventionally referred to as "schwa-verbs," regardless of the actual ending. (In Chadic languages, the central vowel transcribed as -**ə** is typically pronounced as a high vowel, phonetically akin either to [-i] or to [-u].) In Bole, for example, the **a**-class is represented by such verbs as **pata** 'go out', whereas schwa-verbs, which end in -**u**, are represented by such verbs as **poru** 'say' or **wùndu** 'call'.

Another common feature of Chadic languages is the existence of adverbial-like extensions indicating such notions as action away, action toward the speaker, totality of action, completeness of action, partitive, etc. In some languages, for example, Tera, these extensions are adverbial particles totally separable from the verb (comparable to English *out* in *turn out (the light)*), e.g., **mbukə ɓara** 'throw away'; cf. **mbukə** 'throw'. In others, for example, Margi, they are derivational formatives (comparable to German *ver* in *verschenken* 'give away'), e.g., **kwàsənyà** 'eat up'; cf. **kwàsə** 'eat'. In Chadic, these extensions tend to combine freely with basic verbs (subject to semantic appropriateness) and are able to co-occur with one another.

The historical VCE model is a reformulation of the Hausa grade system along the lines of the normal Chadic pattern. There are two primary factors that explain why the Hausa verbal system at first looks so different from that found typically in other Chadic languages. The first is that the erstwhile extensions have become so reduced phonologically that they have become fused into the verb. (It is much easier to recognize that Tera ɓara, as in **mbukə ɓara** 'throw away', is an extension than it is with the Hausa final -ē)^{HL} that one finds in **sayè** 'buy all' < **sàyā** 'buy'). The second factor is that a long-standing analytical error in representing Hausa verbs has hidden the basic -a/schwa vowel class contrast. The general convention among Hausa grammarians and lexicographers has been to treat the A-form, i.e., the form when no object is expressed, as the basic, underlying citation form. As a result, both gr1 verbs, like **dafà** 'cook', and gr2 verbs, like **kàrɓā** 'receive', appear to be -ā final. From a Chadic perspective, however, the more appropriate form to take as representing the underlying shape of the verb is the one that occurs before direct object nouns, which in Hausa is the C-form. In the case of gr2 verbs, the final vowel that appears here is -**i**, e.g., **tā kàrɓi kuɗī** 'She received money.' This can be contrasted with gr1 verbs where the final vowel is -**a**, e.g., **yā dafà àbinci** 'He cooked food.' Thus one finds that the fundamental distinction between basic gr2 verbs and basic gr1 verbs is a reflex of the widespread Chadic lexical opposition between verbs ending in -**i** (i.e., schwa-verbs) and those ending in -**a** (i.e., **a**-verbs).

°AN: Viewed historically, the identification of the C-form as the underlying form is unassailably true. This is independent of the question whether such an analysis does or does not still hold up synchronically.

16.2.1. Basic verb classes

The assignment of Hausa verbs into lexically basic classes according to the quality of the final vowel (-**i** or -**a**) is represented in table 31, where transitive verbs are listed in the C-form. (I illustrate polysyllabic verbs with two-syllable verbs only.) Note that monosyllabic verbs, which pose a problem for the classic grade system, fall naturally into this categorization.

Table 31: Basic verb classes: VCE model

Tone	-**i**	-**a**
H (Monosyllabic)	**ci** eat	**jā** pull
H-L	**fāɗì** fall (= gr3b)	**dafà** cook (= gr1)
L-H	**sàyi** buy (= gr2)	**fìta** go out (= gr3)

°AN: The long /ā/ found with monosyllabic Cā verbs has a phonological/prosodic explanation and does not affect the basic categorization.

In this model, a verb like **fìta**, for example, is a monomorphemic word that happens to end in the vowel /a/. Contrary to the grade system analysis, the final /a/ in this word is not interpreted as a separate formative, i.e., **fìta** is *not* lexically composed of √**fit** + -**a**. Similarly, **ci** (which happens to be monosyllabic), **fāɗì**, and **sàyi** are normal schwa-verbs ending in -**i**; they cannot be decomposed into a root √**c**-, √**fāɗ**-, or √**say**- plus a morpheme -**i**.

Because the final vowel with basic verbs is lexically significant, one would expect to find verbs contrasting on the basis of this element. This, as pointed out earlier, does occur. Examples (with citations in the C-form):

gamà v1	finish, complete	vs.	**gàmi** v2	please, suit, satisfy
rainà v1	despise, belittle	vs.	**ràini** v2	tend, look after
sakà v1	put sth somewhere	vs.	**sàki** v2	release, divorce

Whereas the final vowel was (and is) lexically distinctive in verbs, tone probably was not.

°AN: This analysis is at variance from the model presented in Newman (1973). It is this modification that has necessitated the terminological change from the VTE (vowel tone extension) system to the VCE (vowel-class extension) system.

Monosyllabic verbs all have H tone. Disyllabic verbs do exhibit tonal differences, i.e., one now finds both H-L and L-H, but this surface difference, originally at least, was not lexical. Rather, it appears to have been determined by transitivity. With schwa-verbs, the tone pattern was L-H with transitive verbs (e.g., **fàdi** 'tell') and H-L with intransitives (e.g., **fāɗì** 'fall'). With a-verbs, one found the opposite, i.e., H-L with transitive verbs (e.g., **dakà** 'pound') and L-H with intransitives (e.g., **nùka** 'become ripe'). A verb that was neutral with regard to transitivity, i.e., occurred both as a transitive and as an intransitive, thus appeared with the two different tone patterns, e.g., **cìka** 'be filled' (intr.) vs. **cikà** 'fill' (tr.); **haifù** (with -**i** → -**u** conditioned by the labial consonant) 'give birth' (intr.), e.g., **tā haifù** 'She has given birth' vs. **hàifi** 'give birth to' (tr.), e.g., **tā hàifi ɗā namijì** 'She has given birth to a son.'

°AN: In the earlier analysis, I had cited the irregular verbs **sanì** 'know' and **barì** 'let' as exemplifying the class of H-L transitive schwa-verbs. This was clearly a conceptual error. The H-L tone of these verbs appears only in the A-form, which we know does *not* represent the underlying form. The C-forms of these verbs, namely, **san** and **bař**, are clipped verb forms derived from L-H **sàni** and **bàri**, respectively.

There are a small number of **a**-final intransitives with H-H rather than L-H tone e.g., **sūma** 'faint', **ƙaura** 'migrate', but these do not require that one accept the idea of tone historically being lexically distinctive. Rather, these words have two reasonable alternative explanations, both of which are consistent with the idea that the deviation from the expected L-H tone is secondary. The first explanation is phonological conditioning, based on the fact that these H-H final-**a** intransitives (like **tsīra** 'escape') all have a heavy initial-syllable as opposed to the L-H (= gr3) verbs (like **shìga** 'enter'), almost all of which have a light first syllable. The second explanation (originally suggested, I believe, by Parsons) is that these H-H intransitive verbs constitute back-formations from H-H verbal nouns, e.g., **tsīra** 'escape' < **tsīrā** 'escaping' (m.).

Synchronically one finds a considerable number of H-L **a**-verbs (i.e., gr1 verbs) that are intransitive. I would contend, nonetheless, that basic intransitive **a**-verbs were originally L-H and that the intransitive gr1 verbs that now occur all reflect subsequent secondary developments.

16.2.2. Extensions

In addition to having basic verbs, where the final vowel is part of the underlying representation, Hausa has morphologically derived verbs, where the final vowel (or -VC) is a tone-integrating extensional suffix. These suffixes are added to the basic verbs. (As is the norm with tone-integrating suffixes, the tone of the stem and the final vowel—except in the case of monosyllabic words—are overridden.) The stems with the extensional suffixes make up the secondary grades (namely, grades 4, 5, 6, and 7). Examples:

sàyi	buy + -e)^{HL} totality $\Rightarrow$	**sayè**	buy all (v4)
fìta	go out + -ař)^H efferential $\Rightarrow$	**fitař**	take out (v5)
ci	eat + -ař)^H efferential $\Rightarrow$	**ciyař**	feed (v5)
jā	pull + -(w)ō)^H ventive $\Rightarrow$	**jāwō**	pull here (v6)
fāɗì	fall + -ō)^H ventive $\Rightarrow$	**fāɗō**	fall this way (v6)
dafà	cook + -u)^{LH} sustentative $\Rightarrow$	**dàfu**	be well cooked (v7)

Because the final vowel in basic verbs is an intrinsic part of the stem, the "same" verb should not occur both as an **i**-verb and as an **a**-verb. But in fact, it is very common for the same lexical verb to operate a pair of basic grades like gr2 (or gr3b) (final-**i**) as well as gr1 (final-**a**), e.g.,

zân àri (v2) **wasu lìttàttàfai**	I'll borrow some books.
vs. **zân arà̀** (v1) **mukù wasu lìttàttàfai**	I'll lend you some books.
yā fàɗi (v2) **làbāřì**	He told the news.
vs. **yā faɗà̀** (v1) **matà làbāřì**	He told her the news.
yā hàřbi (v2) **tsuntsū**	He shot a bird.
vs. **yā hařbà** (v1) **bindigà̀**	He shot a gun.
yā fāɗì (v3b)	He fell.
vs. **yā fāɗà̀** (v1) **ruwa**	He fell into the water.
yā yànki (v2) **nāmà̀**	He cut off a piece of meat.
vs. **yā yankà** (v1) **ràgō**	He slaughtered a ram.

yā hàɓi (v2) **gwāzā**   He dug out cocoyams.

vs. yā haɓà (v1) **rāmì**   He dug a hole.

The explanation for the apparent contrast is that in such pairs as the above, both verb forms are not really basic. Rather, one verb is basic and the other contains a derivational extension, which, because of the extreme phonological reduction that has characterized Hausa extensions, now consists solely of a final vowel that is identical in shape with a basic vowel. There are at least two such "hidden extensions" that can be identified.

The first is the "applicative," which serves to direct the action of the verb onto the object (either direct or very often indirect) or onto a location. This extension ends in -a)^{HL} and thus has fallen together with basic a-verbs to make up the form class that now constitutes gr1. A verb like **arà** 'lend to' is not a basic a-verb, as it first appears but rather is a derived verb made up of the basic i-verb **àri** 'borrow' plus the applicative extension -a)^{HL}. Similarly, **fāɗà** 'fall into sth', an intransitive a-ending verb with H-L tone, is not a true a-verb but rather is a derived verb made up of **fāɗi** 'fall' plus the applicative extension -a)^{HL}.

> °AN: In principle there is no reason why the applicative could not be added to a basic a-verb, although there would be no way to see it. Since underlying gr2 i-verbs so often add the applicative extension before indirect objects, it would be reasonable to hypothesize that the same is happening with gr1 a-verbs, i.e., **tā dafà** (a-verb) **àbinci** 'She cooked food', but **tā dafà** (a-verb plus applicative) **masà àbinci** 'She cooked him food' (see Newman 1991a).

The second "hidden extension" is the "partitive-displacive," which indicates that the action affects a part of the object or involves removal or displacement of the object. This extension ends in -i)^{LH} and thus has fallen together with basic i-verbs to make up the form class that now constitutes gr2. In the pair **haɓà** 'dig' and **hàɓi** 'dig out or up', the former is a basic a-verb, whereas the latter is a derived verb containing the extensional suffix -i)^{LH}. Similarly, **yànki** 'cut off some' is a derived partitive and not a basic i-verb.

16.2.3. Grade system and VCE system contrasted

The contrast between the classic grade system and the historically based VCE system is illustrated in the diagrams in fig. 7 on the following page.

[References: There is an extensive literature on the Hausa grade system. The following selected references are essential reading for anyone who wishes to study the matter in greater detail. (a) General: Abdoulaye (1992); Newman (1973); Parsons (1960b); (b) Grade 2: Lukas (1963); Pilszczikowa (1969); (c) Grade 4: Furniss (1981, 1983); Jaggar (1988a, 1992b); Newman (1977b); (c) Grade 5: Bagari (1977b); Frajzyngier (1985); Garba (1982); Gouffé (1962); Newman (1983); Parsons 1962, 1971/72); (d) Grade 7: Caron (1983, 1991); Jaggar (1981)]

Figure 7: Grade system and VCE system contrasted

GRADE SYSTEM

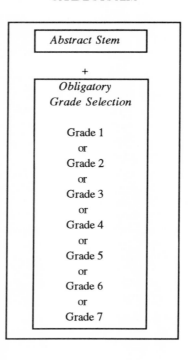

VCE SYSTEM

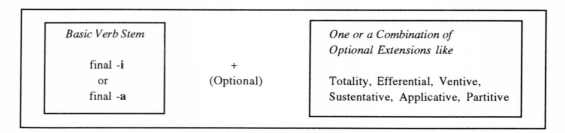

75. Verb Subcategorization

SYNTACTICALLY, verbs can be divided into the five major categories: (a) transitive, (b) intransitive, (c) dative, (d) sociative, and (e) efferential. (In this section, I shall use the term *verb* throughout whether the verb appears as a finite verb or as a morphological verbal noun (nominalized verb) derived from a verb.) These divisions cut across the classification into grades (noted v1, v2, etc.; see chap. **74**). Transitive verbs, for example, are found in grades 0, 1, 2, 4, 5, 5d [dv], and 6, whereas grade 1 includes transitive, intransitive, dative, and sociative verbs. It is important to remember that this is a syntactic classification and that individual lexemes may function as members of a number of different classes.

1. TRANSITIVE VERBS

1.1. Neutral/unmarked
Transitive verbs contain an underlying direct object. In the neutral, unmarked case, the syntactic direct object is the thematic patient. Grade 2 verbs are all transitive, as are all (most?) 5d verbs. Verbs in grades 3 and 7 are never transitive. The other grades (i.e., 0, 1, 4, 5, and 6) include, but are not limited to, transitive verbs. Examples:

Tankò yâ sàyi àtàmfā (v2)	Tanko will probably buy wax print cloth.
wà ya hàr̃bi bàrēwā? (v2)	Who shot the gazelle?
kadà kà tàimàkē sù! (v2)	Don't help them!
kàrē bài shā ruwân ba (v0)	The dog did not drink the water.
munà jîn yunwà (v0)	We are feeling hungry.
màtātā tanà dafà àbinci (v1)	My wife is cooking food.
akàn būɗè ƙōfà dà ƙarfè tar̃à (v4)	One opens the door at nine o'clock.
nā gaishē kà (v5)	I greet you.
sun fiddà ta (v5d)	They took it out.
kàwō kùjèrū! (v6)	Bring chairs!

Transitive verbs may appear on the surface without an immediately following overt d.o., either because the d.o. has been fronted or because it is omitted but understood from the context. Examples:

birì nē ya hàr̃bā	It was a monkey he shot.	mè ka kàrɓā?	What did you receive?
Tankò yâ sàyā	Tanko will likely buy (it).	yā kàmātà mù kòyā	We ought to learn (it).

1.2. Phrasal VPs with **yi** *'do' + a dynamic noun*
The pro-verb **yi** 'do' occurs commonly with a dynamic noun as direct object to indicate what in English would be expressed by an intransitive verb. Grammatically, however, these verb phrases consist of a transitive verb plus a direct object, e.g.,

yā yi aikì   He worked. (lit. he.comp do work)
kadà kà yi wàsā!   Don't play! (lit. don't you do play)
zā mù yi hīřa   We will have a chat. (lit. fut we do chatting)

In nonfinite constructions, as used, for example, in the continuous, the verbal noun corresponding to **yi**
may be, and typically is, deleted. Examples:

yā iyà (yîn) aikì   He can work.   wàsā sukè (yî)   It's playing they're doing.

The verb may also be deleted even in finite constructions when followed by an indirect object, although
this is not as common as the nonfinite VN deletion, e.g.,

yā (yi) wà Mūsā aikì   He worked for Musa.   sun (yi) masà màganà   They spoke to him.

1.3. Applicatives

Applicatives, i.e., grade 1 verbs with an applicative extension, differ from neutral transitives in two
respects. First, the d.o. is often semantically an instrumental rather than a thematic patient. Second, the
verb normally requires that a third argument be expressed in addition to the subject and the d.o. This third
argument is commonly an indirect object, but it may also be a locative or a prepositional phrase.
Examples:

wannàn mùtumìn yā sōkà [wà ràƙumī]$_{i.o.}$ wuƙā   This man stabbed the camel with a knife.
(lit. …stabbed to camel knife) (cf. the neutral transitive sentence with the v2: **wannàn mùtumìn yā sòki
ràƙumī dà wuƙā** (lit. …stabbed camel with knife)
nā tsōkànā [masà]$_{i.o.}$ tsinkē à ido   I poked him in the eye with a stick.
(lit. …poked to.him stick at eye)
an shiřɓùnà mâi [à jìkinsà]$_{loc}$ They applied lotion on him. (lit. on his body)
= an shiřɓùnā [masà]$_{i.o.}$ mâi (lit. …applied to.him oil)
tā baɗà yājì [à tuwō]$_{loc}$ = tā baɗà [wà tuwō]$_{i.o.}$ yājì She sprinkled spices on the *tuwo*.
yā aikà yārò [kàsuwā]$_{loc}$ He sent the boy to the market.
yā aikà wàsīƙà gà Bintà   He sent a letter to Binta.
cf. yā àiki yārò   He sent the boy. (with the transitive v2 verb)
cf. yā aikà dà wàsīƙà   He sent a letter. (with the sociative v1 verb)

> °AN: With the gr1 verb **aikà** 'to send', some speakers now allow deletion of the sociative
> preposition **dà** before the object being sent, i.e., **yā aikà wàsīƙà** = **yā aikà dà wàsīƙà** 'He sent a
> letter.' The bare gr1 verb can also be used when the d.o. is the person being sent, but such sentences
> presuppose a place or purpose related to the sending, e.g., **yā aikà yārò** (**don yà sayō masà Fantà**)
> 'He sent the boy (in order that he buy him a Fanta).'

1.4. Three-place verbs with i.o.

Apart from the syntactic applicatives just described above, most verbs, whether transitive or
intransitive, treat the indirect object as an optional element expressing benèfactive, dative, malefactive,
etc., e.g.,

màtātā tanà dafà [wà màlàmai]$_{i.o.}$ àbinci   My wife is cooking food for the teachers.
àbōkīnā zâi nēmam [makà]$_{i.o.}$ aikì   My friend will look for work for you.
yā sācè [minì]$_{i.o.}$ kuɗī   He stole the money from me.

Some normal transitive verbs with a patient as direct object require that the sentence contain an indirect object as well. These will be represented as verb + IOM. (The IOM (indirect object marker) is /wà/ before noun objects (= /mà/ in WH) and **ma-** before pronoun objects.) (a) Many of these are applicative grade 1 verbs, where the i.o. is the dative recipient (e.g., **gayà** + IOM 'tell', **kallàfā** + IOM 'impose sth. on s.o.', **kōyà** + IOM 'teach to', **rântā** + IOM 'lend to' (esp. money), **sunnà** + IOM 'give sth. secretly to s.o.', **'yam** + IOM 'give a little bit of to' (esp. food or drink). (b) Some are verbs that indicate doing the action to the patient (= i.o.) in a severe or excessive manner, e.g., **daɓà** + IOM 'do forcefully, apply a lot of', **gallà** + IOM 'do something severely', **shirgà** + IOM 'do much of sth. bad, inflict'. (c) Others are verbs used in idiomatic verbal constructions (see chap. 36) of the form V + i.o. + d.o., where the d.o. is fixed, e.g., **baƙàntā** + i.o. **râi** 'displease, make sad', **gamè** + i.o. **kâi** 'conspire against', **kashè** + i.o. **idò** 'dazzle', **ƙurà** + i.o. **idò** 'stare at'. Examples:

(a) **nā gayà masà làbārìn**	I told him the news.
(not ****nā gayà làbārìn** I told the news.)	
nā rântā masà fâm biyu	I lent him 2 pounds.
(not ****nā rântà fâm biyu** I lent 2 pounds.) (cf. **nā rànci fâm biyu** I borrowed 2 pounds.)	
yā kōyà wà bàtūrè Hausa	He taught Hausa to the European.
(not ****yā kōyà Hausa** He taught Hausa, for which one must use the gr5: **yā kōyaɍ dà Hausa**)	
(b) **an daɓà masà wuƙā**	He's been stabbed severely.
yā shirgà minì ƙaryā	He told me a whopping lie.
(c) **wannàn yā baƙàntā minì râi**	This displeased me.
haskên yā kashè wà fāsinjōjī idò	The light blinded the passengers.

The irregular verb **bā/bai** 'give to' is intrinsically a three-place verb. It is unusual in that it behaves differently depending on whether the recipient is a noun or a pronoun. If the recipient is a personal pronoun, it appears structurally as the direct object of **bā**. Nominal recipients, on the other hand, appear as indirect objects (marked either by **wà** or by a floating L tone (ˋ), which is derived from **wà**), e.g.,

yā bâ (= bai wà) Tankò kuɗī	He gave Tanko money.
cf. **yā bā nì kuɗī**	He gave me money. (not ****yā bā/bai minì kuɗī**)

◊HN: The contrast between the double object construction in **zā tà bā nì hùlā** 'She will give me a cap' (not ****zā tà bā minì hùlā**) and the simple transitive construction with a noun indirect object in **zā tà bai wà (= bâ) Mūsā hùlā** 'She will give Musa a cap' reflects a widespread Chadic pattern that can be reconstructed for Proto-Chadic. In this pattern, indirect object pronouns are suffixed directly to verbs without the use of an overt particle, whereas noun indirect objects, which usually follow the direct object, require a prepositionlike particle (like the present-day **wà** (<***gà**)) (see Newman 1982).

1.5. Double object verbs
With most 3-place verbs, the first object is expressed as an i.o. and the second as a d.o., e.g., **nā gayà** [masà]$_{i.o.}$ [làbārìn]$_{d.o.}$ 'I told him the news.' A small number of verbs, which I am calling double object verbs (= ditransitive verbs), allow (or require) two successive objects, where the first is syntactically a d.o. and not an i.o., e.g.,

sun biyā Mūsā kuɗī	They paid Musa money.
kadà kà rôƙi Bàlā gōrò!	Don't ask Bala (for) kolanuts!
nā tayà shi dalà biyu	I offered to pay him two dollars (for it).

Bìntà tā fi Kànde tsawō	Binta is taller than Kande.
(lit. Binta she.comp exceed Kande height)	
tā sâ mālàmařtà fushī	She made her teacher angry.
(lit. she.comp cause teacher.of.her anger)	
àlƙālī yā ci Sulè tàrā	The judge fined Sule.
(lit. the judge he.comp eat Sule fine)	
Kànde tā kāsà Bìntà tsawō	Kande is not as tall as Binta
(lit. Kande she.comp fail Binta height)	
Abdù yā kirā Jummai kāřùwà	Abdu called Jummai a whore.
bà à naɗà Gàmbo sarkī ba	They didn't appoint Gambo (as) chief.

Some of the double object verbs can occur as 2-place transitive verbs with either of the objects functioning as the direct object, e.g.,

sun biyā Mūsā	They paid Musa.	**sun biyā kuɗī**	They paid the money.
kadà kà ròƙi Bàlā!	Don't beg Bala!	**kadà kà ròƙi gōřò!**	Don't beg for kolanuts!

In double object constructions, it is clear that the first object is the true syntactic d.o. and that the second has the status of an oblique object. For example, if the first object is moved, with the result that the second object immediately follows the verb, a finite verb takes the A (non-pre-object) form and not the C (pre-d.o.) form. Similarly, the verb or verbal noun in a nonfinite VP appears as it would if there were no following d.o., e.g.,

Kànde cè Bìntà ta ɗarà (v1-A) **tsawō**
　　　It is Kande that Binta is a little taller than. (*not* ****Kànde cè Bìntà ta ɗarà** (v1-C) **tsawō**)

wândà akà sākè naɗàwā sarkī	the one whom they again appointed emir
not ****wândà akà sākè naɗà sarkī**	
cf. **an sākè naɗà wānè sarkī**	They again appointed so-and-so emir.
su wầ kukè biyầ kuɗîn?	Whom (pl.) are you paying the money?
not ****su wầ kukè biyàn kuɗîn?**	

Note also that it is only the true d.o. and not the second object that can undergo passivization and be made the subject of a gr7 verb, e.g.,

Abdù bā yằ ròƙuwā gōřò à hālin yànzu.	Abdu cannot be asked for kolanuts now.
not ****gōřò bā yằ ròƙuwā Abdù à hālin yànzu**	Kolanuts cannot be asked of Abdu now.
Shatù bā tằ ɗàukuwā mahaukacìyā	Shatu can't be taken for a fool.

When semantically appropriate, double object constructions can also have an indirect object.

Mūsā zâi biyā [minì] Sulè fâm biyu	Musa will pay Sule two pounds for me.
an naɗầ [manà] Gàmbo sarkī	They appointed Gambo chief for us.

Although such sentences as the above are considered to be grammatical, they are felt to be clumsy and thus the indirect object tends to be avoided by means of some appropriate paraphrase, for example, by means of a prepositional phrase, e.g., **Mūsā zâi biyā Sulè fâm biyu [don nī]** 'Musa will pay Sule two pounds [on my behalf].'

2. INTRANSITIVE VERBS

Intransitive verbs are intrinsic 1-place verbs that *may not* take a direct object. All gr3 and gr7 verbs are intransitive. Gr4 verbs are commonly (but not exclusively) intransitive. Grades 0, 1, and 6 contain some intransitive verbs, whereas grades 2, 5d, and (generally speaking) 5 do not, e.g.,

bùkātàr̃sà tā biyā (v0)	His needs have been fulfilled.
kà dākàtā kàɗan! (v1)	Wait a little!
kùnkurū yā dùlmuyà (v3)	The tortoise sank.
mālàm yā tsūfa (v3a)	The teacher has aged.
Bellò bà zâi tāshì ba (v3b)	Bello won't get up.
kwalabâr̃ tā fashè (v4)	The bottle broke.
yāròn yā far̃faɗō (v6)	The boy revived.
mōtà̃ tā gyàru (v7)	The car has been well repaired.

The intransitives subdivide into three main categories depending on the thematic role of the subject: (a) intransitives with an actor/undergoer subject; (b) intransitives with a patient subject ("unaccusatives"); and (c) intransitives with an affected subject ("passives") or lexical reflexives.

2.1. Intransitives with actor/undergoer subject

These are intransitive verbs, whose subject is either the undergoer of the action, e.g., **mutù** 'die', or the doer of the action, e.g., **shìga** 'enter'. This latter category includes basic motion verbs, such as **shìga**, as well as some gr1 activity verbs derived from corresponding transitive verbs, e.g., **taimàkā** 'help'. Examples:

yārò̃ yā fāɗì (v3b)	The boy fell down.
fàr̃fēsà̃ yā dāwō (v6)	The professor came back.
tā haifù (v3b)	She gave birth.
cf. tā hàifi ɗā na-mijì (v2-tr.)	She bore a male child.
nā nēmà nā nēmà̃ àmmā inâ! (v1)	I tried and tried, but no way!
cf. nā nèmi aikì (v2-tr.)	I sought work.
nā hangà̃ àmmā bàn ga kōwā ba (v1)	I looked (from a distance) but I didn't see anyone.
cf. mun hàngi mayàk̃ā can nēsà (v2-tr.)	We saw warriors there in the distance.

Intransitives in this class generally transitivize by use of the efferential extension (gr5), e.g.,

yārò̃ yā tùfātà (v3)	The boy got dressed.
cf. kàkā tā tufātar̃ dà yāròn (v5)	Grandmother dressed the boy.
màge tā shìga cikin ɗākì (v3)	The cat entered the room.
cf. nā shigar̃ dà màge cikin ɗākì (v5)	I brought the cat in the room.

Motion verbs indicating 'to a place' express the locative goal immediately after the verb without the use of a preposition, e.g.,

yā kyàutu kà kōmà̃ makar̃antā	It is appropriate that you return to school.
cf. tā kōmà̃ dàgà makar̃antā	She returned from school.
tā jē kàsuwā — She went to market.	**zā sù zō ōfìs** — They will come to the office.

A motion verb cannot be followed directly by a noun indicating a person; rather, one has to use a locative noun (plus linker), like **wurin** (lit. place of), e.g., **mù tàfi wurin dàr̃ektà** 'Let's to to the director' (lit. we.sub go place.of director).

2.2. Intransitives with patient subject ("unaccusatives")

These are verbs whose grammatical subjects are the underlying objects of corresponding transitive verbs, e.g., **tùlū yā fashè** 'The water pot broke', cf. **yā fasà tùlū** 'He broke the water pot.' The subject is affected by the action of the verb without the implication of an agent. Verbs with patient subjects (= "unaccusative" verbs) are found in grades 3 and 4; their transitive counterparts are usually gr1.

bùhū yā cìka dà gyàɗā (v3)	The sack filled up with peanuts.
cf. **yār̃ò yā cikà bùhū dà gyàɗā** (v1)	The boy filled up the sack with peanuts.
shìnkāfā tā ɗùmāmà (v3)	The rice warmed up.
cf. **yā ɗumàmà shìnkāfā** (v1)	He warmed up the rice.
dar̃mà bà tà narkè ba (v4)	The lead didn't melt.
cf. **bài narkà dar̃mà ba** (v1)	He didn't melt the lead.
ruwân yā tàfasà (v3)	The water boiled.
cf. **sun tafàsà ruwā** (v1)	They boiled water.
sàndā tā karyè (v4)	The stick broke.
cf. **yā karyà sàndā** (v1)	He broke the stick.

2.3. Intransitives with affected subject ("passives") and lexical reflexives

Most gr7 intransitive verbs are agentless passives, i.e., the subject is (entirely) affected by the action of an assumed agent that, however, is not normally expressed, e.g., **mōtà tā gyàru** 'The car was well repaired (by someone unnamed)'; cf. the nonpassive gr4 intransitive **mùtûm yā warkè** 'The man recovered.' In the continuous TAM, these verbs connote the possibility or potentiality of the action being done by someone, e.g., **mōtàr̃ bā tà gyàruwā** 'The car is not repairable.' Grade 7 also includes some lexical reflexives, namely, intransitives with plural subjects in which the subject is both the doer and the undergoer of the action, e.g., **mun gàmu** 'We met' (i.e., we met each other). These intransitive lexical reflexives all enter into corresponding sociative constructions, e.g., **nā gàmu dà shī** 'I met (with) him.' Examples:

tàfiyà Marādī tā fàsu	The trip to Maradi was called off.
tùlū yā fàsu	The water pot was broken (by s.o.).
cf. **tùlū yā fashè** (v4)	The water pot broke.
wannàn hanyà bā tà bìyuwā gà mânyan mōtōcī	This road is impassable for heavy trucks.
sunà tàruwā à ƙōfàr̃ fādà	They are assembling at the front of the palace.

3. DATIVE VERBS

The term *dative verb* (vdat) is used for 2-place verbs whose patient is expressed as an indirect object rather than as a direct object. This class includes the irregular verbs **cim mà** 'achieve, overtake' and **im mà** 'control', which have **mà** rather than **wà** as the pre-noun i.o. marker, and a small number of mostly gr1 and gr4 verbs, e.g., **amìncē** 'trust'; **bâutā** 'worship, serve faithfully'; **bijìrē** 'desert, betray'; **bōtsàrē** 'defy s.o.'; **gallàzā** 'persecute, harass, torture'; **girmè** 'be older than'; **gōdè** 'thank'; **kangàrē** 'defy, rebel against'; **ƙauràcē** 'avoid, keep away from; boycott'; **ƙuntàtā** 'pester or badger s.o.'; **tāsar̃** 'attack'; **tsāwàtā** 'scold, give a warning to'; **tsīnè** 'curse'; **yabà** 'recommend, appreciate'. Examples:

yā cim mà būrìnsà	He achieved his goal.
dà kyaȓ mukà im masà	It was with difficulty that we controlled him.
sunà ƙauràcē wà jūnā	They are avoiding each other.
iyàyensà sun tsīnè masà	His parents cursed him.
yanà bâutā wà iskōkī	He worships spirits.
mālàm yā tsāwàtā wà àlmàjìȓai	The teacher scolded the pupils.
gàrin nàn yā girmè wà bīȓnin Kàdūna	This town is older than Kaduna.
talakāwā sunà nēman kangàrē wà kàntōmà	

    The common people are on the verge of defying the administrator.

The verb **gōdè** 'thank' is normally a dative verb whose object is an i.o. The noun **Allàh** 'God', however, optionally (and commonly) appears as a direct object, e.g.,

nā gōdè makà	I thank you. (not **nā gōdè ka)
kà gōdè wà bàbankà!	Thank your father!
mun gōdè wà Allàh = mun gōdè Allàh	We thank God.

4. SOCIATIVE VERBS

Sociatives are complex verbs composed of a verb stem plus the preposition **dà** 'with', e.g., **lùȓa dà** 'look after, take notice of'.

    °AN: Abdoulaye (1996) has shown that from certain syntactic points of view, a sequence of V + **dà** + NP can be thought of as [V + **dà**]$_{VP}$ + NP (i.e., a complex verb plus an object) rather than V + [**dà** + NP]$_{pp}$ (i.e., a verb followed by a prepositional phrase). There are, nevertheless, good morphological and syntactic reasons for etymologically equating the sociative **dà** with the preposition 'with'.

The verb preceding the **dà** may be (a) a simple stem, generally belonging to grades 0, 1, 3, 4, or 7, e.g., **kàmu dà** 'be infected with', or (b) a phrasal verb, often made up of the pro-verb **yi** 'do' plus a noun or an ideophone, e.g., **yi shirì dà** 'be on good terms with' (lit. do preparation with), **yi tiȓ dà** 'disapprove of' (lit. do expression-of-annoyance with). Statives, i.e., adverbial forms derived from verbs, also enter into sociative constructions (see §67:2.1.1), e.g., **làbce dà** 'be laden with'. The following is a list of some of the more common sociative verbs and verb phrases:

(a) **aikà dà** send sth; **amìncē dà** agree with; **dācè dà** suit, be appropriate; **dàmu dà** be bothered by, worried about; **fàhimtà dà** understand; **gànà dà** meet, chat with; **gaisà dà** greet; **gàji dà** be tired of; **gàmsu dà** be pleased with; **gàmu dà** meet s.o.; **ji dà** feel about, feel for; **jimà dà** pass by (of time); **karà dà** clash with; **kàmu dà** be infected with; **kōmà dà** return sth.; **kulà dà** attend to (= **kùla dà**); **ƙārà dà** do more of; **lùȓa dà** look after, take notice of; **màntā dà** forget; **matsà dà** bring close; **ràbu dà** part company with, divorce; **sàbà dà** be accustomed to; **shàgaltà dà** be carried away with; **shàƙu dà** be close friends with; **tunà dà** remember; **wucè dà** bring in; **yabà dà** praise; **yàrda dà** trust, accept
(b) **ci gàba dà** proceed, continue; **ci karò dà** run/bump into someone; **shā bambam dà** differ from, miss; **yi àmfànī dà** make use of; **yi aȓbà dà** meet unexpectedly; **yi bìȓis dà** ignore completely; **yi gàràjē dà** do sth hastily; **yi kàmā dà** resemble; **yi màganà dà** talk with; **yi na'àm dà** agree with; **yi ȓab dà** catch suddenly; **yi shirì dà** be on good terms with; **yi wàtsī dà** throw away, reject

The irregular **san dà** 'be aware of, know of' (< **sanì** 'know') is essentially equivalent to the stative **sàne dà**, e.g., **nā san dà ita = inà sàne dà ita** 'I know about it/ I know of her.'

Although the **dà** in a sociative construction is closely bound to the verb, it remains a distinct entity and does not constitute an affixed or cliticized element that is attached to the verb stem. For example, it takes an independent pronoun as object and not a direct object pronoun, e.g.,

nā aikà dà <u>sū</u>	I sent them. (cf. **nā aikà <u>su</u> kàsuwā** I sent them to market.)
yā ràbu dà <u>ita</u>	He divorced her. (cf. **yā gan <u>tà</u>** He saw her.)
bàri mù yi bìřis dà <u>shī</u>	Let's ignore him. (cf. **mù kirā <u>shì</u>** Let's call him.)

The verb before **dà** behaves as would be expected of an A-form, i.e., the form used when not followed by an object. In nonfinite constructions, this often means adding the weak verbal noun suffix `-wā`, e.g.,

munà ta gaisàwā dà mutànē	We are continuously greeting the people. (< **gaisà dà**)
bā à sàbàwā dà wàhalà	One doesn't get accustomed to trouble. (< **sàbà dà**)
jinjìrîn dà takè kulàwā (=kùlā) dà shī	The baby she is looking after.
cf. **jinjìrîn dà ta kulà (= kùla) dà shī**	The baby she looked after.
nā fàrà amìncêwā dà sū	I began to rely on them.
mutànē dà yawà sunà kàmuwā dà AIDS	Many people are becoming infected with AIDS.
inà jî dà shī	I am fond of him.

An exception to the general rule is the fixed phrase **cê dà** 'call (name)', where the verb in a nonfinite position does not add the expected verbal noun ending, e.g.,

anà cê dà shī Mūsā He is called Musa. (*not* ****anà cêwā dà shī Mūsā**)

Under conditions of focus or question formation, some sociatives allow the **dà** to be fronted and separated from its verb, e.g.,

dà wà ka tunà?	Who did you remember?
cf. **nā tunà dà Audù**	I remembered Audu.
dà Lādì mukà gaisà	It was with Ladi we exchanged greetings.
cf. **mun gaisà dà Lādì**	We exchanged greetings with Ladi.

More commonly, however, only the object is fronted, its original position following **dà** being filled by a resumptive independent pronoun, e.g.,

wà ka tunà dà shī?	Who did you remember?
Lādì cē mukà gaisà dà ita	It was with Ladi we exchanged greetings.

A sociative verb differs from a simple verb followed by a prepositional phrase containing **dà** in two main respects. First, from a semantic point of view, the object of a sociative verb construction is the thematic patient. By contrast, the object of the true preposition **dà** is commonly an instrumental or a comitative.

mun gabzà dà sū	We clashed with them.
(= **mun gàbjē sù** with the transitive gr2 verb)	
kadà kà mântā dà àlkawàřinmù!	Don't forget our appointment!

(= **kadà kà mântà àlkawàřinmù** with the transitive gr1 verb)

tā yi wà Lādì wàtsī dà kāyā   She threw away Ladi's goods.

yā ràbu dà ita   He divorced her.

(similar to **yā sàkē tà** with the transitive gr2 verb)

jiyà na yi ařbà̀ dà tsōhon manajà   Yesterday I unexpectedly ran into the former manager.

sun kōmà̀ dà mōtà̀   They returned the car. (sociative) *or* They returned by car. (instrumental)

cf. **sun kōmà̀ Kanò̀ dà Lādì**   She and Ladi returned to Kano.

(lit. they.comp return Kano with Ladi) (comitative)

Second, with sociatives built on motion verbs, **dà** and its object precede the locative. With intransitive verbs, on the other hand, the locative goal invariably precedes the prepositional **dà** + NP phrase. Compare the following sentence pairs, which structurally are different although semantically they are very similar:

yanà̀ wucèwā dà kāyân ɗākì̀   He is taking the goods into the room. (sociative)

cf. **yanà̀ wucèwā ɗākì̀ dà kāyân**   He is passing by the room with the goods. (intr. plus pp)

kà kōmà̀ dà kwalabā kàntī!   Return the bottle to the shop! (sociative)

cf. **kà kōmà̀ kàntī dà kwalabā!**   Go back to the shop with the bottle! (intr. plus pp)

5. EFFERENTIAL VERBS (GRADE 5)

The label *efferential verb* refers to grade 5 verbs composed of a verb stem (with or without the suffix -**ař**) plus the formative **dà**, which is used with an overt object (see §74:9). Since the thematic object is expressed as an oblique rather than as a direct object, pronominal objects require the independent pronoun set, e.g.,

yā ciyař dà ìyālìnsà   He provided for (lit. fed) his family.

kadà kà fitař dà kujèrā!   Don't take out the chair!

sun zub dà mâi   They poured out the oil.

sun fid dà ita   They took it out.

°AN: As used here, "efferential" describes a *syntactic* verb category characterized by the presence of the particle **dà**. The term *efferential* is used elsewhere as a morphological/semantic grade label for all gr5 (and dialectal gr5d) verbs whether they employ **dà** or not. For example, the gr5 verb in **yā gayař dà ita** 'He greeted her' belongs to the "efferential" syntactic subcategory, whereas the semantically equivalent efferential gr5 B-form verb in **yā gaishē tà** 'He greeted her' is syntactically a straightforward transitive verb, as is the equivalent gr5d verb in **yā gaidà̀ ta**.

5.1. Differences between sociatives and efferentials

Syntactically, efferentials are similar to sociatives in their use of a formative **dà** and the status of objects as obliques. The efferentials, however, differ from sociatives in a number of ways.

   (a) Sociatives have a word boundary between the verb and the preposition **dà**. As a result, in nonfinite environments (e.g., in sentences with the continuous TAMs), the verb takes the normal verbal noun form required in the non-object A context (e.g., vowel lengthening with gr3 verbs, addition of `-wā` with gr1 or gr4 verbs, etc.). The **dà** that accompanies a gr5 efferential verb, on the other hand, is treated as a clitic (indicated here by means of a hyphen), and thus when **dà** is present, the verb does *not* add the verbal noun formative `-wā`, which is, however, used in the A-form where **dà** is absent, e.g.,

(sociative) **bā à sābàwā dà wàhalà**	One doesn't get accustomed to trouble. (< **sābà dà**)
(efferential) **bā à zubař-dà mâi mài kyâu**	One doesn't pour out good oil.
not ****bā à zubâřwā dà mâi mài kyâu**, cf. **bā à zubâřwā**	One doesn't pour (it) out.
(sociative) **tanà lùřa dà yârā**	She is looking after the children. (< **lùřa dà**)
(efferential) **tanà tsōratař-dà yârā**	She is frightening off the children.
cf. **yârā nè takè tsōratâřwā**	It is children she is frightening.

(b) If the object of a sociative is front-shifted (for reasons of focus, interrogative, relativization, etc.) the **dà** usually remains in situ and a resumptive pronoun is left in its place. If the object of an efferential verb is moved, the **dà** is deleted/omitted.

(sociative): **Audù yā sābà dà kàrên**	Audu has become used to the dog.
mè ya sābà dà shī?	What has he become used to? (not ****mè ya sābà?**)
(efferential): **yārinyà tā zubař dà shàrā**	The girl threw out the trash.
mè ta zubař?	What did she throw out?
(sociative): **sun yabà dà matàimàkin shùgàbā**	They praised the vice president.
matàimàkin shùgàbân dà sukà yabà dà shī	the vice president whom they praised.
(efferential): **zā sù sayař dà àkuyà**	They will sell the goat.
àkuyàř dà zā sù sayař	the goat that they will sell

°AN: The description of "**dà** deletion" with the gr5 verbs, although common, is inexact. A better way to view the alternation found in such sentences as **sun zubař dà mâi** 'They poured out oil' vs. **mâi nē sukà zubař** 'It is oil they poured out' is to say that **dà** is inserted only at a late stage under certain specific conditions (see discussion note in §74:9.3).

(c) Some sociatives allow fronting of the **dà** + NP phrase as a whole. Gr5 efferential verbs do not, e.g.,

(sociative): **dà wà ka tunà?**	Whom did you remember?
cf. **nā tunà dà Audù**	I remembered Audu.
(efferential): **wà ka tsōratař?**	Whom did you frighten off? (not ****dà wà ka tsōratař?**)
cf. **nā tsōratař dà yârò**	I frightened off the boy.

(d) Sociatives with indirect objects have the structure Verb i.o. **dà** + NP, whether the i.o. is a noun or a pronoun. Gr5 efferential verbs with pronoun indirect objects also have this structure. If the indirect object is a noun, however, a different structure is commonly used. Either the **dà** is dropped, or else it immediately follows the i.o. marker. Examples:

(sociative): **yā kulà wà Mūsā dà dōkì**   He looked after the horse for Musa.
(efferential): **yā ciyař wà Mūsā dōkì** = **yā ciyař wà dà Mūsā dōkì**
    He fed the horse for Musa.
(sociative) **kà matsà wà màkānikè dà mōtà!**   Bring the car closer to/for the mechanic!
(efferential) **sun sayař wà màkānikè mōtà** = **sun sayař wà dà màkānikè mōtà**
    They sold the car to the mechanic.

ΔDN: Apparently, some speakers allow optional deletion of the sociative **dà** when an i.o. is expressed, e.g., **yā kulà wà Mūsā dà dōkì** = **yā kulà wà Mūsā dōkì** 'He looked after the horse for Musa.' It is not clear how common this is.

5.2. *Grade 5/6 ventive/efferential verbs*

Grade 5/6 ventive/efferential verbs are gr6 stems built on gr5 verbs, e.g., **fitō dà** 'bring out' (cf. the normal gr5 **fitař dà** 'take out'). They have gr6 morphology, i.e., they end in -ō and have all H tone, but, like gr5 verbs, they incorporate efferential semantics and function syntactically as efferential **dà** verbs. These grade 5/6 verbs with **dà** can be contrasted with similar-looking sociatives and intransitives.

(a) Unlike sociatives and intransitives, grade 5/6 ventive/efferential verbs in nonfinite VPs may appear without the ˋwā verbal noun formative, e.g.,

sunà ɓullō dà dàbāřà	They are introducing a plan. (gr5/6)
≠ **sunà ɓullôwā dà dàbāřà**	They are coming out with a plan. (gr6 sociative)
wà yakè fitō dà kāyā?	Who is bringing out the load? (gr5/6)
cf. **wà yakè fitař dà kāyā?**	Who is taking out the load (gr5)
cf. **wà yakè fitôwā dà kāyā?**	Who is coming out with the load? (gr6 intransitive)

(b) Unlike sociatives, these verbs do not allow fronting of the **dà** + NP phrase. However, some of these verbs differ from regular gr5 verbs in requiring **dà** plus a resumptive pronoun after the verb, e.g.,

tā kařkatō dà fitilàř	She tilted the lamp.
fitilà ta kařkatō	It was a lamp she tilted. not ****dà fitilà ta kařkatō**
sunà fitō dà kāyân	They are bringing out goods.
mè sukè fitō-dà shī?	What are they bringing out?

76. Verb Suffixes: Historical Remnants

MANY verbs contain a historically remnant -CV suffix that now functions as a semantically empty, integral part of the verb. The length of the suffixal vowel is determined by grade assignment, transitivity, etc. (For convenience, the vowel is cited as short.) Some of the suffixes appear to have intrinsic tone; others are treated as toneless.

In a few cases the suffixal nature of the ending is still observable in the language because of synchronic alternations or morpho-semantically related lexical items. In other cases, the identification of the ending as a suffix is supported by comparative/historical evidence. In most cases, however, the ending is simply presumed to be an erstwhile suffix—whether it turns out to be so or not—based on its common occurrence and overall phonotactic patterning. The -**yà** suffix apart, words with the presumed suffixes are either polysyllabic or else disyllabic with a heavy initial syllable, typically CVC-. Where the initial syllable is CVV, it often can be shown to be derived from CVC (or at least can be presumed to be so). There are eight suffixes that recur frequently enough to be readily identifiable and that are described here. These are -**yà**, -**kà**, -**ga**, -**nà**, -**là**, -**sa**, -**ɗa**, and -**ta**, (Presumably there are/were other verb suffixes as well, which will be uncovered by subsequent research, but their status is too tenuous to warrant inclusion in the list at this time.)

1. -yà

This is a commonly occurring ending, which is found in over sixty verbs. It is the only one of the remnant suffixes whose suffixal status is still clearly recognizable synchronically. The suffix -**yà** has (or can be assumed to have had) underlying L tone and the resulting verb displays an alternating (L)-H-L tone pattern. What this means is that disyllabic verbs ending in -**yà** are assigned H-L tone and generally operate as grade 1 verbs, e.g., **shiryà** v1 'prepare' (cf. **dafà** v1 'cook'), whereas trisyllabic verbs ending in -**yà** are normally assigned L-H-L tone and operate as grade 2 verbs if transitive, e.g., **tsìnkāyà** v2 'espy' (cf. **càkumà** v2 'grab') or as grade 3 verbs if intransitive, e.g., **dùlmuyà** v3 'sink' (cf. **zàbuřà** v3 'jump up').

> °AN: [i] Hausaists normally think of tone and final vowels as being determined by the verb's grade, which is morpho-syntactically assigned. In the case of verbs with the remnant suffixes, the opposite seems to be the case, i.e., it is the accident of form that dictates grade assignment and not vice versa.
> [ii] I am unable to account for the form of the vowel, if present, that occurs before the -**yà**.

Here is a sample list of common verbs with fully frozen final -**yà**. (Note: Verbs that now primarily operate gr4 will appear with final -**ye(e)** rather than -**yà**.)

amàyē v4 vomit up; **dàgwiyà** v2 gnaw at, eat much (meat); **dàlayà** v2 pare; **dùlmuyà** v3 sink; **ɗàurayà** v2 plate with silver, rinse; **fèrayà** paring (VN of v2 form, cf. **fērè** pare); **gàurayà** v3 become mixed; **gìciyà** v3 lie across (cf. VN. **gicî** crossing over); **karyà** v1 break, snap; **kàrayà** v3 lose hope (doublet of the preceding); **kāsàyē** v4 defile with excrement (cf. **kāshî** excrement); **ƙìdāyà** v2 count out; **mùsāyà** v2 exchange one thing for another (cf. PC ***masə** buy); **rìnjāyà** v2 overpower, get better of; **sauyà** v1 change, exchange; **shiryà** v1 prepare, arrange (cf. VN **shirî** preparing); **sùlmuyà** v3 fall off, slip off; **sùnkuyà** v3 bend down, stoop down; **tàmbayà** v2 ask; **tsìnkāyà** v2 espy, wait for; **tsùnguyà** v2 pinch off sth (= **tsùngulà**)

In the following examples, the stem with **-yà** coexists for many speakers as an equivalent alternative to the basic verb without the suffix. Alternatively, the **-yà** form with some words exists as a dialect variant (indicated [dv]). This free variation is particularly common with (but not limited to) monoverbs and H-H **-ā** verbs (both classified as grade 0). The assignment of the **-yà** stem to gr1 or gr2 or gr3 is determined by the resultant tonal pattern of the verb and its valency. (Grade 4 represents a secondary derivation operating on the **-yà** stem.) Examples:

ajìyē v4 = **ajè** v4 put away; **biɗîyē** [dv] v4 = **bìɗā** seek v2 (cf. the VN **bìɗiyà** built on the gr2 stem); **dàwayà** v3 (= **dàwai**) [dv] go back, cf. **dāwō** v6 return here; **hàɗiyà** v2 = **haɗè** v4 [dv] swallow; **naɗîyē** [dv] v4 = **naɗè** v4 roll up; **tsânyē** v4 = **tsanè** v4 become partially dry; **zōzàyē** v4 = **zōjè** (< //**zōzè**//) v4 damage fence, erode (cf. the VN **zòzayà** built on the gr2 stem) **jāyà** v1 = **jā** v0 pull; **jiyà** v1 = **ji** v0 hear; **ƙiyà** v1 = **ƙi** v0 hate **jìrāyà** v2 = **jirā** v0 wait for; **kìrāyà** v2 = **kirā** v0 call; **rìgāyà** v2 = **rigā** v0 precede, have already done

The irregular verbs **tàfi** and **gàji** are presumably clipped forms of extended gr3 stems containing the suffix **-yà**, i.e., //**tàfiyà**// and //**gàjiyà**//. These suffixal stems are used in various secondary derivations, e.g., **tàfiyà** f. 'going', **gàjìyu** gr7 'be dead tired' (not ****gàju** or ****gàzu**); **tàfîye-tàfîye** pl. 'travels' (not ****tàfe-tàfe**).

2. -kà

Like the **-yà** suffix, the **-kà** suffix carries its own tone, which serves to determine grade assignment. This **-kà** ending is also a widely attested suffix, being found in over fifty verbs, e.g.,

ɓàrakà v3 = **ɓarkè** v4 split	**dafkà** v1 pile up; wound seriously
ɗaukà (< ***ɗàwukà**) v2 take	**ɗinkà** v1 sew
fàɗakà v3 = **faɽkà** v1 wake up (cf. **faɽfaɗō** v6 revive, recover) (< PC ***faɗ-** wake up)	
faskà v1 [dv] rip (cf. SH **fàɽkā** v2 rip and remove)	**girkà** v1 put pot on fire, cook
hàɓakà v3 swell, expand (cf. **haɓî** swelling of animal's udder just prior to giving birth)	
haikà v1 climb over (= **hayà**)	**haskà** v1 light, illuminate
narkè v4 melt	**ninkà** v1 fold in two
shūkà v1 (= **shifkà** [dv]) plant (< PC ***sip-**)	**surkà** v1 add cold water to hot
tsaikà v1 [dv] stand, wait (= **tsayà**)	**tsinkè** v4 snap
wankà v1 wash	**wàrakà** v3 = **warkè** v4 get well
yankà v1 cut, slaughter (cf. **yanyànā** v1 cut in strips, pieces)	

A notable exception to the expected L tone on **-kà** is the word **sàuka** v3 (< ***sàfka**) 'get down'. This word is also unusual in having the wrong syllable weight for a basic gr3 verb: the norm is to have a light first syllable. One might hypothesize that its original form was ***saf-kà** (v1) and that it switched to gr3 by analogy with other basic, semantically similar gr3 intransitive verbs like **fìta** 'go out' and **shìga** 'enter'; but this is pure speculation.

In the case of **sakà** v1 = **sâ** 'put' (= **sânyā**) and **zakà** v3b [dv] = **zō** 'come (go)' it is not clear whether the **-kà** is a suffix or whether it represents an original part of the basic lexical root.

3. -ga

The suffix **-ga**, which is found in under twenty examples. occurs much less frequently than **-kà** It is possibly the voiced counterpart of **-kà**, the two originally being allomorphs of the same suffix, i.e., **-ga** occurred if the preceding abutting consonant was a voiced obstruent, **-kà** occurred elsewhere. Note, however, that the inherent low tone found with **-kà** does not appear as regularly with **-ga**. Examples:

buřgà v1   whisk with swizzle-stick (cf. **bùřgā** v2   threaten, intimidate psn)
ɓàzgā v2   tear off, e.g., a branch (This v2 is a derived partitive.)
dàbugà v2 [dv] pester s.o. by following him/her around
dîbgā v2   thrash, repulse an enemy   **fizgà** v1   tug, snatch away
hàngā v2   espy   **hàrgā** v2   wolf down food
ƙirgà v1   count (cf. **ƙìdāyà** v2   count, calculate with the same *ƙ-d root)
rūgà v1   flee   **shirgà** v1   pile on
sùngā v2 [dv]   wound with a spear   **tsařgà** v1 [dv]   spit in thin stream
waigà v1   turn head around and look (= **waiwàyā**)   **wuřgà** v1   throw a missile at s.o.
zabgà v1   wound s.o.   **zargà/zàrgā** v1/v2   put on noose, accuse

◊HN: Given the rule that abutting obstruents must both be either voiced or voiceless, we can assume that **wuřgà**, for example, came from *wudgà and not from *wutga. Because we know from other forms that **ƙirgà** comes from *ƙidgà, it should have rolled /ř/ rather than the flap /r/. It is possible that the words **hàrgā**, **shirgà**, and **zargà** historically had a */d/ in the coda of the first syllable and thus also reflect a previously overlooked secondary historical change of /ř/ to /r/ under conditions yet to be determined. If this is not the case, we have a problem explaining how it is that both **-ga** and **-kà** occur after liquids (and nasals) if one is assuming that they originally were phonologically conditioned allomorphs of the same suffix.

4. -nà

The **-nà** suffix is found with some twenty-five verbs. It commonly abuts with a preceding /n/ resulting in a surface geminate. Examples:

aunà v1   measure, weigh (cf. VN **awò**   weighing)   **binnè** v4   bury (cf. VN **bisò** [dv]   burying)
ɓìncinà v2   pinch off some   **càkunà** v2   provoke (= [dv] **càkusà**)
cařnà v1   fire, shoot a long way (= **callà**)   **cinnà** v1   stuff in
cūnà v1   egg on (< *cig-na ?)   **dòsanà** v2   obtain (fire)
dainà v1   cease   **kunnà** v1   light lamp or fire
mannà v1   adhere to, stick to   **mùntsunà** v2   pinch, take a pinch of
rainà v1   have contempt for   **tsòkanà** v2   poke, prod
sunnà v1   give surreptitiously, infect (= **sundà** [dv])
yànƙwanà v3   became emaciated (= **yankwàdē** v4)
zaunà (= **zamnà**) v1   sit (cf. **zama** = **zàmanà** v3   become, happen)

5. -là

About twenty-five disyllabic verbs contain a geminate /ll/ preceding the final vowel, e.g., **ɓallà** v1 'knot, tie'. Most have H-L tone and are gr1. Because geminates are uncommon in nonderived words in Hausa, we can assume that these CVllV words contain a remnant suffix. In some cases we may be dealing with a *-là suffix, to which the abutting root consonant assimilated and geminated. (Note that //n.l// → /ll/ is quite general in Hausa, see §54:6.1.2.) In other cases, however, the suffix was possibly something other than -là (perhaps -nà, or -rà) and the assimilation was to a root final /l/. In the list that follows, I shall simply present examples of common verbs that contain final /-lla(a)/ without attempting to sort out the individual etymological histories.

billà v1	stretch cap with hands	bullà v1	add indigo powder to dye pits
ɓallà v1	knot (but v2 = v4 untie)	ɓùlla v3	appear
ɗallà v1	project by springlike action	fallà v1	run away (= falfàlā)
gillà v1	pinch off a big piece of sth, (with ƙaryā) concoct a lie		
ƙullà v1	knot together (= ƙudùrā)	ƙwallà v1	burst out crying, shine brightly
millà v1	project a missile long way, go a long way, do too much		
tillà v1	pierce hole in pot	wullà v1	pass by
callà v1	fire, shoot a long way = caᵲnà (both from *//cad-// or *//car-// + -là or -nà ?)		

There are also a few trisyllabic words with final -la without gemination, which support the idea of an original suffix of that shape, e.g.,

cāɓùlā v1	make knife notchy, render sloppy (= cāɓà)
cākùlā v1	mix round and round with spoon (= cākùɗā)
tsùngulà v2	pinch off sth (= tsùnguyà)

6. -sa

A small number of doublets plus a few other examples point to the existence of a suffix -sa (with underlying tone unclear). Examples:

càkusà v2 [dv]	provoke (= càkunà v2)
cikàsà v1	fulfill, add to, increase (partially = cikà v1 fill)
cūsà v1	stuff in (< *cik-sa ?) (related to preceding?)
gaisà v1	exchange greetings (cf. gayà v1 tell)
ƙāràsà v1	end, finish sth (cf. ƙàrè v4 end, finish)
lumshè v4	cloud over (cf. lùllùmī (< //lùm-lùmī//) being clouded over)
rūshè v4 (< *ripsè)	collapse (= ribɗè v4)
targashè [dv]	a sprain (VN form) (= targaɗè)

◊HN: The interesting historical question here is what relation there is, if any, between this suffix and the grade 5 ending, which historically was *-as, i.e., are these erstwhile "efferential" verbs in which the extension has become frozen as a stem formative? This certainly seems to be the case with the verb **gaisà**, which synchronically has a related gr5 form in which the /s/ (→ ᵲ in final position) belongs to the gr5 extension, not to the stem, e.g., **yā gay-aᵲ (< gay-as) dà tsòfàffī** 'He greeted the elders.'

7. -ɗa

The suffixal nature of the -ɗa ending is less evident than with the other frozen suffixes in the sense that there are no synchronic alternations and only a few doublets to point to (e.g., **yankwàɗē = yanḳwànē** 'become emaciated'). Nevertheless, it does occur quite often and its status as a suffix has some empirical support. (Parsons (1975: 424–25) proposed a semantic characterization of -ɗa, namely, "displacement or disalignment," which may nor may not hold up.) The -ɗa suffix does not appear to have an inherent tone; rather it gets its tone from the grade form in which it occurs, which is most often gr1. Examples:

bankàɗā v1   lift up edge of sth
cākùɗā v1   mix up with a spoon (= **cākùlā** v1)
faɽɗà v1   slit open, **fàɽɗā** v2   hoe up peanuts
haɽɗà v1   interlace
kalmàɗā v1   bend, go off on a tangent
muɽɗà v1   twist, wring
ribɗè [dv] v4   collapse (= **rūshè** v4) (< *rip-sè)
shūɗè v4   pass through, pass by (< **shìga** enter + -ɗa + gr4 ?)
tankàɗā v1   sift, knock over
tazgàɗā v1   tilt / **tàzgaɗà** v3   be tilted
turbùɗa v1   put in hot ashes to cook, bury
zunkùɗā v1   hitch up on back (e.g., load or baby)

bauɗè v4   swerve, dodge
cūɗà v1   knead, massage
guɽɗè v4   sprain, dislocate
jiɽɗè v4   dislocate, loosen from the ground
kuɽɗà v1   squeeze through a narrow place
murgùɗā v1   twist out of shape, distort
shimfìɗā v1   spread out (e.g., mat)

targaɗè VN   a sprain (= **targashè** [dv])
tunkùɗā v1   push aside
zākùɗā v1 (= **zauɗà** v1)   move aside

8. -ta

Synchronically, Hausa has a productive suffix -ta (or -nta) that forms verbs from nouns (see chap. **79**), e.g., **hanzàrtā** 'hasten' < **hanzarī** 'speed, haste'; **dùhuntà** 'become dark' < **duhù** 'darkness'. In addition, one finds a large number of CVCCV and trisyllabic verbs with final -ta (but *not* -nta) in which the -ta looks in some ways like a suffix although it cannot be identified as the verbalizer. The tone is determined by the grade form. (Note that verbs in grade 4 will appear with final -cē.) Examples:

dākàtā v1   wait (cf. VN **dākò** waiting)
kaftà v1   dig ground for planting (cf. Kanakuru **kàpe** plant)
kùɓutà v3   slip away
ḳyastà v1   strike match or flint
ràntā v2   borrow (money)
saɽcè v4   comb hair
yàfatà v2   beckon
wafcè v4   grab from

fuɽtà v1   mention
ḳìftā v2   wink at
mântà v1   forget. (cf. Kanakuru **monè**)
rikìtā v1   confuse
tsìntā v2   pick up, find by chance
yantà v1   prepare thatch
zântā v1   converse

[References: Jungraithmayr (1970); Lemeshko (1967); Parsons (1975)]

77. Verbal Nouns

IN Hausa scholarship, the term *verbal noun* has been used to describe a variety of nominalized forms derived from or related to verbs, e.g., **kōmôwā** f. 'returning' (cf. **kōmō** 'return here'), **sàyē** m. 'buying' (cf. **sàyā** 'buy'), **aurē** m. 'marrying, marriage' (cf. **àurā** 'marry'), **ginī̀** m. 'building, a building' (cf. **ginà̀** 'build'), **shārā** f. 'sweeping, trash' (cf. **shārè̀** 'sweep'). There exists considerable disagreement about the classification of these "verbal nouns" partly because of differences in the criteria that have been used. Some scholars, for example, have based their analysis of verbal nouns on syntactic criteria, others on (morpho)phonological criteria, and others on a mix of the two. The situation is admittedly complicated because the syntactic classes and the morphological classes do not match, i.e., they are essentially independent classes that intersect rather than coincide. Nevertheless, once the crosscutting nature of the classes is understood and kept in mind, the analysis of verbal nouns, while far from simple, is not intractable.

1. VERBAL NOUNS

The major *syntactic* cut is between "verbal nouns" (VN), in the sense to be defined here, and "deverbal nouns" (DVN). Deverbal nouns, e.g., **dàshē** 'a seedling' < **dasà̀** 'to plant', which are described in chap. **22**, are nouns that are morphologically derived from (or related to) lexical verbs but that function syntactically like ordinary common nouns. Verbal nouns, e.g., **dasà̀wā** 'planting', on the other hand, function as present participles or gerunds in environments, e.g., with a continuous TAM, where a nonfinite form is required in place of a regular verb. (It is perhaps useful to think of VNs as being comparable to English '-ing' forms, although they do not always translate as such.) Examples:

tanà̀ [sàyen]$_{VN}$ nāmà̀	She is buying meat.
cf. tā [sàyi]$_V$ nāmà̀	She bought meat.
bā sà̀ [shân]$_{VN}$ giyà̀	They don't drink beer. *or* They are not drinking beer.
cf. bà̀ zā sù [shā]$_V$ giyà̀ ba	They will not drink beer.
yā ƙi [zaunà̀wā]$_{VN}$	He refused to sit. (lit. he.comp refuse sitting)
cf. yā [zaunà̀]$_V$	He sat.
kù dainà̀ [tàmbayàr̃]$_{VN}$ sà̀	(You pl.) stop asking him.
cf. kù [tàmbàyē]$_V$ shì	(You pl.) ask him.
[kòyon]$_{VN}$ Hausa bâ shi dà wùyā	Learning Hausa is not difficult.
cf. inà̀ sô ìn [kòyi]$_V$ Hausa	I want to learn (lit. that I learn) Hausa.

1.1. Finite vs. nonfinite VP environments

The syntactic use of verbal nouns depends critically on the distinction between two fundamental verb phrase environment types, namely, the finite verb phrase environment and the nonfinite verb phrase environment.

1.1.1. Finite verb phrase environment

The finite environment is one in which (a) the verb is either in the imperative or in a tensed clause having a TAM belonging to the set of noncontinuous TAMs, i.e., the completive, the negative-completive, the preterite, the future, the potential, the habitual, the rhetorical, and the subjunctive; or (b) the verb precedes an indirect object (regardless of the TAM). This finite environment *requires* the use of a finite verb (abbreviated simply as V), e.g.,

(a) **yā [zàbuřà]$_V$**	He jumped up.
kadà tà [tafàsà]$_V$ ruwā	She shouldn't boil water.
zâi [fēďè]$_V$ ràgôn	He will flay the ram.
[nùnà]$_V$ dōgôn!	Show the tall one!
[zàunā]$_V$!	Sit down!
(b) **mun [nēmà]$_V$ masà aikì**	We sought work for him.
munà [nēmà]$_V$ masà aikì	We are seeking work for him.
cf. **munà [nēman]$_{VN}$ aikì**	We are seeking work.
kà dingà [kirā]$_V$ minì shī!	Keep on calling him for me!
cf. **kà dingà [kirànsà]$_{VN}$!**	Keep on calling him!

1.1.2. Nonfinite verb phrase environment

The nonfinite verb environment includes all other verbal environments. These include (a) the position following a continuous TAM (General, Rel, or Neg) or, in some dialects, the allative, or (b) the position following an aspectual verb. It also includes (c) environments in which the VP functions in a nominal slot such as subject or object. In these nonfinite environments, the VP must be either an infinitive phrase (IP) (which internally contains a finite verb) or a verbal noun, depending on the verb grade and, with certain grades, on whether the VP contains a direct object or not. Gr1, gr4, gr5 (including gr5d), and gr6 allow the use of an infinitive phrase; other grades, namely, gr0, gr2, gr3, and gr7, require a verbal noun, e.g.,

yanà [zàbuřà]$_{VN}$	He is jumping up.
yanà [fīďàř]$_{VN}$ ràgō	He is flaying a ram.
cf. **yanà [fēďè]$_V$ manà ràgō**	He is flaying a ram for us.
wà yakè [gyāran]$_{VN}$ mōtàř?	Who is repairing the car?
cf. the equivalent **wà yakè [[gyārà]$_V$ mōtàř]$_{IP}$?**	Who is repairing the car? (gr1)
sun ƙi [kòyō]$_{VN}$	They refused to learn. (lit. they refused learning)
yanà dà wùyař [sayâřwā]$_{VN}$	It is difficult to sell.
cf. **[[sayař]$_V$ dà littāfì mài tsàdā]$_{IP}$ yanà dà wùyā**	
Selling an expensive book is difficult.	
yā hanà ni [aron]$_{VN}$ kèkensà	He prevented me from borrowing his bicycle.
[[hařbìn]$_{VN}$ gīwā] yā buřgè ni	Shooting the elephant amazed me.
[[fìtař]$_{VN}$ sà] kè dà wùyā sai na ji ƙārā	He had just gone out when I heard a scream.
(lit. [[going out] his] was difficult then I heard scream)	

1.2. *Weak vs. strong VNs*

Syntactically VNs fall into two classes, weak and strong, depending on their morphosyntactic behavior in relation to direct objects.

Weak VNs, all of which are formed with the suffix ⸌-wā, occur only when no object is expressed, either because the underlying object has been moved or deleted or because the verb is intransitive, e.g., **bā mà kōmôwā** 'We are not returning';   **mè takè ďaurèwā?** 'What is she tying up?' **sunà kařàntâwā**

'They are reading (it)'; cf. **sunà kaṛàntà littāfì** (*not* ****sunà kaṛàntâwā littāfì**) 'They are reading the book.'

°AN: Numerous scholars, going back to Abraham (1941), if not before, have proposed that all verb forms in a nonfinite environment, such as following a continuous TAM, should be analyzed as verbal nouns. Thus **kaṛàntà** in **sunà kaṛàntà littāfì** 'They are reading the book', for example, is viewed as a verbal noun that just happens to be identical to the finite verb. Some scholars (see Tuller 1986, for example) go even further and suggest that **kaṛàntà** in such a sentence is synchronically derived from the underlying verbal noun **kaṛàntâwā** by deletion of the ꞌ-wā suffix. I find nothing to recommend this approach. In the first place, this analysis requires that putative verbal nouns like **kaṛàntà** undergo exactly the same vowel length and tone alternations in the A/B/C/D contexts (see §74:1) as do true finite verbs. In the second place, it forces one into the untenable position that whereas all other verbal nouns (i.e., 'true' verbal nouns) require a genitive linker before the thematic object, these supposed verbal nouns do not. The straightforward and, I would say, correct analysis is the one presented here, namely, that weak verbal nouns with ꞌ-wā are syntactically restricted to VPs with no following object expressed and that the grade 1, 4, 5, and 6 forms following a continuous TAM that look and behave like ordinary verbs do so because they in fact *are* finite verbs pure and simple, albeit occurring in an infinitive phrase.

Strong verbal nouns, which take a variety of shapes other than ꞌ-wā, occur whether they are followed by a direct object or not. When followed by an object, a strong VN obligatorily takes a linker. If the thematic direct object is a pronoun, it belongs to the genitive set, e.g., **tanà kòyō** 'She is learning', **tanà kòyo-n Hausa** 'She is learning Hausa'; **yā dingà sūkà** 'He kept on criticizing', **yā dingà sūkà-n-tà** 'He kept on criticizing her.' A VP composed of a verbal noun followed by an object has the same surface structure as a possessive NP phrase, i.e., noun + linker + NP. Thus **haṛbì-n-sà bâ shi dà kyâu**, for example, could mean either 'Shooting him was not good' or 'His shooting (that he did) was not good.'

1.3. Stem-derived vs. base-derived verbal nouns

Some verbal nouns are derived from verb stems; these are termed "stem-derived verbal nouns" (SDVN). Others are derived from verbal bases (devoid of final vowel and tone); these are termed "base-derived verbal nouns" (BDVN). Weak verbal nouns are all built on occurring verb stems, i.e., they are SDVNs. For example, **kāwôwā** 'bringing' is an inflected form of the gr6 stem **kāwō** 'bring'. Some strong verbal nouns are also built on verb stems complete with grade endings. For example, **shìgā** 'entering' is derived from the gr3 stem **shìga** 'enter', and **cî** 'eating' is derived from the gr0 stem **ci** 'eat'. Other strong verbal nouns, however, are built on an underlying verb base rather than on any overt grade stem, i.e., they are BDVNs, e.g., **cikò** 'filling' derives from the base //cik-// rather than from the spelled-out gr1 stem **cikà** 'fill (sth)' or the gr3 stem **cìka** 'get filled'; similarly, **fîrà** 'paring' derives from the base //fīr-// rather than from the occurring gr4 stem **fērè** 'pare'.

1.3.1. Stem-derived verbal nouns (SDVN)

The formation of SDVNs is normally straightforward, i.e., given a stem of a particular grade, the shape of the corresponding VN is determined by regular morphological rules (to be described below). For example, monosyllabic H-tone verbs ending in short -i have verbal nouns that end in a long -ī and have falling tone, e.g., **bi** 'follow' ⇒ **bî** 'following', whereas gr3 verbs simply lengthen the final vowel, e.g., **fìta** 'go out' ⇒ **fìtā** 'going out', etc. The verb stem that is altered into a verbal noun may be simple, as in the previous examples, or pluractional, e.g., **fiffitō** v6/plurac. 'come out (many people)' ⇒ **fiffitôwā** 'coming out (many people)'; **jajjā** v0/plurac. 'pull many' ⇒ **jajjâ** 'pulling many'.

As a result of historical changes, the relation between synchronically extant verbs and their verbal nouns has in some cases become skewed. What one finds are gr1 and gr4 verbs optionally employing the

SDVN of an original gr2 verb, which may or may not occur synchronically, e.g., **an tājè** (v4) **gāshì** 'One combed out hair', cf. **anà tàzaṝ** (SDVN of erstwhile gr2) **gāshì** = **anà tājè** (gr4) **gāshì** 'One is combing out hair.'

With few exceptions, stem-derived verbal nouns ending in -ā are feminine. Examples:

VERB		*SDVN of original gr2*
cinkìsā v1	stuff	**cìnkisà**
fallàsā v1	shame by disclosing a secret	**fàllasà**
giṝgìzā v1	shake to and fro	**gìṝgizà**
hūɗà̀ v1	make ridges on farm	**hùɗà**
sussùkā v1	thresh corn	**sùssukà**
baibàyē v4	thatch a roof	**bàibayà**
cāshè̀ v4	thresh grain	**cà̀sā**
dabaibàyē v4	hobble the forefeet	**dàbàibayà**
ɗauràyē v4	rinse	**ɗàurayà**
shārè̀ v4	sweep	**shà̀rā**
tācè̀ v4	filter	**tà̀tā**

1.3.2. Base-derived verbal nouns (BDVN)

BDVNs are derived in the lexicon from a verbal *base* rather being derived from a full verb stem. For example, **haṝbì** 'shooting, hunting' is a BDVN derived from the abstract base //haṝb-// 'shoot, hunt', and not from the gr1 stem **haṝbā** 'shoot a weapon' nor the gr2 stem **hàṝbā** 'shoot sth.' The BDVN **cafiyā** 'catching' is related to **cafè** 'catch' but is not derived directly from it. The BDVN **jīfà** 'throwing' derives from the base //jīf-// 'throw', an ablauted form of the verb stem //jēf-//; it is not a derived form of the gr1 stem **jēfā** 'throw' nor of the gr2 stem **jèfā** 'throw at'. Similarly, **awò** 'weighing', which is built on a base //aw-//, is related to but is not derived from the gr1 verb **aunà** 'weigh'.

With some verbs (most of which are gr2), one *must* use the corresponding BDVN in nonfinite environments, e.g., **tanà zāgìn** (BDVN) **mijìntà** 'She is insulting her husband' (cf. **tā zàgi** (v2) **mijìntà** 'She insulted her husband'). With others, again mostly gr2, the BDVN is not totally obligatory but it is usually chosen, e.g., **yāròn dà sukè cētō** (BDVN) 'the boy they are rescuing' (= but more common than **yāròn dà sukè cētā** (SDVN of gr2). Examples:

VERB		*BDVN*	*VERB*		*BDVN*
àurā v2	marry	**aurē**	**kòyā** v2	learn	**kòyō**
bùgā v2	beat	**bugù**	**làllāsà̀** v2	coax	**lallāshì**
cètā v2	rescue	**cètō**	**nèmā** v2	seek	**nēmā**
cìzā v2	bite	**cīzò̀**	**rìƙā** v2, **rìƙè̀** v4	grasp	**rìƙò̀**
ɗèbā/ɗībà v2	take/fetch	**ɗībà**	**ròƙā** v2	beg	**ròƙō**
duddùƙā v1	crouch	**dùddùƙē**	**ròrā** v2	harvest	**rōrò**
fàkā v2	ambush	**fàkō**	**sàmā/sàmù** v2	get	**sāmù**
gìrbā v2	reap	**girbì**	**sàyā** v2	buy	**sàyē**
jèfā v2, **jéfā** v1	throw	**jīfà**	**zàgā** v2	insult	**zāgì**
gàṝgaɗà̀ v2	warn	**gàṝgàɗī**	**zàtā** v2	think	**zàtō**

◊HN: With the now obligatory BDVN (of gr2 verbs at least), we can assume that the BDVN totally supplanted an existing SDVN, i.e., originally, all verbs probably had corresponding SDVNs. Thus, alongside the now required **munà sàyen** (BDVN) **nāmà** 'We are buying meat', one also would have had *munà sàyaṝ (SDVN) **nāmà**; alongside **tanà zāgìn** (BDVN) **mijìntà** 'She is insulting her husband', one also would have had *tanà zàgař (SDVN) mijìntà, etc. Some modern-day SH speakers do, in fact, use these forms, although rarely so.

With many verbs, the BDVN exists as an essentially equivalent alternative to the corresponding finite verb or SDVN, e.g.,

yanà awòn (BDVN) hatsī =	yanà aunà (v1) hatsī	He is weighing the corn.
tanà bàkàcen (BDVN) dāwà =	tanà bākàcè (v4) dāwà	She is winnowing guinea-
corn.		
sunà ɗinkìn (BDVN) hùlā =	sunà ɗinkà (v1) hùlā	They are embroidering caps.
mun fārà fīràř (BDVN) àbîn =	mun fārà fērè (v4) àbîn	We started paring the thing.
munà hòron (BDVN) -sù =	munà hòrař (v2-SDVN) -sù	We are punishing them.
tanà mārìn (BDVN) yārò =	tanà màrař (v2-SDVN) yārò	She is slapping the boy.
yanà ambaton (BDVN) màganàř =	yanà àmbatàř (v2-SDVN) màganàř	
He is mentioning the matter.		

°AN: In Abraham's dictionary (1962), BDVNs are referred to as "secondary verbal nouns" only when they serve as alternatives to finite verbs or SDVNs. Other scholars, e.g., Gouffé (1981b) and Abraham himself in other places, have used the term "secondary verbal noun" as essentially equivalent to my BDVN, regardless of whether the verbal noun occurs obligatorily or as an alternative to some other form. This "secondary verbal noun" stands in opposition to "primary verbal noun," which is essentially equivalent to my SDVN. Because of the confusion about the meaning of the term "secondary verbal noun," I have decided to drop it in favor of the terminology proposed here.

With an object expressed, the alternative structures are more or less equivalent in meaning. When the object is not expressed (and sometimes even when the object is expressed), sentences with a BDVN often connote a more permanent activity as opposed to sentences with a weak verbal noun or a strong SDVN, where the underlying object is implied, e.g.,

yanà gyāran (BDVN) mōtà = yanà gyārà (v1) mōtà   He is repairing the car.
but yanà gyārā (BDVN)   He is doing repair work. ≠ yanà gyāràwā (v1-weak VN) He is repairing (it).
tanà niƙàn (BDVN) masàřā = tanà niƙà (v1) masàřā   She grinds / is grinding maize.
but tanà niƙà (BDVN)   She grinds. (e.g., for money) ≠ tanà niƙàwā (v1-weak VN) She is grinding (it).
sunà zàɓen (BDVN) hākìmī = sunà zàɓař (v2-SDVN) hākìmī   They are choosing the headman.
but sunà zàɓē (BDVN)   They are having an election. ≠ sunà zàɓā (v2-SDVN) They are chosing (him).

The classification of verbal nouns on the basis of the two parameters weak vs. strong and stem-derived vs. base-derived is illustrated in table 32:

Table 32: Classification of verbal nouns

	Weak	Strong
Stem-derived	(`-wā) kōmôwā returning here	(`-:) cî eating
Base-derived		-ē)^LH shàfē wiping

2. DEVERBAL NOUNS

The term *deverbal noun* (DVN) is used to cover nominal forms derived from verbs that describe an activity or concrete thing resulting from the activity of the source verb (see chap. **22**). These morphologically have the shape of verbal nouns, but *syntactically* they function just like ordinary common nouns, e.g.,

dàkē (DVN)	type of ink (< **dakà** pound), cf. **shàfē** wiping, VN of **shāfà** wipe
mahò̀ (DVN)	a patch on a garment (< **mafè** mend), cf. **awò̀** weighing, VN of **aunà** weigh
askā (DVN)	razor (< **askè** shave), cf. **nēmā** seeking, VN of **nèmā** seek
tayì̀ (DVN)	an offer (< **tayà** offer), cf. **hàrbì̀** shooting, VN of **hàrbā/harbà** shoot

Also included as DVNs are verbal derivatives containing the feminative suffixes -**iyā** and -**uwā**, e.g., **wāshiyā** 'ransacking' (< **wāshè** 'ransack'); **rakiyà̀** 'accompanying, accompaniment' (< **rakà** 'accompany'); **rantsuwā** 'oath, swearing' (< **rantsè** 'swear').

In terms of subcategorization, DVNs are like simple nouns in that they may be dynamic, i.e., denote an activity, e.g., **ƙīrà̀** 'manufacturing', or nondynamic, i.e., denote an object or idea or event, e.g., **shà̀rā** 'garbage, trash'. When denoting things, DVNs potentially take the full range of determiners and modifiers available to common nouns and they may have overt plurals, e.g., **askā** 'razor' (< **askè** 'shave'), pl. **asàkē**; **shirì̀** 'radio or TV program' (< **shiryà̀** 'prepare'), pl. **shìrye-shìrye**. Many nominalized verb forms exist both as DVNs and as active participial VNs, e.g., **aikìnsà gyārā nè̀** 'His work is repairing' (DVN)', cf. **yanà̀ gyāran mōtà̀** 'He is repairing the car' (VN); **àkwai bàbban ginì̀ cân** 'There is a large building over there' (DVN), cf. **sunà̀ ginìn gidā** 'They are building a house' (VN).

Verbal nouns ending in vowels other than -**ā** are masculine, as is the norm with regular common nouns. Those ending in -**iyā** or -**uwā**, the feminative suffixes, are naturally feminine. With other DVNs ending in -**ā**, however, the gender is lexically specific and not predictable, as is also typical of normal nouns. Some are feminine, e.g., **hàrārā** f. 'glaring sideways at s.o.'; **jīmà̀** f. 'tanning, a tanned hide'; **sanɗā** f. 'stalking'; **sātà̀** f. 'stealing, theft'; **sūyā** f. 'frying, pieces of fried meat'. Others, however, are masculine, e.g., **gyārā** m. 'repairing, repairs'; **haƙà̀** m. 'digging, a hole'; **jīfà̀** m. 'throwing, a throw'; **nōmā** m. 'farming'; **sūkā** m. 'criticizing, criticism'.

One should note that there are many other nominalization processes in Hausa by which nouns are derived from verbs apart from those forming DVNs as defined here, e.g., **farkō** 'a beginning' (< **fārà̀** 'begin'); **fashe** 'egg-breaking game' (< **fasà̀** 'break/shatter'); **ɗinkau** 'sewing for payment' (< **ɗinkà̀** 'sew'); **kàɗe-kàɗe** 'drumming' (< **kaɗà̀** 'beat (a drum))'. These derivatives are presented elsewhere in various sections on nominal derivation. The term *deverbal noun* has been reserved strictly for the derivatives that share the morphological formation rules with the VNs, plus the related words with the feminative endings -**iyā** and -**uwā**.

3. THE FORM OF VERBAL NOUNS AND DEVERBAL NOUNS

This section describes the *form* of nominalized verbs whether they function as active (present participial-like) verbal nouns or as deverbal nouns.

3.1. Weak verbal nouns with Ꞌ-wā

The suffix Ꞌ-**wā** forms inflected VNs (and some DVNs) from verb stems in grades 1, 4, 5, 5d [WH], 6, and (probably) grade 7 (see below §3.1.1). It is also used with the irregular verb **kai** 'take'. All verbal nouns with Ꞌ-**wā** are feminine.

This (ˋ-wā)^{LH} formative is a tone non-integrating L-H suffix consisting of the syllable -wā, which has H tone, preceded by a floating L tone that attaches to the final syllable of the verb. The suffix is added to the A-form of the verb, i.e., the stem form that is used when the verb is not followed by an object. If the final tone of the verb is L, the attachment of the floating L operates vacuously; if the final tone of the verb is H, the resulting HL on the syllable is realized as a fall. Examples:

bugà v1 + ˋwā →	bugàwā	beating	kařàntā v1 + ˋwā →	kařàntâwā	reading
fashè v4 + ˋwā →	fashèwā	smashing	Ƙētàrē v4 + ˋwā →	Ƙētàrêwā	crossing
cê v4 + ˋwā →	cêwā	saying	cìdà v5d + ˋwā →	cìdàwā	feeding [WH]
kōyař v5 + ˋwā →	kōyâřwā	teaching	tsōratař v5 + ˋwā →	tsōratâřwā	frightening
kōmō v6 + ˋwā →	kōmôwā	returning here	kai v* + ˋwā →	kâiwā	taking
iyà v1	be able to + ˋwā →	iyàwā		ability, mastery	
sāsàntā v1	reconcile + ˋwā →	sāsàntâwā		reconciliation	
Ƙwarè v4	be an expert + ˋwā →	Ƙwarèwā		expertise	
sanař v5	inform + ˋwā →	sanâřwā		an announcement	

3.1.1. Verbal nouns of grade 7

Grade 7 verbs, all of which are intransitive (with a passive or affected subject meaning), end in short /u/, e.g., tàru 'meet', dînku 'be well sewn'. When the ˋwā suffix is added to this monomoraic short vowel, the floating L tone has nothing to attach to and thus is dropped. (The tone cannot dock because the syllable to which it is to be attached is light, and complex tones in Hausa occur only on heavy syllables.) The syllable preceding the -wā thus appears with H rather than falling tone. Examples: (Note that VNs of gr7 verbs are often best glossed as '-able'.)

bùlbùlu + ˋwā →	bùlbùluwā	be pourable	dînku + ˋwā →	dînkuwā	be sewable
gyàru + ˋwā →	gyàruwā	be repairable	ràsu die + ˋwā →	ràsuwā	death
shàwu + ˋwā →	shàwuwā	be drinkable			
shàƙu	be close friends + ˋwā → shàƙuwā	intimacy			

The final -**uwā** of gr7 VNs can be phonologically simplified to -**ō**, e.g., **dînkuwā** 'be sewable' (→) **dînkō**, **ràbuwā** 'be separable' (→) **ràbō**, **shầwuwā** 'be drinkable' (→) **shầwō**, etc. This reduced form is seldom seen in written Hausa; however, it was noted long ago by Abraham (1959b: 129) and all Hausa speakers with whom I consulted recognized the -**ō** variant and found it to be perfectly normal in everyday spoken language.

3.1.2. Simplification of the falling tone (dialect variants)

When the suffix **ˋ-wā** is added to a word ending in a high-tone heavy syllable, the result is a falling tone, e.g., **jāwō** 'pull (here)' + **ˋ-wā** → **jāwôwā** 'pulling (here)', **bincìkē** 'investigate' + **ˋ-wā** → **bincìkêwā** 'investigating'. In WH dialects this F tone on the penultimate syllable is generally eliminated. With weak verbal nouns corresponding to (H)-H-L-H (gr1 and gr4) verbs, the F-H on the last two syllables simplifies to H-L, e.g.,

SH	WH	
kařàntâwā	**kařàntāwầ**	reading
ɓētàrêwā	**ɓētàrēwầ**	crossing
lugulgùdâwā	**lugulgùdāwầ**	kneading

The verbal nouns of level H-tone gr6 verbs display three different patterns in different subdialects, in all of which the F tone is eliminated. In Dogondoutchi, H-F-H simplifies to H-L-H. In Ader, final F-H becomes H-L, as with gr1 and gr4 verbs. Finally, Maradi uses both of the above strategies. With trisyllabic verbs (i.e., disyllabic stems plus the suffix), it behaves like Dogondoutchi and simplifies H-F-H to H-L-H; with longer words it follows the Ader pattern and simplifies ...H-F-H to ...H-H-L. (In all of the examples, the corresponding SH form has F-H on the last two syllables.)

a. Dogondoutchi: **hitòwā** coming out; **hissuwòwā** bringing out; **lugulgudòwā** kneading (and bringing)

b. Ader: **kāwōwầ** bringing; **lugulgudōwầ** kneading (and bringing)

c. Maradi: [i] **sayòwā** buying and bringing; **kōmòwā** returning here

[ii] **řubūtōwầ** writing; **zāburōwầ** leaping up; **lugulgudōwầ** kneading (and bringing)

3.2. Non ˋ-wā stem-derived verbal nouns

Verbs belong to grades 0, 2, 3 (including 3a and 3b), and a few irregular verbs have stem-derived verbal nouns other than ˋ-wā. There are four different formations depending on the grade.

°AN: These SDVNs (plus, for Gouffé, the gr7 verbal nouns) constitute what some scholars have labeled as "primary verbal nouns."

3.2.1. Ø (gr2)

The regular SDVN of grade 2 verbs is identical in shape with the A-form (the citation/non-object form) of the finite verb, i.e., one has a zero suffix, e.g., **fànsā** v2-A 'redeem', **fànsā** VN 'redeeming'; **tàmbayầ** v2-A 'ask', **tàmbayầ** VN 'asking'. Most of these SDVNs are feminine. A few, e.g., **kàrɓā** 'receiving' and **daukầ** 'taking', are optionally masculine. Examples:

àbîn dà takè kàrɓā (VN)   the thing she is receiving, cf. **àbîn dà ta kàrɓā** (v2)   the thing she received
tanầ kàrɓan (VN) **kudî**   She is receiving money. cf. **tā kàrɓi** (v2) **kudî**   She received money.
mùtumìn dà sukè cùtā (VN)   the man they are deceiving,
cf. **mùtumìn dà sukà cùtā** (v2)   the man they cheated

wà kakè màrā? (VN)	Who are you slapping?
cf. wà zā kà màrā? (v2)	Who are you going to slap?
bā sà càccakàřkù (VN)	They are not poking/provoking you.
cf. bà zā sù càccàkē (v2) kù ba	They won't poke/provoke you.

nā iyà ɗaukà (VN) I am able to take it. cf. bàn ɗaukà (v2) ba I didn't take it.

◊HN: Historically, gr2 verbs formed corresponding SDVNs by means of a suffix -ā)$^{LH(L)}$. As described in §74:16.2, finite gr2 verbs originally ended in -i and had a set L-H tone pattern (Newman 1973). The L-H-L tone now characteristic of the A-form of polysyllabic verbs came from the tone associated with the suffix, e.g., *zùngùri 'poke' + ā)^{LHL} > zùngurà 'poking'. Later, the verbal noun form was adopted as the A-form of the finite verb, such that the two forms are now identical, i.e., it is the A-form that comes from the verbal noun rather than vice versa! Significantly, the extension of verbal nouns to A-form usage has also taken place sporadically with some BDVNS, e.g., yā faɗì 'He told (it)' < faɗì (BDVN) 'telling' (cf. yā fàɗā with the regular A-form); yā sāmù 'He got it' < sāmù (BDVN) 'getting'; yā ɗībà 'He dipped (it) out' < ɗībà (BDVN) 'dipping' (cf. yā ɗèbi ruwā 'He dipped out water' with the finite v2 C-form verb preceding the noun d.o.); mù barì 'Let's leave (it)' < barì 'leaving' (BDVN).

ΔDN: In the dialect of Maradi, the VN corresponding to many disyllabic gr2 verbs has H-H rather than L-H tone, i.e., the VN and the finite verb A-form are not identical, e.g., kùrɓā v2-A 'sip, drink a bit', VN kurɓā (cf. SH kùrɓā); tsòtsā v2-A 'suck', VN tsōtsā (cf. SH tsòtsā). This is probably an innovation reflecting the influence of the H-H base-derived verbal nouns (see §3.3.5 below).

Many gr2 verbs use a base-derived verbal noun (BDVN) as an equivalent (often preferred) alternative to the regular SDVN formation, e.g., yanà mārìn yārò = yanà màrař yārò 'He is slapping the boy.' Other examples include:

ambatō (BDVN) =	àmbatà (v2.SDVN)	mentioning
faɗì (BDVN) =	fàɗā (v2.SDVN)	telling
hàrārā m. (BDVN) =	hàrārà f. (v2.SDVN)	glancing disapprovingly
kwàcē (BDVN) =	kwàtā (v2.SDVN)	seizing, snatching

In a number of cases, the BDVN has completely or essentially driven out the SDVN, e.g., yanà nēman (BDVN) gyàɗā 'He is looking for peanuts', not **yanà nèmař (SDVN) gyàɗā. Common examples include the following:

aurē BDVN of àurā	marry	girbì BDVN of gìrbā	reap
kòyō BDVN of kòyā	learn	sàyē BDVN of sàyā	buy

Interestingly, pluractionals of gr2 verbs (and the irregular verb hau 'mount, climb up', hawā (BDVN)) tend to use SDVNs even in those cases where the simple verbs require or strongly prefer BDVNs, e.g.,

yanà sàssayàř (SDVN) kāyā irì-irì He is buying all kinds of goods. Preferred over ??yanà sàssàyen (BDVN)...; but not **yanà sàyař (SDVN) kāyā, for which one must say yanà sàyen (BDVN) kāyā He is buying goods.

yanà ta fàffaɗàř (SDVN) màganà He is continuing to speak, not **yanà ta faffaɗìn (BDVN) màganà

sunà ta kwàkkōyàř (SDVN) abūbuwà da yawà They are in the process of learning lots of things. Preferred over ??sunà ta kwàkkòyon (BDVN)...

cf. sunà ta kòyon (BDVN) Tūřancī They are learning English; not **yanà kòyař (SDVN)...

sunằ hàhhawằȓ (SDVN) dawākī   They are riding horses. Preferred over **sunằ hahhawan** (BDVN) dawākī. (cf. also **hàhhawằȓ jinī**   high blood pressure, not ****hahhawan jinī**)

In other cases, however, a pluractional BDVN is required to match the required simple BDVN, e.g., **sunằ jijjīfàn** (BDVN) **ɓàrāwòn** 'They were continually pelting the thief', not ****sunằ jàjjēfàȓ** (SDVN)...; **munằ ta nannēmansù** (BDVN) 'We went on seeking them', not ****munằ ta nànnēmàȓsù** (SDVN).

3.2.2. Grade switching (grade 2)

Gr2 VNs generally correspond to synchronically occurring gr2 finite verb stems. In some cases this verbal noun type is used—as a preferred or even obligatorily alternative—even though the corresponding verb now normally operates gr1 or gr4. For example, the VN of the gr1 verb **hūɗằ** 'make farm ridges' is **hùɗā** (f.), which is derived in a morphologically regular manner from a synchronically nonoccurring gr2 verb stem ****hùɗā**. Additional examples:

ɓàmɓarằ	tearing off, stripping off, VN of **ɓamɓàrē** v4 tear/strip off
ɓàrzā	grinding coarsely; corn that has been ground, VN of **ɓarzằ** v1 grind coarsely
càsā	threshing; threshed grain, VN of **cāshè** v4 thresh
ɗàurayằ	rinsing, dishes, VN of **ɗauràyē** v4 rinse
fàllasằ	disclosing a secret to cause s.o. shame, VN of **fallàsā** v1 disclose a secret...
ƙyàfā	drying meat before roasting, VN of **ƙyāfè** v4 dry meat...
ƙìdìddigằ	calculating, statistics, VN of **ƙididdìgā** v1 calculate
tàtā	filtering; liquid to be filtered, VN of **tācè** v4 filter

Such "grade switching" is particularly evident with erstwhile VNs that are now lexically frozen as concrete DVNs, e.g.,

mōlaƙằ f.	a dent, cf. **mōlàƙē** v4 to dent
mùrzā f.	a massage, cf. **murzằ** v1 to massage
shanyằ f.	cloth, sth. spread out to dry, cf. **shânyā** v1 spread sth out to dry
yằtsinằ f.	grimace, cf. **yātsìnē** v4 make a grimace

°AN: The word **shanyằ** with surface H-L tone derives from a tritonal word ***shàńyằ** with the normal L-H-L pattern of trisyllabic gr2 verbs. (The simplification of the LH on a single syllable to H is phonologically automatic.) Compare the corresponding H-L-H gr1 verb **shânyā**, where the three tones are still evident.

Although VNs with the suffix -ā)$^{LH(L)}$ are usually identical (in SH at least) to the corresponding gr2 A-forms (or the presumed gr2 A-forms if the verb is now operating another grade), this is not always the case. Rather, one finds a number of trisyllabic VNs that are segmentally fuller than the synchronically occurring gr2 stems. In some cases the VN exhibits an unreduced internal consonant and/or vowel; in other cases it contains a remnant verbal suffix /-yà/, e.g.,

ɓàrakằ f.	a rip; place where stitching has come apart; breach of trust, rift, cf. **ɓarkằ** v1 rip open
ɗàmarā f.	a belt (esp. for amulets), cf. **ɗaurè** (< **ɗamrè**) v4 tie (e.g., sth around waist)
bìɗiyằ f.	seeking, cf. **bìɗā** v2 seek
fèrayằ f.	paring, sth that was or is to be pared, cf. **fērè** v4 pare
kàrayằ f.	a bone fracture; having second thoughts, cf. **karyè** v4 break; **kàrayà** v3 regret

3.2.3. :) (grade 3)

Grade 3 verbs (including gr3a and gr3b) form corresponding verbal nouns by lengthening the final vowel. Tone is not affected. Here are examples of VNs of regular gr3 verbs, all of which are feminine.

tanằ shìgā (VN)	She is entering. cf. **ta kàn shìga** (v3) She habitually enters.
sàukā dai (VN) **tanằ dà wùyā**	As for getting down, it was difficult.
cf. **bàri ìn sàuka** (v3)	Let me get down.
ba yằ nùnā (VN)	It is not ripening. cf. **bài nùna** (v3) ba It didn't ripen.
yā dingà zàzzằbuřằ (VN)	He kept on jumping up. cf. **zâi zàzzằbuřà** (v3) He will jump up.
dànganằ (VN and DVN)	being resigned; resignation, cf. **dànganà** (v3) be resigned to
wàdātằ (VN and DVN)	becoming wealthy; wealth, contentment
cf. **wàdātà** (v3)	become wealthy, be contented

◊HN: Historically, the vowel lengthening in these verbal nouns may be a reflex of the same *-ā VN suffix found with gr2 verbs, i.e., **shìgā** 'entering' < *shìga v3 'enter' + -ā, etc., cf. **mằrā** 'slapping' < *màri v2 'slap' + -ā. One problem with adopting this analysis (at the synchronic, if not at the historical, level) is that it fails to account for the vowel lengthening with gr3a verbs where /ā/ doesn't appear, e.g., **gudù** 'running' < **gudù** 'run from'. Alternatively, one could suggest that the lengthening historically was simply a function of the categorial change from verb (where short final vowels were found) to common noun (where long vowels were the norm). In other words, the change from [shìga]$_V$ 'enter' to *[shìga]$_N$ 'entering' originally involved "zero derivation," the overt phonological marking, i.e., the vowel lengthening, being a secondary development.

3.2.4. Grade switching (grade 3)

As was the case with gr2 VNs, there are a few regularly formed gr3 verbal noun forms that serve as VNs (or DVNs) of gr1 and gr4 verbs. With gr3 verbs, however, the grade switch is uncommon whereas with gr2 the switch is far from infrequent. Examples:

fìyāyằ f.	mildew, cf. **fìyằyē** v4 become mildewed
hàuhawằ f.	rising up, cf. **hahhau** (plurational of **hau** v* rise)
ràgaitằ f.	aimless wandering, cf. **ràgàicē** v4 wander aimlessly

Two verbs use extended stems as the basis for the verbal noun but clipped stems in the verb form.

gàjiyằ (VN) (< *gàjiyà v3)	tiredness, cf. **gàji** v* be(come) tired
tàfìyằ (VN) (< *tàfìyà v3)	going, cf. **tàfi** v* go

Verbal nouns of the small H-H a-final gr3a verb grade are also formed by vowel lengthening. About two-thirds of these are masculine; the others are either feminine, e.g., **cāřā** f. 'cock's crow' < **cāřa** 'to crow' (which only some speakers accept as a verb); **fařgā** f. 'realizing' < **fařga** 'realize, understand'; and **ƙārā** 'complaint, lawsuit' f. < **ƙāra** 'complain', or have variable gender, e.g., **ƙaurā** m. or f. 'migrating'.

yanằ kwānā (VN)	He is spending the night. cf. **yā kwāna** (v3a) He spent the night.
ba yằ tsūfā (VN)	He is not aging. cf. **yā tsūfa** (v3a) He has aged.
sūmantà yā gìgītā ni (VN)	Her fainting frightened me. cf. **tâ sūma** (v3a) She is likely to faint.
sunằ girmā (VN)	They are growing up. cf. **sun girma** (v3a) They have grown up.
mù yi ta ƙaurā! (VN)	Let's keep on migrating! cf. **kadà kù ƙaura!** (v3a) Don't migrate!
sunằ wằsan ɓūyā (VN)	They are playing hide and seek. cf. **sun ɓūya** They hid.

◊HN: Etymologically the relation between gr3a verbs and their corresponding VNs is not the same as that which holds with regular gr3 verbs. Regular gr3 VNs are morphologically derived forms created by a rule that lengthens the final vowel of the underlying verb stem, e.g., **shìga** + : → **shìgā** 'entering'. With the gr3a verbs, on the other hand, it is likely that the VN was in origin a BDVN belonging to the H-H -**ā** class (§3.3.5) and that the finite verb was created through analogical vowel shortening by a process of back-formation, e.g., **sūmā** m. 'fainting' ⇒ **sūma** v3a 'faint'; **girmā** m. 'size, status, prestige' (< **gìrmā** v2 'be older than') ⇒ **girma** v3a 'grow up'.

The VNs of the irregular H-H verbs **zama** 'become, live' (VN **zamā**) and **kusa** 'draw near, be about to' (VN **kusā**) are also masculine, e.g., **zaman gàrin nàn yanà dà zāfī** 'Living in this city is difficult.'

°AN: Although **kusā** with the long final vowel can be described as the regular verbal noun of **kusa**, it is actually hard to instantiate because it is either followed by an object, in which case it takes a linker, e.g., **yanà kusan gamàwā** 'He is about to finish it', or is replaced by a related verb form, thus ****watàn azùmī yanà kusā** 'The month of fasting is approaching' would normally be expressed as **watàn azùmī yanà kusātôwā** with the gr6 extended verb form **kusātō**. (Note that **watàn azùmī yā kusa** 'The month of fasting is upon us', with the finite verb, is fine.)

Most gr3b verbs, i.e., the small set of intransitive H-L verbs ending in short /i/, /u/, or /a/, and the irregular verb **ƙòshi** 'be replete' also form VNs by vowel lengthening, e.g.,

tā fārà tāshì (VN)	She started to get up. cf. **kadà kì tāshì!** (v3b) Don't get up!
munà gudù (VN)	We are running. cf. **mun gudù** We ran away.
ɓācì (VN)	spoiling, cf. **ɓācì** spoil
ɓatà (VN)	getting lost, cf. **ɓatà** get lost
yanà ƙòshī (VN)	He is becoming full. cf. **nā ƙòshi** I'm full. (i.e., have eaten enough)

3.2.5. -ā (grade 3b)

Instead of lengthening the final vowel, three gr3b verbs add a toneless suffix -**ā**. The surface form results from glide epenthesis and tonal adjustment rules. The one example with an initial light syllable becomes H-H-L; the two words with an initial heavy syllable become H-L-H. These three VNs are feminine. In forming the verbal noun, the verb **fāɗì** behaves as if its stem-final vowel were -**u** rather than -**i**, e.g.,

haihù	give birth + -ā →	**haihùwā** (VN)	giving birth
mutù	die + -ā →	**mutuwà** (VN)	dying, death
fāɗì (stem //fāɗu//)	fall + -ā →	**fāɗùwā** (VN)	falling

3.2.6. -:)ᴸ (grade 0)

Grade 0 verbs, i.e., monosyllabic verbs with H tone (*monoverbs*) and the CVCā H-tone verbs (pseudo-monoverbs), form VNs by means of a suffix -:, i.e., final vowel lengthening with a floating low tone. The suffix is added to simple stems and to pluractional stems. If the final vowel of the stem is already long, the lengthening functions vacuously. The attachment of the L tone to the preceding H produces a fall. All gr0 VNs are masculine regardless of the final vowel. Examples:

bi + ˋ: → **bî**	following	**bibbi** + ˋ: → **bibbî**	keep on following
ci + ˋ: → **cî**	eating	**cicci** + ˋ: → **ciccî**	eating often, much
shā + ˋ: → **shâ**	drinking	**shasshā** + ˋ: → **shasshâ**	drinking often
jā + ˋ: → **jâ**	pulling	**sō** + ˋ: → **sô**	loving, love

°AN: Before pause, monoverbs with a long vowel, e.g., **jā**, phonetically have a half-long vowel followed by a glottal stop, i.e., [ja·?]. In prepausal environments, the corresponding VNs with the falling tone, e.g., **jâ**, have normal long vowels without glottal closure.

The verbal noun of **zō** 'come' is **zuwầ** m. The verb **jē** 'go' does not have a corresponding VN; rather, one has to use **tàfiyầ** f., the VN of **tàfi** 'go'.

With the three H-H nouns ending in -ā, which normally pattern with monoverbs, the floating L tone of the VN suffix replaces the H tone of the stem rather than being attached to it. The result is an H-L pattern spread over two syllables as compared with the monoverb VNs where the H-L pattern is crowded onto one syllable. As with the monoverb VNs, these VNs are masculine. Examples:

biyā + ˋ: → **biyầ**	paying, e.g., **tanầ biyànsà**	She is paying him.
cf. **tā biyā shì**	She paid him.	
jirā + ˋ: → **jirầ**	waiting for	
kirā + ˋ: → **kirầ**	calling; **kikkirā** + ˋ: → **kikkirầ**	calling many/often

The verb **rigā** 'precede' differs from the above three verbs in using a finite verb form rather than a verbal noun in nonfinite environments, e.g.,

tanầ rigā shì zuwầ ōfìs She is preceding him to the office. *not* ****tanầ rigànsà zuwầ ōfìs**

ΔDN: In Skt, the expected VN is in fact used, e.g., **tanầ rigànshì zuwầ ōfìs** 'She is preceding him to the office.'

3.3. Base-derived verbal nouns (BDVN)
Base-derived verbal nouns are formed by adding a tone-integrating affix to a verbal *base*, which, being devoid of tone and final vowel, is not in any particular grade. There are seven classes of base-derived verbal nouns, all of which generally include deverbal nouns (i.e., common nouns) as well as active verbal nouns.

3.3.1. Class 1: -ī
Verbal nouns with final -ī constitute the largest derivational VN class, with roughly one-quarter of all such verbal nouns. As is true of all VNs ending in vowels other than -ā, VNs of this shape are masculine. With disyllabic words, the tone is typically H-L, e.g.,

cūrì	kneading; a kneaded ball	**datsì**	a blockage, dam
ɗinkì	sewing	**gashì**	grilling (meat)
gwajì	testing; a test, demonstration	**kaɗì**	churning, beating; spinning cotton
lāfì	hemming; a hem	**sārì**	buying wholesale for resale
tūkì	stirring, driving	**wāshì**	sharpening; item to be sharpened

Irregular: **ɗab'ì** printing, publishing (base //ɗab'-//) cf. **ɗabbà'ā** print
shirì preparing (base //shir-//), cf. **shiryầ** prepare

In a few cases, the VNs now function as alternative A-forms of finite verbs, e.g.,

yā faɗì =	**yā fàɗā**	He told (it). (cf. VN **faɗì** telling)
tā sakì =	**tā sàkā**	She let (it) go. (cf. VN **sakì** releasing)

The very common irregular verbs **barì** 'leave, let' and **sanì** 'know' obligatorily use the -ì verbal noun form as the A form:

bā mà barìnsù (VN)	We are not leaving them. cf. **bà zā mù barì ba**	We will not leave (it).
sanìnā (VN) bâ yawà	My knowledge is not much. cf. **nā sanì mànà**	I know (it) indeed.

There are only some ten disyllabic -ì verbal nouns with L-H tone. Apart from **yàrɓì** 'flicking away sth sticky', these normally do not function as active VNs. Rather, these forms are now lexicalized DVNs with, in some cases, very specific meanings.

fèshì	splash(ing), esp. of rain	**kằkì**	phlegm (cf. **kākè** spit out phlegm)
tòfì	type of traditional therapy (cf. **tōfà** spit)	**tòyì**	burning, e.g., of a farm to clear it
tsàřgì	apprehension, misgiving (cf. **tsàřgā** ostracize, show dislike toward s.o.)		
wàtsì	dispersal, rejection, disregarding	**yàrɓì**	flicking away sth sticky
yàshì	sand (cf. **yàsā** clean out a well)	**zàrgì**	accusation, reproach, blame

°AN: The words **kwâncī** 'hatching of eggs' (cf. **kwântā** 'lie down) and **amai** 'vomiting' (cf. **amằyē** vomit') are reduced trisyllabic words and not tonally irregular disyllabic forms.
◊HN: There are probably additional L-H ì-final nouns that originally were VNs but that have not been identified as such. Possible candidates would be such words as **tsằkì** 'contemptuous clucking sound' and **hàkì** 'panting'.

Most of the polysyllabic -ì verbal nouns are lexicalized DVNs. The most common tone pattern is H-L-H (or, in one case, L-H-L-H). Examples:

āgàjī	helping, assistance	**dākàcī**	waiting for
dangwàrī	rapping the head with knuckles, a rap	**mallàkī**	possession
rāzànī	terror	**tabbàcī**	certainty
tunkùyī	butting	**zāwàyī**	diarrhea
dàbaibàyī	hobbling rope		

The tone patterns H-H-H and L-(H)-H-H occur about ten times each. Examples:

ařmashī	beautifying, improvement	**lallāshī**	coaxing
sakacī	slackness, carelessness	**yayyafī**	drizzle
hàrgitsī	turmoil, disarray	**kùmburī**	a swelling
tàřnaƙī	hobbling a horse or donkey	**yùnƙurī**	straining every nerve
rùguntsumī	quarrel or fight that has escalated into a brawl		

Only three verbal nouns (all DVNs) have L-L-H tone.

gàřgàɗī	warning	**ràiràyī**	fine sand (cf. **ràirayà** sift)
tàusàyī	mercy, sympathy (cf. **tausàyā wà** sympathize with)		

3.3.2. Class 2: -ū

There are only some eleven or so -ū final VNs. Seven have H-L tone whereas four, all ending in -tū, have (L)-L-H tone. Examples (complete):

H-L: **bugǔ** beating, a punch; **dāmǔ** pestering; **kāmǔ** catching, an arrest; **musǔ** denial, contradiction, argument; **sāmǔ** getting, wealth; **tumǔ** heads of newly ripened millet; **yāgǔ** tearing, a fingernail scratch

L-H: **kàftū** hacking with shovel or hoe, a hacking tool for farm work; **ƙyàstū** striking flint, the steel for striking a fire; **làbtū** loading heavily, the load; **rùbùtū** writing

> °AN: I have not included **gudǔ** 'running' in the list above because I am assuming that it is an SDVN from the gr3b verb **gudù** 'run away'; but this may be wrong.
>
> ◊HN: Etymologically the final -ū in the H-L words is probably the same as the H-L -ī verbal noun suffix, i.e., there was a change of -ī to -ū phonologically conditioned by the preceding /u/ vowel or by the labial properties of the /m/. (In the case of **yāgǔ**, the underlying velar consonant was most likely labialized, i.e., /gw/.) It is curious that the L-H words all end in a syllable having the same segmental shape (-tū). This would suggest that these words, one of which, **rùbùtū**, is a loanword from Kanuri , were formed by means of a now defunct tone-integrating suffix -tū)^LH rather than with the semi-productive verbal noun suffix -ū)^HL. The problem with this analysis, however, is that it runs up against the identification of the final -ta one finds in **labtà** 'load heavily', etc., as a frozen verb suffix (see §76:8).

The VN form **sāmǔ** is now standardly used as the A-form of the gr2 verb, e.g., **mun sāmǔ** 'We got (it)', cf. the pre-pronoun B form **mun sàmē tà** 'We got her.' In the C-form one gets either final -i or final -u, e.g., **mun sàmi** (= **sàmu**) **àbinci** 'We got some food.'

3.3.3. Class 3: -ē

Verbal nouns with final -ē)^LH constitute the second largest derivational VN class. The regular L-H tone pattern applies to polysyllabic as well as to disyllabic words. Some four exceptional items have all H tone, one of which is archaic and not known by modern SH speakers. Examples:

L-H: **dàshē** transplanting; a seedling; **hàngē** seeing sth from afar; **ƙìfcē** winking; **sàyē** buying; **tsìmē** ink made by steeping; **bìncìkē** investigating, investigation; **fàskàrē** splitting wood, the split wood; **ràrràfē** crawling; **ƙùdùndùnē** lying down curled up; **tàgàngànē** sitting with legs apart

H-H: **aurē** marriage (cf. **aùrā** marry); **haifē** [archaic] resourcefulness (cf. **hàifā** give birth to); **haskē** light, brightness (cf. **haskà** light up); **ƙwāƙulē** scraping sth out of a container (cf. **ƙwàƙulà** scrape out)

Note that there there is also a distinct class of nondynamic deverbal nouns with final -ē and H-L tone (see §22:2.2), e.g., **dunƙulè** 'a kneaded ball' (< **dunƙulā** 'knead into a ball').

3.3.4. Class 4: -ō

With -ō VNs, of which there are about fifty-five, tone is lexically determined and totally unpredictable. With disyllabic words, H-L and L-H are equally common patterns; the H-H pattern is limited to five words (listed in full below).

H-L: **awò** measuring, weighing (base //aw-//), cf. **aunà** measure, weigh; **bisò** [WH] burying (base //bis-//), cf. SH **binnè** (< *bis-nè) bury; **cīzò** biting; **dākò** waiting for (base //dāk-//) (cf. **dàkatà** wait for); **gādò** inheriting, inheritance; **kitsò** a braid, coiffure

L-H: **hòrō** punishing, discipline; **kòyō** learning; **yàbō** praising, praise; **zùbō** fading from washing

H-H: **arō** borrowing, a loan; **ɓōyō** hiding; **gōyō** carrying sth or s.o. on the back, a baby; **kallō** looking, a gaze; **tsawō** height, length

◊HN: The word **tsawō** is presumably a verbal noun derived from **tsayà** 'stand, stop'. Synchronically, the change of /y/ to /w/ before /ō/ is not an automatic change. Thus, this item must have become lexicalized at a fairly early date.

There are under ten polysyllabic VNs ending in -ō. These exhibit a variety of tone patterns, e.g.,

ambatō H-H-H   mentioning, a mention;   **dàgwàlgwàlō** L-L-H   messy food or water;   **dògarō** L-H-H (= **dōgarō** H-H-H [Skt])   dependence;   **dùrƙùsō** L-L-H   posture of kneeling;   **kwaikwayō** H-H-H   imitating, imitation;   **sàurārō** L-H-H (= **sàuràrō** L-L-H)   listening;   **tsùgùnō** L-L-H   squatting, shitting;   **wàwasò** L-H-L   scrambling for sth

The word **cùnkōsō** 'crowding, congestion', cf. **cunkùsā** (= **cinkìsā**) 'to stuff', is unusual in undergoing an internal vowel change in addition to the suffix.

3.3.5. Class 5: -ā

Disyllabic VNs ending in -ā appear with two tone patterns: H-H, the somewhat more common pattern, and H-L. This VN class has variable gender. The majority of these words are feminine, as one might expect from the -ā final vowel, but a good third of them are masculine. With the H-L tone pattern, masculine gender is restricted to words with a light first syllable.

H-H: **dūbā** m.   looking, fortune telling;   **girkā** f.   initiation into a *bori* cult;   **gyārā** m. repairing;   **hawā** m.   mounting, riding, a durbar; a steep place (cf. **hau**   mount, ride);   **nēmā** m.   seeking;   **rawā** f. dancing (cf. **rawàr̃ dà**   shake);   **tātā** f.   filtering, refining oil;   **tsāgā** f.   cracks, facial marks;   **wankā** m. bathing;   **yankā** m.   slaughtering, sth slaughtered;   **yantā** f.   thatching, thatching grass
H-L: **būsā** f.   blowing (a musical instrument);   **dakà** m.   pounding;   **niƙà** m.   grinding, thing (to be) ground;   **sāƙà** f.   weaving, honeycomb;   **sātà** f.   stealing, theft;   **shūkà** f.   planting, a plant;   **zugà** f. provocation, incitement

The tone pattern L-H-H appears to be the norm for trisyllabic VNs of this class. There is one example each of H-H-L and L-L-H. All of the trisyllabic words are feminine.

hàrārā   giving s.o. a disapproving side glance;   **ƙìdāyā**   counting, census;   **mùsāyā**   exchanging, an exchange;   **fassar̃à** H-H-L   translation;   **fìfītā** L-L-H   fanning (= [dv] **fītā**)

3.3.6. Class 6: Ablaut)^HL   (ī...-ā / ū...-ā)

A number of disyllabic verbs with a mid vowel in the first syllable have VNs with a corresponding high vowel in the first syllable. The vowel /ē/ is replaced by /ī/ and /ō/ is replaced by /ū/. In addition to the ablaut, there is an -ā suffix with a set H-L tone pattern. As in the case with the -ā verbal nouns in the preceding class, some of these VNs are masculine and some are feminine.

dībà m.	take, fetch (cf. **dèbā** v2)	**fīɗà** f.	flaying (cf. **fēɗè** v4)
fīrà f.	paring (cf. **fērè** v4)	**jīfà** m.	throwing, a throw (cf. **jèfā** v2 and **jēfà** v1)
jīmà f.	tanning, a hide (cf. **jēmà** v1)	**ƙīrà** f.	forging, manufactured item (cf. **ƙērà** v1)
rīɗà f.	scraping (cf. **rèɗà** v2)	**rīgà** f.	washing rice to remove stones (cf. **rēgè** v4)
shīƙà f.	winnowing (cf. **shèƙā** v2)	**tsīfà** f.	combing out (cf. **tsēfè** v4)

°AN: [i] The VN form **dībà** is now standardly used as the A-form of the finite gr2 verb, e.g., **tā dībà** 'She dipped (it) out', cf. **tā dèbi ruwā** 'She dipped out some water.'

[ii] In addition to **shề𝆒ā** 'winnow', there is a phonologically identical verb **shề𝆒ā** 'inhale'. The ablauted form **shī𝆒ằ** only serves as the VN of the first of the two homophonous verbs.

dūkằ m.	beating (cf. **dồkā** v1)	**gūgằ** f.	rubbing, ironing (cf. **gōgề** v4)
kūɗằ f.	sharpening by beating (cf. **kōɗằ** v1)	**𝆒ūnằ** m.	burning heat (cf. **𝆒ōnằ** v1)
sūkằ m.	stabbing, criticism (cf. **sồkā** v2)	**sūsằ** f.	scratching an itch (cf. **sōsằ** v1)
sūyằ f.	frying, fried meat (cf. **sōyằ** v1)	**tūyằ** f.	deep frying (cf. **tōyằ** v1)

◊HN: Historically, the vowel in the initial syllable of the verb was probably /ī/ or /ū/ as it still is in the verbal noun. The VN would have been formed simply by adding a suffix -ā with H-L tone. Subsequently, the vowel in the verb lowered to the corresponding mid vowel, under as yet unknown conditions, resulting in the vowel alternation seen in such examples as **sūsằ** 'scratching' vs. **sōsằ** 'scratch'. In other words, what has to be described synchronically as an ō ⇒ ū or -ē ⇒ -ī morphological raising rule was historically a *-ū > ō or *-ī > -ē (morpho)phonological change.

3.3.7. Class 7: -**iyā** and -**uwā**

This formation class includes two subclasses, one, which is quite numerous, using the suffix -**iyā**, and one, quite small, using the suffix -**uwā**.

3.3.7.1. The -**iyā** suffix used in this class can be identified with the formally identical -**iyā** feminative suffix, i.e., originally these words were presumably the feminine counterparts of masculine verbal nouns ending in a front vowel. In a few cases the noun is built on a reduplicated pluractional form of the verb rather than the simple verb. These derivatives sometimes function as active VNs; mostly, however, they appear as DVNs, sometimes as gerundive dynamic nouns indicting actions, sometimes as nouns indicating concrete things or events that are related in some way to the action of the underlying verb. How close the meaning of the noun is to the source verb depends on how lexicalized the noun has become.

There are some sixty or so common verbal nouns formed with the -**iyā** suffix. Most (about fifty) have all H tone. Some eight words have L-H-H tone; three words, all with a light initial syllable, have H-H-L tone. Examples:

H-H-H: **bauɗiyā** dodging (cf. **bauɗề** dodge); **cāshiyā** speeding up (by musicians); telling a friend off for a misdeed (cf. **cāshề** thresh, speed up); **dāgiyā** perseverance (cf. **dāgề** persevere); **gar̃gājiyā** olden times (< plurac. form of **gàdā** inherit); **kakkafiyā** deep mud (< plurac. form of **kafề** get stuck); **nāniyā** (= **nānì**) mending, a patch (cf. **nānề** mend); **tāriyā** spinning, big spool of thread (cf. **tārằ** collect); **tōshiyā** bribe (cf. **tōshề** block up a hole); **wāshiyā** ransacking (cf. **wāshề** ransack); **zū𝆒iyā** sliding back (physically or in speech) (cf. **zū𝆒ề** dodge)

L-H-H: **gồdiyā** thanks (cf. **gōdề** thank); **kwànciyā** lying down (cf. **kwântā** lie down); **yàdiyā** [Skt] lighting a torch (cf. **yādằ** light); **yàɗiyā** a twining plant or the food made from its leaves (cf. **yāɗằ** spread)

H-H-L: **cigiyằ** searching for sth, lost and found property (< //cig-//, cf. the denominal verb **cigìtā** search for); **rakiyằ** accompanying, accompaniment (cf. **rakằ** accompany); **sakiyằ** puncturing out puss from abcess (cf. **sàkāsakì** release, let go)

◊HN: [i] On the model of feminative nouns that have a similar shape, e.g., **kibiyằ** 'arrow (< *kibì + -ā), we can hypothesize that these -**iyā** VNs were derived by addition of the feminative suffix -ā to i-final H-L verbal nouns belonging to the class that includes **ginì** 'building', **ɗinkì** 'sewing', **sakì** 'releasing', etc., i.e., *rakiyằ < *rakì + ā. Originally *sakì m. 'releasing' and *sakì (later **sakiyằ**) f. 'puncturing an abcess' would have been a doublet distinguished only by gender.

[ii] The verb **cigìtā** (<//**cigiy-ta**//) 'search for', with the -TA verbalizer suffix, is presumably derived from the nominal **cigiyà** (< ***cigì** + **ā**), which itself is derived from a now nonoccurring verb base *//**cig**-//. (There is also a tonally variant form **cìgiyà**, which looks like a regular SDVN of a gr2 verb.) This development of a verb being derived from a verbal noun ultimately going back to an original verb can also be seen, for example, in **aikàtā** 'do work', which is derived from **aikì** m. 'work', which itself is a nominalized form of the verb **àikā** 'send'.

There are a few VNs that at first sight appear to have the -**iyā** suffix but that in reality do not, e.g.,

tàfiyà	going, cf. **tàfi** go	**gàjiyà**	tiredness, cf. **gàji** tire
bìɗiyà	seeking, cf. **bìɗā** seek	**fèrayà**	paring, cf. **fèrè** pare

In all of these cases what one really has is an SDVN formed (synchronically or historically) from an extended verb containing a remnant verbal suffix /-**yà**/ i.e., **tàfiyà** comes not from a base //**taf**-// but from a gr3 verb stem */**tàfiyà**/; similarly, **fèrayà** 'paring' comes not from a base //**fèr**-// 'pare' but from a gr2 verb stem /**fèrayà**/.

3.3.7.2. There is a small class (about ten words) of verbal nouns that end in -**uwā**. The -**uwā** suffix can be identified with a formally identical feminative suffix. Like the -**iyā** words, most derivatives with -**uwā** function as DVNs rather than active VNs. It is not clear why this -**uwā** class should be so small as compared with the corresponding -**iyā** class, but it is probably related to the fact that nominalized verbs with final -**ī** and -**ē** are much more common than those with final -**ū** and -**ō**. The tone pattern of -**uwā** words is all H. In two cases the /**u**/ is dropped and the suffix appears as -**wā**. Examples (complete):

ɗīmuwā losing one's bearings (cf. **ɗīmàucē** lose one's bearings); **gaisuwā** greeting; **kāmuwā** seized property; **mantuwā** forgetfulness, forgetting; **maisuwā** [WH] vomit(ing) (< efferential base //**mays**-// return sth < **mayà** return); **rāmuwā** retaliation, revenge, restitution; **rantsuwā** oath, swearing; **tsar̄tuwā** spitting; **tsintuwā** luckily finding sth, the thing found; **baiwā** gift, betrothal (< ***bayuwā**, cf. **bai** give); **tsaiwā** (= [Kts] **tsayuwā**) alignment, posture (cf. **tsayà** stand)

There are four verbal nouns ending in -**uwā** that do not have all high tone:

mutuwà dying, death (cf. **mutù** die); **fāɗùwā** falling, failure (cf. **fāɗì** fall); **haihùwā** giving birth (cf. **haihù** give birth); **zuwà** coming (cf. **zō** come)

These words should not be thought of as containing the derivational -**uwā** suffix. Rather, the first three, at least, are better thought of as inflectional VNs formed by the addition of -**ā** to the verb stem. The exact derivation of **zuwà** 'coming' is not yet known, but it also should not be grouped with the -**uwā** words.

    The phonological similarity of such words as **ràsuwā** 'death', **kàfuwā** 'establishment', and **àukuwā** 'an event, a happening' and the BDVNs with -**uwā** like **mantuwā** 'forgetfulness, forgetting' is accidental. The former are regular VNs of gr7 verbs containing the weak VN suffix `-**wā** whereas the latter are base-derived words containing the -**uwā** suffix.

3.3.7.3. Two deverbal nouns end in -**ōwā** and have L-H-L tone. It is not clear how they fit into the overall picture.

cìkōwà	crowd, overcrowding (cf. **cìka / cikà** fill up (v3 / v1))
ràgōwà	remainder, reduction (cf. **ragè** remain, be left over)

3.4. Multiple BDVNs

Many verbs have BDVNs as an alternative to semantically equivalent SDVNs or in addition to occurring SDVNs but with a difference in meaning. One also finds verbs with variant BDVNs belonging to different formation classes. In these cases, there is usually a difference in meaning and/or function. For example, one of the BDVNs may function as an active participial VN whereas the other may function only as a concrete noun, or they all may be essentially nounlike but with distinct semantic properties. Here is a representative list:

askì	a shave, haircut	**askā**	razor, penknife
dashì	transplanting	**dàshē**	seed
datsì	blockage, obstacle	**datsiyā**	dam
fashì	robbery	**fàsō**	cracking of heels due to cold (< **fasà** shatter)
girkì	cooking, a meal	**girkā**	initiation into a *bori* cult
kōyì	emulation	**kòyō**	learning (VN) (< **kòyā** learn, copy)
sakì	a divorce	**sàkē**	slackness
sāƙì	a woven cloth	**sāƙà**	weaving, honeycomb
tākì = tākù	a step	**tàkō**	hoof, foot
tārì	heap, crowd	**tàrō**	a meeting, assembly
tsimì	a medicinal drink	**tsìmē**	ink made by steeping
tsìnkàyē	seeing from afar	**tsìnkāyà**	seeing from afar; foresight
tsùgùnē	act of squatting	**tsùgùnō**	shitting
turkè	tethering post	**turkā**	fattening an animal for slaughter (< **turkè** tether)
wankì	washing; the laundry; **wànkē**	ink made from soot on cooking pot; **wankā**	a bath
yankì	strip of cloth; province, region, state; **yànkē** grass cut after first month of rains; a shortcut; **yankā** slaughtering (VN), sth slaughtered (used in **sūnan yankā** Islamic name)		
zubì	one's contribution to a pool; (bank) deposit; casting in metal; preparing indigo infusion in a dye pit; **zùbō** fading of colors from washing		

The following pair illustrates a subtle meaning difference between two BDVNs used in a cognate accusative construction (see §**13**:3):

nā zàɓi na zàɓē	I chose those available to be chosen.
nā zàɓi na zāɓì	I chose those worthy of being chosen.

[References: Gouffé (1981b), esp. §3, "Le nom verbal en haoussa: essai de mise au point"; Parsons (1981), esp. pp. 208–34, 251–86]

78. Verbal Sentences: Simple Syntax

HAUSA is a straightforward SVO (subject-verb-object) language. Surface deviations from this order are primarily due to focus and topicalization (see chaps. **28** and **72**). The core of a simple tensed verbal sentence consists of the subject (SBJ) (which may be null), the person-aspect-complex (PAC), and the verb phrase (VP). (The VP may optionally be followed by adverbial modifiers.) Examples:

[Maryàm]_{SBJ} [takàn]_{PAC} [dafà àbinci]_{VP}   Maryam customarily cooks food.
[yârā]_{SBJ} [sun]_{PAC} [kōmằ gidā]_{VP} jiyà dà sāfe   The children came home yesterday morning.
[Gàmbo]_{SBJ} [zâi]_{PAC} [gayà manà làbāřìn]_{VP}   Gambo will tell us the news.
[dà nī dà shī]_{SBJ} [munằ]_{PAC} [gōgè mōtằ]_{VP} dà mâi He and I are polishing the car with oil.

Imperative sentences, which are nontensed, lack the SBJ and the PAC, e.g.,

[shìgō]_{VP}! Come in!   [kàshè wutā]_{VP}! Turn out the light! (lit. kill fire)

1. SUBJECT

The subject can be a single NP, like **Maryàm** 'Maryam', **kōwā** 'everyone', **waɗànnân** 'these', or it can consist of conjoined (or disjoined) NPs, like **yārò dà yārinyằ** 'a boy and a girl', **kai dà Mūsā** 'you and Musa', **(kō) zākì kō dằmisà** '(either) a lion or a leopard'. The subject can also be a verbal noun (phrase) or an infinitive phrase, e.g., [haƙàn gwâl]_{SBJ} **yanā dà wùyā** 'Mining gold is difficult', [faràntà matà râi]_{SBJ} **yā yi kyâu** 'To make her happy is good.'

    If the underlying subject is a simple personal pronoun, it is obligatorily deleted, i.e., Hausa is a "pro-drop" language. The person and number of the erstwhile subject are reflected in the weak subject pronoun in the PAC.

*[sū]_{SBJ} [zā sù]_{PAC} dāwō ⟹   [Ø]_{SBJ} zā sù dāwō   They will return.
[they] [fut 3p] return   [Ø] [fut 3p] return
*[nī]_{SBJ} [nā]_{PAC} san amsằ ⟹   [Ø]_{SBJ} [nā]_{PAC} san amsằ   I know the answer.
[I] [1s.comp] know answer   [Ø] [1s.comp] know answer
*[ita]_{SBJ} [tanằ]_{PAC} hūtằwā ⟹   [Ø]_{SBJ} [tanằ]_{PAC} hūtằwā   She is resting.
[she] [3f.cont] resting   [Ø] [3f.cont] resting

If the underlying pronoun is modified, conjoined with another word, or separated from the PAC by a modal particle, it remains in the sentence and appears as an independent pronoun, e.g.,

[kē dà kikè gwànā]_{SBJ} [kin]_{PAC} fi mù sanì   You (f.) who are an expert know more than we do.
[ita kântà]_{SBJ} [zā tà]_{PAC} řubùtà takàřdâř   She herself is going to write the letter.

[nī dà shī]_{SBJ} [mun]_{PAC} jē kàsuwā tàre   He and I (we) went to market together.

[nī kuma]_{SBJ} [nā]_{PAC} iyà hawansà   I also am able to ride it.

Single independent pronouns that translate into English as focused subjects syntactically occupy the focus slot and thus they are not deleted, e.g.,

«sū (nè)» [Ø]_{SBJ} [zā sù]_{PAC} dāwō   *They* (i.e., it is they who) will return.

«mū (nè)» [Ø]_{SBJ} [mukà]_{PAC} san amsà   *We* (i.e., it is we who) know the answer.

2. PERSON-ASPECT-COMPLEX (PAC)

The person-aspect-complex (PAC) (which is comparable to INFL in general theoretical linguistic terminology) consists of two components: a weak subject pronoun (wsp), which agrees in number and gender with the underlying subject, and a marker of tense/aspect/mood (TAM), which in some cases is phonologically zero (see §70:1). The order of elements is usually wsp + TAM (e.g., **ta.kàn** '3f.habitual'), although in a few conjugational forms, the future and the allative, it is reversed (e.g., **zā sù** 'future 3p'). In certain specific contexts, the PAC allows deletion of either the wsp or of the TAM, but not both, e.g.,

mātan nàn [Ø nằ]_{PAC} shân wàhalằ

    These women are suffering.

mātan nàn [zā sù]_{PAC} būɗè tāgằ [Ø sù]_{PAC} kuma shārè ɗākìn

    These women are going to open the window and sweep the room.

3. VERB PHRASE (VP)

The verb phrase (VP) consists of a VERB (a category that includes finite verbs as well as verbal nouns derived from verbs (see chap. **77**)), followed by possible objects or locative goals, e.g.,

mùtûm yā [ginà gidā]_{VP}   The man [built a house].

sōjà yā [hàr̃bē shì]_{VP}   A soldier [shot him].

tā [tsūfa]_{VP}   She [has aged].

mun [tàfi Kanò]_{VP}   We [went to Kano].

cf. munằ [tàfiyằ Kanò]_{VP}   We [are going to Kano].

sun [fārà kashè kar̃nukàn]_{VP}   They [began to kill the dogs].

yanằ [nēman aikì]_{VP}   He is [seeking work].

(where **nēman** is the verbal noun **nēmā** plus the linker **-n**)

sunằ [sàtàr̃ wākē]_{VP}   They are [stealing beans].

(where **sàtàr̃** is the verbal noun **sātằ** plus the linker -**r̃**)

munằ [dāwôwā]_{VP}   We are [returning].

(where **dāwôwā** is the verbal noun of **dāwō**)

On the surface, VPs sometimes lack a VERB and consist solely of an object or objects, e.g., **sunằ kòkawā** 'They are wrestling' (where **kòkawā** is a noun, not a verb); **takàn musù tsāwā** 'She is in the habit of reprimanding them' (lit. she.hab to.them thunder). These sentences are presumed to contain the syntactically required underlying VERB (**yi** 'do'), which can be, and commonly is, deleted under appropriate conditions (see §58:3).

3.1. Objects

Objects can be either direct or indirect. A direct object can be essentially any kind of NP, i.e., anything from a simple noun or pronoun to an infinitive phrase to a full sentence, e.g.,

kā ga [Bellò]$_{d.o.}$?   Did you see [Bello]?
zā tà tàimàkē [mù]$_{d.o.}$ She will help [us].
yā hanà [kìɗe-kìɗe dà bùshe-bùshe]$_{d.o.}$ He prohibited [music].
(lit. [drummings and blowings])
sun dingà [kāwō manà àbinci]$_{d.o.}$ They continued [to bring us food].
inà sô(n) [mù jē kànti mù sayō kāyā irì irì]$_{d.o.}$
    I want [that we go to the store and buy all kinds of goods].

Some verbs allow double direct objects, e.g.,

Garbà yā ɗauki Tankò mahàukàcī   Garba considers Tanko a fool.

Indirect objects, which syntactically make use of the markers **ma-** (before personal pronouns) and **wà** (elsewhere), are allowed with intransitive as well as transitive verbs. They occur immediately after the verb and before other arguments in the VP. Thus, when a sentence has both direct and indirect objects, the order is necessarily i.o. + d.o., e.g.,

tōcìlàn tā macè [minì]$_{i.o.}$ The flashlight died on me.
wà ya sayō [makà]$_{i.o.}$ [fentì]$_{d.o.}$?   Who bought you paint?
ɗàlibai sun faɗà [wà mālàminsù]$_{i.o.}$ [làbārì]$_{d.o.}$ The students told their teacher a story.
yā rubùtā [manà]$_{i.o.}$ dà tàfìrētà   He wrote (it) for us with a typewriter.

By contrast, prepositional phrases (pp) with **gà** (= **gàrē** before pronoun objects), which semantically are often equivalent to i.o.'s, occur after the d.o., e.g.,

yā faɗi [làbārì]$_{d.o}$ [gà bàƙìn dà sukà zō wajensà]$_{pp}$
    He told the news to the strangers who came to him.

3.2. Locative goals

Locative goals, which constitute core arguments in the VP, occur immediately after the VERB (unless an i.o. intervenes) and before adverbial modifiers, e.g.,

nâ jē [makarantā]$_{loc}$ gòbe dà sāfe   I will be going to school tomorrow morning.
zō [nân]$_{loc}$ maza maza!   Come here quickly!
yā shigam [manà]$_{i.o.}$ [ɗākìn$_{loc}$ bà don kōmē ba sai sātà
    He entered our room (lit. enter to.us room) for no reason except theft.

3.3. VP modifiers

3.3.1. Post-VERB modifiers

Most verbal modifiers—whether simple adverbs, prepositional phrases, ideophones, or what have you—follow the VP, e.g.,

[kāwō takàrdâr] [gòbe]!   Bring the letter tomorrow!
yārò yā [yi aikì] [à kàntī jiyà dà sāfe]   The boy worked at the store yesterday morning.

tanà [shìgā ɗākìn] [sànnu sànnu]	She was entering the room slowly.
sun [tàfi kàsuwā] [dà kāwùnsù]	They went to the market with their uncle.
kù [cikà bùhū] [dà gyàɗā]!	You (pl.) fill the sack with peanuts!
zân [haṛbè̀ shi] [dà bindigà̀]	I'll shoot him dead with a gun.
wata gadà̀ tā [rūshè̀] [kusa dà Kanò̀]	A bridge collapsed close to Kano.
Sāni yā [gayà̀ minì] [à àsìṛce]	Sani told me on the sly.
nā [gàji] [tiƙis]	I'm completely exhausted.

3.3.2. Pre-VERB modifiers

Although modifiers typically occur later in the sentence after the VP, there are a few special items that can occur between the PAC and the VERB. These include grammatical words like **kō** 'even' (usually used in the negative), the diminutive **ɗan** 'little', the quantifier **yawàn** 'a lot of', and various modal particles. Examples:

bā sà̀ <u>kō</u> sôn buṛōdì dà ruwā	They do not even want bread and water.
bài <u>kō</u> dùbē mù ba	He didn't even look at us.
Kànde tā <u>ɗan</u> tàimàkē nì	Kande helped me a little.
yanà̀ <u>yawàn</u> mārìntà	He is slapping her a lot.
= yanà̀ mārìntà <u>dà̀ yawà̀</u> (with the normal prepositional phrase in post-VP position)	
màkānikè̀ yā <u>fa</u> gyārà mōtàṛ	The mechanic indeed repaired the car.
= (more or less) **màkānikè̀ yā gyārà mōtàṛ <u>fa</u>**	

79. Verbalizer -TA

THE very productive suffix {-TA} (with variant surface forms) serves to derive verbs from nouns or adjectives (or occasionally adverbs), e.g.,

gubà	poison	**gubàntā**	to poison	**gàjērē**	short	**gajàrtā**	shorten
ɗālìbī	student	**ɗālìbcē**	become a student	**fushī**	anger	**fùsātà**	become angry

The nature and length of the final vowel and the tone are determined by the grade that the resulting verb operates and not by the suffix itself. (If the verb ends in a front vowel, the suffixal /t/ will naturally appear as /c/.) The verbalizing formative itself does not dictate which grade the resulting verb will operate. Rather the assignment seems to be determined by syntactic/semantic characteristics of the grades. Transitive verbs tend to go into either gr1 or gr2, less often into gr4. Intransitive verbs are usually assigned to gr3 or gr4. (Although gr1 does contain a number of intransitive verbs, derived intransitives tend not to go into that grade.) Verbs that can occur both transitively and intransitively operate transitive/intransitive grade pairs, the most common pairings being gr1/gr3 or gr1/gr4, less often gr2/gr4, and rarely gr2/gr3. An example of a gr1/gr4 tr./intr. pair would be **gwāmùntā** gr1 'render knock-kneed', **gwāmùncē** gr4 'become knock-kneed', both < **gwāmè** 'knock-kneed'. In the examples in this section, verbs will be presented in one commonly used grade, with the understanding that most of the -TA derivatives may also occur in other grades as well.

1. FORM

The suffixal morpheme {-TA} has two primary allomorphs, each of which has phonological subvariants. These are -**Vnta** and -(**a**)**ta**, the latter being the more common. The choice between the two allomorphs is determined in part by the phonological shape of the underlying noun or adjective, but generally speaking, the choice seems to be lexically specific and not predictable.

1.1. -Vnta

Some fifty, mostly disyllabic, nouns and adjectives create corresponding verbs by means of a suffix containing /Vn/ before the -ta. With most words, the suffix has the form -**anta**. Many, but not all, stems ending in /-ū/—including a few that now end in -ō but that historically ended in -ū (see §34:2.2)—have /u/ as the initial vowel of the suffix. Examples.

(a) **àsùbantà** v2 arrive early < **àsùbâ** early morning; **faràntā** v1 whiten, make happy < **farī** white; **hūtsàncē** v4 become cantankerous < **hūtsū** cantankerous; **jàgòrantà** v2 lead, guide < **jàgòrà** a guide; **ƙàlùbàlantà** v2 challenge, provoke < **ƙàlūbàlē** a challenge; **nìsantà** v3 be away from < **nīsā** distance; **'yântā** v1 free a slave < **'yā** freemen

(b) bằɓuntằ v2   be a guest of, pay a visit to < bằɓō guest (< *bằɓu); dùhuntằ v3   become dark <
duhừ darkness; gurgừncē v4   become lame < gurgừ cripple; sābừntā v1   renew < sābō new (<
*sābu)

The following words contain /un/ even though the stem does not end in a back-rounded vowel:

| gwāmừntā v1 | render knock-kneed < | gwāmề | knock-kneed |
| màtuntà v3 | become a (mature) woman < | màtā | woman/wife |

The word mūgừ 'evil' undergoes irregular shortening of the initial syllable in the derived form, a feature
also found in its other derivatives:

mugừncē v4   become bad, slander < mūgừ evil (cf. mùgừntā evilness)

1.2. -(a)ta

This suffix, which is the more common of the two verbalizer allomorphs, occurs in two subvariants: -ta
and -a(a)ta (the latter displaying conditioned variation in the length of the suffix-initial vowel).

1.2.1. -ta

Trisyllabic (and a few quadrisyllabic) stems drop the final vowel and attach -ta directly. The direct
attachment of -ta also applies to disyllabic stems (and one monosyllabic stem) that are C-final or end in
a diphthong. (In the case of base-final /m/, there is individual and dialectal variation as to whether the
/m/ assimilates to the /t/ and becomes /n/ or not.) Examples:

hanzàrtā v1   hasten < hanzarī speed, haste; hàɾamtà v3   be unlawful < hàɾâm unlawful according
to Islam; jàhiltà v2   be unaware of or ignorant about < jàhìlī ignorant psn; kàɗaità v3   be alone <
kaɗai only; kurừntā v1   deafen, make deaf < kurmā (base //kurum-//) deaf psn; kyâutā v1   do good
to < kyâu good; ɓàzantà v3   be filthy, terrible < ɓàzāmī filth; la'ìfcē v4   become impotent <
la'ìfī impotent (man); màraità v3   become an orphan < màrāyà orphan; Mùsừluntà v3   become a
Muslim < Mùsừlmī (base //Musulum-//) Muslim; tīlàstā v1 (with i.o.)   to force < tīlàs perforce
Irregular: àɾzuɾtà v3   become prosperous < aɾzìkī wealth
ùmaɾtà v2   order, command < ùmàɾnī an order, command

> ◊HN: The form àɾzuɾtà (which the dictionaries give as àɾzutà) is probably a back-
> formation/reanalysis from àɾzuttà with a geminate /tt/, which is derived by assimilation from
> *àɾziktà. The form ùmaɾtà is derived from the base //umaɾ-//, (cf. Arabic 'amr) and not from the
> extant noun ùmàɾnī, which contains a frozen -nī suffix, perhaps borrowed from Kanuri amarnyi
> 'my permission' (cf. Skinner 1996: 277).

In the verb talàutā (< *talàktā) v1 'impoverish' < talàkà 'common man', the abutting sequence of /k/ +
/t/ changes to /u/ + /t/ in accordance with Klingenheben's Law. By contrast, bilabial obstruents + /t/
stay as such and do not change to /u/ in this derivation.

> °AN: The dictionaries list another example that exemplifies the operation of Klingenheben's Law in
> this derivation, namely, cìnūtā (< *cìniktà) v2 'obtain by trading' < cìnikī 'trading'. This verb is
> no longer in general use in SH.

Reduplicated noun stems with the final two syllables identical preserve the final vowel and add -**ta**. Stems with three identical syllables add the suffix to a two-syllable base, e.g.,

(a) **daidàitā** v1	straighten, arrange, become straight < **daidai** correct	
jājàtā v1	color sth red < **jā** red (< *jājā)	
kurūrùtā v1	exaggerate, overstate sth < **kùrūruwà** (base //kùrūrù//) yelling	
lālàcē v4; **lālàtā** v1	spoil; lead someone astray < archaic **lâlā** indolence	
waiwàitā v1	consider as a rumor < **waiwai** rumor, hearsay	
(b) **shāshàtā** v1	treat s.o. as a fool < **shāshàshā** fool	
sūsùcē v4	come to naught < **sūsùsū** fool	

In a number of cases, especially with reduplicated stems, the presumed stem to which the suffix is added is no longer attested as such as an independent synchronic form. Here are some examples with frozen -**ta**:

ɓalɓàlcē v4	waste away < ?		**nānàtā** v1	do or say repeatedly < ?
càncantà v2	deserve < ?		**rīrìtā** v1	treat gently out of love < ?
fāfàtā v1	have a hard time < ?		**wàiwaità** v2	look back for s.o. (= **waigà** v1)
kaikàitā v1	slant, tilt, tip < ?		**zàƙwàiƙwatà** v3	be very eager (= **zàƙu** v7)
ƙūƙùtā v1	strive hard < ?			

The following words, which one might expect to utilize the -**ata** variant (see following section), drop the final vowel and add -**ta** directly:

bâutā v1	serve <	**bāwà**	slave (cf. **bàutā** slavery)	
cùtā (< *ciuta < *ciwta) v2	harm <	**cīwò**	sickness	
gyârtā v1	repair <	**gyārā**	repairing (< **gyārà** v1 repair)	
kwântā v1	lie down <	**kwānā**	spending the night	

1.2.2. -a(a)ta

Disyllabic words (or trisyllabic words with a feminative suffix that is removed in forming the base) drop the lexical-final vowel and add -**a(a)ta**. The length of the suffix-initial vowel /a(a)/ is determined by syllable-weight polarity. If the base has a heavy first syllable, the suffix appears as -**ata**. This produces an alternating heavy-light rhythmic foot in the first two syllables. Examples:

bākàcē v4	winnow < **bàkā** tray
daɽnàcē v4	surround with a fence < **dàɽnī** fence
gàyyatà v2	invite < **gàyyā** invitation, esp. to do communal work
gwammàcē v4	be preferable < **gwàmmà/gwamma** it would be better if...
fàratā v3	behave boastfully < **fàriyà** boastfulness
iyākàcē v4	restrict < **iyàkā** boundary (The initial /i/ is ignored.)
sammàcē v4	bewitch < **sammù** a spell
tsòratà v2; **tsōràtā** v1	be afraid of; frighten < **tsòrō** fright
zàmbatà v2	cheat, satirize s.o. < **zàmbō** cheating
Irregular: **sàllātà** (= **sàllatà**) v2	perform prayer on s.o. < **sallà** prayer
sùmbātà (= **sùmbatà**) v2	kiss < **sumbā** a kiss

Disyllabic words with a light first syllable add the suffix -**āta**, thereby producing an alternating light-heavy rhythmic foot in the first two syllables. Examples:

bàrátà v2	obtain by begging	< **barǎ** begging
fùsàtà v3; fusǎtā v1	become angry; anger s.o.	< **fushī** anger
kùsátā v2	to approach	< **kusa** near
tsiyǎtā v1	impoverish	< **tsìyā** poverty
wàdátà v3	become wealthy, satisfied	< **wàdā** wealth, contentment

The verbs **yawàitā** 'increase, multiply' < **yawǎ** 'quantity, abundance' and **tsiràitā** 'undress' < **tsìrárà** 'naked' (base //tsir-//) add a suffix having the form -**aita**, with an /ai/ diphthong in place of the usual monophthongal long /ā/.

°AN/◊HN: The abstract form corresponding to **tsìrárà** is **tsiraicì** 'nakedness' also with /ai/. This suggests that the historically original form of the base word was probably *tsìrāyà, i.e., **tsiràitā** is a regular trisyllabic formation with -**ta** (cf. **màraitā** 'be an orphan' < **màrāyǎ** 'orphan') rather than an irregular -**ata** form. The form **yawàitā** 'increase', on the other hand, probably is a true example of sporadic diphthongization, the (dissimilatory) conditioning factor being the /w/ in the preceding syllable, cf. the WH dialect form **ɗìyautà** 'become free' < **ɗiyā** 'freemen', where the /ā/ of -**āta** diphthongizes to /au/ following the base-final /y/.

2. VERBALIZATION OF VERBAL NOUNS AND DEVERBAL NOUNS

Nouns derived from verbs that have achieved a certain lexical independence from the verb, i.e., are not perceived simply as regular participial verbal noun forms, can be turned back into verbs by the use of the verbalizer suffix. The result is an interesting derivational cycle of verb > noun > verb, e.g., **kàllā** 'look at' > **kallō** 'looking at, watching' > **kàllatà** 'look at'. In some cases the two verbs occupying different points in the derivational sequence coexist with essentially the same meaning. In other cases, the presumed original verb either has been lost or has semantically diverged from the -TA verb. Examples:

aikàtā v1	to do, accomplish	< **aikì** work < **àikā** v2 send
ɓaɽnàtā v1	to damage	< **ɓaɽnā** damage < **ɓātà** v1 spoil
cigìtā v1	search for	< **cigiyà** searching for (< ***cìgā** v2 search for)
gyârtā v1	repair	< **gyārā** repairing < **gyārǎ** v1 repair
jìrātà v2	wait for s.o./sth	< **jirǎ** waiting < **jirā** v0 wait
kàlatà v2	glean	< **kālā** gleanings (< ***kàlā** v2 glean)
kīwàtā v1	tend	< **kīwǒ** tending < **kiyàyē** v4 look after
nùfátā v2	intend	< **nufì** intention < **nùfā** v2 intend

3. ALTERNATIVE FORMS

The choice between the allomorphs -**Vnta** and -(**a**)**ta** is to a great extent lexically specific and not predictable. For example, one gets **baɽàntā** 'blacken' (< **baɽī** 'black'), not ****baɽàtā**, but **fusàtā** 'make angry' (< **fushī** 'anger'), not ****fusàntā**. Not surprisingly, some stems allow formations with either allomorph, the two forms sometimes being dialect variants, in other cases synchronically coexisting variants. In the examples, the preferred variant in SH is given first:

cìnìkantà = **cìnūtà** [dv] trade (buy and sell); **gōràtā** = **gōràntā** mock s.o. over a past gift or favor; **ƙàyàta** = **ƙàyàntā** beautify, adorn; **shāshàtā** = **shāshàntā** treat s.o. as a fool; **sùmbàtà** / **sùmbatà** = **sùmbantà** kiss; **tufátaɽ (dà)** = **tufantaɽ (dà)** clothe

80. Writing Systems: Orthography

1. INTRODUCTION

HAUSA has two writing systems. One of them, termed **bōkò** (< English 'book'?), is based on the Roman alphabet. This was introduced by the British (and French) colonial governments at the beginning of the twentieth century. It is the system now used in the schools, on road signs and billboards, in the major newspapers and magazines, and in most books. The other, termed **àjàmi**, is based on the Arabic alphabet. This was developed at beginning of the nineteenth century, if not earlier, by traditional Hausa scholars who were literate in Arabic. It is still used for communication among people without Western education, for teachers and students in Koranic schools, and for the writings of various people with a traditionalist bent, such as certain poets.

> °AN: Interestingly, the Hausa translation of the Koran, *Alkur'ani mai Girma*. Madras: Continental Book Centre (1986), is in Roman rather than Arabic script.

2. ROMAN SCRIPT (bōkò)

2.1. Inventory
The Roman script makes use of the following alphabetic letters, which were established as the basis of the orthography in the mid 1930s.

', a, b, ɓ, c, d, ɗ, e, f, g, h, i, j, k, ƙ, l, m, n, o , (p), r, s, t, u, w, y, 'y, z

In pronouncing the letters of the alphabet the consonants are all followed by /a/, e.g., **ba, ɓa, ca, da, ɗa, fa**, etc. The vowels are pronounced with their phonological values, e.g., **a** is pronounced /a/ as in **nāmà** 'meat', **i** is pronounced /i/ as in **kīfī** fish', etc.

The apostrophe represents glottal stop. It is written within a word but not in word-initial position, e.g., /sā'à/ 'time, luck', is spelled **sa'a**, /'aurē/ 'marriage' is spelled **aure**, and / 'àl'amàrī/ 'event' is spelled **al'amari**.

> °AN: Curiously, there is no mention of / ' / in the *Official Guide to Hausa Orthography* (1979). It neither appears in the table of consonants nor is it discussed anywhere.

The "hooked" letters **ɓ, ɗ,** and **ƙ** are now recognized as separate letters distinct from their nonglottalized counterparts. They are thus usually written as such, although one still finds publications (including major newspapers) where the special characters are absent and thus the letters are printed without the hooks, e.g., **barawo** 'thief' instead of **ɓarawo**. The hooked letters became the norm in the late 1930s. Before then, scholars noted these letters by means of a subscript dot (e.g., **ḍ**) or by an apostrophe, which appeared before **b** and **d** and after **k**, i.e., **'b, 'd, k'** (as in the classic dictionary of Bargery 1934).

The apostrophe is still employed in the case of the glottalized 'y, and also for the ejective c' that is found in some WH dialects.

◊HN: Before the adoption of the hooked letters, the dictionaries (e.g., Bargery 1934) did not separate the glottalized and nonglottalized letters for purposes of alphabetization, a practice continued by Abraham (e.g., Abraham and Kano 1949) even though he did use the hooked letters. In more recent dictionaries, e.g., Newman and Newman (1977), Mijingini (1987), and Garba (1990), the hooked letters are alphabetized as totally independent consonants following their plain counterparts.

The digraph **ts**, which represents an ejective sibilant, phonologically belongs to the same glottalized class as the hooked letters although it is not represented in the same fashion. It is sometimes treated as a distinct letter (in line with its phonological status) and thus alphabetized as a separate unit consonant, e.g., Mijingini (1987); but it is usually treated as a sequence of two letters and alphabetized among the **t**'s, thereby following the practice that is normal with such English (and French) digraphs as **th** or **ch**. Like **ts**, the digraph **sh** (which represents the palatal fricative [š] as in English 'shush') is listed in *The Official Guide to Hausa Orthography* as a distinct alphabetic letter and is generally taught as such in literacy programs. For purposes of alphabetization, however, it is usually treated as a sequence of two letters.

The digraphs involving **w** and **y**, e.g., **gw, gy, fy, kw, ƙy**, etc., are typically treated as sequences of letters for orthographic purposes, notwithstanding their phonemic status.

°AN: The problem of how to deal with digraphs extends to major world languages. The long established convention in Spanish, for example, was to treat **ch** and **ll** as distinct letters. Partially due to issues related to computerization, the Association of Spanish Language Academies decided to eliminate these unit "letters" from the Spanish alphabet and treat **ch** and **ll** as sequences of **c + h** and **l + l** respectively. Spain and seventeen other Spanish-speaking countries voted in favor of the change; Ecuador voted against, and Nicaragua, Panama, and Uruguay abstained.

The letter **c** represents the English sound **ch** (as in 'church'). In early written works, it was represented as **ch** as it is in English.

The letter **g** always represents the "hard" /g/ as in 'goat'. The [j] sound that one finds in English words such as 'gem' is represented by the letter /**j**/.

In SH, the letter **p** is restricted to use with foreign proper names, e.g., **Japan, Pakistan, Pele** (the football player). In Hausa in Niger, it is also found in recent loanwords from French, e.g., **parmi** 'driver's license' (Fr. permis); **pil** 'flashlight battery' (Fr. pile).

The letter **r** represents both the flap /r/ and the rolled /r̃/; the phonemic distinction is not noted orthographically, e.g., **far̃kà** 'wake up' and **sarkī** 'chief' are both written with the same **r**, i.e., **farka** and **sarki**, respectively.

In some dialects of Hausa both **m** and **n** in final position are pronounced as [ŋ]. Nevertheless, etymological spelling with **m** and **n** is normally employed, e.g., [mālàŋ] 'teacher' and [gidâŋ] 'the house' are spelled **malam** and **gidan** respectively.

The vowel letters represent both the short and the long counterparts. The phonemic length distinction is not noted, e.g., **farī** 'white' and **fār̃ì** 'beginning' are both written **fari**. The pronunciation of short /e/ and /o/ in closed syllables as [a] is usually not indicated, e.g., [sāban gàrī] 'new town' is usually written **sabon gari**, similarly, [zōbànsà] 'his ring' is written **zobensa**. (There are a few exceptions, e.g., the function word **don** 'in order to', which in Niger is spelled **dan**.)

The diphthongs **ai** and **au** are treated as sequences of letters. The diphthongal spelling is the accepted convention even though many linguists—wrongly in my opinion—phonemically analyze them as /ay/ and /aw/. (An attempt in Niger in the 1960s to write the diphthongs as **ay** and **aw** was subsequently abandoned.)

Tone is totally ignored in the written language, e.g., **gōrà** 'bamboo staff' and **gòrā** 'large calabash' are both written **gora**; similarly, **tà tàfi** 'She should go' and **tâ tàfi** 'She is likely to go' are both written **ta tafi**.

On the whole, spelling is phonemic and matches pronunciation. In a few cases, however, especially with proper names, conventional spellings exist that have become standard, e.g., **Allah** = / 'allā̀/, **Ahmadu** = / 'àmadù/, **Mustapha** = /mustàfā/.

2.2. Spelling rules
With abutting glottalized consonants, only the second is overtly marked, e.g., [riɓɗā̀] 'beat' is spelled **ribɗa**.

With geminate consonants represented by digraphs, only the first letter of the consonant is doubled, e.g., /bùsashshē/ 'dried' is spelled **busasshe**, **gyagygyàrā** 'repair many' is spelled **gyaggyara**.

In the case of the genitive linker -n/-r̃ the spelling is morphological rather than phonological, i.e., assimilations are not shown, e.g., /rìgan nàn/ 'this gown' (lit. gown.of here) is written **rigar nan**, and /gidammù/ 'our house' (lit. house.of.us) is written **gidanmu**.

2.3. Word divisions
Generally speaking the orthographic word divisions coincide with the sense of the linguist and the intuition of native speakers about what should and what should not be written separately or together. There are, however, a number of problematic areas and for these arbitrary conventions have been established. Here are examples of some orthographic rules: (a) Weak subject pronouns are to be written as separate words even though they tend to be attracted to the verb, especially if the verb is monosyllabic, e.g., **ya bi hanya** 'He followed the road' (often seen as ****yabi hanya**). (b) The negative marker **bà** and a following L-tone weak subject pronoun are to be written as two words, e.g., **ba ta zo ba** 'She didn't come' (where /bàtà/ in fact constitutes a phonological word), except in the case of the contracted monosyllabic variants **ban** 'neg.I' and **bai** 'neg.he'. (c) The same rule holds for the future marker plus wsp, e.g., **za ta zo** 'She will come', but **zan** 'fut.I' and **zai** 'fut.he'. (d) Apart from the future, weak subject pronouns plus TAM markers are written as one word, e.g., **muna** 'we.cont', **muke** 'we.Rcont1' (= /mukḗ/ 'Rcont1' and /mukè/ 'Rcont2', with the vowel length distinction not indicated orthographically), **mukan** 'we.hab', **muka** 'we.pret'. (e) The indirect object marker **wà** is to be written separate from the verb even though phonologically they tend to bond to one another, e.g., **Dauda ne ya gaya wa** 'It was Dauda he told it to' (*not* ****Dauda ne ya gayawa**). (f) The possessive clitics **tatà** and **tasà** are to be written as separate words, but the reduced forms -r̃**tà** and -r̃**sà** are written attached to the head noun, e.g., **'ya tata** (i.e., /'yātatà/) 'her daughter' = /'yar̃tà/. (g) Fully reduplicated words such as pseudoplurals of diversity and ideophonic adjectives are written with a hyphen, e.g., **r̃ùbùce-r̃ùbùce** 'writings', **goro r̃uɓu-r̃uɓu** 'large and round kolanuts', but reduplicated attenuated adjectives or distributives are written without a hyphen, e.g., **mota fara fara** 'a whitish car', **dala goma goma** 'ten dollars each'. (h) Bound possessive pronouns functioning as thematic objects of verbal nouns are to be written as separate words but the morphologically identical forms functioning as possessives are to be written bound to the head, e.g., **suna ɗinkin ta** 'They are sewing it', cf. **ɗinkinta** 'her sewing'.

°AN: Principle (h) is the one orthographic convention that I have systematically ignored in this grammar. This is because it runs counter to the reality that the genitive pronouns are *all* bound clitics dependent on their hosts and cannot stand as independent words regardless of their thematic function. The proposed convention particularly fails when the a feminine verbal noun has as its object a first person pronoun, e.g., **yana karɓa ta** 'He is accepting me', where **ta** is made to look like a peculiar, gender-specific, first person pronoun when in fact the /t/ is the feminine linker and the pronoun is /a/.

One area in which the orthographic rules have yet to be established firmly concerns compounds, which are extremely common in the language. The general practice seems to be to write noun.of noun or adjective.of noun compounds as separate words, e.g., **gidan sauro** 'mosquito net' (lit. house.of mosquito), **farin jini** 'popularity' (lit. white.of blood), but verb + noun compounds with hyphens, e.g., **a-ci-balbal** 'an oil- burning lamp' (lit. it burns *balbal* (describes flickering), **kas-dafi** 'potion that makes one impervious to poison' (lit. kill poison).

2.4. Capitalization and punctuation

Hausa has essentially taken over the English system lock, stock, and barrel, i.e., capital letters are used at the beginning of a sentence and for proper nouns, and commas, question marks, etc., are used as in English, e.g., **Yaro ya ce, "Ta tafi Kano da Kande ran Talata."** 'The boy said, "She went to Kano with Kande on Tuesday" .' The major deviation from English concerning capitalization is in writing the first person pronoun **ni** or **na** 'I' with lower case /n/. A common shorthand convention in representing compound names is the use of a single letter plus / in place of the first part of a compound, e.g., **Abdullahi K/Hausa = Abdullahi Kafin-Hausa, Muhammadu D/Tofa = Muhammadu Dawakin-Tofa.**

3. ARABIC SCRIPT (àjàmi)

Before the British takeover of northern Nigeria at the beginning of the twentieth century, Hausa was already a written language employing Arabic script (termed **àjàmi**). As a result, the early dictionaries of Hausa, e.g., Mischlich (1906), Robinson (1899–1900), Le Roux (1886), all represented the Hausa entries in both scripts.

°AN: Most Hausas, being Muslim, learn Arabic script very early in Koranic school. Thus one finds that even young, Western-educated people continue to learn **àjàmi** in spite of a century-long official government policy discouraging **àjàmi** in favor of Roman script.

A considerable quantity of early **àjàmi** writings exist (or existed). For example, the important three-volume collection of Hausa folktales and stories that were published in Roman script by Edgar (1911–1913), and translated into English by Skinner (1969, 1977), consisted of a transliteration of materials written by educated Hausas in **àjàmi**. Around this same period, or even earlier, Robinson (1896) and Rattray (1913) published significant collections of Hausa written materials including the original **àjàmi** versions. Over the past quarter of a century, large collections of poetry and historical texts written in **àjàmi** have been presented and analyzed in the works of scholars specializing in Hausa literature and oral history such as Piłaszewicz (e.g., 1981, 1992).

3.1. Alphabet

For purposes of representing the needs of Hausa, the Arabic script is subject to a few modifications, but these are minor. The standard **àjàmi** alphabet is presented in such scholarly volumes as Mischlich (1906) and Skinner (1969) and in little Hausa language primers like *Ka Koya wa Kanka Karatun Ajami [Teach Yourself Ajami]*, Wusasa; C.M.S., 1971). The chart below in table 33 is reproduced from Rattray (1913), pp. xix–xxiii:

Table 33: Ajami alphabet

Hausa Name of Letter.	Letter. Standing alone.	Connected with following.	Connected on both sides.	Connected with preceding.	Pronunciation in Hausa.	Remarks.
Alif	ا	ا	ا		—	The bearer of vowel-sounds only, as is also *ain*, really consonants.
Alif baki (black alif)				ﺎ		
Ba guje	ب				*b*	*Guje*, lit. *ba* with the twirl.
Ba		ﺑ	ﺒ	ﺐ		
Ta guje	ت				*t*	Lit. *ta* with the twirl.
Ta		ﺗ	ﺘ	ﺖ		
Tsha guje	ث				*tsch*	Lit. *tsch* with the twirl.
Tsha		ﺛ	ﺜ	ﺚ		
Jim karami kōma bāya	ج				*j*	Lit. small *j* with a twirl be-[hind.
Jim karami		ﺟ				Lit. small *j*.
Jim sābe			ﺠ			Lit. *j* with the part projecting.
Jim sābe kōma bāya				ﺞ		Lit. *j* with the part projecting and a twirl behind.
Ha karami kōma bāya	ح				*h*	Lit. little *h* pointing back-[wards.
Ha karami		ﺣ				Lit. little *h*.
Ha sābe			ﺤ	ﺢ		Lit. *h* with the part projecting.
Ha sābe kōma bāya						Lit. *h* with the part pointing backwards.

HAUSA NAME OF LETTER.	LETTER.				Pronunciation in Hausa.	REMARKS.
	Standing alone.	Connected with following.	Connected on both sides.	Connected with preceding.		
Ha mai-rua kōma bāya	ح				*h* (as in Scotch *loch*)	Lit. *h* with the water (i.e. drop, dot) and pointing backwards.
Ha mai-rua		خ				*h* with the (drop of) water.
Ha sābe mai-rua			ـخـ			*h* with the projecting part and dot.
Ha sābe mai-rua kōma bāya				ـخ		*h* with the projecting part pointing backwards.
Dal	د	د	ـد	ـد	*d*	
Zal	ذ	ذ	ـذ	ـذ	*z*	
Ra	ر	ر	ـر	ـر	*r*	
Zaira	ز	ز	ـز	ـز	*z*	
Tsa mal hannu	ط	ط	ـط	ـط	*ts*	
Zadi	ظ	ظ	ـظ	ـظ	*z*	
Kaf lāsan	ك	ک	ـکـ	ـک	*k*	
Lam arat	ل				*l*	
Lam		ل				
Lam jaye			ـل			
Lam arat				ـل		
Mim arat	م				*m*	
Mim		مـ				
Mim jaye			ـمـ			
Mim arat				م		

HAUSA NAME OF LETTER.	LETTER.				Pronunciation in Hausa.	REMARKS.
	Standing alone.	Connected with following.	Connected on both sides.	Connected with preceding.		
Nun arat	ن				*n*	
Nun guda		ن	ن			
Nun arat				ن		
Sodi arat	ص				*s*	
Sodi		ص	ص			
Sodi arat				ص		
Lodi arat	ض				*l*	
Lodi		ض	ض			
Lodi arat				ض		
						Like *alif* bearer of vowel-sounds.
Ain baki wōfi kōma bāya	ع				—	Lit. *ain* with the open mouth and the twirl backwards.
Ain baki wōfi		ع				*Ain* with the open mouth.
Ain likāfa			ع			Stirrup *ain*.
Ain likāfa kōma bāya				ع		Stirrup *ain* with the twirl back.
Angai baki wōfi kōma bāya	غ				*g*	*Angai* with the open mouth and the backward twirl.
Angai baki wōfi		غ				*Angai* with the open mouth.
Angai likāfa			غ			Stirrup *angai*.
Angai likāfa kōma bāya				غ		Stirrup *angai* with the backward twirl.
Fa guje	ف				*f*	*f* with the twirl.
Fa		ف	ف			
Fa guje				ف		

HAUSA NAME OF LETTER.	LETTER.				Pronunciation in Hausa.	REMARKS.
	Standing alone.	Connected with following.	Connected on both sides.	Connected with preceding.		
Kaſ wau	ڧ				*k* (gut-tural)	*Mai-rua*, lit. with the water, i.e. drop, dot.
Kaſ mai-rua		ڧ	ڧ			
Kaſ wau				ڧ		
Sin arat	س				*s*	
Sin		سـ	ـسـ			
Sin arat				ـس		
Schin mai-rua arat	ش				*sch*	*Mai-rua*, *vide* above, *Kaf.*
Schin mai-rua		شـ	ـشـ			
Schin mai-rua arat				ـش		
Ha kuri	۶				*h*	
Ha baba		ھ	ھ			
Ha kuri				ـۀ		
Wau	و	و	ۅ	ۅ	*w*	
Ya arat	ي				*y*	
Ya		يـ	ـئـ			
Ya arat				ـي		

The vowel-signs in Hausa are :

1. ⏑ (above the line) called *wasali bisa* = a.
2. ⏑ (below the line)   ,,   *wasali kasa* = i.
3. ⏑ (below the line)   ,,   *guda casa* = e.
4. ⏑ (above the line)   ,,   *rufua*   = o or u.

Long vowels are distinguished from short vowels in writing as in pronunciation, and the length of a vowel is of such importance that the meaning of a word is often entirely changed, or the tense of a verb altered according as a vowel is long or short.

Long vowels are distinguished from short in writing in the following manner :

1. A long *ā* sound by an *alif* following the *wasali bisa* (⏑).
2. A long *i* sound by a *ya* following the *wasali kasa* (⏑).
3. A long *ē* sound by a *ya* following the *guda kasa* (⏑).
4. A long *ō* or *ū* sound by a *wau* following the *rufua* (⏑).

EXAMPLES :

LONG VOWELS	SHORT VOWELS
1. بَا = bā	1. بَ = bă
2. بِي = bi	2. بِ = bĭ
3. بَى = bē	3. بَ = bĕ
4. بُو = bō or bū	4. بُ = bŏ or bŭ

DIPHTHONGS

There are three diphthongs in Hausa ; they are written and pronounced as follows :

1. يَ = *ai* (like *i* in nice).
2. وَ = *au* (like *ow* in how).
3. يَ = *oi* (like *oy* in boy).

3.2. Sample texts

Below I provide two sample texts in **àjàmi**. These are accompanied by the same texts in Roman orthography (with some accommodation to modern-day practice, although preserving dialectal distinctiveness) along with the original translations.

3.2.1. Ajami text from Robinson (1897, 5th edition 1959, pp. 145ff.)

THE CAPTURE OF KHARTUM AND THE
DEATH OF GENERAL GORDON.[1]

رَانَا دَاكَكَمَشِ اَنِّيي يَك تُنْدَ سَابِى حَلْمَرِيْثِى

بَابُو زَمْنَوَا • مُتَّدِنْ بَاشَا اَنْـكَشِنسُ • مُتَّدِنْ مَهَد

كُمَا اَنْـكَشِنْسُ دَيَو حَلْدَرِى حَلَّاصَبَا • مُتَّدِنْ بَاشَا

سُنْكَبَرْ وَنِ وُرِى سُنْكَنُرْ وِرْنْ مَهَد سُنْكَثِىْ

مُنْغَجِى بَابُو بُتَوَا يَوْ كُنْشِنُمْ كَدَنْ كُنْتَبِى غَدَا

دَدَرِىْ بَاشَا يَغُدُ • مَهَد يَثِىْ تُو حَكَ ذَامِيى

مُسَمْبِشِ • مَهَد يَبَاسُ دُكِيَا يَثِىْ كُتَبِى اِنْ

كُنْسُو كُزُونَ ثِكَنْ سَنْسَنِنَا اِنْ بَكُسُوبَا كُتَبِى

غَرِنْكَ • سُكَييى مَرْنَ • يَكَوُو شَانُو اَكِيَنْكَ دَرَفْمِى

اَكِيَنْكَ يَكَوُو كُزِ دَيَو يَبَا مَاسُقَاطَ يَثِىْ تُو وَنَنْ

[1] A description by a Hausa native in the Mahdi's camp.

بَانِيسو شِكُوَانَا سَىْ مُنْتشِ دَعكُنْ اَللَّه . سَعَنَنْبَ
اَكَتشِى دَاصَب يَسَا مُتْبِىْ سُكَتْبِى غَبَزْ غْخَرْتُمْ
وَدَنُسْ كُمَا غَارْبُوَا مَهدِ شِنْدَعْ كُدُو . مَهدِ يَتَاشِى
اَكِيى بُوسَا دُكَ سُكَتْبِى ذُوَ غْخَرْتُمْ مُتْبِنْ خَرْتُمْ
سُكَتَاشِى اَكَغُمْ اَنَبطَ وَنْ دَوَنْ سُنَبُغْنْ بِنْدِغَا
حَلدَرِىْ . سُنَبْطَ بَا سَايَا شِغَبَا . اَنْبطَ حَرْ غَرِ
يَوِبِى دَجِجِبِ مَهدِ يَشْغَ غَرِ مُتْبِنْ بَاشَا دَسْكِبِى
حَكَننْ دُنْيَرُسْ تَبْنِىْ . كَدَنْ مُتْبِنْ مَهدِ سُكَسُوكِى
مُتُمْ يَكَنِيسَهَ بِفْدِغَ . سُكَكَمْ مُتُمْ كَمَنْ عَشرِنْ .
بَاشَا يَبْنِىْ بَا ذَاشِغُدُو بَا حَرْ اَكَكَمَشِ . اَنَبُغْنشِ
دَبِنْدِغَ اَكَسَارْنشِ دَتَقُوبِ . مَهدِ يَبْنِىْ اَكُو كَنْسَ
اَكَسْرِنشِ اَكَدَوْكِى نَامَنْسَ اَكِجِبْفَشِ شَكَنْ رُوَا
اَكَكَوُورْ كَنْسَ وُرِنْ مَهدِ . مَهدِ يَبْنِىْ اَرْبِى
عِدَاِنْسَ يَبْنِىْ كُنِيِى مُوغُنْ اَبْ دُومِ كُكَكِشبْشِ .
يَيِى فُثِ يَتَاشِى يَكُوهُو سَنْسَنِ دَمَرِيْنِىْ .

3.2.1.1. Transliteration into Roman script:

Rana aka kama shi an yi yaƙi tun da safe hal marece babu zamnawa. Mutanen Basha an kashe su; mutanen Mahadi kuma an kashe su da yawa hal dare hal assuba. Mutanen Basha sunka bar wani wuri sunka zo wurin Mahadi sunka ce mun gaji babu futawa yau ku cishe mu. Kadan kun tafi gida da dare Basha ya gudu. Mahadi ya ce to haka za mu yi mu same shi. Mahadi ya ba su dukiya ya ce ku tafi in kun so ku zauna a cikin sansanina in ba ku so ba ku tafi garinku. Suka yi murna. Ya kawo shanu aka yanka da raƙumi aka yanka ya kawo kurɗi da yawa ya ba masu faɗa ya ce to wannan ba ni so shi kwana sai mun ci shi da ikon Allah. Sa'an nan fa aka tashi da assuba ya sa mutane sunka tafi gabas ga Khartum waɗansu kuma ga arewa. Mahadi shina daga kudu. Mahadi ya tashi aka yi busa, duka suka tafi zuwa ga Khartum, mutanen Khartum suka tashi aka gamu ana faɗa wannan da wannan suna bugun bindiga hal dare. Suna faɗa ba su iya shiga ba. Ana faɗa har gari ya waye da jijjifi Mahadi ya shiga gari mutanen Basha da suka ji haka nan zuciyarsu ta ɓace. Kadan mutanen Mahadi suka soki mutum yakan yas da bindiga. Suka kama mutum kaman ashirin. Basha ya ce ba za shi gudu ba har aka kama shi. An buge shi da bindiga aka sare shi da takobi. Mahadi ya ce a kawo kansa aka sare shi aka ɗauki namansa aka jefa shi cikin ruwa. Aka kawo kansa wurin Mahadi. Mahadi ya ce a rufe idanunsa ya ce kun yi mugun abu, don mi kuka kashe shi? Ya yi fushi ya tashi ya komo sansani da marece.

3.2.2.2. Translation:

On the day on which the city was captured the fight was carried on from morning till night without any respite. Many of the Pasha's men [Pasha = General Gordon] and many of the Mahdi's men were killed. [This went on] till evening, till the early dawn. The Pasha's men left a certain place and came to the place where the Mahdi was and said, we are tired and have had no rest today; give us something to eat. If you come to the house tonight the Pasha will run away. The Mahdi said, it is well; we will do so; we will capture him. The Mahdi gave them goods; he said, go if you wish, or stay in my camp if you do not wish to go to your own town. They rejoiced; he brought them cattle, they were killed; a camel also was killed [for eating[. He brought much money, he gave it to the soldiers. He said, it is well; I do not wish that he [the Pasha] should sleep before we capture him, by the power of God.

Then they rose up in the early morning. He caused his men to go to the east towards Khartoum, others to the north, the Mahdi himself was at the south. He rose up and blew a trumpet, they all went to Khartoum. The men of Khartoum rose up; they met, they fought one with another. They fire guns, they fight till the evening, they are not able to enter. The fight went on till break of day, till the early dawn; [then] the Mahdi entered the town.

When the Pasha's men heard this their heart failed. When the Mahdi's men pierced anyone [with a spear] he threw away his gun. About twenty men captured the Pasha. He said that he would not run away till he was captured. He was shot with a gun, he was cut with a sword. The Mahdi said that his head was to be brought, it was cut off and taken; his body was thrown into the water; his head was taken to the place where the Mahdi was. The Mahdi said, let his eyes be shut. He said, you have done a wicked thing; why did you kill him? He was angry; he rose up; he returned to the camp in the evening.

3.2.2. Ajami text from Rattray (1913, vol. 2, pp. 188ff.)

مستعقمن للسّى أحدم ۰۰ كمتمدم بسشوا ۰ مش ۰ ق آل امش راياش
آل شّا بلج محواللّ أبّى لا وتّى ۰ تشّى أحم مه ديّه مه ديّو مه اسعقن
متلمئى بّسوالبى ۰ قامّا آميايّنك زا قموا مش مّمن تّا مّى
بّسشّى تّا مّن تته مه متكّى آل آران بّه سّه وتى ۰۰ اسعفّى
ومّع امن ۰ لسما زه سا قّمّى ۰ السّى كمّه ا درز ۰ ميقلّما
مّى ۰۰ اذان ۰ هجم كتّى ۰۰ ميلميى شمّا من ش زا قموا مّا ربّى
أبّيو ۰ كموللّشّحمّ آى باتكّمّو ۰ مه أتّقّن آمّ بلم
مّه ۰۰ آمّسّى مّيجعايى ۰۰ تّمّتّى ۰۰ قمّه ميّن زعّتيبجّوا
۰۰ مّش ميّه اعمّ ۰ اسعقّمّن مّا مّسا دم ۰۰ لا وتّى ۰۰

شيبكّمّن

3.2.1.1. Transliteration into Roman script:

Wannan fasali ne na hukuncin suna. Idan matambayi ya tambaye ka, ina wadda ake zana sunan jinjiri, ka ce: Ana zana sunan jinjiri da safe. Rana da ta haihu, idan ta kewayo, mutane su taru liman shi ce: "mu yi salati goma goma ga Annabi." Idan suka gama shi ce: "Allahumma salli ala Muhammadin. Wa ala ali Muhammadin. Warham Muhammadin wa ali Muhammadin. Wa barik ala Muhammadin. Wa ala ali Muhammadin. Kama sallaita wa rahimta wa barakta ala Ibrahima wa ala ali Ibrahima fil'alamina innaka hamidun majidun." Sannan shi yi fatiha uku shi ce: "samaina mauludu". Idan namiji ne shi ce Ibrahima ko Muhammadu ko wani suna. Idan mace ce shi ce Fadimatu ko Hadijatu. Sannan shi yi addu'a, kaman da ya so, shi ce: "Allah shi raya shi, Allah shi ba uwa da uba lafiya." Shi yi addu'a da yawa sannan mutane su watse. Amma an yanka rago tun mutane ba su taru ba. Sa'an nan a zana suna, sa'an nan wanzamai su taru, mata su yi buki, idan mai gata ne. Idan marece ya yi naman rago a rarraba a bai wa kowa sadaka. Ita kuwa matar nan ana ba ta abinci mai dadi, tana ci har jinin haifuwa shi zuba duka, sa'an nan ta samu lafiya. Shi ke nan.

3.2.1.2. Translation:

This is a description of a naming ceremony. If a questioner asked you what was done at the naming of the infant you say, An infant is named on the morning of the day she [the mother] bears it; when that day comes around [i.e. in a week] people assemble. The priest says, "Let us offer up prayers ten times to the Prophet." When they have finished he says [in Arabic] "Oh God be gracious to Muhammad and the family of Muhammad and have mercy on Muhammad and the family of Muhammad and bless Muhammad and the family of Muhammad even as thou wast gracious to, merciful towards, and didst bless Abraham and Abraham's family in the world, verily thou art praiseworthy and glorious." Then he repeats three verses [of the Koran] and says, "We name the child." If it is a male child, he says Abraham or Muhammad or some other name, if it is a girl he says Fatima or Hadijatu. Then he gives a prayer if he wishes, he says "May Allah prolong his life; may Allah give (his) mother and father health." He prays many times and then the people disperse. Now a ram has been slaughtered before the people had assembled. After that they name the child. Then the barbers assemble and the women make a feast, if the man was of a wealthy family. When evening comes, the ram's meat is divided up and given to everyone as alms. And as for her, this wife, she is given the choicest food to eat until all the afterbirth has come away. By that time she has regained her health. That is it.

[References: (1939. *Hausa...*); (1979. *Karatu...*); (1980. *Rapport...*); East (n.d.); Furniss (1991b); Gregersen (1977); Yahaya (1982)]

Bibliography

ABBREVIATIONS

AAL	*Afroasiatic Linguistics*
AAP	*Afrikanistische Arbeitspapiere*
ABU	Ahmadu Bello University [Zaria]
ALS	*African Language Studies*
AuÜ	*Afrika und Übersee*
BLS	*Proceedings of the Berkeley Linguistics Society*
BUK	Bayero University [Kano]
CELHTO	Centre d'Études Linguistiques et Historiques par Traditional Orale [Niamey]
CSNL	Centre for the Study of Nigerian Languages, Bayero University
FWP	*Studies in Hausa Language and Linguistics. In Honour of F. W. Parsons*, ed. by Graham Furniss and Philip J. Jaggar. London: Kegan Paul International
GLECS	*Comptes rendus du groupe linguistique d'études chamito-sémitiques*
HN	*Harsunan Nijeriya*
JAL	*Journal of African Languages*
JALL	*Journal of African Languages and Linguistics*
JWAL	*Journal of West African Languages*
PCL	*Papers in Chadic Linguistics*, ed. by Paul Newman and Roxana Ma Newman. Leiden: Afrika-Studiecentrum
SAL	*Studies in African Linguistics*
SOAS	School of Oriental and African Studies, University of London
UCLA	University of California at Los Angeles

1939. "Hausa orthography." *Africa* 11:505–7.

1979. *Karatu da Rubutu a Harshen Hausa: Jagorar Ka'idojin Rubutun Hausa: The Official Guide to Hausa Orthography*. Ikeja: Thomas Nelson (Nigeria).

1980. *Rapport final: Réunion d'experts sur l'harmonisation de l'orthographe de la langue hawsa*. Niamey: CELHTO.

Abdoulaye, Mahamane L. 1991. "Derived direct objects in Hausa." *JWAL* 21(1):75–90.

———. 1992. *Aspects of Hausa Morphosyntax in Role and Reference Grammar*. Ph.D. dissertation, State University of New York at Buffalo.

———. 1993. "Three topic constructions in Hausa." Unpublished ms.

———. 1996. "Efferential 'verb + dà' constructions in Hausa." *JALL* 17:113–51.

Abraham, R. C. 1934. *The Principles of Hausa*. Kaduna: Government Printer.

———. 1941. *A Modern Grammar of Spoken Hausa*. London: Crown Agents for the Colonies.

———. 1959a. *Hausa Literature and the Hausa Sound System*. London: University of London Press.

———. 1959b. *The Language of the Hausa People*. London: University of London Press.

————. 1962. *Dictionary of the Hausa Language.* 2nd ed. London: University of London Press.

Abraham, R. C., and Mai Kano. 1949. *Dictionary of the Hausa Language.* 1st ed. London: Crown Agents for the Colonies.

Abubakar, Abdulhamid. 1983/85. "Another look at Hausa diphthongs." *HN* 13:1–20.

Ahmad, Mustapha. 1994. *Aspects of Hausa Compounding.* Ph.D. dissertation, Indiana University.

Ahmad, Mustapha, and Robert Botne. 1992. *Hausa Reading Kit: Graded Texts for Elementary and Intermediate University Students.* Bloomington: African Studies Program, Indiana University.

Ahmed, Umaru, and Bello Daura. 1970. *An Introduction to Classical Hausa and the Major Dialects.* Zaria: NNPC.

Al-Hassan, Bello S. Y. 1983. "Intensivization: A Study of the Phonology and Semantics of a Category of Hausa Reduplicants." M.A. thesis, ABU.

Alidou, Ousseina Dioula. 1992. "The reflexives and reciprocals in Hausa and binding theory." Unpublished ms., Indiana University.

————. 1997. *A Phonological Study of Language Games in Six Languages of Niger.* Ph.D. dissertation, Indiana University.

Ames, David W., Edgar A. Gregersen, and Thomas Neugebauer. 1971. "**Taaken sàmàarii**: A drum language of Hausa youth." *Africa* 49:12–31.

Amfani, Ahmad H. 1984. "Abstract Nouns of Games in Hausa." M.A. thesis, SOAS.

Attouman, Mahaman Bachir. 1987. "La modalité d'incompatibilité-dominance en hawsa: **ìnáa** X **ìnáa** Y." *SAL* 18:239–48.

Awde, Nicholas. 1996. *Hausa-English English-Hausa Dictionary.* (Hippocrene Practical Dictionary.) New York: Hippocrene Books.

Baba, Ahmad Tela. 1998. "The use of -**ii** ending Hausa verbal exclamatory expressions in response to a presupposed syntactic construction." *AAP* 53:81–89.

Bagari, Dauda M. 1977a. "Causatives in Hausa." *HN* 7:61–74.

————. 1977b. "Reanalyzing the Hausa causative morpheme." In *PCL*, pp. 1–11.

————. 1982. "Some aspects of Guddiranci." In *The Chad Languages in the Hamitosemitic-Nigritic Border Area*, ed. Herrmann Jungraithmayr, pp. 244–53. (Marburger Studien zur Afrika- und Asienkunde, Serie A, Afrika, 27.) Berlin: Dietrich Reimer.

————. [1984]. "Yaren Guddiranci" [the Guddiri dialect]. In *Studies in Hausa Language, Literature and Culture: Proceedings of the First Hausa International Conference, July 7–10, 1978*, ed. Ibrahim Yaro Yahaya and Abba Rufa'i, pp. 43–46. Kano: CSNL.

————. 1987. *Hausa Subordinate Adverbial Clauses: Syntax and Semantics.* Rabat [Morocco]: El Maarif Al Jadida.

Baldi, Sergio. 1988. *A First Ethnolinguistic Comparison of Arabic Loanwords Common to Hausa and Swahili.* (Supplement 57 to *Annali dell'Istituto Orientale di Napoli* 48/4.) Naples: Istituto Universitario Orientale.

————. 1995. "On Arabic loans in Hausa and Kanuri." In *Studia Chadica et Hamitosemitica: Akten des Internationalen Symposions zur Tschadsprachenforschung*, ed. by Dymitr Ibriszimow and Rudolf Leger, with the assistance of Gerald Schmitt, pp. 252–78. Cologne: Rüdiger Köppe.

Bargery, G. P. 1934. *A Hausa–English Dictionary and English–Hausa Vocabulary.* London: Oxford University Press. (Reprint with a lexical supplement and new introduction by Neil Skinner. Zaria: ABU Press, 1993).

Barth, Heinrich. 1862–1866. *Collection of Vocabularies of Central-African Languages [Sammlung und Bearbeitung zentralafrikanischer Vokabularien].* Gotha: Justus Perthes.

Bature, Abdullahi. 1985. "The Semantic Scope of Negation in Hausa." M.A. thesis, BUK.

————. 1991. *Thematic Arguments and Semantic Roles in Hausa: Morphosyntax and Lexical Semantics Interface.* Ph.D. dissertation, Stanford University.

Bello, Ahmadu. 1992. *The Dialects of Hausa*. Enugu (Nigeria): Fourth Dimension Publishing.

Bross, Michael. 1995. "Toponymie als Zeugen der Vergangenheit: Untersuchungen im nordnigerianischen Bergland der Hausa." In *Mensch und Natur in Westafrika*, ed. by Karsten Brunk and Ursula Greinert-Byer, pp. 223–30. (Berichte des Sonderforschungsbereichs 268, 5.) Frankfurt: Goethe-Universität.

Buba, Malami. 1997a. *Deixis (Demonstratives and Adverbials) in Hausa*. Ph.D. dissertation, SOAS.

———. 1997b. "The deictic particle ɗi-n in Hausa." *African Languages and Cultures* 10:29–45.

Carnochan, Jack. 1951. "A study of quantity in Hausa." *Bulletin of the School of Oriental and African Studies* 13:1032–44.

———. 1952. "Glottalization in Hausa." *Transactions of the Philological Society*, pp. 78–109.

———. 1957. "Gemination in Hausa." In *Studies in Linguistic Analysis*, pp. 149–81. *Transactions of the Philological Society*, special edition.

Caron, Bernard. 1983. "Causatif et extension verbale en -k- en haoussa de l'Ader." *Bulletin des Études Africaines de l'Inalco* 3(5):21–41.

———. 1990a. "La négation en haoussa." *Linguistique Africaine* 4:31–46.

———. 1990b. "Note sur le *ba* final de l'accompli négatif en haoussa." In *Études tchadiques: Verbes monoradicaux*, ed. Herrmann Jungraithmayr and Henry Tourneux, pp. 245–51. Paris: Geuthner; GET-LACITO.

———. 1991. *Le haoussa de l'Ader*. (Sprache und Oralität in Afrika, 10.) Berlin: Dietrich Reimer.

Caron, Bernard, and Ahmed H. Amfani. 1997. *Dictionnaire Français-Haoussa suivi d'un index Haoussa-Français*. Paris: Karthala.

Cole, Desmond T. 1955. *An Introduction to Tswana Grammar*. Cape Town: Longman.

Cowan, J Ronayne, and Russell G. Schuh. 1976. *Spoken Hausa*. Ithaca: Spoken Language Services.

Daba, Habib Ahmed. 1987. *Sociolinguistic Study of Address Terms in Hausa*. Ph.D. dissertation, University of Wisconsin.

Delafosse, Maurice. 1901. *Manuel de langue haoussa ou Chrestomatie haoussa, précédé d'un abrégé de grammaire et suivi d'un vocabulaire*. Paris: J. Maisonneuve.

Dikko, Inuwa, and Usman Maccido. 1991. *Kamus na Adon Maganar Hausa* [Dictionary of Hausa Idioms]. Zaria: NNPC.

Dimmendaal, Gerrit J. 1989. "Complementizers in Hausa." In *Current Progress in Chadic Linguistics*, ed. Zygmunt Frajzyngier, pp. 87–110. Amsterdam: John Benjamins.

East, Rupert M. n.d. *Hausa Spelling*. 2nd ed. Zaria: NORLA (North Regional Literature Agency).

Edgar, Frank W. 1911–13. *Littafi na Tatsuniyoyi na Hausa*. [Hausa Folktales]. 3 vols. Belfast: W. Erskine Mayne.

El-Shazly, Moh. Helal Ahmed Sheref. 1987. *The Provenance of Arabic Loan-words in Hausa: A Phonological and Semantic Study*. Ph.D. dissertation, SOAS.

Eulenberg, John B. 1971. "A new look at predicating particles in Hausa." *SAL* 2:105–15.

———. 1972. *Complementation Phenomena in Hausa*. Ph.D. dissertation, University of California at San Diego.

———. 1974. "How morphological alternations in Hausa conspire to make it a more efficient channel of communication." In *Third Annual Conference on African Linguistics*, ed. Erhard Voeltz, pp. 197–201. (I.U. Publications, African Series, 7.) Bloomington: Indiana University.

Frajzyngier, Zygmunt. 1965. "An analysis of intensive forms in Hausa." *Rocznik Orientalistyczny* 29(2):31–51.

———. 1977. "On the intransitive copy pronouns in Chadic." In *Papers from the Eighth Conference on African Linguistics*, ed. Martin Mould and Thomas J. Hinnebusch, pp. 73–84. (*SAL*, Supplement 7.) Los Angeles: Department of Linguistics, UCLA.

————. 1982. "On the form and function of pre-pronominal markers in Chadic." *Bulletin of the School of Oriental and African Studies* 45:323–42.

————. 1985. "'Causative' and 'benefactive' in Chadic." *AuÜ* 68:23–42.

————. 1991. "The de dicto domain in language." In *Approaches to Grammaticalization*, ed. Elizabeth C. Traugott and Bernd Heine, pp. 220–51. Amsterdam: John Benjamins.

Furniss, Graham. 1981. "Hausa disyllabic verbs: Comments on base forms and extensions." *SAL* 12:97–129.

————. 1983. "The 4th grade of the verb in Hausa." In *Studies in Chadic and Afroasiatic Linguistics*, ed. Ekkehard Wolff and Hilke Meyer-Bahlburg, pp. 287–300. Hamburg: Helmut Buske.

————. 1991. *Second Level Hausa: Grammar in Action.* London: SOAS.

Galadanci, Muhammad Kabir Mahmud. 1969. *The Simple Nominal Phrase in Hausa.* Ph.D. dissertation, SOAS.

————. 1971. "Ideophones in Hausa." *HN* 1:12–26.

————. 1972. "The structure and syntactic function of compound nouns in Hausa." *Anthropological Linguistics* 14:147–54.

Garba, Calvin Y. 1990. *Kamus na Harshen Hausa* [Dictionary of the Hausa Language]. Ibadan: Evans Brothers (Nigeria).

Garba, Mohammed Magashi. 1982. *Morphology of the Hausa Verbs: A Case Grammar Analysis.* Ph.D. dissertation, BUK.

Gital, Garba Mohammed. 1987. "Typology of Dative Ordering: A Case Study of Bausanci Dative Movement in Hausa Dialectology." M.A. thesis, BUK.

Goerner, Margaret, Yousef Salman, and Peter B. Armitage. 1966. *Two Essays on Arabic Loanwords in Hausa.* (Occasional Paper 7.) Zaria: ABU.

Gouffé, Claude. 1962. "Observations sur le degré causatif dans un parler haoussa du Niger." *JAL* 1:182–200.

————. 1963/66. "Les problèmes de l'aspect en haoussa. I - Introduction. Le problème de l'aoriste et de l'accompli II." *GLECS* 10:151–65.

————. 1965. "La lexicographie du haoussa et le préalable phonologique." *JAL* 4:191–210.

————. 1966/67. "Les problèmes de l'aspect en haoussa. II - Le problème de l'inaccompli I et II." *GLECS* 11:29–67.

————. 1967. "Problèmes de toponymie haoussa: Les noms de villages de la région de Maradi." *Revue Internationale d'Onomastique* 19:95–127.

————. 1967/68. "Les problèmes de l'aspect en haoussa. III - L'inaccompli négatif et l'ingressif." *GLECS* 12:27–51.

————. 1969. "À propos de haoussa ['y]." *Word* 25:131–39.

————. 1971. "Observations sur les emprunts au français dans les parlers haoussa du Niger." In *Actes du 8e congrès de la Société Linguistique de l'Afrique Occidentale*, pp. 443–81. (Annales de l'Université d'Abidjan, Série H.) Abidjan.

————. 1974. "Contacts de vocabulaire entre le haoussa et le touareg." In *Actes du premier congrès international de linguistique sémitique et chamito-sémitique*, ed. André Caquot and David Cohen, pp. 357–80. The Hague: Mouton.

————. 1975a. "Noms vernaculaires d'animaux et ethnozoologie: Le point de vue du linguiste (lexicologie haoussa)." In *L'homme et l'animal*, pp. 273–82. (1er Colloque d'Ethnozoologie.) Paris: Inst. Inter. Ethnosciences.

————. 1975b. "Redoublement et réduplication en haoussa: Formes et fonctions." *Bulletin de la Société de Linguistique de Paris* 70(1):291–319.

————. 1978. "Linguistique tchadique." In *Annuaire 1977/1978. École Pratique des Hautes Études*, pp. 249–92 (+ foldout table). Paris: La Sorbonne.

———. 1981a. "La langue haoussa." In *Les langues dans le monde ancien et moderne. I. Les langues de l'Afrique subsaharienne*, ed. Gabriel Manessy, pp. 415–28 [chapter 3]. Paris: CNRS.

———. 1981b. "Linguistique tchadique." In *Annuaire 1978/1979. École Pratique des Hautes Études*, pp. 226–51. Paris: La Sorbonne.

———. 1982. "Notes de morpho-syntaxe haoussa. Note n° 1 – Le nom verbal primaire en -**aa** du 'degré 7'." *Bulletin des études africaines de l'Inalco* 2(3):97–104.

Grabna, Joanna, and Nina Pawlak. 1989. "The verbal bases of compound words in Hausa." *Hausa Studies* [Warsaw] 2:1–28.

Greenberg, Joseph H. 1941. "Some problems in Hausa phonology." *Language* 17:316–23.

———. 1947. "Arabic loan-words in Hausa." *Word* 3:85–97.

———. 1960a. "An Afro-Asiatic pattern of gender and number agreement." *Journal of the American Oriental Society* 80:317–21.

———. 1960b. "Linguistic evidence for the influence of the Kanuri on the Hausa." *Journal of African History* 1:205–12.

———. 1963. *The Languages of Africa*. Bloomington: Indiana University.

———. 1978. "How does a language acquire gender markers?" In *Universals of Human Language. Vol. 3: Word Structure*, ed. J. H. Greenberg, pp. 47–82. Stanford: Stanford University Press.

Gregersen, Edgar A. 1967. "Some competing analyses in Hausa." *JAL* 6:42–57.

Herms, Irmtraud. 1987. *Wörterbuch Hausa-Deutsch*. Leipzig: VEB Verlag Enzyklopädie.

Hill, Clifford A. 1976. "Negation in Hausa and principles of information processing: Secondary signalling and surface bracketing." *Columbia University Working Papers in Linguistics* 3:59–74.

Hiskett, Mervyn. 1965. "The historical background to the naturalization of Arabic loan-words in Hausa." *ALS* 6:18–27.

Hodge, Carleton T. 1970. "The linguistic cycle." *Language Sciences* [Indiana] 13:1–7.

———. 1971. "Afroasiatic S-causative." *Language Sciences* [Indiana] 15:41–43.

Hodge, Carleton T., and Ibrahim Umaru. 1963. *Hausa Basic Course*. Washington, D.C.: Foreign Service Institute.

Hoffmann, Carl. 1963. *A Grammar of the Margi Language*. London: Oxford University Press.

———. 1970. "Ancient Benue-Congo loans in Chadic." *Africana Marburgensia* 3(2):3–23.

Hoskison, James T. 1983. *A Grammar and Dictionary of the Gude Language*. Ph.D. dissertation, Ohio State University.

Hunter, Linda. 1979. "Dila da zarɓe: A visual display of Hausa intonation." *Études linguistiques* [Niamey] 1(2):11–31.

Hyman, Larry M., and Russell G. Schuh. 1974. "Universals of tone rules: Evidence from West Africa." *Linguistic Inquiry* 5:81–115.

Ikara, Bashir A. 1975. *English as a Factor in the Process of Language Modernization: A Study of the Impact of English on the Hausa Language*. Ph.D. dissertation, University of Leeds.

Inkelas, Sharon. 1988. "Prosodic constraints on syntax: Hausa **fa**." In *Proceedings of the Seventh West Coast Conference on Formal Linguistics (WCCFL)*, ed. Hagit Borer, pp. 375–89. Stanford: Stanford Linguistics Association.

Inkelas, Sharon, and William R. Leben. 1990. "Where phonology and phonetics intersect: The case of Hausa intonation." In *Between the Grammar and the Physics of Speech*, ed. Mary E. Beckman and John Kingston, pp. 17–34. (Papers in Laboratory Phonology.) New York: Cambridge University Press.

Inkelas, Sharon, William R. Leben, and Mark Cobler. 1987. "The phonology of intonation in Hausa." *Proceedings of the Annual Meeting of the North Eastern Linguistic Society* 17:327–41.

Jaggar, Philip J. 1976. "Thematic emphasis in Hausa." *HN* 6:63–74.

———. 1977. "The nature and function of auxiliary verbs in Hausa." In *PCL*, pp. 57–87.

————. 1978. "'And what about...?' — Topicalisation in Hausa." *SAL* 9:69–81.

————. 1981. "Some Unusual Lexical Passives in Hausa." M.A. thesis, UCLA.

————. 1982. "Monoverbal imperative formation in Hausa: A striking case of analogical realignment." *JALL* 4:133–56.

————. 1985. *Factors Governing the Morphological Coding of Referents in Hausa Narrative Discourse.* Ph.D. dissertation, UCLA.

————. 1988a. "Affected-subject ('grade 7') verbs in Hausa: What are they and where do they come from?" In *Passive and Voice*, ed. Masayoshi Shibatani, pp. 387–416. (Typological Studies in Language, 16.) Amsterdam: John Benjamins.

————. 1988b. "Discourse-deployability and indefinite NP-marking in Hausa: A demonstration of the universal 'categoriality hypothesis'." In *FWP*, pp. 45–61.

————. 1991. "Some 'unexpected' form–meaning correspondences between Hausa (West Chadic-A) and Guruntum (gùrdùN) (West Chadic-B): How do we explain them?" In *Unwritten Testimonies of the African Past*, ed. Stanisław Piłaszewicz and Eugeniusz Rzewuski, pp. 45–59. (Orientalia Varsoviensia 2.) Warsaw: Wydawnictwa Uniwersytetu Warszawskiego.

————. 1992a. *An Advanced Hausa Reader with Grammatical Notes and Exercises.* London: SOAS.

————. 1992b. "R. C. Abraham's early insights into Hausa pre-dativel verb forms." In *Papers in Honour of R. C. Abraham (1890–1963)*, ed. Philip J. Jaggar, pp. 51–66. London: SOAS.

———— (ed.). 1992c. *Papers in Honour of R. C. Abraham (1890–1963).* London: SOAS.

————. 1996. *Hausa Newspaper Reader.* (Publications of the African Language Project.) Kensington, Md.: Dunwoody.

————. 1998. "Restrictive vs. nonrestrictive relative clauses in Hausa: Where morphosyntax and semantics meet." *SAL* 27:199–238.

————. 1999. "Reflexives in Hausa." In *Von Aegypten zum Tschadsee. Eine linguistische Reise durch Afrika. Festschrift für Herrmann Jungraithmayr zum 65. Geburtstag*, ed. Dymitr Ibriszimow, Rudolf Leger, und Uwe Seibert (in press).

Jaggar, Philip J., and Malami Buba. 1994. "The space and time adverbials NAN/CAN in Hausa: Cracking the deictic code." *Language Sciences* 16:387–421.

Jaggar, Philip J., and Muhammed M. Munkaila. 1995. "Evidence against the proposal that the Hausa pre-dativel final -R verb = the 'grade 5' final -R/-S verb (and an alternative analysis)." In *Studia Chadica et Hamitosemitica: Akten des Internationalen Symposions zur Tschadsprachenforschung*, ed. Dymitr Ibriszimow, Rudolf Leger, and with the assistance of Gerald Schmitt, pp. 289–304. Cologne: Rüdiger Köppe.

Junaidu, Ismail. 1987. *Topicalization in Hausa.* Ph.D. dissertation, Indiana University.

Jungraithmayr, Herrmann. 1970. "On root augmentation in Hausa." *JAL* 9:83–88.

Jungraithmayr, Herrmann, and Abakar Adams. 1992. *Lexique migama: Migama–français et français–migama (Guéra, Tchad), avec une introduction grammaticale.* (Sprache und Oralität in Afrika, 17.) Berlin: Dietrich Reimer.

Jungraithmayr, Herrmann, and Dymitr Ibriszimow. 1994. *Chadic Lexical Roots.* Vol. 1: *Tentative Reconstruction, Grading, Distribution and Comments.* Vol. 2: *Documentation.* (Sprache und Oralität in Afrika, 20.) Berlin: Dietrich Reimer.

Jungraithmayr, Herrmann, and W. J. G. Möhlig. 1976. *Einführung in die Hausa-Sprache (Kursus für Kolleg und Sprachlabor).* (Marburger Studien zur Afrika- und Asienkunde, Serie A, Afrika, 7.) Berlin: Dietrich Reimer. (3rd ed., 1986)

Kirk-Greene, A. H. M. 1964. *A Preliminary Inquiry into Hausa Onomatology: Three Studies in the Origins of Personal, Title and Place Names.* (Research Memorandum.) Zaria: Institute of Administration, ABU.

————. 1966. *Hausa Ba Dabo Ba Ne: A Collection of 500 Proverbs.* Ibadan: Oxford University Press.

Kirk-Greene, Anthony, and Paul Newman. 1971. *West African Travels and Adventures: Two Autobiographical Narratives from Northern Nigeria.* New Haven: Yale University Press.

Klingenheben, August. 1920. *Die lautliche Gestalt des Hausadialekts von Katagum.* Inaugural dissertation, University of Leipzig.

——. 1927/28. "Die Silbenauslautgesetze des Hausa." *Zeitschrift für Eingeborenen-Sprachen* 18:272–97.

Koops, Robert. 1991. "Purpose / reason marking in Chadic." In *Études tchadiques: La phrase complexe,* ed. Herrmann Jungraithmayr and Henry Tourneux, pp. 103–25. Paris: Geuthner.

Korshunova, G. P., and B. A. Uspensky. 1993. "On the parts of speech typology in Hausa: The problem of the adjective." *St. Petersburg Journal of African Studies* 1:41–59.

Kraft, Charles H. 1963. *A Study of Hausa Syntax.* 3 vols. Hartford: Hartford Seminary Foundation.

——. 1970. Hausa **sai** and **dà** — a couple of overworked particles." *JAL* 9:92–109.

——. 1974. "Reconstruction of Chadic pronouns I: Possessive, object, and independent sets – an interim report." In *Third Annual Conference on African Linguistics,* ed. Erhard Voeltz, pp. 69–94. (I.U. Publications, African Series, 7.) Bloomington: Indiana University.

Kraft, Charles H., and A. H. M. Kirk-Greene. 1973. *Hausa.* (Teach Yourself Books.) London: Hodder and Stoughton.

Kraft, Charles H., and Marguerite G. Kraft. 1973. *Introductory Hausa.* Berkeley and Los Angeles: University of California Press.

Lass, Roger. 1990. "How to do things with junk: Exaptation in language evolution." *Journal of Linguistics* 26:79–102.

Leben, William R. 1971. "The morphophonemics of tone in Hausa." In *Papers in African Linguistics,* ed. C.-W. Kim and Herbert Stahlke, pp. 201–18. Edmonton: Linguistic Research.

——. 1996. "Tonal feet and the adaptation of English borrowings in Hausa." *SAL* 25:139–54.

Leben, William R., et al. 1991a. *Hausar Yau da Kullum: Intermediate and Advanced Lessons in Hausa Language and Culture.* Stanford: Center for the Study of Language and Information for the Stanford Linguistics Association.

——. 1991b. *Workbook. Hausar Yau da Kullum: Intermediate and Advanced Lessons in Hausa Language and Culture.* Stanford: Center for the Study of Language and Information for the Stanford Linguistics Association.

Lemeshko, B. G. 1967. "La racine et le thème du verbe dans la langue haoussa." In *II Congrès International des Africanistes. Communications de la Délégation de l'URSS,* pp. 3–5. Moscow.

Le Roux, J. M. 1886. *Essai de dictionnaire français–haoussa et haoussa–français.* Algiers: Adolphe Jourdan.

Leslau, Wolf. 1962. "A prefix ḥ in Egyptian, modern South Arabian and Hausa." *Africa* 32:65–68.

Lindau, Mona. 1984. "Phonetic differences in glottalic consonants." *Journal of Phonetics* 12:147–55.

——. 1986. "Testing a model of intonation in a tone language." *Journal of the Acoustical Society of American* 80:757–64.

Lindau, Mona, Kjell Norlin, and Jan-Olof Svantesson. 1990. "Some cross linguistic differences in diphthongs." *Journal of the International Phonetic Association* 20(1):10–14.

Lindsey, Geoffrey, Katrina Hayward, and Andrew Haruna. 1992. "Hausa glottalic consonants: A laryngographic study." *Bulletin of the School of Oriental and African Studies* 55:511–27

Lukas, Johannes. 1955. "Über die Verwendung der Partikel **sai** im Haussa." In *Afrikanistische Studien [Festschrift Westermann],* ed. J. Lukas, pp. 108–17. Berlin: Akademie-Verlag.

——. 1963. "Der II. Stamm des Verbums im Hausa." *AuÜ* 47:162–86.

——. 1970/71–1971/72. "Die Personalia und das primäre Verb im Bolanci (Nordnigerien), Mit Beiträgen über das Karekare." *AuÜ* 54:237–86, 55:114–39.

Malka, Jean-Guy. 1978. "Nazarin bambance-bambancen da ke tsakanin Daidaitacciyar Hausa (Nijeriya) da Hausar Filinge (Jumhuriyar Nijar) ta fuskar tsarin fannin furuci" [A contrastive study of Standard Hausa (Nigeria) with the Hausa dialect of Filingué (Niger) with regard to phonology]. *Harshe* [Zaria] 1:19–51.

Matsushita, Shuji. 1995. "/aC/ as a focus marker in Sokoto Hausa (Sakkwatancii)." In *Studia Chadica et Hamitosemitica: Akten des Internationalen Symposions zur Tschadsprachenforschung*, ed. Dymitr Ibriszimow, Rudolf Leger and with the assistance of Gerald Schmitt, pp. 305–8. Cologne: Rüdiger Köppe.

McConvell, Patrick. 1973. *Cleft Sentences in Hausa? A Syntactic Study of Focus*. Ph.D. dissertation, SOAS.

———. 1977. "Relativisation and the ordering of cross-reference rules in Hausa." *SAL* 8:1–31.

McIntyre, J. A. 1988a. "A NAg-ging question in Hausa: Remarks on the syntax and semantics of the plural noun of agent." In *FWP*, pp. 78–88.

———. 1988b. "Remarks on the short form of the noun of agent in Hausa." *AuÜ* 71:229–44.

———. 1990. "Is Hausa **jee** a grade 4 verb?" *AAP* 22:5–17.

———. 1992. "Dialect or idiolect: The speaker of *Spoken Hausa*." *Hausa Dialectology Newsletter* 2:28–31.

———. 1995. "It's still NAg-ging: Compounds in Hausa." *AuÜ* 78:239–59.

Meyers, Laura F. 1974. "The particles **sai** and **har**: Only, even and until in Hausa." In *Third Annual Conference on African Linguistics*, ed. Erhard Voeltz, pp. 213–21. (I.U. Publications, African Series, 7.) Bloomington: Indiana University.

———. 1976. *Aspects of Hausa Tone*. (UCLA Working Papers in Phonetics, 32.) Los Angeles: Department of Linguistics, UCLA.

Migeod, F. W. H. 1914. *A Grammar of the Hausa Language*. London: Kegan Paul, Trench, Trübner & Co.

Mijinguini, Abdou. 1986. "À propos des profusatifs en hausa." *Les Cahiers du CELHTO* 4:423–41.

———. 1994. *Karamin Kamus na Hausa zuwa Faransanci* [Concise Hausa–French Dictionary]. Niamey: CELHTO.

Miller, Jennifer, and Paul Tench. 1980. "Aspects of Hausa intonation, 1: Utterances in isolation. *Journal of the International Phonetic Association* 10:45–63.

———. 1982. Aspects of Hausa intonation, 2: Continuous text. *Journal of the International Phonetic Association* 12:78–93.

Mischlich, Adam. 1906. *Wörterbuch der Hausasprache*. (Lehrbücher des Seminars für Orientalische Sprachen, 20.) Berlin: Dietrich Reimer.

———. 1911. *Lehrbuch der Hausa-Sprache*. 2nd ed. Berlin: Dietrich Reimer.

Mohammed, Aliyu. 1991. "The tense system of Hausa." *AAP* 27:65–97.

Moore, Mary Jo. 1968. "The Ideophone in Hausa." M.A. thesis, Michigan State University.

Muhammad, Dalhatu. 1968. "A Brief Critical Review of the Treatment of Hausa Intonation." Diploma thesis, University of Ibadan.

Muhammad, Liman. 1968. *Hausa in the Modern World*. (ABU, Department of Languages, Occasional Paper, 8.) Zaria: ABU.

Munkaila, Muhammed M. 1990. *Indirect Object Constructions in Hausa*. Ph.D. dissertation, SOAS.

Newman, Paul. 1968. "Ideophones from a syntactic point of view." *JWAL* 5:107–17.

———. 1970. *A Grammar of Tera: Transformational Syntax and Texts*. (University of California Publications in Linguistics, 57.) Berkeley and Los Angeles: University of California Press.

———. 1971a. "The Hausa negative markers." *SAL* 2:183–95.

———. 1971b. "Transitive and intransitive in Chadic languages." In *Afrikanische Sprachen und Kulturen – Ein Querschnitt [Festschrift Lukas]*, ed. Veronika Six et al., pp. 188–200. (Hamburger Beiträge zur Afrika-Kunde, 14.) Hamburg: Deutsches Institut für Afrika-Forschung.

————. 1972a. "Study Kanakuru, understand Hausa." *HN* 2:1–13.

————. 1972b. "Syllable weight as a phonological variable." *SAL* 3:301–23.

————. 1973. "Grades, vowel-tone classes and extensions in the Hausa verbal system." *SAL* 4:297–346.

————. 1974. *The Kanakuru Language.* (West African Language Monographs, 9.) Leeds: Institute of Modern English Language Studies, University of Leeds and West African Linguistic Society.

————. 1975. "Proto-Chadic verb classes." *Folia Orientalia* 16:65–84.

————. 1976. "The origin of Hausa /h/." In *Papers in African Linguistics in Honor of Wm. E. Welmers*, ed. Larry M. Hyman, Leon C. Jacobson, and Russell G. Schuh, pp. 165–75. (*SAL*, Supplement 6.) Los Angeles: Department of Linguistics, UCLA.

————. 1977a. "Chadic classification and reconstructions." *AAL* 5:1–42.

————. 1977b. "Chadic extensions and pre-dative verb forms in Hausa." *SAL* 8:275–97.

————. 1979a. "Explaining Hausa feminines." *SAL* 10:197–226.

————. 1979b. "The historical development of medial /ee/ and /oo/ in Hausa." *JALL* 1:172–88.

————. 1980a. *The Classification of Chadic within Afroasiatic.* Leiden: Universitaire Pers.

————. 1980b. "The two R's in Hausa." *ALS* 17:77–87.

————. 1982. "Grammatical restructuring in Hausa: Indirect objects and possessives."*JALL* 4:59–73.

————. 1983. "The efferential (alias 'causative') in Hausa." In *Studies in Chadic and Afroasiatic Linguistics*, ed. Ekkehard Wolff and Hilke Meyer-Bahlburg, pp. 397–418. Hamburg: Helmut Buske.

————. 1984a. "Ethnonyms in Hausa." *SAL* 15:301–20.

————. 1984b. "Methodological pitfalls in Chadic-Afroasiatic comparisons." In *Current Progress in Afro-Asiatic Linguistics: Papers of the Third International Hamito-Semitic Congress*, ed. James Bynon, pp. 161–66. (Current Issues in Linguistic Theory, 28.) Amsterdam: John Benjamins.

————. 1985. "Tone splitting and Gwandara ethnohistory." In *Précis from the Fifteenth Conference on African Linguistics*, ed. Russell G. Schuh, pp. 233–37. (*SAL*, Supplement 9.) Los Angeles: Department of Linguistics, UCLA.

————. 1986a. "Reduplicated nouns in Hausa." *JALL* 8:115–32.

————. 1986b. "Tone and affixation in Hausa." *SAL* 17:249–67.

————. 1988. "O shush! An exclamatory construction in Hausa." In *FWP*, pp. 89–98.

————. 1989a. "The historical change from suffixal to prefixal reduplication in Hausa pluractional verbs." *JALL* 11:37–44.

————. 1989b. "Reduplication and tone in Hausa ideophones." *BLS* 15:248–55.

————. 1990a. "Internal evidence for final vowel lowering in Hausa." *SAL* 21:251–55.

————. 1990b. *Nominal and Verbal Plurality in Chadic.* (Publications in African Languages and Linguistics, 12.) Dordrecht: Foris.

————. 1991a. "A century and a half of Hausa language studies." In *Nigerian Languages: Yesterday, Today and Tomorrow*, ed. Abba Rufa'i, pp. 1–18. Kano: CSNL.

————. 1991b. "Facts count: An empiricist looks at indirect objects in Hausa." *BLS* 17S:155–65.

————. 1991c. "Historical decay and growth in the Hausa lexicon." In *Semitic Studies in Honor of Wolf Leslau*, ed. Alan S. Kaye, pp. 1131–39. Wiesbaden: Harrassowitz.

————. 1992a. "The development of falling contours from tone bending in Hausa." *BLS* 18S:128–33.

————. 1992b. "The drift from the coda into the syllable nucleus in Hausa." *Diachronica* 9:227–38.

————. 1992c. "The previous reference marker in Hausa: R. C. Abraham's insights and new analyses." In *Papers in Honour of R. C. Abraham (1890–1963)*, ed. Philip J. Jaggar, pp. 67–77. (*African Languages and Cultures*, Supplement 1.) London: SOAS.

————. 1995. "Hausa tonology: Complexities in an 'easy' tone language." In *The Handbook of Phonological Theory*, ed. John Goldsmith, pp. 762–81. Oxford: Blackwell.

———. 1996. *Hausa and the Chadic Language Family: A Bibliography.* (African Linguistic Bibliographies, 6.) Cologne: Rüdiger Köppe.

———. 1999. "The cognate accusative in Hausa." In *Von Aegypten zum Tschadsee: Eine linguistische Reise durch Afrika. Festschrift für Herrmann Jungraithmayr zum 65. Geburtstag,* ed. Dymitr Ibriszimow, Rudolf Leger, and Uwe Seibert (in press).

———. n.d. "The historical development of double negatives." Unpublished ms. (Preliminary version presented at the Twelfth International Conference on Historical Linguistics, Manchester, 1995).

Newman, Paul, and Mustapha Ahmad. 1992. "Hypocoristic names in Hausa." *Anthropological Linguistics* 34:159–72.

Newman, Paul, and Philip J. Jaggar. 1989a. "Low tone raising in Hausa: A critical assessment." *SAL* 20:227–51.

———. 1989b. LTR: A reply to Schuh." *SAL* 20:263–64.

Newman, Paul, and Roxana Ma. 1966. Comparative Chadic: Phonology and lexicon." *JAL* 5:218–51.

Newman, Paul, and Roxana Ma Newman. 1977. *Modern Hausa–English Dictionary (Sabon Kamus na Hausa zuwa Turanci).* Ibadan and Zaria: University Press (Nigeria).

———. 1981. "The question morpheme *q* in Hausa." *AuÜ* 64:35–46.

Newman, Paul, and Bello Ahmad Salim. 1981. "Hausa diphthongs." *Lingua* 55:101–21.

Newman, Paul, and Russell G. Schuh. 1974. "The Hausa aspect system." *AAL* 1(1):1–39.

Newman, Roxana Ma. 1974. "Dictionaries of the Hausa language." *HN* 4:1–25.

———. 1976. "The two relative continuous markers in Hausa." In *Papers in African Linguistics in Honor of Wm. E. Welmers,* ed. Larry M. Hyman, Leon C. Jacobson, and Russell G. Schuh, pp. 177–90. (*SAL,* Supplement 6.) Los Angeles: Department of Linguistics, UCLA.

———. 1984. "Denominative adverbs in Hausa." *AuÜ* 67:161–74.

———. 1988. "Augmentative adjectives in Hausa." In *FWP,* pp. 99–116.

———. 1990. *An English–Hausa Dictionary.* New Haven: Yale University Press.

Newman, Roxana Ma, and Vincent J. van Heuven. 1981. "An acoustic and phonological study of pre-pausal vowel length in Hausa." *JALL* 3:1–18.

Parsons, F. W. 1955. "Abstract nouns of sensory quality and their derivatives in Hausa." In *Afrikanistische Studien [Festschrift Westermann],* ed. J. Lukas, pp. 373–404. Berlin: Akademie-Verlag.

———. 1960a. "An introduction to gender in Hausa." *ALS* 1:117–36.

———. 1960b. "The verbal system in Hausa." *AuÜ* 44:1–36.

———. 1961. "The operation of gender in Hausa: The personal pronoun and genitive copula." *ALS* 2:100–124.

———. 1962. "Further observations on the 'causative' grade of the verb in Hausa." *JAL* 1:253–72.

———. 1963. "The operation of gender in Hausa: Stabilizer, dependent nominals and qualifiers." *ALS* 4:166–207.

———. 1970. "Is Hausa really a Chadic language? Some problems of comparative phonology." *ALS* 11:272–88.

———. 1971/72. "Suppletion and neutralization in the verbal system of Hausa." *AuÜ* 55:49–97, 188–208.

———. 1975. "Hausa and Chadic." In *Hamito-Semitica,* ed. James and Theodora Bynon, pp. 421–55. The Hague: Mouton.

———. 1981. *Writings on Hausa Grammar: The Collected Papers of F. W. Parsons,* ed. Graham Furniss. Ann Arbor, Mich.: UMI Books on Demand.

Pawlak, Nina. 1975. "The semantic problems of 'intensive' forms in Hausa verbs." *Africana Bulletin* [Warsaw] 23:139–49.

Piłaszewicz, Stanisław. 1981. *Alhadżi Umaru (1858–1934) – Poeta ludu Xausa: Studium historiczno-literackie [Alhaji Umaru, poet of the Hausa people: A historical-literary study].* (Rozprawy Uniwersitetu Warszawskiego.) Warsaw: Wydawnictwo Uniwersiteta Warszawskiego.

———. 1992. *The Zabarma Conquest of North-West Ghana and Upper Volta: A Hausa Narrative "Histories of Samory and Babatu and Others" by Mallam Abu.* (Rozprawy Uniwersitetu Warszawskiego.) Warsaw: Polish Scientific Publishers.

Pilszczikowa, Nina. 1960. "Les verbes auxiliaires en haoussa." *Rocznik Orientalistyczny* 23(2):101–18.

———. 1969. *The Changing Form (Grade 2) of the Verb in Hausa.* Warsaw: Państowowe Wydawnictwo Naukowe.

Prietze, Rudolf. 1908. "Die spezifischen Verstärkungsadverbien im Haussa und Kanuri." *Mitteilungen des Seminars für Orientalische Sprachen* [Berlin] 11(3):307–17.

Quirk, Randolph, Sidney Greenbaum, Geoffrey Leech, and Jan Svartvik. 1985. *A Comprehensive Grammar of the English Language.* London: Longman.

Rattray, R. Sutherland. 1913. *Hausa Folk-lore Customs, Proverbs, Etc.* 2 vols. Oxford: Clarendon.

Robinson, Charles H. 1896. *Specimens of Hausa Literature.* Cambridge: Cambridge University Press.

———. 1897. *Hausa Grammar (with Exercises, Readings and Vocabularies, and Specimens of Hausa Script).* 1st ed. London: Kegan Paul, Trench, Trübner & Co.

———. 1899–1900. *Dictionary of the Hausa Language.* Cambridge: Cambridge University Press.

Rufa'i, Abba. 1977. *Grammatical Agreement in Hausa.* Ph.D. dissertation, Georgetown University.

———. 1983. "Defining and non-defining relative clauses in Hausa." In *Studies in Chadic and Afroasiatic Linguistics*, ed. by Ekkehard Wolff and Hilke Meyer-Bahlburg, pp. 419–27. Hamburg: Helmut Buske.

Salim, Bello A. 1980. "A note on the Hausa voiceless labials." *SAL* 11:257–60.

———. 1981. *Linguistic Borrowing as External Evidence on Phonology: The Assimilation of English Loanwords in Hausa.* Ph.D. dissertation, University of York.

Sani, Mu'azu A. Z. 1983. *An Introductory Phonology of Hausa (for Schools).* Kano: CSNL.

Schachter, Paul. 1966. "A generative account of Hausa **ne/ce**." *JAL* 5:34–53.

———. 1973. "Focus and relativization." *Language* 49:19–46.

Schmaling, Constanze. 1991. "Modalpartikeln im Hausa: 'Gishirin Hausa'." M.A. thesis, Universität Hamburg.

Schön, James Frederick. 1843. *Vocabulary of the Haussa Language. Phrases, and Specimens of Translations, to which are prefixed, the Grammatical Elements of the Haussa Language.* London: Church Missionary Society.

———. 1862. *Grammar of the Hausa Language.* London: Church Missionary House.

———. 1876. *Dictionary of the Hausa Language, with appendices of Hausa literature.* London: Church Missionary House.

———. 1885. *Magána Hausa [Hausa speech].* London: Society for Promoting Christian Knowledge.

Schubert, Klaus. 1971–72. "Zur Bedeutung und Anwendung der Verbalparadigmen im Hausa und Kanuri." *AuÜ* 55:1–49, 208–27; 56:90–118.

Schuh, Russell G. 1974a. "A note on inalienable possession in Hausa." *JWAL* 9(2):113–14.

———. 1974b. "Sound change as rule simplification? A study of consonant weakening in Kanakuru and in Hausa." In *Third Annual Conference on African Linguistics*, ed. Erhard Voeltz, pp. 95–101. (I.U. Publications, African Series, 7.) Bloomington: Indiana University.

———. 1976. "The history of Hausa nasals." In *Papers in African Linguistics in Honor of Wm. E. Welmers*, ed. Larry M. Hyman, Leon C. Jacobson, and Russell G. Schuh, pp. 221–32. (*SAL*, Supplement 6.) Los Angeles: Department of Linguistics, UCLA.

———. 1977a. "Bade/Ngizim determiner system." *AAL* 4(3):1–74.

———. 1977b. "West Chadic verb classes." In *PCL*, pp. 143–66.

———. 1984. "West Chadic vowel correspondences." In *Current Progress in Afro-Asiatic Linguistics: Papers of the Third International Hamito-Semitic Congress*, ed. James Bynon, pp. 167–223. (Current Issues in Linguistic Theory, 28.) Amsterdam: John Benjamins.

———. 1989a. "Gender and number in Miya." In *Current Progress in Chadic Linguistics*, ed. Zygmunt Frajzyngier, pp. 171–81. (Current Issues in Linguistic Theory, 62.) Amsterdam: John Benjamins.

———. 1989b. "Long vowels and diphthongs in Miya and Hausa." In *Current Approaches to African Linguistics (Vol. 5)*, ed. Paul Newman and Robert D. Botne, pp. 35–43. Dordrecht: Foris.

———. 1989c. "The reality of 'Hausa low tone raising': A response to Newman & Jaggar." *SAL* 20:253–62.

———. 1993. "Ma'anonin hange cikakke na Hausa" [The meanings of the perfective tense in Hausa]. In *Nazari a kan Harshe da Adabi da Al'adu na Hausa*. Vol. 3. Ed. Abba Rufa'i, Ibrahim Yaro Yahaya, and Abdu Yahya Bichi, pp. 39–58. Kano: CSNL.

———. 1998. *A Grammar of Miya*. (University of California Publications in Linguistics, 130.) Berkeley and Los Angeles: University of California Press.

Schwartz, Linda. 1989. "Thematic linking in Hausa asymmetric coordination." *SAL* 20:29–62.

———. 1991. "Category asymmetries in Hausa asymmetric coordination." *BLS* 17S:222–30.

Schwartz, Linda, Paul Newman, and Sammani Sani. 1988. "Agreement and scope of modification in Hausa coordinate structures." *Proceedings of the Chicago Linguistics Society* 24(2):278–90.

Skinner, Neil. 1968. *Hausa-English Pocket Dictionary*. 2nd ed. Ikeja: Longmans of Nigeria.

——— (trans. & ed.). 1969. *Hausa Tales and Traditions: An English Translation of Tatsuniyoyi na Hausa, originally compiled by Frank Edgar*. London: Cass.

———. 1972. *Hausa for Beginners*. 3rd ed. Zaria: NNPC.

——— (trans. & ed.). 1977. *Hausa Tales and Traditions: An English Translation of Tatsuniyoyi na Hausa, originally compiled by Frank Edgar*. Vols. 2–3. Madison: University of Wisconsin Press.

———. 1996. *Hausa Comparative Dictionary*. (Westafrikanische Studien: Frankfurter Beiträge zur Sprach- und Kulturgeschichte, 11.) Cologne: Rüdiger Köppe.

Swets, Francine. 1989. "Grade 2 Verbs with Indirect Objects in the Dogondoutchi Dialect of Hausa." M.A. thesis, University of Leiden.

Taylor, F. W. 1923. *A Practical Hausa Grammar*. Oxford: Clarendon. (2nd ed., 1959, London: Oxford University Press).

Tuller, Laurice A. 1986. *Bijective Relations in Universal Grammar and the Syntax of Hausa*. Ph.D. dissertation, UCLA.

———. 1989. "AGR-drop and VP focus-fronting in Hausa." In *Current Approaches to African Linguistics (Vol. 6)*, ed. Isabelle Haïk and Laurice Tuller, pp. 319–34. Dordrecht: Foris.

———. 1997. "Les 'ICP' en tchadique." In *Les pronoms: Morphologie, syntaxe et typologie*, ed. Anne Zribi-Hertz, pp. 213–29. Vincennes: Presses Universitaires de Vincennes.

Voigt, Rainer M. 1983. "Zu den 'unbestimmten' Vokalen des Hausa." *Africana Marburgensia* 16(1):57–67.

Wängler, Hans-Heinrich. 1963. *Zur Tonologie des Hausa*. Berlin: Akademie-Verlag.

Westermann, Diedrich. 1911. *Die Sprache der Haussa in Zentralafrika*. Berlin: Dietrich Reimer.

Williams, Wayne R. 1970. "Syntax and Meaning of Hausa Ideophones: A New Approach." M.A. thesis, University of Wisconsin.

Wolff, H. Ekkehard. 1992. "Hausa-Plurale in diachronischer Perspektive: Hinweise auf frühen Sprachkontakt?" In *Komparative Afrikanistik*, ed. E. Ebermann, E. R. Sommerauer, and K. É. Thomanek, pp. 405–21. Vienna: Afro-Pub.

———. 1993. *Referenzgrammatik des Hausa*. (Hamburger Beiträge zur Afrikanistik, 2.) Münster: LIT.

Wysocka, Ewa. 1989. "Modernization of the Hausa vocabulary or how the son became a policeman." *Hausa Studies* [Warsaw] 2:29–35.

Yahaya, Ibrahim Yaro, and Sammani Sani. [1979]. *Sunayen Hausawa na Gargajiya da Ire-Iren Abincin Hausawa* [Traditional Hausa Names and Kinds of Hausa Foods]. Kano: BUK.

Yalwa, Lawan Danladi. 1992. "Distribution of Pronouns and Anaphora in Hausa." M.A. thesis, UCLA.

———. 1994. "Complementation of Hausa aspectual verbs." *Kansas Working Papers in Linguistics* 19(1):185–215.

———. 1995. *Issues in Hausa Complementation*. Ph.D. dissertation, UCLA.

Index